Inside the e-Pages for *The St. Martin's Guide*

W9-AAL-060

To access the e-Pages that accompany this text, visit **bedfordstmartins.com/theguide/epages**. Students who do not buy a new book can purchase access to e-Pages at this site.

The St. Martin's
Guide to Writing

SHORT TENTH EDITION

The St. Martin's Guide to Writing

Rise B. Axelrod
University of California, Riverside

Charles R. Cooper
University of California, San Diego

Bedford / St. Martin's
Boston • New York

For Bedford/St. Martin's

Senior Developmental Editor: Jane Carter
Production Editor: Peter Jacoby
Senior Production Supervisor: Jennifer Peterson
Executive Marketing Manager: Molly Parke
Editorial Assistant: Amy Saxon
Copy Editor: Diana Puglisi George
Indexer: Melanie Belkin
Photo Researcher: Debbie Needleman
Permissions Manager: Kalina K. Ingham
Art Director: Lucy Krikorian
Text Design: Jerilyn Bockorick
Cover Design: Marine Bouvier Miller
Composition: Cenveo Publisher Services
Printing and Binding: RR Donnelley and Sons

President, Bedford/St. Martin's: Denise B. Wydra
Presidents, Macmillan Higher Education: Joan E. Feinberg and Tom Scotty
Editor in Chief: Karen S. Henry
Director of Development: Erica T. Appel
Director of Marketing: Karen R. Soeltz
Production Director: Susan W. Brown
Associate Production Director: Elise S. Kaiser
Managing Editor: Shuli Traub

Manufactured in the United States of America.

8 7 6 5 4 3
f e d c b a

For information, write: Bedford/St. Martin's, 75 Arlington Street, Boston, MA 02116   (617-399-4000)

ISBN 978-1-4576-3250-1 (paperback with Handbook)
ISBN 978-1-4576-0442-3 (hardcover with Handbook)
ISBN 978-1-4576-4081-0 (loose-leaf edition with Handbook)
ISBN 978-1-4576-0450-8 (paperback without Handbook)

Advisory Board

We owe an enormous debt to all the rhetoricians and composition specialists whose theory, research, and pedagogy have informed *The St. Martin's Guide to Writing*. We would be adding many pages if we were to name everyone to whom we are indebted.

The members of the advisory board for the tenth edition, a group of dedicated composition instructors from across the country, have provided us with extensive insights and suggestions for the chapters in Part One and have given us the benefit of their advice on new features. *The St. Martin's Guide to Writing* has been greatly enhanced by their contributions.

Lisa Bickmore
Salt Lake Community College

Mary Brantley
Holmes Community College–Ridgeland

Jo Ann Buck
Guilford Technical Community College

Wallace Cleaves
University of California–Riverside

Leona Fisher
Chaffey College

Gwen Graham
Holmes Junior College–Grenada

Lesa Hildebrand
Triton College

Stephanie Kay
University of California–Riverside

Donna Nelson-Beene
Bowling Green State University

Gail Odette
Baton Rouge Community College

Gray Scott
Texas Woman's University

David Taylor
St. Louis Community College

Preface

When we first wrote *The St. Martin's Guide to Writing*, our goal was to provide students with the clear guidance and practical strategies they needed to harness their potential as writers—an achievement that will be key to their success in college, at work, and in the wider world. We also wanted to provide instructors with the hands-on tools they needed to help their students write with a clear understanding of their rhetorical situation. Our goals have remained the same, and so *The St. Martin's Guide* retains the core features that over the years have drawn so many instructors and programs to the *Guide*. But now it also includes many new features that we believe will keep the *Guide* the most practical hands-on text for teachers and students.

Core Features of the *Guide*

The St. Martin's Guide retains its emphasis on active learning—learning by doing   by providing practical guides to writing, promoting genre awareness to aid the transfer of writing skills from one genre or context to another, and integrating reading and writing through hands-on activities of critical thinking, reading, and analysis.

Practical Guides to Writing

Each chapter in Part One offers practical, flexible guides that help students draft and revise essays in a variety of analytical and argumentative genres. Commonsensical and easy to follow, these writing guides teach students to

- assess the rhetorical situation, focusing on their purpose and audience, with special attention to the genre and medium in which they are writing;
- ask probing analytical questions;
- practice finding answers through various kinds of research, including memory search, field research, and traditional source-based research.

These flexible guides to writing begin with a **Starting Points** chart to offer students multiple ways of finding the help they need when they need it. Each also includes a **Critical Reading Guide** to help students assess their own writing and the writing of their classmates and a **Troubleshooting Guide** to help students find ways to improve their drafts. All these guides are organized and color-coded to emphasize the genre's basic features. In short, the guides to writing help students make their writing thoughtful, clear, organized, and compelling—in a word, effective for the rhetorical situation.

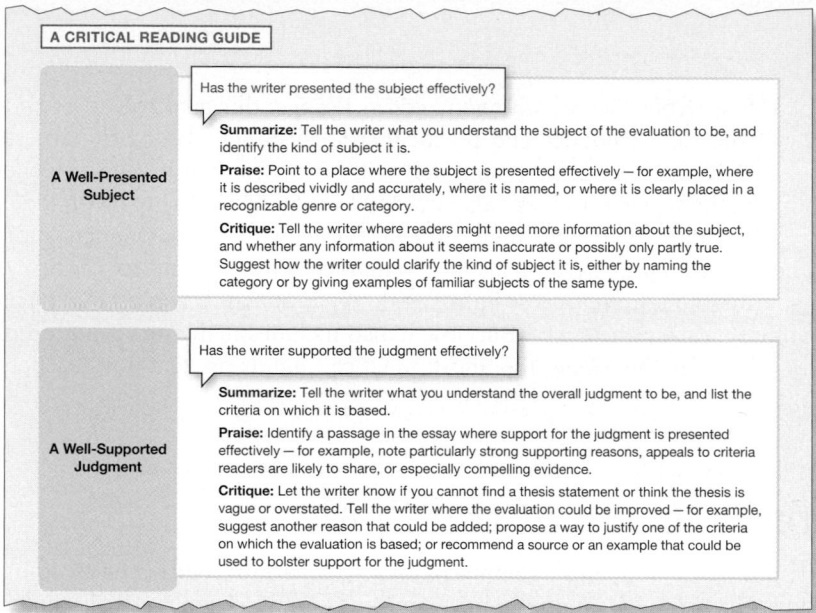

Genre Awareness

Each chapter in Part One introduces a genre of writing. By working through several genres, students learn how writers employ the basic features and strategies of a genre to achieve their purpose with their readers. The Arguing a Position essay, for example, teaches students to examine critically their views on a controversial issue, as well as those of their prospective readers, with an eye toward developing an argument that not only is well reasoned and well supported but also responds constructively to readers' likely questions and concerns. The Finding Common Ground essay teaches students how to analyze opposing arguments on a controversial issue—unpacking the ways writers use the classical appeals of logos, ethos, and pathos to promote their underlying values and beliefs. Whereas the primary purpose in Arguing a Position is persuasive, to convince readers to take seriously the writer's point of view, the primary purpose in a Finding Common Ground essay is analytical, to explain the basis for divergent points of view and determine where, if anywhere, compromise might be forged. Studying multiple genres—as well as multiple examples of each genre—helps students understand that genre is not simply a way for rhetoricians to classify texts or for teachers to construct assignments. More important, genre awareness helps them understand how we actually communicate with one another in a variety of contexts and situations. Genre awareness makes us better communicators, better readers and writers, in whatever medium we are using.

Systematic Integration of Critical Reading and Reflective Writing

Students are asked to read and analyze essays in the genre they are learning to write. The activities following the professional reading selections prompt students to read actively by asking them to reflect on the essay and connect it to their own experience, and to read like a writer, paying attention to the strategies the writer uses to convey his or her ideas and connect with readers.

What's New

Although the tenth edition of *The St. Martin's Guide to Writing* builds on the success of previous editions, many of the strategies the *Guide* employs have changed in order to connect more effectively with a new generation of teachers and students. Even in the years since the publication of the ninth edition, there have been the increasingly burdensome demands on the time, attention, and energy of teachers and students and the tremendous growth in access to high-speed Internet. So the guiding principle for the tenth edition has been to maximize **active learning** by enhancing the book's **visual rhetoric,** giving students more opportunities for **hands-on learning,** and providing students and instructors with **more readings** and more interactive activities than ever before: more showing, more doing, more options, more learning.

 ### More Readings in the e-Pages

The *Guide* is the first rhetoric to integrate **e-Pages** that come alive online with video, Web sites, podcasts, and more. An electronic extension of the printed page, e-Pages make it possible for us to include more reading selections in the *Guide* than ever before. The e-Pages for *The St. Martin's Guide,* Tenth Edition, include the following:

- **Ten more student essays.** Each is accompanied by a headnote identifying the student writer and describing the assignment that the essay was written to fulfill, are available free through the e-Pages. (Additional student essays are also available on the book's companion site and in *Sticks and Stones,* a collection of student essays from across the country that is available free to adopters.)
- **Twenty-one more professional readings** take advantage of what the Web can do to give instructors more choices than ever before. Each reading is accompanied by a headnote describing the writer and the venue in which the selection originally appeared, and each is followed by an Analyze & Write activity that

asks students to think and write about how the selection employs a basic feature of the genre. A Consider Possible Topics feature is also included to help students identify topics about which they could write.

Shankar Vedantam | *The Telescope Effect*

 SHANKAR VEDANTAM is a National Public Radio correspondent and a journalist for the *Philadelphia Inquirer, Slate,* and the *Washington Post*. He has been honored with fellowships and awards by Harvard University, the World Health Organization, the Society of Professional Journalists, and the American Public Health Association. In addition to his many articles, Vedantam writes plays and fiction, including his short story collection, *The Ghosts of Kashmir* (2005). "The Telescope Effect" is excerpted from his book *The Hidden Brain: How Our Unconscious Minds Elect Presidents, Control Markets, Wage Wars, and Save Our Lives* (2010). The photograph of the rescued dog, Hokget, which appears in the reading selection on p. 416, is from the *Honolulu Star-Bulletin*. As you read, consider the following questions:

- How does Vedantam engage readers' interest in the opening paragraphs?
- How might including a photograph of the dog affect readers' perspective?

1   The *Insiko 1907* was a tramp tanker that roamed the Pacific Ocean. Its twelve-man Taiwanese crew hunted the seas for fishing fleets in need of fuel; the *Insiko* had a cargo of tens of thousands of gallons of diesel. It was supposed to be an Indonesian ship, except that it was not registered in Indonesia because its owner, who lived in China, did not bother with taxes. In terms of international law, the *Insiko 1907* was stateless, a two-hundred-sixty-foot microscopic speck on the largest ocean on earth. On March 13, 2002, a fire broke out in the *Insiko*'s engine room. . . . The ship was about eight hundred miles south of Hawaii's Big Island, and adrift. Its crew could not call on anyone for help, and no one who could help knew of the *Insiko*'s existence, let alone its problems.[1]

2   Drawn by wind and currents, the *Insiko* eventually got within two hundred twenty miles of Hawaii, where it was spotted by a cruise ship called the *Norwegian Star* on April 2. The cruise ship diverted course, rescued the Taiwanese crew, and radioed the United States Coast Guard. But as the *Norwegian Star* pulled away from the *Insiko* and steamed toward Hawaii, a few passengers on the cruise ship heard the sound of barking. The captain's puppy had been left behind on the tanker.

3   It is not entirely clear why the cruise ship did not rescue the Jack Russell mixed terrier, or why the Taiwanese crew did not insist on it. . . . Whatever the reason, the burned-out tanker and its lonely inhabitant were abandoned on the terrible immensity of the Pacific. The *Norwegian Star* made a stop at Maui. A passenger who heard the barking dog called the Hawaiian Humane Society in Honolulu. . . . The Humane Society alerted fishing boats about the lost tanker. Media reports began appearing about the terrier, whose name was Hokget.

4   Something about a lost puppy on an abandoned ship on the Pacific gripped people's imaginations. Money poured into the Humane Society to fund a rescue. One check was for five thousand dollars. . . . "It was just about a dog," [Hawaiian Humane Society president Pamela] Burns told me. . . . "This was an opportunity for people to feel good about rescuing a dog. People poured out their support. A handful of people were incensed. These people said, 'You should be giving money to the homeless.'" But Burns felt the great thing about America was that people were free to give money to whatever cause they cared about, and people cared about Hokget. . . .

5   On April 26, nearly one and a half months after the puppy's ordeal began, the *American Quest* found the *Insiko* and boarded the tanker. The forty-pound female pup was still alive, and hiding in a pile of

---

You and your students can access the e-Pages by navigating to the *Student Site for The St. Martin's Guide to Writing*—**bedfordstmartins.com/theguide**—or by typing the following URL into the address bar of a Web browser: **bedfordstmartins.com /theguide/epages**.

Students receive automatic access with the purchase of a new book. If the activation code printed on the inside back cover of the student edition has expired, students can purchase access at the student site. Instructors can access the e-Pages by visiting **bedfordstmartins.com/theguide/epages** and following the instructions there.

Active Learning

Leaner chapters make it easier for instructors to get and keep students reading and to focus their attention on what matters most. This edition of *The St. Martin's Guide to Writing* is tighter and more focused than ever.

A **new design** helps guide students through the chapters, with **headings** that show students where they are, where they've been, and where they're going in the chapter and **that help students identify the activities** and **understand the purpose they serve in active learning**.

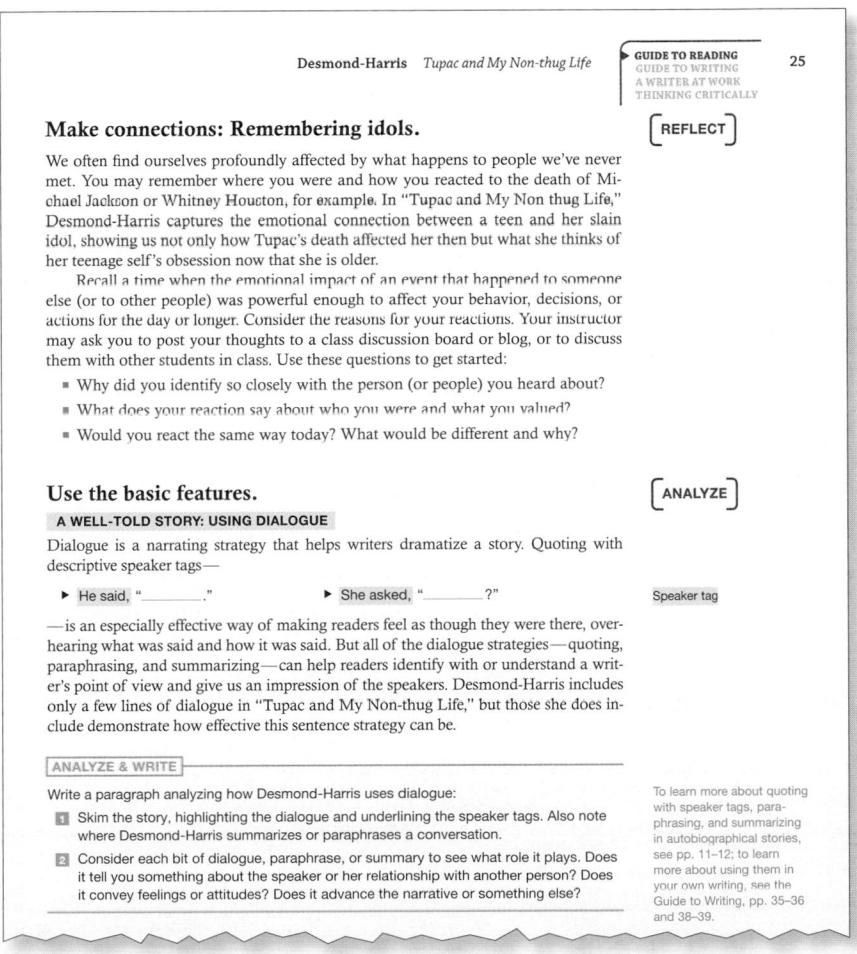

Desmond-Harris *Tupac and My Non-thug Life*   ▸ **GUIDE TO READING**   25
GUIDE TO WRITING
A WRITER AT WORK
THINKING CRITICALLY

Make connections: Remembering idols.

[REFLECT]

We often find ourselves profoundly affected by what happens to people we've never met. You may remember where you were and how you reacted to the death of Michael Jackson or Whitney Houston, for example. In "Tupac and My Non-thug Life," Desmond-Harris captures the emotional connection between a teen and her slain idol, showing us not only how Tupac's death affected her then but what she thinks of her teenage self's obsession now that she is older.

Recall a time when the emotional impact of an event that happened to someone else (or to other people) was powerful enough to affect your behavior, decisions, or actions for the day or longer. Consider the reasons for your reactions. Your instructor may ask you to post your thoughts to a class discussion board or blog, or to discuss them with other students in class. Use these questions to get started:

- Why did you identify so closely with the person (or people) you heard about?
- What does your reaction say about who you were and what you valued?
- Would you react the same way today? What would be different and why?

Use the basic features.

[ANALYZE]

A WELL-TOLD STORY: USING DIALOGUE

Dialogue is a narrating strategy that helps writers dramatize a story. Quoting with descriptive speaker tags—

- ▸ He said, "_____."
- ▸ She asked, "_____?"

Speaker tag

—is an especially effective way of making readers feel as though they were there, overhearing what was said and how it was said. But all of the dialogue strategies—quoting, paraphrasing, and summarizing—can help readers identify with or understand a writer's point of view and give us an impression of the speakers. Desmond-Harris includes only a few lines of dialogue in "Tupac and My Non-thug Life," but those she does include demonstrate how effective this sentence strategy can be.

ANALYZE & WRITE

Write a paragraph analyzing how Desmond-Harris uses dialogue:

1. Skim the story, highlighting the dialogue and underlining the speaker tags. Also note where Desmond-Harris summarizes or paraphrases a conversation.

2. Consider each bit of dialogue, paraphrase, or summary to see what role it plays. Does it tell you something about the speaker or her relationship with another person? Does it convey feelings or attitudes? Does it advance the narrative or something else?

To learn more about quoting with speaker tags, paraphrasing, and summarizing in autobiographical stories, see pp. 11–12; to learn more about using them in your own writing, see the Guide to Writing, pp. 35–36 and 38–39.

A **mini table of contents** and a **Starting Points** chart at the opening of each Guide to Writing section in Part One help students find the information they need. Starting Points, **Critical Reading,** and **Troubleshooting** guides use speech bubbles to prompt students to reflect on, interrogate, and revise their writing on their own.

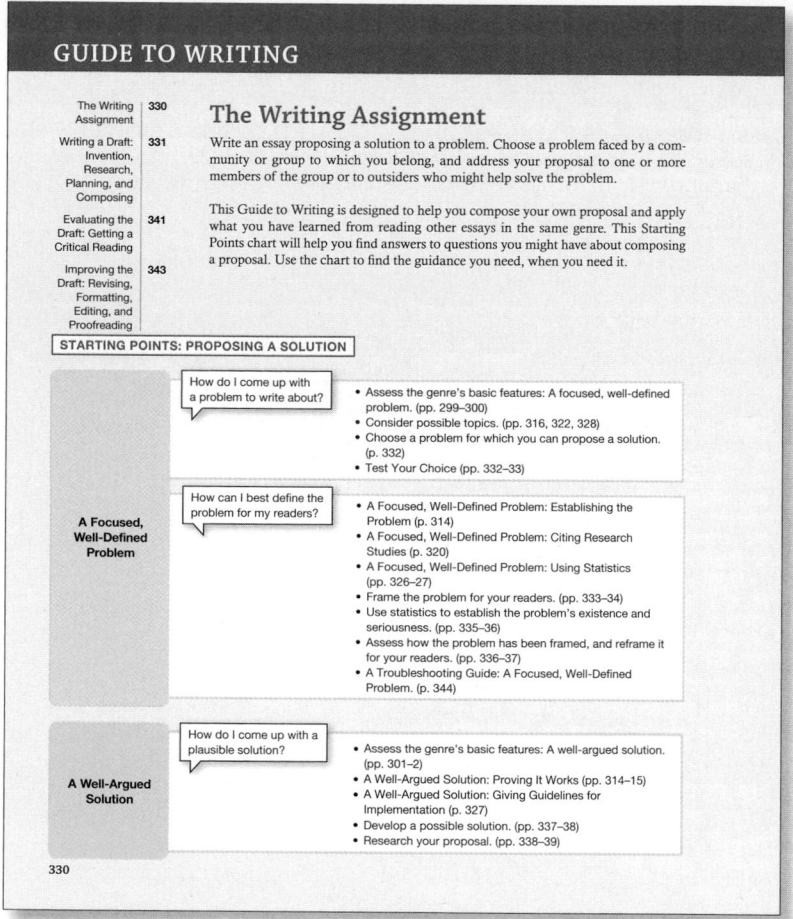

Color-coded highlighting and annotations *show* students the techniques writers use to communicate effectively with their readers.

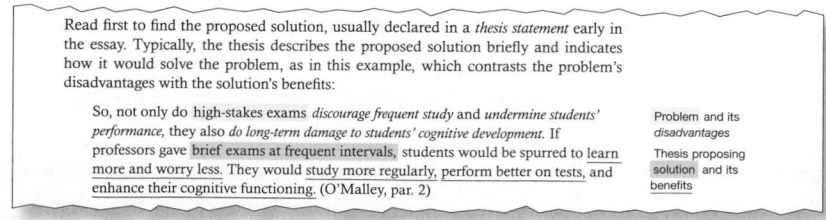

Integrated sentence strategies foreground the sentence patterns writers use to communicate effectively with their readers. Examples from the reading selections demonstrate the flexibility of the pattern.

A FOCUSED, WELL-PRESENTED ISSUE: REFRAMING THROUGH CONTRAST

Writers sometimes have to remind their readers why an issue is controversial. Beginning with the title, Solove works to undermine the widely held assumption that the erosion of privacy should not be a concern. He does this primarily by contrasting two different ways of thinking about threats to privacy, which he calls Orwellian and Kafkaesque, based on the novels *1984,* by George Orwell, and *The Trial,* by Franz Kafka. To present this contrast, Solove uses sentence patterns like these:

▶ Not _____, but _____.

▶ _____ focus on _____, which is characterized by _____, and they don't even notice _____, which is characterized by _____.

Here are a couple of examples from Solove's position argument:

> The problems are not just Orwellian but Kafkaesque. (par. 10)

> Legal and policy solutions focus too much on the problems under the Orwellian metaphor—those of surveillance—and aren't adequately addressing the Kafkaesque problems—those of information processing. (par. 9)

In the Guide to Writing, **sentence strategies are integrated into the Ways In activities** to invite students to use them for their own rhetorical purpose and to make them their own as they revise.

⠿ Frame the problem for your readers.

Once you have made a preliminary choice of a problem, consider what you know about it, what research will help you explore what others think about it, and how you can interest your readers in solving it. Then determine how you can frame or reframe it in a way that appeals to readers' values and concerns. Use the questions and sentence strategies that follow as a jumping-off point; you can make them your own as you revise later.

To learn more about conducting surveys and interviews, consult Chapter 24, pp. 684–88. For advice on listing, cubing, and free-writing, see Chapter 11, pp. 510, 514–15.

WHAT IS THE PROBLEM?	WHY SHOULD READERS CARE?
What do I already know about the problem?	**How can I convince readers the problem is real and deserves attention?**
Brainstorm a list: Spend 10 minutes listing everything you know about the problem. Write quickly, leaving judgment aside for the moment. After the 10 minutes are up, you can review your list and highlight or star the most promising information.	**Give an example to make the problem specific:**
	▶ Recently, _____ has been [in the news/ in movies/a political issue] because of [name event].
Use cubing: Probe the problem from a variety of perspectives:	Example:
• Describe the problem.	Lately, the issue of bullying has been in the news, sparked by the suicide of Tyler Clementi . . . , a gay college student who was a victim of cyber-bullying. (Bornstein, par. 1)
• Compare the problem to other, similar problems, or contrast it with other, related problems.	

WAYS IN

Greater attention to the writing situation helps students transfer the skills they're learning to other courses and contexts: **Practicing the Genre** activities at the beginning of the chapter encourage students to explore the genre collaboratively. **Playing with Genre** boxes at the end of each Guide to Reading section encourage students to consider the effects of genre. **A new chapter on writing in business and scientific** genres encourages students to consider how genre drives design and formatting.

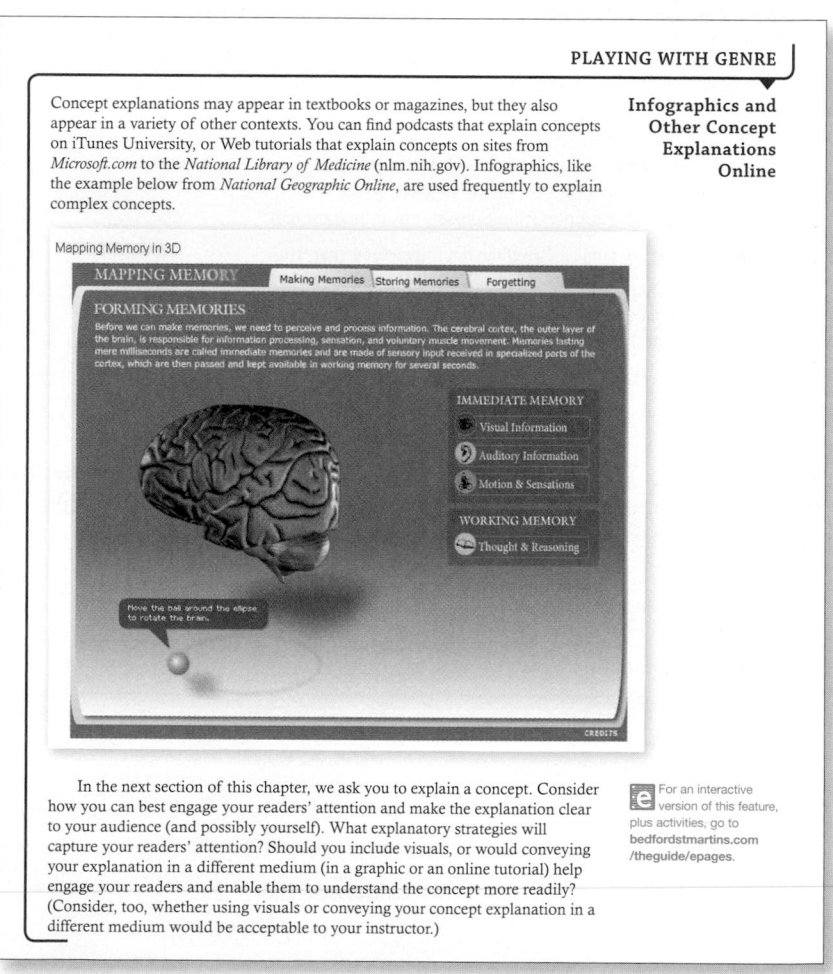

PLAYING WITH GENRE

Infographics and Other Concept Explanations Online

Concept explanations may appear in textbooks or magazines, but they also appear in a variety of other contexts. You can find podcasts that explain concepts on iTunes University, or Web tutorials that explain concepts on sites from *Microsoft.com* to the *National Library of Medicine* (nlm.nih.gov). Infographics, like the example below from *National Geographic Online*, are used frequently to explain complex concepts.

In the next section of this chapter, we ask you to explain a concept. Consider how you can best engage your readers' attention and make the explanation clear to your audience (and possibly yourself). What explanatory strategies will capture your readers' attention? Should you include visuals, or would conveying your explanation in a different medium (in a graphic or an online tutorial) help engage your readers and enable them to understand the concept more readily? (Consider, too, whether using visuals or conveying your concept explanation in a different medium would be acceptable to your instructor.)

For an interactive version of this feature, plus activities, go to bedfordstmartins.com /theguide/epages.

More Options

With the tenth edition, the full version of *The St. Martin's Guide to Writing* is now available in a wider variety of formats than ever before, including **hardcover,**

paperback, loose-leaf, and **e-book** versions. (For a full list of options, visit us online at **bedfordstmartins.com/theguide/catalog.**)

Council of Writing Program Administrators (WPA) Outcomes Statement

The St. Martin's Guide to Writing, Tenth Edition, helps students build proficiency in the four categories of learning that writing programs across the country use to assess their students' work: rhetorical knowledge; critical thinking, reading, and writing; writing processes; and knowledge of conventions. The chart below shows in detail how *The St. Martin's Guide* helps students develop these proficiencies.

DESIRED STUDENT OUTCOMES	RELEVANT FEATURES OF *THE ST. MARTIN'S GUIDE*
Rhetorical Knowledge	
Focus on a purpose	Each writing assignment chapter in Part One offers extensive discussion of the purpose(s) for the genre of writing covered in that chapter.
Respond to the needs of different audiences	Each chapter in Part One discusses the need to consider one's audience for the particular genre covered in that chapter. In Chapters 6–10, which cover argument, there is also extensive discussion of the need to anticipate opposing positions and readers' objections to the writer's thesis.
Respond appropriately to different kinds of rhetorical situations	Each chapter in Part One gives detailed advice on responding to a particular rhetorical situation, from remembering an event (Chapter 2) to analyzing stories (Chapter 10).
Use conventions of format and structure appropriate to the rhetorical situation	Each chapter in Part One points out features of effectively structured writing, and the Guides to Writing help students systematically develop their own effective structures. Document design is covered in the Guide to Writing in each of these chapters, as well as in a dedicated Chapter 21, "Designing Documents," and in a new Chapter 22, "Writing in Business and Scientific Genres."
Adopt appropriate voice, tone, and level of formality	Many of the Sentence Strategies in each chapter in Part One deal with these issues. Also, see purpose and audience coverage mentioned previously.
Understand how genres shape reading and writing	Each chapter in Part One offers student and professional readings accompanied by annotations, questions, and commentary that draw students' attention to the key features of the genre and stimulate ideas for writing. Each chapter's Guide to Writing offers detailed, step-by-step advice for writing in the genre and for offering constructive peer criticism. In addition, In College Courses, In the Community, and In the Workplace sections, which open each Part One chapter, as well as Playing with Genre at the end of each Guide to Reading, show how the various genres are used outside the composition course.

(continued)

DESIRED STUDENT OUTCOMES	RELEVANT FEATURES OF *THE ST. MARTIN'S GUIDE*
Rhetorical Knowledge (continued)	
Write in several genres	The Guides to Writing in each of the nine chapters in Part One offer specific advice on writing to remember an event; to profile a person, activity, or place; to explain a concept; to analyze opposing positions and find common ground; to argue a position; to propose a solution; to justify an evaluation; to speculate about causes; and to analyze literature. In addition, Chapter 22 covers business and scientific genres, and Chapters 23–26 cover research strategies that many students will use while writing in the genres covered in Part One.
Critical Thinking, Reading, and Writing	
Use writing and reading for inquiry, learning, thinking, and communicating	Each Writing Assignment chapter in Part One emphasizes the connection between reading and writing in a particular genre: Each chapter begins with a group of readings whose apparatus introduces students to thinking about the features of the genre; then a Guide to Writing leads them through the process of applying these features to an essay of their own. Chapter 11, "A Catalog of Invention Strategies," and Chapter 12, "A Catalog of Reading Strategies," prompt students to engage actively in invention and reading. Other Part Two chapters include coverage of specific invention, reading, and writing strategies useful in a variety of genres.
Understand a writing assignment as a series of tasks, including finding, evaluating, analyzing, and synthesizing appropriate primary and secondary sources	The Guides to Writing in each chapter in Part One break writing assignments down into doable focused thinking and writing activities that engage students in the recursive process of invention and research to find, analyze, and synthesize information and ideas. Research sections teach specific strategies of evaluating and integrating source material. Chapter 12, "A Catalog of Reading Strategies," covers various strategies useful in working with sources, including annotating, summarizing, and synthesizing. Chapter 26, "Using Sources to Support Your Ideas," offers detailed coverage of finding, evaluating, using, and acknowledging primary and secondary sources, while Chapter 23, "Planning a Research Project," instructs students on creating an annotated bibliography.
Integrate their own ideas with those of others	Chapter 26, "Using Sources to Support Your Ideas," offers detailed advice on how to integrate and introduce quotations, how to cite paraphrases and summaries so as to distinguish them from the writer's own ideas, and how to avoid plagiarism. Sentence strategies and research coverage in several Part One chapters offer additional support.
Understand the relationships among language, knowledge, and power	Make Connections, a recurring section in the apparatus following the professional readings in Part One chapters, encourages students to put what they've read in the context of the world they live in. These preliminary reflections come into play in the Guides to Writing, in which students are asked to draw on their experiences in college, community, and career in order to begin writing. Thinking Critically sections, which conclude Part One chapters, ask students to reconsider what they have learned, often in a social/political context.

DESIRED STUDENT OUTCOMES	RELEVANT FEATURES OF *THE ST. MARTIN'S GUIDE*
Processes	
Be aware that it usually takes multiple drafts to create and complete a successful text	The need for a critical reading of a draft and for revision is emphasized in Chapter 1 as well as in the Guides to Writing in each chapter of Part One. Case studies of particular students' writing processes are offered in Writer at Work sections in each Part One chapter.
Develop flexible strategies for generating ideas, revising, editing, and proofreading	The Guides to Writing in each Part One chapter offer genre-specific coverage of invention and research, getting a critical reading of a draft, revising, editing, and proofreading. Also in each Part One chapter, Ways In invention activities encourage students to start from their strengths, and Starting Points and Troubleshooting charts offer specific, targeted advice for students with different challenges. A dedicated Chapter 11, "A Catalog of Invention Strategies," offers numerous helpful suggestions for idea generation.
Understand writing as an open process that permits writers to use later invention and rethinking to revise their work	The Guides to Writing in each Part One chapter offer extensive, genre-specific advice on rethinking and revising at multiple stages. Ways In activities, Starting Points charts, and Troubleshooting charts in Part One chapters encourage students to discover, review, and revise their own process(es) of writing.
Understand the collaborative and social aspects of writing processes	Each chapter in Part One includes several opportunities for and guides to collaboration: Practicing activities at the beginning of the chapter, Make Connections activities after the readings, and, in the Guides to Writing, Test Your Choice activities and the Critical Reading Guide.
Learn to critique their own and others' works	The Critical Reading Guide and Revising sections in the Guides to Writing in each Part One chapter offer students specific advice on constructively criticizing — and praising — their own work and the work of their classmates. Peer review is also covered in depth in Chapter 32, "Working with Others."
Learn to balance the advantages of relying on others with the responsibility of doing their part	This goal is implicit in several collaborative activities: Practicing activities at the beginning of the chapter, Make Connections activities after the readings, and, in the Guides to Writing, Test Your Choice activities and the Critical Reading Guide. Group work is also covered in depth in Chapter 32, "Working with Others."
Use a variety of technologies to address a range of audiences	Each chapter in Part One includes e-Pages, as well as Playing with Genre boxes that demonstrate how purpose and medium interact. Sidebars provide information and advice about grammar- and spell-checkers and software-based commenting tools. See also Chapters 24 and 25 for extensive coverage of finding, evaluating, and using print and electronic resources and of responsibly using the Internet, e-mail, and online communities for research, and Chapter 22, which offers advice on creating Web sites. Finally, the *Guide*'s electronic ancillaries include a robust companion Web site and an e-book.

(continued)

DESIRED STUDENT OUTCOMES	RELEVANT FEATURES OF *THE ST. MARTIN'S GUIDE*
Knowledge of Conventions	
Learn common formats for different kinds of texts	Document design is covered in a dedicated Chapter 21 as well as in two sections in each of the Writing Assignment chapters in Part One. Examples of specific formats for a range of texts appear on pp. 731–38 (research paper); p. 653 (memo); p. 655 (business letter); p. 656 (e-mail); p. 658 (résumé); p. 660 (job application letter); pp. 662–63 (lab report); and pp. 649–50 (table, diagram, graph, chart, map, and other figures).
Develop knowledge of genre conventions ranging from structure and paragraphing to tone and mechanics	Each chapter in Part One presents several basic features of a specific genre, which are introduced up front and then consistently reinforced throughout the chapter. Genre-specific issues of structure, paragraphing, tone, and mechanics are also addressed in the Sentence Strategies and Editing and Proofreading sections of each Guide to Writing.
Practice appropriate means of documenting their work	Chapter 26 offers detailed advice on how to integrate and introduce quotations, how to cite paraphrases and summaries so as to distinguish them from the writer's own ideas, and how to avoid plagiarism. Chapters 27 and 28 offer coverage of MLA and APA documentation in addition to an annotated sample student research paper. Chapter 20, "Analyzing Visuals," also offers a complete student paper with MLA documentation. In addition, research sections in each Guide to Writing in the Part One chapters help students with the details of using and appropriately documenting sources by providing genre-specific examples of what (and what not) to do.
Control such surface features as syntax, grammar, punctuation, and spelling	Genre-specific editing and proofreading advice is given in the Editing and Proofreading section in each chapter in Part One. The full version of the *Guide* also includes a concise yet remarkably comprehensive handbook that covers syntax, grammar, punctuation, and spelling.

Acknowledgments

We owe an enormous debt to all the rhetoricians and composition specialists whose theory, research, and pedagogy have informed *The St. Martin's Guide to Writing*. We would be adding many pages to an already long book if we were to name everyone to whom we are indebted; suffice it to say that we have been eclectic in our borrowing.

We must also acknowledge immeasurable lessons learned from all the writers, professional and student alike, whose work we analyzed and whose writing we used in this and earlier editions.

So many instructors and students have contributed ideas and criticism over the years. The members of the advisory board for the tenth edition, a group of dedicated composition instructors from across the country, have provided us with extensive insights and suggestions on the ninth edition and have given us the benefit of their advice on new readings and other new features for the tenth edition. For their many contributions, we would like to thank Lisa Bickmore, Salt Lake Community College; Mary Brantley, Holmes Community College–Ridgeland; Jo Ann Buck, Guilford Technical Community College; Wallace Cleaves, University of California–Riverside; Leona Fisher, Chaffey College; Gwen Graham, Holmes Junior College–Grenada; Lesa Hildebrand, Triton College; Stephanie Kay, University of California–Riverside; Donna Nelson-Beene, Bowling Green State University; Gail Odette, Baton Rouge Community College; Gray Scott, Texas Woman's University; and David Taylor, St. Louis Community College.

Many other instructors have also helped us improve the book. For responding to detailed questionnaires about the ninth edition, we thank Yolanda Ainsworth, University of Texas at El Paso; Kara Poe Alexander, Baylor University; Amy Azul, Mt. San Antonio College; Melissa Batai, Triton College; Jacqueline Blackwell, Thomas Nelson Community College; Vanessa M. Cavett, Holmes Community College–Ridgeland Sherry Cisler, Arizona State University; Susan Marie Cruea, Bowling Green State University; James Dail, Riverside Community College; Heath A. Diehl, Bowling Green State University; Leona Fisher, Chaffey College; MacGregor Frank, Guilford Technical Community College; Patricia L. Golder, Victor Valley College; Valerie A. Gray, Harrisburg Area Community College; David R. Hammontree, Jackson Community College; Anne Helms, Alamance Community College; Lesa Hildebrand, Triton College; Richard Hishmeh, Palomar College; Dawn Hubbell-Staeble, Bowling Green State University; Rick Jones, South Suburban College; Lucinda Ligget, Ivy Tech Community College; Gwen W. Macallister, Covenant College; Kate McConnell, Ivy Tech Community College; Sara E. McFarland, Northwestern State University; Linda McHenry, Fort Hays State University; C. Liegh McInnis, Jackson State University; David Michael Merchant, Louisiana Tech University; Caroline Nobile, Edinboro University of Pennsylvania; Jennifer L. Odom, John Tyler Community College; Clayann Gilliam Panetta, Christian Brothers University; Gordon Petry, Bradley University; Kim Salrin, Bradley University; Marguerite Anne Samuels, Cecil College; Graham (Gray) Scott, Texas Woman's University; Frank Shimerdla, Metropolitan Community College; Wanda Synstelien, Southwest Minnesota State University; Ruthe Thompson, Southwest Minnesota State University; Patrick Tompkins, John Tyler Community College; Susan Waldman, Leeward Community and College; and Carmen Wong, John Tyler Community College.

For helping us select new readings and providing feedback on our revisions, we thank Yolanda Ainsworth, University of Texas at El Paso; John Alberti, Northern Kentucky University; Kara Poe Alexander, Baylor University; James Allen, College of DuPage; Laura Baltuska, South Suburban College; Ka'ran Bechet-Benjamin, Thomas Nelson Community College; Paul Beehler, University of California–Riverside; Tammie Bob, College of DuPage; Kristin Brunnemer, Pierce College; Cagle, University of Nevada–Las Vegas; Gary Cale, Jackson Community College; Stacey Coulter, Holmes Community College; Steven P. Deaton, Holmes Community College–Ridgeland; Darren DeFrain, Wichita State University; Tammy DiBenedetto, Riverside College; Joanne Diddlemeyer, Tidewater Community College; Marilu dos

Santos, South Suburban College; Anne Dvorak, Metropolitan Community College–Longview; Christopher Ervin, Western Kentucky University; Janis Flint-Ferguson, Gordon College; MacGregor Frank, Guilford Technical Community College; Linda Gannon, College of Southern Nevada; Valerie Gray, Harrisburg Area Community College; Kathleen Gurnett, University of California–Riverside; Anne Helms, Alamance Community College; Lesa Hildebrand, Triton College; Dawn Hubbell-Staeble, Bowling Green State University; Kim Jameson, Oklahoma City Community College; Peggy Jolly, University of Alabama at Birmingham; Rick Jones, South Suburban College; Nadene Keene, Indiana University–Kokomo; Jessica Kidd, University of Alabama; Lucinda Ligget, Ivy Tech Community College; Carol Marion, Guilford Technical Community College; Linda Matthews, South Suburban College; Kate McConnell, Ivy Tech Community College; Sarah E. McFarland, Northwestern State University; Mary McMullen-Light, Metropolitan Community College–Longview; David Michael Merchant, Louisiana Tech University; Troy Nordman, Butler Community College; Gail Odette, Baton Rouge Community College; Matt Oliver, Old Dominion University; Staci Perryman-Clark, Western Michigan University; Kathryn Raign, University of North Texas; Amanda Rzicznek, Bowling Green State University; Kym Snelling, Metropolitan Community College; Cathy Stablein, College of DuPage; Bonnie Startt, Tidewater Community College; Candace Stewart, Ohio State University; Elissa Weeks Stogner, Loyola University; Deana St. Peter, Guilford Technical Community College; Jamey Trotter, Arapahoe Community College; Janice Vierk, Metropolitan Community College; Melanie Wagner, Lake-Sumter Community College; Gwenna Weshinskey, College of DuPage; Jeana West, Murray State College; Brian Whaley, Utah Valley University; Lynn Wolstadt, South Suburban College; and Hui Wu, University of Texas at Tyler.

For this new edition of the *Guide,* we also gratefully acknowledge the special contributions of Gray Scott, who made recommendations of reading selections, helped draft some of the reading apparatus, and was generally available as a sounding board and a font of good advice; Natasha Cooper, Syracuse University, who provided expert advice on the revised coverage of research; Christine Garbett, Bowling Green State University, who wrote all comprehension quizzes for the reading selections that appear on the Web site and in the instructor's manual; Beth Castrodale, who helped find e-Pages selections and wrote the apparatus to accompany them; and Leona Fisher, who revised and updated the instructor's manual. Finally, we are especially grateful to the student authors for allowing us to use their work in *Sticks and Stones* and the *Guide*.

We want to thank many people at Bedford/St. Martin's, especially Senior Editor Jane Carter, without whom this book would not have been written; Peter Jacoby, who worked miracles keeping all the details straight and keeping us on schedule; Kimberly Hampton, without whom we would have no e-Pages or x-Book; and Amy Saxon, who single-handedly managed the reviewing process, while also editing many of the book's ancillaries, including *Sticks and Stones* and the *Guide* Web site.

Diana George made many valuable contributions to this revision with her careful copyediting, as did Jamie Thaman and Lori Lewis with their meticulous proofreading, and Melanie Belkin, with her indexing of the text. Sue Brown, Shuli Traub, and Jenny Peterson kept the whole process running smoothly.

Thanks also to the immensely talented design team—book designer Jerilyn Bockorick as well as Bedford/St. Martin's art directors, Lucy Krikorian and Anna Palchik—for making the tenth edition the most beautiful and most functional yet. Our gratitude also goes to Linda Winters and Barbara Hernandez for their hard work clearing permissions, and Martha Friedman and Debbie Needleman for their imaginative photo research and quick work clearing permissions for the e-Pages.

We also want to thank Erica Appel, Director of Development; Karen Henry, Editor in Chief; and Leasa Burton, Senior Executive Editor—all of whom offered valued advice at many critical stages in the process. Thanks as well to Joan Feinberg and Tom Scotty for their adroit leadership of Macmillan Higher Education, Denise Wydra for her skillful guidance of Bedford/St. Martin's, and Marketing Director Karen Soeltz and Executive Marketing Manager Molly Parke—along with the extraordinarily talented and hardworking sales staff—for their tireless efforts on behalf of the *Guide*.

Rise dedicates this book to two young women whose writing she very much looks forward to reading: Amalia Serenity Axelrod-Delcampo and Sophie Amistad Axelrod-Delcampo.

You Get More Choices for *The St. Martin's Guide to Writing*

Bedford/St. Martin's offers resources and format choices that help you and your students get even more out of the book and your course. To learn more about or order any of the following products, contact your Bedford/St. Martin's sales representative, e-mail sales support (sales_support@bfwpub.com), or visit **bedfordstmartins.com/theguide/catalog**.

Choose from Alternative Formats of *The St. Martin's Guide*

Bedford/St. Martin's offers a range of affordable formats, allowing students to choose the one that works for them. For details, visit **bedfordstmartins.com/theguide/formats**.

- *Hardcover or paperback, with or without Handbook*   For the first time, *The St. Martin's Guide to Writing* (with Handbook) is available as both a hardcover (cloth) or paperback. To order the hardcover edition (with Handbook), use ISBN 978-1-4576-0442-3; to order the paperback edition (with Handbook), use ISBN 978-1-4576-3250-1. To order *The St. Martin's Guide to Writing,* Short Tenth Edition (without Handbook), use ISBN 978-1-4576-0450-8.

- *Loose-leaf edition*   The loose-leaf edition does not have a traditional binding; its pages are loose and two-hole punched to provide flexibility and a low price to students. To order the loose-leaf edition, use ISBN 978-1-4576-4081-0.

- *E-book options*   *The St. Martin's Guide to Writing* is now available as an **x-Book** that integrates extra interactive content (like reading quizzes and student models) with social tools, letting instructors and students get into your book in a whole new way. Pages come alive with activities that students can complete online and multimodal readings with video, animation, audio, and interactive elements. To learn more about the new x-Book, visit **bedfordstmartins.com/xbook**.

  The St. Martin's Guide is also available as a Bedford e-Book to Go and in **other popular e-book formats** for computers, tablets, and e-readers. For more details, visit **bedfordstmartins.com/ebooks**.

Choose the Flexible Bedford e-Portfolio

Make it easy for students to showcase their work, whether for their class, their job, or their friends. With straightforward, flexible assessment tools, instructors can easily map rubrics and learning outcomes to student work or simply invite students to start their collections. Visit **bedfordstmartins.com/eportfolio**.

Watch Peer Review in Action

Eli Review gives teachers a real-time window into what's happening in drafts and feedback. *Eli* helps writers shape concrete revision plans and motivates reviewers to up their game. Visit **bedfordstmartins.com/eli**.

Bring It All Together with the *x-Book for The St. Martin's Guide*

Bedford's new x-Book integrates the tools and content that writers—and their teachers—need to develop and assess their work. The *x-Book for The St. Martin's Guide* includes LearningCurve adaptive quizzing, multimodal readings, and additional quizzes and resources that can be added to your table of contents.

Select Value Packages

Add more value to your text by packaging one of the following resources with *The St. Martin's Guide to Writing*, Tenth Edition or Short Tenth Edition. To learn more about package options for any of the following products, contact your Bedford/St. Martin's sales representative or visit **bedfordstmartins.com/theguide/catalog**.

Re:Writing Plus. Because composition is getting redefined—when, where, and how we see it—Bedford/St. Martin's is committed to developing new kinds of tools for the changing classroom. The first-ever peer review game; videos of real writers talking about the writing process; the most innovative and interactive help with writing a paragraph; tutorials and practice with writing and research that show how they work in your students' real-world experience; hundreds of models of writing across the disciplines; and hundreds of readings: These resources meet composition where it happens,—online, all the time. To order *Re:Writing Plus* packaged with the *St. Martin's Guide*, please use the following ISBNs:

- Tenth Edition (paper),
  ISBN 978-1-4576-4618-8
- Short Tenth Edition,
  ISBN 978-1-4576-4613-3
- Tenth Edition (cloth),
  ISBN 978-1-4576-4612-6
- Tenth Edition (loose-leaf),
  ISBN 978-1-4576-4753-6

VideoCentral: English **(Access Card).** At 142 videos and counting, *VideoCentral: English* is the premiere collection of video content for the English classroom. With content drawn from interviews that have literally spanned the nation, our videos include some of the best writers across the literary realm, the media industries, and the academic world—writers like Ha Jin, Chitra Banerjee Divakaruni, and Frank McCourt. And they include students across the disciplines who are learning how important writing is for their success in college and beyond. Topics include every stage of the writing process, the elements of each genre, and the ways that writing has been shaped by media and technology.

- Tenth Edition (paper),
  ISBN 978-1-4576-4620-1
- Short Tenth Edition,
  ISBN 978-1-4576-4619-5
- Tenth Edition (cloth),
  ISBN 978-1-4576-4621-8
- Tenth Edition (loose-leaf),
  ISBN 978-1-4576-4751-2

i-series. Add more value to your text by choosing one of the following tutorial series, free when packaged with *The St. Martin's Guide to Writing*. This popular series presents multimedia tutorials in a flexible format—because are things you can't do in a book. To learn more about package options for any of the following products, contact your Bedford/St. Martin's sales representative or visit **bedfordstmartins .com/theguide**.

ix: visualizing composition 2.0 (available online) helps students put into practice key rhetorical and visual concepts.

- Tenth Edition (paper),
  ISBN 978-1-4576-4625-6
- Tenth Edition (cloth),
  ISBN 978-1-4576-4626-3
- Short Tenth Edition,
  ISBN 978-1-4576-4627-0
- Tenth Edition (loose-leaf),
  ISBN 978-1-4576-4749-9

i-claim: visualizing argument 2.0 (available online) offers a new way to see argument—with six multimodal tutorials, an illustrated glossary, more than fifty multimedia arguments, and integrated gradebook reporting.

- Tenth Edition (paper),
  ISBN 978-1-4576-4623-2
- Tenth Edition (cloth),
  ISBN 978-1-4576-4624-9
- Short Tenth Edition,
  ISBN 978-1-4576-4622-5
- Tenth Edition (loose-leaf),
  ISBN 978-1-4576-4752-9

i-cite: visualizing sources (available online as part of *Re:Writing Plus*) brings research to life through an animated introduction, four tutorials, and hands-on source practice.

- Tenth Edition (paper),
  ISBN 978-1-4576-4630-0
- Tenth Edition (cloth),
  ISBN 978-1-4576-4632-4
- Short Tenth Edition,
  ISBN 978-1-4576-4629-4
- Tenth Edition (loose-leaf),
  ISBN 978-1-4576-4748-2

***Sticks and Stones and Other Student Essays,* Eighth Edition.** A collection of more than forty essays written by students across the nation using earlier editions of the *Guide*. Each essay is accompanied by a headnote that spotlights some of the ways the writer uses the genre successfully, invites students to notice other achievements, and supplies context where necessary. *Sticks and Stones* is available for **free** when packaged with new copies of the *Guide*.

- Tenth Edition (paper),
  ISBN 978-1-4576-5438-1
- Tenth Edition (cloth),
  ISBN 978-1-4576-5415-2
- Short Tenth Edition,
  ISBN 978-1-4576-5416-9
- Tenth Edition (loose-leaf),
  ISBN 978-1-4576-5437-4

Access Free and Open Resources for Students at bedfordstmartins.com/theguide

The **student site** offers free and open resources for *The St. Martin's Guide to Writing,* including the following:

- Grammar, writing, and research exercises from *Exercise Central* and Diana Hacker, plus writing exercises and Andrea Lunsford's list of the top twenty most common errors college writers make and how to correct them
- Videos of real writers
- Tutorials on designing documents, creating a Web site, avoiding plagiarism, and more
- Research resources, such as help citing sources or building a bibliography
- *Marriage 101 and Other Student Essays,* an online reader
- Document design resources

Bedford/St. Martin's Supports Instructors

You have a lot to do in your course. Bedford/St. Martin's wants to make it easy for you to find the support you need—and to get it quickly.

Instructor's Manual. Available in print (ISBN 978-1-4576-1261-9) or downloadable from our catalog or the instructor's site (**bedfordstmartins.com/theguide**), the manual features detailed plans for every chapter in the book; comprehension quizzes for every professional reading, both in the print book and in the e-Pages; strategies for teaching with *The St. Martin's Guide to Writing;* best practices for assessment; an updated bibliography in composition studies; and more.

More Resources for Instructors Teaching with *The St. Martin's Guide to Writing*, Tenth Edition. Bedford/St. Martin's supports classroom instruction with Power Point presentations offering lists of important features for each genre, critical reading guides, readings on topics from detecting plagiarism to strategies for judging teaching methods, and additional exercises for use with *The St. Martin's Guide,* Tenth Edition (with Handbook). To access these resources, visit the instructor's side of the *Guide's* Web site at **bedfordstmartins.com/theguide**.

The Elements of Teaching Writing: A Resource for Instructors in All Disciplines. Written by Katherine Gottschalk and Keith Hjortshoj, *The Elements of Teaching Writing* (ISBN 978-0-312-40683-7). provides time-saving strategies and practical guidance in a brief reference form. Drawing on their extensive experience training instructors in all disciplines to incorporate writing into their courses, Gottschalk and Hjortshoj offer reliable advice, accommodating a wide range of teaching styles and class sizes, about how to design effective writing assignments and how to respond to and evaluate student writing in any course.

TeachingCentral (**bedfordstmartins.com/teachingcentral**). Designed for the convenience of instructors, this rich Web site lists and describes Bedford/St. Martin's acclaimed print series of free professional sourcebooks, background readings, and bibliographies for teachers. In addition, *TeachingCentral* offers a host of free online resources, including the following:

- *Bits,* a blog that collects creative ideas for teaching composition from a community of teachers, scholars, authors, and editors; instructors are free to take, use, adapt, and pass the ideas around, in addition to sharing new suggestions
- *Just-in-Time Teaching* and **Adjunct Central**—downloadable syllabi, handouts, exercises, activities, assignments, teaching tips, and more, organized by resource type and by topic
- *Take 20*—a sixty-minute film for teachers, by teachers, in which twenty-two writing teachers answer twenty questions on current practices and emerging ideas in composition

Bedford Coursepacks. Available for the most common course management systems—Blackboard, Canvas, Angel, Desire2Learn, Sakai, and Moodle—Bedford coursepacks allow you to download Bedford/St. Martin's digital materials for your course easily and quickly. Visit **bedfordstmartins.com/coursepacks** for more information.

Contents

3 | Writing Profiles 58

5 Finding Common Ground 172

6 | Arguing a Position 242

9 | Speculating about Causes   402

PART 2 Critical Thinking Strategies

PART 6   Writing and Speaking to Wider Audiences

The St. Martin's Guide to Writing

1

Introduction:
Thinking about Writing

More people are writing today than ever before, and many are switching comfortably from one genre or medium to another—from tweeting to blogging to creating multimedia Web pages. Learning to be effective as a writer is a continuous process as you find yourself in new writing situations using new technologies and trying to anticipate the concerns of different audiences. "The illiterate of the 21st century will not be those who cannot read and write," futurist Alvin Toffler predicted, "but those who cannot learn, unlearn, and relearn."

Learning anything—especially learning to communicate in new ways—benefits from what we call reflection, thinking critically about *how* as well as *what* you are learning. Extensive research confirms what writers have known for a long time: that reflection makes learning easier and faster. In fact, recent studies show that writing even a few sentences about your thoughts and feelings before a high-stress paper or exam helps students reduce stress and boost performance. That is why in this chapter and throughout this book, we ask you to think about your experience as a writer, and we recommend using writing to explore and develop your ideas. The activities that conclude this chapter invite you to compose a **literacy narrative,** a multifaceted exploration of yourself as a writer.

To get started thinking about writing, we will look at some of the important contributions writing makes. Then, we'll preview how *The St. Martin's Guide to Writing* can help you become a better, more confident, and more versatile writer.

Why Write?

"Why write?" is an important basic question, especially today, when many people assume technology has eliminated the need to learn to write well. Obviously, writing enables you to communicate, but it also helps you think and learn, enhances your chances of success, contributes to your personal development, and strengthens your relationships.

Write to communicate effectively in different rhetorical situations.

Writing is a powerful means of communicating with diverse audiences in different genres and media. We use the term **rhetorical situation** to emphasize the fact that writing is social and purposeful. The rhetorical situation includes four interrelated factors:

Why?	Your *purpose* for writing
Who?	The *audience* you are addressing
What?	The *genre* or type of text you are writing
How?	The *medium* in which your text will be read

Writing with an awareness of the rhetorical situation means writing not only to express yourself but also to reach out to your readers (audience) by engaging their interest and responding to their concerns. You write to influence how your readers think and feel about a subject and, depending on the genre, perhaps also to inspire them to action.

Writing with genre awareness affects your composing decisions—what you write about (subject choice), the claims you make (thesis), how you support those claims (reasons and evidence), and how you organize it all. **Genres** are simply ways of categorizing texts—for example, we can distinguish between fiction and nonfiction; subdivide fiction into romance, mystery, and science fiction genres; or break down mystery even further into hard-boiled detective, police procedural, true crime, and classic whodunit genres. Each genre has a set of conventions or **basic features** readers expect texts in that genre to use. Although individual texts within the same genre vary a great deal—for example, no two *proposals*, even those arguing for the same solution, will be identical—they nonetheless follow a general pattern that provides a certain amount of predictability. Without such predictability, communication would be difficult, if not impossible. But these conventional patterns should not be thought of as recipes. Conventions are broad frameworks within which writers are free to be creative. Most writers, in fact, find that working within a framework makes creativity possible. Depending on the formality of the rhetorical situation and the audience's openness to innovation, writers may also play with genre conventions, remixing features of different genres to form new mash-ups, as you will see in the Playing with Genre sections of each Part One chapter.

Like genre, the medium in which you are working also affects many of your design and content choices. For example, written texts can use color, type fonts, charts, diagrams, and still images to heighten the visual impact of the text, delivering information vividly and persuasively. If you are composing Web pages or apps, you have many more options to make your text truly multimedia—for example, by adding hyperlinks, animation, audio, video, and interactivity to your written text.

Write to think.

The very act of writing—crafting and combining sentences—helps you think creatively and logically. You create new ideas by putting words together to make meaningful sentences and by linking sentences with *logical transitions,* like *however* or *because,* to form a coherent chain of meaning. Many writers equate thinking with writing: "How can I tell what I think," the novelist E. M. Forster famously wrote, "till I see what I say?" Other writers have echoed the same idea. Columnist Anna Quindlen, for example, put it this way: "As a writer, I would find out most clearly what I thought, and what I only thought I thought, when I saw it written down." Finally, here's the way physicist James Van Allen explained the connection between writing and thinking: "The mere process of writing is one of the most powerful tools we have for clarifying our own thinking."

> "How can I tell what I think," the novelist E. M. Forster famously wrote, "till I see what I say?"

Write to learn.

As a student, you are probably keenly aware of the many ways writing can help you do well in courses throughout the curriculum. The physical act of writing—from simply making notes as you read, to listing main points, to summarizing—is a potent memory aid. Writing down your rudimentary ideas and posing questions can lead to deeper understanding. *Analyzing* and *synthesizing* ideas and information from different sources can extend your learning. Most important, thinking about what you are learning and how—what are called *methodologies* in many disciplines—can open up new directions for further learning.

Write to succeed.

Writing contributes to success in school and at work. We've already suggested some of the ways writing can both help you think analytically and logically and aid your learning and remembering. In school, you need to use writing to demonstrate your learning. You will be asked to write essays *explaining* and *applying concepts* and to construct academic *arguments* using sources and other kinds of evidence. Your skill at doing these things will most likely affect your grades. Writing also helps in practical ways as you apply for internships, admission to professional school, and a job. At work, you may need to write for a variety of rhetorical situations—for example, to *evaluate* staff you supervise, to collaborate with colleagues *proposing* a new project, to e-mail suggestions for resolving conflicts or ideas about new initiatives, or to prepare year-end reports *justifying* expenditures and priorities. Just as your achievement in school is influenced by your ability to write well, so, too, may your professional success depend on your ability to write effectively to different audiences in varied genres and media.

Write to know yourself and connect to other people.

Writing can help you grow as an individual and also help you maintain and build relationships with friends and colleagues. Journal writing has long been used as a means of self-discovery. Many people blog for the same reason. Becoming an author confers *authority,* giving you confidence to assert your ideas and opinions. Whether you're tweeting to let friends know what's happening, posting comments on a Web site, taking part in a class discussion, or participating in political debate and decision making, writing enables you to offer your own point of view and invites others to share theirs in return.

How *The St. Martin's Guide to Writing* Helps You Learn to Write

There are many myths about writing and writers. Perhaps the most enduring myth is that people who are good at writing do not have to learn to write — they just naturally know how. Writing may be easier and more rewarding for some people, but no one is born knowing how to write. Writing must be learned. To learn to write, as Stephen King explained, "you must do two things above all others: read a lot and write a lot." That is precisely how *The St. Martin's Guide to Writing* works — by providing both a Guide to Reading and a Guide to Writing for each genre you will be writing.

> To learn to write, as Stephen King explained, "you must do two things above all others: read a lot and write a lot."

Learn to write by using the Guides to Reading.

These guides teach you to analyze how texts work in particular rhetorical situations. By analyzing several texts in the genre you will be writing in, you can see how writers employ the genre's basic features differently to achieve their purpose with their audience. In other words, you will see in action the many strategies writers can use to achieve their goals.

Learn to write by using the Guides to Writing.

These guides help you apply to your own writing what you are learning from reading and analyzing examples of the genre. They provide a scaffold to support your writing as you develop a repertoire of strategies for using the genre's basic features to achieve your purpose with your audience.

Each Guide to Writing begins with a Starting Points chart that will enable you to find answers to your composing questions. You can follow your own course, dipping into the Guide for help when you need it, or you can follow the sequence of exploratory activities, from Writing a Draft through Evaluating the Draft to Improving the Draft. Although many people assume that good writers begin with their first sentence and go right through to their last sentence, professional writers know that writing is a process of discovery. Most writers begin with preliminary planning and exploratory writing that at some point turns into a rough draft. Then, as the draft takes shape, they may reconsider the organization, do additional research to fill in gaps, rewrite passages that need clarification, or continue drafting. Essayist Dave Barry describes his typical writing process this way: "It's a matter of piling a little piece here and a little piece there, fitting them together, going on to the next part, then going back and gradually shaping the whole piece into something."

A challenge for most writers comes when they have a draft but don't know how to improve it. It is sometimes hard for them to see what a draft actually says as opposed to what they want to convey. Instructors often set aside class time for a draft workshop or ask students to do an online peer critique. Each chapter's Guide to Writing includes a Critical Reading Guide for this purpose. You may find that reading someone else's draft can be especially helpful to you as a writer because it's often easier to recognize problems and see how to fix them in someone else's draft than it is to see similar problems in your own writing. The Critical Reading Guide is also keyed to a Troubleshooting Guide that will help you find ways to revise and improve your draft. The Guide to Writing also includes advice on proofreading and editing that you can use to check for sentence-level errors.

> Essayist Dave Barry describes his typical writing process this way: "It's a matter of piling a little piece here and a little piece there, fitting them together, going on to the next part, then going back and gradually shaping the whole piece into something."

THINKING CRITICALLY

In addition to modeling good writing and providing guides for reading and writing, *The St. Martin's Guide to Writing* helps you think critically about your writing. Each writing assignment chapter in Part One of the *Guide* includes many opportunities for you to think critically and reflect on your understanding of the rhetorical situation in which you are writing. In addition, a section titled Thinking Critically concludes each chapter, giving you an opportunity to look back and reflect on how you used your writing process creatively and how you expanded your understanding of the genre. The following activity gives you the opportunity to reflect on your own experience with reading and writing, your own literacy narrative. Why not start now to become a better writer by thinking critically about your own experience?

REFLECTION

A Literacy Narrative
Write several pages telling about your experience with writing. Consider the following suggestions:

- Recall an early experience of writing: What did you write? Did anyone read it? What kind of feedback did you get? How did you feel about yourself?
- Think of a turning point when your attitude toward writing changed or crystallized. What happened? What changed?

- Recall a person — a teacher, a classmate, a family member, a published writer, or someone else — who influenced your writing, for good or ill. How was your writing affected?

- Cast yourself as the main character of a story about writing. How would you describe yourself — as a talented writer, as someone who struggles to write well, or somewhere in between? Consider your trajectory, or *narrative arc*: Over the years, would you say you have showed steady improvement? Ups and downs? More downs than ups? A decline?

- Think about literacy more broadly and write about how you acquired academic literacy (perhaps focusing on how you learned to think, talk, and write as a scientist or a historian), workplace literacy (perhaps focusing on how you learned to communicate effectively with customers or managers), sports literacy (perhaps as a player, coach, or fan), music literacy (perhaps as a performer or composer), community literacy (perhaps focusing on how you learned to communicate with people of different ages or with people who speak different languages or dialects), or any other kind of literacy you have mastered.

PART 1
Writing
Activities

2
Remembering an Event

Writing about the memorable events and people in our lives can be exhilarating. This kind of writing can lead us to think deeply about why certain experiences are meaningful and continue to touch us. It can help us understand the cultural influences that helped shape who we are and what we value. It can also give us an opportunity to represent ourselves and connect with others. In college courses, we can use our experience to better understand what we are studying; in the community, we can use personal stories for inspiration; and in the workplace, we can use experience to catalyze needed change.

IN COLLEGE COURSES

For a linguistics course, a student writes an essay analyzing a recent conversation with her brother in light of a book she read for the class: Deborah Tannen's *Gender and Discourse*, in which Tannen argues that when discussing problems, women tend to focus on the problem and their feelings about it, while men typically cut short talk about feelings and focus on possible solutions. The student begins her essay by reconstructing the conversation with her brother, quoting some dialogue from her diary and paraphrasing other parts from memory. Then she analyzes the conversation. Using Tannen's ideas, she discovers that what bothered her about the conversation was less its content than her brother's way of communicating.

IN THE COMMUNITY

As part of a local history series in a newspaper serving a small western ranching community, an amateur historian helps an elderly rancher write about the winter of 1938, when a six-foot snowfall isolated the rancher's family for nearly a month. The rancher talks about how he, his wife, and the couple's infant son survived, including an account of how he snowshoed eight miles to get word to relatives. The details the rancher includes, like the suspenseful description of his exhausting trek, make the event vivid and dramatic for the newspaper's readers.

IN THE WORKPLACE

A respected longtime regional manager gives the keynote speech at the highway department's statewide meeting on workplace safety. He opens his speech with a dramatic recounting of a confrontation he had with a disgruntled employee who complained bitterly about his work schedule and threatened the safety of the manager and his family. Setting the scene (a lonely office after hours) to help audience members enter into his experience, he describes the taste of fear in his mouth and his relief when a contractor entered the office. The manager follows the anecdote with data showing the frequency of such workplace incidents nationwide and concludes by calling for new departmental guidelines on how to defuse such confrontations effectively.

In this chapter, we ask you to write about a remembered event that will engage readers and that has significance for you. From reading and analyzing the selections in the Guide to Reading that follows, you will learn how to make your own story interesting, even exciting, to read. The Guide to Writing later in the chapter will support you as you compose your remembered event essay, showing you ways to use the basic features of the genre to tell your story vividly and dramatically, entertaining readers but also giving them insight into the event's significance—its meaning and importance—in your life.

| PRACTICING THE GENRE |

Telling a Story

The success of remembered event writing depends on how well the story is told. Some memorable events are inherently dramatic, but most are not. The challenge is to make the story entertaining and meaningful for readers. The most effective autobiographical stories make readers care about the storyteller and curious to know what happened. To practice creating an engaging story based on a memorable event in your life, get together with two or three other students and follow these guidelines:

Part 1.   Choose a memorable event that you feel comfortable describing to this group. (Make sure you can tell your story in just a few minutes.) Take five minutes to sketch out a plan: Think about what makes the event memorable (for example, a conflict with someone else or within yourself, the strong or mixed feelings it evokes, the cultural attitudes it reflects). What will be the turning point, or climax, of the story, and how will you build up to it? Then take turns telling your stories.

Part 2.   After telling your stories, discuss what you learned about the genre:

- **What did you learn about the genre from others' stories?** To think about purpose and audience in the genre of autobiography, tell each other what struck you most on hearing each other's stories. For example, identify something in the story that was moving, suspenseful, edgy, or funny. What in the story, if anything, helped you identify or sympathize with the storyteller? What do you think the point or significance of the story is — in other words, what makes the event so memorable?

- **What did you learn about the genre from constructing your own autobiographical story?** With the others in your group, compare your thoughts on what was easiest and hardest about telling the story: for example, choosing an event, portraying the conflict and making the story dramatic, selecting what to put in and leave out, or letting the story speak for itself without explaining.

Analyzing Remembered Event Essays

As you read the selections in this chapter, you will see how different authors craft stories about an important event in their lives. Analyzing how these writers tell a dramatic, well-focused story, use vivid, specific description to enliven their writing, and choose the details and words that enable them to convey their perspective on the event will help you see how you can employ these same techniques when writing your own autobiographical story.

Determine the writer's purpose and audience.

Many people write about important events in their lives to archive their memories and to learn something about themselves. Keep in mind, however, that unless you are writing in your diary, remembered event writing is a public genre meant to be read by others. So it is important to think about self-presentation as well as self-discovery.

Memorable events are by definition full of potential meaning, and insightful readers often see larger themes or deeper implications—what we call **significance**—beyond those the writer consciously intends to communicate or even acknowledges. This richness of meaning makes autobiographical writing fascinating to read and to write. When reading the selections about remembered events that follow, ask yourself the following questions about the writer's purpose and audience:

- What seems to be the writer's main *purpose*—for example, to understand what happened and why, perhaps to confront unconscious and possibly uncomplimentary motives; to relive an intense experience, perhaps to work through complex and ambivalent feelings; to win over readers, perhaps to justify or rationalize choices made, actions taken, or words used; to reflect on cultural attitudes at the time the event occurred, perhaps in contrast to current ways of thinking?

- What does the author assume about the *audience*—for example, that readers will have had similar experiences and therefore appreciate what the writer went through and not judge the writer too harshly; that they will see the writer as innocent, well meaning, a victim, or something else; that readers will laugh with and not at the writer, seeing the writer's failings as amusing foibles and not serious shortcomings; that readers will reflect on the cultural context in which the event occurred and how it influenced the writer?

Assess the genre's basic features.

As you read remembered event essays in this chapter, you will see how different authors incorporate the basic features of the genre. The examples that follow are taken from the reading selections that appear later in this Guide to Reading.

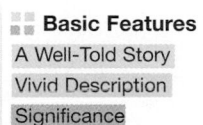

Basic Features
A Well-Told Story
Vivid Description
Significance

A WELL-TOLD STORY

Read first to enjoy the story. The best autobiographical stories are first and foremost a pleasure to read.

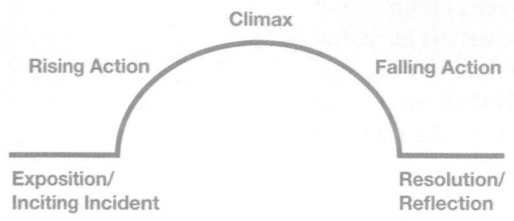

Exposition/Inciting Incident: Background information, scene setting, or an introduction to the characters *or* an initial conflict or problem that sets off the action, arousing curiosity and suspense

Rising Action: The developing crisis, possibly leading to other conflicts and complications

Climax: The emotional high point, often a turning point marking a change for good or ill

Falling Action: Resolution of tension and unraveling of conflicts; may include a final surprise

Resolution/Reflection: Conflicts come to an end but may not be fully resolved, and writer reflects on the event's meaning and importance—its significance

FIGURE 2.1   Dramatic Arc
The shape of the arc varies. Not all stories devote the same amount of space to each element, and some may omit an element or include more than one.

Examine the story to see if it is well told. Does it let readers into the narrator's point of view, enabling us to empathize with the writer? Does it arouse curiosity and suspense by structuring the narrative around conflict? Does it lead to a change or discovery of some kind? These elements can be visualized in the form of a **dramatic arc** (see Figure 2.1), which you can analyze to see how a narrative creates and resolves dramatic tension.

Look also to see how *dialogue* is used to portray people, help readers understand their point of view, and heighten the drama. There are three ways to present dialogue: by quoting, paraphrasing, or summarizing. **Quoting** dramatizes the dialogue through a combination of actual spoken words and descriptive *speaker tags* that surround them:

Speaker tag   "You stupid kids," he began perfunctorily. (Dillard, par. 18)

Paraphrasing reports the content of what was said but doesn't quote the actual words or use quotation marks:

Ernie said he was going to take a quick look in the cave and invited me to come along. I politely declined. (Ruprecht, par. 5)

Summarizing gives the gist without the detail:

I was read my rights and questioned. (Brandt, par. 19)

VIVID DESCRIPTION OF PEOPLE AND PLACES

Look for descriptions of people and places to see how the describing strategies of *naming, detailing,* and *comparing* are used to portray vividly what people look like and how they dress, gesture, and talk as well as to convey graphic sensory images showing what the narrator saw, heard, smelled, touched, and tasted. For example, take a look at Desmond-Harris's description of people and Dillard's description of a place:

My hair has recently been straightened with my first (and last) relaxer and a Gold 'N Hot flatiron on too high a setting. Hers is slicked back with the mixture of Herbal Essences and Blue Magic that we formulated in a bathroom laboratory. (Desmond-Harris, par. 6)

The cars' tires laid behind them on the snowy street a complex trail of beige chunks like crenellated castle walls. I had stepped on some earlier; they squeaked. (Dillard, par. 5)

Naming
Detailing
Comparing

For more on describing strategies, see Chapter 15.

AUTOBIOGRAPHICAL SIGNIFICANCE

Read finally to understand the story's autobiographical significance. This is the point the writer is trying to make—the purpose for writing to a particular audience. Notice how writers convey mixed or ambivalent feelings, how they acknowledge still-unresolved conflict, how they avoid making the story seem clichéd or sentimental.

To convey the richness of meaning that makes the event worth writing about, writers tell as well as show

- by *remembering feelings and thoughts* from the time the event took place:

  The thought of going to jail terrified me. . . . I felt alone and scared." (Brandt, par. 17)

  It was an immense discovery, pounding into my hot head with every sliding, joyous step, that this ordinary adult evidently knew what I thought only children . . . knew. (Dillard, par. 13)

- by reflecting on the past from the *present perspective*:

  I mourned Tupac's death then, and continue to mourn him now, because his music represents the years when I was both forced and privileged to confront what it meant to be black. (Desmond-Harris, par. 9)

- by choosing details and words that create a *dominant impression*: Brandt, for example, describes her rapidly changing feelings: naïve optimism, fear, humiliation, excitement, shame, worry, relief. This cinematic technique of quick cuts from one feeling or thought to another conveys the volatility of her emotions.

Readings

Jean Brandt | *Calling Home*

AS A FIRST-YEAR college student, Jean Brandt wrote about a memorable event that occurred when she was thirteen. Reflecting on how she felt at the time, Brandt writes, "I was afraid, embarrassed, worried, mad." In disclosing her tumultuous and contradictory remembered feelings, Brandt makes her story dramatic and resonant. Even if readers have not had a similar experience, they are likely to empathize with Brandt and grasp the significance of this event in her life.

To learn about Brandt's process of writing this essay, turn to A Writer at Work on pp. 51–56. How did trying out dialogues help Brandt discover the central conflict and significance of her story?

As you read, do the following:

- Look for places where Brandt lets us know how she felt at the time the event occurred.
- Identify the parts of the dramatic arc that she emphasizes or complicates, that she downplays or eliminates.
- Consider the questions in the margin. Your instructor may ask you to post answers to these questions to a class blog or discussion board or bring them to class.

⠿ Basic Features
Well-Told Story
Vivid Description
Significance

1   As we all piled into the car, I knew it was going to be a fabulous day. My grand-mother was visiting for the holidays; and she and I, along with my older brother and sister, Louis and Susan, were setting off for a day of last-minute Christmas shopping. On the way to the mall, we sang Christmas carols, chattered, and laughed. With Christmas only two days away, we were caught up with holiday spirit. I felt light-headed and full of joy. I loved shopping — especially at Christmas.

How well do these descriptive details help you visualize the scene?

2   The shopping center was swarming with frantic last-minute shoppers like our-selves. We went first to the General Store, my favorite. It carried mostly knickknacks and other useless items which nobody needs but buys anyway. I was thirteen years old at the time, and things like buttons and calendars and posters would catch my fancy. This day was no different. The object of my desire was a 75-cent Snoopy button. Snoopy was the latest. If you owned anything with the Peanuts on it, you were "in." But since I was supposed to be shopping for gifts for other people and not myself, I couldn't decide what to do. I went in search of my sister for her opinion. I pushed my way through throngs of people to the back of the store where I found Susan. I asked her if she thought I should buy the button. She said it was cute and if I wanted it to go ahead and buy it.

What is your first impression of Brandt?

3   When I got back to the Snoopy section, I took one look at the lines at the cashiers and knew I didn't want to wait thirty minutes to buy an item worth less than one dollar. I walked back to the basket where I found the button and was about to drop it when suddenly, instead, I took a quick glance around, assured myself no one could see, and slipped the button into the pocket of my sweatshirt.

How do these action verbs (highlighted) and dialogue contribute to the drama?

4   I hesitated for a moment, but once the item was in my pocket, there was no turn-ing back. I had never before stolen anything; but what was done was done. A few sec-onds later, my sister appeared and asked, "So, did you decide to buy the button?"

5   "No, I guess not." I hoped my voice didn't quaver. As we headed for the entrance, my heart began to race. I just had to get out of that store. Only a few more yards to go and I'd be safe. As we crossed the threshold, I heaved a sigh of relief. I was home free. I thought about how sly I had been and I felt proud of my accomplishment.

6   An unexpected tap on my shoulder startled me. I whirled around to find a middle-aged man, dressed in street clothes, flashing some type of badge and politely asking me to empty my pockets. Where did this man come from? How did he know? I was so sure that no one had seen me! On the verge of panicking, I told myself that all I had to do was give this man his button back, say I was sorry, and go on my way. After all, it was only a 75-cent item.

7   Next thing I knew, he was talking about calling the police and having me arrested and thrown in jail, as if he had just nabbed a professional thief instead of a terrified kid. I couldn't believe what he was saying.

8   "Jean, what's going on?"

9   The sound of my sister's voice eased the pressure a bit. She always managed to get me out of trouble. She would come through this time too.

10   "Excuse me. Are you a relative of this young girl?"

11   "Yes, I'm her sister. What's the problem?"

12   "Well, I just caught her shoplifting and I'm afraid I'll have to call the police."

13   "What did she take?"

14   "This button."

15   "A button? You are having a thirteen-year-old arrested for stealing a button?"

16   "I'm sorry, but she broke the law."

17   The man led us through the store and into an office, where we waited for the police officers to arrive. Susan had found my grandmother and brother, who, still shocked, didn't say a word. The thought of going to jail terrified me, not because of jail itself, but because of the encounter with my parents afterward. Not more than ten minutes later, two officers arrived and placed me under arrest. They said that I was to be taken to the station alone. Then, they handcuffed me and led me out of the store. I felt alone and scared. I had counted on my sister being with me, but now I had to muster up the courage to face this ordeal all by myself.

How does your understanding of Brandt deepen or change through what she reveals about her feelings and thoughts?

18   As the officers led me through the mall, I sensed a hundred pairs of eyes staring at me. My face flushed and I broke out in a sweat. Now everyone knew I was a criminal. In their eyes I was a juvenile delinquent, and thank God the cops were getting me off the streets. The worst part was thinking my grandmother might be having the same thoughts. The humiliation at that moment was overwhelming. I felt like Hester Prynne being put on public display for everyone to ridicule.

19   That short walk through the mall seemed to take hours. But once we reached the squad car, time raced by. I was read my rights and questioned. We were at the police station within minutes. Everything happened so fast I didn't have a chance to feel remorse for my crime. Instead, I viewed what was happening to me as if it were a movie. Being searched, although embarrassing, somehow seemed to be exciting. All the movies and television programs I had seen were actually coming to life. This is what it was really like. But why were criminals always portrayed as frightened and regretful? I was having fun. I thought I had nothing to fear — until I was allowed my one phone call. I was trembling as I dialed home. I didn't know what I was going to say to my parents, especially my mother.

20   "Hi, Dad, this is Jean."

21   "We've been waiting for you to call."

22   "Did Susie tell you what happened?"

How does this dialogue add to the drama?

23   "Yeah, but we haven't told your mother. I think you should tell her what you did and where you are."

24   "You mean she doesn't even know where I am?"

25   "No, I want you to explain it to her."

26   There was a pause as he called my mother to the phone. For the first time that night, I was close to tears. I wished I had never stolen that stupid pin. I wanted to give the phone to one of the officers because I was too ashamed to tell my mother the truth, but I had no choice.

27   "Jean, where are you?"

28   "I'm, umm, in jail."

29   "Why? What for?"

30   "Shoplifting."

31   "Oh no, Jean. Why? Why did you do it?"

32   "I don't know. No reason. I just did it."

33 "I don't understand. What did you take? Why did you do it? You had plenty of money with you."

34 "I know but I just did it. I can't explain why. Mom, I'm sorry."

35 "I'm afraid sorry isn't enough. I'm horribly disappointed in you."

36 Long after we got off the phone, while I sat in an empty jail cell, waiting for my parents to pick me up, I could still distinctly hear the disappointment and hurt in my mother's voice. I cried. The tears weren't for me but for her and the pain I had put her through. I felt like a terrible human being. I would rather have stayed in jail than confront my mom right then. I dreaded each passing minute that brought our encounter closer. When the officer came to release me, I hesitated, actually not wanting to leave. We went to the front desk, where I had to sign a form to retrieve my belongings. I saw my parents a few yards away and my heart raced. A large knot formed in my stomach. I fought back the tears.

37 Not a word was spoken as we walked to the car. Slowly, I sank into the back seat anticipating the scolding. Expecting harsh tones, I was relieved to hear almost the opposite from my father.

38 "I'm not going to punish you and I'll tell you why. Although I think what you did was wrong, I think what the police did was more wrong. There's no excuse for locking a thirteen-year-old behind bars. That doesn't mean I condone what you did, but I think you've been punished enough already."

39 As I looked from my father's eyes to my mother's, I knew this ordeal was over. Although it would never be forgotten, the incident was not mentioned again.

> What is the effect of interweaving storytelling and describing with remembering thoughts and feelings in this paragraph?

> What do you learn from Brandt's account of her father's reaction?

> How well does this final paragraph help you understand the event's significance?

> For an additional student reading, go to **bedfordstmartins.com /theguide/epages**.

Annie Dillard | *An American Childhood*

ANNIE DILLARD, professor emeritus at Wesleyan University, won the Pulitzer Prize for nonfiction writing in 1975 with her first book, *Pilgrim at Tinker Creek* (1974). Since then, she has written eleven other books in a variety of genres. They include *Teaching a Stone to Talk* (1988), *The Writing Life* (1990), *The Living* (1993), *Mornings Like This* (1996), and *The Maytrees* (2007). Dillard also wrote an autobiography of her early years, *An American Childhood* (1987), from which the following selection comes.

As you read, consider Dillard's opening paragraphs:

- Why do you think Dillard chose to introduce the event with this reflection when she could have begun with paragraph 3?

- How do the opening paragraphs prepare readers to understand the event's significance?

1   Some boys taught me to play football. This was fine sport. You thought up a new strategy for every play and whispered it to the others. You went out for a pass, fooling everyone. Best, you got to throw yourself mightily at someone's running legs. Either you brought him down or you hit the ground flat out on your chin, with your arms empty before you. It was all or nothing. If you hesitated in fear, you would miss and get hurt: you would take a hard fall while the kid got away, or you would get kicked in the face while the kid got away. But if you flung yourself wholeheartedly at the back of his knees — if you gathered and joined body and soul and pointed them diving fearlessly — then you likely wouldn't get hurt, and you'd stop the ball. Your fate, and your team's score, depended on your concentration and courage. Nothing girls did could compare with it.

2   Boys welcomed me at baseball, too, for I had, through enthusiastic practice, what was weirdly known as a boy's arm. In winter, in the snow, there was neither baseball nor football, so the boys and I threw snowballs at passing cars. I got in trouble throwing snowballs, and have seldom been happier since.

3   On one weekday morning after Christmas, six inches of new snow had just fallen. We were standing up to our boot tops in snow on a front yard on trafficked Reynolds Street, waiting for cars. The cars traveled Reynolds Street slowly and evenly; they were targets all but wrapped in red ribbons, cream puffs. We couldn't miss.

4   I was seven; the boys were eight, nine, and ten. The oldest two Fahey boys were there — Mikey and Peter — polite blond boys who lived near me on Lloyd Street, and who already had four brothers and sisters. My parents approved Mikey and Peter Fahey. Chickie McBride was there, a tough kid, and Billy Paul and Mackie Kean too, from across Reynolds, where the boys grew up dark and furious, grew up skinny, knowing, and skilled. We had all drifted from our houses that morning looking for action, and had found it here on Reynolds Street.

5   It was cloudy but cold. The cars' tires laid behind them on the snowy street a complex trail of beige chunks like crenellated castle walls. I had stepped on some earlier; they squeaked. We could not have wished for more traffic. When a car came, we all popped it one. In the intervals between cars we reverted to the natural solitude of children.

6   I started making an iceball — a perfect iceball, from perfectly white snow, perfectly spherical, and squeezed perfectly translucent so no snow remained all the way through. (The Fahey boys and I considered it unfair actually to throw an iceball at somebody, but it had been known to happen.)

7   I had just embarked on the iceball project when we heard tire chains come clanking from afar. A black Buick was moving toward us down the street. We all spread out, banged together some regular snowballs, took aim, and, when the Buick drew nigh, fired.

8   A soft snowball hit the driver's windshield right before the driver's face. It made a smashed star with a hump in the middle.

9   Often, of course, we hit our target, but this time, the only time in all of life, the car pulled over and stopped. Its wide black door opened; a man got out of it, running. He didn't even close the car door.

10   He ran after us, and we ran away from him, up the snowy Reynolds sidewalk. At the corner, I looked back; incredibly, he was still after us. He was in city clothes: a suit and tie, street shoes. Any normal adult would have quit, having sprung us into flight and made his point. This man was gaining on us. He was a thin man, all action. All of a sudden, we were running for our lives.

11   Wordless, we split up. We were on our turf; we could lose ourselves in the neighborhood backyards, everyone

for himself. I paused and considered. Everyone had vanished except Mikey Fahey, who was just rounding the corner of a yellow brick house. Poor Mikey, I trailed him. The driver of the Buick sensibly picked the two of us to follow. The man apparently had all day.

12 He chased Mikey and me around the yellow house and up a backyard path we knew by heart: under a low tree, up a bank, through a hedge, down some snowy steps, and across the grocery store's delivery driveway. We smashed through a gap in another hedge, entered a scruffy backyard and ran around its back porch and tight between houses to Edgerton Avenue; we ran across Edgerton to an alley and up our own sliding woodpile to the Halls' front yard; he kept coming. We ran up Lloyd Street and wound through mazy backyards toward the steep hilltop at Willard and Lang.

13 He chased us silently, block after block. He chased us silently over picket fences, through thorny hedges, between houses, around garbage cans, and across streets. Every time I glanced back, choking for breath, I expected he would have quit. He must have been as breathless as we were. His jacket strained over his body. It was an immense discovery, pounding into my hot head with every sliding, joyous step, that this ordinary adult evidently knew what I thought only children who trained at football knew: that you have to fling yourself at what you're doing, you have to point yourself, forget yourself, aim, dive.

14 Mikey and I had nowhere to go, in our own neighborhood or out of it, but away from this man who was chasing us. He impelled us forward; we compelled him to follow our route. The air was cold; every breath tore my throat. We kept running, block after block; we kept improvising, backyard after backyard, running a frantic course and choosing it simultaneously, failing always to find small places or hard places to slow him down, and discovering always, exhilarated, dismayed, that only bare speed could save us—for he would never give up, this man—and we were losing speed.

15 He chased us through the backyard labyrinths of ten blocks before he caught us by our jackets. He caught us and we all stopped.

16 We three stood staggering, half blinded, coughing, in an obscure hilltop backyard: a man in his twenties, a boy, a girl. He had released our jackets,

our pursuer, our captor, our hero: he knew we weren't going anywhere. We all played by the rules. Mikey and I unzipped our jackets. I pulled off my sopping mittens. Our tracks multiplied in the backyard's new snow. We had been breaking new snow all morning. We didn't look at each other. I was cherishing my excitement. The man's lower pants legs were wet; his cuffs were full of snow, and there was a prow of snow beneath them on his shoes and socks. Some trees bordered the little flat backyard, some messy winter trees. There was no one around: a clearing in a grove, and we the only players.

17 It was a long time before he could speak. I had some difficulty at first recalling why we were there. My lips felt swollen; I couldn't see out of the sides of my eyes; I kept coughing.

18 "You stupid kids," he began perfunctorily.

19 We listened perfunctorily indeed, if we listened at all, for the chewing out was redundant, a mere formality, and beside the point. The point was that he had chased us passionately without giving up, and so he had caught us. Now he came down to earth. I wanted the glory to last forever.

20 But how could the glory have lasted forever? We could have run through every backyard in North America until we got to Panama. But when he trapped us at the lip of the Panama Canal, what precisely could he have done to prolong the drama of the chase and cap its glory? I brooded about this for the next few years. He could only have fried Mikey Fahey and me in boiling oil, say, or dismembered us piecemeal, or staked us to anthills. None of which I really wanted, and none of which any adult was likely to do, even in the spirit of fun. He could only chew us out there in the Panamanian jungle, after months or years of exalting pursuit. He could only begin, "You stupid kids," and continue in his ordinary Pittsburgh accent with his normal righteous anger and the usual common sense.

21 If in that snowy backyard the driver of the black Buick had cut off our heads, Mikey's and mine, I would have died happy, for nothing has required so much of me since as being chased all over Pittsburgh in the middle of winter—running terrified, exhausted—by this sainted, skinny, furious redheaded man who wished to have a word with us. I don't know how he found his way back to his car.

<table>
<tr><td>

REFLECT

</td><td>

Make connections: Acting fearlessly.

At the beginning of the essay, Dillard tells about being taught by the neighborhood boys the joy of playing football, particularly the "all or nothing" of diving "fearlessly" (par. 1). Recall an occasion when you had an opportunity to dive fearlessly into an activity that posed some challenge or risk or required special effort. For example, you may have been challenged, like Dillard, by your teammates at a football game or by a group of volunteers helping during a natural disaster. Or you may have felt pressured by friends to do something that went against your better judgment, was illegal, or was dangerous. Your instructor may ask you to post your thoughts to a class discussion board or to discuss them with other students in class. Use these questions to get started:

- What made you embrace the challenge or resist it? What do you think your choice tells about you at the time of the event?

- Dillard uses the value term *courage* to describe the fearless behavior she learned playing football. What value term would you use to describe your experience? For example, were you being *selfless* or *self-serving; responsible* or *irresponsible*; *a follower, a leader,* or *a self-reliant individual*?

</td></tr>
</table>

ANALYZE

Use the basic features.

A WELL-TOLD STORY: CONSTRUCTING AN ACTION SEQUENCE

For more on narrative action, see Chapter 14.

Throughout the excerpt from *An American Childhood,* Dillard combines *action verbs* and *prepositional phrases* to create compelling *action sequences.* Consider this example:

Action verb

Prepositional phrases

He chased Mikey and me around the yellow house and up a backyard path we knew by heart: under a low tree, up a bank, through a hedge, down some snowy steps, and across the grocery store's delivery driveway. (par. 12)

ANALYZE & WRITE

Write a paragraph analyzing Dillard's action sequences:

1. Skim paragraphs 11–13, circling the action verbs and underlining the prepositional phrases.

2. Think about how this series of prepositional phrases contributes to the effectiveness of the scene.

VIVID DESCRIPTION OF PEOPLE AND PLACES: USING NAMES AND DETAILS

To learn more about the describing strategies of naming and detailing, see Chapter 15, pp. 574–77.

Describing—naming objects and detailing their colors, shape, size, textures, and other qualities—is an important strategy in remembered event writing. Writers use this strategy to create vivid images of the scene in which the story takes place. They also use describing to give readers thumbnail portraits of people.

| ANALYZE & WRITE |

Write a paragraph analyzing Dillard's use of naming and detailing:

1 Reread paragraph 4, noting the names of her friends and underlining the details she gives to describe each boy. How do these details help you imagine what each boy was like?

2 Look closely at Dillard's description of an iceball to see how she uses these describing strategies:

> I started making an iceball —a perfect iceball, from perfectly white snow, perfectly spherical, and squeezed perfectly translucent so no snow remained all the way through. (par. 6)

Naming

Detailing

What attributes of the iceball does she point out? Why do you think she repeats the words *perfect* and *perfectly*? Notice also that in the next sentence, she tells us that it was against the rules to throw an iceball at someone. So why do you imagine she tries to make such a "perfect" iceball?

AUTOBIOGRAPHICAL SIGNIFICANCE: SHOWING AND TELLING

Writers use both *showing* and *telling* to convey significance. **Showing,** through the careful choice of words and details, creates an overall or dominant impression. **Telling** presents the narrator's remembered feelings and thoughts together with her present perspective on what happened and why it is significant.

To alert readers that they are telling, not showing, writers may announce their experience by using a verb like *felt* or a noun like *thought*:

▶ I felt _____. (Example: "I felt alone and scared" [Brandt, par. 17])   Verb

▶ The thought of _____. (Example: "The thought of going to jail terrified me" [Brandt, par. 17])   Noun

A more direct strategy is to choose words that tell readers which emotion or thought was experienced:

▶ The [terror/exhilaration/excitement] was _____. (Example: "The humiliation of that moment was overwhelming" [Brandt, par. 18])

Writers may also use **stream of consciousness,** which captures remembered thoughts and feelings by relating what went through the narrator's mind at the time. The following example re-creates the mash-up of feelings and thoughts, seemingly uncensored, that went through Jean Brandt's mind as she was being stopped for shoplifting:

> Where did this man come from? How did he know? I was so sure that no one had seen me! . . . I told myself that all I had to do was give this man his button back, say I was sorry, and go on my way. After all, it was only a 75-cent item. (par. 6)

Much of the telling in autobiographical stories includes what the writer remembers thinking and feeling at the time the incident occurred. But writers also occasionally insert comments telling what they think and feel now, from the **present perspective,** as they look back and reflect on the event's significance.

ANALYZE & WRITE

Write a paragraph or two analyzing Dillard's use of showing and telling to create autobiographical significance:

1 Skim paragraphs 7, 10, 13, 16, 18, and 20–21, highlighting the details Dillard uses to describe the man, how he dresses, the car he drives, and especially the way he talks when he catches her and her friend. What is the dominant impression you get of the man from these details, and what do they suggest about why he chases the kids?

2 Review paragraphs 13–21, adding notes where Dillard tells us what she thought and felt at the time. Notice also how Dillard conveys her present perspective—for example, by using adult vocabulary such as "perfunctorily," "redundant," and "mere formality" (par. 19). Highlight any other details that help convey Dillard's adult authorial voice. What does Dillard's telling add to the dominant impression, and how does it help you better understand the event's significance?

[RESPOND]

Consider possible topics: Remembering unexpected adult actions and reactions.

Like Dillard, you could write about a time when an adult did something entirely unexpected during your childhood; an action that seemed dangerous or threatening to you; or something humorous, kind, or generous. Consider unpredictable actions of adults in your immediate or extended family, adults you had come to know outside your family, and strangers. As you consider these possible topics, think about your purpose and audience: What would you want your instructor and classmates to learn about you from reading about this event?

Jenée Desmond-Harris | *Tupac and My Non-thug Life*

JENÉE DESMOND-HARRIS is a staff writer at the *Root*, an online magazine dedicated to African American news and culture. She writes about the intersection of race, politics, and culture in a variety of formats, including personal essays. She has also contributed to *Time* magazine, MSNBC's *Powerwall*, and *xoJane* on topics ranging from her relationship with her grandmother, to the political significance of Michelle Obama's hair, to the stereotypes that hinder giving to black-teen mentoring programs. She has provided television commentary on CNN, MSNBC, and Current TV. Desmond-Harris is a graduate of Howard University and Harvard Law School. The following selection was published in the *Root* in 2011. It chronicles Desmond-Harris's reaction to the murder of gangsta rap icon Tupac Shakur in a Las Vegas drive-by shooting in 1996. She mentions Tupac's mother,

Afeni, as well as the "East Coast–West Coast war"—the rivalry between Tupac and the Notorious B.I.G. (Biggie), who was suspected of being involved in Tupac's murder.

As you read, consider the photograph that appeared in the *Root* article and that is reproduced here:

- What does it capture about the fifteen-year-old Desmond-Harris?
- What does its inclusion say about Desmond-Harris's perspective on her adolescent self and the event she recollects?

1   I learned about Tupac's death when I got home from cheerleading practice that Friday afternoon in September 1996. I was a sophomore in high school in Mill Valley, Calif. I remember trotting up my apartment building's stairs, physically tired but buzzing with the frenetic energy and possibilities for change that accompany fall and a new school year. I'd been cautiously allowing myself to think during the walk home about a topic that felt frighteningly taboo (at least in my world, where discussion of race was avoided as delicately as obesity or mental illness): what it meant to be biracial and on the school's mostly white cheerleading team instead of the mostly black dance team. I remember acknowledging, to the sound of an 8-count that still pounded in my head as I walked through the door, that I didn't really have a choice: I could memorize a series of stiff and precise motions but couldn't actually dance.

2   My private musings on identity and belonging—not original in the least, but novel to me—were interrupted when my mom heard me slam the front door and drop my bags: "*Your friend died!*" she called out from another room. Confused silence. "*You know, that rapper you and Thea love so much!*"

Mourning a Death in Vegas

3   The news was turned on, with coverage of the deadly Vegas shooting. Phone calls were made. Ultimately my best friend, Thea, and I were left to our own 15-year-old devices to mourn that weekend. Her mother and stepfather were out of town. Their expansive, million-dollar home was perched on a hillside less than an hour from Tupac's former stomping grounds in Oakland and Marin City. Of course, her home was also worlds away from both places.

4   We couldn't "pour out" much alcohol undetected for a libation, so we limited ourselves to doing somber shots of liqueur from a well stocked cabinet. One each. Tipsy, in a high-ceilinged kitchen surrounded by hardwood floors and Zen flower arrangements, we baked cookies for his mother. We packed them up to ship to Afeni with a handmade card. ("Did we really do that?" I asked Thea this week. I wanted to ensure that this story, which people who know me now find hilarious, hadn't morphed into some sort of personal urban legend over the past 15 years. "Yes," she said. "We put them in a lovely tin.")

5   On a sound system that echoed through speakers perched discreetly throughout the airy house, we played "Life Goes On" on a loop and sobbed. We analyzed lyrics for premonitions of the tragedy. We, of course, cursed Biggie. Who knew that the East Coast–West Coast war had two earnest soldiers in flannel pajamas, lying on a king-size bed decorated with pink toe shoes that dangled from one of its posts? There, we studied our pictures of Tupac and re-created his tattoos on each other's body with a Sharpie. I got "Thug Life" on my stomach. I gave Thea "Exodus 1811" inside a giant cross. Both are flanked by "West Side."

6   A snapshot taken that Monday on our high school's front lawn (seen here) shows the two of us lying side by side, shirts lifted to display the tributes in black marker.

The author (left) with her friend Thea

Despite our best efforts, it's the innocent, bubbly lettering of notes passed in class and of poster boards made for social studies presentations. My hair has recently been straightened with my first (and last) relaxer and a Gold 'N Hot flatiron on too high a setting. Hers is slicked back with the mixture of Herbal Essences and Blue Magic that we formulated in a bathroom laboratory.

7 My rainbow-striped tee and her white wifebeater capture a transition between our skater-inspired Salvation Army shopping phase and the next one, during which we'd wear the same jeans slung from our hip bones, revealing peeks of flat stomach, but transforming ourselves from Alternative Nation to MTV Jams imitators. We would get bubble coats in primary colors that Christmas and start using silver eyeliner, trying—and failing—to look something like Aaliyah.[1]

Mixed Identities: Tupac and Me

8 Did we take ourselves seriously? Did we feel a real stake in the life of this "hard-core" gangsta rapper, and a real loss in his death? We did, even though we were two mixed-race girls raised by our white moms in a privileged community where we could easily rattle off the names of the small handful of other kids in town who also had one black parent: Sienna. Rashea. Brandon. Aaron. Sudan. Akio. Lauren. Alicia. Even though the most subversive thing we did was make prank calls. Even though we hadn't yet met our first boyfriends, and Shock G's proclamations about putting satin on people's panties sent us into absolute giggling fits. And even though we'd been so delicately cared for, nurtured and protected from any of life's hard edges—with special efforts made to shield us from those involving race—that we sometimes felt ready to explode with boredom. Or maybe because of all that.

9 I mourned Tupac's death then, and continue to mourn him now, because his music represents the years when I was both forced and privileged to confront what it meant to be black. That time, like his music, was about exploring the contradictory textures of this identity: The ambience and indulgence of the fun side, as in

"California Love" and "Picture Me Rollin'." But also the burdensome anxiety and outright anger—"Brenda's Got a Baby," "Changes" and "Hit 'Em Up."

10 For Thea and me, his songs were the musical score to our transition to high school, where there emerged a vague, lunchtime geography to race: White kids perched on a sloping green lawn and the benches above it. Below, black kids sat on a wall outside the gym. The bottom of the hill beckoned. Thea, more outgoing, with more admirers among the boys, stepped down boldly, and I followed timidly. Our formal invitations came in the form of unsolicited hall passes to go to Black Student Union meetings during free periods. We were assigned to recite Maya Angelou's "Phenomenal Woman" at the Black History Month assembly.

11 Tupac was the literal sound track when our school's basketball team would come charging onto the court, and our ragtag group of cheerleaders kicked furiously to "Toss It Up" in a humid gymnasium. Those were the games when we might breathlessly join the dance team after our cheer during time-outs if they did the single "African step" we'd mastered for BSU performances.

Everything Black—and Cool

12 . . . Blackness became something cool, something to which we had brand-new access. We flaunted it, buying Kwanzaa candles and insisting on celebrating privately (really, just lighting the candles and excluding our friends) at a sleepover. We memorized "I Get Around"[2] and took turns singing verses to each other as we drove through Marin County suburbs in Thea's green Toyota station wagon. Because he was with us through all of this, we were in love with Tupac and wanted to embody him. On Halloween, Thea donned a bald cap and a do-rag, penciled in her already-full eyebrows and was a dead ringer.

13 Tupac's music, while full of social commentary (and now even on the Vatican's playlist), probably wasn't made to be a treatise on racial identity. Surely it wasn't created to accompany two girls (*little* girls, really) as they embarked on a coming-of-age journey. But it was there for us when we desperately needed it.

---

[1] A hit rhythm-and-blues and hip-hop recording artist. Aaliyah Dana Haughton died in a plane crash at age twenty-two. [Editor's note]

[2] Tupac Shakur's first top-twenty single, released in 1993 on *Strictly 4 My N.I.G.G.A.Z.*, Shakur's second studio album. [Editor's note]

Make connections: Remembering idols.

We often find ourselves profoundly affected by what happens to people we've never met. You may remember where you were and how you reacted to the death of Michael Jackson or Whitney Houston, for example. In "Tupac and My Non-thug Life," Desmond-Harris captures the emotional connection between a teen and her slain idol, showing us not only how Tupac's death affected her then but what she thinks of her teenage self's obsession now that she is older.

Recall a time when the emotional impact of an event that happened to someone else (or to other people) was powerful enough to affect your behavior, decisions, or actions for the day or longer. Consider the reasons for your reactions. Your instructor may ask you to post your thoughts to a class discussion board or blog, or to discuss them with other students in class. Use these questions to get started:

- Why did you identify so closely with the person (or people) you heard about?

- What does your reaction say about who you were and what you valued?

- Would you react the same way today? What would be different and why?

Use the basic features.

A WELL-TOLD STORY: USING DIALOGUE

Dialogue is a narrating strategy that helps writers dramatize a story. Quoting with descriptive speaker tags—

▶ He said, "_____."   ▶ She asked, "_____?"   Speaker tag

—is an especially effective way of making readers feel as though they were there, overhearing what was said and how it was said. But all of the dialogue strategies—quoting, paraphrasing, and summarizing—can help readers identify with or understand a writer's point of view and give us an impression of the speakers. Desmond-Harris includes only a few lines of dialogue in "Tupac and My Non-thug Life," but those she does include demonstrate how effective this sentence strategy can be.

ANALYZE & WRITE

Write a paragraph analyzing how Desmond-Harris uses dialogue:

1. Skim the story, highlighting the dialogue and underlining the speaker tags. Also note where Desmond-Harris summarizes or paraphrases a conversation.

2. Consider each bit of dialogue, paraphrase, or summary to see what role it plays. Does it tell you something about the speaker or her relationship with another person? Does it convey feelings or attitudes? Does it advance the narrative or something else?

To learn more about quoting with speaker tags, paraphrasing, and summarizing in autobiographical stories, see pp. 11–12; to learn more about using them in your own writing, see the Guide to Writing, pp. 35–36 and 38–39.

VIVID DESCRIPTION OF PEOPLE AND PLACES: USING VISUALS AND BRAND NAMES

Desmond-Harris provides lots of concrete details to enliven her narrative. She also uses a photo and refers to brand names to convey to readers an exact sense of what the girls were like. Notice that she recounts the Sharpie tattooing and then actually shows us a photo of the girls displaying their tattoos. But Desmond-Harris does not let the photo speak for itself; instead, she describes the picture, pointing out features, such as their hairstyles and outfits, that mark their identity. Consider the references to particular styles and brand names (such as "our skater-inspired Salvation Army shopping phase") that tag the various roles they were trying on at that time of their lives (par. 7).

ANALYZE & WRITE

Write a paragraph or two analyzing Desmond-Harris's use of a photograph and brand names to enhance her descriptions:

1. Skim paragraphs 5–7, highlighting the specific details in the photo that Desmond-Harris points out as well as the brand names (usually capitalized) and the modifiers that make them more specific (as in *skater-inspired*).

2. Look closely at the photograph itself, and consider its purpose: Why do you think Desmond-Harris included it? What does the photograph contribute or show us that the text alone does not convey?

3. Consider the effect that the photo and the brand names have on you as a reader (or might have on readers of about Desmond-Harris's age). How do they help readers envision these girls? What is the dominant impression you get of the young Desmond-Harris from these descriptive details? Where, if anywhere, in this passage do you detect the adult author's self-irony?

For more on analyzing visuals, see Chapter 20.

AUTOBIOGRAPHICAL SIGNIFICANCE: HANDLING COMPLEX EMOTIONS

Remembered events that have lasting significance nearly always involve mixed or ambivalent feelings. Therefore, readers expect and appreciate some degree of complexity. Multiple layers of meaning make autobiographical stories more, not less, interesting. Significance that seems simplistic or predictable makes stories less successful.

ANALYZE & WRITE

Write a paragraph or two analyzing Desmond-Harris's handling of the complex personal and cultural significance of her remembered event:

1. Skim the last two sections (pars. 8–13), noting passages where Desmond-Harris tells readers her remembered feelings and thoughts at the time and her present perspective as an adult reflecting on the experience. Consider Desmond-Harris's dual perspective—that of the fifteen-year-old experiencing the event and the thirty-year-old writing about it. How does she use this dual perspective to convey complexity?

2. Look closely at paragraph 8, and highlight the following sentence strategies:

- Rhetorical questions (questions writers answer themselves)
- Repeated words and phrases
- Stylistic sentence fragments (incomplete sentences used for special effect)

What effect do these sentence strategies have on readers? How do they help convey the significance of the event?

To learn more about correcting sentence fragments, turn to the Handbook in the comprehensive edition or e-book; for practice correcting sentence fragments, go to **bedfordstmartins.com/ theguide/exercisecentral** and click on Sentence Boundaries in the Handbook section.

Note that in academic writing, stylistic fragments may be frowned on; one of the instructor's purposes in assigning a writing project is to teach students to use formal academic writing conventions, and it may not be clear from the context whether the student is using a fragment purposely for rhetorical effect or whether the student does not know how to identify and correct sentence fragments.

Consider possible topics: Recognizing a public event as a turning point.

[RESPOND]

Like Desmond-Harris, you could write about how a public event, like a celebrity death or marriage, an act of heroism or charity, or even the passage of a law helped (or forced) you to confront an aspect of your identity. Consider the complexities of your reaction—the significance the event had for you at the time and the significance the event has for you now. You might make a list of physical traits, as well as beliefs about or aspects of your sense of identity that changed as a result of the event.

Tom Ruprecht | *In Too Deep*

TOM RUPRECHT is the author of the book *George W. Bush: An Unauthorized Oral History* (2007) and was a writer for the television show *Late Night with David Letterman*. With Craig Finn, from the band the Hold Steady, he co-wrote a film adaptation of *Fargo Rock City* based on the book by Chuck Klosterman. His writing has also appeared in periodicals, including the *Wall Street Journal* and the *New York Times Magazine*, where "In Too Deep" appeared in 2011.

Throughout the reading selection, Ruprecht refers to events that readers of the *New York Times Magazine* in 2011 would probably have been aware of: that Osama Bin Laden was assumed to have taken refuge in a cave following the U.S. invasion of Afghanistan in 2001; that Aron Ralston amputated his own arm to escape a half-ton boulder pinning him to a canyon wall (an event that was depicted in the 2010 film *127 Hours,* starring James Franco); that the 2010 rescue of thirty-three Chilean miners trapped underground for six weeks was greeted with worldwide jubilation. As you read, consider Ruprecht's use of current events:

- What effect would the references to these events have had on his original audience when this article was published in 2011?
- What effect do these references have on you now?

1 It's impossible to look cool when you're part of a tour group. Instead of bravely exploring on your own, you've chosen to be led around like a frightened kindergartner. My wife and I were on a tour bus while in Hawaii recently, and our guide made me feel even more uncool because he was very rugged and handsome.

After a couple of hours, he announced we were stopping for what he called "snack break," as if we actually were kindergartners. He then mentioned that down a nearby path there was a cave we could check out. Not being a terrorist mastermind, I've never had a huge desire to hang out in a cave. But the opinion of absolute strangers means a lot to me, and I was desperate to differentiate myself from the other travelers in this cool, rugged guide's eyes.

2   "I'm going to the cave," I declared and marched down the path to check out its mouth. The mouth. That's as far as I was willing to go.

3   When I arrived, I found another guy from the group standing there.

4   "Hey, I'm Ernie. I'm a spelunker."

5   Ernie said he was going to take a quick look in the cave and invited me to come along. I politely declined. He insisted. I thought of my dad, who has encouraged me to say "yes!" to every opportunity while traveling. During a trip to Puerto Rico in the '70s, it was this *carpe diem* spirit that led my dad to play tennis all week long with the adult-film star Harry Reems—the same Harry Reems who was in *Deep Throat* (not that you recognized the name, dear reader), though true aficionados prefer his later work, in films like *For Your Thighs Only*. So I entered the mouth of the cave.

6   Thirty feet in, I began telling Ernie we should probably head back. But he simply rushed ahead, and because he had the flashlight, I had no choice but to follow. I soon found myself slithering through tight spaces in order to get to slightly tighter places. I panicked. It was only a matter of time before I would be wedged between rocks. I began looking around for a knife, so I could pre-emptively chop off my arm like James Franco in that movie I was too scared to see.

7   Things Ernie did made me question his spelunking expertise. For instance, there was a weird greenish-whitish substance on the cave's roof. "That's probably sodium," Ernie said, and he swabbed a finger on the slimy substance and stuck it in his mouth. He muttered, "That's not sodium." I believe it was Ernie's pride that kept him from adding, "I think it's bat guano."

8   We were a good mile inside the cave when Ernie looked at me, gave a little laugh and then turned off the flashlight. A mile deep in the cave. "Scared?" he whispered. Then he chuckled, turned the flashlight back on and said, "Nah, the thing you should really be worried about is what would happen if there were an earthquake right now." Seeing my terrified expression, Ernie said, "Oh, hadn't you thought about that?" I had to get out of there. People were waiting for us. More important, my wife was above ground chatting with a ruggedly handsome tour guide. I implored Ernie to turn back. He reluctantly agreed. On the way, we came upon a fork in the cave. I asked if we should go to the right or the left. Ernie, the great spelunker, replied: "Oh, I have a terrible sense of direction." So Ernie had me choose. I, of course, picked the wrong way. We wandered aimlessly for 10 minutes, wondering if we were passing the same generic rocks we passed on the way in or if we were passing slightly different generic rocks. If only there had been a spelunker there, I would have asked him.

9   Eventually Ernie's spelunking expertise did kick in. He realized we were headed down the wrong path. We doubled back, took the other path and, finally, saw a sliver of sunlight. I popped out of the cave, expecting a welcome worthy of a Chilean miner. Instead I was greeted by 11 annoyed people whose trip Ernie and I had hindered. As my wife hugged me, she whispered, "People are kinda mad."

10   The guide reprimanded us for endangering our lives and delaying the others. But as we started back to the bus, he pulled Ernie and me aside and said in a low voice, "Don't tell anybody, but I think what you guys did was seriously kick-ass!" The rest of the day I walked around with a happy smile, like the proudest little kindergartner you've ever seen.

[REFLECT]   # Make connections: Using humor.

Ruprecht's story is often funny, and he's frequently the butt of his own jokes. At the same time, he presents himself as unabashedly proud of his admittedly juvenile behavior. In other words, Ruprecht has it both ways by using humor. On the one hand, humor is tricky to pull off, especially self-deprecating humor, because it can be annoying. On the other hand, writing without humor or self-irony can seem pompous or self-important, especially when you are recalling a time when you acted foolishly or embarrassed yourself. Take a moment to recall an event in your life that you could write about, and consider how you could tell this story effectively using humor.

Your instructor may ask you to post your thoughts to a class discussion board or blog, or to discuss them with other students in class. Use these questions to get started:

- Which aspect of your story is funny? Is the situation funny, or did you do or say something silly? Would you use irony or satire to expose your own or someone else's folly?

- Consider whether humor played a role in any of the other readings in this chapter—and, if so, whether the humor was used effectively.

- Reconsider Ruprecht's use of humor in light of your answers. How effectively do you think he uses humor to tell his story?

Use the basic features.

[ANALYZE]

A WELL-TOLD STORY: UNDERSTANDING THE DRAMATIC ORGANIZATION OF A STORY

To keep readers' interest, even the most exciting remembered events need to be organized in a way that builds suspense and tension. But if you compare the dramatic structure of Dillard's story to Brandt's, for example, you will see that writers may not always devote the same amount of space to the same elements of a story. Take another look at Figure 2.1 (p. 12), showing the parts of a dramatic arc. Recall that after several paragraphs of exposition, Dillard devotes most of the story to the rising action, as the man chases Dillard and Mikey relentlessly through streets and backyards. The climax comes when he catches the children, but the story ends with no falling action other than a line of dialogue and the writer's thoughts for a quick resolution. Brandt has a more complicated rising action that includes the mini-climaxes of getting caught and getting arrested before the final confrontation with her parents, followed by falling action and a briefly stated resolution.

[ANALYZE & WRITE]

Write a paragraph or two analyzing the dramatic arc of Ruprecht's story:

1. Skim the selection and note in the margin where you find the exposition, rising action, climax, falling action, and resolution, or whether any of them is omitted.

2. How effective are Ruprecht's choices about how to plot his narrative? How does Ruprecht's emphasis differ from that of Brandt or Dillard?

3. Describe how useful the dramatic arc was for you in terms of understanding Ruprecht's narrative technique. Did it help you understand how Ruprecht created (or undermined) tension, for example?

VIVID DESCRIPTION OF PEOPLE AND PLACES: USING FIGURES OF SPEECH

Writers often use figures of speech based on comparison to enrich their descriptions. **Comparisons** make descriptions more evocative by associating characteristics from one thing with those of the thing to which it is being compared. You're probably familiar with similes and metaphors. Here are two examples from Brandt's essay:

> I felt like Hester Prynne being put on public display for everyone to ridicule. (par. 18)   Simile

> The shopping center was swarming with frantic last-minute shoppers. (par. 2)   Metaphor

In comparing herself to Hester Prynne, a character in a novel, Brandt also uses a kind of comparison called an **allusion,** an indirect reference to a literary work.

Finally, in the next example, Brandt combines simile with **hyperbole,** a figure of speech that uses exaggeration:

Next thing I knew, he was talking about calling the police and having me arrested and thrown in jail, as if he had just nabbed a professional thief instead of a terrified kid. (par. 7)

Hyperbole

ANALYZE & WRITE

Write a paragraph or two analyzing Ruprecht's use of figures of speech:

1. Reread Ruprecht's story, looking for places in which he uses simile, metaphor, allusion, hyperbole, or another figure of speech.

2. Consider the role that figurative language plays in making the description in this selection vivid. What effect does it have on you as a reader? How appropriate is it given the target audience for this selection? (Remember that it was originally published in the *New York Times Magazine*.)

AUTOBIOGRAPHICAL SIGNIFICANCE: COMING FULL CIRCLE

Sometimes stories about remembered events echo something in the ending that was introduced in the beginning. Brandt's story, for example, begins and ends in a car. In the beginning, there is singing, chatter, and good cheer. She is full of anticipation ("I knew it was going to be a fabulous day"). In the end, she is in another car, "anticipating the scolding" that will be followed by years of silence. This is repetition with a difference that sheds new light on the event's significance.

ANALYZE & WRITE

Write a paragraph or two analyzing how Ruprecht's story comes full circle:

1. Skim paragraph 1, highlighting Ruprecht's references to his desire to "look cool," his admiration for the "rugged and handsome" guide, and his feeling that he is being condescended to—treated "as if we actually were kindergartners."

2. Reread paragraphs 8–10, noting the repetition of these themes. Consider whether this is repetition with a difference or repetition that reinforces the same themes Ruprecht introduced in the opening paragraph.

[RESPOND]

Consider possible topics: Being "In Too Deep."

Most of us, like Ruprecht, have at some point experienced the feeling of being "in too deep." Like him, you might write about a time when you got yourself into a situation you did not feel competent to handle. (Conversely, you could write about an event that proved you more capable than you expected.) Ruprecht's story also suggests other possibilities: You could write about a time when you tried something new, feared for your life, let the opinions of others influence your decisions, trusted someone who (like Ernie) might not have deserved that trust, or behaved foolishly.

For more remembered events, including a multimodal selection, go to **bedfordstmartins .com/theguide/epages.**

Remembered events appear regularly in newspaper columns and blog posts and even in cartoons and graphic memoirs. The cartoon reproduced here, called "Treasure," from Kate Beaton's *Hark! A Vagrant* series, neatly conveys the basic features of the genre: It tells a compelling story, vividly describes the writer and her younger self through simple but evocative drawings, and clearly conveys the autobiographical significance of digging up the "treasures" her younger self had buried. The cartoon also deftly captures the tension between what the writer felt as a child and what she feels now on remembering the day she buried her treasures.

In the next section of this chapter, we ask you to craft your own remembered event story. As you draft your story, consider how you can most effectively create suspense or curiosity and convey your point of view; describe vividly the people and places involved, using specific details and sensory imagery; and convey the significance of the event, both what it meant to you when it happened and what it means to you now. Consider, too, whether using visuals or multimedia or conveying your story in words and pictures, as Beaton docs, would help your readers more fully grasp the significance of your remembered event. (Remember to consider, too, whether a remembered event conveyed in words and pictures would be appropriate to your purpose and audience.)

For an interactive version of this feature, plus activities, go to **bedfordstmartins .com/theguide/epages**.

The Writing Assignment

Write an essay about an event in your life that will engage readers and that will, at the same time, help them understand the significance of the event. Tell your story dramatically and vividly.

This Guide to Writing is designed to help you compose your own remembered event essay and apply what you have learned from reading other essays in the same genre. The following Starting Points chart will help you find answers to many of the questions you might have about composing a remembered event essay. Use the chart to find the guidance you need, when you need it.

STARTING POINTS: REMEMBERING AN EVENT

A Well-Told Story

How can I come up with an event to write about?

- Consider possible topics. (pp. 22, 27, 30)
- Choose an event to write about. (p. 34)
- Test Your Choice (p. 35)

How can I interest my audience and hold its attention?

- Shape your story. (pp. 35–36)
- Organize your story to enhance the drama. (pp. 36–37)
- Test Your Choice (p. 37)
- Write the opening sentences. (pp. 43–44)

How can I make the story of my event dramatic?

- Assess the genre's basic features: A well-told story. (pp. 11–12)
- A Well-Told Story: Constructing an Action Sequence (p. 20)
- A Well-Told Story: Using Dialogue (p. 25)
- Shape your story. (pp. 35–36)
- Organize your story to enhance the drama. (pp. 36–37)
- Use dialogue to tell your story. (pp. 38–39)

How should I organize my story?

- Assess the genre's basic features: A well-told story. (pp. 11–12)
- Autobiographical Significance: Coming Full Circle (p. 30)
- Organize your story to enhance the drama. (pp. 36–37)
- Choose your tense and plan time cues. (p. 38)

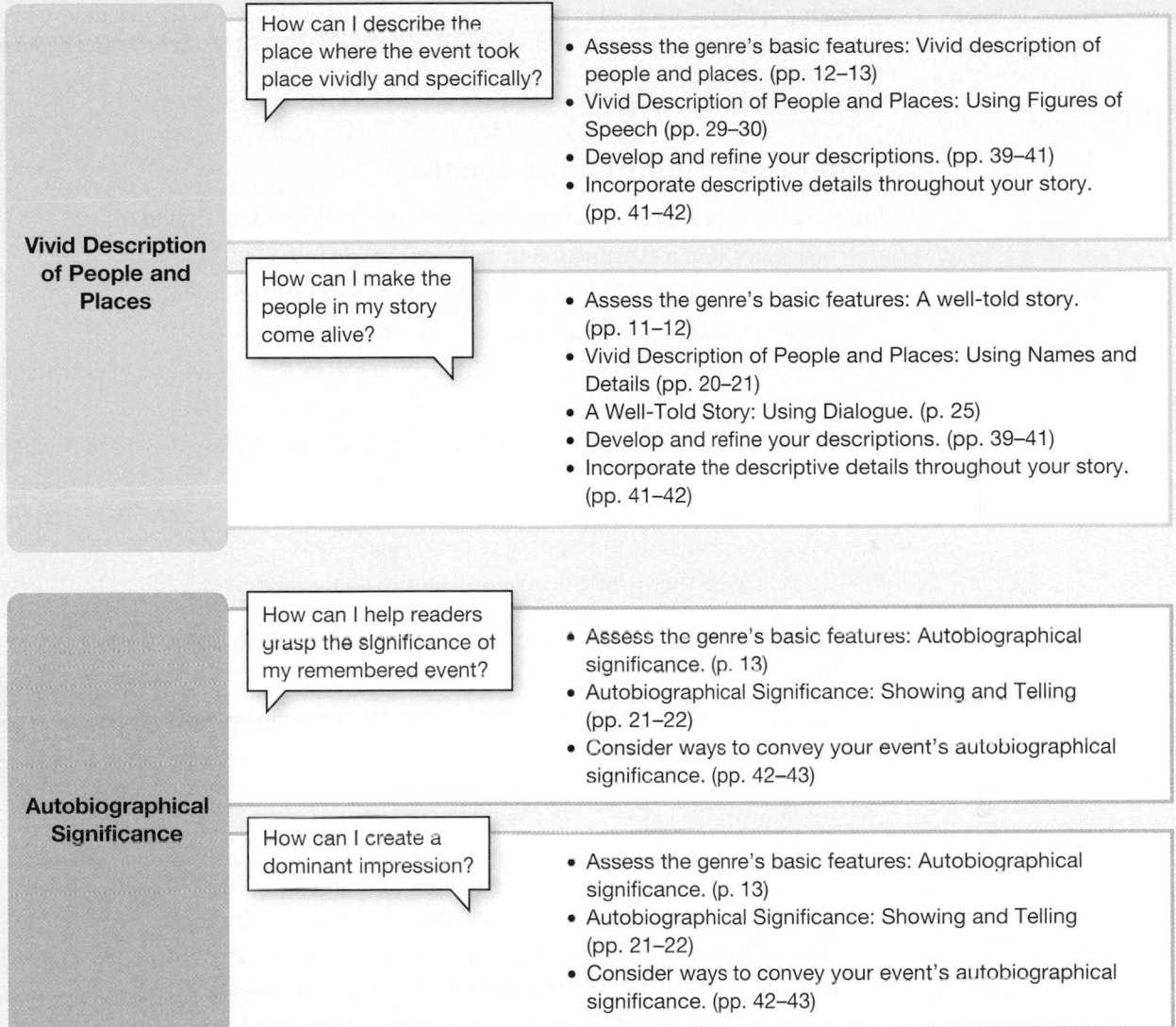

Vivid Description of People and Places

How can I describe the place where the event took place vividly and specifically?

- Assess the genre's basic features: Vivid description of people and places. (pp. 12–13)
- Vivid Description of People and Places: Using Figures of Speech (pp. 29–30)
- Develop and refine your descriptions. (pp. 39–41)
- Incorporate descriptive details throughout your story. (pp. 41–42)

How can I make the people in my story come alive?

- Assess the genre's basic features: A well-told story. (pp. 11–12)
- Vivid Description of People and Places: Using Names and Details (pp. 20–21)
- A Well-Told Story: Using Dialogue. (p. 25)
- Develop and refine your descriptions. (pp. 39–41)
- Incorporate the descriptive details throughout your story. (pp. 41–42)

Autobiographical Significance

How can I help readers grasp the significance of my remembered event?

- Assess the genre's basic features: Autobiographical significance. (p. 13)
- Autobiographical Significance: Showing and Telling (pp. 21–22)
- Consider ways to convey your event's autobiographical significance. (pp. 42–43)

How can I create a dominant impression?

- Assess the genre's basic features: Autobiographical significance. (p. 13)
- Autobiographical Significance: Showing and Telling (pp. 21–22)
- Consider ways to convey your event's autobiographical significance. (pp. 42–43)

To learn about using the *Guide* e-book for invention and drafting, go to **bedfordstmartins.com /theguide**.

Writing a Draft: Invention, Research, Planning, and Composing

The activities in this section will help you choose an event to write about and develop it into a well-told, vivid, significant story. Your writing in response to many of these activities can be used in a rough draft that you will be able to improve after receiving feedback from your classmates and instructor. Do the activities in any order that makes sense to you (and your instructor), and return to them as needed as you revise.

Choose an event to write about.

To make a compelling story, the event you choose to write about should

- take place over a short period of time (preferably just a few hours);
- center on a conflict (an internal struggle or an external confrontation);
- disclose something significant about your life;
- reveal complex or ambivalent feelings (rather than superficial and sentimental ones).

Make a list of events that fit the bill. If you're like most people, you may have trouble coming up with events to write about. To get your juices flowing, try the following:

- Review the Consider Possible Topics sections on pp. 22, 27, and 30, or reread any notes you made in response to those suggestions.
- Consult Web sites where people post stories about their lives, such as the Story Preservation Initiative, the Sixties Project, or StoryCorps. Try also typing *memory project, survivor stories,* or a similar word string into the search box of your browser.

If you need more ideas, the following may give you a jumping-off point:

- A difficult situation (for example, when you had to make a tough choice and face the consequences, or when you let someone down or someone you admired let you down)
- An occasion when things did not turn out as expected (for example, when you expected to be criticized but were praised or ignored instead, or when you were convinced you would succeed but failed)
- An incident that changed you or that revealed an aspect of your personality (such as initiative, insecurity, ambition, jealousy, or heroism)
- An incident in which a conflict or a serious misunderstanding with someone made you feel unjustly treated or caused you to mistreat someone else
- An experience that made you reexamine a basic value or belief (such as a time when you were expected to do something that went against your values or had to make a decision about which you were deeply conflicted)
- An encounter with another person that led you to consider seriously someone else's point of view, that changed the way you viewed yourself, or that altered your ideas about how you fit into a group or community
- An event that revealed to you other people's surprising assumptions about you (as a student, friend, colleague, or worker)

After you have made a tentative choice, ask yourself the following questions:

- Will I be able to reconstruct enough of the story and describe the place and people in vivid detail to make my story dramatic and create a dominant impression?

- Do I feel drawn toward understanding what this event meant to me then and what it means to me now? (You may not yet know what the significance of the event is, but you should feel compelled to explore it.)

- Do I feel comfortable writing about this event for my instructor and classmates? This isn't a diary entry, after all. You are going to share your writing with others and should be comfortable doing so.

If you lose confidence in your choice, return to your list and choose another event.

:: Shape your story.

Once you have selected an event, consider how you might structure your story to make it compelling. To do this, first create a *quick sketch* or *outline* of what happened during the event. Sketch out the moments in simple, chronological order. You can fill in details and revise later.

Once you have a quick sketch of the event, use the following questions and advice to help you put your ideas in writing. (Some writers may prefer to work out the dramatic structure of the story before developing the key moments. If that is true of you, move on to the next section, "Organize your story to enhance the drama," and come back to this section later on.)

WHAT DOES MY STORY NEED?	HOW CAN I INTEREST READERS?
Compare your story sketch with the dramatic arc in Figure 2.1 (p. 12):	Analyze your audience:
Sketch out the backstory, or exposition, your readers will need to understand what happened.	Consider who will be reading your story and what aspect of the story they will find most interesting. Often, it's the conflict, but it could be the setting or the activity you were taking part in.
▶ In (year), while I was (_____ing) in (location), _____ .	Pick a moment in your story that you think might hook readers, such as a bit of dialogue or an inciting incident, and try writing about that moment.
▶ John knew all about _____ because he was a/an _____, an expert on _____ .	
▶ In past years, I had previously _____ .	

WAYS IN

(continued)

Practice writing the "inciting incident," the conflict that triggers the story. To dramatize it, try using narrative actions and dialogue, including speaker tags and quotation marks.

Prep. phrase

Action verbs

> A black Buick was moving toward us down the street. We all spread out, banged together some regular snowballs, took aim, and, when the Buick drew nigh, fired. (Dillard, par. 7)

> "I'm going to the cave," I declared and marched down the path to check out its mouth. (Ruprecht, par. 2)

Dramatize the moment of surprise, confrontation, crisis, or discovery that may become the climax of your story, using narrative action and dialogue.

> He chased us through the backyard labyrinths of ten blocks before he caught us by our jackets. He caught us and we all stopped. . . . "You stupid kids," he began perfunctorily. (Dillard, pars. 15, 18)

Augment your memory by asking people who were there what they remember; look through family photographs, yearbooks, e-mails, or videos, and write briefly about what you found:

> A snapshot taken that Monday on our high school's front lawn (seen here) shows the two of us lying side by side, shirts lifted to display the tributes in black marker. (Desmond-Harris, par. 6)

> My private musings on identity and belonging—not original in the least, but novel to me—were interrupted when my mom heard me slam the front door and drop my bags: "*Your friend died!*" she called out from another room. Confused silence. "*You know, that rapper you and Thea love so much!*" (Desmond-Harris, par. 2)

As an alternative, practice opening your story with an observation that connects with your theme or your motives at the time, as Ruprecht does.

> It's impossible to look cool when you're part of a tour group. (Ruprecht, par. 1)

Or practice opening with exposition, as Dillard does.

> Some boys taught me to play football. (Dillard, par. 1)

Experiment with ways to end your story so that the ending refers to something from the beginning—repetition with a difference.

> Instead of bravely exploring on your own, you've chosen to be led around like a frightened kindergartner. (Ruprecht, par. 1)

> The rest of the day I walked around with a happy smile, like the proudest little kindergartner you've ever seen. (Ruprecht, par. 10)

⠿ Organize your story to enhance the drama.

Once you have sketched out your event and (perhaps) done some writing to help you focus on key moments, you may be ready to revisit the structure of your story. Think about how you can structure it to make it more exciting or moving for your readers. Following are organizational plans based on the dramatic arc in Figure 2.1 (p. 12) that you can use or modify to fit your needs.

If your readers are likely to understand the setting and activities described in the story, you might think about opening directly with the conflict's inciting incident:

I. **Inciting Incident:** Hook readers' attention by showing immediately how the conflict or problem started.

II. **Exposition:** Then rewind a bit to tell us what you had been doing when the event happened, and how you ended up in that situation.

III. **Rising Action:** Return to the main action, showing how the crisis developed or worsened.

IV. **Climax:** Describe the most critical moment of the event.

V. **Falling Action:** Narrate what happened after the climax.

VI. **Resolution/Reflection:** Tell how the event ended, and reflect on its autobiographical significance. What impact has this event had on you?

If the situation you were in when the conflict or problem developed is one that might be interesting to readers or might require some explanation, you might open with exposition:

I. **Exposition:** Tell us what you were doing when the event happened, and how you got there.

II. **Inciting Incident:** Show us how the conflict or problem started.

III. **Rising Action:** Show how the crisis developed or worsened.

IV. **Climax:** Describe the most critical moment of the event.

V. **Falling Action:** Narrate what happened after the climax.

VI. **Resolution/Reflection:** Tell us how the event ended, and reflect on its autobiographical significance. What impact has this event had on you?

If you have drafted parts of your story already (based on the "Ways In" section on pp. 35–36 or other writing you have done), try putting it all together now, so you can see what details your story still needs. You can always change the organization and move the scenes around as you continue drafting and revising.

TEST YOUR CHOICE

Get together with two or three other students to try out your story. Your classmates' reactions will help you determine whether you are telling it in an interesting or exciting way.

Storytellers.   Take turns telling your stories briefly. Try to pique your listeners' curiosity and build suspense, and watch your audience to see if your story is having the desired reaction.

Listeners.   Briefly tell each storyteller what you found most intriguing about the story. For example, consider these questions:

- Were you eager to know how the story would turn out?
- What was the inciting incident? Did it seem sufficient to motivate the climax?
- Was there a clear conflict that seemed important enough to write about?

⠿ Choose your tense and plan time cues.

To prevent readers from becoming confused about the sequence of actions in time, writers use a combination of verb tenses and transitional words and phrases related to time. Although writing about your remembered event in the present tense can give your narrative a sense of immediacy, *writing about the event itself in the past tense will make it easier to manage your other tenses.* For example, you may need to talk about what happened before the event took place or how you feel about the event now, as Desmond-Harris does here:

Past tense for event

Present tense for current reflection

I mourned Tupac's death then, and continue to mourn him now, because his music represents the years when I was both forced and privileged to confront what it meant to be black. (par. 9)

Managing the tenses for these breaks from the timeline can be tough if you aren't already writing most of the story in the past tense. Try rewriting the preceding sentence with the event described in the present tense: "I mourn Tupac's death, and . . ." Can you see how to do it? Most writers write about past events in the past tense because it makes these moves much easier.

Cite calendar *or* clock time *to establish when the event took place and help readers follow the action over time.* Writers often situate the event in terms of the date or time. Brandt, for example, establishes in the opening paragraph that the event occurred when she went to the mall for "a day of last-minute Christmas shopping." Dillard also identifies when the event took place and how old she was at the time: "On one weekday morning after Christmas. . . . I was seven." (pars. 3, 4).

Use transitions of time, such as *after, before, in the meantime,* and *simultaneously, to help readers follow a sequence of actions.* In the following example, *when* signals that one action followed another:

Transition of time

First action

Second action

When I got back to the Snoopy section, I took one look at the lines. (Brandt, par. 3)

In the following example, *as* indicates that the first action occurred at the same time as the second action.

As we all piled into the car, I knew it was going to be a fabulous day.
(Brandt, par. 1)

For more on transitions of time, see also p. 557 in Chapter 13 and pp. 563–64 in Chapter 14.

⠿ Use dialogue to tell your story.

Although writers may not remember exactly what was said, they often reconstruct dialogue through quotation, paraphrase, or summary. Quotation emphasizes a conversation, while paraphrase or summary enables you to move past less important conversations quickly.

When you quote, enclose the words, phrases, or sentences within quotation marks. Each time a new speaker is quoted, start a new paragraph:

"Excuse me. Are you a relative of this young girl?"

"Yes, I'm her sister. What's the problem?"

"Well, I just caught her shoplifting and I'm afraid I'll have to call the police." (Brandt, pars. 10–12)

Security guard

Brandt's sister

Security guard

In the example above, Brandt is careful to let readers know who is speaking by having the security guard ask Jean's sister if she's a relative, and by having her sister identify herself as such. In addition, writers can indicate who is speaking in the paragraphs that precede the dialogue:

There was a pause as he called my mother to the phone. For the first time that night, I was close to tears. I wished I had never stolen that stupid pin. I wanted to give the phone to one of the officers because I was too ashamed to tell my mother the truth, but I had no choice.

"Jean, where are you?"

"I'm, umm, in jail." (Brandt, pars. 26–28)

References to *mother* prepare us for mother's line

Reference to *Jean* prepares us for Jean's reply

I'm tells us it is Jean's turn again

You can also use **speaker tags** to identify the speaker:

"You stupid kids," he began perfunctorily. (Dillard, par. 18)

("Did we really do that?" I asked Thea this week. . . . "Yes," she said. "We put them in a lovely tin.") (Desmond-Harris, par. 4)

To learn more about using speaker tags, see pp. 12, 25, and 35–36 in this chapter and pp. 95–96 in Chapter 3.

Use paraphrase to repeat the substance of what was said in your own words:

Next thing I knew, he was talking about calling the police and having me arrested and thrown in jail. (Brandt, par. 7)

The guide reprimanded us for endangering our lives and delaying the others. (Ruprecht, par. 10)

To learn more about quoting, paraphrasing, and summarizing, see Chapter 26, pp. 701–8.

Use summary to convey the gist of the discussion without the details of what was said:

I implored Ernie to turn back. He reluctantly agreed. (Ruprecht, par. 8)

:: Develop and refine your descriptions.

To be effective, a remembered event should include specific details about the people and places involved. Describe people in detail—what they looked like and how they dressed, talked, and gestured. Describe the setting—what you saw, heard, smelled, touched, and tasted. Once you've described the people and places involved, try incorporating them into the action. The following activities will help you get started.

HOW CAN I MAKE MY DESCRIPTIONS OF PEOPLE AND PLACES MORE VIVID?

- Consult *memorabilia,* like scrapbooks or souvenirs (ticket stubs, T-shirts), for details you may have forgotten.
- Look at *photographs* from your own albums, visit the Facebook pages of key people, or consult Google Earth views to sharpen your descriptions. Consider scanning, uploading, or attaching images of the memorabilia to your essay.
- Come up with a list of *names* or *nouns* to describe the most important people and locations in the story.

People	**Places**
Consider the job(s) they have, the roles they play, their facial features or accents, articles of clothing they wore, or items they carried.	Consider the type of location (clothing store, funeral parlor), the architectural features it had, or what it was near.

> *Brandt's security guard:* man, street clothes, badge.
>
> *Dillard's pursuer:* man, driver, city clothes, suit and tie, street shoes, jacket; *after the pursuit:* cuffs full of snow, prow of snow on shoes and socks, Pittsburgh accent.

> *Brandt's store:* General Store, knickknacks, buttons, calendars, posters, lines at the cashiers, basket, threshold, office.
>
> *Dillard's neighborhood:* Reynolds Street, cars' tires, trail of chunks, sidewalk, house, path, tree, hedge, bank, grocery store driveway, porch, gap in hedge, alley, woodpile, backyards, hilltop.

- Come up with a list of *narrative actions* that remind you of the ways people acted, moved, and talked or that capture what was happening in the setting.

People	**Places**
Brandt's security guard: tapped shoulder, flashed badge.	*Brandt's shopping center:* was swarming with frantic last-minute shoppers.
Ruprecht's Ernie: insisted, rushed, swabbed, muttered.	*Ruprecht's cave:* slithering through tight spaces.

- Use detailing to flesh out descriptions.

People	**Places**
Brandt's security guard: unexpected tap, middle-aged man, some type of badge, politely asking.	*Brandt's store:* other useless items, 75-cent Snoopy button.
Dillard's pursuer: thin man, red-headed, chased silently, pants legs were wet.	*Desmond-Harris's friend's house:* well-stocked liquor cabinet, high-ceilinged kitchen, speakers perched discreetly.

- Use similes or metaphors to compare people or places with other people or things.

People

Desmond-Harris and her friend Thea: were two earnest soldiers in the East Coast–West Coast war.

Ruprecht: felt like a kindergartner.

Places

Dillard's neighborhood: a complex trail of beige chunks like crenellated castle walls; mazy backyards.

Remember that you can rearrange the components of your description in any way that makes sense to you.

Incorporate descriptive details throughout your story.

Look over the details you've generated, your organizational plan, and any sections you've already drafted, and weave the descriptive details into your action sequences. Because readers often skip lengthy descriptions, spreading the details out over the whole story may work best.

HOW CAN I WORK DESCRIPTIONS INTO MY ACTION SEQUENCES?

1. Begin with a simple sentence—an independent clause consisting of a subject (noun or pronoun) and a verb, for example:

   Amalia and Sophie ran.

2. **To describe people,** add descriptive naming and detailing as well as narrative actions to show what the people said and did, as in this example:

   Yelling "Grandma!" at the top of their lungs, the curly-headed five-year-old twins, Amalia and Sophie, ran to their laughing curly-headed grandmother, who was getting out of a silver hybrid sedan.

   | Narrative actions
   | Independent clause
   | Descriptive naming and detailing

   Here's an example from Jean Brandt's essay (par. 6):

   I whirled around to find a middle-aged man, dressed in street clothes, flashing some type of badge and politely asking me to empty my pockets.

   | Independent clause
   | Descriptive naming and detailing
   | Narrative actions

3. **To describe the place,** add descriptive naming, detailing, and comparing along with narrative actions, including prepositional phrases to show where each object is located in the scene, as in this example (with only the new information marked):

   Yelling "Grandma!" at the top of their lungs, Amalia and Sophie ran to their laughing grandmother, a tall, thin woman getting out of a silver hybrid sedan she

   | Narrative actions

   (continued)

WAYS IN

Descriptive naming and detailing

had just parked at the yellow loading-only zone in front of the old-fashioned yellow-clapboard elementary school.

Here's an example from Annie Dillard's essay (par. 12):

Descriptive naming and detailing

Narrative actions

He chased Mikey and me around the yellow house and up a backyard path we knew by heart: under a low tree, up a bank, through a hedge, down some snowy steps, and across the grocery store's delivery driveway.

▪▪ Consider ways to convey your event's autobiographical significance.

The following activities should help you move from the notes you already have to some strategies for showing and telling readers why your event matters to you. Often, your word choices—what you focus on and how you describe it, especially the comparisons you draw—can tell readers a lot about your feelings. It might also help to move back and forth between your memory of the experience and how you see it now, examining changes in your attitude toward the event and your younger self.

WAYS IN

HOW CAN I CONVEY THE AUTOBIOGRAPHICAL SIGNIFICANCE OF MY STORY?

Revisit your purpose and audience

Who are your readers, and what do you want them to think, feel, or believe about you or the event? The following sentence strategy can help you come up with an answer:

▶ Aside from my classmates and instructor, the people I imagine being most interested in what I'm saying would fit this description: _____. I think they will be most surprised by _____. I hope that when they are done reading they will think of me as _____ and be more aware that _____.

Think about your main point

What do you want your readers to understand or believe after reading your story?

▶ When readers finish my story, they will better appreciate how [society and culture/an individual person/the human condition] _____.

Explore the significance of your story's conflict

How does the event reflect what you were going through, and how can you dramatize what occurred? Following are some sentence strategies you may use to start generating ideas, though you may want to revise or restructure them before including them in your paper.

▶ During this event, I found myself locked in conflict with _____. (Elaborate.)

▶ Although I struggled with [a factor outside myself], I also was at war with myself while it happened: I kept wondering, should I _____ or should I _____? (Elaborate.)

Consider the dominant impression you want to convey

Write for a few minutes about the kind of impression (of the setting, of the characters) you are hoping to create. What mood (scary, lighthearted, gloomy) do you want to convey? If you were filming the event, what would the lighting be like? What sound track would you use?

Now reread the writing you have already done. Identify any details that might undermine or contradict the dominant impression. Can you strengthen the dominant impression you want to convey by deleting or replacing any words that carry the wrong connotation (or associations)? Or are these contradictions actually part of the dominant impression and complex significance you want to convey? If so, consider how you could emphasize or deepen the complexity and ambivalence you felt at the time or feel now as you reflect on the event.

Explore how you felt at the time

Write for a few minutes, exploring how you felt and what you thought at the time the event occurred (for example, angry, subdued, in control, vulnerable, proud, embarrassed, or a combination of feelings). The following sentence strategies may help you put your feelings into words:

▶ As the event started [or during or right after the event], I felt _____ and _____. I hoped others would think of me as _____.

▶ I showed or expressed these feelings by _____.

Explore your present perspective

Write for a few minutes, exploring what you think about the event now. What can you say or show that will let readers know what you think and feel as you look back? The following sentence strategies may help you put your feelings into words:

▶ My feelings since the event [have/have not] changed in the following ways: _____.

▶ At the time, I had been going through _____, which may have affected my experience by _____.

▶ Looking back at the event, I realize I was probably trying to _____, though I didn't appreciate that fact at the time.

Write the opening sentences.

Review what you have already written to see if you have something that would work to launch your story. If not, experiment with ways to begin, and review the readings to see how they begin. Here are some additional ideas:

- A graphic description of a place or person
- A startling action that you or someone else took
- A telling bit of dialogue
- Your present reflections on your past self or on the context of the event

Don't agonize over the first sentences, because you may think of better approaches after you've written a rough draft.

Draft your story.

By this point, you have done a lot of writing

- to develop a plan for a well-told story;
- to come up with vivid details to help your readers imagine what happened;
- to think of strategies for showing or telling the autobiographical significance of your event;
- to try out a way to launch your story.

Now stitch that material together to create a draft. The next two parts of this Guide to Writing will help you evaluate and improve your draft.

Evaluating the Draft: Getting a Critical Reading

Your instructor may arrange a peer review session in class or online where you can exchange drafts with your classmates and give each other a thoughtful critical reading, pointing out what works well and suggesting ways to improve the draft. A good critical reading does three things:

1. It lets the writer know how clear, vivid, and meaningful the story seems to readers.
2. It praises what works best.
3. It indicates where the draft could be improved and makes suggestions on how to improve it.

A CRITICAL READING GUIDE

How effectively does the writer tell the story?

A Well-Told Story

Summarize: Circle or highlight the inciting incident and the climax of the story.

Praise: Give an example in the story where the storytelling is especially effective — for example, a place where the story seems to flow smoothly and maintain the reader's interest, or where narrative action is compelling or exciting.

Critique: Tell the writer where the storytelling could be improved — for example, where the suspense slackens, the story lacks tension or conflict, or the chronology is confusing.

Vivid Description of People and Places

Do the descriptions help you imagine what happened?

Summarize: Choose a passage of description and analyze how and how well it uses the describing strategies of naming, detailing, and comparing.

Praise: Identify a description that is particularly vivid — for example, a graphic sensory description or an apt comparison that makes a person or place come alive.

Critique: Tell the writer where the description could be improved — for example, where objects in the scene are not named or described with enough specific detail (colors, sounds, smells, textures), or where the description is sparse. Note any description that contradicts the dominant impression; it may suggest how the significance can be made more complex and interesting.

Autobiographical Significance

Is it clear why the event was important to the author?

Summarize: Briefly describe the story's dominant impression, and tell the writer why you think the event was significant.

Praise: Give an example where the significance comes across effectively — for example, where remembered feelings are expressed poignantly, where the present perspective seems insightful, or where the description creates a strong dominant impression that clarifies the significance.

Critique: Tell the writer where the significance could be strengthened — for example, if the conflict is too easily resolved, if a moral seems tacked on at the end, or if more interesting meanings could be drawn out of the experience.

For a printable version of this Critical Reading Guide, go to **bedfordstmartins .com/theguide**.

Before concluding your peer review, be sure to address any of the writer's concerns that have not been discussed already.

Making Comments Electronically   Most word processing software offers features that allow you to insert comments directly into the text of someone else's document. Many readers prefer to make their comments this way because it tends to be faster than writing on hard copy and space is virtually unlimited; it also eliminates the process of deciphering handwritten comments. Where such features are not available, simply typing comments directly into a document in a contrasting color can provide the same advantages.

Improving the Draft: Revising, Formatting, Editing, and Proofreading

Start improving your draft by reflecting on what you have written thus far:

- Review critical reading comments from your classmates, instructor, or writing center tutor. What are your readers getting at?

- Take another look at your notes and ideas. What else should you consider?
- Review your draft. What else can you do to make your story compelling?

Revise your draft.

If your readers are having difficulty with your draft, try some of the strategies listed in the Troubleshooting Guide below. They can help you fine-tune your presentation of the genre's basic features.

A TROUBLESHOOTING GUIDE

A Well-Told Story

> My readers tell me that the story starts too slowly.

- Shorten the exposition, spread it out more within the story, or move it to a later part of the story.
- Move a bit of dialogue or narrative action up front.
- Start with something surprising but critical to the story.
- Begin with a flashback or flashforward.

> My readers find the chronology confusing.

- Add or change time transitions.
- Look for inadvertent tense shifts and fix them.

> My readers feel that the suspense slackens or that the story lacks drama.

- Add remembered feelings and thoughts to heighten anticipation.
- Add dialogue and narrative action to emphasize critical moments in the story.
- Cut or shorten background exposition and unnecessary description.
- Build rising action in stages, with multiple high points.

> My readers find the conflict vague or unconnected to the autobiographical significance.

- Think about the conflict's multiple and possibly contradictory meanings.
- Add remembered feelings or thoughts to suggest multiple meanings, and cut those that don't clarify the significance.
- Add your present perspective to make the significance clearer and bring out the implications.
- Add dialogue or narrative action to clarify the conflict.

Vivid Description of People and Places

My readers feel that the people in the story don't come alive.

- Add details about distinctive physical features or mannerisms.
- Add speaker tags that characterize people and show their feelings.
- Read your dialogue aloud, and revise to make the language more natural and appropriate to the person.

My readers have trouble visualizing the places I describe.

- Name objects in the scene.
- Add sensory details (colors, sounds, smells, textures).
- Use a comparison — metaphor or simile — to evoke a particular mood or attitude.
- Add a visual — a photograph or other memorabilia.

My readers feel that some descriptions weaken the dominant impression.

- Omit unnecessary details.
- Add adjectives, similes, or metaphors to strengthen the dominant impression.
- Rethink the impression you want your writing to convey and the significance it suggests.

Autobiographical Significance

My readers do not identify or sympathize with me.

- Add background details or explain the context.
- Reveal the cultural influences acting on you or emphasize the historical period in which the event occurred.
- Show readers how you have changed or were affected by the experience.

My readers don't understand the significance of the story.

- Use irony or humor to contrast your present perspective with your past behavior, feelings, or attitudes.
- Show that the event ended but that the conflict was not resolved.
- Use dialogue to show how your relationship with people in your story changed.
- Indicate how the event continues to influence your thoughts or actions.

My readers think the significance seems too pat or simplistic.

- Develop contradictions or show ambivalence to enrich the implications.
- Use humor to comment ironically on your past behavior or current contradictory feelings.
- Stress the social or cultural dimensions of the event.
- Revise Hollywood-movie clichés, simple resolutions, or tagged-on morals.

Think about design.

For an electronic version of the Troubleshooting Guide, go to **bedfordstmartins .com/theguide.**

Remembered event writing appears in a wide variety of contexts and genres outside of college classrooms. For example, a grandparent might write a letter to entertain her grandchild with family stories from the past, and a CEO might give a speech to inspire employees to come up with the next great idea. Each context and genre requires different design decisions to tell the story vividly and engagingly for readers. In the example below, a regional newspaper publishes a story about a farmer's experience during the record-breaking blizzard of 1938 to commemorate this historic event. It is designed to entertain and inform readers about local history.

Headline conveys key elements of the story

Story begins with a quotation to draw readers in and highlight its autobiographical significance

Exposition: Provides background, sets the scene, and suggests the problem to come

Rising action: The crisis develops

A well-told story in a newspaper begins with the most important or exciting information, with later sections on inside pages

The Rocky Valley Times

Special Supplement, Volume XCII, Number 2   January 14, 2006

This Sunday marks the 68th anniversary of the legendary "Storm of the Century" that blitzed the Rocky Valley area with up to 8 feet of snow in just a few hours.

In this era of cell phones and fax machines, it's all too easy to forget the danger and difficulties the regions' widely scattered settlers faced at that time.

In this special 6-page supplement, we salute the resourceful individuals who "made it through" and helped to establish our community as we know it today.
—The Editor

INSIDE
The General Store, 2
An Engineer's Tale, 2
Women Saved Lives, 2
Born During Storm, 3
Animals in Snowstorm, 4
Forecast Went Wrong, 5
Logger's Perspective, 5
Happen Today? 6

RANCHER REMEMBERS THE STORM OF THE CENTURY
By George Valentino

"It was only a few days, but it seemed like a lifetime."

Jim and Anne Austin were new to Rocky Valley, and when it became clear that a major blizzard was imminent, relatives urged the couple and their two young children to stay in town lest supplies become scarce. But Austin and Anne had lived off the land for years, and had weathered storms before.

Anne Austin standing on the roof of the Austin home after the 1938 snowstorm.

They felt safest returning to their ranch to tend their livestock. They were confident they had enough food, water, and candles at the ranch to carry them through any storm. Nothing in their past experience had prepared the couple, however, for the onslaught of what quickly came to be known as "the storm of the century." In a recent interview for the *Times*, Austin unfolded an inspiring tale of resourcefulness and courage in a desperate situation.

The date was January 1938. Young Jim Jr. was only two, and Mark was just a few months old. Austin remembered that, despite the frigid temperature, the children were happy and excited on the ride home from town as the first few flakes of snow started to fall—innocently enough, it seemed at first.

While Anne put the children to bed, Austin went about his usual evening chores. "Within the span of a few hours, the wind started to blow quite a bit harder," he recalls, "but the animals were calm and comfortable in their quarters. Anne and I retired for the night without suspicion about what was to come."

Anne checked on Mark "at about 2:45 in the morning," Austin recalls wryly, "and when she came back down the hall, I knew something was wrong just from the look on her face. She said—and this is what I'll never forget—that Mark was crying because there were snowdrifts up to the windowsills." The snow was blocking the scant light from the moon, leaving the room in total darkness. SEE STORM, 4

Photograph with caption enhances the verbal description

Notice that although it demonstrates many of the genre's key features, this remembered event essay also makes use of design elements that are appropriate to the type of publication in which it appears, such as a headline, the author's byline, the sidebar providing context for the story, and a "continued" line directing readers to the inside page where the story goes on.

Edit and proofread your draft.

Three problems commonly appear in essays about remembered events: misused words and expressions, incorrectly punctuated or formatted dialogue, and misused past-perfect verbs. The following guidelines will help you check your essay for these common errors.

Using the Right Word or Expression

The Problem   Many familiar sayings and expressions are frequently heard but not often seen in writing, so writers often mistake the expression. Consider the following sentences:

> Chock it up to my upbringing, but having several children play butt naked around my feet certainly curved my appetite for parenthood.

> The deer was still jerking in its death throws, but for all intensive purposes it was dead.

Within those two sentences are five commonly mangled expressions. To the ear, they may sound right, but in each case the author has heard the expression incorrectly and written down the wrong words.

Note: the expressions should be: chalk it up, buck naked, curbed my appetite, death throes, for all intents and purposes.

The Correction   You can find and debug these kinds of errors by following these steps:

1. Highlight or circle common expressions of two or more words in your writing project (especially those you've heard before but haven't seen in writing).
2. Check each expression in a dictionary or in a list of frequently misused words.
3. Consider revising the expression: If you have heard the expression so often that it "sounds right," it may be a cliché. A fresh expression will be more powerful.

The Problem   Early drafts often include vague or overly general word choices and flabby sentences. Cutting words that add little, making verbs active, and replacing weak word choices with stronger ones can greatly increase the power of a remembered event essay.

The Correction   The following three steps can help you tighten your language and make it more powerful.

1. Circle empty intensifiers, such as *just, very, certain,* and *really*. Now reread each sentence, omitting the circled word. If the sentence still makes sense without the word, delete it.

A Note on Grammar and Spelling Checkers

These tools can be helpful, but don't rely on them exclusively to catch errors in your text: Spelling checkers cannot catch misspellings that are themselves words, such as *to* for *too*. Grammar checkers miss some problems, sometimes give faulty advice for fixing problems, and can flag correct items as wrong. Use these tools as a second line of defense after your own (and, ideally, another reader's) proofreading and editing efforts.

For practice correcting word choice problems, go to **bedfordstmartins .com/theguide/exercise central** and click on Word Choice in the Handbook section.

A glossary of frequently misused words appears at the end of the full edition of this book (pp. H-112–H-115) and in the e-book, accessible at **bedfordstmartins .com/theguide**.

2. Circle all forms of the verb *to be* (such as *am, is, are, was,* and *were*). Now reread each sentence that includes a circled word, and ask yourself, "Could I revise the sentence or combine it with another sentence to create an active construction?" Examples:

▶ The dog ~~was barking. He~~ took off after Jasper, as he raced toward
   barking^

   Third Avenue.

▶ ~~The rope was tied~~ around the oak in the front yard.
   Sarah double-knotted the rope^

3. Review your descriptions, highlighting or underlining adjectives, adverbs, and prepositional phrases. Now reread them, imagining a more specific noun or verb that could convey the same idea in fewer words.

▶ ~~A large, black truck moved quickly~~ across the parking lot.
   A Humvee sped^

Dialogue Issues

For practice correcting problems punctuating quotations, go to **bedfordstmartins.com /theguide/exercisecentral** and click on Punctuation in the Handbook section.

The Problem   Remembered event essays often include dialogue, but writers sometimes have trouble using the conventions of dialogue correctly. One common problem occurs with punctuation marks:

- In American English, the opening quotation mark hugs the first word of the quotation. Commas belong inside the closing quotation mark, but end punctuation can go inside or outside the closing quotation mark, depending on whether the end punctuation belongs to the quotation or the end of the sentence.
- Speaker tags reflect what the speaker was thinking, feeling, or doing.
- A new paragraph is typically used to indicate a change in speaker.

The Correction   Revise the punctuation, add speaker tags, or start a new paragraph as needed:

▶ "⌈Jean, what's going on^?"/ my sister asked?.^

▶ "Jean, what's going on?" my sister ~~questioned~~.
   asked

▶ A few seconds later, my sister appeared and asked, "So, did you decide to buy the

   button?"^¶ "No, I guess not."

Using the Past Perfect

The Problem   Remembered event essays often mention events that occurred before the main action. To convey this sequence of events, writers use the past-perfect tense rather than the simple past tense:

Past Perfect	Simple Past
had traveled	traveled
had been	was
had begun	began

Failing to use the past perfect when it is needed can make your meaning unclear. (What happened when, exactly?)

The Correction   Check places where you recount events to verify that you are using the past perfect to indicate actions that had already been completed at the time of another past action (she *had finished* her work when we saw her).

> *had*
> ▶ I ʌhad three people in the car, something my father told me not to do that very morning.

> *had run*
> ▶ Coach Kernow told me I ran faster than ever before.
> ʌ

For practice correcting tense problems, go to **bedfordstmartins /theguide/exercisecentral** and click on Grammatical Sentences in the Handbook section.

Note for Multilingual Writers   It is important to remember that the past perfect is formed with *had* followed by a past participle. Past participles usually end in *-ed, -d, -en, -n,* or *-t—worked, hoped, eaten, taken, bent—*although some are irregular (such as *begun* or *chosen*).

> *spoken*
> ▶ Before Tania went to Moscow last year, she had not really speak Russian.
> ʌ

A WRITER AT WORK

Jean Brandt's Essay

In this section, we look at the writing process that Jean Brandt followed in composing her essay, "Calling Home." You will see the writing that became her first draft, and you can compare her first draft with the final draft that appears on pp. 14–17.

Brandt started out by drafting dialogue and exploring her past and present perspectives. This writing took up about nine pages, but it only required about two hours spread over four days for her to produce it. She began by choosing an event, reimagining the place with specific sensory details, and recalling the other people involved.

Creating a Dialogue

She also wrote two dialogues, one with her sister, Sue, and the other with her father. Following is the dialogue between her and her sister.

SUE: Jean, why did you do it?

ME: I don't know. I guess I didn't want to wait in that long line. Sue, what am I going to tell Mom and Dad?

SUE: Don't worry about that yet, the detective might not really call the police.

ME: I can't believe I was stupid enough to take it.

SUE: I know. I've been there before. Now when he comes back, try crying and acting like you're really upset. Tell him how sorry you are and that it was the first time you ever stole something, but make sure you cry. It got me off the hook once.

ME: I don't think I can force myself to cry. I'm not really that upset. I don't think the shock's worn off. I'm more worried about Mom.

SUE: Who knows? Maybe she won't have to find out.

ME: God, I hope not. Hey, where's Louie and Grandma? Grandma doesn't know about this, does she?

SUE: No, I sort of told Lou what was going on so he's just taking Grandma around shopping.

ME: Isn't she wondering where we are?

SUE: I told him to tell her we would meet them in an hour.

ME: How am I ever going to face her? Mom and Dad might possibly understand or at least get over it, but Grandma? This is gonna kill her.

SUE: Don't worry about that right now. Here comes the detective. Now try to look like you're sorry. Try to cry.

Brandt wrote this dialogue quickly, trying to capture the language of excited talk, keeping the exchanges brief. She included a version of this dialogue in her first draft (see pp. 54–55) but excluded it from the final essay. Even though she eventually decided to leave it out, this dialogue helped her work out her thoughts about the event and enabled her to evaluate how to dramatize it.

Recalling Remembered Feelings and Thoughts

In an attempt to bring the autobiographical significance of the event into focus, Brandt explored her remembered as well as her current feelings and thoughts about the experience:

> Being arrested for shoplifting was significant because it changed some of my basic attitudes. Since that night I've never again considered stealing anything. This event would reveal how my attitude toward the law and other people has changed from disrespectful to very respectful.

Reading this statement might lead us to expect a moralistic story of how someone learned something the hard way. As we look at the subsequent invention activities, however, we see how her focus shifts to her relations with other people.

> I was scared, humiliated, and confused. I was terrified when I realized what was happening. I can still see the manager and his badge and remember what I felt when I knew who he was. I just couldn't believe it. I didn't want to run. I felt there wasn't anything I could do—I was afraid, embarrassed, worried, mad that it happened. I didn't show my feelings at all. I tried to look very calm on the outside, but inside I was extremely nervous. The nervousness might have come through in my voice a little. I wanted the people around me to think I was tough and that I could handle the situation. I was really disappointed with myself. Getting arrested made me realize how wrong

my actions were. I felt very ashamed. Afterward I had to talk to my father about it. I
didn't say much of anything except that I was wrong and I was sorry. The immediate
consequence was being taken to jail and then later having to call my parents and tell
them what happened. I hated to call my parents. That was the hardest part. I remember
how much I dreaded that. My mom was really hurt.

Naming specific feelings, Brandt focuses here on the difference between what she felt
and how she acted. She remembers her humiliation at being arrested as well as the
terrible moment when she had to tell her parents. As we will see, this concern with
her parents' reaction, more than her own humiliation, becomes the focus of her remembered feelings and thoughts.

Exploring Her Present Perspective

In exploring her first response to the event, Brandt wrote quickly, jotting down memories as they came to mind. Next, she reread this first exploration and attempted to state
briefly what the incident revealed about her:

> I think it reveals that I was not a hard-core criminal. I was trying to live up to
> Robin Files's (supposedly my best girlfriend) expectations, even though I actually knew
> that what I was doing was wrong.

Stopping to focus her thoughts like this helped Brandt see the point of what she had
just written and discover the autobiographical significance of the event. Next, she
wrote about her present perspective on the event.

> At first I was ashamed to tell anyone that I had been arrested. It was as if
> I couldn't admit it myself. Now I'm glad it happened, because who knows where I'd be
> now if I hadn't been caught. I still don't tell many people about it. Never before have
> I written about it. I think my response was appropriate. If I'd broken down and cried, it
> wouldn't have helped me any, so it's better that I reacted calmly. My actions and re-
> sponses show that I was trying to be tough. I thought that that was the way to gain
> respectability. If I were to get arrested now (of course it wouldn't be for shoplifting),
> I think I'd react the same way because it doesn't do any good to get emotional. My cur-
> rent feelings are ones of appreciation. I feel lucky because I was set straight early. Now
> I can look back on it and laugh, but at the same time know how serious it was. I am
> emotionally distant now because I can view the event objectively rather than subjec-
> tively. My feelings are settled now. I don't get upset thinking about it. I don't feel angry
> at the manager or the police. I think I was more upset about my parents than about
> what was happening to me. After the first part of it was over I mainly worried about
> what my parents would think.

In writing about her present perspective, Brandt reassures herself that she feels comfortable enough to write for class about this event: She no longer feels humiliated,
embarrassed, or angry. She is obviously pleased to recall that she did not lose control
and show her true feelings. Staying calm, not getting emotional, looking tough — these
are the personal qualities Brandt wants others to see in her. Exploring her present
perspective seems to have led to a new, respectable self-image she can proudly display
to her readers:

My present perspective shows that I'm a reasonable person. I can admit when I'm wrong and accept the punishment that is due me. I find that I can be concerned about others even when I'm in trouble.

Clarifying Purpose and Audience

Next, Brandt reflected on what she had written and restated the event's significance, with particular emphasis on her readers' likely reactions:

The event was important because it entirely changed one aspect of my character. I will be disclosing that I was once a thief, and I think many of my readers will be able to identify with my story, even though they won't admit it.

This writing reveals that Brandt is now confident that she has chosen an event with personal significance. She knows what she will be disclosing about herself and feels comfortable doing it. In her brief focusing statements, she begins by moralizing ("my attitude . . . changed") and blaming others ("Robin Files") but concludes by acknowledging what she did. She is now prepared to disclose it to readers ("I was once a thief"). Also, she thinks readers will like her story because she suspects many of them will recall doing something illegal and feeling guilty about it, even if they never got caught.

The First Draft

The day after completing the writing that appears on pp. 51–54, Brandt reviewed her invention and composed her first draft on a word processor. It took her about an hour to write the draft, and she wrote steadily without doing a lot of rearranging or correcting of obvious typos and grammatical errors. She knew this would not be her only draft.

1   It was two days before Christmas and my older sister and brother, my grandmother, and I were rushing around doing last-minute shopping. After going to a few stores we decided to go to Lakewood Center shopping mall. It was packed with other frantic shoppers like ourselves from one end to the other. The first store we went to (the first and last for me) was the General Store. The General Store is your typical gift shop. They mainly have the cutesy knick-knacks, posters, frames and that sort. The store is decorated to resemble an old-time western general store but the appearance doesn't quite come off.

2   We were all browsing around and I saw a basket of buttons so I went to see what the different ones were. One of the first ones I noticed was a Snoopy button. I'm not sure what it said on it, something funny I'm sure and besides I was in love with anything Snoopy when I was 13. I took it out of the basket and showed it to my sister and she said "Why don't you buy it?" I thought about it but the lines at the cashiers were outrageous and I didn't think it was worth it for a 75 cent item. Instead I figured just take it and I did. I thought I was so sly about it. I casually slipped it into my pocket and assumed I was home free since no one pounced on me.

3   Everyone was ready to leave this shop so we made our way through the crowds to the entrance. My grandmother and sister were ahead of my brother and I. They were almost to the entrance of May Co. and we were about 5 to 10 yards behind when I felt this tap on my shoulder. I turned around already terror struck, and this man was flashing some kind of badge in my face. It happened so fast I didn't know what was going on. Louie finally noticed I wasn't with him and came back for me. Jack explained I was being arrested for shoplifting and if my parents were here then Louie should go find them. Louie ran to get Susie and told her about it but kept it from Grandma.

4   By the time Sue got back to the General Store I was in the back office and Jack was calling the police. I was a little scared but not really. It was sort of exciting. My sister was telling me to try and cry but I couldn't. About 20 minutes later two cops came and handcuffed me, led me through the mall outside to the police car. I was kind of embarrassed when they took me through the mall in front of all those people. When they got me in the car they began questioning me, while driving me to the police station. Questions just to fill out the report — age, sex, address, color of eyes, etc.

5   Then when they were finished they began talking about Jack and what a nuisance he was. I gathered that Jack had every single person who shoplifted, no matter what their age, arrested. The police were getting really fed up with it because it was a nuisance for them to have to come way out to the mall for something as petty as that. To hear the police talk about my "crime" that way felt good because it was like what I did wasn't really so bad. It made me feel a bit relieved. When we walked into the station I remember the desk sergeant joking with the arresting officers about "well we got another one of Jack's hardened criminals." Again, I felt my crime lacked any seriousness at all.

6   Next they handcuffed me to a table and questioned me further and then I had to phone my mom. That was the worst. I never was so humiliated in my life. Hearing the disappointment in her voice was worse punishment than the cops could ever give me.

Brandt's first draft establishes the main sequence of actions. About a third of it is devoted to the store manager, an emphasis that disappears by the final draft. What ends up having prominence in the final draft — Brandt's feelings about telling her parents and her conversations with them — appears here only in a few lines at the very end. But mentioning the interaction suggests its eventual importance.

Critical Reading and Revision

Brandt revised this first draft for another student to read critically. In this session, the reader told Brandt how much he liked her story and admired her frankness. However, he did not encourage her to develop the dramatic possibilities in calling her parents and meeting them afterward. In fact, he encouraged her to keep the dialogue with the police officers about the manager and to include what the manager said to the police.

In her final version, "Calling Home," Brandt did not take her reader's advice. She reduces the role of the police officers, eliminating any dialogue with them. She greatly expands the role of her parents: The last third of the essay is now focused on her remembered feelings about calling them and seeing them afterward. In terms of dramatic importance, the phone call home now equals the arrest. When we recall Brandt's earliest writings, we can see that she was headed toward this conclusion all along, but she needed to reflect on her experience, write two drafts, get a critical reading and think about it, and write a final revision to get there.

THINKING CRITICALLY

To think critically means to use all of the knowledge you have acquired from the information in this chapter, your own writing, the writing of other students, and class discussions to reflect deeply on your work for this assignment and the genre (or type) of writing you have produced. The benefit of thinking critically is proven and important: Thinking critically about what you have learned will help you remember it longer, ensuring that you will be able to put it to good use well beyond this writing course.

Reflecting on What You Have Learned

In this chapter, you have learned a great deal about this genre from reading several autobiographical stories and writing one of your own. To consolidate your learning, reflect not only on what you learned but also on how you learned it.

| ANALYZE & WRITE |

Write a blog post, a letter to your instructor or a classmate, or an e-mail message to a student who will take this course next term, using the writing prompt that seems most productive for you:

- Explain how what you wanted your readers to learn about you from reading your story influenced one of your decisions as a writer, such as how you used the dramatic arc to shape your story around a conflict, how you used dialogue to intensify the drama and convey the significance, or how you integrated your remembered thoughts and feelings into your storytelling.

- Discuss what you learned about yourself as a writer in the process of writing this essay. For example, what part of the process did you find most challenging, or did you try anything new, like getting a critical reading of your draft or outlining your draft in order to revise it? If so, how well did it work?

- If you were to give advice to a fellow student who was about to write a remembered event essay, what would you say?

- Which of the readings (in this chapter or elsewhere) influenced your choice of an event to write about or how you told the story? Explain the influence, citing specific examples comparing the two.

- If you got good advice from a critical reader, explain exactly how the person helped you — perhaps by questioning the conflict in a way that enabled you to develop your story's significance, or by pointing out passages that needed clearer time markers to better orient readers.

Reflecting on the Genre

We've said throughout this chapter that writing a remembered event essay leads to self-discovery, but what do we mean by the "self"? Should we think of the self as our "true" essence or as the different roles we play in different situations? If we accept the idea of an essential self, writing about significant events in our lives can help us in the search to discover who we truly are. Given this idea of the self, we might see Jean Brandt, for example, as searching to understand whether she is the kind of person who breaks the law and only cares when she is caught and has to face her parents' disapproval. If, on the other hand, we accept the idea that the various roles we play are ways we construct the self in different situations, then writing about a remembered event allows us to examine a side of our personality and the influences that shaped it. This view of the self assumes that we present different self images to different people in different situations. Given this idea, we might see Brandt as presenting her sassy teenage side to the police but keeping her vulnerability hidden from them and perhaps also from her family, with some painful loss of intimacy.

| ANALYZE & WRITE |

Write a page or two explaining how the genre prompts you to think about self-discovery. In your discussion, you might consider one or more of the following:

1. **Consider how your remembered event essay might be an exercise in self-discovery.** Planning and writing your essay, did you see yourself as discovering your true self or examining how you reacted in a particular situation? Do you think your essay reveals your single, essential, true self, or does it show only an aspect of the person you understand yourself to be?

2. **Write a page or so explaining your ideas about self-discovery and truth in remembered event essays.** Connect your ideas to your own essay and to the readings in this chapter.

3
Writing Profiles

Profiles are analytical, informative, and thought-provoking portraits of a person or place, or of an activity that brings people together. They may be cultural ethnographies, ranging from a day-in-the-life to extended immersion studies of communities or people at work and at play. They are intensively researched, centering on the field research techniques of colorful observations and edifying interviews. As a result, profiles are always entertaining to read, sometimes amusing, and often compelling. Whether written in a college course, for the broader community, or about the workplace, at their best profiles bring their subjects to life, taking us behind the scenes.

IN COLLEGE COURSES

A college student who plans to become a teacher visits a middle school class to study how a group of sixth graders collaborate on a project. During multiple visits, she makes notes of her observations and her interviews with the students and their teacher. To keep the focus on the children's activities, she reports as a spectator, weaving her insights about their collaborative process into a detailed narrative of a typical half-hour session. As she writes, the central idea emerges that the success of their collaboration depends on the children's frequent talk—both planning what to do next and reflecting on what they have already accomplished. After completing her ethnographic profile, she posts it on the class bulletin board for her classmates and others interested in collaborative learning.

IN THE COMMUNITY

A newspaper reporter is assigned to write a profile of a mural project recently commissioned by the city of Los Angeles, so he visits the studio of the local artist in charge of the project. They discuss the specifics of the mural project and the artist's views of other civic art projects, and the artist invites the reporter to spend the following day at the site. The next day, the artist puts the reporter to work alongside two volunteers. The reporter intends to use his firsthand experience, interviews with volunteers, and photos of the project to describe the painting from a participant-observer's point of view. Later, writing copy for the Sunday paper, the reporter organizes the profile around the artist's goals for the project, the experience of volunteers, and the mural's importance as civic art.

IN THE WORKPLACE

For a company newsletter, a public-relations officer profiles the corporation's new chief executive officer (CEO). He follows the CEO from meeting to meeting, taking photographs and observing her interactions with colleagues. Between meetings, he interviews her about her management philosophy and her five-year plan for the corporation. Immediately after the interviews, he makes notes and writes down questions to ask as follow-up. A day later, the CEO invites the writer to visit her at home. He watches her help her daughter with homework, chats with her husband, and takes more photographs. The writer decides to illustrate the profile with images of the CEO at her desk working and with her daughter. As he reports on some of the challenges she anticipates for the corporation, he tries to convey the confidence she shows both at work and at home.

In this chapter, we ask you to write a profile. Whether you choose something you know well or something you want to learn about, focus on it as if for the first time, and choose details that will not only make it come alive for your readers but also show them why your subject is intriguing and important. As you write your profile, consider how you can most effectively convey your insights to your readers. Consider, too, whether using visuals or multimedia would help your readers more fully grasp your subject.

PRACTICING THE GENRE

Conducting an Interview

Part 1.   Get together in a small group to practice interviewing, a crucial skill in profile writing. Have one group member take the role of the interviewee and the rest of the group taking turns as interviewers. (Choose as the interviewee a group member who is knowledgeable about a subject, such as a sport, a type of music or video game, an academic subject, or a kind of work.) Interviewers should take a couple of minutes to prepare questions and then spend five minutes taking turns asking questions. Listen to what is being said, and respond with follow-up questions as needed. All interviewers should take notes on what is being said (quoting or summarizing) plus any details about the way it is said (Is it sarcastic, excited, uncertain?) that could give readers a sense of the interviewee's attitude.

Part 2.   Discuss what you learned about profiles and about conducting an interview:

- **What did you learn about profiles?** For a profile to be effective, it must depict the subject vividly and be thought provoking. Assume that other members of your class do not know much about the subject, and take turns identifying one thing the interviewee said — for example, an illuminating fact, an amusing anecdote, or a surprising judgment — that would engage readers' interest. What other questions would readers want answered?

- **What did you learn about conducting an interview?** Compare your thoughts with those of the others in your group on what was easiest and hardest—for example, preparing questions, listening and following up, taking notes, or considering what to include in your profile.

Analyzing Profiles

As you read the selections in this chapter, you will see how different authors create a compelling profile. Analyzing how they describe and report on what they observed, how they organize the profile (as a guided tour, a story, or an array of topics), the role they take (as spectators or participant-observers), and the dominant impression they create will help you see how you can employ these same techniques to convey your perspective on the subject to your readers.

Determine the writer's purpose and audience.

Although crafting a profile usually helps writers come to understand the people, places, and activities they are studying, most write profiles to impart their own special understanding or insight. When reading the profiles that follow, ask yourself questions like these about the writer's purpose and audience:

- What seems to be the writer's main *purpose*—for example, to inform readers about some aspect of everyday life (the places and activities around us that we rarely get to know intimately); to give readers a behind-the-scenes look at an intriguing or unusual activity; to surprise readers by presenting unusual subjects or familiar ones in new ways; to offer a new way to look at and think about the cultural significance of the subject; or to bridge the distance between outsiders' preconceptions and the lived experience of people as they try to communicate, construct their identities, and define their values?

- What does the author assume about the *audience*—for example, that audience members know nothing or very little about the subject; that they will be interested and possibly amused by a particular aspect of the subject; or that they will be intrigued by the perspective the writer takes or fascinated by certain quotes or descriptive details?

Assess the genre's basic features.

Use the following to help you analyze and evaluate how profile writers employ the genre's basic features. The examples are drawn from the reading selections in this chapter.

> **Basic Features**
> Detailed Information
> A Clear, Logical Organization
> Writer's Role
> Perspective on the Subject

DETAILED INFORMATION ABOUT THE SUBJECT

Read first to learn about the subject. Much of the pleasure of reading a profile comes from the way the writer interweaves bits of information into a tapestry of lively narrative, arresting quotations, and vivid descriptions.

Examine the describing strategies of *naming, detailing,* and *comparing* to see how they create a vivid image, as in Brian Cable's description of coffins on display:

> We passed into a bright, fluorescent-lit "**display room**." Inside were thirty **coffins**. . . . Like new cars on the showroom floor . . . (Cable, par. 18)

> **Naming**
> Detailing
> Comparing

Although most information in a profile comes from observation (and is therefore described), information may also come from interviews and background research. To present information from sources, profile writers rely on three basic strategies—quotation, paraphrase, and summary:

QUOTATION	"We're in *Ripley's Believe It or Not,* along with another funeral home whose owners' names are Baggit and Sackit," Howard told me, without cracking a smile. (Cable, par. 14)
PARAPHRASE	Goodbody Mortuary, upon notification of someone's death, will remove the remains from the hospital or home. They then prepare the body for viewing, whereupon features distorted by illness or accident are restored to their natural condition. (Cable, par. 6)
SUMMARY	I came across several articles describing the causes of a farmworker shortage. The stories cited an aging workforce, immigration crackdowns, and long delays at the border that discourage workers with green cards. (Thompson, par. 5)

See Chapters 27 and 28 to learn about the conventions for citing and documenting sources in two popular academic styles.

Profile writers nearly always research the subject thoroughly. Convention dictates that selections published in popular publications like magazines, blogs, and general-interest books not cite their sources. Not so for academic or scholarly essays: Unless the information is widely known by educated adults, most instructors require you to cite your sources and provide a list of references or works cited.

A CLEAR, LOGICAL ORGANIZATION

Profiles can be organized narratively, as a guided tour of a place or as a story, or they can be organized as an array of topics. In narratives, look for time markers, such as narrative actions, which combine actors (nouns and pronouns) with action verbs; prepositional phrases, which locate objects in space or actions in time; verb tenses, which show how actions relate in time; calendar and clock time; and transitions of time and space.

NARRATIVE ACTIONS	I climbed the stone steps to the entrance. (Cable, par. 4)
PREPOSITIONAL PHRASES	Half a mile down the road, behind a fence coiled with razor wire, Lionel Dufour, proprietor of Farm Fresh Food Supplier . . . (Edge, par. 3) On my first day . . . (Thompson, par. 6)
VERB TENSES	I bend over, noticing that most of the crew has turned to watch. (Thompson, par. 8)
CALENDER AND CLOCK TIME	It's now 3:00. (Coyne, par. 19) His crew packed lips today. Yesterday, it was pickled sausage; the day before that, pig feet. Tomorrow, it's pickled pig lips again. (Edge, par. 4)
TRANSITIONS OF TIME	When I chomp down . . . (Edge, par. 18) Next, he . . . he then . . . (Thompson, par. 7)
TRANSITIONS OF SPACE	Across the aisle . . . Around the corner . . . (Edge, par. 4) Ahead of us . . . (Cable, par. 15)

To learn more about these narrating strategies, see Chapter 14.

In topical sections, look for *logical transitions* such as these that announce a

To learn more about cueing
the reader, see Chapter 13.

CONTRADICTION	. . . but it's widely assumed . . . (Thompson, par. 5)
	On the contrary, his bitterness . . . (Coyne, par. 13)
CAUSE	Because of their difference in skin color, there would be . . . (Coyne, par. 11)
CONCLUSION	So I am to be very careful and precise . . . (Thompson, par. 12)
SPECULATION	Perhaps such an air of comfort makes it easier for the family to give up their loved one. (Cable, par. 24)

Whereas a narrative tour or story may be more engaging, a topical organization may deliver information more efficiently. As you read the profiles in this chapter, consider the writer's decision on how to organize the information. What was gained and lost, if anything?

THE WRITER'S ROLE

Look also at the role that the writer assumes in relation to his or her subject:

- As a **spectator** or **detached observer,** the writer's position is like that of the reader — an outsider looking in on the people and their activities (such as the college student in the first scenario, p. 58, and Brian Cable in his profile below).

- As a **participant observer,** the writer participates in the activity being profiled and acquires insider knowledge (such as Gabriel Thompson in his profile, pp. 81–84).

Sometimes writers use both the spectator and the participant role, as John T. Edge and Amanda Coyne do in their profiles on pp. 69–71 and 75–78, respectively.

A PERSPECTIVE ON THE SUBJECT

All of the basic features listed previously — detailed information, the way the information is organized, and the writer's role — develop the writer's **perspective on the subject,** the main idea or cultural significance that the writer wants readers to take away from reading the profile. Profiles create a dominant impression through their description and narration. But they also analyze and interpret the subject, conveying their perspective explicitly through commentary as well as implicitly through tone (such as irony).

Readings

Brian Cable | *The Last Stop*

THIS PROFILE of a neighborhood mortuary was originally written when Brian Cable was a first-year college student. "Death," as he explains in the opening sentence, "is a subject largely ignored by the living," so it is not surprising that he notices people averting

To learn how Cable con-
ducted his interview with
the funeral director and
wrote up his notes, turn
to A Writer at Work on pp.
110–14. Compare the write-
up to pars. 5–22 of the
profile, where Cable reports
on what he learned from his
interview. How did writing
up his notes help him draft
part of the essay?

A recent photo of Goodbody Mortuary, the subject of Cable's profile. Does this photo match Cable's description? How would the addition of such a photo, or other photos of the mortuary, have strengthened Cable's profile?

their eyes as they walk past the mortuary on a busy commercial street. Cable, however, walks in and takes readers on a guided tour of the premises. As he presents information he learned from observing how the mortuary works — from the reception room up front to the embalming room in back — and from interviewing the people who work there, Cable invites us to reflect on our own feelings and cultural attitudes about death.

As you read, do the following:

- Notice how Cable uses humor to defuse the inherent seriousness of his subject.
- Consider the questions in the margin. Your instructor may ask you to post your answers to a class blog or discussion board or to bring them to class.

:: Basic Features
Detailed Information
A Clear, Logical Organization
Writer's Role
Perspective on the Subject

> Let us endeavor so to live that when we come to die even the undertaker will be sorry.
>
> — Mark Twain, *Pudd'nhead Wilson*

1   Death is a subject largely ignored by the living. We don't discuss it much, not as children (when Grandpa dies, he is said to be "going away"), not as adults, not even as senior citizens. Throughout our lives, death remains intensely private. The death of a loved one can be very painful, partly because of the sense of loss, but also because someone else's mortality reminds us all too vividly of our own.

Cable tells us what he expected. How does the opening — including the title and epigraph (introductory quote) — influence what you expect from his profile?

2   More than a few people avert their eyes as they walk past the dusty-pink building that houses the Goodbody Mortuary. It looks a bit like a church — tall, with gothic arches and stained glass — and somewhat like an apartment complex — low, with many windows stamped out of red brick.

3   It wasn't at all what I had expected. I thought it would be more like Forest Lawn, serene with lush green lawns and meticulously groomed gardens, a place set apart from the hustle of day-to-day life. Here instead was an odd pink structure set in the middle of a business district. On top of the Goodbody Mortuary sign was a large electric clock. What the hell, I thought. Mortuary are concerned with time, too.

What organizational plan for the profile emerges in pars. 4 and 5?

4   I was apprehensive as I climbed the stone steps to the entrance. I feared rejection or, worse, an invitation to come and stay. The door was massive, yet it swung open easily

on well-oiled hinges. "Come in," said the sign. "We're always open." Inside was a cool and quiet reception room. Curtains were drawn against the outside glare, cutting the light down to a soft glow.

5   I found the funeral director in the main lobby, adjacent to the reception room. Like most people, I had preconceptions about what an undertaker looked like. Mr. Deaver fulfilled my expectations entirely. Tall and thin, he even had beady eyes and a bony face. A low, slanted forehead gave way to a beaked nose. His skin, scrubbed of all color, contrasted sharply with his jet black hair. He was wearing a starched white shirt, gray pants, and black shoes. Indeed, he looked like death on two legs.

6   He proved an amiable sort, however, and was easy to talk to. As funeral director, Mr. Deaver ("Call me Howard") was responsible for a wide range of services. Goodbody Mortuary, upon notification of someone's death, will remove the remains from the hospital or home. They then prepare the body for viewing, whereupon features distorted by illness or accident are restored to their natural condition. The body is embalmed and then placed in a casket selected by the family of the deceased. Services are held in one of three chapels at the mortuary, and afterward the casket is placed in a "visitation room," where family and friends can pay their last respects. Goodbody also makes arrangements for the purchase of a burial site and transports the body there for burial.

7   All this information Howard related in a well-practiced, professional manner. It was obvious he was used to explaining the specifics of his profession. We sat alone in the lobby. His desk was bone clean, no pencils or paper, nothing — just a telephone. He did all his paperwork at home; as it turned out, he and his wife lived right upstairs. The phone rang. As he listened, he bit his lips and squeezed his Adam's apple somewhat nervously.

8   "I think we'll be able to get him in by Friday. No, no, the family wants him cremated."

9   His tone was that of a broker conferring on the Dow Jones. Directly behind him was a sign announcing "Visa and Master Charge Welcome Here." It was tacked to the wall, right next to a crucifix.

10   "Some people have the idea that we are bereavement specialists, that we can handle emotional problems which follow a death: Only a trained therapist can do that. We provide services for the dead, not counseling for the living."

What does the detailed description of Deaver in pars. 5 and 6 contribute to Cable's profile of the mortuary?

What role has Cable adopted in writing the profile? When does it become clear?

Why do you think Cable summarizes the information in par. 6 instead of quoting Howard?

What does this observation reveal about Cable's perspective?

Why do you think Cable quotes Howard in par. 10 instead of paraphrasing or summarizing?

11   Physical comfort was the one thing they did provide for the living. The lobby was modestly but comfortably furnished. There were several couches, in colors ranging from earth brown to pastel blue, and a coffee table in front of each one. On one table lay some magazines and a vase of flowers. Another supported an aquarium. Paintings of pastoral scenes hung on every wall. The lobby looked more or less like that of an old hotel. Nothing seemed to match, but it had a homey, lived-in look.

> What does this observation contribute to the dominant impression?

12   "The last time the Goodbodies decorated was in '59, I believe. It still makes people feel welcome."

13   And so "Goodbody" was not a name made up to attract customers but the owner's family name. The Goodbody family started the business way back in 1915. Today, they do over five hundred services a year.

14   "We're in *Ripley's Believe It or Not*, along with another funeral home whose owners' names are Baggit and Sackit," Howard told me, without cracking a smile.

15   I followed him through an arched doorway into a chapel that smelled musty and old. The only illumination came from sunlight filtered through a stained glass ceiling. Ahead of us lay a casket. I could see that it contained a man dressed in a black suit. Wooden benches ran on either side of an aisle that led to the body. I got no closer. From the red roses across the dead man's chest, it was apparent that services had already been held.

> How does Cable make the transition from topic to topic in pars. 15–18?

16   "It was a large service," remarked Howard. "Look at that casket — a beautiful work of craftsmanship."

17   I guess it was. Death may be the great leveler, but one's coffin quickly reestablishes one's status.

18   We passed into a bright, fluorescent-lit "display room." Inside were thirty coffins, lids open, patiently awaiting inspection. Like new cars on the showroom floor, they gleamed with high-gloss finishes.

19   "We have models for every price range."

> What does the comparison to a new-car showroom in pars. 18–21 reveal about Cable's perspective?

20   Indeed, there was a wide variety. They came in all colors and various materials. Some were little more than cloth-covered cardboard boxes, others were made of wood, and a few were made of steel, copper, or bronze. Howard told me prices started at $500 and averaged about $1,800. He motioned toward the center of the room: "The top of the line."

21   This was a solid bronze casket, its seams electronically welded to resist corrosion. Moisture-proof and air-tight, it could be hermetically sealed off from all outside elements. Its handles were plated with 14-karat gold. The Promethean casket made by the Batesville Casket Company is the choice of celebrities and the very wealthy. The price: a cool $25,000.

Fig. 1   "The top of the line." The Promethean casket that Michael Jackson was buried in.

22   A proper funeral remains a measure of respect for the deceased. But it is expensive. In the United States, the amount spent annually on funerals is around $12 billion (Grassley). Among ceremonial expenditures, funerals are second only to weddings. As a result, practices are changing. Howard has been in this business for forty years. He remembers a time when everyone was buried. Nowadays, with burials costing more than $7,000 a shot (Grassley), people often opt instead for cremation — as Howard put it, "a cheap, quick, and easy means of disposal." In some areas of the country, according to Howard, the cremation rate is now over 60 percent. Observing this trend, one might wonder whether burials are becoming obsolete. Do burials serve an important role in society?

23   For Tim, Goodbody's licensed mortician, the answer is very definitely yes. Burials will remain in common practice, according to the slender embalmer with the disarming smile, because they allow family and friends to view the deceased. Painful as it may be, such an experience brings home the finality of death. "Something deep within us demands a confrontation with death," Tim explained. "A last look assures us that the person we loved is, indeed, gone forever."

> Where does the information in pars. 22–23 come from? How can you tell?

> Why do you think Cable uses a rhetorical question here?

24 Apparently, we also need to be assured that the body will be laid to rest in comfort and peace. The average casket, with its innerspring mattress and pleated satin lining, is surprisingly roomy and luxurious. Perhaps such an air of comfort makes it easier for the family to give up their loved one. In addition, the burial site fixes the deceased in the survivors' memory, like a new address. Cremation provides none of these comforts.

25 Tim started out as a clerk in a funeral home but then studied to become a mortician. "It was a profession I could live with," he told me with a sly grin. Mortuary science might be described as a cross between pre-med and cosmetology, with courses in anatomy and embalming as well as in restorative art.

26 Tim let me see the preparation, or embalming, room, a white-walled chamber about the size of an operating room. Against the wall was a large sink with elbow taps and a draining board. In the center of the room stood a table with equipment for preparing the arterial embalming fluid, which consists primarily of formaldehyde, a preservative, and phenol, a disinfectant. This mixture sanitizes and also gives better color to the skin. Facial features can then be "set" to achieve a restful expression. Missing eyes, ears, and even noses can be replaced.

27 I asked Tim if his job ever depressed him. He bridled at the question: "No, it doesn't depress me at all. I do what I can for people and take satisfaction in enabling relatives to see their loved ones as they were in life." He said that he felt people were becoming more aware of the public service his profession provides. Grade-school classes now visit funeral homes as often as they do police stations and museums. The mortician is no longer regarded as a minister of death.

28 Before leaving, I wanted to see a body up close. I thought I could be indifferent after all I had seen and heard, but I wasn't sure. Cautiously, I reached out and touched the skin. It felt cold and firm, not unlike clay. As I walked out, I felt glad to have satisfied my curiosity about dead bodies, but all too happy to let someone else handle them.

Works Cited

Grassley, Chuck. "Opening Statement of Chairman Grassley." U.S. Senate Special Committee on Aging. 21 Sept. 2000. Web. 6 Jan. 2012.

Twain, Mark. *Pudd'nhead Wilson*. New York: Pocket Books, 2004: 45. Print.

Whose perspective does this statement reflect? How do you know?

Is Tim's definition of mortuary science helpful? Why or why not?

Which information in par. 26 comes from observation and which comes from interviewing Tim? How do you know?

How effective is this ending?

For an additional student reading, go to bedfordstmartins.com /theguide/epages.

John T. Edge | *I'm Not Leaving Until I Eat This Thing*

JOHN T. EDGE directs the Southern Foodways Symposium, which is part of the Center for the Study of Southern Culture at the University of Mississippi, and edits the *Encyclopedia of Southern Culture*. He has written *Truck Food Cookbook* (2012); *A Gracious Plenty: Recipes and Recollections from the American South* (1999); *Southern Belly* (2000), a portrait of southern food told through profiles of people and places; and a series of books on specific foods, including *Fried Chicken* (2004), *Apple Pie* (2004), and *Hamburgers and Fries* (2005). In addition to appearing on several radio and television programs, such as *Iron Chef* and NPR's *All Things Considered,* Edge writes columns for a number of newspapers and magazines, including the *New York Times, Garden and Gun, Gourmet,* and the *Oxford American,* in which this profile originally appeared.

As you read, consider how Edge uses his own experience of trying to eat a pickled pig lip to introduce readers to Farm Fresh Food Supplier, a family business that produces pickled meat products:

- What do you learn about this popular bar snack food?
- What do you learn about the family and its business?

1 It's just past 4:00 on a Thursday afternoon in June at Jesse's Place, a country juke 17 miles south of the Mississippi line and three miles west of Amite, Louisiana. The air conditioner hacks and spits forth torrents of Arctic air, but the heat of summer can't be kept at bay. It seeps around the splintered doorjambs and settles in, transforming the squat particleboard-plastered roadhouse into a sauna. Slowly, the dank barroom fills with grease-smeared mechanics from the truck stop up the road and farmers straight from the fields, the soles of their brogans thick with dirt clods. A few weary souls make their way over from the nearby sawmill. I sit alone at the bar, one empty bottle of Bud in front of me, a second in my hand. I drain the beer, order a third, and stare down at the pink juice spreading outward from a crumpled foil pouch and onto the bar.

2 *I'm not leaving until I eat this thing,* I tell myself.

3 Half a mile down the road, behind a fence coiled with razor wire, Lionel Dufour, proprietor of Farm Fresh Food Supplier, is loading up the last truck of the day, wheeling case after case of pickled pork offal out of his cinder-block processing plant and into a semi-trailer bound for Hattiesburg, Mississippi.

4 His crew packed lips today. Yesterday, it was pickled sausage; the day before that, pig feet. Tomorrow, it's pickled pig lips again. Lionel has been on the job since 2:45 in the morning, when he came in to light the boilers. Damon Landry, chief cook and maintenance man, came in at 4:30. By 7:30, the production line was at full tilt: six women in white smocks and blue bouffant caps, slicing ragged white fat from the lips, tossing the good parts in glass jars, the bad parts in barrels bound for the rendering plant. Across the aisle, filled jars clatter by on a conveyor belt as a worker tops them off with a Kool-Aid-red slurry of hot sauce, vinegar, salt, and food coloring. Around the corner, the jars are capped, affixed with a label, and stored in pasteboard boxes to await shipping.

5 Unlike most offal—euphemistically called "variety meats"—lips belie their provenance. Brains, milky white and globular, look like brains. Feet, the ghosts of their cloven hoofs protruding, look like feet. Testicles look like, well, testicles. But lips are different.

Loosed from the snout, trimmed of their fat, and dyed a preternatural pink, they look more like candy than like carrion.

6   At Farm Fresh, no swine root in an adjacent feedlot. No viscera-strewn killing floor lurks just out of sight, down a darkened hallway. These pigs died long ago at some Midwestern abattoir. By the time the lips arrive in Amite, they are, in essence, pig Popsicles, 50-pound blocks of offal and ice.

7   "Lips are all meat," Lionel told me earlier in the day. "No gristle, no bone, no nothing. They're bar food, hot and vinegary, great with a beer. Used to be the lips ended up in sausages, headcheese, those sorts of things. A lot of them still do."

8   Lionel, a 50-year-old father of three with quick, intelligent eyes set deep in a face the color of cordovan, is a veteran of nearly 40 years in the pickled pig lips business. "I started out with my daddy when I wasn't much more than 10," Lionel told me, his shy smile framed by a coarse black mustache flecked with whispers of gray. "The meatpacking business he owned had gone broke back when I was 6, and he was peddling out of the back of his car, selling dried shrimp, napkins, straws, tubes of plastic cups, pig feet, pig lips, whatever the bar owners needed. He sold to black bars, white bars, sweet shops, snowball stands, you name it. We made the rounds together after I got

"Lips are all meat," Lionel told me earlier in the day. "No gristle, no bone, no nothing. They're bar food, hot and vinegary, great with a beer."

out of school, sometimes staying out till two or three in the morning. I remember bringing my toy cars to this one joint and racing them around the floor with the bar owner's son while my daddy and his father did business."

9   For years after the demise of that first meatpacking company, the Dufour family sold someone else's product. "We used to buy lips from Dennis Di Salvo's company down in Belle Chasse," recalled Lionel. "As far as I can tell, his mother was the one who came up with the idea to pickle and pack lips back in the '50s, back when she was working for a company called Three Little Pigs over in Houma. But pretty soon, we were selling so many lips that we had to almost beg Di Salvo's for product. That's when we started cooking up our own," he told me, gesturing toward the cast-iron kettle that hangs from the rafters by the front door of the plant. "My daddy started cooking lips in that very pot."

10   Lionel now cooks lips in 11 retrofitted milk tanks, dull stainless-steel cauldrons shaped like oversized cradles. But little else has changed. Though Lionel's father has passed away, Farm Fresh remains a family-focused company. His wife, Kathy, keeps the books. His daughter, Dana, a button-cute college student who has won numerous beauty titles, takes to the road in the summer, selling lips to convenience stores and wholesalers. Soon, after he graduates from business school, Lionel's younger son, Matt, will take over operations at the plant. And his older son, a veterinarian, lent his name to one of Farm Fresh's top sellers, Jason's Pickled Pig Lips.

11   "We do our best to corner the market on lips," Lionel told me, his voice tinged with bravado. "Sometimes they're hard to get from the packing houses. You gotta kill a lot of pigs to get enough lips to keep us going. I've got new customers calling every day; it's all I can do to keep up with demand, but I bust my ass to keep up. I do what I can for my family — and for my customers.

12   "When my customers tell me something," he continued, "just like when my daddy told me something, I listen. If my customers wanted me to dye the lips

green, I'd ask, 'What shade?' As it is, every few years we'll do some red and some blue for the Fourth of July. This year we did jars full of Mardi Gras lips — half purple, half gold," Lionel recalled with a chuckle. "I guess we'd had a few beers when we came up with that one."

13   Meanwhile, back at Jesse's Place, I finish my third Bud, order my fourth. *Now,* I tell myself, my courage bolstered by booze, *I'm ready to eat a lip.*

14   They may have looked like candy in the plant, but in the barroom they're carrion once again. I poke and prod the six-inch arc of pink flesh, peering up from my reverie just in time to catch the barkeep's wife, Audrey, staring straight at me. She fixes me with a look just this side of pity and asks, "You gonna eat that thing or make love to it?"

15   Her nephew, Jerry, sidles up to a bar stool on my left. "A lot of people like 'em with chips," he says with a nod toward the pink juice pooling on the bar in front of me. I offer to buy him a lip, and Audrey fishes one from a jar behind the counter, wraps it in tinfoil, and places the whole affair on a paper towel in front of him.

16   I take stock of my own cowardice, and, following Jerry's lead, reach for a bag of potato chips, tear open the top with my teeth, and toss the quivering hunk of hog flesh into the shiny interior of the bag, slick with grease and dusted with salt. Vinegar vapors tickle my nostrils. I stifle a gag that rolls from the back of my throat, swallow hard, and pray that the urge to vomit passes.

17   With a smash of my hand, the potato chips are reduced to a pulp, and I feel the cold lump of the lip beneath my fist. I clasp the bag shut and shake it hard in an effort to ensure chip coverage in all the nooks and crannies of the lip. The technique that Jerry uses — and I mimic — is not unlike that employed by home cooks mixing up a mess of Shake 'n Bake chicken.

18   I pull from the bag a coral crescent of meat now crusted with blond bits of potato chips. When I chomp down, the soft flesh dissolves between my teeth. It tastes like a flaccid cracklin', unmistakably porcine, and not altogether bad. The chips help, providing texture where there was none. Slowly, my brow unfurrows, my stomach ceases its fluttering.

19   Sensing my relief, Jerry leans over and peers into my bag. "Kind of look like Frosted Flakes, don't they?" he says, by way of describing the chips rapidly turning to mush in the pickling juice. I offer the bag to Jerry, order yet another beer, and turn to eye the pig feet floating in a murky jar by the cash register, their blunt tips bobbing up through a pasty white film.

Make connections: Aversion to new foods.

⎡ REFLECT ⎤

Edge uses the words *courage* (par. 13) and *cowardice* (par. 16) to describe his squeamishness about eating a pickled pig lip. And when he finally eats a bite, he feels queasy. Although his nausea is undoubtedly real, it may be caused more by anxiety than by anything sickening in the food itself.

Consider the kinds of food you feel uncomfortable eating — foods that you have anxiety about eating, foods that gross you out, or foods that you stay away from for some other reason, such as a religious dietary restriction or a moral conviction. Your instructor may ask you to post your thoughts on a class discussion board or to discuss them with other students in class. Use these questions to get started:

- What role do factors such as family, ethnic, or religious traditions play in your food choices? If your food aversions are unusual in your family or community, consider how other family or community members regard your choice — for example, as a quirk or as a rejection of something they value. If you find it hard to try foods from different cultures, why do you think that is?

- Early in the essay, Edge makes clear that he is squeamish about eating a pickled pig lip even though he is a Southerner and it is a popular southern delicacy. How does his difficulty eating the pig lip set him apart from the other people in the bar? What else separates him from them?

[**ANALYZE**]   ## Use the basic features.

DETAILED INFORMATION ABOUT THE SUBJECT: DESCRIBING THE PLACE AND PEOPLE

To learn more about the descriptive strategies of naming and detailing, see Chapter 15, pp. 574–77. For more on analyzing a photograph, see Chapter 20, pp. 628–29.

An effective description names the observable features of the subject, details the subject by explaining what it is or what its parts or features are, and compares the subject with something else to explain what it is like. The comparisons may be similes, which explicitly compare items using words such as *like* or *as*: The pig lips "look more like candy than like carrion" (par. 5). Or the comparisons may be metaphors, which compare the subject with something else without using words such as *like* or *as*: "The air conditioner . . . spits forth torrents of Arctic air" (par. 1). The choices a writer makes about the details to include and the words to use in creating the description work together to create a **dominant impression** that conveys the writer's perspective—what we call **showing.**

[ANALYZE & WRITE]────────────────────────────────

Write a couple of paragraphs analyzing Edge's descriptions:

1 For paragraphs 5–7, 14, and 16–18, choose a few examples of especially vivid naming and detailing. Also highlight one or two comparisons—similes or metaphors—that work particularly well. What makes these examples so effective?

2 If you have never seen a pickled pig lip, what more do you need to know to imagine what it looks, smells, and tastes like, or how it feels and sounds when you chomp down on it? Which details make a lip seem appealing to you? Which ones make it seem unappealing?

3 Consider the photograph Edge includes in his essay, and explain what it contributes to the dominant impression. Edge could have used a full-body photograph of a pig or a photograph of the pig lips themselves. What does the choice of visual suggest about the writer's perspective?

A CLEAR, LOGICAL ORGANIZATION: TAKING READERS ON A TOUR

Profiles may be organized **topically,** with the writer moving through a series of topics about the subject. They may be organized **narratively,** with the writer taking readers on a tour of the place, pointing out interesting sights and commenting as they move through space. (Brian Cable's profile of the Goodbody Mortuary is a good example of narrative organization.) Or, like Edge, they may combine strategies.

ANALYZE & WRITE

Write a paragraph or two analyzing the organization of Edge's profile:

1. Skim paragraphs 3–12, and note in the margin where Edge presents the following topics: the production process, the various products produced by Farm Fresh, the source of the products, and the history of the Farm Fresh business.

2. Reread paragraphs 16–18, and highlight places where the sequence of actions involved in eating a pig lip are narrated.

3. Explain what, if anything, you learn from Edge's narrative that you couldn't find out from the topics he presents in paragraphs 3–12.

THE WRITER'S ROLE: ACTING AS A SPECTATOR

Profile writers can adopt the role of a spectator or the role of a participant. In the student essay at the beginning of this section, Cable takes on the role of a spectator when he talks to Howard and Tim and takes a tour of the Goodbody Mortuary. To become a participant, Cable would have had to help the funeral director or embalmer in his daily activities.

ANALYZE & WRITE

Analyze Edge's dual roles of spectator and participant in "I'm Not Leaving Until I Eat This Thing," and then write a few paragraphs explaining what the two roles contribute to his profile:

1. Skim the essay, and note in the margin where Edge uses the spectator role and where he uses the participant role.

2. Give an example of each role, and explain how the examples show which role he is using.

3. What does adopting each role enable Edge to do?

A PERSPECTIVE ON THE SUBJECT: SHOWING AND TELLING

Profile writers do not simply present information about their subject; they also offer their insights on it. They do so through their decisions about what to show the reader. For example, by comparing the display of caskets to shiny new cars in a showroom, Cable reveals his perspective on Americans' denial of death and their inclination to profit from it. They may also *tell* readers what they are thinking. Cable conveys his perspective with comments such as, "The death of a loved one can be very painful, partly because . . . someone else's mortality reminds us all too vividly of our own" (par. 1). A writer's tone can also be telling—for example, Cable's use of humor.

ANALYZE & WRITE

Write a paragraph or two analyzing Edge's use of telling to convey his perspective:

1. Reread paragraph 1, and highlight the descriptions of the patrons of Jesse's Place, noting particularly information suggesting the kinds of work they do and their socioeconomic class.

2. Skim paragraph 15, where Jerry shows Edge how people like to eat pickled pig lips.

3. Explain Edge's perspective on this popular Southern bar snack and how it may reflect his own class position.

[RESPOND]

Consider possible topics: Writing about a specialty restaurant, manufacturer, or store.

Consider writing about a place that serves, produces, or sells something unusual, perhaps something that, like Edge, you could try yourself for the purpose of further informing and engaging your readers. There are many possibilities: a producer or packager of a special ethnic or regional food or a local café that serves it, a licensed acupuncture clinic, a caterer, a novelty and toy balloon store, a microbrewery, a boat builder, a talent agency, a manufacturer of ornamental iron, a bead store, a nail salon, a pet fish and aquarium supplier, a detailing shop, a tattoo parlor, a scrap metal recycler, a fly-fishing shop, a handwriting analyst, a dog- or cat-sitting service. If none of these appeals to you, try browsing the Yellow Pages in print or online at Yellow.com. Remember that relating your experience with the service or product is a good idea but not a requirement for a successful profile.

Amanda Coyne | *The Long Good-Bye: Mother's Day in Federal Prison*

AMANDA COYNE earned a master of fine arts degree in creative writing at the University of Iowa, where she was the recipient of an Iowa Arts Fellowship. She is the cofounder and writer of the *Alaska Dispatch,* an award-winning online news site. Her work has appeared in such publications as *Harper's,* the *New York Times Magazine, Bust, Newsweek,* and the *Guardian.* Most recently, she is the coauthor with her husband of a book about oil and politics in Alaska entitled *Crude Awakening: Money, Mavericks, and Mayhem in Alaska* (2011).

"The Long Good-Bye," her first piece of published writing, originally appeared in *Harper's.* This selection takes a more ethnographic turn than the other profiles in this chapter in that Coyne uses direct observation and interview to study the behavior of a particular community. In this profile, Coyne examines women who have been in-carcerated and separated from their children to see how the mothers and children ne-gotiate their difficult relationships.

As you read, think about what you learn about the stresses on these parent-child relationships:

- What stresses seem to affect the family relationships described in this profile?
- What do you think is the author's attitude toward these stresses? How can you tell what she thinks and feels?

1 You can spot the convict-moms here in the visiting room by the way they hold and touch their children and by the single flower that is perched in front of them — a rose, a tulip, a daffodil. Many of these mothers have untied the bow that attaches the flower to its silver-and-red cellophane wrapper and are using one of the many empty soda cans at hand as a vase. They sit proudly before their flower-in-a-Coke-can, amid Hershey bar wrap-pers, half-eaten Ding Dongs, and empty paper coffee cups. Occasionally, a mother will pick up her present and bring it to her nose when one of the bearers of the single flower — her child — asks if she likes it. And the mother will respond the way that mothers always have and always will respond when presented with a gift on this day. "Oh, I just love it. It's perfect. I'll put it in the middle of my Bible." Or, "I'll put it on my desk, right next to your school picture." And always: "It's the best one here."

2 But most of what is being smelled today is the chil-dren themselves. While the other adults are plunking coins into the vending machines, the mothers take deep whiffs from the backs of their children's necks, or kiss and smell the backs of their knees, or take off their shoes and tickle their feet and then pull them close to their noses. They hold them tight and take in their own second scent — the scent assuring them that these are still their children and that they still belong to them.

3 The visitors are allowed to bring in pockets full of coins, and today that Mother's Day flower, and I know from previous visits to my older sister here at the Federal Prison Camp for women in Pekin, Illinois, that there is always an aberrant urge to gather immedi-ately around the vending machines. The sandwiches are stale, the coffee weak, the candy bars the ones we always pass up in a convenience store. But after we hand the children over to their mothers, we gravitate toward those machines. Like milling in the kitchen at a party. We all do it, and nobody knows why. Polite conversation ensues around the microwave while the popcorn is popping and the processed-chicken sand-wiches are being heated. We ask one another where we are from, how long a drive we had. An occasional whistle through the teeth, a shake of the head. "My, my, long way from home, huh?" "Staying at the Super 8 right up the road. Not a bad place." "Stayed at the Econo Lodge last time. Wasn't a good place at all." Never asking the questions we really want to ask: "What's she in for?" "How much time's she got left?" You never ask in the waiting room of a doctor's office either. Eventually, all of us — fathers, mothers, sisters, brothers, a few boyfriends, and very few husbands — return to the queen of the day, sitting at a fold-out table loaded with snacks, prepared for five or so hours of attempted normal conversation.

4 Most of the inmates are elaborately dressed, many in prison-crafted dresses and sweaters in bright blues and pinks. They wear meticulously applied makeup in corresponding hues, and their hair is re-plete with loops and curls — hair that only women with the time have the time for. Some of the better seamstresses have crocheted vests and purses to match their outfits. Although the world outside would never accuse these women of making haute-couture fashion statements, the fathers and the sons and the boyfriends and the very few husbands think they look beautiful, and they tell them so repeatedly. And I can imagine the hours spent preparing for this visit — hours of nee-dles and hooks clicking over brightly colored yards of yarn. The hours of discussing, dissecting, and brag-ging about these visitors — especially the men. Hours

spent in the other world behind the door where we're not allowed, sharing lipsticks and mascaras, and unraveling the occasional hair-tangled hot roller, and the brushing out and lifting and teasing . . . and the giggles that abruptly change into tears without warning—things that define any female-only world. Even, or especially, if that world is a female federal prison camp.

5   While my sister Jennifer is with her son in the playroom, an inmate's mother comes over to introduce herself to my younger sister, Charity, my brother, John, and me. She tells us about visiting her daughter in a higher-security prison before she was transferred here. The woman looks old and tired, and her shoulders sag under the weight of her recently acquired bitterness.

6   "Pit of fire," she says, shaking her head. "Like a pit of fire straight from hell. Never seen anything like it. Like something out of an old movie about prisons." Her voice is getting louder and she looks at each of us with pleading eyes. "My *daughter* was there. Don't even get me started on that place. Women die there."

7   John and Charity and I silently exchange glances.

8   "My daughter would come to the visiting room with a black eye and I'd think, 'All she did was sit in the car while her boyfriend ran into the house.' She didn't even touch the stuff. Never even handled it."

9   She continues to stare at us, each in turn. "Ten years. That boyfriend talked and he got three years. She didn't know anything. Had nothing to tell them. They gave her ten years. They called it conspiracy. Conspiracy? Aren't there real criminals out there?" She asks this with hands outstretched, waiting for an answer that none of us can give her.

10   The woman's daughter, the conspirator, is chasing her son through the maze of chairs and tables and through the other children. She's a twenty-four-year-old blonde, whom I'll call Stephanie, with Dorothy Hamill hair and matching dimples. She looks like any girl you might see in any shopping mall in middle America. She catches her chocolate-brown son and tickles him, and they laugh and trip and fall together onto the floor and laugh harder.

11   Had it not been for that wait in the car, this scene would be taking place at home, in a duplex Stephanie would rent while trying to finish her two-year degree in dental hygiene or respiratory therapy at the local community college. The duplex would be spotless, with a blown-up picture of her and her son over the couch and ceramic unicorns and horses occupying the shelves of the entertainment center. She would make sure that her son went to school every day with stylishly floppy pants, scrubbed teeth, and a good breakfast in his belly. Because of their difference in skin color, there would be occasional tension—caused by the strange looks from strangers, teachers, other mothers, and the bullies on the playground, who would chant after they knocked him down, "Your Momma's white, your Momma's white." But if she were home, their weekends and evenings would be spent together transcending those looks and healing those bruises. Now, however, their time is spent eating visiting-room junk food and his school days are spent fighting the boys in the playground who chant, "Your Momma's in prison, your Momma's in prison."

12   He will be ten when his mother is released, the same age my nephew will be when his mother is let out. But Jennifer, my sister, was able to spend the first five years of Toby's life with him. Stephanie had Ellie after she was incarcerated. They let her hold him for eighteen hours, then sent her back to prison. She has done the "tour," and her son is a well-traveled six-year-old. He has spent weekends visiting his mother in prisons in Kentucky, Texas, Connecticut (the Pit of Fire), and now at last here, the camp—minimum security, Pekin, Illinois.

13   Ellie looks older than his age. But his shoulders do not droop like his grandmother's. On the contrary, his bitterness lifts them and his chin higher than a child's should be, and the childlike, wide-eyed curiosity has been replaced by defiance. You can see his emerging hostility as he and his mother play together. She tells him to pick up the toy that he threw, say, or to put the deck of cards away. His face turns sullen, but she persists. She takes him by the shoulders and looks him in the eye, and he uses one of his hands to swat at her. She grabs the hand and he swats with the other. Eventually, she pulls him toward her and smells the top of his head, and she picks up the cards or the toy herself. After all, it is Mother's Day and she sees him so rarely. But her acquiescence makes him angrier, and he stalks out of the playroom with his shoulders thrown back.

14   Toby, my brother and sister and I assure one another, will not have these resentments. He is better taken care of than most. He is living with relatives in

Wisconsin. Good, solid, middle-class, churchgoing relatives. And when he visits us, his aunts and his uncle, we take him out for adventures where we walk down the alley of a city and pretend that we are being chased by the "bad guys." We buy him fast food, and his uncle, John, keeps him up well past his bedtime enthralling him with stories of the monkeys he met in India. A perfect mix, we try to convince one another. Until we take him to see his mother and on the drive back he asks the question that most confuses him, and no doubt all the other children who spend much of their lives in prison visiting rooms: "Is my Mommy a bad guy?" It is the question that most seriously disorders his five-year-old need to clearly separate right from wrong. And because our own need is perhaps just as great, it is the question that haunts us as well.

15   Now, however, the answer is relatively simple. In a few years, it won't be. In a few years we will have to explain mandatory minimums, and the war on drugs, and the murky conspiracy laws, and the enormous amount of money and time that federal agents pump into imprisoning low-level drug dealers and those who happen to be their friends and their lovers. In a few years he might have the reasoning skills to ask why so many armed robbers and rapists and child-molesters and, indeed, murderers are punished less severely than his mother. When he is older, we will somehow have to explain to him the difference between federal crimes, which don't allow for parole, and state crimes, which do. We will have to explain that his mother was taken from him for five years not because she was a drug dealer but because she made four phone calls for someone she loved.

16   But we also know it is vitally important that we explain all this without betraying our bitterness. We understand the danger of abstract anger, of being disillusioned with your country, and, most of all, we do not want him to inherit that legacy. We would still like him to be raised as we were, with the idea that we live in the best country in the world with the best legal system in the world—a legal system carefully designed to be immune to political mood swings and public hysteria; a system that promises to fit the punishment to the crime. We want him to be a good citizen. We want him to have absolute faith that he lives in a fair

country, a country that watches over and protects its most vulnerable citizens: its women and children.

17   So for now we simply say, "Toby, your mother isn't bad, she just did a bad thing. Like when you put rocks in the lawn mower's gas tank. You weren't bad then, you just did a bad thing."

18   Once, after being given this weak explanation, he said, "I wish I could have done something really bad, like my Mommy. So I could go to prison too and be with her."

19   It's now 3:00. Visiting ends at 3:30. The kids are getting cranky, and the adults are both exhausted and wired from too many hours of conversation, too much coffee and candy. The fathers, mothers, sisters, brothers, and the few boyfriends, and the very few husbands are beginning to show signs of gathering the trash. The mothers of the infants are giving their heads one last whiff before tucking them and their paraphernalia into their respective carrying cases. The visitors meander toward the door, leaving the older children with their mothers for one last word. But the mothers never say what they want to say to their children. They say things like, "Do well in school," "Be nice to your sister," "Be good for Aunt Berry, or Grandma." They don't say, "I'm sorry I'm sorry I'm sorry. I love you more than anything else in the world and I think about you every minute and I worry about you with a pain that shoots straight to my heart, a pain so great I think I will just burst when I think of you alone, without me. I'm sorry."

20   We are standing in front of the double glass doors that lead to the outside world. My older sister holds her son, rocking him gently. They are both crying. We give her a look and she puts him down. Charity and I grasp each of his small hands, and the four of us walk through the doors. As we're walking out, my brother sings one of his banana songs to Toby.

21   "Take me out to the — " and Toby yells out, "Banana store!"

22   "Buy me some — "

23   "Bananas!!"

24   "I don't care if I ever come back. For it's root, root, root for the — "

25   "Monkey team!"

26   I turn back and see a line of women standing behind the glass wall. Some of them are crying, but

> *"Is my Mommy a bad guy?" It is the question that most seriously disorders his five-year-old need to clearly separate right from wrong.*

many simply stare with dazed eyes. Stephanie is holding both of her son's hands in hers and speaking urgently to him. He is struggling, and his head is twisting violently back and forth. He frees one of his hands from her grasp, balls up his fist, and punches her in the face. Then he walks with purpose through the glass doors and out the exit. I look back at her. She is still in a crouched position. She stares, unblinking, through those doors. Her hands have left her face and are hanging on either side of her. I look away, but before I do, I see drops of blood drip from her nose, down her chin, and onto the shiny marble floor.

[REFLECT]   # Make connections: Unfair punishment.

Coyne reflects near the end of the essay that she wishes her nephew Toby would "have absolute faith that he lives in a fair country" (par. 16). Yet she expects that, like Stephanie's son, Ellie, Toby will become bitter and angry when he understands that "his mother was taken from him for five years not because she was a drug dealer but because she made four phone calls for someone she loved" (par. 15).

Think about an occasion when you were punished harshly—for breaking a school rule, perhaps, or neglecting to fulfill an expectation of your parents. Although you willingly admit having done it, you may still feel that the punishment was unjustified. Consider what you did and why you think the punishment was unfair. Your instructor may ask you to post your thoughts on a class discussion board or to discuss them with other students in class. Use these questions to get started:

- Why do you think the punishment was unfair? For example, were the rules or expectations that you broke unclear or unreasonable? Were they applied to everyone or applied selectively or at the whim of those in power?

- Coyne uses the value term *unfair* to describe what's wrong with the punishment her sister and some of the other women received. Why do you think Coyne believes her sister's punishment is unfair? Why does Stephanie's mother think Stephanie's punishment was unfair? Do you agree or disagree?

[ANALYZE]   # Use the basic features.

DETAILED INFORMATION ABOUT THE SUBJECT: USING ANECDOTES

Including **anecdotes**—brief narratives about one-time events—can be a powerful way to convey detailed information about a subject. Coyne, for example, exposes the effects of separation on mothers and children through powerful anecdotes portraying what happened between Stephanie and her son, Ellie, during their visit.

ANALYZE & WRITE

Write a few paragraphs analyzing Coyne's use of anecdotes to present information:

1. Reread paragraphs 13 and 26, underlining the words that Coyne uses to present Ellie's actions and putting brackets around the words Coyne uses to present his mother's reactions.

2. What do you learn from these anecdotes about the effects on Stephanie and Ellie of enforced separation?

A CLEAR, LOGICAL ORGANIZATION: NARRATING A DAY IN THE LIFE

Coyne uses narrative as a kind of exoskeleton, a shell within which to hold the information and ideas she wants to present to her readers. The occasion is specific: visiting hours at the Federal Prison on Mother's Day. The opening paragraphs situate the profile in time and space, and the concluding paragraphs—signaled with the time marker "It's now 3:00. Visiting ends at 3:30" (par. 19)—recount what happened at the end of the visit. Within this narrative framework, however, Coyne does not follow a strict chronological order. Some events occur at the same time as other events. For example, paragraphs 1 to 3 present actions that occur at the same time: while mothers are getting reacquainted with their children (pars. 1 and 2), the family members are using the vending machines and chatting with one another (par. 3).

ANALYZE & WRITE

Write a couple of paragraphs analyzing Coyne's use of narrative organization:

1 Reread the essay, noting in the margin when the events are happening in relation to the events in earlier paragraphs and highlighting any time markers, such as prepositional phrases locating actions in time, clock time, or verb tenses (past, present, future, and so on).

2 Coyne could have organized her essay topically, by presenting a series of insights and impressions from the many visits she has made instead of focusing on one Mother's Day. How does her choice help you understand the situation of the women and their families?

THE WRITER'S ROLE: ALTERNATING PARTICIPANT AND SPECTATOR ROLES

Instead of choosing between the roles of participant-observer or spectator, writers may also alternate between these two roles, as Coyne does in "The Long Good-Bye." Notice how Coyne uses pronouns (first-, second-, and third-person) to let readers know which role she is taking.

The **spectator,** or **eyewitness,** role shows what is unfolding before the writer's eyes.

> You can spot the convict-moms here in the visiting room by the way they hold and touch their children. (par. 1)

2nd-person pronoun

3rd-person pronouns

The participant-observer role puts Coyne and the other adult visitors into the scene.

> I know from previous visits to my older sister. (par. 3)

1st-person pronouns

ANALYZE & WRITE

Write a couple of paragraphs analyzing how Coyne uses these two roles:

1 Analyze the rest of paragraphs 1 and 3, highlighting the first-, second-, and third-person pronouns.

> **2** Look closely at the way the pronouns are used. Note, for example, that writers seldom use the second-person pronoun *you*; why do you think Coyne uses it here? Who is Coyne referring to with the first-person plural pronoun *we*?
>
> **3** Consider the effect that alternating between spectator and participant roles has on the reader. How would your experience as a reader be different if Coyne had stuck with one role or the other? Also think about how alternating the roles helps convey her perspective — for example, how the pronouns align the speaker with certain people and distance her from others (*us* versus *them*).

A PERSPECTIVE ON THE SUBJECT: USING CONTRAST AND JUXTAPOSITION

Profiles may offer a clear perspective on a subject, but unlike an argument for a position or a justification of an evaluation, which tell readers directly what the writer thinks and why, profiles may be more effective when they provide information and ideas that allow readers to draw their own conclusions. One strategy is to use transitions that point out different elements and identify the contrast between them.

To learn more about transitions, see Chapter 13; transitions indicating a contrasting or opposing view are listed on p. 556.

> They may have looked like candy in the plant, but in the barroom they're carrion once again. (Edge, par. 14)

A related strategy is to juxtapose (place next to one another) contrasting elements without explaining the relationship between them:

> They were candy in the plant. They're carrion here.

ANALYZE & WRITE

Write a couple of paragraphs analyzing how Coyne uses transitions indicating contrast and juxtaposition to convey her perspective:

1 Skim Coyne's profile, highlighting the transitional words and phrases that indicate contrast. Analyze at least one of the contrasts you've found. What is being contrasted? How does the transition help you understand?

2 Note in the margin which paragraphs focus on Coyne's sister Jennifer and her son, Toby, and which focus on Stephanie and her son, Ellie. What differences between the two families does Coyne emphasize? Contrasts tend to be worth pointing out when there are also important similarities. What similarities do you think Coyne wants readers to think about?

3 Consider how Coyne's use of contrast and juxtaposition—between people, between the world of the prison and the world outside, and between what is and what could have been—helps convey her perspective on the plight of women like her sister and children like her nephew.

[RESPOND]

Consider possible topics: Profiling one instance of a recurring event.

Like Coyne, you can also profile an activity occurring over a short period of time, in a relatively small space, involving only a few people. Consider, for example, profiling a team practicing, a musical group rehearsing, or researchers working together in a lab. Try to make more than one observational visit to see the group in action, and arrange to talk with people on every visit, perhaps capturing a few digital images you could use to help you prepare the profile and possibly also to illustrate it.

Gabriel Thompson | *A Gringo in the Lettuce Fields*

GABRIEL THOMPSON has worked as a community organizer and written extensively about the lives of undocumented immigrants in the United States. He has published numerous articles in periodicals such as *New York* magazine, the *New York Times,* and the *Nation*. His books include *There's No José Here: Following the Hidden Lives of Mexican Immigrants* (2006), *Calling All Radicals: How Grassroots Organizers Can Help Save Our Democracy* (2007), and *Working in the Shadows: A Year of Doing the Jobs (Most) Americans Won't Do* (2010), from which the following selection is taken. The photograph showing lettuce cutters at work (p. 82) is from Thompson's blog, *Working in the Shadows*.

"A Gringo in the Lettuce Fields" falls into the category of immersion journalism, a cultural ethnography that uses undercover participant observation over an extended period of time to get an insider's view of a particular community. As you read, consider the ethical implications of this kind of profile:

- What does Thompson's outsider status enable him to understand—or prevent him from understanding—about the community?

- How does Thompson avoid—or fail to avoid—stereotyping or exploiting the group being profiled?

- Toward the end, Thompson tells us that one of the workers "guesses" that he "joined the crew . . . to write about it" (par. 17). Not all participant-observers go undercover; why do you think Thompson chose to do so? What concerns would you have if you were the writer or if you were a member of the group being profiled?

1   I wake up staring into the bluest blue I've ever seen. I must have fallen into a deep sleep because I need several seconds to realize that I'm looking at the Arizona sky, that the pillow beneath my head is a large clump of dirt, and that a near-stranger named Manuel is standing over me, smiling. I pull myself to a sitting position. To my left, in the distance, a Border Patrol helicopter is hovering. To my right is Mexico, separated by only a few fields of lettuce. *"Buenos días,"* Manuel says.

2   I stand up gingerly. It's only my third day in the fields, but already my 30-year-old body is failing me. I feel like someone has dropped a log on my back. And then piled that log onto a truck with many other logs, and driven that truck over my thighs. "Let's go," I say, trying to sound energetic as I fall in line behind Manuel, stumbling across rows of lettuce and thinking about "the five-day rule." The five-day rule, according to Manuel, is simple: Survive the first five days and you'll be fine. He's been a farmworker for almost two decades, so he should know. I'm on day three of five—the goal is within sight. Of course, another way to look at my situation is that I'm on day three of what I promised myself would be a two-month immersion in the work life of the people who do a job that most Americans won't do. But thinking about the next seven weeks doesn't benefit anyone. *Day three of five.*

3 "Manuel! Gabriel! Let's go! *¡Vámonos!*" yells Pedro, our foreman. Our short break is over. Two dozen crew members standing near the lettuce machine are already putting on gloves and sharpening knives. Manuel and I hustle toward the machine, grab our own knives from a box of chlorinated water, and set up in neighboring rows, just as the machine starts moving slowly down another endless field.

4 Since the early 1980s, Yuma, Ariz., has been the "winter lettuce capital" of America. Each winter, when the weather turns cold in Salinas, California — the heart of the nation's lettuce industry — temperatures in sunny Yuma are still in the 70s and 80s. At the height of Yuma's growing season, the fields surrounding the city produce virtually all of the iceberg lettuce and 90 percent of the leafy green vegetables consumed in the United States and Canada.

5 America's lettuce industry actually needs people like me. Before applying for fieldwork at the local Dole headquarters, I came across several articles describing the causes of a farmworker shortage. The stories cited an aging workforce, immigration crackdowns, and long delays at the border that discourage workers with green cards who would otherwise commute to the fields from their Mexican homes.[1] Wages have been rising somewhat in response to the demand for laborers (one prominent member of the local growers association tells me average pay is now between $10 and $12 an hour), but it's widely assumed that most U.S. citizens wouldn't do the work at any price. Arizona's own Senator John McCain created a stir in 2006 when he issued a challenge to a group of union members in Washington, D.C. "I'll offer anybody here $50 an hour if you'll go pick lettuce in Yuma this season, and pick for the whole season," he said. Amid jeers, he didn't back down, telling the audience, "You can't do it, my friends."

6 On my first day I discover that even putting on a lettuce cutter's uniform is challenging (no fieldworkers, I learn, "pick" lettuce). First, I'm handed a pair of black galoshes to go over my shoes. Next comes the *gancho,* an S-shaped hook that slips over my belt to hold packets of plastic bags. A white glove goes on my right hand, a gray glove, supposedly designed to offer protection from cuts, goes on my left. Over the cloth gloves I pull on a pair of latex gloves. I put on a black hairnet, my baseball cap, and a pair of protective sunglasses. Adding to my belt a long leather sheath, I'm good to go. I feel ridiculous.

7 The crew is already working in the field when Pedro walks me out to them and introduces me to Manuel. Manuel is holding an 18-inch knife in his hand. "Manuel has been cutting for many years, so watch him to see how it's done," Pedro says. Then he walks away. Manuel resumes cutting, following a machine that rolls along just ahead of the crew. Every several seconds Manuel bends down, grabs a head of iceberg lettuce with his left hand, and makes a quick cut with the knife in his right hand, separating the lettuce from its roots. Next, he lifts the lettuce to his stomach and makes a second cut, trimming the trunk. He shakes the lettuce, letting the outer leaves fall to the ground. With the blade still in his hand, he then brings the lettuce toward the *gancho* at his waist, and with a flick of the wrist the head is bagged and dropped onto one of the machine's extensions. Manuel does this over and over again, explaining each movement. "It's not so hard," he says. Five minutes later, Pedro reappears and tells me to grab a knife. Manuel points to a head of lettuce. "Try this one," he says.

---

[1] A green card is an immigration document that allows noncitizens to work legally in the United States, whether they live here or commute across the border. Undocumented workers (or illegal immigrants, depending on your position) lack green cards. [Editor's note]

Thompson *A Gringo in the Lettuce Fields* ▶ **GUIDE TO READING**
GUIDE TO WRITING
A WRITER AT WORK
THINKING CRITICALLY

83

8 I bend over, noticing that most of the crew has turned to watch. I take my knife and make a tentative sawing motion where I assume the trunk to be, though I'm really just guessing. Grabbing the head with my left hand, I straighten up, doing my best to imitate Manuel. Only my lettuce head doesn't move; it's still securely connected to the soil. Pedro steps in. "When you make the first cut, it is like you are stabbing the lettuce." He makes a quick jabbing action. "You want to aim for the center of the lettuce, where the trunk is," he says.

9 Ten minutes later, after a couple of other discouraging moments, I've cut maybe 20 heads of lettuce and am already feeling pretty accomplished. I'm not perfect: If I don't stoop far enough, my stab—instead of landing an inch above the ground—goes right through the head of lettuce, ruining it entirely. The greatest difficulty, though, is in the trimming. I had no idea that a head of lettuce was so humongous. In order to get it into a shape that can be bagged, I trim and trim and trim, but it's taking me upward of a minute to do what Manuel does in several seconds.

10 Pedro offers me a suggestion. "Act like the lettuce is a bomb," he says. "Imagine you've only got five seconds to get rid of it."

11 Surprisingly, that thought seems to work, and I'm able to greatly increase my speed. For a minute or two I feel euphoric. "Look at me!" I want to shout at Pedro; I'm in the zone. But the woman who is packing the lettuce into boxes soon swivels around to face me. "Look, this lettuce is no good." She's right: I've cut the trunk too high, breaking off dozens of good leaves, which will quickly turn brown because they're attached to nothing. With her left hand she holds the bag up, and with her right she smashes it violently, making a loud pop. She turns the bag over and the massacred lettuce falls to the ground. She does the same for the three other bags I've placed on the extension. "It's okay," Manuel tells me. "You shouldn't try to go too fast when you're beginning." Pedro seconds him. "That's right. Make sure the cuts are precise and that you don't rush."

12 So I am to be very careful and precise, while also treating the lettuce like a bomb that must be tossed aside after five seconds.

13 That first week on the job was one thing. By midway into week two, it isn't clear to me what more I can do to keep up with the rest of the crew. I know the techniques by this time and am moving as fast as my body will permit. Yet I need to somehow *double* my current output to hold my own. I'm able to cut only one row at a time while Manuel is cutting two. Our fastest cutter, Julio, meanwhile can handle three. But how someone could cut two rows for an hour—much less an entire day—is beyond me. "Oh, you will get it," Pedro tells me one day. "You will most definitely get it." Maybe he's trying to be hopeful or inspiring, but it comes across as a threat.

14 That feeling aside, what strikes me about our 31-member crew is how quickly they have welcomed me as one of their own. I encountered some suspicion at first, but it didn't last. Simply showing up on the second day seemed to be proof enough that I was there to work. When I faltered in the field and fell behind, hands would come across from adjacent rows to grab a head or two of my lettuce so I could catch up. People whose names I didn't yet know would ask me how I was holding up, reminding me that it would get easier as time went by. If I took a seat alone during a break, someone would call me into their group and offer a homemade taco or two.

15 Two months in, I make the mistake of calling in sick one Thursday. The day before, I put my left hand too low on a head of lettuce. When I punched my blade through the stem, the knife struck my middle finger. Thanks to the gloves, my skin wasn't even broken, but the finger instantly turned purple. I took two painkillers to get through the afternoon, but when I wake the next morning it is still throbbing. With one call to an answering machine that morning, and another the next day, I create my own four-day weekend.

16 The surprise is that when I return on Monday, feeling recuperated, I wind up having the hardest day of my brief career in lettuce. Within hours, my hands feel weaker than ever. By quitting time—some 10 hours after our day started—I feel like I'm going to vomit from exhaustion. A theory forms in my mind. Early in the season—say, after the first week—a farmworker's body gets thoroughly broken down. Back, legs, and arms grow sore, hands and feet swell up. A tolerance for the pain is developed, though, and two-day weekends provide just enough time for the body to recover from the trauma. My four-day break had been too long; my body actually began to recuperate, and it wanted more time to continue. Instead, it was thrown right back into the mix and rebelled. Only on my second day back did my body recover that middle ground. "I don't think the

soreness goes away," I say to Manuel and two other co-workers one day. "You just forget what it's like not to be sore." Manuel, who's 37, considers this. "That's true, that's true," he says. "It always takes a few weeks at the end of the year to get back to normal, to recover."

17   An older co-worker, Mateo, is the one who eventually guesses that I have joined the crew because I want to write about it. "That is good," he says over coffee at his home one Sunday. "Americans should know the hard work that Mexicans do in this country."

18   Mateo is an unusual case. There aren't many other farmworkers who are still in the fields when they reach their 50s. It's simply not possible to do this work for decades and not suffer a permanently hunched back, or crooked fingers, or hands so swollen that they look as if someone has attached a valve to a finger and pumped vigorously. The punishing nature of the work helps explain why farmworkers don't live very long; the National Migrant Resources Program puts their life expectancy at 49 years.

19   "Are you cutting two rows yet?" Mateo asks me. "Yes, more or less," I say. "I thought I'd be better by now." Mateo shakes his head. "It takes a long time to learn how to really cut lettuce. It's not something that you learn after only one season. Three, maybe four seasons—then you start understanding how to really work with lettuce."

[REFLECT]   # Make connections: Switching perspectives.

Thompson joins a community of lettuce cutters to write about their work from the inside. Have you ever experienced an unfamiliar activity or culture? Perhaps you visited relatives in another country, joined a friend's family for an event, or tried out an unfamiliar sport or hobby with a group of experts. Consider what you learned about the culture, the participants, and yourself. Your instructor may ask you to post your thoughts about the experience on a class discussion board or to discuss them with other students in class. Use these questions to get started:

- How fully were you able to immerse yourself in the community? What, if anything, held you back? How did the group members treat you—for example, welcome you warmly, keep you at arm's length, or make you earn their respect?

- How valuable are such immersion experiences to the individual observing, to the group being observed, and to readers in general? What ethical challenges do you see with this kind of participant observation, especially if the writer is undercover, hiding his true purpose, as Thompson was?

- Suppose Thompson wanted to join a community of which you are a member in order to write about it—such as a religious group, sports team, fraternity, or sorority. What elements of Thompson's profile, if any, would cause you to trust or distrust his reporting?

[ANALYZE]   # Use the basic features.

DETAILED INFORMATION ABOUT THE SUBJECT: USING QUOTATION, PARAPHRASE, AND SUMMARY

Profile writers—like all writers—depend on the three basic strategies for presenting source material: quoting, paraphrasing, and summarizing. Each strategy has advantages and disadvantages. It's obvious why Cable chose this quotation: "We're in *Ripley's Believe It or Not,* along with another funeral home whose owners' names are Baggit and Sackit" (par. 14). But decisions about what to quote and what to paraphrase or summarize are not always that easy.

ANALYZE & WRITE

Write a few paragraphs analyzing Thompson's decisions about how to present information from different sources:

1 Skim the essay to find at least one example of a quotation and one paraphrase or summary of information gleaned from an interview or from background research.

2 Why do you think Thompson chooses to quote certain things and paraphrase or summarize other things? What could be a good rule of thumb for you to apply when deciding whether to quote, paraphrase, or summarize? (Note that when writing for an academic audience (in a paper for a class or in a scholarly publication, all source material—whether it is quoted, paraphrased, or summarized — should be cited.)

To learn more about quotation, paraphrase, and summary, see Chapter 26, pp. 701–08.

A CLEAR, LOGICAL ORGANIZATION: NARRATING AN EXTENDED PERIOD

Some profile writers do field research, observing and interviewing over an extended period of time. As an immersive journalist, Thompson spent more than two months as a member of one crew. To give readers a sense of the chronology of events, he uses time markers (such as calendar and clock time, transitions like *next,* and prepositional phrases such as *on my first day*). These cues are especially useful because Thompson's narrative does not always follow a straightforward chronology.

For more on time markers, see pp. 62–63 and Chapter 14, pp. 561–66.

ANALYZE & WRITE

Write a few paragraphs analyzing Thompson's use of time markers and process narration:

1 Skim the profile, highlighting the time markers. Why do you imagine Thompson decided not to follow a linear chronology? How well does he use time markers to keep readers from becoming confused?

2 Why do you think Thompson devotes so much space (pars. 6–12) to narrating the process of cutting lettuce? What does this detailed depiction provide to readers?

For more on process narration, see Chapter 14.

THE WRITER'S ROLE: PARTICIPATING IN A GROUP

Thompson acts as both a participant and an observer: He does not watch lettuce cutters from the sidelines but works among them for two months. His informal interviews take place during work or on breaks (even at the homes of his coworkers during the weekend). Nevertheless, there is a significant difference between a two-month experiment and a personal account written by a lettuce cutter like Mateo after a lifetime on the job. A profile writer may participate but is always an outsider looking in.

ANALYZE & WRITE

Write a paragraph or two analyzing Thompson's use of the participant-observer role:

1 Skim the text, highlighting each time Thompson

■ reminds readers of his status as an outsider (for example, when he refers to a coworker as a "near-stranger" [par. 1]);

- tells readers about something he thinks will be unfamiliar to them (for example, when he explains that people do not "'pick' lettuce" [par. 6]);

- calls attention to his own incompetence or failings (for example, when he describes his first attempt to cut lettuce [par. 8]).

2 Why do you think Thompson tells us about his errors and reminds us that he is an outsider? What effect are these moves likely to have on his audience?

3 How do the writers whose profiles appear in this chapter use their outsider status to connect with readers? What are the advantages, if any, of adopting the participant-observer role (as Thompson does) instead of the spectator role (as Cable does)?

A PERSPECTIVE ON THE SUBJECT: PROFILING A CONTROVERSIAL SUBJECT

Two of the profiles in this chapter touch on a controversial subject about which people have strong opinions. Cable addresses the commercialization of death, and Coyne, the unfairness of the legal system. While profiles do not engage such debates head on, the way essays arguing a position do, they do offer a perspective on an issue. In doing so, they provide readers with certain kinds of information that they might not get from more explicit arguments.

ANALYZE & WRITE

Write a few paragraphs analyzing Thompson's perspective:

1 Start by identifying the subject of the profile. Point to a couple of specific passages in the text that tell you what the subject is.

2 Identify Thompson's perspective on the subject. Consider the title of the profile ("A Gringo in the Lettuce Fields") and the title of the book from which it is excerpted, *Working in the Shadows: A Year of Doing the Jobs (Most) Americans Won't Do*. What do these titles tell you about Thompson's perspective?

3 What do you think Thompson wants readers to take away from the profile? How does the political debate raging in this country about undocumented (or illegal) immigration affect how you understand the subject and perspective of this profile?

[RESPOND]   # Consider possible topics: Immersing yourself.

For more profiles, including a multimodal selection, go to **bedford stmartins.com/theguide /epages**.

Thompson's experience suggests two possible avenues for research: You could embed yourself in a group, participating alongside group members, and then write about that experience. For example, you might join a club on campus or try an unusual sport. Alternatively, you could observe life in an unfamiliar group, watching how a meeting or event unfolds, interviewing members to learn about their practices, and conducting additional research to learn about the group.

Profiles may be written as essays for a college class or for a magazine, but profiles appear in many other media as well. Extended profiles occur in documentary films. Brief profiles appear on TV shows, like *Undercover Boss* and *Dirty Jobs*. This still photograph shows *Dirty Jobs* host Mike Rowe as a participant-observer in an episode in which he takes on the job of a skull cleaner, someone who makes bones ready for collectors and museums. (Here he is removing flesh-eating beetles from the skull of a horse.) Documentaries, from *God Bless Ozzy Osbourne* to *Sicko,* not only provide detailed information but also show a clear perspective on the subject and, especially in the case of Michael Moore's documentaries, like *Sicko,* a role for the writer, who appears in his own films.

Profiles in the Media

For an interactive version of this feature, plus activities, go to **bedfordstmartins.com /theguide/epages**.

In the next section of this chapter, we ask you to create a profile of an activity, a place, a person, or a group of people in your community. Look for a fresh angle that will help your readers understand the significance of, and gain a new perspective on, your subject. Consider how you can best capture what's special about your subject and engage your readers. What language or details will bring your subject to life for your readers? Should you include visuals, or would conveying your profile in another medium (a video on YouTube) help engage your readers and enable them to grasp your subject more fully? Consider, too, whether creating a profile with images or in a different medium would be acceptable to your instructor.

The Writing Assignment

Write a profile on an intriguing person, a group of people, a place, or an activity in your community. Observe your subject closely, and then present what you have learned in a way that both informs and engages readers.

This Guide to Writing is designed to help you compose your own profile essay and apply what you have learned from reading other profiles. This Starting Points chart will help you find answers to questions you might have about composing a profile. Use the chart to help you find the guidance you need, when you need it.

STARTING POINTS: WRITING A PROFILE

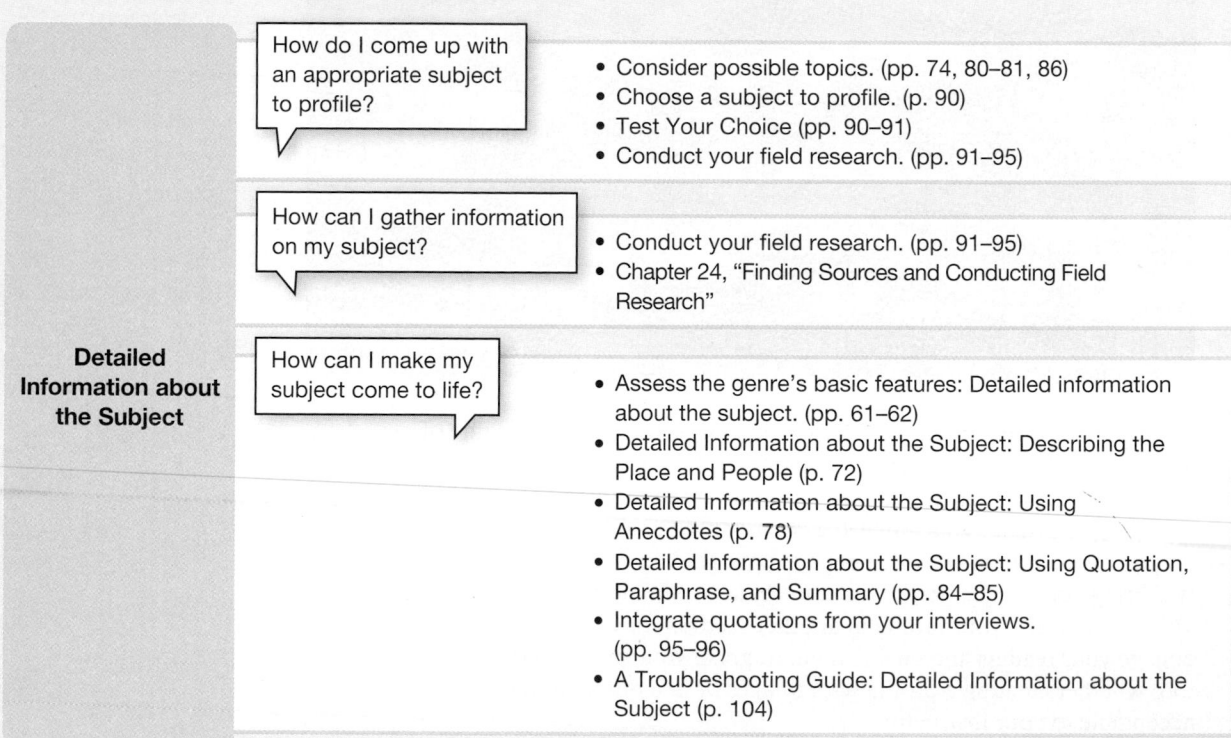

Detailed Information about the Subject

How do I come up with an appropriate subject to profile?

- Consider possible topics. (pp. 74, 80–81, 86)
- Choose a subject to profile. (p. 90)
- Test Your Choice (pp. 90–91)
- Conduct your field research. (pp. 91–95)

How can I gather information on my subject?

- Conduct your field research. (pp. 91–95)
- Chapter 24, "Finding Sources and Conducting Field Research"

How can I make my subject come to life?

- Assess the genre's basic features: Detailed information about the subject. (pp. 61–62)
- Detailed Information about the Subject: Describing the Place and People (p. 72)
- Detailed Information about the Subject: Using Anecdotes (p. 78)
- Detailed Information about the Subject: Using Quotation, Paraphrase, and Summary (pp. 84–85)
- Integrate quotations from your interviews. (pp. 95–96)
- A Troubleshooting Guide: Detailed Information about the Subject (p. 104)

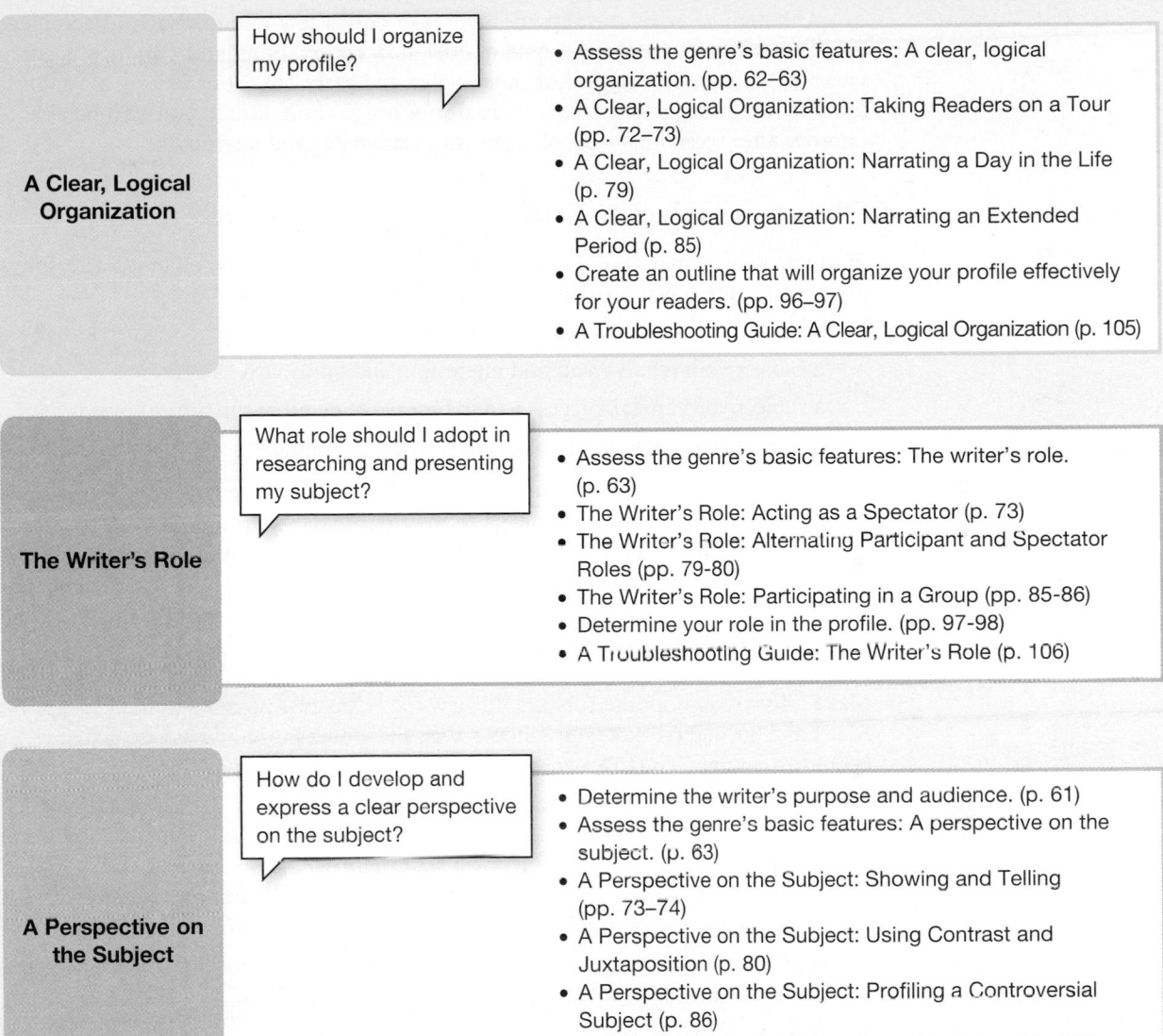

A Clear, Logical Organization

How should I organize my profile?

- Assess the genre's basic features: A clear, logical organization. (pp. 62–63)
- A Clear, Logical Organization: Taking Readers on a Tour (pp. 72–73)
- A Clear, Logical Organization: Narrating a Day in the Life (p. 79)
- A Clear, Logical Organization: Narrating an Extended Period (p. 85)
- Create an outline that will organize your profile effectively for your readers. (pp. 96–97)
- A Troubleshooting Guide: A Clear, Logical Organization (p. 105)

The Writer's Role

What role should I adopt in researching and presenting my subject?

- Assess the genre's basic features: The writer's role. (p. 63)
- The Writer's Role: Acting as a Spectator (p. 73)
- The Writer's Role: Alternating Participant and Spectator Roles (pp. 79-80)
- The Writer's Role: Participating in a Group (pp. 85-86)
- Determine your role in the profile. (pp. 97-98)
- A Troubleshooting Guide: The Writer's Role (p. 106)

A Perspective on the Subject

How do I develop and express a clear perspective on the subject?

- Determine the writer's purpose and audience. (p. 61)
- Assess the genre's basic features: A perspective on the subject. (p. 63)
- A Perspective on the Subject: Showing and Telling (pp. 73–74)
- A Perspective on the Subject: Using Contrast and Juxtaposition (p. 80)
- A Perspective on the Subject: Profiling a Controversial Subject (p. 86)
- Develop your perspective on the subject. (pp. 98–100)
- A Troubleshooting Guide: A Perspective on the Subject (p. 106)

Writing a Draft: Invention, Research, Planning, and Composing

To learn about using the *Guide* e-book for invention and drafting, go to **bedford-stmartins.com/theguide**.

The activities in this section will help you choose a subject to profile and develop your perspective on the subject. Do the activities in any order that makes sense to you (and your instructor), and return to them as needed as you revise.

Although some of the activities will take only a few minutes each to complete, the essential field research — making detailed observations and conducting interviews — will take a good deal of time to plan and carry out. Your writing in response to many of these activities can be used in a rough draft, which you will be able to improve after receiving feedback from your classmates and instructor.

⠿ Choose a subject to profile.

To create an informative and engaging profile, your subject — whether it's a person, a group of people, a place, or an activity — should be

- a subject that sparks your interest or curiosity;
- a subject your readers will find interesting and informative;
- a subject you can gain access to and observe in detail in the time allowed;
- a subject about which (or with whom) you can conduct in-depth interviews.

Note: Whenever you write a profile, consider carefully the ethics involved in such research: You will want to be careful to treat participants fairly and with respect in the way you both approach and depict them. Discuss the ethical implications of your research with your instructor, and think carefully about the goals of your research and the effect it will have on others. You may also need to obtain permission from your school's ethics review board.

Make a list of appropriate subjects. Review the "Consider possible topics" on pp. 74, 80–81 and 86, and consult your school's Web site to find intriguing places, activities, or people on campus. The following ideas may suggest additional possibilities to consider:

- A place where people come together because they are of the same age, gender, sexual orientation, or ethnic group (for example, a foreign language–speaking dorm or fraternity or sorority), or a place where people of different ages, genders, sexual orientations, or ethnic groups have formed a community (for example, a Sunday morning pickup basketball game in the park, LGBT club, or barbershop)
- A place where people are trained for a certain kind of work (for example, a police academy, cosmetology program, truck driving school, or boxing ring)
- A group of people working together for a particular purpose (for example, students and their teacher preparing for the academic decathlon competition, employees working together to produce something, law students and their professor working to help prisoners on death row, or scientists collaborating on a research project)

TEST YOUR CHOICE

After you have made a tentative choice, ask yourself the following questions:

1 Do I feel curious about the subject?

2 Am I confident that I will be able to make the subject interesting for my readers?

3 Do I believe that I can research this subject sufficiently in the time I have?

Then get together with two or three other students:

Presenters.   Take turns identifying your subjects. Explain your interest in the subject, and speculate about why you think it will interest readers.

Listeners.   Briefly tell each presenter what you already know about his or her subject, if anything, and what might make it interesting to readers.

:: Conduct your field research.

To write an effective profile, you must conduct field research—interviews and observations—to collect detailed, firsthand information about your subject. The following activities will help you plan and carry out your field research.

To learn more about conducting observations and making interviews, see Chapter 24, pp. 682–86.

Many writers begin with observations to get the lay of the land and identify people to interview, but you can start with interviews. You may even be able to make observations and conduct interviews during the same visit. Regardless of how you start your field research, come prepared: Dress appropriately, and bring preliminary questions and equipment for taking notes (be sure to ask permission before recording or filming).

HOW CAN I MANAGE MY TIME?

WAYS IN

One of the best strategies for scheduling your time so that everything gets done by your deadline is *backward planning*.

1. Buy or make a calendar (in print or online).

2. Write the date the project is due and any other interim due dates (such as the date that your first draft is due) on the calendar. (Some writers like to give themselves a personal due date — the day before the official due date — so they have some wiggle room.)

3. Move backward through the calendar, writing in due dates for other parts of the project:

    - Interview and observation write-ups completed (organize your scribbled and abbreviated notes into logical categories, add reflections or additional thoughts, and type your notes in complete sentences)

    - All field research completed

    - Follow-up observations or interviews completed

    - Initial interviews and observations conducted (leave at least a week for this process)

    - Interviews and observations scheduled (leave at least several days for this process)

(continued)

A Sample Schedule

October						
Sunday	**Monday**	**Tuesday**	**Wednesday**	**Thursday**	**Friday**	**Saturday**
	1 Arrange interviews & observations	2	3	4 ⟶	5 Research interview subject, locations	6
7	8 Conduct interviews & observations	9	10	11	12 ⟶	13
14	15	16 Write-ups completed	17	18	19 First draft due	20 Conduct any extra research
21	22 Call/E-mail with follow-up questions	23 Revise draft	24	25	26 ⟶ Revised draft due	27
28	29	30	31			

WAYS IN ⟶

HOW DO I SET UP AND PREPARE FOR INTERVIEWS AND OBSERVATIONS?

1. Make a list of people you would like to interview or places you would like to observe. Include a number of possibilities in case your first choice doesn't work out.

2. Write out your intentions and goals, so you can explain them clearly to others.

3. Call or e-mail for an appointment with your interview subject, or make arrangements to visit the site. Explain who you are and what you are doing. Student research projects are often embraced, but be prepared for your request to be rejected.

   Note: Be sure to arrange your interview or site visit as soon as possible. The most common error students report making on this assignment is waiting too long to make that first call. Be aware, too, that the people and places you contact may not respond immediately (or at all); be sure to follow up if you have not gotten an answer to your request within a few days.

4. Make notes about what you expect to learn before you write interview questions, interview your subject, or visit your site. Writing a paragraph or two responding to the following questions might help:

Interview

- How would I define or describe the subject?
- What is the subject's purpose or function?
- Who or what seems to be associated with it?
- Why do I assume it will be interesting to me and to my readers?
- What do I hope to learn about it?

Observation

- How would I define or describe my subject?
- What typically takes place at this location?
- Who will I likely observe?
- Why will my readers be interested in this location or the people who frequent it?
- How will my presence affect those I am observing?
- What do I expect to learn about my subject?

5. Write some interview questions in advance, or ask yourself some questions to help you determine how best to conduct the observation.

Interview

Ask for stories:

▶ Tell me how you got into _____ .

▶ Tell me about something that surprised, pleased, frustrated you _____ .

Give subjects a chance to correct misconceptions, including your own:

▶ What myths about _____ would you most like to bust?

Ask for their thoughts about the subject's past and future:

▶ How has _____ changed over the years, and where do you think it's going?

Observation

Should I observe from different vantage points or from the same location?

Should I visit the location at different times of day or days of the week, or would it be better to visit at the same time every day?

Should I focus on specific people, or should I identify roles and focus on people as they adopt those roles?

6. Conduct some preliminary research on your subject or related subjects if possible, and revise your questions or plans accordingly.

HOW DO I CONDUCT INTERVIEWS?

Take notes

- Clearly distinguish *quotations* from paraphrases/summaries by inserting quotation marks where needed.

- Make an audio recording of what people say, if allowed, but also take notes. If you're worried about keeping pace with a pen, politely ask interviewees to speak slowly, repeat themselves, or confirm your quotations. (Interviewees often fear being misquoted and will usually appreciate your being careful.)

- In addition to writing down what your subject says, describe the interviewee's tone, gestures, and mannerisms.

- To generate *anecdotes,* ask how the interviewee first got involved; if there was a key event worth noting; what most concerns the interviewee; what has been the biggest influence, for good or ill.

- To elicit *process narratives,* ask how something works; what happens if it breaks; whether it was always done the same way; how it has changed; how it could be improved.

- To *classify, compare,* or *contrast,* ask what kind of thing it is; how it's like and unlike others of its kind; how it compares to what it was like in the past.

- To help you with your perspective, ask why the subject is important, how it contributes to the community, or how it could be improved. Ask who would disagree with these perspectives.

- Finally, ask for the interviewee's preferences for handling follow-up questions you might have later.

HOW DO I CONDUCT OBSERVATIONS?

Take notes

- Note your surroundings, using all of your senses: sight, hearing, smell, taste, touch.

- Describe the place from multiple vantage points, noting furnishings, decor, and so on, and sketch the layout.

- Describe people's appearance, dress, gestures, and actions.

- Make a record of interesting overheard conversation.

- Note your reactions and ideas, especially in relation to your preconceptions. What surprises you?

- If you can get permission, look closely over the shoulders of people who are centrally involved.

Consider your perspective

- If you are new to the subject and would like to have a participant-observer role, ask permission to take part in a small way for a limited time.

- If you are an insider, find a new angle so that you learn something new. (For example, if you're on the football team, focus on the cheerleaders or the people who maintain the field.)

Collect artifacts, or take videos or photos

- Collect any brochures or other written material you might be able to use, either to prepare for interviews or to include in your essay.

- Consider taking photographs or videos, if allowed. Try a pan shot scanning the scene from side to side or a tracking shot indicating what you see as you enter or tour the place.

Reflect on the interview

Review your notes for five minutes after the interview. Focus on first impressions. Mark promising material, such as

- anything that calls into question your or your readers' likely preconceptions;
- sensory details that could paint a vivid portrait of the place, people, and activity;
- quotable phrases that could help you capture the tone or mood of the subject;
- questions you still need answered.

Write up your interview

Write a few paragraphs, deciding what to quote, summarize, paraphrase, or omit. Describe the person's tone of voice, gestures, and appearance, as well as details you noticed about the place. You may use some of this material later in your draft. If your interviewee said you could follow up to check facts, e-mail or call with requests for clarification or questions.

Consider another interview

You might also arrange to talk to another person who has different kinds of information to share.

Reflect on your observations

Take five minutes right after your visit to think about what you observed, and write a few sentences about your impressions of the subject:

▶ The most interesting aspect of the subject is _____ because _____ .

▶ Although my visit confirmed that _____ , I was surprised to learn that _____ .

▶ My dominant impression of the subject is

_____ .

Write up your observations

Write a few paragraphs reporting on your visit. This write-up may produce language you can use in your draft. It will also help you think about how to describe your subject, what dominant impression you want to create, and the perspective your profile should take.

Consider a follow-up observation

Consider a follow-up visit, possibly combined with an interview. Examine other aspects of the place or activity, and try to answer questions you still have. Does the impression you had on the first visit still hold?

Integrate quotations from your interviews.

Good profiles quote sources so readers can hear what people have to say in their own voices. As you write, choose quotations from your notes to reveal the style and character of the people you interviewed, and integrate these quotations smoothly into your sentences.

When you quote someone directly (rather than paraphrasing or summarizing), you'll need to identify the speaker. The principal way to do so is with a speaker tag. You may rely on an all-purpose verb (such as *says*) or a more descriptive verb (such as *yells out*) to help readers imagine speakers' attitudes and personal styles:

"Try this one," he says. (Thompson, par. 7)

"Take me out to the" — and Toby yells out, "Banana store!" (Coyne, par. 21)

You may also add a word or phrase to a speaker tag to describe the speaker or to reveal more about how, where, when, or why the speaker speaks:

"We're in *Ripley's Believe It or Not,* along with another funeral home whose owners' names are Baggit and Sackit," Howard told me, without cracking a smile. (Cable, par. 14)

Once, after being given this weak explanation, he said, "I wish I could have done something really bad, like my Mommy. So I could go to prison too and be with her." (Coyne, par. 18)

In addition to being carefully introduced, quotations must be precisely punctuated. Fortunately, there are only two general rules:

For more on integrating quotations, go to **bedfordstmartins.com /theguide** and click on Bedford Research Room; see also Chapter 26, pp. 700–6.

1. Enclose all quotations in quotation marks. These always come in pairs: one at the beginning, and one at the end of the quotation.

2. Separate the quotation from its speaker tag with appropriate punctuation, usually a comma. But if you have more than one sentence (as in the last example above), be careful to punctuate the separate sentences properly.

▦ Create an outline that will organize your profile effectively for your readers.

For more on clustering and outlining, see Chapter 11, pp. 510–14.

Outlining what you have can help you organize the profile effectively for your audience. Compare the following possible outlines to see how you might organize your essay, depending on whether you prefer a narrative or a topical plan. Even if you wish to blend features of both outlines, seeing how each basic plan works can help you combine them.

If you plan to arrange your material *narratively as a tour,* plot the key events on a timeline. The following suggests one way to organize a narrative profile of a place:

I. **Begin by describing the place from the outside.**

II. **Present background information.**

III. **Describe what you see as you enter.**

IV. **Introduce the people and activities.**

V. **Tour the place, describing what you see as you move from one part to the next.**

VI. **Fill in information wherever you can, and comment about the place or the people.**

VII. **Conclude with reflections on what you have learned about the place.**

If you plan to arrange your material *topically,* use *clustering* or *outlining* to help you divide and group related information. Here is a suggested outline for a topical profile about a person:

I. **Begin with a vivid image of the person in action.**

II. **Present the first topic.** (A topic could be a characteristic of the person or one aspect of his or her work.) Use dialogue, description, narration, process description, evaluation, or interpretation to illustrate this topic.

III. **Present the second topic.** Use dialogue, description, narration, process description, evaluation, or interpretation to illustrate this topic.

IV. **Present the third topic** (and continue as above until you have presented all topics).

V. **Conclude with a bit of action or dialogue.**

Writing a Draft   GUIDE TO READING
GUIDE TO WRITING
A WRITER AT WORK
THINKING CRITICALLY   97

The tentative plan you choose should reflect the possibilities in your material as well as your purpose and your understanding of your audience. As you begin drafting, you will almost certainly discover new ways of organizing parts of your material.

Consider document design.

Think about whether visual or audio elements — photographs; postcards; menus; or snippets from films, television programs, or songs — would strengthen your profile. If you can recall profiles you've seen in magazines, on Web pages, or on television shows, what visual or audio elements were used to create a strong sense of the subject? Profiles don't require such elements to be effective, but they can be helpful.

Note: Be sure to cite the source of visual or audio elements you didn't create, and get permission from the source if your profile is going to be published on a Web site that is not password protected.

Consider also whether your readers might benefit from design features such as headings, bulleted or numbered lists, or other typographic elements that can make an essay easier to follow.

Determine your role in the profile.

Based on your work so far, decide whether you want to adopt a participant-observer role, a spectator role, or some blend of the two. All three options can be engaging and help readers identify with you. The following questions can help you choose, and the sentence strategies will give you some tools for expressing these roles in your paper.

WAYS IN

WHAT ARE THE ADVANTAGES AND DRAWBACKS OF A PARTICIPANT-OBSERVER ROLE?	WHAT ARE THE ADVANTAGES AND DRAWBACKS OF A SPECTATOR ROLE?
Advantages	**Advantages**
The participant-observer role is a good way to profile physical activities that readers won't know unless you describe them in detail.	The spectator role is a good way to profile places or people. By focusing attention on the subject rather than yourself, you improve the clarity of the picture.
▶ As I tried to _____ like the _____, I was surprised to find that _____.	▶ On the other side of _____, a _____ [appeared/came into view/did something].
▶ I picked up the _____. It felt like _____ to the touch, and [smelled/tasted/sounded] like _____.	▶ [Person] talked as he _____ -ed. "_____," he said. "_____."
▶ After _____ [hours/minutes/days] of _____, I felt like _____.	▶ _____ing [at/down/along/with/on] _____, [person] remarked that _____.

(continued)

If you try to do what the people you're observing do, readers can imagine going through the same experience.

The participant-observer role enables you to explore the effect your actions might have had on the scene.

▶ I interrupted _____ as [he/she] _____ to ask why _____ .

▶ I can't be sure whether that interruption led to _____ , but I think _____ .

▶ The _____ is [impressive/strange/easy to miss], with [its/his/her] _____ , _____ , and _____ .

If you describe a place readers may never have been, they can see it through your eyes as you learn about it and look over the shoulders of the people there.

The spectator role enables you to build an aura of objectivity—you're just reporting what you saw and heard.

▶ _____ makes [person] angry. [She/he] says it's because: "_____ ."

Disadvantages

The participant-observer role can become distracting if it's overdone—the profile starts to feel like it's about you, rather than the subject. This is particularly true when you are profiling is a person or place.

Disadvantages

The spectator role can feel detached, particularly if you are profiling a physical or difficult activity.

WHAT ARE THE ADVANTAGES AND DRAWBACKS TO ALTERNATING BETWEEN PARTICIPANT AND SPECTATOR ROLES?

Advantages

You gain the best of both worlds: By switching back and forth, as Cable and Coyne do, you make activities come alive while portraying places and people without much interference from you.

▶ [Above/around/before] me, [activity happened]. I tried to _____ [an object or activity], and found it _____ . "_____ ," [person] said, watching, "_____ ."

Disadvantages

It can be challenging to juggle both roles. When it's not handled well, the result can be confusing to readers.

⊞ Develop your perspective on the subject.

The following activities will help you deepen your analysis and think of ways to help your readers gain a better understanding of your subject's cultural significance. Complete them in any order that seems helpful to you, and try using the sentence strategies to come up with ideas.

WAYS IN

HOW CAN I DEVELOP A PERSPECTIVE FOR MY PROFILE?

Explore your perspective

Write for five minutes exploring your perspective on the subject — what about the subject seems important and meaningful?

> If you are focusing on a place, ask yourself what you find interesting about its culture: What rituals or habits are practiced there? Who visits it? What is its function in the community?

▶ Without [name of place], [life/business/academics] would be different in [name of community or larger place], according to [interview subject]: [type of people] would/ would no longer _____ because _____ .

> If you are focusing on an activity, consider how it has changed over time, for good or ill; how outsiders are initiated into the activity; who benefits from it; and what its value is for the community.

▶ Although [activity] might seem _____ , it's important to _____ because _____ , says [interviewee]. _____ , in particular, benefit from it in the following ways: _____ .

▶ [Activity] today is [somewhat/very] different from [activity] [in the past/long ago/just a few years ago]: Instead of _____ , a change brought on by _____ , those interested in participating are in for _____ .

> If you are focusing on a person or group, ask yourself what sense of identity they have; what customs and ways of communicating they have; what their values and attitudes are; what they think about social hierarchies or gender differences; and how they see their role in the community.

▶ Despite common assumptions that _____ , [subject] thinks of [himself/herself] as _____ , an identity that comes across [in/through] _____ .

▶ [She/he] cares less about _____ than about _____ , to the point of _____ .

Define your purpose for your readers

Write for five minutes exploring what you want your readers to learn about the subject. Use these sentence strategies to help you clarify your thinking:

▶ In addition to my teacher and classmates, I envision my ideal readers as _____ .

▶ They probably know _____ about my subject and have these opinions: _____ .

▶ They would be most surprised to learn _____ and most interested in the following facets of the subject: _____ .

▶ I can help change their opinions of the subject by _____ and get them to think about the subject's social and cultural significance by _____ .

(continued)

▶ What I've learned about the subject implies _____ about our shared values and concerns, and I can help readers understand this by _____.

Consider your main point

Review what you have written, and add a couple of sentences summarizing the main idea you want readers to take away from your profile. Readers don't expect a profile to have an explicit thesis statement, as they do an argumentative essay, but the descriptive details and other information need to work together to convey the main idea.

Clarify the dominant impression

Although you need to create a dominant impression, readers appreciate profiles that reveal the richness and complexity of a subject. Even as Cable shows that the Goodbody Mortuary is guided by commercialism, he also gets readers to think about cultural attitudes toward death, perhaps exemplified in his own complex feelings. To create a dominant impression, try reviewing your notes and write-ups, highlighting in one color the descriptive language that supports the dominant impression you want your essay to create. Then highlight in a second color any descriptions that seem to create a different impression. Finally, write for a few minutes exploring how these different impressions relate to one another. Consider whether they reveal complexity in the subject or ambivalence in your perspective that could be developed further in your essay. You might start with one of the following sentence strategies and elaborate from there.

▶ Although [subject] clearly seemed _____, I couldn't [shake the feeling that/ignore/stop thinking about] _____.

▶ Although [subject] [tries to/pretends to/has made progress toward] _____, [overall/for the most part/primarily] [he/she/it] _____.

Present the information

Review the notes from your interviews and observations, noting which information you should include in your draft and how you might present it. Consider including the following:

- Definitions of key terms
- Comparisons or contrasts that make information clearer or more memorable
- Lists or categories that organize information
- Ways to show processes or causes and effects vividly
- Quotes that reveal the character of the speaker as well as something about the subject

Evaluating the Draft

GUIDE TO READING
GUIDE TO WRITING
A WRITER AT WORK
THINKING CRITICALLY

101

Write the opening sentences.

You could try out one or two different ways of beginning your essay — possibly from the list that follows — but don't agonize over the first sentences because you are likely to discover the best way to begin only as you draft your essay. Review your invention writing to see if you have already written something that would work to launch your essay. To engage your readers' interest from the start, consider the following opening strategies:

- A surprising statement
- A remarkable thought or occasion that triggers your observational visit (like Cable)
- A vivid description (like Coyne and Thompson)
- An arresting quotation
- A fascinating bit of information
- An amusing anecdote

Draft your profile.

By this point, you have done a lot of research and writing

- to develop something interesting to say about a subject;
- to devise a plan for presenting that information;
- to identify a role for yourself in the essay;
- to explore your perspective on the subject.

Now stitch that material together to create a draft. As you do so, you will notice that some of the sentences you have written based on the sentence strategies in this chapter feel awkward or forced. Revise them, keeping the content but putting the ideas into words and sentence structures that feel natural to you. The next two parts of this Guide to Writing will help you evaluate and improve your draft.

Evaluating the Draft: Getting a Critical Reading

Your instructor may arrange a peer review session in class or online, where you can exchange drafts with your classmates and give one another a thoughtful critical reading, pointing out what works well and suggesting ways to improve the draft. A good critical reading does three things:

1. It lets the writer know how well the reader understands the point of the essay.
2. It praises what works best.
3. It indicates where the draft could be improved and makes suggestions on how to improve it.

A CRITICAL READING GUIDE

Detailed Information about the Subject

Does the writer portray the subject in enough well-chosen detail to show us why it's interesting?

Summarize: Tell the writer one thing you learned about the subject from reading the essay.

Praise: Point out one passage where the description seems especially vivid, a quotation stands out, or another writing strategy works particularly well to present information.

Critique: Point out one passage where description could be added or where the description could be made more vivid, where a quotation that falls flat should be paraphrased or summarized, or where another writing strategy could be used.

A Clear, Logical Organization

Is the profile easy to follow?

Summarize: Identify the kind of organization — narrative, topical, or a blend of the two — that the writer uses.

Praise: Comment on the cues the writer gives that make the profile easy to follow. For example, point to a place where one topic leads logically to the next or where transitions help you follow the tour or narrative. Also, indicate what in the opening paragraphs grabs your attention or why you think the ending works well.

Critique: Point to information that seems out of place or instances where the chronology is confusing. If you think the opening or ending could be improved, suggest an alternative passage in the essay that could work as an opening or an ending.

The Writer's Role

Is the author's role, whether spectator, participant-observer, or both, clear?

Summarize: Identify the role the writer adopts.

Praise: Point to a passage where the spectator or participant-observer role enables you to identify with the writer, enhancing the essay's immediacy or interest.

Critique: Point out any problems with the role — for example, if the participant-observer role becomes distracting, or if the spectator role seems too distant.

Improving the Draft   GUIDE TO READING
GUIDE TO WRITING
A WRITER AT WORK
THINKING CRITICALLY   103

A Perspective on the Subject

Does the author have a clear point of view on the subject?

Summarize: State briefly what you believe to be the writer's perspective on the subject and the dominant impression you get from the essay.

Praise: Give an example where you have a strong sense of the writer's perspective through a comment, description, quotation, or bit of information.

Critique: Tell the writer if the essay does not have a clear perspective or convey a dominant impression. To help him or her find one, explain what interests you about the subject and what you think is important. If you see contradictions in the draft that could be developed to make the profile more complex and illuminating, briefly explain.

Before concluding your review, be sure to address any of the writer's concerns that have not already been addressed.

Making Comments Electronically Most word processing software offers features that allow you to insert comments directly into the text of someone else's document. Many readers prefer to make their comments this way because it tends to be faster than writing on hard copy, and space is virtually unlimited; it also eliminates the process of deciphering handwritten comments. Where such features are not available, simply typing comments directly into a document in a contrasting color can provide the same advantages.

For a printable version of this Critical Reading Guide, go to **bedfordstmartins .com/theguide**.

Improving the Draft: Revising, Formatting, Editing, and Proofreading

Start improving your draft by reflecting on what you have written thus far:

- Review critical reading comments from your classmates, instructor, or writing center tutor. What are your readers getting at?
- Take another look at the notes from your interviews, observations, and earlier writing activities. What else should you consider?
- Review your draft. What else can you do to make your profile compelling?

Revise your draft.

If your readers are having difficulty with your draft, try some of the strategies listed in the Troubleshooting Guide that follows. It can help you fine-tune your presentation of the genre's basic features.

A TROUBLESHOOTING GUIDE

Detailed Information about the Subject

My readers tell me the people do not come alive.

- Describe a physical feature, a mannerism, or an emotional reaction that will help readers imagine or identify with the person.
- Include speaker tags that characterize how people talk.
- Paraphrase long, dry quotations that convey basic information.
- Use short quotations that reveal character or the way someone speaks.
- Make comparisons.
- Use anecdotes or action sequences to show the person in action.

My readers say the place is hard to visualize.

- Name objects in the scene.
- Add sensory detail — sight, sound, smell, taste, touch, temperature.
- Make comparisons.
- Consider adding a visual — a photograph or sketch, for example.

My readers say there is too much information — it is not clear what is important.

- Prioritize based on the perspective and dominant impression you want to convey, cutting information that does not reinforce or complicates that perspective.
- Break up long blocks of informational text with quotations, narration of events, or examples.
- Vary the writing strategies used to present the information: Switch from raw factual reporting to comparisons, examples, or process descriptions.
- Consider which parts of the profile would be more engaging if presented through dialogue or summarized more succinctly.

My readers say visuals could be added or improved.

- Use a photo, a map, a drawing, a cartoon, or any other visual that might make the place or people easier to imagine or the information more understandable.
- Consider adding textual references to any images in your essay or positioning images more effectively.

Improving the Draft

GUIDE TO READING
GUIDE TO WRITING
A WRITER AT WORK
THINKING CRITICALLY

105

A Clear, Logical Organization

My readers say the narrative plan drags or rambles.

- Try adding drama through dialogue or action sequences.
- Summarize or paraphrase any dialogue that seems dry or uninteresting.
- Give the narrative shape: Establish a conflict, build tension toward a climax, and resolve it.
- Make sure the narrative unfolds or develops and has a clear direction.

My readers say my topically arranged essay seems disorganized or out of balance.

- Rearrange topics into new patterns, choosing the structure that makes the most sense for your subject. (Describe a place from outside to inside or from biggest to smallest; describe a process from start to finish or from cause to effect).
- Add clearer, more explicit transitions or topic sentences.
- Move, remove, or condense information to restore balance.

My readers say the opening fails to engage their attention.

- Consider alternatives: Think of a question, an engaging image, or dialogue you could open with.
- Go back to your notes for other ideas.
- Recall how the writers in this chapter open their profiles: Cable stands on the street in front of the mortuary; Thompson awakens in the lettuce fields, his break over.

My readers say that transitions are missing or are confusing.

- Look for connections between ideas, and try to use those connections to help readers move from point to point.
- Add appropriate transitional words or phrases.

My readers say the ending seems weak.

- Consider ending earlier or moving a striking insight to the end. (Often first drafts hit a great ending point and then keep going. Deleting the last few sentences often improves papers.)
- Consider ending by reminding readers of something from the beginning.
- Recall how the writers in this chapter end their profiles: Cable touches the cold flesh of a cadaver; Coyne watches a mother bleed after being punched by her son.

My readers say the visual features are not effective.

- Consider adding textual references to any images in your essay or positioning images more effectively.
- Think of other design features — drawings, lists, tables, graphs, cartoons, headings — that might make the place and people easier to imagine or the information more understandable.

The Writer's Role

My readers say the spectator role is too distant.

- Consider placing yourself in the scene as you describe it.
- Add your thoughts and reactions to one of the interviews.

My readers say my approach to participation is distracting.

- Bring other people forward by adding material about them.
- Reduce the material about yourself.

A Perspective on the Subject

My readers say the perspective or dominant impression is unclear.

- Try stating your perspective by adding your thoughts or someone else's.
- Make sure the descriptive and narrative details reinforce the dominant impression you want to convey.
- If your perspective is complex, you may need to discuss more directly the contradictions or complications you see in the subject.

My readers don't find my perspective interesting.

- An "uninteresting" perspective is sometimes an unclear one. Check with your readers to see whether they understood it. If they didn't, follow the tips above.
- Readers sometimes say a perspective is "uninteresting" if it's too simple or obvious. Go back through your notes, looking for contradictions, other perspectives, surprises, or anything else that might help you complicate the perspective you are presenting.

For an electronic version of the Troubleshooting Guide, go to **bedfordstmartins .com/theguide**.

Think about design.

Profiles appear in a wide variety of contexts and genres. (Three examples appear in the scenarios at the beginning of this chapter.) The following example (a screenshot of an online profile) is from the project highlighted in the "In College Courses" scenario (p. 58). The student designed her work to inform others interested in collaborative learning (including her classmates) about the sixth graders she studied. Notice that while her profile demonstrates many of the genre's key features, it also makes use of Web design to indicate separate Web pages and a link to the author's own profile.

Contents link and list of topics in navigation make the organization clear.

Findings page provides detailed information about research.

Gallery provides visual information about sixth graders.

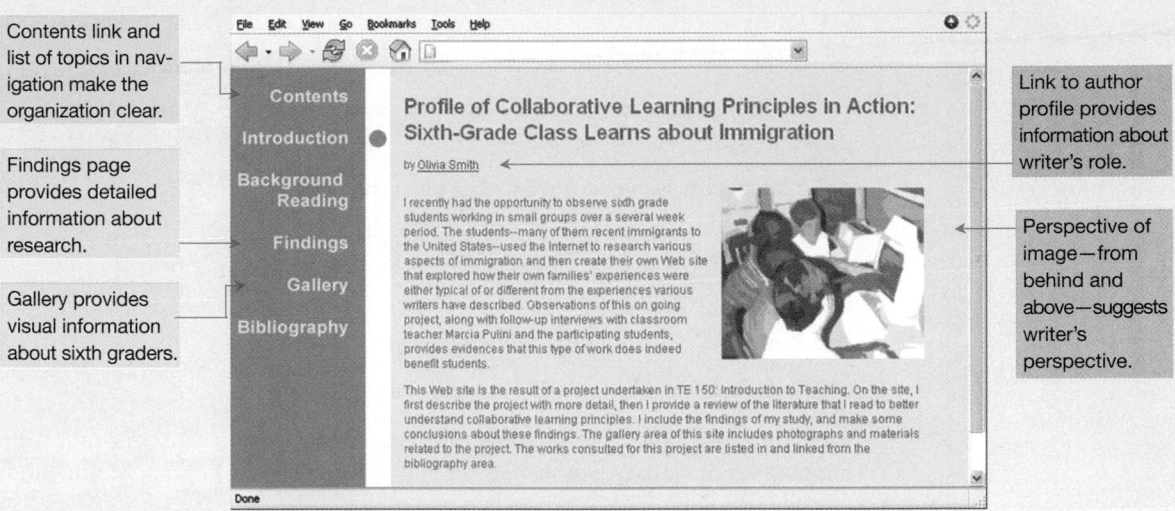

Link to author profile provides information about writer's role.

Perspective of image—from behind and above—suggests writer's perspective.

For more practice correcting punctuation problems, go to **bedfordstmartins.com /theguide/exercisecentral** and click on Punctuation in the Handbook section.

Edit and proofread your draft.

Several errors often occur in profiles, including problems with the punctuation of quotations and the integration of *participial phrases*. The following guidelines will help you check your essay for these common errors.

Checking the Punctuation of Quotations

Because most profiles are based in part on interviews, you have probably quoted one or more people in your essay. When you proofread your writing, check to make sure you have observed the strict conventions for punctuating quotations:

What to Check For

- All quotations should have quotation marks at the beginning and the end.

  ▶ "What exactly is civil litigation?" I asked.

- Commas and periods go *inside* quotation marks.

  ▶ "I'm here to see Anna Post," I replied nervously.

  ▶ Tony explained, "Fraternity boys just wouldn't feel comfortable at the Chez Moi Café."

- Question marks and exclamation points go *inside* closing quotation marks if they are part of the quotation, *outside* if they are not.

  ▶ After a pause, the patient asked, "Where do I sign?"

  ▶ Willie insisted, "You can *too* learn to play Super Mario!"

▸ When was the last time someone you just ticketed said to you, "Thank you, Officer, for doing a great job?"?

■ Use commas with speaker tags (*he said, she asked*) that accompany direct quotations.

▸ "This sound system costs only four thousand dollars," Jorge said.

▸ I asked, "So where were these clothes from originally?"

Integrating Participial Phrases

The Problem   Consider the following sentence:

▸ Snoring blissfully, <u>Bob</u> reclined in his chair.

You know that "Snoring blissfully" applies to Bob, because in English, modifying phrases or clauses like *snoring blissfully* are understood to apply to the nouns they precede or follow. That's why, when you read

▸ Exhausted after 28 hours of studying, <u>Regina</u> sighed loudly.

you know that Regina studied for twenty-eight hours. So what does the following sentence, taken from a 2003 government press release, mean?

▸ Suspected to have been started by an arsonist, <u>the fire investigation team</u> . . . continues its search for the person(s) responsible.

—that the fire investigation team was started by an arsonist? That may not be what the author of this sentence meant, but that's what the sentence says. This kind of error—called a *dangling modifier* — can confuse readers (or make them chuckle).

The Correction   When editing or proofreading your writing, look for modifying clauses or phrases. In each case, ask yourself whether the person or thing performing the action in the modifier is named immediately before or after the modifier. If it isn't, you have several options for fixing the error:

Change the subject of the sentence.

▸ Suspected to have been started by an arsonist, <u>the fire</u> burned nearly 60,000 acres before being brought under control.

Change the modifier.

▸ Suspecting that an arsonist started the fire, <u>the fire investigation team</u> . . . continues its search for the person(s) responsible.

Move the modifying phrase or clause.

▸ The fire investigation team continues its investigation into the <u>fire</u>, suspected to have been started by an arsonist.

For more practice correcting dangling modifiers, go to **bedfordstmartins.com** **/theguide/exercisecentral** and click on Effective Sentences/Modifiers in the Handbook section

A Note on Grammar and Spelling Checkers

These tools can be helpful, but don't rely on them exclusively to catch errors in your text: Spelling checkers cannot catch misspellings that are themselves words, such as *to* for *too*. Grammar checkers miss some problems, sometimes give faulty advice for fixing problems, and can flag correct items as wrong. Use these tools as a second line of defense after your own (and, ideally, another reader's) proofreading and editing efforts.

Improving the Draft

GUIDE TO READING
GUIDE TO WRITING
A WRITER AT WORK
THINKING CRITICALLY

109

A Common Problem for Multilingual Writers: Adjective Order

The Problem   In trying to present the subject of your profile vividly and in detail, you have probably included many descriptive adjectives. When you include more than one adjective in front of a noun, you may have difficulty sequencing them. For example, do you write *a large old ceramic pot* or *an old large ceramic pot*?

The Correction   The following list shows the order in which adjectives are ordinarily arranged in front of a noun:

1. *Amount* (a/an, the, six)
2. *Evaluation* (good, beautiful, ugly, serious)
3. *Size* (large, small, tremendous)
4. *Shape, length* (round, long, short)
5. *Age* (young, new, old)
6. *Color* (red, black, green)
7. *Origin* (Asian, Brazilian, German)
8. *Material* (wood, cotton, gold)
9. Noun used as an adjective (computer [as in *computer program*], cake [as in *cake pan*])

   1.   3.   6.

Seventeen small green buds appeared on my birch sapling.

            1. 2.   5.   6.   9.

He tossed his daughter a nice new yellow tennis ball.

  1.   4.   7.   8.

The slender German-made gold watch cost a great deal of money.

For more practice correcting adjective order, go to **bedfordstmartins.com /theguide/exercisecentral** and click on Troublespots in the Handbook section.

Brian Cable's Interview Notes and Write-Up

Most profile writers take notes when interviewing people. Later, they may summarize their notes in a short write-up. In this section, you will see some of the interview notes and a write-up that Brian Cable prepared for his mortuary profile, "The Last Stop," printed on pp. 63–68.

Cable arranged to tour the mortuary and conduct interviews with the funeral director and mortician. Before each interview, he wrote out a few questions at the top of a sheet of paper and then divided it into two columns; he used the left-hand column for descriptive details and personal impressions, and the right-hand column for the information he got directly from the person he interviewed. Following are Cable's notes and write-up for his interview with the funeral director, Howard Deaver.

Cable used three questions to guide his interview with Howard and then took brief notes during the interview. He did not concern himself too much with notetaking because he planned to spend a half hour directly afterward to complete his notes. He focused his attention on Howard, trying to keep the interview comfortable and conversational and jotting down just enough to jog his memory and catch especially meaningful quotations. A typescript of Cable's interview notes follows.

The Interview Notes

Questions

1. How do families of the deceased view the mortuary business?
2. How is the concept of death approached?
3. How did you get into this business?

Descriptive Details & Personal Impressions	Information
weird-looking	Howard Deaver, funeral director,
tall	Goodbody Mortuary
long fingers	"Call me Howard"
big ears	How things work: Notification, pick up
low, sloping forehead	body at home or hospital, prepare for
like stereotype — skin colorless	viewing, restore distorted features —
	accident or illness, embalm, casket —
	family selects, chapel services (3 in bldg.),
	visitation room — pay respects, family & friends.

Brian Cable's Interview Notes and Write-Up

GUIDE TO READING
GUIDE TO WRITING
A WRITER AT WORK
THINKING CRITICALLY

111

	Can't answer questions about death — "Not bereavement specialists. Don't handle emotional problems. Only a trained therapist can do that." "We provide services for dead, not counseling for the living." (great quote) Concept of death has changed in last 40 yrs (how long he's been in the business)
plays with lips blinks plays with Adam's apple desk empty — phone, no paper or pen	Phone call (interruption) "I think we'll be able to get him in on Friday. No, no, the family wants him cremated." Ask about Neptune Society — cremation Cremation "Cheap, quick, easy means of disposal."
angry disdainful of the Neptune Society	Recent phenomenon. Neptune Society — erroneous claim to be only one. "We've offered them since the beginning. It's only now it's come into vogue." Trend now back toward burial. Cremation still popular in sophisticated areas 60% in Marin Co. and Florida Ask about paperwork — does it upstairs, lives there with wife, Nancy.
musty, old stained glass sunlight filtered	Tour around (happy to show me around) Chapel — large service just done, Italian.
man in black suit roses wooden benches	"Not a religious institution — a business." casket — "beautiful craftsmanship" — admires, expensive
contrast brightness fluorescent lights Plexiglas stands	Display room — caskets, about 30 of them Loves to talk about caskets "models in every price range" glossy (like cars in a showroom) cardboard box, steel, copper, bronze starting at $500, averaging $1,800. Top of line: bronze, electronically welded, no corrosion — $25,000

Cable's interview notes include many descriptive details of Howard as well as of various rooms in the mortuary. Though most entries are short and sketchy, much of the language found its way into the final essay. In describing Howard, for example, Cable noted that he fits the stereotype of the cadaverous undertaker, a fact that Cable emphasized in his essay.

He put quotation marks around Howard's actual words, some of them written in complete sentences, others in fragments. We will see how Cable filled these quotes in when he wrote up the interview. In only a few instances did he take down more than he could use. Even though profile writers want good quotes, they should not use quotes to present information that can be more effectively expressed in their own words. In profiles, writers use direct quotation both to provide information and to capture the mood or character of the person speaking.

As you can see, Howard was not able to answer Cable's questions about the families of the deceased and their attitudes toward death or mortuaries. The gap between these questions and Howard's responses led Cable to recognize one of his own misperceptions about mortuaries — that they serve the living by helping people adjust to the death of loved ones. This misperception would become an important theme of his essay.

Immediately after the interview, Cable filled in his notes with details while they were still fresh in his mind. Next, he took some time to reflect on what he had learned from his interview with Howard. Here are some of his thoughts:

> I was surprised by how much Howard looked like the undertakers in scary movies. Even though he couldn't answer some of my questions, he was friendly enough. It's obviously a business for him (he loves to talk about caskets and to point out all their features, like a car dealer kicking a tire). Best quote: "We offer services to the dead, not counseling to the living." I have to bring up these issues in my interview with the mortician.

The Interview Write-Up

Writing up an account of the interview a short time afterward helped Cable fill in more details and reflect further on what he had learned. His write-up shows him already beginning to organize the information he had gained from his interview with the funeral director.

I. His physical appearance.

> Tall, skinny, with beady blue eyes embedded in his bony face. I was shocked to see that he looks just like the undertakers in scary movies. His skin is white and colorless, from lack of sunshine. He has a long nose and a low, sloping forehead. He was wearing a clean white shirt. A most unusual man — have you ever seen those Ames Home Loan commercials? But he was friendly, and happy to talk with me. "Would I answer some questions? Sure."

Brian Cable's Interview Notes and Write-Up

GUIDE TO READING
GUIDE TO WRITING
A WRITER AT WORK
THINKING CRITICALLY

113

II. What people want from a mortuary.

A. Well first of all, he couldn't answer my second question, about how families cope with the loss of a loved one. "You'd have to talk to a psychologist about that," he said. He did tell me how the concept of death has changed over the last ten or so years.

B. He has been in the business for forty years(!). One look at him and you'd be convinced he'd been there at least that long. He told me that in the old times, everyone was buried. Embalmed, put in a casket, and paid final homage before being shipped underground forever. Nowadays, many people choose to be cremated instead. Hence comes the success of the Neptune Society and others specializing in cremation. You can have your ashes dumped anywhere. "Not that we don't offer cremation services. We've offered them since the beginning," he added with a look of disdain. It's just that they've become so popular recently because they offer a "quick, easy, and efficient means of disposal." Cheap too — I think it is a reflection of a "no nonsense" society. The Neptune Society has become so successful because it claims to be the only one to offer cremations as an alternative to expensive burial. "We've offered it all along. It's just only now come into vogue."

Sophisticated areas (I felt "progressive" would be more accurate) like Marin County have a cremation rate of over 60 percent. The phone rang. "Excuse me," he said. As he talked on the phone, I noticed how he played with his lips, pursing and squeezing them. He was blinking a lot, too. I meant to ask him how he got into this business, but I forgot. I did find out his name and title: Mr. Howard Deaver, funeral director of Goodbody Mortuary (no kidding, that's the real name). He lives on the premises, upstairs with his wife. I doubt if he ever leaves the place.

III. It's a business!

Some people have the idea that mortuaries offer counseling and peace of mind — a place where everyone is sympathetic and ready to offer advice. "In some mortuaries, this is true. But by and large, this is a business. We offer services to the dead, not counseling to the living." I too had expected to feel an awestruck respect for the dead upon entering the building. I had also expected green lawns, ponds with ducks, fountains, flowers, peacefulness — you know, a "Forest Lawn" type deal. But it was only a tall, Catholic-looking building. "Mortuaries do not sell plots for burial," he was saying. "Cemeteries do that, after we embalm the body and select a casket. We're not a religious institution." He seemed hung up on caskets — though maybe he was just trying to impress upon me the differences between caskets. "Oh, they're very important. A good casket is a sign of respect. Sometimes if the family doesn't have enough money, we rent them a nice one. People pay for what they get just like any other business." I wondered when you had to return the casket you rented.

I wanted to take a look around. He was happy to give me a tour. We visited several chapels and visiting rooms   places where the deceased "lie in state" to be "visited" by family and friends. I saw an old lady in a "fairly decent casket," as Mr. Deaver called it. Again I was impressed by the simple businesslike nature of it all. Oh yes, the rooms were elaborately decorated, with lots of shrines and stained glass, but these things were for the customers' benefit. "Sometimes we have up to eight or nine corpses here at one time, sometimes none. We have to have enough rooms to accommodate." Simple enough, yet I never realized how much trouble people were after they died. So much money, time, and effort go into their funerals.

As I prepared to leave, he gave me his card. He'd be happy to see me again, or maybe I could talk to someone else. I said I was going to interview the mortician on another day. I shook his hand. His fingers were long and his skin was warm.

Writing up the interview helped Cable probe his subject more deeply. It also helped him express a humorous attitude toward his subject. Cable's interview notes and write-up were quite informal; later, he integrated this material more formally into his full profile of the mortuary.

THINKING CRITICALLY

To think critically means to use all of the knowledge you have acquired from the information in this chapter, your own writing, the writing and responses of other students, and class discussions to reflect deeply on your work for this assignment and the genre (or type) of writing you have produced. The benefit of thinking critically is proven and important: Thinking critically about what you have learned will help you remember it longer, ensuring that you will be able to put it to good use well beyond this writing course.

Reflecting on What You Have Learned

In this chapter, you have learned a great deal about this genre by reading several profiles and writing one of your own. To consolidate your learning, reflect not only on what you learned but on how you learned it.

ANALYZE & WRITE

Write a blog post, a letter to your instructor or a classmate, or an e-mail message to a student who will take this course next term, using the writing prompt that seems most productive for you:

- Explain how your purpose and audience — what you wanted your readers to learn about your subject from reading your profile — influenced *one* of your decisions as a writer, such as what kinds of descriptive detail you included, what method of organization you used, or the role you adopted in writing about your subject.

Reflecting on the Genre

GUIDE TO READING
GUIDE TO WRITING
A WRITER AT WORK
THINKING CRITICALLY

115

- Discuss what you learned about yourself as a writer in the process of writing this profile. For example, what part of the process did you find most challenging? Did you try anything new, like getting a critical reading of your draft or outlining your draft in order to revise it? If so, how well did it work?

- If you were to give advice to a fellow student who was about to write a profile, what would
you say?

- Which of the readings in this chapter influenced your essay? Explain the influence, citing specific examples from your profile and the reading.

- If you got good advice from a critical reader, explain exactly how the person helped you — perhaps by questioning your perspective in a way that enabled you to refocus your profile's dominant impression, or by pointing out passages that needed more information or clearer chronology to better orient readers.

Reflecting on the Genre

Profiles broaden our view of the world by entertaining and informing us with portraits of people, places, or activities. But even effective profiles sometimes offer a limited view of their subjects. For example, the impulse to entertain readers may lead a profile writer to focus exclusively on the dramatic, colorful, or humorous aspects of a person, place, or activity, ignoring the equally important humdrum, routine, or otherwise less appealing aspects. Imagine a profile that focuses on the dramatic moments in an emergency-room doctor's shift but ignores the routine cases and the slow periods when nothing much is happening. Such a profile would provide a limited and distorted picture of an emergency-room doctor's work. In addition, by focusing on the dramatic or glamorous aspects of a subject, profile writers tend to ignore economic or social consequences and to slight supporting players. Profiling the highly praised chef in a trendy new restaurant, a writer might not ask who the kitchen workers and waitstaff are, how the chef treats them, or how much they are paid.

ANALYZE & WRITE

Write a page or two explaining how the genre prompts you to think about the subject of a profile. In your discussion, you might consider one or more of the following:

1. **Consider whether any of the profiles you have read glamorize or sensationalize their subjects.** Do they ignore less colorful but centrally important people or everyday activities? Is this a problem with your own profile?

2. **Write a page or so explaining what the omissions signify.** What do they suggest about the readers' desires to be entertained and the profile writer's reluctance to present the subject in a more complete way?

4
Explaining a Concept

Concepts are central to the understanding of virtually every subject—in the community, at work, and especially in college. Much of your reading and writing as a student involves learning the concepts that are the building blocks of academic subjects. Concepts include principles or ideals (such as *equal justice* or *the American dream*), theories (such as *relativity* or *evolution*), ideas (such as *commodification* or *states' rights*), conditions (such as *state of flow* or *paranoia*), phenomena (such as *quarks* or *inflation*), and processes (such as *high-intensity interval training* or *socialization*). To communicate effectively and efficiently about a particular subject—whether you are writing to insiders or to novices—you need to be able to use and explain concepts clearly and compellingly.

IN COLLEGE COURSES

For a cultural studies course, a student responds to a writing assignment to analyze the politics of sexuality in advertising. She decides to use the concept of framing she had learned in her first-year composition course the previous term. After reviewing her old class notes, she researches *cultural framing theory* in relation to sexual politics. She finds several sources and cites them to explain the concept. Then, she uses cultural framing to analyze a couple of advertisements she downloaded from the Web. Finally, she posts to her class Web site the final paper, along with the advertisements she analyzed.

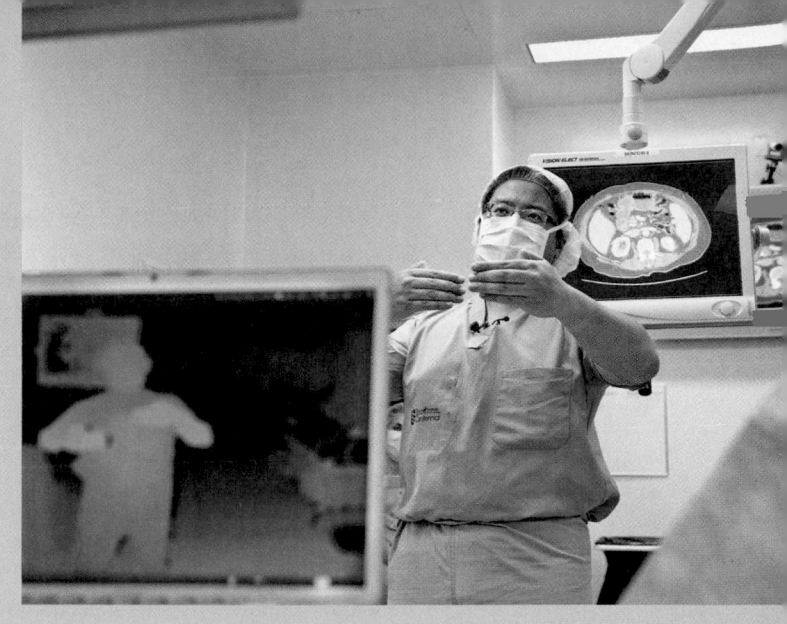

IN THE COMMUNITY

A manager at a marketing research firm gives a presentation on *surveying,* an important research method, to fifth-grade science students. She begins by having students fill out a brief survey on their television-watching habits, and then asks them to speculate on what they expect their answers to show and how this data might be used by advertisers and programmers. Then, with the students' help, she selects the variables that seem significant: the respondents' gender, the number of hours spent watching television, and the types of shows watched. At the next class, she distributes graphs detailing her analysis and asks the students to see whether the results match their assumptions. She concludes by passing out a quiz to find out how much the students have learned about surveys.

IN THE WORKPLACE

At a seminar for small business owners with minimal knowledge of programming, a technology consultant gives a multimedia presentation on what has been called the *Kinect effect*. He begins by explaining what Kinect is and how it works, showing two clips from the film *Minority Report* to illustrate Kinect's gesture-driven 3-D imaging (multitouch computer interface) and personalized advertising (retina-scanning talking billboards). Then he demonstrates some of its many potential medical uses—for example, enabling surgeons to use gesture to examine a patient's MRI scans during surgery or providing navigational assistance for the visually impaired.

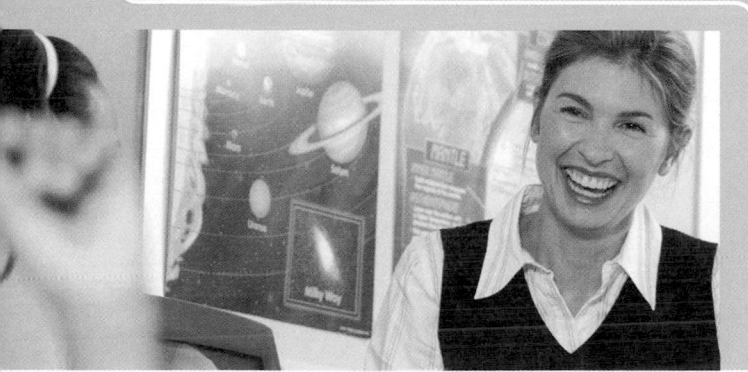

In this chapter, we ask you to explain a concept that is unfamiliar to your readers. Whether you tackle a concept you've studied in college or choose one from your work or your favorite sport, you need to answer your readers' inevitable "So what?" Why should they want to understand the concept? Analyzing the selections in the Guide to Reading that follows will help you learn how to make your concept explanation interesting as well as informative. The Guide to Writing later in the chapter will show you ways to use the basic features of the genre, including how to use visuals and multimedia, to make an unfamiliar concept appealing and understandable to your readers.

PRACTICING THE GENRE

Explaining an Academic Concept

Part 1. Get together in a small group to practice explaining a concept. First, think of a concept you recently learned in one of your courses. Next, take a few minutes to plan how you will explain it to group members who may not know anything about the subject. Consider whether it would be helpful to identify the course and the context in which you learned it, to give your listeners a dictionary definition, to tell them what kind of concept it is, to compare it to something they may already know, to give them an example, or to explain why the concept is important or useful. Then, take two or three minutes each to explain your concept.

Part 2. Discuss what you learned about explaining concepts:

- **What did you learn from others' explanations?** To think about purpose and audience in explaining a concept, tell one another whether you felt the "So what?" question was adequately answered: What, if anything, piqued your interest or made you feel that the concept might be worth learning about? If you were to try to explain the concept to someone else, what would you be able to say?

- **What did you learn by constructing your own explanation?** Compare your thoughts with others in your group about what was easiest and hardest about explaining a concept—for example, choosing a concept you understood well enough to explain to others; making it interesting, important, or useful; or deciding what to say about it in the time you had.

Analyzing Concept Explanations

As you read the selections in this chapter, you will see how different authors explain concepts. Analyzing how these writers focus their explanations, organize their writing, use examples and other writing strategies, and integrate sources will help you see how you can employ these techniques to make your own explanation of a concept clear and compelling for your readers.

Determine the writer's purpose and audience.

How well a writer explains a concept can demonstrate how well the writer understands the concept. That is why this kind of writing is so frequently assigned in college courses. But it is also a popular genre outside of the classroom, where writers typically know more about the subject than their readers do. It is especially important to anticipate readers' "So what?" question and excite their curiosity. When reading the concept explanations that follow, ask questions like these about the writer's purpose and audience:

- What seems to be the writer's main *purpose* in explaining this concept—for example, to inform readers about an important idea or theory, to show how a concept has promoted original thinking and research in an area of study, to better understand the concept by explaining it to others, or to demonstrate knowledge of the concept and the ability to apply it?

- What does the writer assume about the *audience*—for example, that readers will be unfamiliar with the concept and need an introduction that will capture their interest, that readers will know something about the concept but want to learn more about it, or that the primary reader will be an instructor who knows more about the concept than the writer does and who is evaluating the writer's knowledge?

Assess the genre's basic features.

Use the following to help you analyze and evaluate how writers of concept explanations employ the genre's basic features. The examples are drawn from the reading selections in this chapter.

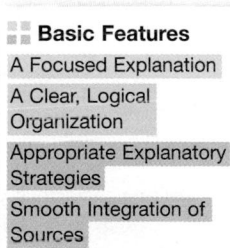

Basic Features
A Focused Explanation
A Clear, Logical Organization
Appropriate Explanatory Strategies
Smooth Integration of Sources

A FOCUSED EXPLANATION

Read first to identify the concept. Then ask yourself, "What is the focus or main point?" This point is the *thesis* of a concept explanation, comparable to what we call autobiographical significance in remembered event essays and perspective in profiles. The point answers the "So what?" question: Why are you telling me about this concept? Why is it interesting or important?

Focusing requires that there be thoughtful selection of what to include and what to leave out. For college writing and some other contexts, the focus may be dictated by a specific question or prompt. For example, Patricia Lyu's instructor asked students to do two things: explain a concept they had learned about in a course, and apply that concept to a passage in *The Things They Carried,* a book the class was reading. In the textbook for her Introduction to Psychology course, Lyu had recently read about infant attachment and the research that had been done to establish the concept in the field of developmental psychology. She saw immediately how the concept could be applied to *The Things They Carried,* in particular to explain Dobbins's "peculiar" attachment to "his girlfriend's pantyhose" (Lyu, par. 11).

A CLEAR, LOGICAL ORGANIZATION

Effective concept explanations have to be clearly and logically organized. As you read the essays in this chapter, notice how each writer develops a plan that does the following:

- States the thesis or main point early on

  > *Concept*
  >
  > *Main point*

  Let's put love under a microscope. . . . When rigorous people with Ph.D.s after their names do that, what they see is not some silly senseless thing. No, their probe reveals that love rests firmly on foundations of evolution, biology, and chemistry. (Toufexis, pars. 1-2)

- Divides the information into clearly distinguishable topics and forecasts them

  > *Rhetorical questions often announce the topics*

  How does that bond develop and how does it affect romantic relationships later in life? John Bowlby and Mary Ainsworth's theory of attachment answers both of these questions. (Lyu, par. 1)

- Guides readers by providing cues or road signs

  > *Logical transitions often used in topic sentences*

  Thus, Harlow's research validated attachment theory . . .

  As an adult, however, . . .

  > *Topic sentence may summarize topic of preceding paragraph and introduce topic of current paragraph*

  Moreover, . . . (Lyu, pars. 8, 11, 12)

  If, in nature's design, romantic love is not eternal, neither is it exclusive. (Toufexis, par. 8)

APPROPRIATE EXPLANATORY STRATEGIES

For more on writing strategies such as definition and classification, see Chapters 14–19.

Writers explaining a concept typically use a variety of writing strategies, such as *definition, classification, comparison-contrast, example, illustration,* and *cause-effect:*

Defining characteristic *Term to be defined*	**DEFINITION**	Each person carries in his or her mind a unique subliminal guide to the ideal partner, a "love map,". . . (Toufexis, par. 17)
Cue signaling classification	**CLASSIFICATION**	From this research, Ainsworth identified three basic types of attachment that children form with their primary caregiver: *secure, anxious* (or *anxious-resistant*), and *avoidant.* (Lyu, par. 4)
Juxtaposition	**COMPARISON-CONTRAST**	Shyness and introversion are not the same thing. Shy people fear negative judgment; introverts simply prefer quiet, minimally stimulating environments. (Cain, par. 9)

Analyzing Concept Explanations

GUIDE TO READING
GUIDE TO WRITING
A WRITER AT WORK
THINKING CRITICALLY

121

In contrast, . . . (Cain, par. 19) Cues

The genetic component of intelligence . . . functions less like the genes that control for eye color and more like the complex of interacting genes that affect weight and height. (Hurley, par. 17)

EXAMPLE We find them in recent history, in figures like Charles Darwin, Marcel Proust and Albert Einstein, and, in contemporary times, think of Google's Larry Page, or Harry Potter's creator, J. K. Rowling. (Cain, par. 11) Cues

Examples

Anxiety . . . can serve an important social purpose; for example, . . . (Cain, par. 22)

Despite . . . side effects—nausea, loss of sex drive, seizures—drugs like Zoloft . . . (Cain, par. 3)

ILLUSTRATION (WITH VISUAL) The infant monkeys were separated from their biological mothers and raised by a surrogate mother made of wood and covered with terry cloth or made from uncovered heavy wire (see fig. 2). (Lyu, par. 7) Reference to a visual in the text

CAUSE-EFFECT How, then, could watching black cats . . . increase . . . fluid intelligence? Because the deceptively simple game . . . targets "working" memory. (Hurley, par. 6) Cues

SMOOTH INTEGRATION OF SOURCES

Although writers often draw on their own experiences and observations in explaining a concept, they almost always conduct research into their subject. As you read, think about how the writer establishes her or his authority by smoothly integrating information from sources into the explanation. Does the writer quote, paraphrase, or summarize the source material? How does the writer establish the source's expertise and credibility?

QUOTE The association between infant attachment and adult relationships was first investigated in Cindy Hazan and Phillip Shaver's appropriately titled breakthrough study, "Romantic Love Conceptualized as an Attachment Process." Since then, attachment theory "has become one of the major frameworks for the study of romantic relationships" (Fraley and Shaver 132). This expansion of the concept of attachment should be no surprise given that Bowlby himself described the formation of attachment as "falling in love" (qtd. in Cassidy 5). (Lyu, par. 11) Signal phrase plus background

Parenthetical citation (qtd. in = quoted in)

PARAPHRASE It is the difference between passionate and compassionate love, observes Walsh, a psychobiologist at Boise State University in Idaho. (Toufexis, par. 14)

SUMMARY   In a 2008 study, Susanne Jaeggi and Martin Buschkuehl, now of the University of Maryland, found that young adults . . . showed improvement in a fundamental cognitive ability known as "fluid" intelligence. (Hurley, par. 4)

How writers treat sources depends on the writing situation. Certain formal situations, such as college assignments or scholarly publications, require writers to cite sources in the text and document them in a bibliography (called a list of **works cited** in many humanities disciplines and a list of **references** in the sciences and social sciences). Students and scholars are expected to cite their sources formally because readers judge their work in part by what the writers have read and how they have used their reading and also so that those interested can locate the sources and read more about the topic for themselves. (See student Patricia Lyu's essay, pp. 123–28, for an example of academic citation.) For more informal writing—magazine and newspaper articles, for example—readers do not expect references or publication information to appear in the article, but they do expect sources to be identified and their expertise established in some way. (See the articles by Toufexis, Hurley, and Cain, on pp. 129–31, 135–38, and 142–45, respectively, for examples of informal citation.)

Readings

Patricia Lyu | *Attachment: Someone to Watch over You*

To learn about how Patricia Lyu used sources to support her own ideas, turn to A Writer at Work on pp. 169–70. How did she contextualize sources to show their relevance? How did she combine summary and quotation to integrate source material into her essay and avoid simply stringing quotations together?

ORIGINALLY, Patricia Lyu wrote this essay explaining the concept of infant attachment for her composition course. You will see that following her instructor's recommendation, Lyu chose a concept she had learned about in another course, Introduction to Psychology, and she quotes from that course's textbook. She also uses a number of other sources, including articles and books, some of which she accessed through the library's Web site and others that she found in print in the library. As you read, consider the following questions as well as those in the margin:

• How effectively does Lyu integrate source material into her own sentences?

• What strategies does she use to cite her sources? Why do you think citing sources this way is expected in most college papers?

Lyu   *Attachment: Someone to Watch over You*

GUIDE TO READING
GUIDE TO WRITING
A WRITER AT WORK
THINKING CRITICALLY

123

Basic Features
A Focused Explanation
A Clear, Logical
Organization
Appropriate Explanatory
Strategies
Smooth Integration of
Sources

"Babies are such nice ways to start people."

—Don Herrold

1   Fortunately, most people agree with humorist Don Herrold, because infants depend for their well-being, indeed for their very survival, on the goodwill of others. Developmental psychologists have wondered about the bond that needs to form between newborns and caregivers in order for infants to survive and thrive. How does that bond develop and how does it affect romantic relationships later in life? John Bowlby and Mary Ainsworth's theory of attachment answers both of these questions.

2   Bowlby theorized that humans have evolved in ways that made infants and caretakers "biologically predisposed" to send and receive signals ("attachment behaviors" such as crying, smiling, and cooing) that bring the child into close contact with the caretaker, which assures the child's safety, feeding, and likelihood of surviving to reproductive age (Cassidy 4–5). According to psychology professor R. Chris Fraley's "A Brief Overview of Adult Attachment Theory and Research," children develop what Bowlby called an "attachment behavioral system." This system ensures that the attachment object (usually a parent or primary caregiver) will be physically present and attentive to the child's needs. But attachment does not end in childhood. As Bowlby famously stated, it continues to play an important role throughout life, from "the cradle to the grave" (qtd. in Fraley 3). Attachment begins in need and is intensified by fear. As we will see, Tim O'Brien's character Henry Dobbins in *The Things They Carried* provides a fascinating example of how the trauma of war affects adult attachment behavior and may even help explain religious faith.

3   Bowlby's understanding of attachment came from observations after World War II of children separated from parents or other primary caregivers. He saw that "separation anxiety" — being physically apart from the caregiver or perceiving the "threat" of separation — "activates the attachment system" (Kobak and Madsen 30). In his "Overview," Fraley describes the way the attachment system works and also illustrates it with the flowchart shown in fig. 1:

> the attachment system essentially "asks" the following fundamental question: "Is the attachment figure nearby, accessible, and attentive?" If the child perceives the answer to this question to be "yes," he or she feels loved,

What strategies does Lyu use in the epigraph and opening paragraphs to introduce the concept to readers? How well do they work to engage readers and give them a map to follow the analysis?

secure, and confident, and, behaviorally, is likely to explore his or her environment, play with others, and be sociable. If, however, the child perceives the answer to this question to be "no," the child experiences anxiety and, behaviorally, is likely to exhibit attachment behaviors ranging from simple visual searching on the low extreme to active following and vocal signaling on the other (1–2).

> How effectively does Lyu integrate information from sources to support her explanation?

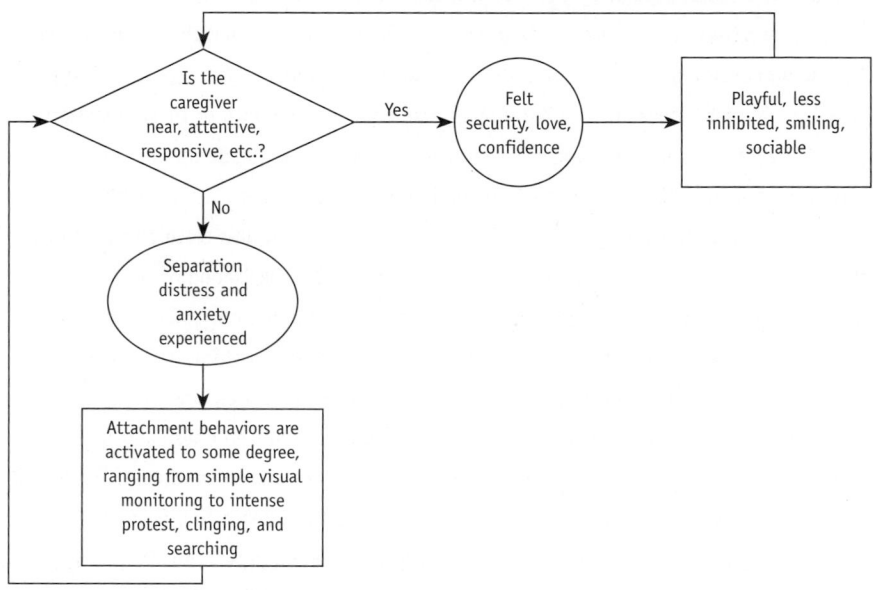

Fig. 1. The attachment behavioral system

> How well do the figures that appear here and elsewhere in the paper help explain the concept of attachment?

4   Developmental psychologist Mary Ainsworth "contributed the concept of the attachment figure as a secure base from which an infant can explore the world" (Bretherton 759). She also designed a series of experiments using "the strange situation" in which researchers watched twelve- to twenty-month-old children through a one-way mirror as they played in an unfamiliar laboratory playroom, first while their attachment figure was with them and then as the caregiver stepped out of the room for a few moments. From this research, Ainsworth identified three basic types of attachment that children form with their primary caregiver: *secure, anxious* (or *anxious-resistant*), and *avoidant* (Fraley 4).

> How does Lyu use Ainsworth's categories to organize this section of her paper?

5   The secure child cries when the caregiver leaves, but goes to the caregiver and calms down when he or she returns. According to Ainsworth, these children feel secure

because their primary caregiver has been reliably responsive to their needs over the course of their short lives.

6   Ainsworth classifies the other two styles of attachment as insecure compared to the first attachment style. Anxious children may be clingy, get very upset when the caregiver leaves, and seem afraid of the stranger. They do not calm down when the caregiver returns, crying inconsolably and seeming very mad at the caregiver. Avoidant children ignore the caregiver when he or she returns. They seem emotionally distant and may even move away from him or her to play with toys.

7   Attachment theory was revolutionary: "Before widespread acceptance of Bowlby's theory, psychologists viewed attachment as a secondary drive, derived from primary drives like hunger" ("Attachment" 1). Harry Harlow's primate research lent support to attachment theory, showing that infant monkeys bond to whatever is soft and cuddly. A psychologist at the Primate Laboratory at the University of Wisconsin, Harlow conducted a series of famous and rather disturbing experiments with infant monkeys. The infant monkeys were separated from their biological mothers and raised by a surrogate mother made of wood and covered with terry cloth or made from uncovered heavy wire (see fig. 2). Kimble, Garmezy, and Zigler, in their introductory psychology textbook, describe Harlow's research this way:

> In one experiment, both types of surrogates were present in the cage, but only one was equipped with a nipple from which the infant could nurse. Some infants received nourishment from the wire mother, and others were fed from the cloth mother. Even when the wire mother was the source of nourishment, the infant monkey spent a greater amount of time clinging to the cloth surrogate. (21)

8   Thus, Harlow's research validated attachment theory by showing that the infant monkeys attached themselves to the more cuddly terry cloth "surrogate" even if it did not have a bottle and therefore could not feed them. Harlow demonstrated that attachment, the need for closeness and comfort, is as strong as the need for food.

9   In other experiments, he also showed that fear is a strong motivator of attachment, leading the infant monkeys to seek consolation from the surrogate. In these experiments, Harlow put a strange object in the cage. If the surrogate was absent or if only the wire surrogate was present, the baby monkey would be afraid, often crying, sucking its thumb, and hiding in the corner. But if the terry cloth surrogate was present, the monkey would run to

How effectively does Lyu transition to and demonstrate the relevance of Harlow's research to the concept of attachment?

Fig. 2. Harlow's infant monkey cuddling the cloth surrogate and turning its back on the wire surrogate with the bottle.

it, cling for a while, and then, apparently reassured, venture out again to explore the cage and confront the intruder. The conclusion drawn from this research is that the attachment figure provides security, especially in times of fear.

10   The original research on attachment, plus Harlow's monkey experiments, underlines the idea that "the attachment and fear systems are intertwined" (Cassidy 8). During a time of war, fear obviously is intensified, especially for soldiers in harm's way. Therefore, we can see how applying the concept of attachment to *The Things They Carried* can be illuminating. It is especially helpful in understanding Henry Dobbins's peculiar habit of wearing "his girlfriend's pantyhose around his neck before heading out on ambush" (O'Brien 117). Fear triggers Dobbins's attachment behavior. Like Harlow's monkey, he seeks comfort from his attachment figure.

> How does Lyu signal the reader that she is shifting from a discussion of infant attachment to a discussion of attachment in adult relationships?

11   As an adult, however, Dobbins's attachment figure is the object of his romantic love, his girlfriend. The association between infant attachment and adult relationships was first investigated in Cindy Hazan and Phillip Shaver's appropriately titled breakthrough study, "Romantic Love Conceptualized as an Attachment Process." Since then, attachment theory "has become one of the major frameworks for the study of romantic relationships" (Fraley and Shaver 132). This expansion of the concept of

Lyu *Attachment: Someone to Watch over You*

GUIDE TO READING
GUIDE TO WRITING
A WRITER AT WORK
THINKING CRITICALLY

127

attachment should be no surprise given that Bowlby himself described the formation of attachment as "falling in love" (qtd. in Cassidy 5).

12   Moreover, O'Brien's description of Dobbins's behavior shows that for adults under extreme duress, the attachment process includes the use of substitutes. For Dobbins, in the absence of his girlfriend, her stockings serve as a substitute attachment object, Dobbins's security blanket: "He sometimes slept with the stockings up against his face, the way an infant sleeps with a flannel blanket, secure and peaceful. More than anything, though, the stockings were a talisman for him. They kept him safe" (117–18).

> How effectively does this quotation support Lyu's claim about Dobbins?

13   O'Brien makes the further point that the power of the security object comes from Dobbins's unwavering faith in it: "he believed firmly and absolutely in the protective power of the stockings. They were like body armor" (118). Even after his girlfriend abandons him, Dobbins's faith is not shaken because the object itself had taken her place in his attachment system. Dobbins clearly has a very secure attachment style.

14   Through Dobbins's example, we can see that O'Brien appears to be making a connection between having absolute confidence in one's attachment figure and having strong religious beliefs. By calling the stockings Dobbins's "talisman" and emphasizing their magical powers, O'Brien makes the connection explicit. Dobbins's faith, in fact, is so strong that it seems to be contagious. The other soldiers somehow "came to appreciate the mystery of it" (118). Ultimately, we as readers also become invested in this belief system because, as O'Brien tells us: "Dobbins was invulnerable. Never wounded. Never a scratch" (118). The example of Henry Dobbins suggests that attachment is not only the evolutionary mechanism by which helpless infants survive, but it may also be a precursor to religious belief, the faith that someone is watching over you.

> What does Lyu achieve in this conclusion? How does it work for you?

Works Cited

"Attachment." *Gale Encyclopedia of Psychology. Encyclopedia.com*, 2001. Web. 5 Mar. 2012.

Bretherton, Inge. "The Origins of Attachment Theory: John Bowlby and Mary Ainsworth." *Developmental Psychology* 28 (1992): 759–75. Print.

Cassidy, Jude. "The Nature of the Child's Ties." *Handbook of Attachment: Theory, Research, and Clinical Applications*. Ed. Jude Cassidy and Phillip R. Shaver. 2nd ed. New York: Guilford, 2008. 3–22. Print.

Fraley, R. Chris. "A Brief Overview of Adult Attachment Theory and Research." *Dept. of Psychology*. University of Illinois, 2010. Web. 5 Mar. 2012.

> What makes Lyu's sources seem authoritative (or not)?

What can you learn about creating a list of works cited from this example?

Fraley, R. Chris, and Phillip R. Shaver. "Adult Romantic Attachment: Theoretical Developments, Emerging Controversies, and Unanswered Questions." *Review of General Psychology* 4.2 (2000): 132–54. *PsycArticles*. Web. 5 Mar. 2012.

Hazan, Cindy, and Phillip Shaver. "Romantic Love Conceptualized as an Attachment Process." *Journal of Personality and Social Psychology* 52.3 (1987): 511–24. *PsycArticles*. Web. 4 Mar. 2012.

Kimble, Gregory, Norman Garmezy, and Edward Zigler. *Principles of General Psychology,* 5th ed. New York: Wiley, 1980. Print.

Kobak, Roger, and Stephanie Madsen. "Disruptions in Attachment Bonds." *Handbook of Attachment: Theory, Research, and Clinical Applications.* Ed. Jude Cassidy and Phillip R. Shaver. 2nd ed. New York: Guilford, 2008. 23–47. Print.

O'Brien, Tim. *The Things They Carried.* Boston: Houghton, 1990. Print.

Passman, Richard H. "Security Objects." *Gale Encyclopedia of Psychology. Encyclopedia .com,* 2001. 5 Mar. 2012.

For an additional student reading, go to **bedfordstmartins.com/ theguide/epages**.

Anastasia Toufexis | *Love: The Right Chemistry*

ANASTASIA TOUFEXIS has been an associate editor of *Time,* senior editor of *Discover,* and editor in chief of *Psychology Today*. She has written on subjects as diverse as medicine, health and fitness, law, the environment, education, science, and national and world news. Toufexis has won a number of awards for her writing, including a Knight-Wallace Fellowship at the University of Michigan and an Ocean Science Journalism Fellowship at Woods Hole Oceanographic Institution. She has also lectured on science writing at Columbia University, the University of North Carolina, and the School of Visual Arts in New York. As you read, consider these questions:

• How would you describe the tone Toufexis adopts in this essay, at least in the beginning? How effective do you think this tone was for her original *Time* magazine readers? How appropriate would it be for a college paper?

- Given her purpose and audience, how helpful is the visual in helping readers understand her rather technical explanation?

Love is a romantic designation for a most ordinary biological—or, shall we say, chemical?—process. A lot of nonsense is talked and written about it.

—Greta Garbo to Melvyn Douglas in *Ninotchka*

1 O.K., let's cut out all this nonsense about romantic love. Let's bring some scientific precision to the party. Let's put love under a microscope.

2 When rigorous people with Ph.D.s after their names do that, what they see is not some silly, senseless thing. No, their probe reveals that love rests firmly on the foundations of evolution, biology and chemistry. What seems on the surface to be irrational, intoxicated behavior is in fact part of nature's master strategy—a vital force that has helped humans survive, thrive and multiply through thousands of years. Says Michael Mills, a psychology professor at Loyola Marymount University in Los Angeles: "Love is our ancestors whispering in our ears."

3 It was on the plains of Africa about 4 million years ago, in the early days of the human species, that the notion of romantic love probably first began to blossom or at least that the first cascades of neurochemicals began flowing from the brain to the bloodstream to produce goofy grins and sweaty palms as men and women gazed deeply into each other's eyes. When mankind graduated from scuttling around on all fours to walking on two legs, this change made the whole person visible to fellow human beings for the first time. Sexual organs were in full display, as were other characteristics, from the color of eyes to the span of shoulders. As never before, each individual had a unique allure.

4 When the sparks flew, new ways of making love enabled sex to become a romantic encounter, not just a reproductive act. Although mounting mates from the rear was, and still is, the method favored among most animals, humans began to enjoy face-to-face couplings; both looks and personal attraction became a much greater part of the equation.

5 Romance served the evolutionary purpose of pulling males and females into long-term partnership, which was essential to child rearing. On open grasslands, one parent would have a hard—and dangerous—time handling a child while foraging for food. "If a woman was carrying the equivalent of a 20-lb. bowling ball in one arm and a pile of sticks in the other, it was ecologically critical to pair up with a mate to rear the young," explains anthropologist Helen Fisher, author of *Anatomy of Love*.

6 While Western culture holds fast to the idea that true love flames forever (the movie *Bram Stoker's Dracula* has the Count carrying the torch beyond the grave), nature apparently meant passions to sputter out in something like four years. Primitive pairs stayed together just "long enough to rear one child through infancy," says Fisher. Then each would find a new partner and start all over again.

7 What Fisher calls the "four-year itch" shows up unmistakably in today's divorce statistics. In most of the 62 cultures she has studied, divorce rates peak around the fourth year of marriage. Additional youngsters help keep pairs together longer. If, say, a couple have another child three years after the first, as often occurs, then their union can be expected to last about four more years. That makes them ripe for the more familiar phenomenon portrayed in the Marilyn Monroe classic *The Seven-Year Itch*.

8 If, in nature's design, romantic love is not eternal, neither is it exclusive. Less than 5% of mammals form rigorously faithful pairs. From the earliest days, contends Fisher, the human pattern has been "monogamy with clandestine adultery." Occasional flings upped the chances that new combinations of genes would be passed on to the next generation. Men who sought new partners had more children. Contrary to common assumptions, women were just as likely to stray. "As long as prehistoric females were secretive about their extramarital affairs," argues Fisher, "they could garner extra resources, life insurance, better genes and more varied DNA for their biological futures. . . ."

If, in nature's design, romantic love is not eternal, neither is it exclusive.

9 Lovers often claim that they feel as if they are being swept away. They're not mistaken; they are literally flooded by chemicals, research suggests. A meeting of eyes, a touch of hands or a whiff of scent sets off a flood that starts in the brain and races along the nerves and through the blood. The results are familiar: flushed

skin, sweaty palms, heavy breathing. If love looks suspiciously like stress, the reason is simple: the chemical pathways are identical.

10   Above all, there is the sheer euphoria of falling in love—a not-so-surprising reaction, considering that many of the substances swamping the newly smitten are chemical cousins of amphetamines. They include dopamine, norepinephrine and especially phenylethylamine (PEA). Cole Porter knew what he was talking about when he wrote, "I get a kick out of you." "Love is a natural high," observes Anthony Walsh, author of *The Science of Love: Understanding Love and Its Effects on Mind and Body.* "PEA gives you that silly smile that you flash at strangers. When we meet someone who is attractive to us, the whistle blows at the PEA factory."

11   But phenylethylamine highs don't last forever, a fact that lends support to arguments that passionate romantic love is short-lived. As with any amphetamine, the body builds up a tolerance to PEA; thus it takes more and more of the substance to produce love's special kick. After two to three years, the body simply can't crank up the needed amount of PEA. And chewing on chocolate doesn't help, despite popular belief. The candy is high in PEA, but it fails to boost the body's supply.

12   Fizzling chemicals spell the end of delirious passion; for many people that marks the end of the liaison as well. It is particularly true for those whom Dr. Michael Liebowitz of the New York State Psychiatric Institute terms "attraction junkies." They crave the intoxication of falling in love so much that they move frantically from affair to affair just as soon as the first rush of infatuation fades.

13   Still, many romances clearly endure beyond the first years. What accounts for that? Another set of chemicals, of course. The continued presence of a partner gradually steps up production in the brain of endorphins. Unlike the fizzy amphetamines, these are

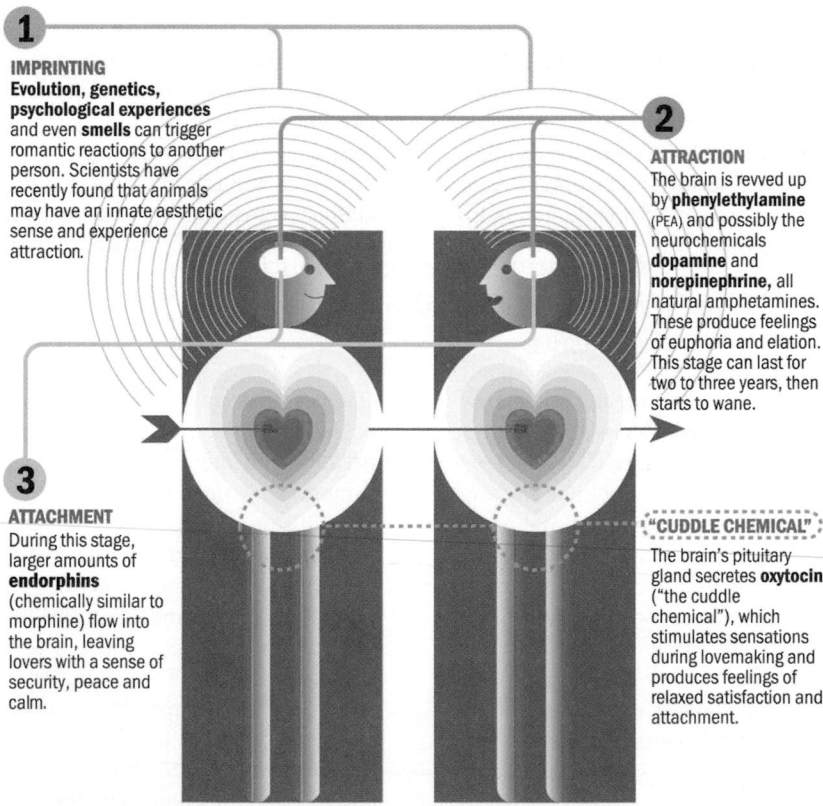

1

IMPRINTING
Evolution, genetics, psychological experiences and even **smells** can trigger romantic reactions to another person. Scientists have recently found that animals may have an innate aesthetic sense and experience attraction.

2

ATTRACTION
The brain is revved up by **phenylethylamine** (PEA) and possibly the neurochemicals **dopamine** and **norepinephrine,** all natural amphetamines. These produce feelings of euphoria and elation. This stage can last for two to three years, then starts to wane.

3

ATTACHMENT
During this stage, larger amounts of **endorphins** (chemically similar to morphine) flow into the brain, leaving lovers with a sense of security, peace and calm.

"CUDDLE CHEMICAL"
The brain's pituitary gland secretes **oxytocin** ("the cuddle chemical"), which stimulates sensations during lovemaking and produces feelings of relaxed satisfaction and attachment.

Toufexis *Love: The Right Chemistry*

GUIDE TO READING
GUIDE TO WRITING
A WRITER AT WORK
THINKING CRITICALLY

131

soothing substances. Natural pain-killers, they give lovers a sense of security, peace and calm. "That is one reason why it feels so horrible when we're abandoned or a lover dies," notes Fisher. "We don't have our daily hit of narcotics."

14   Researchers see a contrast between the heated infatuation induced by PEA, along with other amphetamine-like chemicals, and the more intimate attachment fostered and prolonged by endorphins. "Early love is when you love the way the other person makes you feel," explains psychiatrist Mark Goulston of the University of California, Los Angeles. "Mature love is when you love the person as he or she is." It is the difference between passionate and compassionate love, observes Walsh, a psychobiologist at Boise State University in Idaho. "It's Bon Jovi vs. Beethoven."

15   Oxytocin is another chemical that has recently been implicated in love. Produced by the brain, it sensitizes nerves and stimulates muscle contraction. In women it helps uterine contractions during childbirth as well as production of breast milk, and seems to inspire mothers to nuzzle their infants. Scientists speculate that oxytocin might encourage similar cuddling between adult women and men. The versatile chemical may also enhance orgasms. In one study of men, oxytocin increased to three to five times its normal level during climax, and it may soar even higher in women.

16   Chemicals may help explain (at least to scientists) the feelings of passion and compassion, but why do people tend to fall in love with one partner rather than a myriad of others? Once again, it's partly a function of evolution and biology. "Men are looking for maximal fertility in a mate," says Loyola Marymount's Mills. "That is in large part why females in the prime childbearing ages of 17 to 28 are so desirable." Men can size up youth and vitality in a glance, and studies indeed show that men fall in love quite rapidly. Women tumble more slowly, to a large degree because their requirements are more complex; they need more time to check the guy out. "Age is not vital," notes Mills, "but the ability to provide security, father children, share resources and hold a high status in society are all key factors."

17   Still, that does not explain why the way Mary walks and laughs makes Bill dizzy with desire while Marcia's gait and giggle leave him cold. "Nature has wired us for one special person," suggests Walsh, romantically. He rejects the idea that a woman or a man can be in love with two people at the same time. Each person carries in his or her mind a unique subliminal guide to the ideal partner, a "love map," to borrow a term coined by sexologist John Money of Johns Hopkins University.

18   Drawn from the people and experiences of childhood, the map is a record of whatever we found enticing and exciting—or disturbing and disgusting. Small feet, curly hair. The way our mothers patted our head or how our fathers told a joke. A fireman's uniform, a doctor's stethoscope. All the information gathered while growing up is imprinted in the brain's circuitry by adolescence. Partners never meet each and every requirement, but a sufficient number of matches can light up the wires and signal, "It's love." Not every partner will be like the last one, since lovers may have different combinations of the characteristics favored by the map.

19   O.K., that's the scientific point of view. Satisfied? Probably not. To most people—with or without Ph.D.s—love will always be more than the sum of its natural parts. It's a commingling of body and soul, reality and imagination, poetry and phenylethylamine. In our deepest hearts, most of us harbor the hope that love will never fully yield up its secrets, that it will always elude our grasp.

Make connections: How love works.

[REFLECT]

The chemistry of love is easily summarized: Amphetamines fuel romance; endorphins and oxytocin sustain lasting relationships. As Toufexis makes clear, however, these chemical reactions do not explain why people are attracted to each other in the first place. Rather, she claims that an attraction occurs because each of us carries a "unique subliminal guide," or "love map" (par. 17), that leads us unerringly to a partner.

Make a short list of the qualities in a partner that would appear on your "love map," and then consider Toufexis's explanation. Your instructor may ask you to post your thoughts on a class discussion board or to discuss them with other students in class. Use these questions to get started:

- What role do factors such as family, friends, community, the media, and advertising play in constructing your love map?

- Why do you think Toufexis ignores the topic of sexual orientation?

- According to Toufexis, men typically look for "maximal fertility," whereas women look for security, resources, status, and a willingness to father children (par. 16). Does this explanation seem convincing to you? Why or why not?

ANALYZE   Use the basic features.

A FOCUSED EXPLANATION: EXCLUDING OTHER TOPICS

In writing about a concept as broad as love, Toufexis has to find a way to narrow her focus. Writers choose a focus in part by considering the **rhetorical situation**—the purpose, audience, and genre—in which they are writing. Student Patricia Lyu is limited by the fact that she is writing in response to her instructor's assignment. As a science writer for *Time* magazine, Toufexis probably also had an assignment to report on current scientific research. The question is, though, how does she make the science interesting to her readers?

ANALYZE & WRITE

Write a paragraph analyzing how Toufexis focuses her explanation:

1. What is the focus or main point of Toufexis's essay? How do you think she answers readers' potential "So what?" question?

2. How do the title, epigraph, and opening paragraphs help you identify this focus or main point?

3. How do you think Toufexis's purpose, audience, and genre (an article for a popular newsmagazine) affected the focus she was assigned or chose?

A CLEAR, LOGICAL ORGANIZATION: CUEING THE READER

Experienced writers know that readers often have trouble making their way through new and difficult material. To avoid having them give up in frustration, writers strive to construct a reader-friendly organization: They include a thesis statement that asserts the focus or main point—the answer to the "So what?" question. In addition writers sometimes include a *forecasting statement,* which alerts readers to the main topics to be discussed, and include *transitional words and phrases* to guide readers from topic to topic.

ANALYZE & WRITE

Write a paragraph or two analyzing the strategies Toufexis uses to organize her essay for readers:

1. Skim the essay, and note in the margin where she announces her concept and forecasts the topics she uses to organize her explanation. Then highlight the passage where she discusses each topic. How well does her forecast work to make her essay readable?

2. Study how Toufexis connects the topic of "love maps" (pars. 17–18) to the topics she discussed earlier in the essay. Identify any sentences that connect the two parts of the article, and assess how well they work.

APPROPRIATE EXPLANATORY STRATEGIES: USING VISUALS

Patricia Lyu, like Toufexis, uses a flowchart to show the stages of a process she is describing in her essay. In Lyu's case, the visual comes from one of her sources. In contrast, Toufexis's visual was most likely created after her article was written, by the magazine's art editor, Nigel Holmes. Notice also that whereas Lyu, following a convention of academic writing, refers in the text of her essay to her visuals, labels them "Fig. 1" and "Fig. 2," and includes captions, Toufexis does not refer to the visual in her text, and the visual does not have a caption.

ANALYZE & WRITE

Write a paragraph or two analyzing Toufexis's use of the visual:

1. Analyze the visual included in Toufexis's *Time* magazine article. Consider it apart from the rest of the article. What can you learn from the visual itself? What makes it easy or hard to read?

2. Skim Toufexis's essay to mark where she discusses each of the stages in the process described in the flowchart. Considering her original audience, how well does the flowchart work as a map to help readers navigate through the somewhat technical content of her explanation? Would it have been helpful had Toufexis referred to and labeled the visual?

SMOOTH INTEGRATION OF SOURCES: ESTABLISHING CREDIBILITY

To establish their authority on the subject, writers need to convince readers that the information they are using is authoritative. They can do this in a number of ways, but giving the professional credentials of their sources is a conventional strategy.

Write a paragraph or two analyzing how Toufexis establishes the credentials of her sources:

1 Skim the essay, underlining the name of each source she mentions. Then go back through the essay to highlight each source's credentials. When Toufexis provides credentials, what kinds of information does she include?

2 Consider the effectiveness of Toufexis's strategies for letting readers know the qualifications of her sources. Given her original audience (*Time* magazine readers), how well do you think she establishes her sources' credentials? If she were writing for an academic audience (for example, for your class), what would she have to add?

RESPOND

Consider possible topics: Examining other aspects of love.

Like Toufexis, you could write an essay about love or romance, but you could choose a different focus—for example, the history of romantic love (how did the concept of romantic love develop in the West, and when did it become the basis of marriage?), love's cultural characteristics (how is love regarded by different American ethnic groups or in world cultures?), its excesses or extremes (what is sex addiction?), or the phases of falling in and out of love (what is infatuation?). You could also consider writing about other concepts involving personal relationships, such as jealousy, codependency, stereotyping, or homophobia.

Dan Hurley | *Can You Make Yourself Smarter?*

DAN HURLEY writes books and articles on science for both specialists and general readers. His books include *Diabetes Rising: How a Rare Disease Became a Modern Pandemic and What to Do About It* (2010) and *Natural Causes: Death, Lies, and Politics in America's Vitamin and Herbal Supplement Industry* (2006). Among the medical newspapers he contributes to are *General Surgery News* and *Neurology Today*. In 1995, he won an award for investigative journalism for an article he published in *Psychology Today* on the violent mentally ill. He is currently working on a book on intelligence. The article below was published in the *New York Times* in 2011. Although Hurley did not include references (as is customary when writing in popular periodicals like newspapers and magazines), we have added them so readers interested in this topic can explore it in greater depth. As you read, consider the following:

- How would you describe Hurley's tone in this essay? For example, are there any passages where the tone seems conversational, stuffy, stiff, sarcastic, angry, amused, or anything else?

- How appropriate do you think Hurley's tone is given the rhetorical situation in which he is writing? How might he have modified his tone if the article was intended not for the general public, but for either an academic audience of researchers or for a group of students concerned about their test scores?

1 Early on a drab afternoon in January, a dozen third graders from the working-class suburb of Chicago Heights, Ill., burst into the Mac Lab on the ground floor of Washington-McKinley School in a blur of blue pants, blue vests and white shirts. Minutes later, they were hunkered down in front of the Apple computers lining the room's perimeter, hoping to do what was, until recently, considered impossible: increase their intelligence through training.

2 "Can somebody raise their hand," asked Kate Wulfson, the instructor, "and explain to me how you get points?" On each of the children's monitors, there was a cartoon image of a haunted house, with bats and a crescent moon in a midnight blue sky. Every few seconds, a black cat appeared in one of the house's five windows, then vanished. The exercise was divided into levels. On Level 1, the children earned a point by remembering which window the cat was just in. Easy. But the game is progressive: the cats keep coming, and the kids have to keep watching and remembering. "And here's where it gets confusing," Wulfson continued. "If you get to Level 2, you have to remember where the cat was two windows ago. The time before last. For Level 3, you have to remember where it was three times ago. Level 4 is four times ago. That's hard. You have to keep track. O.K., ready? Once we start, anyone who talks loses a star."

3 So began 10 minutes of a remarkably demanding concentration game. At Level 2, even adults find the task somewhat taxing. Almost no one gets past Level 3 without training. But most people who stick with the game do get better with practice. This isn't surprising: practice improves performance on almost every task humans engage in, whether it's learning to read or playing horseshoes.

4 What is surprising is what else it improved. In a 2008 study, Susanne Jaeggi and Martin Buschkuehl, now of the University of Maryland, found that young adults who practiced a stripped-down, less cartoonish version of the game also showed improvement in a fundamental cognitive ability known as "fluid" intelligence: the capacity to solve novel problems, to learn, to reason, to see connections and to get to the bottom of things (Jaeggi et al.). The implication was that playing the game literally makes people smarter.

5 Psychologists have long regarded intelligence as coming in two flavors: crystallized intelligence, the treasure trove of stored-up information and how-to knowledge (the

sort of thing tested on "Jeopardy!" or put to use when you ride a bicycle); and fluid intelligence. Crystallized intelligence grows as you age; fluid intelligence has long been known to peak in early adulthood, around college age, and then to decline gradually. And unlike physical conditioning, which can transform 98-pound weaklings into hunks, fluid intelligence has always been considered impervious to training. That, after all, is the premise of I.Q. tests, or at least the portion that measures fluid intelligence: we can test you now and predict all sorts of things in the future, because fluid intelligence supposedly sets in early and is fairly immutable. While parents, teachers and others play an essential role in establishing an environment in which a child's intellect can grow, even Tiger Mothers generally expect only higher grades will come from their children's diligence—not better brains.

6 How, then, could watching black cats in a haunted house possibly increase something as profound as fluid intelligence? Because the deceptively simple game, it turns out, targets the most elemental of cognitive skills: "working" memory. What long-term memory is to crystallized intelligence, working memory is to fluid intelligence. Working memory is more than just the ability to remember a telephone number long enough to dial it; it's the capacity to manipulate the information you're holding in your head—to add or subtract those numbers, place them in reverse order or sort them from high to low. Understanding a metaphor or an analogy is equally dependent on working memory; you can't follow even a simple statement like "See Jane run" if you can't put together how "see" and "Jane" connect with "run." Without it, you can't make sense of anything.

7 Over the past three decades, theorists and researchers alike have made significant headway in understanding how working memory functions. They have developed a variety of sensitive tests to measure it and determine its relationship to fluid intelligence. Then, in 2008, Jaeggi turned one of these tests of working memory into a training task for building it up, in the same way that push-ups can be used both as a measure of physical fitness and as a strength-building task. "We see attention and working memory as the cardiovascular function of the brain," Jaeggi says. "If you train your attention and working memory, you increase your basic cognitive skills that help you for many different complex tasks."

8 Jaeggi's study has been widely influential. Since its publication, others have achieved results similar to

Jaeggi's not only in elementary-school children but also in preschoolers, college students and the elderly. The training tasks generally require only 15 to 25 minutes of work per day, five days a week, and have been found to improve scores on tests of fluid intelligence in as little as four weeks. Follow-up studies linking that improvement to real-world gains in schooling and job performance are just getting under way. But already, people with disorders including attention-deficit hyperactivity disorder (A.D.H.D.) and traumatic brain injury have seen benefits from training. Gains can persist for up to eight months after treatment.

9 In a town like Chicago Heights, where only 16 percent of high schoolers met the Illinois version of the No Child Left Behind standards in 2011, finding a clear way to increase cognitive abilities has obvious appeal. But it has other uses too, at all ages and aptitudes. Even high-level professionals have begun training their working memory in hopes of boosting their fluid intelligence—and, with it, their job performance. If the effect is real—if fluid intelligence can be raised in just a few minutes a day, even by a bit, and not just on a test but in real life—then it would seem to offer, as Jaeggi's 2008 study concluded with Spock-like understatement, "a wide range of applications." (Jaeggi et al. 1)

10 Since the first reliable intelligence test was created just over a hundred years ago, researchers have searched for a way to increase scores meaningfully, with little success. The track record was so dismal that by 2002, when Jaeggi and her research partner (and now her husband), Martin Buschkuehl, came across a study claiming to have done so, they simply didn't believe it. The study, by a Swedish neuroscientist named Torkel Klingberg, involved just 14 children, all with A.D.H.D. (Klingberg). Half participated in computerized tasks designed to strengthen their working memory, while the other half played less challenging computer games. After just five weeks, Klingberg found that those who played the working-memory games fidgeted less and moved about less. More remarkable, they also scored higher on one of the single best measures of fluid intelligence, the Raven's Progressive Matrices. Improvement in working memory, in other words, transferred to improvement on a task the children weren't training for. . . .

11 "At that time there was pretty much no evidence whatsoever that you can train on one particular task and get transfer to another task that was totally different,"

Jaeggi says. That is, while most skills improve with practice, the improvement is generally domain-specific: you don't get better at Sudoku by doing crosswords. And fluid intelligence was not just another skill; it was the ultimate cognitive ability underlying all mental skills, and supposedly immune from the usual benefits of practice. To find that training on a working-memory task could result in an increase in fluid intelligence would be cognitive psychology's equivalent of discovering particles traveling faster than light.

12 Together, Jaeggi and Buschkuehl decided to see if they could replicate the Klingberg transfer effect. To do so, they used the N-back test as the basis of a training regimen. As seen in the game played by the children at Washington-McKinley, N-back challenges users to remember something — the location of a cat or the sound of a particular letter — that is presented immediately before (1-back), the time before last (2-back), the time before that (3-back), and so on. If you do well at 2-back, the computer moves you up to 3-back. Do well at that, and you'll jump to 4-back. On the other hand, if you do poorly at any level, you're nudged down a level. The point is to keep the game just challenging enough that you stay fully engaged.

13 To make it harder, Jaeggi and Buschkuehl used what's called the dual N-back task. As a random sequence of letters is heard over earphones, a square appears on a computer screen moving, apparently at random, among eight possible spots on a grid. Your mission is to keep track of both the letters and the squares. (See figure 1.) So, for example, at the 3-back level, you would press one button on the keyboard if you recall that a spoken letter is the same one that was spoken three times ago, while simultaneously pressing another key if the square on the screen is in the same place as it was three times ago. The point of making the task more difficult is to overwhelm the usual task-specific strategies that people develop with games like chess and Scrabble. "We wanted to train underlying attention and working-memory skills," Jaeggi says. Jaeggi and Buschkuehl gave progressive matrix tests to students at Bern and then asked them to practice the dual N-back for 20 to 25 minutes a day. When they retested them at the end of a few weeks, they were surprised and delighted to find significant improvement. Jaeggi and Buschkuehl later expanded the study as postdoctoral fellows at the University of Michigan, in the laboratory of John Jonides, professor of psychology and neuroscience.

Fig. 1. Games based on N-back tests require players to remember the location of a symbol or the sound of a particular letter presented just before (1-back), the time before last (2-back), the time before that (3-back) and so on. Some researchers say that playing games like this may actually make us smarter. (To play a free, online version of the N-back game, go to http://www.soakyourhead.com/dual-n-back.aspx)

The N-Back Game

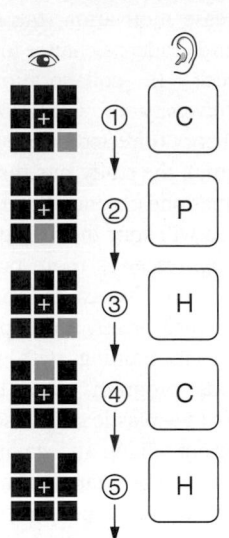

"Those two things, working memory and cognitive control, I think, are at the heart of intellectual functioning," Jonides told me when I met with him, Jaeggi and Buschkuehl in their basement office. "They are part of what differentiates us from other species. They allow us to selectively process information from the environment, and to use that information to do all kinds of problem-solving and reasoning."

14 When they finally published their study, in a May 2008 issue of *Proceedings of the National Academy of Sciences,* the results were striking (Jaeggi et al., "Improving"). Before training, participants were able to correctly answer between 9 and 10 of the matrix questions. Afterward, the 34 young adults who participated in dual N-back training for 12 weeks correctly answered approximately one extra matrix item, while those who trained for 17 weeks were able to answer about three more correctly. After 19 weeks, the improvement was 4.4 additional matrix questions. "It's not just a little bit higher," Jaeggi says. "It's a large effect."

15 The study did have its shortcomings. "We used just one reasoning task to measure their performance," she says. "We showed improvements in this one fluid-reasoning task, which is usually highly correlated with other measures as well." Whether the improved scores on the Raven's would translate into school grades, job performance and real-world gains remained to be seen.

Even so, accompanying the paper's publication in *Proceedings* was a commentary titled, "Increasing Fluid Intelligence Is Possible After All," in which the senior psychologist Robert J. Sternberg (now provost at Oklahoma State University) called Jaeggi's and Buschkuehl's research "pioneering" (Sternberg 6792). The study, he wrote, "seems, in some measure, to resolve the debate over whether fluid intelligence is, in at least some meaningful measure, trainable."

16 For some, the debate is far from settled. Randall Engle, a leading intelligence researcher at the Georgia Tech School of Psychology, views the proposition that I.Q. can be increased through training with a skepticism verging on disdain. . . . The most prominent takedown of I.Q. training came in June 2010, when the neuroscientist Adrian Owen published the results of an experiment conducted in coordination with the BBC television show "Bang Goes the Theory." After inviting British viewers to participate, Owen recruited 11,430 of them to take a battery of I.Q. tests before and after a six-week online program designed to replicate commercially available "brain building" software. (The N-back was not among the tasks offered.) "Although improvements were observed in every one of the cognitive tasks that were trained," he concluded in the journal *Nature,* "no evidence was found for transfer effects to untrained tasks, even when those tasks were cognitively closely related" (775).

17 But even Owen, reached by telephone, told me that he respects Jaeggi's studies and looks forward to seeing others like it. If before Jaeggi's study, scientists' attempts to raise I.Q. were largely unsuccessful, other lines of evidence have long supported the view that intelligence is far from immutable. While studies of twins suggest that intelligence has a fixed genetic component, at least 20 to 50 percent of the variation in I.Q. is due to other factors, whether social, school or family-based. Even more telling, average I.Q.'s have been rising steadily for a century as access to schooling and technology expands, a phenomenon known as the Flynn Effect. As Jaeggi and others see it, the genetic component of intelligence is undeniable, but it functions less like the genes that control for eye color and more like the complex of interacting genes that affect weight and height (both of which have also been rising, on average, for decades). . . .

18 Torkel Klingberg, meanwhile, has continued studying the effects of training children with his own variety of

working-memory tasks. In October 2010, a company he founded to offer those tasks as a package through psychologists and other training professionals, was bought by Pearson Education, the world's largest provider of educational assessment tools (Cogmed). Despite continuing academic debates, other commercial enterprises are rushing in to offer an array of "brain building" games that make bold promises to improve all kinds of cognitive abilities. Within a block of each other in downtown San Francisco are two of the best known. Posit Science, among the oldest in the field, remains relatively small, giving special attention to those with cognitive disorders. Lumosity began in 2007 and is now by far the biggest of the services, with more than 20 million subscribers. Its games include a sleeker, more entertaining version of the N-back task.

19   In Chicago Heights, the magic was definitely not happening for one boy staring blankly at the black cats in the Mac Lab. Sipping from a juice box he held in one hand, jabbing at a computer key over and over with the other, he periodically sneaked a peak at his instructor, a look of abject boredom on his freckled face. "That's the biggest challenge we have as researchers in this field," Jaeggi told me, "to get people engaged and motivated to play our working-memory game and to really stick with it. Some people say it's hard and really frustrating and really challenging and tiring."

20   In a follow-up to their 2008 study in young adults, Jaeggi, Buschkuehl and their colleagues published a paper last year that described the effects of N-back training in 76 elementary- and middle-school children from a broad range of social and economic backgrounds (Jaeggi et al., "Short- and Long-Term"). Only those children who improved substantially on the N-back training had gains in fluid intelligence. But their improvement wasn't linked to how high they originally scored on Raven's; children at all levels of cognitive ability improved. And those gains persisted for three months after the training ended, a heartening sign of possible long-term benefits. Although it's unknown how much longer the improvement in fluid intelligence will last, Jaeggi doubts the effects will be permanent without continued practice. "Do we think they're now smarter for the rest of their lives by just four weeks of training?" she asks. "We probably don't think so. We think of it like physical training: if you go running for a month, you increase your fitness. But does it stay like that for the rest of your life? Probably not.". . .

21   Of course, in order to improve, you need to do the training. For some, whether brilliant or not so much,

training may simply be too hard—or too boring. To increase motivation, the study in Chicago Heights offers third graders a chance to win a $10 prepaid Visa card each week. In collaboration with researchers from the University of Chicago's Initiative on Chicago Price Theory (directed by Steven D. Levitt, of "Freakonomics" fame), the study pits the kids against one another, sometimes one on one, sometimes in groups, to see if competition will spur them to try harder. Each week, whichever group receives more points on the N-back is rewarded with the Visa cards. To isolate the motivating effects of the cash prizes, a group of fourth graders is undergoing N-back training with the same black-cats-in-haunted-house program, but with no Visa cards, only inexpensive prizes—plastic sunglasses, inflatable globes—as a reward for not talking and staying in their seats.

22   The boy tapping randomly at his computer without even paying attention to the game? He was in the fourth-grade class. Although the study is not yet complete, perhaps it will show that the opportunity to increase intelligence is not motivation enough. Just like physical exercise, cognitive exercises may prove to be up against something even more resistant to training than fluid intelligence: human nature.

Works Cited

Cogmed Working Memory Training. Torkel Klingberg, Pearson Assessments. 2011. Web. 14 Aug. 2012.

Engle, Randall. Personal interview. N.d.

Jaeggi, Susanne M. Personal interview. N.d.

Jaeggi, Susanne M., Buschkuehl, Martin, Jonides, John, and Perrig, Walter J. "Improving Fluid Intelligence with Training on Working Memory." *Proceedings of the National Academy of Sciences of the United States of America* 105.19 (2008): 6829–33. Web. 14, Aug. 2012.

Jaeggi, Susanne M., Buschkuehl, Martin, Jonides, John, and Priti Shah. "Short- and long-term benefits of cognitive training." *Proceedings of the National Academy of Sciences of the United States of America* 108:25 (2011): 10081-86. Web. 14, Aug. 2012.

Klingberg, Torkel, Forssberg, Hans, and Westerberg, Helena. "Training of Working Memory in Children with ADHD." *Journal of Clinical and Experimental Neuropsychology,* 24.6 (2002): 781–91. *Academic Search Complete.* Web. 14 Aug. 2012.

Make connections: Brain training games.

[REFLECT]

The N-back game is only one of many kinds of so-called brain training games that test your memory, reflexes, concentration, and problem-solving skills. In *What Video Games Have to Teach Us about Learning,* sociolinguist James Paul Gee argues that video games provide a hands-on, customized learning environment in which players develop skills and teach themselves how to be more adept, independent learners. Think about your experience playing video games or other games (Risk, poker), and consider whether they helped you develop your memory or thinking abilities. Your instructor may ask you to post your thoughts on a class discussion board or to discuss them with other students in class. Use these questions to get started:

- Can you think of at least one way in which a game you played has helped you, in Jaeggi's words, develop "the capacity to solve novel problems, to learn, to reason, to see connections" (par. 4)?

- How important do you think "working" memory ("the capacity to manipulate the information you're holding in your head—to add or subtract . . . numbers, place them in reverse order or sort them from high to low" [par. 6]) is in mastering the brain training games with which you are familiar?

- What other abilities seem important—such as creativity, logical reasoning, or sustained attention?

Use the basic features.

[ANALYZE]

A FOCUSED EXPLANATION: USING AN EXAMPLE

Examples often play a central role in writing about concepts because concepts are general and abstract, and examples help to make them specific and concrete. Examples can also be very useful tools for focusing an explanation. Patricia Lyu, for instance, uses the examples of three researchers—John Bowlby, Mary Ainsworth, and Harry Harlow—in addition to the example of Henry Dobbins from *The Things They Carried* to explain the concept of attachment.

| ANALYZE & WRITE |

Write a paragraph or two analyzing Hurley's use of the example introduced in the opening paragraphs describing Susanne Jaeggi and Martin Buschkuehl's N-back game research to focus his explanation and illustrate the concept of fluid intelligence:

1 Skim paragraphs 2, 12, and 13, look at Figure 1, and read the caption accompanying the figure. How does this text and the figure, which was a sidebar included in the original *New York Times* article, help readers understand the N-back game and its significance?

2 Consider how N-back game research answers the "So what?" question readers of concept explanations inevitably ask. In other words, how does it provide a focus for Hurley's explanation of the concept and help readers grasp why the concept is important?

3 Reread paragraphs 15–20, where Hurley acknowledges the controversy surrounding research of this kind. Why do you imagine Hurley includes information about the "debate" in his explanation (par. 15)?

A CLEAR, LOGICAL ORGANIZATION: USING REPETITION TO CREATE COHESION

Cohesive devices help readers move from paragraph to paragraph and section to section without losing the thread. The most familiar cohesive device is probably the transitional word or phrase (*however, next*), which alerts readers to the logical relationship among ideas. A less familiar, but equally effective strategy, is to repeat key terms and their synonyms or to use pronouns (*it, they*) to refer to the key term. A third strategy is to provide cohesion through referring back to earlier examples, often bringing a selection full circle by referring to an opening example at the end of the essay. Lyu, for example, introduces Tim O'Brien's character Henry Dobbins in her introduction and comes back to him in her conclusion.

ANALYZE & WRITE

Write a paragraph or two analyzing how Hurley creates cohesion in "Can You Make Yourself Smarter?"

1 Reread paragraphs 1–4, 9, and 19–22. How does Hurley use the example of Chicago Heights to lend cohesion to his essay? How effectively does this strategy help readers navigate this essay and understand its main point?

2 Select a series of 3–4 paragraphs and analyze how Hurley knits the paragraphs together. Can you identify any repeated words or concepts or any pronouns that refer back to terms in the preceding paragraph? Did he use transitional words or phrases to link one paragraph to the next?

APPROPRIATE EXPLANATORY STRATEGIES: USING A VARIETY OF STRATEGIES

Writers typically use several different kinds of strategies to explain a concept. Patricia Lyu, for example, *defines* the concept of attachment, *classifies* children's behavior into groups to delineate the types of attachment shown in the "strange situation," *narrates* the process of the experiments Ainsworth and Harlow conducted, and *shows the cause-effect relationship* between fear and the need for attachment. Here are examples of sentence patterns Lyu uses to present these types of explanatory strategies:

DEFINITION	He saw that "separation anxiety"—being physically apart from the caregiver or perceiving the "threat" of separation . . . (Kobak and Madsen 30). (par. 3)
CLASSIFICATION	Ainsworth identified three basic types of attachment . . . *secure, anxious* (or *anxious-resistant*), and *avoidant* (Fraley 4). (par. 4)
PROCESS NARRATION	Harlow conducted a series of famous and rather disturbing experiments with infant monkeys. The infant monkeys were separated from their biological mothers and raised by a surrogate mother . . . made from uncovered heavy wire. (par. 7)

CAUSE-EFFECT REASONING   In other experiments, he also showed that fear is a strong motivator of attachment, leading the infant monkeys to seek consolation from the surrogate. (par. 9)

| ANALYZE & WRITE |

Write a paragraph or two analyzing how Hurley uses definition, classification, process narration, and cause-effect reasoning to explain fluid intelligence:

1. Skim Hurley's essay looking for and highlighting an example of each of these explanatory strategies.

2. Select one strategy that you think is particularly effective and explain why you think it works so well. What does the strategy contribute to the explanation of fluid intelligence?

SMOOTH INTEGRATION OF SOURCES: CITING SOURCES FOR ACADEMIC CONTEXTS

Writers of concept explanations nearly always conduct research, incorporate information from sources (summaries, paraphrases, and quotations) into their writing, and identify their sources so that readers can identify them as experts. Toufexis, for example, identifies Michael Mills as "a psychology professor at Loyola Marymount University in Los Angeles" and quotes him as saying "Love is our ancestors whispering in our ears" (par. 2).

| ANALYZE & WRITE |

Write a paragraph or two analyzing the kinds of material Dan Hurley incorporates from sources and how he identifies his sources so that his readers know that they can be trusted:

1. Skim the essay, highlighting places where Hurley quotes, paraphrases, or summarizes information from sources, and consider the information Hurley provides to identify those sources. What information does he provide, and how does this information help readers know the source is trustworthy?

2. Now skim the essay looking for places where Hurley quotes the researchers. Pay particular attention to the quotations in paragraphs 2, 7, 9, 11, 13–16, and 19–20. Why do you think Hurley decided to use their exact words in these places, rather than merely summarizing their ideas? Can you determine which of the quotations come from published sources and which come from interviews? Can you tell from the text itself or from the citations we added? Consider whether it is important to know if the quotations come from published sources or from the interviews the writer conducted himself.

3. What do you think is the purpose of citing sources—including interviews— particularly for academic audiences? Why is simply identifying sources with a word or two in the text generally sufficient for nonacademic situations? Given your experience reading online, do you think hyperlinks serve a similar purpose to formal citations? Why or why not?

Consider possible topics: Examining other aspects of intelligence.

Because behavioral research can help us understand ourselves in new ways, essays that shed light on psychological phenomena can be fascinating to readers. A writer could explore other aspects of intelligence, such as emotional intelligence, ambient intelligence, or chunking. Related concepts include the theory of mind, self-concept, and identity. Consider entering the concept you are seeking to explain into the search field of a database in the social sciences, like *PsycArticles* or *Social Sciences Full Text,* to find an interesting topic you might never have thought of on your own.

Susan Cain | *Shyness: Evolutionary Tactic?*

SUSAN CAIN is the author of the book *Quiet: The Power of Introverts in a World That Can't Stop Talking* (2012). She also writes a popular blog about introversion and has contributed to the magazine *Psychology Today* on this topic. The selection that appears here was originally published in the *New York Times.* As you read, consider these questions:

- Notice the title of this reading and the title of Cain's book. What do these titles lead you to expect? How accurate is your prediction?
- Given that this selection was first published in a newspaper, consider how effective the opening paragraph is as a hook to catch readers' attention.

1   A beautiful woman lowers her eyes demurely beneath a hat. In an earlier era, her gaze might have signaled a mysterious allure. But this is a 2003 advertisement for Zoloft, a selective serotonin reuptake inhibitor (SSRI) approved by the FDA to treat social anxiety disorder. "Is she just shy? Or is it Social Anxiety Disorder?" reads the caption, suggesting that the young woman is not alluring at all. She is sick.

2   But is she?

3   It is possible that the lovely young woman has a life-wrecking form of social anxiety. There are people too afraid of disapproval to venture out for a job interview, a date or even a meal in public. Despite the risk of serious side effects—nausea, loss of sex drive, seizures—drugs like Zoloft can be a godsend for this group.

4   But the ad's insinuation aside, it's also possible the young woman is "just shy," or introverted—traits our society disfavors. One way we manifest this bias is by encouraging perfectly healthy shy people to see themselves as ill.

5   This does us all a grave disservice, because shyness and introversion—or more precisely, the careful, sensitive temperament from which both often spring—are not just normal. They are valuable. And they may be essential to the survival of our species.

6   Theoretically, shyness and social anxiety disorder are easily distinguishable. But a blurry line divides the two. Imagine that the woman in the ad enjoys a steady paycheck, a strong marriage and a small circle of close friends—a good life by most measures—except that she avoids a needed promotion because she's nervous about leading meetings. She often criticizes herself for feeling too shy to speak up.

> *Shyness and introversion . . . are not just normal. They are valuable. And they may be essential to the survival of our species.*

7   What do you think now? Is she ill, or does she simply need public-speaking training?

8   Before 1980, this would have seemed a strange question. Social anxiety disorder did not officially exist until it appeared in that year's Diagnostic and Statistical Manual, the DSM-III, the psychiatrist's bible of mental disorders, under the name "social phobia." It was not widely known until the 1990s, when pharmaceutical companies received FDA approval to treat social anxiety with SSRI's and poured tens of millions of dollars into advertising its existence. The current version of the Diagnostic and Statistical Manual, the DSM-IV, acknowledges that stage fright (and shyness in social situations) is common and not necessarily a sign of illness. But it also says that diagnosis is warranted when anxiety "interferes significantly" with work performance or if the sufferer shows "marked distress" about it. According to this definition, the answer to our question is clear: the young woman in the ad is indeed sick.

9   The DSM inevitably reflects cultural attitudes; it used to identify homosexuality as a disease, too. Though the DSM did not set out to pathologize shyness, it risks doing so, and has twice come close to identifying introversion as a disorder, too. (Shyness and introversion are not the same thing. Shy people fear negative judgment; introverts simply prefer quiet, minimally stimulating environments.)

10   But shyness and introversion share an undervalued status in a world that prizes extroversion. Children's classroom desks are now often arranged in pods, because group participation supposedly leads to better learning; in one school I visited, a sign announcing "Rules for Group Work" included, "You can't ask a teacher for help unless everyone in your group has the same question." Many adults work for organizations that now assign work in teams, in offices without walls, for supervisors who value "people skills" above all. As a society, we prefer action to contemplation, risk-taking to heed-taking, certainty to doubt. Studies show that we rank fast and frequent talkers as more competent, likable and even smarter than slow ones. As the psychologists William Hart and Dolores Albarracin point out, phrases like "get active," "get moving," "do something" and similar calls to action surface repeatedly in recent books.

11   Yet shy and introverted people have been part of our species for a very long time, often in leadership positions. We find them in the Bible ("Who am I, that I should go unto Pharaoh?" asked Moses, whom the Book of Numbers describes as "very meek, above all the men which were upon the face of the earth.") We find them in recent history, in figures like Charles Darwin, Marcel Proust and Albert Einstein, and, in contemporary times: think of Google's Larry Page, or Harry Potter's creator, J. K. Rowling.

12   In the science journalist Winifred Gallagher's words: "The glory of the disposition that stops to consider stimuli rather than rushing to engage with them is its long association with intellectual and artistic achievement. Neither $E = mc^2$ nor *Paradise Lost* was dashed off by a party animal."

13   We even find "introverts" in the animal kingdom, where 15 percent to 20 percent of many species are watchful, slow-to-warm-up types who stick to the sidelines (sometimes called "sitters") while the other 80 percent are "rovers" who sally forth without paying much attention to their surroundings. Sitters and rovers favor different survival strategies, which could be summed up as the sitter's "Look before you leap" versus the rover's inclination to "Just do it!" Each strategy reaps different rewards.

14   In an illustrative experiment, David Sloan Wilson, a Binghamton evolutionary biologist, dropped metal traps into a pond of pumpkinseed sunfish. The "rover" fish couldn't help but investigate—and were immediately caught. But the "sitter" fish stayed back, making it impossible for Professor Wilson to capture them. Had Professor Wilson's traps posed a real threat, only the sitters would have survived. But had the sitters taken Zoloft and become more like bold rovers, the entire family of pumpkinseed sunfish would have been wiped out. "Anxiety" about the trap saved the fishes' lives.

15   Next, Professor Wilson used fishing nets to catch both types of fish; when he carried them back to his lab, he noted that the rovers quickly acclimated to their new environment and started eating a full five days earlier than their sitter brethren. In this situation, the rovers were the likely survivors. "There is no single best . . . [animal] personality," Professor Wilson concludes in his book, *Evolution for Everyone,* "but rather a diversity of personalities maintained by natural selection."

16   The same might be said of humans, 15 percent to 20 percent of whom are also born with sitter-like temperaments that predispose them to shyness and introversion. (The overall incidence of shyness and introversion is higher—40 percent of the population for shyness, according to the psychology professor

Jonathan Cheek, and 50 percent for introversion. Conversely, some born sitters never become shy or introverted at all.)

17   Once you know about sitters and rovers, you see them everywhere, especially among young children. Drop in on your local Mommy and Me music class: there are the sitters, intently watching the action from their mothers' laps, while the rovers march around the room banging their drums and shaking their maracas.

18   Relaxed and exploratory, the rovers have fun, make friends and will take risks, both rewarding and dangerous ones, as they grow. According to Daniel Nettle, a Newcastle University evolutionary psychologist, extroverts are more likely than introverts to be hospitalized as a result of an injury, have affairs (men) and change relationships (women). One study of bus drivers even found that accidents are more likely to occur when extroverts are at the wheel.

19   In contrast, sitter children are careful and astute, and tend to learn by observing instead of by acting. They notice scary things more than other children do, but they also notice more things in general. Studies dating all the way back to the 1960s by the psychologists Jerome Kagan and Ellen Siegelman found that cautious, solitary children playing matching games spent more time considering all the alternatives than impulsive children did, actually using more eye movements to make decisions. Recent studies by a group of scientists at Stony Brook University and at Chinese universities using functional MRI technology echoed this research, finding that adults with sitter-like temperaments looked longer at pairs of photos with subtle differences and showed more activity in brain regions that make associations between the photos and other stored information in the brain.

20   Once they reach school age, many sitter children use such traits to great effect. Introverts, who tend to digest information thoroughly, stay on task, and work accurately, earn disproportionate numbers of National Merit Scholarship finalist positions and Phi Beta Kappa keys, according to the Center for Applications of Psychological Type, a research arm for the Myers-Briggs personality type indicator—even though their IQ scores are no higher than those of extroverts. Another study, by the psychologists Eric Rolfhus and Philip Ackerman, tested 141 college students' knowledge of 20 different subjects, from art to astronomy to statistics, and found that the introverts knew more than the extroverts about 19 subjects—presumably, the researchers concluded, because the more time people spend socializing, the less time they have for learning.

21   The psychologist Gregory Feist found that many of the most creative people in a range of fields are introverts who are comfortable working in solitary conditions in which they can focus attention inward. Steve Wozniak, the engineer who founded Apple with Steve Jobs, is a prime example: Mr. Wozniak describes his creative process as an exercise in solitude. "Most inventors and engineers I've met are like me," he writes in "iWoz," his autobiography. "They're shy and they live in their heads. They're almost like artists. In fact, the very best of them are artists. And artists work best alone. . . . Not on a committee. Not on a team."

22   Sitters' temperaments also confer more subtle advantages. Anxiety, it seems, can serve an important social purpose; for example, it plays a key role in the development of some children's consciences. When caregivers rebuke them for acting up, they become anxious, and since anxiety is unpleasant, they tend to develop pro-social behaviors. Shy children are often easier to socialize and more conscientious, according to the developmental psychologist Grazyna Kochanska. By six they're less likely than their peers to cheat or break rules, even when they think they can't be caught, according to one study. By seven they're more likely to be described by their parents as having high levels of moral traits such as empathy.

23   When I shared this information with the mother of a "sitter" daughter, her reaction was mixed. "That is all very nice," she said, "but how will it help her in the tough real world?" But sensitivity, if it is not excessive and is properly nurtured, can be a catalyst for empathy and even leadership. Eleanor Roosevelt, for example, was a courageous leader who was very likely a sitter. Painfully shy and serious as a child, she grew up to be a woman who could not look away from other people's suffering—and who urged her husband, the constitutionally buoyant F.D.R., to do the same; the man who had nothing to fear but fear itself relied, paradoxically, on a woman deeply acquainted with it.

24   Another advantage sitters bring to leadership is a willingness to listen to and implement other people's ideas. A groundbreaking study led by the Wharton management professor Adam Grant, to be published

this month in *The Academy of Management Journal*, found that introverts outperform extroverts when leading teams of proactive workers—the kinds of employees who take initiative and are disposed to dream up better ways of doing things. Professor Grant notes that business self-help guides often suggest that introverted leaders practice their communication skills and smile more. But, he told me, it may be extrovert leaders who need to change, to listen more and say less.

25   What would the world look like if all our sitters chose to medicate themselves? The day may come when we have pills that "cure" shyness and turn introverts into social butterflies—without the side effects and other drawbacks of today's medications. (A recent study suggests that today's SSRI's not only relieve social anxiety but also induce extroverted behavior.) The day may come—and might be here already—when people are as comfortable changing their psyches as the color of their hair. If we continue to confuse shyness with sickness, we may find ourselves in a world of all rovers and no sitters, of all yang and no yin.

26   As a sitter who enjoys an engaged, productive life, and a professional speaking career, but still experiences the occasional knock-kneed moment, I can understand why caring physicians prescribe available medicine and encourage effective non-pharmaceutical treatments such as cognitive-behavioral therapy.

27   But even non-medical treatments emphasize what is wrong with the people who use them. They don't focus on what is right. Perhaps we need to rethink our approach to social anxiety: to address the pain, but to respect the temperament that underlies it. The act of treating shyness as an illness obscures the value of that temperament. Ridding people of social unease need not involve pathologizing their fundamental nature, but rather urging them to use its gifts.

28   It's time for the young woman in the Zoloft ad to rediscover her allure.

Make connections: What's wrong with being quiet?   [REFLECT]

Cain asserts that "shyness and introversion share an undervalued status in a world that prizes extroversion. . . . As a society, we prefer action to contemplation, risk-taking to heed taking, certainty to doubt" (par. 10). To explore these categories of introversion and extroversion and to test Cain's assertion about society's valuing one personality type over the other, think of someone you would describe as introverted and someone else who seems to be extroverted. (Include yourself, if you like.) What in particular leads you to classify these individuals as introverts or extroverts? Consider whether personality type has any effect on how other people react to them or whether they are more or less successful in school or in social or work contexts. Your instructor may ask you to post your thoughts on a class discussion board or to discuss them with other students in class. Use these questions to get you started:

- What do you think are the defining characteristics of these two personality types?
- Which, if any, of these characteristics seem to be overvalued or devalued? By whom and in what contexts? Why?
- Cain raises a question about the way psychiatrists and the pharmaceutical industry may be pathologizing shyness or introversion—in other words, "encouraging perfectly healthy shy people to see themselves as ill" (par. 4). What do you think about this issue?

[ANALYZE] # Use the basic features.

A FOCUSED EXPLANATION: PRESENTING ESTABLISHED INFORMATION AND YOUR OWN IDEAS

Writing for her instructor and classmates in an English class, Patricia Lyu can assume that the psychological concept she is explaining is unfamiliar to her audience, and because it is a topic in her Introduction to Psychology textbook, she can be confident that it is widely accepted and a basic building block of the field. However, when she applies the concept to a book her readers know well and uses the concept to interpret Henry Dobbins's "peculiar habit" in *The Things They Carried* (par. 10), Lyu's purpose becomes more complicated. She is not only reporting established information about a concept but also presenting her own ideas. Her readers are not likely to question the concept, as long as she provides authoritative sources to back it up, but they may very well question her application of the concept. Therefore, Lyu needs to provide evidence, quoting from *The Things They Carried* to convince readers that her use of the concept makes sense and that it helps to explain Dobbins's behavior. Concept explanations nearly always entail this kind of shift from reporting established information to presenting the writer's own ideas about the concept and offering supportive evidence.

| ANALYZE & WRITE |

Write a paragraph or two analyzing how Cain reports information and also presents her own ideas:

1 Reread paragraph 5, in which Cain states her thesis. How does the phrase between dashes in the first sentence ("or more precisely, the careful, sensitive temperament from which both often spring") help to unify the different phenomena she describes in this article?

2 Consider the second and third sentences in paragraph 5. How do these sentences help convey Cain's purpose?

3 Skim the rest of the article, looking for places where Cain restates the ideas she conveys in sentences 2 and 3 of paragraph 5. Highlight the words and phrases that restate this theme.

4 Consider how effective Cain's tactics are: After reading the article, do you know what shyness is? Are you persuaded that it is underrated? Why or why not?

A CLEAR, LOGICAL ORGANIZATION: CREATING CLOSURE

Patricia Lyu refers to British psychologist John Bowlby near the beginning and the end of her paper. In paragraph 2, she introduces the concept of attachment as a survival strategy, and then in paragraph 10, she notes Bowlby's assessment of attachment as "intertwined" with fear. With these two references to Bowlby, Lyu creates a sense of closure, a sense that readers have come full circle. Cain also uses this strategy.

ANALYZE & WRITE

Write a paragraph or two analyzing how Cain creates a sense of closure in her article:

1 Skim paragraphs 1–8 and 25–28 to remind yourself of how Cain begins and ends the reading selection. What image does she start with? What image does she end with? How does she make sense of this image for her readers? What context does she put it in?

2 Notice the pronouns she uses: *she, we, us, they, I.* How does the shift—from talking about the shy, the introverted, the "sitters," in the third person (*she/he/they*) to talking about them in the first person (*I/we*)—change the context in which the Zoloft ad is presented? How does this shift in the pronouns Cain uses add or detract from the sense of closure?

APPROPRIATE EXPLANATORY STRATEGIES: USING COMPARISON-CONTRAST

Writers explaining concepts often use comparison and contrast. Research has shown that seeing how unfamiliar concepts are similar to or different from concepts we already know facilitates the learning of new concepts. Even when both concepts are unfamiliar, comparing foregrounds commonalities, while contrasting makes visible inconsistencies we might not otherwise notice.

Writers employ many strategies to signal comparisons and contrasts, including words that emphasize similarity or difference, and repeating sentence patterns to highlight the differences:

COMPARISONS   . . . in the same way that push-ups can be used both as a measure of physical fitness and as a strength-building task. (Hurley, par. 7)

In the same way: words emphasizing similarity

CONTRASTS   "Early love is when you love the way the other person makes you feel." . . . "Mature love is when you love the person as he or she is." It is the difference between passionate and compassionate love. . . . "It's Bon Jovi vs. Beethoven." (Toufexis, par. 14)

Repeated sentence pattern highlights the contrast

ANALYZE & WRITE

Write a paragraph or two analyzing Cain's strategies for showing contrast:

1 Find and highlight two or three of the sentence patterns Cain uses for cueing contrast in paragraphs 3–4, 9, 10, 13, 18, and 19.

2 Analyze what is being contrasted and how each contrast works.

3 Why do you think Cain uses contrast so often in this essay?

To learn more about comparing and contrasting, see Chapter 18.

SMOOTH INTEGRATION OF SOURCES: USING EVIDENCE FROM A SOURCE TO SUPPORT A CLAIM

Cain's article first appeared in the *New York Times*. So, like Toufexis and Hurley, whose articles were originally published in popular periodicals, Cain names her sources and mentions their credentials but does not cite them as you must do when writing a paper for a class. While Cain does not cite her sources formally, as academic writing requires, she does integrate her sources effectively by

- Making a claim of her own
- Showing how the evidence she provides supports her claim
- Naming her source author(s) in a signal phrase (name plus an appropriate verb) and mentioning his, her, or their credentials
- Providing appropriate, relevant supporting evidence

Look at how Cain achieves these goals:

Cain's idea

Research findings supporting Cain's idea

Author credentials and signal phrase

Links Cain's idea and research findings

> *As a society, we prefer action to contemplation, risk-taking to heed-taking, certainty to doubt.* Studies show that we rank fast and frequent talkers as more competent, likable and even smarter than slow ones. As the psychologists William Hart and Dolores Albarracin point out, phrases like "get active," "get moving," "do something" and similar calls to action surface repeatedly in recent books. (par. 10)

ANALYZE & WRITE

Write a paragraph analyzing how Cain integrates source material elsewhere in her article:

1 Examine paragraphs 18–19 or 20–21 to see how Cain uses a pattern similar to the one described above.

2 Find and mark the elements: Cain's idea; the name(s) and credentials of the source or sources; what the source found; text linking the source's findings to the original idea or extending the idea in some way.

3 When writers use information from sources, why do you think they often begin by stating their own idea (even if they got the idea from a source)? What do you think would be the effect on readers if the opening sentence of paragraph 18 or 20 began with the source instead of with Cain's topic sentence?

[RESPOND]

Consider possible topics: Correcting a misunderstood concept.

For more concept explanations, including a multimodal selection, go to bedfordstmartins.com /theguide/epages.

Cain writes in this article about a concept she thinks has been misunderstood or mis-used. Consider other concepts that you think need clarification. For example, you might consider concepts such as *attention-deficit hyperactivity disorder* (*ADHD*), *autism spectrum,* or *transgender*. Alternatively, you might consider contested political concepts such as *liberal, conservative, corporate personhood, American exceptionalism,* or *regime change*.

Concept explanations may appear in textbooks or magazines, but they also appear in a variety of other contexts. You can find podcasts that explain concepts on iTunes University, or Web tutorials that explain concepts on sites from *Microsoft.com* to the *National Library of Medicine* (nlm.nih.gov). Infographics, like the example below from *National Geographic Online*, are used frequently to explain complex concepts.

Infographics and Other Concept Explanations Online

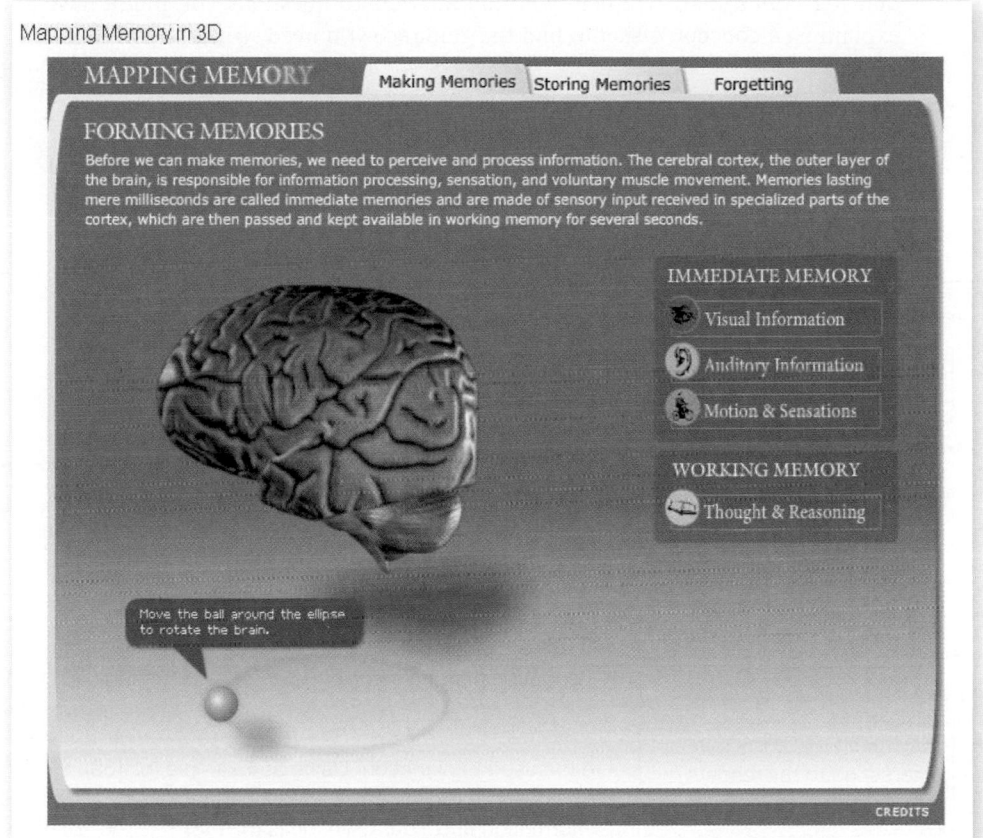

Mapping Memory in 3D

MAPPING MEMORY | Making Memories | Storing Memories | Forgetting

FORMING MEMORIES

Before we can make memories, we need to perceive and process information. The cerebral cortex, the outer layer of the brain, is responsible for information processing, sensation, and voluntary muscle movement. Memories lasting mere milliseconds are called immediate memories and are made of sensory input received in specialized parts of the cortex, which are then passed and kept available in working memory for several seconds.

IMMEDIATE MEMORY

Visual Information

Auditory Information

Motion & Sensations

WORKING MEMORY

Thought & Reasoning

Move the ball around the ellipse to rotate the brain.

CREDITS

In the next section of this chapter, we ask you to explain a concept. Consider how you can best engage your readers' attention and make the explanation clear to your audience (and possibly yourself). What explanatory strategies will capture your readers' attention? Should you include visuals, or would conveying your explanation in a different medium (in a graphic or an online tutorial) help engage your readers and enable them to understand the concept more readily? (Consider, too, whether using visuals or conveying your concept explanation in a different medium would be acceptable to your instructor.)

For an interactive version of this feature, plus activities, go to **bedfordstmartins.com /theguide/epages**.

GUIDE TO WRITING

The Writing Assignment

Write an essay explaining an important and interesting concept, one you already know well or are just learning about. Consider what your readers are likely to know and think about the concept, what you might want them to learn about it, and whether you can research it sufficiently in the time you have.

This Guide to Writing is designed to help you compose your own concept explanation and apply what you have learned from reading other concept explanations. This Starting Points chart will help you find answers to questions you might have about explaining a concept. Use it to find the guidance you need, when you need it.

STARTING POINTS: EXPLAINING A CONCEPT

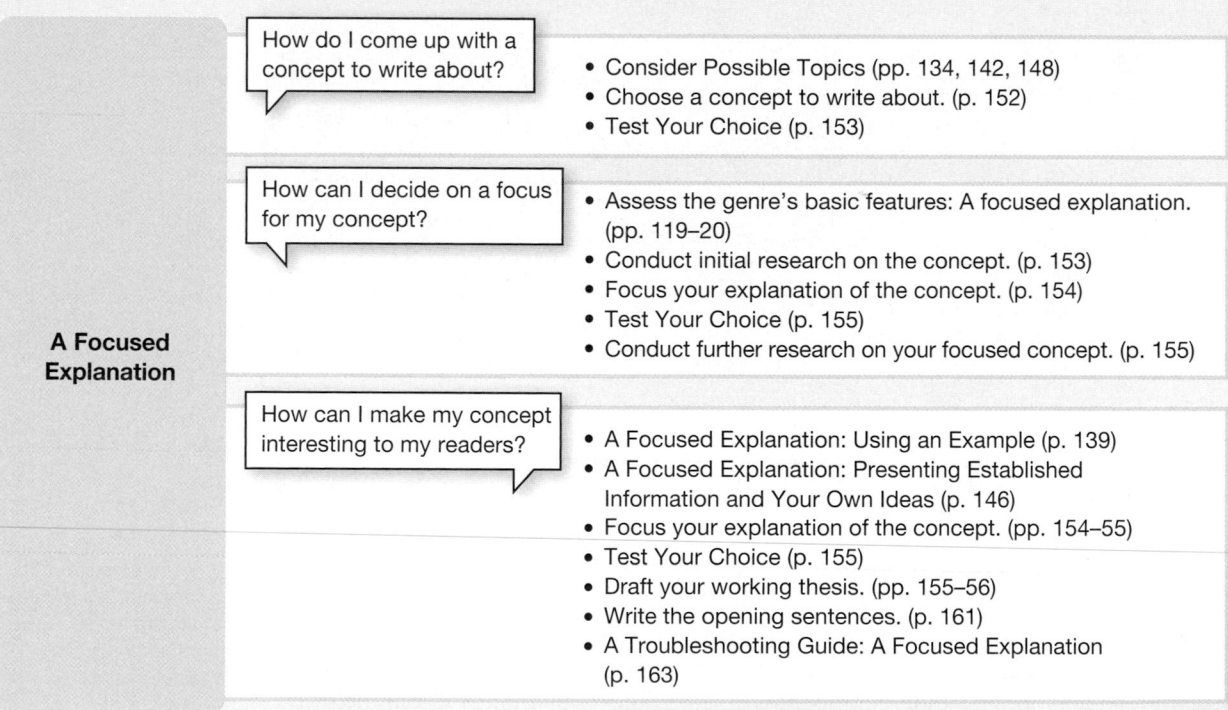

A Focused Explanation

How do I come up with a concept to write about?
- Consider Possible Topics (pp. 134, 142, 148)
- Choose a concept to write about. (p. 152)
- Test Your Choice (p. 153)

How can I decide on a focus for my concept?
- Assess the genre's basic features: A focused explanation. (pp. 119–20)
- Conduct initial research on the concept. (p. 153)
- Focus your explanation of the concept. (p. 154)
- Test Your Choice (p. 155)
- Conduct further research on your focused concept. (p. 155)

How can I make my concept interesting to my readers?
- A Focused Explanation: Using an Example (p. 139)
- A Focused Explanation: Presenting Established Information and Your Own Ideas (p. 146)
- Focus your explanation of the concept. (pp. 154–55)
- Test Your Choice (p. 155)
- Draft your working thesis. (pp. 155–56)
- Write the opening sentences. (p. 161)
- A Troubleshooting Guide: A Focused Explanation (p. 163)

The Writing Assignment

GUIDE TO READING
GUIDE TO WRITING
A WRITER AT WORK
THINKING CRITICALLY

151

A Clear, Logical Organization

How should I organize my explanation so that it's logical and easy to read?

- Assess the genre's basic features: A clear, logical organization. (p. 120)
- A Clear, Logical Organization: Creating Closure (pp. 146–47)
- Organize your concept explanation effectively for your readers. (p. 156)
- A Troubleshooting Guide: A Clear, Logical Organization (p. 164)

What kinds of cues should I provide?

- Assess the genre's basic features: A clear, logical organization. (p. 120)
- A Clear, Logical Organization: Cueing the Reader (pp. 132–33)
- A Clear, Logical Organization: Using Repetition to Create Cohesion (p. 140)
- Draft your working thesis. (pp. 155–56)
- Design your writing project. (p. 157)

Appropriate Explanatory Strategies

What's the best way to explain my concept? What writing strategies should I use?

- Assess the genre's basic features: Appropriate explanatory strategies. (pp. 120–21)
- Appropriate Explanatory Strategies: Using Visuals (p. 133)
- Appropriate Explanatory Strategies: Using a Variety of Strategies (p. 140)
- Appropriate Explanatory Strategies: Using Comparison-Contrast (p. 147)
- Consider the explanatory strategies you should use. (pp. 157–58)
- Use summaries, paraphrases, and quotations from sources to support your points. (p. 158)
- Use visuals or multimedia illustrations to enhance your explanation. (pp. 158–59)
- A Troubleshooting Guide: Appropriate Explanatory Strategies (p. 165)

Smooth Integration of Sources

How should I integrate sources so that they support my argument?

- Assess the genre's basic features: Smooth integration of sources. (pp. 121–22)
- Use appositives to integrate sources. (p. 159)
- Use descriptive verbs in signal phrases to introduce information from sources. (p. 160)
- A Troubleshooting Guide: Smooth Integration of Sources (p. 166)

To learn about using the *Guide* e-book for invention and drafting, go to **bedfordstmartins.com/theguide**.

Writing a Draft: Invention, Research, Planning, and Composing

The activities in this section will help you choose a concept and develop an explanation that will appeal to your readers, using appropriate explanatory strategies as well as photographs, tables, charts, and other illustrations. Do the activities in any order that makes sense to you (and your instructor), and return to them as needed as you revise. They are easy to complete and should take only a few minutes each. Spreading them out over several days will stimulate your creativity, enabling you to find a concept and strategies for explaining it that work for you and your readers. Remember to keep good notes: You'll need them when you draft and revise.

Choose a concept to write about.

Come up with a list of possible concepts you might write about. For the best results, your concept should be one that

- you understand well or feel eager to learn more about;
- you think is important and will interest your readers;
- you can research sufficiently in the allotted time;
- you can explain clearly in the length prescribed by your instructor.

To get your juices flowing, review the Consider Possible Topics activities on pages 134, 142, and 148 or reread notes you made in response to those suggestions. The following list suggests some good concepts:

College Courses

- **Literature and cultural studies:** irony, semiotics, dystopia, canon, postmodernism, realism, genre, connotation
- **Psychology and sociology:** assimilation/accommodation, social cognition, emotional intelligence, the Stroop effect, trauma, theory of mind, deviance, ethnocentrism, social stratification, acculturation, cultural relativism, patriarchy
- **Biology, nursing, and the physical sciences:** morphogenesis, electron transport, phagocytosis, homozygosity, diffusion, mass, energy, gravity, entropy, communicable diseases, epidemiology, toxicology, holistic medicine, pathogen

Community

- **Identity and community:** multiculturalism, racism, social contract, community policing, social Darwinism, identity politics, public space
- **Environment:** fracking, toxic waste, endangered species, sustainability

Workplace and Business Management

- **Work:** private and public sector, minimum wage, affirmative action, glass ceiling, downsizing, collective bargaining, robotics

- **Management and finance:** risk management, leveraged buyout, deregulation, branding, economy of scale, monopoly capitalism, socially conscious investing

---

TEST YOUR CHOICE

To decide whether to proceed with this concept, ask yourself the following questions:

- Can I answer my readers' inevitable "So what?" question and make the concept seem interesting and worth knowing about?
- Am I interested in the concept and can I focus my explanation?
- Do I know enough about the concept now, or can I research it in the time I have?

⁙ Conduct initial research on the concept.

You will need to research your concept in three stages:

1. Gain an overview of the concept.
2. Identify an aspect of the concept to focus on.
3. Conduct enough research to learn about this aspect of the concept.

The following activities will help you begin putting your ideas into words that you may be able to use as you draft.

WHAT DO I ALREADY KNOW?	WHAT DO I NEED TO LEARN?

WHAT DO I ALREADY KNOW?

Describe what you already know about the concept, reviewing textbooks and lecture notes as needed.

Why have you chosen the concept and why do you find it interesting?

- ▶ My concept is important/useful for the study of _____ because _____ .

Explain the concept briefly, using as a starting point the sentence strategies below.

- ▶ My concept can be divided into _____ categories: _____ , _____ , _____ .
- ▶ Examples of my concept include _____ , _____ , and _____ .
- ▶ My concept is a _____ [member of a larger category] that is/does/has _____ [defining characteristics].
- ▶ My concept is [similar to/different from] _____ in these ways: _____ .

WHAT DO I NEED TO LEARN?

Conduct a search on your concept using a reference database such as the Gale Virtual Reference Library or Web of Science. After reading several articles, list the following:

- *Names* of experts on your subject
- Terms, phrases, or synonyms that you might use as *search terms* later
- *Interesting aspects* of the concept that you might want to focus on

Conduct a search for relevant books on your topic, and then click on each library record to find additional subject terms.

Enter the word *overview* or *definition* with the name of your concept into a search engine, and skim the top ten search results to get a general sense of your topic. Bookmark useful links, or save a copy (*.edu, .gov,* or *.org* sites are more likely to be reliable than *.com* sites).

WAYS IN

:: **Focus your explanation of the concept.**

You cannot realistically explain every aspect of your concept thoroughly in a short writing project. Instead, focus on an aspect of the concept that interests you and will interest your readers. The following activities will help you choose a tentative focus, which you will likely refine as you do further research and writing.

WAYS IN

> **WHAT MAKES THE CONCEPT INTERESTING TO ME AND MY READERS?**
>
> ■ List two or three aspects of your concept that interest you, and then answer these questions:
>   - Why does it interest you?
>   - How is it relevant to your life, family, community, work, or studies?
>   - What do you already know about this aspect of the concept? What would you like to learn about it?
>
> ■ Ask yourself questions about your concept:
>   - What is it similar to?
>   - How is it different from related concepts?
>   - What parts or features distinguish it from other concepts?
>   - What are its cultural or historical contexts?
>
> ■ Write for five minutes about your concept, focusing on what you already know.
>
> ■ Analyze your audience by brainstorming answers to the following questions:
>   - Who are your readers, and what is the context in which they will be reading your explanation? What aspects of the concept do you think they would want to know about?
>   - How would you answer your readers' "So what?" question? Think of at least one aspect of the concept that is relevant to their life, family, community, work, or studies.
>   - What are your readers likely to know about the concept, about related concepts, or about the subject in general? How can you build on what they already know?
>   - If you suspect your readers are likely to have faulty assumptions, misunderstandings, or outdated ideas about the concept (or about the subject in general), how can you clarify the concept for them?
>
> ■ After completing the activities above, choose an aspect of your concept on which to focus, and write a sentence explaining why it interests you and why it will interest your audience.

Writing a Draft

GUIDE TO READING
GUIDE TO WRITING
A WRITER AT WORK
THINKING CRITICALLY

155

If you find that you don't have enough to write about, return to the previous section (pp. 153–54) to conduct additional research, broaden your concept by adding cultural or historical contexts, or check sources or class readings to look for broader concepts of which your concept is a part.

TEST YOUR CHOICE

Get together with two or three other students to test your choice:

Presenters   Briefly describe your intended audience, identify the aspect of the concept that you will focus on, and explain what you find interesting or relevant about it and what you think your readers will find interesting or relevant. (If your listeners do not find your focus appropriate or interesting, consider returning to your list of possible concepts and repeating the activities above.)

Listeners   Briefly tell the presenter whether the focus sounds appropriate and interesting for the intended audience. Share what you think readers are likely to know about the concept and what information might be especially interesting to them.

▓ Conduct further research on your focused concept.

Your instructor may expect you to do in-depth research or may limit the number and type of sources you can use. Readers will want to be sure that your sources are reliable and perhaps read your sources for themselves.

To learn more about finding and developing sources, see Chapter 24, pp. 674–82; evaluating your sources, see Chapter 25; citing sources, see Chapter 27 (MLA style) or Chapter 28 (APA style).

▓ Draft your working thesis.

An essay explaining a concept is made up of three basic parts:

- An attempt to engage readers' interest
- A thesis statement, announcing the concept and its focus, and forecasting the main topics
- Information about the concept, organized by topic

You may want to draft a working thesis statement and other parts of your explanation before deciding on an opening that will engage readers' attention. If, however, you prefer to sketch out an opening first, turn to the section "Write the opening sentences" (p. 161), and return to this section later.

The thesis statement in a concept explanation announces the concept to be explained and identifies the aspect of the concept that the writer will focus on. It may also forecast the topics to be explored. Here's an example of a thesis statement from "Love: The Right Chemistry" (pp. 129–31):

O.K., let's cut out all this nonsense about romantic love. Let's bring some scientific precision to the party. Let's put love under a microscope.

Concept

Focus

Forecast
topics

When rigorous people with Ph.D.s after their names do that, what they see is not some silly, senseless thing. No, their probe reveals that love rests firmly on the foundations of evolution, biology and chemistry. (Toufexis, pars. 1–2)

To draft your thesis statement, consider using some of your writing from the Ways In activities in the section "Focus your explanation of the concept" (pp. 154–55). Alternatively, simply state directly the concept you will explain and the approach you will take. You may also want to forecast the topics you will cover.

⠸ Organize your concept explanation effectively for your readers.

Once you have drafted a working thesis, you may want to devise a tentative outline drawing on your invention and research notes. An effective outline for a concept explanation should be divided into separate topics that are conceptually parallel. Patricia Lyu, for example, forecasts her topics in two *rhetorical questions:* "How does that bond develop and how does it affect romantic relationships later in life?" (par. 1) From this sentence, readers know what she will focus on. Toufexis focuses on the scientific foundations of love, and so she divides the topics she will cover into evolution, biology, and chemistry. Once you have decided on your topics, present them in a logical order (for example, from most familiar to least familiar).

Below is a simple *scratch outline* for an essay explaining a concept, which you may use as a starting point:

I. **Introduction:** Attempts to gain readers' interest in the concept, but may not name the concept immediately.

II. **Thesis:** This part is usually a single sentence that identifies the concept. But it may be several sentences, including a brief definition, an example, or another strategy to clarify the focus. It may also include a forecast listing the topics that will be addressed later.

III. **Topic 1:** For each topic, note the explanatory strategies you will use, the source materials you will include, and any visuals you already have or need to find.

IV. **Topic 2:**

V. **Topic 3 (etc.):**

VI. **Conclusion:** Might summarize information, give advice about how to use or apply the information, or speculate about the future of the concept.

Use your outline to guide your drafting, but do not feel tied to it. You may figure out a better way to sequence your topics as you write.

Writing a Draft

GUIDE TO READING
GUIDE TO WRITING
A WRITER AT WORK
THINKING CRITICALLY

157

:: Design your writing project.

Consider whether you want to use headings to indicate the topic to be discussed; bullets or numbers to highlight lists; and tables, graphics, or other visuals to make your explanation clearer.

To learn more about designing documents, see Chapter 21.

:: Consider the explanatory strategies you should use.

To explain your concept, consider how you would define it, examples you can provide to help readers understand it, how it is similar to or different from other related concepts, how it happens or gets done, and what its causes or effects are. Keep in mind that your goal is not only to inform your readers but also to engage their interest. The following activities provide sentence strategies you may use to explore the best ways to explain your concept, and they may also get you started drafting your essay.

WAYS IN

WHAT WRITING STRATEGIES CAN I USE TO EXPLAIN MY FOCUSED CONCEPT?

What are the concept's defining characteristics? What broader class does it belong to, and how does it differ from other members of its class? (*definition*)

▶ [Concept] is a _____ in which _____ [list defining characteristics].

What examples or anecdotes can make the concept less abstract and more understandable? (*example*)

▶ [Experts/scientists/etc.] first became aware of [concept] in [year], when _____ (citation).

▶ Interest in [concept] has been [rising/declining/steady] [because of/in spite of] [recent examples/a shortage of recent examples] like _____, _____, and _____.

How is this concept like or unlike related concepts with which your readers may be more familiar? (*comparison and contrast*)

▶ Many people think the term [concept] means _____, but it might be more accurate to say it means _____.

▶ [Concept] is similar in some ways to [similar concept]: [list areas of similarity]. However, unlike [similar concept], it [list areas of difference].

▶ [Concept], a kind of [grown-up, children's, bigger, smaller, local, international, or other adjective] version of [similar concept], [is/does/has] _____.

How can an explanation of this concept be divided into parts to make it easier for readers to understand? (*classification*)

▶ Experts like [name of expert] say there are [number] [categories, types, subtypes, versions] of [concept], ranging from _____ to _____ (citation).

(continued)

How does this concept happen, or how does one go about doing it? (*process narration*)

▶ To perform [concept or task related to concept], a [person, performer, participant, etc.] starts by _____. Then [he/she/it] must [verb], [verb], and [verb]. [Insert or remove sections as necessary.] The process ends when [he/she/it] [verb].

What are this concept's known causes or effects? (*cause and effect*)

▶ [Concept or concept-related result] happens because _____.

▶ Before [concept or concept-related result] can [happen/take place/occur], [identify a condition that has to be met first]. However, [that condition] isn't enough by itself: [second condition] must also [happen/take place/be established].

▶ Experts disagree over the causes of [concept]. Some, like [name 1], believe _____ (citation). Others, like [name 2], contend that _____ (citation).

▪▪ Use summaries, paraphrases, and quotations from sources to support your points.

Summaries, paraphrases, and quotations from sources are frequently used to explain concepts or reinforce an explanation. Chapter 26 (in Part 4, "Research Strategies"), explains how to write an effective summary or paraphrase and to decide when to summarize, paraphrase, or quote from a source. But keep the following in mind:

- Use *summary* to give the gist of a research report or other information.
- Use *paraphrase* to provide specific details or examples when the language of the source is not especially memorable.
- Use *quotation* to emphasize source material that is particularly vivid or clear, to convey an expert's voice, or to discuss the source's choice of words.

In academic writing projects, you will need to cite the sources of all summaries, paraphrases, and quotations.

Also remember that your readers will want you to explain how the ideas from the sources you cite reinforce the points you are making. So make sure you comment on sources, making the relationship between your own ideas and the supporting information from sources absolutely clear. (For help with integrating information from sources, see p. 159.)

▪▪ Use visuals or multimedia illustrations to enhance your explanation.

Concept explanations do not require illustrations, but they can be an effective tool. The medium in which your concept explanation appears will determine the types of illustrations you can use. For example, papers can include visual images such as photographs and flowcharts. Web pages can include music, film clips, and animated graphs. Oral presentations can use the Web or presentation slides (such as PowerPoint).

When deciding whether to include illustrations, consider whether you can create your own graphics (for example, using spreadsheet software to create bar graphs or pie charts) or whether you will need to borrow materials that others have created (for example, downloading materials from the Internet, taking screenshots from Web sites or DVDs, or scanning visuals from books or magazines). Borrowed material must be cited, including the sources of data you use to create graphs and tables. If your writing is going to be published on a Web site that is not password protected, you also need to obtain permission from the source.

Use appositives to integrate sources.

When you write your essay, you'll have to tell readers about the credentials of experts you quote, paraphrase, and summarize. Instead of providing this information in separate sentences, you can use an *appositive* to embed this information smoothly and clearly into another sentence.

For more on appositives, go to **bedfordstmartins .com/theguide** and type "Appositives" in the search box.

An **appositive** is a noun or pronoun that, along with modifiers, gives more information about another noun or pronoun. Here is an example from one of the reading selections earlier in the chapter:

"Love is a natural high," observes Anthony Walsh, author of *The Science of Love: Understanding Love and Its Effects on Mind and Body.* (Toufexis, par. 10)

Noun

Appositive

By placing the credentials right after the expert's name, these sentences provide readers with the information they need, exactly where they need it.

Appositives can also be used for many different purposes, as these examples suggest:

TO DEFINE A KEY TERM	Each person carries in his or her mind a unique subliminal guide to the ideal partner, a "love map." (Toufexis, par. 17)
TO IDENTIFY PEOPLE AND THINGS	Randall Engle, a leading intelligence researcher at the Georgia Tech School of Psychology, views the proposition that I.Q. can be increased through training with a skepticism verging on disdain. (Hurley, par. 16)
TO GIVE EXAMPLES	Despite the risk of serious side effects—nausea, loss of sex drive, seizures—drugs like Zoloft can be a godsend for this group. (Cain, par. 3)

Notice that the last example uses dashes instead of commas to set off the appositive from the rest of the sentence. Although commas are more common, dashes are often used if the writer wants to give the appositive more emphasis or if the appositive itself contains commas, as in the last example above.

:: Use descriptive verbs in signal phrases to introduce information from sources.

When introducing quotations, paraphrases, or summaries, writers often use a **signal phrase**—the source author's name plus an appropriate verb—to alert readers to the fact that they are borrowing someone else's words or ideas. Often the verb is neutral, as with the following two examples (the verbs are italicized):

> "That is one reason why it feels so horrible when we're abandoned or a lover dies," *notes* Fisher. (Toufexis, par. 13)

Signal phrase

> "It's not just a little bit higher," Jaeggi says. "It's a large effect." (Hurley, par. 14)

Sometimes, however, the verb may be more descriptive—even evaluative:

> "As long as prehistoric females were secretive about their extramarital affairs," *argues* Fisher, "they could garner extra resources, life insurance, better genes and more varied DNA for their biological futures. . . ." (Toufexis, par. 8)

The verb *argues* emphasizes the fact that what is being reported is an interpretation that others may disagree with. As you refer to sources in your concept explanation, choose carefully among a wide variety of precise verbs to introduce your sources. Here are a number of possibilities: *suggests, reveals, questions, brings into focus, finds, notices, observes, underscores.*

For more about integrating sources into your sentences and constructing signal phrases, see Chapter 26.

In academic writing, merely mentioning the author's name in a signal phrase is not sufficient. In most cases, you must also include in-text citations that provide the page number from which the borrowed material is taken and include full bibliographic information in a list of works cited or references, so readers can trace the source for themselves. Writers may also include the source author's name in a signal phrase. But often the information provided in parentheses following the borrowed passage is sufficient, particularly if the source author has already been identified or if the source's identity is not relevant (as when citing facts):

Parenthetical citation

> The original research on attachment, plus Harlow's monkey experiments, underlines the idea that "the attachment and fear systems are intertwined" (Cassidy 8). During a time of war, fear obviously is intensified, especially for soldiers in harm's way. Therefore, we can see how applying the concept of attachment to *The Things They Carried* can be illuminating. It is especially helpful in understanding Henry Dobbins's peculiar habit of wearing "his girlfriend's pantyhose around his neck before heading out on ambush" (O'Brien 117). Fear triggers Dobbins's attachment behavior. Like Harlow's monkey, he seeks comfort from his attachment figure. (Lyu, par. 10)

Evaluating the Draft

GUIDE TO READING
GUIDE TO WRITING
A WRITER AT WORK
THINKING CRITICALLY

161

Write the opening sentences.

Review your invention writing to see if you have already written something that would work to launch your essay, or try out one or two ways of beginning your essay—possibly from the list that follows:

- A surprising or provocative quotation (like Toufexis and Lyu)
- An anecdote illustrating the concept (like Hurley)
- A concrete example (like Cain)
- A paradox or surprising aspect of the concept
- A comparison or contrast that relates the concept to something readers know

Your goal should be to engage your readers' interest from the start, but do not agonize over the first sentences, because you are likely to discover the best way to begin only after you have written a rough draft.

Draft your explanation.

By this point, you have done a lot of research and writing to

- focus your explanation and develop a working thesis statement;
- try out writing strategies that can help you explain your concept;
- create an outline for presenting that information;
- come up with ways to smoothly integrate your sources;
- consider opening sentences.

Now stitch that material together to create a draft. As you do so, you will notice that some of the sentences you have written based on the sentence strategies in this chapter feel awkward or forced. If so, revise them, retaining the content but experimenting with new ways to present them. The next two parts of this Guide to Writing will help you evaluate and improve your draft.

Evaluating the Draft: Getting a Critical Reading

Your instructor may arrange a peer review session in class or online, where you can exchange drafts with your classmates and give one another a thoughtful critical reading, pointing out what works well and suggesting ways to improve the draft. A good critical reading does three things:

1. It lets the writer know how well the reader understands the point of the essay.
2. It praises what works best.
3. It indicates where the draft could be improved and makes suggestions on how to improve it.

A CRITICAL READING GUIDE

A Focused Explanation

Is the explanation focused?

Summarize: Tell the writer, in one sentence, what you understand the concept to mean and why it is important or useful.

Praise: Give an example of something in the draft that you think will especially interest the intended readers.

Critique: Tell the writer about any confusion or uncertainty you have about the concept's meaning, importance, or usefulness. Indicate if the focus could be clearer or more appropriate for the intended readers or if the explanation could have a more interesting focus.

A Clear, Logical Organization

Is the explanation easy to follow?

Summarize: Look at the way the essay is organized by making a scratch outline.

Praise: Give an example of where the essay succeeds in being readable — for instance, in its overall organization, forecast of topics, or use of transitions.

Critique: Identify places where readability could be improved — for example, the beginning made more appealing, a topic sentence made clearer, or transitions or headings added.

Appropriate Explanatory Strategies

Is the concept explained effectively?

Summarize: Note which explanatory strategies the writer uses, such as definition, comparison, example, cause-effect, or process analysis.

Praise: Point to an explanatory strategy that is especially effective, and highlight research that is particularly helpful in explaining the concept.

Critique: Point to any places where a definition is needed, where more (or better) examples might help, or where another explanatory strategy could be improved or added. Note where a visual (such as a flowchart or graph) would make the explanation clearer.

Smooth Integration of Sources

Are the sources incorporated into the essay effectively?

Summarize: Note each source mentioned in the text, and check to make sure it appears in the list of works cited, if there is one. Highlight signal phrases and in-text citations, and identify appositives used to provide experts' credentials.

Praise: Give an example of the effective use of sources — a particularly well-integrated quotation, paraphrase, or summary that supports and illustrates the point. Note any especially descriptive verbs used to introduce information.

Critique: Point out where experts' credentials are needed. Indicate quotations, paraphrases, or summaries that could be more smoothly integrated or more fully interpreted or explained. Suggest verbs in signal phrases that may be more appropriate.

Improving the Draft

GUIDE TO READING
GUIDE TO WRITING
A WRITER AT WORK
THINKING CRITICALLY

163

Before concluding your review, be sure to address any of the writer's concerns that have not already been addressed.

Making Comments Electronically   Most word processing software offers features that allow you to insert comments directly into the text of someone else's document. Many readers prefer to make their comments this way because it tends to be faster than writing on hard copy, and space is virtually unlimited; it also eliminates the process of deciphering handwritten comments. Where such features are not available, simply typing comments directly into a document in a contrasting color can provide the same advantages.

For a printable version of this Critical Reading Guide, go to **bedfordstmartins .com/theguide**.

Improving the Draft: Revising, Formatting, Editing, and Proofreading

Start improving your draft by reflecting on what you have written thus far:

- Review critical reading comments from your classmates, instructor, or writing center tutor. What are your readers getting at?
- Take another look at the notes from your earlier research and writing activities. What else should you consider?
- Review your draft. What else can you do to make your explanation effective?

Revise your draft.

If your readers are having difficulty with your draft, or if you think there is room for improvement, try some of the strategies listed in the Troubleshooting Guide that follows. It can help you fine-tune your presentation of the genre's basic features:

A TROUBLESHOOTING GUIDE

A Focused Explanation

I don't have enough to write about. (The focus is too narrow.)

- Broaden your concept by adding cultural or historical comparisons and contrasts.
- Look up your concept using reference sources to find additional subject terms for larger concepts that include it.
- Conduct a Web search using the name of your concept and *overview* or *definition*. Use the Advanced Search feature to focus on sites with an *.edu, .gov,* or *.org* domain.
- If your concept comes from another course you are taking, check your textbook or lecture notes for broader, related topics.

A Focused Explanation

Readers don't find my focus interesting.

- Conduct additional research, focusing on finding information likely to be of value and interest to your readers.
- Consider how you can answer your readers' "So what?" question. Show them, perhaps, how they could use the concept; build on their interests or what they already know; or clarify their mistaken, faulty, or outdated assumptions or ideas.
- Consider using humor, anecdotes, or visuals to engage readers' interest.
- Ask yourself whether the focus is interesting to you. If it isn't, choose a different focus. If it is, ask yourself how you can communicate your enthusiasm to your readers — perhaps with anecdotes, examples, or illustrations.

A Clear, Logical Organization

The organization is not clear and logical.

- Reread your thesis statement to be sure that it clearly announces the concept and forecasts the topics in the order they appear in the essay.
- Outline your material to be sure that it is divided into separate topics that are conceptually parallel and presented in a logical order.
- Look for topic sentences in each paragraph. (If you find them difficult to locate, your reader will, too.) Clarify where necessary.

The beginning does not draw readers in.

- Review your opening paragraphs to be sure that you clearly introduce your concept and your focus.
- Try starting with an anecdote, an interesting quotation, a surprising aspect of the concept, a concrete example, or a similar lead-in.
- Consider stating explicitly what makes the concept worth thinking about and how it relates to your readers' interests.

The essay doesn't flow smoothly from one part to the next.

- Outline your essay, dividing it into major parts — introduction, main topics, and conclusion. Reread the end of each major part and the beginning of the next to make sure you have provided transitional cues (for example, the strategic repetition of words or phrases; use of synonyms; rhetorical questions). If there are none, add some.
- Consider adding headings to make the topical sections easier to identify.

The ending falls flat.

- Consider ending by speculating on what the future will bring — how the concept might be redefined, for example.
- Consider relating the ending to the beginning — for example, by recalling an example or a comparison.

Appropriate Explanatory Strategies

> Readers don't understand my explanation.

- Consider whether you have used the most appropriate writing strategies for your topic — defining, classifying, comparing and contrasting, narrating, illustrating, describing, or explaining cause and effect.
- Recheck your definitions for clarity. Be sure that you have explicitly defined any key terms your readers might not know.
- Consider forecasting the topics you will cover explicitly.
- Add transitional cues (transitional words and phrases, strategic repetition, rhetorical questions, etc.).
- Add headings and bulleted or numbered lists to help readers follow the discussion.

> Readers want more information about certain aspects of the concept.

- Expand or clarify definitions by adding examples or using appositives.
- Add examples or comparisons and contrasts to relate the concept to something readers already know.
- Conduct additional research on your topic, and cite it in your essay.

> Readers want visuals to help them understand certain aspects of the concept.

- Check whether your sources use visuals (tables, graphs, drawings, photographs, and the like) that might be appropriate for your explanation. (If you are publishing your concept explanation online, consider video clips, audio files, and animated graphics as well.)
- Consider drafting your own charts, tables, or graphs, or adding your own photographs or illustrations.

> Summaries lack oomph; paraphrases are too complicated; quotations are too long or uninteresting.

- Revise the summaries to emphasize a single key idea.
- Restate the paraphrases more succinctly, omitting irrelevant details. Consider quoting important words.
- Use ellipses to tighten the quotations to emphasize the memorable words.

> Readers aren't sure how source information supports my explanation of the concept.

- Check to be sure that you have appropriately commented on all cited material, making its relation to your own ideas absolutely clear.
- Expand or clarify accounts of research that your readers find unconvincing on grounds apart from the credibility of the source.

Smooth Integration of Sources

> Quotes, summaries, and/or paraphrases don't flow smoothly with the rest of the essay.

- Reread all passages where you quote outside sources. Ask yourself whether you provide enough context for the quotation or establish clearly enough the credentials of the source author.
- Use signal phrases to place sources in context. Consider using descriptive verbs in signal phrases to give your readers more information about what your source is saying and why you are referring to it.
- Use appositives to integrate information about your sources smoothly and clearly.

> Readers are concerned that my list of sources is too limited.

- Do additional research to balance your list, taking particular care that you have an adequate number of scholarly sources.
- If you have difficulty finding appropriate material, ask your instructor or a reference librarian for help.

> My readers wonder whether my sources are credible.

- Clearly identify all sources, and fully state the credentials of all cited authorities, using appositives where appropriate.
- Eliminate sources that are clearly identified and well integrated but not considered relevant, credible, or otherwise appropriate.

For an electronic version of this Troubleshooting Guide, go to **bedfordstmartins .com/theguide**.

Think about design.

When formatting your concept explanation, consider the design that is appropriate to your context and genre, and follow the formatting requirements that your readers expect. Patricia Lyu followed MLA style, as is appropriate for her composition class.

Leave 1-inch margins on all sides

Include last name and page number 1/2 inch from the top of the page

Indent block quotations 1 inch from the margin

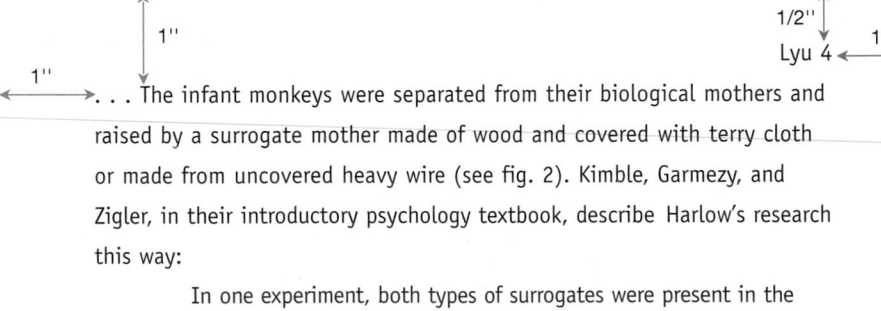

1"

1/2"   1"

Lyu 4

1"

. . . The infant monkeys were separated from their biological mothers and raised by a surrogate mother made of wood and covered with terry cloth or made from uncovered heavy wire (see fig. 2). Kimble, Garmezy, and Zigler, in their introductory psychology textbook, describe Harlow's research this way:

> In one experiment, both types of surrogates were present in the cage, but only one was equipped with a nipple. . . . (21)

1"

Improving the Draft

GUIDE TO READING
GUIDE TO WRITING
A WRITER AT WORK
THINKING CRITICALLY

167

Fig. 2. Harlow's infant monkey cuddling the cloth surrogate and turning its back on the wire surrogate with the bottle.

Label and number all figures, and include a caption

Edit and proofread your draft.

Two kinds of errors occur often in concept explanations: mixed constructions and missing or unnecessary commas around adjective clauses. The following guidelines will help you check your essay for these common errors.

Avoiding Mixed Constructions

What Is a Mixed Construction? A **mixed construction** in a sentence is a combination of structures that don't work together properly according to the rules of logic or English grammar. Mixed constructions often occur when a writer attributes information to a source, defines a term, or provides an explanation. In particular, watch out for definitions that include *is when* or *is where* and explanations that include *the reason . . . is because,* which are likely to be both illogical and ungrammatical.

The Problem Sentences are logically or grammatically incoherent.

The Correction Replace *when* or *where* with a noun that renames the subject or with an adjective that describes the subject.

> ▶ Depression is ~~where~~ people feel sad, guilty, or worthless, and lack energy or focus.
> *a disorder in which*

Delete either *the reason . . . is* or *because.*

> ▶ ~~The reasons~~ ponds become meadows ~~is~~ because plant life collects in the bottom.
> *P*

Check subjects and predicates to make sure they are logically and grammatically matched, and delete any redundant expressions.

A Note on Grammar and Spelling Checkers

These tools can be helpful, but don't rely on them exclusively to catch errors in your text: Spelling checkers cannot catch misspellings that are themselves words, such as *to* or *too.* Grammar checkers miss some problems, sometimes give faulty advice for fixing problems, and can flag correct items as wrong. Use these tools as a second line of defense after your own (and, ideally, another reader's) proofreading and editing efforts.

For more practice correcting mixed construction errors, go to **bedfordstmartins .com/theguide/ exercisecentral** and click on Effective Sentences in the Handbook section.

▶ ~~According to Eleanor Smith,~~ she said that the best movie of the year was *Queen Margot.*

▶ According to Eleanor Smith, ~~she said that~~ the best movie of the year was *Queen Margot.*

Using Punctuation with Adjective Clauses

What Is an Adjective Clause?   **An adjective clause** includes both a subject and a verb, gives information about a noun or a pronoun and often begins with *who, which,* or *that*:

For more practice correcting comma problems, go to bedfordstmartins.com /theguide/exercisecentral and click on Punctuation in the Handbook section.

▶ It is common for schizophrenics to have delusions $\overbrace{\textit{that they are being persecuted.}}^{\text{adjective clause}}$
 subj.   verb

Because adjective clauses add information about the nouns they follow — defining, illustrating, or explaining — they can be useful in writing that explains a concept.

The Problem   Adjective clauses may or may not need to be set off with a comma or commas. To decide, determine whether the clause is essential to the meaning of the sentence. Essential clauses should *not* be set off with commas; nonessential clauses *must* be set off with commas.

The Correction   Mentally delete the clause. If taking out the clause does not change the basic meaning of the sentence or make it unclear, add a comma or commas.

▶ Postpartum neurosis‚which can last for two weeks or longer‚can adversely affect a mother's ability to care for her infant.

If the clause follows a proper noun, add a comma or commas.

▶ Nanotechnologists defer to K. Eric Drexler‚who speculates imaginatively about the use of nonmachines.

If taking out the clause changes the basic meaning of the sentence or makes it unclear, do *not* add a comma or commas.

▶ Seasonal affective disorders are mood disturbances/ that occur in fall/winter.

Patricia Lyu's Use of Sources

This section describes how student writer Patricia Lyu selected information from a source and integrated it into one part of her explanation of attachment. The following excerpt from Lyu's essay illustrates a sound strategy for integrating sources into your essay, relying on them fully—as you nearly always must do in explanatory writing—and yet making them your own. Most of the information Lyu uses in this passage comes from an online report by psychologist R. Chris Fraley at the University of Illinois. Given her purpose—to identify the three types of attachment delineated by psychologist Mary Ainsworth—Lyu selects only a limited amount of information from Fraley's publication.

Lyu relies on paraphrase to present the information she learned primarily from Fraley's publication. When you **paraphrase,** you construct your own sentences but rely necessarily on the key words in your source. In the following comparison, the paraphrased sections are highlighted in yellow and key words are underlined:

Patricia Lyu

. . . From this research, Ainsworth identified three basic types ("attachment styles") of attachment bond that children form with their primary caregiver: *secure, anxious* (or *anxious-resistant*), and *avoidant* (Fraley 4).

The secure child cries when the caregiver leaves but goes to the caregiver and calms down when he or she returns. According to Ainsworth, these children feel secure because their primary caregiver has been reliably responsive to their needs over the course of their short lives.

Ainsworth classifies the other two styles of attachment as insecure compared to the first attachment style. Anxious children may be clingy, get very upset when the caregiver leaves, and seem afraid of the stranger. They do not calm down when the caregiver returns, crying inconsolably and seeming very mad at the caregiver. Avoidant children ignore the caregiver when he or she returns. They seem emotionally distant and may even move away from him or her to play with toys.

R. Chris Fraley

In the strange situation, most children (i.e., about 60%) behave in the way implied by Bowlby's "normative" theory. They become upset when the parent leaves the room, but, when he or she returns, they actively seek the parent and are easily comforted by him or her. Children who exhibit this pattern of behavior are often called secure. Other children (about 20% or less) are ill-at-ease initially, and, upon separation, become extremely distressed. Importantly, when reunited with their parents, these children have a difficult time being soothed, and often exhibit conflicting behaviors that suggest they want to be comforted, but that they also want to "punish" the parent for leaving. These children are often called **anxious-resistant**. The third pattern of attachment that Ainsworth and her colleagues documented is called **avoidant.** Avoidant children (about 20%) don't appear too distressed by the separation, and, upon reunion, actively avoid seeking contact with their parent, sometimes turning their attention to play objects on the laboratory floor.

Lyu's writing illustrates a careful balance between a writer's ideas and information gleaned from her source; she is careful not to let the sources take over the explanation. For the material cited from Fraley, she includes a parenthetical citation. Because

Fraley is reporting information about Ainsworth's experiment that is widely known and reported, Lyu uses Ainsworth's name in the text—"According to Ainsworth"—and does not need to cite Fraley.

THINKING CRITICALLY

To think critically means to use all of the knowledge you have acquired from the information in this chapter, your own writing, the writing and responses of other students, and class discussions to reflect deeply on your work for this assignment and the genre (or type) of writing you have produced. The benefit of thinking critically is proven and important: Thinking critically about what you have learned will help you remember it longer, ensuring that you will be able to put it to good use well beyond this writing course.

Reflecting on What You Have Learned

In this chapter, you have learned a great deal about this genre from reading several explanations of a concept and writing a concept explanation of your own. To consolidate your learning, reflect not only on what you learned but also on how you learned it.

ANALYZE & WRITE

Write a blog post, a letter to your instructor or a classmate, or an e-mail message to a student who will take this course next term, using the writing prompt that seems most productive for you:

- Explain how your purpose and audience — what you wanted your readers to learn from reading your concept explanation — influenced *one* of your decisions as a writer, such as how you focused the concept, how you organized your explanation, how you used writing strategies to convey information, or how you integrated sources into your essay.

- If you were to give advice to a fellow student who was about to write a concept explanation, what would you say?

- Which of the readings in this chapter influenced your essay? Explain the influence, citing specific examples from your essay and the reading.

- If you got good advice from a critical reader, explain exactly how the person helped you — perhaps by questioning your definitions, your use of visuals, the way you began or ended your essay, or the kinds of sources you used.

Reflecting on the Genre

GUIDE TO READING
GUIDE TO WRITING
A WRITER AT WORK
THINKING CRITICALLY

171

- Discuss what you learned about yourself as a writer in the process of writing this essay. For example, what part of the process did you find most challenging? Did you try anything new like getting a critical reading of your draft or outlining your draft in order to revise it?

Reflecting on the Genre

Writers explaining concepts typically present knowledge as established and uncontested. They presume to be unbiased and objective, and they assume that readers will not doubt or challenge the truth or the value of the knowledge they present. This stance encourages readers to feel confident about the validity of the explanation. But should explanatory writing always be accepted at face value? Textbooks and reference materials, in particular, sometimes present a simplified or limited view of knowledge in an academic discipline. Because they must be highly selective, they necessarily leave out certain sources of information and types of knowledge.

ANALYZE & WRITE

Write a page or two considering how concept explanations may distort knowledge. In your discussion, you might consider one or more of the following:

1. **Consider the claim that concept explanations attempt to present their information as uncontested truths.** Identify a reading in this chapter that particularly seems to support this claim, and then think about how it does so. Do the same for a chapter or section in a textbook you are reading for another course.

2. **Write a page or two explaining your initial assumptions about the knowledge or information you presented about the concept in your essay.** When you were doing research on the concept, did you discover that some of the information was being challenged by experts? Or did the body of knowledge seem settled and established? Did you at any point think that your readers might question any of the information you were presenting? How did you decide what information might seem new or even surprising to readers? Did you feel comfortable in your roles as the selector and giver of knowledge?

5

Finding Common Ground

Common ground essays analyze opposing arguments to identify potential areas of agreement based on shared concerns and values as well as overlapping interests and priorities. Taking an impartial view of an ongoing debate, writers strive not only to understand why people disagree but also to find points on which they may agree. Whether written for a college course, for the community, or for the workplace, common ground essays avoid the trap of thinking in terms of winners and losers. Instead, they try to bridge differences by forging constructive answers to challenging issues.

IN COLLEGE COURSES

For a course in scientific research ethics, a biology major writes a paper on the debate over stem cell research. She explains that groups with seemingly irreconcilable differences have agreed to a compromise drafted by the National Institutes of Health (NIH) limiting research to stem cells from embryos that would have been destroyed because they are no longer needed for in vitro fertilization. The student points out that there are still serious disagreements: for example, some scientists argue that banning techniques like therapeutic cloning or somatic cell nuclear transfer is a major impediment to research, and the National Right to Life Committee opposes the new guidelines as "part of an incremental strategy to desensitize the public." Nevertheless, she concludes, the fact that many people support the guidelines represents a path toward an eventual resolution of the issue.

IN THE COMMUNITY

The chair of the School Uniform Committee of a middle school's Parent Teacher Association (PTA) writes a blog post reporting on a recent meeting about whether to adopt school uniforms. She begins by summarizing the inconsistent findings of published research. Then she explains that although disagreement continues on the advantages and disadvantages of school uniforms, there was agreement that reducing distinctions of social class and forestalling gang violence are worthy goals. She reports that a compromise—substituting ordinary casual clothes for expensive formal uniforms while also banning gang colors—was proposed and appeared to win support from people on different sides of the issue.

IN THE WORKPLACE

Population growth and haphazard development threaten a watershed that supplies local communities and supports endangered species. Longtime residents, developers, and county planning officials agree to hire a consulting firm to write a report that analyzes the positions of the stakeholders and outlines a plan for development. The consulting firm analyzes the competing needs and recommends changes to the developer's original proposal, calling for higher-density development that would be situated away from the endangered watershed, cost less to build, and be easier to support with transportation and utilities.

In this chapter, we ask you to analyze the points of disagreement and potential agreement in opposing arguments on a controversial issue. From reading and examining the selections in the Guide to Reading that follows, you will learn how writers present an issue and the opposing positions with fairness and accuracy, how they analyze the opposing arguments, and how they organize their analyses clearly and logically. The Guide to Writing later in the chapter will show you ways to write your own impartial analysis of opposing positions.

PRACTICING THE GENRE

Finding Common Ground

To get a sense of what is involved in trying to find common ground on a controversial issue, get together with two or three students to explore the possibilities for agreement among those who argue about an issue.

Part 1.   As a group, choose a controversial issue with which you are all familiar, such as whether there should be a community service requirement for graduation, whether college athletes should be paid, or whether a college education, like kindergarten through twelfth grade, should be free to everyone who qualifies. Then discuss why people usually disagree about the issue and the aspects of the issue on which they might agree. Consider, for example, whether any basic values, needs, interests, or concerns are likely to be shared by people with otherwise opposing viewpoints. (You do not need to have an opinion on this issue yourself; you simply need to recall or guess what others have said or would say.)

Part 2.   Discuss what you learned about analyzing opposing arguments and trying to find common ground:

- Was it easier to think of points of disagreement or points of potential agreement?
- Why do you think that when people debate controversial issues such as the one you analyzed, they tend to emphasize the disagreement and ignore what people hold in common?
- What benefits, if any, would result from people spending time looking for areas on which they could agree (or building agreement through compromise), rather than focusing so much of their attention on areas of disagreement?

Analyzing Opposing Positions to Find Common Ground

As you read the selections in this chapter, you will see how different authors find common ground. Analyzing how these writers lay out the opposing positions for their readers, dissect the arguments to identify priorities and common values, maintain their impartiality, and organize their writing will help you see how you can employ similar strategies to make your own common ground analysis clear and compelling for your readers.

Determine the writer's purpose and audience.

College courses throughout the curriculum require students to *analyze* and *synthesize* opposing points of view because these are essential critical thinking skills necessary for research, reading, and writing. Still, common ground essays may be written for a variety of purposes and audiences. As you read the common ground essays in this chapter, ask yourself the following questions:

- What seems to be the writer's main *purpose*—for example, to inform readers about a controversial issue, to clarify different points of view on the issue and the kinds of arguments people typically use to support their position, to analyze the important points of disagreement, or to suggest where there may be potential for compromise based on shared values or interests?

- What does the author assume about the *audience*—for example, that audience members will be unfamiliar with the issue, meaning that the essay will serve as an introduction; that they will know something about the arguments typically made on the issue but will think agreement is impossible; or that they will have strong opinions themselves on the issue?

Assess the genre's basic features.

Use the following to help you analyze and evaluate how writers seeking common ground employ the genre's basic features. The strategies they typically use to make their essays insightful and impartial are illustrated below with examples from the readings in this chapter as well as sentence strategies you can experiment with later as you write your own common ground essay.

> **Basic Features**
> An Informative Introduction
> A Probing Analysis
> A Fair and Impartial Presentation
> A Clear, Logical Organization

AN INFORMATIVE INTRODUCTION TO THE ISSUE AND OPPOSING POSITIONS

Read first to see how the writer presents the issue. Consider, for example, whether the writer assumes that readers are already well informed about the issue or need background information, and whether they will be interested in the issue or will need to have their interest piqued. To inform and interest readers, writers often provide the historical context, using a simple sentence strategy like this:

▶ In [year(s)], when _____ [describe events or provide historical context], [name authors] voiced strong opinions about _____ [name controversy].

In the following example, Jeremy Bernard provides the historical context for the controversy over the use of steroids in Major League Baseball. Notice how Bernard introduces the two authors whose texts his common ground essay analyzes.

Historical context

Authors' names

Credentials

Publication

> The age of innocence in baseball seems to have ended in the 1990s when "the Steroid Era" began and players from Mark McGwire to Roger Clemens, Barry Bonds, and Alex Rodriguez were identified as using performance enhancing drugs (PEDs). . . . In 2006, the concern was so great that George Mitchell, the former Senate Majority Leader and peace negotiator, was enlisted to investigate . . . . An opposing position has been presented by respected baseball authority Eric Walker on his Web site *Steroids, Other "Drugs," and Baseball.* (Bernard, pars. 1–3)

To grab readers' attention, notice that Bernard includes the names of some of the most famous baseball players who were caught up in the steroids scandal: sluggers Mark McGwire and Barry Bonds, award-winning pitcher Roger Clemens, and one of the best all-around players, Alex Rodriguez.

A PROBING ANALYSIS

Look for passages where the opposing arguments are presented. To present the arguments clearly and accurately, writers of common ground analyses usually rely heavily on quotation, although they may also use **summary** (giving the gist of the writer's argument) and **paraphrase** (putting the writer's argument into their own words), as we can see in this example where student Betsy Samson uses all three strategies:

Paraphrase

Summary

Quotation

> Chua's main argument is that children of Chinese immigrants usually are high-achieving because their parents are proud to be helicopter parents intensely involved in every aspect of their children's lives. More importantly, as Chua's anecdote about her daughter Lulu's effort to learn to play a difficult piano piece demonstrates. . . . [A]s Chua explains at the end of her article: "the Chinese believe that the best way to protect their children is . . . letting them see what they're capable of, and arming them with skills, work habits and inner confidence" (par. 35). (Samson, par. 5)

Examine the analysis of the points of disagreement and potential agreement in the common ground essays that follow, and ask yourself how well the analysis helps you understand the motivating factors underlying the arguments. For example, see if basic values are discussed, and look for words that indicate an opposing or contrasting view, a concession, or a rebuttal:

Basic value

Cue: opposing view, concession, or rebuttal

> You'd think anyone interested in sports would value fairness. But fairness turns out to be rather complicated, at least for Walker. For Mitchell, it's pretty straightforward. As I explained earlier, Mitchell claims performance enhancing substances are wrong simply because . . . Walker concedes this point . . . However, Walker disagrees . . . . (Bernard, pars. 8–9)

Or look at the explanation of the writers' priorities, as in this example that highlights Betsy Samson's cueing words:

> While Chua's goal is to raise children who are "successful" (par. 1), Rosin believes "happiness" is more important than success (par. 12). In fact, Rosin claims that "success will not make you happy" (par. 12). (Samson, par. 9)

Remember that although writers search for common ground, they do not always find it. Determine whether the potential agreement the writer identifies seems likely, and note whether the writer adds qualifying words to soften any claims, as in these examples:

> Indeed, they appear to prepare the way for a potentially productive common-ground-building discussion when they conclude . . . (Mae, par. 9)

> The fact that Rosin seems to accept Chua's justification provides a basis for potential compromise between their opposing viewpoints.
>   Another basis for possible compromise is . . . (Samson, pars. 10–11)

For a complete list of motivating factors, turn to Analyze the Opposing Argument Essays on pp. 199–201.

Qualifying words

A FAIR AND IMPARTIAL PRESENTATION

Determine whether the writer comes across as fair and impartial in presenting the opposing points of view. To win and hold readers' confidence, the writer normally does the following:

- Represents the opposing sides fairly and accurately
- Refrains from taking a position on the issue
- Avoids judging either side's arguments
- Gives roughly equal attention to the opposing viewpoints

One strategy writers use to maintain their impartiality is to use quotations to present criticism, rather than presenting criticism in their own words. For example, Bernard quotes the *Mitchell Report* directly rather than paraphrasing the report:

> "The minority of players who used [performance enhancing] substances were wrong," the *Mitchell Report* concludes. (Bernard, par. 2)

Quotation

He also quotes ethicist Dr. Norman Fost, critiquing Mitchell's argument about unfairness:

> Fost asserts in "Steroid Hysteria: Unpacking the Claims" that "even if steroids did have . . . dire effects, it wouldn't follow that a competent adult should be prohibited from assuming those risks in exchange for the possible benefits. We allow adults to do things that are far riskier than even the most extreme claims about steroids, such as race car driving, and even playing football." (Bernard, par. 6)

Writers also maintain an impartial stance by using neutral language to describe the views they are analyzing and the proponents of those views. Betsy Samson, for example, describes Chua simply as a "Yale law professor" and Rosin as "a contributing editor for the *Atlantic*" (par. 3), avoiding any terms that could be perceived as critical or dismissive. She uses neutral verbs such as *outlines, believes,* and *claims* when describing the views espoused by the writers of the articles she is analyzing.

A CLEAR, LOGICAL ORGANIZATION

Examine the strategies the writer uses to make the points of agreement and disagreement clear and easy to follow, such as providing a clear *thesis* and *forecasting* statement announcing the areas of agreement and disagreement that the essay will focus on, as in this example from Bernard's essay:

Announces agreement

Transition signaling shift

Announces disagreement

They agree that the medical evidence is inconclusive. More importantly, they agree that there is a risk of side effects from PEDs. They agree that the medical risks to adolescents are, as Walker puts it, "substantial and potentially grave." But they disagree on the significance of the risks to adults, and they disagree on who should decide whether the risks are worth taking. (Bernard, par. 4)

Check to see whether the key terms used in the thesis and forecasting statement (or synonyms) are used again in topic sentences or headings. For example, Bernard uses the key term *health risk* both in a heading and in the topic sentence used to introduce the discussion of that risk:

Key term

HEADING	Should PEDs Be Banned from Baseball Because They Constitute a Significant Health Risk?
TOPIC SENTENCE	The health risks of using PEDs . . . (Bernard, par. 4)

(He used "medical risks" earlier.) Because common ground analyses are usually organized as a *comparison and contrast* between two opposing points of view, writers typically use the author's name to identify each viewpoint. In addition, they use *logical transitions* indicating comparison (*like, similarly, as well as*) and contrast (*whereas, but, although*) to make clear to readers the important similarities and differences between the two authors' positions on the issue.

Readings

Jeremy Bernard | *Lost Innocence*

AS AN AVID BASEBALL FAN, Jeremy Bernard has closely followed the many steroid scandals, so he asked his instructor if he could write about the issue. He planned to use as his two main texts George Mitchell's report and a Web site written in response to it. Even though these two texts were too long and complex for Bernard to cover in depth, his instructor gave him permission to use them if he met two criteria: his essay stayed within the page limit, and he refrained from stating his own position on the issue. (His instructor gave Bernard the opportunity to argue for one position or the other in his next essay, a position paper.) As you read, consider the following:

Links to Bernard's key sources are available online at **bedfordstmartins.com/theguide**.

- Does Bernard successfully keep his opinion to himself in this essay? Point to any places where you think he reveals his own position.

- How effective do you think Bernard is in finding common ground between Mitchell and Walker?

Bernard   *Lost Innocence*

GUIDE TO READING
GUIDE TO WRITING
A WRITER AT WORK
THINKING CRITICALLY

179

Basic Features

An Informative
Introduction

A Probing Analysis

A Fair and Impartial
Presentation

A Clear, Logical
Organization

In a nation committed to better living through chemistry — where Viagra-enabled men pursue silicone-contoured women — the national pastime has a problem of illicit chemical enhancement.

— George Will

1   Many American writers have waxed poetic about baseball. Walt Whitman, the great nineteenth-century poet, sang its praises: "It's our game — the American game." "More than anything," remarked Pete Hamill, the twentieth-century journalist and novelist, "it's a game of innocence" (Andrijeski). The age of innocence in baseball seems to have ended in the 1990s when "the Steroid Era" began and players from Mark McGwire to Roger Clemens, Barry Bonds, and Alex Rodriguez were identified as using performance enhancing drugs (PEDs). Such substances as anabolic steroids and human growth hormone are a concern in other sports as well, but the steroid scandal has been especially painful in baseball, possibly because of its special status as America's national pastime. As Daniel de la Rosa put it: "Baseball is part of the soul and fabric of the United States" ("Steroids").

2   In 2006, the concern was so great that George Mitchell, the former Senate Majority Leader and peace negotiator, was enlisted to investigate. "The minority of players who used [performance enhancing] substances were wrong," the *Mitchell Report* concludes. "They violated federal law and baseball policy, and they distorted the fairness of competition by trying to gain an unfair advantage over the majority of players who followed the law and the rules" (310).

3   An opposing position has been presented by respected baseball authority Eric Walker on his Web site *Steroids, Other "Drugs," and Baseball*. Walker concedes that using PEDs is against the law and against the rules of baseball. But he argues that the real issue is whether PEDs ought to be "illegal and banned" by Major League Baseball (MLB). He addresses many of Mitchell's arguments, but I will focus here on two of Mitchell's main reasons supporting the ban on PEDs: the health risk and fairness.

Should PEDs Be Banned from Baseball Because
They Constitute a Significant Health Risk?

4   The health risks of using PEDs would seem to be a question of fact on which everyone should be able to agree. Mitchell and Walker do agree, but not on everything. They agree that the medical evidence is inconclusive. More importantly, they agree that

Why does Bernard begin with the epigraph and quotes by Whitman and Hamill?

Why is this information worth presenting to readers?

How does Bernard frame the debate in pars. 2 and 3? How fair does he seem?

Skim the essay to see how Bernard uses key terms to forecast his main points.

How do the repeated words and sentence structure help readers understand the two positions?

there is a risk of side effects from PEDs. They agree that the medical risks to adolescents are, as Walker puts it, "substantial and potentially grave." But they disagree on the significance of the risks to adults, and they disagree on who should decide whether the risks are worth taking.

5   Mitchell and Walker consider the medical evidence for a variety of PEDs. They each cite reputable scientists and research studies. While Walker concludes that "PEDs are by no means guaranteed harmless," he argues that the side effects tend to be mild and reversible. Mitchell takes a more negative view, arguing that there is "sufficient data to conclude that there is an association between steroid abuse and significant adverse side effects" (6). Nevertheless, it is notable that when discussing each of the possible side effects, he is careful to use hedging words like *can* and *may* and to acknowledge that clinical trial data is limited. So it's possible that Mitchell and Walker are closer on the health risks than their arguments suggest.

6   However, Mitchell and Walker seem to be miles apart when it comes to the question of who should decide whether the risks are worth taking. Walker argues that adults ought to have the responsibility to decide for themselves. To support this ethical argument, Walker cites authorities such as Dr. Norman Fost, Director of the Program in Medical Ethics at the University of Wisconsin. Fost asserts in "Steroid Hysteria: Unpacking the Claims" that "even if steroids did have . . . dire effects, it wouldn't follow that a competent adult should be prohibited from assuming those risks in exchange for the possible benefits. We allow adults to do things that are far riskier than even the most extreme claims about steroids, such as race car driving, and even playing football."

7   Although Mitchell does not address this ethical question directly, he clearly thinks Major League Baseball should make the decision for the players by banning PEDs. While Mitchell expresses other ethical concerns (discussed in the sections below), he seems not to have considered the ethics of who should decide whether the risks are worth taking. Perhaps he and Walker would be able to find common ground if they discussed this question directly and if the players themselves made their opinions known.

Should PEDs Be Banned from Baseball Because They Give an Unfair Advantage to Athletes Willing to Take the Risk?

8   You'd think anyone interested in sports would value fairness. But fairness turns out to be rather complicated, at least for Walker. For Mitchell, it's pretty straightforward.

Where does Bernard choose to quote and paraphrase? Are these choices appropriate?

What do these highlighted transitions signal?

How does citing Fost get at a potential basis for agreement between Walker and Mitchell?

How does Bernard avoid taking a position here?

How do the headings help you as a reader?

How effectively does Bernard transition to and introduce his second point?

As I explained earlier, Mitchell claims performance enhancing substances are wrong simply because they give some players an "unfair advantage" over those who play by the rules (310). Walker concedes this point. In fact, he says "that is why PEDs are banned."

9   However, Walker disagrees with Mitchell's way of defining "a level playing field" as one where "success and advancement . . . is the result of ability and hard work" (Mitchell 5). According to Walker, Mitchell makes a false distinction between what is natural and unnatural. Whereas certain aids to performance — such as better bats, chemical-filled drinks like Gatorade, Tommy John and Lasik surgery — are considered natural and therefore allowable, other aids — particularly PEDs — are deemed unnatural and banned. To support his argument, Walker cites Fost again. "Here's what Fost wrote in 'Steroid Hysteria': 'There is no coherent argument to support the view that enhancing performance is unfair. If it were, we should ban coaching and training. Competition can be unfair if there is unequal access to such enhancements.'"

10   In other words, unequal access is the key to the unfairness argument. On this point, Mitchell and Walker seem to agree. The argument is really about making sure that there is a level playing field. Mitchell puts his finger on it when he explains that

> the illegal use of these substances by some players is unfair to the majority of players who do not use them. These players have a right to expect a level playing field where success and advancement to the major leagues is the result of ability and hard work. They should not be forced to choose between joining the ranks of those who illegally use these substances or falling short of their ambition to succeed at the major league level. (5)

Ethicists call this a coercion argument. "Steroids are coercive," Fost explains, because "if your opponents use them, you have to" as well or you risk losing. Walker has a simple solution: allow PEDs to be "equally available to any who might want them." He argues that there are lots of requirements or expectations that athletes regularly make choices about. He sees "no logical or ethical distinction between — just for example — killer workouts and PEDs." Therefore, Walker concludes, each athlete has to decide for him- or herself what's "appropriate or necessary."

11   Mitchell, on the other hand, assumes it should be the responsibility of Major League Baseball to set rules that protect the athletes and protect the sport. He

---

How do the highlighted transitions help you as a reader?

Why does Bernard indent this quotation?

How effectively does Bernard analyze the argument about fairness?

acknowledges that players "are responsible for their actions" (311). But he insists that "Commissioners, club officials, the Players Association, and players" should share "responsibility for the steroids era" and "should join in" the "effort to bring the era of steroids and human growth hormone to an end" (311). To initiate a new era, the Baseball Hall of Fame has launched a national education outreach program that encourages individuals to sign a pledge to remain free of performance enhancing substances (National). By saying that everyone involved in Major League Baseball shares some responsibility for its future well being, Mitchell appears also to be reaching out to critics like Walker who share a common love of the sport. It seems that they may not really be that far apart after all.

How effective is this way of ending the essay?

What can you learn from these citations for your own essay?

Works Cited

Andrijeski, Peter. *Pete's Baseball Quotes*. Peter Andrijeski, n.d. Web. 24 Apr. 2009.

de la Rosa, Daniel. "Steroids in Baseball: The Detritus of a Dark Era." *Bleacher Report*. Bleacher Report, 14 Jan. 2012. Web. 23 Apr. 2012.

Fost, Norman. "Steroid Hysteria: Unpacking the Claims." *Virtual Mentor* 7.11 (Nov. 2005): n. pag. Web. 24 Apr. 2009.

Mitchell, George J. *Report to the Commissioner of Baseball of an Independent Investigation into the Illegal Use of Steroids and Other Performance Enhancing Substances by Players in Major League Baseball*. Office of the Commissioner of Baseball, 2007. Web. 25 Apr. 2009.

National Baseball Hall of Fame. "'Be a Superior Example' Encourages Individuals of All Ages to Sign Pledge." *National Baseball Hall of Fame and Museum*. National Baseball Hall of Fame, 8 Feb. 2012. Web. 23 Apr. 2012.

Walker, Eric. *Steroids, Other "Drugs," and Baseball*. The Owlcroft Company, 2008. Web. 23 Apr. 2009.

Will, George. "George Will Quotes." *The Baseball Almanac*. Baseball Almanac, 2009. Web. 25 Apr. 2009.

Betsy Samson | *Does Mother Know Best?*

A PSYCHOLOGY MAJOR with an interest in child development, Betsy Samson wanted to analyze two controversial articles about parenting that were published in the *Wall Street Journal*. In addition to focusing her analysis on these two articles, by Amy Chua and Hanna Rosin, Samson draws on several other sources about "helicopter parenting"— a parenting style that includes close interaction between parents and children, even as the "child" enters adulthood. As you read, consider these questions:

Samson's key sources appear on pp. 219–27.

- According to Samson's quote from College Parents of America, "Many parents 'virtually walk through the day with their [child] (via cell phone, texting, Twitter, or Facebook)'" (par. 2). In your experience, how common is this phenomenon?
- What do you think are the advantages and/or disadvantages of such close contact between parents and their college-age children?

1   When we are infants, we are completely dependent on our parents. We need them to make every decision for us. But as we grow older, we want to become independent, making more and more decisions for ourselves. This process of seeking autonomy (or self-rule) apparently begins in earnest in what is commonly called "the terrible twos" and often reaches a high point in adolescent rebellion. By the time we go to college, most of us expect to be treated like adults.

2   But nowadays even college students tend to maintain close contact with their parents. According to College Parents of America, many parents "virtually walk through the day with their [child] (via cell phone, texting, Twitter, or Facebook)" ("Affirming" 1). These parents are often called "helicopter parents," using a term made popular by Foster Cline and Jim Fay in their 1990 book *Parenting with Love and Logic*. They describe helicopter parents as "[hovering] over and [rescuing] their children whenever trouble arises" (23). Hovering is seen by social historian Barbara Dafoe Whitehead as a positive characteristic of helicopter parenting: she says that this "high level of oversight and supervision, keeping tabs on the kids but not interfering in every activity or decision" makes helicopter parenting "a positive style of child-rearing" (qtd. in Aucoin). Rescuing, however, is considered a negative characteristic because, as Whitehead explains, it does not allow "kids the freedom to make a decision and live with its consequences."

3   How much influence should parents have in their children's decision making as kids get older? When does parental influence cross the line and, however well-intentioned,

become detrimental? These are questions that parents and children wrestle with constantly, which is perhaps part of the reason their answers can provoke such intense reactions. The perennial debate about parenting styles heated up when the *Wall Street Journal* ran an excerpt from Yale law professor Amy Chua's new book *Battle Hymn of the Tiger Mother*. A number of outraged responses were subsequently published, including one in the *Wall Street Journal* by Hanna Rosin, a contributing editor for the *Atlantic*. Chua's article is provocatively titled "Why Chinese Mothers Are Superior," and Rosin's response is ironically titled "Mother Inferior?" Chua and Rosin take a very different approach to parenting, but their goals may be closer than they think. Both can be categorized as helicopter parents who are trying in their own way to help their children become happy, fulfilled adults.

4   Chua's article outlines her "Chinese parenting" philosophy and practice, contrasting them with typical "Western" views of parenting. Chua is careful to acknowledge that these terms are broad generalizations, even "stereotypes" (par. 4), and that both "Chinese" and "Western" parents actually "come in all varieties" (par. 2). Putting aside what she calls "our squeamishness about cultural stereotypes," Chua claims that "there are tons of studies . . . showing marked and quantifiable differences between Chinese and Westerners" regarding parenting (par. 4). She refers to one study, although she doesn't give a citation. It is also worth noting that within Chua's own family, Chinese and Western viewpoints are represented by herself and her husband respectively.

5   Chua's main argument is that children of Chinese immigrants usually are high-achieving because their parents are proud to be helicopter parents intensely involved in every aspect of their children's lives. More importantly, as Chua's anecdote about her daughter Lulu's effort to learn to play a difficult piano piece demonstrates, children raised the Chinese way succeed because their parents force them to drill until they achieve mastery. Chua's helicoptering, then, certainly involves hovering but does not include rescuing. In fact, it's aim is the opposite, as Chua explains at the end of her article: "the Chinese believe that the best way to protect their children is . . . letting them see what they're capable of, and arming them with skills, work habits and inner confidence" (par. 35).

6   Rosin begins her article by describing her own parenting style as the opposite of Chua's. Whereas Chua calls herself a "Tiger Mother," Rosin shows that she herself is

a pussycat who happily wastes time "playing useless board games" with her children (par. 1). Although she identifies herself as "the weak-willed, pathetic Western parent that Ms. Chua describes," Rosin argues assertively for her nurturing approach to parenting (par. 2). Like Chua, Rosin can be categorized as a helicopter parent. Rosin claims not to pay the same "vigilant attention" Chua does, but she admits to some degree of hovering — apparently spent playing with her children and driving them to extracurricular activities (par. 3).

7   Also like Chua, Rosin does not appear to rescue her children, possibly because she doesn't need to. Indeed, Rosin seems to be concerned that her children are, if anything, too obedient: "In my household, it's a struggle to get my children to steal a cookie from the cookie jar without immediately confessing" (par. 10). Rosin complains that regardless of whether they are raised in the traditional Chinese or contemporary American way, many children today are being raised to be "dutiful proto-adults, always responsible and good, incapable of proper childhood rebellion" (par. 4).

8   The idea that "childhood rebellion" is "proper" and ought to be encouraged, not discouraged, surely separates Rosin from Chua. Chua speculates that the Chinese tradition of "Confucian filial piety" explains, at least in part, "the understanding" that Chinese children owe their parents absolute obedience (par. 14). This notion of "proper" rebellion is the crux of Rosin's disagreement with Chua:

> Ms. Chua has the diagnosis of American childhood exactly backward. What privileged American children need is not more skills and rules and math drills. They need to lighten up and roam free, to express themselves in ways not dictated by their uptight, over-invested parents. (par. 4)

Rosin sounds a lot like Huck Finn in her traditional American idea that "childhood should be full of spontaneity, freedom, discovery and experience" (par. 15).

9   Both authors believe, as Chua says, that like all "decent parents" they "want to do what's best for their children," but they appear to have very different ideas about what is "best" (par. 34). While Chua's goal is to raise children who are "successful" (par. 1), Rosin believes "happiness" is more important than success (par. 12). In fact, Rosin claims that "success will not make you happy" (par. 12). Chua, on the other hand, states that the measure of children's success is "academic achievement" (par. 4). In this opinion, Chua

is aligning herself with Chinese American immigrant mothers who responded to a survey. Like them, Chua thinks that children's academic success is also the primary measure of a parent's effectiveness: "if children did not excel at school then . . . parents 'were not doing their job'" (par. 4). According to Chua, the same survey reports that while "almost 70% of the Western mothers said either that 'stressing academic success is not good for children' or that 'parents need to foster the idea that learning is fun,'" "roughly 0% of the Chinese mothers felt the same way" (par. 4). Rosin doesn't directly address the question of academic achievement, but she does assert that "it is better to have a happy, moderately successful child than a miserable high-achiever" (par. 12).

10   Although Rosin sets up an opposition between happiness and success, she concedes that "Ms. Chua's most compelling argument is that happiness comes from mastery" (par. 9). This is a crucial point of agreement between Rosin and Chua for two reasons. First of all, Chua concedes the value of happiness as a worthwhile goal. Second, Rosin concedes Chua's argument that "nothing is fun until you're good at it" (Rosin, par. 9). Chua's justification for overriding her children's preferences is based on the observation that children inevitably want to avoid hard work and the corollary assumption that practice and perseverance are necessary to excel at anything (par. 5). The fact that Rosin seems to accept Chua's justification provides a basis for potential compromise between their opposing viewpoints.

11   Another basis for possible compromise is Rosin's agreement with Chua's analysis that Western parents have "conflicted feelings about achievement" (Rosin, par. 13). Rosin goes so far as to admit that she does "not have the guts or the tools" to do what Chua does to help her children fulfill their potential. Furthermore, Rosin speculates that "a large part of the fascination with Ms. Chua's book" is that other Western parents, like herself, find Chua's book "more seductive" — and perhaps also more complex — than the "distilled media version" (including the excerpt published in the *Wall Street Journal*) makes it appear (par. 5). Rosin implies that Chua is intentionally exaggerating her approach and ultimately may be somewhat "more pussycat" than tiger mother.

12   Finally, it may be worth pointing out that Chua and Rosin both assume that their behavior, whether tasking their children with math puzzles and piano practice or playing games that foster imagination, plays an essential formative role in their children's development. However, some research in developmental psychology — such as that reported

in Judith Rich Harris's controversial book *The Nurture Assumption* — suggests that hered-
ity and peer group interactions may play a role equal to, or perhaps even greater than,
that of parenting practices.

Works Cited

Aucoin, Don. "For Some, Helicopter Parenting Delivers Benefits." *Boston Globe*. Boston
Globe, 3 Mar. 2009. Web. 8 Feb. 2012.

Chua, Amy. "Why Chinese Mothers Are Superior." *Wall Street Journal*. Dow Jones, 8 Jan.
2011. Web. 8 Feb. 2012.

Cline, Foster, and Jim Fay. *Parenting with Love and Logic*. Colorado Springs: Piñon Press,
1990. Print.

College Parents of America. "Affirming 'Helicopter Parents': Redefining the Title." College
Parents of America. College Parents of America, n.d. Web. 8 Feb. 2012.

Harris, Judith Rich. *The Nurture Assumption: Why Children Turn Out the Way They Do*. New
York: Free Press, 2009. Print.

Rosin, Hanna. "Mother Inferior?" *Wall Street Journal*. Dow Jones, 15 Jan. 2011. Web. 8
Feb. 2012.

Make connections: Parenting styles.

REFLECT

According to social historian Barbara Dafoe Whitehead, "keeping tabs" on children
even when they are in college is a characteristic of good parenting as long as children
have "the freedom to make a decision and live with its consequences" (qtd. in Samson,
par. 2). To think about parenting styles, reflect on your own experience as well as your
observations of other parent-child relationships. Your instructor may ask you to post
your thoughts on a class discussion board or to discuss them with other students
in class. Use these questions to get started:

- If you have experienced or witnessed helicopter parenting, what do you think are
  its defining characteristics?

- Do you agree or disagree with Whitehead's opinion that "hovering" is good as
  long as it does not interfere with children's decision making, especially as they
  get older?

- How do Chua's and Rosin's different parenting styles compare to your own
  experience?

[ANALYZE]   ## Use the basic features.

AN INFORMATIVE INTRODUCTION TO THE ISSUE AND OPPOSING POSITIONS: PROVIDING BACKGROUND INFORMATION

Amy Chua's *Wall Street Journal* article, with its challenging title and tone, helped popularize her memoir *Battle Hymn of the Tiger Mother*. It fueled controversy, generating many reviews and opinion pieces—including Rosin's—in newspapers, on blogs, and on talk shows. Writing only a short time after Chua's article was published, Samson could assume that many of her readers would be likely to know about the controversy. Nevertheless, she begins by providing some background information to help readers think about the issue.

ANALYZE & WRITE

Write a few paragraphs analyzing and evaluating how Samson introduces the issue:

1 How does discussing what she calls the child's "process of seeking autonomy" (par. 1) help Samson engage readers' interest in parenting styles? (You may assume that her audience includes both her instructor and other first-year writing students.)

2 Notice that in paragraph 2 Samson provides information about helicopter parenting from two different sources, Cline and Fay, and Whitehead (quoted in Aucoin). How effectively does this information contextualize the debate between Chua and Rosin?

A PROBING ANALYSIS: EXPLORING POINTS OF POSSIBLE AGREEMENT

In paragraphs 7 and 8, Samson focuses her analysis on Rosin's and Chua's different cultural traditions—what she calls "the crux" of their disagreement. But then, in paragraphs 9–11, Samson identifies points on which she thinks there may be the possibility of agreement.

ANALYZE & WRITE

Write a couple of paragraphs evaluating how effectively Samson analyzes the potential for common ground between Chua's and Rosin's positions:

1 Reread paragraphs 9–10, in which Samson discusses the authors' ideas about success and happiness. On what basis does Samson think there may be room here for agreement?

2 How does Samson's analysis in paragraph 11 bolster her idea that there may be some potential for compromise between Rosin's and Chua's viewpoints?

A FAIR AND IMPARTIAL PRESENTATION: CHOICE OF VERBS

Writers of common ground essays try to use descriptive but unbiased language when they introduce quotations. For example, Jeremy Bernard uses verbs like *concludes, argues, cites, expresses,* and *assumes.* Melissa Mae, whose essay appears on pp. 190–93, uses *writes, thinks, asserts, argues,* and *labels.* With these descriptive verbs, Bernard and Mae do not reveal their attitude toward the authors or what they wrote. They express no judgments but act as impartial reporters.

Mae   *Laying Claim to a Higher Morality*

GUIDE TO READING
GUIDE TO WRITING
A WRITER AT WORK
THINKING CRITICALLY

189

ANALYZE & WRITE

Write a few paragraphs analyzing and assessing Samson's fairness and impartiality:

1. Skim Samson's essay, noting the verbs she uses to introduce quotations from Chua and Rosin.

2. Consider whether the verbs Samson uses present Chua's and Rosin's ideas fairly and impartially.

3. Where, if anywhere, do you think Samson implies her own opinion or evaluates the authors she's analyzing? How can you tell?

A CLEAR, LOGICAL ORGANIZATION: USING TRANSITIONS

To help readers track the points of agreement and disagreement, writers of common ground essays rely heavily on transitions that identify similarities and differences in the texts being analyzed.

ANALYZE & WRITE

Write a few paragraphs analyzing the effectiveness of Samson's use of transitions to make her analysis clear and easy to follow:

1. Skim Samson's essay, circling the transitions she uses to signal similarities and differences between Chua's and Rosin's arguments.

2. Assess how well these transitions work to keep you oriented as you read the essay. What would you change, if anything, to make the essay easier to follow?

Consider possible topics: Debates about cultural issues.

[RESPOND]

According to Samson, the crux of the disagreement between Chua and Rosin on parenting stems from their different cultural traditions. You might consider other debates that are affected by cultural values, such as same-sex marriage, abortion, and contraception.

Melissa Mae | *Laying Claim to a Higher Morality*

CONCERNED ABOUT both terrorism and our treatment of terror suspects, Melissa Mae asked her instructor if she could analyze the controversy about the U.S. government's treatment of detainees suspected of terrorism. She read two published essays on torture recommended by her instructor, one coauthored by law professor Mirko Bagaric and law lecturer Julie Clarke, the other by retired Army chaplain Kermit D. Johnson. Mae decided to focus her essay more on their commonalities than on the obvious differences between them. As you read this essay, consider these questions:

- How well does Mae succeed in finding areas of potential common ground between the authors she is analyzing?

Links to Mae's key sources are available online at **bedfordstmartins.com /theguide**.

- How effectively does Mae maintain a neutral tone in presenting these different points of view on such a highly emotional issue? Point to any places where her position is evident, and indicate how you identified it.

1   In 2004, when the abuse of detainees at Abu Ghraib became known, many Americans became concerned that the government was using torture as part of its interrogation of war-on-terror detainees. Although the government denied a torture program existed, we now know that the Bush Administration did order what they called "enhanced interrogation techniques" such as waterboarding and sleep deprivation. The debate over whether these techniques constitute torture continues today.

2   In 2005 and 2006, when Kermit D. Johnson wrote "Inhuman Behavior" and Mirko Bagaric and Julie Clarke wrote "A Case for Torture," this debate was just heating up. Bagaric and Clarke, professor and lecturer, respectively, in the law faculty at Australia's Deakin University, argued that torture is necessary in extreme circumstances to save innocent lives. Major Johnson, a retired Army chaplain, wrote that torture should never be used for any reason whatsoever. Although their positions appear to be diametrically opposed, some common ground exists, because the authors of both essays share a goal—the preservation of human life—as well as a belief in the importance of morality.

3   The authors of both essays present their positions on torture as the surest way to save lives. Bagaric and Clarke write specifically about the lives of innocent victims threatened by hostage-takers or terrorists and claim that the use of torture in such cases to forestall the loss of innocent life is "universally accepted" as "self-defense." Whereas Bagaric and Clarke think saving lives justifies torture, however, Johnson believes renouncing torture saves lives. Johnson asserts: "A clear-cut repudiation of torture or abuse is . . . essential to the safety of the troops" (26), who need to be able to "claim the full protection of the Geneva Conventions . . . when they are captured, in this or any war" (27).

4   This underlying shared value—human life is precious—represents one important aspect of common ground between the two positions. In addition to this, however, the authors of both essays agree that torture is ultimately a moral issue, and that morality is

worth arguing about. For Bagaric and Clarke, torture is morally defensible under certain, extreme circumstances when it "is the only means, due to the immediacy of the situation, to save the life of an innocent person"; in effect, Bagaric and Clarke argue that the end justifies the means. Johnson argues against this common claim, writing that "whenever we torture or mistreat prisoners, we are capitulating morally to the enemy—in fact, adopting the terrorist ethic that the end justifies the means" (26). Bagaric and Clarke, in their turn, anticipate Johnson's argument and refute it by arguing that those who believe (as Johnson does) that "torture is always wrong" are "misguided." Bagaric and Clarke label Johnson's kind of thinking "absolutist," and claim it is a "distorted" moral judgment.

5   It is not surprising that, as a chaplain, Johnson would adopt a religious perspective on morality. Likewise, it should not be surprising that, as faculty at a law school, Bagaric and Clarke would take a more pragmatic and legalistic perspective. It is hard to imagine how they could bridge their differences when their moral perspectives are so different, but perhaps the answer lies in the real-world application of their principles.

6   The authors of these essays refer to the kind of situation typically raised when a justification for torture is debated: Bagaric and Clarke call it "the hostage scenario," and Johnson refers to it as the "scenario about a ticking time bomb" (26). As the Parents Television Council has demonstrated (see fig. 1), scenes of torture dominated television in the period the authors were writing about, and may have had a profound influence on the persuasive power of the scenario.

7   Johnson rejects the scenario outright as an unrealistic "Hollywood drama" (26). Bagaric and Clarke's take on it is somewhat more complicated. First, Bagaric and Clarke ask the rhetorical question: "Will a real-life situation actually occur where the only option is between torturing a wrongdoer or saving an innocent person?" They initially answer, "Perhaps not." Then, however, they offer the real-life example of Douglas Wood, a 63-year-old engineer taken hostage in Iraq and held for six weeks until he was rescued by U.S. and Iraqi soldiers.

8   At first glance, they seem to offer this example to refute Johnson's claim that such scenarios don't occur in real life. However, a news report about the rescue of

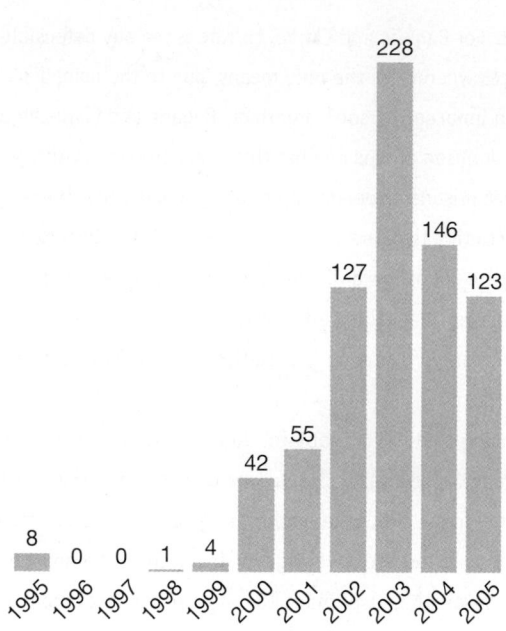

Fig. 1. Parents Television Council, "Scenes of Torture on Primetime Network TV"; rpt. in "Primetime Torture," *Human Rights First* (Human Rights First, 2009; web; n. pag.).

Wood published in the *Age,* where Bagaric and Clarke's essay was also published, says that the soldiers "effectively 'stumbled across Wood' during a 'routine' raid on a suspected insurgent weapons cache" ("Firefight"). The report's wording suggests that the Wood example does not really fit the Hollywood-style hostage scenario; Wood's rescuers appear to have acted on information they got from ordinary informants rather than through torture.

9   By using this example, rather than one that fits the ticking time bomb scenario, Bagaric and Clarke seem to be conceding that such scenarios are exceedingly rare. Indeed, they appear to prepare the way for a potentially productive common-ground-building discussion when they conclude: "Even if a real-life situation where torture is justifiable does not eventuate, the above argument in favour of torture in limited

circumstances needs to be made because it will encourage the community to think more carefully about moral judgments."

10   Although Bagaric and Clarke continue to take a situational view of torture (considering the morality of an act in light of its particular situation) and Johnson does not waver in seeing torture in terms of moral absolutes, a discussion about real-world applications of their principles could allow them to find common ground. Because they all value the preservation of life, they already have a basis for mutual respect and might be motivated to work together to find ways of acting for the greatest good—to "lay claim to a higher morality" (26).

Works Cited

Bagaric, Mirko, and Julie Clarke. "A Case for Torture." *theage.com.au*. The Age, 17 May 2005. Web. 1 May 2009.

"Firefight as Wood Rescued." *theage.com.au*. The Age, 16 June 2005. Web. 2 May 2009.

Johnson, Kermit D. "Inhuman Behavior: A Chaplain's View of Torture." *Christian Century* 18 Apr. 2006: 26–27. *Academic Search Premier*. Web. 2 May 2009.

Make connections: Hollywood and the ticking time bomb scenario.

[REFLECT]

The post-9/11 television series *24* brought the ticking time bomb scenario into our homes weekly. Other popular programs such as *Lost* and *Law & Order*, as well as many films, have also shown scenes of torture.

In her essay, Mae includes a bar graph she found on the Web site *Human Rights First* to show how prevalent scenes of torture became during the period her authors are writing about, and she asks us to think about whether the hostage and ticking time bomb scenarios so often used to justify torture are Hollywood fantasies or real-life situations.

To judge Mae's essay against your own experience, consider the films and television shows you have seen where someone is tortured. Was the torturer the "good guy" or the "bad guy"? Was the torture quick and effective? Was it depicted as justifiable, even patriotic? Your instructor may ask you to post your thoughts on a class discussion board or to discuss them with other students in class. Use these questions to get started:

- Have your views on torture been influenced by the way torture has been portrayed on television and in film?
- How do you think torture should be portrayed, if at all?

ANALYZE

Use the basic features.

AN INFORMATIVE INTRODUCTION TO THE ISSUE AND OPPOSING POSITIONS: PLACING THE ISSUE IN A HISTORICAL CONTEXT

Common ground essays often situate the issue in time, as Jeremy Bernard does when he locates the end of baseball's "age of innocence" and the beginning of "the Steroid Era" in the 1990s and suggests that the issue came to a head in 2006 with the *Mitchell Report*. Common ground essays may also provide details about the historical context so readers can better understand the issue and the opposing positions.

ANALYZE & WRITE

Write a couple of paragraphs analyzing how Mae contextualizes her issue and opposing positions:

1. Reread paragraph 1. Why do you think Mae chose to mention Abu Ghraib? What, if anything, do you know about it? How does referring to Abu Ghraib help provide historical context for readers?

2. In paragraphs 2 and 5, Mae introduces the authors whose arguments she is analyzing. How does the information she provides contextualize the issue for readers and help them understand the different points of view?

A PROBING ANALYSIS: EXPLORING MORAL ARGUMENTS

Although common ground essays seek ways to bridge differences, sometimes the analysis does nothing more than reveal how deep the disagreement is because it is based on fundamentally different values or ways of thinking about the issue.

ANALYZE & WRITE

Write a couple of paragraphs examining Mae's analysis:

1. What does Mae mean when she characterizes Johnson as "seeing torture in terms of moral absolutes" and Bagaric and Clarke as taking "a situational view of torture" (par. 10)? How does this characterization help explain why Mae cannot find common ground between her authors?

2. How does Mae use the news report about the Douglas Wood hostage situation and the ticking time bomb scenario to analyze the main differences in their points of view?

A FAIR AND IMPARTIAL PRESENTATION: USING AUTHORITIES

Writers try to adopt an impartial stance when analyzing opposing arguments. One method Jeremy Bernard uses is to quote an authority (for example, in pars. 9 and 10) to critique one of the authors he is analyzing, rather than doing so directly himself.

ANALYZE & WRITE

Write a paragraph analyzing and evaluating Mae's stance:

1 Reread paragraphs 7–9, in which Mae presents information on the Douglas Wood hostage situation.

2 How does the Wood example help Mae remain impartial as she questions Bagaric and Clarke's argument? How effective is this strategy?

A CLEAR, LOGICAL ORGANIZATION: USING VISUALS

Writers of common ground essays usually try to make the analysis clear and direct. Fairly early in the essay, they typically state the essay's thesis about the possibility of finding common ground and forecast the main points of disagreement and agreement. They may also include graphics to help convey data clearly and concisely.

ANALYZE & WRITE

Write a couple of paragraphs analyzing how clearly and logically Mae presents the issue to her readers:

1 Skim paragraph 2 and highlight Mae's thesis statement. What are the two topics Mae plans to discuss in the essay?

2 Skim the rest of the essay and note where these two topics are brought up again.

3 Consider the ticking time bomb (or hostage) scenario in relation to the two topics Mae focuses on. How does this scenario help illuminate these two topics? How does the graph help convey information and illuminate these topics? What element(s) of Mae's subject does the graph illuminate?

Consider possible topics: Debates about current political issues.

RESPOND

To find issues that are currently under discussion, look at the op-ed, opinion and editorial pages of newspapers and blogs. For example, through your campus library, you might be able to use databases such as LexisNexis Academic to search for newspaper editorials.

For an additional student reading, go to **bedfordstmartins .com/theguide/epages**.

PLAYING WITH GENRE

Talk Shows and Blogs

Efforts to find common ground require the full expression of opposing viewpoints. Perhaps the most familiar expression of opposing viewpoints comes from television talk shows like *Washington Week, Real Time with Bill Maher,* and *The View,* which explicitly present opposing views as context for a wide-ranging discussion of current issues. Online, sites such as *Bloggingheads.tv* and *Opposing Views* (www.opposingviews.com) offer commentary from experts with opposing perspectives on current issues.

Will Wilkinson (*The Fly Bottle, The Economist*) and Jonathan Haidt (University of Virginia, *The Righteous Mind*)

- Self-righteous liberals think it's OK to eat dogs   6:55
- Who says morality has a single foundation?   10:48
- Should we let parents treat kids as they please?   6:09
- Why America is so religious   4:09
- Why are Europeans getting happier?   6:08
- How moral truth is like the market value of gold   8:17

PLAY ENTIRE VIDEO

While these media projects vary in their commitment to a "fair and unbiased" presentation, most of them do exhibit the other basic features common to searches for common ground: an introduction to the issue that highlights points of similarity and difference, a presentation of the views by the people who hold them, and a structure (of the show or site and the host's commentary) that provides a perceptible, if not always logical, organization.

As you work on your own common ground analysis, you might want to consult some of these media projects, both for factual information and for inspiration. If the format in which you are working allows for it—if, for example, you are creating a poster, Web site, or video—consider taking advantage of the strategies available to those working in multimedia. For example, you could embed videos of experts articulating their positions or artifacts relevant to the positions you are explaining. (Always remember to document properly any material you might use that was created by someone else.)

 For an interactive version of this feature, plus activities, go to
bedfordstmartins.com/theguide/epages.

The Writing Assignment

Write an essay analyzing two or more essays taking different positions on an issue. You may also draw on other sources for background information or context. Your purpose is to analyze the position essays to understand their authors' main points of disagreement and to suggest ways to build common ground based on shared values, concerns, needs, and interests.

This Guide to Writing is designed to help you compose your own common ground essay and apply what you have learned from reading other essays in the same genre. This Starting Points chart will help you find answers to questions you might have about composing an essay finding common ground. Use the chart to find the guidance you need, when you need it.

STARTING POINTS: FINDING COMMON GROUND

An Informative Introduction to the Issue and Opposing Positions

How do I come up with an issue to write about?

- Consider possible topics. (pp. 189, 195)
- Choose opposing argument essays to write about. (pp. 198–99)
- Test Your Choice (p. 201)

How can I interest my readers in the issue?

- Determine the writer's purpose and audience. (p. 175)
- Assess the genre's basic features: An informative introduction to the issue and opposing positions. (pp. 175–76)
- An Informative Introduction to the Issue and Opposing Positions: Providing Background Information (p. 188)
- An Informative Introduction to the Issue and Opposing Positions: Placing the Issue in a Historical Context (p. 194)
- Think about your readers. (pp. 201–2)
- Research the issue. (p. 202)
- Write the opening sentences. (pp. 206–7)

How can I give readers an overview of the debate?

- Assess the genre's basic features: An informative introduction to the issue and opposing positions. (pp. 175–76)
- Research the issue. (p. 202)
- Present the issue to your readers. (p. 202)

A Probing Analysis

How do I identify the areas of disagreement and possible areas of common ground?

- Assess the genre's basic features: A probing analysis. (pp. 176–77)
- A Probing Analysis: Exploring Points of Possible Agreement (p. 188)
- A Probing Analysis: Exploring Moral Arguments (p. 194)
- Analyze the opposing argument essays. (pp. 199–201)
- Develop your analysis (pp. 202–3)
- Test Your Analysis (p. 203)
- Formulate a working thesis statement. (pp. 203–4)

A Fair and Impartial Presentation

How do I avoid entering the debate myself?

- Assess the genre's basic features: A fair and impartial presentation. (p. 177)
- A Fair and Impartial Presentation: Choice of Verbs (pp. 188–89)
- A Fair and Impartial Presentation: Using Authorities (p. 195)
- Consider your tone. (p. 204)
- Weave quoted material into your own sentences. (pp. 204–5)

A Clear, Logical Organization

How can I make my essay clear?

- Assess the genre's basic features: A clear, logical organization. (pp. 177–78)
- A Clear, Logical Organization: Using Transitions (p. 189)
- A Clear, Logical Organization: Using Visuals (p. 195)
- Create an outline that will organize your analysis effectively for your readers. (pp. 205–6)

Writing a Draft: Invention, Research, Planning, and Composing

The activities in this section will help you choose argument essays to write about and assist you in developing your analysis of the arguments. Do the activities in any order that makes sense to you (and your instructor), and return to them as needed as you revise. Your writing in response to many of these activities can be used in a rough draft that you will be able to improve after receiving feedback from your classmates and instructor.

For more on searching databases, see Chapter 24, pp. 674–79.

▪▪ Choose opposing argument essays to write about.

Access the e-Pages and Web site at **bedfordstmartins.com /theguide**.

Your instructor may ask you to write on one of the debates from the appendix to this chapter or from the e-Pages and companion Web site for this book. If you are permitted to find your own opposing argument essays to write about, you could begin

Writing a Draft   GUIDE TO READING
GUIDE TO WRITING
A WRITER AT WORK
THINKING CRITICALLY   **199**

by reviewing the Consider Possible Topics activities following the readings (pp. 189, 195). Alternatively, you might search for op-ed articles in newspapers and blogs, using LexisNexis Academic or other databases accessible through your college library. Your instructor also may invite you to survey such Web sites as procon.org or controversialissues.org, or to find articles on the Room for Debate page on the *New York Times*'s Web site (nytimes.com/roomfordebate).

When choosing opposing argument essays, it can help if one writer is responding to the other (as in Samson's choice of Chua and Rosin and Bernard's choice of Mitchell and Walker). However, it is not a requirement that the arguments refer explicitly to each other. What is necessary is that they both

- address the same controversial issue;
- take different positions on the issue and offer thoughtful arguments supporting their position;
- articulate clear disagreements but also have the potential for common ground — possibly in shared values, priorities, or concerns; and
- be interesting to you and your readers, and worth the time and effort you will need to invest.

Analyze the opposing argument essays.

The following activities will help you identify the basic features of the opposing arguments you are analyzing and assist you in identifying motivating factors underlying the points of disagreement and potential agreement you find in the essays. Your instructor may ask you to use the first Ways In activity to annotate the essays as you read them, and then to complete the Annotations Chart, which will help you organize and draft your common ground analysis. Keep in mind that most writers need to reread parts of the opposing argument essays more than once.

HOW CAN I ANALYZE EACH ARGUMENT ESSAY?

WAYS IN

1. Start by reading each essay, highlighting and labeling in the margin where you find the following basic features of the argument:
   - **Issue**   Where the writer introduces the issue
   - **Position**   Where the writer's position or opinion on the issue is stated (thesis statement)
   - **Support**   Where the writer offers supporting reasons and evidence for the position
   - **Concession/Refutation**   Where, if anywhere, the writer **concedes** (accepts) or **refutes** (argues against) other points of view on the issue
2. Make a note on the essay where you detect any of these underlying motivating factors:
   - **Values—moral, ethical, or religious principles** (for example, fairness, justice, equality, "do unto others")

- **Ideas** and **ideals** (for example, ideas about democracy, such as every adult has the right to vote and to freedom of speech)
- **Needs** and **interests** (for example, food, shelter, work, respect, privacy, choice)
- **Fears** and **concerns** (for example, regarding safety, abuse of power, consequences of actions taken or not taken)
- **Goals and priorities** about what is most important or urgent (for example, whether obedience to authority is more important than independent thinking, whether global warming ought to be a concern)

3. Fill in the Annotations Chart that follows by entering your notes and paragraph numbers for each essay you've analyzed. Creating a chart will make it easy for you to locate points of agreement and disagreement. (Remember that you may have to leave some sections blank because you may not find examples of all the features or motivating factors in each argument essay you analyze.)

An electronic version of the chart is available on the companion Web site at **bedfordstmartins.com/theguide**.

For an example of annotating and the annotations chart, see A Writer at Work, pp. 213-15.

Annotations Chart			
		Essay 1	*Essay 2*
Features of the argument	Issue		
	Position (thesis)		
	Supporting reasons and evidence		
	Refutation and/or concession		
Motivating factors	Values		
	Ideas and ideals		

Motivating factors	Needs and interests		
	Fears and concerns		
	Goals and priorities		
Other factors			

TEST YOUR CHOICE

After analyzing the argument essays, ask yourself the following questions:

1 Do I understand the opposing positions and their supporting arguments?

2 Have I been able to find a potential basis for agreement in motivating factors such as basic values or ideals, shared interests or concerns, or common goals that drive the arguments?

If you cannot answer *yes* to both of these questions, you may want to consider choosing a different set of essays to write about, or discuss them with your instructor.

∷ Think about your readers.

Now that you have analyzed the opposing argument essays, take a few minutes to think about your readers. The following questions will help you identify them and develop a better understanding of whether the topic will interest them (or how difficult it will be for you to interest them):

- Who are my readers?
- What are they likely to know about the issue and the arguments surrounding it?

- What do they need to know about the history or context of the issue?
- How can I interest them in the issue — for example, by connecting it to their experience or concerns, or by citing statistics or relating vivid anecdotes?

Research the issue.

Researching the history of the issue and how people have written about it may help you introduce it in a way that will interest your readers in your analysis. To find background information on your topic or authors, enter keywords or phrases related to the issue or the authors' names into the search box of one of the following:

- An all-purpose database, such as *Academic OneFile* (InfoTrac) or *Academic Search Complete* (EBSCOHost), to find relevant articles in magazines and journals. Ask a librarian if you need help selecting an appropriate database.
- A search engine like Google
- Your library's catalog, to locate books on the issue or books written by the authors of the arguments you are analyzing

To learn more about searching a database, a library catalog, or the Web, consult Chapter 24, pp. 674–82.

It may help to gather some background information about the issue and the authors, but do not spend too much time on research, because your essay should focus on your close analysis of the opposing argument essays.

Present the issue to your readers.

Having thought about your readers and possibly having done some background research, write a sentence or two introducing the issue. For example, you could begin by giving the historical context of the issue, using a sentence strategy like this:

▶ Prior to _____ [date], _____ [topic] was considered _____, but after _____ [date or event], it became highly controversial.

Jeremy Bernard uses this strategy when he presents quotations describing baseball as "a game of innocence" and then writes:

> The age of innocence in baseball seems to have ended in the 1990s when "the Steroid Era" began and players from Mark McGwire to Roger Clemens, Barry Bonds, and Alex Rodriguez were identified as using performance enhancing drugs (PEDs). (par. 1)

Another possible strategy is to pose rhetorical questions, like those Betsy Samson uses to present the issue of helicopter parenting:

> How much influence should parents have in their children's decision making as kids get older? When does parental influence cross the line and, however well-intentioned, become detrimental? These are questions that parents and children wrestle with constantly. (par. 3)

Develop your analysis.

The following Ways In activity will help you develop your analysis of the points of agreement and disagreement. You may use the sentence strategies as a jumping-off point — you can always revise them later — or you can use language of your own from the start.

HOW CAN I PRESENT MY ANALYSIS OF THE OPPOSING ARGUMENTS?

WAYS IN

Write a paragraph presenting each important point of disagreement or agreement:

1. Summarize or paraphrase the disagreement or potential agreement.

   ▶ [Author X] takes the position that _____ because _____. [In contrast/ Similarly], [author Y] thinks _____ because _____.

2. Choose quotations from each writer to analyze and compare their perspectives.

   ▶ [Author X] claims: [quotation].

   ▶ X's use of [quoted word or phrase] shows that _____ [name motivating factor] is central to [her/his] way of thinking about the issue.

   ▶ [Author Y's] argument that [quotation], [however/also], shows that [she/he] values _____ more highly than _____.

3. Explain what you think are the different or similar motivating factors influencing the writers' perspectives, and why you think so.

   ▶ Whereas [author X's] argument is based on _____ [name motivating factor], [author Y's] is primarily concerned with [name motivating factor].

   ▶ Like [author X], [author Y] is primarily concerned about _____ [motivating factor].

TEST YOUR ANALYSIS

Present to two other students the areas of agreement you have come up with:

Presenters.   Briefly summarize the opposing views on the issue, and then explain the motivating factor (such as a shared value or common concern) that you think could be the basis for agreement. (You may use the sentence strategies you devised in the preceding Ways In activity to help you articulate your views, or you can use language of your own.)

Listeners.   Tell the presenter whether the motivating factor seems to be a likely basis for agreement. If you have any questions, comments, or insights, share your thoughts with the presenter.

▪▪ Formulate a working thesis statement.

Write one or more sentences that could serve as a thesis statement for your essay. Although you will probably need to clarify your thesis statement as you draft your essay, trying to state it now will give you focus and direction as you plan and draft your essay. These sentences from the end of paragraph 3 in Betsy Samson's essay assert her thesis:

> Chua and Rosin take a very different approach to parenting, but their goals may be closer than they think. Both can be categorized as helicopter parents who are trying in their own way to help their children become happy, fulfilled adults.

As you write your own tentative thesis statement, think about how you could help readers see the important ways the writers disagree and possibly the basis on which they might be able to agree. You may also need to qualify your thesis with words like *often, sometimes,* or *in part.*

∷ Define your purpose for your readers.

Given who your readers are and what they are likely to think about the issue and opposing arguments, try now to define your purpose in finding common ground for these particular readers by considering the following questions:

- If my readers are likely to favor one side in the debate, how can I interest them in my effort to find possible areas of agreement? For example, what motivating factors are likely to influence their thinking?
- If my readers are unfamiliar with the issue, how can I make my analysis of the potential for common ground interesting?

∷ Consider your tone.

To earn their readers' confidence, writers of essays finding common ground must come across as impartial. To achieve this, writers should give roughly equal attention to both positions and avoid taking a position on the issue. In addition, they should carefully assess the words they use to describe the positions, their proponents, or the actions of the proponents. Consider the following sentence from paragraph 5 of Betsy Samson's essay (pp. 183–87):

> More importantly, as Chua's anecdote about her daughter Lulu's effort to learn to play a difficult piano piece demonstrates, children raised the Chinese way succeed because their parents force them to drill until they achieve mastery. (par. 5)

Except perhaps for "force," Samson has carefully chosen words with neutral connotations; were the highlighted words in Samson's sentence to be replaced by words that have a more negative connotation, the tone would become more critical of Chua:

> More importantly, as Chua's anecdote about her daughter Lulu's painful struggle to learn to play a demanding piano piece demonstrates, children raised the Chinese way succeed because their parents force them to drill until they achieve mastery. (par. 5)

As you write (and revise) your common ground essay, consider the connotation of the words you use to describe the positions and the proponents of those positions, and make sure to choose neutral words.

∷ Weave quoted material into your own sentences.

Your essay seeking common ground is based on your analysis of sources: the opposing argument essays you are analyzing and your background research on the issue. In order to present the issue and the arguments fairly and impartially, you are likely to include

Writing a Draft

GUIDE TO READING
GUIDE TO WRITING
A WRITER AT WORK
THINKING CRITICALLY

205

quotations throughout your common ground essay, and you have many options for integrating quotations smoothly into your analysis. Here are a few:

Create a clause beginning with *that*:

> Johnson argues against this common claim, writing that "whenever we torture or mistreat prisoners, we are . . . " (26). (Mae, par. 4)

> But he insists that "Commissioners, club officials, the Players Association, and players" should . . . (311). (Bernard, par. 11)

Introduce the quotation with a colon:

> Walt Whitman, the great nineteenth-century poet, sang its praises: "It's our game — the American game." (Bernard, par. 1)

> Indeed, Rosin seems to be concerned that her children are, if anything, too obedient: "In my household, it's a struggle to get my children to steal a cookie from the cookie jar without immediately confessing" (par. 10). (Samson, par. 7)

Weave quoted words or short phrases into your own sentence:

> The idea that "childhood rebellion" is "proper" and ought to be encouraged, not discouraged, surely separates Rosin from Chua. (Samson, par. 8)

> Johnson rejects the scenario outright as an unrealistic "Hollywood drama" (26). (Mae, par. 7)

For more help on integrating sources in your writing, turn to Chapter 26.

:: Create an outline that will organize your analysis effectively for your readers.

Whether you have rough notes or a complete draft, making an outline of what you have written can help you organize the essay effectively for your audience. Your outline will differ depending on your audience and purpose. Using headings in the form of questions, Jeremy Bernard's outline (at left) is organized around topics under which each author's arguments are presented. Betsy Samson's outline (at right) is organized around points of agreement and disagreement on the central question.

Jeremy Bernard's Outline (Emphasizes Topics)

I. **Introduction of the issue:** Should PEDs be banned by major league baseball?

II. **Introduction of opposing positions: Should performance enhancing drugs be illegal/banned?**

> Yes — George Mitchell, the MLB-sponsored *Mitchell Report*

Betsy Samson's Outline (Emphasizes Points of Agreement and Disagreement)

I. **Introduction:** From dependence in infancy to independence as adults; definition and role of helicopter parenting

> Issue: Should parents control their children's decisions?

No—Eric Walker's independent Web site, *Steroids, Other "Drugs," and Baseball*

III. **Heading 1:** Should PEDs be banned because their health risk is significant?

Points of agreement:

- Medical evidence inconclusive
- Risk of side effects exists
- Risk to adolescents particularly serious

Points of disagreement:

- Risk to adults—Mitchell: Grave; Walker: Not grave
- Choice—Mitchell: Adults should be prohibited from undergoing risk; Walker: Adults should be allowed to choose.

IV. **Heading 2:** Should PEDs be banned because players who take them have an unfair advantage?

Points of Agreement:

- Use of PEDs gives athletes an advantage
- Unequal access is unfair, not a level playing field

Points of Disagreement:

- Whose responsibility?—Mitchell: MLB should set rules; Walker: Athletes should decide for themselves.
- Distinction between "natural" and "unnatural"—Mitchell: Distinction is clear and should be maintained; Walker: Distinction is arbitrary and needs rethinking.

V. **Conclusion:** Possibility of common ground based on shared love of baseball

II. **Introduction to Issue: Should parents control their children's decisions?**

Yes—Amy Chua, "Why Chinese Mothers Are Superior," *Wall Street Journal*

No—Hanna Rosin, "Mother Inferior?" *Wall Street Journal* (response to Chua)

III. **Points of agreement**

- Parents are influential in their children's lives
- Parents want to do what's best for their kids

IV. **Points of disagreement**

- Parents should
  - make decisions for their children (Chua)
  - support their children as they learn to make their own decisions (Rosin)
- Parents should make sure their children
  - attain mastery (Chua)
  - find happiness and personal satisfaction (Rosin)

V. **Conclusion**

- Summarize Chua's argument for heavy parental involvement vs. Rosin's argument for child-directed parental involvement
- Common ground:
  - Shared value of acting in the best interest of child
  - Cultural/situational cues influencing parenting techniques

Write the opening sentences.

You might want to review your invention writing to see whether you have already written something that would work to launch your essay, or you could try out one or two ways of beginning your essay from the list that follows. But do not agonize over the first sentences, because you are likely to discover the best way to begin only as you revise your rough draft.

The following opening strategies may help to engage your readers' interest:

Evaluating the Draft

GUIDE TO READING
GUIDE TO WRITING
A WRITER AT WORK
THINKING CRITICALLY

207

- An interesting and relevant quotation (like Bernard)
- An assertion of the topic's larger cultural relevance (like Bernard and Samson)
- An assertion of the issue's significance (like Mae)
- An anecdote or statistic to show how the issue affects readers

Draft your essay finding common ground.

By this point, you have done a lot of writing to

- analyze the opposing arguments;
- present those arguments to your readers;
- formulate a working thesis; and
- integrate quotations.

Now stitch that material together to create a draft. The next two parts of this Guide to Writing will help you evaluate and improve the draft you write.

Evaluating the Draft: Getting a Critical Reading

Your instructor may arrange a peer review session in class or online, where you can exchange drafts with your classmates and give each other a thoughtful critical reading, pointing out what works well and suggesting ways to improve the draft. A good critical reading does three things:

1. It lets the writer know how well the reader understands the point of the essay.
2. It praises what works best.
3. It indicates where the draft could be improved and makes suggestions on how to improve it.

One strategy for evaluating a draft is to use the basic features of the common ground essay as a guide.

A CRITICAL READING GUIDE

An Informative Introduction to the Issue and Opposing Positions

Has the writer explained the issue and opposing positions clearly and in a way that will engage readers' interest?

Summarize: Briefly tell the writer what you understand the issue to be and what the opposing positions are.

Praise: Indicate where the writer does a good job explaining the issue, introducing the authors, or engaging readers' interest.

Critique: Describe any confusion or uncertainty you have about the issue, about why it is important, or about the positions the essays being analyzed take on it.

A Probing Analysis

Is the writer's analysis of the points of disagreement and potential agreement interesting and insightful?

Summarize: Tell the writer what you understand to be the points of disagreement and the areas of potential agreement.

Praise: Identify one or two passages where the analysis seems especially effective — for example, where the opposing arguments are shown to be based on similar motivating factors, such as a shared value or common concern.

Critique: Identify places where additional details, an example or illustration, or more explanation would make the analysis clearer. Let the writer know if you detect any other motivating factors that might be used to establish common ground.

A Fair and Impartial Presentation

Has the writer represented the opposing arguments in a balanced, unbiased way?

Summarize: Circle the words used to describe the proponents, and underline the words used to describe their views.

Praise: Note any passages where the writer comes across as being especially fair and impartial.

Critique: Tell the writer if the authors and their positions are presented unfairly or if one side seems to be favored over the other. Identify passages that seem critical of the proponents or their views, and suggest ways the writer could make the point less negatively, such as by using quotations to state criticisms or replacing negative words with neutral ones.

A Clear, Logical Organization

Is the essay clear and readable?

Summarize: Underline the thesis, and circle key terms that forecast the topics the essay will focus on. Then circle those key terms when they appear elsewhere in the essay.

Praise: Pick one or two places where the essay is especially clear and easy to follow — for example, where the writer has repeated key terms or synonyms for them effectively, or where the writer has used comparative transitions, such as *both* or *as well as* to signal similarity and *whereas* or *although* to signal differences.

Critique: Let the writer know where the readability could be improved — for example, where a topic sentence could be clearer or where a transition is needed. Suggest a better beginning or a more effective ending.

For a printable version of this Critical Reading Guide, go to **bedfordstmartins .com/theguide**.

Before concluding your review, be sure to address any of the writer's concerns that have not been addressed already.

Making Comments Electronically   Most word processing software offers features that allow you to insert comments directly into the text of someone else's document. Many readers prefer to make their comments this way because it tends to be faster than writing on hard copy and space is virtually unlimited; it also eliminates the process of deciphering handwritten comments. Where such features are not available, simply typing comments directly into a document in a contrasting color can provide the same advantages.

Improving the Draft: Revising, Formatting, Editing, and Proofreading

Start improving your draft by reflecting on what you have written thus far:

- Consider critical reading comments from your classmates, instructor, or writing center tutor: What basic problems do your readers identify?
- Look back at your invention writing: What else could you add to the draft?
- Review your draft: What can you do to present your analysis more clearly and to make it more penetrating?

Revise your draft.

If your readers are having difficulty with your draft, or if you think there is room for improvement, try some of the strategies listed in the Troubleshooting Guide that follows. It can help you fine-tune your presentation of the genre's basic features.

A TROUBLESHOOTING GUIDE

An Informative Introduction to the Issue and Opposing Positions	**My readers are not clear about the issue or the opposing positions.** • State the issue explicitly as a question. • Explain the issue in more depth, perhaps providing an example to show why it's important. • Use a transition (such as *whereas* or *although*) to sharpen the contrast between the opposing positions. • Consider adding a graph or other visual to represent the issue or opposing positions. **My readers are not interested or do not appreciate the issue's importance.** • Add information showing the impact of the issue or how it affects people's lives. • Contextualize the issue in history, politics, or culture. • Quote notable authorities to emphasize the issue's importance. • Cite polls or research studies, or use graphics to convey statistical information demonstrating the widespread impact of the issue.

A Probing Analysis

> My readers do not understand my analysis.

- Determine whether you are trying to cover too many points.
- Explain in more detail the points that are harder for readers to grasp.
- Consider emphasizing the less obvious points of agreement.

> My analysis seems more like a summary of the arguments than a probing analysis.

- Ask yourself why the writer makes a particular kind of argument rather than another kind of argument.
- Consider how the writer's profession or biography could explain why a particular motivating factor (such as a moral value or idea) has so much persuasive power.
- Think about the social and political situation in which each essay was originally written and how the writer was trying to appeal to readers.
- Examine the concessions and refutations of opposing views to see where there might be room for agreement.

A Fair and Impartial Presentation

> My presentation is not impartial or balanced.

- Give equal space to both arguments.
- Make sure that you are representing each writer accurately and fairly by relying more on quoting than summarizing or paraphrasing.
- Consider your word choices, replacing judgmental words with neutral ones.

A Clear, Logical Organization

> My readers are confused by my essay or find it difficult to read.

- Consider adding a forecasting statement to preview the topics you discuss.
- Add topic sentences or repeat key terms in topic sentences.
- Add transitions to signal comparisons or contrasts.

Improving the Draft

GUIDE TO READING
GUIDE TO WRITING
A WRITER AT WORK
THINKING CRITICALLY

211

Think about design.

Because essays finding common ground must avoid the appearance of bias, they rely heavily on quotations to convey the positions of the proponents and to articulate criticisms of those positions. Notice how Jeremy Bernard integrates longer and shorter quotations to articulate the positions and criticisms of those positions.

9   However, Walker disagrees with Mitchell's way of defining "a level playing field" as one where "success and advancement . . . is the result of ability and hard work" (Mitchell 5). According to Walker, Mitchell makes a false distinction between what is natural and unnatural. Whereas certain aids to performance — such as better bats, chemical-filled drinks like Gatorade, Tommy John and Lasik surgery — are considered natural and therefore allowable, other aids — particularly PEDs — are deemed unnatural and banned. To support his argument, Walker cites Fost again. "Here's what Fost wrote in 'Steroid Hysteria': 'There is no coherent argument to support the view that enhancing performance is unfair. If it were, we should ban coaching and training. Competition can be unfair if there is unequal access to such enhancements.'"

Uses quotations to articulate positions and criticisms

Uses quotation marks and integrates shorter quotations into his own sentences

10   In other words, unequal access is the key to the unfairness argument. On this point, Mitchell and Walker seem to agree. The argument is really about making sure that there is a level playing field. Mitchell puts his finger on it when he explains that

1/2" ←→ the illegal use of these substances by some players is unfair to the majority of players who do not use them. These players have a right to expect a level playing field where success and advancement to the major leagues is the result of ability and hard work. They should not be forced to choose between joining the ranks of those who illegally use these substances or falling short of their ambition to succeed at the major league level. (5)

Omits quotation marks and indents longer quotations (over 4 lines in MLA style; over 40 words in APA style) a half inch from the left margin

Ethicists call this a coercion argument. "Steroids are coercive," Fost explains, because "if your opponents use them, you have to" as well or you risk losing. Walker has a simple solution: allow PEDs to be "equally available to any who might want them." He argues that there are lots of requirements or expectations that athletes regularly make choices about. He sees "no logical or ethical distinction between — just for example — killer workouts and PEDs." Therefore, Walker concludes, each athlete has to decide for him- or herself what's "appropriate or necessary."

For practice, go to bedfordstmartins.com /theguide/exercisecentral and click on Commas around Interrupting Phrases.

Edit and proofread your draft.

Our research indicates that particular errors occur often in common ground essays: incorrect comma usage in sentences with interrupting phrases, and vague pronoun reference. The following guidelines will help you check your essay for these common errors.

Using Commas around Interrupting Phrases

What is an *interrupting phrase*? When writers are analyzing opposing positions, they need to supply a great deal of information precisely and accurately. They add much of this information in phrases that interrupt the flow of a sentence, as in the following example:

> The concern was so great that George Mitchell, the former Senate Majority Leader and peace negotiator, was enlisted to investigate. (Bernard, par. 2)

Such interrupting phrases, as they are called, are typically set off with commas.

The Problem   Forgetting to set off an interrupting phrase with commas can make sentences unclear or difficult to read.

How to Correct It   Add a comma on either side of an interrupting phrase.

▶ Live Nation‸ without hesitating‸ paid $350 million to buy HOB Entertainment, which owns the popular House of Blues clubs.

▶ Virtual football‸ to hold on to its fans and gain more‸ soon has to move beyond solitary players to teams of players on the Internet.

Correcting Vague Pronoun Reference

The Problem   **Pronouns** replace and refer to nouns, making writing more efficient and cohesive. If the reference is vague, however, this advantage is lost. A common problem is vague use of *this, that, it,* or *which*.

How to Correct It   Scan your writing for pronouns, taking special note of places where you use *this, that, it,* or *which*. Check to be sure that what *this, that, it, which,* or another pronoun refers to is crystal clear. If it is not, revise your sentence.

▶ Television evangelists seem to be perpetually raising money‚⁄。 ~~which~~ makes some ^This habit^

viewers question their motives.

▶ By the late 1960s, plate tectonics emerged as a new area of study. Tectonics was

based on the notion of the earth's crust as a collection of plates or land masses

Betsy Samson's Analysis of Opposing Argument Essays

GUIDE TO READING
GUIDE TO WRITING
A WRITER AT WORK
THINKING CRITICALLY

213

startling new geological theory

above and below sea level, constantly in motion. This took a while for most people to

accept, ~~because of its unexpected novelty.~~

▶ Inside the Summit Tunnel, the Chinese laborers were using as much as

500 kegs a day of costly black powder to blast their way through the

The unexpected expense

solid rock. It was straining the Central Pacific's budget.

For practice, go to
**bedfordstmartins.com
/theguide/exercisecentral**
and click on Vague Pronoun
Reference.

A WRITER AT WORK

Betsy Samson's Analysis of Opposing Argument Essays

Betsy Samson's common ground essay "Does Mother Know Best?" (pp. 183–87) analyzes the arguments in two essays taking opposing positions on parenting: Amy Chua's "Why Chinese Mothers Are Superior" and Hanna Rosin's response, "Mother Inferior?" (You can find these essays in the appendix at the end of this chapter on pp. 219–22 and 222–25.)

Using the Analyze the Opposing Argument Essays section of the Guide to Writing (pp. 199–201), Samson read the two essays carefully. She annotated as she read, highlighting the text and making marginal notes that identify the basic features of the arguments and their motivating factors. Below is paragraph 5 from Chua's essay with Samson's annotations, followed by Samson's annotations chart showing how she recorded the results of her analysis of Chua's and Rosin's essays.

Annotations

What Chinese parents understand is that nothing is fun until you're good at it. To get good at anything you have to work, and children on their own never want to work, which is why it is crucial to override their preferences. This often requires fortitude on the part of the parents because the child will resist; things are always hardest at the beginning, which is where Western parents tend to give up. But if done properly, the Chinese strategy produces a virtuous circle. Tenacious practice, practice, practice is crucial for excellence; rote repetition is underrated in America. Once a child starts to excel at something—whether it's math, piano, pitching or ballet—he or she gets praise, admiration and satisfaction This builds confidence and makes the once not-fun activity fun. This in turn makes it easier for the parent to get the child to work even more.

Can't let children make their own choices

Chua's position: virtuous circle strategy necessary

Virtuous not vicious circle: work → success → confidence → more work

Charting the Annotations

Here you can see how Samson filled in the Annotations Chart based on her analysis of Chua's and Rosin's essays. Note that she doesn't fill in every cell in the chart, nor does she devote the same amount of space to each element. To show students how people annotate differently, your instructor might invite you to compare your annotated text and annotations chart to those of other students.

Betsy Samson's Annotations Chart			
		Essay 1: Chua	*Essay 2: Rosin*
Features of the argument	Issue	Chinese parenting techniques better than Western (pars. 1–4) Examples show Chua's "strict" parenting (2)	Western parenting techniques better than Chinese (pars. 1–4) Examples show Rosin fits Chua's stereotype of Western parent (1–3)
	Position (thesis)	Chinese virtuous circle strategy: work → success → confidence → willingness to "work even more" (5). This is "how Chinese parents raise such stereotypically successful kids." (1)	"In fact, I think Ms. Chua has the diagnosis of American childhood exactly backward. What privileged American children need is not more skills and rules and math drills. They need to lighten up and roam free, to express themselves in ways not dictated by their uptight, over-invested parents." (4)
	Supporting reasons and evidence	Reason #1: Because Chinese parents assume child's "strength," they tell truth & demand hard work & success. Contrast: b/c Western parents anxious about child's self-esteem, they give false praise & children settle for less (11–14) Reason #2: Because "Chinese parents believe . . . kids owe them everything," they demand their children make them proud. (15–16)	Reason #1: Because holding children to "impossibly high standards" is damaging. Evidence—"horror stories of child prodigies gone bad"; Chua's admission that she's "'not good at enjoying life'" (5) Reason #2: Because children forced to practice too hard on something that they have neither passion nor talent for grow to hate what they have mastered. Evidence: her friend & Andre Agassi (6–8)
		Reason #3: Because "Chinese parents . . . know what is best," they "override . . . children's own desires and preferences." (16) Evidence: Anecdote about Lulu supports all three reasons (18–32)	

Betsy Samson's Analysis of Opposing Argument Essays

GUIDE TO READING
GUIDE TO WRITING
A WRITER AT WORK
THINKING CRITICALLY

215

	Refutation and/or concession	Concedes she may have been wrong (Lulu anecdote: "even I began to have doubts") (30) Concedes that Western parenting style means well ("All decent parents want to do what's best for their children. The Chinese just have a totally different idea of how to do that.") (34)	Concedes parents should encourage/push kids to work at a goal, but also refutes Chua's claim that parents know best what should be the goal (8) Concedes "Chua's most compelling argument is that happiness comes from mastery," but also refutes Chua's use of harsh criticism (9) Refutes Chua's claim that "'Children on their own never want to work.'" (10) Concedes Chua's claim about Western parents' "'conflicted feelings about achievement'" (13)
Motivating factors	Values	Studies comparing parents' values: "Chinese mothers . . . believe . . . 'academic achievement reflects successful parenting.'" Contrast: Western parents think "'stressing academic success is not good for children'" & "'parents need to foster the idea that learning is fun.'" (4) "Confucian filial piety"—kids owe parents (14) Chinese parents "would give up anything for their children" (17)	Shares Chua's "mother-in-law's belief that childhood should be full of 'spontaneity, freedom, discovery and experience'" (15) Values "proper childhood rebellion" (4) Rejects Chua's goal to "perfect our children" (14)
	Ideas and ideals		
	Needs and interests		
	Fears and concerns	Concern: children will not work hard enough to succeed (11–13)	Concern: children will not be happy (12)
	Priorities and agendas	Priority: "best way to protect their children is . . . letting them see what they're capable of, and arming them with skills, work habits and inner confidence" (35)	Priority: to help children "navigate" life's difficulties (11)

To think critically means to use all of the knowledge you have acquired from the information in this chapter, your own writing, the writing of other students, and class discussions to reflect deeply on your work for this assignment and the genre (or type) of writing you have produced. The benefit of thinking critically is proven and important: Thinking critically about what you have learned will help you remember it longer, ensuring that you will be able to put it to good use well beyond this writing course.

Reflecting on What You Have Learned

In this chapter, you have learned a great deal about this genre from reading several essays that find common ground and from writing a common ground essay of your own. To consolidate your learning, reflect not only on what you learned but also on how you learned it.

ANALYZE & WRITE

Write a blog post, a letter to your instructor, or an e-mail message to a student who will take this course next term, using the writing prompt below that seems most productive for you:

- Explain how your purpose and audience influenced *one* of your decisions as a writer, such as how you presented the subject, the strategies you used in justifying your evaluation, or the ways in which you attempted to counter possible objections.

- Discuss what you learned about yourself as a writer in the process of writing this essay. For example, what part of the process did you find most challenging? Did you try anything new, like getting a critical reading of your draft or outlining your draft in order to revise it?

- If you were to give advice to a friend who was about to write an essay finding common ground, what would you say?

- Which of the readings in this chapter influenced your essay? Explain the influence, citing specific examples from your essay and from the reading.

- If you got good advice from a critical reader, explain exactly how the person helped you — perhaps by questioning the way you addressed your audience or the kinds of evidence you offered in support of your position.

Reflecting on the Genre

Essays that analyze points of disagreement and possible agreement help us understand complex issues and discover ways to move forward constructively. They are especially important in a democracy because they enable us to perform our role as citizens conscientiously.

One of the greatest challenges of analyzing opposing arguments is to represent each viewpoint accurately and fairly. Writers wrestle with the requirement that analysis be impartial. They often make a distinction between objectivity and impartiality: To be objective assumes that it is possible for a writer not only to be balanced but also to be detached, somehow removed from or raised above the controversy. To be impartial, in contrast, means to be fair or even-handed in presenting different views. While objectivity may not be possible, writers can strive to be fair in the way they represent different viewpoints, giving each side its voice and avoiding judgmental language.

| ANALYZE & WRITE |

Write a page or two about your own experience of analyzing an argument fairly and impartially. In your discussion, you might do either or both of the following:

1. **Consider how challenging it was to make your analysis fair and impartial.** As you were analyzing the arguments and writing your finding common ground essay, in what ways, if any, did you have difficulty maintaining your impartiality? How did you try to make sure you were being fair? What strategies did you use in your writing to come across to readers as a trustworthy analyst?

2. **Think about the goal of trying to be fair and impartial as an analyst.** Based on your own experience as a writer of a finding common ground essay (as well as other writing you may have done in the past), what have you learned about the goal of trying to be fair and impartial? Is it an achievable goal? Is it a worthwhile goal? Why or why not? Add to your discussion any ideas you have from your experience as a consumer of analytical writing and talk. How critical are you as a reader or listener? How important do you think it is for you as a citizen and student to feel confident that the analysis you are consuming is fair, unbiased, impartial, even objective? Be sure to distinguish between op-ed style commentary, intended to express opinions and judgments, and journalism or academic analysis, intended to be fair and impartial.

APPENDIX

Following are three clusters of essays taking positions on two different issues: parenting, helmet use among athletes, and compensating organ donors. These clusters include two argument essays and one informative essay that may be used for background. You may read the first cluster to compare the arguments by Chua and Rosin with Betsy Samson's representation of them in her essay "Does Mother Know Best?" (pp. 183–87). You may select from the essays in this appendix, along with essays on several other debate topics that are available in the e-Pages or that you can link to from the book's companion site.

To access more debate clusters, go to **bedfordstmartins .com/theguide**.

Understanding the Issue of Parenting Style

With the publication of Amy Chua's opinion essay "Why Chinese Mothers Are Superior" in the *Wall Street Journal* and the publicity surrounding the publication of her comic memoir *Battle Hymn of the Tiger Mother,* the controversy over parenting styles reached a fever pitch in 2011. The debate over parenting styles, however, has a long history in developmental psychology. In the early 1970s, for example, developmental psychologist Diana Baumrind identified three general parenting styles: authoritative, authoritarian, and permissive. The term *helicopter parenting,* as Betsy Samson points out, was popularized by Foster Cline and Jim Fay's 1990 book *Parenting with Love and Logic.* A *Time* magazine cover story in 2009 by Nancy Gibbs, "The Growing Backlash against Overparenting," describes what she calls "a new revolution . . . rolling back the almost comical overprotectiveness and overinvestment of moms and dads."

Amy Chua | *Why Chinese Mothers Are Superior*

AMY CHUA has a bachelor of arts and a doctorate in law from Harvard University, and she is the John M. Duff, Jr. Professor of Law at Yale Law School, where she earned the Distinguished Teaching Award in 2002–2003. She has written several books, including *Day of Empire: How Hyperpowers Rise to Global Dominance—and Why They Fall* (2007) and *World on Fire: How Exporting Free Market Democracy Breeds Ethnic Hatred and Global Instability* (2002). The following selection, excerpted from her comic memoir *Battle Hymn of the Tiger Mother* (2011), appeared in the *Wall Street Journal*.

1 A lot of people wonder how Chinese parents raise such stereotypically successful kids. They wonder what these parents do to produce so many math whizzes and music prodigies, what it's like inside the family, and whether they could do it too. Well, I can tell them, because I've done it. Here are some things my daughters, Sophia and Louisa, were never allowed to do:

- attend a sleepover
- have a playdate
- be in a school play
- complain about not being in a school play
- watch TV or play computer games
- choose their own extracurricular activities
- get any grade less than an A
- not be the No. 1 student in every subject except gym and drama
- play any instrument other than the piano or violin
- not play the piano or violin.

2 I'm using the term "Chinese mother" loosely. I know some Korean, Indian, Jamaican, Irish and Ghanaian parents who qualify too. Conversely, I know some mothers of Chinese heritage, almost always born in the West, who are not Chinese mothers, by choice or otherwise. I'm also using the term "Western parents" loosely. Western parents come in all varieties.

3 All the same, even when Western parents think they're being strict, they usually don't come close to being Chinese mothers. For example, my Western friends who consider themselves strict make their children practice their instruments 30 minutes every day. An hour at most. For a Chinese mother, the first hour is the easy part. It's hours two and three that get tough.

4 Despite our squeamishness about cultural stereotypes, there are tons of studies out there showing marked and quantifiable differences between Chinese and Westerners when it comes to parenting. In one study of 50 Western American mothers and 48 Chinese immigrant mothers, almost 70% of the Western mothers said either that "stressing academic success is not good for children" or that "parents need to foster the idea that learning is fun." By contrast, roughly 0% of the Chinese mothers felt the same way. Instead, the vast majority of the Chinese mothers said that they believe their children can be "the best" students, that "academic achievement reflects successful parenting," and that if children did not excel at school then there was "a problem" and parents "were not doing their job." Other studies indicate that compared to Western parents, Chinese parents spend

Chua at home with her daughters, Louisa (left) and Sophia (right)

approximately 10 times as long every day drilling academic activities with their children. By contrast, Western kids are more likely to participate in sports teams.

5   What Chinese parents understand is that nothing is fun until you're good at it. To get good at anything you have to work, and children on their own never want to work, which is why it is crucial to override their preferences. This often requires fortitude on the part of the parents because the child will resist; things are always hardest at the beginning, which is where Western parents tend to give up. But if done properly, the Chinese strategy produces a virtuous circle. Tenacious practice, practice, practice is crucial for excellence; rote repetition is underrated in America. Once a child starts to excel at something—whether it's math, piano, pitching or ballet—he or she gets praise, admiration and satisfaction. This builds confidence and makes the once not-fun activity fun. This in turn makes it easier for the parent to get the child to work even more.

"Mean me with Lulu in hotel room with score taped to the TV!"

6   Chinese parents can get away with things that Western parents can't. Once when I was young—maybe more than once—when I was extremely disrespectful to my mother, my father angrily called me "garbage" in our native Hokkien dialect. It worked really well. I felt terrible and deeply ashamed of what I had done. But it didn't damage my self-esteem or anything like that. I knew exactly how highly he thought of me. I didn't actually think I was worthless or feel like a piece of garbage.

7   As an adult, I once did the same thing to Sophia, calling her garbage in English when she acted extremely disrespectfully toward me. When I mentioned that I had

done this at a dinner party, I was immediately ostracized. One guest named Marcy got so upset she broke down in tears and had to leave early. My friend Susan, the host, tried to rehabilitate me with the remaining guests.

8   The fact is that Chinese parents can do things that would seem unimaginable—even legally actionable—to Westerners. Chinese mothers can say to their daughters, "Hey fatty—lose some weight." By contrast, Western parents have to tiptoe around the issue, talking in terms of "health" and never ever mentioning the *f*-word, and their kids still end up in therapy for eating disorders and negative self-image. (I also once heard a Western father toast his adult daughter by calling her "beautiful and incredibly competent." She later told me that made her feel like garbage.)

9   Chinese parents can order their kids to get straight As. Western parents can only ask their kids to try their best. Chinese parents can say, "You're lazy. All your classmates are getting ahead of you." By contrast, Western parents have to struggle with their own conflicted feelings about achievement, and try to persuade themselves that they're not disappointed about how their kids turned out.

10   I've thought long and hard about how Chinese parents can get away with what they do. I think there are three big differences between the Chinese and Western parental mind-sets.

11   First, I've noticed that Western parents are extremely anxious about their children's self-esteem. They worry about how their children will feel if they fail at something, and they constantly try to reassure their children about how good they are notwithstanding a mediocre performance on a test or at a recital. In other words, Western parents are concerned about their children's psyches. Chinese parents aren't. They assume strength, not fragility, and as a result they behave very differently.

12   For example, if a child comes home with an A-minus on a test, a Western parent will most likely praise the child. The Chinese mother will gasp in horror and ask what went wrong. If the child comes home with a B on the test, some Western parents will still praise the child. Other Western parents will sit their child down and express disapproval, but they will be careful not to make their child feel inadequate or insecure, and they will not call their child "stupid," "worthless" or "a disgrace." Privately, the Western parents may worry that their child does not test well or have aptitude in the subject or that

there is something wrong with the curriculum and possibly the whole school. If the child's grades do not improve, they may eventually schedule a meeting with the school principal to challenge the way the subject is being taught or to call into question the teacher's credentials.

13   If a Chinese child gets a B—which would never happen—there would first be a screaming, hair-tearing explosion. The devastated Chinese mother would then get dozens, maybe hundreds of practice tests and work through them with her child for as long as it takes to get the grade up to an A. Chinese parents demand perfect grades because they believe that their child can get them. If their child doesn't get them, the Chinese parent assumes it's because the child didn't work hard enough. That's why the solution to substandard performance is always to excoriate, punish and shame the child. The Chinese parent believes that their child will be strong enough to take the shaming and to improve from it. (And when Chinese kids do excel, there is plenty of ego-inflating parental praise lavished in the privacy of the home.)

14   Second, Chinese parents believe that their kids owe them everything. The reason for this is a little unclear, but it's probably a combination of Confucian filial piety and the fact that the parents have sacrificed and done so much for their children. (And it's true that Chinese mothers get in the trenches, putting in long grueling hours personally tutoring, training, interrogating and spying on their kids.) Anyway, the understanding is that Chinese children must spend their lives repaying their parents by obeying them and making them proud.

15   By contrast, I don't think most Westerners have the same view of children being permanently indebted to their parents. My husband, Jed, actually has the opposite view. "Children don't choose their parents," he once said to me. "They don't even choose to be born. It's parents who foist life on their kids, so it's the parents' responsibility to provide for them. Kids don't owe their parents anything. Their duty will be to their own kids." This strikes me as a terrible deal for the Western parent.

16   Third, Chinese parents believe that they know what is best for their children and therefore override all of their children's own desires and preferences. That's why Chinese daughters can't have boyfriends in high school and why Chinese kids can't go to sleepaway camp. It's also why no Chinese kid would ever dare say to their mother, "I got a part in the school play! I'm Villager Number Six. I'll have to stay after school for rehearsal every day from 3:00 to 7:00, and I'll also need a ride on weekends." God help any Chinese kid who tried that one.

17   Don't get me wrong: It's not that Chinese parents don't care about their children. Just the opposite. They would give up anything for their children. It's just an entirely different parenting model.

18   Here's a story in favor of coercion, Chinese-style. Lulu was about 7, still playing two instruments, and working on a piano piece called "The Little White Donkey" by the French composer Jacques Ibert. The piece is really cute—you can just imagine a little donkey ambling along a country road with its master—but it's also incredibly difficult for young players because the two hands have to keep schizophrenically different rhythms.

19   Lulu couldn't do it. We worked on it nonstop for a week, drilling each of her hands separately, over and over. But whenever we tried putting the hands together, one always morphed into the other, and everything fell apart. Finally, the day before her lesson, Lulu announced in exasperation that she was giving up and stomped off.

20   "Get back to the piano now," I ordered.

21   "You can't make me."

22   "Oh yes, I can."

23   Back at the piano, Lulu made me pay. She punched, thrashed and kicked. She grabbed the music score and tore it to shreds. I taped the score back together and encased it in a plastic shield so that it could never be destroyed again. Then I hauled Lulu's dollhouse to the car and told her I'd donate it to the Salvation Army piece by piece if she didn't have "The Little White Donkey" perfect by the next day. When Lulu said, "I thought you were going to the Salvation Army, why are you still here?" I threatened her with no lunch, no dinner, no Christmas or Hanukkah presents, no birthday parties for two, three, four years. When she still kept playing it wrong, I told her she was purposely working herself into a frenzy because she was secretly afraid she couldn't do it. I told her to stop being lazy, cowardly, self-indulgent and pathetic.

24   Jed took me aside. He told me to stop insulting Lulu—which I wasn't even doing, I was just motivating her—and that he didn't think threatening Lulu was helpful. Also, he said, maybe Lulu really just couldn't do the technique—perhaps she didn't have the coordination yet—had I considered that possibility?

25 "You just don't believe in her," I accused.

26 "That's ridiculous," Jed said scornfully. "Of course I do."

27 "Sophia could play the piece when she was this age."

28 "But Lulu and Sophia are different people," Jed pointed out.

29 "Oh no, not this," I said, rolling my eyes. "Everyone is special in their special own way," I mimicked sarcastically. "Even losers are special in their own special way. Well don't worry, you don't have to lift a finger. I'm willing to put in as long as it takes, and I'm happy to be the one hated. And you can be the one they adore because you make them pancakes and take them to Yankees games."

30 I rolled up my sleeves and went back to Lulu. I used every weapon and tactic I could think of. We worked right through dinner into the night, and I wouldn't let Lulu get up, not for water, not even to go to the bathroom. The house became a war zone, and I lost my voice yelling, but still there seemed to be only negative progress, and even I began to have doubts.

31 Then, out of the blue, Lulu did it. Her hands suddenly came together—her right and left hands each doing their own imperturbable thing—just like that. Lulu realized it the same time I did. I held my breath. She tried it tentatively again. Then she played it more confidently and faster, and still the rhythm held. A moment later, she was beaming.

32 "Mommy, look—it's easy!" After that, she wanted to play the piece over and over and wouldn't leave the piano.

That night, she came to sleep in my bed, and we snuggled and hugged, cracking each other up. When she performed "The Little White Donkey" at a recital a few weeks later, parents came up to me and said, "What a perfect piece for Lulu—it's so spunky and so her."

33 Even Jed gave me credit for that one. Western parents worry a lot about their children's self-esteem. But as a parent, one of the worst things you can do for your child's self-esteem is to let them give up. On the flip side, there's nothing better for building confidence than learning you can do something you thought you couldn't.

34 There are all these new books out there portraying Asian mothers as scheming, callous, overdriven people indifferent to their kids' true interests. For their part, many Chinese secretly believe that they care more about their children and are willing to sacrifice much more for them than Westerners, who seem perfectly content to let their children turn out badly. I think it's a misunderstanding on both sides. All decent parents want to do what's best for their children. The Chinese just have a totally different idea of how to do that.

35 Western parents try to respect their children's individuality, encouraging them to pursue their true passions, supporting their choices, and providing positive reinforcement and a nurturing environment. By contrast, the Chinese believe that the best way to protect their children is by preparing them for the future, letting them see what they're capable of, and arming them with skills, work habits and inner confidence that no one can ever take away.

Hanna Rosin | *Mother Inferior?*

HANNA ROSIN was born in Israel and raised in Queens, one of New York City's five boroughs, by her taxi-driver father, about whom she wrote fondly in *New York* magazine. Rosin cofounded the women's Web site *DoubleX* and is a senior editor at the *Atlantic*. In 2010, she delivered a presentation for TED, a nonprofit organization "devoted to ideas worth spreading," on the "rise of women"—the theme of her article "The End of Men," which appeared in the *Atlantic* in 2010, and a forthcoming book. She has also appeared on *The Daily Show with Jon Stewart* and *The Colbert Report*. Her book *God's Harvard: A Christian College on a Mission to Save America* (2007) profiles the evangelical Patrick Henry College. The article that follows is her response to Amy Chua's "Why Chinese Mothers Are Superior"; it appeared in the *Wall Street Journal* in 2011, a week after Ms. Chua's article ran.

1 The other day I was playing a game called "Kids on Stage" with my 2-year-old. I had to act out "tiger," so I got down on all fours and roared. He laughed, so I roared even louder, which only made him laugh more. Eventually he came up to me, patted my head and said "kitty kat" with benevolent condescension. This perfectly sums up my status in the animal pack of mothers defined by Amy Chua's *Battle Hymn of the Tiger Mother*. There are the fierce tigers who churn out child prodigies, and then there are the pussycats who waste their afternoons playing useless board games and get bested by their own toddlers.

Hanna Rosin at home with Jacob (left), Gideon (on Rosin's lap), and Noa (right).

2 In pretty much every way, I am the weak-willed, pathetic Western parent that Ms. Chua describes. My children go on playdates and sleepovers; in fact I wish they would go on more of them. When they give me lopsided, hastily drawn birthday cards, I praise them as if they were Matisse, sometimes with tears in my eyes. (Ms. Chua threw back one quickly scribbled birthday card, saying "I reject this," and told her daughters they could do better.) My middle son is skilled at precisely the two extracurricular activities Ms. Chua most mocks: He just got a minor part in the school play as a fisherman, and he is a master of the drums, the instrument that she claims leads directly to using drugs (I'm not sure if she is joking or not).

3 I would be thrilled, of course, if my eldest child made it to Carnegie Hall at 14, which is the great crescendo of the Chua family story (although I would make sure to tell my other two children that they were fabulous in other ways!). But the chances that I would threaten to burn all her stuffed animals unless she played a piano piece perfectly, or to donate her favorite doll house to the Salvation Army piece by piece, as Ms. Chua did with her daughter, are exactly zero. It's not merely that such vigilant attention to how my daughter spends every minute of her afternoon is time-consuming and exhausting; after all, it takes time to play "Kids on Stage" and to drive to drum lessons, too. It's more that I don't have it in me. I just don't have the demented drive to pull it off.

4 Many American parents will read *Battle Hymn of the Tiger Mother* and feel somewhat defensive and regretful. *Well, I do make my Johnny practice his guitar twice a week! Or, Look, I have this nice discipline chart on my refrigerator with frowny faces for when he's rude at dinner!* But I don't feel all that defensive. In fact, I think Ms. Chua has the diagnosis of American childhood exactly backward. What privileged American children need is not more skills and rules and math drills. They need to lighten up and roam free, to express themselves in ways not dictated by their uptight, over-invested parents. Like Ms. Chua, many American parents suffer from the delusion that, with careful enough control, a child can be made perfect. Ms. Chua does it with Suzuki piano books and insults, while many of my friends do it with organic baby food and playrooms filled with carefully curated wooden toys. In both cases, the result is the same: an excess of children who are dutiful proto-adults, always responsible and good, incapable of proper childhood rebellion.

5 In the days since Ms. Chua's book has come out, the media have brought up horror stories of child prodigies gone bad, including [a] 16-year-old who stabbed her mother to death[1] after complaining that her Chinese immigrant parents held her to impossibly high standards. Most prodigy stories, I imagine, involve more complicated emotions. (The Amy Chua of the book, by the way, is more seductive than the distilled media version. She is remarkably self-aware. "The truth is, I'm not good at enjoying life," she writes, and she never hesitates to tell stories that she knows make her look beastly. It's worth noting that, in TV and radio interviews about the book, she's been trending more pussycat).[2]

6 I have a good friend who was raised by a Chinese-style mother, although her parents were actually

German. Her mother pushed her to practice the violin for eight hours a day, and she rarely saw other people her age. Now she is my age, and she does not hate her mother or even resent her. She is grateful to her mother for instilling in her a drive and focus that she otherwise would have lacked. What she does hate is music, because it carries for her associations of loneliness and torture. She hasn't picked up the violin in a decade, and these days, she says, classical music leaves her cold. It's not an uncommon sentiment among prodigies: "I hate tennis," Andre Agassi says on the first page of his autobiography, *Open,* "hate it with a dark and secret passion, and always have."

7   The oddest part of Ms. Chua's parenting prescription is that it exists wholly apart from any passion or innate talent. The Chua women rarely express pure love of music; instead they express joy at having mastered it. Ms. Chua writes that she listened to CDs of Itzhak Perlman to figure out "why he sounded so good." This conception of child prodigies is not just Chinese. It is the extreme expression of the modern egalitarian notion of genius, as described by Malcolm Gladwell in *Outliers.* Anyone can be a genius, if they just put in 10,000 hours of practice! It doesn't matter if they can carry a tune or have especially limber fingers. They don't even have to like music.

8   But why not wait for your children to show some small spark of talent or interest in an activity before you force them to work at it for hours a day? What would be so bad if they followed their own interests and became an expert flutist, or a soccer star or even a master tightrope walker? What's so special about the violin and the piano?

9   Ms. Chua's most compelling argument is that happiness comes from mastery. "What Chinese parents understand is that nothing is fun until you're good at it." There is some truth to this, of course. But there is no reason to believe that calling your child "lazy" or "stupid" or "worthless" is a better way to motivate her to be good than some other more gentle but persistent mode. There is a vast world between perfection and loserdom. With her own children, Ms. Chua does not just want them to be good at what they do; she wants them to be better than everyone else.

10   "Children on their own never want to work," Ms. Chua writes, but in my experience this is not at all true. Left to their own devices, many children of this

generation still have giant superegos and a mad drive to succeed. They want to run faster than their siblings, be smarter than their classmates and save the world from environmental disaster. In my household, it's a struggle to get my children to steal a cookie from the cookie jar without immediately confessing.

11   Before I had children, I worried about all the wrong things. I was raised by (immigrant) parents who did not have a lot of money, and so I spent my childhood roaming the streets of Queens looking for an open handball court. My children, by contrast, have been raised by relatively well-off parents who can afford to send them to good schools and drum lessons. I wanted them to be coddled and never to experience hardship. But childhood, like life, doesn't work that way. Privilege does not shield a child from being painfully shy or awkward around peers or generally ostracized. There are a thousand ways a child's life can be difficult, and it's a parent's job to help them navigate through them.

12   Because Ms. Chua really likes bullet points, I will offer some of my own:

- Success will not make you happy.
- Happiness is the great human quest.
- Children have to find happiness themselves.
- It is better to have a happy, moderately successful child than a miserable high-achiever.

13   "Western parents," Ms. Chua writes, "have to struggle with their own conflicted feelings about achievement, and try and persuade themselves that they're not disappointed about how their kids turned out." With that, she really has our number. At the present moment in Western parenting, we believe that our children are special and entitled, but we do not have the guts or the tools to make that reality true for them. This explains, I think, a large part of the fascination with Ms. Chua's book.

14   But *Battle Hymn of the Tiger Mother* will lead us down the wrong path. The answer is not to aim for more effective child-perfecting techniques; it is to give up altogether on trying to perfect our children. Now I look upon those aimless days wandering the streets of Queens with fondness, because my life since then, starting the moment I entered a competitive high school, has been one ladder rung after another.

15   In her book, Ms. Chua refers, with some disdain, to her mother-in-law's belief that childhood should be full of "spontaneity, freedom, discovery and experience."

My mother-in-law believes that, too, and she is especially gifted at facilitating it with whatever tools are at hand: a cardboard box, some pots and pans, torn envelopes. One afternoon I watched her play with my then 2-year-old daughter for hours with some elephant toothpick holders and Play-Doh. I suppose that I could quantify what my daughter learned in those few hours: the letter *E*, the meaning of "pachyderm," who Hannibal was and how to love her grandmother 2% more. But the real point is that they earned themselves knee scabs marching across those imaginary Alps, and pretty soon it was time for a nap.

Links

1. Greene, Richard Allen. "Killer Daughter Case Ignites US Debate." *BBC News*. BBC, 3 May 2006. Web. 26 Apr. 2012.
2. "Parenting Today: Raising Successful Kids 'The Chinese Way.'" *Today.com*. MSNBC.com, 11 Jan. 2011. Web. 26 Apr. 2012.

Don Aucoin | *For Some, Helicopter Parenting Delivers Benefits*

DON AUCOIN is the chief theater critic of the *Boston Globe* and a coauthor of *Last Lion: The Fall and Rise of Ted Kennedy*. He has been a TV critic, a political reporter, and a feature writer. In 2000, Aucoin was one of twelve U.S. journalists selected to be a Nieman Fellow at Harvard University. He wrote this article for the *Globe* in 2009.

1   According to the image cemented in the public mind, helicopter parents hover over their children (hence the name). All through high school and even after the "kids" have turned 18, 19, 20, and beyond, helicopter parents try to micromanage their lives. Eyebrow-raising stories abound of the mother who accompanies her 24-year-old son to a job fair or the father who writes a college essay for his 19-year-old daughter.

2   But wait. Beyond such undeniable excesses, a quiet reappraisal of helicopter parents is underway. Some researchers have begun to argue that late adolescence and young adulthood are such minefields today—emotional, social, sexual, logistical, psychological—that there are valid reasons for parents to remain deeply involved in their children's lives even after the kids are, technically speaking, adults. Moreover, they say, with the economy in a deep swoon, helicopter parents may have a vital role to play as career counselors or even as providers of financial aid to their offspring.

3   "There is this stereotypical, oversensationalized, negative portrait, where they use 'over-parenting' and 'helicopter parenting' synonymously," says Barbara Dafoe Whitehead, a social historian and author who studies family issues. "Over-parenting is not letting your kids take the consequences of their actions, swooping down to rescue them, and the result would be a spoiled brat. But helicopter parenting is entirely different, and I think it is a positive style of child-rearing."

4   Pattie Knight concurs. Even though Knight's twin daughters, Symphony and Kymberlee, are 19 and attending college, Knight remains deeply involved in their day-to-day lives. She goes shopping with them. She gives them advice about their relationships. She weighs in when they are worried about an upcoming test or wondering which class to take. She helps decorate their dorm rooms. One night a week, when Symphony gets off work from her part-time job, Knight drives from her Newton home to downtown Boston, picks her up, and transports her back to Pine Manor College.

5   Some of Knight's friends roll their eyes at how much she does for her daughters, and she acknowledges it can be excessive at times. For example, by her count she and Symphony spoke on the phone 144 times in January, though she notes her daughter did most of the

Pattie Knight with her twin daughters, Symphony and Kymberlee

calling. "Even their boyfriends call me, Lord have mercy," Knight says with a laugh. But the bottom line to Knight is that her style is helping her to forge a close and lasting bond with her daughters. "The thing that I like about our relationship is that whenever they're nervous or unsure about a decision they're about to make, that's when they need me," she says.

6   That reflects what Stephanie Coontz, director of research at the Council on Contemporary Families, sees as an unacknowledged dividend to helicopter parenting that is becoming more apparent: namely, the enduring friendship often forged between the generations, in contrast to the "generation gap" of old. "Obviously, there are horrible extremes that helicopter parents can go to, where they don't allow their children to succeed or fail on their own," Coontz says. "But in the majority of cases, this increased closeness between parents and kids is found among healthy students, not unhealthy ones." That was what Jillian Kinzie found—to her astonishment—when she helped conduct a national survey in 2007 at 750 colleges and universities.

7   When Kinzie, the associate director of Indiana University's Center for Postsecondary Research, first saw the results of a question about helicopter parenting on the survey, her immediate reaction was: "This can't be right. We have to go back and look at this again." The survey found that college students whose parents fit the survey's definition of helicopter parents—they had met frequently with campus officials to discuss issues involving their children—were more engaged in learning and reported greater satisfaction with their colleges, even though they had slightly lower grades than other students. "They tended to have more interactions with the faculty, they tended to be involved in active learning, collaborative learning, more often than their peers," Kinzie says. "I have to admit I was surprised. I had the same negative ideas about helicopter parenting. But perhaps these are students who needed a little support to get over a hurdle, and their parents intervened, and perhaps helped those students stay in college.

8   "Perhaps I'm less concerned about these helicopter parents than I used to be."

9   Still, there is far from a consensus that helicopter parenting is a plus, especially when it involves older children. Whitehead defines helicopter parenting as a "high level of oversight and supervision, keeping tabs on the kids but not interfering in every activity or decision," and she defines over-parenting as "intrusive involvement, never allowing the kids the freedom to make a decision and live with its consequences." Inevitably, that means the line between helicopter parenting and over-parenting is a porous one, often crossed.

10   Susan Newman, the author of *Nobody's Baby Now: Reinventing Your Adult Relationship with Your Mother and Father,* maintains that helicopter parents "do their children an extreme disservice. . . . When parents are making decisions for their children all the time and protecting them, when they get out on their own they don't know a thing about disappointment," Newman says. "I've seen a lot of these children who are parented in the helicopter manner who can't make a decision. They are calling home constantly: 'I don't get along with my roommate, what should I do? My roommate ate my food, what should I do?'" In one case, Newman says, the college-age daughter of a helicopter parent she knows called home to ask her mother whether she should have sex with a particular young man.

11   Such extremes are easy to find and hard to defend. But changing economic circumstances—namely, the recession—may give helicopter parenting more legitimacy. Financial independence will become even harder for young adults, especially since so many of them are leaving college burdened by tens of thousands of dollars in debt. So they may increasingly rely on their parents for monetary support or a temporary place to live, or both. "Younger generations have always been poor, but rarely have they been so much in debt at 21 as this generation," observes Whitehead.

12   Sara Christie of Swampscott does not necessarily embrace the term *"helicopter parent,"* and says she tries to give her 16-year-old son Steve space, privacy, and room to

grow. But she makes no apologies for her close and vigilant relationship with him. They are "friends" on Facebook; she still makes sure that he wears a helmet while bicycling and skateboarding; and if she thinks it necessary she will text him in school to find out "what class he's in, how's it going, does he need a ride later."

13   And when Steve goes to college in two years? "I want to be very involved," Christie answers, then pauses before acknowledging: "I just learned something, answering that question. . . . I feel confident that I can and will be involved with my son on a daily basis, even if he goes to college far away," Christie says. "That means a lot to me."

Understanding the Issue of Sports Helmet Use

Concern about the damaging effects of concussions and the efficacy of sports helmets has been growing in recent years. In 2011, the *American Journal of Sports Medicine* published a study that found an annual increase of 15.5 percent in concussions for high school sports over the eleven-year period from 1997–1998 to 2007–2008. For boys, football was responsible for more than half of the concussions, and for girls, it was soccer. In professional football, the National Football League (NFL) issued its first guidelines regarding concussions in 2009 and has revised those guidelines periodically—banning blindside hits to the head, imposing large fines on players responsible for helmet-to-helmet hits, mandating baseline neurological testing, and requiring players with concussion symptoms during a game to be examined by a doctor. Research indicates that although helmets reduce skull fractures and head-injury fatalities, they do not do much to prevent concussions from small as well as big hits. In 2012, former players sued the NFL for fraud and negligence, charging that the NFL downplayed the risks of multiple concussions and discredited valid research linking concussions with brain injury and dementia.

Nate Jackson | *The NFL's Head Cases*

NATE JACKSON played professional football from 2003 to 2009, first as a wide receiver and then as a tight end for the Denver Broncos. He contributes regularly to *Slate's* Sports Nut column and writes for *Deadspin,* a site covering "sports gossip, athlete culture, and other things you won't find on any other sports-oriented site." The article reprinted here appeared in the *New York Times's* Opinion section in October 2010, just as the issue of helmet-to-helmet collisions was gaining traction.

1   After an unusually large number of brain-jarring tackles last week, the National Football League[1] went on the offensive against players. Commissioner Roger Goodell doled out a total of $175,000 in fines to three players and threatened future suspensions[2] for what a league official called "devastating" hits to the head.

2   As someone who played in the NFL for six years, I'm all for reducing reckless play as much as possible. But the league's effort to police particular kinds of hits raises plenty of questions. For instance, what if I lead with my head to make a tackle and knock myself out? Do I get suspended for that? What if I lead with my

head and no one gets hurt? What if I hit an opponent with my shoulder and knock him out? What if I hit him in the rib cage and puncture his lung? What if we're both going for the ball and I catch him under the chin with my helmet? What if he dies?

3   The truth is that NFL players have been using their heads as weapons since they first donned pads as children. It's the nature of the sport. Sure, coaches tell you to wrap up an opponent with your arms, to keep your head up, to see what you hit. But when a player is moving forward, his knees are bent and his body is leaning forward. The head leads no matter what.

4   Some say players should block and tackle with the shoulder pads instead. Doing that means choosing a side, trying to hit an opponent with the left or right shoulder. That technique will get you cut by any professional team before you can begin to perfect it. It uses only half of your body and half of your strength, and it removes your arms from the equation. In a head-first hit, the arms are free to follow the first contact with a bear hug that brings the opponent to the ground.

5   In my first two seasons in the NFL, I played wide receiver, so I rarely had to concern myself with blocking or tackling. Then I was moved to tight end, where I quickly learned that to have any chance of containing the large men across the line of scrimmage, I had to hit them square in the face with my helmet. "Put a hat on him," coaches implore.

6   I felt woozy or "saw stars" plenty of times, but that didn't stop me, because using my head was the only effective technique. It was either lead with my head or get trampled. On kickoff returns, I had to sprint back 30 yards, whip around, size up the man I was assigned to block and take his helmet directly in my face. Avoid that contact and your manhood is questioned. The brain cells I lost on plays like that were of less concern to me than being called out in meetings by coaches.

7   While only the most violent, dramatic and egregious hits make the highlights, there are probably six or seven helmet-to-helmet hits on every play in the NFL The offensive and defensive linemen are smacking heads, running backs are colliding with linebackers, tight ends are blocking defensive ends, safeties are flying in to make tackles.

8   Before the 1950s, when they wore soft helmets without face masks, players didn't lead with their heads. They dived at opponents' legs and corralled them with their arms. Leading with the head meant facial disfigurement and lots of stitches. But once leather was replaced by hard plastic, enclosing the head in protective armor, all bets were off. Couple that with the size of today's players and the speed of the modern game, and you have a recipe for cerebellum custard.

9   I understand the NFL's desire to protect "defenseless" players. But how do we define *defenseless*? Someone who isn't paying attention? Someone who doesn't see you? There are instances where it's obvious, like a player jogging on the opposite side of the field from the action. The NFL already does a good job of penalizing those types of hits.

10   But when a receiver is trying to catch a ball or avoid being tackled, the height of his head is constantly changing, often making it impossible for a defensive player to judge the point of impact. One of the players fined by the NFL last week, James Harrison of the Pittsburgh Steelers, was right to say that the penalties handicap his playing style. Maybe a new helmet design would help, something that would better protect the skull and brain but also offer a more forgiving outer surface. The NFL could also try educating coaches, who now believe that a headless hit is an ineffectual one, about the perils of head-first tackling, in hopes that over time safer techniques would become the norm. Or maybe the league should do away with helmets altogether and return to its early "rag days," bloody noses and all.

11   But stiffer on-field penalties, fines, suspensions, seminars, summit meetings, press releases—these are knee-jerk public-relations reactions that will do little. The only way to prevent head injuries in football is no more football. It is a violent game by design. The use of helmets plays a critical role in creating that violence. The players understand the risks, and the fans enjoy watching them take those risks. Changing the rules enough to truly safeguard against head injuries would change the game beyond recognition. It wouldn't be football anymore.

Links

1. "National Football League Labor Dispute." *New York Times*. New York Times, n.d. Web. 25 Apr. 2012.
2. National Football League. "Goodell Issues Memo Enforcing Player Safety Rules." *NFL.com*. NFL Enterprises, LLC, 20 Oct. 2011. Web. 25 Apr. 2012.

David Weisman | *Disposable Heroes*

DAVID WEISMAN is a neurologist in Pennsylvania. He contributes to *Seed* magazine on issues related to the brain. This article appeared on seedmagazine.com in January 2011, just before the close of the regular football season.

1   In an ancient Aztec cultural practice, priests would choose a man to represent one of their gods, Tezcatlipoca. The man would be worshiped as a god for a year, but at a preordained date, the priests would sacrifice him, sometimes cannibalizing his body. Each year the priests turned from the sacrifice to select a new "god," repeating the cycle of reverence and destruction.

2   I wonder what the Aztecs would make of the view in front of me. I am in a sports bar with my family, eating after a walk around town. The other patrons' eyes mostly rest, enthralled, on the many football games televised before them.

3   One can't avoid watching the flatscreens that hang off every wall, or the brutal athleticism they capture. Throughout each play, the players' heads can be seen as shells traveling at a certain vector, pinballing with others, sometimes whipping to sudden impacts with the ground. Force equals mass times acceleration. Masses hit each other with high velocities, creating sudden and twisting accelerations, and the forces proportionally rise. No human rule trumps physics.

4   The high-definition flatscreen TVs show it all, but don't provide a deeper, more physiological look. Inside a football helmet is a skull, and inside each skull is a free-floating brain. Inside the brain are billions of neurons, chattering with each other in a code we scarcely understand, wired to each other with long and slender projections called axons. An internal scaffolding structure holds each axon in place. The axons crisscross the brain, side to side, forwards and backwards, up and down.

5   As force is applied to the brain, a shockwave ripples through. If large enough, the shock tears the axons and can result in catastrophic injury. Smaller forces stun the neurons, their electrical firing decreases, and symptoms of concussion occur. The player may go limp, or stumble and appear unfocused. He is usually amnestic of the event. If the force is milder, none of these symptoms may manifest, but the changes are still felt in the long and slender axons. Their supporting scaffolds, on a human scale akin to bridges from San Francisco to Taipei and Perth to Cape Town, experience an earthquake.

6   Over and over, every head blow stresses the scaffolding. A protein called tau normally stabilizes the scaffolds, but the tau proteins become dysfunctional, pathologic, then malignant. The tau binds together, twists in on itself, assembles into sharp aggregates that poke holes in the fragile cell wall and kill the neuron. A neuron goes silent, its axonal bridge crumbles. As the brain digests the dead neuron, it leaves behind the twisted skeleton of the tau aggregate, a "tangle."

7   Other than the injuries that are so obvious they leave the player unconscious, impaired, or dead, we do not know exactly how harmful low-velocity impacts are. We see the ice above the water—in the form of a stunned and staggering player—but we're starting to realize how deep the risk extends. Emerging data shows low-force head blows produce tau pathologies. Over time the minor head injuries combine and the tau can turn malignant. When enough cells die, symptoms begin. It is now known as chronic traumatic encephalopathy (CTE). It was "dementia pugilistica" when I was in med school, falsely implying a restriction to boxers, as in the later *Rocky* movies. Before that it was called "punch drunk." Just as "shell-shock" came before "Post-Traumatic Stress Disorder," these are different names for the same problem. It leaves victims with cognitive and emotional derangements, prone to odd behaviors, suicide, and dementia. There is no treatment. In the parlance of the announcers, you can't unring the bell.

8   Knowing all this, I can hardly watch the game, but I can't stop myself from watching either. The plays on the bar's screens are a thrilling combination of grace, toughness, and skill, and the sport is easily seen as a

metaphor for all that is great in humans. But within this escapism it's easy to forget that football is only a game, albeit one with real-world sacrifices and consequences.

9   Consider the case of Owen Thomas, a University of Pennsylvania football player who committed suicide, and whose parents afterward came forward to expose the truth behind the tragedy. Thomas's brain carried an amount of skeleton tangles that would be expected in mild dementia. His impact burden was small, and he may never have even suffered a concussion, yet at only 21 years of age, his brain showed tangles, which have become the signature injury from repetitive head traumas. Tangles are a signature for which football carries a pen full of ink.

10   From junior-high football and even earlier, boys are told to hit hard. Even though they may never suffer a concussion, they do suffer head blow after head blow. It seems no one is safe, and the level of risk is unknown. Mr. Thomas did not

"Better helmets" are a laughable solution.

have unique neuropathology; there are other deceased players who have displayed similar symptoms: Chris Henry, John Glenn Grimsley, and Justin Strzelczyk, to name just a few. There are likely to be many more still unrecognized and, judging from the bizarre behavior of others still living, more to come. As of now, the youngest case was an 18-year-old player. It seems the more football players' brains come under neuropathologists' microscopes, the more pathology they display.

11   Perhaps it is wrong to directly compare football to a dead religion that sacrificed young men and ate them. But it is easy to do partially because the Aztecs were honest: one year as an enslaved god, then death. We don't have the data, so we can't offer a timeline, or a reasonable cap on concussions, or guess at the probabilities of a player losing his mind in the next year, three years, or three decades.

12   Why not?

13   There is something sacrosanct about the game itself. It celebrates our ideals of battle and victory. It touches the divine, and not in just the inhuman abilities and sizes of the players. The numbers of fans bear this out. They not only find entertainment; they invest their passions in it. Many fans, in all outward appearances, worship the players, and treat the teams as a personal, religious, and tribal brand. Better than discussions with in-laws over Thanksgiving dinner, where all these aphasic dogmas compete, in the matter of football, one clearly wins. Religion, ethnicity, and team are even explicitly linked in some colleges: Go Irish!*

14   A touch of the divine may explain why Mr. Thomas's death and neuropathology have been met with words of no consequence, no change, and certainly no moratorium. Currently the NFL takes "no position" on low-velocity head impacts—impacts that, though they do not cause concussions, can cause CTE. Proposals so far have been designed around a single desire: Do not upset the boat. "Better helmets" are a laughable solution, as if any helmet could eliminate the full inertial force of a charging offensive lineman. Who knows, it might be paradoxically more sensible to have worse helmets, so the players routinely feel the impact's force as nature intended, and consequently modulate their play. Sensors to measure helmet force and accelerations are the best start in a good-faith effort to collect data, but without medical outcomes, the numbers have no context. One NFL study will compare 120 retired players with 60 players with no game time. The study's design is telling: a "placebo" group with nearly the same exposure, chosen to deliver negative results.

15   There is a "head, neck, and spine committee" that tries to keep things as safe as possible, akin to making a playground safe without getting rid of the hungry Grizzly bears. There is a new, moderately sensible policy about visible concussions: When symptoms surface in a player, that player cannot get on the field for one day, and the player must be examined and cleared by a neurologist before suiting up again.

16   How like theology it all is. With no effects on low-impact injuries, these words, studies, and positions allow fans to feel better about their revered amusement. The thousands of coaches, vendors, journalists, and merchandisers turn to their next tasks. Among all those who don't wear the helmets, there is a serious moral hazard.

17   In my business, medicine, if a product caused a brain disease or death, then we would immediately work to define the risk. We would get the numbers, quantifying

---

*A reference to the Fighting Irish, the football team of the Catholic University of Notre Dame. [Editor's note]

how many individuals are harmed compared to how many are exposed or treated. We would quantitatively define any resulting neurological damage and deficits, and try to define safe behavioral thresholds. Finally, we would perform a calculation: Do the risks of the product or behavior in question outweigh its benefits? Medicine is hardly perfect in this regard, and in the places it fails to quantify risk, faith-based reasoning reigns: witness herbal supplements.

18   But risk can be downplayed, especially if the culture doesn't want to hear it. Adherents assign infinite benefit to something seen as divine. In relation, any evil can be permitted. Outright denial is the chief danger and most common tactic in the face of anything that might disrupt wishful thinking. A perceived immunity to risk is rarely an actual immunity to risk.

19   It is temporal distance from the human-sacrificing Aztecs that allows us to find their practice abhorrent, an example of a culture worshiping death and false celebrity. They were unable to elevate their culture out of Stone-Age technologies, unable to address their problems. Because they could not improve themselves with new medicines and new technologies, or put an end to their puny internecine wars, their empire came to an end. Yet they found their behavior reasonable. They were invested in their religion and culture, and found themselves as normal as we find ourselves.

20   We also declare ourselves different and more civilized than those today who watch dogs fight to the death, and those who in the ancient world watched gladiator death matches. We like to imagine there is a comfortable margin. After all, most of us watch these events via divine technology, each of us a modern Zeus, removed from visceral immediacy in the Olympus of our living rooms. But our view is suspect. The TV's divine eye feeds an unchanged, insatiable, human lust for blood sport, death, and celebrity. When considering the victims, Owen Thomas and others like him, it is difficult to distinguish between their game and those we pretend to be so different.

21   What is the good? And where does it lie? I do not know. I am not a moral philosopher. Nor am I a fan, nor one whose salary depends upon not understanding football's risks. I am a neurologist. Perhaps I place too great a value on brains, not enough on selling cars and beer, and not enough on divine amusements.

22   Other societies display barbarism, which is supported by seemingly sacrosanct cultural inertias. People fight cocks, kill albinos, or mutilate genitals. You can usually find internal efforts to stop these abominations. The efforts seem a far fringe and minority view. This isn't, however, such a far fringe view for football. The American Academy of Pediatrics' guideline on concussions has this to say, "When in doubt, sit it out." Most see the wisdom when applied to concussed individuals. Current data introduces doubt into the perceived safety of multiple low-velocity impacts. It is reasonable to apply the same guideline to football in general, from junior high to college and beyond.

23   I don't anticipate action, even to sit out developing brains until we know more. Nor do I predict a ban on tackles, a weight limit, or an upper limit of traumatic exposure. What does it say about a society without support for a moratorium or limitations on this game? The silence is unflattering, as millions turn to their TVs.

Lane Wallace | *Do Sports Helmets Help or Hurt?*

 LANE WALLACE is an adventure writer and pilot, who contributes regularly to *Sport Aviation* magazine and is an honorary member of the United States Air Force Society of Wild Weasels. She has written a number of books, including *Flights of Discovery* (2006) and *Wild Blue Wonders: Exploring the Magic of Flight* (2001). Her latest book is *Unforgettable: My 10 Best Flights* (2009). The following article appeared in the *Atlantic* in February 2011.

1 After years of too little attention, the subject of head injuries in sports, and how to prevent them, is now what Twitter would call a "trending topic." First came the turnaround in attitudes toward NFL player head injuries, and the helmet-to-helmet tackles and hits that increase the risk of those injuries. Then came the discussion about skier Lindsey Vonn's continued participation in the World Cup last week, despite clear indications and admissions on her part that she was still skiing behind the course and "in a fog" after suffering a concussion in a training accident. And now, there's the U.S. lacrosse league debating whether or not the girls—who now only have to wear protective eye gear—should be required to wear helmets as well.

2 Girls' lacrosse has dramatically different rules than the boys' game: body checks are illegal, as are certain stick checks, and there is a regulated safety zone around each girl's head. Nevertheless, research quoted in a *New York Times* article[1] today concluded that when it comes to concussions, lacrosse ranks third in female sports (behind basketball and soccer). In addition, despite the less-aggressive nature and rules of the girls' game, girls' lacrosse has an in-game concussion rate only 15 percent lower than the boys.

3 Improving safety has had more to do with changing a group's culture and attitudes about high-risk activities than with any technological advance. So if concussions are an issue in girls' lacrosse, the argument goes, we should require girls to wear more protective headgear. After all, the boys' helmets, intended to reduce skull fracture and intracranial bleeding, are thought to reduce the number of concussions, as well.

Improving safety has had more to do with changing a group's culture and attitudes about high-risk activities than with any technological advance.

4 But does the addition of extra safety gear actually reduce the risk of the injuries it is designed to prevent? Well, yes . . . and no. Which is what fuels the debate on the issue. Taken by itself, it's easy enough to prove that wearing a helmet, like wearing a seat belt, decreases the chance or severity of injury in an impact. But humans are far more complex creatures than crash test dummies. And so the true impact of safety equipment becomes far more complex, as well.

5 In his 1995 book *Risk*,[2] British researcher John Adams spelled out several reasons why safety equipment does not always increase safety the way its designers or legislators think it will. The first is a phenomenon called "risk compensation," in which humans respond to additional safety equipment by taking greater risks than they did when they felt less protected. For example, Adams said, while seat belts unquestionably gave a person better protection if they were in a collision, the chances of being in a collision went up in places with seat belt laws, because seat-belted drivers took more risks in how they drove.

6 For all the time and discussion space we devote to the goal of eliminating accidents or injuries, Adams suggests that people have "risk thermostats," and that we all adjust our behavior to maintain the level of risk in our lives that we find acceptable. We all compensate for the extra margin provided by safety equipment to some degree, and some of us will push the new boundaries further than others. All of which means that safety equipment often doesn't make as much of a difference as its proponents believe it will.

7 Indeed, there are many who argue that mandatory helmets, and increasingly strong helmets, have actually exacerbated the problem of head injury in sports ranging from boys' lacrosse and ice hockey to professional football. So perhaps helmets for female lacrosse players really *are* a bad idea, as U.S. Lacrosse (the sport's governing body) argues.

8 So what's the solution? In many cases, improving safety has had more to do with changing a group's culture and attitudes about high-risk activities than it does any specific technological advance—especially in individual sports or hobbies.

9 A prominent example is the Cirrus Design company (a company profiled by James Fallows in his *Atlantic* article[3] and subsequent book[4] *Free Flight*). In an effort to build a safer aircraft, Cirrus included a full-airplane parachute and vastly improved "glass" cockpit displays in its Cirrus airplane. But when the airplane was first introduced, it actually had a significantly higher-than-average fatality rate, because pilots—comforted by the extra technology and safety systems—"compensated" by pushing the aircraft into weather they wouldn't otherwise have undertaken. In the end, the company was able to bring its accident rates down by requiring additional training and working to change the culture of its buyers—at least to some degree.

10   The field of SCUBA diving also vastly reduced its accident rate over several decades by changing its group attitudes toward risk. Once upon a time, diving was a macho sport where the toughest regularly pushed the limits. Today, attitudes about pushing the limits have changed. Dive without a buddy, push your depth or time limits, and a diver today is likely to be seen as stupid, not brave.

11   Notably, the NFL is now taking a similar approach toward head injuries. Instead of simply improving the cushioning in players' helmets, the NFL is trying to change the league's culture, rules and consequences related to hits to the head, or tackles "leading" with a player's helmet. How well that works remains to be seen, of course. But the popular image and standard for what's "admirable" and "acceptable" in tackling technique has already changed dramatically, even in the breathtakingly short span of a single season.

12   But girls' lacrosse already has a restrictive set of rules regarding contact. And most of the concussions its players suffer come from accidental contact and falls, not intentionally aggressive maneuvering. So is it a different case? Could helmets actually make it safer?

13   "I think helmets encourage you to push the limits of whatever the rules are," one high school athlete responded, when I asked the question. "If you're only allowed one kind of hit, you'll hit as hard as you can in that one way. But given that girls' lacrosse has so many rules restricting contact, [helmets] might actually help."

14   Of course, given the complexities of how humans assess and respond to risk, and the fact that lacrosse players are unlikely to be timid or risk-adverse by nature, it's also a fair bet that whatever safety margin helmets provide would—at best—be narrowed by some amount by compensating behavior on the part of the players. Which means at some point in the future, U.S. Lacrosse, like Cirrus and the NFL, may find itself compensating for that compensation through more complex solutions than the seemingly simple answer of a helmet.

Links

1. Schwarz, Alan. "A Case against Helmets in Lacrosse." *New York Times*. New York Times, 16 Feb. 2011. Web. 25 Apr. 2012.
2. Adams, John. *Risk*. London: Routledge, 1995. Print.
3. Fallows, James. "Discouraging News Out of Oshkosh." *Atlantic*. The Atlantic Monthly Group, 31 July 2009. Web. 25 Apr. 2012.
4. Fallows, James. *Free Flight: From Airline Hell to a New Age of Travel*. New York: PublicAffairs, 2001. Print.

Understanding the Issue of Compensating Organ Donors

The issue of compensating organ donors is fraught ethically, geopolitically, and economically. Obviously, one needs to have died to donate certain organs, such as the heart, but for other organs, like kidneys, healthy individuals can apparently live a long life after donating. Throughout the world, demand for organs far exceeds the supply. The shortage of organs has led to an international organ trade, sometimes called transplant tourism. A number of nations—including India, Pakistan, and Peru—are commonly known as organ-exporting countries, whereas the United States, Saudi Arabia, and Australia are some of the major organ-importing countries. The question of whether organ donors should be compensated—and, if so, how—has become increasingly heated. In 1999, Nancy Scheper-Hughes, an anthropology professor at the University of California, Berkeley, helped launch Organs Watch, which tracks the global organ market. She also coedited the essay collection *Commodifying*

Bodies (2003), which examines global attitudes and practices about organ donation. There have been several public debates on the issue, such as one aired in 2008 on National Public Radio and another printed in 2010 in the *New York Times* Room for Debate series.

Sally Satel | *Yuan a Kidney?*

SALLY SATEL received a donor kidney in 2006, after living with renal failure for two years. She wrote about her experience in an article published in the *New York Times*. A psychiatrist, Satel publishes regularly on health care. Her books include *When Altruism Isn't Enough: The Case for Compensating Kidney Donors* (2009), *The Health Disparity Myth* (2006), and *One Nation under Therapy* (2005). She is a resident scholar at the conservative American Enterprise Institute. The following article appeared in *Slate* magazine in 2011.

1   China's record on organ trafficking is by now a well-known international horror story. The vast majority of organs transplanted each year in Chinese hospitals are taken from executed criminals—and allegedly from political detainees, such as members of the Falun Gong; charges that are currently under investigation[1] by the U.N. Human Rights Council and Amnesty International. Now, paradoxically, China is proposing forward-thinking transplant policies; commendable laws that, if properly carried out, challenge the status quo and major international health organizations.

2   China's black market is why paying patients—citizens as well as foreigners—can get a new kidney or liver in a matter of days or weeks. Such lightning speed is unheard of in countries without black markets in organs; in countries that rely solely on altruistic giving, the wait for a deceased-donor organ is years long. In major cities in the United States, for example, it is not unusual for patients on dialysis to wait eight or 10 years before a kidney becomes available—a wait that only about half can survive.

3   Last winter, a 26-year-old migrant worker from Hunan made headlines in the Chinese press because he wanted to sell a kidney to pay off gambling debts. A black-market broker promised him 40,000 yuan (about $6,000), but at the last minute the migrant worker got cold feet. According to the man's story, the broker then took him to a small hospital[2] and bound him to an operating table, where a nurse sedated him and surgeons removed his left kidney. Authorities are now investigating, but China's thriving kidney trade makes accounts like these sound quite plausible.

4   In 2007, China began licensing transplant centers in an effort to raise standards of practice and regulate performance. Only 163 of the more than 600 centers qualified and are now authorized to perform transplants, the vice minister of health, Huang Jiefu, told the *Lancet* in an article published earlier this month.[3] Huang, who is regarded as uncommonly open about his aversion to using prisoners as the major source of transplantable organs, still acknowledges that the market is far from moribund. Indeed, the same *Lancet* article notes that transplant specialists in the United States and Europe say they still occasionally see patients who report having purchased their transplants in China.

5   Meanwhile, the need for organs remains vast. The Chinese population itself drives a demand because the country has virtually no culture of altruistic deceased organ donation. Last year, roughly 1.5 million Chinese needed kidneys, livers, lungs, and hearts, but only 10,000 received them—the vast majority through illicit means.

6   Even in countries with much better records of deceased organ donation, the shortfalls are dramatic. In desperation, patients go underground. The World Health

Organization estimates that 5 to 10 percent of the roughly 60,000 kidney transplant operations performed worldwide each year are obtained in the shady organ bazaars of Northern Africa, Asia, Eastern Europe, and South America.

7   Thus, we face a dual tragedy: On one side, thousands of patients who die each year waiting for a kidney; on the other, a human rights fiasco in which corrupt brokers deceive indigent donors about the nature of surgery, cheat them out of payment, and ignore their post-surgical needs.

8   Last month, China's health ministry announced a proposal that could expand the pool of organs available for transplant surgeries. Huang told the Chinese press that his office was considering several possible incentives. These include tax rebates, deduction of transplant-related hospital fees, medical insurance, tuition waivers for donors' family members, or deduction of burial fees for people who donated in death.

9   Unfortunately, much of the international transplant establishment — including the World Health Organization, the Transplantation Society, and the World Medical Association — focuses exclusively on obliterating illicit organ sales. While this may seem like a reasonable approach to abhorrent practices, in reality it is a lethal prescription.

10   Efforts to stamp out corruption either drive it further underground or cause unauthorized markets to pop up elsewhere. And the organ trade, like a vampire, is hard to kill. When the Turkish authorities clamped down on illicit sales about six years ago, patients from the Middle East who had traveled there for kidneys rerouted to the Philippines. Then in 2008, the president of the Philippines banned foreigners from receiving transplants. Fewer transplants were conducted with the tragic and predictable trade-off that patients either died or went elsewhere, perhaps to Lima, Peru; Cairo; or Pristina, Kosovo.

11   Paying for organs is not "opportunistic human cannibalism,"[4] as Jeremy Chapman, the past president of the international, Montreal-based Transplantation Society, puts it. The patient is no predator; he is as desperate to save his life as an impoverished donor is to salvage his own.

12   Nor are organ sales "a filthy business in the same subcategory as the sex trade and child pornography,"[5]

as nephrologist Gabriel Danovitch of the University of California at Los Angeles has claimed. Prostitution and child pornography — legal or not — debase everyone involved. Organs, by contrast, are the rare trafficked good that saves lives. And if the vendors were able to engage in licit, safe, transparent, and regulated transactions, they too could improve their welfare.

13   But alas, this sensible vision runs afoul of ideology. "Altruism is the bioethical foundation [for obtaining organs]," affirmed a 2009 report by Council of Europe and the United Nations. "Organs should not give rise to financial gain."

14   Why not? It is all too easy to romanticize altruism. The "gift of life" is indeed precious. I received it from a friend in 2006. But I am not so naive about my good fortune as to ignore the reality that altruism is not producing enough organs. Government-sponsored compensation of healthy individuals who are willing to give one of their kidneys to save the life of a dying stranger is the best solution.

Paying for organs is not "opportunistic human cannibalism."

15   In-kind benefits such as those China is considering, paired with lengthy medical screening, would be unattractive to desperate people (who might otherwise rush to donate for a large sum of instant cash). This should allay concerns that poorer citizens would be effectively forced to donate.

16   But coming from a government that has legitimized organ harvesting from detained individuals, China's proposals may be rejected out of hand by the international medical community. Understandably so. After all, China's transplant practices are profoundly opaque, with few details on clinical protocols or outcomes published in the medical literature except in the breach.

17   If China is serious about creating an incentive program, transparency and accountability will be vital to its integrity and safety. Transactions on a black market are dangerous because they are illicit, not because they are transactions.

18   A number of countries recognize this and have carefully modified their laws to permit donor enrichment. Singapore, for example, helps cover health insurance costs for living kidney donors. In Manila, a major transplant center offered business grants and home-improvement packages to donors. That government-approved program lasted four years until 2008, when it was dismantled by

the Philippine government under pressure from the World Health Organization.

19 In Israel, citizens who register to become posthumous donors get slight priority on the waiting list for organs, if they ever need one. Israeli families may also now accept up to $13,400 to "memorialize" the deceased donor with, for example, a scholarship in his name. More controversially, Iran pays cash to kidney donors. China's initiative, should it be undertaken with requisite oversight, would be unprecedented in scope and in range of benefits offered to donors.

20 These countries' efforts are being studied by the Nuffield Council on Bioethics, a British ethics think tank that's pondering how the United Kingdom can increase organ donation. It's considering a broad range of potential actions, from the innocuous (an official "thank you" to the donor) to the audacious (creating a free market in body parts). The council will release its report in the fall.

21 No one seriously thinks the council will opt for unfettered sales, but the bottom line of any serious consideration is inescapably this: The only way to save lives and starve underground markets abroad is to provide more transplants at home. And the only way to do that is to break radically — and ethically — with a status quo that forbids an informed donor to be rewarded for saving the life of a stranger.

Links

1. Falun Gong Human Rights Working Group, "United Nations Human Rights Special Rapporteurs Reiterate Findings on China's Organ Harvesting from Falun Gong Practitioners." *Information Daily*. Egovmonitor.com, 9 May 2008. Web. 25 Apr. 2012.
2. Aihua, Wang, Yuchen, Lai, and Di, Wu. "Illegal Organ Deals Strike Fear into Hearts of Chinese." *English.news.cn*, Xinhua, 8 June 2011. Web. 25 Apr. 2012.
3. Alcorn, Ted. "China's Organ Transplant System in Transition." *Lancet*. Elsevier Limited, 4 June 2011. Web. 25 Apr. 2012. DOI: 10.1016/S0140-6736(11)60794-0
4. Satel, Sally. "Is It Ever Right to Buy or Sell Human Organs?" *New Internationalist*. New Internationist, Oct. 2010. Web. 25 Apr. 2012.
5. Smith, Michael. "Desperate Americans Buy Kidneys from Peru Poor in Fatal Trade." Bloomberg Markets Magazine. Bloomberg LP, 12 May 2011. Web. 25 Apr. 2012.

National Kidney Foundation | *Financial Incentives for Organ Donation*

THE NONPROFIT National Kidney Foundation works to prevent kidney disease, promote research and education related to kidney disease, and fund services for those people affected by kidney disease. It publishes the *American Journal of Kidney Diseases* among other journals and newspapers. The position statement that follows was adopted in 2003 and is posted to the National Kidney Foundation's Web site.

1 The National Kidney Foundation opposes all efforts to legalize payments for human organs for use in transplantation and urges the federal government to retain the prohibition against the purchase of organs that is codified in Title III of the National Organ Transplant Act of 1984.

2 Offering direct or indirect economic benefits in exchange for organ donation is inconsistent with our values as a society. Any attempt to assign a monetary value to the human body, or body parts, either arbitrarily, or through market forces, diminishes human dignity. By treating the body as property, in the hope of

increasing organ supply, we risk devaluating the very human life we seek to save. Providing any form of compensation for organs may be an affront to the thousands of donor families and living donors who have already made an altruistic gift of life and it could alienate Americans who are prepared to donate life-saving organs out of humanitarian concern. In addition, it disregards families who are unable to donate organs but do consent to tissue donation.

3   Offering money for organs can be viewed as an attempt to coerce economically disadvantaged Americans to participate in organ donation. Furthermore, since the economically disadvantaged have been shown to be less likely to be organ transplant candidates, financial incentives for organ donation could be characterized as exploitation.

4   While payment for organs has real potential to undermine the transplant system in this country, its ability to increase the supply of organs for transplantation is questionable. In a recent survey of families who refused to donate organs of their loved ones who have died, 92% said that payment would not have persuaded them to donate. Public opinion polls and focus groups have disclosed that many Americans are not inclined to be organ donors because they distrust the U.S. health care system, in general, and, in particular, because they are concerned that the health care of potential organ donors might be compromised if their donor status were known. A program of financial incentives for organ donation is not likely to change these perceptions and, indeed, may aggravate mistrust. This is true even with the suggested subterfuge of paying the money to funeral homes. That strategy would most likely simply raise the price of a funeral without benefiting the family at all. Making financial incentives available at the time of death opens the possibility of creating new sources of tension and dissension between family members who are faced with the option of organ

> *The National Kidney Foundation believes that payment for organs is wrong.*

donation. Finally, a program of financial incentives for organ donation could expose transplant recipients to unnecessary risks because living donors and donor families would have an incentive to withhold information concerning the donor's health status so that they can be assured a financial benefit.

5   Proponents of financial incentives for organ donation assert that a demonstration project is necessary to confirm or refute the types of concerns mentioned above. The American Medical Association, the United Network for Organ Sharing and the Ethics Committee of the American Society of Transplant Surgeons have called for pilot studies of financial incentives. Conversely, the National Kidney Foundation maintains that it would not be feasible to design a pilot project that would definitively demonstrate the efficacy of financial incentives for organ donation. Moreover, the implementation of a pilot project would have the same corrosive effect on the ethical, moral and social fabric of this country that a formal change in policy would have. Finally, a demonstration project is objectionable because it will be difficult to revert to an altruistic system once payment is initiated, even if it becomes evident that financial incentives don't have a positive impact on organ donation.

6   The National Kidney Foundation believes that payment for organs is wrong. Such a practice should not be started or tested since its negative message could not be undone if, as research indicates, it will not work. The headline "Local Family Offered Money for Loved One's Organs" should never appear.

7   The National Kidney Foundation remains committed to doing everything that can rightly be done to alleviate the critical organ shortage. However, better understanding by the public, better practices from medical and procurement professionals, better organ preserving-care for post-transplant patients and increased living donation will help, not money. Any attempt to pay families to say yes is wrong.

Scott Carney | *Inside the Business of Selling Human Body Parts*

SCOTT CARNEY, an investigative journalist, has published articles in publications from *Mother Jones* to *Foreign Policy*. His work often focuses on South Asia, including India, which he first visited as a college student in 1998. The following information, which appeared in more visual form in *Wired* magazine, is based on research for his book *The Red Market* (2011).

1   Is the human body sacred? Or is it a commodity ready to be chopped up and exposed to the forces of supply and demand? The answer is a matter of perspective. Our own body is a temple. But when we need a spare part, suddenly we're surprisingly open to a transaction. To a person looking for a kidney, a scientist trying to learn anatomy, a beauty parlor customer looking for the perfect 'do, there's no substitute for a piece of someone else.

2   The problem is, demand for replacement flesh grossly outstrips supply. In the US and like-minded countries, it's illegal to sell body parts[1]—they can be taken only from those who filled out a donor card before they died or who are willing to give up an organ out of sheer benevolence. This means there isn't enough tissue to go around. So, as with any outlawed or heavily regulated resource, a bustling underground trade has formed.

3   Sometimes the market in body parts is exploitive: Desperate people are paid tiny sums for huge donations. Other times it is ghoulish: Pieces are stolen from the recently dead. And every so often, the resource grab is lethal—people are simply killed for their organs. Welcome to the red market.

BLOOD

Price	India (per pint)	$25
	U.S. (per pint)	$337
Source	Legal	Blood donors
	Illegal	Paid blood donors, blood farmers

Description: Until the 1970s, for-profit blood-collection centers were located in almost every poor neighborhood, somewhat like payday loan centers are today. This changed after a study showed that paid donations encourage lax standards. As a result, the rules were modified and blood and organs can no longer be sold. At least not here. In the developing world, there are still profits to be made. In 2008, blood thieves in India were busted for keeping people prisoner and milking their blood up to three times a week. Some captives had been held for more than two years.

---

[1] Major, Rupert W. L. "Paying Kidney Donors: Time to Follow Iran?" *McGill Journal of Medicine.* 11 (1): 67–69. Web.

HAIR

Price	$308	
	Average U.S. retail (for a set of extensions)	
Source	**Legal**	Indian temples, donations, direct sales
	Illegal	N/A

Description: Every year, millions of pounds of hair are given to the Lord Venkateswara at the Tirumala temple in South India. The temple sells these donations to the West, where they become raw material for the US hair-extension industry. Indian hair is valued for its length and the fact that the average Indian doesn't use damaging products. The temple makes about $12 million a year in sales, which translates to hundreds of millions at the salon level. There are also secondary markets for human hair. Lesser manes, for example, are sent to factories and boiled down into enzymes that help soften the dough of many baked goods.

CORNEAS

Price	$24,400	
	Implanted (in the U.S.)	
Source	**Legal**	Deceased donors
	Illegal	Mortuaries

Description: Corneas are relatively easy to transplant and easy to ship. This makes for a brisk international market, and cryo packages zip across the globe to needy eyeballs everywhere. Donation rates exceed demand in the US, so we are actually a net exporter of corneas. But overseas, the market is far from orderly. In 2001, a former Chinese surgeon testified before the US Congress that he had harvested hundreds of corneas (along with kidneys and skin) from more than a hundred executed Chinese prisoners. The United Nations has discussed trying to put an end to international organ brokering, but so far the global market remains unregulated.

HEARTS

Price	**Legal**	$997,700
	Illegal	$119,000
Source	**Legal**	Deceased donors
	Illegal	Chinese prisoners

Description: Black-market heart transplants are extremely rare, if only because putting in a new ticker requires a state-of-the-art medical facility, and these tend to be highly fastidious about organ donation. While one hospital manager in Saudi Arabia told *Wired* that there's a black market for transplants in that country, there is no evidence of an actual operation ever taking place. The few known nonconsensual donations that do occur once again tend to come from Chinese prisoners and Falun Gong practitioners, according to the UN.

LIVERS

Price	**Legal**	$557,100
	Illegal	$157,000
Source	**Legal**	Living donors, deceased donors
	Illegal	Executed prisoners, Filipino slum dwellers

Description: The liver is amazingly resilient;[2] even a badly damaged one can fully regenerate on its own. But when there's an excessive buildup of scar tissue, a person will need a transplant. The good news is that a patient may not need a whole new organ: Because of the liver's fortitude, just a healthy lobe may be enough. This means living donors are possible. The bad news is that, for the living donor, recovery can be excruciating, so donors aren't common. Executed Chinese prisoners are one source of black-market livers. Or organ brokers can set you up in the Philippines, where illicit donations likely come from those desperate for cash.

[2] Edwards, Steven. "Adult Stem Cells Regenerate Liver Tissue." *Wired.* Condé Nast, 27 Mar. 2007. Web. 26 June 2012.

KIDNEYS

Price	India	$15,000
	China	$62,000
	U.S.	$262,900
Source	Legal	Living donors, deceased donors
	Illegal	Paid donors, executed prisoners

Description: Don't have years to wait for a kidney in the US? Finding an international source is easy. In fact, two US insurance companies will sometimes even pay for you to go abroad. Outside the US, however, a kidney's origin can be difficult to discern. According to a Council of Europe report, for example, a clinic with ties to senior Kosovo officials engaged in an organ harvesting ring as recently as 2008. And in China, an investigation found that people on death row are routinely tested, typed, and held for on-demand "donations." Then there are India, Pakistan, and Indonesia, where slum dwellers are lured into selling their innards for a pittance.

EGGS

Price	U.S.	$12,400 per IVF cycle (in the U.S.)
Source	Legal	Egg donors
	Illegal	Egg sellers

Description: Egg donation is legal in the US, but getting one (or more) is going to cost you in fees and hospital charges. That said, would-be buyers can also look abroad for deals. The Mediterranean island nation of Cyprus is one destination with a burgeoning illegal trade in human eggs. Clinics there have flown in impoverished women from Russia and Ukraine for aggressive egg harvesting, returning them before complications can arise. The deal can save a client up to 40 percent on in vitro fertilization services. Other egg-harvesting programs in Romania, Spain, and Israel offer similar deals.

WOMB RENTALS

Price	India	$20,000–30,000
	U.S.	$80,000–150,000
Source	Legal	Fertility clinics
	Illegal	Fertility clinics

Description: India—the outsourcing capital of the world—is the go-to place for getting someone else to grow you a child. Tucked away in an industrial dairy town in Gujarat, for example, the Akanksha Infertility Clinic offers a complete surrogacy program for just $23,000—a fraction of what people pay in the West. The clinic achieves a surprisingly high success rate by transferring five or six embryos to women who sign up for the program (sometimes resulting in sets of twins and the prenatal developmental complications they entail) and by keeping the surrogates on lockdown for the nine months that they gestate.

PLASTINATES

Price	$45,730–77,560 per body	
Source	Legal	Donated cadavers
	Illegal	Chinese prisoners

Description: In the late 1970s, Gunther von Hagens revolutionized the study of anatomy by changing the way specimens were prepared. Instead of immersing dead bodies in a preservative, he replaced their fat and water with polymer, turning corpses into plastic statues. Plastination exposed the body's internal structures and greatly enhanced researchers' ability to study them. It also led to several traveling exhibition shows. An investigation into those shows revealed that many bodies were likely coming from executed prisoners.

LIGAMENTS AND BONES

Price	$5,465 for an ACL reconstruction	
Source	Legal	Deceased donors
	Illegal	Mortuaries

Description: Most organs become useless soon after the owner dies. The key exceptions are ligaments and bone. Funeral parlors in the US have been implicated in stealing these less perishable body parts and selling them without permission to tissue banks. According to a recent criminal investigation, for example, between 2004 and 2005 a company named Biomedical Tissue Services illicitly harvested 244 bodies from Philadelphia mortuaries. Since tissue banks are not set up to monitor whether parts come from fraudulent sources, it is difficult to know how many donation recipients carry contraband inside their bodies.

SKIN

Price	$10 per square inch	
Source	Legal	Deceased donors
	Illegal	Mortuaries

Description: If a burn or an ulcer leaves a hole in your body that's too big to stitch, the best option is to patch it up with extra skin—preferably your own. In a pinch, however, someone else's will do. There aren't a lot of people willing to donate living skin, so most grafts are taken from dead bodies—either legally from organ donors or, like ligaments and bone, illegally from funeral parlors. The danger of cadaver harvesting is that the skin is not always as sanitary as it should be. In the Biomedical Tissue Services case, workers hacked at body after body without washing their hands, sending potentially infected samples to tissue banks.

SKELETONS

Price	$2,993–5,500	
Source	Legal	Donated cadavers
	Illegal	Indian graves

Description: There was a time when every doctor in training received a full set of human bones along with their first-year textbooks. These bones usually came from Calcutta, which produced almost 60,000 skeletons a year. But in 1985 the practice of exporting human parts was banned, and there aren't a lot of good, legal sources of medical skeletons anymore. Today, black-market skeletons pilfered from graves in India are cleaned in acid baths, smuggled out of the country, and sold at a premium through brokers in Canada.

6
Arguing a Position

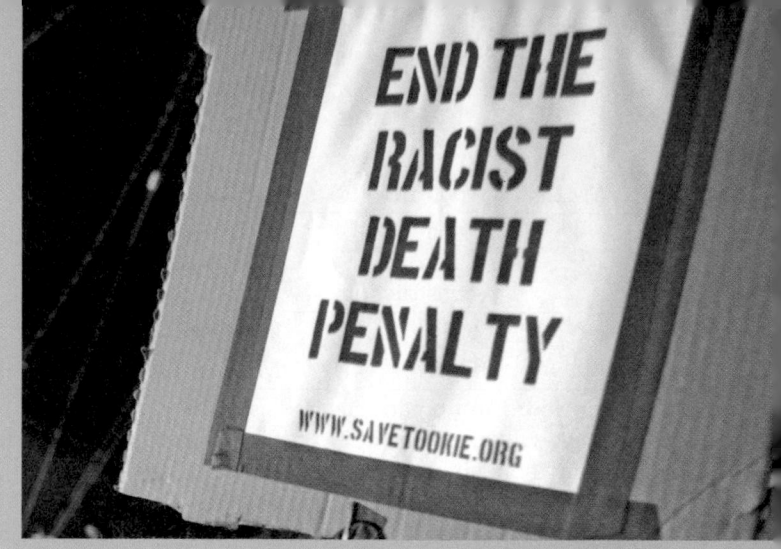

Because of the in-your-face kind of arguing in blogs and on talk shows, you may associate arguing to support your position on a controversial issue with quarreling. Although this kind of "argument" lets people vent strong feelings, it seldom leads them to consider seriously other points of view or to think critically about their own reasons or underlying values. A more thoughtful, deliberative kind of position argument, one that depends on a critical analysis of an issue, on giving logical reasons rather than raising voices, is more likely to convince others in the workplace, in the community, and especially in college courses to accept—or even to take seriously—a controversial position.

IN COLLEGE COURSES

For a law and society course, a student writes an essay analyzing racial discrepancies in sentencing, especially in death-penalty cases. She cites studies that have found, surprisingly, that the race of the murder victim, not the perpetrator, is the crucial factor: If the victim is white, the defendant is more likely to receive the death sentence. Based on her research, she argues that the main reason for this disparity is due not to the decision of the jury but to the decision of prosecutors who seek the death penalty more often when the murder victim is white. She concludes that although there is no evidence that sentencing decisions are racially discriminatory, outcomes often are, and this fact makes people think the justice system is unjust.

IN THE COMMUNITY

In an open letter, a group of parents asks the school board to institute a Peacemakers program at the local middle school. The group's impassioned letter begins with anecdotal reports of bullying at the school to underscore the need for action and to appeal to board members' compassion. It then describes the Peacemakers program and details the negotiation procedure children are taught. It acknowledges that the program will add to the school's budget, but it claims that the negotiation skills the children will learn will help them now and throughout their lives.

IN THE WORKPLACE

At a business conference, a consultant makes a presentation arguing that adopting sustainable business practices is good for business. He displays poll results showing that two-thirds of businesses see sustainability as a necessity to compete in the global marketplace—up more than 50 percent from the previous year—and that a third increased profits as a direct result of their sustainability efforts. Citing several examples, he shows how companies can develop a strategic sustainability plan such as by changing performance reviews or compensation packages to reward employees who implement sustainability practices and achieve goals. He concludes by urging audience members to log on to his blog to read inspiring examples and to add their own.

In this chapter, we ask you to write about your position on a controversial issue for the purpose of convincing readers to adopt your point of view or at least to consider it seriously. Analyzing the selections in the Guide to Reading that follows, you will learn how writers engage their readers' attention and make a compelling argument. As you read, consider whether visuals would help readers more fully grasp the issue or accept the position.

PRACTICING THE GENRE

Debating a Position

To get a sense of what's involved in arguing a position, get together with two or three students to discuss an issue you have strong feelings about. Here are some guidelines to follow:

Part 1.   As a group, think of a college issue you all know and care about, or choose one from the following list:

- Should admission to college be based solely on high school grade point average?
- Should there be a community service requirement for graduation from college?
- Should college students be required to take courses outside of their major?
- Should the federal government subsidize everyone's college education?
- Should drinking alcohol on college campuses be permitted?
- Should college athletes be paid?

First, identify your purpose and audience: Is your goal to convince readers to change their minds, confirm their opinions, or move them to action? Who constitutes your audience — college administrators, parents, or fellow students — and what values or interests do you think they will find most important? What values or interests are most important to you?

Second, divide into two teams — those in favor and those opposed (at least, for this activity) — and take a few minutes to think of reasons why your audience should accept your position.

Third, take turns presenting your argument.

Part 2.   Reflect on what you learned, and discuss these questions in your group:

- How did clarifying your purpose and knowing whether you were addressing administrators, parents, or students affect which reasons you used and how you presented them?
- Why did you expect your audience to find these particular reasons convincing?

Your instructor may ask you to write about what you learned and present your conclusions to the rest of the class.

Analyzing Position Arguments

As you read the selections in this chapter, you will see how different authors argue a position. Analyzing how these writers present and support their position, respond to opposing views, and organize their writing will also help you see how you can employ these techniques to make your own position argument clear and compelling for your readers.

Determine the writer's purpose and audience.

Although arguing a position helps writers clarify their own reasons for taking that particular position, writers typically aim to influence others. When reading the position arguments that follow, ask yourself these questions about the writer's purpose and audience:

- What seems to be the writer's main *purpose* in arguing for a position—for example, to change readers' minds by convincing them to look at the issue in a new way, to confirm readers' opinions by providing them with authoritative arguments, to move readers to take action by stressing the urgency or seriousness of the issue, or to remind readers what is at stake and establish common ground on which people might be able to agree?

- What does the writer assume about the *audience*—for example, that audience members are already knowledgeable about the issue, that they will be only mildly interested and need to be inspired to care about the issue, or that they have strong convictions and are likely to have serious objections to the writer's position?

Assess the genre's basic features.

Use the following to help you analyze and evaluate how writers of position arguments use the genre's basic features. The strategies position writers typically use to make a convincing case are illustrated below with examples from the readings in this chapter as well as sentence strategies you can experiment with later, as you write your own position argument.

> **Basic Features**
> A Focused, Well-Presented Issue
> A Well-Supported Position
> An Effective Response to Opposing Views
> A Clear, Logical Organization

A FOCUSED, WELL-PRESENTED ISSUE

Read first to see how the issue is presented and to determine whether it is clearly focused and well presented, given the writer's purpose and original audience. To identify the issue, look at the title and the opening paragraphs. The title of Daniel J. Solove's position argument (pp. 266–67), for example, identifies both the topic and his position:

> Why Privacy Matters Even If You Have "Nothing to Hide"

Topic

Position

For current, hotly debated issues, the title may be enough to identify the issue for readers, and writers may use their opening paragraphs merely to remind readers about what is at stake or what the position is that they oppose, using a simple sentence pattern like this:

> ▶ When [issue/event] happens, most people think _____, but I think _____.

245

For example, Solove uses this strategy in his position paper about privacy:

> When the government gathers or analyzes personal information, many people say . . . (par. 1)

His "but I think . . ." response to the common view takes up the bulk of the essay.

When writers know the issue will be unfamiliar to their audience, they need to establish its significance, as student Jessica Statsky does in her position essay:

> "Organized sports for young people have become an institution in North America," reports sports journalist Steve Silverman, attracting more than 44 million youngsters according to a recent survey by the National Council of Youth Sports ("History"). (par. 1)

To establish the significance of the issue, Statsky quotes a respected authority and also cites statistics.

To present their positions effectively, writers must focus on a specific aspect of their issue, one they can address fully in the space allowed. An issue like the death penalty, for example, is too complex to be tackled fully in a relatively brief space. So writers must focus on one aspect of the issue. A writer taking a position on the death penalty might address the more specific question of whether race influences prosecutors to seek the death penalty, as does the student in the In College Courses scenario on page 242. Similarly, Richard Estrada addresses the complex issue of racial stereotyping by focusing on sports mascots (pp. 255–57).

Also consider how the writer frames the issue. **Framing an issue** is like cropping and resizing a photograph to focus the viewer's eye on one part of the picture (see Figure 6.1). Writers typically frame the issue in a way that sets the stage for their argument and promotes their point of view, usually by suggesting that particular values are at stake or by raising in readers' minds certain concerns. As you read, notice how each writer frames the issue, asking yourself questions like these:

FIGURE 6.1
Framing an issue.
By cropping this photograph of a protest march to focus on the little boy, the photographer's message is softened when framed in terms of saving the planet for this child.

- Who does the writer associate with each position, and how does the writer characterize their views? For example, does one side appear thoughtful, moderate, and knowledgeable, and the other side extreme, unreasonable, or self-interested? What does the writer suggest is really at stake, and for whom?

- How does the way the writer frames the issue affect your own thinking about it? If the issue was unfamiliar to you before reading the essay, what did the writer lead you to think and feel about it? If you were already familiar with the issue, which of your preconceptions were reinforced and which were challenged by the writer's way of framing the issue?

Analyzing Position Arguments   ▶ **GUIDE TO READING**
GUIDE TO WRITING
A WRITER AT WORK
THINKING CRITICALLY   **247**

A WELL-SUPPORTED POSITION

To argue effectively, writers need to *assert an arguable **position***—that is, an opinion, not a fact that can be proved or disproved or a belief taken on faith—that can be supported with convincing *reasons* and trustworthy *evidence*. Read first to identify the position, usually declared in a *thesis statement* early in the essay. Then determine whether the position is clear and appropriately qualified (for example, using words like *may* and specifying conditions). Notice, for example, how Jessica Statsky states her thesis:

> When overzealous parents and coaches impose adult standards on children's sports, the result can be activities that are neither satisfying nor beneficial to children.
>
>   I am concerned about all organized sports activities for children between the ages of six and twelve. (pars. 1–2)

Qualifying terms

Then examine the main reasons and the evidence the writer provides, making sure that the reasons clearly support the writer's position and that the evidence (such as statistics, research studies, or authorities) is credible. (Writers of position arguments often *forecast* the reasons they will develop; to see how Statsky does this, see the section that follows on organization.) Look for sentence strategies like these that introduce supporting reasons:

▶ What makes _____ [problematic/praiseworthy] is _____.

Position

Reason

EXAMPLE   What makes naming teams after ethnic groups . . . reprehensible is that politically impotent groups continue to be targeted, while politically powerful ones who bite back are left alone. (Estrada, par. 11)

▶ Because _____, I [support/oppose] _____.

EXAMPLE   This statistic illustrates another reason I oppose competitive sports for children: because they are so highly selective, very few children get to participate. (Statsky, par. 7)

Position

Reason

The following examples demonstrate some approaches to introducing supporting evidence:

> 24 percent . . . worked . . . five to seven days. . . . There is just no way such amounts of work will not interfere with school work, especially homework. In an informal survey . . . , 58 percent of seniors acknowledged that their jobs interfere with their school work. (Etzioni, par. 13)

Statistics

Reason

> Leonard Koppett in *Sports Illusion, Sports Reality* claims that . . . , sometimes resulting in lifelong injuries (294). (Statsky, par. 3)

Authority

Reason

Position arguments are most convincing when writers are able to appeal to readers on three levels:

- **Logos:** Appeal to readers' intellect, presenting them with logical reasoning and reliable evidence.
- **Ethos:** Appeal to readers' perception of the writer's credibility and fairness.
- **Pathos:** Appeal to readers' values and feelings.

To learn more about evaluating sources, see Chapter 12.

To learn more about constructing an argument, see Chapter 19.

When reading a position argument (or writing your own), consider how well the writer has used these appeals. Ask yourself questions like these: Is the argument logical and reasonable (logos)? Does the writer appear credible and trustworthy (pathos)? Are the values and feelings sincere or manipulative (ethos)?

AN EFFECTIVE RESPONSE TO OPPOSING VIEWS

An effective argument anticipates readers' objections and opposing arguments and refutes or concedes them. Writers **refute** (argue against) opposing views when they can show that the opposing view is weak or flawed. A typical refutation states the problem with the opposing view and then explains why the view is problematic, using sentence strategies like these:

▶ One problem with [opposing view] is that _____.

▶ Some claim [opposing view], but in reality _____.

Notice that writers often introduce the refutation with a *transition* that indicates *contrast,* such as *but, although, nevertheless,* or *however:*

> Yet another problem with government gathering and use of personal data is distortion. Although personal information can reveal quite a lot about people's personalities and activities, it often fails to reflect the whole person. It can paint a distorted picture. (Solove, par. 14)

Transition
Refutation

Writers may also **concede** (accept) valid objections, concerns, or reasons. A typical way of conceding is to use sentence strategies like these:

▶ I agree that _____.

▶ _____ is certainly an important factor.

Here is an example from Jessica Statsky's essay (pp. 250–55):

> Some children *want* to play competitive sports; they are not being forced to play. These children are eager to learn skills, to enjoy the camaraderie of the team, and earn self-respect by trying hard to benefit their team. I acknowledge that some children may benefit from playing competitive sports. (par. 12)

Concession

Conceding a strong opposing view reassures readers that the writer shares their values and builds a bridge of common concerns.

Frequently, though, writers reach out to readers by making a concession but then go on to point out where they differ. We call this the **concession-refutation move.** Writers making the concession-refutation move often employ sentence patterns like these, which include transitions that indicate contrast, like *but, although, nevertheless,* or *however,* to indicate that an exception or refinement is coming.

▶ _____ may be true for _____, *but* not for _____.

▶ *Although* _____, I think _____.

▶ _____ insists that _____. *Nevertheless,* in spite of her good intentions, _____.

Analyzing Position Arguments

GUIDE TO READING
GUIDE TO WRITING
A WRITER AT WORK
THINKING CRITICALLY

249

Here's an example:

> By no means were such names originally meant to disparage Native Americans. The noble symbols of the Redskins or college football's Florida State Seminoles or the Illinois Illini are meant to be strong and proud. Yet, ultimately, the practice of using a people as mascots is dehumanizing. (Estrada, par. 4)

Concession

Refutation

While reading position arguments, assess the effectiveness of the responses:

- Do the concessions seem significant or trivial, genuine or insincere? Do they add to or detract from the writer's credibility (ethos)?

- Do the refutations appeal to shared values (pathos) or question readers' priorities? Do they offer compelling reasons and credible evidence (logos) or simply make unsubstantiated assertions? Do they draw on authorities whose expertise is established (ethos) or merely refer vaguely to "some" or "many" people with whom they agree? Do they misrepresent the opposition (committing a *straw man fallacy*) or attack people personally (committing an *ad hominem fallacy*)?

To learn more about logical fallacies, see Chapter 19, pp. 620–21.

A CLEAR, LOGICAL ORGANIZATION

When reading a position argument, first *look for a thesis statement that directly asserts the writer's position*. For example, Amitai Etzioni begins with an alarming sentence that states in a surprising way what he goes on to clarify in the next sentence:

> McDonald's is bad for your kids. I do not mean the flat patties and the white-flour buns; I refer to the jobs teen-agers undertake, mass-producing these choice items. (par. 1)

In addition to asserting the thesis, writers sometimes preview the reasons in the same order they will bring them up later in the essay, as in this example of a *forecasting statement* by Jessica Statsky:

> . . . too often played to adult standards, which are developmentally inappropriate for children and can be both physically and psychologically harmful. Furthermore, because they . . . , they are actually counterproductive for developing either future players or fans. Finally, because they . . . *provide occasions for some parents and coaches to place their own fantasies and needs ahead of children's welfare.* (par. 2)

Transition
Reason 1
Reason 2
Reason 3

Notice also where the writer uses *logical transitions:* to indicate supporting evidence (*because*), exceptions (*however*), concessions (*admittedly*), refutations (*on the other hand*), or conclusions (*therefore*) as well as to list reasons (*first, finally*). Transitions may be useful in a forecasting statement, as in the preceding example, or in the *topic sentence* of a paragraph or group of paragraphs, as in the following examples from Solove's position argument:

To learn more about these cues, see Chapter 13, pp. 555–58.

> One such harm, for example, . . . Another potential problem with . . . is . . . A related problem involves. . . . Yet another problem. . . . (pars. 11–14)

Finally, check for logical fallacies—such as *oversimplifying, personal attack* (ad hominem), *slanting,* and *false analogy.*

Readings

Jessica Statsky | *Children Need to Play, Not Compete*

To see how Jessica Statsky developed her response to readers' likely objections, see A Writer at Work on pp. 292–94. If you could have given Statsky advice in a peer review of her drafts, what objections would you have advised her to respond to, and how do you think she could have responded?

THIS ESSAY by Jessica Statsky about children's competitive sports was written for a college composition course. When you were a child, you may have had experience playing competitive sports, in or out of school, for example in Peewee Football, Little League Baseball, American Youth Soccer, or some other organization. Or you may have had relatives or friends who were deeply involved in sports. As you read, consider the following:

- In your experience and observation, was winning unduly emphasized or was more value placed on having a good time, learning to get along with others, developing athletic skills, or something else altogether?

- The questions in the margin: Your instructor may ask you to post your answers to a class blog or discussion board or to bring them to class.

▪▪ **Basic Features**
A Focused, Well-Presented Issue
A Well-Supported Position
An Effective Response to Opposing Views
A Clear, Logical Organization

How does Statsky present the issue in a way that prepares readers for her argument?

How does she qualify her position in par. 2?

What reasons does she forecast here, and in which paragraphs does she discuss each reason? Do her reasons appeal primarily to readers' intellect (logos), to their sense of fairness and what's credible (pathos), or to their feelings (ethos)?

1   "Organized sports for young people have become an institution in North America," reports sports journalist Steve Silverman, attracting more than 44 million youngsters according to a recent survey by the National Council of Youth Sports ("History"). Though many adults regard Little League Baseball and Peewee Football as a basic part of childhood, the games are not always joyous ones. When overzealous parents and coaches impose adult standards on children's sports, the result can be activities that are neither satisfying nor beneficial to children.

2   I am concerned about all organized sports activities for children between the ages of six and twelve. The damage I see results from noncontact as well as contact sports, from sports organized locally as well as those organized nationally. Highly organized competitive sports such as Peewee Football and Little League Baseball are too often played to adult standards, which are developmentally inappropriate for children and can be both physically and psychologically harmful. Furthermore, because they eliminate many children from organized sports before they are ready to compete, they are actually counterproductive for developing either future players or fans. Finally, because they emphasize competition and winning, they unfortunately provide occasions for some parents and coaches to place their own fantasies and needs ahead of children's welfare.

3   One readily understandable danger of overly competitive sports is that they entice children into physical actions that are bad for growing bodies. "There is a growing epidemic of preventable youth sports injuries," according to the STOP Sports Injuries campaign. "Among athletes ages 5 to 14, 28 percent of football players, 25 percent of baseball players, 22 percent of soccer players, 15 percent of basketball players, and 12 percent of softball players were injured while playing their respective sports." Although the official Little League Web site acknowledges that children do risk injury playing baseball, it insists that "severe injuries . . . are infrequent," the risk "far less than the risk of riding a skateboard, a bicycle, or even the school bus" ("What about My Child?"). Nevertheless, Leonard Koppett in *Sports Illusion, Sports Reality* claims that a twelve-year-old trying to throw a curve ball, for example, may put abnormal strain on developing arm and shoulder muscles, sometimes resulting in lifelong injuries (294). Contact sports like football can be even more hazardous. Thomas Tutko, a psychology professor at San Jose State University and coauthor of the book *Winning Is Everything and Other American Myths*, writes:

> I am strongly opposed to young kids playing tackle football. It is not the
> right stage of development for them to be taught to crash into other kids.
> Kids under the age of fourteen are not by nature physical. Their main
> concern is self-preservation. They don't want to meet head on and slam
> into each other. But tackle football absolutely requires that they try to hit
> each other as hard as they can. And it is too traumatic for young kids.
> (qtd. in Tosches A1)

4   As Tutko indicates, even when children are not injured, fear of being hurt detracts from their enjoyment of the sport. The Little League Web site ranks fear of injury as the seventh of seven reasons children quit ("What about My Child?"). One mother of an eight-year-old Peewee Football player explained, "The kids get so scared. They get hit once and they don't want anything to do with football anymore. They'll sit on the bench and pretend their leg hurts..." (qtd. in Tosches A1). Some children are driven to even more desperate measures. For example, in one Peewee Football game, a reporter watched the following scene as a player took himself out of the game:

How does Statsky try to establish the credibility of her sources in pars. 3–5 (ethos)?

Why do you think she uses block quotations instead of integrating these quotes into her own sentences?

"Coach, my tummy hurts. I can't play," he said. The coach told the player to get back onto the field. "There's nothing wrong with your stomach," he said. When the coach turned his head the seven-year-old stuck a finger down his throat and made himself vomit. When the coach turned back, the boy pointed to the ground and told him, "Yes there is, coach. See?" (Tosches A33)

5   Besides physical hazards and anxieties, competitive sports pose psychological dangers for children. Martin Rablovsky, a former sports editor for the *New York Times*, says that in all his years of watching young children play organized sports, he has noticed very few of them smiling. "I've seen children enjoying a spontaneous pre-practice scrimmage become somber and serious when the coach's whistle blows," Rablovsky says. "The spirit of play suddenly disappears, and sport becomes joblike" (qtd. in Coakley 94). The primary goal of a professional athlete — winning — is not appropriate for children. Their goals should be having fun, learning, and being with friends. Although winning does add to the fun, too many adults lose sight of what matters and make winning the most important goal. Several studies have shown that when children are asked whether they would rather be warming the bench on a winning team or playing regularly on a losing team, about 90 percent choose the latter (Smith, Smith, and Smoll 11).

How does Statsky try to refute this objection?

6   Winning and losing may be an inevitable part of adult life, but they should not be part of childhood. Too much competition too early in life can affect a child's development. Children are easily influenced, and when they sense that their competence and worth are based on their ability to live up to their parents' and coaches' high expectations — and on their ability to win — they can become discouraged and depressed. Little League advises parents to "keep winning in perspective" ("Your Role"), noting that the most common reasons children give for quitting, aside from change in interest, are lack of playing time, failure and fear of failure, disapproval by significant others, and psychological stress ("What about My Child?"). According to Dr. Glyn C. Roberts, a professor of kinesiology at the Institute of Child Behavior and Development at the University of Illinois, 80 to 90 percent of children who play competitive sports at a young age drop out by sixteen (Kutner).

How effective do you think Statsky's argument in par. 7 is? Why?

7   This statistic illustrates another reason I oppose competitive sports for children: because they are so highly selective, very few children get to participate. Far

too soon, a few children are singled out for their athletic promise, while many others, who may be on the verge of developing the necessary strength and ability, are screened out and discouraged from trying out again. Like adults, children fear failure, and so even those with good physical skills may stay away because they lack self-confidence. Consequently, teams lose many promising players who with some encouragement and experience might have become stars. The problem is that many parent-sponsored, out-of-school programs give more importance to having a winning team than to developing children's physical skills and self-esteem.

8   Indeed, it is no secret that too often scorekeeping, league standings, and the drive to win bring out the worst in adults who are more absorbed in living out their own fantasies than in enhancing the quality of the experience for children (Smith, Smith, and Smoll 9). Recent newspaper articles on children's sports contain plenty of horror stories. *Los Angeles Times* reporter Rich Tosches, for example, tells the story of a brawl among seventy-five parents following a Peewee Football game (A33). As a result of the brawl, which began when a parent from one team confronted a player from the other team, the teams are now thinking of hiring security guards for future games. Another example is provided by a *Los Angeles Times* editorial about a Little League manager who intimidated the opposing team by setting fire to one of their team's jerseys on the pitcher's mound before the game began. As the editorial writer commented, the manager showed his young team that "intimidation could substitute for playing well" ("The Bad News").

9   Although not all parents or coaches behave so inappropriately, the seriousness of the problem is illustrated by the fact that Adelphi University in Garden City, New York, offers a sports psychology workshop for Little League coaches, designed to balance their "animal instincts" with "educational theory" in hopes of reducing the "screaming and hollering," in the words of Harold Weisman, manager of sixteen Little Leagues in New York City (Schmitt). In a three-and-one-half-hour Sunday morning workshop, coaches learn how to make practices more fun, treat injuries, deal with irate parents, and be "more sensitive to their young players' fears, emotional frailties, and need for recognition." Little League is to be credited with recognizing the need for such workshops.

In criticizing some parents' behavior in pars. 8–9, Statsky risks alienating her readers. How effective is this part of her argument?

How effective is Statsky's use of concession and refutation here?

10   Some parents would no doubt argue that children cannot start too soon preparing to live in a competitive free-market economy. After all, secondary schools and colleges require students to compete for grades, and college admission is extremely competitive. And it is perfectly obvious how important competitive skills are in finding a job. Yet the ability to cooperate is also important for success in life. Before children are psychologically ready for competition, maybe we should emphasize cooperation and individual performance in team sports rather than winning.

11   Many people are ready for such an emphasis. In 1988, one New York Little League official who had attended the Adelphi workshop tried to ban scoring from six- to eight-year-olds' games — but parents wouldn't support him (Schmitt). An innovative children's sports program in New York City, City Sports for Kids, emphasizes fitness, self-esteem, and sportsmanship. In this program's basketball games, every member on a team plays at least two of six eight-minute periods. The basket is seven feet from the floor, rather than ten feet, and a player can score a point just by hitting the rim (Bloch). I believe this kind of local program should replace overly competitive programs like Peewee Football and Little League Baseball. As one coach explains, significant improvements can result from a few simple rule changes, such as including every player in the batting order and giving every player, regardless of age or ability, the opportunity to play at least four innings a game (Frank).

How effectively does Statsky conclude her argument?

12   Some children *want* to play competitive sports; they are not being forced to play. These children are eager to learn skills, to enjoy the camaraderie of the team, and earn self-respect by trying hard to benefit their team. I acknowledge that some children may benefit from playing competitive sports. While some children do benefit from these programs, however, many more would benefit from programs that avoid the excesses and dangers of many competitive sports programs and instead emphasize fitness, cooperation, sportsmanship, and individual performance.

Works Cited

Are Statsky's sources adequate to support her position, in number and kind? Has she documented them clearly and accurately?

"The Bad News Pyromaniacs?" Editorial. *Los Angeles Times* 16 June 1990: B6. *LexisNexis*. Web. 16 May 2008.

Bloch, Gordon B. "Thrill of Victory Is Secondary to Fun." *New York Times* 2 Apr. 1990, late ed.: C12. *LexisNexis*. Web. 14 May 2008.

Coakley, Jay J. *Sport in Society: Issues and Controversies*. St. Louis: Mosby, 1982. Print.

Frank, L. "Contributions from Parents and Coaches." *CYB Message Board*. AOL, 8 July
    1997. Web. 14 May 2008.

Koppett, Leonard. *Sports Illusion, Sports Reality*. Boston: Houghton, 1981. Print.

Kutner, Lawrence. "Athletics, through a Child's Eyes." *New York Times* 23 Mar. 1989,
    late ed.: C8. *LexisNexis*. Web. 15 May 2008.

Schmitt, Eric. "Psychologists Take Seat on Little League Bench." *New York Times*
    14 Mar. 1988, late ed.: B2. *LexisNexis*. Web. 14 May 2008.

Silverman, Steve. "The History of Youth Sports." Livestrong.com. Demand Media,
    Inc., 26 May 2011. Web. 10 Dec. 2011.

Smith, Nathan, Ronald Smith, and Frank Smoll. *Kidsports: A Survival Guide for
    Parents*. Reading: Addison, 1983. Print.

STOPSportsInjuries.org. American Orthopaedic Society for Sports Medicine, n.d. Web.
    10 Dec. 2011.

Tosches, Rich. "Peewee Football: Is It Time to Blow the Whistle?" *Los Angeles Times* 3
    Dec. 1988: A1+. *LexisNexis*. Web. 22 May 2008.

"What about My Child?" *Little League Online*. Little League Baseball, Incorporated,
    1999. Web. 30 May 2008.

"Your Role as a Little League Parent." *Little League Online*. Little League Baseball,
    Incorporated, 1999. Web. 30 May 2008.

For an additional
student reading, go to
bedfordstmartins.com
/theguide/epages.

Richard Estrada | *Sticks and Stones and Sports Team Names*

RICHARD ESTRADA was best known as a thoughtful, independent-minded commentator on immigration and social issues. He was the associate editor of the *Dallas Morning News* editorial page and a syndicated columnist whose essays appeared regularly in the *Washington Post,* the *Los Angeles Times,* and other major newspapers. Before joining the *Dallas Morning News* in 1988, Estrada worked as a congressional staff member and as a researcher at the Center for Immigration Studies in Washington, D.C. In the 1990s, he was appointed to the U.S.

Commission on Immigration Reform. The Richard Estrada Fellowship in Immigration Studies was established in his honor following his death in 1999.

In this essay, Estrada addresses the issue of whether sports teams should use names and images associated with Native Americans. Some schools (like Stanford) changed their team's name voluntarily. In 2005, the National Collegiate Athletic Association (NCAA) required colleges to evaluate the potential offensiveness of their team name, symbol, or mascot and to get permission from the affected group. But in some regions the issue remains controversial: In North Dakota, for example, the state university tried to drop its Fighting Sioux moniker; in 2011 the state legislature blocked the move and then repealed the decision; and finally in 2012 voters decided the issue, supporting the university's decision by an overwhelming 67 percent. As you read, consider the following questions:

- How does Estrada try to establish *common ground* that could potentially bring different readers together?

- How effective is Estrada's strategy of seeking common ground with his intended readers or with you?

1   When I was a kid living in Baltimore in the late 1950s, there was only one professional sports team worth following. Anyone who ever saw the movie *Diner* knows which one it was. Back when we liked Ike, the Colts were the gods of the gridiron and Memorial Stadium was their Mount Olympus.

2   Ah, yes: The Colts. The Lions. Da Bears. Back when defensive tackle Big Daddy Lipscomb was letting running backs know exactly what time it was, a young fan could easily forget that in a game where men were men, the teams they played on were not invariably named after animals. Among others, the Packers, the Steelers and the distant 49ers were cases in point. But in the roll call of pro teams, one name in particular always discomfited me: the Washington Redskins. Still, however willing I may have been to go along with the name as a kid, as an adult I have concluded that using an ethnic group essentially as a sports mascot is wrong.

3   The Redskins and the Kansas City Chiefs, along with baseball teams like the Atlanta Braves and the Cleveland Indians, should find other names that avoid highlighting ethnicity.

4   By no means were such names originally meant to disparage Native Americans. The noble symbols of the Redskins or college football's Florida State Seminoles or the Illinois Illini are meant to be strong and proud. Yet, ultimately, the practice of using a people as mascots is dehumanizing. It sets them apart from the rest of society. It promotes the politics of racial aggrievement at a moment when our storehouse is running over with it.

5   The World Series between the Cleveland Indians and the Atlanta Braves re-ignited the debate. In the chill night air of October, tomahawk chops and war chants suddenly became far more familiar to millions of fans, along with the ridiculous and offensive cartoon logo of Cleveland's "Chief Wahoo."

6   The defenders of team names that use variations on the Indian theme argue that tradition should not be sacrificed at the altar of political correctness. In truth, the nation's No. 1 P.C. [politically correct] school, Stanford University, helped matters some when it changed its team nickname from "the Indians" to "the Cardinals." To be sure, Stanford did the right thing, but the school's status as P.C. without peer tainted the decision for those who still need to do the right thing.

7   Another argument is that ethnic group leaders are too inclined to cry wolf in alleging racial insensitivity. Often, this is the case. But no one should overlook genuine cases of political insensitivity in an attempt to avoid accusations of hypersensitivity and political correctness.

The practice of using a people as mascots is dehumanizing.

8   The real world is different from the world of sports entertainment. I recently heard a father who happened to be a Native American complain on the radio that his child was being pressured into participating in celebrations of Braves baseball. At his kid's school, certain days are set aside on which all children are told to dress in Indian garb and celebrate with tomahawk chops and the like.

9   That father should be forgiven for not wanting his family to serve as somebody's mascot. The desire to avoid ridicule is legitimate and understandable. Nobody likes to be trivialized or deprived of their dignity. This has nothing to do with political correctness and the provocations of militant leaders.

10   Against this backdrop, the decision by newspapers in Minneapolis, Seattle and Portland to ban references to Native American nicknames is more reasonable than some might think.

11   What makes naming teams after ethnic groups, particularly minorities, reprehensible is that politically impotent groups continue to be targeted, while politically powerful ones who bite back are left alone. How long does anyone think the name "Washington Blackskins" would last? Or how about "the New York Jews"?

12   With no fewer than 10 Latino ballplayers on the Cleveland Indians' roster, the team could change its name to "the Banditos." The trouble is, they would be missing the point: Latinos would correctly object to that stereotype, just as they rightly protested against Frito-Lay's use of the "Frito Bandito" character years ago.

13   It seems to me that what Native Americans are saying is that what would be intolerable for Jews, blacks, Latinos and others is no less offensive to them. Theirs is a request not only for dignified treatment, but for fair treatment as well. For America to ignore the complaints of a numerically small segment of the population because it is small is neither dignified nor fair.

Make connections: The power of naming.

[REFLECT]

As children, we may say, "Sticks and stones will break my bones, but words will never hurt me." Most children, however, recognize the power of naming, especially when that naming is intended to make them feel different or inferior.

To judge Estrada's argument, reflect on your own observation of and personal experience with name-calling. Your instructor may ask you to post your thoughts on a class discussion board or to discuss them with other students in class. Use these questions to get you started:

- Make a list of words sometimes used to refer to groups with which you identify—for example, words associated with your ethnicity, religion, gender, sexual orientation, or geographic region.

- Which of these words are potentially hurtful or demeaning? How does the identity of the person who uses the word or the situation in which the word is used affect its power?

- How does name-calling compare to what Estrada calls "the practice of using a people as mascots," a practice he calls "dehumanizing" (par. 4)?

[ANALYZE]   # Use the basic features.

A FOCUSED, WELL-PRESENTED ISSUE: FRAMING AN ARGUMENT FOR YOUR AUDIENCE

Disagreement over controversial issues often depends on a difference of values and concerns. To argue effectively, writers must anticipate what their readers are likely to think about the issue, and they must frame (or reframe) the issue to influence how their readers think about it. In "Sticks and Stones and Sports Team Names," Estrada refers in paragraph 6 to the way in which the issue of sports teams' names has already been framed by political conservatives, who use the label "political correctness" to belittle concerns about the issue. This label makes it sound as though those who object are just being overly sensitive. Estrada reframes the issue, changing it from a story about oversensitivity to a story about bullying.

ANALYZE & WRITE

Write a few paragraphs analyzing more fully how Estrada frames the issue of sports team names for his readers:

1. What does Estrada do to construct a story about bullying? For example, how does the title, Estrada's remembered experience (pars. 1–2), the anecdote (par. 8), or another aspect of the argument tell this story?

2. Why do you think Estrada thought making the issue about bullying, instead of oversensitivity, would be likely to make his readers more receptive to his argument?

3. If you were arguing your own position on this issue, how would you frame it to induce your classmates to be receptive to your argument? Why do you think this way of framing the issue would appeal to your classmates?

A WELL-SUPPORTED POSITION: USING ANECDOTES AND EXAMPLES

Anecdotes (brief stories) and *examples* can be especially effective as evidence because they appeal to readers' values and feelings. Jessica Statsky, for instance, relates an anecdote about a seven-year-old Peewee Football player who made himself vomit to avoid playing. This anecdote delivers the message powerfully, but it also runs the risk of being perceived by readers as exaggerated or emotionally manipulative. Examples can also bring home the writer's claims, making them more concrete, graphic, and convincing, as Statsky does when she reports "a brawl among seventy-five parents following a Peewee Football game" (par. 8). Because examples are isolated instances, however, they do not necessarily prove the general rule. To get around this, Statsky introduces this example as one of many "horror stories" to suggest that it is not all that unusual, but a fairly typical incident that should be taken seriously as evidence to support her position.

For more on recognizing emotional manipulation, see Chapter 12, pp. 541–42.

ANALYZE & WRITE

Write a paragraph analyzing and evaluating Estrada's use of anecdotes and examples:

1 Highlight the anecdotes and examples — both real and hypothetical — Estrada uses to support his position.

2 Why do you think, given his original newspaper readers, that Estrada thought these anecdotes and examples would be compelling? How effective are they for you?

AN EFFECTIVE RESPONSE: CONCEDING AND/OR REFUTING

Writers of position essays try to anticipate other widely held positions on the issue as well as objections and questions readers might raises, because doing so enhances the writer's credibility (or ethos) and strengthens the argument. They may concede, refute, or combine the two strategies in a concession-refutation move. To review examples of these response strategies and criteria to assess their effectiveness, look back at pp. 248–49 in the Guide to Reading.

ANALYZE & WRITE

Write a paragraph or two analyzing and evaluating how Estrada concedes and refutes criticism:

1 Skim Estrada's essay, marking where he uses either concession or refutation, or where he makes the concession-refutation move. How can you identify which strategy he is using?

2 Analyze and evaluate one of the examples you found: What values does Estrada assume underlie his readers' point of view? How does his way of responding attempt to bridge the gap between his readers' and his own points of view?

3 How do you think you would respond if you were arguing your own position on this issue?

A CLEAR, LOGICAL ORGANIZATION: USING KEY WORDS

One of the strategies Jessica Statsky uses to make her argument coherent is to introduce key words in the thesis and forecasting statement, and to repeat them or their synonyms when they reappear later in the essay. For example, in paragraph 2, Statsky identifies one of her main reasons for opposing competitive sports for young children—namely, that they can be "physically and psychologically harmful." In paragraphs 3–5, Statsky discusses first the risk of actual physical injury and then the psychological fear of being hurt. In these paragraphs, Statsky repeats the key words *physical* and *psychological,* as well as synonyms for *harm* such as *injury* and *hurt.* The repetition of these key words and synonyms makes it easy for readers to follow this part of her argument.

Write a paragraph analyzing and evaluating the effectiveness with which Estrada repeats key words or their synonyms:

1 Reread paragraph 2, in which Estrada first states his thesis. What key words does he use to assert his moral opposition to the practice of using ethnic group names and images for sports teams?

2 Find other places in the essay where Estrada uses synonyms or related words for these key words to indicate why he thinks the practice is morally wrong.

3 How do these strategies work to make the essay clear and coherent?

RESPOND

Consider possible topics: Issues concerning fairness.

List some issues that involve what you believe to be unfair treatment of any group. For example, should a law be passed to make English the official language in this country, requiring that election ballots and drivers' tests be printed only in English? Should teenagers be required to get their parents' permission to obtain birth-control information and contraception? What is affirmative action, and should it be used in college admissions for underrepresented groups? Should schools create and enforce guidelines to protect individuals from bullying and discrimination? Should everyone, regardless of their sexual orientation, be allowed to marry?

Amitai Etzioni | *Working at McDonald's*

AMITAI ETZIONI is a sociologist who has taught at Columbia, Harvard, and George Washington Universities, where he currently directs the Institute for Communitarian Policy Studies. He has written numerous articles and more than two dozen books reflecting his commitment to peace in a nuclear age—for example, *Winning without War* (1964); overcoming excessive individualism through communitarianism—for example, *The Spirit of Community: The Reinvention of American Society* (1983); limiting the erosion of privacy in an age of technological surveillance—for example, *The Limits of Privacy* (2004); and, most recently, rethinking foreign policy in an age of terrorism—for example, *Security First: For a Muscular, Moral Foreign Policy* (2007). The following reading was originally published on the opinion page of the *Miami Herald* newspaper. As you read, consider the following:

- What may Etzioni's teenage son Dari, who helped his father write the essay, have contributed?

- What have you learned from the various summer and school-year jobs you have held?

1 McDonald's is bad for your kids. I do not mean the flat patties and the white-flour buns; I refer to the jobs teen-agers undertake, mass-producing these choice items.

2 As many as two-thirds of America's high school juniors and seniors now hold down part-time paying jobs, according to studies. Many of these are in fast-food chains, of which McDonald's is the pioneer, trend-setter and symbol.

3 At first, such jobs may seem right out of the Founding Fathers' educational manual for how to bring up self-reliant, work-ethic-driven, productive youngsters. But in fact, these jobs undermine school attendance and involvement, impart few skills that will be useful in later life, and simultaneously skew the values of teen-agers — especially their ideas about the worth of a dollar.

4 It has been a longstanding American tradition that youngsters ought to get paying jobs. In folklore, few pursuits are more deeply revered than the news-paper route and the sidewalk lemonade stand. Here the youngsters are to learn how sweet are the fruits of labor and self-discipline (papers are delivered early in the morning, rain or shine), and the ways of trade (if you price your lemonade too high or too low . . .).

5 Roy Rogers, Baskin Robbins, Kentucky Fried Chicken, et al. may at first seem nothing but a vast extension of the lemonade stand. They provide very large numbers of teen jobs, provide regular employment, pay quite well compared to many other teen jobs and, in the modern equivalent of toiling over a hot stove, test one's stamina.

6 Closer examination, however, finds the McDonald's kind of job highly uneducational in several ways. Far from providing opportunities for entrepreneurship (the lemonade stand) or self-discipline, self-supervision and self-scheduling (the paper route), most teen jobs these days are highly structured — what social scientists call "highly routinized."

7 True, you still have to have the gumption to get yourself over to the hamburger stand, but once you don the prescribed uniform, your task is spelled out in minute detail. The franchise prescribes the shape of the coffee cups; the weight, size, shape and color of the patties; and the texture of the napkins (if any). Fresh coffee is to be made every eight minutes. And so on. There is no room for initiative, creativity, or even elementary rearrangements. These are breeding grounds for robots working for yesterday's assembly lines, not tomorrow's high-tech posts.

8 There are very few studies on the matter. One of the few is a 1984 study by Ivan Charper and Bryan Shore Fraser. The study relies mainly on what teen-agers write in response to questionnaires rather than actual observations of fast-food jobs. The authors argue that the employees develop many skills such as how to operate a food-preparation machine and a cash register. However, little attention is paid to how long it takes to acquire such a skill, or what its significance is.

9 What does it matter if you spend 20 minutes to learn to use a cash register, and then — "operate" it? What "skill" have you acquired? It is a long way from learning to work with a lathe or carpenter tools in the olden days or to program computers in the modern age.

10 A 1980 study by A. V. Harrell and P. W. Wirtz found that, among those students who worked at least 25 hours per week while in school, their unemployment rate four years later was half of that of seniors who did not work. This is an impressive statistic. It must be seen, though, together with the finding that many who begin as part-time employees in fast-food chains drop out of high school and are gobbled up in the world of low-skill jobs.

11 Some say that while these jobs are rather unsuited for college-bound, white, middle-class youngsters, they are "ideal" for lower-class, "non-academic," minority youngsters. Indeed, minorities are "over-represented" in these jobs (21 percent of fast-food employees). While it is true that these places provide income, work and even some training to such youngsters, they also tend to perpetuate their disadvantaged status. They provide no career ladders, few marketable skills, and undermine school attendance and involvement.

12 The hours are often long. Among those 14 to 17, a third of fast-food employees (including some school

> *Far from providing opportunities for entrepreneurship . . . most teen jobs these days are highly structured.*

dropouts) labor more than 30 hours per week, according to the Charper-Fraser study. Only 20 percent work 15 hours or less. The rest: between 15 and 30 hours.

13 Often the stores close late, and after closing one must clean up and tally up. In affluent Montgomery County, Md., where child labor would not seem to be a widespread economic necessity, 24 percent of the seniors at one high school in 1985 worked as much as five to seven days a week; 27 percent, three to five. There is just no way such amounts of work will not interfere with school work, especially homework. In an informal survey published in the most recent yearbook of the high school, 58 percent of seniors acknowledged that their jobs interfere with their school work.

14 The Charper-Fraser study sees merit in learning teamwork and working under supervision. The authors have a point here. However, it must be noted that such learning is not automatically educational or wholesome. For example, much of the supervision in fast-food places leans toward teaching one the wrong kinds of compliance: blind obedience, or shared alienation with the "boss."

15 Supervision is often both tight and woefully inappropriate. Today, fast-food chains and other such places of work (record shops, bowling alleys) keep costs down by having teens supervise teens with often no adult on the premises.

16 There is no father or mother figure with which to identify, to emulate, to provide a role model and guidance. The work-culture varies from one place to another: Sometimes it is a tightly run shop (must keep the cash registers ringing); sometimes a rather loose pot party interrupted by customers. However, only rarely is there a master to learn from, or much worth learning. Indeed, far from being places where solid adult work values are being transmitted, these are places where all too often delinquent teen values dominate. Typically, when my son Oren was dishing out ice cream for Baskin Robbins in upper Manhattan, his fellow teen-workers considered him a sucker for not helping himself to the till. Most youngsters felt they were entitled to $50 severance "pay" on their last day on the job.

17 The pay, oddly, is the part of the teen work-world that is most difficult to evaluate. The lemonade stand or paper route money was for your allowance. In the old days, apprentices learning a trade from a master contributed most, if not all, of their income to their parents' household. Today, the teen pay may be low by adult standards, but it is often, especially in the middle class, spent largely or wholly by the teens. That is, the youngsters live free at home ("after all, they are high school kids") and are left with very substantial sums of money.

18 Where this money goes is not quite clear. Some use it to support themselves, especially among the poor. More middle-class kids set some money aside to help pay for college, or save it for a major purchase — often a car. But large amounts seem to flow to pay for an early introduction into the most trite aspects of American consumerism: flimsy punk clothes, trinkets and whatever else is the last fast-moving teen craze.

19 One may say that this is only fair and square; they are being good American consumers and spend their money on what turns them on. At least, a cynic might add, these funds do not go into illicit drugs and booze. On the other hand, an educator might bemoan that these young, yet unformed individuals, so early in life driven to buy objects of no intrinsic educational, cultural or social merit, learn so quickly the dubious merit of keeping up with the Joneses in ever-changing fads, promoted by mass merchandising.

20 Many teens find the instant reward of money, and the youth status symbols it buys, much more alluring than credits in calculus courses, European history or foreign languages. No wonder quite a few would rather skip school—and certainly homework — and instead work longer at a Burger King. Thus, most teen work these days is not providing early lessons in the work ethic; it fosters escape from school and responsibilities, quick gratification and a short cut to the consumeristic aspects of adult life.

21 Thus, parents should look at teen employment not as automatically educational. It is an activity — like sports — that can be turned into an educational opportunity. But it can also easily be abused. Youngsters must learn to balance the quest for income with the needs to keep growing and pursue other endeavors that do not pay off instantly—above all education.

22 Go back to school.

Make connections: useful job skills.

Etzioni argues that fast-food jobs do not qualify as meaningful work experience because they do not teach young people the skills and habits they will need for fulfilling careers: "entrepreneurship . . . or self-discipline, self-supervision and self-scheduling" (par. 6).

To judge Etzioni's argument against your own experience, consider what you have learned from your own summer and after-school jobs, either paid or volunteer. Your instructor may ask you to post your thoughts on a class discussion board or to discuss them with other students in class. Use these questions to get started:

- Which, if any, of the skills and habits Etzioni lists as important did you practice at your job or through the activities in which you participated?

- Why do you think these skills and habits are worth learning? If you think other skills and habits are as important or even more important, explain what they are and why you think so.

Use the basic features.

A FOCUSED, WELL-PRESENTED ISSUE: FRAMING AN ARGUMENT FOR A DIVERSE GROUP OF READERS

When Jessica Statsky wrote "Children Need to Play, Not Compete," she knew she would be addressing her classmates. But writers of position essays do not always have such a homogeneous audience. Often, they have to direct their argument to a diverse group of readers, many of whom do not share their concerns or values. From the first sentence, it is clear that Etzioni's primary audience is the parents of teenagers, but his concluding sentence is a direct address to the teenagers themselves: "Go back to school."

ANALYZE & WRITE

Write a paragraph or two analyzing and evaluating how Etzioni presents the issue to a diverse group of readers:

1 Reread paragraphs 1–7, highlighting the qualities—values and skills—associated with traditional jobs (the newspaper route and lemonade stand of yesteryear) and with today's McDonald's-type jobs, at least according to Etzioni. How does Etzioni use these values and skills to lead parents to reconsider their assumption that McDonald's-type jobs are good for their kids?

2 As we point out in the headnote, Etzioni's teenage son Dari helped him write the essay. Skim the essay looking for places where Etzioni appeals to teenagers themselves. Notice, for example, how he represents teenagers' experience and values. Explain how effective you think Etzioni's appeal would be to teenage readers and how effective you think it would be for you and your classmates.

A WELL-SUPPORTED POSITION: USING STATISTICS

Statistics—numerical data about a given population sample—are often used to support position arguments because readers tend to find statistical evidence especially convincing. Numbers can seem impressive—as, for example, when Jessica Statsky refers to the research finding that about 90 percent of children would choose to play regularly on a losing team rather than sit on the bench of a winning team (par. 5). Readers are likely to accept such a high percentage at face value because they would probably share the preference for playing over watching. However, without knowing the size of the sample (90 percent of 10 people, 100 people, or 10,000 people?), it is impossible to judge the significance of the statistic. Moreover, without knowing who the researchers are and how their research was funded and conducted, it is also difficult to judge the credibility of the statistic. That's why most critical readers want to know the source of statistics to see whether the research is **peer-reviewed**—that is, whether it has been evaluated by other researchers knowledgeable about the subject and able to judge the reliability of its findings.

ANALYZE & WRITE

Write a couple of paragraphs analyzing and evaluating Etzioni's use of statistics, and write a paragraph explaining how you could use statistics to enhance your credibility with readers:

1 Reread paragraphs 8–14, and highlight the statistics Etzioni uses. What is each statistic being used to illustrate or prove?

2 Identify what you would need to know about these research studies before you could accept their statistics as credible. Consider also what you would need to know about Etzioni himself before you could decide whether to rely on statistics he calls "impressive" (par. 10). How does your personal experience and observation influence your decision?

3 Based on this analysis, explain how you think you should present statistics that you want your readers to accept as trustworthy.

AN EFFECTIVE RESPONSE: PRESENTING AND REINTERPRETING EVIDENCE TO UNDERMINE OBJECTIONS

At key points throughout his essay, Etzioni acknowledges readers' likely objections and then responds to them. One strategy Etzioni uses is to cite research that appears to undermine his claim and then offer a new interpretation of that evidence. For example, he cites a study by Harrell and Wirtz (par. 10) that links work as a student with greater likelihood of employment later on. He then reinterprets the data from this study to show that the high likelihood of future employment could be an indication that workers in fast-food restaurants are more likely to drop out of school rather than an indication that workers are learning important employment skills. This strategy of presenting and reinterpreting evidence can be especially effective in academic writing, as Etzioni (a professor of sociology) well knows.

ANALYZE & WRITE

Write a couple of paragraphs analyzing and evaluating Etzioni's use of this strategy elsewhere in his essay:

1. Reread paragraphs 8–9, in which Etzioni responds to the claim that employees in McDonald's-type jobs develop many useful skills.

2. Reread paragraphs 14–16, in which Etzioni discusses the benefits and shortcomings of various kinds of on-the-job supervision.

3. Identify the claim that appears in the research Etzioni cites, point out how Etzioni reinterprets it, and explain whether you find his reinterpretation persuasive.

A CLEAR, LOGICAL ORGANIZATION: PROVIDING CUES FOR READERS

Writers of position arguments generally try to make their writing logical and easy to follow. Providing **cues,** or road signs—for example, by forecasting their reasons in a thesis statement early in the argument, using topic sentences to announce each reason as it is supported, and employing transitions (such as *furthermore, in addition,* and *finally*) to guide readers from one point to another—can be helpful, especially in newspaper articles, the readers of which do not want to spend a lot of time deciphering arguments.

ANALYZE & WRITE

Write a paragraph analyzing and evaluating the cueing strategies Etzioni uses to help his readers follow his argument:

1. Find and highlight his thesis statement, the cues forecasting his reasons, the transitions he provides, and any other cueing devices Etzioni uses.

2. Identify the paragraphs in which Etzioni develops each of his reasons.

3. Explain how Etzioni helps readers track his reasons and how effective his cues are.

Consider possible topics: Issues facing students.

[RESPOND]

Etzioni focuses on a single kind of part-time work, takes a position on how worthwhile it is, and recommends against it. You could write a similar kind of essay. For example, you could take a position for or against students' participating in other kinds of part-time work or recreation during the high school or college academic year or over the summer—for example, playing on a sports team, volunteering, completing an internship, studying a musical instrument or a foreign language, or taking an elective class. If you work to support yourself and pay for college, you could focus on why the job either strengthens or weakens you as a person, given your life and career goals. Writing for other students, you would either recommend the job or activity to them or discourage them from pursuing it, giving reasons and support for your position.

Daniel J. Solove | *Why Privacy Matters Even If You Have "Nothing to Hide"*

DANIEL J. SOLOVE is the John Marshall Harlan Research Professor of Law at the George Washington University Law School. In addition to writing numerous books and articles on issues of privacy and the Internet, Solove is the founder of a company that provides privacy and data security training to corporations and universities. Among his books are *The Future of Reputation: Gossip, Rumor, and Privacy on the Internet* (2007), which won Fordham University's McGannon Award for Social and Ethical Relevance in Communications Policy Research, and *Nothing to Hide: The False Tradeoff between Privacy and Security* (2011). An earlier and longer version of this essay in a law review journal included citations that had to be eliminated for publication in the *Chronicle of Higher Education* in 2011, but we have restored them so that you can see how Solove uses a variety of sources to support his position. As you read, consider the following:

- The sources cited in the opening paragraphs: How do they contribute to your understanding of why many people think privacy is not something they should be concerned about?

- Do you use Internet privacy settings, and should you be concerned about protecting your privacy on social networking and other Web sites?

1 When the government gathers or analyzes personal information, many people say they're not worried. "I've got nothing to hide," they declare. "Only if you're doing something wrong should you worry, and then you don't deserve to keep it private." The nothing-to-hide argument pervades discussions about privacy. The data-security expert Bruce Schneier calls it the "most common retort against privacy advocates." The legal scholar Geoffrey Stone refers to it as an "all-too-common refrain." In its most compelling form, it is an argument that the privacy interest is generally minimal, thus making the contest with security concerns a foreordained victory for security.

2 The nothing-to-hide argument is everywhere. In Britain, for example, the government has installed millions of public-surveillance cameras in cities and towns, which are watched by officials via closed-circuit television. In a campaign slogan for the program, the government declares: "If you've got nothing to hide, you've got nothing to fear" (Rosen 36). Variations of nothing-to-hide arguments frequently appear in blogs, letters to the editor, television news interviews, and other forums.

One blogger in the United States, in reference to profiling people for national-security purposes, declares: "I don't mind people wanting to find out things about me, I've got nothing to hide! Which is why I support [the government's] efforts to find terrorists by monitoring our phone calls!" (greatcarrieoakey).

3 On the surface, it seems easy to dismiss the nothing-to-hide argument. Everybody probably has something to hide from somebody. As Aleksandr Solzhenitsyn declared, "Everyone is guilty of something or has something to conceal. All one has to do is look hard enough to find what it is" (192). . . . One can usually think of something that even the most open person would want to hide. As a commenter to my blog post noted, "If you have nothing to hide, then that quite literally means you are willing to let me photograph you naked? And I get full rights to that photograph—so I can show it to your neighbors?" (Andrew) . . .

4 But such responses attack the nothing-to-hide argument only in its most extreme form, which isn't particularly strong. In a less extreme form, the nothing-to-hide argument refers not to all personal information but only

to the type of data the government is likely to collect. Retorts to the nothing-to-hide argument about exposing people's naked bodies or their deepest secrets are relevant only if the government is likely to gather this kind of information. In many instances, hardly anyone will see the information, and it won't be disclosed to the public. Thus, some might argue, the privacy interest is minimal, and the security interest in preventing terrorism is much more important. In this less extreme form, the nothing-to-hide argument is a formidable one. However, it stems from certain faulty assumptions about privacy and its value. . . .

5   Most attempts to understand privacy do so by attempting to locate its essence—its core characteristics or the common denominator that links together the various things we classify under the rubric of "privacy." Privacy, however, is too complex a concept to be reduced to a singular essence. It is a plurality of different things that do not share any one element but nevertheless bear a resemblance to one another. For example, privacy can be invaded by the disclosure of your deepest secrets. It might also be invaded if you're watched by a peeping Tom, even if no secrets are ever revealed. With the disclosure of secrets, the harm is that your concealed information is spread to others. With the peeping Tom, the harm is that you're being watched. You'd probably find that creepy regardless of whether the peeper finds out anything sensitive or discloses any information to others. There are many other forms of invasion of privacy, such as blackmail and the improper use of your personal data. Your privacy can also be invaded if the government compiles an extensive dossier about you. Privacy, in other words, involves so many things that it is impossible to reduce them all to one simple idea. And we need not do so. . . .

6   To describe the problems created by the collection and use of personal data, many commentators use a metaphor based on George Orwell's *Nineteen Eighty-Four*. Orwell depicted a harrowing totalitarian society ruled by a government called Big Brother that watches its citizens obsessively and demands strict discipline. The Orwell metaphor, which focuses on the harms of surveillance (such as inhibition and social control), might be apt to describe government monitoring of citizens. But much of the data gathered in computer databases, such

> *The problem with the nothing-to-hide argument is the underlying assumption that privacy is about hiding bad things.*

as one's race, birth date, gender, address, or marital status, isn't particularly sensitive. Many people don't care about concealing the hotels they stay at, the cars they own, or the kind of beverages they drink. Frequently, though not always, people wouldn't be inhibited or embarrassed if others knew this information.

7   Another metaphor better captures the problems: Franz Kafka's *The Trial*. Kafka's novel centers around a man who is arrested but not informed why. He desperately tries to find out what triggered his arrest and what's in store for him. He finds out that a mysterious court system has a dossier on him and is investigating him, but he's unable to learn much more. *The Trial* depicts a bureaucracy with inscrutable purposes that uses people's information to make important decisions about them, yet denies the people the ability to participate in how their information is used.

8   The problems portrayed by the Kafkaesque metaphor are of a different sort than the problems caused by surveillance. They often do not result in inhibition. Instead they are problems of information processing—the storage, use, or analysis of data—rather than of information collection. They affect the power relationships between people and the institutions of the modern state. They not only frustrate the individual by creating a sense of helplessness and powerlessness, but also affect social structure by altering the kind of relationships people have with the institutions that make important decisions about their lives.

9   Legal and policy solutions focus too much on the problems under the Orwellian metaphor—those of surveillance—and aren't adequately addressing the Kafkaesque problems—those of information processing. The difficulty is that commentators are trying to conceive of the problems caused by databases in terms of surveillance when, in fact, those problems are different. Commentators often attempt to refute the nothing-to-hide argument by pointing to things people want to hide. But the problem with the nothing-to-hide argument is the underlying assumption that privacy is about hiding bad things. By accepting this assumption, we concede far too much ground and invite an unproductive discussion about information that people would very likely want to hide. As the computer-security specialist

Schneier aptly notes, the nothing-to-hide argument stems from a faulty "premise that privacy is about hiding a wrong." Surveillance, for example, can inhibit such lawful activities as free speech, free association, and other First Amendment rights essential for democracy.

10   The deeper problem with the nothing-to-hide argument is that it myopically views privacy as a form of secrecy. In contrast, understanding privacy as a plurality of related issues demonstrates that the disclosure of bad things is just one among many difficulties caused by government security measures. To return to my discussion of literary metaphors, the problems are not just Orwellian but Kafkaesque. Government information-gathering programs are problematic even if no information that people want to hide is uncovered. In *The Trial,* the problem is not inhibited behavior but rather a suffocating powerlessness and vulnerability created by the court system's use of personal data and its denial to the protagonist of any knowledge of or participation in the process. The harms are bureaucratic ones—indifference, error, abuse, frustration, and lack of transparency and accountability.

11   One such harm, for example, which I call aggregation, emerges from the fusion of small bits of seemingly innocuous data. When combined, the information becomes much more telling. By joining pieces of information we might not take pains to guard, the government can glean information about us that we might indeed wish to conceal. For example, suppose you bought a book about cancer. This purchase isn't very revealing on its own, for it indicates just an interest in the disease. Suppose you bought a wig. The purchase of a wig, by itself, could be for a number of reasons. But combine those two pieces of information, and now the inference can be made that you have cancer and are undergoing chemotherapy. That might be a fact you wouldn't mind sharing, but you'd certainly want to have the choice.

12   Another potential problem with the government's harvest of personal data is one I call exclusion. Exclusion occurs when people are prevented from having knowledge about how information about them is being used, and when they are barred from accessing and correcting errors in that data. Many government national-security measures involve maintaining a huge database of information that individuals cannot access. Indeed, because they involve national security, the very existence of these programs is often kept secret. This kind of information processing, which blocks subjects'

knowledge and involvement, is a kind of due-process problem. It is a structural problem, involving the way people are treated by government institutions and creating a power imbalance between people and the government. To what extent should government officials have such a significant power over citizens? This issue isn't about what information people want to hide but about the power and the structure of government.

13   A related problem involves secondary use. Secondary use is the exploitation of data obtained for one purpose for an unrelated purpose without the subject's consent. How long will personal data be stored? How will the information be used? What could it be used for in the future? The potential uses of any piece of personal information are vast. Without limits on or accountability for how that information is used, it is hard for people to assess the dangers of the data's being in the government's control.

14   Yet another problem with government gathering and use of personal data is distortion. Although personal information can reveal quite a lot about people's personalities and activities, it often fails to reflect the whole person. It can paint a distorted picture, especially since records are reductive—they often capture information in a standardized format with many details omitted. For example, suppose government officials learn that a person has bought a number of books on how to manufacture methamphetamine. That information makes them suspect that he's building a meth lab. What is missing from the records is the full story: The person is writing a novel about a character who makes meth. When he bought the books, he didn't consider how suspicious the purchase might appear to government officials, and his records didn't reveal the reason for the purchases. Should he have to worry about government scrutiny of all his purchases and actions? Should he have to be concerned that he'll wind up on a suspicious-persons list? Even if he isn't doing anything wrong, he may want to keep his records away from government officials who might make faulty inferences from them. He might not want to have to worry about how everything he does will be perceived by officials nervously monitoring for criminal activity. He might not want to have a computer flag him as suspicious because he has an unusual pattern of behavior. . . .

15   Privacy is rarely lost in one fell swoop. It is usually eroded over time, little bits dissolving almost imperceptibly

until we finally begin to notice how much is gone. When the government starts monitoring the phone numbers people call, many may shrug their shoulders and say, "Ah, it's just numbers, that's all." Then the government might start monitoring some phone calls. "It's just a few phone calls, nothing more." The government might install more video cameras in public places. "So what? Some more cameras watching in a few more places. No big deal." The increase in cameras might lead to a more elaborate network of video surveillance. Satellite surveillance might be added to help track people's movements. The government might start analyzing people's bank records. "It's just my deposits and some of the bills I pay—no problem." The government may then start combing through credit-card records, then expand to Internet-service providers' records, health records, employment records, and more. Each step may seem incremental, but after a while, the government will be watching and knowing everything about us.

16   "My life's an open book," people might say. "I've got nothing to hide." But now the government has large dossiers of everyone's activities, interests, reading habits, finances, and health. What if the government leaks the information to the public? What if the government mistakenly determines that based on your pattern of

> *Privacy is rarely lost in one fell swoop. It is usually eroded over time, little bits dissolving almost imperceptibly until we finally begin to notice how much is gone.*

activities, you're likely to engage in a criminal act? What if it denies you the right to fly? What if the government thinks your financial transactions look odd—even if you've done nothing wrong—and freezes your accounts? What if the government doesn't protect your information with adequate security, and an identity thief obtains it and uses it to defraud you? Even if you have nothing to hide, the government can cause you a lot of harm. . . .

Works Cited

Andrew. Weblog comment. *Concurring Opinions.* 16 Oct. 2006. Web. 24 May 2012.

greatcarrieoakey. "Reach For The Stars!" *Blogspot.com.* 14 May 2006. Web. 24 May 2012.

Rosen, Jeffrey. *The Naked Crowd: Reclaiming Security and Freedom in an Anxious Age.* New York: Random House, 2004. Print.

Schneier, Bruce. "The Eternal Value of Privacy." *Wired.* 18 May 2006. Web. 24 May 2012.

Solzhenitsyn, Aleksandr. *Cancer Ward.* Trans. Nicholas Bethell and David Burg. New York: Farrar, Straus and Giroux, 1969. Print.

Stone, Geoffrey R. "Freedom and Public Responsibility." *Chicago Tribune* 21 May 2006: 11. Print.

Make connections: Privacy concerns on the Internet.   `REFLECT`

Whereas Solove's position argument focuses on concerns about government collection and use of personal information, many people today are concerned as well about corporate collection and use of personal information. For example, students about to graduate from college have been surprised to discover that potential employers search blogs and social media Web sites to gather information about job candidates and to check their résumés. Corporations also use data mining to personalize advertising, sending diaper coupons, for example, to women in their thirties who have recently bought diaper bags or baby monitors online. (You may recall the talking billboards depicted in the film *Minority Report:* "John Anderton! You could use a Guinness right about now.")

Think about the implications of corporate data mining, and reflect on how this could affect your own sense of online privacy. Your instructor may ask you to post your thoughts on a class discussion board or to discuss them with other students in class. Use these questions to get started:

- How, if at all, do you manage the privacy preferences or settings on sites you use? Do you ever de-friend people or click the "do not track" tool when you have the opportunity to do so? Would you untag photos or delete comments on social networking sites like Facebook that you didn't want potential employers to see?

- Do you think you should be concerned or learn more about privacy problems, such as identity theft, cyberstalking, or personalized advertising?

- What are the advantages and disadvantages of corporate data mining? Have targeted advertisements been a boon to you, or are you distressed about a corporation's knowing so much about you?

[ANALYZE]   # Use the basic features.

A FOCUSED, WELL-PRESENTED ISSUE: REFRAMING THROUGH CONTRAST

Writers sometimes have to remind their readers why an issue is controversial. Beginning with the title, Solove works to undermine the widely held assumption that the erosion of privacy should not be a concern. He does this primarily by contrasting two different ways of thinking about threats to privacy, which he calls Orwellian and Kafkaesque, based on the novels *1984,* by George Orwell, and *The Trial,* by Franz Kafka. To present this contrast, Solove uses sentence patterns like these:

- ▶ Not _____ , but _____ .

- ▶ _____ focus on _____ , which is characterized by _____ , and they don't even notice _____ , which is characterized by _____ .

Here are a couple of examples from Solove's position argument:

> The problems are not just Orwellian but Kafkaesque. (par. 10)

> Legal and policy solutions focus too much on the problems under the Orwellian metaphor—those of surveillance—and aren't adequately addressing the Kafkaesque problems—those of information processing. (par. 9)

| ANALYZE & WRITE |

Write a few paragraphs analyzing and evaluating the effectiveness of Solove's use of contrast to reframe the issue for readers:

1 Notice how Solove uses sources in his first two paragraphs. Given his purpose to reframe a commonly held view of privacy, why do you think he begins this way?

2 Reread paragraphs 6–7 to see how Solove explains the two contrasting metaphors. Then skim paragraphs 8–10, highlighting any sentence patterns used to mark the contrast.

3 Has Solove's reframing of the discussion affected your understanding of privacy and your concerns about its loss? Why or why not?

A WELL-SUPPORTED POSITION: USING SOURCES

Writers of position arguments often quote, paraphrase, and summarize sources. Usually, they use sources to support their positions, as Jessica Statsky does in her argument about children's sports. Sometimes, however, they use sources to highlight opposing positions to which they will respond, as Solove does on occasion in this essay.

In the following example, Solove signals his opinion through the words he chooses to characterize the source:

> As the computer-security specialist Schneier aptly notes, the nothing-to-hide argument stems from a faulty "premise that privacy is about hiding a wrong." (par. 9)

Elsewhere, readers have to work a little harder to determine how Solove is using the source.

Solove also uses what we might call **hypothetical quotations**—sentences that quote not what someone actually said but what they *might* have said:

> Many people say they're not worried. "I've got nothing to hide," they declare. "Only if you're doing something wrong should you worry, and then you don't deserve to keep it private." (par. 1)

> "My life's an open book," people might say. "I've got nothing to hide." (par. 16)

You can tell from a signal phrase like "people might say" or "many people say" that no actual person made the statement, but Solove does not always supply such cues.

To learn more about using patterns of opposition to read critically, see Chapter 12, pp. 537–38.

Signal phrase

Hypothetical quotation

| ANALYZE & WRITE |

Write a couple of paragraphs analyzing and evaluating Solove's use of quotations:

1. Find and mark the quotations, noting which actually quote someone and which are hypothetical.

2. Identify the quotations — real or hypothetical — that Solove agrees with and those that represent an opposing view.

3. Consider how effective Solove's quoting strategy was likely to have been, given his purpose and audience. (Remember that this article appeared in the *Chronicle of Higher Education,* a weekly newspaper for college faculty and administrators.) How effective did you find his quoting strategy?

AN EFFECTIVE RESPONSE: REFUTING BY DEMONSTRATING THE EFFECTS

As his title suggests, Solove refutes the claim that privacy does not matter "if you have 'nothing to hide.'" His primary way of refuting the nothing-to-hide argument is to argue that the collection and use of personal information (the cause) has negative effects, which he sometimes calls "problems" and sometimes calls "harms" (pars. 5 and 6).

Write a few paragraphs analyzing and evaluating Solove's use of cause and effect reasoning to refute the claim that privacy only matters if you have something to hide:

1 Reread paragraphs 6–14, noting where Solove discusses potential problems or harms that could result from the collection of personal data.

2 Choose one of these harms, and examine Solove's argument more closely. How does he support this part of the argument — for example, what are his reasons, his evidence, the values and beliefs he uses to appeal to his audience?

3 How effective are Solove's reasons and evidence for you? How effective might they have been for his original audience?

A CLEAR, LOGICAL ORGANIZATION: USING CUEING DEVICES

Solove uses a number of cueing devices to help readers keep track of his argument. Perhaps the most obvious and helpful cues are the topic sentences that begin each paragraph and the logical transitions ("One such harm . . . ," "Another potential problem . . . ," "A related problem . . . ," "Yet another problem . . ." [pars. 11–14]) that signal connections between and within paragraphs. In addition, Solove uses rhetorical questions, such as the series of "What if" questions in the final paragraph.

Write a few paragraphs analyzing and evaluating the effectiveness of Solove's use of cueing devices to help readers follow his argument:

1 Choose a couple of paragraphs that seem to you to use topic sentences and logical transitions effectively. Look closely at the way Solove uses these cueing devices, and determine what makes them so effective.

2 Highlight the rhetorical questions posed in paragraphs 12–14 and 16. Why do you imagine Solove uses so many of them, especially in the final paragraph? Given his purpose and audience, how effective do you think these rhetorical questions were likely to have been? How effective do you find them?

[RESPOND]

Consider possible topics: Issues concerning privacy.

Solove focuses on one concern about the erosion of privacy. You could write a similar type of essay, taking a position on issues such as state laws requiring women to have ultrasounds before terminating a pregnancy; airport security requiring passengers either to go through a full-body scanner or to submit to a "pat-down" before boarding a flight; cell phones making it possible for individuals to be located and tracked without their consent or knowledge; or houses, offices, and even people on the street being depicted on Google Maps without their knowledge or consent.

For more reading selections, including a multimodal selection, go to **bedfordstmartins.com /theguide/epages**.

Public Service Announcements

Reasoned arguments about controversial issues appear every day in classrooms, but they also appear in newspaper editorials, blogs, and sometimes even in advertisements. Consider, for example, the public service announcement (PSA) reproduced here.

Using a single image and relatively few words, this PSA makes a surprisingly effective argument: Even a couple of beers can be a recipe for disaster, given the right conditions, so don't drink and drive. The appealing visual, the familiar recipe format, and the use of realistic language expressing a seemingly moderate perspective ("It's only another beer"; "just a few") reach out to average adults, who likely do not think of themselves as reckless or irresponsible, and remind them that it can be a short step from an ordinary evening relaxing with coworkers to a catastrophic accident.

In this chapter, we ask you to argue for a controversial position. As you compose your argument, consider how you can most effectively capture your readers' attention and convince them to take your point of view seriously. Consider, too, whether using visual or multimedia support or the conventions of another genre would help your readers more fully grasp and more immediately accept your position.

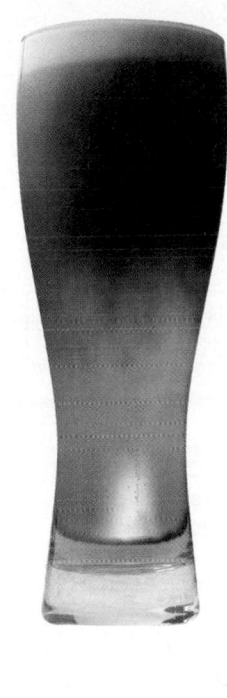

The "It's Only Another Beer"
Black and Tan

8 oz. pilsner lager
8 oz. stout lager
1 frosty mug
1 icy road
1 pick-up truck
1 10-hour day
1 tired worker
A few rounds with the guys

Mix ingredients.
Add 1 totalled vehicle.

Never underestimate 'just a few.'
Buzzed driving is drunk driving.

U.S. Department of Transportation

For an interactive version of this feature, plus activities, go to **bedfordstmartins.com/theguide/epages**.

The Writing Assignment

Write an essay arguing a controversial position: Start by learning more about the issue and the debate surrounding it, and then take a position. Present the issue so readers recognize that it merits their attention, and develop a well-supported argument that will confirm, challenge, or change your readers' views.

This Guide to Writing is designed to help you compose your own position argument and apply what you have learned from reading other position arguments. This Starting Points chart will help you find answers to questions you might have about composing a position argument. Use the chart to find the guidance you need, when you need it.

STARTING POINTS: ARGUING A POSITION

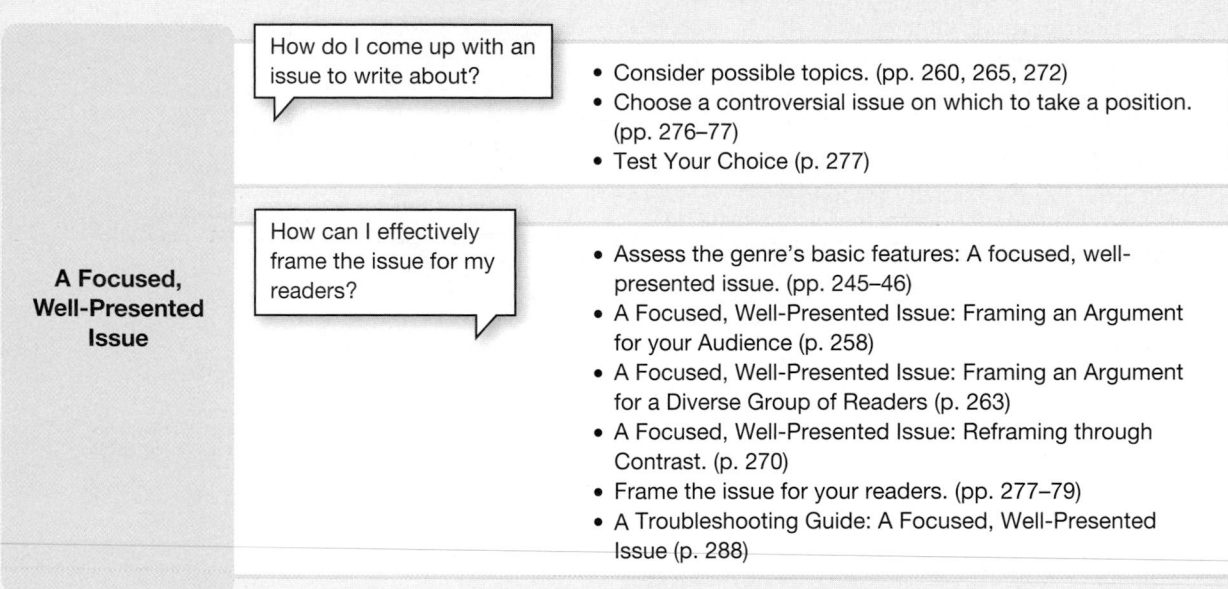

How do I come up with an issue to write about?

- Consider possible topics. (pp. 260, 265, 272)
- Choose a controversial issue on which to take a position. (pp. 276–77)
- Test Your Choice (p. 277)

A Focused, Well-Presented Issue

How can I effectively frame the issue for my readers?

- Assess the genre's basic features: A focused, well-presented issue. (pp. 245–46)
- A Focused, Well-Presented Issue: Framing an Argument for your Audience (p. 258)
- A Focused, Well-Presented Issue: Framing an Argument for a Diverse Group of Readers (p. 263)
- A Focused, Well-Presented Issue: Reframing through Contrast. (p. 270)
- Frame the issue for your readers. (pp. 277–79)
- A Troubleshooting Guide: A Focused, Well-Presented Issue (p. 288)

A Well-Supported Position

How do I come up with a plausible position?

- Assess the genre's basic features: A well-supported position. (pp. 247–48)
- Formulate a working thesis stating your position. (p. 279)
- Develop the reasons supporting your position. (p. 280)
- Research your position. (pp. 280–81)
- Use sources to reinforce your credibility. (pp. 281–82)

How do I come up with reasons and evidence supporting my position?

- A Well-Supported Position: Using Anecdotes and Examples (pp. 258–59)
- A Well-Supported Position: Using Statistics (p. 264)
- A Well-Supported Position: Using Sources (p. 271)
- Formulate a working thesis stating your position (p. 279)
- Develop the reasons supporting your position. (p. 280)
- Research your position. (pp. 280–81)

An Effective Response to Opposing Views

How do I respond to possible objections to my position?

- Assess the genre's basic features: An effective response to opposing views. (pp. 248–49)
- An Effective Response: Conceding and/or Refuting (p. 259)
- Identify and respond to your readers' likely reasons and objections. (pp. 282–84)
- Write the opening sentences. (pp. 285–86)

How do I respond to possible alternative positions?

- Assess the genre's basic feature: An effective response to opposing views (pp. 248–49)
- An Effective Response: Conceding and/or Refuting (p. 259)
- An Effective Response: Presenting and Reinterpreting Evidence to Undermine Objections (pp. 264–65)
- An Effective Response: Refuting by Demonstrating the Effects (pp. 271–72)
- Research your position. (pp. 280–81)
- Identify and respond to your readers' likely reasons and objections. (pp. 282–84)

(continued)

A Clear, Logical Organization

How can I help my readers follow my argument?

- Assess the genre's basic features: A clear, logical organization. (p. 249)
- A Clear, Logical Organization: Using Key Words (pp. 259–60)
- A Clear, Logical Organization: Providing Cues for Readers (p. 265)
- A Clear, Logical Organization: Using Cueing Devices (p. 272)
- Create an outline that will organize your argument effectively for your readers. (p. 284)
- A Troubleshooting Guide: A Clear, Logical Organization (p. 289)
- Think about design (pp. 289–90)

Writing a Draft: Invention, Research, Planning, and Composing

The activities in this section will help you choose and research an issue as well as develop and organize an argument for your position. Do the activities in any order that makes sense to you (and your instructor), and return to them as needed as you revise. Your writing in response to many of these activities can be used in a rough draft that you will be able to improve after receiving feedback from your classmates and instructor.

Choose a controversial issue on which to take a position.

When choosing an issue, keep in mind that the issue must be

- controversial—an issue that people disagree about;
- arguable—a matter of opinion on which there is no absolute proof or authority;
- one that you can research, as necessary, in the time you have; and
- one that you care about.

Choosing an issue about which you have special interest or knowledge usually works best. For example, if you are thinking of addressing an issue of national concern, focus on a local or at least a specific aspect of it: For example, instead of addressing censorship in general, write about a recent lawmaker's effort to propose a law censoring the Internet, a city council attempt to block access to Internet sites at the public library, or a school board's ban on certain textbooks.

You may already have an issue in mind. If you do, skip to Test Your Choice (p. 277). If you do not, the topics that follow, in addition to those following the readings (pp. 260, 265, 272), may suggest an issue you can make your own:

Issues Related to School

- Should particular courses, community service, or an internship be a graduation requirement at your high school or college?

- Should students attending public colleges be required to pay higher tuition fees if they have been full-time students but have not graduated within four years?
- Should your large lecture or online courses have frequent (weekly or biweekly) exams instead of only a midterm and final?

Issues Related to Your Community

- Should children raised in this country whose parents entered illegally be given an opportunity to become citizens upon finishing college or serving in the military?
- Should the racial, ethnic, or gender makeup of the police force resemble the makeup of the community it serves?
- Should the football conference your school (or another school in the area) participates in be allowed to expand?

Issues Related to Work

- Should you look primarily for a job that is well paid or for a job that is personally fulfilling or socially responsible?
- Should public employees be allowed to unionize and to bargain collectively for improved working conditions, pay, or pensions?
- Should the state or federal government provide job training for those who are unemployed but able to work?

TEST YOUR CHOICE

Ask yourself the following questions:

- Does the issue matter to me and to my readers? If the issue is not currently one of widespread concern, would I be able to argue convincingly at the beginning of my essay that it *ought* to be of concern?
- Do I know enough about the issue to take a position that I can support effectively, or can I learn what I need to know in the time I have?
- Have I begun to understand the issue well enough to frame or reframe it in a way that might open readers to my point of view?
- What can I realistically hope to achieve with my readers — convince them to adopt my point of view; get them to reconsider what's at stake; show them that arguments they trust are unfair, inaccurate, or logically flawed?

As you plan and draft your argument, you will probably want to consider these questions. If at any point you cannot answer them with a confident *yes*, you may want to consider modifying your position on the issue or choosing a different issue to write about. If you have serious doubts, discuss them with your instructor.

Frame the issue for your readers.

Once you have made a preliminary choice of an issue, consider how you can frame (or reframe) it so that readers who support opposing positions will listen to your argument. To do this, consider how the issue has been debated in the past and what your readers are likely to think. Use the following questions and sentence strategies to help you put your ideas in writing.

WAYS IN

HOW CAN I EXPLORE THE ISSUE?

What groups or notable individuals have shaped the debate on this issue? What positions have they taken?

▶ It may surprise you that _____ is a controversial issue. Although many people take _____ for granted, [individuals/groups] oppose it on the grounds that _____.

▶ Whereas supporters of _____ have argued that _____, opponents such as [list individuals/groups] contend that _____.

How has the issue, or people's opinions about the issue, changed? What makes the issue important now?

▶ [Recent research reports/incidents reported in the news] have changed some people's minds on this issue. Instead of assuming _____, many people now think _____.

▶ The debate over whether _____ should _____ was initially concerned with _____, but now the main concern seems to be that _____.

WHAT DO MY READERS THINK?

What values and concerns do I and my readers share regarding the issue?

▶ Concern about _____ leads many of us to oppose _____. We worry that _____ will happen if _____.

▶ _____ is a basic human right that needs to be protected. But what does it mean in everyday practice when _____?

What fundamental differences in worldview or experience might keep me and my readers from agreeing?

▶ Those who disagree about _____ often see it as a choice between _____ and _____. But both are important. We don't have to choose between them because _____.

▶ While others may view it as a matter of _____, for me, the issue hinges on _____.

▶ According to _____, what's at stake in this issue is _____. For me, however, what is most important is _____.

HOW CAN I FRAME THE ISSUE EFFECTIVELY?

Once you have a good idea of how the issue has been debated and what your readers think, use these sentence strategies to frame the issue for your readers.

What is the issue, and why should my readers be concerned about it?

▶ I'm concerned about _____ because _____.

EXAMPLE   I'm concerned about the high cost of tuition at state colleges like ours because students are having to borrow more money to pay for their education than they will be able to repay.

Why are popular approaches or attitudes inappropriate or inadequate?

▶ Although some argue _____, I think _____ because _____.

EXAMPLE   Although some argue that college football players should be paid, I think the current system should be maintained because it is only the money earned from football that enables our school to fund other, less lucrative sports programs.

TEST YOUR CHOICE

Ask two or three other students to consider the way you have framed your issue.

Presenters. Briefly explain the values and concerns you think are at stake. (The sentence strategies in the Ways In section can help you articulate your position and approach.)

Listeners. Tell the presenter what response this way of framing the issue elicits from you and why. Use language that follows as a model for structuring your response, or use language of your own.

- ▶ I'm [also/not] concerned about the high cost of tuition because _____ .

- ▶ I [agree/disagree] that college football players should not be paid because _____ .

▪▪ Formulate a working thesis stating your position.

You may already have a position on the issue; if so, try drafting a working thesis statement now. (Alternatively, if you prefer to conduct research or develop your argument before trying to formulate a thesis, skip this activity and return to it when you're ready.) As you develop your argument, rework this assertion to make it a compelling thesis statement by sharpening the language and perhaps forecasting your reasons. You may also need to qualify it, with words like *often*, *sometimes*, or *in part*.

HOW CAN I DEVISE AN ARGUABLE THESIS?

A good strategy is to begin by describing the issue, possibly indicating where others stand on it or what's at stake, and then saying what you think. These sentence strategies may help you get started:

- ▶ On this issue, X and Y say _____ . Although I understand and to some degree sympathize with their point of view, this is ultimately a question of _____ . What's at stake is not _____ but _____ . Therefore, we must _____ .

- ▶ This issue is dividing our community. Some people argue _____ . Others contend _____ . And still others believe _____ . It is in all of our interests to _____ , however, because _____ .

- ▶ Conventional wisdom is that _____ . But I take a different view: _____ .

WAYS IN

Develop the reasons supporting your position.

For more idea-generating strategies, see Chapter 11.

The following activities will help you find plausible reasons and evidence for your position. Begin by writing down what you already know. You can do some focused research later to fill in the details, or skip ahead to conduct research now.

WAYS IN

HOW CAN I COME UP WITH REASONS THAT SUPPORT MY POSITION?

One way to generate ideas is to write steadily for at least five minutes exploring your reasons. Ask yourself questions like these:

- How can I show readers that my reasons lead logically to my position?
- In addition to appealing to readers' intellect (logos), how can I convince my readers that I am trustworthy (ethos) or appeal to their feelings (pathos)?

At this point, don't worry about the exact language you will use in your final draft. Instead, just write the reasons you hold your position and the evidence (such as anecdotes, examples, statistics, expert testimony) that supports it. Keep your readers in mind—what would they find most convincing?

If you prefer to brainstorm a list of reasons, try this:

- Start by writing your position at the top of the page.
- List as many potential reasons as you can think of to support your position. (Don't judge at this point.).
- Make notes about the kinds of evidence you would need to show how each reason supports your position. You may be able to use this list and you notes as a starting point for further research and drafting.

Research your position.

Do some research to find out how others have argued in support of your position:

- Try entering keywords or phrases related to the issue or your position in the search box of an all-purpose database, such as *Academic OneFile* (InfoTrac) or *Academic Search Complete* (EBSCOHost), to find relevant articles in magazines and journals, or use the database Lexis/Nexis to find articles in newspapers. For example, Jessica Statsky could have tried a combination of keywords, such as *children's sports,* or variations on her terms (*youth sports*) to find relevant articles. A similar search of your library's catalog could also be conducted to locate books and other resources on your topic.

To learn more about searching a database or catalog, consult Chapter 24, pp. 674–79.

To learn more about finding government documents, consult Chapter 24, p. 679.

- If you think your issue has been dealt with by a government agency, explore the state, local, or tribal sections of USA.gov—the U.S. government's official Web portal—or visit the Library of Congress page on state government information (www.loc.gov/rr/news/stategov/stategov.html) and follow the links.

Writing a Draft

GUIDE TO READING
GUIDE TO WRITING
A WRITER AT WORK
THINKING CRITICALLY

281

Remember to bookmark promising sites and to record the URL and information you will need to cite and document any sources or visuals you use.

To learn more about documenting sources, consult Chapter 27, pp. 709–38, or Chapter 28, pp. 739–50.

:: Use sources to reinforce your credibility.

How you represent your sources can quickly establish your credibility (ethos)—or the reverse. For example, by briefly describing the author's credentials the first time you *summarize, paraphrase,* or *quote* from a source, you establish the source's authority and demonstrate that you have selected sources appropriately:

> Martin Rablovsky, a former sports editor for the *New York Times,* says that in all his years of watching young children play organized sports, he has noticed very few of them smiling. "I've seen children enjoying a spontaneous pre-practice scrimmage become somber and serious when the coach's whistle blows," Rablovsky says . . . (qtd. in Coakley 94).

Signal phrase & author's credentials

Source summary

In-text citation follows quotation

Quotations can also reinforce the accuracy of your summary or paraphrase and establish your fairness to opposing points of view. In the following sentence, Jessica Statsky demonstrates her fairness by quoting from the Web site of the Little League, a well-known organization, and she establishes her credibility by demonstrating that even those who disagree with her recognize that injuries occur:

> Although the official Little League Web site acknowledges that children do risk injury playing baseball, it insists that "severe injuries . . . are infrequent," the risk "far less than the risk of riding a skateboard, a bicycle, or even the school bus" ("What about My Child?").

Statsky's introduction: Summarizes source

In-text citation follows quotation

In both of these examples from "Children Need to Play, Not Compete" (pars. 5 and 3, respectively), Statsky introduces the source to her readers, explaining the relevance of the source material, including the author's credentials, for readers rather than leaving them to figure out its relevance for themselves.

Whenever you borrow information from sources, be sure to double check that you are summarizing, paraphrasing, and quoting accurately and fairly. Compare Statsky's sentence with the source passage (that follows). (The portions she uses are highlighted.) Notice that she has inserted ellipsis (. . .) to indicate that she has left out words from her source's second sentence.

Source

> Injuries seem to be inevitable in any rigorous activity, especially if players are new to the sport and unfamiliar with its demands. But because of the safety precautions taken in Little League, severe injuries such as bone fractures are infrequent. Most injuries are sprains and strains, abrasions and cuts and bruises. The risk of serious injury in Little League Baseball is far less than the risk of riding a skateboard, a bicycle, or even the school bus.

For more on integrating language from sources into your own sentences and avoiding plagiarism, see Chapter 26, pp. 698–708; for additional help avoiding plagiarism, go to **bedford-stmartins.com/theguide** and click on the Avoiding Plagiarism Tutorial.

In both of the preceding examples, Statsky uses quotation marks to indicate that she is borrowing the words of a source and provides an in-text citation so that readers can locate the sources in her list of works cited. Doing both is essential to avoiding plagiarism; one or the other is not enough.

Identify and respond to your readers' likely reasons and objections.

The following activity will help you anticipate reasons your readers may use to support their argument or objections they may have. You may want to return to this activity as you do additional research and learn more about the issue and the arguments people make. Use the research strategies on pp. 280–81 or consult Chapter 24, "Finding Sources and Conducting Field Research."

WAYS IN

For more logical fallacies see Chapter 19, pp. 620–21.

HOW CAN I FIGURE OUT WHAT MY READERS WILL BE CONCERNED ABOUT?

1. Start by listing the reasons you expect your readers to have for their position and the objections (including those based on logical fallacies) you expect them to raise to your argument. To think of readers' concerns, consider how you differ on values, beliefs, and priorities.

2. Analyze your list of readers' likely reasons and objections. Which can you refute, and how? Which may you need to concede?

HOW CAN I RESPOND TO READERS' REASONS AND OBJECTIONS?

Now, choose a reason or objection, and try out a response:

1. Summarize it accurately and fairly. (Do not commit the "straw man" fallacy of knocking down something that no one really takes seriously.)

2. Decide whether you can refute it, need to concede it, or can refute part and concede part.

Try sentence strategies like these to refute, concede, or concede and refute reasons supporting readers' arguments or their objections to your argument:

To Refute

Reason or Objection Lacks Credible Support

▶ My opponents cite research to support their [reason/objection], but the credibility of that research is questionable because _____ . In contrast, reliable research by _____ shows _____ .

Writing a Draft

GUIDE TO READING
GUIDE TO WRITING
A WRITER AT WORK
THINKING CRITICALLY

283

▶ This [reason/objection] seems plausible because it is consistent with our preconceptions. Nevertheless, evidence shows ＿＿＿＿＿.

Readers' Values and Concerns Are Better Served by Your Position

▶ Some insist ＿＿＿＿. Still, in spite of their good intentions, ＿＿＿＿ would
[take away a basic right/make things even worse].

▶ X and Y think this issue is about ＿＿＿＿. But what is really at stake here is

＿＿＿＿.

Reasoning Is Flawed

▶ Proponents object to my argument on the grounds that ＿＿＿＿. However, they
are confusing results with causes. What I am arguing is ＿＿＿＿.

▶ Polls show that most people favor ＿＿＿＿, but an opinion's popularity does
not make it true or right.

▶ While most would agree that ＿＿＿＿, it does not necessarily follow that

＿＿＿＿.

Times Have Changed

▶ One common complaint is ＿＿＿＿. In recent years, however, ＿＿＿＿.

To Concede

Accept an Objection Well Taken

▶ To be sure, ＿＿＿＿ is true.

▶ Granted, ＿＿＿＿ must be taken into consideration.

Qualify on Common Ground

▶ Some people argue that ＿＿＿＿. I understand this reservation, and therefore,
I think we should ＿＿＿＿.

Refocus Your Argument

▶ A common concern about this issue is ＿＿＿＿. That's why my argument focuses
on [a different aspect of the issue].

To Concede and Refute

And Instead of *Or*

▶ I agree that ＿＿＿＿ is important, and so is ＿＿＿＿.

Yes, But

▶ I agree that ＿＿＿＿ is important, but my opponents also need to consider

＿＿＿＿.

(continued)

On the One Hand . . . On the Other Hand

▶ On the one hand, I accept X's argument that ＿＿＿＿＿, but on the other hand, I still think ＿＿＿＿ is ultimately more important because ＿＿＿＿.

Note: If a reason or an objection seems so damaging that you cannot refute it convincingly or concede it without undermining your own argument, discuss with your instructor how you could modify your position or whether you should choose a new issue to write about. If you do not know enough about readers' views to anticipate their reasons or likely objections to your argument, do more research.

Create an outline that will organize your argument effectively for your readers.

Whether you have rough notes or a complete draft, making an outline of what you have written can help you organize the essay effectively for your audience. Compare the possible outlines that follow to see how you might organize your essay depending on whether your readers primarily agree or disagree with you.

Readers Primarily Agree with You

Strengthen their convictions by organizing your argument around a series of reasons backed by supporting evidence or by refuting opposing arguments point by point:

I. **Presentation of the issue**

II. **Thesis statement:** A direct statement of your position

III. **Your most plausible reasons and evidence**

IV. **Concession or refutation of opposing reasons or objections to your argument**

V. **Conclusion:** Reaffirmation of your position

Readers Primarily Disagree with You

Begin by emphasizing common ground, and make a concession to show that you have considered the opposing position carefully and with an open mind:

I. **Presentation of the issue:** Reframe the issue in terms of common values

II. **Concession:** Acknowledge the wisdom of an aspect of the opposing position

III. **Thesis statement:** A direct statement of your position, qualified as necessary

IV. **Your most plausible reasons and evidence**

V. **Conclusion:** Reiteration of shared values

For more on outlining, see Chapter 11, pp. 510–14.

Whatever organizational strategy you adopt, do not hesitate to change your outline as necessary while drafting and revising. For instance, you might find it more effective to hold back on presenting your own position until you have discussed unacceptable alternatives. Or you might find a more powerful way to order the reasons for supporting your position. The purpose of an outline is to identify the basic components of your argument and to help you organize them effectively, not to lock you into a particular structure.

:: Consider document design.

Think about whether visual or audio elements—photographs, graphics, snippets of interviews with experts—would strengthen your position argument. If you can recall position arguments you've read in newspapers (op-eds and editorials generally argue for positions), on Web pages, and on blogs, what visual or audio elements were used to establish the writer's credibility and to appeal to the reader logically, ethically, or emotionally? Position arguments do not require visual or audio examples to be effective, but these elements can be helpful.

Note: Be sure to cite the source of visual or audio elements you didn't create, and get permission from the source if your essay is going to be published on a Web site that will be accessible outside of your class or college.

Consider also whether your readers might benefit from design features such as headings, bulleted or numbered lists, or other typographic elements that can make your argument easier to follow.

Write the opening sentences.

Notice how the writers of the selections in this chapter have used their opening sentences to frame or reframe the issue for their readers while also grabbing their attention:

- Jessica Statsky provides statistics to help readers understand the importance of her topic:

  "Organized sports for young people have become an institution in North America," reports sports journalist Steve Silverman, attracting more than 44 million youngsters according to a recent survey by the National Council of Youth Sports ("History"). (p. 250)

- Richard Estrada uses personal reminiscence to make the issue less abstract and more tangible:

  When I was a kid living in Baltimore in the late 1950s . . . (p. 256)

- Amitai Etzioni uses a surprising statement to capture readers' attention:

  McDonald's is bad for your kids. (p. 261)

- Daniel J. Solove uses a hypothetical quotation to indicate how people typically think about the issue:

  When the government gathers or analyzes personal information, many people say they're not worried. "I've got nothing to hide," they declare. (p. 266)

Additional strategies you could try include comparing your issue to a different issue about which your readers may agree or using a rhetorical question to arouse your readers' concerns about the issue. To engage your readers and set the stage for your position, try reworking your framing sentences (p. 278) and using them to open your essay, but do not agonize over the first sentences because you are likely to discover the best way to begin only after you have written a rough draft.

Draft your position argument.

By this point, you have done a lot of writing to

- Devise a focused, well-presented issue and take a position on it
- Frame your issue so that readers will be open to your argument
- Support your position with reasons and evidence your readers will find persuasive
- Refute or concede alternative viewpoints on the issue
- Organize your ideas to make them clear, logical, and effective for readers

Now stitch that material together to create a draft. The next two parts of this Guide to Writing will help you evaluate and improve that draft.

Evaluating the Draft: Getting a Critical Reading

Your instructor may arrange a peer review session in class or online, where you can exchange drafts with your classmates and give each other a thoughtful critical reading—pointing out what works well and suggesting ways to improve the draft. A good critical reading does three things:

1. It lets the writer know how the reader understands the point of the argument.
2. It praises what works best.
3. It indicates where the draft could be improved and makes suggestions how to improve it.

One strategy for evaluating a draft is to use the basic features of a position argument as a guide.

A CRITICAL READING GUIDE

A Focused, Well-Presented Issue

How well does the writer present the issue?

Summarize: Tell the writer what you understand the issue to be. If you were already familiar with it and understand it differently, briefly explain.

Praise: Give an example from the essay where the issue and its significance come across effectively.

Critique: Tell the writer where more information about the issue is needed, where more might be done to establish its seriousness, or how the issue could be framed or reframed in a way that would better prepare readers for the argument.

A Well-Supported Position

How well does the writer argue in support of the position?

Summarize: Underline the thesis statement and the main reasons.

Praise: Give an example in the essay where the argument is especially effective; for example, indicate which reason is especially convincing or which supporting evidence is particularly compelling.

Critique: Tell the writer where the argument could be strengthened; for example, indicate how the thesis statement could be made clearer or more appropriately qualified, how the argument could be developed, or where additional support is needed.

An Effective Response to Opposing Views

How effectively has the writer responded to others' reasons and likely objections?

Summarize: Identify where the writer responds to a reason others use to support their argument or an objection they have to the writer's argument.

Praise: Give an example in the essay where a concession seems particularly well done or a refutation is convincing.

Critique: Tell the writer how a concession or refutation could be made more effective, a reason or objection the writer should respond to, or where common ground could be found.

A Clear, Logical Organization

How clearly and logically has the writer organized the argument?

Summarize: Find the sentence(s) in which the writer states the thesis and forecasts supporting reasons, as well as transitions or repeated key words and phrases.

Praise: Give an example of how or where the essay succeeds in being especially easy to read, perhaps in its overall organization, clear presentation of the thesis, clear transitions, or effective opening or closing.

Critique: Tell the writer where the readability could be improved. Can you, for example, suggest better forecasting or clearer transitions? If the overall organization of the essay needs work, make suggestions for rearranging parts or strengthening connections.

Before concluding your peer review, be sure to address any of the writer's concerns that have not been discussed already.

For a printable version of this Critical Reading Guide, go to **bedfordstmartins .com/theguide**.

Making Comments Electronically   Most word processing software offers features that allow you to insert comments directly into the text of someone else's document. Many readers prefer to make their comments this way because it tends to be faster than writing on hard copy and space is virtually unlimited; it also eliminates the process of deciphering handwritten comments. Where such features are not available, simply typing comments directly into a document in a contrasting color can provide the same advantages.

Improving the Draft: Revising, Formatting, Editing, and Proofreading

Start improving your draft by reflecting on what you have written thus far:

- Review critical reading comments from your classmates, instructor, or writing center tutor: What problems are your readers identifying?
- Consider your invention writing: What else should you consider?
- Review your draft: What can you do to support your position more effectively?

Revise your draft.

If your readers are having difficulty with your draft, or if you think there is room for improvement, try some of the strategies listed in the Troubleshooting Guide that follows. It can help you fine-tune your presentation of the genre's basic features.

A TROUBLESHOOTING GUIDE

A Focused, Well-Presented Issue

My readers don't get the point.

- Quote experts or add information—statistics, examples, anecdotes, and so on—to help readers understand what's at stake.
- Consider adding visuals, graphs, tables, or charts to present the issue more clearly.

My readers have a different perspective on the issue than I do.

- Show the limitations of how the issue has traditionally been understood.
- Reframe the issue by showing how it relates to values, concerns, needs, and priorities you share with readers.
- Give concrete examples or anecdotes, facts, and details that could help readers see the issue as you see it.

A Well-Supported Position

My readers do not find my argument clear and/or persuasive.

- Revisit your thesis statement to make sure your position is stated clearly and directly.
- Reconsider your reasons, or explain how they support your position.
- Add supporting evidence—statistics, examples, authorities, and so on.
- Consider adding visuals, graphs, tables, or charts to support your argument.
- Strengthen the logical, ethical, and/or emotional appeals of your argument.
- Try outlining your argument; if your organization is weak or illogical, or if your transitional strategies are not working, try reorganizing the material, adding transitional words and phrases, or repeating key words strategically.

Improving the Draft

GUIDE TO READING
GUIDE TO WRITING
A WRITER AT WORK
THINKING CRITICALLY

289

An Effective Response to Opposing Views	My readers question my response to opposing arguments or objections to my argument. • If your refutation is weak, strengthen it with additional or more compelling reasons and evidence. • If your concession weakens your argument, qualify your position with words like *sometimes* or *often*. • Consider adding a refutation to your concession.
A Clear, Logical Organization	My readers are confused by my essay or find it difficult to read. • Outline your essay. If necessary, move, add, or delete sections to strengthen coherence. • Consider adding a forecasting statement with key terms that are repeated in topic sentences throughout the essay. • Check for appropriate transitions between sentences, paragraphs, and major sections of your essay. • Review your opening and closing paragraphs. Be sure that your thesis is clearly expressed and that you reaffirm your position in your closing.

Think about design.

For an electronic version of this Troubleshooting Guide, go to **bedfordstmartins .com/theguide**.

Formatting and design requirements differ depending on the context and genre in which your position argument appears. Whether you are writing for a college course, a community organization, or your workplace, though, you may want to consider including graphics that will help your readers grasp evidence or a key point immediately. The pie chart below is from the project highlighted in the In College Courses scenario on p. 242.

Race of Defendants Executed

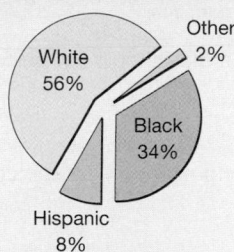

Other 2%
White 56%
Black 34%
Hispanic 8%

• White: 724
• Black: 442
• Hispanic: 99
• Other: 24

Race of Victims in Death Penalty Cases

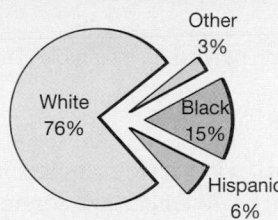

Other 3%
White 76%
Black 15%
Hispanic 6%

Over 75% of the murder victims in cases resulting in an execution were white, even though nationally only 50% of murder victims generally are white.

The writer included this graphic to bring home starkly to her readers—her instructor and classmates—the racial disparity in death penalty cases. A graphic like this one will appeal to readers logically, but it may also make an ethical appeal (appeal to readers' sense of fairness).

Edit and proofread your draft.

Students frequently struggle to maintain a neutral tone when arguing a position they hold dearly. Our research also indicates that incorrect comma usage in sentences with *coordinating conjunctions* and punctuation errors in sentences that use *conjunctive adverbs* are common in position arguments. The following guidelines will help you check your essay for these common errors.

Editing for Tone

To demonstrate that you are treating alternative viewpoints fairly, use words with a positive or neutral connotation (emotional resonance) and avoid name-calling.

> ▶ Too often . . . the drive to win ~~turns~~ parents ~~into monsters threatening~~ umpires.
>   *encourages*   *to threaten*

As you edit your position argument, also watch out for language that is puffed up or pompous:

> ▶ A coach who had attended the Adelphi workshop tried to ~~operationalize~~ what he had
>   *put into practice*
>
> learned there, but the players' ~~progenitors~~ would not support him.
>   *parents*

Using Commas before Coordinating Conjunctions

In essays that argue a position, writers often use coordinating conjunctions (*and, but, for, or, nor, so,* and *yet*) to join related **independent clauses**—groups of words that can stand alone as complete sentences—to create *compound sentences*. Consider this example from Jessica Statsky's essay:

Compound sentence: two independent clauses linked by a coordinating conjunction

> ┌──────── independent clause 1 ────────┐ ┌─ coord. conj. ─┐
>   ┌─ independent clause 2 ─┐
> ▶ Winning and losing may be an inevitable part of adult life, but they should not be part
>   └──────────┘   comma
> of childhood. (par. 6)

In this sentence, Statsky links two complete ideas of equal importance with the coordinating conjunction *but* to emphasize contrast.

The Problem   Two common errors occur in sentences like these:

1. A comma may be left out when two independent clauses are linked by a coordinating conjunction.

2. A comma may be inserted before the coordinating conjunction when one of the sentence parts is not an independent clause.

The Correction   Add a comma before coordinating conjunctions that join two independent clauses, as in the following example:

> ▶ The new immigration laws will bring in more skilled people but their presence will take jobs away from other Americans.

Omit the comma when coordinating conjunctions join phrases that are not independent clauses:

> ▶ We need people with special talents/ and diverse skills to make the United States a stronger nation.

For practice, go to **bedfordstmartins.com /theguide/exercisecentral** and click on Semicolons in the Handbook section.

Avoiding Comma Splices When Using Conjunctive Adverbs to Link Independent Clauses

Conjunctive adverbs (such as *consequently, furthermore, however, moreover, therefore,* and *thus*) indicate the logical relationships among ideas. For example, words like *thus* and *therefore* are used to alert readers that a conclusion is coming, and words like *furthermore* and *moreover* are used to alert readers to expect additional ideas on the same topic. When writers take a position, they often use conjunctive adverbs to link independent clauses.

Consider this example:

> ┌─────────── independent clause 1 ───────────┐   conj. adv.
> ▶ Children watching television recognize violence but not its intention ; thus, they
>   ┌──── independent clause 2 ────┐   semicolon   comma
>   become desensitized to violence.

In this sentence, the writer uses the word *thus* to indicate that he is drawing a conclusion.

The Problem   A *comma splice* is one error that often occurs when writers use a comma before a conjunctive adverb linking two independent clauses.

The Correction   Use a semicolon before and a comma after a conjunctive adverb when it links two independent clauses:

> ▶ The recent vote on increasing student fees produced a disappointing turnout/ moreover,
>
>   the presence of campaign literature on ballot tables violated voting procedures.

Make sure that both parts of the sentence are independent clauses before inserting a semicolon, a conjunctive adverb, and a comma to link them. If one or both parts cannot stand alone, add a subject, a verb, or both as needed to avoid a *sentence fragment:*

>   *they do not recognize*
> ▶ Children watching television recognize violence; however, not its intention.
>   ^

Alternatively, you may replace the semicolon, conjunctive adverb, and comma with a coordinating conjunction:

>   *but*
> ▶ Children watching television recognize violence/ however, not its intention.
>   ^

For practice, go to **bedfordstmartins.com /theguide/exercisecentral** and click on Coordinating Ideas with Semicolons and Conjunctive Adverbs.

A Note on Grammar and Spelling Checkers

These tools can be helpful, but do not rely on them exclusively to catch errors in your text: Spelling checkers cannot catch misspellings that are themselves words, such as *to* for *too.* Grammar checkers miss some problems, sometimes give faulty advice for fixing problems, and can flag correct items as wrong. Use these tools as a second line of defense after your own (and, ideally, another reader's) editing and proofreading efforts.

For practice, go to
**bedfordstmartins.com
/theguide/exercisecentral**
and click on Word Choice in
the Handbook section.

**A Common Problem for Multilingual Writers:
Subtle Differences in Meaning**

Because the distinctions in meaning among some common conjunctive adverbs are subtle, nonnative speakers often have difficulty using them accurately. For example, the difference between *however* and *nevertheless* is small; each is used to introduce a contrasting statement. But *nevertheless* emphasizes the contrast, whereas *however* softens it. Check usage of such terms in an English dictionary rather than a bilingual one. *The American Heritage Dictionary of the English Language* has special usage notes to help distinguish frequently confused words.

A WRITER AT WORK

Jessica Statsky's Response to Opposing Positions

In this section, we look at how Jessica Statsky tried to anticipate opposing positions and respond to them. To understand Statsky's thinking about possible opposing positions, look first at the invention writing she did while analyzing her potential readers.

Three potential
groups of readers

Two groups of
parents

> I think I will write mainly to parents who are considering letting their children get involved in competitive sports and to those whose children are already on teams and who don't know about the possible dangers. Parents who are really into competition and winning probably couldn't be swayed by my arguments anyway. I don't know how to reach coaches (but aren't they also parents?) or league organizers. I'll tell parents some horror stories and present solid evidence from psychologists that competitive sports can really harm children under the age of twelve. I think they'll be impressed with this scientific evidence.
>
> I share with parents one important value: the best interests of children. Competition really works against children's best interests. Maybe parents' magazines (don't know of any specific ones) publish essays like mine.

Notice that Statsky lists three potential groups of readers here, but she is already leaning toward making parents her primary audience. Moreover, she divides these parents into two camps: those who are new to organized sports and unaware of the adverse effects of competition, and those who are really into winning. Statsky decides early on against trying to change the minds of parents who place great value on winning. But as you will see in the next excerpt from her invention writing, Statsky gave a lot of thought to the position these parents would likely favor.

Listing Reasons for the Opposing Position

In continuing her invention writing, Statsky listed the following reasons she thought others might have for their position that organized competitive sports teach young children valuable skills:

--because competition teaches children how to succeed in later life

--because competition--especially winning--is fun

--because competition boosts children's self-esteem

--because competition gives children an incentive to excel

This list appears to pose serious challenges to Statsky's argument, but she benefited by considering the reasons her readers might give for opposing her position before she drafted her essay. By preparing this list, she gained insight into how she had to develop her own argument in light of these predictable arguments, and she could begin thinking about which reasons she might concede and which she had to refute. Her essay ultimately gained authority because she could demonstrate a good understanding of the opposing arguments that might be offered by her primary readers—parents who have not considered the dangers of competition for young children.

Conceding a Plausible Reason

Looking over her list of reasons, Statsky decided that she could accommodate readers by conceding that competitive sports can sometimes be fun for children—at least for those who win. Here are her invention notes:

It is true that children do sometimes enjoy getting prizes and being recognized as winners in competitions adults set up for them. I remember feeling very excited when our sixth-grade relay team won a race at our school's sports day. And I felt really good when I would occasionally win the candy bar for being the last one standing in classroom spelling contests. But when I think about these events, it's the activity itself I remember as the main fun, not the winning. I think I can concede that winning is exciting to six- to twelve-year-olds, while arguing that it's not as important as adults might think. I hope this will win me some friends among readers who are undecided about my position.

We can see this concession in paragraph 5 of Statsky's revised essay (p. 252), in which she concedes that sports should be fun but quotes an authority who argues that even fun is jeopardized when competition becomes intense.

Refuting an Implausible Reason

Statsky recognized that she had to attempt to refute the other objections in her list. She chose the first reason in her list and tried out the following refutation:

It irritates me that adults are so eager to make first and second graders go into training for getting and keeping jobs as adults. I don't see why the pressures on adults need to be put on children. Anyway, both my parents tell me that in their jobs, cooperation and teamwork are keys to success. You can't get ahead unless you're effective in working with others. Maybe we should be training children and even high school and college students in the skills necessary for cooperation, rather than competition. Sports and physical activity are important for children, but elementary schools should emphasize achievement rather than competition--race against the clock rather than against each other. Rewards could be given for gains in speed or strength instead of for defeating somebody in a competition.

This brief invention activity led to the argument in paragraph 10 of the revised essay (p. 254), in which Statsky acknowledges the importance of competition for success in school and work, but goes on to argue that cooperation is also important. To support this part of her argument, she gives examples in paragraph 11 of sports programs that emphasize cooperation over competition.

You can see from Statsky's revised essay that her refutation of this opposing argument runs through her entire essay. The invention activities Statsky did advanced her thinking about her readers and purpose; they also brought an early, productive focus to her research on competition in children's sports.

THINKING CRITICALLY

To think critically means to use all of the knowledge you have acquired from the information in this chapter, your own writing, the writing of other students, and class discussions to reflect deeply on your work for this assignment and the genre (or type) of writing you have produced. The benefit of thinking critically is proven and important: Thinking critically about what you have learned will help you remember it longer, ensuring that you will be able to put it to good use well beyond this writing course.

Reflecting on What You Have Learned

In this chapter, you have learned a great deal about arguing for a position from reading several position arguments and from writing one of your own. To consolidate your learning, reflect not only on what you learned but also on how you learned it.

─────── ANALYZE & WRITE ───────────────────────────────

Write a blog post to classmates, a letter to your instructor, or an e-mail message to a student who will take this course next term, using the writing prompt that seems most productive for you:

- Explain how your purpose and audience influenced one of your decisions as a writer, such as how you presented the issue, the strategies you used in arguing your position, or the ways in which you attempted to counter possible objections.

Reflecting on the Genre   GUIDE TO READING
GUIDE TO WRITING
A WRITER AT WORK
THINKING CRITICALLY   295

- Discuss what you learned about yourself as a writer in the process of writing this essay. For example, what part of the process did you find most challenging? Did you try anything new, like getting a critical reading of your draft or outlining your draft in order to revise it?

- Choose one of the readings in this chapter and explain how it influenced your essay. Be sure to cite specific examples from your essay and the reading.

- If you got good advice from a critical reader, explain exactly how the person helped you—perhaps by questioning the way you addressed your audience or the kinds of evidence you offered in support of your position.

Reflecting on the Genre

While you were writing your position argument, we encouraged you to frame your position in terms of values you share with your readers and to provide logical reasons and evidence in support of your position. However, some critics argue that privileging reasoned argument over other ways of arguing is merely a means to control dissent. Instead of expressing what may be legitimate outrage and inciting public concern through passionate language, dissenters are urged to be dispassionate and reasonable even though they are arguing with people whose views they find repugnant. In the end, trying to present a well-reasoned, well-supported argument may serve to maintain the status quo by silencing the more radical voices within the community. What do you think about this controversy?

ANALYZE & WRITE

Write a page or two explaining your ideas about whether the genre's requirement that writers give reasons and support suppresses dissent. Connect your ideas to your own position argument and to the readings in this chapter. In your discussion, you might consider one or more of the following questions:

1. **In your own experience of arguing a position on a controversial issue, did having to give reasons and support discourage you from choosing any particular issue or from expressing strong feelings?** Reflect on the issues you listed as possible subjects for your essay and how you made your choice. Did you reject any issues because you could not come up with reasons and support for your position? When you made your choice, did you think about whether you could be dispassionate and reasonable about it?

2. **Consider the readings in this chapter and the position arguments you read by other students in the class.** Do you think any of these writers felt limited by the need to give reasons and support for their position? Which of the essays you read, if any, seemed to you to express strong feelings about the issue? Which, if any, seemed dispassionate?

3. **Consider the kind of arguing you typically witness in the media — radio, television, newspapers, magazines, the Internet.** In the media, have giving reasons and support and anticipating readers' objections been replaced with a more contentious, in-your-face style of arguing? Think of media examples of these two different ways of arguing. What do these examples lead you to conclude about the contention that reasoned argument can stifle dissent?

7 Proposing a Solution

A proposal urges readers to take action to solve a problem. To be convincing, proposals need to demonstrate that the problem must be solved and that the proposed solution is the best available option. In college, proposals may be written to solve campus problems, such as residence hall noise, or they may be more specialized, such as research proposals to seek funding to investigate how to preserve indigenous languages. Workplace proposals may be addressed to the company's management (such as the need for investment in new technology) or to another company seeking a contract to perform certain services. In the community, proposals seek to get things done, from a neighborhood proposal for a traffic signal at a dangerous intersection to a congressional recommendation to improve the health care system.

IN COLLEGE COURSES

For an early childhood education class, a student writes a proposal that Congress require broadcast networks to provide programming to help preschool children learn English. He establishes the need for such regulation by citing statistics showing that the children of non-English-speaking parents are less likely than the children of English speakers to attend preschool. To lend credibility to his proposal, he cites a researcher specializing in the impact of media on children's language acquisition and interviews via e-mail the programming coordinator for a national network. He counters possible objections of impracticality by citing two model programs, public television's *Sesame Street* and cable's *Mi Casita* (*My Little House*). He concludes by reminding his readers—not only his instructor but also his local Congressional representative—that those who use publicly owned airwaves are required by law to serve the public interest.

IN THE COMMUNITY

A social services administrator in a large city becomes concerned about a rise in the number of adolescents in jail. To help solve this problem, he proposes that his department intervene at the first sign of delinquent behavior in eight- to twelve-year-olds. He describes the consequences of jailing young criminals, focusing on the cost of incarceration and the high rate of recidivism (the return to criminal activity), and he provides statistics and case histories showing the positive effects of intervention for very young first offenders. He then discusses the major components of his program: finding mentors for struggling adolescents and placing social workers with troubled families. The administrator acknowledges the costs of the program but points to savings if incarceration rates are lowered.

IN THE WORKPLACE

A truck driver notices that her employer is unable to find enough short-haul drivers for deliveries. To solve this problem, she suggests in an e-mail message to her boss that the company initiate a training program to bring more women into the workforce. By interviewing other female truck drivers, she had learned that women tend to be turned off by the male-dominated truck-driving schools, so she proposes that qualified recruits be placed with experienced drivers serving as paid mentors. She recognizes that the program must not adversely affect the company's bottom line, so she suggests that the cost of the mentorship be offset by a rookie-driver tuition fee. She concludes by pointing out that the company would not only get the skilled drivers it needs at no cost but also create an incentive (additional income) for experienced drivers to remain with the company.

In this chapter, we ask you to identify a problem you care about and write a proposal to solve it. Analyzing the reading selections that follow will help you learn how to make a convincing case for the solution you propose. The Guide to Writing later in the chapter will show you ways to use the basic features of the genre to make your proposal inventive as well as practical.

PRACTICING THE GENRE

Arguing That a Solution Is Feasible

Proposals often succeed or fail on the strength of the argument that the proposed solution is feasible. To practice making a feasibility argument, get together with two or three other students and follow these guidelines:

Part 1.   Begin by identifying a problem you face as a student in one of your college courses (this course or a different one). Next, discuss the problem in your group, and choose one of the following solutions (or think of another solution). The instructor should:

- drop one of the assigned books;
- offer special study sessions;
- post study sheets on the readings.

Then discuss the following questions to determine how you could demonstrate to the instructor that your solution is feasible:

- Is it doable? List specific steps that the instructor would need to take.
- Is it worth doing? Identify what implementing the solution would cost the instructor (in terms of time, for example) compared to how much it would benefit the students (in terms of learning, for example).
- Would it work? To prove it would actually help solve the problem, you could show that it eliminates a cause of the problem or that it has worked elsewhere, for example.

Part 2.   As a group, discuss what you learned from this activity.

- Which part of the argument — identifying a problem, finding a solution, or arguing that the solution is doable, is worth doing, and would work — was easiest? hardest?
- If the instructor objected that your proposed solution would be unfair to those students who are doing well in the course, how could you respond in a way that assures the instructor that it would be fair?
- Imagine that you were writing this proposal to a different audience — for example, a group of professors at a conference about undergraduate teaching or an administrator who controls the budget or schedule. How might you change your argument or the way you present it for a different audience?

Analyzing Proposals

As you read the selections in this chapter, you will see how different authors propose a solution. Analyzing how these writers define their problems, argue for their solutions, respond to opposing views, and organize their writing will help you see how you can use these techniques to make your own proposals clear and compelling for your readers.

Determine the writer's purpose and audience.

When reading the proposals in this chapter, ask yourself the following questions about the writer's purpose and audience:

- What seems to be the writer's main *purpose*—for example, to convince readers that the problem truly exists and needs immediate action; to persuade readers that the writer's proposed solution is better than alternative solutions; or to rekindle readers' interest in a long-standing problem?

- What does the writer assume about the *audience*—for example, that readers will be unaware of the problem; that they will recognize the existence of the problem but fail to take it seriously; that they will think the problem has already been solved; or that they will prefer an alternative solution?

Assess the genre's basic features.

Use the following to help you analyze and evaluate how proposal writers use the genre's basic features. The writing strategies they typically use to convince readers to adopt the proposed solution are illustrated below with examples from the readings in this chapter as well as sentence strategies you can experiment with later, as you write your own proposal.

> ▥ **Basic Features**
> A Focused, Well-Defined Problem
> A Well-Argued Solution
> An Effective Response to Objections and Alternative Solutions
> A Clear, Logical Organization

A FOCUSED, WELL-DEFINED PROBLEM

Read first to see how the writer defines or frames the problem. Framing a problem is a way of preparing readers for the proposed solution by focusing on the aspect of the problem the proposal tries to solve. In "More Testing, More Learning," for example, student Patrick O'Malley frames the problem in terms of the detrimental effects of high-stakes exams on students' learning. If O'Malley were writing to students instead of their teachers, he might have framed the problem in terms of students' poor study habits or procrastination. By framing the problem as he did, he indicates that teachers, rather than students, have the ability to solve the problem and tries to convince readers that it is real and serious. Consider, for example, how (and how well) the writer frames the problem

- by recounting *anecdotes* or constructing *scenarios* to show how the problem affects people

EXAMPLE   It's late at night. The final's tomorrow. (O'Malley, par. 1)

▓ by giving *examples* to make the problem less abstract

EXAMPLE   [Tyler Clementi was] a victim of cyber-bullying. (Bornstein, par. 1)

▓ by listing the negative *effects* of the problem

Cause
Transition
Effect

EXAMPLE   As a result of the unaffordable and low quality nature of child care in this country, a disturbing number of today's children are left home alone. (Kornbluh, par. 13)

▓ by describing the ongoing discussion of the problem and debate over solutions

EXAMPLE   The obesity epidemic has inspired calls for public health measures to prevent diet-related diseases. (Brownell and Frieden, par. 1)

Probably the most convincing strategy writers use to demonstrate the severity of the problem is to cite *research studies* and *statistics*. As you read, look for source material, and notice whether the writer emphasizes the credibility of the research by including the expert's name and credentials or by identifying the publication in which the study appeared at the beginning of the sentence in which the study is mentioned:

Placement emphasizes credibility of expert/publication

▶ A study published in [name of journal or university press] shows that _____.

EXAMPLE   A 2006 study reported in the journal *Psychological Science* concluded that "taking repeated tests . . . leads to better . . . retention" . . . according to the study's coauthors, Henry L. Roediger and Jeffrey Karpicke (ScienceWatch.com, 2008). (O'Malley, par. 4)

▶ [Name], [title] at [institution], has found that _____.

EXAMPLE   Ervin Staub, professor emeritus of psychology at the University of Massachusetts, has studied . . . and found that . . . ("Biographical Note"). (Bornstein, par. 9)

Alternatively, the writer may emphasize the source material by putting the information about the study up front and identifying the source later in the sentence or in the parenthetical citation, as in the following:

Placement emphasizes study

▶ _____ percent of [group studied] [believe/work/struggle] _____.

EXAMPLE   Fifty-nine percent of these caregivers either work or have worked while providing care ("Caregiving"). (Kornbluh, par. 8)

▶ [Research findings] show that _____ (source).

EXAMPLE   Moreover, many employees . . . lack the ability to take a day off to care for a family member (Lovell). (Kornbluh, par. 2)

Then assess whether the problem is focused enough to have been treated in the depth needed to achieve the writer's purpose with the original audience. To make their proposal manageable, writers concentrate on one aspect of a broad problem—for example, Brownell and Frieden focus on sugar-sweetened beverages, which they claim "may be the single largest driver of the obesity epidemic" (par. 2).

Analyzing Proposals

▶ **GUIDE TO READING**
GUIDE TO WRITING
A WRITER AT WORK
THINKING CRITICALLY

301

A WELL-ARGUED SOLUTION

To argue convincingly for a solution to a problem, writers need to *make clear exactly what is being proposed and offer supporting reasons and evidence* showing that the proposed solution

- will help solve the problem;
- can be implemented;
- is worth the expense, time, and effort to do so.

Read first to find the proposed solution, usually declared in a *thesis statement* early in the essay. Typically, the thesis describes the proposed solution briefly and indicates how it would solve the problem, as in this example, which contrasts the problem's disadvantages with the solution's benefits:

> So, not only do high-stakes exams *discourage frequent study* and *undermine students' performance,* they also *do long-term damage to students' cognitive development.* If professors gave brief exams at frequent intervals, students would be spurred to learn more and worry less. They would study more regularly, perform better on tests, and enhance their cognitive functioning. (O'Malley, par. 2)

Problem and its *disadvantages*

Thesis proposing solution and its benefits

Then check to see how the writer presents the *supporting reasons* and *evidence,* and consider how compelling the argument is likely to be, given the writer's purpose and audience. The following sentence strategies and accompanying examples suggest the kinds of reasons and evidence proposal writers often employ to present their argument, as well as the writing strategies they represent:

- The proposed solution would reduce or eliminate a major cause of the problem and would (or could) have beneficial effects:

Cause/effect

▶ As research shows, [the proposed solution] would [stop something harmful, change habits, reverse a decline] and would [lead to/encourage] ....

EXAMPLE   A review conducted by Yale University's Rudd Center for Food Policy and Obesity suggested that . . . a tax on sugared beverages would encourage consumers to switch to more healthful beverages, which would lead to reduced caloric intake and less weight gain. (Brownell and Frieden, par. 3)

- A similar solution has worked elsewhere:

Comparison

▶ [Solution X] has worked for [problem Y], so it could work for this problem as well.

EXAMPLE   Taxes on tobacco products have been highly effective in reducing consumption, and data indicate that higher prices also reduce soda consumption. (Brownell and Frieden, par. 3)

▶ Research shows that [program Y] has been effective in [solving/causing] ....

EXAMPLE   It seems that it's not only possible to make people kinder, it's possible to do it systematically at scale—at least with school children. That's what one organization based in Toronto called Roots of Empathy has done. (Bornstein, par. 4)

Process analysis

- The necessary steps to put the solution into practice can be taken without excessive cost or inconvenience:

  ▶ [The solution] is easy to implement: first do _____ and then do _____.

  EXAMPLE   Ideally, a professor would give an in-class test or quiz after each unit. . . . These exams should be given weekly or at least twice monthly. . . . Exams should take no more than 15 or 20 minutes. (O'Malley, par. 3)

Statistics

- Stakeholders could come together behind the proposal:

  ▶ Statistical surveys suggest that [the solution] will appeal to those who are concerned about _____ as well as those worried about _____ because [it would alleviate both groups' concerns/is in the best interests of everyone].

  EXAMPLE   This should be a popular priority. A recent poll found that 77 percent of likely voters feel . . . Eighty-four percent of voters agree that . . . (Kornbluh, par. 15)

AN EFFECTIVE RESPONSE TO OBJECTIONS AND ALTERNATIVE SOLUTIONS

Writers proposing solutions need to *anticipate and respond to readers' likely objections and to the alternative solutions readers may prefer*. Writers typically respond in one or more of the following ways:

- By **conceding** (accepting) a valid objection and modifying the argument to accommodate it
- By **refuting** (arguing against) criticism—for example, by demonstrating that an objection is without merit or arguing that an alternative solution would be more costly or less likely to solve the problem than the proposed solution

A typical way of conceding is to use a sentence strategy like this:

  ▶ To accommodate [critic A's concern], instead of doing _____, you could do _____.

Before writing his proposal, student Patrick O'Malley interviewed professors so that he could respond to their objections. Notice how his concession is really a compromise designed to convince readers of his proposal's flexibility:

> If weekly exams still seem too time-consuming to some professors, their frequency could be reduced to every other week or their length to 5 or 10 minutes. In courses where multiple-choice exams are appropriate, several questions could be designed to take only a few minutes to answer. (O'Malley, par. 9)

A typical refutation summarizes the objection or alternative solution and then explains why the criticism is problematic. Proposal writers refute objections and

Analyzing Proposals

GUIDE TO READING
GUIDE TO WRITING
A WRITER AT WORK
THINKING CRITICALLY

303

alternative solutions more often than they concede. Following are common sentence strategies used to refute objections and alternative solutions:

▶ Some object that the proposed solution would [cost too much/cause too much disruption]. However, when you take into consideration the fact that [inaction would cost even more/cause more disruption than doing nothing], you have to conclude that ....

▶ Although X and Y prefer [alternative approach], my solution would be [less expensive/ easier to implement] because ....

Here are a few examples showing how the proposals in this chapter refute objections or alternative solutions. Notice that proposal writers often introduce the refutation with a *transition* that indicates contrast, such as *but, although, nevertheless,* or *however.*

Some believe that . . . From the student's perspective, however, this time is well spent. (O'Malley, par. 9)

Some argue that . . . , but several considerations support . . . The first is . . . The second consideration is . . . A third consideration is . . . (Brownell and Frieden, par. 5)

The typical institutional response to bullying is to get tough. . . . But programs like the one I want to discuss today show the potential of augmenting our innate impulses to care for one another instead of just falling back on punishment as a deterrent. (Bornstein, par. 2)

> Contrasts alternative and proposed solutions

When reading a proposal, consider whether the writer presents others' views fairly and accurately and whether the writer's rebuttal is likely to be convincing to readers. Pay special attention to the writer's tone in responding to other views, noting any place the tone seems sarcastic or dismissive and considering whether such a tone would be effective given the writer's purpose and audience.

> To learn more about constructing arguments, see Chapter 19.

A CLEAR, LOGICAL ORGANIZATION

Look for cues or signposts that help readers identify the parts of the proposal. Identify the topic and find the thesis, which in a proposal asserts the solution. Bornstein identifies the topic in his title— "Fighting Bullying with Babies"—and asserts his thesis in paragraph 4:

It seems that it's not only possible to make people kinder, it's possible to do it systematically at scale—at least with school children.

Look also for topic sentences, particularly those that announce the parts of the proposal argument. Notice also any transitions and how they function. For example, all of the transitions in the following topic sentences (*another, moreover, still,* and *furthermore*) indicate items in a list. Other transitions you can expect in proposals signal causes or effects (*because, as a result*), exceptions (*but*), concessions (*although*), refutations (*however*), emphasis (*more important*), conclusions (*then, therefore*), and enumerations (*first, second*). Here are the beginnings of several topic sentences from O'Malley's essay:

Transitions

The main reason professors should give frequent exams is that . . . (par. 4)

Another, closely related argument in favor of multiple exams is that . . . (par. 6)

Moreover, professors object to frequent exams because . . . (par. 10)

Still another solution might be to . . . (par. 12)

Furthermore, professors could . . . (par. 13)

Finally, if headings or visuals (such as flowcharts, graphs, tables, photographs, or cartoons) are included, determine how they contribute. Notice whether visuals are referred to in the text and whether they have titles or captions.

Readings

Patrick O'Malley | *More Testing, More Learning*

To learn about how O'Malley responds to professors' likely objections to his proposed solution and argues against their preferred solutions to the problem, look at A Writer at Work on pp. 347–48.

FRUSTRATED BY what he calls "high-stakes exams," Patrick O'Malley wrote the following proposal while he was a first-year college student. To conduct research into opposing viewpoints, O'Malley interviewed two professors (his writing instructor and the writing program director), talked with several students, and read published research on testing. He cited his sources using APA style, as his instructor had requested.

As you read, consider the questions in the margin. Your instructor may ask you to post your answers or bring them to class. Also consider the following:

- How does O'Malley respond to likely objections?
- How does he respond to preferred alternative solutions?

Basic Features
A Focused, Well-Defined Problem
A Well-Argued Solution
An Effective Response to Objections and Alternative Solutions
A Clear, Logical Organization

What is the function of the opening paragraph?

How does framing the problem this way set up the solution?

1   It's late at night. The final's tomorrow. You got a C on the midterm, so this one will make or break you. Will it be like the midterm? Did you study enough? Did you study the right things? It's too late to drop the course. So what happens if you fail? No time to worry about that now—you've got a ton of notes to go over.

2   Although this last-minute anxiety about midterm and final exams is only too familiar to most college students, many professors may not realize how such major, infrequent, high-stakes exams work against the best interests of students both psychologically and cognitively. They cause unnecessary amounts of stress, placing too much importance on one or two days in the students' entire term, judging ability on a

single or dual performance. Reporting on recent research at Cornell University Medical School, Sian Beilock, a psychology professor at the University of Chicago, points out that "stressing about doing well on an important exam can backfire, leading students to 'choke under pressure' or to score less well than they might otherwise score if the stakes weren't so high." Moreover, Cornell's research using fMRI brain scans shows that "the pressures of a big test can reach beyond the exam itself—stunting the cognitive systems that support the attention and memory skills every day" (Beilock 2010). So, not only do high-stakes exams discourage frequent study and undermine students' performance, they also do long-term damage to students' cognitive development. If professors gave brief exams at frequent intervals, students would be spurred to learn more and worry less. They would study more regularly, perform better on tests, and enhance their cognitive functioning.

> How does O'Malley use the key terms introduced here throughout the essay?

3   Ideally, a professor would give an in-class test or quiz after each unit, chapter, or focus of study, depending on the type of class and course material. A physics class might require a test on concepts after every chapter covered, while a history class could necessitate quizzes covering certain time periods or major events. These exams should be given weekly or at least twice monthly. Whenever possible, they should consist of two or three essay questions rather than many multiple-choice or short-answer questions. To preserve class time for lecture and discussion, exams should take no more than 15 or 20 minutes.

> What does par. 3 contribute to the argument?

4   The main reason professors should give frequent exams is that when they do and when they provide feedback to students on how well they are doing, students learn more in the course and perform better on major exams, projects, and papers. It makes sense that in a challenging course containing a great deal of material, students will learn more of it and put it to better use if they have to apply or "practice" it frequently on exams, which also helps them find out how much they are learning and what they need to go over again. A 2006 study reported in the journal *Psychological Science* concluded that "taking repeated tests on material leads to better long-term retention than repeated studying," according to the study's coauthors, Henry L. Roediger and Jeffrey Karpicke (ScienceWatch.com, 2008). When asked what the impact of this breakthrough research would be, they responded: "We hope that this research may be picked up in educational circles as a way to improve educational practices, both for students in the classroom

> How does O'Malley introduce this reason? What kinds of support does he offer?

and as a study strategy outside of class." The new field of mind, brain, and education research advocates the use of "retrieval testing." For example, research by Karpicke and Blunt (2011) published in *Science* found that testing was more effective than other, more traditional methods of studying both for comprehension and for analysis. Why retrieval testing works is not known. UCLA psychologist Robert Bjork speculates that it may be effective because "when we use our memories by retrieving things, we change our access" to that information. "What we recall," therefore, "becomes more recallable in the future" (qtd. in Belluck, 2011).

5   Many students already recognize the value of frequent testing, but their reason is that they need the professor's feedback. A Harvard study notes students' "strong preference for frequent evaluation in a course." Harvard students feel they learn least in courses that have "only a midterm and a final exam, with no other personal evaluation." Students believe they learn most in courses with "many opportunities to see how they are doing" (Light, 1990, p. 32). In a review of a number of studies of student learning, Frederiksen (1984) reports that students who take weekly quizzes achieve higher scores on final exams than students who take only a midterm exam and that testing increases retention of material tested.

6   Another, closely related argument in favor of multiple exams is that they encourage students to improve their study habits. Greater frequency in test taking means greater frequency in studying for tests. Students prone to cramming will be required — or at least strongly motivated — to open their textbooks and notebooks more often, making them less likely to resort to long, kamikaze nights of studying for major exams. Since there is so much to be learned in the typical course, it makes sense that frequent, careful study and review are highly beneficial. But students need motivation to study regularly, and nothing works like an exam. If students had frequent exams in all their courses, they would have to schedule study time each week and would gradually develop a habit of frequent study. It might be argued that students are adults who have to learn how to manage their own lives, but learning history or physics is more complicated than learning to drive a car or balance a checkbook. Students need coaching and practice in learning. The right way to learn new material needs to become a habit, and I believe that frequent exams are key to developing good habits of study and learning. The Harvard study concludes that "tying regular evaluation to good course

How does O'Malley integrate and cite sources in pars. 4 and 5?

How does O'Malley support this reason? Why does he include it?

How does O'Malley introduce and respond to this possible objection?

organization enables students to plan their work more than a few days in advance. If quizzes and homework are scheduled on specific days, students plan their work to capitalize on them" (Light, 1990, p. 33).

7   By encouraging regular study habits, frequent exams would also decrease anxiety by reducing the procrastination that produces anxiety. Students would benefit psychologically if they were not subjected to the emotional ups and downs caused by major exams, when after being virtually worry-free for weeks they are suddenly ready to check into the psychiatric ward. Researchers at the University of Vermont found a strong relationship among procrastination, anxiety, and achievement. Students who regularly put off studying for exams had continuing high anxiety and lower grades than students who procrastinated less. The researchers found that even "low" procrastinators did not study regularly and recommended that professors give frequent assignments and exams to reduce procrastination and increase achievement (Rothblum, Solomon, & Murakami, 1986, pp. 393–394).

> How effectively does O'Malley use this source?

8   Research supports my proposed solution to the problem I have described. Common sense as well as my experience and that of many of my friends support it. Why, then, do so few professors give frequent brief exams?

> What is the purpose of this question?

9   Some believe that such exams take up too much of the limited class time available to cover the material in the course. Most courses meet 150 minutes a week — three times a week for 50 minutes each time. A 20-minute weekly exam might take 30 minutes to administer, and that is one-fifth of each week's class time. From the student's perspective, however, this time is well spent. Better learning and greater confidence about the course seem a good trade-off for another 30 minutes of lecture. Moreover, time lost to lecturing or discussion could easily be made up in students' learning on their own through careful regular study for the weekly exams. If weekly exams still seem too time-consuming to some professors, their frequency could be reduced to every other week or their length to 5 or 10 minutes. In courses where multiple-choice exams are appropriate, several questions could be designed to take only a few minutes to answer.

10   Moreover, professors object to frequent exams because they take too much time to read and grade. In a 20-minute essay exam, a well-prepared student can easily write two pages. A relatively small class of 30 students might then produce 60 pages, no small amount of material to read each week. A large class of 100 or more students would

> How does O'Malley argue against possible objections in pars. 9 and 10?

produce an insurmountable pile of material. There are a number of responses to this objection. Again, professors could give exams every other week or make them very short. Instead of reading them closely, they could skim them quickly to see whether students understand an idea or can apply it to an unfamiliar problem; and instead of numerical or letter grades, they could give a plus, check, or minus. Exams could be collected and responded to only every third or fourth week. Professors who have readers or teaching assistants could rely on them to grade or check exams. And the Scantron machine is always available for instant grading of multiple-choice exams. Finally, frequent exams could be given *in place of* a midterm exam or out-of-class essay assignment.

11   Since frequent exams seem to some professors to create too many problems, however, it is reasonable to consider alternative ways to achieve the same goals. One alternative solution is to implement a program that would improve study skills. While such a program might teach students how to study for exams, it cannot prevent procrastination or reduce "large test anxiety" by a substantial amount. One research team studying anxiety and test performance found that study skills training was not effective in reducing anxiety or improving performance (Dendato & Diener, 1986, p. 134). This team, which also reviewed other research that reached the same conclusion, did find that a combination of "cognitive/relaxation therapy" and study skills training was effective. This possible solution seems complicated, however, not to mention time-consuming and expensive. It seems much easier and more effective to change the cause of the bad habit rather than treat the habit itself. That is, it would make more sense to solve the problem at its root: the method of learning and evaluation.

12   Still another solution might be to provide frequent study questions for students to answer. These would no doubt be helpful in focusing students' time studying, but students would probably not actually write out the answers unless they were required to. To get students to complete the questions in a timely way, professors would have to collect and check the answers. In that case, however, they might as well devote the time to grading an exam. Even if it asks the same questions, a scheduled exam is preferable to a set of study questions because it takes far less time to write in class, compared to the time students would devote to responding to questions at home. In-class exams also ensure that each student produces his or her own work.

How effectively does O'Malley present alternative solutions in pars. 11 and 12?

How do the highlighted words and phrases make the argument easy to follow?

13   Furthermore, professors could help students prepare for midterm and final exams by providing sets of questions from which the exam questions will be selected or announcing possible exam topics at the beginning of the course. This solution would have the advantage of reducing students' anxiety about learning every fact in the textbook, and it would clarify the course goals, but it would not motivate students to study carefully each new unit, concept, or text chapter in the course. I see this as a way of complementing frequent exams, not as substituting for them.

14   From the evidence and from my talks with professors and students, I see frequent, brief in-class exams as the only way to improve students' study habits and learning, reduce their anxiety and procrastination, and increase their satisfaction with college. These exams are not a panacea, but only more parking spaces and a winning football team would do as much to improve college life. Professors can't do much about parking or football, but they can give more frequent exams. Campus administrators should get behind this effort, and professors should get together to consider giving exams more frequently. It would make a difference.

How effective is this conclusion?

References

Deilock, S. (2010, September 3). Stressing about a high-stakes exam carries consequences beyond the test [Web log post]. Retrieved from http://www.psychologytoday.com /blog/choke/201009/stressing-about-high-stakes-exam-carries-consequences -beyond-the-test

Belluck, P. (2011, January 20). To really learn, quit studying and take a test. *The New York Times*. Retrieved from http://www.nytimes.com

Dendato, K. M., & Diener, D. (1986). Effectiveness of cognitive/relaxation therapy and study skills training in reducing self-reported anxiety and improving the academic performance of test-anxious students. *The Journal of Counseling Psychology, 33*, 131–135.

Frederiksen, N. (1984). The real test bias: Influences of testing on teaching and learning. *American Psychologist, 39*, 193–202.

Karpicke, J. D., & Blunt, J. R. (2011, January 30). Retrieval practice produces more learning than elaborative studying with concept mapping. *Science Online* doi: 10.1126/science.1199327

Light, R. J. (1990). *Explorations with students and faculty about teaching, learning, and student life*. Cambridge, MA: Harvard University Graduate School of Education and Kennedy School of Government.

Rothblum, E. D., Solomon, L., & Murakami, J. (1986). Affective, cognitive, and behavioral differences between high and low procrastinators. *Journal of Counseling Psychology, 33*, 387–394.

ScienceWatch.com (2008, February). Henry L. Roediger and Jeff Karpicke talk with ScienceWatch.com and answer a few questions about this month's fast breaking paper in the field of psychiatry/psychology [Interview]. Retrieved from http://sciencewatch.com/dr/fbp/2008/08febfbp/08febfbpRoedigerETAL

For an additional student reading, go to **bedfordstmartins.com/theguide/epages**.

David Bornstein | *Fighting Bullying with Babies*

DAVID BORNSTEIN has written popular books about solving social problems, including *How to Change the World: Social Entrepreneurs and the Power of New Ideas* (2007) and *Social Entrepreneurship: What Everyone Needs to Know* (2010). The recipient of several awards (for example, from Duke University's Fuqua School of Business), Bornstein co-wrote the PBS documentary *To Our Credit* and founded Dowser.org. The following proposal, "Fighting Bullying with Babies," originally appeared in Bornstein's *New York Times* blog *Fixes* in November 2010. We have converted Bornstein's links to in-text citations and have provided a list of the links at the end of the selection. We have also included photographs from the Roots of Empathy site that appeared in Borstein's blog post.

As you read, think about Bornstein's goal as described on the Dowser Web site to "present the world through a 'solution frame,' rather than a 'problem frame,'" and consider the following questions:

- What is the tone created by his opening journalistic hook: "Imagine there was a cure for meanness. Well, maybe there is"?

- How does the reference in the next sentence to the Tyler Clementi suicide affect the tone created by the hook? Point to any other passages where the tone seems to change or seems surprising.

- Given his purpose and original *New York Times* blog audience, what do you imagine Bornstein is trying to achieve with tone in this kind of proposal?

1   I magine there was a cure for meanness. Well, maybe there is. Lately, the issue of bullying has been in the news, sparked by the suicide of Tyler Clementi ("Tyler"), a gay college student who was a victim of cyber-bullying, and by a widely circulated *New York Times* article that focused on "mean girl" bullying in kindergarten (Paul). The federal government has identified bullying as a national problem. In August, it organized the first-ever "Bullying Prevention Summit," and it is now rolling out an anti-bullying campaign aimed at 5- to 8-year old children (White House). This past month the Department of Education released a guidance letter ("Guidance") urging schools, colleges and universities to take bullying seriously, or face potential legal consequences.

2   The typical institutional response to bullying is to get tough. In the Tyler Clementi case, prosecutors are considering bringing hate-crime charges (Dolnick).[1] But programs like the one I want to discuss today show the potential of augmenting our innate impulses to care for one another instead of just falling back on punishment as a deterrent. And what's the secret formula? A baby.

> *Tough kids smile, disruptive kids focus, shy kids open up.*

3   We know that humans are hardwired to be aggressive and selfish. But a growing body of research is demonstrating that there is also a biological basis for human compassion (Angier). Brain scans reveal that when we contemplate violence done to others we activate the same regions in our brains that fire up when mothers gaze at their children, suggesting that caring for strangers may be instinctual. When we help others, areas of the brain associated with pleasure also light up. Research by Felix Warneken and Michael Tomasello indicates that toddlers as young as 18 months behave altruistically. (If you want to feel good, watch one of their 15-second video clips [Warneken]. . . .)

4   More important, we are beginning to understand how to nurture this biological potential. It seems that it's not only possible to make people kinder, it's possible to do it systematically at scale—at least with school children. That's what one organization based in Toronto called Roots of Empathy has done. Roots of Empathy was founded in 1996 by Mary Gordon, an educator who had built Canada's largest network of school-based parenting and family-literacy centers after having worked with neglectful and abusive parents (Toronto District School Board). Gordon had found many of them to be lacking in empathy for their children. They hadn't developed the skill because they hadn't experienced or witnessed it sufficiently themselves. She envisioned Roots as a seriously proactive parent education program—one that would begin when the mothers- and fathers-to-be were in kindergarten. Since then, Roots has worked with more than 12,600 classes across Canada, and in recent years, the program has expanded to the Isle of Man, the United Kingdom, New Zealand, and the United States, where it currently operates in Seattle. Researchers have found that the program increases kindness and acceptance of others and decreases negative aggression.

5   Here's how it works: Roots arranges monthly class visits by a mother and her baby (who must be between two and four months old at the beginning of the school year). Each month, for nine months, a trained instructor guides a classroom using a standard curriculum that involves three 40-minute visits—a previsit, a baby visit, and a post-visit. The program runs from kindergarten to seventh grade. During the baby visits, the children sit around the baby and mother (sometimes it's a father) on a green blanket (which represents new life and nature) and they try to understand the baby's feelings. The instructor helps by labeling them. "It's a launch pad for them to understand their own feelings and the feelings of others," explains Gordon. "It carries over to the rest of class" (Gordon).

6   I have visited several public schools in low-income neighborhoods in Toronto to observe Roots of Empathy's work. What I find most fascinating is how the baby actually changes the children's behavior. Teachers have confirmed my impressions: tough kids smile, disruptive kids focus, shy kids open up. In a seventh grade class, I found 12-year-olds unabashedly singing nursery rhymes. The baby seems to act like a heart-softening magnet. No one fully understands why. Kimberly Schonert-Reichl, an applied developmental psychologist who is a professor at the University of British Columbia, has evaluated Roots of Empathy in four studies. "Do kids become more

---

[1]Tyler Clementi's roommate, Dharun Ravi, was found guilty in March 2010 of fifteen counts, including invasion of privacy, tampering with evidence, and bias intimidation. [Editor's note]

Photographs from the Roots of Empathy Web site showing the program in action

empathic and understanding? Do they become less aggressive and kinder to each other? The answer is yes and yes," she explained. "The question is why?" (Schonert-Reichl).

7   C. Sue Carter, a neurobiologist based at the University of Illinois at Chicago, who has conducted pioneering research into the effects of oxytocin, a hormone that has been linked with caring and trusting behavior, suspects that biology is playing a role in the program's impact (Angier). "This may be an oxytocin story," Carter told me. "I believe that being around the baby is somehow putting the children in a biologically different place. We don't know what that place is because we haven't measured it. However, if it works here as it does in other animals, we would guess that exposure to an infant would create a physiological state in which the children would be more social."

8   To parent well, you must try to imagine what your baby is experiencing. So the kids do a lot of "perspective taking." When the baby is too small to raise its own head, for example, the instructor asks the children to lay their heads on the blanket and look around from there. Perspective taking is the cognitive dimension of empathy—and like any skill it takes practice to master. Children learn strategies for comforting a crying baby. They learn that one must never shake a baby. They discover that everyone comes into the world with a different temperament, including themselves and their classmates. They see how hard it can be to be a parent, which helps them empathize with their own mothers and fathers. And they marvel at how capacity develops.

Each month, the baby does something that it couldn't do during its last visit: roll over, crawl, sit up, maybe even begin walking. Witnessing the baby's triumphs— even something as small as picking up a rattle for the first time—the children will often cheer.

9   Ervin Staub, professor emeritus of psychology at the University of Massachusetts, has studied altruism in children and found that the best way to create a caring climate is to engage children collectively in an activity that benefits another human being ("Biographical Note"). In Roots, children are enlisted in each class to do something to care for the baby, whether it is to sing a song, speak in a gentle voice, or make a "wishing tree." The results can be dramatic. In a study of first- to third-grade classrooms, Schonert-Reichl focused on the subset of kids who exhibited "proactive aggression"—the deliberate and cold-blooded aggression of bullies who prey on vulnerable kids (Schonert-Reichl et al.). Of those who participated in the Roots program, 88 percent decreased this form of behavior over the school year, while in the control group, only 9 percent did, and many actually increased it. Schonert-Reichl has reproduced these findings with fourth to seventh grade children in a randomized controlled trial. She also found that Roots produced significant drops in "relational aggression"— things like gossiping, excluding others, and backstabbing. Research also found a sharp increase in children's parenting knowledge. "Empathy can't be taught, but it can be caught," Gordon often says—and not just by children. "Programmatically my biggest surprise was that not only did empathy increase in children, but it

increased in their teachers," she added. "And that, to me, was glorious, because teachers hold such sway over children."

10   When the program was implemented on a large scale across the province of Manitoba—it's now in 300 classrooms there—it achieved an "effect size" that Rob Santos, the scientific director of Healthy Child Manitoba, said translates to reducing the proportion of students who get into fights from 15 percent to 8 percent, close to a 50 percent reduction (Healthy Child Manitoba). "For a program that costs only hundreds of dollars per child, the cost-benefit of preventing later problems that cost thousands of dollars per child, is obvious," said Santos. Follow up studies have found that outcomes are maintained or enhanced three years after the program ends. "When you've got emotion and cognition happening at the same time, that's deep learning," explains Gordon. "That's learning that will last."

Links

Angier, Natalie. "The Biology Behind the Milk of Human Kindness." *New York Times*. New York Times, 23 Nov. 2009. Web. 27 Mar. 2012.

Carter, Sue C. Personal interview. N.d.

Dolnick, Sam. "2 Linked to Suicide Case Withdraw from Rutgers." *New York Times*. New York Times, 29 Oct. 2010. Web. 27 Mar. 2012.

Gordon, Mary. Personal interview. N.d.

Healthy Child Manitoba. "Putting Children and Families First." Province of Manitoba, n.d. Web. 27 Mar. 2012.

Paul, Pamela. "The Playground Gets Even Tougher." *New York Times*. New York Times, 8 Oct. 2010. Web. 27 Mar. 2012.

"Roots of Empathy: From Research to Recognition." *Roots of Empathy*. Roots of Empathy, 2012. 27 Mar. 2012.

Schonert-Reichl, Kimberly. Personal interview. N.d.

Schonert-Reichl, Kimberly, et al. "Contextual Considerations in the Evaluation of a School-Based Social Emotional Competence Program." American Educational Research Association, April 2009. Print.

Staub, Ervin. "Biographical Note." *Ervinstaub.com*. Ervinstaub.com, n.d. Web. 27 Mar. 2012.

Toronto District School Board. "Parenting and Family Literacy Centres." Toronto District School Board, n.d. Web. 27 Mar. 2012.

"Tyler Clementi." Times Topics. *New York Times*. New York Times, 16 Mar. 2012. Web. 27 Mar. 2012.

United States. Dept. of Education. "Guidance Targeting Harassment Outlines Local and Federal Responsibility." *Ed.gov*. Dept. of Education, 26 Oct. 2010. Web. 27 Mar. 2012.

———. Dept. of Health and Human Services. "Stop Bullying Now." *TFK Extra!*. Health Resources and Services Administration, Dept. of Health and Human Services, n.d. Web. 27 Mar. 2012.

———. White House Conference on Bullying Prevention. *White House*. White House, 14 Oct. 2010. Web. 27 Mar. 2012.

Warneken, Felix. "Videoclips." Dept. of Developmental and Comparative Psychology, Max Planck Institute for Evolutionary Anthropology. Max Planck Institute, n.d. Web. 27 Mar. 2012.

Warneken, Felix, and Michael Tomasello. "Altruistic Helping in Human Infants and Young Chimpanzees." *Science* 311.5765 (2006): 1301–3. *Academic Search Complete*. Web. 27 Mar. 2012.

Make connections: Thinking about perspective taking.

[**REFLECT**]

One of the ways of developing empathy seems to be through "perspective taking," which Bornstein calls "the cognitive dimension of empathy" (par. 8). Think about your own observation and personal experience with perspective taking. Your instructor may ask you to post your thoughts on a class discussion board or to discuss them with other students in class. Use the following suggestions to get started:

- Think of a situation in which you conflicted with someone, such as a sibling, parent, coworker, teacher, or classmate. Reflect on how you felt at the time of the conflict. Then put yourself in the position of the other person and try to imagine how he or she may have felt.

- Consider the insights, if any, you gained from perspective taking in this case. Do you think perspective taking could help while in the middle of a conflict, or do you need distance to empathize with someone else's point of view?

[ANALYZE]   # Use the basic features.

A FOCUSED, WELL-DEFINED PROBLEM: ESTABLISHING THE PROBLEM

Every proposal begins with a problem. Student Patrick O'Malley (pp. 304–10) uses his title ("More Testing, More Learning") to hint at both the problem he will identify and the solution he will offer and to capture his readers' attention. He uses a scenario, dramatized by a series of *rhetorical questions,* to frame the problem, and he follows that with citations of research reports that help establish the problem's seriousness. Bornstein's title ("Fighting Bullying with Babies") is designed to surprise readers, and his first two sentences serve as a hook, drawing readers in by his bold claim to find a "cure" for "meanness."

ANALYZE & WRITE

Write a few paragraphs analyzing the strategies Bornstein uses to frame the problem of bullying and establish its seriousness and to evaluate how effective these strategies would be for Bornstein's readers:

1 Skim paragraph 1. In addition to referring to the Tyler Clementi case, with which his original *New York Times* readers would certainly have been familiar, why do you think Bornstein also refers to the article on the "mean girl" bullying in kindergarten? What do these two examples have in common?

2 Why do you think Bornstein refers to a White House summit and the Department of Education's "guidance letter"? How do these references help him frame the problem and excite readers' interest in the solution he describes?

3 Bornstein does not directly define *bullying*. Assuming that bullying is a rather wide and varied class of behaviors, how important is it that Bornstein clarify what he means by *bullying*? How does he give readers a sense of what bullying involves?

A WELL-ARGUED SOLUTION: PROVING IT WORKS

Arguing in support of a proposed solution requires evidence that the solution will help solve the problem and that it is feasible (doable and cost-effective). O'Malley cites a number of studies to support his claim that frequent testing reduces anxiety and increases learning.

| ANALYZE & WRITE |

Write a few paragraphs analyzing and evaluating Bornstein's use of evidence, particularly his use of the Roots of Empathy program, to support his claim:

1 Skim paragraph 5. How does the Roots of Empathy program demonstrate that the proposed solution is feasible and easily implemented? What details about how the program works does Bornstein share with readers?

2 How effectively do you think the information Bornstein provides, including photographs, will convince readers that the Roots of Empathy program will work and that it can be implemented broadly, in a cost-effective way?

AN EFFECTIVE RESPONSE TO OBJECTIONS AND ALTERNATIVE SOLUTIONS: REJECTING THE STANDARD SOLUTION

In addition to arguing for the proposed solution, proposal writers also need to show that their solution is preferable to alternatives their readers might favor. Patrick O'Malley, for example, identifies several alternative solutions his intended audience (instructors) might bring up, including implementing programs to improve students' study skills, giving students study questions, and handing out possible exam topics to help students prepare. He concedes the benefits of some of these solutions, but he also points out their shortcomings, showing how his solution is better.

| ANALYZE & WRITE |

Write a paragraph analyzing and evaluating how Bornstein anticipates and responds to alternative solutions:

1 Reread the opening paragraphs to identify the actions that have been taken to address the problem of bullying. Consider the words Bornstein uses and the details he provides to describe these programs.

2 Now skim paragraphs 4–10, in which Bornstein describes the Roots of Empathy program. Consider the words he uses and the details he provides about that program. How does he contrast his solution to the alternatives?

3 Given your analysis of Bornstein's choice of words and details, how evenhanded is he in his evaluation of alternative solutions? How persuasive is the solution he offers?

A CLEAR, LOGICAL ORGANIZATION: USING TOPIC SENTENCES

Topic sentences can be especially helpful to readers trying to follow the logic of a proposal. O'Malley, for example, uses topic sentences to introduce the reasons in favor of frequent exams, to identify the reasons opponents offer against frequent exams, and to respond to alternative solutions. He uses transitions such as "The main reason" (par. 4), "Another, closely related argument" (par. 6), and "Moreover" (par. 10), and repeats the key words "frequent exams" and "solution" to guide readers.

Write a couple of paragraphs analyzing and evaluating Bornstein's use of topic sentences to help readers follow his argument:

1 Reread paragraphs 7–9 to see how Bornstein answers the rhetorical question "Why does the solution work?" Look particularly at each of the topic sentences in these paragraphs to see how Bornstein announces the answers.

2 Now review paragraph 3 to see how Bornstein previews two of these answers.

3 Given Bornstein's purpose and audience, how clear and comprehensible is the logic of this proposal argument? If you were to give Bornstein advice on revising this proposal for an audience of college students, what, if anything, would you recommend?

[RESPOND]   ## Consider possible topics: Tweaking others' solutions.

The idea behind much of Bornstein's work, as he explains on his Dowser Web site, is to show "Who's solving what and how" with the aim of inspiring creative problem solving in others. Instead of beginning with a problem and then trying to come up with a solution, reflect on solutions with which you are familiar, and then consider how those solutions could be tweaked to help solve another problem. The Roots of Empathy program, for example, might suggest other problems that could be helped by giving people an opportunity to try out a different perspective. Another example featured on the Dowser site that could offer a model to solve problems is Community Spokes, an after-school program that teaches students to fix bicycles in their community. How could this program be adapted to teach other practical, possibly even money-making, skills to children?

**Kelly D. Brownell
and Thomas R. Frieden**

Ounces of Prevention—The Public Policy Case for Taxes on Sugared Beverages

KELLY D. BROWNELL is a professor of psychology as well as a professor of epidemiology and public health at Yale, where he is also director of the Rudd Center for Food Policy and Obesity. An international expert who has published numerous books and articles, including *Food Fight: The Inside Story of the Food Industry, America's Obesity Crisis, and What We Can Do About It* (2003), Brownell received the 2012 American Psychological Association Award for Outstanding Lifetime Contributions to Psychology. He was also featured in the Academy Award–nominated film *Super Size Me*.

THOMAS R. FRIEDEN, a physician specializing in public health, is the director of the U.S. Centers for Disease Control and Prevention (CDC) and served for several years as the health commissioner for the City of New York.

Brownell and Frieden's proposal "Ounces of Prevention — The Public Policy Case for Taxes on Sugared Beverages" was originally published in 2009 in the highly respected *New England Journal of Medicine,* which calls itself "the most widely read, cited, and influential general medical periodical in the world." In fact, research published there is often referred to widely throughout the media.

As you read, consider the effect that Brownell and Frieden's use of graphs and formal citation of sources has on their credibility:

- How do the graphs help establish the seriousness of the problem? How do they also help demonstrate the feasibility of the solution the authors propose?

- How do the citations help persuade you to accept the authors' solution? What effect might they have had on their original readers? (Note that the authors use neither of the two citation styles covered in Part 4 of this text. Instead, they use one common to medical journals and publications of the U.S. National Library of Medicine.)

Sugar, rum, and tobacco are commodities which are nowhere necessaries of life, which are become objects of almost universal consumption, and which are therefore extremely proper subjects of taxation.

— Adam Smith, *The Wealth of Nations,* 1776

1   The obesity epidemic has inspired calls for public health measures to prevent diet-related diseases. One controversial idea is now the subject of public debate: food taxes. Forty states already have small taxes on sugared beverages and snack foods, but in the past year, Maine and New York have proposed large taxes on sugared beverages, and similar discussions have begun in other states. The size of the taxes, their potential for generating revenue and reducing consumption, and vigorous opposition by the beverage industry have resulted in substantial controversy. Because excess consumption of unhealthful foods underlies many leading causes of death, food taxes at local, state, and national levels are likely to remain part of political and public health discourse.

2   Sugar-sweetened beverages (soda sweetened with sugar, corn syrup, or other caloric sweeteners and other carbonated and uncarbonated drinks, such as sports and energy drinks) may be the single largest driver of the obesity epidemic. A recent meta-analysis found that the intake of sugared beverages is associated with increased body weight, poor nutrition, and displacement of more healthful beverages; increasing consumption increases risk for obesity and diabetes; the strongest effects are seen in studies with the best methods (e.g., longitudinal and interventional vs. correlational studies);* and interventional studies show that reduced intake of soft drinks improves health.[1] Studies that do not support a relationship between consumption of sugared beverages and health outcomes tend to be conducted by authors supported by the beverage industry.[2] Sugared beverages are marketed extensively to children and adolescents, and in the mid-1990s, children's intake of sugared beverages surpassed that of milk. In the past decade, per capita intake of calories from sugar-sweetened beverages has increased by nearly 30 percent (see bar graph Daily Caloric Intake from Sugar-Sweetened Drinks in the

---

*In a *longitudinal* study, researchers observe changes taking place over a long period of time; in an *interventional* study, investigators give research subjects a measured amount of whatever is being studied and note its effects; and in a *correlational* study, researchers examine statistics to see if two or more variables have a mathematically significant similarity. [Editor's note]

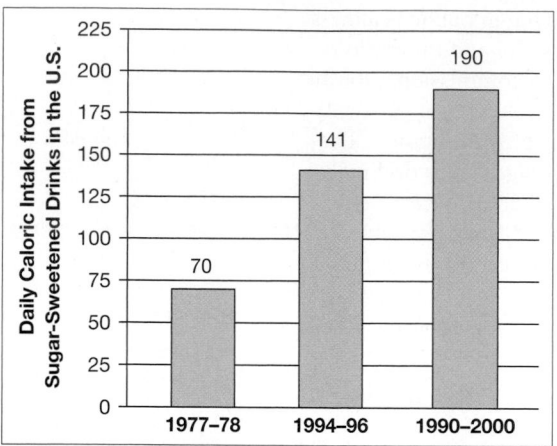

Daily Caloric Intake from Sugar-Sweetened Drinks in the United States.
Data are from Nielsen and Popkin.[3]

United States);[3] beverages now account for 10 to 15 percent of the calories consumed by children and adolescents. For each extra can or glass of sugared beverage consumed per day, the likelihood of a child's becoming obese increases by 60 percent.[4]

3   Taxes on tobacco products have been highly effective in reducing consumption, and data indicate that higher prices also reduce soda consumption. A review conducted by Yale University's Rudd Center for Food Policy and Obesity suggested that for every 10 percent increase in price, consumption decreases by 7.8 percent. An industry trade publication reported even larger reductions: as prices of carbonated soft drinks increased by 6.8 percent, sales dropped by 7.8 percent, and as

Coca-Cola prices increased by 12 percent, sales dropped by 14.6 percent.[5] Such studies—and the economic principles that support their findings—suggest that a tax on sugared beverages would encourage consumers to switch to more healthful beverages, which would lead to reduced caloric intake and less weight gain.

4   The increasing affordability of soda—and the decreasing affordability of fresh fruits and vegetables (see line graph)—probably contributes to the rise in obesity in the United States. In 2008, a group of child and health care advocates in New York proposed a one-penny-per-ounce excise tax on sugared beverages, which would be expected to reduce consumption by 13 percent—about two servings per week per person. Even if one quarter of the calories consumed from sugared beverages are replaced by other food, the decrease in consumption would lead to an estimated reduction of 8,000 calories per person per year—slightly more than 2 pounds each year for the average person. Such a reduction in calorie consumption would be expected to substantially reduce the risk of obesity and diabetes and may also reduce the risk of heart disease and other conditions.

5   Some argue that government should not interfere in the market and that products and prices will change as consumers demand more healthful food, but several considerations support government action. The first is externality—costs to parties not directly involved in a transaction. The contribution of unhealthful diets to health care costs is already high and is increasing—an estimated $79 billion is spent annually for overweight and obesity alone—and approximately half of these costs are paid by Medicare and Medicaid, at taxpayers'

Relative Price Changes for Fresh Fruits and Vegetables, Sugar and Sweets, and Carbonated Drinks, 1978–2009.
Data are from the Bureau of Labor Statistics and represent the U.S. city averages for all urban consumers in January of each year.

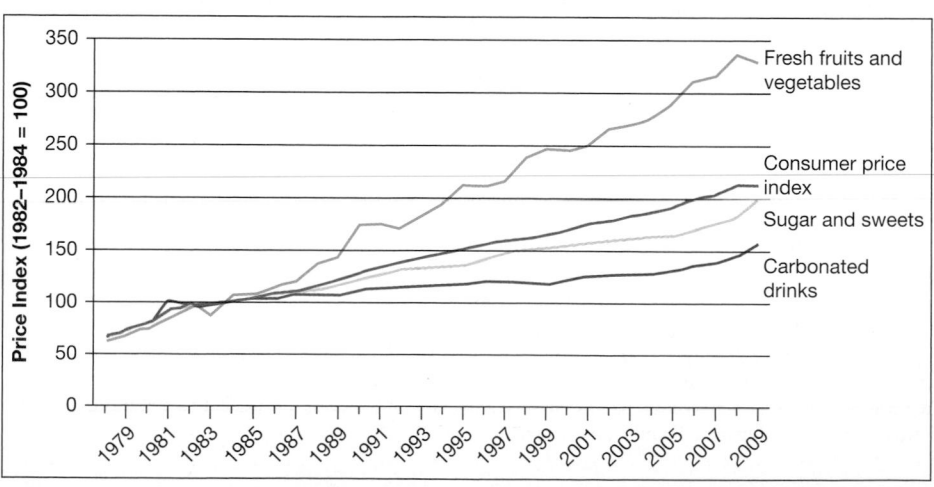

expense. Diet-related diseases also cost society in terms of decreased work productivity, increased absenteeism, poorer school performance, and reduced fitness on the part of military recruits, among other negative effects. The second consideration is information asymmetry between the parties to a transaction. In the case of sugared beverages, marketers commonly make health claims (e.g., that such beverages provide energy or vitamins) and use techniques that exploit the cognitive vulnerabilities of young children, who often cannot distinguish a television program from an advertisement. A third consideration is revenue generation, which can further increase the societal benefits of a tax on soft drinks. A penny-per-ounce excise tax would raise an estimated $1.2 billion in New York State alone. In times of economic hardship, taxes that both generate this much revenue and promote health are better options than revenue initiatives that may have adverse effects.

6   Objections have certainly been raised: that such a tax would be regressive, that food taxes are not comparable to tobacco or alcohol taxes because people must eat to survive, that it is unfair to single out one type of food for taxation, and that the tax will not solve the obesity problem. But the poor are disproportionately affected by diet-related diseases and would derive the greatest benefit from reduced consumption; sugared beverages are not necessary for survival; Americans consume about 250 to 300 more calories daily today than they did several decades ago, and nearly half this increase is accounted for by consumption of sugared beverages; and though no single intervention will solve the obesity problem, that is hardly a reason to take no action.

7   The full impact of public policies becomes apparent only after they take effect. We can estimate changes in sugared-drink consumption that would be prompted by a tax, but accompanying changes in the consumption of other foods or beverages are more difficult to predict. One question is whether the proportions of calories consumed in liquid and solid foods would change. And shifts among beverages would have different effects depending on whether consumers substituted water, milk, diet drinks, or equivalent generic brands of sugared drinks.

8   Effects will also vary depending on whether the tax is designed to reduce consumption, generate revenue, or both; the size of the tax; whether the revenue is earmarked for programs related to nutrition and health; and where in the production and distribution chain the tax is applied. Given the heavy consumption of sugared beverages, even small taxes will generate substantial revenue, but only heftier taxes will significantly reduce consumption. Sales taxes are the most common form of food tax, but because they are levied as a percentage of the retail price, they encourage the purchase of less-expensive brands or larger containers. Excise taxes structured as a fixed cost per ounce provide an incentive to buy less and hence would be much more effective in reducing consumption and improving health. In addition, manufacturers generally pass the cost of an excise tax along to their customers, including it in the price consumers see when they are making their selection, whereas sales taxes are seen only at the cash register.

9   Although a tax on sugared beverages would have health benefits regardless of how the revenue was used, the popularity of such a proposal increases greatly if revenues are used for programs to prevent childhood obesity, such as media campaigns, facilities and programs for physical activity, and healthier food in schools. Poll results show that support of a tax on sugared beverages ranges from 37 to 72 percent; a poll of New York residents found that 52 percent supported a "soda tax," but the number rose to 72 percent when respondents were told that the revenue would be used for obesity prevention. Perhaps the most defensible approach is to use revenue to subsidize the purchase of healthful foods. The public would then see a relationship between tax and benefit, and any regressive effects would be counteracted by the reduced costs of healthful food.

10   A penny-per-ounce excise tax could reduce consumption of sugared beverages by more than 10 percent. It is difficult to imagine producing behavior change of this magnitude through education alone, even if government devoted massive resources to the task. In contrast, a sales tax on sugared drinks would generate considerable revenue, and as with the tax on tobacco, it could become a key tool in efforts to improve health.

References

1. Vartanian LR, Schwartz MB, Brownell KD. Effects of soft drink consumption on nutrition and health: a systematic review and meta-analysis. Am J Public Health 2007;97:667–675.

2. Forshee RA, Anderson PA, Storey ML. Sugar-sweetened beverages and body mass index in children and adolescents: a meta-analysis. Am J Clin Nutr 2008;87:1662–71.

3. Nielsen SJ, Popkin BM. Changes in beverage intake between 1977 and 2001. Am J Prev Med 2004;27:205–210.
4. Ludwig DS, Peterson KE, Gortmaker SL. Relation between consumption of sugar-sweetened drinks and childhood obesity: a prospective, observational analysis. Lancet 2001;357:505–508.
5. Elasticity: big price increases cause Coke volume to plummet. Beverage Digest. November 21, 2008:3–4.

[REFLECT] ## Make connections: Government problem solving.

Brownell and Frieden explicitly argue in favor of the federal and/or state government taking action to address public health problems such as those related to obesity and smoking. Imposing taxes is one thing government can do. Another action is to require that foods be labeled with accurate nutritional information.

Write a few paragraphs considering the right and responsibility of government to solve public health problems. Your instructor may ask you to post your thoughts on a class discussion board or to discuss them with other students in class. Use these questions to get started:

- Consider what actions government *could* take to address public health problems and whether government *should* take such actions.

- Think about how you would respond to Brownell and Frieden's argument that "though no single intervention will solve the obesity problem, that is hardly a reason to take no action" (par. 6).

[ANALYZE] ## Use the basic features.

A FOCUSED, WELL-DEFINED PROBLEM: CITING RESEARCH STUDIES

Brownell and Frieden identify the problem for which they are proposing a solution in broad terms as the "obesity epidemic" (par. 1). However, they frame the issue by focusing on "sugar-sweetened beverages" (par. 2). To support a causal connection between consuming sugar-sweetened beverages and obesity, they cite research studies.

ANALYZE & WRITE

Write a few paragraphs analyzing more closely how Brownell and Frieden use research to establish a causal connection between sweetened drinks and obesity:

1. Skim paragraph 3 to identify the findings Brownell and Frieden summarize there. Note that these are the findings of a "meta-analysis," which compares different studies researching the same question.

2. Consider how effectively, if at all, these findings support Brownell and Frieden's argument about a cause-effect relationship between consuming sugar-sweetened beverages and obesity.

3. Think about what kinds of studies were done and consider how Brownell and Frieden rate these different kinds of studies. Why might it be helpful for Brownell and Frieden's readers from the *New England Journal of Medicine* to know the kinds of studies that have been used and which ones employ "the best methods" and get "the strongest effects"?

A WELL-ARGUED SOLUTION: USING COMPARISON-CONTRAST AND CLASSIFICATION

Like O'Malley, Brownell and Frieden use their title to announce the solution they are proposing: the imposition of a tax on certain beverages. They use writing strategies such as comparison-contrast and classification to support their claims. Even the epigraph quoting Adam Smith, the father of free market economics, is a kind of comparison in that it implicitly associates a figure linked to conservative politics with their position, which would generally be considered liberal.

ANALYZE & WRITE

Write a few paragraphs analyzing and evaluating how Brownell and Frieden use comparison and contrast and classification strategies to support their proposal:

1 Reread paragraphs 3–4. How do Brownell and Frieden use comparison and contrast there to argue for a tax on sweetened beverages?

2 Reread paragraphs 8–9. How do they use classification there?

3 Consider the strengths and weaknesses of using these two strategies to support their proposed solution. How are these two writing strategies effective ways of supporting their position? What other strategies might work better?

AN EFFECTIVE RESPONSE TO OBJECTIONS AND ALTERNATIVE SOLUTIONS: HANDLING OBJECTIONS

Proposal writers usually try to anticipate readers' objections and questions and concede or refute them. How writers handle objections and questions affects their credibility with readers, who usually expect writers to be respectful of other points of view and to take criticism seriously while still arguing assertively for their solution. Brownell and Frieden anticipate and respond to five objections they would expect their readers to raise.

ANALYZE & WRITE

Write a couple of paragraphs analyzing and evaluating how Brownell and Frieden respond to objections:

1 Reread paragraph 5. First, summarize the objection and their argument refuting it. Then evaluate their response: How effective is their refutation likely to be with their readers?

2 Reread paragraph 6, in which the authors respond to a number of objections. What cues do they provide to help you follow their argument?

3 Given their purpose and audience, why do you think Brownell and Frieden focus so much attention on the first objection and group the other objections together in a single paragraph?

4 How would you describe the tone of Brownell and Frieden's refutation? How is their credibility with readers likely to be affected by the way they respond to objections?

To learn more about using graphics, see Chapter 21, pp. 647–51.

A CLEAR, LOGICAL ORGANIZATION: USING GRAPHS

Brownell and Frieden include two graphs in their proposal—a bar graph and a line graph. Bar graphs and line graphs can be used to display numerical and statistical information at different points in time and also to compare groups or data sets by using different color bars or lines.

ANALYZE & WRITE

Write a paragraph analyzing and evaluating how well Brownell and Frieden integrate these graphs:

1 Highlight the sentences in paragraphs 2 and 4 in which Brownell and Frieden introduce each graph. How else do they integrate the graphs into their argument?

2 Consider the sections in which these graphs appear. How might the graphs help demarcate sections and move readers from one section to the next?

3 Look closely at the graphs themselves to see how the information is presented. What do the graphs contribute? Given Brownell and Frieden's purpose and audience, why do you think they chose to include these graphs?

RESPOND

Consider possible topics: Improving a group to which you belong.

Consider making a proposal to improve the operation of an organization, a business, or a club to which you belong. For example, you might propose that your college keep administrative offices open in the evenings or on weekends to accommodate working students, or that a child-care center be opened for students who are parents of young children. For a business, you might propose a system to handle customer complaints or a fairer way for employees to arrange their schedules. If you belong to a club that has a problem with the collection of dues, you might propose a new collection system or suggest alternative ways of raising money.

Karen Kornbluh | *Win-Win Flexibility*

KAREN KORNBLUH worked in the private sector as an economist and management consultant before becoming deputy chief of staff at the U.S. Treasury Department. She currently serves as the ambassador and U.S. permanent representative to the international Organization for Economic Co-operation and Development. As founder and director of the Work and Family Program of the New America Foundation—a nonprofit, nonpartisan institute that sponsors research and conferences on public policy issues—Kornbluh led an effort to change the American workplace to accommodate what she calls the "juggler family," in which parents have to juggle their time among caring for their children, their elderly parents, and their work. Kornbluh's book *Running Harder to Stay in Place: The Growth of Family Work Hours and Incomes* was published by the New America Foundation in 2005. Kornbluh's articles have appeared in such distinguished venues as the *New York Times,* the *Washington Post,* and the *Atlantic Monthly*. "Win-Win Flexibility" was first published by the Work and Family Program in 2005. As you read, consider who Kornbluh's audience is for this proposal:

- What type of reader do you think made up Kornbluh's (and the New America Foundation's) intended audience?

- Given this audience, why do you think Kornbluh characterizes her proposal as "win-win"?

Introduction

1 Today fully 70 percent of families with children are headed by two working parents or by an unmarried working parent. The "traditional family" of the breadwinner and homemaker has been replaced by the "juggler family," in which no one is home full-time. Two-parent families are working 10 more hours a week than in 1979 (Bernstein and Kornbluh).

2 To be decent parents, caregivers, and members of their communities, workers now need greater flexibility than they once did. Yet good part-time or flex-time jobs remain rare. Whereas companies have embraced flexibility in virtually every other aspect of their businesses (inventory control, production schedules, financing), full-time workers' schedules remain largely inflexible. Employers often demand workers be available around the clock. Moreover, many employees have no right to a minimum number of sick or vacation days; almost two-thirds of all workers—and an even larger percentage of low-income parents—lack the ability to take a day off to care for a family member (Lovell). The Family and Medical Leave Act (FMLA) of 1993 finally guaranteed that workers at large companies could take a leave of absence for the birth or adoption of a baby, or for the illness of a family member. Yet that guaranteed leave is unpaid.

3 Many businesses are finding ways to give their most valued employees flexibility but, all too often, workers who need flexibility find themselves shunted into part-time, temporary, on-call, or contract jobs with reduced wages and career opportunities— and, often, no benefits. A full quarter of American workers are in these jobs. Only 15 percent of women and 12 percent of men in such jobs receive health insurance from their employers (Wenger). A number of European countries provide workers the right to a part-time schedule and all have enacted legislation to implement a European Union directive to prohibit discrimination against part-time workers.

4 In America, employers are required to accommodate the needs of employees with disabilities—even if that means providing a part-time or flexible schedule. Employers may also provide religious accommodations for employees by offering a part-time or flexible schedule. At the same time, employers have no obligation to allow parents or employees caring for sick relatives to work part-time or flexible schedules, even if the cost to the employer would be inconsequential.

5 In the 21st century global economy, America needs a new approach that allows businesses to gain flexibility in staffing without sacrificing their competitiveness and enables workers to gain control over their work-lives without sacrificing their economic security. This win-win flexibility arrangement will not be the same in every company, nor even for each employee working within the same organization. Each case will be different. But flexibility will not come for all employees without some education, prodding, and leadership. So, employers and employees must be required to come to the table to work out a solution that benefits everyone. American businesses must be educated on strategies for giving employees flexibility without sacrificing productivity or morale. And businesses should be recognized and rewarded when they do so.

6 America is a nation that continually rises to the occasion. At the dawn of a new century, we face many challenges. One of these is helping families to raise our next generation in an increasingly demanding global economy. This is a challenge America must meet with imagination and determination.

Background: The Need for Workplace Flexibility

7 Between 1970 and 2000, the percentage of mothers in the workforce rose from 38 to 67 percent (Smolensky and Gootman). Moreover, the number of hours worked by dual-income families has increased dramatically. Couples with children worked a full 60 hours a week in 1979. By 2000 they were working 70 hours a week (Bernstein and Kornbluh). And more parents than ever are working long hours. In 2000, nearly 1 out of every 8 couples with children was putting in 100 hours a week or more on the job, compared to only 1 out of 12 families in 1970 (Jacobs and Gerson).

8 In addition to working parents, there are over 44.4 million Americans who provide care to another adult, often an older relative. Fifty-nine percent of these caregivers either work or have worked while providing care ("Caregiving").

9 In a 2002 report by the Families and Work Institute, 45 percent of employees reported that work and family responsibilities interfered with each other "a lot" or "some" and 67 percent of employed parents report that they do not have enough time with their children (Galinsky, Bond, and Hill).

10 Over half of workers today have no control over scheduling alternative start and end times at work (Galinsky, Bond, and Hill). According to a recent study by the Institute for Women's Policy Research, 49 percent of workers—over 59 million Americans—lack basic paid sick days for themselves. And almost two-thirds of all workers—and an even larger percentage of low-income parents—lack the ability to take a day off to care for a family member (Lovell). Thirteen percent of non-poor workers with caregiving responsibilities lack paid vacation leave, while 28 percent of poor caregivers lack any paid vacation time (Heymann). Research has shown that flexible arrangements and benefits tend to be more accessible in larger and more profitable firms, and then to the most valued professional and managerial workers in those firms (Golden). Parents with young children and working welfare recipients—the workers who need access to paid leave the most—are the least likely to have these benefits, according to research from the Urban Institute (Ross Phillips).

11 In the US, only 5 percent of workers have access to a job that provides paid parental leave. The Family and Medical Leave Act grants the right to 12 weeks of unpaid leave for the birth or adoption of a child or for the serious illness of the worker or a worker's family member. But the law does not apply to employees who work in companies with fewer than 50 people, employees who have worked for less than a year at their place of employment, or employees who work fewer than 1,250 hours a year. Consequently, only 45 percent of parents working in the private sector are eligible to take even this unpaid time off (Smolensky and Gootman).

12 Workers often buy flexibility by sacrificing job security, benefits, and pay. Part-time workers are less likely to have employer-provided health insurance or pensions and their hourly wages are lower. One study in 2002 found that 43 percent of employed parents said that using flexibility would jeopardize their advancement (Galinsky, Bond, and Hill).

13 Children, in particular, pay a heavy price for workplace inflexibility (Waters Boots). Almost 60 percent of child care arrangements are of poor or mediocre quality (Smolensky and Gootman). Children in low-income families are even less likely to be in good or excellent care settings. Full-day child care easily costs $4,000 to $10,000 per year—approaching the price of college tuition at a public university. As a result of the unaffordable and low quality nature of child care in this country, a disturbing number of today's children are left home alone: Over 3.3 million children ages 6–12 are home alone after school each day (Vandivere et al.).

14 Many enlightened businesses are showing the way forward to a 21st century flexible workplace. Currently, however, businesses have little incentive to provide families with the flexibility they need. We need to level the playing field and remove the competitive disadvantages for all businesses that do provide workplace flexibility.

15 This should be a popular priority. A recent poll found that 77 percent of likely voters feel that it is difficult for families to earn enough and still have time to be with their families. Eighty-four percent of voters agree that children are being shortchanged when their parents have to work long hours. . . .

Proposal: Win-Win Flexibility

16 A win-win approach in the US to flexibility . . . might function as follows. It would be "soft touch" at first—requiring a process and giving business an out if it would

Kornbluh   *Win-Win Flexibility*

GUIDE TO READING
GUIDE TO WRITING
A WRITER AT WORK
THINKING CRITICALLY

325

be costly to implement—with a high-profile public education campaign on the importance of workplace flexibility to American business, American families, and American society. A survey at the end of the second year would determine whether a stricter approach is needed.

17   Employees would have the right to make a formal request to their employers for flexibility in the number of hours worked, the times worked, and/or the ability to work from home. Examples of such flexibility would include part-time, annualized hours,[1] compressed hours,[2] flex-time,[3] job-sharing, shift working, staggered hours, and telecommuting.

18   The employee would be required to make a written application providing details on the change in work, the effect on the employer, and solutions to any problems caused to the employer. The employer would be required to meet with the employee and give the employee a decision on the request within two weeks, as well as provide an opportunity for an internal appeal within one month from the initial request.

19   The employee request would be granted unless the employer demonstrated it would require significant difficulty or expense entailing more than ordinary costs, decreased job efficiency, impairment of worker safety, infringement of other employees' rights, or conflict with another law or regulation.

20   The employer would be required to provide an employee working a flexible schedule with the same hourly pay and proportionate health, pension, vacation, holiday, and FMLA benefits that the employee received before working flexibly and would be required thereafter to advance the employee at the same rate as full-time employees.

21   *Who would be covered:* Parents (including parents, legal guardians, foster parents) and other caregivers at first. Eventually all workers should be eligible in our flexible, 24×7 economy. During the initial period, it will be necessary to define non-parental "caregivers." One proposal is to define them as immediate relatives or other caregivers of "certified care recipients" (defined as those whom a doctor certifies as having three or more limitations that impede daily functioning—using diagnostic criteria such as Activities of Daily Living [ADL]/ Instrumental Activities of Daily Living [IADL]—for at least 180 consecutive days). . . .

22   *Public Education:* Critical to the success of the proposal will be public education along the lines of the education that the government and business schools conducted in the 1980s about the need for American business to adopt higher quality standards to compete against Japanese business. A Malcolm Baldridge—like award[4] should be created for companies that make flexibility win-win. A public education campaign conducted by the Department of Labor should encourage small businesses to adopt best practices of win-win flexibility. Tax credits could be used in the first year to reward early adopters.

Works Cited

Bernstein, Jared, and Karen Kornbluh. *Running Faster to Stay in Place: The Growth of Family Work Hours and Incomes.* Washington: New America Foundation, 2005. *New America Foundation.* Web. 22 May 2008.

Galinsky, Ellen, James Bond, and Jeffrey E. Hill. *Workplace Flexibility: What Is It? Who Has It? Who Wants It? Does It Make a Difference?* New York: Families and Work Institute, 2004. Print.

Golden, Lonnie. *The Time Bandit: What U.S. Workers Surrender to Get Greater Flexibility in Work Schedules.* Washington: Economic Policy Institute, 2000. *Economic Policy Institute.* Web. 18 May 2008.

Heymann, Jody. *The Widening Gap: Why America's Working Families Are in Jeopardy—and What Can Be Done About It.* New York: Basic, 2000. Print.

Jacobs, Jerry, and Kathleen Gerson. *The Time Divide: Work, Family and Gender Inequality.* Cambridge: Harvard UP, 2004. Print.

Lovell, Vickey. *No Time to Be Sick: Why Everyone Suffers When Workers Don't Have Paid Sick Leave.* Washington: Institute for Women's Policy Research, 2004. *Institute for Women's Policy Research.* Web. 20 May 2008.

---

[1] *Annualized hours* means working different numbers of hours a week but a fixed annual total. [Editor's note]

[2] *Compressed hours* means working more hours a day in exchange for working fewer days a week. [Editor's note]

[3] *Flex-time* means working on an adjustable daily schedule. [Editor's note]

[4] The Malcolm Baldridge National Quality Award is given by the U.S. President to outstanding businesses. [Editor's note]

National Alliance for Caregiving and AARP.
Caregiving in the U.S. Bethesda: NAC, 2004.
National Alliance for Caregiving. Web. 20 May 2008.

Ross Phillips, Katherin. *Getting Time Off: Access to Leave among Working Parents.* Washington: Urban Institute, 2004. *Urban Institute.* Web. 21 May 2008. New Federalism: National Survey of America's Families B-57.

Smolensky, Eugene, and Jennifer A. Gootman, eds. *Working Families and Growing Kids: Caring for Children and Adolescents.* Washington: The National Academies P, 2004. Print.

Vandivere, Sharon, et al. *Unsupervised Time: Family and Child Factors Associated with Self-Care.* Washington: Urban Institute, 2003. *Urban Institute.* Web. 21 May 2008. Assessing the New Federalism 71.

Waters Boots, Shelley. *The Way We Work: How Children and Their Families Fare in a 21st Century Workplace.* Washington: New America Foundation, 2004. *New America Foundation.* Web. 22 May 2008.

Wenger, Jeffrey. *Share of Workers in "Nonstandard" Jobs Declines.* Briefing Paper. Washington: Economic Policy Institute, 2003. *Economic Policy Institute.* Web. 18 May 2008.

REFLECT

Make connections: The problem of child care.

Kornbluh asserts in paragraph 13 that it is the children in juggler families who "pay a heavy price." She is particularly critical of child care, which she says is very expensive and low quality. She also cites research indicating that many six- to twelve-year-old children are latchkey kids, "home alone after school each day" (par. 13).

Consider whether your family should be classified as a "juggler" or as a "traditional family" (par. 1). If you are a parent, you might compare the family in which you grew up to the family in which you are a parent and reflect on your personal experience as a child or as a parent. Your instructor may ask you to post your thoughts on a class discussion board or to discuss them with other students during class time. Use the following questions to get started:

- Assess the strengths and weaknesses of your family's arrangements for child care. In your view, how could they be improved? Kornbluh appears to assume that being "home alone" is bad for six- to twelve-year-old children. At what age do you think children can take care of themselves?

- Consider also your family's work situation and whether the kinds of flexibility Kornbluh suggests, such as working part-time, working more hours each day but fewer days per week, being able to adjust your daily schedule, or telecommuting, would be feasible. Which, if any, of these suggestions would help your family and fit your family's workplace conditions?

ANALYZE

Use the basic features.

A FOCUSED, WELL-DEFINED PROBLEM: USING STATISTICS

For problems that are new to readers, writers not only need to explain the problem but also need to convince readers that it exists and is serious enough to justify the actions the writer thinks are necessary to solve it. Kornbluh assumes readers will not be familiar with the problem she is writing about or take it seriously, so she spends the first part of her essay introducing the problem and the second part establishing the problem's existence and seriousness.

ANALYZE & WRITE

Write a couple of paragraphs analyzing and evaluating Kornbluh's use of statistics to present the problem:

1 Reread Kornbluh's opening paragraph. Given that her audience probably combines people in business, labor, and government, what makes the statistics she cites there effective or ineffective?

2 Now reread paragraph 7. Notice that Kornbluh cites statistics from two different time periods in this paragraph. How does this comparison contribute to Kornbluh's presentation of the problem?

3 Finally, skim Kornbluh's proposal to find places where she cites the raw number together with the percentage. Here's one example:

> According to a recent study by the Institute for Women's Policy Research, 49 percent of workers — over 59 million Americans — lack basic paid sick days for themselves. (par. 10)

How, if at all, does giving statistics in both forms help readers? In addition to clarity, for what other reasons might Kornbluh have stated the number in two different ways?

A WELL-ARGUED SOLUTION: GIVING GUIDELINES FOR IMPLEMENTATION

Patrick O'Malley identifies his proposed solution in his title, as does Kornbluh. But whereas O'Malley tries to convince his readers that more frequent exams would indeed help solve the problem he has defined, Kornbluh can safely assume her readers will appreciate that her proposed solution — a flexible work schedule — would help solve the problem. Although she does not have to demonstrate that her proposed solution would solve the problem, Kornbluh does have to convince readers that her proposed solution is feasible — that it could be implemented at little cost and within a reasonable time.

ANALYZE & WRITE

Write a few paragraphs analyzing how Kornbluh argues that her solution is feasible:

1 Reread paragraph 5. Kornbluh states that the "flexibility arrangement will not be the same in every company, nor even for each employee working within the same organization." Given her audience — which includes employers as well as employees — why do you think she includes this statement? How worrisome or reassuring is this statement likely to be?

2 Skim paragraphs 16–22, in which Kornbluh sets out the guidelines for what employees and employers should do to implement her solution. Notice the *would*, *should*, and *could* verb forms she uses, and consider why she uses them.

3 What, if anything, do you think is missing from Kornbluh's description of how to implement her solution? What difficulties would need to be overcome?

AN EFFECTIVE RESPONSE TO OBJECTIONS AND ALTERNATIVE SOLUTIONS: ANTICIPATING ALTERNATIVES

Proposal writers need to anticipate alternative solutions their readers may prefer. O'Malley, for example, brings up several alternatives to improve students' study skills, such as giving students frequent study questions and handing out possible exam topics to help students prepare. He acknowledges the benefits of some of these solutions but also points out their shortcomings, arguing that his solution is preferable to the alternatives.

┌─ ANALYZE & WRITE ───

Write a few paragraphs analyzing how Kornbluh responds to alternative solutions and an objection to her proposed solution:

1. Reread paragraphs 2–3 and 10–12. Identify the alternative solutions readers could claim are already in place to solve the problem of the "juggler family." How does Kornbluh try to refute these alternative solutions. Is she successful?

2. Reread paragraph 21, in which Kornbluh anticipates an objection. What is the objection, and how does she handle it? How effective is her response in allaying readers' concerns?

3. Now assess the effectiveness of Kornbluh's refutation of the alternative solution and the effectiveness of her response to the objection she anticipates. Has Kornbluh done enough to anticipate and respond to objections and alternative solutions? Why or why not?

A CLEAR, LOGICAL ORGANIZATION: USING HEADINGS

Writers sometimes use headings to make it easy for readers to follow a complicated proposal. In long proposals, headings can be especially helpful. But what do they add to a short essay like this one?

┌─ ANALYZE & WRITE ───

Write a couple of paragraphs analyzing and evaluating Kornbluh's use of headings:

1. Highlight each heading.

2. Examine the role each heading plays in relation to the paragraphs that follow it. Look particularly at the relationship between the heading and the topic sentences.

3. Why do you think Kornbluh chose to include these headings? Do they help make the proposal logical and easy to follow? How would omitting the headings affect readers?

For more reading selections, including a multimodal selection, go to **bedfordstmartins.com/theguide/epages**.

[RESPOND]

Consider possible topics: Improving living or working conditions.

If you are interested in the problem Kornbluh describes, you might suggest other ways of helping parents juggle their work and family responsibilities. For example, consider writing a proposal for increasing opportunities for one or more parents to work at home via telecommuting. Alternatively, you might consider a proposal to improve the living or working conditions of a group of people. Focus on a problem a particular category of people face. For example, think of ways to help elderly and infirm people in your community who need transportation, or elementary-school kids who have no after-school programs. Alternatively, devise solutions to problems that affect college students—for example, the creation of job-training or referral programs to help college students find work on or near campus, or recycling and "green" energy solutions that will help students living in dorms limit their impact on the environment.

Proposals for solving problems can take many forms. Proposals to obtain funding usually include a statement of the problem, the proposed solution, and the methods for achieving the solution. These are often used in government and the academic world to present possible solutions to problems like rising costs or lower-than-expected graduation rates. These kinds of proposals are usually written in a dispassionate tone and often use the third-person point of view (*The organization provides services to . . .*) or the passive voice (*Services are provided to . . .*).

Proposals in Public Service Announcements

Less formal proposals may be conveyed in self-help manuals (like *The Secret* or *The Seven Habits of Highly Effective People*) and even in public service announcements (like the one shown here). Informal proposals use a casual tone and may use the first person (*I*) or second person (*you*). They are likely to use writing strategies like comparison or contrast to make the proposed solution seem familiar. This public service announcement uses a visual comparison, equating take-out lunch with money (what usually travels in the back of an armored car); it uses the green of cash and some of the decorations that appear on money in the bottom third of the ad to emphasize the connection; and it uses the second person (*you*) to address the reader directly.

While self-help manuals and advertisements may not exhibit all the basic features of formal proposals, the best ones use images and text efficiently to define a problem (such as poor money management) and suggest a feasible solution (such as packing a lunch).

For an interactive version of this feature, plus activities, go to **bedfordstmartins.com /theguide/epages**.

That 9 dollar lunch is worth more than you think. Like 19,000 dollars more.

Pack your own lunch instead of going out. $6 saved a day x 5 days a week x 10 years x 6% interest = $19,592. That could be money in your pocket. Small changes today. Big bucks tomorrow. Go to feedthepig.org for free savings tips.

GUIDE TO WRITING

The Writing Assignment

Write an essay proposing a solution to a problem. Choose a problem faced by a community or group to which you belong, and address your proposal to one or more members of the group or to outsiders who might help solve the problem.

This Guide to Writing is designed to help you compose your own proposal and apply what you have learned from reading other essays in the same genre. This Starting Points chart will help you find answers to questions you might have about composing a proposal. Use the chart to find the guidance you need, when you need it.

STARTING POINTS: PROPOSING A SOLUTION

How do I come up with a problem to write about?

- Assess the genre's basic features: A focused, well-defined problem. (pp. 299–300)
- Consider possible topics. (pp. 316, 322, 328)
- Choose a problem for which you can propose a solution. (p. 332)
- Test Your Choice (pp. 332–33)

A Focused, Well-Defined Problem

How can I best define the problem for my readers?

- A Focused, Well-Defined Problem: Establishing the Problem (p. 314)
- A Focused, Well-Defined Problem: Citing Research Studies (p. 320)
- A Focused, Well-Defined Problem: Using Statistics (pp. 326–27)
- Frame the problem for your readers. (pp. 333–34)
- Use statistics to establish the problem's existence and seriousness. (pp. 335–36)
- Assess how the problem has been framed, and reframe it for your readers. (pp. 336–37)
- A Troubleshooting Guide: A Focused, Well-Defined Problem. (p. 344)

A Well-Argued Solution

How do I come up with a plausible solution?

- Assess the genre's basic features: A well-argued solution. (pp. 301–2)
- A Well-Argued Solution: Proving It Works (pp. 314–15)
- A Well-Argued Solution: Giving Guidelines for Implementation (p. 327)
- Develop a possible solution. (pp. 337–38)
- Research your proposal. (pp. 338–39)

A Well-Argued Solution

How do I construct an argument supporting my solution?

- Assess the genre's basic features: A well-argued solution. (pp. 301–2)
- A Well-Argued Solution: Using Comparison-Contrast and Classification (p. 321)
- Explain your solution. (p. 338)
- Research your proposal. (pp. 338–39)
- A Troubleshooting Guide: A Well-Argued Solution (p. 344)

An Effective Response to Objections and Alternative Solutions

How do I respond to possible objections to my solution?

- Assess the genre's basic features: An effective response to objections and alternative solutions. (pp. 302–3)
- An Effective Response to Objections and Alternative Solutions: Handling Objections (p. 321)
- Develop a response to objections or alternative solutions. (pp. 339–40)

How do I respond to possible alternative solutions?

- Assess the genre's basic features: An effective response to objections and alternative solutions. (pp. 302–3)
- An Effective Response to Objections and Alternative Solutions: Rejecting the Standard Solution (p. 315)
- An Effective Response to Objections and Alternative Solutions: Anticipating Alternatives (pp. 327–28)
- Develop a response to objections or alternative solutions. (pp. 339–40).

A Clear, Logical Organization

How can I help my readers follow my argument?

- Assess the genre's basic features: A clear, logical organization. (pp. 303–4)
- A Clear, Logical Organization: Using Topic Sentences (pp. 315–16)
- A Clear, Logical Organization: Using Graphs (p. 322)
- A Clear, Logical Organization: Using Headings (p. 328)
- Create an outline that will organize your proposal effectively for your readers. (pp. 340–41)
- A Troubleshooting Guide: A Clear, Logical Organization (p. 344)

Writing a Draft: Invention, Research, Planning, and Composing

The activities in this section will help you choose and research a problem as well as develop and organize an argument for your proposed solution. Do the activities in any order that makes sense to you (and your instructor), and return to them as needed as you revise. Your writing in response to many of these activities can be used in a rough draft that you will be able to improve after receiving feedback from your classmates and instructor.

Choose a problem for which you can propose a solution.

When choosing a problem, keep in mind that it must be

- important to you and of concern to your readers;
- solvable, at least in part;
- one that you can research sufficiently in the time you have.

Choosing a problem affecting a group to which you belong (for example, as a classmate, teammate, participant in an online game site, or garage band member) or a place at which you have worked (a coffee shop, community pool, or radio station) gives you an advantage: You can write as an expert. You know the history of the problem, you know who to interview, and perhaps you have already thought about possible solutions. Moreover, you know who to address and how to persuade that audience to take action on your proposed solution.

If you already have a problem and possible solution(s) in mind, skip to Test Your Choice below. If you need to find a problem, consider the possible topics following the readings and the suggestions in the following chart. Keeping a chart like this could help you get started exploring creative solutions to real-life problems.

	Problems	**Possible Solutions**
School	Can't get into required courses	Make them large lecture courses.
		Make them online or hybrid courses.
		Give priority to majors.
Community	No safe place for children to play	Use school yards for after-school sports.
		Get high school students or senior citizens to tutor kids.
		Make pocket parks for neighborhood play.
		Offer programs for kids at branch libraries.
Work	Inadequate training for new staff	Make a training video or Web site.
		Assign experienced workers to mentor trainees (for bonus pay)

TEST YOUR CHOICE

After you have made a provisional choice, ask yourself the following questions:

- Do I understand the problem well enough to convince my readers that it really exists and is worth their attention?
- Do I have some ideas about how to solve this problem?
- Do I know enough about the problem, or can I learn what I need to know in the time allotted?

To try out your choice of a problem, get together with two or three other students:

Presenters.   Take turns identifying the problem you're thinking of writing about.

Listeners.   Briefly tell each presenter whether the problem seems important, and why.

As you plan and draft your proposal, you may need to reconsider your choice (for example, if you discover you don't have any good ideas about how to solve the problem) and either refocus it or choose a different problem to write about. If you have serious doubts about your choice, discuss them with your instructor before starting over with a new problem.

:: Frame the problem for your readers.

Once you have made a preliminary choice of a problem, consider what you know about it, what research will help you explore what others think about it, and how you can interest your readers in solving it. Then determine how you can frame or reframe it in a way that appeals to readers' values and concerns. Use the questions and sentence strategies that follow as a jumping-off point; you can make them your own as you revise later.

To learn more about conducting surveys and interviews, consult Chapter 24, pp. 684–88. For advice on listing, cubing, and freewriting, see Chapter 11, pp. 510, 514–15.

WAYS IN

WHAT IS THE PROBLEM?

What do I already know about the problem?

Brainstorm a list: Spend 10 minutes listing everything you know about the problem. Write quickly, leaving judgment aside for the moment. After the 10 minutes are up, you can review your list and highlight or star the most promising information.

Use cubing: Probe the problem from a variety of perspectives:

- Describe the problem.
- Compare the problem to other, similar problems, or contrast it with other, related problems.
- Connect the problem to other problems in your experience.
- Analyze the problem to identify its parts, its causes, or its effects.
- Apply the problem to a real-life situation.

Freewrite: Write without stopping for 5 or 10 minutes about the problem. Don't stop to reflect or consider; if you hit a roadblock, just

WHY SHOULD READERS CARE?

How can I convince readers the problem is real and deserves attention?

Give an example to make the problem specific:

▶ Recently, _____ has been [in the news/ in movies/a political issue] because of [name event].

Example:
Lately, the issue of bullying has been in the news, sparked by the suicide of Tyler Clementi . . . , a gay college student who was a victim of cyber-bullying. (Bornstein, par. 1)

Use a scenario or anecdote to dramatize the problem:

▶ [Describe time and place.] [Describe problem related to time or place.]

Example:
It's late at night. The final's tomorrow. You got a C on the midterm, so this one will make or break you. (O'Malley, par. 1)

(continued)

keep coming back to the problem. At the end of the specified time, review your writing and highlight or underline promising ideas.

What do others think about the problem? Conduct surveys:

- Talk to a variety of students at your school (your friends and others).
- Discuss the problem with neighbors or survey shoppers at a local mall.
- Discuss the problem with coworkers or people who work at similar jobs.

Conduct interviews:

- Interview faculty experts.
- Discuss the issue with businesspeople in the community.
- Interview local officials (members of the city council, the fire chief, the local labor union representative).

What do most of my readers already think about the problem?

- ▶ Many complain about _____ but do nothing because solving it seems [too hard/too costly].
- ▶ Some think _____ is [someone else's responsibility/not that big of a problem].
- ▶ Others see _____ as a matter of [fairness/human decency].

Who suffers from the problem?

- ▶ Studies have shown that _____ mostly affects [name group(s)].

Example:
> Research has shown that . . . parents with young children and working welfare recipients—the workers who need access to paid leave the most—are the least likely to have these benefits. . . . Children, in particular, pay a heavy price. (Kornbluh, pars. 10, 13)

Cite statistics to show the severity of the problem:

- ▶ It has recently been reported that _____ percent of [name group] are [specify problem].

Example:
> Today fully 70 percent of families with children . . . are working 10 more hours a week than in 1979 (Bernstein and Kornbluh). (Kornbluh, par. 1)

Describe the problem's negative consequences:

- ▶ According to [name expert/study], [state problem] is affecting [name affected group]: [insert quote from expert.]

Example:
> Sian Beilock, a psychology professor at the University of Chicago, points out that "stressing about doing well on an important exam can backfire, leading students to 'choke under pressure' or to score less well than they might otherwise score if the stakes weren't so high." (O'Malley, par. 2)

Why should readers care about solving the problem?

- ▶ We're all in this together. _____ is not a win-lose proposition. If [name group] loses, we all lose.
- ▶ If we don't try to solve _____, no one else will.
- ▶ Doing nothing will only make _____ worse.
- ▶ We have a moral responsibility to do something about _____ .

Writing a Draft

GUIDE TO READING
GUIDE TO WRITING
A WRITER AT WORK
THINKING CRITICALLY

335

| TEST YOUR CHOICE |

Ask two or three other students to help you develop your plan to define the problem.

Presenters. Briefly explain how you are thinking of framing or reframing the problem for your audience. Use the following language as a model for presenting your problem, or use language of your own.

▶ I plan to define the problem [not as _____ but as _____ /in terms of _____] because I think my readers [describe briefly] will share my [concerns, values, or priorities].

Listeners. Tell the presenter what response this way of framing the problem elicits from you and why. You may also explain how you think other readers might respond. Use the following language as a model for structuring your response, or use your own words.

▶ I'm [also/not] concerned about _____ because [state reasons].

▶ I [agree/disagree] that _____ because [state reasons].

Use statistics to establish the problem's existence and seriousness.

Statistics can be helpful in establishing that a problem exists and is serious. (In fact, using statistics is offered as an option in the preceding Ways In box.) To define her problem, Kornbluh uses statistics in three different forms: percentages, numbers, and proportions.

> Between 1970 and 2000, the percentage of mothers in the workforce rose from 38 to 67 percent (Smolensky and Gootman). Moreover, the number of hours worked by dual-income families has increased dramatically. Couples with children worked a full 60 hours a week in 1979. By 2000 they were working 70 hours a week (Bernstein and Kornbluh). And more parents than ever are working long hours. In 2000, nearly 1 out of every 8 couples with children was putting in 100 hours a week or more on the job, compared to only 1 out of 12 families in 1970 (Jacobs and Gerson). (par. 7)

percentage

number

proportion

Percentages can seem quite impressive, but sometimes without the raw numbers readers may not appreciate just how remarkable the percentages really are. In the following example, readers can see at a glance that the percentage Kornbluh cites is truly significant:

> In addition to working parents, there are over 44.4 million Americans who provide care to another adult, often an older relative. Fifty-nine percent of these caregivers either work or have worked while providing care ("Caregiving"). (par. 8)

To establish that there is a widespread perception among working parents that the problem is serious, Kornbluh cites survey results:

In a 2002 report by the Families and Work Institute, 45 percent of employees reported that work and family responsibilities interfered with each other "a lot" or "some" and 67 percent of employed parents report that they do not have enough time with their children (Galinsky, Bond, and Hill). (par. 9)

This example shows that nearly half of all employees have had difficulty juggling work and family responsibilities. The readers Kornbluh is addressing—employers—are likely to find this statistic important because it suggests that their employees are spending time worrying about or attending to family responsibilities instead of focusing on work.

For statistics to be persuasive, they must be from sources that readers consider reliable. Researchers' trustworthiness, in turn, depends on their credentials as experts in the field they are investigating and also on the degree to which they are disinterested, or free from bias. Kornbluh provides a list of works cited that readers can follow up on to check whether the sources are indeed reliable. The fact that some of her sources are books published by major publishers (Harvard University Press and Basic Books, for example) helps establish their credibility. Other sources she cites are research institutes (such as the New America Foundation, Economic Policy Institute, and Families and Work Institute), which readers can easily check out. Another factor that adds to the appearance of reliability is that Kornbluh cites statistics from a range of sources instead of relying on only one or two. Moreover, the statistics are current and clearly relevant to her argument.

To find statistics relating to the problem (or possible solution) you are writing about, explore the state, local, or tribal sections of USA.gov, the U.S. government's official Web portal, or visit the Library of Congress page "State Government Information," www.loc.gov/rr/news/stategov/stategov.html, and follow the links. In particular, visit the U.S. Census Bureau's Web site (www.census.gov), which offers reliable statistics on a wide variety of issues.

To learn more about assessing reliability, consult Chapter 25, pp. 692–96.

To learn more about finding government documents, see Chapter 24, p. 679.

⁝ Assess how the problem has been framed, and reframe it for your readers.

Once you have a good idea of what you and your readers think about the problem, consider how others have framed the problem and how you might be able to reframe it for your readers.

WAYS IN

HOW HAS THE PROBLEM BEEN FRAMED?	HOW CAN I REFRAME THE PROBLEM?
Sink or Swim Argument	**Teaching Should Not Be Punitive Argument**
Example: Providing tutoring for students who are failing a course is wrong because students should do what they need to do to pass the course or face the consequences. That's the way the system is supposed to work.	**Example:** Providing tutoring for students who are failing a course assumes the purpose of education is learning, not testing for its own sake or punishing those who have not done well.

Don't Reward Failure Argument	**Encourage Success Argument**
Example: Providing tutoring for students who are failing a course is like a welfare system that makes underprepared students dependent and second-class citizens.	**Example:** Providing tutoring for students who are failing a course encourages students to work hard and value doing well in school.
Reverse Discrimination Argument	**Level Playing Ground Argument**
Example: Providing tutoring for students who are failing a course is unfair to the other students who don't need assistance.	**Example:** Providing tutoring for students who are failing a course is a way to make up for inadequacies in previous schooling.
Win-Lose Argument	**Win-Win Argument**
Example: Providing tutoring for students who are failing a course ignores the fact that grades should fall on a bell curve—that is, an equal proportion of students should get an *F* as get an *A*.	**Example:** Providing tutoring for students who are failing a course assumes that it would be a good thing if every student earned an *A*. Providing tutoring enhances learning.

Develop a possible solution.

The following activities will help you devise a solution and develop an argument to support it. If you have already found a solution, you may want to skip this activity and go directly to the Explain Your Solution section (p. 338).

HOW CAN I SOLVE THIS PROBLEM?

One way to generate ideas is to write steadily for at least five minutes, exploring some of the possible ways of solving the problem. Consider using the following approaches as a jumping-off point:

- **Adapt a solution that has been tried or proposed for a similar problem.**

  Example: Bornstein's solution to bullying is to teach children empathy, as the Roots of Empathy program does.

- **Focus on eliminating a cause or minimizing an effect of the problem.**

  Example: O'Malley's solution to stressful high-stakes exams is to eliminate the cause of the stress by inducing instructors to give more frequent low-stakes exams.

- **See the problem as part of a larger system, and explore solutions to the system.**

  Example: Kornbluh's solution is for employers to work with employees to enhance job flexibility.

WAYS IN

(continued)

- **Focus on solving a small part of the problem.**

  Example: Brownell and Frieden's solution to obesity is to reduce the consumption of sugared beverages through taxation.

- **Look at the problem from different points of view.**

  Example: Consider what students, teachers, parents, or administrators might think could be done to help solve the problem.

- **Think of a specific example of the problem, and consider how you could solve it.**

  Example: O'Malley could have focus on solving the problem of high-stakes exams in his biology course.

For more idea-generating strategies, see Chapter 11.

Explain your solution.

You may yet know for certain whether you will be able to construct a convincing argument to support your solution, but you should choose a solution that you feel motivated to pursue. Use the questions and sentence strategies that follow to help you put your ideas in writing. You will likely want to revise what you come up with later, but the questions and sentence strategies below may provide a convenient jumping-off point.

WAYS IN

HOW CAN I EXPLAIN HOW MY SOLUTION WOULD HELP SOLVE THE PROBLEM?	HOW CAN I EXPLAIN THAT MY SOLUTION IS FEASIBLE?
It would eliminate a cause of the problem.	**It could be implemented.**
▶ Research shows it would reduce _____.	Describe the major stages or steps necessary to carry out your solution.
It has worked elsewhere.	**We can afford it.**
▶ It works in _____, _____, and _____, as studies evaluating it show.	Explain what it would cost to put the solution into practice.
It would change people's behavior.	**It would not take too much time.**
▶ _____ would [discourage/encourage] people to _____.	Create a rough schedule or timeline to show how long it would take to make the necessary arrangements.

Research your proposal.

You may have already begun researching the problem and familiarizing yourself with alternative solutions that have been offered, or you may have ideas about what you need to research. If you are proposing a solution to a problem about which others have written, use the following research strategies to help you find out what solutions others have proposed or tried. You may also use these strategies to find out how others have defined the problem and demonstrated its seriousness.

- Enter keywords or phrases related to your solution (or problem) into the search box of an all-purpose database, such as *Academic OneFile* (InfoTrac) or *Academic Search Complete* (EBSCOHost), to find relevant articles in magazines and journals; in the database Lexis/Nexis to find articles in newspapers; or in library catalogs to find books and other resources. (Database names may change, and what is available will differ from school to school. Some libraries may even combine all three into one search link on the library's home page. Ask a librarian if you need help.) Patrick O'Malley could have tried a combination of keywords, such as *learning* and *test anxiety,* or variations on his terms (*frequent testing, improve retention*) to find relevant articles.

- Bookmark or keep a record of the URLs of promising sites, and download or copy information you could use in your essay. When available, download PDF files rather than HTML files, because these are likely to include visuals, such as graphs and charts. If you copy and paste relevant information into your notes, be careful to distinguish all material from sources from your own ideas.

- Remember to record source information and to cite and document any sources you use, including visuals and interviews.

For more about searching for information, consult Chapter 24. For more about avoiding plagiarism, see Chapter 26, pp. 698–700. For more about documenting sources, consult Chapter 27 (MLA style) or Chapter 28 (APA style).

▓ Develop a response to objections or alternative solutions.

The topics you considered when developing an argument for your solution may be the same topics you need to consider when developing a response to likely criticisms of your proposal—answering possible objections to your solution or alternative solutions readers may prefer. The following sentence strategies may help you start drafting an effective response.

HOW CAN I DRAFT A REFUTATION OR CONCESSION?

To draft a refutation, try beginning with sentence strategies like these:

- ▶ Some people think we can't afford to do [name solution], but it would only cost $_____$ to put my solution in place compared to $ _____$, the cost of [doing nothing/implementing an alternative solution].

- ▶ Although it might take [number of months/years] to implement this solution, it would actually take longer to implement [alternative solution].

- ▶ There are critics who think that only a few people would benefit from solving this problem, but _____ would benefit because _____ .

- ▶ Some may suggest that I favor this solution because I would benefit personally; however, the fact is we would all benefit because _____ .

WAYS IN

(continued)

▶ Some may claim that this solution has been tried and hasn't worked. But research shows that [explain how proposed solution has worked] **or** my solution differs from past experiments in these important ways: _____, _____, and _____ .

To draft a concession, try beginning with sentence strategies like these:

▶ I agree with those who [claim X/object on X grounds]; therefore, instead of _____, I think we should pursue _____ .

▶ If _____ seems too [time-consuming/expensive], let's try _____ .

▶ Where _____ is a concern, I think [name alternative] should be followed.

▶ Although _____ is the best way to deal with a problem like this, under [describe special circumstances], I agree that _____ should be done.

⸬ Create an outline that will organize your proposal effectively for your readers.

For more on outlining, see Chapter 11, pp. 510–14.

Whether you have rough notes or a complete draft, making an outline of what you have written can help you organize your essay effectively for your audience. Compare the possible outlines below to see how you might organize the essay depending on whether your readers agree that a serious problem exists and are open to your solution—or not.

If you are writing primarily for readers who *acknowledge that the problem exists and are open to your solution:*

  I. Introduce the problem, concluding with a thesis statement asserting your solution.

 II. Demonstrate the problem's seriousness: Frame the problem in a way that prepares readers for the solution.

III. Describe the proposed solution: Show what could be done to implement it.

IV. Refute objections.

 V. Conclude: Urge action on your solution.

If you are writing primarily for readers who *do not recognize the problem or are likely to prefer alternative solutions:*

  I. Reframe the problem: Identify common ground, and acknowledge alternative ways readers might see the problem.

 II. Concede strengths, but emphasize the weaknesses of alternative solution(s) that readers might prefer.

III. Describe the proposed solution: Give reasons and provide evidence to demonstrate that it is preferable to the alternative(s).

IV. Refute objections.

 V. Conclude: Reiterate shared values.

Whatever organizational strategy you adopt, do not hesitate to change your outline as necessary while drafting and revising. For instance, you might find it more effective to hold back on presenting your solution until you have discussed unacceptable alternatives. The purpose of an outline is to identify the basic components of your proposal and to help you organize it effectively, not to lock you into a particular structure.

Write the opening sentences.

Review your invention writing to see if you have already written something that would work to launch your essay, or try out one or two ways of beginning your essay—possibly from the list that follows:

- A scenario (like O'Malley)
- Statistics (like Kornbluh)
- News events demonstrating the seriousness of the problem (like Bornstein)
- A quotation that highlights support for your solution (like Brownell and Frieden)
- A comparison with other places where the solution has been tried successfully
- A preview of the negative consequences if the problem goes unsolved

Draft your proposal.

By this point, you have done a lot of research and writing to

- focus and define a problem, and develop a solution to it;
- support your solution with reasons and evidence your readers will find persuasive;
- refute or concede objections and alternative solutions;
- organize your ideas to make them clear, logical, and effective for readers.

Now stitch that material together to create a draft. The next two parts of this Guide to Writing will help you evaluate and improve that draft.

Evaluating the Draft: Getting a Critical Reading

Your instructor may arrange a peer review session in class or online, where you can exchange drafts with your classmates and give each other a thoughtful critical reading, pointing out what works well and suggesting ways to improve the draft. A good critical reading does three things:

1. It lets the writer know how well the reader understands the point of the draft.
2. It praises what works best.
3. It indicates where the draft could be improved and makes suggestions on how to improve it.

You can use the Critical Reading Guide on the next page to guide your discussion.

A CRITICAL READING GUIDE

A Focused, Well-Defined Problem

> Has the writer framed the problem effectively?

Summarize: Tell the writer what you understand the problem to be.

Praise: Give an example where the problem and its significance come across effectively such as where an example dramatizes the problem or statistics establish its significance.

Critique: Tell the writer where readers might need more information about the problem's causes and consequences, or where more might be done to establish its seriousness.

A Well-Argued Solution

> Has the writer argued effectively for the solution?

Summarize: Tell the writer what you understand the proposed solution to be.

Praise: Give an example in the essay where support for the solution is presented especially effectively—for example, note particularly strong reasons, writing strategies that engage readers, or design or visual elements that make the solution clear and accessible.

Critique: Tell the writer where the argument for the solution could be strengthened—for example, where steps for implementation could be laid out more clearly, where the practicality of the solution could be established more convincingly, or where additional support for reasons should be added.

An Effective Response to Objections and Alternative Solutions

> Has the writer responded effectively to objections or alternative solutions?

Summarize: Tell the writer what you understand to be the objections or alternative solutions that he or she is responding to.

Praise: Give an example in the essay where the writer concedes or refutes a likely objection to the argument effectively, and where reasons showing the limitations of alternative solutions are most effectively presented.

Critique: Tell the writer where concessions and refutations could be more convincing, where possible objections or reservations should be taken into account or alternative solutions should be discussed, where reasons for not accepting other solutions need to be strengthened, or where common ground should be sought with advocates of other positions.

Improving the Draft

GUIDE TO READING
GUIDE TO WRITING
A WRITER AT WORK
THINKING CRITICALLY

343

A Clear, Logical Organization

Is the proposal clearly and logically organized?

Summarize: Underline the sentence(s) in which the writer establishes the problem and proposes a solution. Also identify the places where the writer forecasts the argument, supplies topic sentences, and uses transitions or repeats key words and phrases.

Praise: Give an example of how the essay succeeds in being readable—for example, in its overall organization, its use of forecasting statements or key terms introduced in its thesis and strategically repeated elsewhere, its use of topic sentences or transitions, or an especially effective opening or closing.

Critique: Tell the writer where the readability could be improved. For example, point to places where using key terms would help or where a topic sentence could be made clearer, where the use of transitions could be improved or added, or indicate whether the beginning or ending could be more effective.

Before concluding your peer review, be sure to address any of the writer's concerns that have not been discussed already.

Making Comments Electronically   Most word processing software offers features that allow you to insert comments directly into the text of someone else's document. Many readers prefer to make their comments this way because it tends to be faster than writing on hard copy and space is virtually unlimited; it also eliminates the process of deciphering handwritten comments. Where such features are not available, simply typing comments directly into a document in a contrasting color can provide the same advantages.

For a printable version of this Critical Reading Guide, go to **bedfordstmartins .com/theguide**.

Improving the Draft: Revising, Formatting, Editing, and Proofreading

Start improving your draft by reflecting on what you have written thus far:

- Review the Test Your Choice responses and critical reading comments from your classmates, instructor, or writing center tutor: What are your readers getting at?
- Take another look at the notes from your earlier research and writing activities: What else should you consider?
- Review your draft: What else can you do to make your proposal more effective?

Revise your draft.

If your readers are having difficulty with your draft, or if you think there is room for improvement, try some of the strategies listed in the Troubleshooting Guide that follows. It can help you fine-tune your presentation of the genre's basic features.

A TROUBLESHOOTING GUIDE

A Focused, Well-Defined Problem

My readers aren't convinced that my problem is serious or even exists.

- Change the way you present the problem to address readers' concerns more directly.
- Add information—statistics, examples, description, and so on—that your audience is likely to find persuasive or that they can relate to.
- Consider adding visuals, such as graphs, tables, or charts, if these would help clarify the problem for your audience.

A Well-Argued Solution

My readers aren't convinced that my solution is a good one.

- Try to make your solution more convincing by discussing similar solutions used successfully elsewhere or by demonstrating more clearly how it will solve the problem.
- Add evidence (such as facts, statistics, and examples) to support your reasons.
- Review the steps needed to enact your solution; if necessary, lay them out more clearly.

An Effective Response to Objections and Alternative Solutions

My readers have raised objections to my solution.

- Cite research studies, statistics, or examples to refute readers' objections.
- Concede valid points or modify your solution to accommodate the criticism.
- If you can neither refute nor accommodate objections, rethink your solution.

My readers have proposed alternative solutions that I don't discuss.

- If possible, establish common ground with those who propose alternative solutions, but show why their solutions will not work as well as yours.
- If you cannot demonstrate that your solution is preferable, consider arguing that both solutions deserve serious consideration.

A Clear, Logical Organization

My readers are confused by my proposal or find it hard to follow.

- Try outlining your proposal to be sure that the overall organization is strong; if it is not, try moving, adding, or deleting sections to strengthen coherence.
- Consider adding a forecasting statement and using key terms in your thesis and repeating them when you discuss your main points.
- Check to see that you use topic sentences to introduce your main points and that you provide appropriate transitions.
- Consider adding headings to make the structure of your proposal clearer.

Improving the Draft

GUIDE TO READING
GUIDE TO WRITING
A WRITER AT WORK
THINKING CRITICALLY

345

Think about design.

Proposals frequently include graphics because they help demonstrate the seriousness of the problem or show that the proposal will have the desired result. The following graphics are from the project highlighted in the In the Workplace scenario (p. 297). It was designed by the truck driver who proposed a solution to the problem of too few short-haul drivers. The line graph demonstrates the trajectory of the demand for short-haul drivers, and the pie charts show that one demographic group—women—is not projected to increase, despite the demand. If you want to show change over time or indicate percentages of groups affected, for example, consider adding a line, bar graph, or pie chart in your proposal.

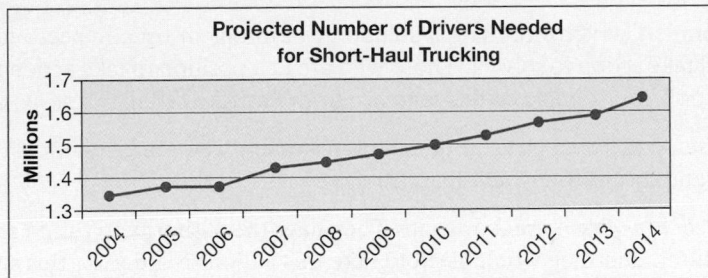

Line graph demonstrates the growing seriousness of the problem

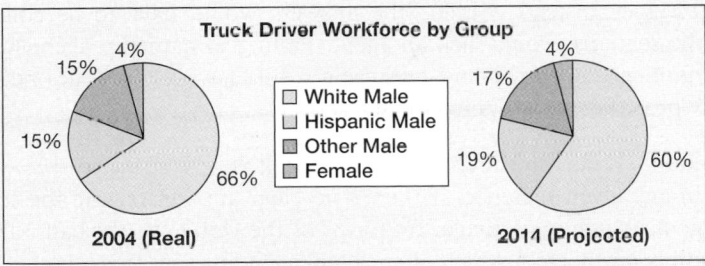

Pie charts highlight an opportunity to solve the problem: increasing the number of women drivers

Edit and proofread your draft.

Several errors occur often in essays that propose solutions: ambiguous use of *this* and *that,* and sentences that lack an agent. The following guidelines will help you check your essay for these common errors.

Avoiding Ambiguous Use of *This* and *That*

The Problem   Because you must frequently refer to the problem and the solution in a proposal, you will often use pronouns to avoid the monotony or wordiness of repeatedly referring to them by name. Using *this* and *that* vaguely to refer to other words or ideas, however, can confuse readers.

The Correction   Add a specific noun after *this* or *that*. For example, in his essay in this chapter, Patrick O'Malley writes:

> Furthermore, professors could help students prepare for midterm and final exams by providing sets of questions from which the exam questions will be selected.

This solution would have the advantage of reducing students' anxiety about learning every fact in the textbook. (par. 13)

O'Malley avoids an ambiguous *this* in the second sentence by adding the noun *solution*. (He might just as well have used *preparation* or *action* or *approach*.) Here's another example:

> Students would not resist a reasonable fee increase of $40 a year if that ^*increase*^ would pay for needed dormitory remodeling.

Revising Sentences That Lack an Agent

The Problem   A writer proposing a solution to a problem usually needs to indicate who should take action to solve it. Those who are in a position to take action are called "agents." Look, for example, at this sentence from Patrick O'Malley's proposal:

> To get students to complete the questions in a timely way, professors would have to collect and check the answers. (par. 12)

In this sentence, *professors* are the agents. They have the authority to assign and collect study questions, and they would need to take this action in order for this solution to be successfully implemented.

Had O'Malley instead written "the answers would have to be collected and checked," the sentence would lack an agent. Failing to name an agent would have made his argument less convincing, because it would have left unclear one of the key parts of any proposal: who is going to take action.

The Correction   When you revise your work, ask yourself *who* or *what* performed the action in any given sentence. If there's no clear answer, rewrite the sentence to give it an agent. Watch in particular for forms of the verb *to be* (the ball *was* dropped, exams should *be* given, etc.), which often signal agentless sentences.

> *Your staff should plan a survey*
> ▶ ~~A survey could be planned~~ to find out more about students' problems in scheduling the courses they need.

> *The registrar should extend*
> ▶ ~~Extending~~ the deadline to mid-quarter. ~~would make sense.~~

Note: Sometimes, however, agentless sentences are appropriate, as when the agent is clear from the context, unknown, or less important than the person or thing acted upon.

A Note on Grammar and Spelling Checkers

These tools can be helpful, but do not rely on them exclusively to catch errors in your text: Spelling checkers cannot catch misspellings that are themselves words, such as *to* for *too*. Grammar checkers miss some problems, sometimes give faulty advice for fixing problems, and can flag correct items as wrong. Use these tools as a second line of defense after your own (and, ideally, another reader's) proofreading and editing efforts.

For practice, go to **bedfordstmartins.com /theguide/exercisecentral** and click on Ambiguous Use of *This* and *That*.

For practice, go to **bedfordstmartins.com /theguide/exercisecentral** and click on Sentences That Lack an Agent.

Patrick O'Malley's Revision Process

This section focuses on student writer Patrick O'Malley's successful efforts to strengthen his argument for the solution he proposes in his essay, "More Testing, More Learning." Compare the following three paragraphs from his draft with paragraphs 4–7 of his final essay on pp. 304–10. As you read, take notes on the differences you observe.

> The predominant reason students perform better with multiple exams is that they improve their study habits. Greater regularity in test taking means greater regularity in studying for tests. Students prone to cramming will be forced to open their textbooks more often, keeping them away from long, "kamikaze" nights of studying. Regularity prepares them for the "real world" where you rarely take on large tasks at long intervals. Several tests also improve study habits by reducing procrastination. An article about procrastination from the *Journal of Counseling Psychology* reports that "students view exams as difficult, important, and anxiety provoking." These symptoms of anxiety leading to procrastination could be solved if individual test importance was lessened, reducing the stress associated with the perceived burden.

> With multiple exams, this anxiety decrease will free students to perform better. Several, less important tests may appear as less of an obstacle, allowing the students to worry less, leaving them free to concentrate on their work without any emotional hindrances. It is proven that "the performance of test-anxious subjects varies inversely with evaluation stress." It would also be to the psychological benefit of students if they were not subjected to the emotional ups and downs of large exams where they are virtually worry-free one moment and ready to check into the psychiatric ward the next.

> Lastly, with multiple exams, students can learn how to perform better on future tests in the class. Regular testing allows them to "practice" the information they learned, thereby improving future test scores. In just two exams, they are not able to learn the instructor's personal examination style, and are not given the chance to adapt their study habits to it. The *American Psychologist* concludes: "It is possible to influence teaching and learning by changing the type of tests."

One difference you may have noted between O'Malley's draft and revised paragraphs is the sequence of reasons he offers.

Draft	Revision
1. Improve study habits	1. Learn more
2. Decrease anxiety and improve performance	2. Perform better on tests
	3. Improve study habits
3. Perform better on future tests	4. Decrease anxiety

O'Malley made learning more his first reason after a classmate commented that professors (the target audience) would probably be more convinced by students' learning than by their improving their study habits or decreasing their anxiety. Here are some other improvements you may have noticed:

- **O'Malley's revised paragraphs are better focused.** For example, in the first draft paragraph, O'Malley switches from study habits to procrastination to anxiety. The revised paragraph (par. 6), by contrast, focuses on study habits. Also, reduced anxiety as a result of less procrastination is discussed in a single paragraph in the revision (par. 7), whereas in the draft it is mixed in with intellectual benefits in the first two paragraphs.

- **O'Malley's language is more precise.** For example, he changes "predominant reason" to "main reason" and "future tests" to "major exams, projects, and papers."

- **O'Malley's supporting evidence is more relevant.** For example, in the first draft paragraph, O'Malley includes a quotation that adds nothing, whereas in the revised paragraph (par. 6) the quotation he uses from the Harvard report provides convincing support for his claims and offers an effective conclusion to the paragraph.

Can you find other examples of better focus, more precise language, or relevant support? Did you notice any other improvements?

THINKING CRITICALLY

To think critically means to use all of the knowledge you have acquired from the information in this chapter, your own writing, the writing of other students, and class discussions to reflect deeply on your work for this assignment and the genre (or type) of writing you have produced. The benefit of thinking critically is proven and important: Thinking critically about what you have learned will help you remember it longer, ensuring that you will be able to put it to good use well beyond this writing course.

Reflecting on What You Have Learned

In this chapter, you have learned a great deal about this genre from reading several proposals and writing one of your own. To consolidate your learning, reflect not only on what you learned but also on how you learned it.

ANALYZE & WRITE

Write a blog post, a letter to your instructor, or an e-mail message to a student who will take this course next term, using the writing prompt below that seems most productive for you:

- Explain how your purpose and audience influenced *one* of your decisions as a writer, such as how you defined the problem, the strategies you used in presenting your solution, or the ways in which you attempted to counter possible objections.

- Discuss what you learned about yourself as a writer in the process of writing this particular essay. For example, what part of the process did you find most challenging? Did you try anything new, like getting a critical reading of your draft or outlining your draft in order to revise it?

- If you were to give advice to a friend who was about to write an essay proposing a solution to a problem, what would you say?

- Which of the readings in this chapter influenced your essay? Explain the influence, citing specific examples from your essay and the reading.

- If you got good advice from a critical reader, explain exactly how the person helped you—perhaps by questioning the way you addressed your audience or the kinds of evidence you offered in support of your proposed solution.

Reflecting on the Genre

No matter how well researched and well argued, many proposals are simply never carried out. In choosing among competing proposals, decision makers—who usually hold the power of the purse strings and necessarily represent a fairly conservative position—often go for the one that is cheapest, most expedient, and least disruptive. They may also choose small, incremental changes over more fundamental, radical solutions. While sometimes the most pragmatic choice, such immediately feasible solutions may merely patch over a problem, failing to solve it structurally. They may even inadvertently maintain the status quo. Worse, they can cause people to give up all attempts to resolve a problem after superficial treatments fail.

ANALYZE & WRITE

Write a page or two explaining how the genre pushes writers to select problems that are easy to solve or that reinforce the status quo. In your discussion, you might consider one or more of the following:

1. **Consider how proposals, because they invite us to select problems that are solvable, might inadvertently push us to focus on minor problems that are only a small part of a major problem.** Do any of the proposals you have read or written reveal this misdirection? If so, what do you think is the major problem in each case? Is the minor problem worth solving as a first step toward solving the major problem, or is it perhaps an unfortunate diversion?

2. **Reflect on arguments that we should not try to solve fundamental social problems by "throwing money at them."** Do you think this objection is a legitimate criticism of most proposals to solve social problems, or is it a justification for allowing the rich and powerful to maintain the status quo? What else, besides money, is required to solve serious social problems? Where are these other resources to come from?

3. **Write a page or two explaining your ideas about the frustrations of effecting real change.** Connect your ideas to your own essay and to the readings in this chapter.

8
Justifying an Evaluation

Before you buy a computer, phone, or video game, do you take a look at the reviews? Brief reviews, written by consumers, are easy to find, but some are more helpful than others. The best reviewers know what they're talking about. They don't just say what they like, they justify *why* they like it, giving examples or other evidence. Moreover, their judgment is based not on individual taste alone but on commonly held standards or criteria. For example, no one would consider it appropriate to judge an action film by its poetic dialogue or its subtle characterizations; instead, they would judge it by whether it delivers an exciting roller-coaster ride. The usefulness of an *evaluation*—be it a brief consumer comment or an expert's detailed review—depends on readers sharing or at least respecting the writer's criteria.

IN COLLEGE COURSES

For a film course, a student writes a review evaluating the last two Harry Potter movies in terms of how effectively they adapt J. K. Rowling's much-loved novel *Harry Potter and the Deathly Hallows* (2007). He compares key scenes in the films (like that in Part 2 in which Bellatrix Lestrange and the other Death Eaters attack Hogwarts in the final battle of the Second Wizarding War) with their counterparts in the novel. To support his judgment, he analyzes the sequence of camera shots and angles, which he illustrates with stills from the film and contrasts with quotations from the novel. In refuting critics who think the movies leave out too much detail, he treats his audience—his instructor and classmates—as if they were knowledgeable about the films and novel, and he is careful not to let his review fall into plot summary. He concludes that while some die-hard Harry Potter fans may be reluctant to sacrifice their vision to the director's, the films effectively capture the bleak mood and nerve-racking excitement of the last Harry Potter novel.

IN THE COMMUNITY

A motorcycle enthusiast evaluates the tour he took of the Harley-Davidson factory in York, Pennsylvania, for his blog. In his post, "Hog Heaven," he concedes that some may get restless waiting to get in—he waited over an hour—but he was entertained while he waited by the great old "hogs" from eras past on display. Most of the post focuses on how informative and exciting the factory tour was: his anticipation while donning safety glasses and headset, the buzz he got from being on the factory floor with over a thousand workers, and the thrill of watching a motorcycle roll off the assembly line. He uses photos from his visit to illustrate his post, and he links to Harley-Davidson's handy Ride Planner to help other enthusiasts plan their own trip.

IN THE WORKPLACE

At a conference on innovations in education, an elementary school teacher gives a presentation evaluating the effectiveness of using *Schoolhouse Rock!* videos to teach math to second graders. She tries to maintain objectivity in her voice that matches the objectivity of her evidence: a comparison of her students' test results with those of other students in her district who did not see the videos. She surmises that the *Schoolhouse Rock!* videos are an effective teaching tool because the witty lyrics and catchy tunes make the information memorable and fun, but she concedes that additional research is needed to rule out other factors, such as her own enthusiasm for the videos or the makeup of her class.

In this chapter, we ask you to choose a subject for evaluation that you can examine closely. Analyzing the selections in the Guide to Reading that follows will help you learn how to use appropriate criteria to support your judgment. The Guide to Writing later in the chapter will show you ways to use the basic features of the genre to make your evaluation interesting and persuasive.

PRACTICING THE GENRE

Choosing Appropriate Criteria and Examples

To practice developing an evaluative argument based on appropriate criteria, get together with two or three other students and follow the guidelines below:

Part 1. Begin by choosing a film everyone in the group has seen fairly recently. It's fine if you differ in your judgment of the film.

Next, discuss how you would classify the film in terms of **genre** (or *type*): comedy, romance, horror, or science fiction, for example. If you think it combines features of different genres, choose the genre you think best fits the film.

Then do the following:

- As a group, agree on one **criterion,** or *standard,* all of you typically use to evaluate a film in this genre. (For example, we usually expect a comedy to be funny.)
- Individually, find an example (such as a scene, a bit of dialogue, or a character) and briefly explain why you think that example supports your judgment that the film either does or does not meet the criterion the group has chosen.

Part 2. As a group, discuss what you learned from this activity:

- Reflect on the process of classifying a film by genre and choosing a criterion you could all agree was appropriate for evaluating a film of that kind. What disagreements or difficulties did your group have?
- Imagine you had an opportunity to post your film review on the Internet or publish it in the school newspaper. Would the criterion you chose still be appropriate for that audience? Would you have to justify it or choose a different criterion that your audience would be more likely to accept?

Analyzing Evaluations

As you read the selections in this chapter, you will see how different authors justify an evaluation. Analyzing how these writers present their subject, assert and justify their judgment, respond to alternative viewpoints, and organize their writing will help you see how you can use these techniques to make your own evaluations clear and compelling for your readers.

Determine the writer's purpose and audience.

Although writing a review usually helps writers better understand the criteria they use when making evaluations, most writers also hope to influence others. When reading the evaluations that follow, ask yourself questions like these about the writer's purpose and audience:

- What seems to be the writer's main *purpose*—for example, to influence readers' judgments and possibly their actions; to inspire readers to think critically about which criteria are appropriate for judging subjects of this kind; or to get readers to look at the subject in a new way?

- What does the writer assume about the *audience*—for example, that readers will accept the writer's judgment; use the review to make their own independent, informed judgments; already have an independent judgment; or have serious objections to the writer's argument?

Assess the genre's basic features.

Use the following to help you analyze and evaluate how reviewers use the genre's basic features. The strategies they typically use to make their evaluations helpful and convincing are illustrated below with examples from the readings in this chapter as well as sentence strategies you can experiment with later as you write your own evaluation.

> **Basic Features**
> A Well-Presented Subject
> A Well-Supported Judgment
> An Effective Response to Objections and Alternative Judgments
> A Clear, Logical Organization

A WELL-PRESENTED SUBJECT

Read first to identify the subject of the review, which is often named in the title (for example, "The Myth of Multitasking") and described briefly in the opening paragraphs. Look also to see how the writer classifies the subject in terms of its genre. Here's an example from the first reading selection in the chapter, by student William Akana:

> From start to finish, *Scott Pilgrim vs. the World* delivers intense action in a hilarious slacker movie that also somehow reimagines romantic comedy. (par. 1)

subgenres

genre

Even if readers don't recognize the title, Akana makes clear that the film he is reviewing combines elements of three different kinds of movies (or subgenres), so readers can determine whether he is using appropriate criteria, as you will see in the next section.

Knowing the genre is also important because readers need different kinds of information for different genres. For example, most readers of film reviews want to know what the story is about but do not want to know how it turns out. Film reviewers, therefore, try not to give too much plot detail, as you can see in this concise plot summary from Akana's essay:

> Pilgrim's life takes a dramatic turn when he falls in love with Ramona Flowers (Mary Elizabeth Winstead), who is, quite literally, the girl of his dreams. However, he soon discovers that Ramona's former lovers have formed a league of evil exes to destroy him, and he is forced to fight to the death to prove his love. (par. 2)

A WELL-SUPPORTED JUDGMENT

Reviewers assert their judgment of the subject, stating whether it is good or bad, better or worse than other things in the same genre. Typically, writers announce their judgment in a *thesis statement* early in the evaluation. Below are a couple of sentence strategies typically used for thesis statements in evaluations, followed by examples from reviews in this chapter:

▶ Other [genre] have [attempted/succeeded at/failed at] _____ [state goal]; what makes [name of subject] [a success/a failure] is _____ and _____ [state specific characteristics].

Genre
Reason
Subject
Judgment
(reasons implied)

EXAMPLE   The games industry has dreamed of creating one thing above all else — a game that is indistinguishable from a film, except that you can control the lead character. *With* LA Noire, *it just might, finally, have found the embodiment of that particular holy grail.* (Boxer, par. 1)

▶ [Subject] can be [appreciated/criticized] for _____ , _____ , and _____ [state/forecast reasons].

Genre
Subject
Judgment
Reasons

EXAMPLE   Although the film is especially targeted for old-school gamers, anime fans, and comic book fanatics, *Scott Pilgrim vs. the World can be appreciated and enjoyed* by all audiences because of its inventive special effects, clever dialogue, and artistic cinematography and editing. (Akana, par. 2)

When reading an evaluation, look for the thesis and examine it to see whether the writer asserts an *overall judgment* and, if so, what it is. Also note the features of the subject that are being praised or criticized and the *reasons* supporting the judgment. Finally, consider whether the reasons are based on criteria you would expect to be used for evaluating something of this kind. For example, one of William Akana's reasons is that the film uses "special effects" that are "inventive." To support this reason, he devotes two paragraphs to detailing some of the film's special effects. He also gives examples of "video-game-like gimmicks" such as "gamertags," describing them and also providing a screen shot to show what they look like (par. 3).

Examples and *visuals* are two common types of evidence reviewers provide. They also may *cite sources*. When reading an evaluation that cites sources, determine whether the writer *quotes, paraphrases,* or *summarizes* the source material. Also notice whether the writer uses a *signal phrase* to identify the source and establish its credibility.

QUOTE   As the educational researchers Patrick Terenzini and Ernest Pascarella concluded after analyzing twenty-six hundred reports on the effects of college on students:

> After taking into account the characteristics, abilities, and backgrounds students bring with them to college, we found that . . . (Gladwell, par. 8)

As neurologist Jordan Grafman told *Time* magazine: "Kids that are instant messaging while doing homework, playing games online and watching TV, I predict, aren't going to do well in the long run." (Rosen, par. 12)

Signal phrase

Quotation (indented)

Signal phrase
Quotation (integrated into sentence)

PARAPHRASE   Psychologist David Meyer at the University of Michigan believes that rather than a bottleneck in the brain, a process of "adaptive executive control" takes place, which "schedules task processes appropriately to obey instructions about their relative priorities and serial order," as he described to the *New Scientist*. Unlike many other researchers who study multitasking, Meyer is optimistic that, with training, the brain can learn to task-switch more effectively, and there is some evidence that certain simple tasks are amenable to such practice. But his research has also found that multitasking contributes to the release of stress hormones and adrenaline, which can cause long-term health problems if not controlled, and contributes to the loss of short-term memory. (Rosen, par. 8)

Signal phrase

For advice on when to indent quotations rather than use quotation marks, see Chapter 26, pp. 705–6.

Notice that the writer has quoted specific words and phrases that would be difficult to paraphrase accurately.

SUMMARIZE   Best-selling business advice author Timothy Ferriss also extols the virtues of "single-tasking" in his book, *The 4-Hour Workweek*. (Rosen, par. 5)

Signal phrase

How writers treat sources depends on the rhetorical situation. Certain formal situations, such as college assignments or scholarly publications, require writers to cite sources in the text and document them in a bibliography (called a list of *works cited* in many humanities disciplines or a list of *references* in the sciences and social sciences), as we can see in Akana's essay. In writing for a general audience—blogs and newspaper articles, for example—readers do not expect references to appear in the article, but they do expect sources to be named and their credentials to be identified in a signal phrase.

For more on citing sources, see Chapters 26, 27, and 28.

Another important strategy reviewers use to support their judgment is *comparison and contrast*. Malcolm Gladwell, for example, sets up his evaluation of the ranking system used by *U.S. News & World Report*'s annual "Best Colleges" guide by comparing it to the system used by *Car and Driver* magazine. Steve Boxer also relies on comparison and contrast in his video-game review:

Comparison cue

From start to finish, *LA Noire* feels like a film—*LA Confidential,* in fact, along with any similarly hard-boiled example of film noir adapted from stories by the likes of Chandler and Hammett. (par. 2)

Contrast cue

LA Noire largely does away with the free-roaming that enhanced the appeal of *Grand Theft Auto* and *Red Dead Redemption.* (par. 11)

AN EFFECTIVE RESPONSE TO OBJECTIONS AND ALTERNATIVE JUDGMENTS

Reviewers occasionally need to respond to objections to their argument or to alternative judgments readers might prefer. Writers may **concede** (accept) or **refute** (argue against) alternatives, providing a transition or other cues to alert readers:

CONCESSION   The one criticism that could be leveled at the game is that the shooting system has been oversimplified so that it feels clunky compared to the likes of *Grand Theft Auto.* (Boxer, par. 10)

Often writers use transitions to indicate a concession:

Transition indicating concession

▶ Of course, _____ is an important factor.

▶ Granted, _____ must be taken into consideration.

REFUTATION   Some reviewers have criticized the film because they think that in the end it fails as a romantic comedy. For example, *Miami Herald* film reviewer Rene Rodriguez argues that the film ultimately fails because of the lack of "chemistry" or "emotional involvement" in the romance between Pilgrim and Ramona. But I agree with *New York Times* reviewer A. O. Scott, who argues that "the movie comes home to the well-known territory of the coming-of-age story, with an account of lessons learned and conflicts resolved." (Akana, par. 9)

The basic structure of a refutation is

Transition indicating opposing or contrasting point

▶ Although _____, I think _____.

▶ X says _____, but I think _____ because _____.

A CLEAR, LOGICAL ORGANIZATION

Read to see if the reviewer provides cues *to help readers follow the logic of the argument.* Notice, for example, if the reasons are *forecast* in the thesis or elsewhere in the opening and, if so, where they are brought up again later in the essay. Here are examples from William Akana's film review:

Thesis with topics forecast

Scott Pilgrim vs. the World can be appreciated and enjoyed by all audiences *because* of its inventive special effects, clever dialogue, and artistic cinematography and editing. (par. 2)

Scott Pilgrim vs. the World shines bright with superb special effects that serve to reinforce the ideas, themes, and style of the film. (par. 3)

Topic sentences
with reasons
forecast

Another strong point of *Scott Pilgrim vs. the World* is its clever and humorous dialogue. (par. 6)

The best attribute by far is the film's creative cinematography and editing. (par. 7)

Notice that, in addition, Akana provides readers with logical transitions—such as *because* to introduce reasons and *another* to indicate the next reason in a list.

Reviewers may also use *headings* to orient readers, as in these examples from Steve Boxer's game review:

See Chapter 13 for more
on strategies for cueing
readers.

Real-life gameplay

LA Noire's gameplay capitalizes cleverly on this breakthrough technology. (par. 5)

Key word in heading

Beautiful pacing

The game's pacing and narrative arc are as impressive as they are believable. (par. 9)

Key word in topic
sentence

Finally, where visuals—such as film stills, cartoons, screen shots, and diagrams—are included, determine how they are integrated into the text. Akana, for example, uses the conventional phrase "see fig. 1" in parentheses following his written description and includes a descriptive caption with the visual. In contrast, Boxer simply intersperses screen shots following his descriptions to illustrate his points.

To see how Akana inte-
grated visuals into his
essay, see pp. 396–97.

Readings

William Akana | Scott Pilgrim vs. the World:
A Hell of a Ride

THIS EVALUATION ESSAY was written by student William Akana for his composition course. The assignment prompt asked students to choose a film and write a review that includes a close analysis of the cinematic techniques used in at least one important scene. Akana's instructor illustrated various cinematic techniques, such as camera angles and movements, and demonstrated how to take screen shots, explaining that students can use visuals for a class project without asking permission, but to publish them they would have to get permission, as we did. As you read, consider these questions as well as those in the margin:

To learn how Akana devel-
oped his thesis and
responses to objections,
turn to A Writer at Work
on pp. 399–400.

- How well do the screen shots illustrate Akana's analysis and support his evaluation?

- How would you describe Akana's tone in this essay? How is his tone affected by the fact that he only uses the first person pronoun "I" to refer to himself only in the opening and closing paragraphs?

Notice that Akana used film stills—screen shots he took from a DVD of the movie—to illustrate his review. Because he used these visuals for a class project and not for public distribution, he did not have to get permission to use them. We did, however.

■■ Basic Features

A Well-Presented Subject

A Well-Supported Judgment

An Effective Response to Objections and Alternative Judgments

A Clear, Logical Organization

How appropriate is this narrative and informality for a film review? For a college paper?

Why do you think Akana gives readers this information?

How well does this thesis statement forecast Akana's argument? Skim the essay, noting where he discusses each of these reasons.

1   As I leaned back in the movie theater seat, accompanied by my friends on a typical Saturday night, I knew I was in for something special. I was reassured; not only had my friends and I reached a unanimous vote to watch *Scott Pilgrim vs. the World*, but two of my friends had already seen the film and were eager to see it again. As soon as *Scott Pilgrim vs. the World* began, with its presentation of the classic Universal Studios introduction in old-timer eight-bit music and pixilated format, I knew I was in for one hell of a ride. From start to finish, *Scott Pilgrim vs. the World* delivers intense action in a hilarious slacker movie that also somehow reimagines romantic comedy.

2   *Scott Pilgrim vs. the World,* released in 2010 by Universal Studios, came into production as a comic book adaptation film under the direction of Edgar Wright (best known for the zombie movie masterpiece *Shaun of the Dead*). Scott Pilgrim (Michael Cera) is a twenty-two-year-old Canadian who plays bass for his indie band, Sex Bob-ombs, located in Toronto, Canada. Pilgrim's life takes a dramatic turn when he falls in love with Ramona Flowers (Mary Elizabeth Winstead), who is, quite literally, the girl of his dreams. However, he soon discovers that Ramona's former lovers have formed a league of evil exes to destroy him, and he is forced to fight to the death to prove his love. Although the film is especially targeted for old-school gamers, anime fans, and comic book fanatics, *Scott Pilgrim vs. the World* can be appreciated and enjoyed by all audiences because of its inventive special effects, clever dialogue, and artistic cinematography and editing.

3   *Scott Pilgrim vs. the World* shines bright with superb special effects that serve to reinforce the ideas, themes, and style of the film. Special effects are plentiful throughout the entire film, ranging from superimposed annotations echoing classic gaming features to artful backgrounds and action sequences modeled on colorful comic book pages. For example, each of the main characters is described for the first time with "gamertags," short-timed boxes of information that include name, age, and rating (see fig. 1).

Akana   Scott Pilgrim vs. the World: *A Hell of a Ride*

▶ **GUIDE TO READING**
GUIDE TO WRITING
A WRITER AT WORK
THINKING CRITICALLY

359

Fig. 1. Screen shot showing gamertags

4   *Scott Pilgrim vs. the World* contains numerous amounts of other fun video-game-like gimmicks that were made possible through special effects. One humorous scene presents a pee bar that depletes as Pilgrim relieves himself. Another scene presents a bass battle between Pilgrim and one of the evil exes in the format of PlayStation's popular Guitar Hero (see fig. 2). It goes without saying that anyone who has ever dabbled in video games will greatly appreciate the gaming-culture inside jokes. As the reviewer for the Web site *Cinema Sight* wrote, this film is intended for "the video game generation" ("Review").

5   Comic book references are also installed using special effects. In almost every battle between Pilgrim and his enemies, comic-book-like backgrounds, added through CGI, enhance the eye-popping fight sequences as characters fly into the air to deliver devastating punches accompanied with traditional onomatopoeic "POWs" and "KAPOWs" (see fig. 3). However, comic book annotations are not reserved merely for fight scenes. Annotations range from even the simplest "RIIIINGs" of a telephone to trails of shouting "AAAAHs" of Pilgrim as he is thrown into the air in battle. To make the film even more visually appealing, *Scott Pilgrim vs. the World* portrays flashbacks using white and black comic strips similar to the original Scott Pilgrim comic books. Special effects play a truly vital part in enlivening the style of the film.

How well do these details and the illustration he chose support Akana's claim that the special effects are "inventive" and "superb"?

Fig. 2. Guitar face-off

6   Another strong point of *Scott Pilgrim vs. the World* is its clever and humorous dialogue. One memorable scene in the film involves Knives Chau (Ellen Wong) and Scott Pilgrim in an awkward situation where Knives states sheepishly: "I've never even

Fig. 3. Comic-book-style annotations

Akana   Scott Pilgrim vs. the World: *A Hell of a Ride*

▶ **GUIDE TO READING**
GUIDE TO WRITING
A WRITER AT WORK
THINKING CRITICALLY

361

kissed a guy." In a supposedly intimate gesture of affection, Pilgrim moves closer only to pause shortly before saying "Hey . . . me neither." Additionally, *Scott Pilgrim vs. the World* is rich in cultural satire that pokes fun at adolescent and young adult behaviors. One scene contains Pilgrim telling Ramona Flowers: "I feel like I'm on drugs when I'm with you, not that I do drugs, unless you do — in which case, I do drugs all the time." Dialogue like this gives the film a raw yet rich sense of humor that is one of the many inventive risks of the film that pay off.

7   The best attribute by far is the film's creative cinematography and editing, which can be illustrated in the ultimate fight scene of the movie. Pilgrim finally confronts his former band members, who are playing in an underground lair for Ramona's seventh evil ex, Gideon (Jason Schwartzman). As Pilgrim admits his faults and proceeds to apologize to the band for former wrongs, the shot assumes a point of view from Pilgrim's perspective looking up to the band on stage. Shortly before Pilgrim is finished, Gideon, sitting on his throne atop a miniature pyramid, interrupts him. The shot quickly cuts to a close-up of Gideon's eyes, emphasizing his anger at Pilgrim. From this point, soft focusing is utilized to blur the background as a tracking shot follows Pilgrim in a medium close-up as he marches to the base of the pyramid. Then, shot reverse shots are used between high- and low-angled frames to illustrate Pilgrim's challenge to Gideon for

8   a final duel.

Gideon, in response to the challenge, asks Pilgrim if he is fighting for Ramona, which leads to a climactic epiphany for Pilgrim as he realizes his true motive, admitting in a tight close-up: "No. I want to fight you for me." As Pilgrim finishes this confession, a deep narrating voice announces that "Scott Pilgrim has earned the power of self-respect," and in turn, he is awarded a magical sword with which he can defeat Gideon. Subsequently, the camera pans from left to right in a subjective shot to illustrate Gideon's goons closing in on Pilgrim. Pilgrim, in a series of fast-paced jump cuts, quickly dispatches the bad guys before charging up the pyramid. After an extended battle, deep focusing is used with a long shot to establish that the hierarchy has changed between hero and villain: Pilgrim is seen standing atop the pyramid, looking down at the kneeling Gideon before Pilgrim kicks him to smithereens.

9   This brilliantly executed scene illustrates the artful cinematography of *Scott Pilgrim vs. the World*. More importantly, it delivers the film's thematic message, which undercuts

How do the highlighted transitions help readers follow Akana's analysis?

For what purposes does Akana use these sources? How effective is his response to an apposing view?

the cliché "love conquers all" and instead focuses on the fresh concept that, in the grand scheme of things, the only person you are fighting for is yourself. Some reviewers have criticized the film because they think that in the end it fails as a romantic comedy. For example, *Miami Herald* film reviewer Rene Rodriguez argues that the film ultimately fails because of the lack of "chemistry" or "emotional involvement" in the romance between Pilgrim and Ramona. But I agree with *New York Times* reviewer A. O. Scott, who argues that "the movie comes home to the well-known territory of the coming-of-age story, with an account of lessons learned and conflicts resolved." Fighting Ramona's exes forces Pilgrim to wake up out of his slacker stupor. Before he can begin a grown-up relationship with Ramona, he has to come to terms with his own failures, especially in relation to his own exes. The film ends, as director Edgar Wright explained in an interview, on the threshold of a new beginning: "Scott and Ramona might not make it past the end credits, or it might be the start of a beautiful relationship" (Cozzalio).

Fig. 4. Threshold of a new beginning?

Works Cited

Cozzalio, Dennis. "Scott Pilgrim's Dreamscape and the Glories of the Wright Stuff II: An interview with director Edgar Wright." *Sergio Leone and the Infield Fly Rule.* SergioLeoneIFR.blogspot.com, 15. Jan. 2011. Web. 30 Mar. 2011.

Rodriguez, Rene. Rev. of *Scott Pilgrim vs. the World*. *Miami Herald*. Miami.com, 11 Aug.
    2010. Web. 28 Mar. 2011.

Scott, A. O. "This Girl Has a Lot of Baggage, and He Must Shoulder the Load." *New York
    Times*. New York Times, 12 Aug. 2010. Web. 29 Mar. 2011.

Rev. of *Scott Pilgrim vs. The World*. *Cinema Sight*. CinemaSight.com, 13 Sept. 2010.
    Web. 30 Mar. 2011.

For an additional
student reading, go to
**bedfordstmartins.com
/theguide/epages**.

Steve Boxer | LA Noire *Review*

STEVE BOXER is a contributor to the British newspaper the *Guardian*, for which he writes video game reviews. Published online as well as in print, the *Guardian* is one of the most widely read English-language newspapers in the world, and it has received many awards. The video games team, which includes Steve Boxer, won the coveted Games Media Award five years in a row. In addition to being an accomplished game reviewer, Boxer describes himself as a general freelance-for-hire writer as well as an electronic-music lover. As you read Boxer's review, consider these questions:

- As a member of an award-winning video game review team, Boxer presumably knows a lot about video games. How does this review display his expertise?

- What adjectives would you use to describe Boxer's tone—for example, formal, conversational, assertive, condescending, authoritative, or tentative?

LA Noire . . . arresting your attention with consummate ease

1   Ever since it first worked out how to assemble pixels so that they resembled something more recognizable than aliens, the games industry has dreamed of creating one thing above all else—a game that is indistinguishable from a film, except that you can control the lead character. With *LA Noire*, it just might, finally, have found the embodiment of that particular holy grail.

2   From start to finish, *LA Noire* feels like a film— *LA Confidential*, in fact, along with any similarly hardboiled example of film noir adapted from stories by the likes of Chandler and Hammett. Set in a gloriously convincing depiction of Los Angeles in 1947 (which is much more attractive than today's L.A.), it casts you as

Cole Phelps, returning war hero turned cop. Instantly, you plunge deeply and satisfyingly into his working life, solving a vast number of cases as he becomes the LAPD's poster-boy, first in Homicide, then in Vice. And your immersion in Phelps's affairs ratchets up even further when he is hung out to dry by his dubious superiors.

3   There have been plenty of games with cinematic pretensions in the past, so what is it that enables *LA Noire* to make a transcendental leap? Inevitably, technology is involved: the new MotionScan system used to capture actors' performances simply produces more convincing facial animation than we have ever seen in a game.

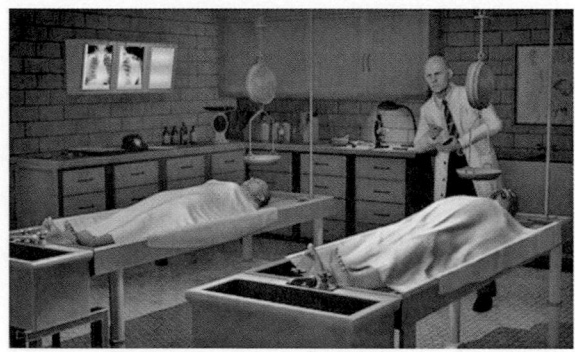

4   Couple that with the obsessive attention to detail for which Rockstar's existing games such as *Grand Theft Auto* and *Red Dead Redemption* are famed, and the end result rings true to a greater extent than anything that has gone before. The familiar need to suspend disbelief has been all but eliminated.

Real-Life Gameplay

5 *LA Noire*'s gameplay capitalizes cleverly on this breakthrough technology. Essentially, it sees you playing through Phelps's working life, doing what you imagine a real-life LAPD detective would have done in 1947. Thus, you have to drive to crime scenes, root around for clues and examine bodies, then follow the resulting leads.

6   It's when you question suspects and witnesses that things get interesting. You have to analyze facial responses and bodily tics like a poker player seeking tells, then choose one of three tones to adopt for each question. These are marked Truth, Doubt and Lying,

but Sympathetic, Dubious and Accusatory would perhaps be more rigorous.

7   If you accuse a suspect of lying, you must back that up by producing evidence (all accessed, along with your records of each case and details of suspects, from your standard cop's notebook). If you don't adopt the correct tone, the character you're quizzing will, at the very least, take longer to give you the crucial information you seek.

8   As you rise through the ranks, you earn Intuition points, which can be cashed in to eliminate one wrong question-tone (or reveal the location of all the clues at a location). Luckily, *LA Noire* is pretty forgiving, so if your body language–assessment skills aren't up to *CSI* standards, you should still get the right result in the end, although you risk a chewing-out from your boss for shoddy police work, which is genuinely mortifying.

Beautiful Pacing

9 The game's pacing and narrative arc are as impressive as they are believable. The bog-standard detective work, fun though it is, is punctuated judiciously by action sequences including car chases, pursuing suspects on foot, climbing around inaccessible areas, puzzle-solving and, of course, shoot-outs. Between cases, you either get a flashback to Phelps's war experiences in Japan or a glimpse into his off-duty life; both those elements end up feeding back into the overarching storyline. The oeuvres of Shelley and even anarchist author Piotr Kropotkin are fed into the mix. Newspapers that you find when hunting for clues trigger yet another backstory (this time involving ongoing LA skullduggery), which yet again intersects with the main storyline in the game's later

stages. A fascinating snapshot of an America struggling to readjust to everyday life in the aftermath of the Second World War emerges. . . .

10   Since you're at the center of proceedings, participating in and dictating the action, the overall effect is powerfully immersive. Cleverly, Rockstar has ensured that *LA Noire* is a thoroughly inclusive game, too. The control system is sufficiently simplified that even the most determined nongamers shouldn't find it intimidating. Indeed, the more hardcore gamers may carp that it isn't sufficiently action-packed or precise. The one criticism that could be leveled at the game is that the shooting system has been oversimplified so that it feels clunky compared to the likes of *Grand Theft Auto*.

Depth and Meatiness

11   *LA Noire* largely does away with the free-roaming that enhanced the appeal of *Grand Theft Auto* and *Red Dead Redemption*. As you drive around, you do occasionally hear of street crimes to which you can respond, and there are hidden vehicles and LA landmarks that completists can collect and visit, but the overwhelming focus is on the main story. So it's a good job that, bucking the modern trend for short single-player games, *LA Noire* is satisfyingly meaty. Rockstar reckons it's roughly equivalent in length to two seasons of a TV series, a claim that feels roughly accurate.

12   Perhaps, then, it would be more accurate to argue that *LA Noire* more closely approximates a television show than a film—it beats any film hands down in terms of the sheer amount of entertainment on offer, which of course is an advantage games have always had over films. It has all the period charm of *Boardwalk Empire* or *Mad Men*—indeed, the role of Phelps is played by *Mad Men*'s Aaron Staton and other digitized *Mad Men* actors crop up sporadically—and it seasons the gameplay with a healthy dash of *CSI*.

13   In the past, games with such overwhelming ambitions have floundered on odd, usually peripheral, aspects that jarred—such as unrealistic animation (and especially facial animation), clunky dialogue, poor virtual camerawork or facile characterization. *LA Noire* is the first game to lack any such element which naggingly reminds you that you're playing a video game, rather than strolling through a film or TV series. That's why it marks a breakthrough for games as a whole—and we can't wait to see what Rockstar does with *LA Noire*'s technology in its other blockbuster franchises.

Make connections: Considering what makes genre fiction interesting.

[REFLECT]

Noir-style fiction in any medium (film, video game, novel, or television) typically tells the story of a private eye or police detective. Boxer suggests that what makes this genre interesting are the multiple levels of conflict and tension in the story.

Choose a genre of fiction you enjoy (such as mystery, science fiction, or comedy), and think about what makes it interesting to you. Your instructor may ask you to post your thoughts on a class discussion board or to discuss them with other students in class. Use these questions to get started:

- Name the fictional genre, and identify a couple of examples.
- Identify what makes fiction in this genre pleasurable for you, drawing on the examples you have chosen. For instance, does it invite viewers or readers to identify with a particular character? Does it offer intricate or suspenseful plots or intriguing settings? Is the setting appealing? Does it offer pure escapist fun, make a cultural critique, or something else?

[ANALYZE] Use the basic features.

A WELL-PRESENTED SUBJECT: DECIDING HOW MUCH TO TELL READERS

As a game reviewer, Boxer is in a rhetorical situation very much like that of a film reviewer, who needs to describe what the film is about without giving away too much and ruining the fun.

ANALYZE & WRITE

Write a few paragraphs analyzing and evaluating the descriptive details Boxer provides about the game:

1 Skim paragraphs 2 and 5–10, highlighting the details Boxer uses to describe the game — for example, setting, characters, and action.

2 From the perspective of someone considering whether to buy the game, which of these details seem likely to be helpful, and which seem unnecessary? What, if anything, does Boxer leave out of his description that you think a reader would want to know in order to make a decision?

3 Given your analysis, what can you conclude about the amount and kind of descriptive detail game and film reviewers should include in their reviews?

A WELL-SUPPORTED JUDGMENT: BASING JUDGMENTS ON CRITERIA

Evaluations usually assert an overall judgment of the subject in the thesis statement, as Boxer does in the opening paragraph, in which he calls *LA Noire* the "embodiment" of the game industry's "holy grail" (par. 1). Calling something the "holy grail" is certainly high praise. Boxer qualifies this claim a bit by using the hedging word "might." Nevertheless, he opens his evaluation by declaring his judgment clearly and forcefully.

To effectively support a judgment, the criteria or standards being used to judge the subject need to be appropriate for the genre, and the writer must show that the standards are indeed being met (or in the case of a negative evaluation, failing to be met). In his review, Boxer asserts that the most important criterion, the "holy grail" the industry has been seeking, is "a game that is indistinguishable from a film, except that you can control the lead character" (par. 1).

Boxer LA Noire *Review*

▶ **GUIDE TO READING**
GUIDE TO WRITING
A WRITER AT WORK
THINKING CRITICALLY

367

ANALYZE & WRITE

Write a few paragraphs analyzing and evaluating how Boxer presents and supports his criteria:

1 How does Boxer support his judgment that *LA Noire* "feels like a film" (par. 2)? To answer this question, analyze the details he provides about the game, the comparisons he makes, and the words he uses that are associated with film.

2 In addition to its seeming like a film, what other criteria does Boxer use to judge *LA Noire*? How appropriate do you think video game enthusiasts would consider these criteria?

3 If you have played *LA Noire,* consider whether you would use the same evaluative criteria Boxer uses. Or think of another video game you know well, and decide what criteria most people would think is appropriate for evaluating that game.

AN EFFECTIVE RESPONSE TO OBJECTIONS AND ALTERNATIVE JUDGMENTS: ANTICIPATING READERS' CONCERNS

Film reviewers may acknowledge on occasion that their opinion differs significantly from the prevailing point of view. Most often, though, writers of evaluations do not engage in debate. They often do, however, try to anticipate and respond to readers' possible questions and concerns. Boxer anticipates potential concerns of two groups of readers: "nongamers" and "hardcore gamers."

ANALYZE & WRITE

Write a few paragraphs analyzing and evaluating how Boxer responds to the possible concerns of nongamers and hardcore gamers:

1 Reread paragraphs 8–11 to identify where Boxer refers to these two groups of readers.

2 Analyze the wording to determine whether Boxer is conceding or refuting criticism that one of these groups may be likely to make about *LA Noire*.

3 Whether you regard yourself as a nongamer, a hardcore gamer, or someone in between, how effective do you think Boxer's response is likely to be for his readers?

A CLEAR, LOGICAL ORGANIZATION: USING VISUALS AND HEADINGS

Visual cues can help readers see at a glance the structure of an argument. Screen shots, for example, are often used in reviews of films, Web sites, and games to illustrate each topic, or element, of the writer's evaluation. Given that his evaluation is based primarily on the idea that *LA Noire* succeeds because it looks and feels like a film, it is logical for Boxer to provide screen shots that show how cinematic the game is, but do these screen shots also help make the organization of the review clear and logical?

Another visual cue Boxer uses is headings. Writers sometimes use headings to make it easy for readers to follow a long and complicated argument. Boxer's review, however, is neither long nor especially complicated. Why do you think he uses headings?

Write a few paragraphs analyzing and evaluating Boxer's use of screen shots and headings:

1 Examine the screen shots Boxer includes, and speculate about why he chose these images. Consider also their order and placement, and determine if they do more than illustrate a point the writer is making.

2 Look closely at the three headings, and consider both the way they are written and their placement in the essay. What purpose do they serve?

[RESPOND] ## Consider possible topics: Evaluating media.

Consider games, Web sites, films, or television programs that you recall especially well and about which you already have a strong opinion. Then consider how you would argue for your judgment. Specifically, what criteria do you think you would use? Why do you assume that your readers would accept these criteria as appropriate for evaluating this subject? (Note that if you were actually to write about this subject, you would need to research it to develop your argument and find supporting details.)

Malcolm Gladwell | *What College Rankings Really Tell Us*

MALCOLM GLADWELL is a staff writer for the *New Yorker* magazine and has written a number of best-selling books, including *Outliers: The Story of Success* (2008) and *Blink: The Power of Thinking without Thinking* (2005). He received the American Sociological Association Award for Excellence in the Reporting of Social Issues and was named one of the hundred most influential people by *Time* magazine. As he explains on his Web site (gladwell.com), giving public readings, particularly to academic audiences, has helped him "re-shape and sharpen [his] arguments."

"What College Rankings Really Tell Us" (2011) evaluates the popular *U.S. News* annual "Best Colleges" guide. You may be familiar with this guide and may have even consulted it when selecting a college. Excerpted from a longer *New Yorker* article, Gladwell's evaluation focuses on the *U.S. News* ranking system. As you read Gladwell's review, consider these questions:

- Note the numbered list of "variables" the *U.S. News* uses to rank colleges. For whom do you suppose *U.S. News*'s criteria are important? Why?

- If they are important for you, why? If they are not important for you, why not? What criteria for choosing a college are important for you?

Gladwell *What College Rankings Really Tell Us*

GUIDE TO READING
GUIDE TO WRITING
A WRITER AT WORK
THINKING CRITICALLY

369

1 *C*ar and Driver conducted a comparison test of three sports cars, the Lotus Evora, the Chevrolet Corvette Grand Sport, and the Porsche Cayman S. . . . Yet when you inspect the magazine's tabulations it is hard to figure out why *Car and Driver* was so sure that the Cayman is better than the Corvette and the Evora. The trouble starts with the fact that the ranking methodology *Car and Driver* used was essentially the same one it uses for all the vehicles it tests—from S.U.V.s to economy sedans. It's not set up for sports cars. Exterior styling, for example, counts for four per cent of the total score. Has anyone buying a sports car ever placed so little value on how it looks? Similarly, the categories of "fun to drive" and "chassis"—which cover the subjective experience of driving the car—count for only eighty-five points out of the total of two hundred and thirty-five. That may make sense for S.U.V. buyers. But, for people interested in Porsches and Corvettes and Lotuses, the subjective experience of driving is surely what matters most. In other words, in trying to come up with a ranking that is heterogeneous—a methodology that is broad enough to cover all vehicles—*Car and Driver* ended up with a system that is absurdly ill-suited to some vehicles. . . .

2 A heterogeneous ranking system works if it focuses just on, say, how much fun a car is to drive, or how good-looking it is, or how beautifully it handles. The magazine's ambition to create a comprehensive ranking system—one that considered cars along twenty-one variables, each weighted according to a secret sauce cooked up by the editors—would also be fine, as long as the cars being compared were truly similar. It's only when one car is thirteen thousand dollars more than another that juggling twenty-one variables starts to break down, because you're faced with the impossible task of deciding how much a difference of that degree ought to matter. A ranking can be heterogeneous, in other words, as long as it doesn't try to be too comprehensive. And it can be comprehensive as long as it doesn't try to measure things that are heterogeneous. But it's an act of real audacity when a ranking system tries to be comprehensive and heterogeneous—which is the first thing to keep in mind in any consideration of *U.S. News & World Report*'s annual "Best Colleges" guide.

3 The *U.S. News* rankings . . . relies on seven weighted variables:

1. Undergraduate academic reputation, 22.5 per cent
2. Graduation and freshman retention rates, 20 per cent
3. Faculty resources, 20 per cent
4. Student selectivity, 15 per cent
5. Financial resources, 10 per cent
6. Graduation rate performance, 7.5 per cent
7. Alumni giving, 5 per cent

From these variables, *U.S. News* generates a score for each institution on a scale of 1 to 100. . . . This ranking system looks a great deal like the *Car and Driver* methodology. It is heterogeneous. It doesn't just compare U.C. Irvine, the University of Washington, the University of Texas–Austin, the University of Wisconsin–Madison, Penn State, and the University of Illinois, Urbana–Champaign—all public institutions of roughly the same size. It aims to compare Penn State—a very large, public, land-grant university with a low tuition and an economically diverse student body, set in a rural valley in central Pennsylvania and famous for its football team—with Yeshiva University, a small, expensive, private Jewish university whose undergraduate program is set on two campuses in Manhattan (one in midtown, for the women, and one far uptown, for the men) and is definitely not famous for its football team.

4 The system is also comprehensive. It doesn't simply compare schools along one dimension—the test scores of incoming freshmen, say, or academic reputation. An algorithm takes a slate of statistics on each college and transforms them into a single score: it tells us that Penn State is a better school than Yeshiva by one point. It is easy to see why the *U.S. News* rankings are so popular. A single score allows us to judge between entities (like Yeshiva and Penn State) that otherwise would be impossible to compare. . . .

5 A comprehensive, heterogeneous ranking system was a stretch for *Car and Driver*—and all it did was rank inanimate objects operated by a single person. The Penn State campus at University Park is a complex institution with dozens of schools and departments, four thousand faculty members, and forty-five thousand students. How on earth does anyone propose to assign a number to something like that?

6 The first difficulty with rankings is that it can be surprisingly hard to measure the variable you want to rank—even in cases where that variable seems perfectly objective. . . . There's no direct way to measure the quality of an institution—how well a college manages to inform, inspire, and challenge its students. So the

U.S. News algorithm relies instead on proxies for quality—and the proxies for educational quality turn out to be flimsy at best.

7   Take the category of "faculty resources," which counts for twenty per cent of an institution's score (number 3 on the chart above). "Research shows that the more satisfied students are about their contact with professors," the College Guide's explanation of the category begins, "the more they will learn and the more likely it is they will graduate." That's true. According to educational researchers, arguably the most important variable in a successful college education is a vague but crucial concept called student "engagement"—that is, the extent to which students immerse themselves in the intellectual and social life of their college—and a major component of engagement is the quality of a student's contacts with faculty. . . . So what proxies does *U.S. News* use to measure this elusive dimension of engagement? The explanation goes on:

> We use six factors from the 2009–10 academic year to assess a school's commitment to instruction. Class size has two components, the proportion of classes with fewer than 20 students (30 percent of the faculty resources score) and the proportion with 50 or more students (10 percent of the score). Faculty salary (35 percent) is the average faculty pay, plus benefits, during the 2008–09 and 2009–10 academic years, adjusted for regional differences in the cost of living. . . . We also weigh the proportion of professors with the highest degree in their fields (15 percent), the student-faculty ratio (5 percent), and the proportion of faculty who are full time (5 percent).

8   This is a puzzling list. Do professors who get paid more money really take their teaching roles more seriously? And why does it matter whether a professor has the highest degree in his or her field? Salaries and degree attainment are known to be predictors of research productivity. But studies show that being oriented toward research has very little to do with being good at teaching. Almost none of the *U.S. News* variables, in fact, seem to be particularly effective proxies for engagement. As the educational researchers Patrick Terenzini and Ernest Pascarella concluded after analyzing twenty-six hundred reports on the effects of college on students:

> After taking into account the characteristics, abilities, and backgrounds students bring with them to college, we found that how much students grow or change has only inconsistent and, perhaps in a practical sense, trivial relationships with such traditional measures of institutional "quality" as educational expenditures per student, student/faculty ratios, faculty salaries, percentage of faculty with the highest degree in their field, faculty research productivity, size of the library, [or] admissions selectivity. . . .

9   There's something missing from that list of variables, of course: it doesn't include price. That is one of the most distinctive features of the *U.S. News* methodology. Both its college rankings and its law-school rankings reward schools for devoting lots of financial resources to educating their students, but not for being affordable. Why? [Director of Data Research Robert] Morse admitted that there was no formal reason for that position. It was just a feeling. "We're not saying that we're measuring educational outcomes," he explained. "We're not saying we're social scientists, or we're subjecting our rankings to some peer-review process. We're just saying we've made this judgment. We're saying we've interviewed a lot of experts, we've developed these academic indicators, and we think these measures measure quality schools."

10   As answers go, that's up there with the parental "Because I said so." But Morse is simply being honest. If we don't understand what the right proxies for college quality are, let alone how to represent those proxies in a comprehensive, heterogeneous grading system, then our rankings are inherently arbitrary. . . . *U.S. News* thinks that schools that spend a lot of money on their students are nicer than those that don't, and that this niceness ought to be factored into the equation of desirability. Plenty of Americans agree: the campus of Vanderbilt University or Williams College is filled

The first difficulty with rankings is that it can be surprisingly hard to measure the variable you want to rank.

with students whose families are largely indifferent to the price their school charges but keenly interested in the flower beds and the spacious suites and the architecturally distinguished lecture halls those high prices make possible. Of course, given that the rising cost of college has become a significant social problem in the United States in recent years, you can make a strong case that a school ought to be rewarded for being affordable. . . .

11   The *U.S. News* rankings turn out to be full of these kinds of implicit ideological choices. One common statistic used to evaluate colleges, for example, is called "graduation rate performance," which compares a school's actual graduation rate with its predicted graduation rate given the socioeconomic status and the test scores of its incoming freshman class. It is a measure of the school's efficacy: it quantifies the impact of a school's culture and teachers and institutional support mechanisms. Tulane, given the qualifications of the students that it admits, ought to have a graduation rate of eighty-seven per cent; its actual 2009 graduation rate was seventy-three per cent. That shortfall suggests that something is amiss at Tulane. Another common statistic for measuring college quality is "student selectivity." This reflects variables such as how many of a college's freshmen were in the top ten per cent of their high-

school class, how high their S.A.T. scores were, and what percentage of applicants a college admits. Selectivity quantifies how accomplished students are when they first arrive on campus.

12   Each of these statistics matters, but for very different reasons. As a society, we probably care more about efficacy: America's future depends on colleges that make sure the students they admit leave with an education and a degree. If you are a bright high-school senior and you're thinking about your own future, though, you may well care more about selectivity, because that relates to the prestige of your degree. . . .

13   There is no right answer to how much weight a ranking system should give to these two competing values. It's a matter of which educational model you value more — and here, once again, *U.S. News* makes its position clear. It gives twice as much weight to selectivity as it does to efficacy. . . .

14   Rankings are not benign. They enshrine very particular ideologies, and, at a time when American higher education is facing a crisis of accessibility and affordability, we have adopted a defacto standard of college quality that is uninterested in both of those factors. And why? Because a group of magazine analysts in an office building in Washington, D.C., decided twenty years ago to value selectivity over efficacy.

Make connections: Ideology underlying judgments.   [REFLECT]

Gladwell asserts that "implicit ideological choices" underlie ranking systems (par. 11). The word *ideology* refers to the values and beliefs that influence people's thinking. An important sign of underlying ideology is the fact that the *U.S. News* rankings leave out how much it costs to go to each college. This omission is significant, especially at a time when there is "a crisis of accessibility and affordability" (par. 14).

To think about the role of ideology in your own choice of a college, reflect on your personal experience as well as your observations of others choosing a college. Your instructor may ask you to post your thoughts on a class discussion board or to discuss them with other students in class. Use these questions to get started:

- What colleges did you consider, and what criteria (cost, location, standing in the *U.S. News* college ranking, and so on) did you use?

- Choose one or two of your criteria, and consider what values and beliefs were behind your choice. For example, was it important to you to attend a college with a winning football team, with a particular religious orientation, with opportunities for undergraduates to do scientific research?

- How would comparing the criteria you used with the criteria your classmates used help you better understand the ideology—values and beliefs—behind your choices?

[ANALYZE]   ## Use the basic features.

A WELL-PRESENTED SUBJECT: INTRODUCING A COMPLICATED SUBJECT

Every year, *U.S. News* publishes a special edition that ranks colleges and universities across the nation. In his essay, Gladwell does not simply evaluate one year's ratings; he evaluates the ranking system itself. But he begins by focusing on the ranking system of another magazine, *Car and Driver*.

| ANALYZE & WRITE |

Write a paragraph or two analyzing and evaluating how Gladwell introduces *U.S. News*'s ranking system:

1 Reread paragraph 1. Why do you think Gladwell begins his evaluation of *U.S. News*'s college ranking system by discussing the system used by another magazine to rank cars? How is Gladwell's evaluation of *Car and Driver*'s ranking system preparing the reader for his evaluation of *U.S. News*'s ranking system?

2 Now reread paragraph 2. What cues does Gladwell provide to help readers follow his transition from the ranking system of *Car and Driver* to that of *U.S. News*?

3 What does Gladwell mean when he describes *U.S. News*'s ranking system as striving to be both comprehensive and heterogeneous?

A WELL-SUPPORTED JUDGMENT: DEFINING CRITERIA

In paragraph 3, Gladwell lists the "seven weighted variables" *U.S. News* uses to represent a school's quality. Then, in paragraph 6, he states his main reason for criticizing any system for ranking colleges: "There's no direct way to measure the quality of an institution. . . . So the *U.S. News* algorithm"—its formula or set of rules—"relies instead on proxies for quality—and the proxies for educational quality turn out to be flimsy at best."

| ANALYZE & WRITE |

Write a few paragraphs analyzing and evaluating how Gladwell supports his claim:

1 Reread paragraphs 7 and 8, in which Gladwell focuses on one criterion — "faculty resources" — from the list of variables *U.S. News* uses to measure a school's quality. Why does *U.S. News* focus on faculty resources, and what do the editors of the magazine use to measure this quality?

2 Now consider Gladwell's claim that faculty resources are an inappropriate criterion for evaluating student engagement. What reasons and evidence does Gladwell supply? Given your own experience as a student, how convincing is this part of his argument?

3 What single criterion would you consider most important in evaluating a school's quality? How would you measure that criterion?

AN EFFECTIVE RESPONSE TO OBJECTIONS AND ALTERNATIVE JUDGMENTS: SINGLING OUT A COMMENT FOR RESPONSE

Because it is a negative evaluation, one could say that Gladwell's entire essay is an implied refutation of those who think well of the *U.S. News* college rankings. However, Gladwell also responds specifically to comments made by Robert Morse, the director of data research for *U.S. News & World Report*.

ANALYZE & WRITE

Write a paragraph analyzing Morse's response to Gladwell and Gladwell's response to Morse:

1 Reread paragraph 9. How would you describe Morse's response to Gladwell's criticism: Which of Gladwell's points does Morse concede or refute? Is his response effective?

2 Now reread paragraphs 10–12. How does Gladwell respond to Morse? How does he concede or refute Morse's response? How would you describe the tone, or emotional resonance, of Gladwell's response? Is he fair, mean, sarcastic, something else?

3 Given Gladwell's purpose and audience, how do you imagine readers would react to Morse's response to criticism as well as to Gladwell's handling of Morse's response? How did you respond?

A CLEAR, LOGICAL ORGANIZATION: USING COMPARISON AND CONTRAST

Lengthy evaluations can be difficult to follow, but writers have a number of strategies at their disposal to help guide readers. They may use transitional words and phrases or numbered lists, as Gladwell does. But they may also use more subtle strategies to help create cohesion. Gladwell, for example, uses comparison and contrast and strategic repetition to help readers follow his analysis.

ANALYZE & WRITE

Write a brief analysis of how Gladwell uses these two strategies:

1 Skim paragraphs 1–3, 5, and 10, noting every place that Gladwell mentions *Car and Driver* or compares *Car and Driver*'s ranking system with the ranking system used by *U.S. News*, and highlight every time Gladwell uses the word *heterogeneous* to describe these ranking systems. Consider the comparison Gladwell is making between *Car and Driver*'s and *U.S. News*'s ranking systems. How does this comparison help him structure his article logically?

2 Skim paragraphs 3, 8, and 11–14, underlining the words *selectivity* and *efficacy*. How does Gladwell use the contrast between selectivity and efficacy? How does this contrast help him guide readers and make his point?

3 Finally, evaluate Gladwell's use of these strategies. How effective were they in helping you follow Gladwell's logic? What, if anything, would you suggest Gladwell do to make his analysis easier to follow?

RESPOND

Consider possible topics: Evaluating a text.

List several texts you would consider evaluating, such as an essay from one of the chapters in this book; a children's book that you read when you were young or that you now read to your own children; a magazine for people interested in a particular topic, like computers or cars; or a scholarly article you read for a research paper. If you choose an argument from Chapters 6–9, you could evaluate its logic, its use of emotional appeals, or its credibility. You need not limit yourself to texts written on paper. You might also evaluate a Web site or blog, a radio or television program or advertisement, or even a work of art (such as a story from Chapter 10 or a multimedia selection from this book's e-Pages). Choose one possibility from your list, and then come up with two or three criteria for evaluation.

Christine Rosen | *The Myth of Multitasking*

CHRISTINE ROSEN has written several books, including *My Fundamentalist Education* (2005) and *The Feminist Dilemma* (2001). She also coedited *Acculturated: 23 Savvy Writers Find Hidden Virtue in Reality TV, Chic Lit, Video Games, and Other Pillars of Pop Culture* (2011). A senior editor of the *New Atlantis: A Journal of Technology and Society,* in which this essay originally appeared, Rosen frequently appears on National Public Radio, CNN, and other news outlets. Her essays have also appeared in such prestigious venues as the *New York Times Magazine, Washington Post, Wall Street Journal,* and *National Review.*

As you read, think about your experience, and the experience of Rosen's other readers, with multitasking:

- How frequently do you multitask, and what effect has multitasking had on your productivity?

- How does Rosen try to get readers to consider the idea that there may be a downside to multitasking?

1 In one of the many letters he wrote to his son in the 1740s, Lord Chesterfield offered the following advice: "There is time enough for everything in the course of the day, if you do but one thing at once, but there is not time enough in the year, if you will do two things at a time." To Chesterfield, singular focus was not merely a practical way to structure one's time; it was a mark of intelligence. "This steady and undissipated attention to one object, is a sure mark of a superior genius; as hurry, bustle, and agitation, are the never-failing symptoms of a weak and frivolous mind."

2 In modern times, hurry, bustle, and agitation have become a regular way of life for many people — so much so that we have embraced a word to describe our efforts to respond to the many pressing demands on our time: *multitasking*. Used for decades to describe the parallel processing abilities of computers, multitasking is now shorthand for the human attempt to do simultaneously as many things as possible, as quickly as possible, preferably marshaling the power of as many technologies as possible.

3 In the late 1990s and early 2000s, one sensed a kind of exuberance about the possibilities of multitasking. Advertisements for new electronic gadgets — particularly the first generation of handheld digital devices — celebrated the notion of using technology to accomplish several things at once. The word *multitasking* began appearing in the "skills" sections of résumés, as office workers restyled themselves as high-tech, high-performing team players. "We have always multitasked — inability to walk and chew gum is a time-honored cause for derision — but never so intensely or self-consciously as now," James Gleick wrote in his 1999 book *Faster*. "We are multitasking connoisseurs — experts in crowding, pressing, packing, and overlapping distinct activities in our all-too-finite moments." An article in the *New York Times Magazine* in 2001 asked, "Who can remember life before multitasking? These days we all do it." The article offered advice on "How to Multitask" with suggestions about giving your brain's "multitasking hot spot" an appropriate workout.

4 But more recently, challenges to the ethos of multitasking have begun to emerge. Numerous studies have shown the sometimes-fatal danger of using cell phones and other electronic devices while driving, for example, and several states have now made that particular form of multitasking illegal. In the business world, where concerns about time-management are perennial, warnings about workplace distractions spawned by a multitasking culture are on the rise. In 2005, the BBC reported on a research study, funded by Hewlett-Packard and conducted by the Institute of Psychiatry at the University of London, that found, "Workers distracted by e-mail and phone calls suffer a fall in IQ more than twice that found in marijuana smokers." The psychologist who led the study called this new "infomania" a serious threat to workplace productivity. One of the *Harvard Business Review*'s "Breakthrough Ideas" for 2007 was Linda Stone's notion of "continuous partial attention," which might be understood as a subspecies of multitasking: using mobile computing power and the Internet, we are "constantly scanning for opportunities and staying on top of contacts, events, and activities in an effort to miss nothing."

> **Numerous studies have shown the sometimes-fatal danger of using cell phones and other electronic devices while driving.**

5 Dr. Edward Hallowell, a Massachusetts-based psychiatrist who specializes in the treatment of attention deficit/hyperactivity disorder and has written a book with the self-explanatory title *CrazyBusy*, has been offering therapies to combat extreme multitasking for years; in his book he calls multitasking a "mythical activity in which people believe they can perform two or more tasks simultaneously." In a 2005 article, he described a new condition, "Attention Deficit Trait," which he claims is rampant in the business world. ADT is "purely a response to the hyperkinetic environment in which we live," writes Hallowell, and its hallmark symptoms mimic those of ADD. "Never in history has the human brain been asked to track so many data points," Hallowell argues, and this challenge "can be controlled only by creatively engineering one's environment and one's emotional and physical health." Limiting multitasking is essential. Best-selling business advice author Timothy Ferriss also extols the virtues of "single-tasking" in his book, *The 4-Hour Workweek*.

6 Multitasking might also be taking a toll on the economy. One study by researchers at the University of California at Irvine monitored interruptions among office workers; they found that workers took an average

of twenty-five minutes to recover from interruptions such as phone calls or answering e-mail and return to their original task. Discussing multitasking with the *New York Times* in 2007, Jonathan B. Spira, an analyst at the business research firm Basex, estimated that extreme multitasking—information overload—costs the U.S. economy $650 billion a year in lost productivity.

Changing Our Brains

7 To better understand the multitasking phenomenon, neurologists and psychologists have studied the workings of the brain. In 1999, Jordan Grafman, chief of cognitive neuroscience at the National Institute of Neurological Disorders and Stroke (part of the National Institutes of Health), used functional magnetic resonance imaging (fMRI) scans to determine that when people engage in "task-switching"—that is, multitasking behavior—the flow of blood increases to a region of the frontal cortex called Brodmann area 10. (The flow of blood to particular regions of the brain is taken as a proxy indication of activity in those regions.) "This is presumably the last part of the brain to evolve, the most mysterious and exciting part," Grafman told the *New York Times* in 2001—adding, with a touch of hyperbole, "It's what makes us most human."

8   It is also what makes multitasking a poor long-term strategy for learning. Other studies, such as those performed by psychologist René Marois of Vanderbilt University, have used fMRI to demonstrate the brain's response to handling multiple tasks. Marois found evidence of a "response selection bottleneck" that occurs when the brain is forced to respond to several stimuli at once. As a result, task-switching leads to time lost as the brain determines which task to perform. Psychologist David Meyer at the University of Michigan believes that rather than a bottleneck in the brain, a process of "adaptive executive control" takes place, which "schedules task processes appropriately to obey instructions about their relative priorities and serial order," as he described to the *New Scientist*. Unlike many other researchers who study multitasking, Meyer is optimistic that, with training, the brain can learn to task-switch more effectively, and there is some evidence that certain simple tasks are amenable to such practice. But his research has also found that multitasking contributes to the release of stress hormones and adrenaline, which can cause long-

term health problems if not controlled, and contributes to the loss of short-term memory.

9   In one recent study, Russell Poldrack, a psychology professor at the University of California, Los Angeles, found that "multitasking adversely affects how you learn. Even if you learn while multitasking, that learning is less flexible and more specialized, so you cannot retrieve the information as easily." His research demonstrates that people use different areas of the brain for learning and storing new information when they are distracted: brain scans of people who are distracted or multitasking show activity in the striatum, a region of the brain involved in learning new skills; brain scans of people who are not distracted show activity in the hippocampus, a region involved in storing and recalling information. Discussing his research on National Public Radio recently, Poldrack warned, "We have to be aware that there is a cost to the way that our society is changing, that humans are not built to work this way. We're really built to focus. And when we sort of force ourselves to multitask, we're driving ourselves to perhaps be less efficient in the long run even though it sometimes feels like we're being more efficient."

10   If, as Poldrack concluded, "multitasking changes the way people learn," what might this mean for today's children and teens, raised with an excess of new entertainment and educational technology, and avidly multitasking at a young age? Poldrack calls this the "million-dollar question." Media multitasking—that is, the simultaneous use of several different media, such as television, the Internet, video games, text messages, telephones, and e-mail—is clearly on the rise, as a 2006 report from the Kaiser Family Foundation showed: in 1999, only 16 percent of the time people spent using any of those media was spent on multiple media at once; by 2005, 26 percent of media time was spent multitasking. "I multitask every single second I am online," confessed one study participant. "At this very moment I am watching TV, checking my e-mail every two minutes, reading a newsgroup about who shot JFK, burning some music to a CD, and writing this message."

11   The Kaiser report noted several factors that increase the likelihood of media multitasking, including "having a computer and being able to see a television from it." Also, "sensation-seeking" personality types are more likely to multitask, as are those living in "a highly

TV-oriented household." The picture that emerges of these pubescent multitasking mavens is of a generation of great technical facility and intelligence but of extreme impatience, unsatisfied with slowness and uncomfortable with silence: "I get bored if it's not all going at once, because everything has gaps—waiting for a website to come up, commercials on TV, etc.," one participant said. The report concludes on a very peculiar note, perhaps intended to be optimistic: "In this media-heavy world, it is likely that brains that are more adept at media multitasking will be passed along and these changes will be naturally selected," the report states. "After all, information is power, and if one can process more information all at once, perhaps one can be more powerful." This is techno-social Darwinism, nature red in pixel and claw.

12   Other experts aren't so sure. As neurologist Jordan Grafman told *Time* magazine: "Kids that are instant messaging while doing homework, playing games online and watching TV, I predict, aren't going to do well in the long run." "I think this generation of kids is guinea pigs," educational psychologist Jane Healy told the *San Francisco Chronicle;* she worries that they might become adults who engage in "very quick but very shallow thinking." Or, as the novelist Walter Kirn suggests in a deft essay in *The Atlantic,* we might be headed for an "Attention-Deficit Recession."

Paying Attention

13 When we talk about multitasking, we are really talking about attention: the art of paying attention, the ability to shift our attention, and, more broadly, to exercise judgment about what objects are worthy of our attention. People who have achieved great things often credit for their success a finely honed skill for paying attention. When asked about his particular genius, Isaac Newton responded that if he had made any discoveries, it was "owing more to patient attention than to any other talent."

14   William James, the great psychologist, wrote at length about the varieties of human attention. In *The Principles of Psychology* (1890), he outlined the differences among "sensorial attention," "intellectual attention," "passive attention," and the like, and noted the "gray chaotic indiscriminateness" of the minds of people who were incapable of paying attention. James compared our stream of thought to a river, and his observations presaged the cognitive "bottlenecks" described later

by neurologists: "On the whole easy simple flowing predominates in it, the drift of things is with the pull of gravity, and effortless attention is the rule," he wrote. "But at intervals an obstruction, a set-back, a log-jam occurs, stops the current, creates an eddy, and makes things temporarily move the other way."

15   To James, steady attention was thus the default condition of a mature mind, an ordinary state undone only by perturbation. To readers a century later, that placid portrayal may seem alien—as though depicting a bygone world. Instead, today's multitasking adult may find something more familiar in James's description of the youthful mind: an "extreme mobility of the attention" that "makes the child seem to belong less to himself than to every object which happens to catch his notice." For some people, James noted, this challenge is never overcome; such people only get their work done "in the interstices of their mind-wandering." Like Chesterfield, James believed that the transition from youthful distraction to mature attention was in large part the result of personal mastery and discipline—and so was illustrative of character. "The faculty of voluntarily bringing back a wandering attention, over and over again," he wrote, "is the very root of judgment, character, and will."

16   Today, our collective will to pay attention seems fairly weak. We require advice books to teach us how to avoid distraction. In the not-too-distant future we may even employ new devices to help us overcome the unintended attention deficits created by today's gadgets. As one *New York Times* article recently suggested, "Further research could help create clever technology, like sensors or smart software that workers could instruct with their preferences and priorities to serve as a high tech 'time nanny' to ease the modern multitasker's plight." Perhaps we will all accept as a matter of course a computer governor—like the devices placed on engines so that people can't drive cars beyond a certain speed. Our technological governors might prompt us with reminders to set mental limits when we try to do too much, too quickly, all at once.

17   Then again, perhaps we will simply adjust and come to accept what James called "acquired inattention." E-mails pouring in, cell phones ringing, televisions blaring, podcasts streaming—all this may become background noise, like the "din of a foundry or factory" that James observed workers could scarcely avoid at first, but which eventually became just another part

of their daily routine. For the younger generation of multitaskers, the great electronic din is an expected part of everyday life. And given what neuroscience and anecdotal evidence have shown us, this state of constant intentional self-distraction could well be of profound detriment to individual and cultural well-being. When people do their work only in the "interstices of their mind-wandering," with crumbs of attention rationed out among many competing tasks, their culture may gain in information, but it will surely weaken in wisdom.

[REFLECT]

Make connections: Advantages and disadvantages of multitasking.

Rosen cites studies that show that multitasking can have a number of negative effects—such as increasing stress and making learning less flexible—and that multitaskers have difficulty focusing attention on a single task and tend to be easily distracted, impatient, and bored. Think about whether your experience with multitasking confirms or contradicts these studies. Your instructor may ask you to post your thoughts on a class discussion board or to discuss them with other students in class. Use these questions to get started:

- What do you see as the advantages and disadvantages of multitasking? Have you experienced any of the negative effects Rosen writes about?

- Do you think multitasking is better for certain kinds of tasks than others? If so, what tasks?

- Under what circumstances, if any, do you practice what Timothy Ferriss calls "single-tasking"? Why might certain kinds of tasks or situations be better for single-tasking than for multitasking?

[ANALYZE]

Use the basic features.

A WELL-PRESENTED SUBJECT: USING DEFINITIONS AND EXAMPLES TO REFRAME THE SUBJECT

Because she is writing an evaluation critical of something she knows most of her readers think well of, Rosen needs to reframe her subject. That is, she needs to reintroduce the phenomenon in a way that leads readers to see that multitasking has serious disadvantages.

To do this, she starts the essay by defining the term: She offers synonyms and related words and phrases, gives examples, and contrasts the term with its opposite ("single-tasking"). Let's look at some of the strategies she uses to define what multitasking is and frame the concept for her readers. (Later, we will examine how she defines what it isn't.)

ANALYZE & WRITE

Write a few paragraphs analyzing and evaluating how Rosen reframes her subject:

1 Reread paragraph 1. How does Rosen introduce the concept of multitasking here? Why does she include the quotation from Lord Chesterfield?

2 Now reread paragraph 2. Notice how Rosen begins the paragraph with words from Chesterfield — "hurry, bustle, and agitation." What effect do you think repeating these words would have on the reader? Notice that she constructs her sentence with *multitasking* at the end, introduced by a colon and in italics. Why do you think she positions the word *multitasking* at the end of the sentence in this way? If you did not know what multitasking is, what would you learn about it from this sentence? Consider how Rosen classifies multitasking in the next sentence. How does explaining the history (or *etymology*) of the word *multitasking* help readers understand its meaning and help the writer reframe the concept?

3 A third defining strategy is to give examples of multitasking. Skim paragraphs 3 and 4, noting where Rosen offers examples. How do these examples help readers understand what she means by multitasking?

4 Consider how well Rosen's definition and examples set up readers for her evaluation of the practice in the rest of the essay. How well do her definition and examples fit your own experience and observation of multitasking? (Do not comment now on how she judges multitasking; focus only on how she defines it.)

A WELL-SUPPORTED JUDGMENT: USING AUTHORITIES AND RESEARCH STUDIES

Rosen relies primarily on authorities and research studies to support her argument about the value of multitasking. Because she is not writing for an academic audience, she does not include formal citations. But she does provide the same kinds of information about her sources that formal citations offer— the source author or lead researcher's name, the title of the publication in which the borrowed material appeared, and the year of publication of the source—so that readers can locate and read the source themselves. Notice in the following examples how Rosen presents this information.

> In one of the many letters he wrote to his son in the 1740s, Lord Chesterfield offered the following advice: "There is time enough for everything." (par. 1)

Bibliographical information

> An article in the *New York Times Magazine* in 2001 asked, "Who can remember life before multitasking? These days we all do it." (par. 3)

> "We have always multitasked . . . but never so intensely or self-consciously as now," James Gleick wrote in his 1999 book *Faster.* "We are multitasking connoisseurs." (par. 3)

Writers often begin with the source's name to provide context and establish credibility. In the third example, Rosen places the source information in the middle of the quotation, possibly because she wants to emphasize the opening phrases of both sentences.

Not all sources are quoted, of course. Writers sometimes summarize the main idea or paraphrase what the source has said:

> One study by researchers at the University of California at Irvine monitored interruptions among office workers; they found that workers took an average of twenty-five minutes to recover from interruptions. (par. 6)

Summary

> The psychologist who led the study called this new "infomania" a serious threat to workplace productivity. (par. 4)

Paraphrase

Studying how writers use strategies like these can help you as you write your own evaluation.

Write a paragraph analyzing and evaluating how Rosen uses material from other authorities and research studies to support her argument:

1 Skim paragraphs 4–9 to highlight the names of authorities and the research studies Rosen cites.

2 Choose two sources, and determine how Rosen uses them to support her judgment about the value of multitasking. Notice how she integrates them into her text.

3 Why might these sources be convincing (or not) for Rosen's readers? How convincing are they for you?

AN EFFECTIVE RESPONSE TO OBJECTIONS AND ALTERNATIVE JUDGMENTS: USING CONTRAST

Writing about a phenomenon her readers have experienced firsthand, Rosen has to assume that many of them will have a judgment of multitasking that differs from the one she is arguing for. Consequently, Rosen's entire essay can be seen as an attempt to refute an alternative judgment.

Rosen tries to convince readers to see multitasking in a new way by contrasting it with its opposite. In the opening paragraph, she uses a sentence strategy like this to present the contrast:

▶ _____ [the opposite of multitasking] is *not only* _____ [name a good quality]; it is *also* _____ [name another good quality].

Opposite of multitasking

Good quality 1

Good quality 2

EXAMPLE   To Chesterfield, singular focus was *not merely* a practical way to structure one's time; it was a mark of intelligence. (par. 1)

To learn more about patterns of opposition, see Chapter 12, pp. 537–38.

Write a couple of paragraphs analyzing and evaluating the effectiveness of Rosen's use of contrast to reframe her readers' ideas and attitudes about multitasking:

1 Skim the essay, highlighting with one color (or underlining) the qualities Rosen associates with multitasking, and highlighting with a different color (or circling) the qualities Rosen associates with the opposite of multitasking.

2 Review the words and phrases Rosen uses to describe multitasking and its opposite. What values and ideas does she attach to these two alternatives?

3 Given her purpose and audience, how well do you think this strategy of using contrast is likely to work? What seems to you to be its strengths and weaknesses?

Rosen *The Myth of Multitasking*

GUIDE TO READING
GUIDE TO WRITING
A WRITER AT WORK
THINKING CRITICALLY

381

A CLEAR, LOGICAL ORGANIZATION: CUEING READERS

Rosen's evaluation is complicated. Not only is she juggling multitasking and singular focus, but she is also referring to a range of sources spanning a long period of time. To make clear which phenomenon and which source she is talking about, Rosen uses a variety of explicit cueing devices, including time references, names and titles, transitions, and headings.

ANALYZE & WRITE

Write a couple of paragraphs analyzing and evaluating Rosen's use of cues to help readers follow her argument:

1. Skim paragraphs 1–4, highlighting dates and other time references Rosen uses to help readers follow the chronology.

2. Reread paragraphs 7–12, in which Rosen introduces a series of research studies. Highlight the name of the lead researcher (Grafman, for example) or the publication in which the report appeared (the Kaiser Family Foundation) and circle the transitional words and phrases she uses (such as "Other studies") to orient readers.

3. Note the two headings she uses. How do these help readers follow her evaluative argument?

Consider possible topics: Evaluating technology.

Choose a contemporary phenomenon to evaluate—for example, an Internet site (such as *Wikipedia*), a social networking site (such as *Facebook* or *Twitter*), or a reality television program (such as *Jersey Shore* or *MythBusters*). Select a phenomenon about which you already have a strong overall judgment and consider the criteria you would use to persuade others to accept your evaluation. Be sure to consider the evidence you could use to support your judgment.

[RESPOND]

For more reading selections, including a multimodal selection, go to **bedfordstmartins.com/theguide/epages**.

PLAYING WITH GENRE

Crowd-Sourced Evaluations

Most of us have opinions about things that interest us—music, TV shows, politicians—and sometimes we even express our likes and dislikes online, at sites like *TripAdvisor* or *Yelp*. Of course, some online reviews offer useful assessments of products and services, while others merely rant and rave. The helpful ones are generally those that offer a well-supported judgment, providing evidence that ranges from concrete examples to reviewer photographs. Just saying that a hotel or restaurant "sucks" isn't enough!

In an interesting acknowledgment that not all online evaluations are created equal, many sites now also encourage visitors to rate reviews, so effective evaluations rise to the top, while troll-like responses fall to the bottom. Sites may also provide an average rating and number of responses (as *Yelp* does), so users can tell whether the rating is based on a large number of responses and whether just a handful of bad ratings are pulling down an average score.

For an interactive version of this feature, plus activities, go to **bedfordstmartins.com/theguide/epages**.

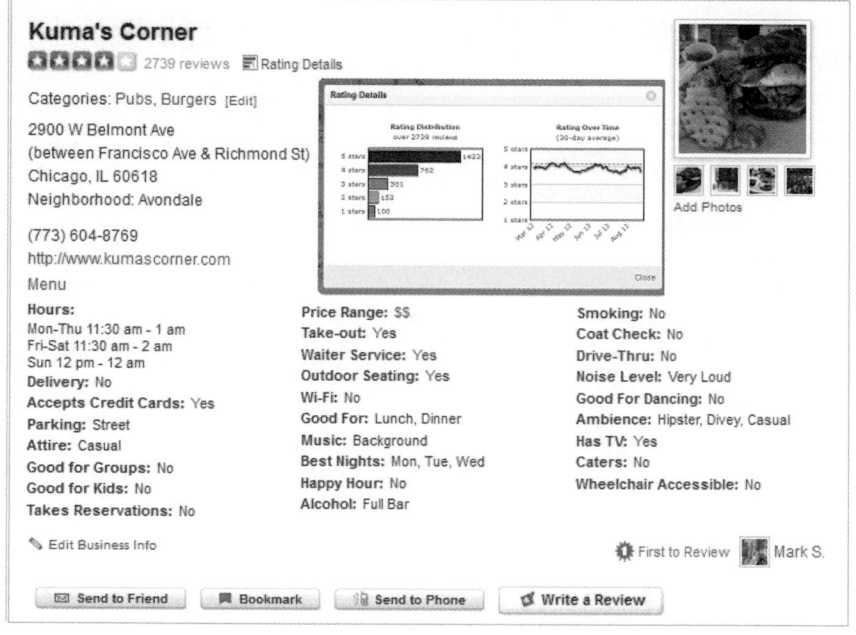

In this chapter, we ask you to evaluate a subject that interests you. As you write your evaluation, consider whether your claim will be more persuasive if you include photographic evidence or statistics from a survey of your own. Take a hint from evaluations in other media to make yours engaging and effective, but evaluate critically the strategies that work well in different genres to make sure they will be appropriate for an academic assignment.

The Writing Assignment

Write an essay evaluating a specific subject. Examine your subject closely, and make a judgment about it. Give reasons for your judgment that are based on widely recognized criteria or standards for evaluating a subject like yours. Support your reasons with examples and other details primarily from your subject.

This Guide to Writing is designed to help you compose your own evaluation and apply what you have learned from reading other essays in the same genre. This Starting Points chart will help you find answers to questions you might have about composing an essay evaluating a subject. Use the chart to find the guidance you need, when you need it.

STARTING POINTS: JUSTIFYING AN EVALUATION

How do I come up with a subject to write about?

- Consider possible topics. (pp. 368, 374, 381)
- Choose a subject to evaluate. (p. 385)
- Test Your Choice (pp. 385–86)
- Assess your subject, and consider how to present it to your readers. (pp. 386–87)

A Well-Presented Subject

How can I present my subject clearly and convincingly?

- Determine the writer's purpose and audience. (p. 353)
- Assess the genre's basic features: A well-presented subject (pp. 353–54)
- A Well-Presented Subject: Deciding How Much To Tell Readers (p. 366)
- A Well-Presented Subject: Introducing a Complicated Subject (p. 372)
- A Well-Presented Subject: Using Definitions and Examples to Reframe the Subject (pp. 378–79)
- Assess your subject, and consider how to present it to your readers. (pp. 386–87)

A Well-Supported Judgment

How do I come up with a thesis statement?

- Assess the genre's basic features: A well-supported judgment. (pp. 354–56)
- Formulate a working thesis stating your overall judgment. (pp. 387–88)

(continued)

383

A Well-Supported Judgment

How do I construct an argument supporting my judgment?

- Assess the genre's basic features: A well-supported judgment (pp. 354–56)
- A Well-Supported Judgment: Basing Judgments on Criteria (pp. 366–67)
- A Well-Supported Judgment: Defining Criteria (pp. 372–73)
- A Well-Supported Judgment: Using Authorities and Research Studies (pp. 379–80)
- Develop the reasons and evidence supporting your judgment. (pp. 388–89)
- Research your evaluation. (p. 389)
- Think about design. (pp. 396–97)

An Effective Response to Objections and Alternative Judgments

How do I respond to possible objections and alternative judgments?

- Assess the genre's basic features: An effective response to objections and alternative judgments (p. 356)
- An Effective Response to Objections and Alternative Judgments: Anticipating Readers' Concerns (p. 367)
- An Effective Response to Objections and Alternative Judgments: Singling Out a Comment for Response (p. 373)
- An Effective Response to Objections and Alternative Judgments: Using Contrast (pp. 380–81)
- Respond to a likely objection or alternative judgment. (pp. 389–91)

A Clear, Logical Organization

How can I help my readers follow my argument?

- Assess the genre's basic features: A clear, logical organization (pp. 356–57)
- A Clear, Logical Organization: Using Visuals and Headings (pp. 367–68)
- A Clear, Logical Organization: Using Comparison and Contrast (pp. 373–74)
- A Clear, Logical Organization: Cueing Readers (p. 381)
- Organize your draft to appeal to your readers. (pp. 391–92)

Writing a Draft: Invention, Research, Planning, and Composing

The activities in this section will help you choose and research a subject as well as develop and organize an evaluative argument. Do the activities in any order that makes sense to you (and your instructor), and return to them as needed as you revise. Your writing in response to many of these activities can be used in a rough

Writing a Draft

GUIDE TO READING
GUIDE TO WRITING
A WRITER AT WORK
THINKING CRITICALLY

385

draft that you will be able to improve after receiving feedback from your classmates and instructor.

⠿ Choose a subject to evaluate.

When choosing a subject for evaluation, keep in mind that it must be

- one that has strengths or weaknesses you could write about;
- one that you can view and review (for example, a location you can visit; a printed text; or a Web site or digital recording from which you can capture stills or video clips to use as examples in a multimedia presentation);
- one typically evaluated according to criteria or standards of judgment that you understand and share with your readers.

You may already have a subject in mind. If you do, skip to Test Your Choice below. If you do not, the following topics, in addition to those following the readings (pp. 368, 374, and 381), may suggest one you can write about effectively.

Subjects Related to School

- Evaluate some aspect of your high school or college—for example, a particular program or major you are considering; a residence hall, library, or lab; the sports facilities or teams; a campus research institute or center; or campus work-study or student support services.
- Evaluate an article, an essay, a textbook, or another book assigned in a course; a campus newspaper blog, editorial, or opinion piece; or a campus performance, exhibit, or film series.

Subjects Related to Your Community

- Evaluate how well one of the following meets the needs of residents of your town or city: public library, health clinic, neighborhood watch or block parent program, meals-on-wheels program, theater, or symphony.
- Evaluate a law or a proposed law, such as the Dream Act, the Stop Online Piracy Act, the Defense of Marriage Act, the balanced budget amendment or the equal rights amendment to the Constitution.

Subjects Related to Work

- Evaluate a job you have had or currently have, or evaluate someone else you have observed closely, such as a coworker or supervisor.
- Evaluate a local job-training program, either one in which you have participated or one that will allow you to observe and interview trainees.

> | TEST YOUR CHOICE |
>
> After you have made a provisional choice, ask yourself the following questions:
>
> - Do I know enough about the subject, or can I learn enough in the time I have?
> - Do I already have a judgment (either tentative or certain) about this subject?

- Do I know what criteria or standards my readers are likely to use for judging something of this kind? Would I use the same criteria?

To try out your choice of a subject and ideas about criteria, get together with two or three other students:

Presenters.   Take turns describing your subject.

Listeners.   Briefly tell the presenter what criteria or standards of judgment you would use to evaluate a subject of this kind.

As you plan and draft your evaluation, you may need to reconsider your choice of subject (for example, if you discover your criteria for evaluating are different from those your readers would use). If you have serious doubts about your choice, discuss them with your instructor before starting over with a new subject.

:: Assess your subject and consider how to present it to your readers.

Once you have made a preliminary choice of a subject, consider how you can frame or reframe it so that readers will be open to your evaluation. To do this, consider first how you regard the subject and what your readers are likely to think. Use the following questions and sentence strategies as a jumping-off point. You can make the sentences you generate your own later, as you revise.

WAYS IN

WHAT DO I THINK?	WHAT DO MY READERS THINK?
List those qualities of your subject that you like and dislike, or list its strengths and weaknesses or advantages and disadvantages.	Who are your readers, and why will they be reading your review? Is the subject new or familiar to them?

WHAT DO I THINK?

List those qualities of your subject that you like and dislike, or list its strengths and weaknesses or advantages and disadvantages.

▶ What makes _____ [good/bad] is _____ , _____ , and _____ .

▶ Although _____ is stellar in [these ways], it falls short in [these other ways].

What genre or kind of subject is it?

▶ The _____ is a [name genre or category of subject, such as romantic comedy or horror movie].

▶ It is an innovative [name category in which the subject belongs] that combines elements of _____ and _____ .

▶ [Subject] is rather unconventional for a [name category in which your subject belongs].

WHAT DO MY READERS THINK?

Who are your readers, and why will they be reading your review? Is the subject new or familiar to them?

▶ My readers are _____ and are probably reading my review [to learn about the subject or to decide whether to see it, play it, or buy it].

▶ My readers will probably be familiar with the subject [and may have heard or read others' evaluations of it]. They may be curious to know what I think because _____ .

How might factors such as the readers' age, gender, cultural background, or work experience affect their judgment of the subject?

▶ [Older/Younger] readers are [less/more] likely to _____ .

Writing a Draft

GUIDE TO READING
GUIDE TO WRITING
A WRITER AT WORK
THINKING CRITICALLY

387

What criteria or standards of judgment do you usually use to evaluate things of this kind?

▶ I expect _____ to be _____ or _____ .

▶ I dislike it when _____ are _____ .

How does your subject compare to other examples of the genre?

▶ Compared to [other subjects], _____ has the [best or worst] _____ [name trait].

▶ The _____ Is like [a comparable subject] in that both [are/do/make] _____ , but this subject is [more/less] _____ .

▶ Whereas other [comparable subjects] can be [faulted/praised for] _____ , this subject _____ .

▶ People who work in _____ or who are familiar with _____ may be [more/less critical, or apply different standards] to a subject like this one.

What criteria or standards of judgment do you expect your readers to use when evaluating subjects of this kind? What other examples of the genre would they be familiar with?

▶ I expect readers to share my criteria.

▶ If they [like/dislike] [comparable subject], they are sure to like/dislike _____ .

▶ Judging [this kind of subject] on the basis of _____ is likely to surprise readers because they probably are more familiar with _____ and _____ .

:: Formulate a working thesis stating your overall judgment.

You may already have a good idea about how you want to assert your thesis: stating whether your subject is good or bad, or better or worse than something else in the same genre or category. Remember that evaluations can be mixed—you can concede shortcomings in a generally favorable review or concede admirable qualities in a mostly negative assessment. If you feel comfortable drafting a working thesis statement now, do so. You may use the following sentence strategies as a jumping-off point—you can always revise them later—or use language of your own. (Alternatively, if you prefer to develop your argument before trying to formulate a thesis, skip this activity now and return to it later.)

As you develop your argument, you may want to rework your thesis to make it more compelling by sharpening the language and perhaps also by forecasting your reasons. You may also need to qualify your judgment with words like *generally, may,* or *in part.*

WAYS IN

HOW CAN I ASSERT A TENTATIVE OVERALL JUDGMENT?

A good strategy is to begin by naming the subject and identifying the kind of subject it is, and then using value terms to state your judgment of the subject's strengths and weaknesses:

▶ _____ is a brilliant embodiment of [the genre/category], especially notable for its superb _____ and thorough _____ .

> ▶ Because I admire [another artist's other work], I expected _____ to be _____. But I was [disappointed/surprised] by _____.

> ▶ _____ has many good qualities including _____ and _____; however, the pluses do not outweigh its one major drawback, namely that _____.

▪▪ Develop the reasons and evidence supporting your judgment.

For more idea-generating strategies, see Chapter 11.

The following activities will help you find reasons and evidence to support your evaluation. Begin by writing down what you already know. You can do some focused research later to fill in the details.

WAYS IN

HOW CAN I COME UP WITH REASONS AND EVIDENCE TO SUPPORT MY JUDGMENT?

List the good and bad qualities of the subject. Begin by reviewing the criteria and the value terms you have already used to describe the good and bad qualities of the subject. These are the potential reasons for your judgment. Try restating them using this basic sentence strategy, which is also illustrated by an example from student William Akana's film review:

> ▶ _____ is [your overall judgment] *because* _____, _____, and _____.

Example:

> *Scott Pilgrim vs. the World* can be appreciated and enjoyed by all audiences *because* of its inventive special effects, clever dialogue, and artistic cinematography and editing. (par. 2)

Write steadily for at least five minutes, developing your reasons. Ask yourself questions like these:

> ▶ Why are the characteristics I'm pointing out for praise or criticism so important in judging my subject?

Example:

> Akana singles out special effects, dialogue, cinematography and editing because of the particular kind of film *Scott Pilgrim vs. the World* is—"a hilarious slacker movie that also somehow reimagines romantic comedy" (par. 1).

> ▶ How can I prove to readers that the value terms I'm using to evaluate these characteristics are fair and accurate?

Example:

> Akana analyzes the film's special effects and gives readers specific examples, including screen shots, to demonstrate that they are indeed "inventive."

Writing a Draft   GUIDE TO READING
GUIDE TO WRITING
A WRITER AT WORK
THINKING CRITICALLY   **389**

Make notes of the evidence you will use to support your judgment. Evidence you might use to support each reason may include the following:

- Examples
- Quotations from authorities
- Textual evidence (quotations, paraphrases, or summaries)
- Images
- Statistics
- Comparisons or contrasts

You may already have some evidence you could use. If you lack evidence for any of your reasons, make a *Research To Do* note for later.

Research your evaluation.

Consult your *Research To Do* notes to determine what you need to find out. If you are evaluating a subject that others have written about, try searching for articles or books on your topic. Enter keywords or phrases related to the subject, genre, or category into the search box of

- an all-purpose database—such as *Academic OneFile* (InfoTrac) or *Academic Search Complete* (EBSCOHost)—to find relevant articles in magazines and journals;
- the database *Lexis/Nexis* to find newspaper reviews;
- a search engine like *Google* or *Yahoo!* (Akana used *Movie Review Query Engine* [mrqe.com] and *Rotten Tomatoes* to find film reviews of *Scott Pilgrim vs. the World*);
- your library's catalog to locate books on your topic.

Turn to databases and search engines for information on more recent items, like films and popular novels; use books, databases, and search engines to find information on classic topics. (Books are more likely to provide in-depth information, but articles in print or online are more likely to be current.)

To learn more about searching a database or catalog, see Chapter 24, pp. 674–75, 677–79.

Respond to a likely objection or alternative judgment.

Start by identifying an objection or an alternative judgment you expect some readers to raise. To come up with likely objections or alternative judgments, you might try the following:

- *Brainstorm* a list on your own or with fellow students.
- *Freewrite* for ten minutes on this topic.
- Conduct research to learn what others have said about your subject.
- Conduct interviews with experts.
- Distribute a survey to a group of people similar to your intended readers.

For more on idea-generating strategies, see Chapter 11; for more on conducting research, see Chapter 24.

Then figure out whether to concede or refute a likely objection or alternative judgment. You may be able simply to acknowledge an objection or alternative judgment. But if the criticism is serious, consider conceding the point and qualifying your judgment. You might also try to refute an objection or alternative judgment by arguing that the standards you are using are appropriate and important. Use the following strategies for generating ideas and sentences as a jumping-off point, and revise them later to make them your own.

WAYS IN →

HOW CAN I RESPOND EFFECTIVELY TO MY READERS?

1. Start by listing objections you expect readers to have as well as their preferred alternative judgments. In the Ways In activity on p. 386, you considered your readers and the criteria they are likely to favor. If their criteria differ from yours, you may need to explain or defend your criteria.

2. Analyze your list of objections and alternative judgments to determine which are likely to be most powerful for your readers.

3. Draft refutations and concession statements:

To Refute

▶ X, reviewer for _____, claims that _____. But I agree with Y, reviewer for _____, who argues that _____.

▶ Some people think _____ is [alternative judgment] because of _____, _____, and _____ [reasons]. Although one can see why they might make this argument, the evidence does not back it up because _____.

▶ Reviewers have remarked that _____ is a pale imitation of [comparable subject]. I disagree. Whereas [comparable subject] is _____, _____ is _____.

▶ This _____ has generated criticism for its supposed _____. But _____ is not _____. Instead, it is _____.

▶ In contrast to popular opinion, a recent study of _____ showed that _____.

To Concede

▶ Indeed, the more hard-core [name enthusiasts] may carp that _____ is not sufficiently [shortcomings].

▶ The one justifiable criticism that could be made against _____ is _____.

▶ As some critics have pointed out, _____ follows the tried-and-true formula of _____.

To Concede and Refute

Frequently, writers concede a point only to come back with a refutation. To make the *concession-refutation move,* follow concessions like those above with sentences that begin with a transition like *but, however, yet,* or *nevertheless,* and then explain why you believe that your interpretation or position is more powerful or compelling.

► As some critics have pointed out, _____ follows the tried-and-true formula of
_____. Still, the [director/writer/artist] is using the formula effectively to _____.

Research Note: You may want to return to this activity after conducting further research. (For example, when he researched published reviews of *Scott Pilgrim*, student William Akana found objections to his argument as well as alternative judgments he could quote and refute.)

For more on the concession-refutation move, see Chapter 6, pp. 248–49, 282–84.

▪ Organize your draft to appeal to your readers.

Whether you have rough notes or a complete draft, making an *outline* of what you have written can help you organize the essay effectively for your audience. An evaluative essay contains as many as four basic parts:

1. Presentation of the subject
2. Judgment of the subject
3. Presentation of reasons and support
4. Consideration of readers' objections and alternative judgments

These parts can be organized in various ways; two options follow:

If you are writing primarily for readers who disagree with your judgment, you could start by showing them what you think they have overlooked or misjudged about the subject. Then you could anticipate and refute their likely objections before presenting your own reasons.

I. **Presentation of the subject:** Reframe subject in terms that support your judgment

II. **Thesis statement:** State your judgment directly

III. **Refutation of alternative judgments**

IV. **First reason and support with refutation of objection**

V. **Second reason and support (and so on)**

VI. **Conclusion:** Reiterate why your judgment is preferable to the alternatives

If you expect some readers to disagree with your judgment even though they share your standards, you could begin by restating these standards and then demonstrate how the subject fails to meet them. Then you could present your reasons and support before responding to alternative judgments.

I. **Presentation of the issue:** Reassert shared criteria

II. **Thesis statement:** State judgment that subject fails to meet shared criteria

III. **First reason and support showing how subject falls short**

IV. **Second reason and support (and so on)**

V. **Refutation of alternative judgment**

VI. **Conclusion:** Reassert judgment based on shared criteria

For more on outlining, see Chapter 11, pp. 510–14.

There are, of course, many other ways to organize an evaluative essay, but these outlines should help you start planning your draft.

Never be a slave to an outline: As you draft, you may see ways to improve your original plan, and you should be ready to revise your outline, shift parts around, or drop or add parts as needed. If you use the outlining function of your word processing program, changing your outline will be simple, and you may be able to write the essay simply by expanding that outline.

Write the opening sentences.

You might want to review your invention writing to see if you have already written something that would work to launch your essay. Alternatively, try one or two options from the following list. But do not agonize over the first sentences, because you are likely to discover the best way to begin only after you have written a rough draft:

- An anecdote (like Akana)
- A surprising or provocative statement (like Boxer)
- A quotation (like Rosen)
- Something comparable that readers are likely to know (like Gladwell)
- Statistics or research study results

Draft your evaluation.

By this point, you have done a lot of writing to

- devise a well-presented subject and made a judgment about it;
- support your judgment with reasons and evidence that your readers will find persuasive;
- refute or concede objections and alternative judgments;
- organize your ideas to make them clear, logical, and effective for readers.

Now stitch that material together to create a draft. The next two parts of this Guide to Writing will help you evaluate and improve that draft.

Evaluating the Draft: Getting a Critical Reading

Your instructor may arrange a peer review session in class or online where you can exchange drafts with your classmates to give each other a thoughtful critical reading, pointing out what works well and suggesting ways to improve the draft. A good critical reading does three things:

1. It lets the writer know how well the reader understands the point of the essay.
2. It praises what works best.
3. It indicates where the draft could be improved and makes suggestions on how to improve it.

One strategy for evaluating a draft is to use the basic features of evaluative essays as a guide.

A CRITICAL READING GUIDE

A Well-Presented Subject

Has the writer presented the subject effectively?

Summarize: Tell the writer what you understand the subject of the evaluation to be, and identify the kind of subject it is.

Praise: Point to a place where the subject is presented effectively — for example, where it is described vividly and accurately, where it is named, or where it is clearly placed in a recognizable genre or category.

Critique: Tell the writer where readers might need more information about the subject, and whether any information about it seems inaccurate or possibly only partly true. Suggest how the writer could clarify the kind of subject it is, either by naming the category or by giving examples of familiar subjects of the same type.

A Well-Supported Judgment

Has the writer supported the judgment effectively?

Summarize: Tell the writer what you understand the overall judgment to be, and list the criteria on which it is based.

Praise: Identify a passage in the essay where support for the judgment is presented effectively — for example, note particularly strong supporting reasons, appeals to criteria readers are likely to share, or especially compelling evidence.

Critique: Let the writer know if you cannot find a thesis statement or think the thesis is vague or overstated. Tell the writer where the evaluation could be improved — for example, suggest another reason that could be added; propose a way to justify one of the criteria on which the evaluation is based; or recommend a source or an example that could be used to bolster support for the judgment.

An Effective Response to Objections and Alternative Judgments

Has the writer responded effectively to objections and alternative judgments?

Summarize: Choose an objection or alternative judgment about the subject, and explain it in your own words.

Praise: Identify a passage in the essay where the writer responds effectively to an objection or alternative judgment. An effective response may include making a concession — for example, agreeing that a subject the writer is primarily criticizing has some good points, or agreeing that the subject has weaknesses as well as strengths.

Critique: Tell the writer where a response is needed or could be made more effective — for example, suggest a likely objection or alternative judgment that should be taken into account, help the writer understand the criteria behind an alternative judgment, or offer an example that could be used to refute an objection.

(continued)

A Clear, Logical Organization

> Is the evaluation clearly and logically organized?

Summarize: Briefly describe the strategies used to make the essay clear and easy to follow.

Praise: Give an example of where the essay succeeds in being readable — in its overall organization, in its clear presentation of the thesis, in its effective opening or closing, or by other means.

Critique: Tell the writer where the readability could be improved. Can you, for example, suggest a better beginning or a more effective ending? If the overall organization of the essay needs work, make suggestions for rearranging parts or strengthening connections.

For a printable version of this Critical Reading Guide, go to **bedfordstmartins .com/theguide**.

Before concluding your peer review, be sure to address any of the writer's concerns that have not been discussed already.

Making Comments Electronically   Most word processing software offers features that allow you to insert comments directly into the text of someone else's document. Many readers prefer to make their comments this way because it tends to be faster than writing on hard copy and space is virtually unlimited; it also eliminates the process of deciphering handwritten comments. Where such features are not available, simply typing comments directly into a document in a contrasting color can provide the same advantages.

Improving the Draft: Revising, Formatting, Editing, and Proofreading

Start improving your draft by reflecting on what you have written thus far:

- Review critical reading comments from your classmates, instructor, or writing center tutor: What are your readers getting at?
- Consider whether you can add any of the notes from your earlier writings: What else should you consider?
- Review your draft: What can you do to present your position more compellingly?

Revise your draft.

If your readers are having difficulty with your draft, or if you think there is room for improvement, try some of the strategies listed in the Troubleshooting Guide that follows. It can help you fine-tune your presentation of the genre's basic features:

Improving the Draft

GUIDE TO READING
GUIDE TO WRITING
A WRITER AT WORK
THINKING CRITICALLY

395

A TROUBLESHOOTING GUIDE

A Well-Presented Subject

> My readers find my subject vague or do not think it has been identified clearly.

- Identify the subject, name the author or director, and give the title.
- Describe the subject — summarize what it is about, cite statistics that establish its importance, or give examples to make it concrete.
- Consider adding visuals — photographs, tables, or charts — to help clarify the subject.

> My readers aren't sure what kind of subject it is.

- Classify the subject by naming the genre or category it fits into.
- Refer to reviews or reviewers of subjects of this kind.
- Compare your subject to other, better-known subjects of the same kind.

A Well-Supported Judgment

> My readers don't find my thesis or overall judgment clear.

- State your thesis early in the essay.
- Clarify the language in your thesis statement to indicate your overall judgment.
- Consider whether your judgment is arguable (not simply a matter of taste). If you cannot provide reasons and support for it, then your judgment probably isn't arguable; ask your instructor about modifying your judgment or writing about a different subject.

> My readers aren't convinced that my evaluation is reasonable and/or persuasive.

- Clarify the criteria on which you base your judgment, and justify them by citing authorities or reviews of similar subjects, making comparisons, or explaining why your criteria are appropriate and perhaps preferable to criteria readers may be more familiar with.
- Add support for your reasons by, for example, quoting respected experts or research studies; providing facts or statistics; giving specific examples; or quoting, summarizing, or paraphrasing the subject of your evaluation.

> My readers don't understand my evaluation.

- Review the way you present your evaluation to make sure that you have explained it clearly and that you state your supporting reasons clearly.
- Outline your argument to be sure that it is clearly organized; if it is not, try rearranging parts or strengthening connections.
- Make sure that you have cut out any irrelevant content, and revise to strengthen the connections among your ideas.

(continued)

An Effective Response to Objections and Alternative Judgments

> My readers raise objections I haven't considered or find fault with my response to alternative judgments.

- If readers raise only a minor concern, you may be able to ignore or dismiss it. (Not every objection requires a response.)
- If readers raise a serious objection, one that undermines your argument, try to refute it by showing that it's not based on widely held or appropriate criteria or that it's based on a misunderstanding of your argument or the subject.
- If readers raise a serious objection that you can't refute, acknowledge it but try to demonstrate that it doesn't invalidate your judgment.

> My readers have proposed alternative judgments or have found fault with how I handle alternatives.

- Address the alternative judgments directly by conceding good or bad qualities of the subject that others focus on, but emphasize that you disagree about the overall value of the subject.
- Point out where you and your readers agree on criteria but disagree on how well the subject meets the criteria.
- Where you disagree with readers on criteria, try to justify the standards you are applying by citing authorities or establishing your own authority.

A Clear, Logical Organization

> My readers find my essay confusing or hard to follow.

- Outline your essay to review its structure, and move, add, or delete sections as necessary to strengthen coherence.
- Consider adding a forecasting statement early in your essay.
- Repeat your key terms or use synonyms of key terms to keep readers oriented.
- Check to see that you introduce your reasons clearly in topic sentences.
- Check to be sure that you provide appropriate transitions between sentences, paragraphs, and sections of your essay, especially at points where your readers have trouble following your argument.
- Review your opening and closing paragraphs to be sure that your overall judgment is clear and appropriately qualified.

Think about design.

Because evaluations depend heavily on excerpts from the subject, they frequently include quotations, paraphrases, or summaries of the subject. When the subject of evaluation is in a visual medium (as with films, television shows, works of art, and Web sites), writers may use movie stills, photographs, or screen shots as evidence to support their claims. Consider how William Akana used film stills from *Scott Pilgrim vs. the World* as evidence to support his claim that this film "can be appreciated and enjoyed by all audiences because of its inventive special effects" (par. 2).

Improving the Draft

GUIDE TO READING
GUIDE TO WRITING
A WRITER AT WORK
THINKING CRITICALLY

397

Scott Pilgrim vs the World shines bright with superb special effects that serve to reinforce the ideas, themes, and style of the film. Special effects are plentiful throughout the entire film, ranging from superimposed annotations echoing classic gaming features to artful backgrounds and action sequences modeled on colorful comic book pages. For example, each of the main characters is described for the first time with "gamertags," short-timed boxes of information that include name, age, and rating (see fig. 1).

Fig. 1. Screen shot showing gamertags

Uses a film still to support his claim that the film offers inventive special effects (film still shows "gamertags")

Connects text discussion to the illustration with a figure callout

Uses a caption to highlight what the illustration shows

Edit and proofread your draft.

Our research indicates that particular errors occur often in essays that justify an evaluation: incomplete and illogical comparisons, and short, choppy sentences. The following guidelines will help you check your essay for these common errors.

Making Complete, Logical, and Grammatically Correct Comparisons

The Problem In essays that justify an evaluation, writers often engage in comparison—showing, for example, that one film is stronger than another, a new recording is inferior to an earlier one, or one restaurant is better than another. When comparisons are expressed incompletely, illogically, or incorrectly, however, the point of the comparison can be dulled or lost completely.

The Correction Reread your comparisons, checking for completeness, logic, and correctness.

A Note on Grammar and Spelling Checkers

These tools can be helpful, but do not rely on them exclusively to catch errors in your text: Spelling checkers cannot catch misspellings that are themselves words, such as *to* for *too*. Grammar checkers miss some problems, sometimes give faulty advice for fixing problems, and can flag correct items as wrong. Use these tools as a second line of defense after your own (and, ideally, another reader's) proofreading and editing efforts.

For practice, go to bedfordstmartins.com /theguide/exercisecentral and click on Comparisons.

A comparison is complete if two terms are introduced, and the relationship between them is clearly expressed:

▶ *Jazz* is as good, *as* if not better than, Morrison's other novels.

▶ I liked the Lispector story because it's so different. *from anything else I've ever read.*

A comparison is logical if the terms compared are parallel (and therefore comparable):

▶ Will Smith's Muhammad Ali is more serious than any *other* role he's played.

▶ Ohio State's offense played much better than Michigan. *Michigan's did.*

Note that *different from* is correct; *different than,* though commonly used, is incorrect:

▶ Carrying herself with a confident and brisk stride, Katherine Parker seems
different *from* than the other women in the office.

▶ Films like *Drive,* which glorify violence for its own sake, are different *from* than
films like *Apocalypse Now,* which use violence to make a moral point.

Combining Sentences

The Problem   When writers justify an evaluation, they generally present their subject in some detail—defining it, describing it, placing it in some context. Inexperienced writers often present such details one after another, in short, choppy sentences. These sentences can be difficult or irritating to read, and they provide the reader with no help in determining how the different details relate to one another.

The Correction   Combine sentences to make your writing more readable and to clarify the relationships among ideas. Two common strategies for sentence combining involve converting full sentences into **appositive phrases** (a noun phrase that renames the noun or pronoun that immediately precedes it) or **verbal phrases** (phrases using words derived from verbs that function as adjectives, adverbs, or nouns). Consider the following example:

▶ In paragraph 5, the details provide a different impression. It is a comic or
perhaps even pathetic impression. The impression comes from *based on* the boy's
attempts to dress up like a real westerner.

From three separate sentences, this writer smoothly combines details about the "different impression" into a single sentence, using an appositive phrase ("a comic or perhaps even pathetic impression") and a verbal phrase ("based on the boy's attempts to dress up like a real westerner").

William Akana's Thesis and Response to Objections

GUIDE TO READING
GUIDE TO WRITING
A WRITER AT WORK
THINKING CRITICALLY

399

Here are two additional examples of the first strategy (conversion into an appositive phrase):

▶ "Something Pacific" was created by Nam June Paik/. ~~He is~~ a Korean artist who is considered a founder of video art.

▶ One of Dylan's songs ~~ridiculed~~ the John Birch Society. ^"Talkin' John Birch Paranoid Blues^." ~~This song was called "Talkin' John Birch Paranoid Blues."~~

Finally, here are two additional examples of the second strategy (conversion into a verbal phrase):

▶ Spider-Man's lifesaving webbing sprung from his wristbands/. _carrying_ ~~They carried~~ Mary Jane Watson and him out of peril.

▶ The coffee bar flanks the bookshelves/. _enticing_ ~~It entices~~ readers to relax with a book.

For practice, go to **bedfordstmartins.com /theguide/exercisecentral** and click on Combining Sentences.

A WRITER AT WORK

William Akana's Thesis and Response to Objections

In this section, we look at how William Akana anticipated his readers' objections. Using the Ways In activities on pp. 386–87, Akana determined that readers would be interested in his review to "learn about whether the movie is worth going to see," although he realized that his instructor would read the review to assess how effectively he used the basic features of evaluative essays and whether he included an insightful analysis of the cinematic techniques used in at least one important scene.

After writing for a few minutes on the first part of the Test Your Choice activity on pp. 385–86, Akana got together with three other students in the class to test out his idea for a subject and his criteria for evaluation. One of his group's members told him that she had gone to see the movie on a date and had found the film lacking as a romantic comedy. Akana realized that this was an objection that he could respond to.

A few days later, Akana received some helpful advice from a student who read his draft. Using the Critical Reading Guide in this chapter (pp. 393–94), the student noted that she could not find a clear statement of his judgment in the draft. She told him that the evidence he provided made it pretty clear that he liked the movie but that she couldn't find where he stated his judgment directly. So he went back to the Ways In activity on drafting a tentative overall judgment (pp. 387–88), and used one of the sentence strategies to help him draft a thesis:

> *Scott Pilgrim vs. the World* is a brilliant embodiment of the slacker film, especially notable for its superb special effects and clever dialogue.

When he finished his first draft, he revisited his thesis to polish it and to add another reason he had been discussing in his supporting paragraphs. He also realized that he needed to acknowledge the target audience but wanted to make sure readers who were *not* video game or anime enthusiasts knew they would also enjoy the movie. Here's the final version of his thesis:

> Although the film is especially targeted for old-school gamers, anime fans, and comic book fanatics, *Scott Pilgrim vs. the World* can be appreciated and enjoyed by all audiences because of its inventive special effects, clever dialogue, and artistic cinematography and editing.

Another student reader noted that Akana's draft provided lots of strong evidence, especially the analysis of film stills, but she found his response to an objection weak and unconvincing. This assessment hit home because Akana had inserted his classmate's criticism—that the movie failed as a romantic comedy—without really thinking about it. To strengthen his response to the criticism, Akana conducted research and found an expert reviewer who agreed with his classmate. He found a review by Rene Rodriguez in the *Miami Herald* that offered a reason why the romance was not convincing, and then he brainstormed his own response—that the romance is really secondary to Pilgrim's personal development. Akana then did more research and found a review that he could use to support this claim. His paragraph (par. 9), which originally focused solely on Rodriguez's criticism of the romance theme, developed into one in which Akana argued what he really believed—that the romance is pretty much beside the point.

THINKING CRITICALLY

To think critically means to use all of the knowledge you have acquired from the information in this chapter, your own writing, the writing of other students, and class discussions to reflect deeply on your work for this assignment and the genre (or type) of writing you have produced. The benefit of thinking critically is proven and important: Thinking critically about what you have learned will help you remember it longer, ensuring that you will be able to put it to good use well beyond this writing course.

Reflecting on What You Have Learned

In this chapter, you have learned a great deal about this genre from reading several essays that justify an evaluation and from writing an evaluation of your own. To consolidate your learning, reflect not only on what you learned but also on how you learned it.

Reflecting on the Genre

GUIDE TO READING
GUIDE TO WRITING
A WRITER AT WORK
THINKING CRITICALLY

401

| ANALYZE & WRITE |

Write a blog post, a letter to your instructor, or an e-mail message to a student who will take this course next term, using the writing prompt that seems most productive for you:

- Explain how your purpose and audience influenced *one* of your decisions as a writer, such as how you presented the subject, the strategies you used in justifying your evaluation, or the ways in which you attempted to counter possible objections.

- Discuss what you learned about yourself as a writer in the process of writing this particular essay. For example, what part of the process did you find most challenging? Did you try anything new, like getting a critical reading of your draft or outlining your draft in order to revise it?

- If you were to give advice to a friend who was about to write an essay justifying an evaluation, what would you say?

- Which of the readings in this chapter influenced your essay? Explain the influence, citing specific examples from your essay and from the reading.

- If you got good advice from a critical reader, explain exactly how the person helped you — perhaps by questioning the way you addressed your audience or the kinds of support you offered in support of your position.

Reflecting on the Genre

Good evaluative writing provides readers with reasons and support for the writer's judgment. However, the writer's personal experiences, cultural background, and political ideology are also reflected in evaluations. Even the most fair-minded evaluators write from the perspective of their ethnicity, religion, gender, age, social class, sexual orientation, academic discipline, and so on. Writers seldom make their assumptions explicit, however. Consequently, while the reasons presented within an evaluation may make it seem fair and objective, the writer's judgment may result from hidden assumptions that even the writer has not examined critically.

| ANALYZE & WRITE |

Write a page or two explaining how the genre disguises the writer's assumptions. In your discussion, you might do one or more of the following:

1. **Identify one of the hidden assumptions of a writer in this chapter.** Think of a personal or cultural factor that may have influenced the writer's judgment of the subject. For example, how do you imagine that Akana's gender may have influenced his judgment of the film *Scott Pilgrim vs. the World*?

2. **Reflect on your own experience of writing an evaluation essay.** How do you think factors such as gender, age, social class, ethnicity, religion, geographical region, or political perspective may have influenced your own evaluation? Recall the subjects that you listed as possibilities for your essay and how you chose one to evaluate. Also recall how you arrived at your overall judgment and how you decided which reasons to use and which not to use in your essay.

3. **Write a page or two explaining your ideas about how hidden assumptions play a role in evaluation essays.** Connect your ideas to the readings in this chapter and to your own essay.

9 Speculating about Causes

As children, we predictably ask "Why?" when we notice something new, unusual, or puzzling. This quest for answers inspires scientific inquiry, which can fully and satisfactorily explain the causes of many things. But for other subjects, the cause—or, more likely, causes—are uncertain and may never be known conclusively. For such subjects, it is helpful to think of *speculating about causes* as a special kind of *argument* that analyzes the evidence for a cause to determine whether it is likely to play an important—perhaps surprising—role in bringing about the effect.

IN COLLEGE COURSES

For a first-year seminar on the environment, a student prepares a research project speculating about what is causing coral reefs to die off. She includes photographs and cites a 2011 study that shows that six hundred square miles of reef have disappeared every year since the late 1960s. She argues that overfishing, runoff from agriculture, and damage from shipping are all contributing factors, but that rising ocean temperatures and increasing carbon dioxide in the atmosphere are more significant factors, apparently caused by climate change. She concedes that some scientists question whether climate change is severe enough to have been responsible for these changes; however, she concludes that rising temperatures and increasing carbon dioxide levels are factors worth studying in greater detail.

IN THE COMMUNITY

In an op-ed for a community newspaper, the captain of a neighborhood watch committee speculates on the causes of the neighborhood's deterioration. He has heard of the "broken windows" effect, the claim that small things like not fixing broken windows or cleaning up graffiti have a snowball effect that accelerates the deterioration of neighborhoods. His research shows that most political scientists and sociologists report a statistical correlation but no definitive cause-effect relationship between things like unrepaired windows and serious crime, so in his op-ed, he is careful not to overstate his claim. But he argues, based on his research and his own long experience in the neighborhood, that letting individual homes deteriorate has a negative effect on the neighborhood. He concludes that it is therefore especially important for neighbors to join together to clean up their block.

IN THE WORKPLACE

After an incident in which her twelve-year-old son is disciplined by a teacher, a science reporter comes up with an idea for an article speculating on the reasons for intolerance of "boyish behavior" in school. After getting the go-ahead from her editor, she reviews recent research in sociological and medical journals, in which she reads that boys are being diagnosed with various behavioral disorders at a far higher rate than girls. She conjectures that adults attempt to stamp out shouting, roughhousing, and other signs of aggression in boys for several reasons: because of concern about bullying; because boys' behavior is perceived as disruptive, especially in group-oriented classrooms; and because boys' fidgeting at their desks is seen as a threat to their eventual success in an economy that increasingly values sitting still and concentrating for seven or more hours a day.

In this chapter, we ask you to choose a subject that does not have a single, definitive cause that everyone accepts as fact, and then to *argue* that one (or more than one) cause is the most plausible culprit, providing *reasons* and *evidence* to support your claim. Analyzing the reading selections that follow will help you learn how to develop your own causal analysis. The Guide to Writing later in the chapter will show you ways to use the basic features of the genre to compose an original, thought-provoking causal argument.

PRACTICING THE GENRE

Arguing That a Cause Is Plausible

Making a cause-effect argument can be quite challenging and usually requires evidence. To think about how you could make a convincing argument, get together with two or three other students and follow these guidelines:

Part 1.   The health effects of smoking are well known—particularly the increased risks of lung cancer and heart disease. Smoking by teenagers has been declining for at least a decade. Using the statistics in the following table, from the annual Monitoring the Future study conducted by University of Michigan researchers, discuss a few possible causes that would help explain why some high school students today choose to smoke cigarettes. (If you have some ideas about why there has been a decline in smoking over the last decade, you could explore causes of that trend instead.)

Percentage of 12th graders reporting that they	2011	1996
are daily smokers	10%	22%
have smoked in the last 30 days	19	34
have ever tried smoking	40	64

Then, pick one of those causes and discuss these questions:

- Who might be interested in knowing about this cause?
- What kinds of supporting evidence would you need to convince this audience that the cause you have identified is plausible?

Part 2.   As a group, discuss what you learned from this activity:

- Think about how your group initially came up with possible causes. For example, did you recall your own experience and observation? Did you consider different categories of causes, such as cultural, biological, psychological, or social?
- When your group was discussing the kinds of supporting evidence needed to make a convincing argument about the cause's plausibility, what did you assume about your audience?

Analyzing Texts Speculating about Causes

As you read the selections in this chapter, you will see how different authors write a provocative causal analysis. Analyzing how these writers present their subjects to their readers, persuade readers that their cause is plausible, respond to alternative viewpoints, and organize their writing will help you see how you can employ similar strategies to make your own causal analysis clear and compelling for your readers.

Determine the writer's purpose and audience.

In speculating about causes, writers exercise their imagination along with their logical thinking skills, but they also want to influence the way their readers think. As you read these texts, ask yourself the following questions about the writer's purpose and audience:

- What seems to be the writer's main *purpose*—for example, to engage readers in thinking about the subject in creative new ways; to convince readers to contemplate causes that have not been considered or taken seriously before; or to persuade readers that certain causes are more likely than others to play a significant role in bringing about the effect?

- What does the writer assume about the *audience*—for example, that readers will already know a lot about the subject or will need to be informed about it; that readers' curiosity will need to be piqued; that readers will be familiar with the usual suspects and perhaps have their preferred causes; or that readers will be curious and open to new ideas?

Assess the genre's basic features.

Use the following to help you analyze and evaluate how writers of causal analyses use the genre's basic features. The strategies they typically use to make their essays insightful and persuasive are illustrated below with examples from the readings in this chapter as well as sentence strategies you can experiment with later, as you write your own causal analysis.

> **Basic Features**
> A Well-Presented Subject
> A Well-Supported Causal Analysis
> An Effective Response to Objections and Alternative Causes
> A Clear, Logical Organization

A WELL-PRESENTED SUBJECT

Look first at the title and the opening paragraphs to see what the subject is and whether it is clearly and vividly established. For example, to establish the subject, a writer may cite statistics or provide graphic illustrations, as in these examples from readings in this chapter:

> The exercise and fitness industry used to cater to a small, select group of hard-core athletes and bodybuilders. Now, physical fitness has an increasingly broad appeal to people of all ages, and the evidence can be seen everywhere. . . . Fitness club membership, according to the International Health, Racquet and Sportsclub Association (IHRSA), jumped from 20 million in 1991 to over 40 million in 2006. . . . It leapt

another 10 percent to 50.2 million in 2010 ("U.S. Health Club Membership"). As of September 30, 2011, as many as 16 percent of Americans were members of a health club ("IHRSA"). (McClain, par. 1)

"Researchers have underestimated the powerful importance of the local environment on eating," said Dr. Paul Rozin, a professor of psychology at the University of Pennsylvania, who studies food preferences. Give moviegoers an extra-large tub of popcorn instead of a container one size smaller and they will eat 45 to 50 percent more, as Dr. Brian Wansink, a professor of nutritional science and marketing at the University of Illinois, showed in one experiment. Even if the popcorn is stale, they will still eat 40 to 45 percent more. (Goode, par. 1)

Next, consider how the writer presents the subject to arouse readers' curiosity. One common approach is to pose the subject directly or indirectly as a *why* question:

Why We Crave Horror Movies

When we [see] a horror movie, we are daring the nightmare. Why? Some of the reasons are simple and obvious. (King, title, par. 2)

Why did so many people come forward to save Hokget? . . . Why did they feel a single abandoned dog on a stateless ship was *their* problem? (Vedantam, par. 11)

Finally, determine how the writer *frames* or *reframes* the subject to lead readers to put aside widely accepted causes and consider new possibilities. Writers often use the following sentence patterns (as shown in the examples included below):

▶ Most people assume _____; however, _____.

EXAMPLE   Saving the dog . . . was an act of pure altruism, and a marker of the remarkable capacity human beings have to empathize with the plight of others. There are a series of disturbing questions, however. (Vedantam, pars. 6–7)

▶ Many people do _____, but the reasons they do it are not what you'd think.

EXAMPLE   We all know why we should exercise, but why join a fitness club? Some of the answers may surprise you. (McClain, par. 4)

A WELL-SUPPORTED CAUSAL ANALYSIS

Find where the writer identifies and discusses each possible cause, and note which one(s) the writer favors as being the most plausible (the most likely to have played a significant role in bringing about the effect) *as well as the most interesting* (possibly because the cause has been overlooked or underappreciated). Then assess the persuasiveness of the supporting evidence:

Examples   From giant sodas to supersize burgers to all-you-can-eat buffets, America's approach to food can be summed up by one word: Big. (Goode, par. 1)

Analyzing Texts Speculating about Causes

GUIDE TO READING
GUIDE TO WRITING
A WRITER AT WORK
THINKING CRITICALLY

407

The evidence for what I am going to call the telescope effect comes from a series of fascinating experiments. (Vedantam, par. 14)

Research studies

In 2006, the Pew Research Center found that 86 percent of adults surveyed thought that "exercising for fitness improves a person's odds of a long and healthy life by 'a lot.' And, about six in ten believe that exercising has 'a lot' of impact on a person's attractiveness" (Table 1). (McClain, par. 3)

Statistics

Also check that the *cause-effect argument* makes sense—in particular, that the cause (or causes) could actually bring about the effect. Note whether either of these logical fallacies or errors of causal analysis have been made:

- **Mistaking chronology for causation:** Assuming that because one thing preceded another, the former caused the latter. (This fallacy is often called by its Latin name, *post hoc, ergo propter hoc,* which means "after this, therefore because of this.")

- **Mistaking correlation for causation:** Assuming that because two things seem to be related or complementary that one thing caused the other. (This fallacy is sometimes called "with this, therefore because of this.")

AN EFFECTIVE RESPONSE TO OBJECTIONS AND ALTERNATIVE CAUSES

Look for places where either objections to the writer's favored causes or alternative causes that readers might prefer are brought up, and assess how well the writer responds to these objections and alternatives—either by conceding *(accepting) or by* refuting *(arguing against) them.*

A common response strategy is to mention the well-known, predictable causes first, but quickly put them aside to make room for a more detailed consideration of the writer's preferred cause. Here are a couple of sentence strategies that you might look for in the reading selections (and use in your own writing), followed by examples of these strategies in context:

▶ .... and .... are the usual suspects, but let's look at a totally new possibility: ....

EXAMPLE   Some of the reasons are simple and obvious. To show that we can, that we are not afraid, that we can ride this roller coaster. . . . We also go to re-establish our feelings of essential normality. . . . And we go to have fun. Ah, but this is where the ground starts to slope away, isn't it? Because this is a very peculiar sort of fun, indeed. The fun comes from seeing others menaced—sometimes killed. (King, pars. 2–5)

Concedes but puts aside

Introduces a surprising new cause

▶ Research shows that [predictable cause] leads to .... , but it also leads to .... [conflicting result].

EXAMPLE   Skepticism about this cause is also evident in research by Laura Brudzynski and William P. Ebben, published in the *International Journal of Exercise Science,* showing that "body image may act as a motivator to exercise" but can also be "a barrier to exercise," particularly for those with a negative body image (15). (McClain, par. 6)

Concedes but then refutes

▶ [Experts argue/Studies demonstrate] that _____ is a key cause of _____ . Some claim that this cannot be proved. [But/still/nevertheless], _____ [evidence in support of cause].

EXAMPLE   She and other experts think it is no coincidence that obesity began rising sharply in the United States at the same time that portion sizes started increasing. But cause and effect cannot be proved. And the food industry rejects the idea of a connection. . . . Still, in cultures where people are thinner, portion sizes appear to be smaller. Take France . . . (Goode, par. 7)

Objection
Refutation

In this last example, Goode responds to the objection that correlation has been mistaken for causation. Notice how she goes on to refute this objection by using comparison and contrast.

A CLEAR, LOGICAL ORGANIZATION

Read to see if the writer provides cues to help readers follow the logic of the causal analysis. Essays speculating about causes tend to be rather complicated because the writer has to establish that the subject exists before presenting causes and arguing for those that are more likely to play an important role. (Notice that Sheila McClain spends her first three paragraphs establishing her subject.) So cues to help readers follow the argument are needed. Notice, for example, whether the writer asserts the preferred cause or causes in a *thesis statement:*

Causes forecast

We all know why we should exercise, but why join a fitness club? Some of the answers may surprise you — such as to be part of a community, to reduce stress, to improve your body image, and simply to have fun. (McClain, par. 4)

Notice, too, whether the writer *repeats* key terms or sentence structures from the forecasting statement in the essay's *topic sentences* to emphasize that another cause, response to objections, or supporting example is coming. Here's an example from "Why We Crave Horror Movies" by Stephen King:

FORECASTING STATEMENT   Why? Some of the reasons are simple and obvious. To show that we can, that we are not afraid, that we can ride this roller coaster. (par. 2)

Repeats sentence structure

TOPIC SENTENCE   We also go to re-establish our feelings of essential normality. (par. 3)

TOPIC SENTENCE   And we go to have fun. (par. 4)

By repeating the same subject (*we*) and an active verb (*can, are, go*), King helps readers identify each new cause.

Writers may also use parallel grammatical structures within a paragraph to help readers recognize a series of supporting examples. Consider this passage from "The Gorge-Yourself Environment" by Erica Goode:

Command form of verb
Future form of verb

Give moviegoers an extra-large tub of popcorn instead of a container one size smaller and they will eat 45 to 50 percent more. . . . Keep a tabletop in the office stocked with cookies and candy, and people will nibble their way through the workday. . . . Reduce prices or offer four-course meals instead of single tasty entrees, and diners will increase their consumption. (par. 1)

Each of these examples provides support for her claim that "environmental factors . . . can influence the amount the average person consumes" (par. 1). Other cues writers may provide to guide readers include the following:

- Introductory material establishing the subject
- A thesis statement and possibly a forecast of the main cause or causes
- Topic sentences announcing each new cause
- Clear transitional words and phrases
- Visuals (such as charts, graphs, and tables) that present information in an easy-to-read format

Readings

Sheila McClain | *The Fitness Culture*

ORIGINALLY WRITTEN by Sheila McClain for her first-year college composition course, this essay speculating about the causes of the fitness culture has been updated to reflect current statistics. Before reading, reflect on your own attitudes about exercise:

- How would you respond to the poll reported on in paragraph 3? How much do you think exercising can impact health and attractiveness?
- What do you do, if anything, to achieve physical fitness? What do your friends typically do?

As you read, consider the questions in the margin. Your instructor may ask you to post your answers to a class discussion board or to answer them in a writing journal.

1   The exercise and fitness industry used to cater to a small, select group of hard-core athletes and bodybuilders. Now, physical fitness has an increasingly broad appeal to people of all ages, and the evidence can be seen everywhere. You cannot turn on the television without seeing an infomercial featuring the latest exercise machine. Sales of fitness equipment for home use—from home gyms to DVDs and fitness games like the Wii Fit—have been booming since the early 1990s. Fitness club membership, according to the International Health, Racquet and Sportsclub Association (IHRSA), jumped

▪▫ Basic Features
A Well-Presented Subject
A Well-Supported Causal Analysis
An Effective Response to Objections and Alternative Causes
A Clear, Logical Organization

from 20 million in 1991 to over 40 million in 2006 ("U.S. Health Club Membership"; see fig. 1). Although club membership did not change significantly between 2006 and 2009, it leapt another 10 percent to 50.2 million in 2010 ("U.S. Health Club Membership"). As of September 30, 2011, as many as 16 percent of Americans were members of a health club ("IHRSA").

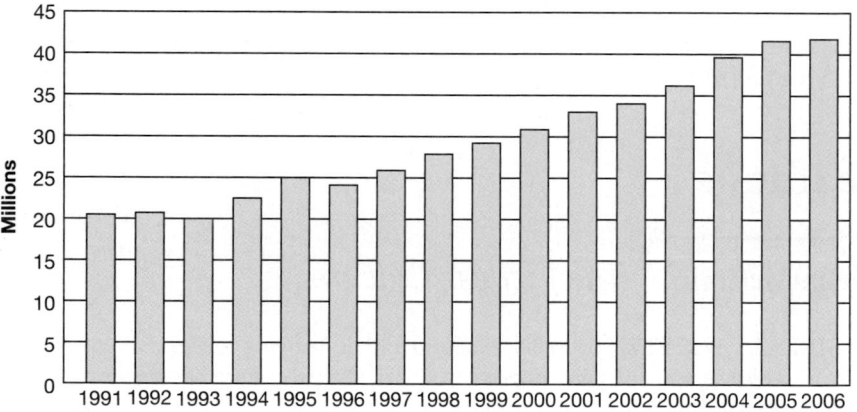

Fig. 1. Number of Health Club Members in the United States by Year (in Millions) (Source: The Active Network 2007, p. 4)

How does McClain establish the fact that the appeal of fitness has increased?

2   Research linking fitness to health and longevity has led to the growth of the "fitness culture" in America. Numerous clinical studies and scientific reports have been publicized confirming that exercise, together with a proper diet, helps prevent heart disease as well as many other serious health problems, and may even reverse the effects of certain ailments. According to Marc Leepson, historian and former staff writer for the *Congressional Quarterly*, "clinical studies in 1989 done by the United States Preventive Services Task Force, a government appointed panel of experts, found 'a strong association between physical activity and decreased risk of several medical conditions, as well as overall mortality'" (Leepson). Subsequent research has just heightened the association between fitness and longevity. A recent study reported in *Circulation: Journal of the American Heart Association* found that keeping fit or becoming more fit, regardless of your weight, can reduce your risk of dying. On the other hand, reducing your fitness correlated with increased risk ("Physical"). The

Take a look at the words and phrases (and synonyms for them) that McClain repeats in par. 2. Why does she repeat them?

federal government has tried to increase awareness about the benefits of fitness, including by promoting workplace wellness programs. "Hundreds of firms established in-house fitness centers or contracted with local gyms," because, as historian Marc Stern points out, exercise was assumed "to increase productivity, reduce absenteeism, enable recruitment and retention, and improve morale" (3–4).

3   As a nation, we have become much more aware of the ways that physical fitness contributes to health and longevity. In 2006, the Pew Research Center found that 86 percent of adults surveyed thought that "exercising for fitness improves a person's odds of a long and healthy life by 'a lot.' And, about six in ten believe that exercising has 'a lot' of impact on a person's attractiveness" (Table 1). Fifty-seven percent claim to do "some kind of exercise program to keep fit." Even so, "among these regular exercisers, about two-thirds (65%) admit that they aren't getting as much exercise as they should."

TABLE 1   The Benefits of Exercise.

How much do you think exercising can impact . . .	a long and healthy life	attractiveness
A lot	86%	59%
A little	11	31
Not at all	1	6
It depends (vol.)	1	2
Don't know	1	2
	100	100

Source: Pew Research Center

> Why does McClain include this table?

4   We all know why we should exercise, but why join a fitness club? Some of the answers may surprise you—such as to be part of a community, to reduce stress, to improve your body image, and simply to have fun. One reason people join fitness clubs is to fulfill the basic human desire for a sense of community and belonging. People today are more likely than in the past to stay at home, as Harvard professor Robert D. Putnam argued in his best-selling book *Bowling Alone: The Collapse and Revival of American Community*. As a result, Americans have become more solitary. At the same

> Why use a rhetorical question here?

time, they are growing more aware that they must stay fit to be healthy and realize that health clubs can have the added advantage of bringing them into contact with other people. Psychology professors Jasper A. J. Smits and Michael W. Otto, in their new book, *Exercise for Mood and Anxiety*, cite research showing that "one of the benefits of regular physical activity is feeling more connected to others" (7). Glenn Colarossi — a widely quoted authority on fitness, who has a master's degree in exercise physiology and is co-owner of the Stamford (Connecticut) Athletic Club—adds his own anecdotal evidence about why people join clubs: "People like to belong to something. They like the support and added incentive of working out with others" (qtd. in Glenn). Furthermore, Catherine Larner, a writer on health and lifestyle issues, considers "increasing one's circle of friends" among the benefits of going to the gym (1). Group exercise also fosters positive peer pressure that keeps people going when they might give up were they exercising alone at home.

How do these sources support McClain's argument?

5   Another even more surprising cause of the popularity of fitness clubs may be the anxiety about terrorism following 9/11. As Mary Sisson notes in an article in *Crain's New York Business,* health club chains saw an increase in revenues immediately after 9/11 and even expanded, one of them opening four new clubs, despite an economic downturn for most other industries. Sisson offers several plausible reasons why fear from the threat of terrorism on top of the normal stresses of modern life cause people to exercise more and to do so together: (1) under stressful conditions, people want the sense of community provided by gyms and classes; (2) working out gives people a sense of empowerment that counteracts feelings of helplessness; (3) traveling less provided many people with more leisure time to fill after 9/11; and (4) people make personal reassessments after a major catastrophe—such as the woman who realized how out-of-shape she was and joined a gym after descending forty flights of stairs to evacuate the World Trade Center.

Why does McClain call this cause "surprising"? How does the source she cites support her argument?

6   Body image is a more predictable cause but may not actually play as central a role as most people think it does. A cynical friend of mine thinks that the fitness culture is fueled by women who are less interested in reducing their stress, improving their health, or joining a community than they are in wanting to look like the idealized images of celebrities and models they see in the media. I tried out this idea on my exercise physiology professor, and she agreed that some people—men as well

How does McClain set aside this predictable cause in favor of her preferred cause?

as women—are motivated to begin exercise programs by the desire to reshape their bodies. The Pew Research Center poll showing people's opinions about the impact of exercising on attractiveness also seems to support this cause (see Table 1). However, my professor doubted that it could explain the huge increase in attendance at health clubs, because research in her field has shown that people with unrealistic goals are more likely to become discouraged easily and drop out of fitness classes (Harton). Skepticism about this cause is also evident in research by Laura Brudzynski and William P. Ebben, published in the *International Journal of Exercise Science,* showing that "body image may act as a motivator to exercise" but can also be "a barrier to exercise," particularly for those with a negative body image (15). So perhaps body image is not as significant a cause as many people assume.

7   A final cause worth noting is that fitness is becoming a lifestyle choice. As attitudes toward exercise are changing, health clubs may be becoming associated with fun instead of hard work. "No pain, no gain" used to be synonymous with exercise. But today exercise comes in many different forms, many of which are more engaging and gentler than in the past. The variety may also appeal to a wider range of people. Consider classes in belly dancing (you know what that is), strip tease aerobics (look it up!), and spinning (indoor group stationary cycling, led by an instructor)—these are just a few examples. David J. Glenn, writing in a business journal, points to the impact of these changing attitudes: "People look to personal fitness as a lifestyle and a way to enjoy life, not as a way to look like Arnold Schwarzenegger." Gabriela Lukas, a New Yorker who has been exercising regularly since 2001, finds it emotionally satisfying and says it makes her "feel alive" (qtd. in Sisson). When people are having fun, they are more likely to stick with exercise long enough to experience the body's release of endorphins commonly known as a "runner's high." More and more people are changing their attitudes about physical fitness as they recognize that they feel better, have more energy, and are actually improving the quality of their lives by exercising regularly.

8   The "fitness culture" in America continues to grow and shows no signs of slowing down anytime soon. As we become increasingly aware of the health benefits of fitness and as we continue to experience stress in our busy lives, we are bound to have even more need of the community support and the good fun of exercising with others at the local gym.

> How do these words and phrases make the argument clear?

> How effective is this way of ending?

What is one thing you learn from this works cited list?

Works Cited

Active Marketing Group. "2007 Health Club Industry Review." *The Active Network*. The Active Network, 2007. Web. 4 Apr. 2012.

Brudzynski, Laura, and William P. Ebben. "Body Image as a Motivator and Barrier to Exercise Participation." *International Journal of Exercise Science* 3(1): 14–24, 2010. *WKU Top Scholar*. Web. 6 Apr. 2012.

Glenn, David J. "Exercise Activities Mellowing Out." *Fairfield County Business Journal* 2 June 2003: 22. *Regional Business News*. Web. 6 Apr. 2012.

Harton, Dorothy. Personal interview. 3 Apr. 2012.

International Health, Racquet & Sportsclub Association. "IHRSA Quarterly Consumer Study Available Free to IHRSA Members." *IHRSA*, 29 Nov. 2011. Web. 8 Apr. 2012.

- - - "U.S. Health Club Membership Exceeds 50 Million, Up 10.8%; Industry Revenue Up 4% as New Members Fuel Growth." *IHRSA,* 5 April 2011. Web. 5 Apr. 2012.

Larner, Catherine. "Will Gym Fix It for You?" *Challenge Newsline* 31.1 (2003): 1–2. *Academic Search Premier*. Web. 6 Apr. 2012.

Leepson, Marc. "Physical Fitness." *CQ Researcher* 2.41 (1992): 953–76. *CQ Researcher*. Web. 9 Apr. 2012.

Pew Research Center. "In the Battle of the Bulge, More Soldiers Than Successes." *Pew Research Center Publications*. Pew Research Center, 26 April 2006. Web. 4 Apr. 2012.

"Physical Fitness Trumps Body Weight in Reducing Death Risks, Study Finds." *Science Daily*. Science Daily, 5 Dec. 2011. Web. 4 Apr. 2012.

Putnam, Robert D. *Bowling Alone: The Collapse and Revival of American Community*. New York: Touchstone-Simon and Schuster, 2001. Print.

Sisson, Mary. "Gyms Dandy." *Crain's New York Business* 26 Aug. 2002: 1–2. *Regional Business News*. Web. 3 Apr. 2012.

Smits, Jasper A. J., and Michael W. Otto. *Exercise for Mood and Anxiety*. New York: Oxford UP, 2011. Print.

Stern, Marc. "The Fitness Movement and the Fitness Center Industry, 1960–2000." *Business and Economic History On-Line* 6 (2008): 1–26. Business History Conference. Web. 5 Apr. 2012.

For an additional student reading, go to bedfordstmartins.com /theguide/epages.

Vedantam   *The Telescope Effect*

GUIDE TO READING
GUIDE TO WRITING
A WRITER AT WORK
THINKING CRITICALLY

415

Shankar Vedantam | *The Telescope Effect*

SHANKAR VEDANTAM is a National Public Radio correspondent and a journalist for the *Philadelphia Inquirer, Slate,* and the *Washington Post*. He has been honored with fellowships and awards by Harvard University, the World Health Organization, the Society of Professional Journalists, and the American Public Health Association. In addition to his many articles, Vedantam writes plays and fiction, including his short story collection, *The Ghosts of Kashmir* (2005). "The Telescope Effect" is excerpted from his book *The Hidden Brain: How Our Unconscious Minds Elect Presidents, Control Markets, Wage Wars, and Save Our Lives* (2010). The photograph of the rescued dog, Hokget, which appears in the reading selection on p. 416, is from the *Honolulu Star-Bulletin*. As you read, consider the following questions:

- How does Vedantam engage readers' interest in the opening paragraphs?
- How might including a photograph of the dog affect readers' perspective?

1   The *Insiko 1907* was a tramp tanker that roamed the Pacific Ocean. Its twelve-man Taiwanese crew hunted the seas for fishing fleets in need of fuel; the *Insiko* had a cargo of tens of thousands of gallons of diesel. It was supposed to be an Indonesian ship, except that it was not registered in Indonesia because its owner, who lived in China, did not bother with taxes. In terms of international law, the *Insiko 1907* was stateless, a two-hundred-sixty-foot microscopic speck on the largest ocean on earth. On March 13, 2002, a fire broke out in the *Insiko*'s engine room. . . . The ship was about eight hundred miles south of Hawaii's Big Island, and adrift. Its crew could not call on anyone for help, and no one who could help knew of the *Insiko*'s existence, let alone its problems.[1]

2   Drawn by wind and currents, the *Insiko* eventually got within two hundred twenty miles of Hawaii, where it was spotted by a cruise ship called the *Norwegian Star* on April 2. The cruise ship diverted course, rescued the Taiwanese crew, and radioed the United States Coast Guard. But as the *Norwegian Star* pulled away from the *Insiko* and steamed toward Hawaii, a few passengers on the cruise ship heard the sound of barking. The captain's puppy had been left behind on the tanker.

3   It is not entirely clear why the cruise ship did not rescue the Jack Russell mixed terrier, or why the Taiwanese crew did not insist on it. . . . Whatever the reason, the burned-out tanker and its lonely inhabitant were abandoned on the terrible immensity of the Pacific. The *Norwegian Star* made a stop at Maui. A passenger who heard the barking dog called the Hawaiian Humane Society in Honolulu. . . . The Humane Society alerted fishing boats about the lost tanker. Media reports began appearing about the terrier, whose name was Hokget.

4   Something about a lost puppy on an abandoned ship on the Pacific gripped people's imaginations. Money poured into the Humane Society to fund a rescue. One check was for five thousand dollars. . . . "It was just about a dog," [Hawaiian Humane Society president Pamela] Burns told me. . . . "This was an opportunity for people to feel good about rescuing a dog. People poured out their support. A handful of people were incensed. These people said, 'You should be giving money to the homeless.'" But Burns felt the great thing about America was that people were free to give money to whatever cause they cared about, and people cared about Hokget. . . .

5   On April 26, nearly one and a half months after the puppy's ordeal began, the *American Quest* found the *Insiko* and boarded the tanker. The forty-pound female pup was still alive, and hiding in a pile of

Hokget, the rescued dog, with Dr. Becky Rhoades, the veterinarian with the Kauai (Hawaii) Humane Society who examined her

tires. It was a hot day, so Brian Murray, the *American Quest*'s salvage supervisor, went in and simply grabbed the terrier by the scruff of her neck. The puppy was terrified and shook for two hours. Her rescuers fed her, bathed her, and applied lotion to her nose, which was sunburned.

6   The story of Hokget's rescue is comical, but it is also touching. Human beings from around the world came together to save a dog. The vast majority of people who sent money to the Humane Society knew they would never personally see Hokget, never have their hands licked in gratitude. Saving the dog, as Pamela Burns suggested to me, was an act of pure altruism, and a marker of the remarkable capacity human beings have to empathize with the plight of others.

7   There are a series of disturbing questions, however. Eight years before Hokget was rescued, the same world that showed extraordinary compassion in the rescue of a dog sat on its hands as a million human beings were killed in Rwanda. . . . The twentieth century reveals a shockingly long list of similar horrors that have been ignored by the world as they unfolded. . . . Why have successive generations of Americans—a people with extraordinary powers of compassion—done so little to halt suffering on such a large scale? . . .

8   There are many explanations for the discrepancy between our response to Hokget and our response to genocide. Some argue that Americans care little about foreign lives—but then what should we make about their willingness to spend thousands of dollars to rescue a dog, a foreign dog on a stateless ship in international waters? Well, perhaps Americans care more about pets than people? But that does not stand up to scrutiny, either. Hokget's rescue was remarkable, but there are countless stories about similar acts of compassion and generosity that people show toward their fellow human beings every day. No, there is something about genocide, about mass death in particular, that seems to trigger inaction.

9   I believe our inability to wrap our minds around large numbers is responsible for our apathy toward mass suffering. We are unconsciously biased in our moral judgment, in much the same way we are biased when we think about risk. Just as we are blasé about heart disease and lackadaisical about suicide, but terrified about psychopaths and terrorists, so also we make systematic errors in thinking about moral questions—especially those involving large numbers of people.

10   The philosopher Peter Singer once devised a dilemma that highlights a central contradiction in our moral reasoning. If you see a child drowning in a pond, and you know you can save the child without any risk to your own life—but you would ruin a fine pair of shoes worth two hundred dollars if you jumped into the water—would you save the child or save your shoes?[2] Most people react incredulously to the question; obviously, a child's life is worth more than a pair of shoes. If this is the case, Singer asked, why do large numbers

of people hesitate to write a check for two hundred dollars to a reputable charity that could save the life of a child halfway around the world—when there are millions of such children who need our help? Even when people are absolutely certain their money will not be wasted and will be used to save a child's life, fewer people are willing to write the check than to leap into the pond.

11   Our moral responsibilities feel different in these situations even though Singer is absolutely right in arguing they are equivalent challenges; one feels immediate and visceral, the other distant and abstract. We feel personally responsible for one child, whereas the other is one of millions who need help. Our responsibility feels diffused when it comes to children in distant places—there are many people who could write that check. But distance and diffusion of responsibility do not explain why we step forward in some cases—why did so many people come forward to save Hokget? Why did they write checks for a dog they would never meet? Why did they feel a single abandoned dog on a stateless ship was *their* problem?

12   I want to offer a disturbing idea. The reason human beings seem to care so little about mass suffering and death is precisely *because* the suffering is happening on a mass scale. The brain is simply not very good at grasping the implications of mass suffering. Americans would be far more likely to step forward if only a few people were suffering, or a single person were in pain. Hokget did not draw our sympathies because we care more about dogs than people; she drew our sympathies because she was a *single* dog lost on the biggest ocean in the world. If the hidden brain biases our perceptions about risk toward exotic threats, it shapes our compassion into a telescope. We are best able to respond when we are focused on a single victim. We don't feel twenty times sadder when we hear that twenty people have died in a disaster than when we hear that one person has died, even though the magnitude of the tragedy *is* twenty times larger. . . . We can certainly reach such a conclusion abstractly, in our conscious minds, but we cannot *feel it viscerally,* because that is the domain of the hidden

I want to offer a disturbing idea. The reason human beings seem to care so little about mass suffering and death is precisely because *the suffering is happening on a mass scale.*

brain, and the hidden brain is simply not calibrated to deal with the difference between a single death and a million deaths.

13   But the paradox does not end there. Even if ten deaths do not make us feel ten times as sad as a single death, shouldn't we feel five times as sad, or even at least twice as sad? There is disturbing evidence that shows that in many situations, not only do we not care twice as much about ten deaths as we do about one, but we may actually care *less.* I strongly suspect that if the *Insiko* had been carrying a hundred dogs, many people would have cared less about their fate than they did about Hokget. A hundred dogs do not have a single face, a single name, a single life story around which we can wrap our imaginations—and our compassion. . . .

14   The evidence for what I am going to call the telescope effect comes from a series of fascinating experiments.[3] At the University of Oregon, the psychologist Paul Slovic asked . . . groups of volunteers to imagine they were running a philanthropic foundation. Would they rather spend ten million dollars to save 10,000 lives from a disease that caused 15,000 deaths a year, or save 20,000 lives from a disease that killed 290,000 people a year? Overwhelmingly, volunteers preferred to spend money saving the ten thousand lives rather than the twenty thousand lives. Rather than tailor their investments to saving the largest number of lives, people sought to save the largest *proportion* of lives among the different groups of victims. An investment directed toward disease A could save two-thirds of the victims, whereas an investment directed at disease B could save "only" seven percent of the victims.

15   We respond to mass suffering in much the same way we respond to most things in our lives. We fall back on rules of thumb, on feelings, on intuitions. People who choose to spend money saving ten thousand lives rather than twenty thousand lives are not bad people. Rather, like those who spend thousands of dollars rescuing a single dog rather than directing the same amount of money to save a dozen dogs, they are merely allowing their hidden brain to guide them.

16   I have often wondered why the hidden brain displays a telescope effect when it comes to compassion. Evolutionary psychology tends to be an armchair sport, so please take my explanation for the paradox as one of several possible answers. The telescope effect may have arisen because evolution has built a powerful bias into us to preferentially love our kith and kin. It is absurd that we spend two hundred dollars on a birthday party for our son or our daughter when we could send the same money to a charity and save the life of a child halfway around the world. How can one child's birthday party mean more to us than another child's life? When we put it in those terms, we sound like terrible human beings. The paradox, as with the rescue of Hokget, is that our impulse springs from love, not callousness. Evolution has built a fierce loyalty toward our children into the deepest strands of our psyche. Without the unthinking telescope effect in the unconscious mind, parents would not devote the immense time and effort it takes to raise children; generations of our ancestors would not have braved danger and cold, predators and hunger, to protect their young. The fact that you and I exist testifies to the utility of having a telescope in the brain that caused our ancestors to care intensely about the good of the few rather than the good of the many.

17   This telescope is activated when we hear a single cry for help—the child drowning in the pond, the puppy abandoned on an ocean. When we think of human suffering on a mass scale, our telescope does not work, because it has not been designed to work in such situations.

18   What makes evolutionary sense rarely makes moral sense. (One paradox of evolution is that ruthless natural selection has produced a species that recoils at the ruthlessness of natural selection.) Humans are the first and only species that is even aware of large-scale suffering taking place in distant lands; the moral telescope in our brain has not had a chance to evolve and catch up with our technological advances. When we are told about a faraway genocide, we can apply only our conscious mind to the challenge. We can reason, but we cannot feel the visceral compassion that is automatically triggered by the child who is drowning right before us. Our conscious minds can tell us that it is absurd to spend a boatload of money to save one life when the same money could be used to save ten—just as it can tell us it is absurd to be more worried about homicide than suicide. But in moral decision-making, as in many other domains of life where we are unaware of how unconscious biases influence us, it is the hidden brain that usually carries the day.

Editor's Notes

1. Chris Lee and George Butler, "Complex Response to Tankship *Insiko 1907*," *Proceedings of the Marine Safety Council,* Vol. 60, No. 1 (January–March 2003), pp. 49–51.
2. Peter Singer has mentioned the story about the drowning child in a number of publications, including his 2009 book, *The Life You Can Save,* Random House, Inc.
3. Paul Slovic, "'If I Look at the Mass I Will Never Act': Psychic Numbing and Genocide," *Judgment and Decision Making,* Vol. 2, No. 2 (April 2007), pp. 79–95.

[REFLECT] **Make connections: Thinking about—and feeling— others' suffering.**

Moral dilemma experiments—scenarios that challenge our ability to decide what is the right thing to do—can be useful in helping us analyze our moral intuitions. Consider one of the moral dilemmas that follow, and then think about how scenarios like these help you to think through a moral decision:

- Vedantam's scenario: Would you have sent money to support the lost dog Hokget's rescue?

- Singer's dilemma: Would you be more likely to ruin expensive shoes to save a drowning child than to send the same amount of money to save an anonymous child halfway around the world?

- Slovic's dilemma: Would you rather spend $10 million to save 10,000 lives from a disease that caused 15,000 deaths a year or save 20,000 lives from a disease that killed 290,000 people a year?

- Sinking Lifeboat dilemma: Your cruise ship has sunk and you are in a dangerously overcrowded lifeboat. One person is gravely ill and not likely to survive the journey. Could you throw the sick person overboard in order to increase the chances of survival of the rest of the people in the lifeboat?

- Runaway Trolley dilemma: A runaway trolley is heading toward a group of people who can't be warned in time. Throwing a switch would shift the train from the track headed toward the group of people to another track on which one person is standing. Only you can divert the trolley by throwing the switch. What would you do?

Your instructor may ask you to post your thoughts on a class discussion board or to discuss them with other students in class. Use these questions to get started:

- What would you do if you were in the situation described in the dilemma? Briefly explain your choice. If you and your classmates are considering the same dilemma, discuss your various responses to it.

- How did you decide what was the right thing to do? For example, how did your feeling of closeness or identification with the potential victims or beneficiaries of your action influence you? How did the magnitude or the consequences of your action or inaction affect your choice?

- What is the value of participating in a thought experiment like this? If, as Vedantam suggests, we tend to respond to others' suffering, especially on a mass scale, with logical or "abstract" thinking, rather than "visceral" or gut feelings, what role did your gut feelings play in the scenario? What role do you think they should play?

Use the basic features.

⌈ANALYZE⌉

A WELL-PRESENTED SUBJECT: USING ANECDOTE TO DRAMATIZE THE SUBJECT

In "The Telescope Effect," Vedantam begins his causal analysis with an *anecdote,* a story about an actual event. Vedantam could have summarized the anecdote about Hokget in a sentence or two:

> A dog was stranded on a ship adrift in the ocean, and after an outpouring of concern, the dog was ultimately rescued.

Instead, he gives readers a brief but dramatic *narrative* about how Hokget got stranded (in pars. 1–3) and rescued (par. 5).

Write a paragraph or two analyzing how Vedantam uses anecdote and examples to support his causal analysis:

1 Reread paragraphs 1–3 and 5, highlighting the details that help to dramatize Hokget's story. What feelings do these narrative details evoke in you as a reader? Given his purpose, why do you think Vedantam would want to arouse readers' feelings at the beginning of his analysis?

2 Reread paragraph 7, contrasting the detail Vedantam provides in telling Hokget's story with the concise way in which he presents the example of the genocide in Rwanda. Why do you think Vedantam says so much about Hokget's story but so little about the Rwandan genocide?

A WELL-SUPPORTED CAUSAL ANALYSIS: USING A SOURCE

Although Vedantam is writing for a general audience, he follows the academic convention of explicitly acknowledging his sources. In fact, Vedantam states at the beginning of paragraph 14 that psychologist Paul Slovic's research provides the main "evidence" supporting his favored cause and cites Slovic's research in the notes.

Write a paragraph or two analyzing how Vedantam uses Slovic's research:

1 Reread paragraph 14. How does Vedantam use Slovic's research to support his causal analysis?

2 Reread paragraphs 12 and 15–18. What could Vedantam have added, if anything, to clarify the connection between Slovic's research and Vedantam's ideas about "the hidden brain" and "the telescope effect."

AN EFFECTIVE RESPONSE: USING COUNTEREXAMPLES

A common strategy writers use to refute alternative causes is to give counterexamples. A counterexample contradicts the causal explanation and shows that the analysis is flawed or at least incomplete. We can see this strategy at work in Vedantam's response to the cause proposed by Pamela Burns, the president of the Hawaiian Humane Society:

Paraphrase of Burns's cause	Saving the dog, as Pamela Burns suggested to me, was an act of pure altruism, and a marker of the remarkable capacity human beings have to empathize with the plight of others.
Transition cueing refutation	There are a series of disturbing questions, <u>however</u>. Eight years before Hokget was rescued, the same world that showed extraordinary compassion in the rescue
Counterexample	of a dog sat on its hands as a million human beings were killed in Rwanda. (pars. 6–7)

ANALYZE & WRITE

Write a paragraph or two analyzing and assessing how Vedantam refutes philosopher Peter Singer's causal analysis:

■1 Reread paragraphs 10 and 11. What example and counterexample does Singer use? How does Vedantam explain what Singer's thought experiment demonstrates?

■2 Now examine paragraph 11, noting where Vedantam appears to accept Singer's causal analysis and also where he cues readers that he is about to question it. How does Vedantam use the counterexample of Hokget to refute Singer's explanation?

■3 How effective is Vedantam's response? Does Singer's thought experiment raise interesting moral issues outside the context of Hogket?

A CLEAR, LOGICAL ORGANIZATION: USING RHETORICAL QUESTIONS

Writers sometimes use *rhetorical questions* to guide readers through a causal argument. In this selection, Vedantam presents several important rhetorical questions, such as these:

> Why have successive generations of Americans . . . done so little to halt suffering on such a large scale? (par. 7)

> Why did so many people come forward to save Hokget? . . . Why did they feel a single abandoned dog on a stateless ship was *their* problem? (par. 11)

ANALYZE & WRITE

Write a paragraph or two analyzing how Vedantam uses rhetorical questions to help readers follow the logic of his causal argument:

■1 Reread paragraphs 7–13, in which Vedantam poses rhetorical questions. What is the "discrepancy" (par. 8) or "paradox" (par. 13) that Vedantam is trying to explain? How do these rhetorical questions convey to readers this central problem?

■2 Skim the rest of the selection, highlighting the other rhetorical questions Vedantam includes. Which are Vedantam's own questions, and which are questions paraphrased from sources? How do these additional rhetorical questions help guide readers' understanding of the subject?

Consider possible topics: Current events.

[RESPOND]

Following Vedantam, you could consider the causes of a current event. For example, think about why people voted a certain way in a recent election, or why a particular news story or YouTube video went viral. Also think about the causes of something ongoing, such as why the risk of auto accidents is higher among teenage drivers than among older motorists, or why the rate of teen pregnancy is the lowest it has been in twenty years.

Stephen King | *Why We Crave Horror Movies*

STEPHEN KING is America's best-known writer of horror fiction. In 2003, he won a Lifetime Achievement Award from the Horror Writers Association, and he has also won many other awards, including the 2003 National Book Foundation Medal for Distinguished Contribution to American Letters. A prolific writer in many genres and media, King has recently published *The Wind through the Keyhole* (2012), the latest in his Dark Tower graphic novel series; *Road Rage* (2012), a comic book series co-written with his son Joe Hill; *11/22/63* (2012), a time-travel novel about the assassination of President John F. Kennedy; and *Stephen King Goes to the Movies* (2009), a short story collection. Many films and television movies have been based on King's work, including the classics *The Shawshank Redemption* (1994) and *Stand by Me* (1986). King offers this wise advice to beginning writers in *On Writing* (2000): "You have to read a lot and write a lot. There's no way around these two things . . . no shortcut."

Introducing horror films on Turner Classic Movies, King recently said, "You can talk to filmmakers and even psychologists who've studied the genre, and even they don't understand what works or what doesn't work. More importantly, they don't understand why it works when it works." Nevertheless, in this classic essay, King speculates about why some of us love horror movies. As you read, consider the following:

- What's your feeling about horror films, roller coasters, or other scary rides? For you personally, what makes them attractive or something to avoid?
- How does King go beyond the obvious in explaining why the culture at large appears never to tire of horror films?

1   I think that we're all mentally ill; those of us outside the asylums only hide it a little better — and maybe not all that much better, after all. We've all known people who talk to themselves, people who sometimes squinch their faces into horrible grimaces when they believe no one is watching, people who have some hysterical fear—of snakes, the dark, the tight place, the long drop . . . and, of course, those final worms and grubs that are waiting so patiently underground.

2   When we [see] a horror movie, we are daring the nightmare. Why? Some of the reasons are simple and obvious. To show that we can, that we are not afraid, that we can ride this roller coaster. Which is not to say that a really good horror movie may not surprise a scream out of us at some point, the way we may scream when the roller coaster twists through a complete 360 or plows through a lake at the bottom of the drop. And horror movies, like roller coasters, have always been the special province of the young; by the time one turns 40 or 50, one's appetite for double twists or 360-degree loops may be considerably depleted.

3   We also go to re-establish our feelings of essential normality; the horror movie is innately conservative, even reactionary. Freda Jackson as the horrible melting woman in *Die, Monster, Die!* confirms for us that no matter how far we may be removed from the beauty of a Robert Redford or a Diana Ross, we are still light-years from true ugliness.

4   And we go to have fun.

5   Ah, but this is where the ground starts to slope away, isn't it? Because this is a very peculiar sort of fun, indeed. The fun comes from seeing others menaced—sometimes killed. One critic has suggested that if pro football has become the voyeur's version of combat, then the horror film has become the modern version of the public lynching.

6   It is true that the mythic, "fairy tale" horror film intends to take away the shades of gray. . . . It urges us to put away our more civilized and adult penchant for analysis and to become children again, seeing things in pure blacks and whites. It may be that horror movies provide psychic relief on this level because this invitation to lapse into simplicity, irrationality, and even outright madness is extended so rarely. We are told we may allow our emotions a free rein . . . or no rein at all.

7   If we are all insane, then sanity becomes a matter of degree. If your insanity leads you to carve up women like Jack the Ripper or the Cleveland Torso Murderer, we clap you away in the funny farm (but neither of those two amateur-night surgeons was ever caught, heh-heh-heh); if, on the other hand, your insanity leads you only to talk to yourself when you're under stress or to pick your nose on your morning bus, then you are left alone to go about your business . . . though it is doubtful that you will ever be invited to the best parties.

8   The potential lyncher is in almost all of us (excluding saints, past and present; but then, most saints have been crazy in their own ways), and every now and then, he has to be let loose to scream and roll around in the grass. Our emotions and our fears form their own body, and we recognize that it demands its own exercise to maintain proper muscle tone. Certain of these emotional muscles are accepted—even exalted—in civilized society; they are, of course, the emotions that tend to maintain the status quo of civilization itself. Love, friendship, loyalty, kindness—these are all the emotions that we applaud, emotions that have been immortalized in the couplets of Hallmark cards and in the verses (I don't dare call it poetry) of Leonard Nimoy.

9   When we exhibit these emotions, society showers us with positive reinforcement; we learn this even before we get out of diapers. When, as children, we hug our rotten little puke of a sister and give her a kiss, all the aunts and uncles smile and twit and cry, "Isn't he the sweetest little thing?" Such coveted treats as chocolate-covered graham crackers often follow. But if we deliberately slam the rotten little puke of a sister's fingers in the door, sanctions follow—angry remonstrance from parents, aunts, and uncles; instead of a chocolate-covered graham cracker, a spanking.

10   But anticivilization emotions don't go away, and they demand periodic exercise. We have such "sick" jokes as "What's the difference between a truckload of bowling balls and a truckload of dead babies?" ("You can't unload a truckload of bowling balls with a pitchfork" . . . a joke, by the way, that I heard originally from a ten-year-old.) Such a joke may surprise a laugh or a grin out of us even as we recoil, a possibility that confirms the thesis: If we share a brotherhood of man, then we also share an insanity of man. None of which is intended as a defense of either the sick joke or insanity but merely as an explanation of why the best horror films, like the best fairy tales, manage to be reactionary, anarchistic, and revolutionary all at the same time.

> *The mythic horror movie, like the sick joke, has a dirty job to do. It deliberately appeals to all that is worst in us.*

11   The mythic horror movie, like the sick joke, has a dirty job to do. It deliberately appeals to all that is worst in us. It is morbidity unchained, our most base instincts let free, our nastiest fantasies realized . . . and it all happens, fittingly enough, in the dark. For those reasons, good liberals often shy away from horror films. For myself, I like to see the most aggressive of them—*Dawn of the Dead*, for instance—as lifting a trap door in the civilized forebrain and throwing a basket of raw meat to the hungry alligators swimming around in that subterranean river beneath.

12   Why bother? Because it keeps them from getting out, man. It keeps them down there and me up here. It was Lennon and McCartney who said that all you need is love, and I would agree with that.

13   As long as you keep the gators fed.

Make connections: Media violence. $\boxed{\text{REFLECT}}$

"The potential lyncher is in almost all of us," says Stephen King, ". . . and every now and then, he has to be let loose to scream and roll around in the grass" (par. 8). King seems to say that horror films perform a social function by allowing us to exercise (or possibly exorcise) our least civilized emotions. In fact, King even argued against a proposed ban on the sale of violent video games to people under the age of eighteen.

To analyze King's ideas about violence in the media, reflect on your own observation and personal experience with film, video games, or other media that may be considered violent. Your instructor may ask you to post your thoughts on a class discussion board or to discuss them with other students in class. Use these questions to get you started:

- King asserts that we all have what he calls "anticivilization emotions" (par. 10). What does King give as an example of these emotions? What have you seen, heard, or felt that suggests you or others harbor such emotions?

- The argument against violence in the media is basically that images of violence—or in the case of video games, performing virtual acts of violence—arouse anticivilization feelings and perhaps even inspire people (especially young people) to commit acts of real violence. King seems to agree that there is a cause-effect relationship, but what does he think is the cause and the effect? What do you think?

- If you think media violence inspires real violence, do you support censorship of movies, television programs, books, or Internet sites that portray violence? If so, should this material be censored just for children or for all viewers? If you oppose outright censorship, do you support movie rating systems or the television V-chip, which gives parents some control over what their children watch? Explain your responses.

⎡ANALYZE⎤ Use the basic features.

A WELL-PRESENTED SUBJECT: REFRAMING THE SUBJECT FOR READERS

Writers try to present their subjects in an intriguing way that makes readers wonder about it. To do so, they typically frame or reframe their subjects, emphasizing new ways of looking at and understanding them. How does King make room for his less predictable causes and convince readers to go along for the ride?

⎡ANALYZE & WRITE⎤

Write a couple of paragraphs analyzing and evaluating how King reframes his subject:

1 The title suggests that the subject of this essay is horror movies, but the key term in the title is the word "crave." Look up the verb *crave* and the related noun *craving* to see what they mean. Also highlight some of the other words and phrases King associates with the appeal of horror movies, such as "mentally ill" and "hysterical fear" (par. 1). How do the words you highlighted relate to the word *crave*?

2 Given these key terms, how would you describe the way King reframes the subject for readers? How do these key terms enable him to plant the seed of his main idea at the very beginning of the essay?

A WELL-SUPPORTED CAUSAL ANALYSIS: USING EXAMPLES AND COMPARISONS

In writing about horror movies, you might expect King to provide a lot of examples of the genre or to go into detail about one or two particularly memorable films. But, interestingly, King names only two films, neither of which is that memorable. By limiting the number and only referring to them briefly, King leaves a lot of space for readers to fill with their own favorite horror movies.

| ANALYZE & WRITE |

Write a couple of paragraphs analyzing and evaluating the examples and comparisons King uses to support his argument and the films that come to mind for you:

1 In addition to horror movies, King gives several other examples. Find one or two of them, and consider how well they confirm his thesis that we all harbor anticivilization emotions.

2 King also compares horror movies to various other things, such as roller coasters (par. 2). Skim the essay, highlighting the comparisons King makes. Then, consider how they help support his causal argument.

3 Taken together, how effective are the examples and comparisons as support for King's analysis? What examples did you think of as you read? How would the reading have been different had King supplied more examples of horror films?

AN EFFECTIVE RESPONSE: PUTTING ASIDE OBVIOUS CAUSES

People analyzing causes sometimes consider an array of possibilities before focusing on one or two serious probabilities. They may concede that these other causes play some role, or they may simply dismiss them as trivial or irrelevant. "Some of the reasons," King explicitly declares, "are simple and obvious" (par. 2).

| ANALYZE & WRITE |

Write a couple of paragraphs analyzing and evaluating how well King uses concession and refutation:

1 Look closely at the causes King considers in the opening paragraphs to determine how he actually responds to them. For example, how does he support the assertion that some of them are "simple and obvious"? What other arguments, if any, does he use to refute them?

2 Given his purpose and audience, why do you think King chooses to begin by presenting reasons he thinks are simple and obvious?

A CLEAR, LOGICAL ORGANIZATION: USING CAUSE-EFFECT SENTENCE STRATEGIES

Writers of essays speculating about causes sometimes rely on certain sentence strategies to present cause-effect relationships:

▶ When _____ happens, _____ is the result.

▶ If [I/he/she/we/they do/say/act] _____, then [others do/say/act] _____.

These two types of sentences can be seen in King's essay:

> When we exhibit these emotions, society showers us with positive reinforcement; we learn this even before we get out of diapers. When, as children, we hug our rotten little puke of a sister and give her a kiss, all the aunts and uncles smile and twit and cry, "Isn't he the sweetest little thing?" Such coveted treats as chocolate-covered graham crackers often follow. But if we deliberately slam the rotten little puke of a sister's fingers in the door, sanctions follow — angry remonstrance from parents, aunts, and uncles; instead of a chocolate-covered graham cracker, a spanking. (par. 9)

Both of these sentence strategies establish a chronological relationship — one thing happens and then another thing happens. They also establish a causal relationship. (Chronology and causality, of course, do not always go together. See p. 407.)

| ANALYZE & WRITE |

Write a paragraph or two analyzing and evaluating how King uses these patterns elsewhere in this reading selection:

1 Skim the essay to find and mark the sentences elsewhere in the essay that use these strategies. How do you know whether they each present a cause-effect relationship as well as a chronological sequence?

2 Why do you think King repeats these sentence strategies so often in this essay? Is this repetition an effective or ineffective strategy?

[RESPOND] **Consider possible topics: Popular culture.**

Following King, you could consider writing about some aspect of popular culture. Consider, for example, why particular social networking sites, apps or video games, or genres of fiction or film are so popular with college students or other demographic groups. Why do ads appealing to sex work so well to sell cars and other consumer products? Why are negative political ads so effective?

Erica Goode | *The Gorge-Yourself Environment*

ERICA GOODE is an award-winning journalist who served as assistant managing editor at *U.S. News & World Report* before joining the *New York Times,* where she covers science and the environment. After earning a master's degree in social psychology, Goode received fellowships from the American Association for the Advancement of Science and the Center for Advanced Study in the Behavioral Sciences at Stanford University. She has won awards for her writing from the National Mental Health Association and the American Psychiatric Association.

Notice that even though writing for a newspaper and, therefore, not using an academic style of citing sources, Goode informs readers about her sources. As you read, consider the following:

- How effectively does Goode establish the credibility of her sources?
- What more, if anything, might she do to demonstrate their reliability? How would she present her sources differently if she were writing for an academic audience?

1 From giant sodas to supersize burgers to all-you-can-eat buffets, America's approach to food can be summed up by one word: Big. Plates are piled high, and few crumbs are left behind. Today's blueberry muffin could, in an earlier era, have fed a family of four. But social norms change. . . . Traditionally, the prescription for shedding extra pounds has been a sensible diet and increased exercise. Losing weight has been viewed as a matter of personal responsibility, a private battle between dieters and their bathroom scales. But a growing number of studies suggests that while willpower obviously plays a role, people do not gorge themselves solely because they lack self-control. Rather, social scientists are finding, a host of environmental factors—among them, portion size, price, . . . the availability of food and the number of food choices presented—can influence the amount the average person consumes. "Researchers have underestimated the powerful importance of the local environment on eating," said Dr. Paul Rozin, a professor of psychology at the University of Pennsylvania, who studies food preferences. Give moviegoers an extra-large tub of popcorn instead of a container one size smaller and they will eat 45 to 50 percent more, as Dr. Brian Wansink, a professor of nutritional science and marketing at the University of Illinois, showed in one experiment. Even if the popcorn is stale, they will still eat 40 to 45 percent more. Keep a tabletop in the office stocked with cookies and candy, and people will nibble their way through the workday, even if they are not hungry. Reduce prices or offer four-course meals instead of single tasty entrees, and diners will increase their consumption.

2 In a culture where serving sizes are mammoth, attractive foods are ubiquitous, bargains are abundant and variety is not just the spice but the staple of life, many researchers say, it is no surprise that waistlines are expanding. Dr. Kelly D. Brownell, a professor of psychology at Yale and an expert on eating disorders, has gone so far as to label American society a "toxic environment" when it comes to food. Health experts and consumer advocates point to the studies of portion size and other environmental influences in arguing that fast-food chains and food manufacturers must bear some of the blame for the country's weight problem. "The food industry has used portion sizes and value marketing as very effective tools to try to increase their sales and profits," said Margo Wootan, the director of nutrition policy at the Center for Science in the Public Interest, an advocacy group financed by private foundations. . . .

3 . . . An increasing number of studies show that how food is served, presented and sold plays at least some role in what and how much people eat. Price is a powerful influence. In a series of studies, researchers at the University of Minnesota have demonstrated that the relative cost of different products has an even more potent effect on food choice than nutritional labeling. Dr. Simone French, an associate professor of epidemiology, and her colleagues manipulated the prices of high-fat and low-fat snacks in vending machines at 12 high schools and 12 workplaces. In some cases, the snacks were labeled to indicate their fat content. "The most interesting finding was that the price changes were whopping in effect," compared with the labels, Dr. French said. Dropping the price of the low-fat snacks by even a nickel spurred more sales. In contrast, orange stickers signaling low-fat content or cartoons promoting the low-fat alternatives had little influence over which snacks were more popular.

4 Packaging can change the amount people consume. Dr. Wansink and his colleagues have showed that, fooled by a visual illusion, people drink more from short, wide glasses than thinner, taller ones, but they think they are drinking less. Having more choices also appears to make people eat more. In one study, Dr. Barbara Rolls,

More Food, More Choices, More Eating. In an affluent society, decisions about what and how much to eat are dictated by many factors besides hunger. Bigger, cheaper, and more varied meals, heavily advertised and widely available, may induce people to eat more than they need to.

whose laboratory at Pennsylvania State University has studied the effects of the environment on eating, found that research subjects ate more when offered sandwiches with four different fillings than they did when they were given sandwiches with their single favorite filling. In another study, participants served a four-course meal with meat, fruit, bread and a pudding—foods with very different tastes, flavors and textures—ate 60 percent more food than those served an equivalent meal of only their favorite course.

5   To anyone who has survived Christmas season at the office, it will come as no surprise that the availability of food has an effect as well. Dr. Wansink and his colleagues varied the placement of chocolate candy in work settings over three weeks. When the candy was in plain sight on workers' desks, they ate an average of nine pieces each. Storing the sweets in a desk drawer reduced consumption to six pieces. And chocolates lurking out of sight, a couple of yards from the desk, cut the number to three pieces per person.

6   Researchers have long suspected that large portions encourage people to eat more, but studies have begun to confirm this suspicion only in the last several years. There is little question that the serving size of many foods has increased since McDonald's introduced its groundbreaking Big Mac in 1968. For her doctoral dissertation, Dr. Lisa Young, now an adjunct assistant professor in the department of nutrition, food studies and public health at New York University, tracked portion sizes in national restaurant chains, in foods like cakes, bread products, steaks and sodas and in cookbook recipes from the 1970's to the late 1990's. The amount of food allotted for one person increased in virtually every category Dr. Young examined. French fries, hamburgers and soda expanded to portions that were two to five times as great as they had been at the beginning of the

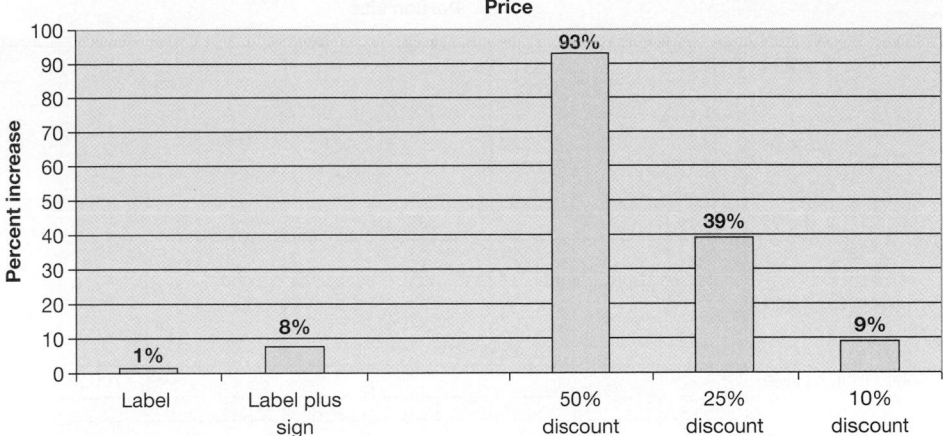

According to a 2001 study on the effects of promotion and price on sales of low-fat foods in vending machines, price was by far the most significant factor in persuading consumers to buy. Source: French et al. (2001)

period Dr. Young studied. Steaks, chocolate bars and bread products grew markedly. Cookbooks specified fewer servings (and correspondingly larger portions) for the same recipe appearing in earlier editions. "Restaurants are using larger dinner plates, bakers are selling larger muffin tins, pizzerias are using larger pans and fast-food companies are using larger drink and French fry containers," Dr. Young wrote in a paper published last year in *The American Journal of Public Health*. Even the cup holders in automobiles have grown larger to make room for giant drinks, Dr. Young noted.

7   She and other experts think it is no coincidence that obesity began rising sharply in the United States at the same time that portion sizes started increasing. But cause and effect cannot be proved. And the food industry rejects the idea of a connection. Mr. Anderson of the restaurant association, for example, says that lack of exercise, poor eating habits and genetic influences are largely responsible for Americans' struggle with extra fat. Still, in cultures where people are thinner, portion sizes appear to be smaller. Take France, where the citizenry is leaner in body mass and where only 7.4 percent of the population is obese, a contrast to America, where 22.3 percent qualify. Examining similar restaurant meals and supermarket foods in Paris and Philadelphia, Dr. Rozin and colleagues at Penn found that the Parisian portions were significantly less hefty. Cookbook portions were

also smaller. Even some items sold at McDonald's—the chicken sandwich, for example—are smaller than their American counterparts.

8   "There is a disconnect between people's understanding of portions and the idea that a larger portion has more calories," said Dr. Marion Nestle, chairwoman of the N.Y.U. nutrition and food policy department and the author of "Food Politics: How the Food Industry Influences Nutrition and Health." The Double Gulp, a 64-ounce soft drink sold by 7-Eleven, Dr. Nestle noted, has close to 800 calories, more than a third of many people's daily requirement, but she said people were often shocked to learn this. And, as studies by Dr. Rolls, Dr. Wansink and others suggest, faced with larger portions, people are likely to consume more, an effect, Dr. Rolls noted, that is not limited to people who are overweight. "Men or women, obese or lean, dieters, nondieters, plate-cleaners, non-plate-cleaners—it's pretty much across the board," she said. In one demonstration of this, Dr. Rolls and her colleagues varied the portions of ziti served at an Italian restaurant, keeping the price for the dish the same but on some days increasing the serving by 50 percent. On the days of the increase, Dr. Rolls said, customers ate 45 percent more, and while diners rated the bigger portion size as a better value, they deemed both servings appropriate. The researchers have also shown that after downing large plates of food, people do not usually compensate by eating less at their next meal. . . .

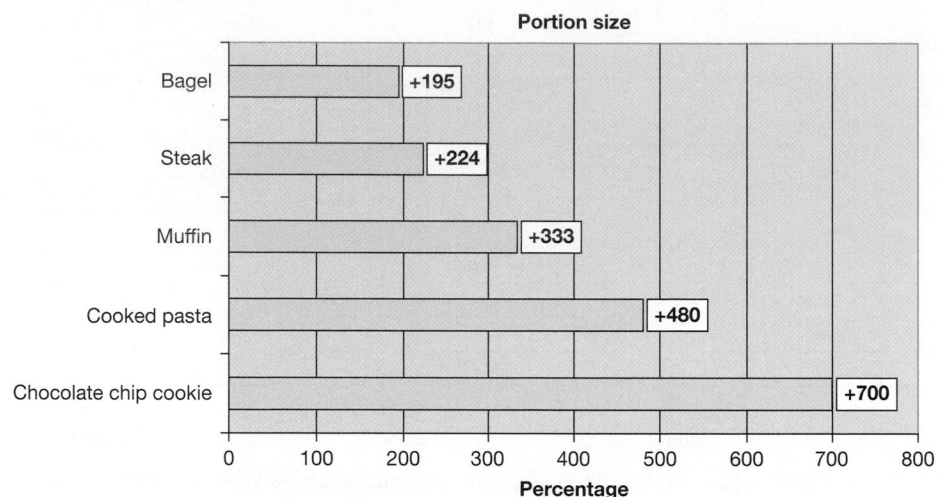

Actual average portion sizes of ready-to-eat foods, compared to USDA recommendations. Source: Young and Nestle (2002)

9   Researchers have yet to cement the link between larger portions and a fatter public. But add up the studies, Dr. Rolls and other experts say, and it is clear Americans might have more success slimming down if plates were not quite so large and a tempting snack did not await on every corner. Obviously, people have responsibility for deciding what to eat and how much, Dr. Rolls said. "The problem is," she said, "they're not very good at it."

[ANALYZE]   ## Make connections: The freshman fifteen.

Have you ever heard of the "freshman fifteen?" The phrase refers to the fact that many college students gain weight in their first year of college. Although most first-year students don't gain fifteen pounds, current research shows that female students gain an average of seven to nine pounds and male students an average of twelve to thirteen pounds during their college career. Some researchers attribute this weight gain to increased alcohol consumption, all-you-can-eat campus cafeterias, around-the-clock socializing, and even the stress of writing papers and studying for exams. These are "environmental" causes similar to those Goode discusses in her essay, such as portion size and price. Other environmental causes might be the kinds of foods available at places where students congregate and socialize—for example, fast-food restaurants, coffee shops, and sports arenas.

Consider your eating habits. Your instructor may ask you to post your thoughts on a class discussion board or to discuss them with other students in class. Use these questions to get started:

- Do you tend to eat and drink more than you normally would when you are with a group of friends? Are the foods you eat more or less healthy when you are with friends?

Goode   *The Gorge-Yourself Environment*

▶ **GUIDE TO READING**
GUIDE TO WRITING
A WRITER AT WORK
THINKING CRITICALLY

431

- Some cities require restaurants to list the calories in the foods they serve; Goode, how-ever, reports University of Minnesota studies showing that nutritional labeling is less of an influence on people than price (par. 3). Would caloric or nutritional information change what you order, or is price, habit, or something else more important?

Use the basic features.

[ANALYZE]

A WELL-PRESENTED SUBJECT: USING EXAMPLES

Giving one or more brief examples can be a quick and effective way to help readers grasp the subject. Sheila McClain opens her essay with several examples to illustrate the pervasiveness of the fitness culture, such as infomercials advertising exercise ma-chines and the popular Wii Fit exercise game (par. 1). Similarly, Stephen King names a couple of classic horror films—*Die, Monster, Die!* and *Dawn of the Dead*—to inspire readers to think of their own favorites.

ANALYZE & WRITE

Write a couple of paragraphs analyzing and evaluating how Goode uses examples to pre-sent her subject:

1. Skim paragraph 1 to highlight the examples of food Goode lists. What do her descrip-tions of these foods have in common?

2. Examine the visual headed "More Food, More Choices, More Eating" on page 428. How do these vivid pictorial examples help Goode present her subject?

A WELL-SUPPORTED CAUSAL ANALYSIS: DEPICTING RESEARCH GRAPHICALLY

Although many writers of causal analyses (like Shankar Vedantam) cite research stud-ies to support their argument, some, like Erica Goode and Sheila McClain, also use visuals to depict some of the research they cite graphically.

ANALYZE & WRITE

Write a couple of paragraphs analyzing and evaluating Goode's use of graphs to supple-ment her written description of the research:

1. Compare the graph headed "Price" (p. 429) with Goode's discussion of Dr. French's research in paragraph 3, and the graph headed "Portion size" (p. 430) with Goode's discussion of Dr. Nestle's research in paragraph 8.

2. Consider what these graphs add to the written text. How do they reinforce or supple-ment the text discussion? (If you think they are merely eye candy for readers, explain why you think so.)

AN EFFECTIVE RESPONSE: ANSWERING AN OBJECTION

Objections sometimes center on the use of evidence. For instance, a source might be critiqued for not being *authoritative* or *credible*. A good way to avoid this kind of criticism of a source is to establish its expertise and independence. It can also help to back up a vulnerable source with other evidence.

ANALYZE & WRITE ├──────────────────────────────────────

Write a couple of paragraphs analyzing and evaluating how Goode handles an objection:

1 Reread paragraph 7 to identify the objection Goode summarizes. On what basis does the food industry object to the findings of researchers like Young and Rolls?

2 Skim paragraphs 7–9 to determine how Goode responds to this criticism.

3 What makes her refutation effective or ineffective?

A CLEAR, LOGICAL ORGANIZATION: FORECASTING CAUSES

Because essays speculating about causes often discuss multiple causes, writers need to help readers follow the argument for each cause. Important strategies for keeping readers oriented include forecasting the causes early in the essay, using *key terms* as labels for the causes, and repeating the same key terms or synonyms for the key terms as each cause is discussed in the essay.

ANALYZE & WRITE ├──────────────────────────────────────

Write a couple of paragraphs analyzing and evaluating how Goode uses these strategies to help readers navigate her argument:

1 Find in the first two paragraphs the forecasting statement in which Goode lists the causes—what she calls "environmental factors"—that she will go on to analyze. Highlight the key terms she uses to label each cause.

2 Skim the essay to locate where these key terms (or related ones) appear later in the essay.

3 Reflect on how these *cueing strategies* help readers follow the argument.

[RESPOND]

Consider possible topics: Social problems.

For more reading selections, including a multimodal selection, go to bedfordstmartins.com /theguide/epages.

Goode is writing about some of the surprising causes of overeating and obesity. You also could consider writing about the causes of a current social problem. Think of topics you may already know something about (even though you may also want to do some research on the topic). Consider, for example, why a school, local business, or team with which you are familiar is or is not successful; why there is an epidemic of bullying in the schools; or why students choose to go to college despite the high cost of tuition and the uncertainty of getting a job.

Speculating on why something happened is a favorite pastime for many, but persuading others to accept your speculations requires evidence. Regardless of the genre in which you present your speculations — a PowerPoint presentation, Facebook update, blog post, or news analysis — graphs, charts, diagrams, and tables can be especially useful in demonstrating a trend. A **line graph** can show change over time, a **bar graph** can make a comparison, and a **pie chart** can demonstrate at a glance how a whole is divided into its parts. A **flowchart** — like the one that follows, showing the sequence of events preceding the 2008 mortgage crisis — can help readers understand how a process occurred. For online arguments speculating about causes, animated line graphs, flowcharts, and even videos (like the one for which we include a static screenshot here) can make the analysis even more compelling.

Graphics and Other Visuals

As you work on your own project, consider using explanatory graphics to present your subject and to support your causal analysis. (If you are writing in an academic setting, don't forget to document any material you borrow from a source, including visuals or the data you use to create your own graphics.)

For an interactive version of this feature, plus activities, go to **bedfordstmartins.com /theguide/epages**.

GUIDE TO WRITING

The Writing Assignment	434
Writing a Draft: Invention, Research, Planning, and Composing	436
Evaluating the Draft: Getting a Critical Reading	446
Improving the Draft: Revising, Formatting, Editing, and Proofreading	448

The Writing Assignment

Write an essay about an important or intriguing subject, and speculate about why it might have occurred. Make sure that it is an appropriate subject for a speculative causal analysis and not simply a report of widely accepted causes. Be sure to demonstrate that the subject exists and to argue for the plausibility of certain causes, while anticipating your readers' likely objections to your argument as well as their preferred alternative causes.

This Guide to Writing is designed to help you compose your own causal analysis and apply what you have learned from reading other selections in the same genre. The Starting Points chart (below) will help you find answers to questions you might have about composing an essay speculating about causes. Use the chart to find the guidance you need, when you need it.

STARTING POINTS: SPECULATING ABOUT CAUSES

A Well-Presented Subject

How do I come up with a subject to write about?
- Consider possible topics. (pp. 421, 426, 432)
- Choose a subject to analyze. (pp. 436–37)
- Test Your Choice (p. 437)

How can I present my subject clearly and effectively?
- Determine the writer's purpose and audience. (p. 405)
- Assess the genre's basic features: A well-presented subject. (pp. 405–6)
- A Well-Presented Subject: Using Anecdote to Dramatize the Subject (pp. 419–20)
- A Well-Presented Subject: Reframing the Subject for Readers (p. 424)
- A Well-Presented Subject: Using Examples (p. 431)
- Present the subject to your readers. (p. 438)
- A Troubleshooting Guide: A Well-Presented Subject (p. 449)

A Well-Supported Causal Analysis

How do I come up with a list of possible causes to explore?
- Present the subject to your readers. (p. 438)
- Analyze possible causes. (p. 439)
- Conduct research. (p. 440)

A Well-Supported Causal Analysis

How can I convince my readers that the causes I identify are plausible?

- Assess the genre's basic features: A well-supported causal analysis. (pp. 406–7)
- A Well-Supported Causal Analysis: Using a Source (p. 420)
- A Well-Supported Causal Analysis: Using Examples and Comparisons (pp. 424–25)
- A Well-Supported Causal Analysis: Depicting Research Graphically (p. 431)
- Analyze possible causes. (p. 439)
- Conduct research. (p. 440)
- Cite a variety of sources to support your causal analysis. (p. 441)
- Formulate a working thesis stating your preferred cause(s). (pp. 441–42)

An Effective Response to Objections and Alternative Causes

How do I deal with my readers' likely objections or alternative causes?

- Assess the genre's basic features: An effective response to objections and alternative causes. (pp. 407–8)
- An Effective Response: Using Counterexamples (pp. 420–21)
- An Effective Response: Putting Aside Obvious Causes (p. 425)
- An Effective Response: Answering an Objection (pp. 431–32)
- Draft a response to objections readers are likely to raise. (pp. 442–43)
- Draft a response to the causes your readers are likely to favor. (pp. 443–44)
- A Troubleshooting Guide: An Effective Response (p. 449)

A Clear, Logical Organization

How can I help my readers follow my argument?

- Assess the genre's basic features: A clear, logical organization. (pp. 408–9)
- A Clear, Logical Organization: Using Rhetorical Questions (p. 421)
- A Clear, Logical Organization: Using Cause-Effect Sentence Strategies (pp. 425–26)
- A Clear, Logical Organization: Forecasting Causes (p. 432)
- Create an outline that will organize your causal analysis effectively for your readers. (p. 445)
- A Troubleshooting Guide: A Clear, Logical Organization (p. 450)

Writing a Draft: Invention, Research, Planning, and Composing

The activities in this section will help you choose and research a subject as well as develop and organize your causal analysis. Do the activities in any order that makes sense to you (and your instructor), and return to them as needed as you revise. Your writing in response to many of these activities can be used in a rough draft that you will be able to improve after receiving feedback from your classmates and instructor.

⠼ Choose a subject to analyze.

When choosing a subject for a causal analysis, keep in mind that it must be

- one that you can show exists (such as with examples or statistics);
- one that has no definitive, proven cause;
- one that you can research, as necessary, in the time you have;
- one that will puzzle—or at least interest—you and your readers.

You may already have a subject in mind and a clear idea of the causes you want to discuss. If so, turn to Test Your Choice (p. 437). If you do not, the subjects that follow, in addition to those following the readings (pp. 421, 426, and 432), may suggest a cause you can analyze effectively:

Subjects Related to School

- Why do some parents choose to homeschool their children, send their children to private instead of public schools, or oppose or advocate for publishing teacher evaluations?
- What are the most or the least popular majors among undergraduates at your college? Why do you think these fields are so popular or unpopular?
- Why did a recent surprising or controversial event happen at your college, such as the closing of the tutoring center or the firing of a coach or popular teacher?

Subjects Related to Your Community

- Why has hooking up replaced dating, or living together replaced getting married, for many young people?
- Why are people more or less politically active nowadays—for example, voting; working for candidates; blogging; or joining Occupy, Tea Party, or other movements?
- Why are people embracing or abandoning social media, getting or removing tattoos or body piercings, or becoming vegetarians or giving up vegetarianism?

Subjects Related to Work

- Why is collaborating with others or being able to communicate clearly in writing especially valuable in the workplace today?

Writing a Draft

GUIDE TO READING
GUIDE TO WRITING
A WRITER AT WORK
THINKING CRITICALLY

437

- Why is the attitude that one should "work to live" more prevalent among young people than the attitude that one should "live to work"?

- Why do employees choose to join or not join a union, or why have so many state legislatures passed so-called right-to-work laws?

Writers often find it helpful to consider several possibilities before choosing a subject. Making a chart listing subjects that interest you and their possible causes can help you decide which subject is most promising.

Subject	Possible Causes
Example: What causes bullies?	Putting down others makes them feel powerful.
	They are mean.
	They are performing for their friends.
	They are sociopaths without empathy for others.
Example: Why do students often procrastinate in writing papers or studying for exams?	They have better things to do.
	They are lazy.
	They are actually using time efficiently.

TEST YOUR CHOICE

After you have made a provisional choice, ask yourself the following questions:

- Do I know enough about the subject, or can I learn enough in the time I have?

- Do I know what causes readers would be likely to think of, and do I have any ideas about what causes might surprise and interest them?

To try out your subject and learn what other people think caused it, get together with two or three other students:

Presenters.   Take turns describing your subject.

Listeners.   Briefly tell each presenter what you think is a likely cause and why you think so.

As you plan and draft your causal analysis, you may need to reconsider your choice of subject (for example, if you cannot find evidence to support the causes you think are most plausible). If you have serious doubts about your choice, discuss them with your instructor before starting over with a new subject.

Research Note

As you begin exploring the subject and its possible causes, you may discover that you need to conduct research before you can go further. If so, skip ahead to the Conduct Research section (p. 440), and return to the activities here later on in the writing process. Alternatively, you may be able simply to make a *Research To Do* list for later.

⠿ Present the subject to your readers.

Once you have made a preliminary choice of a subject and have some idea about its possible causes, consider how you can present the subject in a way that will interest your readers in understanding its causes. To do this, consider what you think about the subject and what your readers are likely to think. Use the questions and sentence strategies that follow to help you put your ideas in writing.

WAYS IN

WHAT DO I THINK?

Why do I find this subject intriguing?

▶ I think .... is important because ....

▶ .... is changing the way we [think/do] ....

▶ .... has widespread effects, such as ....

▶ I know what the obvious causes of .... are, but I'm curious about the underlying [cultural/psychological/ideological] causes because ....

Which possible cause will surprise readers or help them think about the subject in a constructive new way?

▶ I think .... will enable readers to understand ....

▶ Thinking about .... will challenge readers to ....

How do your subject and its causes compare with or contrast to other, more familiar subjects?

▶ .... [name subject] is like .... in that they are both caused by ....

▶ Whereas .... is .... , ... [name subject] is ....

WHAT DO MY READERS THINK?

What will readers know about the subject?

▶ My readers will probably be familiar with .... because ....

▶ .... is likely to be new to my readers, so I will need to show that it is widespread and serious by providing .... [statistics/research studies/examples/anecdotes showing how it affects people].

▶ My readers are likely to be curious about .... because .... [it affects them personally/it raises important moral, psychological, or other questions].

How might readers' age, gender, work, or cultural background affect their thinking?

▶ Readers who [are/have] .... trait may assume that .... is caused by individuals who should have ....

▶ Readers who [are/have] .... trait are likely to think the causes are part of a larger system that involves ....

▶ Readers who have experienced .... may think of .... in terms of ....

What causes are readers likely to know about?

▶ My readers will have heard of .... from .... [name source].

▶ Readers' experience of .... will lead them to assume .... caused ....

Writing a Draft

GUIDE TO READING
GUIDE TO WRITING
A WRITER AT WORK
THINKING CRITICALLY

439

⠿ Analyze possible causes.

The following activity will help you analyze an array of possible causes and decide which ones you could use in your essay. Remember that causal analysis essays often speculate about several possible causes but usually also argue for an especially interesting or plausible cause.

HOW CAN I ANALYZE POSSIBLE CAUSES?

WAYS IN

1. List the possible causes you've identified so far—ones that your readers are likely to think of, that your classmates suggested, that you found doing research, and that you thought of yourself.

2. Write a few sentences about each cause, answering questions like these:

▶ Why do [I/my readers] think _____ could have caused _____?

▶ Is _____ necessary to bring about _____; that is, could _____ not happen without it? Is _____ sufficient—enough in itself—to cause _____?

▶ If _____ is one of several contributing factors, what role does it play? For example, is it a minor or a major cause, an obvious or a hidden cause, a triggering cause (the one that got the cause-effect process started) or a continuing cause (the one that keeps it going)?

▶ What kinds of evidence could I use to argue in favor of or to argue against _____ [cause]? (If you don't already have supporting evidence, make a *Research To Do* note indicating what kind of evidence you need and where you might possibly find it.)

3. Classify the causes you plan to discuss in your essay into three categories: plausible cause(s) you want to argue for, causes your readers may favor that you can concede but put aside as obvious or minor, and causes you should refute because your readers are likely to think they are important.

Plausible cause(s) to argue for	Readers' causes to concede/put aside	Readers' causes to refute

Turn to the Writer at Work on pp. 453–54 to see how Sheila McClain used this activity to analyze her list of possible causes.

Remember that the only category you must include in your essay is the first: one or more causes you will argue played a major, and perhaps surprising, role.

:: **Conduct research.**

If you are analyzing a cause that others have written about, try searching for articles or books on your topic. Enter keywords or phrases related to your cause or subject into the search box of

To learn more about searching a database, consult Chapter 24, pp. 674–75, 677–79.

- an all-purpose database, such as *Academic OneFile* (InfoTrac) or *Academic Search Complete* (EBSCOHost), to find relevant articles in magazines and journals;
- a database like Lexis/Nexis to find articles in newspapers;
- a search engine like *Google* or *Yahoo!* to find relevant Web sites, blogs, podcasts, and discussion lists;
- your library's catalog or *WorldCat,* www.worldcat.org, to find books and other resources on your topic.

To locate numerical or statistical evidence that you could use or to draw graphs or tables, try the following sites:

- USA.gov, the U.S. government's official Web portal, to find information about the federal government
- Library of Congress page on State Government Information, www.loc.gov/rr /news/stategov/stategov.html; follow the links for information on state and local government
- U.S. Census Bureau, www.census.gov, especially the Quick Facts and Fact Finder pages, and the Statistical Abstracts for various years (to compare years), for demographic information
- The Centers for Disease Control and Prevention, www.cdc.gov, especially the FastStats pages, for statistics about diseases and illnesses
- National Center for Education Statistics, nces.ed.gov, for reports, such as *America's Youth: Transitions to Adulthood*

To learn more about finding government documents, consult Chapter 24, p. 679.

- Pew Research Center, www.pewresearch.org, for research data and public opinion polling data
- Rasmussen Reports, www.rasmussenreports.com, for public opinion polling data
- Gallup, www.gallup.com, for public opinion polling data

Bookmark or keep a record of the URLs of promising sites. If you find useful information, you may want to download or copy it to use in your essay. When they are available, download PDF files rather than HTML files, because the PDFs are more likely to include visuals, such as graphs and charts. If you copy and paste relevant information from sources into your notes, be careful to distinguish all source material from your own ideas and to record source information, so you can cite and document any sources you use, including graphics.

Another option is to conduct field research and to use personal experience. Field research, such as interviews, surveys, and direct observation, can offer statistical data and information about public opinion. Your own experience may also provide anecdotal evidence that might interest readers.

⁞⁞ Cite a variety of sources to support your causal analysis.

Writers of essays speculating about causes often rely on evidence from experts to support some causes and refute others. For college assignments, the instructor may require that certain kinds of sources be used and may even specify a minimum number of sources. But for most writing situations, you have to decide whether your sources are appropriate and sufficient. Using too few sources or sources that are too narrow in scope can undercut the effectiveness of your analysis. Consequently, it can be important to offer information from a number of sources and from sources that reflect a variety of areas of expertise.

Look, for example, at the sources Goode uses to support her causal analysis in "The Gorge-Yourself Environment" (pp. 426–30). Because her essay was originally published in a newspaper, she does not include a works cited list or parenthetical citations, but she does identify each of her sources by giving their credentials and academic affiliations: professors from a range of distinguished universities (such as Yale, the University of Pennsylvania, and the University of Minnesota) and different disciplines (such as psychology, nutritional science, marketing, and epidemiology). She uses as support for her analysis the specific findings of a number of academic research projects. In addition, she quotes the director of the Center for Science in the Public Interest advocacy group. The number and variety of expert sources adds to the credibility of Goode's own analysis.

Similarly, student Sheila McClain uses a number of sources to support her causal analysis in "The Fitness Culture" (pp. 409–14). Because she is writing for a class, McClain includes both in-text citations and a list of works cited. Like Goode, she uses *signal phrases* (the author's name and an appropriate verb, plus the author's background where context is needed). McClain uses health club statistics from industry Web sites, but she does not rely solely — or even primarily — on industry or business sources. She also cites independent sources her readers are likely to find credible, such as the Pew Research Center, a university press book, and several newspaper and academic articles. McClain also refers to an interview she did with her exercise physiology professor. The number of sources, their authority, and their variety lend credibility to McClain's own speculations.

As you determine how many and what kinds of sources to cite in your essay, keep in mind that readers of essays speculating about causes are more likely to be persuaded if the sources you rely on are neither too few nor too narrowly focused. If, when you begin to draft, you find that your evidence seems skimpy, you may need to do further research.

⁞⁞ Formulate a working thesis stating your preferred cause(s).

Once you have identified one or more interesting and plausible causes that could be the focus of your analysis, try drafting a working thesis. (Some writers may want to skip this activity now and return to it after they have developed their analysis and completed some research.)

WAYS IN

HOW CAN I ASSERT MY THESIS?

To get an idea about how you might formulate your thesis, take a look at the thesis statements from the reading selections you've studied in this chapter.

> We all know why we should exercise, but why join a fitness club? Some of the answers may surprise you—such as to be part of a community, to reduce stress, to improve your body image, and simply to have fun. (McClain, par. 4)

> I want to offer a disturbing idea. The reason human beings seem to care so little about mass suffering and death is precisely *because* the suffering is happening on a mass scale. The brain is simply not very good at grasping the implications of mass suffering. (Vedantam, par. 12)

> The mythic horror movie, like the sick joke, has a dirty job to do. It deliberately appeals to all that is worst in us. It is morbidity unchained, our most base instincts let free, our nastiest fantasies realized . . . and it all happens, fittingly enough, in the dark. (King, par. 11)

> An increasing number of studies show that how food is served, presented and sold plays at least some role in what and how much people eat. (Goode, par. 3)

Now draft your own thesis statement, using the examples from the readings or the sentence strategies that follow as a jumping-off point. You can put your ideas into your own words now or when you revise:

▶ The reasons for _____ may surprise you, such as _____, _____, and _____ .

▶ The cause(s) of _____ may be [surprising/alarming/disturbing/amazing], but it/they is/are clear: _____ [state cause(s)].

▶ _____ plays a [surprising/alarming/disturbing/amazing] role in [our lives/our families/our communities/our workplaces]: It [does/is/provides] _____ [describe role].

▶ For many years, _____ [name group] has believed that _____ . Now there is research supporting this claim, but not for the reasons you may think. It's not _____ that has been causing this phenomenon but _____ .

:: Draft a response to objections readers are likely to raise.

The following activity will help you respond to possible objections your readers might raise. Start by analyzing the reasons your readers object to your cause, and then consider ways you might refute their objections.

Writing a Draft

GUIDE TO READING
GUIDE TO WRITING
A WRITER AT WORK
THINKING CRITICALLY

443

WAYS IN

HOW CAN I RESPOND EFFECTIVELY TO MY READERS' OBJECTIONS?

1. For each of your preferred causes, consider the questions your readers might raise. Some possibilities include the following:

▶ Even if you can prove that .... [your cause] and .... [your subject] [increased/decreased] at the same time, how do you know .... actually caused ....?

▶ Even if you can prove that .... [your subject] occurred after .... [your cause], how do you know .... actually caused ....?

▶ Could .... [your cause] and .... [your subject] both have been caused by something else altogether?

▶ .... seems to have been a cause of .... [your subject], but was it really a major cause or just one of many contributing causes?

2. Use the following sentence strategies or language of your own to respond to one of these objections:

▶ The objection that .... can be caused by things other than [my cause] may be true. But there is strong evidence showing that [my cause] played a central role by ....

▶ Researchers studying .... have shown a causal connection between [my cause] and [my subject]. They claim [quote/paraphrase/summarize information from source] (cite source).

▶ A large number of people have been polled on this question, and it appears that .... was an important factor in their decision to ....

Research Note

You may need to conduct research to find evidence to support your refutation. If so, revisit the sections Conduct Research and Cite a Variety of Sources to Support Your Causal Analysis.

Draft a response to the causes your readers are likely to favor.

In the preceding activity, you analyzed and drafted a response to the objections your readers are likely to raise. The next activity will help you respond to your readers' preferred causes.

WAYS IN

HOW CAN I RESPOND TO MY READERS' PREFERRED CAUSES?

- **Choose an alternative cause, and summarize it.** Be sure to summarize it accurately and fairly. Do not commit the straw man fallacy of knocking down something that no one really takes seriously.

- **Decide whether you can refute the alternative cause or need to concede it.** Refute the alternative cause if you can show that it lacks credible support or if the reasoning underlying the cause is flawed. Concede it by pointing out that the cause is obvious and setting it aside or by showing that it plays a less important role than the cause you are championing. Try the following sentence strategies, or use language of your own.

To *Refute*

Lacks Credible Support

▶ Just because _____ caused [a similar subject] does not mean that it caused this one. Here's why: _____ .

▶ The [scenario/anecdote] others sometimes give to support this cause certainly helps dramatize _____ , but it doesn't really explain what caused it.

▶ If _____ did cause _____ , then one would expect _____ to happen, but [it hasn't/ the opposite has happened].

Reasoning Is Flawed

Mistakes correlation for causation.

▶ Some argue that _____ caused _____ because _____ [occurred/began rising sharply] at the same time that _____ [occurred/started increasing]. But, in fact, [this is merely a coincidence/both were caused by something else altogether].

Mistakes chronology for causation.

▶ Just because _____ occurred before _____ doesn't prove that _____ caused _____ . [Opponent] has not provided convincing evidence to show how _____ could have caused _____ .

To *Concede*

Set Aside a Well-Known Cause

▶ An obvious explanation is _____ . But if we dig deeper, we find that _____ .

▶ Typical explanations include _____ and _____ , but let's consider a totally different possibility: _____ .

Show That an Alternative Cause Is Minor

▶ _____ is one of the answers but may not play as central a role as most people think it does.

▶ _____ may have kept the process going, but _____ was the trigger: Without it, _____ would never have gotten started.

▶ _____ may have been a factor at the outset, getting the process started, but what keeps it going is _____ .

Writing a Draft

GUIDE TO READING
GUIDE TO WRITING
A WRITER AT WORK
THINKING CRITICALLY

445

▪▪ Create an outline that will organize your causal analysis effectively for your readers.

Whether you have rough notes or a complete draft, making an outline of what you have written can help you organize the essay effectively for your audience. A causal analysis may contain as many as four basic parts:

1. A presentation of the subject
2. Plausible causes, logically sequenced
3. Convincing support for each cause
4. A consideration of readers' questions, objections, and alternative causes

Compare the possible outlines that follow to see how you might organize your essay depending on whether your readers primarily agree with you—or not.

If your readers are *not* likely to favor any alternative causes, you may want to anticipate and respond to their possible objections to your causes.

I. **Presentation of the subject:** Demonstrate that the subject exists and that its causes are uncertain

II. **Thesis and forecasting statement:** Announce the causes you will offer.

III. **First cause with supporting evidence and refutation of objection**

IV. **Second cause with supporting evidence and refutation of objection**

V. **Conclusion:** Reassertion of judgment

If you expect readers *are* likely to favor alternative causes, you may want to concede or refute them before offering your own cause.

I. **Presentation of the subject:** Demonstrate that the subject exists and that its causes are uncertain

II. **Thesis statement:** Acknowledge alternative causes readers are likely to know about

III. **Concession of first alternative cause to set it aside**

IV. **Refutation of second alternative cause with supporting evidence**

V. **Writer's preferred cause with supporting evidence**

VI. **Refutation of objection(s)**

VII. **Conclusion:** Reassertion of judgment based on shared criteria

Whatever organizational strategy you adopt, do not hesitate to change your outline as necessary while drafting and revising. For instance, you might find it more effective to begin with your own preferred cause and to hold back on presenting unacceptable alternatives until you've made the case for the cause you think is most plausible and interesting. The purpose of an outline is to identify the basic components of your analysis and to help you organize them effectively, not to lock you into a particular structure.

For more on outlining, see Chapter 11, pp. 510–14.

Write the opening sentences.

While drafting, do not agonize over the first sentences, because you are likely to discover the best way to begin only after you've written a rough draft. When you feel ready to write your opening, however, you might start by reviewing the ideas and sentences you generated to see if you have something that would work to launch your essay. You might also consider starting with one of the following strategies:

- A surprising assertion (like King)
- A historical perspective (like McClain)
- One or more specific examples (like Goode)
- A scenario or an anecdote (like Vedantam)
- Statistics
- A quotation from a research study

Draft your causal analysis.

By this point, you have done a lot of writing to:

- devise a well-presented subject and analyze its causes;
- support your preferred causes with evidence your readers will find persuasive;
- refute or concede objections and alternative causes;
- organize your ideas to make them clear, logical, and effective for readers.

Now stitch that material together to create a draft. The next two parts of this Guide to Writing will help you evaluate and improve that draft.

Evaluating the Draft: Getting a Critical Reading

Your instructor may arrange a peer review session in class or online, where you can exchange drafts with your classmates and give each other a thoughtful critical reading, pointing out what works well and suggesting ways to improve the draft. A good critical reading does three things:

1. It lets the writer know how well the reader understands the causal analysis.
2. It praises what works best.
3. It indicates where the draft could be improved and makes suggestions for how to improve it.

One strategy for evaluating a draft is to use the basic features of the causal analysis as a guide.

Evaluating the Draft

GUIDE TO READING
GUIDE TO WRITING
A WRITER AT WORK
THINKING CRITICALLY

447

A CRITICAL READING GUIDE

A Well-Presented Subject

How effectively does the writer present the subject?

Summarize: Tell the writer what you understand the subject to be and why he or she thinks it is important and worth analyzing.

Praise: Give an example of something in the draft that you think will especially interest the intended readers and help them understand the subject.

Critique: Tell the writer if you have any confusion or uncertainty about the subject. What further explanation, examples, or statistics do you need to understand it better? If you can think of a more interesting way to present the subject, share your ideas with the writer.

A Well-Supported Causal Analysis

How plausible are the proposed causes, and how well does the writer support the causal analysis?

Summary: Identify the possible causes the writer argues are the most plausible and interesting.

Praise: Tell the writer which cause seems most convincing. Point to any support (such as a particular example, a statistic, a research study, or a graph) that you think is especially strong.

Critique: Tell the writer if any of the causes seem too obvious or minor, and if you think an important cause has been left out. Where the support seems lacking or unconvincing, explain what is missing or seems wrong. If the reasoning seems flawed, what makes you think so?

An Effective Response to Objections and Alternative Causes

How effectively does the writer respond to readers' objections and alternative causes?

Summary: Identify the objections or alternative causes to which the writer responds.

Praise: Point out any response you think is especially effective, and tell the writer what makes you think so. For example, indicate where the support is especially credible and convincing.

Critique: Point to any objections or alternative causes that the writer could have responded to more effectively, and suggest how the response could be improved. Also indicate if the writer has overlooked any serious objections.

(continued)

> How clear and logical is the causal analysis?

A Clear, Logical Organization

Summary: Underline the thesis statement and topic sentences.

Praise: Give an example of where the essay succeeds in being especially clear and easy to follow—for example, in its overall organization, its use of key terms and transitions, or its use of visuals.

Critique: Point to any passages where the writing could be clearer, where topic sentences or transitions could be added, or where key terms could be repeated to make the essay easier to follow. Try suggesting a better beginning or a more effective ending.

For a printable version of this Critical Reading Guide, go to **bedfordstmartins.com /theguide**.

Before concluding your peer review, be sure to address any of the writer's concerns that have not been discussed already.

Making Comments Electronically   Most word processing software offers features that allow you to insert comments directly into the text of someone else's document. Many readers prefer to make their comments this way because it tends to be faster than writing on hard copy and space is virtually unlimited; it also eliminates the process of deciphering handwritten comments. Where such features are not available, simply typing comments directly into a document in a contrasting color can provide the same advantages.

Improving the Draft: Revising, Formatting, Editing, and Proofreading

Start improving your draft by reflecting on what you have written thus far:

- Review critical reading comments from your classmates, instructor, or writing center tutor: What are your readers getting at?
- Consider your invention writing: What else should you consider?
- Review your draft: What can you do to present your causal analysis more compellingly?

Revise your draft.

If your readers are having difficulty with your draft, or if you think there is room for improvement, try some of the strategies listed in the Troubleshooting Guide that follows. It can help you fine-tune your presentation of the genre's basic features.

Improving the Draft

GUIDE TO READING
GUIDE TO WRITING
A WRITER AT WORK
THINKING CRITICALLY

449

A TROUBLESHOOTING GUIDE

A Well-Presented Subject

> My readers don't understand the subject or see why it is important.

- Reconsider what your readers already know, and provide additional background if necessary.
- Try providing examples or an anecdote to interest readers in the subject.
- Quote authorities and explain research findings, including statistics, to demonstrate the subject's importance — that it is widespread and significant.
- Use visuals—graphs, tables, photographs, or screen shots—to make the subject more vivid.
- Review your research to see if you can add anything to help clarify the subject for your readers, or do some additional research.
- Pose the subject directly or indirectly as a *why* question, and then answer it.

A Well-Supported Causal Analysis

> My readers don't understand which of the causes I am arguing are the most plausible.

- Be explicit about which causes are the ones you think are most plausible, and why you think so.
- Use a thesis and forecasting statement followed by topic sentences with key terms to announce your main causes.

> My readers do not find my causal analysis convincing.

- Whenever possible, explain how the cause-effect relationship works, backing up your explanation with appropriate support.
- Cite more credible experts, being sure to give their credentials.
- Cite research studies and statistics rather than limiting yourself to examples and anecdotes.
- Review your sources to make sure they are varied, or do additional focused research to fill in where your analysis is weak.
- Make sure your sources are cited properly.

An Effective Response to Objections and Alternative Causes

> My readers do not think my responses are effective.

- Respond directly to criticism of your reasoning by showing that you are not mistaking correlation or chronology for causation.
- Demonstrate that you understand the complexity of the cause-effect relationship you are analyzing, for example, by indicating how your cause relates to other contributing causes.
- If your readers think you have overlooked an objection, consider it seriously and do further research to respond to it if necessary.

(continued)

A Clear, Logical Organization

> My readers think my analysis is not clear or logical.

- If readers have difficulty finding the thesis statement or topic sentences, consider revising them.
- Add a forecasting statement early in the essay to help guide readers.
- Review your use of transitions, and consider adding transitions to make the logical relationships among sentences and paragraphs clear to readers.
- Refer to visuals explicitly (for example, by adding the direction, "see fig. 1"), and include a caption tying each visual to the text discussion.
- Outline your essay to review its structure, and move, add, or delete sections as necessary to strengthen coherence.

Think about design.

Because causal analyses depend heavily on evidence, especially statistical evidence, to establish the subject and persuade readers to accept the cause(s), writers frequently include graphics—tables and charts. Consider how Sheila McClain uses graphics to establish her subject.

Uses a bar graph (fig. 1) as evidence of the claim that "physical fitness has an increasingly broad appeal"

Connects text discussion to the graph by including "see fig. 1" in text and "Fig. 1" in caption

The exercise and fitness industry used to cater to a small, select group of hard-core athletes and bodybuilders. Now, physical fitness has an increasingly broad appeal to people of all ages, and the evidence can be seen everywhere. . . . Fitness club membership, according to the International Health, Racquet and Sportsclub Association (IHRSA), jumped from 20 million in 1991 to over 40 million in 2006 ("U.S. Health Club Membership"; see fig. 1). Although club membership did not change significantly between 2006 and 2009, it leapt another 10 percent to 50.2 million in 2010 ("U.S. Health Club Membership"). As of September 30, 2011, as many as 16 percent of Americans were members of a health club ("IHRSA").

Edit and proofread your draft.

Two kinds of errors occur often in essays speculating about causes: mechanical errors in using numbers, and use of the wordy and illogical construction *the reason is because.* The following guidelines will help you check your essay for these common errors.

Improving the Draft

GUIDE TO READING
GUIDE TO WRITING
A WRITER AT WORK
THINKING CRITICALLY

451

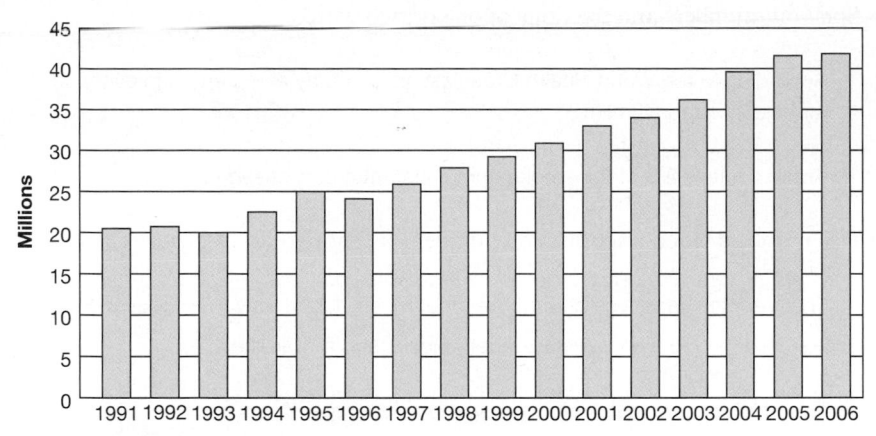

Fig. 1. Number of Health Club Members in the United States by Year (in Millions)
(Source: The Active Network 2007, p. 4)

Uses a bar graph to show the increase in health club memberships over time

Checking Your Use of Numbers

Whether they are indicating the scope of a phenomenon or citing the increase or decrease of a trend, writers who are speculating about causes often cite dates, percentages, fractions, and other numbers. Academic writing prescribes conventional ways of writing such numbers. Look, for example, at these sentences from an essay about increasing reports of sexual harassment in the workplace:

> According to a 1994 survey conducted by the Society for Human Resource Management, the percentage of human resource professionals who have reported that their departments handled at least one sexual harassment complaint rose from 35 percent in 1991 to 65 percent in 1994. The jury awarded Weeks $7.1 million in punitive damages, twice what she sought in her lawsuit.

The writer follows the convention of spelling out numbers (*one*) that can be written as one or two words and using a combination of numerals and words for a large number (*$7.1 million*). (She could also have used numerals for the large number: *$7,100,000.*) She uses numerals for dates and percentages.

The Problem Ignoring the rules for writing dates, percentages, fractions, and other numbers in academic writing can confuse your readers or make them question your attention to detail.

A Note on Grammar and Spelling Checkers

These tools can be helpful, but do not rely on them exclusively to catch errors in your text: Spelling checkers cannot catch misspellings that are themselves words, such as *to* for *too*. Grammar checkers miss some problems, sometimes give faulty advice for fixing problems, and can flag correct items as wrong. Use these tools as a second line of defense after your own (and, ideally, another reader's) proofreading and editing efforts.

The Correction

- Spell out numbers and fractions of one or two words.

  ▶ According to the World Health Organization, as many as ~~1~~ *one* person in every ~~50~~ *fifty* may be infected with HIV.

  ▶ Approximately ~~2/3~~ *two-thirds* of the smoke from a cigarette is released into the air.

- Use numbers when fractions and numbers are more than two words.

  ▶ That year the Japanese automobile industry produced only ~~four thousand eight hundred thirty-seven~~ *4,837* vehicles, mostly trucks and motorbikes.

  ▶ This study shows that Americans spend an average of ~~five and one-third~~ *5⅓* hours a day watching television.

- Write percentages and dates with figures.

  ▶ Comparing 1980 to 1960, we can see that time spent viewing television increased ~~twenty-eight~~ *28* percent.

For practice, go to **bedfordstmartins.com /theguide/exercisecentral** and click on Numbers.

- Spell out numbers that begin a sentence.

  ▶ ~~30~~ *Thirty* percent of commercial real estate in Washington, D.C., is owned by foreigners.

Checking for *Reason Is Because* Constructions

When you speculate about causes, you need to offer reasons and support for your speculations. Consequently, essays that speculate about causes often contain sentences constructed around a *reason is because* pattern, as in the following example:

The *reason* we lost the war *is because* troop morale was down.

The Problem   Since *because* means "for the reason that," such sentences say essentially that "the reason is the reason."

The Correction   Rewrite the sentence so that it uses either *the reason . . . is* or *because,* but not both:

The *reason* we lost the war *is* that troop morale was down.

We lost the war *because* troop morale was down.

▶ Her research suggests that one reason women attend women's colleges is ~~because~~ *that* they want to avoid certain social pressures.

▶ ~~A reason~~ *Older* ~~older~~ Americans watch so much television ~~is because~~ they tend to be sedentary.

Sheila McClain's Analysis of Possible Causes

Using the "Ways In" activity on page 439, Sheila McClain was able to sort through the notes she had made doing preliminary research for her essay "The Fitness Culture" (pp. 409–14). She began with the vague idea that she would examine why fitness has become a priority for many people. But when she did some research on the subject, she found industry statistics from the International Health, Racquet and Sportsclub Association showing a dramatic growth in health club membership. So she decided to narrow the focus of her analysis to why people are increasingly enrolling in health clubs.

Following is the list of possible causes and a few sentences she wrote analyzing each cause. Notice that in a few cases she refers to research she has already found. She also refers to anecdotal evidence from her mother, which she later decided not to use in the essay.

Possible Causes	Analysis of Causes
1. Sense of community in going to the gym	Positive peer pressure keeps people going—they are more likely to exercise on a regular basis and have a greater sense of commitment than if exercising alone. Also, going to a gym substitutes for social activities many people don't have time for. My mom joined a gym because she said it was motivation for her to do something outside of the home and office.
2. Variety of equipment and activities offered by gyms	Traditional exercises are boring and hard work. At a gym, people have the opportunity to work out as strenuously or as gently as they want, depending on the kind of equipment and classes they choose. Many types of exercise offered by gyms, such as aerobics and spinning, are actually fun.
3. Desire to look better	An increasing emphasis on body image in the media is a predictable cause. But when I interviewed Prof. Harton, she said research is surprising; unrealistic goals people have for themselves may be discouraging rather than encouraging. (*Research To Do* note: Find the research she mentioned by Brudzynski and Ebben.)

4. Greater awareness of the benefits of exercise	Government studies on the benefits of physical activity led to greater public awareness of health benefits. Employers have jumped on the bandwagon, encouraged by insurance companies. (See historian Marc Stern's article on the advantages to business if employees stay fit and healthy.)
5. Reaction to 9/11	Definitely a surprising cause. Sisson shows an increase in the number of health clubs since the terrorist attacks on the World Trade Center for several reasons—stress leads people to want to be part of a group, working out can empower people feeling helpless, and the tragedy led people to reassess their lives and look for ways of improving themselves.
6. Changing attitudes toward exercise	Inside and outside of gyms, more people are beginning to recognize the emotional benefits of exercise, the endorphin release known as "runner's high." As Glenn says, exercise is now seen as "a way to enjoy life." (Combine with #2.)

McClain decided she could use all of these causes, although they evolved a good deal as she did additional research and worked through a couple of drafts of her essay. She used cause 4 to introduce the general subject of fitness, but for the focus on health club membership, she began with cause 1—sense of community—because she found a number of sources that made the idea interesting as a cultural phenomenon. Beginning with cause 1 also made a smooth transition to cause 5—9/11—which she knew would surprise readers and could be supported by Sisson's article. Next, she discussed cause 3—body image. This cause turned out to be rather complicated as she thought about it and discussed it with a classmate. McClain's interview with her exercise physiology professor led her to a fascinating article that helped her refute this cause. The last cause she included is a version of 6, combined with 2.

THINKING CRITICALLY

To think critically means to use all of the knowledge you have acquired from the information in this chapter, your own writing, the writing of other students, and class discussions to reflect deeply on your work for this assignment and the genre (or type) of writing you have produced. The benefit of thinking critically is proven and important: Thinking critically about what you have learned will help you remember it longer, ensuring that you will be able to put it to good use well beyond this writing course.

Reflecting on What You Have Learned

In this chapter, you have learned a great deal about the genre from reading several causal analysis essays and from writing one of your own. To consolidate your learning, reflect not only on what you learned but also on how you learned it.

ANALYZE & WRITE

Write a blog post, a letter to your instructor, or an e-mail message to a student who will take this course next term, using the writing prompt that seems most productive for you:

- Explain how your purpose and audience influenced *one* of your decisions as a writer, such as how you explained the subject, how you supported your preferred causes, or how you responded to readers' likely objections.

- Discuss what you learned about yourself as a writer in the process of writing this essay. For example, what part of the process did you find most challenging? Did you try anything new, like getting a critical reading of your draft or outlining your draft in order to revise it?

- If you were to give advice to a friend who was about to write a causal analysis, what would you say?

- Which of the readings in this chapter influenced your essay? Explain the influence, citing specific examples from your essay and the reading.

- If you got good advice from a critical reader, explain exactly how the person helped you—perhaps by questioning your use of support, your use of visuals, the way you began or ended your essay, or the kinds of sources you used.

Reflecting on the Genre

Causal analysis is always shaped by the writer's expertise and special interests. For example, Stephen King—a horror writer—has a personal investment in establishing the horror movie as a legitimate literary and cinematic form; not surprisingly, then, he emphasizes the psychological benefits of horror movies. Erica Goode, whose educational background is in social psychology, is clearly sympathetic to the work of the various psychologists and social scientists she quotes to support her claim that a variety of environmental factors contribute to how much people eat. For reasons of their own, spokespersons for the fast-food industry point to very different factors—such as lack of exercise, poor eating habits, and genetic makeup—for the increasing obesity among Americans.

ANALYZE & WRITE

Write a page or two explaining how causal analyses disguise the writer's assumptions. In your discussion, you might do one or more of the following:

1. **Consider how the readings and your own essay are exercises in exerting authority.** We have said that because causal analysis deals with possibilities instead of certainties, writers must be somewhat tentative about their speculations. However, if causal analysis is to be convincing, it cannot be too timid. Writers who have studied a subject carefully may feel that they are justified in exerting their authority. Compare two or more of the essays by McClain, Vedantam, King, and Goode. Which seems most assertive? What accounts for your response? What seems to you assertive or unassertive about your own essay? Was it your knowledge or your **ideology** (your way of looking at the world), or both, that gave you (or withheld from you) the confidence to be authoritative?

2. **Consider how easy it is to accept a causal analysis.** If not alert, readers may begin to think that the analysis a selection offers is the only possible one. Are any of the selections in this chapter so seductive that you find yourself accepting their causal analyses without question? Explain briefly.

3. **Write a page or two explaining your ideas about authority and ideology in essays speculating about causes.** Connect your ideas to your own essay and to the readings in this chapter.

10
Analyzing Stories

Stories have a special place in most cultures. Sharing stories strengthens the bonds of family and community: Elders relate family and cultural history through stories; children learn lessons through fables and parables; people of all ages use stories to express feelings, work out conflicts, and entertain themselves and others. Reading stories stimulates our feelings and imagination, allowing us to escape our everyday routine and become aware of the wider world around us. Stories can lead us to look at others with sensitivity and, for a brief time, to see the world through another person's eyes. They can also lead us to see ourselves differently, to gain insight into our innermost feelings and thoughts.

The short stories presented in this chapter may in some respects remind you of the essays about remembered events you read and wrote in Chapter 2. As you may recall, essays about remembered events convey *significance* primarily through vivid *descriptive detail* showing people in particular places engaged in some kind of *dramatic action*. Fictional stories work the same way, except that the people in them are called *characters,* places are called *setting,* the dramatic action is called *plot,* and the significance is called *theme* or *meaning.*

Good stories tend to be enigmatic in that they usually do not reveal themselves fully on first reading. That is why it can be so enjoyable and enlightening to analyze stories and discuss them with other readers. Even very short stories can elicit fascinating analyses. For example, Ernest Hemingway wrote this six-word story, which he reportedly claimed was his best work:

For sale: baby shoes, never worn.

Upon first reading, you might think you have gotten everything there is to get from the story. But consider the following questions:

- It looks like an ad, but who would try to sell baby shoes, and why? What is the relationship between the person trying to sell the shoes and the baby for whom the shoes were originally bought?
- If the person is a parent, what does selling the shoes suggest?
- If the person is someone unrelated to the baby, how did that person get the shoes, and why is he or she selling them?
- Could the person selling the shoes be someone who wanted a baby but lost or never had one? Or is he or she more likely to be someone who simply bought the wrong size shoes and didn't return them?
- Who would be a potential buyer for the shoes?

- If the story is about the death of a child, how old was the child, and what were the circumstances of his or her death? If there is no death involved, what *are* the circumstances: Is the baby unable to walk or wear shoes? Was he or she taken away from the person who placed the ad? Or were the shoes simply a bad purchase?

- Where and when was the ad written? (In a country where there are land mines? In a time of severe economic depression?)

- Why is the story so short? Could the brevity say something about emotion? Could the fact that the story is written in the form of an advertisement suggest something about commercialism?

As these questions imply, even the shortest story can be analyzed and discussed in ways that enhance its possible meanings and enrich your reading experience.

In this chapter, we ask you to write an analysis of a story. Analyzing the selections in the Guide to Reading that follows will help you learn the basic features and strategies writers typically use when writing about stories. The readings, as well as the questions and discussion surrounding them, will help you consider strategies you might want to try out when writing your own analysis.

| PRACTICING THE GENRE |

Analyzing a Story Collaboratively

Although writing about stories is an important academic kind of discourse, many people who are not in school enjoy discussing stories and writing about how a story resonates in their lives. That is why book clubs, reading groups, and online discussion forums are so popular. Talking and writing about stories we have read and seen can help us understand why a particular story may be moving or thought-provoking. Sharing the experience with others exposes us to different ways of interpreting and responding to stories — expanding our openness to new perspectives, deepening our insight, and enhancing our pleasure.

To benefit from this kind of discussion with others, work together on an analysis of one story with two or three other students. Here are some guidelines to follow:

Part 1.

- Get together with students who have read the same story from An Anthology of Short Stories that begins on p. 495.

- Begin by discussing one question from the Analyze & Write section following the story your group read. (During the discussion, you may go on to answer other questions as well.)

Part 2.   After you have discussed the story for half of the time allotted for this activity, reflect on the process of analyzing the story in your group:

- Before you began, what were your expectations of how the group would work together? For example, did you think your group should or would agree on one "right answer" to the questions, or did you expect significant disagreement? What actually happened once you began to discuss the story?

- How did the discussion affect your attitude about the story or about the process of analyzing stories? What, if anything, did you learn?

Your instructor may ask you to write about what you learned and to present your conclusions to the rest of the class.

Analyzing Essays That Analyze Stories

In the Readings section of this chapter, you will see how different authors analyze the same short story: "The Use of Force" by William Carlos Williams (pp. 501–3). Examining how these writers present an *arguable thesis* about the story, *support* this thesis, and guide readers through their argument will help you write an insightful *literary analysis* of your own.

Determine the writer's purpose and audience.

When reading the short story analysis essays that appear in this chapter, ask yourself the following questions:

- What seems to be the writer's main *purpose*—for example, to illuminate the story; to change or expand the way readers understand the story; or to impress readers with the writer's insight and close reading?

- What does the writer assume about the *audience*? The short story analyses from this chapter were written by students in a college course in which the entire class had read the same story. These writers assumed that their primary reader, the instructor, not only had read the story but also knew a fair amount about its context and the conversation surrounding it—enough, at least, to be able to judge whether the essayist had read the story with sufficient care and thought. In cases such as these, plot summaries and recitals of well-known facts about the short story and its author are not necessary.

Assess the genre's basic features.

As you read the essays that analyze stories in this chapter, you will see how different writers incorporate the basic features of the genre. The following discussions of these features include examples from the essays as well as sentence strategies you can experiment with later, as you write your own analysis of a story.

> **Basic Features**
> A Clear, Arguable Thesis
> A Well-Supported Argument
> A Clear, Logical Organization

A CLEAR, ARGUABLE THESIS

Read first to find the thesis statement, *which is often one or two sentences long but that may run to several paragraphs.* A good thesis statement in an essay analyzing a story

- asserts the main idea or claim;

- is arguable, not a simple statement of fact (for example, " 'The Use of Force' tells the story of a doctor's visit to a sick little girl") or an obvious conclusion (for example, "The doctor grows frustrated by the little girl's behavior");

- is appropriately qualified, not overgeneralized or exaggerated (for example, "The behavior of the doctor at the center of 'The Use of Force' shows that no medical professional can be trusted");

- is clearly stated, not vague or ambiguous.

Often, the thesis is part of an introduction that is at least a paragraph in length. In most cases, this introduction identifies the story being analyzed by giving the title and author, and it may also provide some historical, biographical, or cultural context. In effective writing, the thesis and other sentences in the opening paragraph (or paragraphs) introduce *key terms* for ideas that are echoed and further developed later in the essay. In this way, the introductory sentences and thesis *forecast* how the argument will be developed.

Inexperienced writers are sometimes afraid to ruin the surprise by forecasting their argument at the beginning of their essays. But explicit forecasting is a convention of literary analysis, similar in purpose to the abstract that precedes many articles in academic journals.

Take a look at Iris Lee's lead-up to the thesis in her essay on "The Use of Force." In it, she introduces key terms that are *repeated* (exactly, closely, or through synonyms) and underscored in her thesis:

Key terms

Thesis

> The Hippocratic Oath binds doctors to practice ethically and, above all, to "do no harm." The doctor narrating William Carlos Williams's short story "The Use of Force" comes dangerously close to breaking that oath, yet ironically is able to justify his actions by invoking his professional image and the pretense of preserving his patient's well-being. As an account of a professional doing harm under the pretense of healing, the story uncovers how a doctor can take advantage of the intimate nature of his work and his professional status to overstep common forms of conduct, to the extent that his actions actually hurt rather than help a patient. In this way, the doctor-narrator actually performs a valuable service by warning readers, indirectly through his story, that blindly trusting members of his profession can have negative consequences. (par. 1)

Sometimes, the thesis of a literary analysis contradicts or complicates a surface reading of a work. Look for sentence strategies like this one:

▶ A [common/superficial] reading of ⸺ [title by author] is that ⸺ [surface reading], but in fact ⸺ [insert your own interpretation].

In Isabella Wright's essay on "The Use of Force," the surface reading actually appears in the sentences leading up to the thesis. A transitional sentence and a transitional word introduce the contradiction/complication that constitutes the thesis:

Surface reading

Transitional sentence
Transitional word
Contradiction/ complication

> By any reasonable standards, the story of a doctor prying a little girl's mouth open as she screams in pain and fear should leave readers feeling nothing but horror and disgust at the doctor's actions. William Carlos Williams's story "The Use of Force" is surprising in that it does not completely condemn the doctor for doing just that. *Instead,* through his actions and words (uttered or thought), readers are able to see the freeing, transformative power of breaking with social conventions. (par. 1)

Analyzing Essays That Analyze Stories

GUIDE TO READING
GUIDE TO WRITING
A WRITER AT WORK
THINKING CRITICALLY

461

A WELL-SUPPORTED ARGUMENT

Consider how the writer provides support for the argument. Because essays analyzing stories usually present new ideas that are not obvious and that readers may disagree with, writers need to make an argument that includes

- *reasons*—the supporting ideas or points that develop the essay's thesis or main claim;
- *evidence* or *examples* from the story;
- *explanations* or *analyses* showing how the examples support the argument.

In addition, writers may provide other kinds of support—for example, *quotations from experts* or historical, biographical, or cultural evidence. But *textual evidence* from the work of literature is the primary support readers expect in literary analysis essays.

Evidence from the text often takes the form of *quotation* of words, phrases, sentences, and, occasionally, even paragraphs. Quoting is the most important method of providing support for essays that analyze short stories, but effective writers do not expect a quotation to do the work by itself. Instead, they analyze the language of the story to show how particular words' *connotations,* their *figurative* use in *images* and *metaphors,* or their *symbolism* enrich the story's meanings.

When reading a literary analysis, look for sentence strategies like this one:

▶ .... [type of evidence from the text], such as "..............." and "..............."
[quotations] [illustrates/demonstrates/shows] .... [analysis].

Now look at the extended example from paragraph 4 of Iris Lee's essay. In this excerpt, Lee supports an assertion about the author's use of "militaristic diction" by quoting from several parts of the story:

Examples of militaristic diction include calling his struggle with the girl a "battle" (502), the tongue depressor a "wooden blade" (503), his bodily effort an "assault" (503). She too is a party in this war, moving from fighting "on the defensive" to surging forward in an attack (503). Such metaphors of fighting and warfare, especially those associated with the doctor and his actions, figuratively convey that his character crosses a crucial boundary. They present the argument that, despite his honorable pretentions, his actions—at least during the height of his conflict with the girl—align more with violence than with healing. The doctor's thoughts even turn more obviously (and more consciously) violent at times, such as when, in a bout of frustration, he wants "to kill" the girl's father, (502) or when he says, "I could have torn the child apart in my own fury and enjoyed it" (503). Although these statements are arguably exaggerated, they, like the metaphors of war, imply a tendency to do harm that goes directly against the narrator's duty as a doctor. While the story's opening introduces him as a person whose occupation is reason to overcome the parents' distrust, by the end of the story he leaves his readers thoroughly horrified by his forceful handling of the little girl. *By investigating the calculated artifice and military metaphors, we might conclude that the narrator is conscious both of his deceptive rhetoric and of the harm it allows him to inflict upon his patient.*

Supporting quotations

Description of evidence

Analysis

Writer's conclusions

In addition to quoting, evidence can also take the form of *summary* or *paraphrase*. Writers can use this type of evidence to set up an extended close textual analysis like that shown on the preceding page. Or they might use summary or paraphrase in brief snippets of analysis, as in sentence strategies like the following:

▶ When [summarize what happens or paraphrase what is said in the story], readers can readily see _____.

For more on quotation, summary, and paraphrase, see Chapter 26, pp. 701–8.

For example, to support her thesis, Isabella Wright summarizes the doctor's conflict with the girl instead of describing it in detail. The summary is introduced by repeating key terms from the thesis statement:

Key terms
Summary

> The doctor also breaks with social conventions by willingly engaging in a physical struggle with the little girl. (par. 5)

A CLEAR, LOGICAL ORGANIZATION

To make the argument in a literary analysis easy to follow, writers usually include some or all of the following:

- *Topic sentences* introducing paragraphs or groups of paragraphs (often using key terms from the thesis statement)
- Key terms—words or phrases—introduced in the thesis or other introductory text as a way of forecasting the development of the argument (see the previous section); these key terms are repeated strategically throughout the essay
- Clear *transitional words* and *phrases* (such as "although," "in addition," and "at the story's beginning")

Writers tend to place topic sentences at or near the beginning of a paragraph because these sentences help readers make sense of the details, examples, and explanations that follow. Often, topic sentences repeat key terms from the thesis or other introductory text. Look, for example, at the first topic sentence of Iris Lee's essay, which repeats key terms from the introduction in paragraph 1.

Key terms

> In the way the story and its characters introduce us to the narrator, we see how people automatically grant a doctor status and privilege based on his profession alone, creating an odd sort of intimacy that is uncommon in ordinary social relations. (par. 2)

The paragraph then gives examples of the extreme politeness the young patient's parents show to the doctor, and in describing and analyzing the scene, Lee repeats the words "privilege" and "intimacy."

Topic sentences can also serve as transitions from one paragraph to the next. In reading literary analyses, look for sentence strategies like the following:

▶ [In comparison with/in contrast to/in addition to/because of] _____ [subject A (discussed in the previous paragraph)], _____ [subject B (discussed in this paragraph)].

Lee *Performing a Doctor's Duty*

GUIDE TO READING
GUIDE TO WRITING
A WRITER AT WORK
THINKING CRITICALLY

463

In her analysis of "The Use of Force," Isabella Wright uses this strategy:

EXAMPLE *In contrast to* the little girl's parents, the doctor breaks social conventions in his interactions with the family and in doing so highlights the absurdity of these rules. (par. 3)

Subject A
Subject B

Notice that Wright repeats the phrase "social conventions," which she introduces in her thesis.

Readings

The following essays by students Iris Lee and Isabella Wright analyze the short story "The Use of Force," by William Carlos Williams (pp. 501–3). As you will see, both Lee and Wright attempt to answer questions that many readers have asked of this story: What is the purpose—aside from vividly describing his anger and frustration—of portraying a doctor's use of force on an uncooperative patient? What larger points are being made? Lee and Wright arrive at different answers to these questions. By reading their essays, you will learn a great deal about how writers argue for their own analysis of a story.

Iris Lee | *Performing a Doctor's Duty*

WRITTEN FOR A FIRST-YEAR COMPOSITION COURSE, this essay by Iris Lee emphasizes the "doctor's duty." As you read, consider the following:

- What, from Lee's perspective, is the doctor's duty, as indicated in the title?
- What evidence from the story does Lee use to support her main idea?

Also consider the questions in the margin. Your instructor may ask you to post your answers to a class blog or discussion board or to bring them to class.

1   The Hippocratic Oath binds doctors to practice ethically and, above all, to "do no harm." The doctor narrating William Carlos Williams's short story "The Use of Force" comes dangerously close to breaking that oath, yet ironically is able to justify his actions by invoking his professional image and the pretense of preserving his patient's well-being. As an account of a professional doing harm under the pretense of healing, the story uncovers how a doctor can take advantage of the intimate nature of his work and his professional status to overstep common forms of conduct, to the extent that

:: Basic Features
A Clear, Arguable Thesis
A Well-Supported Argument
A Clear, Logical Organization

his actions actually hurt rather than help a patient. In this way, the doctor-narrator actually performs a valuable service by warning readers, indirectly through his story, that blindly trusting members of his profession can have negative consequences.

In the way the story and its characters introduce us to the narrator, we see how people automatically grant a doctor status and privilege based on his profession alone, creating an odd sort of intimacy that is uncommon in ordinary social relations. At the story's beginning, the narrator identifies the family he visits as "new patients" (501), and he establishes that they are virtual strangers to him — "all [he] had was the name, Olson" (501). After the mother confirms that he is the doctor, however, she immediately invites him into the most intimate part of her home, the kitchen, where her husband and sick daughter are waiting (501). Later, the mother reassures the child that the doctor is a "nice man" and "won't hurt you," though she can base those assertions only on what little she knows of him: his occupation (502). At the same time, the narrator senses that the family is "very nervous, eyeing me up and down distrustfully" (501). The parents' eagerness in offering their home and hospitality, coupled with the betrayal of their nervousness, hints at the dubious nature of the intimacy between a doctor and his patient. Although the doctor's profession gives him privilege to overstep certain boundaries, the basis of real trust is lacking, thus casting the doctor-patient relationship as something strange and artificial.

The narrator communicates to readers that he perceives both sides of the interaction and also admits to intentionally using the weight of his professional status against the family's natural distrust of outsiders. The young girl, who is not yet "adult" enough to follow social conventions (503), might be read as representing the family's instinct for self-protection. In the face of the child's resistance, the narrator "smiled in [his] best professional manner" (502), trying to invoke the special form of trust that doctors typically assume. The phrase "professional manner" shows that the narrator acknowledges he is using the power of his occupation, while also admitting that his reassuring smile is only part of his professional performance. As the doctor's struggle to examine the little girl's throat becomes more heated, he repeatedly brings up his expert concern to justify his rough actions. He tells readers, "I had to do it . . . for her own protection" (502). Later, he reminds readers (and himself) that "I have seen at least two children lying dead in bed of neglect in such cases, and [feel] that I must get a diagnosis now or never" (503). He also notes that "others must be protected" against the sick child before him (503). The narrator repeatedly

2

3

How do the highlighted transitions help the reader? Is this merely plot summary or does it serve an analytical purpose?

Highlight the topic sentences of paragraphs 3–5. How well do they work?

brings up his duty as a doctor and the privilege that comes with it to defend his use of force. Yet at other points, he admits to having "grown furious" (503), to being unable to "hold [himself] down" (503), and to have "got beyond reason" (503). In acknowledging the loss of his capacity for reason and self-control, he essentially admits that his "professional manner" and attempts to be gentle in getting the girl to follow his commands are empty artifice (502). When these attempts fail, emotion alone drives his actions. In effect, he uses the medical art as a pretense to justify otherwise unacceptable interventions.

4   Beyond admitting his personal motivations in his treatment of the girl, the narrator sketches a more disturbing and potentially incriminating image of himself in his use of militaristic diction, for it aligns his character more with harming than healing — the perfect contradiction of a doctor. Examples of militaristic diction include calling his struggle with the girl a "battle" (502), the tongue depressor a "wooden blade" (503), his bodily effort an "assault" (503). She too is a party in this war, moving from fighting "on the defensive" to surging forward in an attack (503). Such metaphors of fighting and warfare, especially those associated with the doctor and his actions, figuratively convey that his character crosses a crucial boundary. They present the argument that, despite his honorable pretentions, his actions — at least during the height of his conflict with the girl — align more with violence than with healing. The doctor's thoughts even turn more obviously (and more consciously) violent at times, such as when, in a bout of frustration, he wants "to kill" the girl's father (502), or when he says, "I could have torn the child apart in my own fury and enjoyed it" (503). Although these statements are arguably exaggerated or hyperbolic, they, like the metaphors of war, imply a tendency to do harm that goes directly against the narrator's duty as a doctor. While the story's opening introduces him as a person whose occupation is enough to overcome the parents' distrust, by the end of the story he leaves his readers thoroughly horrified by his forceful handling of the little girl. By investigating the calculated artifice and military metaphors, we might conclude that the narrater is conscious both of his deceptive rhetoric and of the harm it allows him to inflict upon his patient.

5   Curiously, the narrator readily pleads guilty on both counts, which leads one to wonder why any person would willingly paint such a damning picture of himself — one that would surely destroy his livelihood. I would argue that the doctor of this story does not take ownership of his despicable actions but uses them to blame the parents

> How clear is Lee's analysis here? How does she support it?

> How well do the quoted words illustrate Lee's analysis?

> Why do you think Lee poses an implied question ("wonder why")? How do her answers ("I would argue") make her analysis deeper?

and more generally to warn against blindly trusting those in positions of authority. Looking back to the story's opening, we note that the narrator presents himself generically. He does not name or describe himself or provide any information beyond the fact that he is a doctor. The lack of specification renders him the "every doctor" and expands the possible reference points for the pronoun "I" as it is used in this story. That is to say, although the story is told in the first person, attaching the actions and events to the singular narrator, that narrator turns himself into a placeholder for every doctor by leaving out all identifying features. I would argue, furthermore, that speaking in the first person, as he must to make his story credible, the narrator offers a cautionary tale about a doctor who exploits the privileges of his profession. The warning implied in the story of a doctor's exploitation of professional privilege is for patients to protect themselves. Thus, through his cautionary tale, the doctor-as-narrator does the opposite of the doctor-as-actor in the story: he performs a doctor's duty to his readers of preventing harm.

6   For readers who distinguish between the different layers of Williams's first-person narrator, the story is ultimately both a damning and a flattering depiction of the doctor figure. The doctor-as-actor in the story becomes a despicable specimen of professionalism corrupted, someone capable of brutality and rhetorical manipulation. Above him stands another — the doctor-as-narrator — who counteracts these crimes through his art. The way he tells the story conveys a powerful story and serious message.

> Why do you think Lee provides so many transitions (highlighted in purple) here?

> What are the strengths of this ending? How could it be improved?

Work Cited

Williams, William Carlos. "The Use of Force." *The St. Martin's Guide to Writing*. Ed. Rise B. Axelrod and Charles R. Cooper. 10th ed. Boston: Bedford/St. Martin's, 2013. 501–03. Print.

Isabella Wright | *"For Heaven's Sake!"*

To learn about how Isabella Wright used the activities in the Analyze the Story section (pp. 475–78), turn to A Writer at Work on pp. 491–95.

USING THE WAYS IN ACTIVITIES in the Guide to Writing section Analyze the Story (pp. 475–78), Isabella Wright explored and wrote about how the doctor's thoughts and actions in "The Use of Force" might be justified. We have not annotated or highlighted this essay, but you may want to do so as you read and as you respond to the Analyze & Write questions in the sections that follow. As you read, notice how Wright's analysis differs from Lee's. Consider which essay you find more convincing and why.

1   By any reasonable standards, the story of a doctor prying a little girl's mouth open as she screams in pain and fear should leave readers feeling nothing but horror and disgust at the doctor's actions. William Carlos Williams's story "The Use of Force" is surprising in that it does not completely condemn the doctor for doing just that. Instead, through his actions and words (utterred or thought), readers are able to see the freeing, transformative power of breaking with social conventions. Thus, they are also encouraged to rethink what is acceptable and unacceptable in polite society.

2   Social conventions and proper conduct are prominent themes in Williams's story, in which the mother and father of the sick little girl are fixated on acting and speaking within the boundaries of politeness. The parents demonstrate this tendency most obviously in how they go out of their way to be respectful to the doctor. Upon his arrival at their home, the mother preemptively says that "[he] must excuse [them]" for bringing him into the kitchen, where they are keeping the child warm (501). There, the father makes an effort to "get up" to greet the doctor (501). The parents' efforts continue and take on even greater urgency when the child is uncooperative with the doctor as he tries to examine her throat. When she succeeds in knocking his glasses to the floor, her parents "almost [turn] themselves inside out in embarrassment and apology" (502). At certain moments, keeping up appearances seems to become disproportionately important, overshadowing their concern for their daughter's well-being. The mother's ultimate argument, meant to be stronger even than her threat to take the girl to the hospital, is to shame her daughter over her discourteous behavior. "Aren't you ashamed to act like that in front of the doctor?" she asks (503). The ending of her statement is key because it raises the question, would the daughter's misbehavior be shameful if no one outside of the family witnessed it? In other words, to what extent should concerns over appearances determine rightful and wrongful conduct?

3   In contrast to the little girl's parents, the doctor breaks social conventions in his interactions with the family and in doing so highlights the absurdity of these rules. From the beginning we see him as someone who pushes aside polite but pointless practices; for example, he "motion[s] for [the father] not to bother" standing for a greeting when it would have disturbed the child on his lap (501). The doctor's disregard for social conventions applies most to his tendency to give voice to thoughts rather than to keep them to himself for fear of sounding rude or causing discomfort. When the mother scolds her daughter for

knocking the glasses off the "nice man" (502), the doctor's reaction borders on outright rudeness: "For heaven's sake, I broke in. Don't call me a nice man to her. I'm here to look at her throat on the chance that she might have diphtheria and possibly die of it" (502).

4   But is the doctor *really* giving voice to such reactions? The absence of quotation marks in the story leaves it uncertain which lines are and are not spoken aloud, creating a thought-provoking ambiguity. For example, does the doctor actually respond with "Oh yeah?" to the mother's threat to take the girl to the hospital, or does he care enough to keep such an irreverent reaction to himself (502)? In any case, readers are presented with the possibility of imagining that all the doctor's thoughts — no matter how offensive, belittling, or inappropriate — are expressed aloud. In fact, the very existence of the text and our reading of it give these thoughts expression, turning a stylistic choice into the ultimate statement on how social considerations limit our actions and expressions.

5   The doctor also breaks with social conventions by willingly engaging in a physical struggle with the little girl. This conflict might be interpreted as a process of reverse socialization or reverse civilization, a transformation that, surprisingly, the story presents as a potentially positive change. While the doctor stoops to the primitive tactics of the little girl, he does not view her in a negative light. To the contrary, from the beginning, he — and, through him, readers — sees the little girl as "unusually attractive" and "strong," with "magnificent blonde hair." This description of her seems almost angelic (501). Through the doctor's conflict with her, his admiration grows. He comes to respect, even "love," the girl for her raw spirit that allows her to "[rise] to magnificent heights" in her struggle against him (502). Such worshipful language — note the repetition of the word "magnificent," for example — leads readers to understand the girl and her strength as something closer to glory and divinity than to savagery. The doctor's entering a similar state might thus be read as his reeducation into a finer, truer self. Indeed, it is at these points in the story when he uses the most sophisticated language and the most involved metaphors. Thus, the story demonstrates, through the doctor's transformation, that the casting off of social conventions might lead not to a reduced state of humanity but to a purer, more admirable state of being.

6   In a story where politeness is made to seem absurd, the doctor's tactless words and his inappropriate use of force actually have the potential to be improvements on his character. By tossing aside social conventions, he brings himself closer to the glorious heights of the little girl, who, from the story's beginning, is magnificent and strong in her stubbornness. In the characters of the mother and father, readers come to understand also that politeness can stand in the way of accomplishing a task or communicating a clear

meaning, and thus the doctor's actions are in the service of honesty and efficiency. Thus framed, the story leads readers to a point where they cannot fully condemn the doctor's outwardly abhorrent actions and instead must reconsider their own metric of what is and is not socially appropriate.

Work Cited

Williams, William Carlos. "The Use of Force." *The St. Martin's Guide to Writing*. Ed. Rise B. Axelrod and Charles R. Cooper. 10th ed. Boston: Bedford/St. Martin's, 2013. 501–03. Print.

For an additional student reading, go to **bedfordstmartins .com/theguide/epages**.

Use the basic features.

[ANALYZE]

A CLEAR, ARGUABLE THESIS: GETTING BENEATH THE SURFACE

Earlier, we discussed how the thesis of a literary analysis can contradict or complicate a surface reading of a work. After asserting her thesis about how "The Use of Force" helps readers see the "freeing, transformative power of breaking with social conventions," Wright supports her thesis with examples from the text and with her own analysis. Often, she returns to a key term from her thesis: "social conventions."

ANALYZE & WRITE

Write a paragraph or two about how well Wright gets below the surface in her reading of "The Use of Force":

1. Reread the thesis statement, and highlight the term "social conventions" whenever it appears later in the essay, paying attention to what Wright says about it in each instance.

2. Do you think Wright's thesis accurately forecasts the argument she develops in the rest of her essay? If not, what changes to the thesis might you suggest?

3. In her discussion of how the doctor breaks with social conventions, do you think Wright makes an adequate case for the "freeing, transformative power" of his thoughts and actions? Why or why not?

A WELL-SUPPORTED ARGUMENT: PAIRING TEXTUAL EVIDENCE WITH ANALYSIS

As we have noted, an essay about a short story relies primarily on textual evidence— gleaned from a close reading of the story—to support the argument. We have also discussed how simply quoting, summarizing, or paraphrasing passages from the text is not enough; instead, effective writing about a literary work must use such evidence in support of an analysis: the writer's original, thoughtful examination of the text. Earlier, we looked at Lee's analysis of militaristic diction in "The Use of Force," an analysis that drew on quotations from the story. Now let's turn to Wright's essay.

ANALYZE & WRITE

Write a paragraph or two about how well Wright uses textual evidence and analysis:

1 Focus on quotations, highlighting the one in the title as well as those in paragraphs 2–5. Consider how — and how well — these quotations support Wright's argument.

2 What improvements might you suggest to the choice of quotations? For example, in paragraph 5, Wright refers to the "most involved metaphors" of the story but does not quote any of them. Which metaphors, if any, might she have quoted? Or is summarizing these parts of the story sufficient to support her analysis?

3 What improvements might you suggest to Wright's analysis of textual evidence? For example, in paragraph 2, Wright discusses how the parents of the sick child go out of their way to be polite and respectful to the doctor. However, read paragraph 3 of the story (p. 501), and consider in what ways this part of the story might complicate Wright's analysis of the parents' behavior.

A CLEAR, LOGICAL ORGANIZATION: COORDINATING KEY WORDS AND TOPIC SENTENCES

As we have seen, writers try to help readers follow their argument by making their plan or organization clear to readers. For example, topic sentences that repeat key terms from the thesis statement help readers connect individual paragraphs to the larger argument the writer is making.

ANALYZE & WRITE

Write a paragraph or two about Wright's use of key words in topic sentences:

1 Underline the topic sentences of paragraphs 2, 3, and 5, and circle any key terms that are repeated in these sentences.

2 Pay special attention to the key terms, noting the way they are used in each topic sentence and built upon in the paragraph. Assess how well each topic sentence helps you follow the argument as it is developed in these paragraphs.

Adaptations, Sequels, and Parodies

While the traditional essay that analyzes short stories has very specific features, responses to short stories and other forms of literature can take many forms, including adaptations, sequels, and parodies. Responses to literature in other media, such as theater, dance, film, and music, are common: The musical *West Side Story,* for example, is an adaptation of Shakespeare's *Romeo and Juliet;* the 2007 opera *Grapes of Wrath* is based on John Steinbeck's novel of the same name; and F. Scott Fitzgerald's *The Great Gatsby* has inspired numerous film versions, including a 3-D version directed by Baz Luhrmann.

Students sometimes interpret stories they have studied by presenting them in different media. The screen shot below is from a video developed by three students—Natalie George, Lacey Patzer, and Sam Williams—for their digital storytelling course. It retells "The Story of an Hour" from Mrs. Mallard's point of view. This screen shot captures a moment not included in Chopin's story (pp. 495–97)—the whispering of Mrs. Mallard's sister and her husband's friend, as they discuss the news of Brently Mallard's death and how to break it to his "widow."

For an interactive version of this feature, go to **bedfordstmartins .com/theguide/epages**.

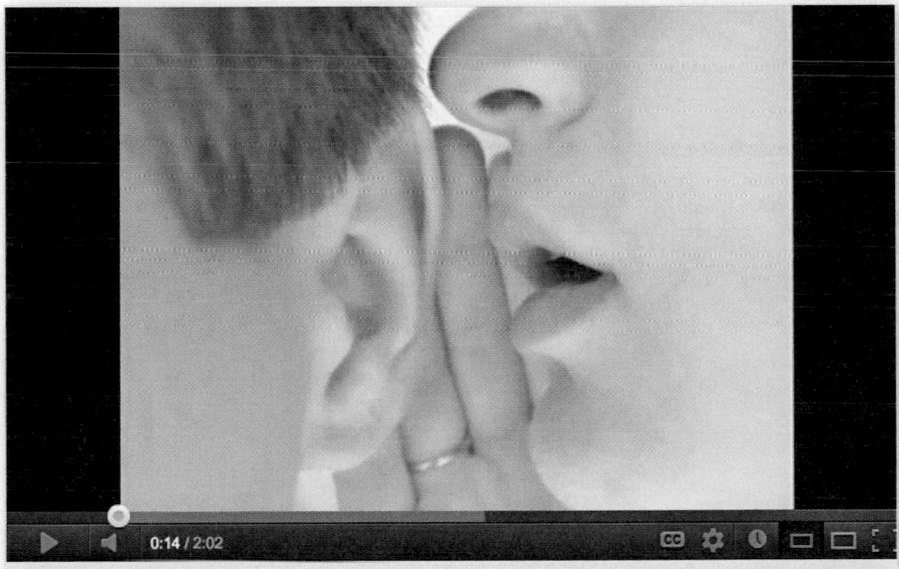

As you work on your own project, you might want to consult some of these alternative forms of response for inspiration. If the format in which you are working allows for it—if, for example, you are creating a poster, Web page, or video—you could take advantage of the strategies available to those working in multimedia, for example, by embedding images or artifacts relevant to the story you are interpreting. (Always remember to document properly any material you might use that was created by someone else.)

The Writing Assignment

Write an essay analyzing one or more aspects of a story. Aim to convince readers that your analysis is interesting and contributes to the conversation about the story. Back up your ideas with supporting quotations and examples from the story.

This Guide to Writing is designed to help you write your own analysis of a story and apply what you have learned from reading other students' essays. This Starting Points chart will help you find answers to questions you might have about analyzing a story. Use the chart to find the guidance you need, when you need it.

STARTING POINTS: ANALYZING STORIES

A Clear, Arguable Thesis

How can I find a good story to write about?

- Find a story to write about. (pp. 473–74)
- Analyze the story. (pp. 475–79)

How do I decide on a main idea and develop a thesis?

- Determine the writer's purpose and audience. (p. 459)
- Assess the genre's basic features: A clear, arguable thesis (pp. 459–60)
- A Clear, Arguable Thesis: Getting Beneath the Surface (pp. 469–70)
- Analyze the story. (pp. 475–79)
- Formulate a working thesis. (pp. 479–81)
- A Troubleshooting Guide: A Clear, Arguable Thesis (p. 487)

A Well-Supported Argument

How do I support my ideas?

- Assess the genre's basic features: A well-supported argument. (pp. 461–62)
- A Well-Supported Argument: Pairing Textual Evidence with Analysis (p. 470)
- Analyze the story. (pp. 475–79)
- Formulate a working thesis. (pp. 479–81)
- Provide support for your argument. (pp. 481–82)
- To build on your support, consider doing outside research. (pp. 482–83)

Writing a Draft

GUIDE TO READING
GUIDE TO WRITING
A WRITER AT WORK
THINKING CRITICALLY

473

A Clear, Logical Organization

How should I organize my argument so that my audience can follow it easily?

- Assess the genre's basic features: A clear, logical organization (pp. 462–63)
- A Clear, Logical Organization: Coordinating Key Words and Topic Sentences (p. 470)
- Create an outline that will organize your argument effectively. (p. 483)
- Draft your analysis. (p. 484)

Writing a Draft: Invention, Research, Planning, and Composing

The activities in this section will help you find a story to write about, analyze it thoughtfully, and develop and organize an essay that argues for the position you are taking on the story. Do the activities in any order that makes sense to you (and your instructor), and return to them as needed as you revise. Your writing in response to many of these activities can be used in a rough draft that you will be able to improve after receiving feedback from your classmates and instructor.

Find a story to write about.

Your instructor may have given you a list of stories to choose from or assigned a particular story for the class to write about. If so, go on to the next section, Analyze the Story (pp. 475–79). If you need to find a story on your own, look for one that meets your instructor's approval and does one or more of the following:

- Deals with a culturally, politically, or historically significant theme
- Surprises or puzzles you with apparent contradictions
- Leads you to wonder what is left out of the story—the backstory or *context*
- Raises questions about characters' motivations, relationships, or development
- Uses conventional story motifs, setting, or other features in unconventional ways
- Resonates emotionally, perhaps giving you insight into human frailty or moral ambiguity

To find a story on your own, browse any literature anthology or short story collection in a library or bookstore, or try one of the following online sites:

- *American Literature* short story library (americanliterature.com)
- *Classic Short Stories* (classicshorts.com)
- *Classic Reader:* Short Stories (classicreader.com/browse/6)
- *Short Story Archive* (shortstoryarchive.com)

You might also consider stories in the following subject areas:

Stories Related to Identity and Community

"The Story of an Hour" (pp. 495–97), "Araby" (pp. 497–500), or "Girl" (pp. 504–5), would make good choices if you are interested in issues of identity and community. If you would like to look further, here are a few other widely anthologized stories you might consider writing about:

"The Monkey Garden," by Sandra Cisneros

"The Open Boat," by Stephen Crane

"Fleur," by Louise Erdrich

"A Rose for Emily," by William Faulkner

"My Kinsman, Major Molineux," by Nathaniel Hawthorne

"A Clean, Well-Lighted Place," by Ernest Hemingway

"The Lottery," by Shirley Jackson

"The Metamorphosis," by Franz Kafka

"The Ones Who Walk Away from Omelas," by Ursula Le Guin

"My Father's Chinese Wives," by Sandra Tsing Loh

"A Pair of Tickets," by Amy Tan

"Everyday Use," by Alice Walker

Stories Related to Work and Career

"The Use of Force" (pp. 501–3) would be one good choice if you are interested in writing about the topic of work and career. Here are some additional stories you might consider for exploring this topic:

"Sonny's Blues," by James Baldwin

"The Yellow Wallpaper," by Charlotte Perkins Gilman

"The Birthmark," by Nathaniel Hawthorne

"Reena," by Paule Marshall

"Shiloh," by Bobbie Ann Mason

"Bartleby the Scrivener," by Herman Melville

"Picasso," by Gertrude Stein

"The Catbird Seat," by James Thurber

"A&P," by John Updike

"Why I Live at the P.O.," by Eudora Welty

Writing a Draft

GUIDE TO READING
GUIDE TO WRITING
A WRITER AT WORK
THINKING CRITICALLY

475

:: Analyze the story.

Use the following suggestions as a way into the story. Try out more than one to discover how different aspects of the story work together and to generate ideas for a thoughtful analysis. To read the story closely and critically, *annotate* it as you work through the suggestions, highlighting key passages and noting your ideas and questions.

For more on annotating, see Chapter 12, pp. 522–28.

WHAT ELEMENTS COULD I ANALYZE, AND WHY?	WHAT APPROACH MIGHT I TAKE?	WHAT SHOULD I ASK MYSELF?
Character You want to know • why a character acts in a particular way; • how gender or ethnicity affects relationships; • whether a character changes or grows; • whether we should approve of a character's actions or accept his or her justifications.	Psychological	Does the character change/learn anything in the course of the story? How does the character relate to other characters? For instance, how does he or she deal with intimacy, commitment, and responsibility? Does the character seem depressed, manic, abusive, fearful, egotistical, or paranoid? Does any other character seem to represent the character's double or opposite?
	Ethical or moral	What are the character's virtues and/or vices? What influences your judgment of the character? Something in the story (such as what the narrator or another character says)? Something you bring to the story (your views of right and wrong, based on your family upbringing or religious teachings)? Something else? Do any of the other characters have different moral values that could be compared or contrasted to the character's values?
	Social or cultural	How does the character fit into and appear to be defined by society, in terms of race, ethnicity, socioeconomic class, sexual orientation, age, or gender?

WAYS IN

(continued)

		Who in the story exercises power over whom? What causes the difference in power? What are the effects of this difference? Does the balance of power change during the story?
Setting You want to know ▪ how much time and place matter; ▪ what the description of the setting symbolizes; ▪ how the setting affects characters.	In relation to the mood, characters, or actions	How does the setting affect the mood? For example, does it create feelings of suspense or foreboding? Are there any cause-effect connections between the setting and what characters are doing, thinking, or feeling?
	Historical or cultural	How does the historical period or cultural context in which the story is set affect what happens and does not happen? How might the story's meaning be different if the historical time or cultural situation were changed?
	Metaphoric or symbolic	Assuming that the setting is a projection of the thoughts and feelings of the narrator, what does the setting tell you about the narrator's state of mind? Assuming that the setting symbolizes the social relations among characters in the story, what does the setting tell you about these relationships? Assuming that the setting stands for something outside the characters' control (such as nature, God, or some aspect of society), what does the setting tell you about the pressures and rules under which the characters function?
Plot Structure You want to know ▪ what the ending means; ▪ whether there is a turning point in the story;	As realistic (resembling real-life experience)	After marking where each new stage of the story begins, how can the sequence of scenes or events be understood? In what ways do subplots mirror, undercut, or comment on the main plot?

Writing a Draft

GUIDE TO READING
GUIDE TO WRITING
A WRITER AT WORK
THINKING CRITICALLY

477

■ how a subplot relates to the main plot.	As surrealistic (having symbolic rather than literal meaning)	Thinking of the story as a series of images (more like a collage or a dream than a realistic portrayal of actual events), what meanings do you find in the arrangement of these images?
Point of View You want to know ■ whether the narrator can be believed; ■ whose values and interests are represented; ■ how readers' sympathies are manipulated.	In terms of what the narrator actually sees	Is the narrator a character in the story or an all-knowing, disembodied voice who knows what every character thinks, feels, and does? What important insights or ideas does the narrator have? How do factors such as the narrator's gender, age, and ethnicity influence what he or she notices as important? Are there things that the narrator is not able to see or that he or she distorts—for example, certain truths about himself or herself, about other characters, or about what happens in the story?
	In terms of how the narrator represents what he or she sees	How would you characterize the narrator's tone at various points in the story? For example, is the tone satirical, celebratory, angry, bitter, or optimistic? What about the narrator (or about the situation) might account for each tone you identify? What special agenda or motive might have led the narrator to this particular way of describing characters and scenes or telling the story?
Literary Motif or Theme You want to know ■ whether the story is about a break with social conventions, the	In terms of a traditional story motif (or an ironic reversal of the tradition)	Could you analyze the text as . . . an initiation (or coming-of-age or rite-of-passage) story? . . . a quest (for love, truth, fame, fortune, or salvation of oneself or the community)?

(continued)

initiation into adulthood, or some other common literary motif; ▪ what the story says about war, poverty, love, alienation, or some other general theme; ▪ how the story illuminates a historical or current issue.	In terms of a common literary theme	. . . a story about a character's disillusionment or fall from innocence? . . . a story about family or surrogate families? . . . a story about storytelling (or some other art) or becoming a writer or an artist? Might you focus on the theme of . . . the American dream? . . . the social construction of femininity or masculinity? . . . race relations in America? . . . alienation? . . . the urban or suburban experience?

In addition to generating ideas by taking one of the approaches listed above, you can consider the details and use those to generate an approach. Or you can list ideas you had while reading the story and use those to locate supporting details. The Ways In box that follows can help you generate ideas using these two approaches.

WAYS IN

HOW CAN I GENERATE IDEAS BY MOVING FROM SPECIFIC DETAILS TO GENERAL IDEAS?

1. Select two or three quotations, and write several sentences answering this question: What idea or ideas does each quotation suggest, and what in the quotation makes you think so?

2. Write a paragraph analyzing one or more patterns you found in the story. Here are a few patterns to help you get started:

   • Imagery (for example, the militaristic images in "The Use of Force" that Lee analyzes)

HOW CAN I GENERATE IDEAS BY MOVING FROM GENERAL IDEAS TO SPECIFIC DETAILS?

1. List ideas you thought of as you analyzed the story, without worrying about how these ideas relate to one another or whether they are contradictory. For example, here are two of Isabella Wright's ideas about the doctor in "The Use of Force" (see A Writer at Work, pp. 491–93).

   He has no time for the social conventions upheld by the parents.

   His break with social conventions feels freeing—maybe even transformative.

Writing a Draft

GUIDE TO READING
GUIDE TO WRITING
A WRITER AT WORK
THINKING CRITICALLY

479

- Characters as contrasts (for example, differences between the parents and the doctor in "The Use of Force" that Wright discusses)
- Events that echo or reverse one another (for example, the doctor's fury echoes the young girl's)

2. Review the story to find quotations or other details you could use to illustrate your ideas.

3. Write for a few minutes about your most interesting ideas and how they connect to one another. For example, in exploring her ideas about "The Use of Force," Wright connected her ideas about breaking social conventions to develop her main claim about the transformative power of disobeying the rules of social behavior.

TEST YOUR CHOICE

Get together with two or three other students who have read your story, and offer responses to one another's ideas.

Presenters.   Take turns telling one another your two or three most promising ideas, giving an example from the story to support each idea.

Listeners.   Briefly respond to each presenter's ideas, identifying what you find interesting in them, what you agree or disagree with, and how the ideas could be extended or complicated productively.

⠿ Formulate a working thesis.

Remember that an arguable thesis is not a simple statement of fact or an obvious conclusion. To get a sense of how you might formulate an arguable thesis, take a look at the thesis statements from the student essays you've studied in this chapter.

> As an account of a professional doing harm under the pretense of healing, the story uncovers how a doctor can take advantage of the intimate nature of his work and his professional status to overstep common forms of conduct, to the extent that his actions actually hurt rather than help a patient. In this way, the doctor-narrator actually performs a valuable service by warning readers, indirectly through his story, that blindly trusting members of his profession can have negative consequences. (Lee, par. 1)

> Through [the doctor's] actions and words (uttered or thought), readers are able to see the freeing, transformative power of breaking with social conventions. Thus, they are also encouraged to rethink what is acceptable and unacceptable in polite society. (Wright, par. 1)

You may have already decided on the main claim you want to make in your short story analysis; if so, try drafting a working thesis statement now. The Ways In activities that follow may help. (Alternatively, if you prefer to develop your analysis before trying to formulate a thesis, skip this activity and return to it when you're ready.)

WAYS IN

HOW CAN I FORMULATE AN ARGUABLE THESIS?

Write for ten minutes about your most promising ideas. After writing, read what you have written and see if you can find one main idea or claim that can serve as the thesis for your essay. Focus your exploratory writing on questions like these:

- How can readers understand a character's internal conflict or apparent change?

- How is the story's theme reflected in the way the story is told, the way the setting is described, how characters relate to one another, or some other aspect of the story?

- How does the language used to describe the setting or the characters' actions illuminate such things as the main character's internal conflict, the relationship between characters, or the theme? (For example, the doctor-patient struggle described in "The Use of Force" forms the basis of Iris Lee's argument that the story warns readers against blindly trusting doctors.)

- What does the trajectory of the story (the plot structure) say about the characters or the culture? (For example, Isabella Wright's analysis of the increasing tension between repression and expression, social conventions and human willfulness, underlies her argument about the value of breaking with these conventions.)

Reread the story with one of the following questions (or a question of your own) in mind, underlining passages or taking notes as you read:

- How do my ideas about the story form links in a chain leading to some general conclusion? For example, Wright links two ideas: (1) pressure to adhere to social conventions and (2) reasons for breaking with these conventions. She is *not* simply retelling the story; she is stating her ideas about what happens in the story.

- How can I present my ideas as a response to a question — either a question my instructor asked or one I composed myself? For example, in their essays, Lee and Wright responded to the first question we posed in the Analyze & Write section for "The Use of Force" (p. 503).

- What, if anything, does the story say about what may be universally true about people and society versus what may result from specific historical, economic, or cultural conditions? About what is usually considered normal versus what is considered abnormal? About how some groups exert power while others may be oppressed or subversive?

Now reread your notes. Do they suggest one main idea or claim that can serve as the thesis for your essay?

Use the sentence strategies that follow as a jumping-off point; put your thesis into your own words when you revise, or use your own words and sentence patterns now:

- Many readers of .... point to .... [state feature(s) of the story], but an important aspect of the story that is often overlooked is ....

- A common (or superficial) reading of .... [name story or character] is that .... [common conclusion], but in fact .... [your own conclusion].

- Through the actions of [name character], [he/she/we] [is/are] led to this [surprising/alarming/disturbing] conclusion: ....

- Through the events unfolded in ...., [the main character/we] [is/are] led to this [surprising/alarming/disturbing] conclusion: ....

⸬ Provide support for your argument.

Look back on the ideas that you have generated so far, and ask yourself these questions:

- How can I present my ideas as reasons supporting my central claim, the essay's thesis? For example, Isabella Wright shaped the ideas she generated moving from general ideas to specific details (pp. 492–93) into reasons supporting her thesis about the value of breaking with social conventions.

- Have I remembered to include my own analysis in the support instead of just retelling the story through quotation, paraphrase, or summary? (If you are unsure, work through the activities in the Ways In box that follows.)

HOW CAN I INTEGRATE EVIDENCE FROM THE STORY?

WAYS IN

As noted earlier, to provide support for a short story analysis, writers may quote, paraphrase, or summarize parts of the story. However, this evidence should be offered in the service of a thoughtful examination of the story and go beyond a simple repetition of description, dialogue, and so on. To effectively integrate material from a story, try these strategies:

- **Use short quotations frequently to support your analysis.** Brief quotations are not in themselves superior to sentence-length and longer quotations, but they allow you to stay focused on your own argument and analysis while bringing in key information or vivid details from the story. Look at these examples from the student essays in this chapter:

  > To the contrary, from the beginning, he—and, through him, readers—sees the little girl as "unusually attractive" and "strong," with "magnificent blonde hair." This description of her seems almost angelic (par. 4). (Wright, par. 5)

(continued)

> Later, the mother reassures the child that the doctor is a "nice man" and "won't hurt you," though she can base those assertions only on what little she knows of him: his occupation (par. 15). (Lee, par. 2)

- **Comment directly on what you have quoted, paraphrased, or summarized so that readers will understand the relevance of this material to your analysis.** These comments should connect the quotation, paraphrase, or summary to the idea you are trying to support. One good strategy is to refer to quotations or paraphrases with *this, these,* or *they* statements, which are italicized in the following examples:

> After quoting the doctor's violent thoughts about the girl, Lee comments, "Although *these statements* are arguably exaggerated or hyperbolic, *they,* like the metaphors of war, imply a tendency *to do harm* that goes directly against the narrator's duty as a doctor" (Lee, par. 4).

> After summarizing the doctor's struggle with the girl, Wright notes, "*This conflict* might be interpreted as a process of reverse socialization or reverse civilization, a transformation that, surprisingly, the story presents as a potentially positive change" (Wright, par. 5).

Another good strategy is to repeat key nouns from quotations, paraphrases, or summaries in your analysis. These nouns are italicized in the following examples:

> After quoting part of the story that refers to the doctor smiling in his "best professional manner," Lee explains that, in using the "phrase '*professional manner,*'" the narrator admits his actions are not sincere but a calculated "*professional* performance." (Lee, par. 3).

> After quoting and paraphrasing information about the parents' politeness to the doctor, Wright observes, "In a story where *politeness* is made to seem absurd, the doctor's tactless words and his inappropriate use of force actually have the potential to be improvements on his character" (Wright, par. 6).

⸬ To build on your support, consider doing outside research.

Many analyses of short stories rely on a close reading of the text alone; the writer's analysis is the only tool brought to bear on the work. Some approaches to analysis, however, also consider biographical information on the author, his or her other works, or various critical responses to the short story in question. If your instructor has asked you to include such information, or if you are curious about some aspect of the text that you do not understand—or that you suspect your readers will not understand—you might want to conduct some research and include your findings in your essay. Here are a few suggestions for getting started:

- Do a *Google* search, using keywords relevant to your analysis. For example, if you want more information about the context of "The Use of Force," you could try keywords such as *diphtheria epidemic.*

- To see what others have said about an author's work, conduct a search using a specialized periodical database, such as the *MLA International Bibliography,* which specializes in academic writing about languages and literature. You should have access to periodical databases through your school's library. If you are not sure how to use them, see Chapter 24, pages 674–75, 678–79. Ask a reference librarian for help if you encounter problems.

As you work, bookmark or keep a record of promising sites. If you download or copy information you could use in your essay, remember to record source information.

Create an outline that will organize your argument effectively.

Whether you have rough notes or a complete draft, making an outline of what you have written can help you organize the essay effectively for your audience. One way to outline a literary analysis is to lay out your argument as a series of *because* sentences. For example, here's how Iris Lee might have outlined her argument:

I. The story performs a valuable service because, through the doctor's actions, readers see that it's unwise to blindly trust members of his profession.

   A. Although he displays his "best professional manner," the doctor does so only because he knows it will encourage the family's deference to him despite his rude and rough behavior.

   B. The doctor shows his untrustworthiness because he seems more interested in harming the girl than healing her.

II. Readers who see the doctor purely as a bad person are wrong because the author presents two sides of him.

   A. The doctor-as-actor deserves our scorn because he is capable of brutality under the guise of professionalism.

   B. The doctor-as-narrator deserves our thanks because he depicts the crimes of the doctor-as-actor, warning readers about the dangers of placing too much trust in medical professionals.

Once you have a working outline, you should not hesitate to change it as necessary while drafting and revising. For instance, you might find you left out an important idea that is needed to make the chain of reasoning complete. Remember that the purpose of an outline is to help you organize your ideas logically, not to lock you into a particular structure.

Write the opening sentences.

The Ways In feature on pp. 480–81 suggests several ways to present an arguable thesis. In writing your introduction, avoid creating a "funnel paragraph," which begins with a broad generalization and then becomes more and more focused and narrow, culminating in what is usually the essay's thesis. The problem with this kind of paragraph structure is that broad generalizations are not very interesting and add nothing to the essay. Look, for example, at the italicized sentences in this modified version of Isabella Wright's opening paragraph:

> *As all of us know, being the subject of a medical examination, especially if you are a child, is rarely fun. Patients can be nervous and uncooperative, and in the worst cases, doctors can act like real jerks.* William Carlos Williams's story "The Use of Force" is surprising in that it does not completely condemn the doctor for doing just that.

It is best to get rid of sentences like these and simply begin by presenting your ideas about the story.

Draft your analysis.

By this point, you have done a lot of writing to

- come up with ideas for your short story analysis;
- draft an arguable thesis;
- provide support for your argument;
- organize your ideas to present them logically to readers.

Now stitch that material together to create a draft. As you write, ask yourself questions like the following:

- Early in my essay, should I name the story and also identify the author?
- How much do I need to tell my readers about what happens in the story? Should I assume, as both Iris Lee and Isabella Wright do, that my readers have read the story?
- Should I consider placing this particular story in the context of the author's other writing or in its historical context?
- How can I revise my topic sentences to use the key terms introduced in my thesis? What synonyms could I use to avoid repeating my key terms too often?
- How can I use logical transitions to help readers see how one point connects to the next? For example, could I use transitions that announce contrasts, such as *but, although,* and *yet*?
- Should I consider ending with a new idea that grows out of my argument? Could I, for example, expand on the cultural or historical implications of my reading of the story?

Evaluating the Draft: Getting a Critical Reading

Your instructor may arrange a peer review session in class or online, where you can exchange drafts with your classmates and give each other a thoughtful critical reading, pointing out what works well and suggesting ways to improve the draft. A good critical reading of a literary analysis does three things:

Evaluating the Draft

GUIDE TO READING
GUIDE TO WRITING
A WRITER AT WORK
THINKING CRITICALLY

485

1. It lets the writer know how well the point of his or her analysis comes across to readers.

2. It praises what works best.

3. It indicates where the draft could be improved and makes suggestions on how to improve it.

One strategy for evaluating a draft is to use the basic features of a literary analysis as a guide.

A CRITICAL READING GUIDE

A Clear, Arguable Thesis

How well does the writer present the thesis?

Summarize: Tell the writer what you understand the essay's thesis to be and what its key terms are.

Praise: Tell the writer what seems most interesting to you about his or her main claim about the story, whether you agree with it or not.

Critique: If you cannot find the thesis statement or cannot identify the key terms, let the writer know. Evaluate the thesis statement on the basis of whether

- it makes an interesting and arguable assertion (rather than making a statement of fact or an obvious point);
- it is clear and precise (neither ambiguous nor vague);
- it is appropriately qualified (neither overgeneralized nor exaggerated).

A Well-Supported Argument

How well does the writer develop and support the argument?

Summarize: Underline the thesis statement and the major support for it. (Often, the major support appears in the topic sentences of paragraphs.)

Praise: Give an example in the essay where support for a reason is presented especially effectively — for instance, note where brief quotations (words and short phrases), a longer quotation, or summaries of particular events are introduced and explained in a way that clearly illustrates a particular point that is being argued.

Critique: Tell the writer where the connection between a reason and its support seems vague, where too much plot is being relayed with no apparent point, or where a quotation is left to speak for itself without explanation. Let the writer know if any part of the argument seems to be undeveloped or does not support the thesis.

(continued)

> Has the writer clearly and logically organized the argument?

A Clear, Logical Organization

Summarize: Underline the sentence(s) in which the writer forecasts supporting reasons, and circle transitions or repeated key words and phrases.

Praise: Give an example of something that makes the essay especially easy to read — where, for example, the key terms introduced in the thesis recur throughout the essay in topic sentences and elsewhere, or where transitions are used logically.

Critique: Tell the writer where readability could be improved. For example, point to places where key terms could be added or where a topic sentence could be made more clearly to indicate where the use of transitions might be improved, or note where transitions are lacking and could be added.

For a printable version of this Critical Reading Guide, go to **bedfordstmartins .com/theguide**.

Before concluding your peer review, be sure to address any of the writer's concerns that have not been discussed already.

Making Comments Electronically   Most word processing software offers features that allow you to insert comments directly into the text of someone else's document. Many readers prefer to make their comments this way because it tends to be faster than writing on hard copy and space is virtually unlimited; it also eliminates the process of deciphering handwritten comments. Where such features are not available, simply typing comments directly into a document in a contrasting color can provide the same advantages.

Improving the Draft: Revising, Formatting, Editing, and Proofreading

Start improving your draft by reflecting on what you have written thus far:

- Review critical reading comments from your classmates, instructor, or writing center tutor: What are your readers getting at?
- Consider your invention writing: What else should you consider?
- Review your draft: What can you do to present your argument more compellingly?

Revise your draft.

If your readers are having difficulty with your draft, or if you think there is room for improvement, try some of the strategies listed in the Troubleshooting Guide that follows. It can help you fine-tune your presentation of the genre's basic features.

A TROUBLESHOOTING GUIDE

A Clear, Arguable Thesis

> My thesis is unclear or overgeneralized.

- Add more explanation.
- Refer to the story specifically.
- Add qualifying words like *some* or *usually*.

> My thesis is not arguable or interesting.

- Respond to a question or class discussion.
- Summarize an alternative argument.
- Try additional suggestions for analysis from the Ways In box on pp. 475–78.

A Well-Supported Argument

> My argument seems superficial or thin.

- Develop your ideas by connecting them.
- Link your ideas to make a chain of reasoning.
- Connect to a literary motif or theme.
- Add textual evidence by quoting, paraphrasing, or summarizing important passages.
- Focus on the writer's choice of words, explaining how particular word choices support your ideas.
- Consider using other kinds of support, such as information about the story's historical or cultural context.

> The connection between a reason and its support seems vague.

- Explain why the support illustrates the point you are making.
- Explain what the quoted words imply — their connotative as well as their denotative meanings.
- Introduce quotations, and follow them with some analysis or explanation.
- Explain more fully and clearly how your reasons relate logically to one another as well as to your thesis.
- Fill in the gaps.
- Use contradictions or gaps to extend or complicate your argument.

(continued)

A Clear, Logical Organization

My essay is hard to follow.

- Repeat key terms from the thesis and other introductory text.
- Provide explicit topic sentences.
- Add logical transitions.

For an electronic version of this Troubleshooting Guide, go to **bedfordstmartins .com/theguide**.

Think about design.

Some literary analyses can be enhanced by visuals—for example, drawings, photographs, tables, or graphs—that provide a historical or social context or some other supporting information.

Suppose in writing about "The Use of Force," for example, you are interested in the history of diphtheria epidemics. In doing research, you might find or construct a timeline showing how many children died over the years from the disease, and include this information in a simple table. If you were writing an analysis of the story "Araby" and taking a biographical approach, you might include this photograph of 17 North Richmond Street in Dublin, Ireland, where Joyce lived during part of his youth. Descriptions of this home are featured in "Araby" as well as in Joyce's books *Portrait of the Artist as a Young Man, Ulysses,* and *Finnegan's Wake.*

As always, consider reviewing other analyses of the short story you are studying or analyses of other stories to see how they use visuals to support and strengthen their arguments. Use the formatting instructions for the style manual your instructor requires to determine matters such as the width of margins, the use of headers and page numbers, and the formatting of your works cited list. (For writing projects in English composition and literature, instructors frequently ask students to follow MLA style.)

Edit and proofread your draft.

Our research has identified several errors that occur often in essays that analyze short stories, including problems with parallelism and the use of ellipsis marks. The following guidelines will help you check your essay for these common errors.

For more on document design, see Chapter 21. For guidelines on formatting a writing project and acknowledging the sources of visuals in MLA style, see Chapter 27.

Using Parallel Structure

The Problem   When you present items as a pair or in a series (for example, *I gave him x and y;* or *I gave him x, y, and z*), you must present the items in the series in the same grammatical form—all nouns, all prepositional phrases, all adverb clauses, and so on.

Improving the Draft

GUIDE TO READING
GUIDE TO WRITING
A WRITER AT WORK
THINKING CRITICALLY

489

Mixing and matching leads to lack of clarity and lessens the impact of your prose. Take as an example one of Iris Lee's first-draft sentences:

> The doctor's actions actually hurt rather than providing any benefit to a patient.

"Hurt" is a one-word verb; "providing any benefit to," which should be a parallel item, combines an -*ing* verb, an adjective, an object, and a preposition. The resulting sentence is unnecessarily complicated and clumsy.

The Correction   Lee eventually edited the sentence as follows:

> ▸ The doctor's actions actually hurt rather than ~~providing any benefit to~~ a patient.
> *help*

The parallelism of *hurt* and *help* puts the verbs in the same form and emphasizes the contrast between these two actions in a way that the first-draft wording did not. For more examples, see the following sentences:

> ▸ This image comes more from ~~his reading~~ than from anything he's observed.
> *what he's read*

> ▸ To Kafka, loneliness, ~~being isolated~~, and regrets are the price of freedom.
> *isolation*

> ▸ Sarah really cares about her brother and ~~to maintain~~ their relationship. She lets
> *values*
>
> us know that she was injured by her mother's abuse but avoids saying what she
>
> felt after the incident, how others reacted to the incident, and ~~that~~ physical pain
> *what*
>
> she endured.

Using Ellipsis Marks Correctly

You will often quote sources when you analyze a story, and you must be careful to use **ellipsis marks** (or **ellipses**) — three spaced periods — to indicate places where you delete material from a quotation. Look, for example, at how Iris Lee, in an early draft of her essay, used ellipsis marks in quoting from "The Use of Force."

Passage from Story	**Quotation with Ellipsis Marks**
When finally I got the wooden spatula behind the last teeth and just the point of it into the mouth cavity, she opened up for an instant but before I could see anything she came down again and gripping the wooden blade between her molars she reduced it to splinters before I could get it out again. . . . (Williams, par. 29)	In describing his attempts to get the wooden spatula into the girl's mouth, the narrator says "she opened up for an instant but . . . came down again and gripping the wooden blade between her molars reduced it to splinters."

A Note on Grammar and Spelling Checkers

These tools can be helpful, but do not rely on them exclusively to catch errors in your text: Spelling checkers cannot catch misspellings that are themselves words, such as *to* for *too*. Grammar checkers miss some problems, sometimes give faulty advice for fixing problems, and can flag correct items as wrong. Use these tools as a second line of defense after your own (and, ideally, another reader's) proofreading and editing efforts.

For practice, go to **bedfordstmartins.com /theguide/exercisecentral** and click on Parallelism.

The Problem   Failing to use ellipsis marks to indicate the omission of material misrepresents the quote, which is a serious breach of convention. Using ellipsis marks incorrectly makes your readers doubt your knowledge of conventions.

The Correction   If you are using MLA style, follow these rules about using ellipsis marks:

- When you delete words from the *middle of a quoted sentence,* add ellipsis marks, and leave a single space before and after each ellipsis point.

- When you delete words from the *end of a quoted sentence* and a grammatically complete sentence remains, add a period after the last word and then three ellipsis marks.

- Leave a single space after the period and each of the first two ellipsis marks. Do not leave a space between the last mark and the closing quotation mark.

- When you delete material from the middle of a passage of *two or more sentences,* use ellipsis marks where the text is omitted and a period after the preceding text if it is a grammatically complete sentence.

- When you delete words from the *beginning of a quoted sentence,* use ellipsis marks only if the remainder of the sentence begins with a capitalized word and is a grammatically complete sentence.

- Single words and brief phrases can be quoted without ellipsis marks.

Examples of sentences edited to show correct usage follow:

For more on using ellipsis marks to indicate a deletion from a quotation, see Chapter 26, p. 702.

▶ The narrator describes his patient as "~~She did not move and seemed, inwardly,~~

~~quiet;~~ an unusually attractive little thing, and as strong as a heifer in appearance.

~~But her face was flushed, she was breathing rapidly, and I realized that she had a~~
          . . .
~~high fever.~~ She had magnificent blonde hair, in profusion."
      ^

▶ According to the narrator, the little girl's mother was "a big startled-looking
          . . .
woman, ~~very clean and apologetic,~~ who merely said, Is this the doctor? and let me in."
       ^

For practice, go to **bedfordstmartins.com /theguide/exercisecentral** and click on Ellipsis Marks.

Isabella Wright's Invention Work

In this section, you will see some of the work that Isabella Wright did in developing her essay analyzing the story "The Use of Force." Using the Guide to Writing in this book, Wright chose the suggestions for interpreting character to guide her analysis of the story. As you will see,

- she annotated a portion of the story focusing on the doctor's first attempts to examine the young patient's throat;
- she wrote to explore her annotations on the passages;
- she listed ideas for formulating her tentative thesis statement.

You will be able to infer from her invention work how her ideas came to form the thesis she developed for her final essay.

Annotating

Wright annotated paragraphs 12–22 of "The Use of Force" as she reread them with the suggestions for analyzing character in mind. The annotated passages are reproduced here. Notice the diversity of her annotations:

- In the text itself, she underlined key words and circled words to be defined.
- In the margin, she defined words, made comments, and posed questions. She also expressed her tentative insights, reactions, and judgments.

---

smile really sincere? 12 Well, I said, suppose we take a look at the throat first. I <u>smiled</u> in my best professional manner and asking for the child's first name I said, come on, Mathilda, open your mouth and let's take a look at your throat.

13 Nothing doing.

14 Aw, come on, I coaxed, just open your mouth wide and let me take a look. <u>Look, I said opening both hands wide, I haven't anything in my hands. Just open up and let me see.</u>

he's trying to come across as unthreatening

mother's politeness continues 15 Such a <u>nice man</u>, put in the mother. Look how kind he is to you. Come on, do what he tells you to. He won't hurt you.

16 At that I <u>ground my teeth in disgust.</u> If only they wouldn't use the word "hurt" I might be able to get somewhere. But I did not allow myself to be hurried or disturbed but speaking quietly and slowly I approached the child again.

not willing to promise he won't hurt girl

unlike parents, child showing her true self 17 As I moved my chair a little nearer suddenly with one catlike movement both her hands clawed instinctively for my eyes and she almost reached them too. In fact she knocked my glasses flying and they fell, though unbroken, several feet away from me on the kitchen floor.

18   Both the mother and father almost turned themselves inside out in <u>embarrassment</u> and <u>apology</u>. You bad girl, said the mother, taking her and shaking her by one arm. Look what you've done. The nice man . . .

parents very embarrassed— concerned with social conventions

19   For heaven's sake, I broke in. Don't call me a nice man to her. I'm here to look at her throat on the chance that she might have (diphtheria) and possibly die of it. But that's nothing to her. Look here, I said to the child, we're going to look at your throat. You're old enough to understand what I'm saying. Will you open it now by yourself or shall we have to open it for you?

Rude. Is he really saying this? No quotation marks

possibly deadly infection

he's losing his patience

20   Not a move. Even her expression hadn't changed. Her breaths however were coming faster and faster. Then the <u>battle</u> began. I had to do it. I had to have a throat culture for <u>her own protection</u>. But first I told the parents that it was entirely up to them. I explained the danger but said that I would not insist on a throat examination so long as they would take the responsibility.

battle of the wills as much as a physical battle?

"her own protection"— he's trying to justify his actions

21   If you don't do what the doctor says you'll have to go to the hospital, the mother admonished her severely.

22   Oh yeah? <u>I had to smile to myself</u>. After all, I had already fallen in love with the savage brat, the parents were contemptible to me. In the ensuing struggle they grew more and more (abject,) crushed, exhausted while she surely rose to magnificent heights of insane fury of effort bred of her terror of me.

Now here's a sincere smile!

hopeless

struggle has transformed him— and his view of her?

As you can see, annotating this section of the story with the suggestions for analyzing character in mind led Wright to notice how much the doctor's direct, and sometimes rude, manner is butting up against the parents' politeness and embarrassment over their child's behavior.

Examining Patterns in the Story

Following the instructions in the Ways In feature for generating ideas by moving from details to general ideas (pp. 478–79), Wright explored a pattern of contrast she saw between the doctor and the parents in the story. Here is what she wrote:

> From the start of this scene, it feels like the whole experience between the doctor and
> the family is going to go from bad to worse. The doctor's smile feels forced, almost as

Isabella Wright's Invention Work

GUIDE TO READING
GUIDE TO WRITING
A WRITER AT WORK
THINKING CRITICALLY

493

if he's warning the little girl that she's in for an unpleasant time. The parents' attempts to smooth things over do nothing but irritate him, and he's actually angered by being referred to as a "nice man." It's as if he has no time for the social conventions so important to the parents; these rules mean nothing to him, much less to the girl. In some ways, the doctor and the girl seem more alike than the doctor and the parents because he and the girl are showing their true selves. For that reason, maybe he even respects her more than he does the parents. The longer the two of them struggle, the more he seems to admire her. From the parents' and the girl's point of view, the experience is pretty clearly a bad one, but perhaps there's something freeing about it from the doctor's perspective.

As Wright wrote about the contrasts between the characters, she became increasingly confident that she not only had an interesting idea but had also one she could find support for in the story.

Listing Ideas

Wright tried out the activity on listing ideas from the Ways In feature on pp. 478–79. In doing so, she drew on both her annotations and on the exploratory writing she did about the doctor and the family (above):

> The doctor comes across in a bad light: He's rude and impatient and able to justify the use of force against the girl.
>
> He has no time for the social conventions upheld by the parents.
>
> He's more annoyed than flattered by the mother's compliments and attempts to smooth things over.
>
> In this way, maybe he is more like the little girl than the parents.
>
> They both seem to be showing their true selves.
>
> In the end, it's hard to condemn the doctor.
>
> His break with social conventions feels freeing—maybe even transformative.

From these ideas about the doctor's behavior and how his views about social conventions differ from those of the parents, Wright was able to devise the thesis statement she eventually used in her essay.

To think critically means to use all of the knowledge you have acquired from the information in this chapter, your own writing, the writing of other students, and class discussions to reflect deeply on your work for this assignment and the genre (or type) of writing you have produced. The benefit of thinking critically is proven and important: Thinking critically about what you have learned will help you remember it longer, ensuring that you will be able to put it to good use well beyond this writing course.

Reflecting on What You Have Learned

In this chapter, you have learned a great deal about arguing for your analysis of a short story by reading two essays in this genre and by writing one of your own. To consolidate your learning, reflect not only on what you learned but also on how you learned it.

ANALYZE & WRITE

Write a blog post to classmates, a letter to your instructor, or an e-mail message to a student who will take this course next term, using the writing prompt that seems most productive for you:

- Explain how your purpose and audience influenced *one* of your decisions as a writer, such as how you chose the suggestions for analysis you used, the key words you used in presenting your thesis, or the quotations you chose to support your argument.

- Discuss what you learned about yourself as a writer in the process of writing this essay. For example, what part of the process did you find most challenging? Did you try anything new, like getting a critical reading of your draft or summarizing an alternative argument to improve your thesis? If so, would you do it again?

- Choose one of the readings in this chapter, and explain how it influenced your essay. Be sure to cite specific examples from your essay and the reading.

- If you got good advice from a critical reader, explain exactly how the person helped you—perhaps by questioning the way you stated your thesis or how you explained one of your reasons.

Reflecting on the Genre

Some genres, like position papers, have a broad general audience, composed of people whose knowledge of current controversial issues varies widely. Other genres, like essays analyzing stories, are highly specialized, read and written by a comparatively small group of people who share certain kinds of knowledge and interests.

Students in English courses learn certain ways of reading and writing about stories, and they also discover what kinds of analyses are likely to interest their readers—people engaged in an ongoing conversation about stories and other works of literature. They need to know some of the specialized vocabulary used in writing about literature, such as *point of view,* as well as the critical approaches to analyzing stories they find useful. English instructors determine which approaches their students need to become familiar with, and they introduce these subjects in lectures and class discussions. They choose stories to read and assign essays to write that will give students opportunities to use these approaches.

ANALYZE & WRITE

Write a page or two about your experience analyzing literature in this course and, if relevant, in other English classes. Connect your ideas to your experience with writing a short story analysis and to the readings in this chapter. In your discussion, you might consider one or more of the following questions:

1 **List some of the subjects you and your classmates discussed in class and wrote about.** Where did these subjects come from — class discussion, the Ways In box on pp. 475–78 in the Guide to Writing, your instructor's questions or lectures, other English classes?

2 **Consider whether any subjects were deemed by your instructor or other students to be uninteresting or not appropriate for analyzing stories.** Why were these subjects rejected? Do you agree with their exclusion?

3 **Did you become part of the conversation about the literature you studied?** If so, what made you feel most connected to the stories (or other works) you read and the discussions about them? If not, can you name anything in particular that made you feel left out?

AN ANTHOLOGY OF SHORT STORIES

In this section, you will find four short stories: "The Story of an Hour," by Kate Chopin; "Araby," by James Joyce; "The Use of Force," by William Carlos Williams; and "Girl" by Jamaica Kincaid. Each is followed by questions to help you get started analyzing the story. The stories are intended for use with the "Practicing the Genre: Analyzing a Story Collaboratively" activity on p. 458. Your instructor may also ask you to choose one of these stories for your essay analyzing a story.

Kate Chopin | *The Story of an Hour*

 KATE CHOPIN (1851–1904) was born in St. Louis and lived in Louisiana until her husband died in 1882, leaving her with six children. Encouraged by friends, Chopin wrote her first novel, *At Fault* (1890), when she was nearly forty years old. She wrote many short stories for such popular magazines as *Century, Harper's,* and *Vogue,* in which "The Story of an Hour" first appeared in 1894. She published two collections of stories and a second novel, her best-known work, *The Awakening* (1899).

1 Knowing that Mrs. Mallard was afflicted with a heart trouble, great care was taken to break to her as gently as possible the news of her husband's death.

2 It was her sister Josephine who told her, in broken sentences; veiled hints that revealed in half concealing. Her husband's friend Richards was there, too, near her. It was he who had been in the newspaper office when intelligence of the railroad disaster was received, with Brently Mallard's name leading the list of "killed." He had only taken the time to assure himself of its truth by a second telegram, and had hastened to forestall any less careful, less tender friend in bearing the sad message.

3 She did not hear the story as many women have heard the same, with a paralyzed inability to accept its significance. She wept at once, with sudden, wild abandonment, in her sister's arms. When the storm of grief had spent itself she went away to her room alone. She would have no one follow her.

4 There stood, facing the open window, a comfortable, roomy armchair. Into this she sank, pressed down by a physical exhaustion that haunted her body and seemed to reach into her soul.

5 She could see in the open square before her house the tops of trees that were all aquiver with the new spring life. The delicious breath of rain was in the air. In the street below a peddler was crying his wares. The notes of a distant song which some one was singing reached her faintly, and countless sparrows were twittering in the eaves.

6 There were patches of blue sky showing here and there through the clouds that had met and piled one above the other in the west facing her window.

7 She sat with her head thrown back upon the cushion of the chair, quite motionless, except when a sob came up into her throat and shook her, as a child who has cried itself to sleep continues to sob in its dreams.

8 She was young, with a fair, calm face, whose lines bespoke repression and even a certain strength. But now there was a dull stare in her eyes, whose gaze was fixed away off yonder on one of those patches of blue sky. It was not a glance of reflection, but rather indicated a suspension of intelligent thought.

9 There was something coming to her and she was waiting for it, fearfully. What was it? She did not know; it was too subtle and elusive to name. But she felt it, creeping out of the sky, reaching toward her through the sounds, the scents, the color that filled the air.

10 Now her bosom rose and fell tumultuously. She was beginning to recognize this thing that was approaching to possess her, and she was striving to beat it back with her will—as powerless as her two white slender hands would have been.

11 When she abandoned herself a little whispered word escaped her slightly parted lips. She said it over and over under her breath: "free, free, free!" The vacant stare and the look of terror that had followed it went from her eyes. They stayed keen and bright. Her pulses beat fast, and the coursing blood warmed and relaxed every inch of her body.

12 She did not stop to ask if it were or were not a monstrous joy that held her. A clear and exalted perception enabled her to dismiss the suggestion as trivial.

13 She knew that she would weep again when she saw the kind, tender hands folded in death; the face that had never looked save with love upon her, fixed and gray and dead. But she saw beyond that bitter moment a long procession of years to come that would belong to her absolutely. And she opened and spread her arms out to them in welcome.

14 There would be no one to live for during those coming years; she would live for herself. There would be no powerful will bending hers in that blind persistence with which men and women believe they have a right to impose a private will upon a fellow-creature. A kind intention or a cruel intention made the act seem no less a crime as she looked upon it in that brief moment of illumination.

15 And yet she had loved him—sometimes. Often she had not. What did it matter! What could love, the unsolved mystery, count for in face of this possession of self-assertion which she suddenly recognized as the strongest impulse of her being!

16 "Free! Body and soul free!" she kept whispering.

17 Josephine was kneeling before the closed door with her lips to the keyhole, imploring for admission. "Louise, open the door! I beg; open the door—you will make yourself ill. What are you doing, Louise? For heaven's sake open the door."

18 "Go away. I am not making myself ill." No; she was drinking in a very elixir of life through that open window.

19   Her fancy was running riot along those days ahead of her. Spring days, and summer days, and all sorts of days that would be her own. She breathed a quick prayer that life might be long. It was only yesterday she had thought with a shudder that life might be long.

20   She arose at length and opened the door to her sister's importunities. There was a feverish triumph in her eyes, and she carried herself unwittingly like a goddess of Victory. She clasped her sister's waist, and together they descended the stairs. Richards stood waiting for them at the bottom.

21   Some one was opening the front door with a latch-key. It was Brently Mallard who entered, a little travel-stained, composedly carrying his gripsack and umbrella. He had been far from the scene of accident, and did not even know there had been one. He stood amazed at Josephine's piercing cry; at Richards' quick motion to screen him from the view of his wife.

22   But Richards was too late.

23   When the doctors came they said she had died of heart disease—of joy that kills.

ANALYZE & WRITE

Use the following questions to begin analyzing "The Story of an Hour":

1 **Irony** refers to a gap or discrepancy between what is said and what is true, or between a result that is expected and what actually happens. In literature, readers often perceive irony that characters are unable to see. What is the central irony of "The Story of an Hour"? To get started, take a look at how the story is framed in the opening and closing paragraphs. What gap or discrepancy do you notice? Do the characters share your insight?

2 What do you learn from the setting and, in particular, the language Chopin uses to describe what Mrs. Mallard experiences when, beginning in paragraph 4, she sits in her armchair, looking out the window?

3 This story was originally published at the end of the nineteenth century. With this context in mind, what do you think Chopin is saying about marriage, gender, power, and sexuality in American society? To get started, you could look at how Richards tries to "screen [Mr. Mallard] from the view of his wife" (par. 21).

James Joyce | *Araby*

JAMES JOYCE (1882–1941), a native of Dublin, Ireland, is considered one of the most influential writers of the early twentieth century. "Araby," one of his most often anthologized stories, first appeared in the collection *Dubliners* in 1914. Like his novel *Portrait of the Artist as a Young Man,* published two years later, it relies on scenes from Joyce's own boyhood.

1 Ｎorth Richmond Street, being blind,[1] was a quiet street except at the hour when the Christian Brothers' School set the boys free. An uninhabited house of two storeys stood at the blind end, detached from its neighbours in a square ground. The other houses of the street, conscious of decent lives within them, gazed at one another with brown imperturbable faces.

2 The former tenant of our house, a priest, had died in the back drawing-room. Air, musty from having been long enclosed, hung in all the rooms, and the waste room behind the kitchen was littered with old useless papers. Among these I found a few paper-covered books, the pages of which were curled and damp: *The Abbot,* by Walter Scott, *The Devout Communicant* and *The Memoirs of Vidocq*.[2] I liked the last best because its leaves were yellow. The wild garden behind the house contained a central apple-tree and a few straggling bushes under one of which I found the late tenant's rusty bicycle-pump. He had been a very charitable priest; in his will he had left all his money to institutions and the furniture of his house to his sister.

3 When the short days of winter came dusk fell before we had well eaten our dinners. When we met in the street the houses had grown sombre. The space of sky above us was the colour of ever-changing violet and towards it the lamps of the street lifted their feeble lanterns. The cold air stung us and we played till our bodies glowed. Our shouts echoed in the silent street. The career of our play brought us through the dark muddy lanes behind the houses where we ran the gauntlet of the rough tribes from the cottages, to the back doors of the dark dripping gardens where odours arose from the ashpits, to the dark odorous stables where a coachman smoothed and combed the horse or shook music from the buckled harness. When we returned to the street light from the kitchen windows had filled the areas. If my uncle was seen turning the corner we hid in the shadow until we had seen him safely housed. Or if Mangan's sister came out on the doorstep to call her brother in to his tea we watched her from our shadow peer up and down the street. We waited to see whether she would remain or go in and, if she remained, we left our shadow and walked up to Mangan's steps resignedly. She was waiting for us, her figure defined by the light from the half-opened door. Her brother always teased her before he obeyed and I stood by the railings looking at her. Her dress swung as she moved her body and the soft rope of her hair tossed from side to side.

4 Every morning I lay on the floor in the front parlour watching her door. The blind was pulled down to within an inch of the sash so that I could not be seen. When she came out on the doorstep my heart leaped. I ran to the hall, seized my books and followed her. I kept her brown figure always in my eye and, when we came near the point at which our ways diverged, I quickened my pace and passed her. This happened morning after morning. I had never spoken to her, except for a few casual words, and yet her name was like a summons to all my foolish blood.

5 Her image accompanied me even in places the most hostile to romance. On Saturday evenings when my aunt went marketing I had to go to carry some of the parcels. We walked through the flaring streets, jostled by drunken men and bargaining women, amid the curses of labourers, the shrill litanies of shop-boys who stood on guard by the barrels of pigs' cheeks, the nasal chanting of street-singers, who sang a *come-all-you* about O'Donovan Rossa,[3] or a ballad about the troubles in our native land. These noises converged in a single sensation of life for me: I imagined that I bore my chalice safely through a throng of foes. Her name sprang to my lips at moments in strange prayers and praises which I myself

---

[1] A dead end. The young Joyce in fact lived for a time on North Richmond Street in Dublin. [Editor's note]

[2] *The Abbot* is a historical romance set in the court of Mary, Queen of Scots, a Catholic, who was beheaded for plotting to assassinate her Protestant cousin, Queen Elizabeth I. *The Devout Communicant* is a collection of religious meditations. *The Memoirs of Vidocq* is a collection of sexually suggestive stories about a French criminal turned detective. [Editor's note]

[3] A contemporary leader of an underground organization opposed to British rule of Ireland. [Editor's note]

did not understand. My eyes were often full of tears (I could not tell why) and at times a flood from my heart seemed to pour itself out into my bosom. I thought little of the future. I did not know whether I would ever speak to her or not or, if I spoke to her, how I could tell her of my confused adoration. But my body was like a harp and her words and gestures were like fingers running upon the wires.

6   One evening I went into the back drawing-room in which the priest had died. It was a dark rainy evening and there was no sound in the house. Through one of the broken panes I heard the rain impinge upon the earth, the fine incessant needles of water playing in the sodden beds. Some distant lamp or lighted window gleamed below me. I was thankful that I could see so little. All my senses seemed to desire to veil themselves and, feeling that I was about to slip from them, I pressed the palms of my hands together until they trembled, murmuring: "*O love! O love!*" many times.

7   At last she spoke to me. When she addressed the first words to me I was so confused that I did not know what to answer. She asked me was I going to Araby. I forgot whether I answered yes or no. It would be a splendid bazaar, she said she would love to go.[4]

8   "And why can't you?" I asked.

9   While she spoke she turned a silver bracelet round and round her wrist. She could not go, she said, because there would be a retreat that week in her convent. Her brother and two other boys were fighting for their caps and I was alone at the railings. She held one of the spikes, bowing her head towards me. The light from the lamp opposite our door caught the white curve of her neck, lit up her hair that rested there and, falling, lit up the hand upon the railing. It fell over one side of her dress and caught the white border of a petticoat, just visible as she stood at ease.

10   "It's well for you," she said.

11   "If I go," I said, "I will bring you something."

12   What innumerable follies laid waste my waking and sleeping thoughts after that evening! I wished to annihilate the tedious intervening days. I chafed against the work of school. At night in my bedroom and by day in the classroom her image came between me and the page I strove to read. The syllables of the word *Araby* were called to me through the silence in which my soul luxuriated and cast an Eastern enchantment over me. I asked for leave to go to the bazaar on Saturday night. My aunt was surprised and hoped it was not some Freemason affair.[5] I answered few questions in class. I watched my master's face pass from amiability to sternness; he hoped I was not beginning to idle. I could not call my wandering thoughts together. I had hardly any patience with the serious work of life which, now that it stood between me and my desire, seemed to me child's play, ugly monotonous child's play.

13   On Saturday morning I reminded my uncle that I wished to go to the bazaar in the evening. He was fussing at the hallstand, looking for the hatbrush, and answered me curtly:

14   "Yes, boy, I know."

15   As he was in the hall I could not go into the front parlour and lie at the window. I left the house in bad humour and walked slowly towards the school. The air was pitilessly raw and already my heart misgave me.

16   When I came home to dinner my uncle had not yet been home. Still it was early. I sat staring at the clock for some time and, when its ticking began to irritate me, I left the room. I mounted the staircase and gained the upper part of the house. The high cold empty gloomy rooms liberated me and I went from room to room singing. From the front window I saw my companions playing below in the street. Their cries reached me weakened and indistinct and, leaning my forehead against the cool glass, I looked over at the dark house where she lived. I may have stood there for an hour, seeing nothing but the brown-clad figure cast by my imagination, touched discreetly by the lamplight at the curved neck, at the hand upon the railings and at the border below the dress.

17   When I came downstairs again I found Mrs. Mercer sitting at the fire. She was an old garrulous woman, a pawnbroker's widow, who collected used stamps for some pious purpose. I had to endure the gossip of the tea-table. The meal was prolonged beyond an hour and

[4] Traveling bazaars featured cafés, shopping stalls, and entertainment. Araby was the name of an English bazaar that visited Dublin when Joyce was a boy. [Editor's note]

[5] The Freemasons is a secretive fraternal order that has a long history and that has traditionally been opposed by the Catholic Church. [Editor's note]

still my uncle did not come. Mrs. Mercer stood up to go: she was sorry she couldn't wait any longer, but it was after eight o'clock and she did not like to be out late, as the night air was bad for her. When she had gone I began to walk up and down the room, clenching my fists. My aunt said:

18   "I'm afraid you may put off your bazaar for this night of Our Lord."

19   At nine o'clock I heard my uncle's latchkey in the halldoor. I heard him talking to himself and heard the hallstand rocking when it had received the weight of his overcoat. I could interpret these signs. When he was midway through his dinner I asked him to give me the money to go to the bazaar. He had forgotten.

20   "The people are in bed and after their first sleep now," he said.

21   I did not smile. My aunt said to him energetically:

22   "Can't you give him the money and let him go? You've kept him late enough as it is."

23   My uncle said he was very sorry he had forgotten. He said he believed in the old saying: "All work and no play makes Jack a dull boy." He asked me where I was going and, when I had told him a second time he asked me did I know *The Arab's Farewell to His Steed*. When I left the kitchen he was about to recite the opening lines of the piece to my aunt.

24   I held a florin tightly in my hand as I strode down Buckingham Street towards the station. The sight of the streets thronged with buyers and glaring with gas recalled to me the purpose of my journey. I took my seat in a third-class carriage of a deserted train. After an intolerable delay the train moved out of the station slowly. It crept onward among ruinous houses and over the twinkling river. At Westland Row Station a crowd of people pressed to the carriage doors; but the porters moved them back, saying that it was a special train for the bazaar. I remained alone in the bare carriage. In a few minutes the train drew up beside an improvised wooden platform. I passed out on to the road and saw by the lighted dial of a clock that it was ten minutes to ten. In front of me was a large building which displayed the magical name.

25   I could not find any sixpenny entrance and, fearing that the bazaar would be closed, I passed in quickly through a turnstile, handing a shilling to a weary-looking man. I found myself in a big hall girdled at half its height by a gallery. Nearly all the stalls were closed and the greater part of the hall was in darkness. I recognised a silence like that which pervades a church after a service. I walked into the centre of the bazaar timidly. A few people were gathered about the stalls which were still open. Before a curtain, over which the words *Café Chantant* [6] were written in coloured lamps, two men were counting money on a salver. I listened to the fall of the coins.

26   Remembering with difficulty why I had come I went over to one of the stalls and examined porcelain vases and flowered tea-sets. At the door of the stall a young lady was talking and laughing with two young gentlemen. I remarked their English accents and listened vaguely to their conversation.

27   "O, I never said such a thing!"

28   "O, but you did!"

29   "O, but I didn't!"

30   "Didn't she say that?"

31   "Yes. I heard her."

32   "O, there's a . . . fib!"

33   Observing me the young lady came over and asked me did I wish to buy anything. The tone of her voice was not encouraging; she seemed to have spoken to me out of a sense of duty. I looked humbly at the great jars that stood like eastern guards at either side of the dark entrance to the stall and murmured:

34   "No, thank you."

35   The young lady changed the position of one of the vases and went back to the two young men. They began to talk of the same subject. Once or twice the young lady glanced at me over her shoulder.

36   I lingered before her stall, though I knew my stay was useless, to make my interest in her wares seem the more real. Then I turned away slowly and walked down the middle of the bazaar. I allowed the two pennies to fall against the sixpence in my pocket. I heard a voice call from one end of the gallery that the light was out. The upper part of the hall was now completely dark.

37   Gazing up into the darkness I saw myself as a creature driven and derided by vanity; and my eyes burned with anguish and anger.

---

[6] Literally, *singing café* (French), a music hall. [Editor's note]

Use the following questions to begin analyzing "Araby":

1 "Araby" can be read as a coming-of-age story about an adolescent boy's first crush. If you read it on this level, what changes would you say the boy goes through? What, if anything, does he learn? To get started, take a look at paragraph 4.

2 The boy describes himself as carrying the "image" of Mangan's sister like a "chalice," "even in places the most hostile to romance," such as the crowded, raucous streets of early twentieth century–Dublin, Ireland (par. 5). How does the boy's experience on Saturday evening shopping trips with his aunt compare to his experience at Araby (par. 25)? What makes the experiences so different?

3 This story is saturated with the culture of Dublin, Ireland, particularly its Catholicism and its attitudes about gender and sexuality. How are these or other important cultural influences expressed in the story? To get started, take a look at paragraph 2.

William Carlos Williams | *The Use of Force*

WILLIAM CARLOS WILLIAMS (1883–1963) is one of the most important poets of the twentieth century, best known for his long poem *Paterson* (1946–1958). He also wrote essays, plays, novels, and short stories. "The Use of Force" was initially published in *The Doctor Stories* (1933), a collection loosely based on Williams's experiences as a pediatrician.

1 They were new patients to me, all I had was the name, Olson. Please come down as soon as you can, my daughter is very sick.

2 When I arrived I was met by the mother, a big startled-looking woman, very clean and apologetic, who merely said, Is this the doctor? and let me in. In the back, she added. You must excuse us, doctor, we have her in the kitchen where it is warm. It is very damp here sometimes.

3 The child was fully dressed and sitting on her father's lap near the kitchen table. He tried to get up, but I motioned for him not to bother, took off my overcoat and started to look things over. I could see that they were all very nervous, eyeing me up and down distrust-fully. As often, in such cases, they weren't telling me more than they had to, it was up to me to tell them; that's why they were spending three dollars on me.

4 The child was fairly eating me up with her cold, steady eyes, and no expression to her face whatever. She did not move and seemed, inwardly, quiet; an unusually attractive little thing, and as strong as a heifer in appearance. But her face was flushed, she was breathing rapidly, and I realized that she had a high fever. She had magnificent blonde hair, in profusion. One of those picture children often reproduced in advertising leaflets and the photogravure sections of the Sunday papers.

5 She's had a fever for three days, began the father, and we don't know what it comes from. My wife has given her things, you know, like people do, but it don't do no good. And there's been a lot of sickness around. So we tho't you better look her over and tell us what is the matter.

6 As doctors often do I took a trial shot at it as a point of departure. Has she had a sore throat?

7 Both parents answered me together, No . . . No, she says her throat don't hurt her.

8 Does your throat hurt you? added the mother to the child. But the little girl's expression didn't change nor did she move her eyes from my face.

9 Have you looked?

10 I tried, said the mother, but I couldn't see.

11 As it happens we had been having a number of cases of diphtheria in the school to which this child went during that month and we were all, quite apparently, thinking of that, though no one had as yet spoken of the thing.

12 Well, I said, suppose we take a look at the throat first. I smiled in my best professional manner and asking for the child's first name I said, come on, Mathilda, open your mouth and let's take a look at your throat.

13 Nothing doing.

14 Aw, come on, I coaxed, just open your mouth wide and let me take a look. Look, I said opening both hands wide, I haven't anything in my hands. Just open up and let me see.

15 Such a nice man, put in the mother. Look how kind he is to you. Come on, do what he tells you to. He won't hurt you.

16 At that I ground my teeth in disgust. If only they wouldn't use the word "hurt" I might be able to get somewhere. But I did not allow myself to be hurried or disturbed but speaking quietly and slowly I approached the child again.

17 As I moved my chair a little nearer suddenly with one catlike movement both her hands clawed instinctively for my eyes and she almost reached them too. In fact she knocked my glasses flying and they fell, though unbroken, several feet away from me on the kitchen floor.

18 Both the mother and father almost turned themselves inside out in embarrassment and apology. You bad girl, said the mother, taking her and

shaking her by one arm. Look what you've done. The nice man . . .

19 For heaven's sake, I broke in. Don't call me a nice man to her. I'm here to look at her throat on the chance that she might have diphtheria and possibly die of it. But that's nothing to her. Look here, I said to the child, we're going to look at your throat. You're old enough to understand what I'm saying. Will you open it now by yourself or shall we have to open it for you?

20 Not a move. Even her expression hadn't changed. Her breaths however were coming faster and faster. Then the battle began. I had to do it. I had to have a throat culture for her own protection. But first I told the parents that it was entirely up to them. I explained the danger but said that I would not insist on a throat examination so long as they would take the responsibility.

21 If you don't do what the doctor says you'll have to go to the hospital, the mother admonished her severely.

22 Oh yeah? I had to smile to myself. After all, I had already fallen in love with the savage brat, the parents were contemptible to me. In the ensuing struggle they grew more and more abject, crushed, exhausted while she surely rose to magnificent heights of insane fury of effort bred of her terror of me.

23 The father tried his best, and he was a big man, but the fact that she was his daughter, his shame at her behavior and his dread of hurting her made him release her just at the critical times when I had almost achieved success, till I wanted to kill him. But his dread also that she might have diphtheria made him tell me to go on, go on though he himself was almost fainting, while the mother moved back and forth behind us raising and lowering her hands in an agony of apprehension.

24 Put her in front of you on your lap, I ordered, and hold both her wrists.

25 But as soon as he did the child let out a scream. Don't, you're hurting me. Let go of my hands. Let them go I tell you. Then she shrieked terrifyingly, hysterically. Stop it! Stop it! You're killing me!

26 Do you think she can stand it, doctor! said the mother.

27 You get out, said the husband to his wife. Do you want her to die of diphtheria?

28 Come on now, hold her, I said.

29 Then I grasped the child's head with my left hand and tried to get the wooden tongue depressor between

her teeth. She fought, with clenched teeth, desperately! But now I also had grown furious—at a child. I tried to hold myself down but I couldn't. I know how to expose a throat for inspection. And I did my best. When finally I got the wooden spatula behind the last teeth and just the point of it into the mouth cavity, she opened up for an instant but before I could see anything she came down again and gripping the wooden blade between her molars she reduced it to splinters before I could get it out again.

30   Aren't you ashamed, the mother yelled at her. Aren't you ashamed to act like that in front of the doctor?

31   Get me a smooth-handled spoon of some sort, I told the mother. We're going through with this. The child's mouth was already bleeding. Her tongue was cut and she was screaming in wild hysterical shrieks. Perhaps I should have desisted and come back in an hour or more. No doubt it would have been better. But I have seen at least two children lying dead in bed of neglect in such cases, and feeling that I must get a diagnosis now or never I went at it again. But the worst of it was that I too had got beyond reason. I could have torn the child apart in my own fury and enjoyed it. It was a pleasure to attack her. My face was burning with it.

32   The damned little brat must be protected against her own idiocy, one says to oneself at such times. Others must be protected against her. It is a social necessity. And all these things are true. But a blind fury, a feeling of adult shame, bred of a longing for muscular release are the operatives. One goes on to the end.

33   In a final unreasoning assault I overpowered the child's neck and jaws. I forced the heavy silver spoon back of her teeth and down her throat till she gagged. And there it was—both tonsils covered with membrane. She had fought valiantly to keep me from knowing her secret. She had been hiding that sore throat for three days at least and lying to her parents in order to escape just such an outcome as this.

34   Now truly she was furious. She had been on the defensive before but now she attacked. Tried to get off her father's lap and fly at me while tears of defeat blinded her eyes.

ANALYZE & WRITE

Use the following questions to begin analyzing "The Use of Force":

1   This story is told from the doctor's point of view. How does he justify his use of force? What are the pros and cons he weighs in using it? To get started, look in particular at paragraph 34.

2   How do the sexual overtones of the story — for example, in the doctor's describing the girl as "an unusually attractive little thing" (par. 4) and admitting "I had already fallen in love with the savage brat" (par. 22) — affect your understanding and judgment of the doctor's and the girl's behavior?

3   Because this story came out of the era of the Great Depression, you might expect it to say something about the impoverished material conditions in which people lived at the time and how these hardships affected them. Are these expectations borne out? What seems to be the economic status of the family and the doctor, and how does class affect what happens in the story? To get started, take a look at paragraphs 2 and 3.

Jamaica Kincaid | *Girl*

JAMAICA KINCAID was born Elaine Potter Richardson in 1949 in St. Johns, Antigua, in the West Indies. As Kincaid's mother had more children, the once-close relationship between mother and daughter became strained, and Kincaid began to feel increasingly restricted by life in Antigua under British rule. At seventeen, she left Antigua to work as an au pair in New York, where she attended night classes and began working as a freelance writer. At the start of her writing career, she changed her name to Jamaica Kincaid to shed the "weights" (as she put it) of her past life. Kincaid's stories have appeared in such prestigious venues as *Rolling Stone,* the *Paris Review,* and the *New Yorker,* where she became a staff writer in 1978. "Girl" was published first in the *New Yorker* and later in Kincaid's first book, *At the Bottom of the River* (1984), an anthology of short stories that won the Morton Dauwen Zabel Award. Her next book, *Annie John* (1985), also a collection of stories, centered on a girl growing up in the West Indies. In addition to two novels—*Lucy* (1990) and *The Autobiography of My Mother* (1996)—Kincaid has published two books of nonfiction: *My Brother* (1997), the story of her brother Devon Drew's short life, and *A Small Place* (2000), an examination of her native Antigua. Kincaid now makes her home in Vermont, where her husband is a composer and professor of music at Bennington College.

As you read "Girl," listen to the rhythms of the language, and consider how the almost poetic litany of instructions reflects and shapes the relationship between mother and daughter.

Wash the white clothes on Monday and put them on the stone heap; wash the color clothes on Tuesday and put them on the clothesline to dry; don't walk barehead in the hot sun; cook pumpkin fritters in very hot sweet oil; soak your little cloths right after you take them off; when buying cotton to make yourself a nice blouse, be sure that it doesn't have gum on it, because that way it won't hold up well after a wash; soak salt fish overnight before you cook it; is it true that you sing benna[1] in Sunday school?; always eat your food in such a way that it won't turn someone else's stomach; on Sundays try to walk like a lady and not like the slut you are so bent on becoming; don't sing benna in Sunday school; you mustn't speak to wharf-rat boys, not even to give directions; don't eat fruits on the street—flies will follow you; *but I don't sing benna on Sundays at all and never in Sunday school;* this is how to sew on a button; this is how to make a button-hole for the button you have just sewed on; this is how to hem a dress when you see the hem coming down and so to prevent yourself from looking like the slut I know you are so bent on becoming; this is how you iron your father's khaki shirt so that it doesn't have a crease; this is how you iron your father's khaki pants so that they don't have a crease; this is how you grow okra—far from the house, because okra tree harbors red ants; when you are growing dasheen,[2] make sure it gets plenty of water or else it makes your throat itch when you are eating it; this is how you sweep a corner; this is how you sweep a whole house; this is how you sweep a yard; this is how you smile to someone you don't like too much; this is how you smile to someone you don't like at all; this is how you smile to someone you like completely; this is how you set a table for tea; this is

---

[1] Calypso, popular Afro-Caribbean music from the West Indies. [Editor's note]
[2] Taro, a starchy root vegetable with edible leaves that is a staple crop of the Caribbean. [Editor's note]

how you set a table for dinner; this is how you set a table for dinner with an important guest; this is how you set a table for lunch; this is how you set a table for breakfast; this is how to behave in the presence of men who don't know you very well, and this way they won't recognize immediately the slut I have warned you against becoming; be sure to wash every day, even if it is with your own spit; don't squat down to play marbles—you are not a boy, you know; don't pick people's flowers—you might catch something; don't throw stones at blackbirds, because it might not be a blackbird at all; this is how to make a bread pudding; this is how to make doukona;[3] this is how to make pepper pot;[4] this is how to make a good medicine for a cold; this is how to make a good medicine to throw away a child before it even becomes a child; this is how to catch a fish; this is how to throw back a fish you don't like, and that way something bad won't fall on you; this is how to bully a man; this is how a man bullies you; this is how to love a man; and if this doesn't work there are other ways, and if they don't work don't feel too bad about giving up; this is how to spit up in the air if you feel like it, and this is how to move quick so that it doesn't fall on you; this is how to make ends meet; always squeeze bread to make sure it's fresh; *but what if the baker won't let me feel the bread?;* you mean to say that after all you are really going to be the kind of woman who the baker won't let near the bread?

ANALYZE & WRITE

Use the following questions to begin analyzing "Girl":

1. This story is told almost exclusively from the mother's point of view; with the exception of two italicized interjections from the daughter ("but I don't sing benna on Sundays at all and never in Sunday school"; "but what if the baker won't let me feel the bread?"), the words are entirely the mother's. How does the language the mother uses, and the instructions she gives, shape your understanding of the mother's character? How would you describe her relationship with her daughter based on her litany of advice?

2. If irony is the discrepancy between the truth and what is said or the gap between what is expected and what actually happens, is "Girl" ironic? Why or why not?

3. Kincaid grew up in St. John's, Antigua, in the 1950s and 1960s, and while the setting is not specified, "Girl" seems to have been set in a similar place and time. What can you infer about the society in which "Girl" is set from the advice the mother gives and the language she uses? How might the story's first readers (subscribers to the *New Yorker* magazine in 1978) have reacted and why? How might your reaction differ from that of the story's initial audience?

For more reading selections, including a multimedia reading, go to **bedfordstmartins .com/theguide/epages**.

---

[3] Spicy pudding made from plantains. [Editor's note]
[4] A West Indian stew that is typically made for special occasions. [Editor's note]

PART 2

Critical Thinking Strategies

11

A Catalog of Invention Strategies

Writers are like scientists: They ask questions, systematically inquiring about how things work, what they are, where they occur, and how more information can be learned about them. Writers are also like artists in that they use what they know and learn to create something new and imaginative.

The invention and inquiry strategies—also known as **heuristics**—described in this chapter are not mysterious or magical. They are available to all writers, and one or more of them may appeal to your common sense and experience. These techniques represent ways creative writers, engineers, scientists, composers—in fact, all of us—solve problems. Once you have mastered these strategies, you can use them to tackle many of the writing situations you will encounter in college, on the job, and in the community.

The strategies for invention and inquiry in this chapter are grouped into two categories:

Mapping: A brief visual representation of your thinking or planning

Writing: The composition of phrases or sentences to discover information and ideas and to make connections among them

These invention and inquiry strategies will help you explore and research a topic fully before you begin drafting, and then help you creatively solve problems as you draft and revise. In this chapter, strategies are arranged alphabetically within each of the two categories.

Mapping

Mapping strategies involve making a visual record of invention and inquiry. In making maps, writers usually use key words and phrases to record material they want to remember, questions they need to answer, and new sources of information they want to check. The maps show the ideas, details, and facts as well as possible ways to connect and focus them. Mapping can be especially useful for working in collaborative writing situations, for preparing oral presentations, and for creating visual aids for written or oral reports. Mapping strategies include *clustering, listing,* and *outlining.*

Create a cluster diagram.

Clustering is a strategy for revealing possible relationships among facts and ideas. Unlike listing (the next mapping strategy), clustering requires a brief period of initial preparation, when you divide your topic into parts or main ideas. Clustering works as follows:

1. In a word or phrase, write your topic in the center of a piece of paper. Circle it.

2. Also in words or phrases, write down the main parts or ideas of your topic. Circle these, and connect them with lines to the topic in the center.

3. Next, write down facts, details, and examples related to these main parts or ideas. Connect them with lines to the relevant main parts or ideas.

Clustering can be useful in the early stages of planning an essay to find subtopics and organize information. You may try out and discard several clusters before finding one that is promising. Many writers also use clustering to plan brief sections of an essay as they are drafting or revising. (A model of clustering is shown in Figure 11.1.)

Software-based diagramming tools

Software vendors have created a variety of electronic tools to help people better visualize complex projects. These flowcharts, webs, and outlines can make it easier for you to see how to proceed at any stage of your project.

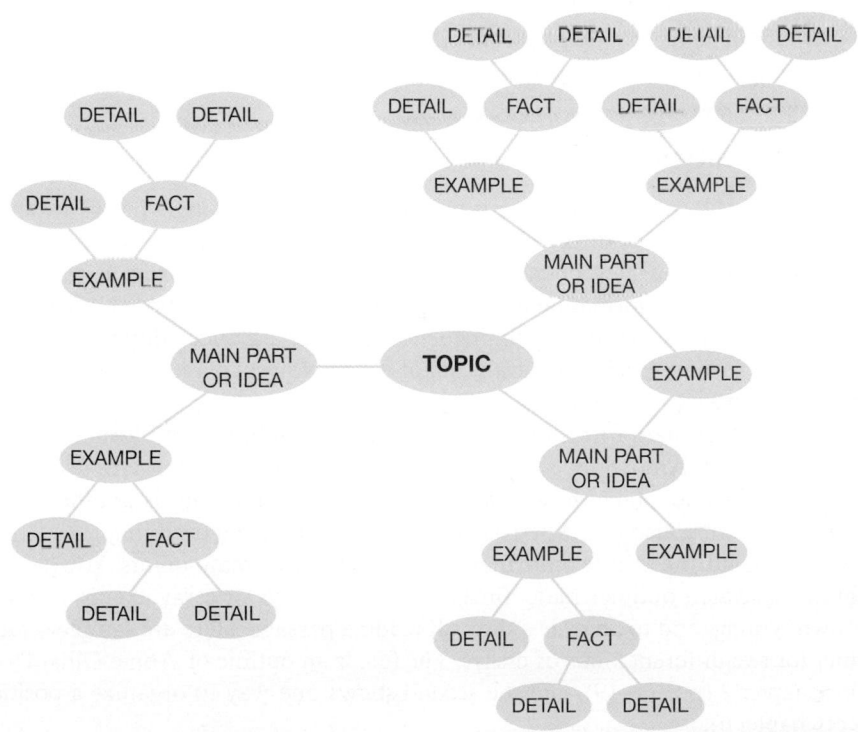

FIGURE 11.1   A Model of Clustering

Make a list.

Listing is a familiar activity. You make shopping lists and lists of errands to do or people to call, but listing can also be a great help in planning an essay. It enables you to recall what you already know about a topic and suggests what else you may need to find out.

A basic activity for all writers, listing is especially useful to those who have little time for planning—for example, reporters facing deadlines and college students taking essay exams. Listing lets you order your ideas quickly. It can also serve as a first step in discovering possible writing topics. Here is how listing works best for invention work:

1. Give your list a title that indicates your main idea or topic.

2. Write as fast as you can, relying on short phrases.

3. Include anything that seems at all useful. Try not to be judgmental at this point.

4. After you have finished or even as you write, reflect on the list, and organize it in the following way:

   - Put an asterisk next to the most promising items.

   - Number key items in order of importance.

   - Put items in related groups.

   - Cross out items that do not seem promising.

   - Add new items.

Create an outline.

Like listing and clustering, **outlining** is both a means of inventing what you want to say in an essay and a way of organizing your ideas and information. As you outline, you nearly always see new possibilities in your subject, discovering new ways of dividing or grouping information and seeing where you need additional information to develop your ideas. Because outlining lets you see at a glance where your essay's strengths and weaknesses lie, outlining can also help you read and revise your essay with a critical eye.

There are two main forms of outlining: informal outlining and formal topic or sentence outlining. Among the several types of informal outlining, *scratch outlines* are perhaps the most adaptable to a variety of situations. Chunking is another useful method. (Clustering also may be considered a type of informal outlining.)

A **scratch outline** is little more than a list of the essay's main points. You have no doubt made scratch outlines many times — to plan essays or essay exams, to revise your own writing, and to analyze a difficult reading passage. Here are sample scratch outlines for two different kinds of essays. The first is an outline of Annie Dillard's essay in Chapter 2 (pp. 17–19), and the second shows one way to organize a position paper (Chapter 6):

Scratch Outline: Essay about a Remembered Event

1. explains what she learned from playing football
2. identifies other sports she learned from boys in the neighborhood
3. sets the scene by describing the time and place of the event
4. describes the boys who were playing with her
5. describes what typically happened: a car would come down the street, they would throw snowballs, and then they would wait for another car
6. describes the iceball-making project she had begun while waiting
7. describes the Buick's approach and how they followed the routine
8. describes the impact of the snowball on the Buick's windshield
9. describes the man's surprising reaction: getting out of the car and running after them
10. narrates the chase and describes the man
11. explains how the kids split up and the man followed her and Mikey
12. narrates the chase and describes how the neighborhood looked as they ran through it
13. continues the narration, describing the way the man threw himself into the chase
14. continues the narration, commenting on her thoughts and feelings
15. narrates the ending or climax of the chase, when the man caught them
16. describes the runners trying to catch their breath
17. describes her own physical state
18. relates the man's words
19. explains her reactions to his words and actions
20. explains her later thoughts and feelings
21. explains her present perspective on this remembered event

Scratch Outline: Essay Arguing a Position

Presentation of the issue

Concession of some aspect of an opposing position

Thesis statement

First reason with support

Second reason with support

(etc.)

Conclusion

Remember that the items in a scratch outline do not necessarily coincide with paragraphs. Sometimes two or more items may be developed in the same paragraph or one item may be covered in two or more paragraphs.

Chunking, a type of scratch outline commonly used by professional writers in business and industry and especially well suited to writing in the electronic age, consists of a set of headings describing the major points to be covered in the final document. What makes chunking distinctive is that the blocks of text— or "chunks"—under each heading are intended to be roughly the same length and scope. These headings can be discussed and passed around among several writers and editors before writing begins, and different chunks may be written by different authors, simply by typing notes into the space under each heading. The list of headings is subject to change during the writing, and new headings may be added or old ones subdivided or discarded as part of the drafting and editing process.

The advantage of chunking in your own writing is that it breaks the large task of drafting into smaller tasks in a simple, evenly balanced way; once the headings are determined, the writing becomes just a matter of filling in the specifics that go in each chunk. Organization tends to improve as you get a sense of the weight of different parts of the document while filling in the blanks. Places where the essay needs more information or there is a problem with pacing tend to stand out because of the chunking structure, and the headings can be either taken out of the finished essay or left in as devices to help guide readers. If they are left in, they should be edited into parallel grammatical form like the items in a formal topic or sentence outline, as discussed below.

Topic outlines and **sentence outlines** are considered more formal than scratch outlines because they follow a conventional format of numbered and lettered headings and subheadings:

I. (Main topic)
   A. (Subtopic of I)
   B.
      1. (Subtopic of I.B)
      2.
         a. (Subtopic of I.B.2)
         b.
            (1) (Subtopic of I.B.2.b)
            (2)
   C.
      1. (Subtopic of I.C)
      2.

The difference between a topic and sentence outline is obvious: Topic outlines simply name the topics and subtopics, whereas sentence outlines use complete or abbreviated sentences. To illustrate, here are two partial formal outlines of an essay arguing a position, Jessica Statsky's "Children Need to Play, Not Compete," from Chapter 6 (pp. 250–55).

Formal Topic Outline

I. Organized sports harmful to children
   A. Harmful physically
      1. Curve ball (Koppett)
      2. Tackle football (Tutko)
   B. Harmful psychologically
      1. Fear of being hurt
         a. Little League Online
         b. Mother
         c. Reporter
      2. Competition
         a. Rablovsky
         b. Studies

Formal Sentence Outline

I. Highly organized competitive sports such as Peewee Football and Little League Baseball can be physically and psychologically harmful to children, as well as counterproductive for developing future players.
   A. Physically harmful because sports entice children into physical actions that are bad for growing bodies.
      1. Koppett claims throwing a curve ball may put abnormal strain on developing arm and shoulder muscles.
      2. Tutko argues that tackle football is too traumatic for young kids.
   B. Psychologically harmful to children for a number of reasons.
      1. Fear of being hurt detracts from their enjoyment of the sport.
         a. Little League Online ranks fear of injury seventh among the seven top reasons children quit.
         b. One mother says, "kids get so scared. . . . They'll sit on the bench and pretend their leg hurts."
         c. A reporter tells about a child who made himself vomit to get out of playing Peewee Football.
      2. Too much competition poses psychological dangers for children.
         a. Rablovsky reports: "The spirit of play suddenly disappears, and sport becomes joblike."
         b. Studies show that children prefer playing on a losing team to "warming the bench on a winning team."

In contrast to an informal outline in which anything goes, a formal outline must follow many conventions. The roman numerals and capital letters are followed by periods. In both topic and sentence outlines, the first word of each item is capitalized, but items in topic outlines do not end with a period as items in sentence outlines do. Every level of a formal outline except the top level (identified by the roman numeral *I*) must include at least two items. Items at the same level of indentation in a topic outline should be grammatically parallel—all beginning with the same part of speech. For example, *I.A* and *I.B* are parallel when they both begin with an adverb (*Physically harmful* and *Psychologically harmful*) or with an adjective (*Harmful physically* and *Harmful psychologically*); they would not be parallel if one began with an adverb (*Physically harmful*) and the other with an adjective (*Harmful psychologically*).

Writing

Unlike most mapping strategies, **writing strategies** invite you to produce complete sentences. Sentences provide considerable generative power. Because they are complete statements, they take you further than listing or clustering. They enable you to explore ideas and define relationships, bring ideas together or show how they differ, and identify causes and effects. Sentences can also help you develop a logical chain of thought.

Some of these invention and inquiry strategies are systematic, while others are more flexible. Even though they call for complete sentences that are related to one another, they do not require preparation or revision. You can use them to develop oral as well as written presentations.

These writing strategies include *cubing, dialoguing, dramatizing, freewriting, keeping a journal, looping,* and *questioning.*

Use cubing.

Cubing is useful for quickly exploring a writing topic, probing it from six different perspectives. It is known as *cubing* because a cube has six sides. These are the six perspectives in cubing:

Describing: What does your subject look like? What size is it? What is its color? Its shape? Its texture? Name its parts.

Comparing: What is your subject similar to? Different from?

Associating: What does your subject make you think of? What connections does it have to anything else in your experience?

Analyzing: What are the origins of your subject? What are the functions or significance of its parts? How are its parts related?

Applying: What can you do with your subject? What uses does it have?

Arguing: What arguments can you make for your subject? Against it?

Here are some guidelines to help you use cubing productively.

1. Select a topic, subject, or part of a subject. This can be a person, a scene, an event, an object, a problem, an idea, or an issue. Hold it in focus.

2. Limit your writing to three to five minutes for each perspective. The whole activity should take no more than half an hour.

3. Keep going until you have written about your subject from all six perspectives. Remember that cubing offers the special advantage of enabling you to generate multiple perspectives quickly.

4. As you write from each perspective, begin with what you know about your subject. However, do not limit yourself to your present knowledge. Indicate what else you would like to know about your subject, and suggest where you might find that information.

5. Reread what you have written. Look for bright spots, surprises. Recall the part that was easiest for you to write. Recall the part where you felt a special momentum and pleasure in writing. Look for an angle or an unexpected insight. These special parts may suggest a focus or topic within a larger subject, or they may provide specific details to include in a draft.

Construct a dialogue.

A *dialogue* is a conversation between two or more people. You can use **dialoguing** to search for topics, find a focus, explore ideas, or consider opposing viewpoints. When you write a dialogue as an invention strategy, you need to make up all parts of the conversation (unless, of course, you are writing collaboratively). To construct a dialogue independently or collaboratively, follow these steps:

1. Write a conversation between two speakers. Label the participants *Speaker A* and *Speaker B,* or make up names for them.

2. If you get stuck, you might have one of the speakers ask the other a question.

3. Write brief responses to keep the conversation moving fast. Do not spend much time planning or rehearsing responses. Write what first occurs to you, just as in a real conversation, in which people take quick turns to prevent any awkward silences.

Dialogues can be especially useful in writing based on personal experience and persuasive essays because they help you remember conversations and anticipate objections.

Use the five elements of dramatizing.

Dramatizing is an invention activity developed by the philosopher Kenneth Burke as a way of thinking about how people interact and as a way of analyzing stories and films.

Thinking about human behavior in dramatic terms can be very productive for writers. Drama has action, actors, setting, motives, and methods. Since stars and acting go together, you can use a five-pointed star to remember these five points of dramatizing: Each point on the star provides a different perspective on human behavior (see Figure 11.2).

Action An action is anything that happens, has happened, will happen, or could happen. Action includes events that are physical

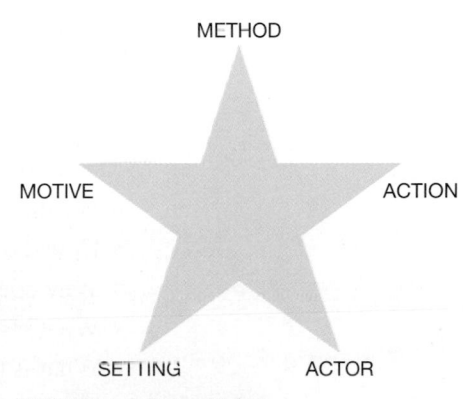

FIGURE 11.2 Dramatizing

(running a marathon), mental (thinking about a book you have read), and emotional (falling in love).

Actor   The actor is involved in the action—either responsible for it or simply affected by it. (The actor does not have to be a person. It can be a force, something that causes an action. For example, if the action is a rise in the price of gasoline, the actor could be increased demand or short supply.) Dramatizing may also include a number of coactors working together or at odds.

Setting   The setting is the situation or background of the action. We usually think of setting as the place and time of an event, but it may also be the historical background of an event or the childhood of a person.

Motive   The motive is the purpose or reason for an action—the actor's intention. Actions may have multiple, even conflicting, motives.

Method   The method explains how an action occurs, including the techniques an actor uses. It refers to whatever makes things happen.

Each of these points suggests a simple invention question:

Action: What?

Actor: Who?

Setting: When and where?

Motive: Why?

Method: How?

This list looks like the questions reporters typically ask. But dramatizing goes further: It enables us to consider relations between and among these five elements. We can think about actors' motives, the effect of the setting on the actors, the relations between actors, and so on.

You can use this invention strategy to learn more about yourself or about other significant people in your life. You can use it as well to explore, interpret, or evaluate characters in stories or movies. Moreover, dramatizing is especially useful in understanding the readers you want to inform or convince.

To use dramatizing, imagine the person you want to understand better in a particular situation. Holding this image in mind, write answers to any questions in the following list that apply. You may draw a blank on some questions, have little to say to some, and find a lot to say to others. Be exploratory and playful with the questions. Write responses quickly, relying on words and phrases, even drawings.

- What is the actor doing?
- How did the actor come to be involved in this situation?
- Why does the actor do what he or she does?
- What else might the actor do?
- What is the actor trying to accomplish?
- How do other actors influence — help or hinder — the main actor?

- What do the actor's actions reveal about him or her?
- What does the actor's language reveal about him or her?
- How does the event's setting influence the actor's actions?
- How does the time of the event influence what the actor does?
- Where does the actor come from?
- How is the actor different now from what he or she used to be?
- What might the actor become?
- How is the actor like or unlike the other actors?

Freewrite for a set amount of time.

Freewriting is a technique that requires you to stop judging what you write and simply let your mind wander in order to generate ideas freely and creatively. Freewriting can be useful for generating ideas on a topic you already know. To freewrite, set a certain amount of time, say five or ten minutes, and then simply write, generating as much text as you can in the allotted time. While freewriting, try not to stop; if you cannot think of anything to say, simply write "don't know what to say" over and over until an idea comes to you. If you find it difficult to avoid editing yourself, try turning down the brightness on your monitor until you can no longer see what it says. A variation on freewriting is **focused freewriting**. In focused freewriting, you begin from a specific topic, returning to the beginning topic whenever you find yourself getting off track.

Keep a journal.

Professional writers often use **journals** to keep notes. Starting one is easy. Buy a special notebook, or open a new file on your computer, and start writing. Here are some possibilities:

- Keep a list of new words and concepts you learn in your courses. You could also write about the progress and direction of your learning in particular courses — the experience of being in the course, your feelings about what is happening, and what you are learning.
- Respond to your reading, both assigned and personal. As you read, write about your personal associations, reflections, reactions, and evaluations. Summarize or copy memorable or especially important passages, and comment on them. (Copying and commenting have been practiced by students and writers for centuries in special journals called *commonplace books*.)
- Write to prepare for particular class meetings. Write about the main ideas you have learned from assigned readings and about the relationship of these new ideas to other ideas in the course. After class, write to summarize what you have learned. List questions you have about the ideas or information discussed in class. Journal writing of this kind involves reflecting, evaluating, interpreting, synthesizing, summarizing, and questioning.

- Record observations and overheard conversations.
- Write for ten or fifteen minutes every day about whatever is on your mind. Focus these meditations on your new experiences as you try to understand, interpret, and reflect on them.
- Write sketches of people who catch your attention.
- Organize your time. Write about your goals and priorities, or list specific things to accomplish and what you plan to do.
- Keep a log over several days or weeks about a particular event unfolding in the news—a sensational trial, an environmental disaster, a political campaign, a campus controversy, or the fortunes of a sports team.

You can use a journal in many ways. All of the writing in your journal has value for learning. You may also be able to use parts of your journal for writing in your other courses.

Use looping.

Looping is especially useful for the first stages of exploring a topic. As its name suggests, **looping** involves writing quickly to explore some aspect of a topic and then looping back to your original starting point or to a new starting point to explore another aspect. Beginning with almost any starting point, looping enables you to find a center of interest and eventually a thesis for your essay. The steps are simple:

1. Write down your area of interest. You may know only that you have to write about another person or a movie or a cultural trend that has caught your attention. Or you may want to search for a topic in a broad historical period or for one related to a major political event. Although you may wander from this topic as you write, you will want to keep coming back to it. Your purpose is to find a focus for writing.

2. Write nonstop for ten minutes. Start with the first thing that comes to mind. Write rapidly, without looking back to reread or to correct anything. *Do not stop writing. Keep your pencil moving or keystrokes clacking.* Continuous writing is the key to looping. If you get stuck for a moment, rewrite the last sentence. Follow diversions and digressions, but keep returning to your topic.

3. After ten minutes, pause to reread what you have written. Decide what is most important—a single insight, a pattern of ideas, an emerging theme, a visual detail, anything at all that stands out. Some writers call this a "center of gravity" or a "hot spot." To complete the first loop, restate this center in a single sentence.

4. Beginning with this sentence, write nonstop for another ten minutes.

5. Summarize in one sentence again to complete the second loop.

6. Keep looping until one of your summary sentences produces a focus or thesis. You may need only two or three loops; you may need more.

Ask questions.

Asking questions about a subject is a way to learn about it and decide what to write. When you first encounter a subject, however, your questions may be scattered. Also, you are not likely to think right away of all the important questions you ought to ask. The advantage of having a basic list of questions for invention, like the ones for cubing and for dramatizing discussed earlier in this chapter, is that it provides a systematic approach to exploring a subject.

The questions that follow come from classical rhetoric (what the Greek philosopher Aristotle called *topics*) and a modern approach to invention called *tagmemics*. Based on the work of linguist Kenneth Pike, tagmemics provides questions about different ways we make sense of the world, the ways we sort and classify experience in order to understand it.

Here are the steps in using questions for invention:

1. In a sentence or two, identify your subject. A subject could be any event, person, problem, project, idea, or issue—in other words, anything you might write about.

2. Start by writing a response to the first question in the following list, and move right through the list. Try to answer each question at least briefly with a word or a phrase. Some questions may invite several sentences or even a page or more of writing. You may draw a blank on a few questions. Skip them. Later, when you have more experience with questions for invention, you can start anywhere in the list.

3. Write your responses quickly, without much planning. Follow digressions or associations. Do not screen anything out. Be playful.

What Is Your Subject?

- What is your subject's name? What other names does it have? What names did it have in the past?
- What aspects of the subject do these different names emphasize?
- Imagine a still photograph or a moving picture of your subject. What would it look like?
- What would you put into a time capsule to stand for your subject?
- What are its causes and effects?
- How would it look from different vantage points or perspectives?
- What particular experiences have you had with the subject? What have you learned?

What Parts or Features Does Your Subject Have, and How Are They Related?

- Name the parts or features of your subject.
- Describe each one, using the questions in the preceding subject list.
- How is each part or feature related to the others?

How Is Your Subject Similar to and Different from Other Subjects?

- What is your subject similar to? In what ways?
- What is your subject different from? In what ways?
- What seems to you most unlike your subject? In what ways? Now, just for fun, note how they are alike.

How Much Can Your Subject Change and Still Remain the Same?

- How has your subject changed from what it once was?
- How is it changing now—moment to moment, day to day, year to year?
- How does each change alter your way of thinking about your subject?
- What are some different forms your subject takes?
- What does it become when it is no longer itself?

Where Does Your Subject Fit in the World?

- When and where did your subject originate?
- What would happen if at some future time your subject ceased to exist?
- When and where do you usually experience your subject?
- What is your subject a part of, and what are the other parts?
- What do other people think of your subject?

12

A Catalog of Reading Strategies

This chapter presents strategies to help you become a thoughtful reader. A thoughtful reader is above all a patient rereader, concerned not only with comprehending and remembering but also with interpreting and evaluating—on the one hand, striving to understand the text on its own terms; on the other hand, taking care to question its ideas.

The reading strategies in this chapter can help you enrich your thinking as a reader and participate in conversations as a writer. These strategies are as follows:

- *Annotating:* Recording your reactions to, interpretations of, and questions about a text as you read it
- *Taking inventory:* Listing and grouping your annotations and other notes to find meaningful patterns
- *Outlining:* Listing the text's main ideas to reveal how it is organized
- *Paraphrasing:* Restating what you have read to clarify or refer to it
- *Summarizing:* Distilling the main ideas or gist of a text
- *Synthesizing:* Integrating into your own writing ideas and information gleaned from different sources
- *Contextualizing:* Placing a text in its historical and cultural context
- *Exploring the significance of figurative language:* Examining how metaphors, similes, and symbols are used in a text to convey meaning and evoke feelings
- *Looking for patterns of opposition:* Inferring the values and assumptions embodied in the language of a text
- *Reflecting on challenges to your beliefs and values:* Examining the bases of your personal responses to a text
- *Evaluating the logic of an argument:* Determining whether an argument is well reasoned and adequately supported
- *Recognizing emotional manipulation:* Identifying texts that unfairly and inappropriately use emotional appeals based on false or exaggerated claims
- *Judging the writer's credibility:* Considering whether writers represent different points of view fairly and know what they are writing about

Although mastering these strategies will not make critical reading easy, it can make your reading much more satisfying and productive and thus help you handle even difficult material with confidence. In addition, these reading strategies will often be useful in your reading outside of school—for instance, these strategies can help you understand, evaluate, and comment on what political figures, advertisers, and competing businesses are saying.

Annotating

Annotating on-screen

Although this discussion of annotating assumes you are reading printed pages, you can also annotate many kinds of text on-screen by using your software's highlighting and commenting functions or simply by typing annotations into the text using a different color or font. If electronic annotation is not possible, print out the text and annotate by hand.

Annotations are the marks—underlines, highlights, and comments—you make directly on the page as you read. Annotating can be used to record immediate reactions and questions, outline and summarize main points, and evaluate and relate the reading to other ideas and points of view. Your annotations can take many forms, such as the following:

- Writing comments, questions, or definitions in the margins
- Underlining or circling words, phrases, or sentences
- Connecting ideas with lines or arrows
- Numbering related points
- Bracketing sections of the text
- Noting anything that strikes you as interesting, important, or questionable

Most readers annotate in layers, adding further annotations on second and third readings. Annotations can be light or heavy, depending on your purpose and the difficulty of the material. Your purpose for reading also determines how you use your annotations.

The following selection, excerpted from Martin Luther King Jr.'s "Letter from Birmingham Jail," illustrates some of the ways you can annotate as you read. Add your own annotations, if you like.

Martin Luther King Jr. | *An Annotated Sample from "Letter from Birmingham Jail"*

MARTIN LUTHER KING JR. (1929–1968) first came to national notice in 1955, when he led a successful boycott against the policy of restricting African American passengers to rear seats on city buses in Montgomery, Alabama, where he was minister of a Baptist church. He subsequently formed the Southern Christian Leadership Conference, which brought people of all races from all over the country to the South to fight nonviolently for racial integration. In 1963, King led demonstrations in Birmingham, Alabama, that were met with violence;

a bomb was detonated in a black church, killing four young girls. King was arrested for his role in organizing the protests, and while in prison, he wrote his "Letter from Birmingham Jail" to justify his strategy of civil disobedience, which he called "nonviolent direct action."

King begins his letter by discussing his disappointment with the lack of support he has received from white moderates, such as the group of clergy who published criticism of his organization in the local newspaper.

Read the following excerpt, paying attention to the following:

- Try to infer what the clergy's specific criticisms might have been.

- Notice the tone King uses. Would you characterize the writing as apologetic, conciliatory, accusatory, or something else?

¶1. *White moderates block progress.*

I must confess that over the past few years I have been gravely 1 disappointed with the white moderate. I have almost reached the regrettable conclusion that the Negro's [great stumbling block in his stride toward freedom] is not the White Citizen's Counciler or the Ku Klux Klanner, but the white moderate, who is more

Contrasts: order vs. justice, negative vs. positive peace, ends vs. means

devoted to "order" than to justice; who prefers a negative peace which is the absence of tension to a positive peace which is the presence of justice; who constantly says: "I agree with you in the goal you seek, but I cannot agree with your methods of direct ac-

(treating others like children)

tion"; who (paternalistically) believes he can set the timetable for another man's freedom; who lives by a mythical concept of time and who constantly advises the Negro to wait for a "more convenient season." Shallow understanding from people of good will

more contrasts

is more frustrating than absolute misunderstanding from people of ill will. (Lukewarm acceptance is much more bewildering than outright rejection.)

¶2. *What the moderates don't understand*

I had hoped that the white moderate would understand that 2 law and order exist for the purpose of establishing justice and that when they fail in this purpose they become the [dangerously struc-

metaphor: law and order = dams (faulty?)

tured dams that block the flow of social progress.] I had hoped that the white moderate would understand that the present tension in the South is a necessary phase of the transition from an [obnoxious

repeats contrast (negative/positive)

negative peace,] in which the Negro passively accepted his unjust plight, to a [substantive and positive peace,] in which all men will respect the dignity and worth of human personality. Actually, we

Tension already exists: We help dispel it. (True?)

who engage in nonviolent direct action are not the creators of tension. We merely bring to the surface the hidden tension that

simile: hidden tension is "like a boil"

is already alive. We bring it out in the open, where it can be seen and dealt with. [Like a boil that can never be cured so long as it is covered up but must be opened with all its ugliness to the natural medicines of air and light, injustice must be exposed, with all the tension its exposure creates, to the light of human conscience and the air of national opinion before it can be cured.]

¶3. Questions clergymen's logic: condemning his actions = condemning robbery victim, Socrates, Jesus.

In your statement you assert that our actions, even though peaceful, must be condemned because they precipitate violence. But is this a logical assertion? Isn't this like condemning a robbed man because his possession of money precipitated the evil act of robbery? Isn't this like condemning Socrates because his unswerving commitment to truth and his philosophical inquiries precipitated the act by the misguided populace in which they made him drink hemlock? Isn't this like condemning Jesus because his unique God-consciousness and never-ceasing devotion to God's will precipitated the evil act of crucifixion? We must come to see that, as the federal courts have consistently affirmed, it is wrong to urge an individual to cease his efforts to gain his basic constitutional rights because the question may precipitate violence. [Society must protect the robbed and punish the robber.] 3

repetition ("Isn't this like . . .")

(Yes!)

example of a white moderate's view

I had also hoped that the white moderate would reject the myth concerning time in relation to the struggle for freedom. I have just received a letter from a white brother in Texas. He writes: "All Christians know that the colored people will receive equal rights eventually, but it is possible that you are in too great a religious hurry. It has taken Christianity almost two thousand years to accomplish what it has. The teachings of Christ take time to come to earth." Such an attitude stems from a tragic misconception of time, from the strangely irrational notion that there is something in the very flow of time that will inevitably cure all ills. Actually, time itself is neutral; it can be used either destructively or constructively. 4

¶4. Time must be used to do right.

More and more I feel that the people of ill will have used time much more effectively than have the people of good will. We will have to repent in this generation not merely for the [hateful words and actions of the bad people] but for the [appalling silence of the good people.] Human progress never rolls in on [wheels of

Silence/passivity is as bad as hateful words and actions.

stop developing

metaphors (song, natural world)

inevitability;] it comes through the tireless efforts of men willing to be co-workers with God, and without this hard work, time itself becomes an ally of the forces of social (stagnation.) [We must use time creatively, in the knowledge that the time is always ripe to do right.] Now is the time to make real the promise of democracy and transform our pending [national elegy] into a creative [psalm of brotherhood.] Now is the time to lift our national policy from the [quicksand of racial injustice] to the [solid rock of human dignity.]

metaphor (mechanical?)

¶5. *Puts self in middle of two extremes: complacency and bitterness.*

You speak of our activity in Birmingham as extreme. At first 5 I was rather disappointed that fellow clergymen would see my nonviolent efforts as those of an extremist. I began thinking about the fact that I stand in the middle of two opposing forces in the Negro community. One is a [force of complacency,] made up in part of Negroes who, as a result of long years of oppression, are so drained of self-respect and a sense of "somebodiness" that they have adjusted to segregation; and in part of a few middle-class Negroes, who because of a degree of academic and economic security and because in some ways they profit by segregation, have become insensitive to the problems of the masses. The other [force is one of bitterness and hatred,] and it comes perilously close to advocating violence. It is expressed in the various black nationalist [groups that are springing up] across the nation, the largest and best-known being Elijah Muhammad's Muslim movement. Nourished by the Negro's frustration over the continued existence of racial discrimination, this movement is made up of people who have lost faith in America, who have absolutely repudiated Christianity, and who have concluded that the white man is an incorrigible "devil."

King accused of being an extremist.

Malcolm X?

¶6. *Offers better choice: nonviolent protest.*

I have tried to stand between these two forces, saying that we 6 need emulate neither the "do-nothingism" of the complacent nor the hatred and despair of the black nationalist. For there is the more excellent way of love and nonviolent protest. I am grateful to God that, through the influence of the Negro church, the way of nonviolence became an integral part of our struggle.

(How did nonviolence become part of King's movement?)

¶7. *Says movement prevents racial violence. (Threat?)*

If this philosophy had not emerged, by now many streets of 7 the South would, I am convinced, be flowing with blood. And I am further convinced that if our white brothers dismiss as "rabble-rousers" and "outside agitators" those of us who employ nonviolent direct action, and if they refuse to support our nonviolent efforts, millions of Negroes will, out of frustration and despair, seek solace *(comfort)* and security in black-nationalist ideologies—a development that would inevitably lead to a frightening racial nightmare.

Oppressed people cannot remain oppressed forever. The 8 yearning for freedom eventually manifests itself, and that is what has happened to the American Negro. Something within has reminded him of his birthright of freedom, and something without has reminded him that it can be gained. Consciously or *(spirit of the times)* unconsciously, he has been caught up by the Zeitgeist, and with his black brothers of Africa and his brown and yellow brothers of Asia, South America and the Caribbean, the United States Negro is moving with a sense of great urgency toward the [promised land of racial justice.] If one recognizes this [vital urge that has engulfed the Negro community,] one should readily understand why public demonstrations are taking place. The Negro has many [pent-up resentments] and latent frustrations, and he must release them. So let him march; let him make prayer pilgrimages to the city hall; let him go on freedom rides—and try to understand why he must do so. If his repressed emotions are not released in nonviolent ways, *Not a threat, but a fact — ?* they will seek expression through violence; this is not a threat but a fact of history. So I have not said to my people: "Get rid of your discontent." Rather, I have tried to say that this normal and *¶8. Discontent is normal, healthy, and historically inevitable, but it must be channeled.* healthy discontent can be [channeled into the creative outlet of nonviolent direct action.] And now this approach is being termed extremist.

But though I was initially disappointed at being categorized as 9 an extremist, as I continued to think about the matter I gradually gained a measure of satisfaction from the label. Was not Jesus an *¶9. Redefines "extremism," embraces "extremist" label.* extremist for love: "Love your enemies, bless them that curse you, do good to them that hate you, and pray for them which despite-fully use you, and persecute you." Was not Amos an extremist for *(Hebrew prophet)* justice: "Let justice roll down like waters and righteousness like an *(Christian apostle)* ever-flowing stream." Was not Paul an extremist for the Christian gospel: "I bear in my body the marks of the Lord Jesus." Was not (Martin Luther) an extremist: "Here I stand; I cannot do otherwise, so help me God." And (John Bunyan:) "I will stay in jail to the end of my days before I make a butchery of my conscience." And (Abraham Lincoln:) "This nation cannot survive half slave and half free." And (Thomas Jefferson:) "We hold these truths to be self-evident, that all men are created equal. . . ." (So the question is not whether we will be extremists, but what kind of extremists we will be.) Will we be extremists for hate or for love? Will we be extremists for the preservation of injustice or for the extension of justice? In that dramatic scene on Calvary's hill three men were crucified. We must never forget that all three were crucified for the same crime — the crime of extremism. Two were extremists for immorality, and thus fell below their environment. The other, (Jesus Christ,) was an extremist for love, truth and goodness, and thereby rose above his environment. Perhaps the South, the (nation and the world are in dire need of creative extremists.)

I had hoped that the white moderate would see this need. 10 Perhaps I was too optimistic; perhaps I expected too much. I suppose I should have realized that few members of the oppressor race can understand the deep groans and passionate yearnings of the oppressed race, and still fewer have the vision to see that [injustice must be rooted out] by strong, persistent and determined action. I am thankful, however, that some of our white brothers in the South have grasped the meaning of this social revolution and committed themselves to it. They are still all too few in quantity, but they are big in quality. Some—such as Ralph McGill, Lillian Smith, Harry Golden, James McBride Dabbs, Ann Braden and Sarah Patton Boyle—have written about our struggle in eloquent and prophetic terms. Others have marched with us down nameless streets of the South. They have (languished) in filthy, roach-infested jails, suffering the abuse and brutality of policemen who view them as "dirty nigger-lovers." Unlike so many of their moderate brothers and sisters, they have recognized the urgency of the moment and sensed the need for [powerful "action" antidotes] to combat the [disease of segregation.]

(founder of Protestantism)

(English preacher)

Compares self to great "extremists"— including Jesus

Disappointed in the white moderate

¶10. Praises whites who have supported movement.

(Who are they?)

(been left unaided)

Metaphor: segregation is a disease.

Annotating

1 Select a reading from chapters 2–9 or from another text, and mark the text using notations like these:

- Circle words to be defined in the margin.
- Underline key words and phrases.
- Bracket important sentences and passages.
- Use lines or arrows to connect ideas or words.

2 Write marginal comments like these:

- Number and summarize each paragraph.
- Define unfamiliar words.
- Note responses and questions.
- Identify interesting writing strategies.
- Point out patterns.

3 Layer additional markings in the text and comments in the margins as you reread for different purposes.

Taking Inventory

Taking inventory helps you analyze your annotations for different purposes. When you take inventory, you make various kinds of lists to explore patterns of meaning you find in the text. For instance, in reading the annotated passage by Martin Luther King Jr., you might have noticed that certain similes and metaphors are used or that many famous people are named. By listing the names (Socrates, Jesus, Luther, Lincoln, and so on) and then grouping them into categories (people who died for their beliefs, leaders, teachers, and religious figures), you could better understand why the writer refers to these particular people. Taking inventory of your annotations can be helpful if you plan to write about a text you are reading.

Taking Inventory

1 Examine the annotations you made in the activity above for patterns or repetitions, such as recurring images, stylistic features, repeated words and phrases, repeated examples or illustrations, and reliance on particular writing strategies.

2 List the items that make up a pattern.

3 Decide what the pattern might reveal about the reading.

Outlining

Outlining is an especially helpful reading strategy for understanding the content and structure of a reading. **Outlining,** which identifies the text's main ideas, may be part of the annotating process, or it may be done separately. Writing an outline in the margins of the text as you read and annotate makes it easier to find information later. Writing an outline on a separate piece of paper gives you more space to work with, and therefore such an outline usually includes more detail.

The key to outlining is distinguishing between the main ideas and the supporting material, such as examples, quotations, comparisons, and reasons. The main ideas form the backbone that holds the various parts of the text together. Outlining the main ideas helps you uncover this structure.

Making an outline, however, is not simple. The reader must exercise judgment in deciding which are the most important ideas. The words used in an outline reflect the reader's interpretation and emphasis. Readers also must decide when to use the writer's words, their own words, or a combination of the two.

For more on the conventions of formal outlines, see Chapter 11, pp. 512–14.

You may make either a formal, multileveled outline or an informal scratch outline. A *formal outline* is harder to make and much more time-consuming than a scratch outline. You might choose to make a formal outline of a reading about which you are writing an in-depth analysis or evaluation. For example, here is a formal outline a student wrote for an essay evaluating the logic of the King excerpt.

Formal Outline of "Letter from Birmingham Jail"

I. "[T]he Negro's great stumbling block in his stride toward freedom is . . . the white moderate . . . " (par. 1).

   A. White moderates are more devoted to "order" than to justice; however,

      1. law and order exist only to establish justice (par. 2).

      2. law and order *without* justice actually threaten social order ("dangerously structured dams" metaphor, par. 2).

   B. White moderates prefer "negative peace" (absence of tension) to "positive peace" (justice); however,

      1. tension already exists; it is not created by movement (par. 2).

      2. tension is a necessary phase in progress to a just society (par. 2).

      3. tension must be allowed outlet if society is to be healthy ("boil" simile, par. 2).

   C. White moderates disagree with methods of movement; however,

      1. nonviolent direct action can't be condemned for violent response to it (analogies: robbed man; Socrates; Jesus, par. 3).

      2. federal courts affirm that those who seek constitutional rights can't be held responsible for violent response (par. 3).

   D. White moderates paternalistically counsel patience, saying time will bring change; however,

      1. time is "neutral"—we are obligated to use it *actively* to achieve justice (par. 4).

      2. the time for action is now (par. 4).

II. Contrary to white moderates' claims, the movement is not "extremist" in the usual sense (par. 5 ff.).
   A. It stands between extremes in black community: passivity, seen in the oppressed and the self-interested middle-class; and violent radicalism, seen in Elijah Muhammad's followers (pars. 5–6).
   B. In its advocacy of love and nonviolent protest, the movement has forestalled bloodshed and kept more blacks from joining radicals (pars. 5–7).
   C. The movement helps blacks channel urge for freedom that's part of historical trend and the prevailing *Zeitgeist* (par. 8).

III. The movement can be defined as extremist if the term is redefined: "Creative extremism" is extremism in the service of love, truth, and goodness (examples of Amos, Paul, Luther, Bunyan, Lincoln, Jefferson, Jesus, par. 9).

IV. Some whites—"few in quantity, but . . . big in quality"—have recognized the truth of the arguments above and, unlike the white moderates, have committed themselves to the movement (par. 10).

A *scratch outline* will not record as much information as a formal outline, but it is sufficient for most reading purposes. To make a scratch outline, you first need to locate the topic of each paragraph in the reading. The topic is usually stated in a word or phrase, and it may be repeated or referred to throughout the paragraph. For example, the opening paragraph of the King excerpt (p. 523) makes clear that its topic is the white moderate.

After you have found the topic of the paragraph, figure out what is being said about it. To return to our example: King immediately establishes the white moderate as the topic of the opening paragraph and at the beginning of the second sentence announces the conclusion he has come to—namely, that the white moderate is "the Negro's great stumbling block in his stride toward freedom." The rest of the paragraph specifies the ways the white moderate blocks progress.

The annotations include a summary of each paragraph's topic. Here is a scratch outline that lists the topics:

Scratch Outline of "Letter from Birmingham Jail"

¶1. White moderates block progress
¶2. What the moderates don't understand
¶3. Questions clergymen's logic
¶4. Time must be used to do right
¶5. Puts self in middle of two extremes: complacency and bitterness
¶6. Offers better choice: nonviolent protest
¶7. Says movement prevents racial violence
¶8. Discontent normal, healthy, and historically inevitable, but it must be channeled
¶9. Redefines "extremism," embraces "extremist" label
¶10. Praises whites who have supported movement

| ANALYZE & WRITE |

Outlining

1. Reread each paragraph of the selection you have been working with in the previous activities in this chapter. Identify the topic and the comments made about the topic. Do not include examples, specific details, quotations, or other explanatory and supporting material.

2. List the author's main ideas in the margin of the text or on a separate piece of paper.

Paraphrasing

Paraphrasing is restating a text you have read by using mostly your own words. It can help you clarify the meaning of an obscure or ambiguous passage. It is one of the three ways of integrating other people's ideas and information into your own writing, along with **quoting** (reproducing exactly the language of the source text) and **summarizing** (distilling the main ideas or gist of the source text). You might choose to paraphrase rather than quote when the source's language is not especially arresting or memorable. You might paraphrase short passages but summarize longer ones.

Following are two passages. The first is from paragraph 2 of the excerpt from King's "Letter." The second passage is a paraphrase of the first:

Original

I had hoped that the white moderate would understand that law and order exist for the purpose of establishing justice and that when they fail in this purpose they become the dangerously structured dams that block the flow of social progress. I had hoped that the white moderate would understand that the present tension in the South is a necessary phase of the transition from an obnoxious negative peace, in which the Negro passively accepted his unjust plight, to a substantive and positive peace, in which all men will respect the dignity and worth of human personality.

Paraphrase

King writes that he had hoped for more understanding from white moderates—specifically that they would recognize that law and order are not ends in themselves but means to the greater end of establishing justice. When law and order do not serve this greater end, they stand in the way of progress. King expected the white moderate to recognize that the current tense situation in the South is part of a transition process that is necessary for progress. The current situation is bad because although there is peace, it is an "obnoxious" and "negative" kind of peace based on blacks passively accepting the injustice of the status quo. A better kind of peace—one that is "substantive," real and not imaginary, as well as "positive"—requires that all people, regardless of race, be valued.

When you compare the paraphrase to the original, you can see that the paraphrase contains all the important information and ideas of the original. Notice also that the paraphrase is somewhat longer than the original, refers to the writer by name, and encloses King's original words in quotation marks. The paraphrase tries to be *neutral,* to avoid inserting the reader's opinions or distorting the original writer's ideas.

ANALYZE & WRITE

Paraphrasing

1 Select an important passage from the selection you have been working with. (The passage need be only two or three sentences.) Then reread the passage, looking up unfamiliar words in a college dictionary.

2 Translate the passage into your own words and sentences, putting quotation marks around any words or phrases you quote from the original.

3 Revise to ensure coherence.

Summarizing

Summarizing is important because it helps you understand and remember what is most significant in a reading. Another advantage of summarizing is that it creates a condensed version of the reading's ideas and information, which you can refer to later or insert into your own writing. Along with quoting and paraphrasing, summarizing enables you to integrate other writers' ideas into your own writing.

A **summary** is a relatively brief restatement, primarily in the reader's own words, of the reading's main ideas. Summaries vary in length, depending on the reader's purpose. Some summaries are very brief — a sentence or even a subordinate clause. For example, if you were referring to the excerpt from "Letter from Birmingham Jail" and simply needed to indicate how it relates to your other sources, your summary might look something like this: "There have always been advocates of extremism in politics. Martin Luther King Jr., in 'Letter from Birmingham Jail,' for instance, defends nonviolent civil disobedience as an extreme but necessary means of bringing about racial justice." If, however, you were surveying the important texts of the civil rights movement, you might write a longer, more detailed summary that not only identifies the reading's main ideas but also shows how the ideas relate to one another.

Many writers find it useful to outline the reading as a preliminary to writing a summary. A paragraph-by-paragraph scratch outline (like the one on p. 530) lists the reading's main ideas in the sequence in which they appear in the original. But summarizing requires more than merely stringing together the entries in an outline, it must fill in the logical connections between the author's ideas. Notice also in the following example that the reader repeats selected words and phrases and refers to the author by name, indicating, with verbs like *expresses, acknowledges,* and *explains*, the writer's purpose and strategy at each point in the argument.

Summary

King expresses his disappointment with white moderates who, by opposing his program of nonviolent direct action, have become a barrier to progress toward racial justice. He acknowledges that his program has raised tension in the South, but he explains that tension is necessary to bring about change. Furthermore, he argues that tension already exists, but because it has been unexpressed, it is unhealthy and potentially dangerous.

He defends his actions against the clergy's criticisms, particularly their argument that he is in too much of a hurry. Responding to charges of extremism, King claims that he has actually prevented racial violence by channeling the natural frustrations of oppressed blacks into nonviolent protest. He asserts that extremism is precisely what is needed now — but it must be creative, rather than destructive, extremism. He concludes by again expressing disappointment with white moderates for not joining his effort as some other whites have.

A summary presents only ideas. Although it may use certain key terms from the source, it does not otherwise attempt to reflect the source's language, imagery, or tone; and it avoids even a hint of agreement or disagreement with the ideas it summarizes. Of course, a writer might summarize ideas in a source like "Letter from Birmingham Jail" to show readers that he or she has read it carefully and then proceed to use the summary to praise, question, or challenge King's argument. In doing so, the writer might quote specific language that reveals word choice, imagery, or tone.

ANALYZE & WRITE

Summarizing

1. Make a scratch outline of the reading you have been working with, or use the outline you created in the activity on page 531.

2. Write a paragraph or more that presents the author's main ideas largely in your own words. Use the outline as a guide, but reread parts of the original text as necessary.

3. To make the summary coherent, fill in connections between the ideas you present.

Synthesizing

Synthesizing involves presenting ideas and information gleaned from different sources. It can help you see how different sources relate to one another. For example, one reading may provide information that fills out the information in another reading, or a reading could present arguments that challenge arguments in another reading.

When you synthesize material from different sources, you construct a conversation among your sources, a conversation in which you also participate. Synthesizing contributes most when writers use sources, not only to support their ideas but to challenge and extend them as well.

In the following example, the reader uses a variety of sources related to the King passage (pp. 523–27) and brings them together around a central idea. Notice how quotation, paraphrase, and summary are all used.

Synthesis

When King defends his campaign of nonviolent direct action against the clergymen's criticism that "our actions, even though peaceful, must be condemned because they precipitate violence" (King excerpt, par. 3), he is using what Vinit Haksar calls Mohandas Gandhi's "safety-valve argument" ("Civil Disobedience and Non-Cooperation" 117). According to Haksar, Gandhi gave a "non-threatening warning of worse things to come" if his demands were not met. King similarly makes clear that advocates of actions more extreme than those he advocates are waiting in the wings: "The other force is one of bitterness and hatred, and it comes perilously close to advocating violence" (King excerpt, par. 5). King identifies this force with Elijah Muhammad, and although he does not name him, King's contemporary readers would have known that he was referring also to his disciple Malcolm X, who, according to Herbert J. Storing, "urged that Negroes take seriously the idea of revolution" ("The Case against Civil Disobedience" 90). In fact, Malcolm X accused King of being a modern-day Uncle Tom, trying "to keep us under control, to keep us passive and peaceful and nonviolent" (*Malcolm X Speaks* 12).

ANALYZE & WRITE

Synthesizing

1. Find and read two or three sources on the topic of the selection you have been working with, annotating the passages that give you ideas about the topic.

2. Look for patterns among your sources, possibly supporting or challenging your ideas or those of other sources.

3. Write a paragraph or more synthesizing your sources, using quotation, paraphrase, and summary to present what they say on the topic.

Contextualizing

All texts reflect historical and cultural assumptions, values, and attitudes that may differ from your own. To read thoughtfully, you need to become aware of these differences. **Contextualizing** is a critical reading strategy that enables you to make inferences about a reading's historical and cultural context and to examine the differences between its context and your own.

The excerpt from King's "Letter from Birmingham Jail" is a good example of a text that benefits from being read contextually. If you knew little about the history of slavery and segregation in the United States, it would be difficult to understand the passion expressed in this passage. To understand the historical and cultural context in which King wrote his "Letter from Birmingham Jail," you could do some library or Internet research. Comparing the situation at the time to situations with which you are familiar would help you understand some of your own attitudes toward King and the civil rights movement.

Here is what one reader wrote to contextualize King's writing:

Notes from a Contextualized Reading

1. I am not old enough to know what it was like in the early 1960s when Dr. King was leading marches and sit-ins, but I have seen television documentaries showing demonstrators being attacked by dogs, doused by fire hoses, beaten and dragged by helmeted police. Such images give me a sense of the violence, fear, and hatred that King was responding to.

   The tension King writes about comes across in his writing. He uses his anger and frustration creatively to inspire his critics. He also threatens them, although he denies it. I saw a film on Malcolm X, so I could see that King was giving white people a choice between his own nonviolent way and Malcolm's more confrontational way.

2. Things have certainly changed since the sixties. Legal segregation has ended, but there are still racists, like the detective in the O. J. Simpson trial. African Americans like Condoleezza Rice and Barack Obama are highly respected and powerful. The civil rights movement is over. So when I'm reading King today, I feel like I'm reading history. But then again, every once in a while there are reports of police brutality because of race (think of Amadou Diallo) and of what we now call hate crimes (Trayvon Martin).

ANALYZE & WRITE

Contextualizing

1. Describe the historical and cultural situation as it is represented in the reading you have been working with and in other sources with which you are familiar. Your knowledge may come from other reading, television or film, school, or elsewhere. (If you know nothing about the historical and cultural context, you could do some library or Internet research.)

2. Compare the historical and cultural situation in which the text was written with your own historical and cultural situation. Consider how your understanding and judgment of the reading are affected by your own context.

Exploring the Significance of Figurative Language

Figurative language—*metaphor, simile,* and *symbolism*—enhances literal meaning by implying abstract ideas through vivid images and by evoking feelings and associations.

Metaphor implicitly compares two different things by identifying them with each other. For instance, when King calls the white moderate "the Negro's great stumbling block in his stride toward freedom" (par. 1), he does not mean that the white moderate literally trips the Negro who is attempting to walk toward freedom. The sentence makes sense only if understood figuratively: The white moderate trips up the Negro by frustrating every effort to achieve justice.

Simile, a more explicit form of comparison, uses the word *like* or *as* to signal the relationship of two seemingly unrelated things. King uses simile when he says that injustice is "like a boil that can never be cured so long as it is covered up" (par. 2). This simile makes several points of comparison between injustice and a boil. It suggests that injustice is a disease of society as a boil is a disease of the skin and that injustice, like a boil, must be exposed or it will fester and infect the entire body.

Symbolism compares two things by making one stand for the other. King uses the white moderate as a symbol for supposed liberals and would-be supporters of civil rights who are actually frustrating the cause.

How these figures of speech are used in a text reveals something of the writer's feelings about the subject. Exploring possible meanings in a text's figurative language involves (1) annotating and then listing the metaphors, similes, and symbols you find in a reading; (2) grouping and labeling the figures of speech that appear to express related feelings or attitudes; and (3) writing to explore the meaning of the patterns you have found.

The following example shows the process of exploring figures of speech in the King excerpt.

Listing Figures of Speech

"stumbling block in his stride toward freedom" (par. 1)
"law and order...become the dangerously structured dams" (2)
"the flow of social progress" (2)
"Like a boil that can never be cured" (2)
"the light of human conscience and the air of national opinion" (2)
"the quicksand of racial injustice" (4)

Grouping and Labeling Figures of Speech

Sickness: "like a boil" (2); "the disease of segregation" (10)
Underground: "hidden tension" (2); "injustice must be exposed" (2); "injustice must be rooted out" (10)
Blockage: "dams," "block the flow" (2); "Human progress never rolls in on wheels of inevitability" (4); "pent-up resentments" (8); "repressed emotions" (8)

Writing to Explore Meaning

The patterns labeled underground and blockage suggest a feeling of frustration. Inertia is a problem; movement forward toward progress or upward toward the promised land is stalled. The strong need to break through the resistance may represent

King's feelings about both his attempt to lead purposeful, effective demonstrations and his effort to write a convincing argument.

The simile of injustice being "like a boil" links the two patterns of underground and sickness, suggesting that something bad, a disease, is inside the people or the society. The cure is to expose or to root out the blocked hatred and injustice as well as to release the tension or emotion that has long been repressed. This implies that repression itself is the evil, not simply what is repressed. Therefore, writing and speaking out through political action may have curative power for individuals and society alike.

ANALYZE & WRITE

Exploring the Significance of Figurative Language

1. Annotate all the figures of speech you find in the reading you have been working with (or another selection) — metaphors, similes, and symbols — and then list them.

2. Group the figures of speech that appear to express related feelings and attitudes, and label each group.

3. Write one or two paragraphs exploring the meaning of these patterns. What do they tell you about the text?

Looking for Patterns of Opposition

All texts carry within themselves voices of opposition. These voices may echo the views and values of readers the writer anticipates or predecessors to whom the writer is responding in some way; they may even reflect the writer's own conflicting values. Careful readers look closely for such a dialogue of opposing voices within the text.

When we think of oppositions, we ordinarily think of polarities: *yes* and *no, up* and *down, black* and *white, new* and *old*. Some oppositions, however, may be more subtle. The excerpt from King's "Letter from Birmingham Jail" is rich in such oppositions: *moderate* versus *extremist, order* versus *justice, direct action* versus *passive acceptance, expression* versus *repression*. These oppositions are not accidental; they form a significant pattern that gives a reader important information about the essay.

A careful reading will show that King always values one of the two terms in an opposition over the other. In the passage, for example, *extremist* is valued over *moderate* (par. 9). This preference for extremism is surprising. The reader should ask why, when white extremists like members of the Ku Klux Klan have committed so many outrages against African Americans, King would prefer extremism. If King is trying to convince his readers to accept his point of view, why would he represent himself as an extremist? Moreover, why would a clergyman advocate extremism instead of moderation?

Studying the **patterns of opposition** in the text enables you to answer these questions. You will see that King sets up this opposition to force his readers to examine their own values and realize that they are in fact misplaced. Instead of working toward justice, he says, those who support law and order maintain the unjust status quo. By getting his readers to think of white moderates as blocking rather than facilitating peaceful change, King brings readers to align themselves with him and perhaps even embrace his strategy of nonviolent resistance.

Looking for patterns of opposition involves annotating words or phrases in the reading that indicate oppositions, listing the opposing terms in pairs, deciding which term in each pair is preferred by the writer, and reflecting on the meaning of the patterns. Here is a partial list of oppositions from the King excerpt, with the preferred terms marked by an asterisk:

Listing Patterns of Opposition

moderate	*extremist
order	*justice
negative peace	*positive peace
absence of justice	*presence of justice
goals	*methods
*direct action	passive acceptance
*exposed tension	hidden tension

ANALYZE & WRITE

Looking for Patterns of Opposition

1. Annotate the selection you have been working with (or another selection) for words or phrases indicating oppositions.

2. List the pairs of oppositions. (You may have to paraphrase or even supply the opposite word or phrase if it is not stated directly in the text.)

3. For each pair of oppositions, put an asterisk next to the term that the writer seems to value or prefer over the other.

4. Study the patterns of opposition. How do they contribute to your understanding of the essay? What do they tell you about what the author wants you to believe?

Reflecting on Challenges to Your Beliefs and Values

To read thoughtfully, you need to scrutinize your own assumptions and attitudes as well as those expressed in the text you are reading. If you are like most readers, however, you will find that your assumptions and attitudes are so ingrained that you are not always fully aware of them. A good strategy for getting at these underlying beliefs and values is to identify and reflect on the ways the text challenges you and how it makes you feel—disturbed, threatened, ashamed, combative, pleased, exuberant, or some other way.

For example, here is what one student wrote about the King passage:

Reflections

In paragraph 1, Dr. King criticizes people who are "more devoted to 'order' than to justice." This criticism upsets me because today I think I would choose order over justice. When I reflect on my feelings and try to figure out where they come from, I realize that what I feel most is fear. I am terrified by the violence in society today. I'm afraid of sociopaths who don't respect the rule of law, much less the value of human life.

I know Dr. King was writing in a time when the law itself was unjust, when order was apparently used to keep people from protesting and changing the law. But things are different now. Today, justice seems to serve criminals more than it serves law-abiding citizens. That's why I'm for order over justice.

ANALYZE & WRITE

Reflecting on Challenges to Your Beliefs and Values

1 Identify challenges by marking the text you have been working with (or another text) where you feel your beliefs and values are being opposed, criticized, or unfairly characterized.

2 Write a few paragraphs reflecting on why you feel challenged. Do not defend your feelings; instead, search your memory to discover where they come from.

Evaluating the Logic of an Argument

An *argument* includes a thesis backed by reasons and support. The **thesis** asserts a position on a controversial issue or a solution to a problem that the writer wants readers to accept. The **reasons** tell readers why they should accept the thesis, and the **support** (such as examples, statistics, authorities, and textual evidence) gives readers grounds for accepting it. For an argument to be considered logically acceptable, it must meet the three conditions of what we call the ABC test:

For more on argument, see Chapter 19.

The ABC Test

A. The reasons and support must be *appropriate* to the thesis.

B. The reasons and support must be *believable*.

C. The reasons and support must be *consistent* with one another as well as *complete*.

Test for appropriateness.

To evaluate the logic of an argument, you first decide whether the argument's reasons and support are appropriate. To test for appropriateness, ask these questions: How does each reason or piece of support relate to the thesis? Is the connection between reasons and support and the thesis clear and compelling?

Readers most often question the appropriateness of reasons and support when the writer argues by analogy or by invoking authority. For example, in paragraph 2, King argues that when law and order fail to establish justice, "they become the dangerously structured dams that block the flow of social progress." The analogy asserts the following logical relationship: Law and order are to progress toward justice what a dam is to water. If you do not accept this analogy, the argument fails the test of appropriateness.

King uses both analogy and authority in paragraph 3: "Isn't this like condemning Socrates because his unswerving commitment to truth and his philosophical inquiries precipitated the act by the misguided populace in which they made him drink hemlock?" Not only must you judge the appropriateness of the analogy comparing the Greeks' condemnation of Socrates to the white moderates' condemnation of King, but you must also judge whether it is appropriate to accept Socrates as an authority. Since Socrates is generally respected for his teachings on justice, his words and actions are likely to be considered appropriate to King's situation in Birmingham.

For more on analogy, see Chapter 18, pp. 605–6. For invoking authorities, see Chapter 19, pp. 614–15.

Test for believability.

Believability is a measure of your willingness to accept as true the reasons and support the writer gives in defense of a thesis.

To test for believability, ask: On what basis am I being asked to believe this reason or support is true? If it cannot be proved true or false, how much weight does it carry?

In judging facts, examples and anecdotes, statistics, and authorities, consider the following points.

Facts are statements that can be proved objectively to be true. The believability of facts depends on their *accuracy* (they should not distort or misrepresent reality), their *completeness* (they should not omit important details), and the *trustworthiness* of their sources (sources should be qualified and unbiased). King, for instance, asserts as fact that the African American will not wait much longer for racial justice (par. 8). His critics might question the factuality of this assertion by asking: Is it true of all African Americans? How does King know what African Americans will and will not do?

Examples and **anecdotes** are particular instances that may or may not make you believe a general statement. The believability of examples depends on their *representativeness* (whether they are truly typical and thus generalizable) and their *specificity* (whether particular details make them seem true to life). Even if a vivid example or gripping anecdote does not convince readers, it usually strengthens argumentative writing by clarifying the meaning and dramatizing the point. In paragraph 5 of the King excerpt, for example, King supports his generalization that some African American extremists are motivated by bitterness and hatred by citing the specific example of Elijah Muhammad's Black Muslim movement. Conversely, in paragraph 9, he refers to Jesus, Paul, Luther, and others as examples of extremists motivated by love and Christianity. These examples support his assertion that extremism is not in itself wrong and that any judgment of extremism must be based on its motivation and cause.

Statistics are numerical data. The believability of statistics depends on the *comparability* of the data (the price of apples in 1985 cannot be compared with the price of apples in 2012 unless the figures are adjusted to account for inflation), the *precision* of the methods employed to gather and analyze data (representative samples should be used and variables accounted for), and the *trustworthiness* of the sources.

Authorities are people to whom the writer attributes expertise on a given subject. Not only must such authorities be appropriate, as mentioned earlier, but they must be credible as well—that is, the reader must accept them as experts on the topic at hand. King cites authorities repeatedly throughout his essay. He refers to religious leaders (Jesus and Luther) as well as to American political leaders (Lincoln and Jefferson). These figures are likely to have a high degree of credibility among King's readers.

Test for consistency and completeness.

In looking for consistency, you should be concerned that all the parts of the argument work together and that they are sufficient to convince readers to accept the thesis or at least take it seriously. To test for consistency and completeness, ask: Are any of the reasons and support contradictory? Do they provide sufficient grounds for accepting the thesis? Does the writer fail to acknowledge, concede, or refute any opposing arguments or important objections?

For more on responding to opposing views, see Chapter 19, pp. 617–20.

A thoughtful reader might regard as contradictory King's characterizing himself first as a moderate and later as an extremist opposed to the forces of violence. (King attempts to reconcile this apparent contradiction by explicitly redefining extremism in par. 9.) Similarly, the fact that King fails to examine and refute every legal recourse available to his cause might allow a critical reader to question the sufficiency of his argument.

| ANALYZE & WRITE |

Evaluating the Logic of an Argument

Use the ABC test on the selection you have been working with (or another selection):

- **A** *Test for appropriateness* by checking that the reasons and support are clearly and directly related to the thesis.

- **B** *Test for believability* by deciding whether you can accept the reasons and support as likely to be true.

- **C** *Test for consistency and completeness* by deciding whether the argument has any contradictions and whether any important objections or opposing views have been ignored.

Recognizing Emotional Manipulation

Writers often try to arouse emotions in readers to excite their interest, make them care, or move them to take action. There is nothing wrong with appealing to readers' emotions. What is wrong is manipulating readers with false or exaggerated appeals. Therefore, you should be suspicious of writing that is overly sentimental, that cites alarming statistics and frightening anecdotes, that demonizes others and identifies itself with revered authorities, or that uses potent symbols (for example, the American flag) or emotionally loaded words (such as *racist*).

King, for example, uses the emotionally loaded word *paternalistically* to refer to the white moderate's belief that "he can set the timetable for another man's freedom" (par. 1). In the same paragraph, King uses symbolism to get an emotional reaction from readers when he compares the white moderate to the "Ku Klux Klanner." To get readers to accept his ideas, he also relies on authorities whose names evoke the greatest respect, such as Jesus and Lincoln. But some readers might object that comparing his own crusade to that of Jesus is pretentious and manipulative. A critical reader might also consider King's discussion of African American extremists in paragraph 7 to be a veiled threat designed to frighten readers into agreement.

ANALYZE & WRITE

Recognizing Emotional Manipulation

1 Annotate places in the text you have been working with (or another text) where you sense emotional appeals are being used.

2 Assess whether any of the emotional appeals are unfairly manipulative.

Judging the Writer's Credibility

Writers try to persuade readers by presenting an image of themselves in their writing that will gain their readers' confidence. This image must be created indirectly, through the arguments, language, and system of values and beliefs expressed or implied in the writing. Writers establish credibility in their writing in three ways:

- By showing their knowledge of the subject
- By building *common ground* with readers
- By responding fairly to objections and opposing arguments

Test for knowledge.

Writers demonstrate their knowledge through the facts and statistics they marshal, the sources they rely on for information, and the scope and depth of their understanding. You may not be sufficiently expert on the subject yourself to know whether the facts are accurate, the sources are reliable, and the understanding is sufficient. You may need to do some research to see what others say about the subject. You can also check credentials—the writer's educational and professional qualifications, the respectability of the publication in which the selection first appeared, and reviews of the writer's work—to determine whether the writer is a respected authority in the field. For example, King brings with him the authority that comes from being a member of the clergy and a respected leader of the Southern Christian Leadership Conference.

Test for common ground.

One way writers can establish **common ground** with their readers is by basing their reasoning on shared values, beliefs, and attitudes. They use language that includes their readers (*we*) and qualify their assertions to keep them from being too extreme. Above all, they acknowledge differences of opinion. You want to notice such appeals.

King creates common ground with readers by using the inclusive pronoun *we,* suggesting shared concerns between himself and his audience. Notice, however, his use of masculine pronouns and other references ("the Negro . . . he," "our brothers"). Although King addressed his letter to male clergy, he intended it to be published in the local newspaper, where it would be read by an audience of both men and women. By using language that excludes women—a common practice at the time the selection was written—King may have missed the opportunity to build common ground with more than half of his readers.

Test for fairness.

Writers reveal their character by how they handle opposing arguments and objections to their argument. As a critical reader, pay particular attention to how writers treat possible differences of opinion. Be suspicious of those who ignore differences and pretend that everyone agrees with their viewpoints. When objections or opposing views are represented, consider whether they have been distorted in any way; if they are refuted, be sure they are challenged fairly—with sound reasoning and solid support.

One way to gauge the author's credibility is to identify the tone of the argument, for it conveys the writer's attitude toward the subject and toward the reader. Is the text angry? Sarcastic? Evenhanded? Shrill? Condescending? Bullying? Do you feel as if the writer is treating the subject—and you, as a reader—with fairness? King's tone might be characterized in different passages as patient (he doesn't lose his temper), respectful (he refers to white moderates as "people of good will"), or pompous (comparing himself to Jesus and Socrates).

ANALYZE & WRITE ┤

Judging the Writer's Credibility

1 Using the selection you have been working with (or another selection), annotate for the writer's knowledge of the subject, how well common ground is established, and whether the writer deals fairly with objections and opposing arguments.

2 Decide what in the essay you find credible and what you question.

PART 3
Writing Strategies

13

Cueing the Reader

Readers need guidance. To guide readers through a piece of writing, a writer can provide five basic kinds of **cues,** or signals:

1. Thesis and forecasting statements, to orient readers to ideas and organization
2. Paragraphing, to group related ideas and details
3. Cohesive devices, to connect ideas to one another and bring about clarity
4. Transitions, to signal relationships or shifts in meaning
5. Headings and subheadings, to group related paragraphs and help readers locate specific information quickly

This chapter illustrates how each of these cueing strategies works.

Orienting Statements

To help readers find their way, especially in difficult and lengthy texts, you can provide two kinds of **orienting statements:** a thesis statement, which declares the main point, and a forecasting statement, which previews subordinate points, showing the order in which they will be discussed in the essay.

Use thesis statements to announce the main idea.

To help readers understand what is being said about a subject, writers often provide a thesis statement early in the essay. The **thesis statement,** which can comprise one or more sentences, operates as a cue by letting readers know which is the most important general idea among the writer's many ideas and observations. In "Love: The Right Chemistry" in Chapter 4, Anastasia Toufexis expresses her thesis in the second paragraph:

> O.K., let's cut out all this nonsense about romantic love. Let's bring some scientific precision to the party. Let's put love under a microscope.
>
> When rigorous people with Ph.D.s after their names do that, what they see is not some silly, senseless thing. No, their probe reveals that love rests firmly on the foundations of evolution, biology and chemistry.

Readers naturally look for something that will tell them the point of an essay, a focus for the many diverse details and ideas they encounter as they read. They expect to find some information early on that will give them a context for reading the essay, particularly if they are reading about a new or difficult subject. Therefore, a thesis statement, like Toufexis's, placed at the beginning of an essay enables readers to anticipate the content of the essay and helps them understand the relationships among its various ideas and details.

Occasionally, however, particularly in fairly short, informal essays and in some autobiographical and argumentative essays, a writer may save a direct statement of the thesis until the conclusion. In "Sticks and Stones and Sports Team Names," for example, from Chapter 6, Richard Estrada explicitly states his thesis in his final paragraph:

> It seems to me that what Native Americans are saying is that what would be intolerable for Jews, blacks, Latinos and others is no less offensive to them. Theirs is a request not only for dignified treatment, but for fair treatment as well. For America to ignore the complaints of a numerically small segment of the population because it is small is neither dignified nor fair.

Ending with the thesis brings together the various strands of information or supporting details introduced over the course of the essay and makes clear the essay's main idea.

Some essays, particularly autobiographical essays, offer no direct thesis statement. Although this can make the point of the essay more difficult to determine, it can be appropriate when the essay is more expressive and personal than it is informative. In all cases, careful writers keep readers' needs and expectations in mind when deciding how—and whether—to state the thesis.

| EXERCISE 13.1 |

In the essay by Jessica Statsky in Chapter 6, underline the thesis statement, the last sentence in paragraph 1. Notice the key terms: "overzealous parents and coaches," "impose adult standards," "children's sports," "activities . . . neither satisfying nor beneficial." Then skim the essay, stopping to read the sentence at the beginning of each paragraph. Also read the last paragraph.

Consider whether the idea in every paragraph's first sentence is anticipated by the thesis's key terms. Consider also the connection between the ideas in the last paragraph and the thesis's key terms. What can you conclude about how a thesis might assert the point of an essay, anticipate the ideas that follow, and help readers relate the ideas to one another?

Use forecasting statements to preview topics.

Some thesis statements include a **forecast,** which overviews the way a thesis will be developed, as in the following example:

> In the three years from 1348 through 1350 the pandemic of plague known as the
> Black Death, or, as the Germans called it, the Great Dying, killed at least a fourth of

the population of Europe. It was undoubtedly the worst disaster that has ever befallen mankind. Today we can have no real conception of the terror under which people lived in the shadow of the plague. For more than two centuries plague has not been a serious threat to mankind in the large, although it is still a grisly presence in parts of the Far East and Africa. Scholars continue to study the Great Dying, however, as a historical example of human behavior under the stress of universal catastrophe. In these days when the threat of plague has been replaced by the threat of mass human extermination by even more rapid means, there has been a sharp renewal of interest in the history of the fourteenth-century calamity. With new perspective, students are investigating its manifold effects: demographic, economic, psychological, moral and religious.

—WILLIAM LANGER, "The Black Death"

> **Thesis forecasts five main categories of effects of the Black Death.**

As a reader would expect, Langer divides his essay into explanations of the research into these five effects, addressing them in the order in which they appear in the forecasting statement.

EXERCISE 13.2

Turn to Patrick O'Malley's essay in Chapter 7, and underline the forecasting statement in paragraph 2. Then skim the essay. Notice whether O'Malley takes up every point he mentions in the forecasting statement and whether he sticks to the order he promises readers. How well does his forecasting statement help you follow his essay? What suggestions for improvement, if any, would you offer him?

Paragraphing

Paragraph cues as obvious as indentation keep readers on track. You can also arrange material in a paragraph to help readers see what is important or significant. For example, you can begin with a topic sentence, help readers see the relationship between the previous paragraph and the present one with an explicit transition, and place the most important information toward the end.

Paragraph indents signal related ideas.

One paragraph cue — the indentation that signals the beginning of a new paragraph — is a relatively modern printing convention. Old manuscripts show that paragraph divisions were not always marked. To make reading easier, scribes and printers began to use the symbol ¶ to mark paragraph breaks, and later, indenting became common practice. Indenting has been abandoned by most online and business writers, who now distinguish one paragraph from another by leaving a line of space between paragraphs.

> For additional visual cues for readers, see Headings and Subheadings on pp. 558–60.

Paragraphing helps readers by signaling when a sequence of related ideas begins and ends. Paragraphing also helps readers judge what is most important in what they are reading. Writers typically emphasize important information by placing it at the two points in the paragraph where readers are most attentive — the beginning and the end.

You can give special emphasis to information by placing it in its own paragraph.

EXERCISE 13.3

Turn again to Patrick O'Malley's essay in Chapter 7, and read paragraphs 4–7 with the following questions in mind: Does all the material in each paragraph seem to be related? Do you feel a sense of closure at the end of each paragraph? Does the last sentence offer the most important or significant or weighty information in the paragraph?

Topic sentences announce the paragraph's focus.

A **topic sentence** lets readers know the focus of a paragraph in simple and direct terms. It is a cueing strategy for the paragraph, much as a thesis or forecasting statement is for the whole essay. Because paragraphing usually signals a shift in focus, readers expect some kind of reorientation in the opening sentence. They need to know whether the new paragraph will introduce another aspect of the topic or develop one already introduced.

Announcing the Topic   Some topic sentences simply announce the topic. Here are some examples taken from Barry Lopez's book *Arctic Dreams:*

> A polar bear walks in a way all its own.

> What is so consistently striking about the way Eskimos used parts of an animal is the breadth of their understanding about what would work.

> The Mediterranean view of the Arctic, down to the time of the Elizabethan mariners, was shaped by two somewhat contradictory thoughts.

The following paragraph shows how one of Lopez's topic sentences (highlighted) is developed:

> What is so consistently striking about the way Eskimos used parts of an animal is the breadth of their understanding about what would work. Knowing that muskox horn is more flexible than caribou antler, they preferred it for making the side prongs of a fish spear. For a waterproof bag in which to carry sinews for clothing repair, they chose salmon skin. They selected the strong, translucent intestine of a bearded seal to make a window for a snowhouse — it would fold up for easy traveling and it would not frost over in cold weather. To make small snares for sea ducks, they needed a springy material that would not rot in salt water — baleen fibers. The down feather of a common eider, tethered at the end of a stick in the snow at an angle, would reveal the exhalation of a quietly surfacing seal. Polar bear bone was used anywhere a stout, sharp point was required, because it is the hardest bone.
>
> —BARRY LOPEZ, *Arctic Dreams*

Turn to Jessica Statsky's essay in Chapter 6. Underline the topic sentence (the first sentence) in paragraphs 3 and 5. Consider how these sentences help you anticipate the paragraph's topic and method of development.

Making a Transition   Not all topic sentences simply point to what will follow. Some also refer to earlier sentences. Such sentences work both as topic sentences, stating the main point of the paragraph, and as *transitions,* linking that paragraph to the previous one. Here are a few topic sentences from "Quilts and Women's Culture," by Elaine Hedges, with transitions highlighted:

> Transitions tie each topic sentence to a previous statement.

Within its broad traditionalism and anonymity, however, variations and distinctions developed.

Regionally, too, distinctions were introduced into quilt making through the interesting process of renaming.

Finally, out of such regional and other variations come individual, signed achievements.

Quilts, then, were an outlet for creative energy, a source and emblem of sisterhood and solidarity, and a graphic response to historical and political change.

Sometimes the first sentence of a paragraph serves as a transition, and a subsequent sentence states the topic, as in the following example:

> Transition sentences

What a convenience, what a relief it will be, they say, never to worry about how to dress for a job interview, a romantic tryst, or a funeral!
   Convenient, perhaps, but not exactly a relief. Such a utopia would give most of us the same kind of chill we feel when a stadium full of Communist-bloc athletes in identical sports outfits, shouting slogans in unison, appears on TV. Most people do not want to be told what to wear any more than they want to be told what to say. In Belfast recently four hundred Irish Republican prisoners "refused to wear any clothes at all, draping themselves day and night in blankets,'' rather than put on prison uniforms. Even the offer of civilian-style dress did not satisfy them; they insisted on wearing their own clothes brought from home, or nothing. Fashion is free speech, and one of the privileges, if not always one of the pleasures, of a free world.

—Alison Lurie, *The Language of Clothes*

Occasionally, whole paragraphs serve as transitions, linking one sequence of paragraphs with those that follow, as in the following:

> Transition paragraph summarizes contrasts and sets up an analysis of the similarities.

Yet it was not all contrast, after all. Different as they were — in background, in personality, in underlying aspiration—these two great soldiers had much in common. Under everything else, they were marvelous fighters. Furthermore, their fighting qualities were really very much alike.

—Bruce Catton, "Grant and Lee: A Study in Contrasts"

EXERCISE 13.5

Turn to Jessica Statsky's essay in Chapter 6 and read paragraphs 3–7. As you read, underline the part of the first sentence in paragraphs 4, 5, and 7 that refers to the previous paragraph, creating a transition from one to the next. Notice the different ways Statsky creates these transitions. Consider whether they are all equally effective.

Positioning the Topic Sentence   Although topic sentences may occur anywhere in a paragraph, stating the topic in the first sentence has the advantage of giving readers a sense of how the paragraph is likely to be developed. The beginning of the paragraph is therefore the most common position.

A topic sentence that does not open a paragraph is most likely to appear at the end. When a topic sentence concludes a paragraph, it usually summarizes or generalizes preceding information:

> Even black Americans sometimes need to be reminded about the deceptiveness of television. Blacks retain their fascination with black characters on TV: Many of us buy *Jet* magazine primarily to read its weekly television feature, which lists every black character (major or minor) to be seen on the screen that week. Yet our fixation with the presence of black characters on TV has blinded us to an important fact that *Cosby,* which began in 1984, and its offshoots over the years demonstrate convincingly: There is very little connection between the social status of black Americans and the fabricated images of black people that Americans consume each day. The representation of blacks on TV is a very poor index to our social advancement or political progress.
> —HENRY LOUIS GATES JR., "TV's Black World Turns—but Stays Unreal"

Topic is not stated until the last sentence.

When a topic sentence is used in a narrative, it often appears as the last sentence as a way to evaluate or reflect on events:

> A cold sun was sliding down a gray fall sky. Some older boys had been playing tackle football in the field we took charge of every weekend. In a few years, they'd be called to Southeast Asia, some of them. Their locations would be tracked with pushpins in red, white, and blue on maps on nearly every kitchen wall. But that afternoon, they were quick as young deer. They leapt and dodged, dove from each other and collided in midair. Bulletlike passes flew to connect them. Or the ball spiraled in a high arc across the frosty sky one to another. In short, they were mindlessly agile in a way that captured as audience every little kid within running distance of the yellow goalposts.
>
> —MARY KARR, *Cherry*

Topic sentence reflects on narrated events described earlier in paragraph.

It is possible for a single topic sentence to introduce two or more paragraphs. Subsequent paragraphs in such a sequence have no separate topic sentences of their own:

> Anthropologists Daniel Maltz and Ruth Borker point out that boys and girls socialize differently. Little girls tend to play in small groups or, even more common, in pairs. Their social life usually centers around a best friend, and friendships are made, maintained, and broken by talk—especially "secrets." If a little girl tells her

Topic sentence states topic of this paragraph and next.

friend's secret to another little girl, she may find herself with a new best friend. The secrets themselves may or may not be important, but the fact of telling them is all-important. It's hard for newcomers to get into these tight groups, but anyone who is admitted is treated as an equal. Girls like to play cooperatively; if they can't cooperate, the group breaks up.

Little boys tend to play in larger groups, often outdoors, and they spend more time doing things than talking. It's easy for boys to get into the group, but not everyone is accepted as an equal. Once in the group, boys must jockey for their status in it. One of the most important ways they do this is through talk: verbal display such as telling stories and jokes, challenging and sidetracking the verbal displays of other boys, and withstanding other boys' challenges in order to maintain their own story — and status. Their talk is often competitive talk about who is best at what.

—Deborah Tannen, *That's Not What I Meant!*

EXERCISE 13.6

Consider the variety and effectiveness of the topic sentences in your most recent essay. Begin by underlining the topic sentence in each paragraph after the first one. The topic sentence may not be the first sentence in a paragraph, though it will often be.

Then double-underline the part of the topic sentence that provides an explicit transition from one paragraph to the next. You may find a transition that is separate from the topic sentence. You may not always find a topic sentence.

Reflect on your topic sentences, and evaluate how well they serve to orient your readers to the sequence of topics or ideas in your essay.

Cohesive Devices

Cohesive devices guide readers, helping them follow your train of thought by connecting key words and phrases throughout a passage. Among such devices are pronoun reference, word repetition, synonyms, sentence structure repetition, and collocation.

Pronouns connect phrases or sentences.

One common cohesive device is *pronoun reference.* As noun substitutes, pronouns refer to nouns that either precede or follow them and thus serve to connect phrases or sentences. The nouns that come before pronouns are called **antecedents.**

In New York from dawn to dusk to dawn, day after day, you can hear the steady rumble of tires against the concrete span of the George Washington Bridge. The bridge is never completely still. It trembles with traffic. It moves in the wind. Its great veins of steel swell when hot and contract when cold; its span often is ten feet closer to the Hudson River in summer than in winter.

—Gay Talese, "New York"

Pronouns form a chain of connection with antecedent.

This example has only one pronoun-antecedent chain, and the antecedent comes first, so all the pronouns refer back to it. When there are multiple pronoun-antecedent chains with references forward as well as back, writers have to make sure that readers will not mistake one pronoun's antecedent for another's.

Word repetition aids cohesion.

To avoid confusion, writers often use *word repetition*. The device of repeating words and phrases is especially helpful if a pronoun might confuse readers:

> Some odd optical property of our highly polarized and unequal society makes the poor almost invisible to their economic superiors. The poor can see the affluent easily enough—on television, for example, or on the covers of magazines. But the affluent rarely see the poor or, if they do catch sight of them in some public space, rarely know what they're seeing, since—thanks to consignment stores and, yes, Wal-Mart—the poor are usually able to disguise themselves as members of the more comfortable classes.
>
> —BARBARA EHRENREICH, *Nickel and Dimed*

Repeated words

In the next example, several overlapping chains of word repetition prevent confusion and help the reader follow the ideas:

> Natural selection is the central concept of Darwinian theory—the fittest survive and spread their favored traits through populations. Natural selection is defined by Spencer's phrase "survival of the fittest," but what does this famous bit of jargon really mean? Who are the fittest? And how is "fitness" defined? We often read that fitness involves no more than "differential reproductive success"—the production of more surviving offspring than other competing members of the population. Whoa! cries Bethell, as many others have before him. This formulation defines fitness in terms of survival only. The crucial phrase of natural selection means no more than "the survival of those who survive"—a vacuous tautology. (A tautology is a phrase—like "my father is a man"—containing no information in the predicate ["a man"] not inherent in the subject ["my father"]. Tautologies are fine as definitions, but not as testable scientific statements—there can be nothing to test in a statement true by definition.)
>
> —STEPHEN JAY GOULD, *Ever Since Darwin*

Repeated words with some variation of form

Synonyms connect ideas.

In addition to word repetition, you can use **synonyms,** words with identical or very similar meanings, to connect important ideas. In the following example, the author develops a careful chain of synonyms and word repetitions:

> Over time, small bits of knowledge about a region accumulate among local residents in the form of stories. These are remembered in the community; even what is unusual does not become lost and therefore irrelevant. These

Synonym sequences:
region, particular landscape
local residents, native

stories, narratives are remembered, does not become lost

intricate, . . . view, complex . . . "reality"

narratives comprise for a **native** an intricate, long-term view of a **particular landscape**. . . . Outside the region this **complex** but easily shared "**reality**" is hard to get across without reducing it to generalities, to misleading or imprecise abstraction.

—BARRY LOPEZ, Arctic Dreams

The result is a coherent paragraph that constantly reinforces the author's point.

Sentence structure repetition emphasizes connections.

Writers occasionally use *sentence structure repetition* to emphasize the connections among their ideas, as in this example:

Repeats the if/then sentence structure

> But the life forms are as much part of the structure of the Earth as any inanimate portion is. It is all an inseparable part of a whole. If any animal is isolated totally from other forms of life, then death by starvation will surely follow. If isolated from water, death by dehydration will follow even faster. If isolated from air, whether free or dissolved in water, death by asphyxiation will follow still faster. If isolated from the Sun, animals will survive for a time, but plants would die, and if all plants died, all animals would starve.

— ISAAC ASIMOV, "The Case against Man"

Collocation creates networks of meaning.

Collocation—the positioning of words together in expected ways around a particular topic—occurs quite naturally to writers and usually forms recognizable networks of meaning for readers. For example, in a paragraph on a high school graduation, a reader might expect to encounter such words as *valedictorian, diploma, commencement, honors, cap* and *gown,* and *senior class.* The paragraph that follows uses five collocation chains:

> housewife, cooking, neighbor, home
> clocks, calculated, progression, precise
> obstinacy, vagaries, problem
> sun, clear days, cloudy ones, sundial, cast its light, angle, seasons, sun, weather
> cooking, fire, matches, hot coals smoldering, ashes, go out, bed-warming pan

The seventeenth-century **housewife** not only had to make do without thermometers, she also had to make do without **clocks**, which were scarce and dear throughout the sixteen hundreds. She **calculated** **cooking** times by the **progression** of the **sun**; her **cooking** must have been more **precise** on **clear days** than on **cloudy ones**. Marks were sometimes painted on the floor, providing her with a rough **sundial**, but she still had to make allowance for the **obstinacy** of the sun in refusing to **cast** its light at the same angle as the seasons changed; but she was used to allowing for the vagaries of sun and weather. She also had a problem starting her fire in the morning; there were no matches. If she had allowed the hot coals smoldering under the ashes to go out, she had to borrow some from a neighbor, carrying them home with care, perhaps in a bed-warming pan.

—WAVERLY ROOT AND RICHARD DE ROUCHEMENT, *Eating in America*

EXERCISE 13.7

Now that you know more about pronoun reference, word repetition, synonyms, sentence structure repetition, and collocation, turn to Brian Cable's essay in Chapter 3 and identify the cohesive devices you find in paragraphs 1–5. Underline each cohesive device you can find; there will be many. You might also want to connect with lines the various pronoun, related-word, and synonym chains you find. You could also try listing the separate collocation chains. Consider how these cohesive devices help you read and make sense of the passage.

EXERCISE 13.8

Choose one of your recent essays, and select any three contiguous paragraphs. Underline every cohesive device you can find; there will be many. Try to connect with lines the various pronoun, related-word, and synonym chains you find. Also try listing the separate collocation chains.

You will be surprised and pleased at how extensively you rely on cohesive ties. Indeed, you could not produce readable text without cohesive ties. Consider these questions relevant to your development as a writer: Are all of your pronoun references clear? Are you straining for synonyms when repeated words would do? Do you ever repeat sentence structures to emphasize connections? Do you trust yourself to put collocation to work?

Transitions

A **transition** serves as a bridge to connect one paragraph, sentence, clause, or word with another. It also identifies the kind of connection by indicating to readers how the item preceding the transition relates to the one that follows it. Transitions help readers anticipate how the next paragraph or sentence will affect the meaning of what they have just read. There are three basic groups of transitions, based on the relationships they indicate: logical, temporal, and spatial.

Transitions emphasize logical relationships.

Transitions help readers follow the *logical relationships* within an argument. How such transitions work is illustrated in this tightly and passionately reasoned paragraph by James Baldwin:

The black man insists, by whatever means he finds at his disposal, that the white man cease to regard him as an exotic rarity and recognize him as a human being. This is a very charged and difficult moment, for there is a great deal of will power involved in the white man's naïveté. Most people are not naturally malicious, and the white man prefers to keep the black man at a certain human remove because it is easier for him thus to preserve his simplicity and to avoid being called to account for crimes committed by his forefathers, or his neighbors. He is inescapably aware, nevertheless, that he is in a better position in the world than black men are, nor can he quite put to death the suspicion that he is hated by black men therefore. He does not wish to be hated, neither does he wish to change places, and at this point in his uneasiness he can scarcely avoid having recourse to those legends which white men have created about black men, the most unusual effect of which is that the white man finds himself enmeshed, so to speak, in his own language which describes hell, as well as the attributes which lead one to hell, as being black as night.

—James Baldwin, "Stranger in the Village"

Transitions Showing Logical Relationships

- *To introduce another item in a series:* first . . . , second; in the second place; for one thing . . . , for another; next; then; furthermore; moreover; in addition; finally; last; also; similarly; besides; and; as well as

- *To introduce an illustration or other specification:* in particular; specifically; for instance; for example; that is; namely

- *To introduce a result or a cause:* consequently; as a result; hence; accordingly; thus; so; therefore; then; because; since; for

- *To introduce a restatement:* that is; in other words; in simpler terms; to put it differently

- *To introduce a conclusion or summary:* in conclusion; finally; all in all; evidently; clearly; actually; to sum up; altogether; of course

- *To introduce an opposing point:* but; however; yet; nevertheless; on the contrary; on the other hand; in contrast; still; neither; nor

- *To introduce a concession to an opposing view:* certainly; naturally; of course; it is true; to be sure; granted

- *To resume the original line of reasoning after a concession:* nonetheless; all the same; even though; still; nevertheless

Transitions can indicate a sequence in time.

In addition to showing logical connections, transitions may indicate **temporal relationships**—a sequence or progression in time—as this example illustrates:

That night, we drank tea and then vodka with lemon peel steeped in it. The four of us talked in Russian and English about mutual friends and American railroads and the Rolling Stones. Seryozha loves the Stones, and his face grew wistful as we spoke about their recent album, *Some Girls*. He played a tape of "Let It Bleed" over and over, until we could translate some difficult phrases for him; after that, he came out with the phrases at intervals during the evening, in a pretty decent imitation of Jagger's Cockney snarl. He was an adroit and oddly formal host, inconspicuously filling our teacups and politely urging us to eat bread and cheese and chocolate. While he talked to us, he teased Anya, calling her "Piglet," and she shook back her bangs and glowered at him. It was clear that theirs was a fiery relationship. After a while, we talked about ourselves. Anya told us about painting and printmaking and about how hard it was to buy supplies in Moscow. There had been something angry in her dark face since the beginning of the evening; I thought at first that it meant she didn't like Americans; but now I realized that it was a constant, barely suppressed rage at her own situation.

— ANDREA LEE, Russian Journal

Transitions to relationships of time

Transitions Showing Temporal Relationships

- *To indicate frequency:* frequently; hourly; often; occasionally; now and then; day after day; every so often; again and again

- *To indicate duration:* during; briefly; for a long time; minute by minute; while

- *To indicate a particular time:* now; then; at that time; in those days; last Sunday; next Christmas; in 2003; at the beginning of August; at six o'clock; first thing in the morning; two months ago; when

- *To indicate the beginning:* at first; in the beginning; since; before then

- *To indicate the middle:* in the meantime; meanwhile; as it was happening; at that moment; at the same time; simultaneously; next; then

- *To indicate the end and beyond:* eventually; finally; at last; in the end; subsequently; later; afterward

Transitions can indicate relationships in space.

Transitions showing **spatial relationships** orient readers to the objects in a scene, as illustrated in these paragraphs:

On Georgia 155, I crossed Troublesome Creek, then went through groves of pecan trees aligned one with the next like fenceposts. The pastures grew a green almost blue, and syrupy water the color of a dusty sunset filled the ponds. Around the farmhouses, from wires strung high above the ground, swayed gourds hollowed out for purple martins.

Transitions to show relationships in space

> The land rose again on the other side of the Chattahoochee River, and Highway 34 went to the ridgetops where long views over the hills opened in all directions. Here was the tail of the Appalachian backbone, its gradual descent to the Gulf. Near the Alabama stateline stood a couple of LAST CHANCE! bars.
>
> — WILLIAM LEAST HEAT MOON, *Blue Highways*

Transitions Showing Spatial Relationships

- *To indicate closeness:* close to; near; next to; alongside; adjacent to; facing
- *To indicate distance:* in the distance; far; beyond; away; there
- *To indicate direction:* up/down; sideways; along; across; to the right/left; in front of/behind; above/below; inside/outside; toward/away from

---

EXERCISE 13.9

Turn to William Akana's essay in Chapter 8 (pp. 358–63). Relying on the lists of transitions just given, underline the transitions in paragraphs 4–6. Consider how the transitions connect the ideas from sentence to sentence. Suggest any further transitions that could be added to make the relationships even clearer.

EXERCISE 13.10

Select a recent essay of your own. Choose at least three paragraphs, and underline the logical, temporal, and spatial transitions. Depending on the kind of writing you were doing, you may find few, if any, transitions in one category or another. For example, an essay speculating about causes may not include any spatial transitions; writing about a remembered event might not contain transitions showing logical relationships.

Consider how your transitions relate the ideas from sentence to sentence. Compare your transitions with those in the lists in this text. Do you find that you are making full use of the repertoire? Do you find gaps between any of your sentences that a well-chosen transition would close?

Headings and Subheadings

Headings and **subheadings** — brief phrases set off from the text in various ways — can provide visible cues to readers about the content and organization of a text. Headings can be distinguished from the text in numerous ways, including the selective use of capital letters, bold or italic type, or different sizes of type. To be most helpful to readers, headings should be phrased similarly and follow a predictable system.

Headings indicate sections and levels.

In this chapter, the headings in the section Paragraphing, beginning on p. 548, provide a good example of a system of headings that can readily be outlined:

Paragraphing
Paragraph cues.
Topic sentence strategies.
Announcing the Topic
Making a Transition
Positioning the Topic Sentence

Notice that in this example, the heading system has three levels. The first-level heading sits on its own line and is set in a large, red font; this heading stands out most visibly among the others. (It is one of five such headings in this chapter.) The second-level heading also sits on its own line but is set in a smaller font (and uses black type). The first of these second-level headings has no subheadings beneath it, while the second has three. These third-level headings, in black, do not sit on their own lines but run into the paragraph they introduce, as you can see if you turn back to pp. 549–51.

To learn more about distinguishing headings from surrounding text and about setting up systems of headings, see p. 644 in Chapter 21, Designing Documents.

All of these headings follow a parallel grammatical structure: "-ing" nouns at the first level; nouns at the second level ("cues" and "strategies"); and "-ing" nouns at the third level.

Headings are not common in all genres.

Headings may not be necessary in short essays: thesis statements, forecasting statements, well-positioned topic sentences, and transition sentences may be all the cues the reader needs. Headings are rare in some genres, such as essays about remembered events (Chapter 2) and essays profiling people and places (Chapter 3). Headings appear more frequently in such genres as concept explanations, finding-common-ground essays, position papers, public policy proposals, evaluations, and causal analyses (Chapters 4–9). Headings are required in résumés and lab reports (Chapter 22).

At least two headings are needed at each level.

Before dividing their essays into sections with headings and subheadings, writers need to make sure their discussion is detailed enough to support at least two headings at each level. The frequency and placement of headings depend entirely on the content and how it is divided and organized. Keep in mind that headings do not reduce the need for other cues to keep readers on track.

EXERCISE 13.11

Turn either to Jeremy Bernard's "Lost Innocence" in Chapter 5 or to Steve Boxer's "*LA Noire* Review" in Chapter 8, and survey that essay's system of headings. If you have not read the essay, read or skim it now. Consider how the headings help readers anticipate what is coming and how the argument is organized. Decide whether the headings substitute for or complement other cues for keeping readers on track. Consider whether the headings are grammatically parallel.

EXERCISE 13.12

Select one of your essays that might benefit from headings. Develop a system of headings, and insert them where appropriate. Be prepared to justify your headings in light of the discussion about headings in this section.

14

Narrating

Narrating is a basic strategy for representing action and events. As the term's Latin root, *gnarus* ("knowing"), implies, narrating helps people make sense of events they are involved in, as well as events they observe or read about. From earliest childhood, we use narrating to help us reflect on what has happened, to explain what is happening, and to imagine what could happen.

Narrating serves many different purposes. It can be used to report on events, present information, illustrate abstract ideas, support arguments, explain procedures, and entertain with stories. This chapter begins by describing and illustrating five basic narrating strategies, it includes two types of process narrative—explanatory and instructional—and it concludes with some sentence strategies you might use to get started drafting a narrative.

Narrating Strategies

Strategies such as calendar and clock time, temporal transitions, verb tense, narrative action, and dialogue give narrative its dynamic quality, the sense of events unfolding in time. They also help readers track the order in which the events occurred and understand how they relate to one another.

Use calendar and clock time to create a sequence of events.

One of the simplest ways of constructing a clear time sequence is to place events on a timeline, with years or precise dates and times clearly marked. Look, for example, at the excerpted portion of a timeline in Figure 14.1, which presents a series of events in the history of flight. A timeline is not itself a narrative, but it shares with narrative two basic elements: Events are presented in chronological order, and each event is "time-stamped," so that readers can clearly understand when events occurred in relation to one another.

Look now at a brief but fully developed narrative reconstructing the discovery of the bacterial cause of stomach ulcers. This narrative was written by Martin J. Blaser for *Scientific American,* a journal read primarily by nonspecialists interested in science. As you read, notice the same narrating strategies you saw in the timeline in Figure 14.1: sequencing events in chronological order and specifying when each event occurred:

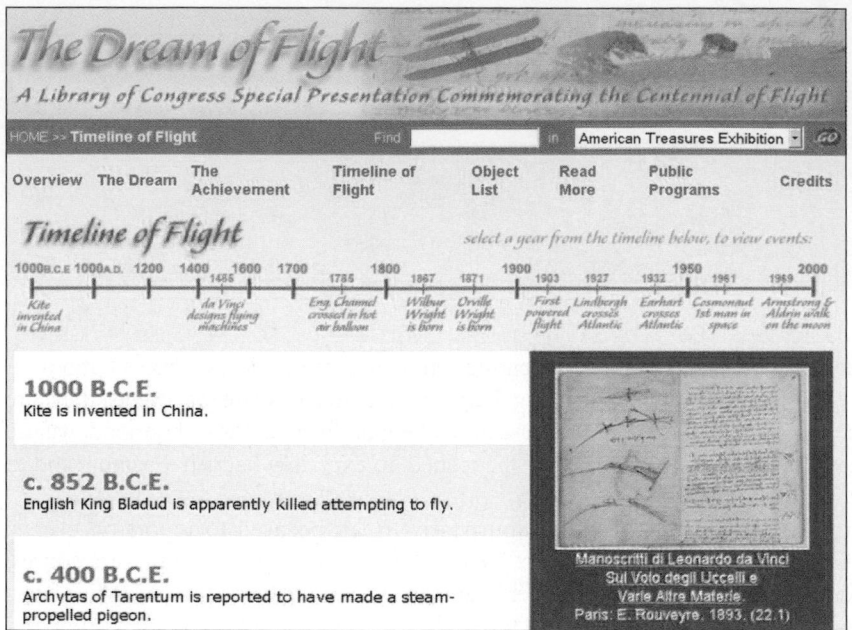

FIGURE 14.1 Chronology of events in the history of flight (Library of Congress)

Blaser cites specific years, months, days, and a holiday to convey the passage of time and indicate when each event occurred.

In 1979 J. Robin Warren, a pathologist at the Royal Perth Hospital in Australia, made a puzzling observation. As he examined tissue specimens from patients who had undergone stomach biopsies, he noticed that several samples had large numbers of curved and spiral-shaped bacteria. Ordinarily, stomach acid would destroy such organisms before they could settle in the stomach. But those Warren saw lay underneath the organ's thick mucus layer—a lining that coats the stomach's tissues and protects them from acid. Warren also noted that the bacteria were present only in tissue samples that were inflamed. Wondering whether the microbes might somehow be related to the irritation, he looked to the literature for clues and learned that German pathologists had witnessed similar organisms a century earlier. Because they could not grow the bacteria in culture, though, their findings had been ignored and then forgotten.

Warren, aided by an enthusiastic young trainee named Barry J. Marshall, also had difficulty growing the unknown bacteria in culture. He began his efforts in 1981. By April 1982 the two men had attempted to culture samples from 30-odd patients—all without success. Then the Easter holidays arrived. The hospital laboratory staff accidentally held some of the culture plates for five days instead of the usual two. On the fifth day, colonies emerged. The workers christened them *Campylobacter pyloridis* because they resembled pathogenic bacteria of the *Campylobacter* genus found in the intestinal tract. Early in 1983 Warren and

Marshall published their first report, and within months scientists around the world had isolated the bacteria.

—Martin J. Blaser, "The Bacteria behind Ulcers"

In addition to calendar time (years, months, days), writers sometimes also refer to clock time (hours, minutes, seconds). Here is a brief narrative from an essay profiling the emergency room at Bellevue Hospital in New York City:

> 9:05 p.m. An ambulance backs into the receiving bay, its red and yellow lights flashing in and out of the lobby. A split second later, the glass doors burst open as a nurse and an attendant roll a mobile stretcher into the lobby. When the nurse screams, "Emergency!" the lobby explodes with activity as the way is cleared to the trauma room. Doctors appear from nowhere and transfer the bloodied body of a black man to the treatment table. Within seconds his clothes are stripped away.
>
> — George Simpson, "The War Room at Bellevue"

The references to clock time establish the sequence and contribute to dramatic intensity.

EXERCISE 14.1

Skim Gabriel Thompson's "A Gringo in the Lettuce Fields" in Chapter 3, and underline the references to calendar and clock time. How do you think these time markers function in the narrative? What do they tell you about the impression Thompson wants to create about that period of his life?

Use temporal transitions to establish an action sequence.

Whereas writers tend to use calendar and clock time sparingly, they regularly use **temporal transitions** such as *when, at that moment, before,* and *while* to establish a clear sequence of actions in narrating onetime or recurring events.

For a more extensive list of transitions showing temporal relationships, see Chapter 13, p. 557.

Onetime Events   To see how temporal transitions work, let us look at the concluding paragraphs of a remembered-event essay in which Russell Baker recounts what happened after his final flight test, his last chance to become a pilot. The "he" Baker refers to is the flight check pilot, T. L. (nicknamed "Total Loss") Smith:

> Back at the flight line, when I'd cut the ignition, he climbed out and tramped back toward the ready room while I waited to sign the plane in. When I got there he was standing at a distance talking to my regular instructor. His talk was being illustrated with hand movements, as pilots' conversations always were, hands executing little loops and rolls in the air. After he did the falling-leaf motion with his hands, he pointed a finger at my instructor's chest, said something I couldn't hear, and trudged off. My instructor, who had flown only with the pre-hangover Baker, was slack-jawed when he approached me.
>
> "Smith just said you gave him the best check flight he's ever had in his life," he said. "What the hell did you do to him up there?"
>
> "I guess I just suddenly learned to fly," I said.
>
> — Russell Baker, "Smooth and Easy"

Baker uses temporal transitions to show what he and Smith were doing after the flight test.

Look closely at the two transitions in the first sentence. The word *when* presents actions in chronological order (first Baker stopped the plane, and then Smith got out). *While* performs a different function, showing that the next two actions occurred at the same time (Baker waited to sign in as the check pilot returned to the ready room). There is nothing complicated or unusual about this set of actions, but it would be hard to represent them in writing without temporal transitions.

Recurring Events   Temporal transitions also enable writers to narrate recurring events. In the following narrative by Monica Sone about her daily life in an internment camp for Japanese Americans during World War II, we can see how transitions (highlighted) help the writer represent actions she routinely performed:

> First I typed on pink, green, blue and white work sheets the hours put in by the 10,000 evacuees, then sorted and alphabetized these sheets, and stacked them away in shoe boxes. My job was excruciatingly dull, but under no circumstances did I want to leave it. The Administration Building was the only place which had modern plumbing and running hot and cold water; in the first few months and every morning, after I had typed for a decent hour, I slipped into the rest room and took a complete sponge bath with scalding hot water. During the remainder of the day, I slipped back into the rest room at inconspicuous intervals, took off my head scarf and wrestled with my scorched hair. I stood upside down over the basin of hot water, soaking my hair, combing, stretching and pulling at it.
>
> — MONICA SONE, "Camp Harmony"

> With the time marker *first*, Sone starts describing her typical work routine. In the third sentence, she tells of her surreptitious actions *in the first few months and every morning.*

EXERCISE 14.2

Turn to Anastasia Toufexis's, "Love: The Right Chemistry" in Chapter 4, pp. 129–31. Read paragraph 3, underlining the temporal transitions Toufexis uses to present the sequence of evolutionary changes that may have contributed to the development of romantic love. How important are these transitions in helping you follow her narrative?

Use verb tense to place actions in time.

In addition to time markers like calendar time and temporal transitions, writers use *verb tense* to represent action in writing and to help readers understand when each action occurred in relation to other actions.

Onetime Events   Writers typically use the past tense to represent onetime events that began and ended in the past. Here is a brief passage from a remembered-person essay by Amy Wu. In addition to the temporal transitions *once* and *when* in the opening sentence, which let readers know that this particular event occurred many years earlier, the writer also uses simple past-tense verbs (highlighted):

> Once, when I was 5 or 6, I interrupted my mother during a dinner with her friends and told her that I disliked the meal. My mother's eyes transformed from serene

> Wu uses the simple past tense to indicate that actions occurred in a linear sequence.

pools of blackness into stormy balls of fire. "Quiet!" she hissed, "do you not know that silent waters run deep?"

— AMY WU, "A Different Kind of Mother"

In the next example, by Chang-Rae Lee, we see how verb tense can be used to show more complicated relationships between past actions that occurred at different times in the past:

> When Uncle Chul amassed the war chest he needed to open the wholesale business he had hoped for, he moved away from New York.
>
> — CHANG-RAE LEE, "Uncle Chul Gets Rich"

Lee employs both the simple past tense (*amassed, needed, moved*) and the past perfect tense (*had hoped*).

You do not have to know that *amassed* is simple past tense and *had hoped* is past perfect tense to know that the uncle's hopes came before the money was amassed. In fact, most readers of English can understand complicated combinations of tenses without knowing their names.

Let us look at another verb tense combination used frequently in narrative: the simple past and the past progressive:

> When Dinah Washington was leaving with some friends, I overheard someone say she was on her way to the Savoy Ballroom where Lionel Hampton was appearing that night — she was then Hamp's vocalist.
>
> — MALCOLM X, *The Autobiography of Malcolm X*

Malcolm X uses the simple past tense (*overheard, was*) and the past progressive tense (*was leaving, was appearing*).

This combination of tenses plus the temporal transition *when* shows that the two actions occurred at the same time in the past. The first action ("Dinah Washington was leaving") continued during the period that the second action ("I overheard") occurred.

Occasionally, writers use the present instead of the past tense to narrate onetime events. Process narratives and profiles typically use the present tense to give the story a sense of "you are there" immediacy:

> Slowly, the dank barroom fills with grease-smeared mechanics from the truck stop up the road and farmers straight from the fields, the soles of their brogans thick with dirt clods. A few weary souls make their way over from the nearby sawmill. I sit alone at the bar, one empty bottle of Bud in front of me, a second in my hand. I drain the beer, order a third, and stare down at the pink juice spreading outward from a crumpled foil pouch and onto the bar.
>
> *I'm not leaving until I eat this thing,* I tell myself.
>
> — JOHN T. EDGE, "I'm Not Leaving Until I Eat This Thing"

Edge uses present-tense verbs to give readers a sense that they are in the room with him.

Recurring Events   Verb tense, usually combined with temporal transitions, can also help writers narrate events that occurred routinely:

> Many times, walking home from work, I would see some unknowing soul venture across that intersection against the light and then freeze in horror when he saw the cars ripping out of the tunnel toward him. . . . Suddenly, the human reflex would take over, and the pedestrian would jackknife first one way, then another, arms

Morris uses the helping verb *would* along with temporal transitions to show recurring actions.

flaying the empty air, and often the car would literally skim the man, brushing by him so close it would touch his coat or his tie. . . . On one occasion, feeling sorry for the person who had brushed against the speeding car, I hurried across the intersection after him to cheer him up a little. Catching up with him down by 32nd I said, "That was good legwork, sir. Excellent moves for a big man!" but the man looked at me with an empty expression in his eyes, and then moved away mechanically and trancelike, heading for the nearest bar.

— Willie Morris, *North toward Home*

Notice also that Morris shifts to the simple past tense when he moves from recurring actions to an action that occurred only once. He signals this shift with the temporal transition *on one occasion.*

EXERCISE 14.3

Turn to Jean Brandt's essay, "Calling Home" in Chapter 2, pp. 14–17. Read paragraph 3, and underline the verbs, beginning with *got, took, knew,* and *didn't want* in the first sentence. Brandt uses verb tense to reconstruct her actions and reflect on their effectiveness. Notice also how verb tense helps you follow the sequence of actions Brandt took.

Use narrative action for vivid sequences.

The narrating strategy we call **narrative action** uses active verbs and modifying phrases and clauses to present action vividly. Narrative action is especially suited to representing the intense, fast-moving, physical actions of sports events. The following example by George Plimpton shows how well narrative actions work to show what happened during a practice scrimmage. Plimpton participated in the Detroit Lions football training camp while writing a book profiling professional football. This is what he experienced:

> Since in the two preceding plays the concentration of the play had been elsewhere, I had felt alone with the flanker. Now, the whole heave of the play was toward me, flooding the zone not only with confused motion but noise—the quick stomp of feet, the creak of football gear, the strained grunts of effort, the faint *ah-ah-ah* of piston-stroke regularity, and the stiff calls of instruction, like exhalations. "Inside, inside! Take him inside!" someone shouted, tearing by me, his cleats thumping in the grass. A call—a parrot squawk—may have erupted from me. My feet splayed in hopeless confusion as Barr came directly toward me, feinting in one direction, and then stopping suddenly, drawing me toward him for the possibility of a buttonhook pass, and as I leaned almost off balance toward him, he turned and came on again, downfield, moving past me at high speed, leaving me poised on one leg, reaching for him, trying to grab at him despite the illegality, anything to keep him from getting by. But he was gone, and by the time I had turned to set out after him, he had ten yards on me, drawing away fast with his sprinter's run, his legs pinwheeling, the row of cleats flicking up a faint wake of dust behind.

> —George Plimpton, *Paper Lion*

Though Plimpton uses active verbs, he describes most of the action through modifying phrases and clauses.

By piling up narrative actions, Plimpton reconstructs for readers the texture and excitement of his experience on the football field. He uses the two most common kinds of modifiers that writers employ to present narrative action:

> ***Participial phrases:*** *tearing by me, stopping suddenly, moving past me at high speed*
>
> ***Absolute phrases:*** *his cleats thumping in the grass, his legs pinwheeling, the row of cleats flicking up a faint wake of dust behind*

Combined with vivid *sensory description* (*the creak of football gear, the strained grunts of effort, the faint* ah-ah-ah *of piston-stroke regularity*), these narrative actions re-create the sights and sounds of people in motion.

EXERCISE 14.4

Turn to paragraph 2 of Amanda Coyne's profile essay "The Long Good-Bye: Mother's Day in Federal Prison" in Chapter 3, pp. 75–78. Underline any narrative actions you find in this brief paragraph. Then reflect on how they help the reader envision the scene in the prison's visiting room.

EXERCISE 14.5

Record several brief—two- or three-minute—televised segments of a fast-moving sports competition, such as a soccer or basketball game. Then review the recording, and choose one segment to narrate using narrative actions to describe in detail what you see.

If you cannot record a televised game, narrate a live-action event (for example, people playing touch football, a dog catching a Frisbee, or a skateboarder or inline skater practicing a trick). As you watch the action, take detailed notes of what you see. Then, based on your notes, write a few sentences using narrative actions to describe the action you witnessed firsthand.

Use dialogue to dramatize events.

Dialogue is most often used in narratives that dramatize events. It reconstructs choice bits of conversation, rather than trying to present an accurate and complete record. In addition to showing people interacting, dialogue can give readers insight into character and relationships. Dialogue may be *quoted* to make it resemble the give-and-take of actual conversation, or it may be *summarized* to give readers the gist of what was said.

The following example from Gary Soto's *Living up the Street* shows how a narrative can combine quoted and summarized dialogue. In this passage, Soto recalls his first experience as a migrant worker in California's San Joaquin Valley:

> "Are you tired?" she asked.
>
> "No, but I got a sliver from the frame," I told her. I showed her the web of skin between my thumb and index finger. She wrinkled her forehead but said it was nothing.
>
> "How many trays did you do?"

Soto uses signal phrases with the first two quotations but not with the third, where it is clear who is speaking. The fourth quotation, "thirty-seven," is preceded by a narrative that tells what Soto did and thought before speaking and is followed by a summary of further conversation.

I looked straight ahead, not answering at first. I recounted in my mind the whole morning of bend, cut, pour again and again, before answering a feeble "thirty-seven." No elaboration, no detail. Without looking at me she told me how she had done field work in Texas and Michigan as a child. But I had a difficult time listening to her stories. I played with my grape knife, stabbing it into the ground, but stopped when Mother reminded me that I had better not lose it. I left the knife sticking up like a small, leafless plant. She then talked about school, the junior high I would be going to that fall, and then about Rick and Debra, how sorry they would be that they hadn't come out to pick grapes because they'd have no new clothes for the school year. She stopped talking when she peeked at her watch, a bandless one she kept in her pocket. She got up with an "Ay, Dios," and told me that we'd work until three, leaving me cutting figures in the sand with my knife and dreading the return to work.

— Gary Soto, "One Last Time"

For more on deciding when to quote, see Chapter 2, pp. 25, 38–39, 50, and Chapter 26, pp. 701–6.

Quoted dialogue is easy to recognize, of course, because of the quotation marks. Summarized dialogue can be harder to identify. In this case, however, Soto embeds *signal phrases* (*she told me* and *she then talked*) in his narrative. Summarizing leaves out information the writer decides readers do not need. In this passage about a remembered event, Soto has chosen to focus on his own feelings and thoughts rather than his mother's.

EXERCISE 14.6

Read the essay "A Gringo in the Lettuce Fields" in Chapter 3, and consider Gabriel Thompson's use of both direct quotation and summaries for reporting speech. When does Thompson choose to quote directly, and why might he have made this decision?

EXERCISE 14.7

If you wrote a remembered-event essay in Chapter 2, pp. 81–84 or wrote a bit of narrative in some other essay, reread your essay, looking for one example of each of the following narrating strategies: calendar and clock time, temporal transitions, past-tense verbs in onetime events, narrative action, and dialogue. Do not worry if you cannot find examples of all of the strategies. Pick one strategy you did use, and comment on what it contributes to your narrative.

Narrating a Process

Process narratives explain how something was done or instruct readers on how it could or should be done. Whether the purpose is explanatory or instructional, process narratives must clearly convey each necessary action and the exact order in which the actions occur.

Use process narratives to explain.

Explanatory process narratives often relate particular experiences or elucidate processes followed by machines or organizations. Let us begin with an excerpt from a remembered-event essay by Mary Mebane. She uses process narrative to let readers know what happened the first time she worked on an assembly line putting tobacco leaves on the conveyor belt:

> The job seemed easy enough as I picked up bundle after bundle of tobacco and put it on the belt, careful to turn the knot end toward me so that it would be placed right to go under the cutting machine. Gradually, as we worked up our tobacco, I had to bend more, for as we emptied the hogshead we had to stoop over to pick up the tobacco, then straighten up and put it on the belt just right. Then I discovered the hard part of the job: the belt kept moving at the same speed all the time and if the leaves were not placed on the belt at the same tempo there would be a big gap where your bundle should have been. So that meant that when you got down lower, you had to bend down, get the tobacco, straighten up fast, make sure it was placed knot end toward you, place it on the belt, and bend down again. Soon you were bending down, up; down, up; down, up. All along the line, heads were bobbing—down, up; down, up—until you finished the barrel. Then you could rest until the men brought you another one.
>
> —MARY MEBANE, "Summer Job"

Temporal transitions and simple past-tense verbs place the actions in time.

Here, narrative actions (*bend down, get the tobacco, straighten up fast*) become a series of staccato movements (*down, up; down, up; down, up*) that emphasize the speed and machinelike actions Mebane had to take to keep up with the conveyor belt.

The next example shows how a laser printer functions:

> To create a page, the computer sends signals to the printer, which shines a laser at a mirror system that scans across a charged drum. Whenever the beam strikes the drum, it removes the charge. The drum then rotates through a toner chamber filled with thermoplastic particles. The toner particles stick to the negatively charged areas of the drum in the pattern of characters, lines, or other elements the computer has transmitted and the laser beam mapped.
>
> Once the drum is coated with toner in the appropriate locations, a piece of paper is pulled across a so-called transfer corona wire, which imparts a positive electrical charge. The paper then passes across the toner-coated drum. The positive charge on the paper attracts the toner in the same position it occupied on the drum. The final phase of the process involves fusing the toner to the paper with a set of high-temperature rollers.
>
> —RICHARD GOLUB AND ERIC BRUS, *Almanac of Science and Technology*

Because the objects performing the action change from sentence to sentence, the writers must construct a clearly marked chain, introducing the object's name in one sentence and repeating the name or using a synonym in the next.

Like Mebane's process narrative, this one sequences the actions chronologically from beginning ("the computer sends signals to the printer") to end ("fusing the toner to the paper"). Temporal transitions (*then, once, then, final*), present-tense verbs, and narrative actions (*sends, shines, scans, strikes*) convey the passage of time and place the actions clearly in this chronological sequence.

Our last explanatory process narrative is a graphic sidebar of the type commonly used in magazines and books. This one comes from a *Newsweek* magazine feature on Matthew Scott, the third person ever to receive a hand transplant. "A Second Hand, A Second Chance," shown in Figure 14.2, illustrates the process narrative.

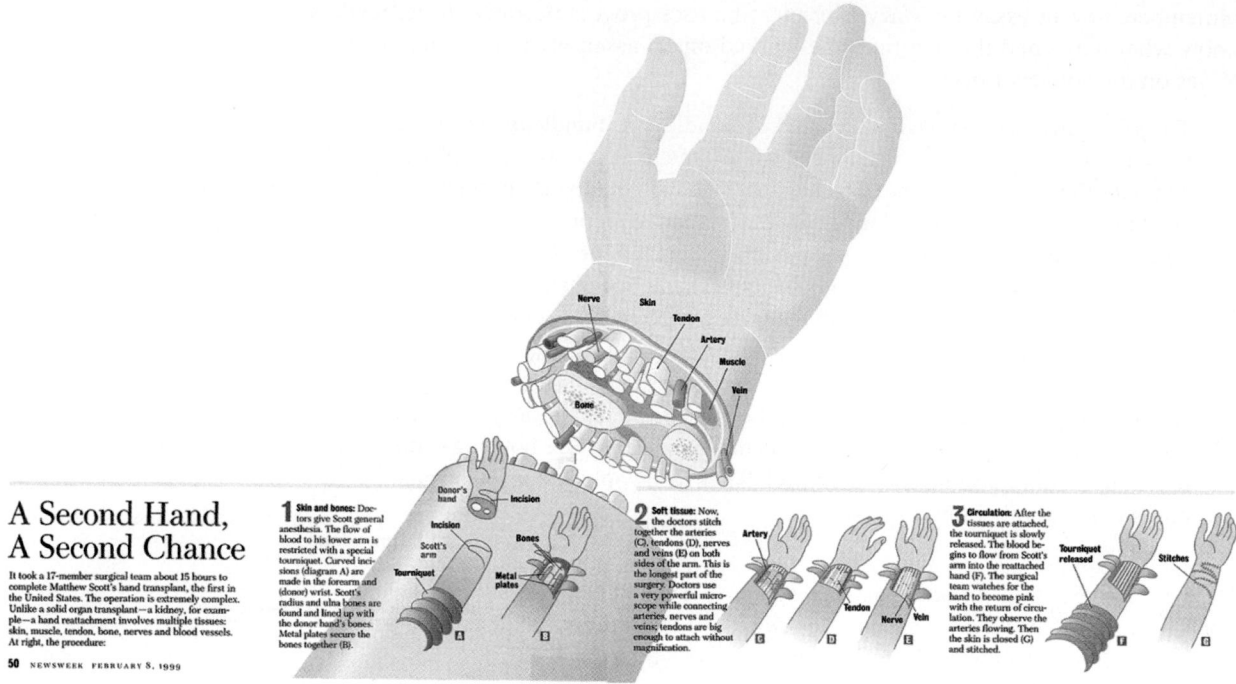

FIGURE 14.2 Presentation of an explanatory process
"A Second Hand, A Second Chance" was designed as a sidebar accompanying a longer article ("To Have and to Hold")
chronicling Matthew Scott's experience as the third person and first American to undergo hand transplant surgery.

Notice that this process narrative integrates writing with graphics. The procedure is divided into three distinct steps, with each step clearly numbered and labeled (*1. Skin and bones*). In each step, the figure captions refer to the graphics with letters—*Curved incisions (diagram A)*. The graphics themselves incorporate labels—*Donor's hand, Incision, Tourniquet released*. The writer uses some basic narrating strategies to present the actions and make clear the sequence in which they were taken: temporal transitions (*now, while, after*), present-tense verbs, and narrative actions, mostly in the form of active verbs (*secure, stitch, watches*). Much is left out, of course. Readers could not duplicate the procedure based on this narrative, but it does give *Newsweek* readers a clear sense of what was done during the fifteen hours of surgery.

EXERCISE 14.8

In Chapter 3, read paragraph 6 (p. 64) of Brian Cable's profile of a local mortuary, "The Last Stop." Here Cable narrates the process that the company follows once it has been notified of a client's death. As you read, look for and mark the narrating strategies discussed in this chapter that Cable uses. Then reflect on how well you think the narrative presents the actions and their sequence.

▪ Replacing Plugs ▪

Replacing a plug with terminal screws

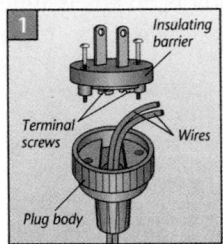 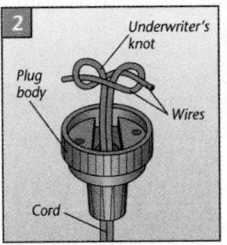 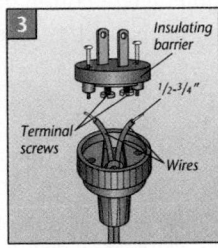 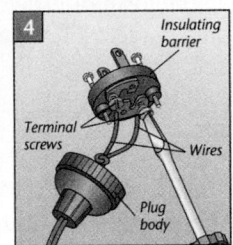

Unscrew and remove the new plug's insulating barrier. Using a utility knife, split the end of the cord to separate the wires; push the cord through the plug body.

Make two loops with the wires, pass the loose ends of the wires through the loops, and pull to form an Underwriter's knot (to prevent strain on connections).

Strip 1/2 to 3/4 inch of insulation off the wire ends, being careful not to nick the wires *(page 159)*. Unscrew the terminal screws to allow space for the wires.

Form loops on wires and wrap them clockwise three-quarters of the way around screws. Tighten the screws, trim excess wire, and reattach the barrier to the body.

Replacing three special types of plugs

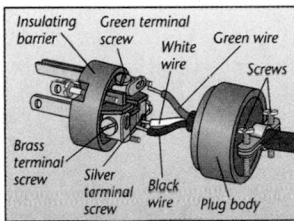 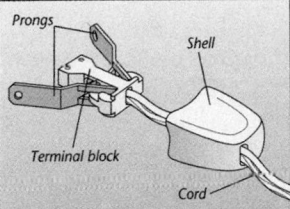 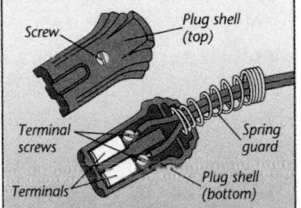

Three prong grounding plug. Unscrew the insulating barrier; push stripped wires through the plug body into the correct terminal slots. Tighten the terminal screws and reassemble the plug.

Self-connecting plug. Push the cord (don't strip it) through the shell and into the terminal block; squeeze the prongs together to grip the cord and slide into the shell.

Female appliance plug. Unscrew the plug shell; feed the cord through the spring guard. Strip the wire ends *(page 159)*, wrap them clockwise around the terminal screws, and tighten; reassemble the plug.

FIGURE 14.3 Replacing plugs

From *Home Repair Handbook* (Menlo Park, CA: Sunset, 1999), 156–57.

Use process narratives to instruct.

Unlike explanatory process narratives, **instructional process narratives** must include all of the information a reader needs to perform the procedure presented. Depending on the reader's experience, the writer might need to define technical terms, list tools that should be used, give background information, and account for alternatives or possible problems.

Figure 14.3 presents a detailed instructional process narrative from the Sunset *Home Repair Handbook,* which gives readers directions for replacing a broken plug in the graphics labeled "Replacing a plug with terminal screws" and "Replacing three special types of plugs." The first of these graphics includes four steps that are clearly numbered, illustrated, and narrated. Each step presents several actions to be taken, and its graphic shows what the plug should look like when these actions have been completed. We can identify the actions by looking at the verbs. Step 1 in "Replacing a plug with terminal screws," for example, instructs readers to take four separate actions, each signaled by the verb (italicized here): "*Unscrew* and *remove* the new plug's

For guidelines on designing your own documents, see Chapter 21.

insulating barrier. Using a utility knife, *split* the end of the cord to *separate* the wires; *push* the cord through the plug body." These are active verbs, and the sentences are in the form of clear and efficient commands. The anonymous authors do not assume that readers know very much, as they label every element of each drawing, including the screws.

EXERCISE 14.9

Write a one- to two-page instructional process narrative that tells readers how to make a peanut butter and jelly sandwich or perform some other equally simple procedure, such as logging on to the Internet, hemming a pair of pants, potting a plant, or filling a fountain pen. Address your narrative to readers who have never done the procedure before.

Sentence Strategies for Narration

When writing about a remembered event, writers often struggle to convey the event's significance. If you are writing about a remembered event, why not try out some of these sentence strategies to help you capture your experience in words, first for yourself and then for your readers? You will probably want to rework these sentences to make them your own, but they may give you a jumping-off point for articulating your thoughts.

To Think about Your Main Point

▶ When readers finish my story, they will better appreciate how [society and culture/an individual person/the human condition] _____ .

To Explore the Significance of Your Story's Conflict

▶ During this event, I found myself locked in conflict with _____ . [Elaborate.]

▶ Although I struggled with [a factor outside myself], I also was _____ . [Elaborate.]

▶ I kept wondering, should I _____ or should I _____ ? [Elaborate.]

To Explore How You Felt at the Time

▶ As the event started [or during or right after the event], I felt _____ and _____ . I hoped others would think of me as _____ .

▶ I showed or expressed these feelings by _____ .

To Explore Your Present Perspective

▶ My feelings since the event [have/have not] changed: _____ . [Elaborate on how your feelings have/have not changed.]

▶ At the time, I had been going through _____ , which may have affected my experience by _____ .

▶ Looking back at the event now, I realize I was probably trying to ...., though I didn't appreciate that fact at the time.

To Alert Readers to What You Were Thinking or Feeling

▶ I felt ....

▶ The thought of .... made me feel ....

▶ The [terror/exhilaration/excitement] was ....

To Make Clear Who Is Speaking and to Convey Their Attitude or Position

▶ He said, " ...."

▶ She asked, " .... ?"

▶ " .... ," he complained.

▶ " .... ," she snapped.

To Sketch Out the Backstory (Exposition) Readers Need to Understand What Happened and Why It Mattered

▶ In [year], while I was .... ing in [location], ...

▶ John knew all about .... because he was [a/an] .... ologist, an expert on ....

▶ In past years, I had previously ....

15

Describing

The word *describing* comes from the Latin *describere,* meaning "to sketch" or "to copy in writing." Written descriptions help readers imagine what is being described. Vivid description creates an intense, distinctive image, one that seems to bring the words on the page to life. Good description can also be evocative, calling up memories or suggesting feelings associated with the subject being described. Writers can use description for many purposes: to give readers an impression of a person or place, to illustrate abstract ideas, to make information memorable, or to support an argument. This chapter presents the three basic descriptive techniques of *naming, detailing,* and *comparing;* it surveys the words writers typically use to evoke vivid sense impressions; it examines how writers use description to create a dominant impression; and it provides some sentence strategies you might use to get started drafting a description.

Naming

For more on naming, see Chapter 2, pp. 12–13, 40–41.

Naming calls readers' attention to observable features of the subject being described. To describe a room, for example, you might name objects you see as you look around, such as a bed, pillows, blankets, a dresser, clothes, books, a CD player, and CDs. These objects suggest what kind of room it is and begin to give readers an impression of what it is like to be in this particular room.

Look closely at the following passage describing a weasel that the writer, Annie Dillard, encountered in the woods:

> He was ten inches long, thin as a curve, a muscled ribbon, brown as fruitwood, soft-furred, alert. His face was fierce, small and pointed as a lizard's; he would have made a good arrowhead. There was just a dot of chin, maybe two brown hairs' worth, and then the pure white fur began that spread down his underside. He had two black eyes I didn't see, any more than you see a window.
>
> — ANNIE DILLARD, *Teaching a Stone to Talk*

With these names, readers can begin to put together a mental image of the animal Dillard is describing. She uses simple, everyday nouns, like *chin,* to identify the weasel's features, not technical words like *maxilla* or *mandible.* The piling up of simple, concrete nouns helps readers imagine what the weasel looked like to Dillard.

Although writers most commonly name what they see, sight is not the only sense contributing to vivid descriptions, as in the following passage:

> When the sun fell across the great white pile of the new Telephone Company building, you could smell the stucco burning as you passed; then some liquid sweetness that came to me from deep in the rings of the freshly cut lumber stacked in the yards, and the fresh plaster and paint on the brand-new storefronts. Rawness, sunshiny rawness down the end streets of the city, as I thought of them then — the hot ash-laden stink of the refuse dumps in my nostrils and the only sound at noon the resonant metal plunk of a tin can I kicked ahead of me as I went my way.
>
> — Alfred Kazin, *A Walker in the City*

Kazin names smells, sounds, tastes, and tactile qualities.

EXERCISE 15.1

Go to a place where you can sit for a while and observe the scene. It might be a landscape or a cityscape, indoors or outdoors, crowded or solitary. For five minutes, list everything in the scene that you can name using nouns. (A simple way to test if a word is a noun is to see if you can put the word *the, a,* or *an* in front of it.) Remember, you can name objects you see (*dog, hydrant*) as well as impressions such as smells or sounds you experience at the place (*stench, hiss*).

Then write a page or so that describes the scene for someone who is not there with you. Write for readers who have never been to this particular place to let them know what to expect when they get there.

EXERCISE 15.2

Turn to Annie Dillard's "An American Childhood" in Chapter 2, pp. 18–19 . Read paragraphs 12 and 13, and underline the names that Dillard uses to describe the circuitous route she runs while the stranger is chasing her. Begin underlining with the words *house, path, tree,* and *bank* in the opening sentence. How do you think the amount of naming Dillard does contributes to the description's vividness — measured by your ability to imagine the chase scene?

Detailing

Naming identifies the notable features of the subject being described; **detailing** makes the features more specific or particularized. Naming answers the questions What is it? and What are its parts or features? Detailing answers questions like these:

For more on detailing, see Chapter 2, pp. 12–14, 39–42.

- What size is it?
- How many are there?
- What is it made of?
- Where is it located?
- What is its condition?
- How is it used?

- Where does it come from?
- What is its effect?
- What is its value?

To add details to names, add modifiers—adjectives and adverbs, phrases and clauses. **Modifiers** make nouns more specific by supplying additional information. Notice how many modifying details Dillard provides in her description of the weasel:

Dillard provides details about size, shape, color, and texture, as well as details that convey subjective information.

> He was ten inches long, thin as a curve, a muscled ribbon, brown as fruitwood, soft-furred, alert. His face was fierce, small and pointed as a lizard's; he would have made a good arrowhead. There was just a dot of chin, maybe two brown hairs' worth, and then the pure white fur began that spread down his underside. He had two black eyes I didn't see, any more than you see a window.
>
> —ANNIE DILLARD, *Teaching a Stone to Talk*

Dillard's details provide information that shows readers what this specific weasel looked like. Other details convey subjective information about Dillard's thoughts and feelings during the encounter. For example, when Dillard writes that the weasel's "face was fierce," she is making a judgment. She uses details like this to make readers see the weasel as a wild animal, not a soft and cuddly pet.

In describing people, writers often combine physical details with details characterizing aspects of the individual's personality. These characterizations or evaluations let readers know something about the writer's thoughts about the person, as the following examples illustrate:

Walker uses both physical description (*fat*) and evaluative details (*funny, beautiful*) to express her feelings about her father. Welty combines physical detail (*higharched bony nose*) with subjective judgment (*bearing-down authority*) to help readers understand her fear.

> My father, a fat, funny man with beautiful eyes and a subversive wit . . .
>
> —ALICE WALKER, "Beauty: When the Other Dancer Is the Self"

> I was afraid of her higharched bony nose, her eyebrows lifted in half-circles above her hooded, brilliant eyes, and of the Kentucky R's in her speech, and the long steps she took in her hightop shoes. I did nothing but fear her bearing-down authority.
>
> —EUDORA WELTY, "Miss Duling"

Sometimes physical details alone can be enough to symbolize a person's character or the writer's feelings toward that person, as in the following passage:

The physical details suggest a powerful and threatening character.

> Rick was not a friendly looking man. He wore only swim trunks, and his short, powerful legs rose up to meet a bulging torso. His big belly was solid. His shoulders, as if to offset his front-heaviness, were thrown back, creating a deep crease of excess muscle from his sides around the small of his back, a crease like a huge frown. His arms were crossed, two medieval maces placed carefully on their racks, ready to be swung at any moment. His round cheeks and chin were darkened by traces of black whiskers. His hair was sparse. Huge, black, mirrored sunglasses replaced his eyes. Below his prominent nose was a thin, sinister mustache. I couldn't believe this menacing-looking man was the legendary jovial Rick.
>
> —BRAD BENIOFF, "Rick"

EXERCISE 15.3

Return to the description you wrote in Exercise 15.1. Put brackets around the details you used to help describe the scene. Add any other details you think of now — details that indicate size, quantity, makeup, location, condition, use, source, effect, value, or any other quality that would make the description more specific and particularized for readers. Then reread your description. What do you think the detailing contributes to the description you wrote?

EXERCISE 15.4

Look again at paragraphs 12 and 13 of Annie Dillard's essay in Chapter 2, pp. 18–19. In Exercise 15.2, you underlined the names Dillard used. Now put brackets around the details. You might begin, for example, with the modifiers *yellow* and *backyard*. How do you think detailing contributes to Dillard's description? How do these details help you imagine Dillard's experience of the chase?

EXERCISE 15.5

Turn to paragraphs 10 and 13 of Amanda Coyne's essay in Chapter 3, pp. 75–78. Read and put brackets around the words that detail the description of Stephanie and her son, Ellie. If you have not read the entire essay, read it now, and consider how Coyne uses these contrasting descriptions of the inmate and her son to emphasize her main point in the essay.

Comparing

In addition to naming and detailing, writers sometimes use *comparing* to make their description more vivid for readers. Look again at Annie Dillard's description of a weasel, paying attention this time to the comparisons:

> He was ten inches long, thin as a curve, a muscled ribbon, brown as fruitwood, soft-furred, alert. His face was fierce, small and pointed as a lizard's; he would have made a good arrowhead. There was just a dot of chin, maybe two brown hairs' worth, and then the pure white fur began that spread down his underside. He had two black eyes I didn't see, any more than you see a window.
>
> — ANNIE DILLARD, *Teaching a Stone to Talk*

Dillard uses similes and metaphors to describe the weasel.

Dillard uses two kinds of comparison in this description: simile and metaphor, both of which point out similarities in things that are essentially dissimilar. A **simile** expresses the similarity directly by using the words *like* or *as* to announce the comparison. A **metaphor,** by contrast, is an implicit comparison in which one thing is described as though it were the other.

Similes and metaphors can enhance the vividness of a description by giving readers additional information to help them picture the subject. For example, Dillard uses the word *thin* to detail the weasel's body shape. But *thin* is a relative term, leading readers to wonder, how thin? Dillard gives readers two images for comparison, a curve and a ribbon, to help them construct a fuller mental image of the weasel.

Comparing can also convey to readers what the writer feels about the subject. The following comparison from Brad Benioff's description of Coach Rick suggests the writer's feelings: "His arms were crossed, two medieval maces placed carefully on their racks, ready to be swung at any moment." Sometimes the similes or metaphors writers use are suggestive but hard to pin down. What do you think Dillard means, for example, by comparing the weasel's eyes to a window: "He had two black eyes I didn't see, any more than you see a window"?

EXERCISE 15.6

Return to the description you wrote in Exercise 15.1 and may have added to in Exercise 15.3. Reread it, and mark any comparing you did. Try to add one or two similes or metaphors to your description. How do you think your use of comparing may help readers imagine the subject or get a sense of what you feel about it?

Using Sensory Description

When writers use **sensory description** to describe animals, people, or scenes, they usually rely on the sense of sight more than the other senses. In general, our vocabulary for reporting what we see is larger and more varied than our vocabulary for reporting other sense impressions. Nevertheless, writers can detail the qualities and attributes of nonvisual sensations — the loudness or tinniness or rumble of an engine, for instance. They can also use comparing to help readers imagine what something sounds, feels, smells, or tastes like.

Describe what you saw.

When people describe what they see, they identify the objects in their field of vision. Here are two brief examples of visual description:

> On Christmas Eve I saw that my mother had outdone herself in creating a strange menu. She was pulling black veins out of the backs of fleshy prawns. The kitchen was littered with appalling mounds of raw food: A slimy rock cod with bulging eyes that pleaded not to be thrown into a pan of hot oil. Tofu, which looked like stacked wedges of rubbery white sponges. A bowl soaking dried fungus back to life. A plate of squid, their backs crisscrossed with knife markings so they resembled bicycle tires.
>
> — Amy Tan, "Fish Cheeks"

Tan uses visual details to depict her mother's kitchen.

> She was thirty-four. She wore a white skirt and yellow sweater and a thin gold necklace, which she held in her fingers, as if holding her own reins, while waiting

Kidder uses visual details to describe Mrs. Zajac, a grade school teacher.

for children to answer. Her hair was black with a hint of Irish red. It was cut short to the tops of her ears, and swept back like a pair of folded wings. She had a delicate cleft chin, and she was short — the children's chairs would have fit her. . . . Her hands kept very busy. They sliced the air and made karate chops to mark off boundaries. They extended straight out like a traffic cop's, halting illegal maneuvers yet to be perpetrated. When they rested momentarily on her hips, her hands looked as if they were in holsters.

— TRACY KIDDER, *Among Schoolchildren*

EXERCISE 15.7

Write a few sentences describing a teacher, friend, or family member. Do not rely on memory for this exercise; describe someone who is before you as you write so that you can describe in detail what you see. Later, when you are alone, reread what you have written, and make any changes you think will help make this visual description more vivid for your readers.

Describe what you heard.

In reporting auditory impressions, writers seldom name sounds without also specifying what the sounds come from: the murmur of a voice, the rustle of the wind, the squeak of a hinge, the sputter of an engine. *Onomatopoeia* is the term for names of sounds that echo the sounds themselves: *squeak, murmur, hiss, boom, plink, tinkle, twang, jangle, rasp, chirr.* Sometimes writers make up words like *sweesh* and *cara-wong* to imitate sounds they wish to describe. Qualitative words like *powerful* and *rich* as well as relative terms like *loud* and *low* often specify sounds further. For detailing sounds, writers sometimes use the technique called *synesthesia,* applying words commonly used to describe one sense to another, such as describing sounds as *sharp* and *soft;* they sometimes also use simile or metaphor to compare one sound to another.

To write about the sounds along Manhattan's Canal Street, Ian Frazier uses many of these describing and naming techniques:

> The traffic on Canal Street never stops. It is a high-energy current jumping constantly between the poles of Brooklyn and New Jersey. It hates to have its flow pinched in the density of Manhattan, hates to stop at intersections. Along Canal Street, it moans and screams. Worn brake shoes of semitrucks go "Ooohhhh nooohhhh" at stoplights, and the sound echoes in the canyons of warehouses and Chinatown tenements. People lean on their horns from one end of Canal Street to the other. They'll honk nonstop for ten minutes at a time, until the horns get tired and out of breath. They'll try different combinations: shave-and-a-hair-cut, long-long-long, short-short-short-long. Some people have musical car horns; a person purchasing a musical car horn seems to be limited to a choice of four tunes — "La Cucaracha," "Theme from *The Godfather,*" "Dixie," and "Hava Nagila."
>
> — IAN FRAZIER, "Canal Street"

Frazier uses metaphor, onomatopoeia, and other vivid detail.

EXERCISE 15.8

Find a noisy spot — a restaurant, a football game, a nursery school, a laundry room — where you can perch for about half an hour. Listen attentively to the sounds of the place, and make notes about what you hear. Then write a page or so describing the place through its sounds.

Describe what you smelled.

The English language has a meager stock of words to express the olfactory sense. In addition to the word *smell,* fewer than a dozen commonly used nouns name this sensation: *odor, scent, vapor, fume, aroma, fragrance, perfume, bouquet, stench,* and *stink.* Although there are other, rarer words like *fetor* and *effluvium,* few writers use them, probably for fear that their readers will not know them. Few verbs describe receiving or sending odors — *smell, sniff, waft* — but a fair number of detailing adjectives are available: *redolent, pungent, aromatic, perfumed, stinking, musty, rancid, putrid, rank, fetid, malodorous, foul, acrid, sweet,* and *cloying.*

Here is an example of how Amanda Coyne, in her essay in Chapter 3, uses smell in a description:

> Occasionally, a mother will pick up her present and bring it to her nose when one of the bearers of the single flower — her child — asks if she likes it. . . . But most of what is being smelled today is the children themselves. While the other adults are plunking coins into the vending machines, the mothers take deep whiffs from the backs of their children's necks, or kiss and smell the backs of their knees, or take off their shoes and tickle their feet and then pull them close to their noses. They hold them tight and take in their own second scent — the scent assuring them that these are still their children and that they still belong to them.
>
> — AMANDA COYNE, "The Long Good-Bye: Mother's Day in Federal Prison"

In the margin: *Coyne uses smell to describe "convict moms" and their children in a prison visiting room.*

In addition to using *smell* as a verb, Coyne describes the repeated action of bringing the object being smelled to the nose, an act that not only signifies the process of smelling but also underscores its intimacy. To further emphasize intimacy, Coyne connects smelling with other intimate acts of kissing, tickling, pulling close, and holding tight.

Because she is not describing her own experience of smell, Coyne does not try to find words to evoke the effect the odor has on her. In the next passage, however, Frank Conroy uses comparing in addition to naming and detailing to describe how the smell of flowers affected him:

> The perfume of the flowers rushed into my brain. A lush aroma, thick with sweetness, thick as blood, and spiced with the clear acid of tropical greenery.
>
> — FRANK CONROY, *Stop-Time*

Naming the objects from which smells come can also be very suggestive:

> The odor of these houses was different, full of fragrances, sweet and nauseating. On 105th Street the smells were of fried lard, of beans and car fumes, of factory

smoke and home-made brew out of backyard stills. There were chicken smells and goat smells in grassless yards filled with engine parts and wire and wood planks, cracked and sprinkled with rusty nails. These were the familiar aromas: the funky earth, animal and mechanical smells which were absent from the homes my mother cleaned.

— Luis J. Rodriguez, *Always Running: Gang Days in L.A.*

EXERCISE 15.9

Turn to John T. Edge's "I'm Not Leaving Until I Eat This Thing" in Chapter 3 (pp. 69–71), and read paragraph 16. Underline the words describing the sense of smell. How do you think this bit of sensory description helps readers imagine the scene?

EXERCISE 15.10

Choose a place with noticeable, distinctive smells where you can stay for ten or fifteen minutes. You may choose an eating place (a cafeteria, a doughnut shop), a place where something is being manufactured (a sawmill, a bakery), or some other place that has strong, identifiable odors (a fishing dock, a garden, a locker room). While you are there, take notes on what you smell, and then write a page or so describing the place primarily through its smells.

Describe tactile sensations.

Relatively few nouns and verbs name tactile sensations besides words like *touch, feel, tickle, brush, scratch, sting, itch,* and *tingle.* Probably as a consequence, writers describing the sense of touch tend not to name the sensation directly or even to report the act of feeling. Nevertheless, a large stock of words describes temperature (*hot, warm, mild, tepid, cold, arctic*), moisture content (*wet, dry, sticky, oily, greasy, moist, crisp*), texture (*gritty, silky, smooth, crinkled, coarse, soft, leathery*), and weight (*heavy, light, ponderous, buoyant, feathery*). Read the following passages with an eye for descriptions of touch:

> A small slab of roughly finished concrete offered a place to stand opposite a square of tar from which a splintered tee protruded.
>
> — William Rintoul, "Breaking One Hundred"

> The earth was moldy, a dense clay. No sun had fallen here for over two centuries. I climbed over the brick retaining wall and crawled toward the sound of the kitten. As I neared, as it sensed my presence was too large to be its mother, it went silent and scrabbled away from the reach of my hand. I brushed fur, though, and that slight warmth filled me with what must have been a mad calm because when the creature squeezed into a bearing wall of piled stones, I inched forward on my stomach.
>
> — Louise Erdrich, "Beneath the House"

Here is an example of a writer recalling a childish fantasy of aggression toward her younger sister. Notice the tactile description she uses:

> She was baby-soft. I thought that I could put my thumb on her nose and push it bonelessly in, indent her face. I could poke dimples into her cheeks. I could work her face around like dough.
>
> — MAXINE HONG KINGSTON, "The Quiet Girl"

EXERCISE 15.11

Do something with your hands, and then write a sentence or two describing the experience of touch. For example, you might pet a dog, dig a hole and put a plant into the earth, make a pizza, sculpt with clay, bathe a baby, or scrub a floor. As you write, notice the words you consider using to describe temperature, moisture content, texture, weight, or any other tactile quality.

EXERCISE 15.12

Turn to Brian Cable's "The Last Stop" in Chapter 3, and read the last paragraph. Underline the language that describes the sense of touch. What does this detail add to your understanding of the scene, and why might Cable have chosen to save it for the last paragraph of his profile?

Describe flavors.

Other than *taste, savor,* and *flavor,* few words name gustatory sensations directly. Certain words do distinguish among types of tastes — *sweet (saccharine, sugary, cloying); sour (acidic, tart); bitter (acrid, biting); salty (briny, brackish)* — and several other words describe specific tastes (*piquant, spicy, pungent, peppery, savory, toothsome*).

In the following passage, M. F. K. Fisher describes the surprisingly "delicious" taste of tar:

> Tar with some dust in it was perhaps even more delicious than dirty chips from the iceman's wagon, largely because if we worked up enough body heat and had the right amount of spit we could keep it melted so that it acted almost like chewing gum, which was forbidden to us as vulgar and bad for the teeth and in general to be shunned. Tar was better than anything ever put out by Wrigley and Beechnut, anyway. It had a high, bright taste. It tasted the way it smelled, but better.
>
> — M. F. K. FISHER, "Prejudice, Hate, and the First World War"

Fisher uses suggestive words not typically associated with taste.

Fisher tries to evoke the sense of taste by comparing tar that acted like chewing gum to actual Wrigley and Beechnut chewing gum. More surprisingly, she compares the taste of tar to its smell.

Ernest Hemingway, in a more conventional passage, tries to describe taste primarily by naming the foods he consumed and giving details that indicate the intensity and quality of the tastes:

As I ate the oysters with their strong taste of the sea and their faint metallic taste that the cold wine washed away, leaving only the sea taste and the succulent texture, and as I drank their cold liquid from each shell and washed it down with the crisp taste of the wine, I lost the empty feeling and began to be happy and to make plans.

— ERNEST HEMINGWAY, A Moveable Feast

> Hemingway combines taste and touch (the feel of the food in his mouth).

Writers often use words like *juicy, chewy,* and *chunky* to evoke both the taste and the feel of food in the mouth.

EXERCISE 15.13

In the manner of Hemingway, take notes as you eat a particular food or an entire meal. Then write a few sentences describing the tastes you experienced.

EXERCISE 15.14

Turn to John T. Edge's "I'm Not Leaving Until I Eat This Thing" in Chapter 3 (pp. 69–71), an essay about pickled pig's lips. Read paragraphs 7 and 18, underlining any language that describes or suggests the sense of taste. How well does this sensory description help you participate in the writer's experience?

Creating a Dominant Impression

The most effective description creates a **dominant impression,** a mood or an atmosphere that reinforces the writer's purpose. Naming, detailing, comparing, and sensory language — all the choices about what to include and what to call things — come together to create this effect, as the following passage by Mary McCarthy illustrates. Notice that McCarthy directly states the idea she is trying to convey in the last sentence of the paragraph:

> Whenever we children came to stay at my grandmother's house, we were put to sleep in the sewing room, a bleak, shabby, utilitarian rectangle, more office than bedroom, more attic than office, that played to the hierarchy of chambers the role of a poor relation. It was a room seldom entered by the other members of the family, seldom swept by the maid, a room without pride; the old sewing machine, some cast-off chairs, a shadeless lamp, rolls of wrapping paper, piles of pins, and remnants of material united with the iron folding cots put out for our use and the bare floor boards to give an impression of intense and ruthless temporality. Thin, white spreads, of the kind used in hospitals and charity institutions, and naked blinds at the windows reminded us of our orphaned condition and of the ephemeral character of our visit; there was nothing here to encourage us to consider this our home.

— MARY MCCARTHY, Memories of a Catholic Girlhood

> McCarthy names objects and provides details that support the overall impression she seeks to convey.

Everything in the room made McCarthy and her brothers feel unwanted, discarded, orphaned. The room itself is described in terms applicable to the children: Like them, it "played to the hierarchy of chambers the role of a poor relation."

Sometimes writers comment directly in a description, as McCarthy does. Often, however, writers want description to speak for itself, as in the following example:

Orwell uses language that *shows* objects and details that convey an impression.

Hanging from the ceiling there was a heavy glass chandelier on which the dust was so thick that it was like fur. And covering most of one wall there was a huge hideous piece of junk, something between a sideboard and a hall-stand, with lots of carving and little drawers and strips of looking-glass, and there was a once-gaudy carpet ringed by the slop-pails of years, and two gilt chairs with burst seats, and one of those old-fashioned armchairs which you slide off when you try to sit on them. The room had been turned into a bedroom by thrusting four squalid beds in among the wreckage.

— GEORGE ORWELL, *The Road to Wigan Pier*

EXERCISE 15.15

Turn to Amanda Coyne's essay in Chapter 3 (pp. 75–78) and read paragraph 3. What seems to you to be the dominant impression of this description? What do you think contributes most to this impression?

Sentence Strategies for Description

Effective descriptions not only create a distinctive image but also contribute to the overall impression the writer wants to convey. To create this overall impression, writers must determine not only what is most relevant, important, or interesting about what they are describing but also what role they are playing. The sentence strategies that follow may provide you with a jumping-off point for writing descriptions that are both powerful and effective. To make these sentences your own, though, you may need to rework them as you revise.

To Reflect on Your Observations

▶ The most interesting aspect of the subject is _____, because _____.

▶ Although my visit confirmed that _____, I was surprised to learn that _____.

▶ My dominant impression of the subject is _____.

To Describe as a Participant

▶ As I tried to _____ like the _____, I was surprised to find that _____.

▶ I picked up the _____. It felt like _____ to the touch, and it [smelled/tasted/sounded] like _____.

▶ After _____ [hours/minutes/days] of _____, I felt like _____ .

▶ I interrupted _____ as [he/she] _____ to ask why _____ . I can't be sure whether that interruption led to _____ , but I think _____ .

To Describe as a Spectator

▶ On the other side of _____ , [a/an] _____ [appeared/came into view/did something].

▶ [Person] talked as he _____ . "_____ ," he said. "_____ ."

▶ _____ ing [at/down/along/with/on] _____ , [person] remarked that _____ .

▶ The _____ is [impressive/strange/easy to miss, etc.], with [its/his/her] _____ , _____ , and _____ .

▶ _____ makes [person] angry. [She/he] says it's because _____ : "_____ ."

▶ Although [subject] [tries to/pretends to/has made progress toward] _____ , [overall/ for the most part/primarily] [he/she/it] _____ .

To Describe as a Participant Observing Other Participants

▶ [Above/around/before] me, _____ [activity] happened. I tried to _____ , and found it _____ . "_____ ," [person] said, watching. "_____ ."

▶ Although [subject] clearly seemed _____ , I couldn't [shake the feeling that/ignore/ stop thinking about] _____ .

16

Defining

Defining is an essential strategy for all writing. Autobiographers, for example, must occasionally define objects, conditions, events, and activities for readers likely to be unfamiliar with particular terms, as in the following example:

Gray defines *psoriasis* in this example of autobiographical writing.

> My father's hands are grotesque. He suffers from psoriasis, a chronic skin disease that covers his massive, thick hands with scaly, reddish patches that periodically flake off, sending tiny pieces of dead skin sailing to the ground.
>
> — Jan Gray, "Father"

When writers share information or explain how to do something, they must often define important terms for readers who are unfamiliar with the subject, as in this example:

Olson defines *shifting baselines* in this example of explanatory writing.

> Shifting baselines are the chronic, slow, hard-to-notice changes in things, from the disappearance of birds and frogs in the countryside to the increased drive time from L.A. to San Diego.
>
> — Randy Olson, "Shifting Baselines: Slow-Motion Disaster below the Waves"

To convince readers of a position or an evaluation or to move them to act on a proposal, a writer must often define concepts important to an argument:

Ehrenreich defines *extreme poverty* in this example of argument.

> You would come across news of a study showing that the percentage of Wisconsin food-stamp families in "extreme poverty" — defined as less than 50 percent of the federal poverty line — has tripled in the last decade to more than 30 percent.
>
> — Barbara Ehrenreich, *Nickel and Dimed*

As these examples illustrate, there are many kinds of definitions and many forms that they can take. Some published essays and reports are primarily concerned with the definition of a little-understood or problematic concept or thing. Usually, however, definition is only a part of an essay. A long piece of writing, like a term paper, textbook, or research report, may include many kinds of brief and extended definitions, all of them integrated with other writing strategies.

This chapter illustrates various types of sentence definitions, the most common in writing. When writers use sentence definitions, they rely on various sentence patterns to provide concise definitions. The chapter also provides illustrations of multi-sentence extended definitions, including definition by word history, or etymology, and by stipulation. It concludes with some sentence strategies you might use to get started drafting a definition.

Sentence Definitions

Coming to a new field of study, institution, or activity for the first time, a participant is often baffled by the many unfamiliar concepts and terms. In college, introductory courses in all the academic disciplines often seem like courses in definitions of new terms. In the same way, newcomers to a sport like sailing or rock climbing often need to learn a great deal of specialized terminology. Writers of textbooks and manuals that cover such topics rely on brief **sentence definitions** to explain terms and concepts. The most obvious strategies simply announce a definition:

> A *karyotype* is a graphic representation of a set of chromosomes.   Definition

> Then, within the first week, the cells begin to *differentiate* — to specialize in structure and function.

> *Posthypnotic suggestions* (suggestions to be carried out after the hypnosis session has ended) have helped alleviate headaches, asthma, warts, and stress-related skin disorders.

Other, less direct strategies for integrating definitions are signaled by *subordinate clauses*:

> During the *oral stage,* which lasts throughout the first 18 months, the infant's sensual pleasures focus on sucking, biting, and chewing.

> *Hemophilia* is called the bleeder's disease because the affected person's blood does not clot.

Another common defining strategy is to use an *appositive*—a brief, inserted word or phrase that presents either the definition or the word to be defined:

> *Taxonomy,* the science of classifying groups (taxa) of organisms in formal groups, is hierarchical.

> The actual exchange of gases takes place in small air sacs, the *alveoli,* which are clustered in branches like grapes around the ends of the smallest bronchioles.

| EXERCISE 16.1 |

Look up any three of the following words or phrases in a dictionary. Define each one in a sentence. Try to use a different sentence pattern for each of your definitions.

bull market	ecumenism	samba
carcinogen	edema	seasonal affective disorder
caricature	harangue	sonnet
clinometer	hyperhidrosis	testosterone
ectomorph	mnemonic	zero-based budgeting

Turn to the essay in Chapter 8 entitled "What College Rankings Really Tell Us" by Malcolm Gladwell (pp. 368–71) and analyze the sentence definition in paragraph 2. Notice the strategy Gladwell relies on. Keeping in mind that Gladwell's purpose is to persuade readers to accept his criticism of the *U.S. News* staff's college rankings, how helpful do you find this sentence definition?

Extended Definitions

At times a writer may need to go further than a brief sentence definition and provide readers with a fuller, **extended definition,** as in the following example:

In Winn's extended definition of *TV addiction,* she compares her subject to drug and alcohol addiction, describes its effects on addicts, and speculates on why breaking the addiction is so difficult.

People often refer to being "hooked on TV." Does this, too, fall into the lighthearted category of cookie eating and other pleasures that people pursue with unusual intensity, or is there a kind of television viewing that falls into the more serious category of destructive addiction? . . .

Let us consider television viewing in the light of the conditions that define serious addictions.

Not unlike drugs or alcohol, the television experience allows the participant to blot out the real world and enter into a pleasurable and passive mental state. The worries and anxieties of reality are as effectively deferred by becoming absorbed in a television program as by going on a "trip" induced by drugs or alcohol. And just as alcoholics are only inchoately aware of their addiction, feeling that they control their drinking more than they really do ("I can cut it out any time I want — I just like to have three or four drinks before dinner"), people similarly overestimate their control over television watching. Even as they put off other activities to spend hour after hour watching television, they feel they could easily resume living in a different, less passive style. But somehow or other while the television set is present in their homes, the click doesn't sound. With television pleasures available, those other experiences seem less attractive, more difficult somehow. . . .

The self-confessed television addict often feels he "ought" to do other things — but the fact that he doesn't read and doesn't plant his garden or sew or crochet or play games or have conversations means that those activities are no longer as desirable as television viewing. In a way a heavy viewer's life is as imbalanced by his television "habit" as a drug addict's or an alcoholic's. He is living in a holding pattern, as it were, passing up the activities that lead to growth or development or a sense of accomplishment. This is one reason people talk about their television viewing so ruefully, so apologetically. They are aware that it is an unproductive experience, that almost any other endeavor is more worthwhile by any human measure.

Finally, it is the adverse effect of television viewing on the lives of so many people that defines it as a serious addiction. The television habit distorts the sense of time. It renders other experiences vague and curiously unreal while taking on a greater reality for itself. It weakens relationships by reducing and sometimes eliminating normal opportunities for talking, for communicating.

And yet television does not satisfy, else why would the viewer continue to watch hour after hour, day after day? "The measure of health," writes Lawrence Kubie, "is flexibility . . . and especially the freedom to cease when sated." But the television viewer can never be sated with his television experiences — they do not provide the true nourishment that satiation requires — and thus he finds that he cannot stop watching.

— Marie Winn, "TV Addiction"

In this example, Marie Winn offers an extended definition of television addiction that begins with a comparison. *Comparison or contrast* is often the most effective way to present an unfamiliar term or concept to readers. The key is to know your readers well enough to find a term nearly all of them will know to compare to the unfamiliar term.

Extended definitions may also include *negative definitions* — explanations of what the thing being defined is *not:*

It's important to be clear about the reverse definition, as well: what dinosaurs are not. Dinosaurs are not lizards, and vice versa. Lizards are scaly reptiles of an ancient bloodline. The oldest lizards antedate the earliest dinosaurs by a full thirty million years. A few large lizards, such as the man-eating Komodo dragon, have been called "relics of the dinosaur age," but this phrase is historically incorrect. No lizard ever evolved the birdlike characteristics peculiar to each and every dinosaur. A big lizard never resembled a small dinosaur except for a few inconsequential details of the teeth. Lizards never walked with the erect, long-striding gait that distinguishes the dinosaur like ground birds today or the birdlike dinosaurs of the Mesozoic.

— Robert T. Bakker, *The Dinosaur Heresies*

Bakker uses a negative definition, explaining that *dinosaurs* are not lizards.

EXERCISE 16.3

Choose one term that names some concept or feature of central importance in an activity or a subject you know well. For example, if you are studying biology, you have probably encountered terms like *morphogenesis* and *ecosystem*. Choose a word with a well-established definition. Write an extended definition of several sentences for this important term. Write for readers your own age who will be encountering the term for the first time when they read your definition.

EXERCISE 16.4

In her essay in Chapter 8, Christine Rosen presents an extended definition. After reading her essay, how would you define *multitasking*? Reread the essay to see which strategies she uses to define the term.

Historical Definitions

Occasionally, a writer will provide a **historical definition,** tracing the evolution of a term from its first use to its adoption into other languages to its shifting meanings over the centuries. Such a strategy can be a rich addition to an essay, bringing surprising depth and resonance to the definition of a concept.

In this example, from a special issue of *Time* magazine on the future uses of cyberspace and its potential impact on the economy, Philip Elmer-DeWitt provides a historical definition of the term *cyberspace*:

> It started, as the big ideas in technology often do, with a science-fiction writer. William Gibson, a young expatriate American living in Canada, was wandering past the video arcades on Vancouver's Granville Street in the early 1980s when something about the way the players were hunched over their glowing screens struck him as odd. "I could see in the physical intensity of their postures how *rapt* the kids were," he says. "It was like a feedback loop, with photons coming off the screens into the kids' eyes, neurons moving through their bodies and electrons moving through the video game. These kids clearly *believed* in the space the games projected."
>
> That image haunted Gibson. He didn't know much about video games or computers — he wrote his breakthrough novel *Neuromancer* (1984) on an ancient manual typewriter — but he knew people who did. And as near as he could tell, everybody who worked much with the machines eventually came to accept, almost as an article of faith, the reality of that imaginary realm. "They develop a belief that there's some kind of *actual space* behind the screen," he says. "Some place that you can't see but you know is there."
>
> Gibson called that place "cyberspace," and used it as the setting for his early novels and short stories. In his fiction, cyberspace is a computer-generated landscape that characters enter by "jacking in" — sometimes by plugging electrodes directly into sockets implanted in the brain. What they see when they get there is a three-dimensional representation of all the information stored in "every computer in the human system" — great warehouses and skyscrapers of data. He describes it in a key passage in *Neuromancer* as a place of "unthinkable complexity," with "lines of light ranged in the nonspace of the mind, clusters and constellations of data. Like city lights, receding. . . ."
>
> In the years since, there have been other names given to that shadowy space where our computer data reside: the Net, the Web, the Cloud, the Matrix, the Metaverse, the Datasphere, the Electronic Frontier, the information superhighway. But Gibson's coinage may prove the most enduring. By 1989 it had been borrowed by the online community to describe not some science-fiction fantasy but today's increasingly interconnected computer systems — especially the millions of computers jacked into the Internet.
>
> — Philip Elmer-DeWitt, "Welcome to Cyberspace"

The historical definition serves Elmer-DeWitt's larger purpose in writing this essay: to help readers acquire a deeper understanding of the new technologies that continue to profoundly affect the ways in which we live our lives.

| EXERCISE 16.5 |

You can consult a historical, or etymological, dictionary, such as the *Oxford English Dictionary, A Dictionary of American English,* or *A Dictionary of Americanisms,* to trace changes in the use of a word over long periods of time or to survey different theories of a word's or phrase's origins. Online you can search the *Phrase Finder,* search the *Urban Dictionary,* or just Google the word or phrase plus definition. Look up the historical definition of any one of the following words — or a word or phrase you're curious about — in one or more sources, and write several sentences on its roots and development.

bedrock	eye-opener	lobbying	rubberneck
bogus	filibuster	lynching	sashay
bushwhack	gerrymander	pep	23 skidoo
dugout	head over heels	podunk	two-bit

Stipulative Definitions

To stipulate means to seek or assert agreement on something. In a **stipulative definition,** the writer declares a certain meaning, generally not one found in the dictionary.

In her autobiography, Annie Dillard defines *football* as she understood it as a nine-year-old:

> Some boys taught me to play football. This was fine sport. You thought up a new strategy for every play and whispered it to the others. You went out for a pass, fooling everyone. Best, you got to throw yourself mightily at someone's running legs. Either you brought him down or you hit the ground flat out on your chin, with your arms empty before you. It was all or nothing. If you hesitated in fear, you would miss and get hurt: you would take a hard fall while the kid got away, or you would get kicked in the face while the kid got away. But if you flung yourself wholeheartedly at the back of his knees — if you gathered and joined body and soul and pointed them diving fearlessly — then you likely wouldn't get hurt, and you'd stop the ball. Your fate, and your team's score, depended on your concentration and courage. Nothing girls did could compare with it.
>
> — ANNIE DILLARD, *An American Childhood*

Dillard provides a stipulative definition of *football* as she understood it when she was nine years old.

For Dillard's complete essay, see Chapter 2, pp. 17–19.

There are recognizable elements of grown-up football in Dillard's definition. Her focus is less on rules and strategy, however, than on the "concentration and courage" required to make a successful tackle and, of course, on the sheer thrill of doing so.

In the next example, the writer stipulates a definition of a term to support an argument:

> Ozone depletion and the greenhouse effect are human disasters. They happen to occur in the environment. But they are urgent because they directly threaten man. A sane environmentalism, the only kind of environmentalism that will win universal public support, begins by unashamedly declaring that nature is here to serve man.

Krauthammer uses his stipulative definition of *environmentalism* to argue for a more realistic approach to protecting the environment.

A sane environmentalism is entirely anthropocentric: it enjoins man to preserve nature, but on the grounds of self-preservation.

A sane environmentalism does not sentimentalize the earth. It does not ask people to sacrifice in the name of other creatures. After all, it is hard enough to ask people to sacrifice in the name of other humans. (Think of the chronic public resistance to foreign aid and welfare.) Ask hardworking voters to sacrifice in the name of the snail darter, and, if they are feeling polite, they will give you a shrug.

— CHARLES KRAUTHAMMER, "Saving Nature, but Only for Man"

EXERCISE 16.6

Look at Karen Kornbluh's essay "Win-Win Flexibility" in Chapter 7 (pp. 321–23). Kornbluh begins the argument with contrasting stipulative definitions of the "traditional" family and the "juggler" family. What is her stipulative definition of each type of family? How does she use these definitions to support her overall argument?

EXERCISE 16.7

Write several sentences of a stipulative definition for one of the following:

1 Define in your own way game shows, soap operas, police dramas, horror movies, or some other form of entertainment. Try for a stipulative definition of what your subject is generally like. In effect, you will be saying to your readers — other students in your class who are familiar with these entertainments — "Let's define it this way for now."

2 Define in your own way some hard-to-define concept, such as "loyalty," "love," "bravery," "shyness," or "masculinity."

3 Think of a new development or phenomenon in contemporary romance, music, television, leisure, fashion, or eating habits, or in your line of work. Invent a name for it, and write a stipulative definition for it.

Sentence Strategies for Definition

Writers frequently include definitions in essays that explain concepts. Essay exams also may require students to define terms. If you need to integrate a definition into an essay or exam, one or more of the following sentence strategies may provide a jumping-off point. Remember to make them your own as you revise.

▶ _____ [phenomenon/event/process] is [a/an] _____ in which _____ [list defining characteristics].

▶ Many people think the term _____ means _____, but it might be more accurate to say it means _____.

▶ What makes _____ a good example of _____ is _____ , _____ , and _____ .

▶ The [subject] _____ is a [name genre or category of subject, such as romantic comedy or horror movie] because _____ .

▶ It is an innovative _____ [name genre or category to which your subject belongs] because it not only includes _____ [name standard features] but also offers _____ [name additional features].

▶ _____ is rather unconventional for [a/an] _____ [name genre or category to which your subject belongs] because _____ .

▶ _____ is a brilliant embodiment of [name genre or category to which your subject belongs], especially notable for its superb _____ and thorough _____ .

17

Classifying

Classifying is an essential writing strategy for thinking about and organizing ideas, information, and experience. The process of **classifying** involves either grouping or dividing. Writers group related items (such as *apples, oranges, bananas, strawberries, cantaloupes,* and *cherries*) and label the general class of items they grouped together (*fruit*). Or they begin classifying with a general class (such as *fruit*) and then divide it into subclasses of particular types (*apples, oranges,* etc.).

This chapter shows how you can organize and illustrate a classification you have read about or constructed yourself, and it concludes with some sentence strategies you might use when classifying information.

Organizing Classification

Classifying in writing serves primarily as a means of **organization**—of creating a framework for the presentation of information, whether in a few paragraphs of an essay or in an entire book. This section surveys several examples of classifying, ranging from a simple two-level classification to a complex multilevel system.

The simplest classification divides a general topic into two subtopics. Here is an example by Edward J. Loughram from a proposal to keep at-risk teenagers out of jail and help them lead productive lives. Before he can present his proposed solution, Loughram has to get readers to see that juvenile offenders are not all the same. He does this by explaining that although statistics show that the number of juvenile offenders is rising, they do not take into account the fact that there are two distinct groups of young people getting into trouble. He classifies juvenile offenders into these two categories to argue that the problem of delinquency can be solved, at least in part, by interrupting the criminal paths of the second group:

> Two primary factors explain the growing numbers of juvenile offenders. First, there is indeed a rise in serious crime among young people, fueled by the steady stream of drugs and weapons into their hands. These dangerous offenders are committed—legitimately—to juvenile-correction agencies for long-term custody or treatment.
>
> But a second, larger group is also contributing to the increase. It consists of 11-, 12-, and 13-year-old first-time offenders who have failed at home, failed in school, and fallen through the cracks of state and community social-service agencies. These are not serious offenders, or even typical delinquents. But they

Loughram's two categories show that the basis for his classification is the seriousness of the crimes.

594

are coming into the correctional system because we have ignored the warning signs among them.

— EDWARD J. LOUGHRAM, "Prevention of Delinquency"

From Loughram's essay, we see how a writer can use a simple two-category classification to advance an argument. The student essay by Sheila McClain (on pp. 409–14 of Chapter 9) offers a somewhat more complex classification to analyze the reasons people join health clubs. The following figure below offers a *tree diagram* of her analysis:

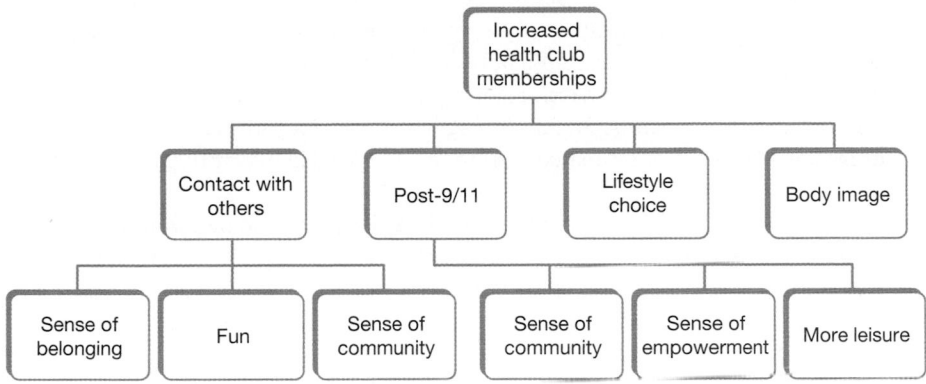

What the tree diagram shows at a glance is that in a classification system, some categories, such as "sense of belonging" and "fun," are on the same level, or *coordinate*. Some are on a higher level, or *superordinate*. And some are on a lower level, or *subordinate*. The highest level represents the most general category, and each lower level identifies increasingly specific types. If McClain took her classification to the most specific level, she would name individuals as examples of people who joined health clubs for each of the reasons she names.

EXERCISE 17.1

Turn to the concept explanation in Chapter 4, "Attachment: Somebody to Watch over You" (pp. 123–28) and make a tree diagram of the classification in paragraphs 4–7. What do you think is Patricia Lyu's basis for classification? Does each item seem to be placed in an appropriate category and at the proper level?

EXERCISE 17.2

Review the essays you have written so far for this class or for another class, looking for an essay in which you used classifying. What was the purpose of your essay and your basis for classifying? Construct a tree diagram of your classification to see whether each item can be placed in an appropriate category and on the proper level.

Illustrating Classification

We used tree diagrams as an *illustration* of the categories and levels of McClain's classification of reasons. Similarly, writers sometimes integrate graphics to make their classification easy for readers to see at a glance.

Here is an example from *Newsweek* magazine in which Sharon Begley and Martha Brant explain the problem of drug abuse by Olympic athletes:

> If doping is, as [the head of IOC's Medical Commission Prince Alexandre] de Merode noticed, suddenly "an important problem," it is partly because the newest doping agents pose the risk of serious health problems, and even death. But the larger reason is that it is ridiculously easy to dope and not get caught. Doping and detection are like an arms race. First, trainers discover a performance-enhancing drug. Then, sports officials develop a test for it. Trainers retaliate by inventing a way to elude the detectors. So far, doping has stayed a lap ahead. "Undetectable drugs are 90 percent of estimated doping cases," says Hein Verbruggen, head of international cycling.
>
> Czech tennis pro Petr Korda tested positive for the steroid nandrolone after the Wimbledon quarterfinals last May, for instance. (Protesting that he did not know how the chemicals got into his system, he avoided the one-year suspension the International Tennis Association is supposed to impose.) But American pro Jim Courier charged that steroids are far from the worst abuse in tennis. " EPO is the problem," Courier told *Newsweek*. "I have pretty strong suspicions that guys are using it on the tour. I see guys who are out there week in and week out without taking rests. EPO can help you when it's the fifth set and you've been playing for four-and-a-half hours." Although the endurance-building effects of EPO last for about two weeks, its use can't be detected in urine at all or in blood for more than a day or so after the athlete stops taking it.
>
> EPO is only one weapon in a pharmaceutical arsenal of performance-enhancing substances flowing through sports. Stimulants like amphetamines, ephedrine and caffeine were the first substances to land on the IOC's list of banned agents, and they're still popular. They provide a quick pop of energy, and so are a favorite of sprinters, cyclists and swimmers. They are an ingredient of many asthma medications. Exercise-induced asthma has inexplicably stricken many Olympians, including 60 percent of the U.S. team in 1994, and medical use of stimulant inhalants is allowed. Are stimulants detectable? Sure, if your trainer's IQ matches his hat size. They clear the urine in hours, so all an athlete has to do is not take them too close to her event. If you've been using too soon before your race, there are always "masking agents." Probenecid, for one, inhibits substances from reaching the urine. And urine tests are all the IOC requires: blood tests, which can detect more substances, are deemed too invasive.
>
> Anabolic steroids, almost all of them derivatives of the hormone testoster-one, are the mothers of all doping agents. They build muscles. By most estimates, an athlete can improve strength at least 5 percent by taking steroids either orally or through injection during high-intensity training. Drug-detection machines, such as the high-resolution mass spectrometer used at the Atlanta Games in 1996,

Begley and Brant classify performance-enhancing drugs into five categories and explain what each type of drug does, how detectable it is, and what its health risks are.

Drug	What Does It Do?	Masking/Detection	Risks
Human growth hormone (hGH)	Stimulates the intracellular breakdown of body fat, allowing more to be used for energy.	This is a natural hormone, so added amounts don't show up in blood or urine tests.	Muscle and bone disfigurement — jutting forehead, elongated jaw. Also: heart and metabolic problems.
Erythropoietin (EPO)	Increases the number of red blood cells without having to "dope" using one's own blood.	It's extremely difficult to detect because the extra blood cells are the athlete's own.	Extra cells can make blood the consistency of yogurt. This can lead to a clot, heart attack or stroke.
Testosterone	Used to build muscles. It lets the body recover quickly from strenuous exercise.	Rules allow up to five times the natural body level, giving athletes latitude.	Unnatural levels can cause heart disease, liver cancer and impotence.
Steroids/ androstenedione	Anabolic steroids are incarnations of testosterone; androstenedione is a precursor molecule.	Water-based steroids (most common) are undetectable in urine after several weeks.	Synthetic testosterone carries the same risks as naturally occurring testosterone.
Stimulants	The first category that the IOC tested for. They delay the symptoms of fatigue.	Stimulants such as amphetamines can be detected; diuretics can dilute them in urine.	Fatigue is the body saying "stop" — overriding that message can be dangerous.

can be tuned to detect any synthetic steroid; the Atlanta lab tested for 100 different types. But the Dr. Feelgoods of sport can tinker with the molecular structure of common steroids, so they slip through. "There are 72 banned steroids," says one American coach who says he developed drug regimes for athletes in Atlanta, "but the testosterone molecule is changeable in millions of ways. All you have to do is make a steroid not on the list." Or, simply by going cold turkey a few weeks before competition, an athlete can get the muscle-bulking effects without getting caught. If that seems too chancy, athletes can use a diuretic. These drugs, which are also banned, dilute the urine. That makes illicit substances virtually undetectable.

   More and more athletes are turning to the source of all steroids: testosterone itself. Natural levels vary, so sports federations and the IOC try to detect doping indirectly. They measure the relative amounts of testosterone and another natural steroid called epitestosterone. In most people, testosterone levels are no more than twice epi levels. But to allow for individual variation, the IOC set the prohibited level at anything over 6 to 1. That means an athlete can dope himself up to, say, five times his normal testosterone levels, and get away with it. How much of an edge would that provide? A male athlete with a typical testosterone/epitestosterone ratio of 1.3 to 1 could boost that to 6 to 1, stay within the IOC limit and improve his performance at least 10 percent. Women, with a natural ratio of 2.5 to 1, could do even better, since they have less testosterone to begin with and so are

The essay's organizational plan is illustrated in the chart; the chart sometimes repeats information in the text but more often complements or adds to the text.

For more information on designing documents with graphics, see Chapter 21, pp. 647–50.

more sensitive to added amounts. Testosterone can give women beards, deep voices and tough skin. It can make men's breasts swell and testicles shrivel.

The doping agents of choice today are substances that cannot be detected in urine: EPO and human growth hormone. Even though the performance-enhancing effects of hGH are unproved, many athletes believe it boosts energy. (Athletes dubbed the Atlanta Olympics "The Growth Hormone Games.") hGH can also cause grotesque skeletal deformations by stimulating abnormal bone growth. EPO, by increasing the production of red blood cells up to tenfold, can turn blood the consistency of yogurt, making it too thick to flow freely. The misuse of EPO has apparently killed at least 18 Dutch and Belgian cyclists since 1987.

— SHARON BEGLEY AND MARTHA BRANT, "The Real Scandal"

Maintaining Clarity and Coherence

The next example illustrates how writers can help readers follow a classification system by maintaining *clarity* and *coherence* — even when the subject is new and difficult. The passage comes from a book on physics by Gary Zukav. He uses classifying to explain the concept of mass. Simply defined, mass in physics is a measure of the matter in an object:

Zukav explains the concept of mass by classifying it into two types— gravitational and inertial—and provides cues to help readers understand the classification.

> There are two kinds of mass, which means that there are two ways of talking about it. The first is gravitational mass. The gravitational mass of an object, roughly speaking, is the weight of the object as measured on a balance scale. Something that weighs three times more than another object has three times more mass. Gravitational mass is the measure of how much force the gravity of the earth exerts on an object. Newton's laws describe the effects of this force, which vary with the distance of the mass from the earth. . . .
>
> The second type of mass is inertial mass. Inertial mass is the measure of the resistance of an object to acceleration (or deceleration, which is negative acceleration). For example, it takes three times more force to move three railroad cars from a standstill to twenty miles per hour (positive acceleration) than it takes to move one railroad car from a standstill to twenty miles per hour. . . . Similarly, once they are moving, it takes three times more force to stop three cars than it takes to stop the single car. This is because the inertial mass of the three railroad cars is three times more than the inertial mass of the single railroad car.
>
> — GARY ZUKAV, *The Dancing Wu Li Masters: An Overview of the New Physics*

From this passage, we can see some of the cues writers use to make a classification clear and coherent. Zukav begins by *forecasting* the classification he will develop (*There are two kinds of mass*). He then introduces each category in its own paragraph, announced with a *transition* (*first* and *second*) and presented in the same sentence pattern (*The first is . . .* and *The second type of mass is . . .*). Careful *cueing* like this can help make a classification clear to readers.

| EXERCISE 17.3 |

Look back at the paragraphs from Patricia Lyu's essay on attachment that you used to make a tree diagram in Exercise 17.1 or at the example by Begley and Brant earlier in this chapter to examine the strategies these authors use to make their classifications clear and coherent. Notice how each category is introduced and how transitions are used to help readers keep track of the categories. What conclusions can you draw about how writers maintain clarity and coherence from your analysis?

| EXERCISE 17.4 |

Look back at the classification you examined in Exercise 17.2 to see how well you were able to maintain clarity and coherence in your classification. What changes would you make, if any, to improve clarity and coherence?

General strategies for coherence are discussed in Chapter 13.

Sentence Strategies for Classification

Many genres invite the use of classification, including concept explanations, proposals, evaluations, and speculations about causes. If classifying ideas, information, or experience will help your readers understand a concept or accept a proposal or an evaluation, use these sentence strategies to begin putting your ideas into words. You will probably want to rework these sentences to make them your own, but they may give you a jumping-off point for articulating your thoughts.

Use Rhetorical Questions to Establish the Categories

▶ How does _____ develop, and how does it continue in _____ [name stage or period]? _____ and _____ [name researchers] provide answers to these questions.

Use Comparison or Contrast to Establish the Categories

▶ _____ is [similar to/different from] _____ in these ways: _____ , _____ , and _____ .

Use Causes and Effects as Categories

▶ Recent research on _____ demonstrates that when _____ [state cause], it often _____ [state effect].

Use Reasons as Categories

▶ What makes _____ [problematic/praiseworthy] is _____ , _____ , and _____ .

▶ I'm [also/not] concerned about _____ [state problem] because _____ , _____ , and _____ [state reasons].

List the Categories

▶ [Topic] can be divided into .... [indicate number] types or categories: .... ,
.... , ... , and ....

▶ Experts like [name of expert] say there are [number] [categories/types/subtypes/
versions] of [concept], ranging from .... to .... (citation).

▶ Experts disagree over the causes of [concept]. Some, like [name 1], believe ....
(citation). Others, like [name 2], contend that .... (citation).

Use Cues to Forecast Categories

▶ [Name researcher] identified three basic [types/categories] of .... The first [type/
category] is .... It [does/is/has] .... [name distinguishing characteristics].
The [second/next] [type/category] is .... It [does/is/has] .... [name
distinguishing characteristics]. The [final/third] [type/category] is .... It [does/
is/has] .... [name distinguishing characteristics].

18

Comparing and Contrasting

Most of us compare things all the time, at work, in school, and in everyday life. You might compare two people you know well, two motorcycles you are considering buying for a cross-country tour, three Stephen King novels, four tomato plants being grown under different laboratory conditions, or two theories about the relationship between inflation and wages. But as soon as you begin to compare two things, you usually begin to contrast them as well, for rarely are two things alike in all respects. The contrasts, or differences, between the two motorcycles are likely to be more enlightening than the similarities, many of which may be so obvious as to need no analysis. **Comparison,** then, brings similar things together for examination, to see how they are alike. **Contrast** is a form of comparison that emphasizes differences. According to research on learning, we acquire new concepts most readily if we can see how they are similar to or different from concepts we already know.

Professional writers say that comparison and contrast is a basic strategy they would not want to be without. Indeed, some writing is essentially extended comparison. But for all kinds of writing situations, writers regularly alternate comparison and contrast with other writing strategies when they present information.

Chances are that you will confront many test questions and essay assignments asking you to compare and contrast — two poems, three presidents, four procedures. This strategy is popular in all academic disciplines, for it is one of the best ways to challenge students intellectually. This chapter shows how you can organize a comparison/contrast, and it concludes with some sentence strategies you might use when comparing or contrasting.

Two Ways of Comparing and Contrasting

There are two ways to organize comparison and contrast in writing: in chunks and in sequence. In **chunking,** each object of the comparison is presented separately; in sequencing, the items are compared point by point. For example, a chunked comparison of two motorcycles would first detail all pertinent features of the Pirsig Z-1700 XL and then consider all features of the Kawazuki 1750XL, whereas a **sequenced comparison** would analyze the Pirsig and the Kawazuki feature by feature. In a chunked comparison, the discussion is organized around each separate item being compared. In a sequenced comparison, it is organized around characteristics of the items being compared.

In the following example of chunked comparison, Jane Tompkins contrasts popular nineteenth-century sentimental novels with the Western novels that provided a reaction against them:

> The female, domestic, "sentimental" religion of the best-selling women writers — Harriet Beecher Stowe, Susan Warner, Maria Cummins, and dozens of others — whose novels spoke to the deepest beliefs and highest ideals of middle-class America, is the real antagonist of the Western.
>
> You can see this simply by comparing the main features of the Western with the sentimental novel. In these books . . . a woman is always the main character, usually a young orphan girl, with several other main characters being women too. Most of the action takes place in private spaces, at home, indoors, in kitchens, parlors, and upstairs chambers. And most of it concerns the interior struggles of the heroine to live up to an ideal of Christian virtue — usually involving uncomplaining submission to difficult and painful circumstances, learning to quell rebellious instincts, and dedicating her life to the service of God through serving others. In these struggles, women give one another a great deal of emotional and material support, and they have close relationships verging on what today we would identify as homosocial and homoerotic. There's a great deal of Bible reading, praying, hymn singing, and drinking of tea. Emotions other than anger are expressed very freely and openly. Often there are long, drawn-out death scenes in which a saintly woman dies a natural death at home. . . .
>
> The elements of the typical Western plot arrange themselves in stark opposition to this pattern, not just vaguely and generally but point for point. First of all, in Westerns (which are generally written by men), the main character is always a full-grown adult male, and almost all of the other characters are men. The action takes place either outdoors — on the prairie, on the main street — or in public places — the saloon, the sheriff's office, the barber shop, the livery stable. The action concerns physical struggles between the hero and a rival or rivals, and culminates in a fight to the death with guns. In the course of these struggles the hero frequently forms a bond with another man — sometimes his rival, more often a comrade — a bond that is more important than any relation he has with a woman and is frequently tinged with homoeroticism. There is very little free expression of the emotions. The hero is a man of few words who expresses himself through physical action — usually fighting. And when death occurs it is never at home in bed but always sudden death, usually murder.
>
> —JANE TOMPKINS, *West of Everything: The Inner Life of Westerns*

Tompkins discusses sentimental novels and Westerns separately, presenting each point of contrast for the two subjects in the same order (chunking).

Tompkins signals the shift from one subject to the other with a transition sentence at the start of the third paragraph.

Schematically, a chunked comparison looks simple enough. As the preceding example shows, it is easy to block off such a discussion in a text and then provide a clean *transition* between the various parts. And yet it can in fact be more complicated for a writer to plan than a sequenced comparison. Sequenced comparison may be closer to the way people perceive and think about similarities or differences in things. For example, you may have realized all at once that two navy blazers are different, but you would identify the specific differences — buttons, tailoring, fabric — one at a time. A sequenced comparison would point to the differences in just this way, one at a time, whereas a chunked comparison would present all the features of one blazer and then do the same for the second. A writer using the chunked strategy, then, must organize all the points of comparison before starting to write and then be sure that the points of comparison are presented in the same order in the discussion of each item being compared. With sequencing, however, the writer can take up each point of comparison as it comes to mind.

In the next example, from a natural history of the earth, David Attenborough uses sequencing to contrast bird wings and airplane wings:

> Bird wings have a much more complex job to do than the wings of an aeroplane, for in addition to supporting the bird they must act as its engine, rowing it through the air. Even so the wing outline of a bird conforms to the same aerodynamic principles as those eventually discovered by man when designing his aeroplanes, and if you know how different kinds of aircraft perform, you can predict the flight capabilities of similarly shaped birds.
>
> Short stubby wings enable a tanager and other forest-living birds to swerve and dodge at speed through the undergrowth just as they helped the fighter planes of the Second World War to make tight turns and aerobatic manoeuvres in a dog-fight. More modern fighters achieve greater speeds by sweeping back their wings while in flight, just as peregrines do when they go into a 130 kph dive, stooping to a kill. Championship gliders have long thin wings so that, having gained height in a thermal up-current, they can soar gently down for hours and an albatross, the largest of flying birds, with a similar wing shape and a span of 3 metres, can patrol the ocean for hours in the same way without a single wing beat. Vultures and hawks circle at very slow speeds supported by a thermal and they have the broad rectangular wings that very slow flying aircraft have. Man has not been able to adapt wings to provide hovering flight. He has only achieved that with the whirling horizontal blades of a helicopter or the downward-pointing engines of a vertical landing jet. Hummingbirds have paralleled even this. They tilt their bodies so that they are almost upright and then beat their wings as fast as 80 times a second producing a similar down-draught of air. So the hummingbird can hover and even fly backwards.
>
> — David Attenborough, *Life on Earth*

Attenborough uses a limited, focused basis for the comparison of bird wings and airplane wings: their shape.

Attenborough finds a valid — and fascinating — basis for comparison between birds and airplanes and develops it in a way that both informs and entertains his readers. A successful comparison always has these qualities: a valid basis for comparison, a limited focus, and information that will catch a reader's attention.

EXERCISE 18.1

Identify the specific items contrasted in Tompkins's passage comparing sentimental novels and Westerns. Number in sequence each contrast, and underline both parts of the contrast. To get started, in the paragraph about sentimental novels, underline "a woman is always the main character, usually a young orphan girl," and number it "1" in the margin. In the paragraph about Westerns, underline "the main character is always a full-grown adult male," and number this "1" also to complete your identification of both parts of the comparison. Then look for contrast 2, underline and number the contrasted items, and so on.

Look over your work and consider the pattern of these contrasts. Were they easy to identify? If so, what made them easy to identify? Was any contrast left incomplete? In general, how successful and informative do you find this set of contrasts?

EXERCISE 18.2

Identify the specific items compared in Attenborough's passage comparing bird wings and aircraft wings. Underline both items, and number the pair in the margin. To get started, underline "tanager" and "fighter planes" in the first sentence of the second paragraph. In the margin, number this pair "1." Then identify pair 2 and so on.

Consider the pattern and ordering of the comparisons you have identified. Were the pairs of items easy to identify? If so, what made them easy to identify? Some comparisons begin by naming a bird, some by identifying a category of aircraft. Did this lack of predictability present problems for you? Do you see any possible justification for the writer's having given up the predictability of always beginning each comparison with either a bird or an aircraft? In general, how successful and informative did you find this comparison?

EXERCISE 18.3

Write a page or so comparing or contrasting any one of the following subjects. Be careful to limit the basis for your comparison, and underline the sentence that states that basis. Use chunking or sequencing to organize the comparison.

- Two ways of achieving the same goal (for example, traveling by bus or subway, or using flattery or persuasion to get what you want)
- A good and bad job interview or date
- Your relationship with two friends or relatives
- Two or more forms of music, dance, film, or computer software
- Two methods of doing some task at home or on the job

EXERCISE 18.4

Read paragraph 14 from "Love: The Right Chemistry" in Chapter 4 (p. 131) and paragraph 6 from "The Gorge-Yourself Environment" in Chapter 9 (p. 428). How is each comparison organized? (It may or may not be neatly chunked or sequenced.) Why do you think the writer organizes the comparison in that way?

Analogy

An **analogy** is a special form of comparison in which one part of the comparison is used simply to explain the other, as in the following example:

> In like manner, geologists will sometimes use the calendar year as a unit to represent the time scale, and in such terms the Precambrian runs from New Year's Day until well after Halloween. Dinosaurs appear in the middle of December and are gone the day after Christmas. The last ice sheet melts on December 31st at one minute before midnight, and the Roman Empire lasts five seconds. With your arms spread wide . . . to represent all time on earth, look at one hand with its line of life. The Cambrian begins in the wrist, and the Permian Extinction is at the outer end of the palm. All of the Cenozoic is in a fingerprint, and in a single stroke with a medium-grained nail file you could eradicate human history. Geologists live with the geologic scale. Individually, they may or may not be alarmed by the rate of exploitation of the things they discover, but, like the environmentalists, they use these repetitive analogies to place the human record in perspective — to see the Age of Reflection, the last few thousand years, as a small bright sparkle at the end of time.
>
> — JOHN McPHEE, *Basin and Range*

McPhee uses two analogies — the twelve-month calendar and the distance along two widespread arms — to explain the duration of geologic time.

Analogies are not limited to abstract, scientific concepts. Writers often use analogies to make nontechnical descriptions and explanations more vivid or to make an imaginative point of comparison that serves a larger argument. Consider the following example:

> But now that government has largely withdrawn its "handouts" [to the welfare poor], now that the overwhelming majority of the poor are out there toiling in Wal-Mart or Wendy's — well, what are we to think of them? Disapproval and condescension no longer apply, so what outlook makes sense?
>
> Guilt, you may be thinking warily. Isn't that what we're supposed to feel? But guilt doesn't go anywhere near far enough; the appropriate emotion is shame — shame at our own dependency, in this case, on the underpaid labor of others. When someone works for less pay than she can live on — when, for example, she goes hungry so that you can eat more cheaply and conveniently — then she has made a great sacrifice for you, she has made you a gift of some part of her abilities, her health, and her life. The "working poor," as they are approvingly termed, are in fact the major philanthropists of our society. They neglect their own children so that the children of others will be cared for; they live in substandard housing so that other homes will be shiny and perfect; they endure privation so that inflation will be low and stock prices high. To be a member of the working poor is to be an anonymous donor, a nameless benefactor, to everyone else. As Gail, one of my restaurant coworkers put it, "you give and you give."
>
> — BARBARA EHRENREICH, *Nickel and Dimed*

Ehrenreich suggests, by analogy, that the working poor in the United States are among society's "major philanthropists."

Analogies are tricky. They can be useful, but analogies rarely are consistently accurate at all major points of comparison. For example, in the preceding analogy, the working poor can be seen as philanthropists in the sense that they have "made a great sacrifice" but not in the sense that they are selflessly sharing their wealth. Analogies can powerfully bring home a point, but skilled writers use them with caution.

Nevertheless, you will run across analogies regularly; indeed, it would be hard to find a book without at least one. For abstract information and in certain writing situations, analogy is often the writing strategy of choice.

| EXERCISE 18.5 |

Write a one-paragraph analogy that explains a principle or process to a reader who is unfamiliar with it. Choose a principle or process that you know well. You might select a basic principle from the natural or social sciences, like dark matter or ethnocentrism; a bodily movement, like running; a physiological process, like digestion; or a process from your job, like assembling a product. Look for something very familiar to compare it with that will help the reader understand the principle or process without a technical explanation.

Sentence Strategies for Comparison and Contrast

Writers frequently use comparison and contrast in writing of almost all genres to present ideas and information. You, too, are likely to use comparison and contrast in your writing, so these sentence strategies may provide a jumping-off point for articulating your thoughts. Remember to make them your own as you revise.

To Define Using Comparison or Contrast

▶ [Topic] is [similar to/different from] _____ in these ways: _____, _____, and _____ .

▶ Many people think that [topic] means _____, but it might be more accurate to say it means _____ .

▶ [Topic] is similar in some ways to [similar concept]: _____ [list areas of similarity]. However, unlike [similar concept], it _____ [list areas of difference].

▶ [Concept], a kind of [grown-up, children's, bigger, smaller, local, international, or other adjective] version of [similar concept], [is/does/has] _____ .

▶ Similarly, _____ .

▶ [In contrast/however/on the other hand], _____ .

▶ [Topic 1] and [topic 2] are frequently confused, but they are not the same; [topic 1] [has/is/does] _____, whereas [topic 2] [has/is/does] _____ .

To Argue Using Comparison or Contrast

▶ Most people assume ⸺⸺⸺; however, ⸺⸺⸺.

▶ ⸺⸺⸺ and ⸺⸺⸺ are the usual suspects, but let's look at a totally new possibility: ⸺⸺⸺.

▶ It's not ⸺⸺⸺ but ⸺⸺⸺.

▶ [People] focus on [X], which is characterized by ⸺⸺⸺, and they don't even notice [Y], which is characterized by ⸺⸺⸺.

▶ Whereas supporters of ⸺⸺⸺ have argued that ⸺⸺⸺, opponents such as [list individuals/groups] contend that ⸺⸺⸺.

▶ Although some argue ⸺⸺⸺, I think ⸺⸺⸺ because ⸺⸺⸺.

▶ On this issue, X and Y say ⸺⸺⸺. Although I understand and to some degree sympathize with their point of view, this is ultimately a question of ⸺⸺⸺. What's at stake is not ⸺⸺⸺ but ⸺⸺⸺. Therefore, we must ⸺⸺⸺.

▶ This issue is dividing our community. Some people argue ⸺⸺⸺. Others contend ⸺⸺⸺. And still others believe ⸺⸺⸺. It is in all of our interests to ⸺⸺⸺, however, because ⸺⸺⸺.

▶ Conventional wisdom is that ⸺⸺⸺. But I take a different view: ⸺⸺⸺.

▶ One common complaint is ⸺⸺⸺. In recent years, however, ⸺⸺⸺.

19

Arguing

This chapter presents the basic strategies for making *arguments* in writing. In it, we focus on asserting a thesis, backing it up with reasons and support, and anticipating readers' questions and objections. It concludes with some sentence strategies you might use when composing an argument.

Asserting a Thesis

Central to any argument is the **thesis**. In a sentence or two, a thesis asserts or states the main point of any argument you want to make. It can be assertive only if you make it clear and direct. The thesis statement usually appears at the beginning of an argument essay.

There are five kinds of argument essays in Part One of this book. Each of these essays requires a special kind of assertion and reasoning:

- *Assertion of opinion:* What is your position on a controversial issue? (Chapter 6, "Arguing a Position")

  > When overzealous parents and coaches impose adult standards on children's sports, the result can be activities that are neither satisfying nor beneficial to children.
  > — JESSICA STATSKY, "Children Need to Play, Not Compete"

Chapters 6–10 contain essays that argue for each of these kinds of assertions, along with guidelines for constructing an argument to support such an assertion.

- *Assertion of policy:* What is your understanding of a problem, and what do you think should be done to solve it? (Chapter 7, "Proposing a Solution")

  > Although this last-minute anxiety about midterm and final exams is only too familiar to most college students, many professors may not realize how such major, infrequent, high-stakes exams work against the best interests of students both psychologically and cognitively. . . . If professors gave brief exams at frequent intervals, students would be spurred to learn more and worry less.
  > — PATRICK O'MALLEY, "More Testing, More Learning"

- *Assertion of evaluation:* What is your judgment of a subject? (Chapter 8, "Justifying an Evaluation")

  > Although the film is especially targeted for old school gamers, anime fans, and comic book fanatics, *Scott Pilgrim vs. the World* can be appreciated and enjoyed by all audiences because of its inventive special effects, clever dialogue, and artistic cinematography and editing.
  > —WILLIAM AKANA, "*Scott Pilgrim vs. the World:* A Hell of a Ride"

- ***Assertion of cause:*** What do you think made a subject the way it is? (Chapter 9, "Speculating about Causes")

  > The mythic horror movie, like the sick joke, has a dirty job to do. It deliberately appeals to all that is worst in us. It is morbidity unchained, our most base instincts let free, our nastiest fantasies realized . . . and it all happens, fittingly enough, in the dark.
  >
  > — STEPHEN KING, "Why We Crave Horror Movies"

- ***Assertion of story analysis:*** What does a story mean, or what is significant about it? (Chapter 10, "Analyzing Stories")

  > As an account of a professional doing harm under the pretense of healing, the story uncovers how a doctor can take advantage of the intimate nature of his work and his professional status to overstep common forms of conduct, to the extent that his actions actually hurt rather than help a patient. In this way, the doctor-narrator actually performs a valuable service by warning readers, indirectly through his story, that blindly trusting members of his profession can have negative consequences.
  >
  > —IRIS LEE, "Performing a Doctor's Duty"

As these different thesis statements indicate, the kind of thesis you assert depends on the occasion for which you are writing and the question you are trying to answer for your readers. Whatever the writing situation, to be effective, every thesis must satisfy the same three standards: It must be *arguable, clear,* and *appropriately qualified.*

Make arguable assertions.

Reasoned argument is called for when informed people disagree over an issue or remain divided over how best to solve a problem, as is so often the case in social and political life. Hence, the thesis statements in reasoned arguments make **arguable assertions**—possibilities or probabilities, not certainties.

Therefore, a statement of fact could not be an arguable thesis statement because facts are easy to verify—whether by checking an authoritative reference book, asking an authority, or observing the fact with your own eyes. For example, these statements assert facts:

> Jem has a Ph.D. in history.
>
> I am less than five feet tall.
>
> Eucalyptus trees were originally imported into California from Australia.

Each of these assertions can be easily verified. To find out Jem's academic degree, you can ask him, among other things. To determine a person's height, you can use a tape measure. To discover where California got its eucalyptus trees, you can search the library or Internet. There is no point in arguing such statements (though you might question the authority of a particular source or the accuracy of someone's measurement). If a writer asserts something as fact and attempts to support the assertion with *authorities* or *statistics,* the resulting essay is not an argument but a *report.*

Like facts, expressions of personal feelings are not arguable assertions. Whereas facts are unarguable because they can be definitively proved true or false, feelings are unarguable because they are purely subjective.

You can declare, for example, that you detest eight o'clock classes, but you cannot offer an argument to support this assertion. All you can do is explain why you feel as you do. If, however, you were to restate the assertion as "Eight o'clock classes are counterproductive," you could then construct an argument that does not depend solely on your subjective feelings, memories, or preferences. Your argument could be based on *reasons* and *support* that apply to others as well as to yourself. For example, you might argue that students' ability to learn is at an especially low ebb immediately after breakfast and provide scientific support for this assertion — in addition, perhaps, to personal experience and reports of interviews with your friends.

Use clear and precise wording.

The way a thesis is worded is as important as its arguability. The wording of a thesis, especially its key terms, must be *clear* and *precise.*

Consider the following assertion: "Democracy is a way of life." The meaning of this claim is uncertain, partly because the word *democracy* is abstract and partly because the phrase *way of life* is inexact. Abstract ideas like democracy, freedom, and patriotism are by their very nature hard to grasp, and they become even less clear with overuse. Too often, such words take on *connotations* that may obscure the meaning you want to emphasize. *Way of life* is fuzzy: What does it mean? Does it refer to daily life, to a general philosophy or attitude toward life, or to something else?

Thus, a thesis is vague if its meaning is unclear; it is ambiguous if it has more than one possible meaning. For example, the statement "My English instructor is mad" can be understood in two ways: The teacher is either angry or insane. Obviously, these are two very different assertions. You would not want readers to think you mean one when you actually mean the other.

Whenever you write argument, you should pay special attention to the way you phrase your thesis and take care to avoid vague and ambiguous language.

Qualify the thesis appropriately.

In addition to being arguable and clear, an argument thesis must make **appropriate qualifications** that suit your writing situation. If you are confident that your case is so strong that readers will accept your argument without question, state your thesis emphatically and unconditionally. If, however, you expect readers to challenge your assumptions or conclusions, you must qualify your statement. Qualifying a thesis makes it more likely that readers will take it seriously. Expressions like *probably, very likely, apparently,* and *it seems* all serve to qualify a thesis.

| EXERCISE 19.1 |

Write an assertion of opinion that states your position on one of the following controversial issues:

- Should English be the official language of the United States and the only language used in local, state, and federal governments' oral and written communications?

- Should teenagers be required to get their parents' permission to obtain birth control information and contraceptives?

- Should high schools or colleges require students to perform community service as a condition for graduation?

- Should marriage between same-sex couples be legal?

Constructing a persuasive argument on any of these issues would obviously require careful deliberation and research. For this exercise, however, all you need to do is construct an arguable, clear, and appropriately qualified thesis.

| EXERCISE 19.2 |

Find the thesis in one of the argument essays in Chapters 6–10. Then decide whether the thesis meets the three requirements: that it be arguable, clear, and appropriately qualified.

| EXERCISE 19.3 |

If you have written or are currently working on one of the argument assignments in Chapters 6–10, consider whether your essay thesis is arguable, clear, and appropriately qualified. If you believe it does not meet these requirements, revise it accordingly.

Giving Reasons and Support

Whether you are arguing a position, proposing a solution, justifying an evaluation, or speculating about causes, you need to give reasons and support for your thesis.

Think of **reasons** as the main points supporting your thesis. Often they answer the question Why do you think so? For example, if you assert among friends that you value a certain movie highly, one of your friends might ask, "Why do you like it so much?" And you might answer, "*Because* it has challenging ideas, unusual camera work, and memorable acting." Similarly, you might oppose restrictions on students' use of offensive language at your college *because* such restrictions would make students reluctant to enter into frank debates, *because* offensive speech is hard to define, and *because* restrictions violate the free-speech clause of the First Amendment. These *because* phrases are your reasons. You may have one or many reasons, depending on your subject and your writing situation.

For your argument to succeed with your readers, you must not only give reasons but also support your reasons. The main kinds of **support** writers use are examples, statistics, authorities, anecdotes, and textual evidence. Following is a discussion and illustration of each kind of support, along with standards for judging its reliability.

Use representative examples for support.

Examples may be used as support in all types of arguments. For examples to be believable and convincing, they must be representative (typical of all the relevant examples you might have chosen), consistent with the experience of your readers (familiar to them and not extreme), and adequate in number (numerous enough to be convincing and yet not likely to overwhelm readers).

The following illustration comes from a book on illiteracy in America by Jonathan Kozol, a prominent educator and writer:

> Kozol presents several examples to support his argument that the human costs of illiteracy are high.

Illiterates cannot read the menu in a restaurant.

They cannot read the cost of items on the menu in the window of the restaurant before they enter.

Illiterates cannot read the letters that their children bring home from their teachers. They cannot study school department circulars that tell them of the courses that their children must be taking if they hope to pass the SAT exams. They cannot help with homework. They cannot write a letter to the teacher. They are afraid to visit in the classroom. They do not want to humiliate their child or themselves.

Illiterates cannot read instructions on a bottle of prescription medicine. They cannot find out when a medicine is past the year of safe consumption; nor can they read of allergenic risks, warnings to diabetics, or the potential sedative effect of certain kinds of nonprescription pills. They cannot observe preventive health care admonitions. They cannot read about "the seven warning signs of cancer" or the indications of blood-sugar fluctuations or the risks of eating certain foods that aggravate the likelihood of cardiac arrest.

— JONATHAN KOZOL, *Illiterate America*

Kozol collected these examples in his many interviews with people who could neither read nor write. Though all of his readers are literate and have presumably never experienced the frustrations of adult illiterates, Kozol assumes they will accept that the experiences are a familiar part of illiterates' lives. Most readers will believe the experiences to be neither atypical nor extreme.

EXERCISE 19.4

Identify the examples in paragraphs 9 and 11 in Jessica Statsky's essay "Children Need to Play, Not Compete" and paragraphs 16–18 in Amitai Etzioni's essay "Working at McDonald's" (both in Chapter 6). If you have not read the essays, pause to skim them so that you can evaluate these examples within the context of the entire essay. How well do the examples meet the standards of representativeness, consistency with experience of readers, and adequacy in number? You will not have all the information you need to evaluate the examples — you rarely do unless you are an expert on the subject — but make a judgment based on the information available to you in the headnotes and the essays.

Use up-to-date, relevant, and accurate statistics.

In many kinds of arguments about economic, educational, or social issues, *statistics* may be essential. When you use statistics in your own arguments, you will want to ensure that they are up-to-date, relevant, and accurate. In addition, take care to select statistics from reliable sources and to cite them from the sources in which they originally appeared if at all possible. For example, you would want to get medical statistics directly from a reputable and authoritative professional periodical like the *New England Journal of Medicine* rather than secondhand from a supermarket tabloid or an unaffiliated Web site, neither of which can be relied on for accuracy. If you are uncertain about the most authoritative sources, ask a reference librarian or a professor who knows your topic.

The following selection, written by a Harvard University professor, comes from an argument speculating about the decline of civic life in the United States. Civic life includes all of the clubs, organizations, and communal activities in which people choose to participate:

> The culprit is television.
>
> First, the timing fits. The long civic generation was the last cohort of Americans to grow up without television, for television flashed into American society like lightning in the 1950s. In 1950 barely 10 percent of American homes had television sets, but by 1959, 90 percent did. . . . The reverberations from this lightning bolt continued for decades, as viewing hours grew by 17–20 percent during the 1960s and by an additional 7–8 percent during the 1970s. In the early years, TV watching was concentrated among the less educated sectors of the population, but during the 1970s the viewing time of the more educated sectors of the population began to converge upward. Television viewing increases with age, particularly upon retirement, but each generation since the introduction of television has begun its life cycle at a higher starting point. By 1995 viewing per TV household was more than 50 percent higher than it had been in the 1950s.
>
> Most studies estimate that the average American now watches roughly four hours per day (excluding periods in which television is merely playing in the background). Even a more conservative estimate of three hours means that television absorbs 40 percent of the average American's free time, an increase of about one-third since 1965. Moreover, multiple sets have proliferated: By the late 1980s three-quarters of all U.S. homes had more than one set, and these numbers too are rising steadily, allowing ever more private viewing. . . . This massive change in the way Americans spend their days and nights occurred precisely during the years of generational civic disengagement.
>
> — ROBERT D. PUTNAM, "The Strange Disappearance of Civic America"

These statistics come primarily from the U.S. Bureau of the Census, a nationwide count of the number of Americans and a survey, in part, of their buying habits, levels of education, and leisure activities. The Census reports are widely considered to be accurate and trustworthy. They qualify as original sources of statistics.

Putnam uses statistics to support his opinion that since the early 1960s, Americans have devoted less and less time to civic life because they are watching more and more television.

Chapter 24, pp.674–82, provides help finding statistical data in the library.

EXERCISE 19.5

In Chapter 6, underline the statistics in paragraphs 5 and 6 of Jessica Statsky's essay. If you have not read the essay, pause to skim it so that you can evaluate the writer's use of statistics within the context of the whole essay. How well do the statistics meet the standards of up-to-dateness, relevance, accuracy, and reliance on the original source? Does the writer indicate where the statistics come from? What do the statistics contribute to the argument?

Cite reputable authorities on relevant topics.

To support an argument, writers often cite experts on the subject. *Quoting, paraphrasing,* or even just referring to a respected **authority** can add to a writer's *credibility*. Authorities must be selected as carefully as are facts and statistics, however. One qualification for authorities is suggested by the way we refer to them: They must be authoritative—that is, trustworthy and reputable. They must also be specially qualified to contribute to the subject you are writing about. For example, a well-known expert on the American presidency might be a perfect choice to support an argument about the achievements of a past president but a poor choice to support an argument on whether adolescents who commit serious crimes should be tried as adults. Finally, qualified authorities must have training at respected institutions or have unique real-world experiences, and they must have a record of research and publications recognized by other authorities.

The following example comes from a *New York Times* article about some parents' and experts' heightened concern over boys' behavior. The author believes that the concern is exaggerated and potentially dangerous. In the full argument, she is particularly concerned about the number of boys who are being given Ritalin, a popular drug for treating attention-deficit hyperactivity disorder (ADHD):

> Today, the world is no longer safe for boys. A boy being a shade too boyish risks finding himself under the scrutiny of parents, teachers, guidance counselors, child therapists—all of them on watch for the early glimmerings of a medical syndrome, a bona fide behavioral disorder. Does the boy disregard authority, make snide comments in class, push other kids around and play hooky? Maybe he has a conduct disorder. Is he fidgety, impulsive, disruptive, easily bored? Perhaps he is suffering from attention-deficit hyperactivity disorder, or ADHD, the disease of the hour and the most frequently diagnosed behavioral disorder of childhood. Does he prefer computer games and goofing off to homework? He might have dyslexia or another learning disorder.

> "There is now an attempt to pathologize what was once considered the normal range of behavior of boys," said Melvin Konner of the departments of anthropology and psychiatry at Emory University in Atlanta. "Today, Tom Sawyer and Huckleberry Finn surely would have been diagnosed with both conduct disorder and ADHD." And both, perhaps, would have been put on Ritalin, the drug of choice for treating attention-deficit disorder.
>
> — Natalie Angier, "Intolerance of Boyish Behavior"

Angier establishes Melvin Konner's professional qualifications by naming the university where he teaches and his areas of study.

In this example, Angier relies on **informal citation** within her essay to introduce Melvin Konner, the authority she quotes, along with a reference to his professional qualifications. Such informal citation is common in newspapers, magazines, and some books intended for general audiences. In other books and in academic contexts, writers use **formal citation,** providing a list of works cited at the end of the essay.

For examples of two formal citation styles often used in college essays, see Chapters 27 and 28.

EXERCISE 19.6

Analyze how authorities are used in paragraphs 4 and 6 of Patrick O'Malley's essay "More Testing, More Learning" in Chapter 7 (pp. 302–8). Begin by underlining the authorities' contributions to these paragraphs, whether through quotation, summary, or paraphrase. On the basis of the evidence you have available, decide to what extent each source is authoritative on the subject: qualified to contribute to the subject, trained appropriately, and recognized widely. How does O'Malley establish each authority's credentials? Then decide what each authority contributes to the argument as a whole. (If you have not read the essay, take time to read or skim it.)

Use vivid, relevant anecdotes.

Anecdotes are brief stories about events or experiences. If they are relevant to the argument, well told, and true to life, they can provide convincing support. To be relevant, an anecdote must strike readers as more than an entertaining diversion; it must seem to make an irreplaceable contribution to an argument. A well-told story is easy to follow, and the people and scenes are described memorably, even vividly. A true-to-life anecdote seems believable, even if the experience is foreign to readers' experiences.

The following anecdote appeared in an argument taking a position on gun control. The writer, an essayist, poet, and environmentalist who is also a rancher in South Dakota, always carries a pistol and believes that other people should have the right to do so:

> One day, while driving to the highway mailbox, I saw a vehicle parked about halfway to the house. Several men were standing in the ditch, relieving themselves. I have no objection to emergency urination; we always need moisture. But I noticed they'd also dumped several dozen beer cans, which can blow into pastures and slash a cow's legs or stomach.
>
> As I drove slowly closer, the men zipped their trousers ostentatiously while walking toward me, and one of them demanded what the hell I wanted.
>
> "This is private land. I'd like you to pick up the beer cans."
>
> "What beer cans?" said the belligerent one, putting both hands on the car door and leaning in my window. His face was inches from mine, and the beer fumes were strong. The others laughed. One tried the passenger door, locked; another put his foot on the hood and rocked the car. They circled, lightly thumping the roof, discussing my good fortune in meeting them and the benefits they were likely to bestow upon me. I felt small and trapped; they knew it.

To support her argument, Hasselstrom tells an engaging anecdote and, in the last paragraph, explains its relevance.

"The ones you just threw out," I said politely.

"I don't see no beer cans. Why don't you get out here and show them to me, honey?" said the belligerent one, reaching for the handle inside my door.

"Right over there," I said, still being polite, "—there and over there." I pointed with the pistol, which had been under my thigh. Within one minute the cans and the men were back in the car and headed down the road.

I believe this incident illustrates several important principles. The men were trespassing and knew it; their judgment may have been impaired by alcohol. Their response to the polite request of a woman alone was to use their size and numbers to inspire fear. The pistol was a response in the same language. Politeness didn't work; I couldn't intimidate them. Out of the car, I'd have been more vulnerable. The pistol just changed the balance of power.

— LINDA M. HASSELSTROM, "Why One Peaceful Woman Carries a Pistol"

See Chapter 14, Narrating, and Chapter 2, Remembering an Event, for more information about narrating anecdotes.

Most readers would readily agree that this anecdote is well told: It has many concrete, memorable details; there is action, suspense, climax, resolution, and even dialogue. It is about a believable, possible experience. Finally, the anecdote is clearly relevant to the author's argument about gun control.

EXERCISE 19.7

Evaluate the way an anecdote is used in paragraph 16 of Amitai Etzioni's essay "Working at McDonald's" in Chapter 6 (pp. 261–62). Consider whether the story is well told and true to life. Decide whether it seems to be relevant to the whole argument. Does the writer make the relevance clear? Does the anecdote support Etzioni's argument?

Use relevant textual evidence.

When you argue claims of value (Chapter 8) and offer an analysis (Chapter 10), **textual evidence** will be very important. In your college courses, if you are asked to evaluate a controversial article, you must quote, paraphrase, or *summarize* passages so that readers can understand why you think the author's argument is or is not credible. If you are analyzing a novel, you must include numerous excerpts to show just how you arrived at your conclusion.

For textual evidence to be considered effective support for an argument, it must be carefully selected to be relevant. You must help readers see the connection between each piece of evidence and the reason it supports. Textual evidence must also be highly selective — that is, chosen from among all the available evidence to provide the support needed without overwhelming the reader or weakening the argument with marginally relevant evidence. Textual evidence usually has more impact if it is balanced between quotation and paraphrase, and quotations must be smoothly *integrated* into the sentences of the argument.

You can read "Araby" in Chapter 10, pp. 497–500.

The following example comes from a student essay in which the writer argues that the main character (referred to as "the boy") in the short story "Araby" by James Joyce is so self-absorbed that he learns nothing about himself or other people:

The story opens and closes with images of blindness — a framing device that shows the boy does not change but ends up with the same lack of understanding that he began with. The street is "blind" with an "uninhabited house . . . at the blind end" (par. 1). As he spies on Mangan's sister, from his own house, the boy intentionally limits what he is able to see by lowering the "blind" until it is only an inch from the window sash (par. 4). At the bazaar in the closing scene, the "light was out," and the upper part of the hall was "completely dark" (par. 36). The boy is left "gazing up into the darkness," seeing nothing but an inner torment that burns his eyes (par. 37).

> Crane cites textual evidence from "Araby" to convince readers to take her argument seriously.

The boy's blindness appears to be caused by his obsession with Mangan's sister. When he tries to read at night, for example, the girl's "image [comes] between [him] and the page," in effect blinding him (par. 12). In fact, he seems blind to everything except this "image" of the "brown-clad figure cast by [his] imagination" (par. 16). The girl's "brown-clad figure" is also associated with the houses on "blind" North Richmond Street, with their "brown imperturbable faces" (par. 1). The houses stare back at the boy, unaffected by his presence and gaze.

— SALLY CRANE, "Gazing into the Darkness"

Notice how the writer quotes selected words and phrases about blindness to support her reasoning that the boy learns nothing because he is blinded. There are twelve smoothly integrated quotations in these two paragraphs, along with a number of paraphrases, all of them relevant. The writer does not assume that the evidence speaks for itself; she comments and interprets throughout.

> For more information on paraphrasing, see pp. 531–32 in Chapter 12 and pp. 706–8 in Chapter 26.

EXERCISE 19.8

Analyze the use of evidence in paragraphs 2 and 3 of Iris Lee's essay "Performing a Doctor's Duty" in Chapter 10 (pp. 463–66). If you have not read this essay, read it now. Identify the quotes and paraphrases Lee uses, and then try to identify the phrases or sentences that comment on or explain this evidence. Consider whether Lee's evidence in these two paragraphs seems relevant to her thesis and reasons, appropriately selective, well balanced between quotes and paraphrases, integrated smoothly into the sentences she creates, and explained helpfully.

Responding to Objections and Alternatives

Asserting a thesis and backing it with reasons and support are essential to a successful argument. Thoughtful writers go further, however, by anticipating and responding to their readers' objections or their alternative position or solutions to a problem.

To respond to objections and alternatives, writers rely on three basic strategies: acknowledging, conceding, and refuting. Writers show they are aware of readers' objections and questions (*acknowledge*), modify their position to accept readers' concerns they think are legitimate (*concede*), or explicitly argue that readers' objections may be invalid or that their concerns may be irrelevant (*refute*). Writers may use one or more of these three strategies in the same essay. Readers find arguments more convincing when writers have anticipated their concerns in these ways.

Acknowledge readers' concerns.

When you **acknowledge** readers' questions or objections, you show that you are aware of their point of view and take it seriously even if you do not agree with it, as in the following example:

> The homeless, it seems, can be roughly divided into two groups: those who have had marginality and homelessness forced upon them and want nothing more than to escape them, and a smaller number who have at least in part chosen marginality, and now accept, or, in a few cases, embrace it.
>
> I understand how dangerous it can be to introduce the idea of choice into a discussion of homelessness. It can all too easily be used for all the wrong reasons by all the wrong people to justify indifference or brutality toward the homeless, or to argue that they are getting only what they deserve.
>
> And I understand, too, how complicated the notion can become: Many of the veterans on the street, or battered women, or abused and runaway children, have chosen this life only as the lesser of evils, and because, in this society, there is often no place else to go.
>
> And finally, I understand how much that happens on the street can combine to create an apparent acceptance of homelessness that is nothing more than the absolute absence of hope.
>
> Nonetheless we must learn to accept that there may indeed be people on the street who have seen so much of our world, or have seen it so clearly, that to live in it becomes impossible.
>
> — PETER MARIN, "Go Ask Alice"

You might think that acknowledging readers' objections in this way—addressing readers directly, listing their possible objections, and discussing each one—would weaken your argument. It might even seem reckless to suggest objections that not all readers would think of. On the contrary, however, most readers respond positively to this strategy because it makes you seem thoughtful and reasonable. By researching your subject and your readers, you will be able to use this strategy confidently in your own argumentative essays. And you will learn to look for it in arguments you read and use it to make judgments about the writer's credibility.

EXERCISE 19.9

Richard Estrada acknowledges readers' concerns in paragraphs 6 and 7 of his essay in Chapter 6 (pp. 256–57). How, specifically, does Estrada attempt to acknowledge his readers' concerns? What do you find most and least successful in his acknowledgment? How does the acknowledgment affect your judgment of the writer's credibility?

Concede readers' concerns.

To argue effectively, you must often take special care to acknowledge readers' objections; questions; and alternative positions, causes, or solutions. Occasionally, however, you

---

Marin acknowledges three doubts his readers may have regarding his argument that some of America's homeless have chosen that way of life.

may have to go even further. Instead of merely acknowledging your readers' concerns, you may decide to accept some of them and incorporate them into your own argument. This strategy, called **concession,** can be very disarming to readers, for it recognizes that opposing views have merit. The following example comes from an essay enthusiastically endorsing e-mail:

> To be sure, egalitarianism has its limits. The ease and economy of sending email, especially to multiple recipients, makes us all vulnerable to any bore, loony, or commercial or political salesman who can get our email address. It's still a lot less intrusive than the telephone, since you can read and answer or ignore email at your own convenience. But as normal people's email starts mounting into the hundreds daily, . . . filtering mechanisms and conventions of etiquette that are still in their primitive stage will be desperately needed.
>
> Another supposed disadvantage of email is that it discourages face-to-face communication. At Microsoft, where people routinely send email back and forth all day to the person in the next office, this is certainly true. Some people believe this tendency has more to do with the underdeveloped social skills of computer geeks than with Microsoft's role in developing the technology email relies on. I wouldn't presume to comment on that. Whether you think email replacing live conversation is a good or bad thing depends, I guess, on how much of a misanthrope you are. I like it.
>
> — MICHAEL KINSLEY, "Email Culture"

After supporting his own reasons for embracing e-mail, Kinsley accommodates readers' likely reservations by conceding that e-mail poses certain problems.

Notice that Kinsley's accommodation or concession is not grudging. He readily concedes that e-mail brings users a lot of unwanted messages and may discourage conversation in the workplace.

EXERCISE 19.10

How does Patrick O'Malley respond to readers' objections and alternatives in paragraphs 9 and 10 of his Chapter 7 essay (pp. 302–7) arguing for more frequent exams? What seems successful or unsuccessful in his argument? How do his efforts to acknowledge readers' concerns or make concessions affect his argument and his credibility?

Refute readers' objections.

Your readers' possible objections and views cannot always be conceded. Sometimes they must be refuted. When you **refute readers' objections,** you assert that they are wrong and argue against them. Refutation does not have to be delivered arrogantly or dismissively, however. Because differences are inevitable, reasoned argument provides a peaceful and constructive way for informed, well-intentioned people who disagree strongly to air their differences.

In the following example, social sciences professor Todd Gitlin refutes one argument for giving college students the opportunity to purchase lecture notes prepared by someone else:

Gitlin first concedes a possible objection, and then even partially agrees with this view. In the second paragraph, however, he begins to refute the objection.

Now, it may well be argued that universities are already shortchanging their students by stuffing them into huge lecture halls where, unlike at rock concerts or basketball games, the lecturer can't even be seen on a giant screen in real time. If they're already shortchanged with impersonal instruction, what's the harm in offering canned lecture notes?

The amphitheater lecture is indeed, for all but the most engaging professors, a lesser form of instruction, and scarcely to be idealized. Still, Education by Download misses one of the keys to learning. Education is a meeting of minds, a process through which the student educes, draws from within, a response to what the teacher teaches.

The very act of taking notes—not reading someone else's notes, no matter how stellar—is a way of engaging the material, wrestling with it, struggling to comprehend or take issue, but in any case entering into the work. The point is to decide, while you are listening, what matters in the presentation. And while I don't believe that most of life consists of showing up, education does begin with that— with immersing yourself in the activity at hand, listening, thinking, judging, offering active responses. A download is a poor substitute.

— Todd Gitlin, "Disappearing Ink"

As this selection illustrates, writers cannot simply dismiss readers' possible concerns with a wave of their hand. Gitlin states a potential objection fully and fairly but then goes on to refute it by claiming that students need to take their own lecture notes to engage and comprehend the material that is being presented to them.

Effective refutation requires a restrained tone and careful argument. Although you may not accept this particular refutation, you can agree that it is well reasoned and supported. You need not feel attacked personally because the writer disagrees with you.

EXERCISE 19.11

Evaluate Kelly D. Brownell and Thomas R. Frieden's use of refutation in paragraphs 5 and 6 of "Ounces of Prevention — The Public Policy Case for Taxes on Sugared Beverages" (Chapter 7, pp. 315–18). How do Brownell and Frieden signal or announce the refutation? How do they support the refutation? What is the tone of the refutation, and how effective do you think the tone would be in convincing readers to take the writers' argument seriously?

Logical Fallacies

Fallacies are errors or flaws in reasoning. Although essentially unsound, fallacious arguments seem superficially plausible and often have great persuasive power. Fallacies are not necessarily deliberate efforts to deceive readers. Writers may introduce a fallacy accidentally by not examining their own reasons or underlying assumptions, by failing to establish solid support, or by using unclear or ambiguous words. Here is a summary of the most common logical fallacies (listed alphabetically):

- *Begging the question:* Arguing that a claim is true by repeating the claim in different words (also called *circular reasoning*)

- *Confusing chronology with causality:* Assuming that because one thing preceded another, the former caused the latter (also called *post hoc, ergo propter hoc*—Latin for "after this, therefore because of this")

- *Either-or reasoning:* Assuming that there are only two sides to a question and representing yours as the only correct one

- *Equivocating:* Misleading or hedging with ambiguous word choices

- *Failing to accept the burden of proof:* Asserting a claim without presenting a reasoned argument to support it

- *False analogy:* Assuming that because one thing resembles another, conclusions drawn from one also apply to the other

- *Hasty generalization:* Offering only weak or limited evidence to support a conclusion

- *Overreliance on authority:* Assuming that something is true simply because an expert says so and ignoring evidence to the contrary

- *Oversimplifying:* Giving easy answers to complicated questions, often by appealing to emotions rather than logic

- *Personal attack:* Demeaning the proponents of a claim instead of refuting their argument (also called *ad hominem*—Latin for "against the man"—*attack*)

- *Red herring:* Attempting to misdirect the discussion by raising an essentially unrelated point

- *Slanting:* Selecting or emphasizing the evidence that supports your claim and suppressing or playing down other evidence

- *Slippery slope:* Pretending that one thing inevitably leads to another

- *Sob story:* Manipulating readers' emotions to lead them to draw unjustified conclusions

- *Straw man:* Directing the argument against a claim that nobody actually makes or that everyone agrees is very weak

Sentence Strategies for Argument

Writers in college courses, in the community, and in the workplace argue to persuade others, so you are likely to write sentences that assert and support a position or that respond to alternative positions and concede or refute objections. Sentence strategies like these may provide a jumping-off point for articulating your thoughts. Of course, you will probably want to rework the sentences they inspire.

To Assert a Position

▶ When [issue/event] happens, most people think _____, but I think _____ because _____ .

▶ [People] focus on [X], which is characterized by _____, and they don't even notice [Y], which is characterized by _____ .

▶ Although many people take _____ for granted, [list individuals/groups] oppose it on the grounds that _____ .

▶ Whereas supporters of _____ have argued that _____, opponents such as [list individuals/groups] contend that _____ .

▶ Though others may view it as a matter of _____, for me, the issue hinges on _____ .

▶ According to _____, what's at stake in this issue is _____ . For me, however, what is most important is _____ .

▶ On this issue, X and Y say _____ . Although I understand and to some degree sympathize with their point of view, this is ultimately a question of _____ . What's at stake is not _____ but _____ . Therefore, we must _____ .

▶ This issue is dividing our community. Some people argue _____ . Others contend _____ . And still others believe _____ . It is in all of our interests to _____, however, because _____ .

▶ Conventional wisdom is that _____ . But I take a different view: _____ .

▶ [Subject] has many good qualities, including _____ and _____; however, the pluses do not outweigh its one major drawback, namely that _____ .

▶ [Subject] is a brilliant embodiment of [genre or category], especially notable for its superb _____ and thorough _____ .

▶ Because I admire [another artist's other work], I expected [subject] to be _____ . But I was [disappointed/surprised] by _____ because _____ .

▶ Many complain about _____ but do nothing because solving it seems [too hard/too costly].

To Support a Position

▶ What makes _____ [problematic/praiseworthy] is _____ .

▶ Because _____, I [support/oppose] _____ .

▶ Studies such as _____ have shown that [problem] mostly affects _____ [name group(s)].

▶ Studies by X, Y, and Z show that [solution] has worked in _____, _____, and _____ .

▶ The reasons for .... may surprise you, such as ...., ..., and
....

▶ The cause(s) of [subject] may be [surprising/alarming/disturbing/amazing], but they are clear: .... [state cause(s) and provide evidence].

▶ [Cause] plays a [surprising/alarming/disturbing/amazing] role in [our lives/our families/our communities/our workplaces]: It [does/is/provides] .... [describe role].

▶ For many years, [name group] has believed that .... Now there is research supporting this claim, but not for the reasons you may think. It's not .... that has been causing this phenomenon but ....

▶ Researchers studying .... have shown a causal connection between .... [my causes] and .... [my subject]. They claim .... [quote/paraphrase/summarize information from source] (cite source).

▶ A large number of people have been polled on this question, and it appears that .... was an important factor in their decision to ....

▶ Reliable research by .... shows ....

To Refute an Opposing Position

▶ One problem with [opposing view] is that ....

▶ Some claim [opposing view], but in reality ....

▶ My opponents cite research to support their argument, but the credibility of that research is questionable because ....

▶ This argument seems plausible because it is consistent with our preconceptions. Nevertheless, evidence shows ....

▶ Activists insist .... Still, in spite of their good intentions, ... would [take away a basic right/make things even worse].

▶ X and Y think this issue is about .... But what is really at stake here is ....

▶ Proponents object to my argument on the grounds that .... However, they are confusing results with causes. What I am arguing is ....

▶ Polls show that most people favor .... , but an opinion's popularity does not make it true or right.

▶ Though most would agree that .... is true, it does not necessarily follow that ....

▶ One common complaint is .... In recent years, however, ...

▶ Some people think we can't afford to do .... [name solution], but it would only cost $ .... [insert dollar amount] to put my solution in place compared to $ .... , the cost of [doing nothing/implementing an alternative solution].

▶ Although it might take _____ [months/years] to implement this solution, it would actually take longer to implement [alternative solution].

▶ Some may suggest that I favor this solution because I would benefit personally; however, the fact is we would all benefit because _____ .

▶ Some may claim that this solution has been tried and hasn't worked. But research shows that _____ [explain how my solution differs from past experiments in several important ways]: _____ , _____ , and _____ (list differences).

▶ X, reviewer for _____ , claims that _____ . But I agree with Y, reviewer for _____ , who argues that _____ .

▶ Some people think [subject] is [alternative judgment] because of _____ , _____ , and _____ [reasons]. Although it is easy to see why they might make this argument, the evidence does not back it up: _____ [explanation].

▶ Reviewers have remarked that [subject] is a pale imitation of [comparable subject]. I disagree. Whereas [comparable subject] is _____ , [subject] is _____ .

▶ This [subject] has generated criticism for its supposed _____ . But [subject] is not _____ . Instead, it is _____ .

▶ A recent study of [subject] showed that _____ .

To Concede an Objection

▶ I agree that _____ .

▶ _____ is certainly an important factor.

▶ To be sure, _____ is true.

▶ Granted, _____ must be taken into consideration.

▶ Some people argue that _____ . I understand this reservation, and therefore, I think we should _____ .

▶ A common concern about this issue is _____ . That's why my argument focuses on [this other aspect] of the issue.

▶ I agree with those who [claim X/object on X grounds]; therefore, instead of [option A], I think we should pursue [option B].

▶ If _____ seems too [time-consuming/expensive], let's try _____ .

▶ Where _____ is a concern, I think [name alternative] should be followed.

▶ Although _____ is the best way to deal with a problem like this, under [describe special circumstances], I agree that _____ should be done.

▶ Indeed, the more hard-core [name enthusiasts] may carp that [subject] is not sufficiently _____ [shortcomings].

▶ The one justifiable criticism that could be made against [subject] is ....

▶ As some critics have pointed out, [subject] does follow the tried-and-true formula of ....

To Concede and Refute an Objection

▶ .... may be true for X but not for Y.

▶ Although ...., I think ....

▶ X and Y insist that .... Nevertheless, in spite of their good intentions, ...

▶ I agree that .... is important, but so is ....

▶ I agree that .... is important, but my opponents need to consider ....

▶ On the one hand, I accept X's argument that ...., but on the other hand, I still think .... is ultimately more important because ....

▶ As some critics have pointed out, [subject] does follow the tried-and-true formula of .... Still, the [director/writer/artist] is using the formula effectively to ....

▶ The objection that [subject] can be caused by things other than [my cause] may be true. But there is strong evidence showing that [my cause] played a central role by ....

▶ Those who disagree about .... often see it as a choice between .... and .... But both are important. We don't have to choose between them because ....

20

Analyzing Visuals

We live in a highly visual world. Every day we are deluged with a seemingly endless stream of images from television, magazines, billboards, books, Web pages, newspapers, flyers, storefront signs, and more, all of them competing for our attention, and all of them loaded with information and ideas. Forms of communication that traditionally used only the written word (letters, books, term papers) or the spoken word (telephone conversations, lectures) are today increasingly enhanced with visual components (PowerPoint slides, cell-phone graphics, video, photos, illustrations, graphs, and the like) for greater impact. And most of us would agree that visuals do, indeed, have an impact: A picture, as the saying goes, is worth a thousand words.

In part because of their potentially powerful effect on us, visuals and visual texts* should be approached the way we approach written texts: analytically and critically. Whether their purpose is to sell us an idea or a car, to spur us to action or inspire us to dream, visuals invite analysis both of their key components and their *rhetorical context*. As we "read" a visual, therefore, we should ask ourselves a series of questions: Who created it? Where was it published? What *audience* is it addressing? What is it trying to get this audience to think and feel about the subject? How does it attempt to achieve this *purpose*?

FIGURE 20.1
Times Square at Dusk

Let's look, for example, at the visual text on the following page: a public service announcement (PSA) from the World Wildlife Fund (WWF).

---

* In this chapter, we use the word *image* to refer primarily to photographs. We use the word *visual* as a broader designation for visual elements of texts (including images, but also such components as diagrams, charts, and graphs), and *visual text* for documents such as ads, brochures, and the like, in which visuals are strongly featured, but which consist of more than a single image.

The central image in this PSA is a photo of an attractive, smiling young couple. Most of us will immediately recognize the dress, posture, and facial expressions of the young man and woman as those of a newly married couple; the photo-mounting corners make the image seem like a real wedding album photo, as opposed to an ad agency's creation (which would be easier to ignore). After noting these things, however, we are immediately struck by what is wrong with the picture: a hurricane rages in the background, blowing hair, clothing, and the bride's veil forcefully to one side showering the bride's pure white dress with spots (of rain? mud?) and threatening to rip the bridal bouquet from her hand.

So what do we make of the disruption of the convention (the traditional wedding photo) on which the PSA image is based? In trying to decide, most of us will look next to the text below the image: "Ignoring global warming won't make it go away." The disjunction between the couple's blissful expression and the storm raging around them turns out to be the point of the PSA: Like the young couple in the picture, the PSA implies, we are all blithely ignoring the impending disaster that global warming represents. The reputable, nonprofit WWF's logo and URL, which constitute its "signature," are meant to be an assurance that this threat is real, and not just an idea a profit-seeking ad agency dreamt up to manipulate us.

FIGURE 20.2
"Wedding," from the WWF's "Beautiful Day U.S." Series

People continue to argue about how urgent the problem of climate change is and what, if anything, we need to do about it. The WWF suggests that, like the clueless young couple, too many of us have adopted a "head-in-the-sand" attitude about the problem. Lest the implied criticism be construed as an outright insult and alienate viewers, the implied connection to the couple also flatters us by implying that we are attractive, hopeful, and well intentioned. Global warming, in the WWF's view, threatens the bright future we all like to imagine we have ahead of us.

Not everyone will be convinced by this PSA to support the work of the WWF, and some viewers may feel manipulated by the visual image. They may disagree that the problem is as dire as the depiction implicitly claims it is. They may feel that our resources and energy would be better directed toward other problems facing the world. Nevertheless, most people would agree that with a single cleverly constructed image, a single line of text, and a logo, the PSA delivers its message clearly and forcefully.

Criteria for Analyzing Visuals

The primary purpose of this chapter is to help you analyze visuals and write about them. In your college courses, some of you will be asked to write entire papers in which you analyze one or more visuals (a painting or a photo, for example). Some of you will write papers in which you include analysis of one or more visual texts within the context of a larger written essay (say, by analyzing the brochures and ads authorized by a political candidate, in an argument about her campaign).

Of course, learning to analyze visuals effectively can also help you gain a more complete understanding of any document that *uses* visuals but that is not entirely or predominantly composed of them. Why did the author of a remembered event essay, for example, choose a particular photo of a person mentioned in the text—does it reinforce the written description, add to it, or contradict it in some way? If there is a caption under the photo, how does it affect the way we

---

CRITERIA FOR ANALYZING VISUALS

KEY COMPONENTS

Composition

- Of what elements is the visual composed?
- What is the focal point—that is, the place your eyes are drawn to?
- From what perspective do you view the focal point? Are you looking straight ahead at it, down at it, or up at it? If the visual is a photograph, what angle was the image shot from—straight ahead, looking down or up?
- What colors are used? Are there obvious special effects employed? Is there a frame, or are there any additional graphical elements? If so, what do these elements contribute to your "reading" of the visual?

People/Other Main Figures

- If people are depicted, how would you describe their age, gender, subculture, ethnicity, profession, level of attractiveness, and socioeconomic class? How do these factors relate to other elements of the image?
- Who is looking at whom? Do the people represented seem conscious of the viewer's gaze?

- What do the facial expressions and body language tell you about power relationships (equal, subordinate, in charge) and attitudes (self-confident, vulnerable, anxious, subservient, angry, aggressive, sad)?

Scene

- If a recognizable scene is depicted, what is its setting? What is in the background and the foreground?
- What has happened just before the image was "shot"? What will happen in the next scene?
- What, if anything, is happening just outside of the visual frame?

Words

- If text is combined with the visual, what role does the text play? Is it a slogan? A famous quote? Lyrics from a well-known song?
- If the text help you interpret the visual's overall meaning, what interpretive clues does it provide?
- What is the tone of the text? Humorous? Elegiac? Ironic?

read it? In a concept explanation, why are illustrations of one process included but not those of another? How well do the charts and graphs work with the text to help us understand the author's explanation? Understanding what visuals can do for a text can also help you effectively integrate images, charts, graphs, and other visuals into your own essays, whatever your topic.

The chart above outlines key criteria for analyzing visuals and provides questions for you to ask about documents that include them.

A Sample Analysis

In a composition class, students were asked to do a short written analysis of a photograph. In looking for ideas, Paul Taylor came across the Library of Congress's *Documenting America*, an exhibit of photographs taken 1935–45. Gordon Parks's

---

Tone

- What tone, or mood, does the visual convey? Is it lighthearted, somber, frightening, shocking, joyful? What elements in the visual (color, composition, words, people, setting) convey this tone?

CONTEXT(S)

Rhetorical Context

- **What is the visual's main purpose?** Are we being asked to buy a product? Form an opinion or judgment about something? Support a political party's candidate? Take some other kind of action?

- **Who is its target audience?** Children? Men? Women? Some sub- or super-set of these groups (e.g., African American men, "tweens," seniors)?

- **Who is the author? Who sponsored its publication?** What background/associations do the author and the sponsoring publication have? What other works have they produced?

- **Where was it published, and in what form?** Online? On television? In print? In a commercial publication (a sales brochure, billboard, ad) or an informational one (newspaper, magazine)?

- **If the visual is embedded within a document that is primarily written text, how do the written text and the visual relate to each other?** Do they convey the same message, or are they at odds in any way? What does the image contribute to the written text? Is it essential or just eye candy?

- *Social Context.* **What is the immediate social and cultural context within which the visual is operating?** If we are being asked to support a certain candidate, for example, how does the visual reinforce or counter what we already know about this candidate? What other social/cultural knowledge does the visual assume its audience already has?

- *Historical Context.* **What historical knowledge does it assume the audience already possesses?** Does the visual refer to other historical images, figures, events, or stories that the audience would recognize? How do these historical references relate to the visual's audience and purpose?

- *Intertextuality.* **How does the visual connect, relate to, or contrast with any other significant texts, visual or otherwise, that you are aware of?** How do such considerations inform your ideas about this particular visual?

FIGURE 20.3   *Ella Watson,* **Gordon Parks (1942)**

FIGURE 20.4   *American Gothic,* **Grant Wood (1930)**

Source: The Art Institute of Chicago. © Figge Art Museum, successors to the estate of Nan Wood Graham/VAGA.

photographs struck Paul as particularly interesting, especially those of Ella Watson, a poorly paid office cleaner employed by the federal government. (See Figure 20.3.)

After studying the photos, Paul read about Parks's first session with Watson:

> My first photograph of [Watson] was unsubtle. I overdid it and posed her, Grant Wood style, before the American flag, a broom in one hand, a mop in the other, staring straight into the camera.[1]

Paul didn't understand Parks's reference to Grant Wood in his description of the photo, so he did an Internet search and discovered that Parks was referring to a classic painting by Wood called *American Gothic* (Figure 20.4). Reading further about the connection, he discovered that Parks's photo of Watson is itself commonly titled *American Gothic* and discussed as a parody of Grant Wood's painting.

---

[1]Gordon Parks, *A Choice of Weapons* (New York: Harper & Row, 1966), 230–31.

After learning about the connection with *American Gothic,* Paul read more about the context of Parks's photos:

> Gordon Parks was born in Kansas in 1912. . . . During the Depression a variety of jobs . . . took him to various parts of the northern United States. He took up photography during his travels. . . . In 1942, an opportunity to work for the Farm Security Administration brought the photographer to the nation's capital; Parks later recalled that "discrimination and bigotry were worse there than any place I had yet seen."[2]

Intrigued by what he had learned so far, Paul decided to delve into Parks's later career. A 2006 obituary of Parks in the *New York Times* reproduced his 1952 photo *Emerging Man,* which Paul decided to analyze for his assignment. First he did additional research on the photo. Then he made notes on his responses to the photo using the criteria for analysis provided on pp. 628–29.

FIGURE 20.5 *Emerging Man,* **Gordon Parks (1952)**

Photograph courtesy of the Gordon Parks Foundation. Copyright © The Gordon Parks Foundation.

---

[2]Martin H. Bush, "A Conversation with Gordon Parks," in *The Photographs of Gordon Parks* (Wichita, KS: Wichita State University, 1983), 36.

PAUL TAYLOR'S ANALYSIS OF *EMERGING MAN*

KEY COMPONENTS OF THE VISUAL

Composition

- **Of what elements is the visual composed?** It's a black-and-white photo showing the top three-quarters of a man's face and his hands (mostly fingers). He appears to be emerging out of the ground--out of a sewer? There's what looks like asphalt in the foreground, and buildings (out of focus) in the far background.

- **What is the focal point—that is, the place your eyes are drawn to?** The focal point is the face of the man staring directly into the camera's lens. There's a shaft of light angled (slightly from the right?) onto the lower-middle part of his face. His eyes appear to glisten slightly. The rest of his face, his hands, and the foreground are in shadow.

- **From what perspective do you view the focal point?** We appear to be looking at him at eye level--weird, since eye level for him is just a few inches from the ground. Was the photographer lying down? The shot is also a close-up--a foot or two from the man's face. Why so close?

- **What colors are used? Are there obvious special effects employed? Is there a frame, or are there any additional graphical elements?** There's no visible frame or any graphic elements. The image is in stark black and white, and there's a "graininess" to it: we can see the texture of the man's skin and the asphalt on the street.

People/Other Main Figures

- **If people are depicted, how would you describe their age, gender, subculture, ethnicity, profession, level of attractiveness, and socioeconomic class?** The man is African American and probably middle-aged (or at least not obviously very young or very old). We can't see his clothing or any other marker of class, profession, etc. The fact that he seems to be emerging from a sewer implies that he's not hugely rich or prominent, of course--a "man of the people"?

- **Who is looking at whom? Do the people represented seem conscious of the viewer's gaze?** The man seems to be looking directly into the camera and at the viewer (who's in the position of the photographer). I guess, yes, he seems to look straight at the viewer--perhaps in a challenging or questioning way.

- **What do the facial expressions and body language tell you about power relationships (equal, subordinate, in charge) and attitudes (self-confident, vulnerable, anxious, subservient, angry, aggressive, sad)?** We can only see his face from the nose up, and his fingertips. It looks like one eyebrow is slightly raised, which might mean he's questioning or skeptical. The expression in his eyes is definitely serious. The position of his fingers implies that he's clutching the rim of the manhole--that, and the title, indicate that he's pulling himself up out of the hole. But since we see only the fingers, not the whole hand, does his hold seem tenuous--he's "holding on by his fingertips"? Not sure.

Scene

- **If a recognizable scene is depicted, what is its setting? What is in the background and the foreground?** It looks like an urban setting (asphalt, manhole cover, buildings, and lights in the blurry distant background). Descriptions of the photo note that Parks shot the image in Harlem. Hazy buildings and objects are in the distance. Only the man's face and fingertips are in focus. The sky behind him is light gray, though--is it dawn?

- **What has happened just before the image was "shot"? What will happen in the next scene?** He appears to be coming up and out of the hole in the ground (the sewer).

- **What, if anything, is happening just outside of the visual frame?** It's not clear. There's no activity in the background at all. It's deserted, except for him.

Words

- **If text is combined with the visual, what role does the text play?** There's no text on or near the image. There is the title, though--*Emerging Man*.

- **Does the text help you interpret the visual's overall meaning?** The title is a literal description, but it might also refer to the civil rights movement--the gradual racial and economic integration--of African Americans into American society.

- **What is the tone of the text?** Hard to say. I guess, assuming wordplay is involved, it's sort of witty (merging traffic?).

Tone

- **What tone, or mood, does the visual convey? What elements in the visual (color, composition, words, people, setting) convey this tone?** The tone is serious, even perhaps a bit spooky. The use of black and white and heavy shadows lends a somewhat ominous feel, though the ray of light on the man's face, the lightness of the sky, and the lights in the background counterbalance this to an extent. The man's expression is somber, though not obviously angry or grief-stricken.

CONTEXT(S)

Rhetorical Context

- **What is the visual's main purpose?** Given Parks's interest in politics and social justice, it seems fair to assume that the image of the man emerging from underground--from the darkness into the light?--is a reference to social progress (civil rights movement) and suggests rebirth of a sort. The use of black and white, while certainly not unusual in photographs of the era, emphasizes the division between black and white that is in part the photo's subject.

- **Who is its target audience?** Because it appeared first in Life, the target audience was mainstream-- a broad cross-section of the magazine-reading U.S. population at mid-twentieth century.

- **Who is the author? Who sponsored its publication?** During this era, Gordon Parks was best known as a photographer whose works documented and commented on social conditions. The fact that this photo was originally published in Life (a mainstream periodical read by white Americans throughout the country) is probably significant.

- **If the visual is embedded within a document that is primarily written text, how do the written text and the visual relate to each other?** The photo accompanied an article about Ellison's *Invisible Man,* a novel about a man who goes underground to escape racism and conflicts within the early civil rights movement. Now the man is reentering mainstream society?

- *Social Context.* **What is the immediate social and cultural context within which the visual is operating?** The civil rights movement was gaining ground in post–World War II society.

- *Historical Context.* **What historical knowledge does it assume the audience already possesses?** For a viewer in 1952, the image would call to mind the current and past situation of African Americans. Uncertainty about what the future would hold (Would the emergence be successful? What kind of man would eventually emerge?) would be a big part of the viewer's response. Viewers today obviously feel less suspense about what would happen in the immediate (post-1952) future. The "vintage" feel of the photo's style and even the man's hair, along with the use of black and white, probably have a "distancing" effect on the viewer today. At the same time, the subject continues to be relevant--most viewers will likely think about the progress we've made in race relations and where we're currently headed.

- *Intertextuality.* **How does the visual connect, relate to, or contrast with any other significant texts, visual or otherwise, that you are aware of?** *Invisible Man,* which I've already discussed, was a best-seller and won the National Book Award in 1953.

After writing and reviewing these notes and doing some further research to fill in gaps in his knowledge about Parks, Ellison, and the civil rights movement, Paul drafted his analysis. He submitted this draft to his peer group for comments, and then revised. His final draft follows.

Taylor 1

Paul Taylor

Professor Stevens

Writing Seminar I

4 October 2012

The Rising

Gordon Parks's 1952 photograph *Emerging Man* (Fig. 1) is as historically significant a reflection of the civil rights movement as are the speeches of Martin Luther King and Malcolm X, the music of Mahalia Jackson, and the books of Ralph Ellison and James Baldwin. Through striking use of black and white--a reflection of the racial divisions plaguing American cities and towns throughout much of the nineteenth and twentieth centuries--and a symbolically potent central subject--an African American man we see literally "emerging" from a city manhole--Parks's photo evokes the centuries of racial and economic marginalization of African Americans, at the same time as it projects a spirit of determination and optimism regarding the civil rights movement's eventual success.

In choosing the starkest of urban settings and giving the image a gritty feel, Parks alerts the viewer to the gravity of his subject and gives

Fig. 1. Gordon Parks, *Emerging Man* (1952)

Fig. 2. Gordon Parks, *Ella Watson* (1942)

it a sense of immediacy. As with the documentary photographs Parks took of office cleaner Ella Watson for the Farm Security Administration in the 1940s--see Fig. 2 for one example--the carefully chosen setting and the spareness of the treatment ensure the viewer's focus on the social statement the artist is making (*Documenting*). Whereas the photos of Ella Watson document a particular woman and the actual conditions of her life and work, however, *Emerging Man* strips away any particulars, including any name for the man, with the result that the photo enters the symbolic or even mythic realm.

The composition of *Emerging Man* makes it impossible for us to focus on anything other than the unnamed subject rising from the manhole--we are, for instance, unable to consider what the weather might be, though we might surmise from the relatively light tone of the sky and the emptiness of the street that it is dawn. Similarly, we are not given any specifics of the setting, which is simply urban and, apart from the central figure, unpopulated. Reducing the elements to their outlines in this way keeps the viewer focused on the grand central theme of the piece: the role of race in mid-twentieth-century America and the future of race relations.

Taylor 3

The fact that the man is looking directly at the camera, in a way that's challenging but not hostile, speaks to the racial optimism of the period among many African Americans and whites alike. President Truman's creation of the President's Committee on Civil Rights in 1946 and his 1948 Executive Order for the integration of all armed services were significant steps toward the emergence of the full-blown civil rights movement, providing hope that African Americans would be able, for perhaps the first time in American history, to look directly into the eyes of their white counterparts and fearlessly emphasize their shared humanity (Leuchtenburg). The "emerging man" seems to be daring us to try to stop his rise from the manhole, his hands gripping its sides, his eyes focused intently on the viewer.

According to several sources, Parks planned and executed the photograph as a photographic counterpart to Ralph Ellison's 1952 *Invisible Man,* a breakthrough novel about race and society that was both a best-seller and a critical success. *Invisible Man* is narrated in the first person by an unnamed African American man who traces his experiences from boyhood. The climax of the novel shows the narrator hunted by policemen controlling a Harlem race riot; escaping down a manhole, the narrator is trapped at first but eventually decides to live permanently underground, hidden from society ("Ralph Ellison"). The correspondences between the photo and the book are apparent. In fact, according to the catalog accompanying an exhibit of Parks's photos selected by the photographer himself before his death in 2006, Ellison actually collaborated on the staging of the photo (*Bare Witness*).

More than just a photographic counterpart, however, it seems that Parks's *Emerging Man* can be read as a sequel to *Invisible Man,* with the emphasis radically shifted from resignation to optimism. The man who had decided to live underground now decides to emerge, and does so with determination. In this compelling photograph, Parks--himself an "emerging man," considering he was the first African American photographer to be hired full-time by the widely respected mainstream *Life* magazine-- created a photograph that celebrated the changing racial landscape in American society.

Taylor 4

Works Cited

Bare Witness: Photographs by Gordon Parks. Catalog. Milan: Skira;
    Stanford, CA: Iris & B. Gerald Cantor Center for Visual Arts at
    Stanford University, 2006. Traditional Fine Arts Organization.
    Resource Library. Web. 29 Sept. 2012.

Documenting America: Photographers on Assignment. 15 Dec. 1998.
    *America from the Great Depression to World War II: Black-and-White
    Photographs from the FSA-OWI, 1935-1945*. Prints and Photographs
    Div., Lib. of Cong. Web. 27 Sept. 2012.

Leuchtenburg, William E. "The Conversion of Harry Truman." *American
    Heritage 42.7* (1991): 55-68. *America: History & Life*. Web. 29 Sept.
    2012.

Parks, Gordon. *Ella Watson*. Aug. 1942. *America from the Great Depression
    to World War II: Black-and-White Photographs from the FSA-OWI,
    1935-1945*. Prints and Photographs Div., Lib. of Cong. Web.
    27 Sept. 2012.

---. *Emerging Man*. 1952. *PhotoMuse*. George Eastman House and ICP,
    n.d. Web. 26 Sept. 2012.

"Ralph Ellison: *Invisible Man*." *Literature and Its Times: Profiles of 300
    Notable Literary Works and the Historical Events That Influenced
    Them*. Ed. Joyce Moss and George Wilson. Vol. 4. Gale Research,
    1997. *Literature Resource Center*. Web. 30 Sept. 2012.

EXERCISE 20.1

Dorothea Lange's *First-Graders at the Weill Public School* shows children of Japanese descent reciting the Pledge of Allegiance in San Francisco, California, in 1942. Following the steps below, write an essay suggesting what the image means.

First-Graders at the Weill Public School, **Dorothea Lange (1942)**

1. Do some research on Lange's work. (Like Paul Taylor, you might start at the Library of Congress's online exhibit *Documenting America,* which features Lange, along with Gordon Parks and other photographers.)

2. Analyze the image using the criteria for analysis presented on pp. 628–29.

3. From this preliminary analysis, develop a tentative thesis that says what the image means and how it communicates that meaning.

4. With this thesis in mind, plan your essay, using your analysis of the image to illustrate your thesis. Be aware that as you draft your essay, your thesis will develop and may even change substantially.

Analyze one of the ads that follow by using the criteria for visual analysis on pp. 628–29. Be sure to consider the role that writing plays in the ad's overall meaning. Write an essay with a thesis that discusses the ad's central meaning and significance.

Magazine Ad for Continental Savings Bank (2008)

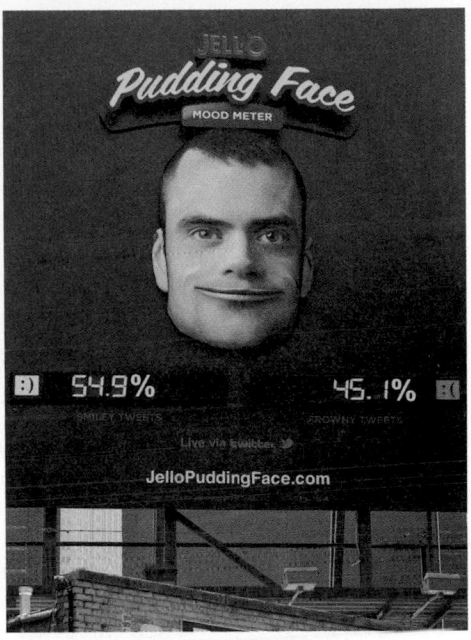

Magazine Ad for Jell-O (2012)

Magazine Ad for Novopelle Laser Hair Removal (2008)
(Text reads: "A closet full of low-cut blouses. Countless hours at the gym. A small fortune in pushup bras. And he can't stop staring at my upper lip.")

Find an ad or public service announcement that you find compelling in its use of visuals. Analyze the ad by using the criteria for visual analysis on pp. 628–29. Be sure to consider the role that writing plays in the ad's overall meaning. Write an essay with a thesis that discusses the ad's central meaning and significance.

21

Designing Documents

The way a document is designed—the arrangement of text, visuals, and white space on a page—has a major impact on the readability of a document and may influence the reader's attitude toward it. This chapter introduces basic components of document design, offers guidelines for designing effective documents, and discusses some common formats for documents you may be asked to create in your college courses or in the workplace. You may also want to look at the Think about Design sections in Chapters 2–10 to learn more about how to format and integrate visuals into college writing projects. In addition, Chapters 27 and 28 include research projects annotated to point out the formatting requirements in MLA and APA style.

The Impact of Document Design

When we read a well-designed document, part of the meaning we take away from it is attributable to design. When we read a poorly designed document, however, it may be difficult to discern its meaning at all. We can probably all agree that effectively written documents are easy to navigate, and their meanings are accessible to the intended audience. Good design should accordingly make readability easier and make the intended meaning clearer and more vivid.

The ways in which design affects the way we read documents can be illustrated fairly simply. Consider the following familiar phrase, rendered in four different ways:

I   l   o   v   e   y   o   u

I love you

The words in each rendering are the same, but the different uses of fonts, colors, and white space encourage us to read them very differently. The first message is vaguely unsettling (is that a ransom note? a message from a stalker?); the second seems conventionally sweet; the third carries no emotional or context clues, but the spacing makes it irritatingly difficult to read; and the fourth offers no tone or context clues at all (though this in itself might strike us as odd, given the meaning of the words). Thus, design does far more than add visual interest: It actually directs how we read and, to a certain extent, determines the meaning we derive from texts.

The freedom you have in terms of using design elements and visuals in your college writing projects will vary quite a bit, depending on your instructors' preferences and the nature of the projects. As you write, however, you should always remain aware of the impact document design can have on your reader. And any time you read a document—whether it is a textbook, a blog, or even an ad on the bus—you should stop to think about how that document was designed and how that design affects your reading of it.

Considering Context, Audience, and Purpose

Context, audience, and *purpose* are the key components to consider in designing any document. For instance, if you are writing an essay for a college course, you can expect that your instructor and your classmates will read it carefully. Your design decisions should therefore make sustained reading as easy as possible; fonts that are too small to read easily or print that is too light to see clearly will make the reader's job unnecessarily difficult. Additionally, instructors usually ask students to submit hard-copy work that is double-spaced text with one-inch margins to give the reviewers room to write comments on the page.*

In most college courses, guidelines on design have traditionally followed a "less is more" rule—written assignments were generally expected to be printed on white, 8.5- by 11-inch paper, and the use of colors, extravagant fonts, sheerly decorative visuals, and the like, was in most cases discouraged. However, in many college classrooms, what constitutes an acceptable course "paper" or project is in transition; many instructors now allow or in some cases require the creation of multimodal projects — Web sites, video, PowerPoint presentations, playlists, and the like—in place of traditional papers.

Developments like these, driven largely by advances in technology, have obviously required some adjustments to traditional notions of acceptable design for college writing. "Less is more" still applies, however, in principle. Good design gives priority to clarity:

---

* It is important to note that MLA, APA, and other style systems have specific rules regarding such things as spacing, margins, and heading formats. Be sure to ask your instructor whether you will be expected to adhere closely to these rules; if so, your choices regarding document design will be limited. For more on MLA and APA style, see pp. 709–50.

Whatever the project, you should use design not for its own sake but to make your points as clearly, effectively, and efficiently as possible.

Of course, the same principle of clarity applies to most *non*academic documents you will write. In writing for nonacademic audiences, however, you cannot necessarily expect all readers to read your writing closely. Some readers may skim through your blog entries looking for interesting points; others might scan a report or memo for information important specifically to them. Design elements such as *headings, bullets,* and *chunking* will help these readers find the information of most interest to them.

Frequently, too, your document design decisions will be predetermined by the kind of document you are preparing. Business letters and memos, for example, traditionally follow specific formats. Because your readers will bring certain expectations to these kinds of documents, altering an established format can cause confusion and should therefore be avoided.

To analyze the context in which a document is read or used, ask yourself the following questions:

- *Where will my document be read?* Will the document be read on paper in a well-lighted, quiet room, or in another context — perhaps on a laptop in a noisy, dimly lit coffee shop?

- *Do my readers have specific expectations for this kind of document?* Am I writing a memo, letter, or report that requires certain design conventions? Does my instructor expect me to follow MLA style, APA style, or another system?

- *How will the information be used?* Are my readers reading to learn or to be entertained? Do I expect them to skim the document or to read it carefully?

Elements of Document Design

Readable *fonts;* informative *headings; bulleted or numbered lists;* and appropriate use of *color, white space,* and *visuals* like photographs, charts, and diagrams all help readers learn from your document.

Choose readable fonts.

Typography is a design term for the letters and symbols that make up the print on a page or a screen. You are already using important aspects of typography when you use capital letters, italics, boldface, or different sizes of type to signal a new sentence, identify the title of a book, or distinguish a heading from body text.

Word processing programs enable you to use dozens of different **fonts,** or typefaces; bold and italic versions of these fonts; and a range of font sizes. Fortunately, you can rely on some simple design principles to make good typographic choices for your documents.

Perhaps the most important advice for working with typography is to choose fonts that are easy to read. Some fonts are meant for decorative or otherwise very minimal use, and are hard to read in extended passages. Font style, font size, and combinations of style and size are features that can add to or detract from readability.

Considering Font Style   For most academic and business writing, you will probably want to choose a traditional font that is easy to read, such as Arial or Times New Roman. This book is set in Calisto. Sentences and paragraphs printed in fonts that imitate *calligraphy* (typically called script fonts) or those that mimic **Handwriting** are not only difficult to read but also too informal in appearance for most academic and business purposes.

Some Fonts Appropriate for Academic and Business Writing

Arial

Georgia

Tahoma

Times New Roman

Verdana

Considering Font Size   To ensure that your documents can be read easily, you also need to choose an appropriate font size (traditionally measured in units called **points**). For most types of academic writing, a 12-point font is standard for the main (body) text. For Web pages, however, you should consider using a slightly larger font to compensate for the difficulty of reading from a computer monitor. For computer-projected displays, you should use an even larger font size (such as 32-point, and typically no smaller than 18-point) to ensure that the text can be read from a distance.

Combining Font Styles and Sizes   Although computers now make hundreds of font styles and sizes available to writers, you should avoid confusing readers with too many different fonts in one document. Limit the fonts in a document to one or two that complement each other well. A common practice, for instance, is to choose one font for all titles and headings (such as Arial, 14-pt, boldface) and another for the body text (such as Times New Roman, 12-pt), as shown in the example here.

This Is an Example Heading

This is body text. This is body text.
This is body text. This is body text.
This is body text. This is body text.

This Is an Example Heading

This is body text. This is body text.
This is body text. This is body text.
This is body text. This is body text.

Use headings to organize your writing.

Titles and headings are often distinguished from body text by boldface, italics, or font size. Headings are helpful in calling attention to certain parts or sections of a piece of writing and in offering readers visual cues to its overall organization. Always check with your instructor about the conventions for using (or not using) these elements in the particular discipline you are studying.

Distinguishing between Headings and Subheadings   Typically, headings for major sections (level-one headings) must have more visual impact than those subdividing these sections (level-two headings), which should be more prominent than headings within the subdivisions (level-three headings). The typography should reflect this hierarchy of headings. Here is one possible system for distinguishing among three levels of headings:

LEVEL-ONE HEADING
Level-Two Heading
Level-Three Heading

Notice that the level-one and level-two headings are given the greatest prominence by the use of boldface and that they are distinguished from one another by the use of all capital letters for the major heading versus capital and lowercase letters for the subheading. The third-level heading, italicized but not boldfaced, is less prominent than the other two headings but can still be readily distinguished from body text. Whatever system you use to distinguish headings and subheadings, be sure to apply it consistently throughout your document.

For more on selecting appropriate headings and subheadings, see Chapter 13, pp. 558–59.

Positioning Headings Consistently   In addition to keeping track of the font size and style of headings, you need to position headings in the same way throughout a piece of writing. You will want to consider the spacing above and below headings and determine whether the headings should be aligned with the left margin, indented a fixed amount of space, or centered. In this book, headings like the one that begins this paragraph—**Positioning Headings Consistently**—are aligned with the left margin and followed by a fixed amount of space.

Using Type Size to Differentiate Headings from Text   In documents that do not need to observe MLA or APA style, which have specific rules about formatting, you may wish to use font size to help make headings visually distinct from the body of the text. If you do so, avoid making the headings too large. To accompany 12-point body text, for instance, a 14-point heading will do. The default settings for heading and body text styles on most word processing and desktop publishing programs are effective, and you may want to use them to autoformat your heading and text styles.

Use lists to highlight steps or key points.

Lists are often an effective way to present information in a logical and visually coherent way. Use a **numbered list** (1, 2, 3) to present the steps in a process or to list items that readers will need to refer to easily (for instance, see the sample e-mail message on p. 656). Use a **bulleted list** (marking each new item with a "bullet"—a dash, circle, or box) to highlight key points when the order of the items is not significant (for instance, see the sample memo on p. 653). Written instructions, such as recipes, are typically formatted using numbered lists, whereas a list of supplies, for example, is more often presented in the form of a bulleted list.

Use colors with care.

Color printers, photocopiers, and online technology facilitate the use of color, but color does not necessarily make text easier to read. In most academic print documents, the only color you should use is black. Though color is typically used more freely in academic writing produced in other media (for example, Web pages or slide-show presentations), it should still be used in moderation and always with the aim of increasing your readers' understanding of what you have to say. Always consider, too, whether your readers might be color-blind and whether they will have access to a full-color version of the document.

Although the slideshow design in Figure 21.1 is visually interesting and the heading is readable, the bulleted text is very hard to read because there is too little contrast between the text color and the background color.

In Figure 21.2, it is clear that the person who created the pie chart carefully chose the colors to represent the different data. What the person did not consider, however, is how the colors would look when printed out on a black-and-white printer. It is nearly impossible to associate the labels with the slices of the pie and thus to read the

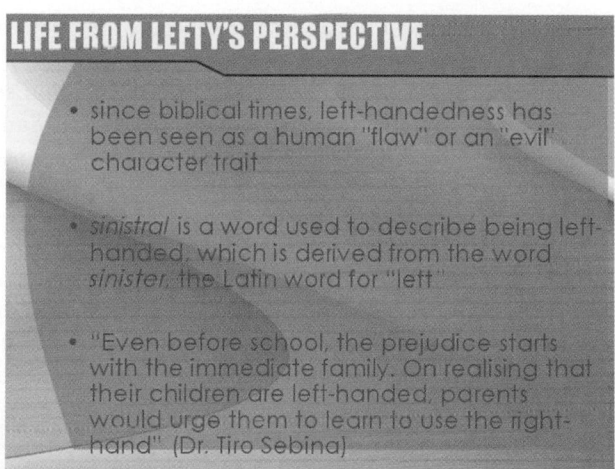

FIGURE 21.1   Document with Too Little Color Contrast

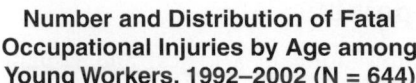

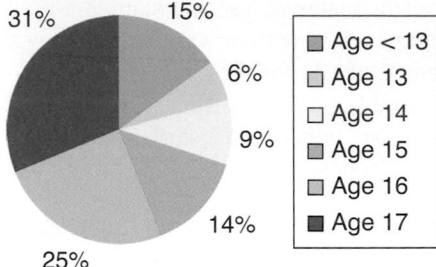 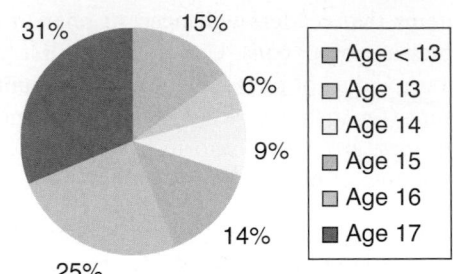

FIGURE 21.2 A Pie Chart That Requires a Color Printer to Be Understandable
Source: National Institute for Occupational Safety and Health, "Data on Young Worker Injuries and Illnesses in Worker Health" (2004).

chart. If your work is likely to be photocopied, consider using patterns to distinguish pie slices or lines and bars in graphs.

Also consider the meanings associated with different colors. For example, in the United States and other Western cultures, white is typically associated with goodness and purity; in China, however, white represents grief and mourning. Although your use of color in an essay, a Web page, or a slideshow presentation might not carry such deep meaning, bear in mind that most people have emotional or psychological responses to colors and color combinations.

Use white space to make text readable.

Another basic element of document design, **white space,** is the open, or blank, space surrounding the text. White space is usually used between a heading and the paragraph that follows the heading. You also use white space when you set the margins on the page, and even when you double-space between lines of text and indent paragraphs. In all of these cases, the space makes your document easier to read. When used generously, white space facilitates reading by keeping the pages of a document uncluttered and by helping the eye find and follow the text.

Chunking   **Chunking,** the breaking up of text into smaller units, also facilitates reading. **Paragraphing** is a form of chunking that divides text into units of closely related information. In most academic essays and reports, text is double-spaced, and paragraphs are distinguished by indenting the first line one-half inch.

In single-spaced text or text that will be read on-screen, you may want to make reading easier by adding extra space between paragraphs rather than indenting the first lines of paragraphs. This format, referred to as **block style,** is often used in memos, letters, and electronic documents. When creating electronic documents, especially

Web pages, you might consider chunking your material into separate "pages" or screens, with links connecting the chunks.

Margins   Adequate margins are an important component of readability. If the margins are too small, your page will seem cluttered. For academic essays, use one-inch margins on all sides unless your instructor (or the style manual you are following) advises differently.

Adding Visuals

Tables, graphs, charts, diagrams, photographs, maps, and screen shots add visual interest and are often more effective in conveying information than prose alone. Be certain, however, that each visual has a valid role to play in your work; if the visual is merely a decoration, leave it out or replace it with a visual that is more appropriate.

You can create visuals on a computer, using the drawing tools of a word processing program, the charting tools of a spreadsheet program, or software specifically designed for creating visuals. You can also download visuals from the Internet or photocopy or scan visuals from print materials. If your essay is going to be posted on the Web on a site that is not password-protected and a visual you want to use is from a source that is copyrighted, you should request written permission from the copyright holder (such as the photographer, publisher, or site sponsor). For any visual that you borrow from or create based on data from a source, be sure to cite the source in the caption, your bibliography, or both, according to the guidelines of the documentation system you are using.

Choose and design visuals with their final use in mind.

Select the types of visuals that will best suit your purpose (see Figure 21.3, pp. 648–49).

Number, title, and label visuals.

Number your visuals in sequential order, and give each one a title. Refer to tables as *Table 1, Table 2,* and so on, and to other types of visuals as *Figure 1, Figure 2,* and so on. (In a long work with chapters or sections, also include the chapter or section number [*Figure 21.1*], as is done here.) In MLA style, use the abbreviation *fig.*

Make sure each visual has a title that reflects its subject (for example, income levels) and its purpose (to compare changes in those income levels over time): *Figure 1. Percentage of U.S. Households in Three Income Ranges, 2000–2012.* MLA style requires that the title be placed above a table and below a figure.

To help readers understand a visual, clearly label all of its parts. For instance, give each of a table's columns a heading, and label each section of a pie chart with the percentage and the item it represents. You may place the label on the chart itself if it is readable, or in a legend next to the chart.

Some visuals may require a caption to provide a fuller description or explanation than the title alone can. (See Figure 21.2, for example.)

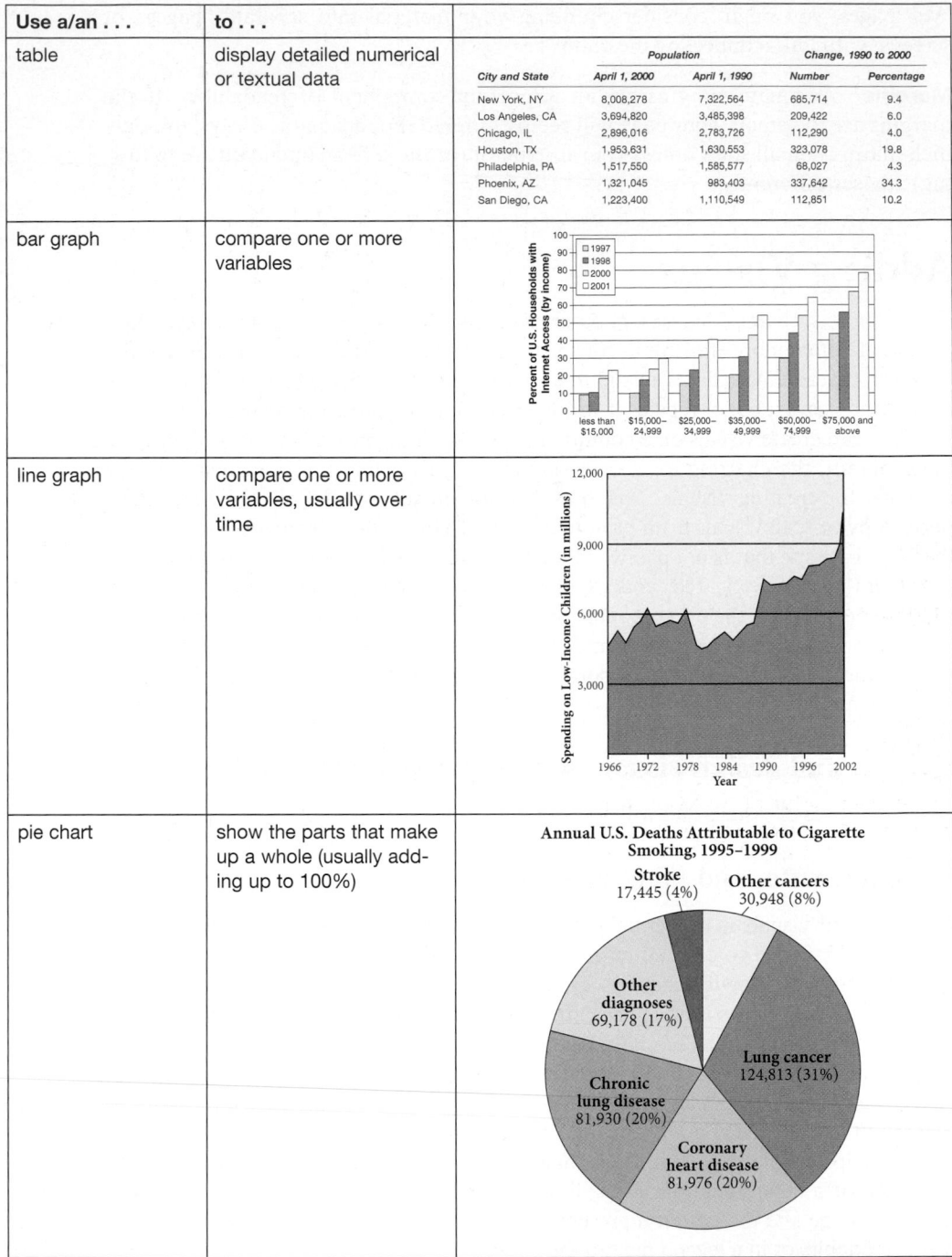

Use a/an . . .	to . . .	
table	display detailed numerical or textual data	
bar graph	compare one or more variables	
line graph	compare one or more variables, usually over time	
pie chart	show the parts that make up a whole (usually adding up to 100%)	

Figure 21.3   When to Use a Visual

flowchart	show a process broken down into steps or stages	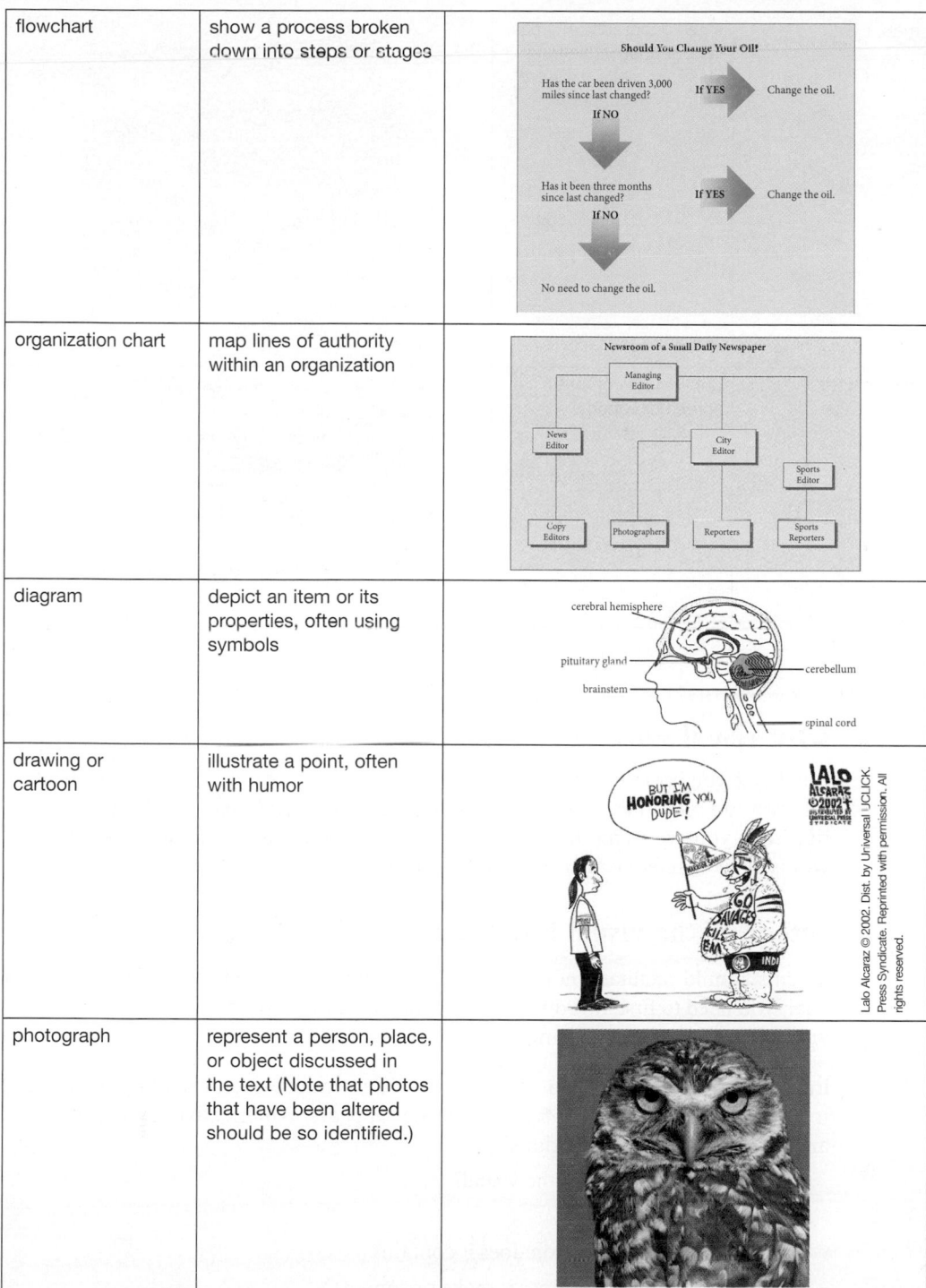
organization chart	map lines of authority within an organization	
diagram	depict an item or its properties, often using symbols	
drawing or cartoon	illustrate a point, often with humor	
photograph	represent a person, place, or object discussed in the text (Note that photos that have been altered should be so identified.)	

(continued)

map	show geographical areas, lay out spatial relationships, or make a historical or political point	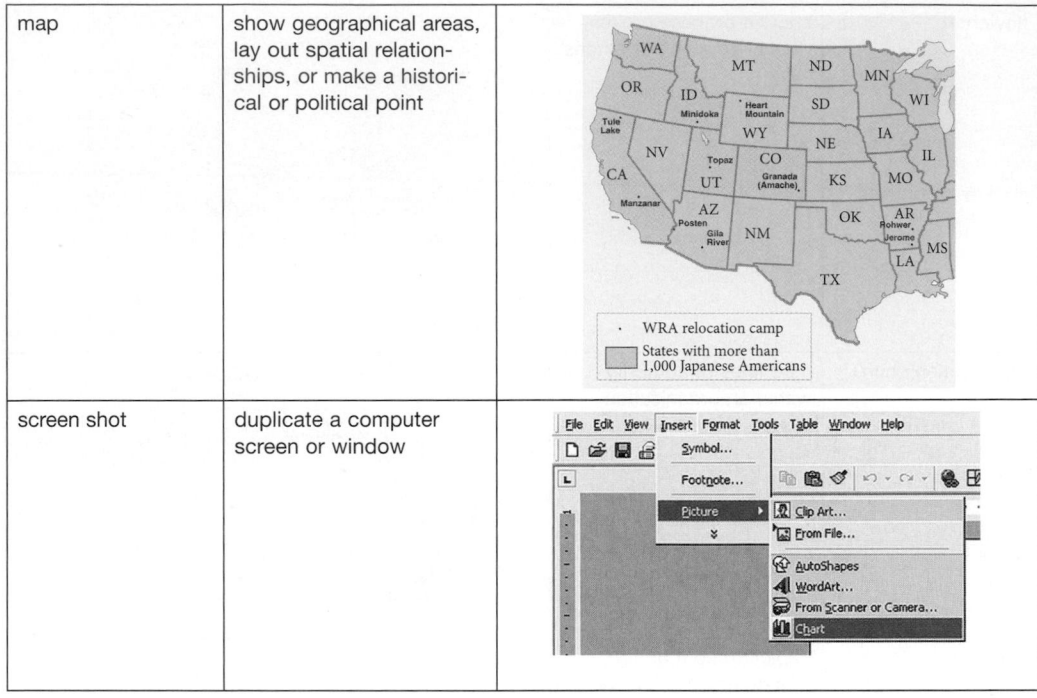
screen shot	duplicate a computer screen or window	

Cite visual sources.

Finally, if you borrow a visual from another source or create a visual from borrowed information, you must cite the source, following the guidelines for the documentation style you are using. In addition, be sure to document the source in your list of works cited or references at the end of your document.

Integrate the visual into the text.

For models demonstrating how to integrate and label visuals in college writing projects, see the student papers in Chapters 3–5, 8–9, and 20.

Visuals should facilitate, not disrupt, the reading of the body text. To achieve this goal, you need to first introduce and discuss the visual in your text and then insert the visual in an appropriate location.

Introducing the Visual   Ideally, you should introduce each visual by referring to it in your text immediately *before* the visual appears. An effective textual reference answers the following questions:

- What is the number of the visual?
- Where is it located?
- What kind of information does it contain?
- What important point does it make or support?

Here is an example of a paragraph that effectively refers to a visual; it is taken from the student paper by Paul Taylor that appears in Chapter 20 (pp. 634–37):

> Gordon Parks's 1952 photograph *Emerging Man* (Fig. 1) is as historically significant a reflection of the civil rights movement as are the speeches of Martin Luther King and Malcolm X, the music of Mahalia Jackson, and the books of Ralph Ellison and James Baldwin. Through striking use of black and white--a reflection of the racial divisions plaguing American cities and towns throughout much of the nineteenth and twentieth centuries--and a symbolically potent central subject--an African American man we see literally "emerging" from a city manhole--Parks's photo evokes the centuries of racial and economic marginalization of African Americans, at the same time as it projects a spirit of determination and optimism regarding the civil rights movement's eventual success.

Placing the Visual in an Appropriate Location   MLA style requires that you place a visual in the body of your text as soon after the discussion as possible, particularly when the reader will need to consult the visual. See, for example, Paul Taylor's paper in the previous chapter (pp. 634–37). (Note that he discusses the figures in the text and places them as close after he first mentions them as he can. He also includes them in his list of works cited (p. 637), with a descriptive title and source information.)

Use common sense when creating visuals on a computer.

If you use a computer program to create visuals, keep this advice in mind:

- *Make the decisions that your computer cannot make for you.* A computer can automatically turn spreadsheet data into a pie chart or bar graph, but only you can decide which visual—or what use of color, if any—is most appropriate for your purpose.

- *Avoid "chart junk."* Many computer programs provide an array of special effects that can be used to alter visuals, including three-dimensional renderings, textured backgrounds, and shadowed text. Such special effects often detract from the intended message of the visual by calling attention to themselves instead. Use them sparingly, and only when they emphasize key information.

- *Use clip art sparingly, if at all.* Clip art consists of icons, symbols, and other simple, typically abstract, copyright-free drawings. Because clip art simplifies ideas, it is of limited use in conveying the complex information contained in most academic writing.

22

Writing in Business and Scientific Genres

Genres are simply categories or types of texts. Movies, for example, may be categorized into genres such as action adventure, romantic comedy, or film noir. Audiences for each of these genres of film have likely seen romantic comedies or noir films in the past, so they bring certain expectations based on that experience to the next romantic comedy or film noir they see. The same is true for genres of printed texts that you are likely to read or create: Many of your decisions—from what to write about (subject choice) to the organizational structure, length, formatting and design—are affected by the audience's genre expectations. While writers usually try to satisfy readers' expectations, genre conventions also provide opportunities for creativity. Depending on the *rhetorical situation* and the audience's openness to innovation, writers may play with genre conventions. But anticipating when your audience will respond to a genre surprise with delight rather than rejection is crucial.

Each of the genres you will encounter in this chapter—from business documents such as résumés and business letters to laboratory reports—are highly conventional genres in which surprises are unlikely to be met with delight. Readers of each of these genres expect writers to get directly to the point in clear, unadorned prose and to follow the format prescribed for the genre. As you examine the documents in this chapter, analyze the way language and design (*typography, color, white space,* and *visuals*) are used to inform and guide readers. What language choices and design features make the documents easy to read? What choices and features make finding specific information within the documents easy? What choices and features make the documents easy to use?

Memos

Memos, such as the one shown in Figure 22.1 (and many others that are now sent by e-mail), are documents sent between employees of the same organization. Typically, memos are

- brief, to the point, and focused on a single subject; if readers will need additional information, memos may refer to other documents, such as reports and spreadsheets, to which the recipients have access (if the memo is sent as an e-mail message, these supporting documents may be attached).

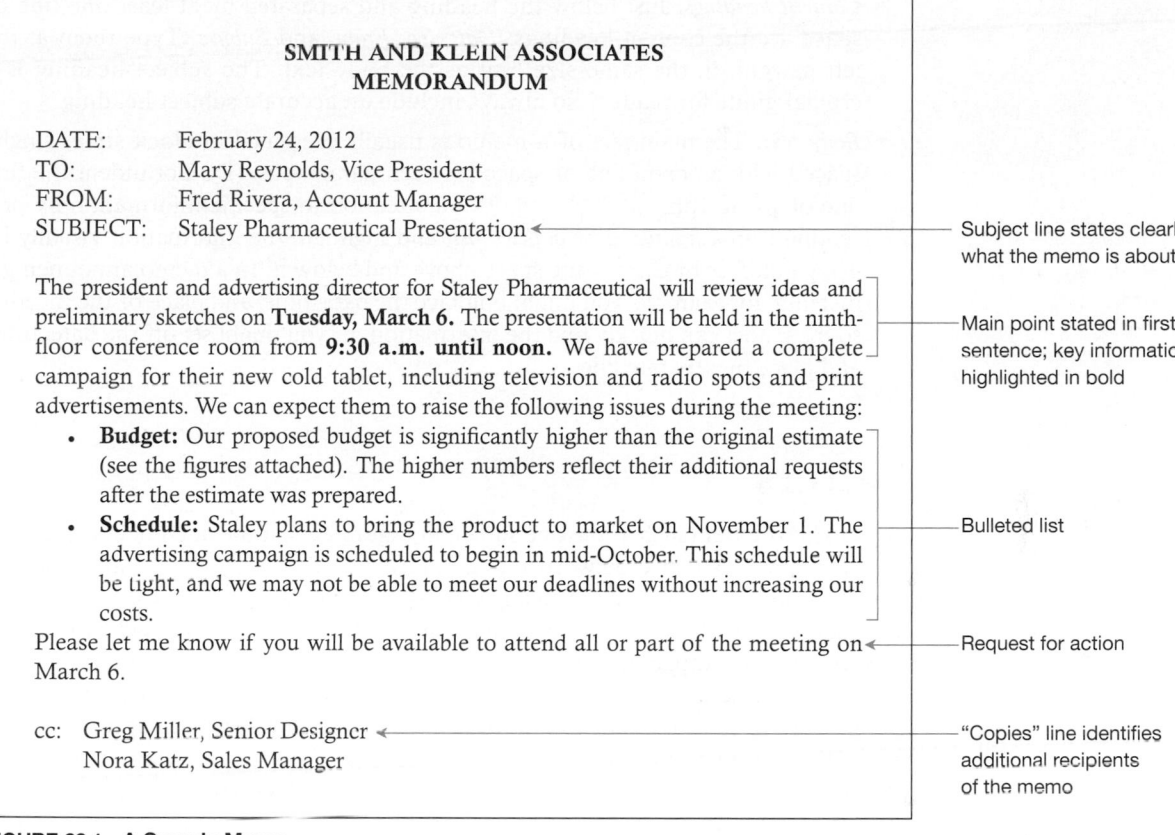

FIGURE 22.1   A Sample Memo

- written in short paragraphs, sometimes of only a single sentence, with the main point stated succinctly in the first paragraph
- framed in terms of how the information contained in the memo will affect its readers; if readers are expected to take action in response to the memo, for example, then the memo should state clearly what readers are to do and when

The following conventions for formatting a memo are well established and should rarely be altered. In addition, some organizations have specific guidelines for memos (such as the use of letterhead).

- ***Heading.*** A memo should carry the major heading *Memorandum* or *Memo.* If you are using letterhead stationery, position the heading just below the letterhead. The heading may be centered on the page or positioned at the left margin (depending on your organization's guidelines). In either case, the heading should be distinguished in some way from the rest of the body text, such as by a large font size, boldface type, or capital letters.

- *Content headings.* Just below the heading and separated by at least one line of space are the content headings: *Date, To, From,* and *Subject*. Type them at the left margin, in the same size font as the body text. The subject heading is a crucial guide for readers, so always include an accurate subject heading.

- *Body text.* The main text of a memo is usually presented in **block style:** single-spaced with an extra line of space between paragraphs. (Do not indent the first line of paragraphs in block style.) Call attention to specific information by presenting it in a *numbered* or *bulleted list,* and highlight the information visually by using boldface or extra white space above and below it. In a memo announcing a meeting, for example, you might boldface the date, time, and place of the meeting so the reader can quickly find the information, or you might set off the date, time, and place on separate lines.

Letters

The **business letter** (such as the one shown in Figure 22.2) is the document most often used for correspondence between representatives of one organization and another, though e-mail messages are increasingly being used in place of business letters. Business letters are written to obtain information about a company's products, to register or respond to a complaint, or to introduce other documents (such as a proposal) that accompany the letter.

Be sure to state the purpose of your letter in the first few lines and to provide supporting information in the paragraphs that follow. Always maintain a courteous and professional tone throughout a business letter. Include enough information to identify clearly any documents you refer to in the letter.

As with memos, the design conventions of business letters are long established:

- **Return address** (included in your company's letterhead or typed at the top of the page), plus any additional contact information for your company

- **Date:** The date, with the name of the month spelled out, follows the return address.

- **Inside address:** Include the name, title, and street address of the recipient, with words like *Street* or *Avenue* spelled out.

- **Salutation:** The convention is to address recipients of business letters as *Dear,* even if you've never met the person before. Use the recipient's title (abbreviated), such as *Gen., Rev., Mr.,* or *Ms.,* and address your letter to a specific person, even if you have to telephone the company to find out the name to use.

- **Body:** Most business letters are written in block style, with the paragraphs flush with the left margin. But look at other business letters from your organization to make sure that this is the preferred style.

- **Closing and signature:** Business letters, even if sent by e-mail, typically conclude with a formal closing, such as *Yours truly* or *Sincerely,* but your relationship with the recipient may influence your choice here. Four lines below the closing, type your full name, and sign the letter above it.

- **Additional information:** If you include items with the letter, such as a proposal or brochure, indicate this with the abbreviation *Enc.* below your name. If other people, such as your boss, will receive a copy of the letter, insert the abbreviation *cc:* followed by the initials of the recipient's name. If you are typing the letter for someone else, include the author's initials (in capital letters), a slash, and the typist's initials (in lowercase letters).

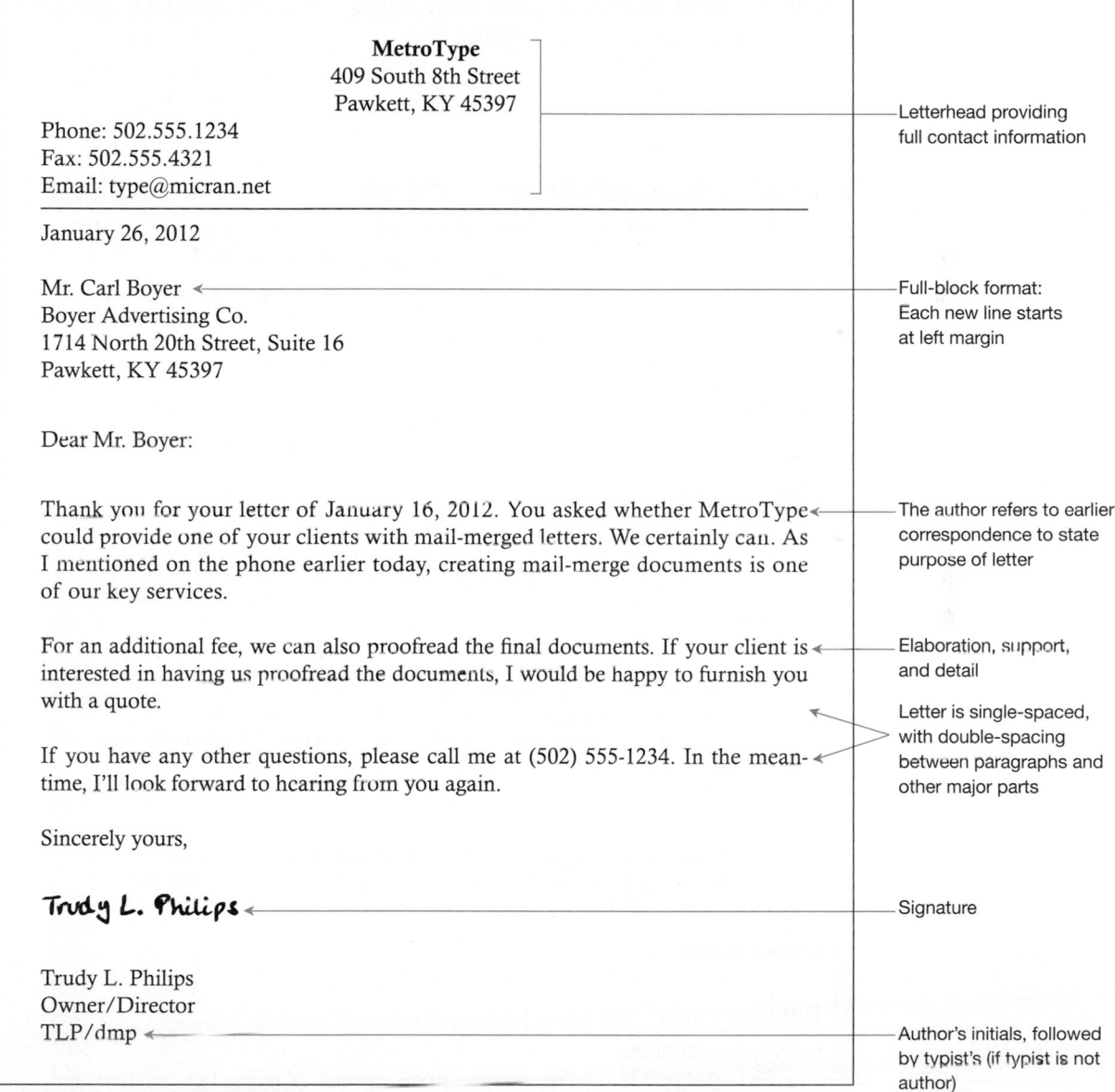

FIGURE 22.2   A Sample Business Letter

E-mail

Many students and instructors rely on **e-mail** to exchange information about assignments and schedules as well as to follow up on class discussions (see Figure 22.3). Like other business correspondence, e-mail messages are usually concise, direct, and limited to a single subject. Although most memos and business letters sent by e-mail should maintain a fairly formal tone, most other e-mail messages may be polite but informal. Because of the deluge of e-mails, e-mail messages should always include a clear, accurate subject line.

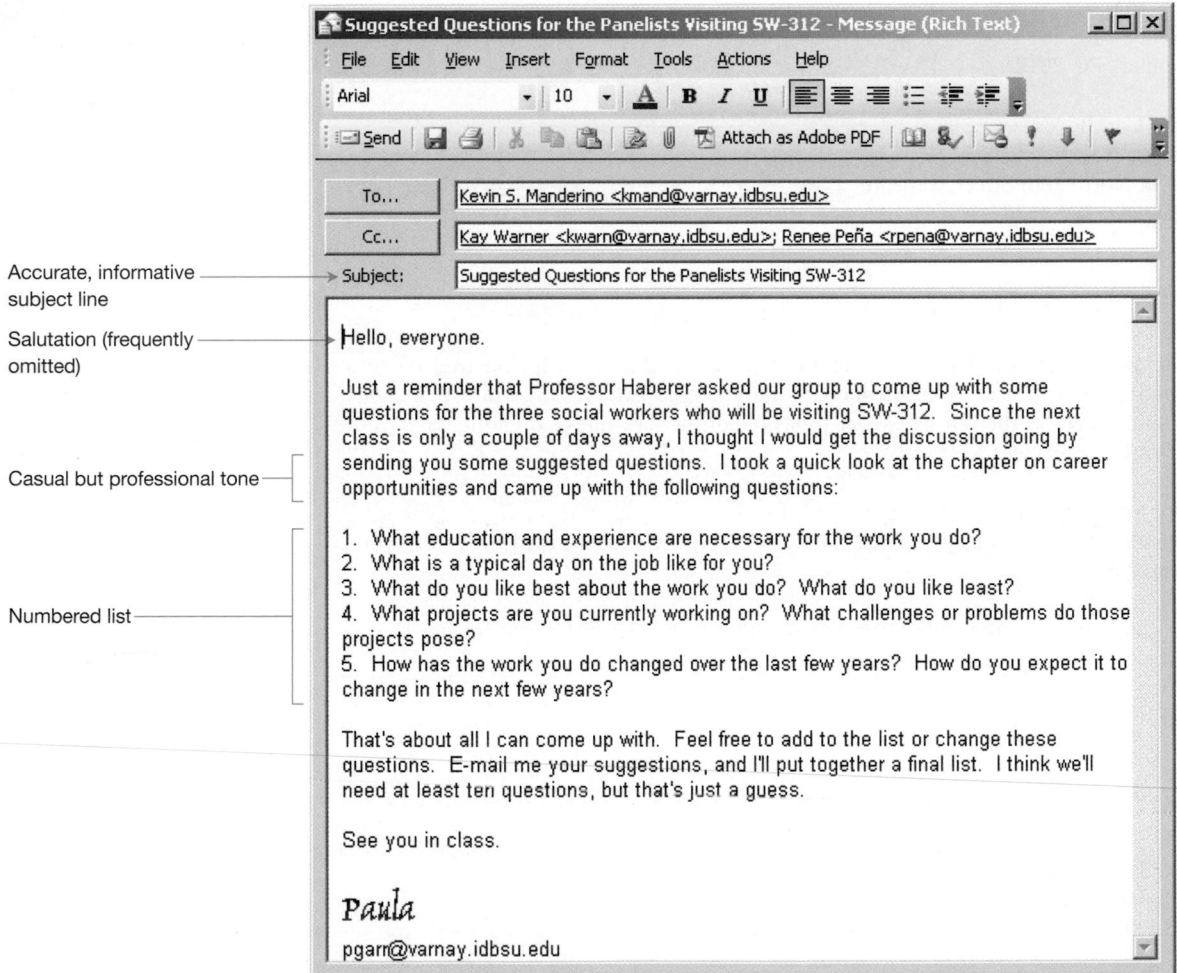

Accurate, informative subject line

Salutation (frequently omitted)

Casual but professional tone

Numbered list

FIGURE 22.3   A Sample E-Mail Message

In many organizations, e-mail messages are replacing memos. When you send a memo electronically, make sure the headings automatically provided by the e-mail program convey the same essential information as the content headings in a traditional memo. If you are part of a large or complex organization, you may want to repeat your name and add such information as your job title, division, and telephone extension in a "signature" at the end of the document.

E-mail is a broader medium of communication than the business memo. Nevertheless, in anything other than quick e-mails to friends, you should maintain a professional tone. Avoid sarcasm and humor, which may not come across as you intend, and be sure to proofread and spell-check your message before sending it. Also, because e-mail messages are accessible to many people besides the intended recipient, always be careful about what you write in an e-mail message.

Though e-mail messages are among the simplest forms of electronic documents, new software programs allow you to attach files, insert hypertext links, and even insert pictures and graphics into your e-mail documents. As a matter of courtesy, check to be sure that the recipient of your e-mail message has the software to read these electronic files before you include them with the message, and pause before sending to make sure the promised attachment is included.

Résumés

A **résumé** is used to acquaint a prospective employer with your work experience, education, and accomplishments. All résumés contain such basic information as your name, address, phone number, and e-mail address.

The résumé is a good example of why the context in which a document is read is so important. An employer may receive dozens of résumés for one position. Your résumé may not be read closely in a first screening. Consequently, your résumé should highlight your important qualifications visually so that the reader can quickly find the pertinent information by scanning the page.

The format of résumés varies among disciplines and professions. Some professions require traditional formatting, while others allow for some flexibility in design. Be sure to research your field and potential employers to see if a particular résumé format is preferred; consider consulting recently published reference books that show examples of good résumés. Also consider whether posting your résumé on a Web site such as *Monster.com* might be advisable. Always tailor your résumé to the job for which you are applying.

Résumés may also vary in terms of what is emphasized — educational or work experience, for example. If you have little work experience, focus your résumé on your grade-point average, the courses you have taken, the projects you have completed, and the applicable skills and abilities you have acquired in college. (For an example of such a résumé, see Figure 22.4.) If you have extensive, relevant, and continuous work experience, consider a reverse-chronological résumé, listing the jobs you have held (beginning with the most recent job) and describing the duties, responsibilities, and accomplishments associated with each one. If you have shifted directions during your adult life, consider organizing your résumé in a way that emphasizes the strengths and skills you have acquired and used in different settings —for instance, your experience speaking in front of groups, handling money, or working with specific software programs.

Kim Hua

Contact information ——————

Current Address: MS 1789, Union College, Union, PA 55342
Permanent Address: 702 Good Street, Borah, ID 83702
Phone: (412) 555-1234 E-mail: khua@mailer.union.edu

EDUCATION

| Union College | Bachelor of Arts, | Anticipated May 2013 |
| Union, PA | Child Development | GPA: 3.7 |

Relevant Courses: Lifespan Human Development, Infancy and Early Childhood, Parent-Child Relations, Fundamentals of Nutrition, Education of the Preschool Child

Relevant Projects: Coordinator, collaborative research project analyzing educational goals for local Head Start program. Lead writer, report on parent-child relations, delivered to the Borah, Idaho, School Board.

CHILD DEVELOPMENT WORK EXPERIENCE

Work experience begins with most current employment ——————→

- *Summer 2012, Union College Child-Care Center, Union College, Union, PA*

  Child Care Provider: Provided educational experiences and daily care for three 2-year-olds and four 3-year-olds. Prepared daily activity agendas.

- *Summer 2011, St. Alphonsus Day Care Center, St. Alphonsus Hospital, Union, PA*

  Child Care Provider: Provided educational experiences and daily care for a group of nine children ages six through ten.

Relevant volunteer work ——————

- *Fall 2010, Governor's Commission for the Prevention of Child Abuse, Union, PA*

  Intern: Located online resources relevant to the prevention of child abuse. Recommended which resources to include in the Web site of the Governor's Commission.

OTHER WORK EXPERIENCE

2010 to present, Union Falls Bed & Breakfast, Union, PA

Other experience showing dependability and responsibility ——————→

Payroll Manager: Maintain daily payroll records for all employees, compile daily and weekly reports of payroll costs for the manager, and ensure compliance with all applicable state and federal laws governing payroll matters.

PROFESSIONAL AFFILIATIONS

Past President, Union College Child and Family Studies Club; Student Member, American Society of Child Care Professionals; Member, National Child Care Providers

---

FIGURE 22.4   A Sample Résumé

Do not include such personal information as your height, weight, and age. Mention personal interests or hobbies only if they are relevant to the position. Finally, proofread your résumé carefully; it must be error-free. Your résumé is the first impression you make on a potential employer. Do everything you can to make a good first impression.

Job-Application Letters

A **job-application letter** (sometimes called a **cover letter**) is sent with a résumé when you apply for a job. The primary purpose of the job-application letter is to persuade your reader that you are a qualified candidate for employment and to introduce your résumé. For college students and recent graduates, most job-application letters (such as the one shown in Figure 22.5) consist of four paragraphs:

1. **Paragraph 1:** Identify the position you are applying for and how you became aware of its availability. If you are not applying for a particular position, the first paragraph expresses your desire to work for the particular organization.

2. **Paragraph 2:** Briefly describe your education, focusing on specific achievements, projects, and relevant coursework.

3. **Paragraph 3:** Briefly describe your work experience, focusing on relevant responsibilities and accomplishments.

   Note that paragraphs 2 and 3 should not merely restate what is in your résumé; rather, they should help persuade your reader that you are qualified for the job.

4. **Paragraph 4:** Express your willingness to provide additional information and to be interviewed at the employer's convenience.

Web Pages

Although Web pages offer the potential for expanded use of color and visuals (including animation and video), the general principles of design used for paper documents can be applied to them. Again, you will want to evaluate the context in which the document will be read. Will your reader be reading from a computer screen or printing the document on paper for reading? If the reading will be taking place on a computer screen, how big is the screen and how good is its resolution? Reading from a computer screen can be more difficult than reading on paper, so you will want to avoid small fonts and confusing backgrounds that distract from the core content.

Web pages and other electronic texts differ from print texts in large part because of the links they can include to additional text or graphics, to other Web pages, or to short clips of video, animation, or sound. As an author, you must consider that because of these links, readers may navigate your text in a nonlinear fashion, starting almost anywhere they like and branching off whenever a link piques their curiosity. To help readers find their way around, Web authors often provide a navigation scheme, usually in the form of site maps or "index" pages.

Modified block format:
Address, date, and signature
block begins five spaces to
the right of center

308 Fairmont Street
Warren, CA 07812
June 9, 2012

Ms. Ronda Green
Software Engineer
Santa Clara Technology
P.O. Box 679
Santa Clara, CA 09145

Dear Ms. Green:

Purpose of the letter

I am responding to your June 8 posting on Monster.com (reference #91921) announcing that Santa Clara Technology is accepting résumés for an entry-level engineer position in the Quality Assurance Department. I think that my experience as an intern in quality assurance and my educational background qualify me for this position.

Education paragraph

As my résumé states, I graduated this past May from the University of Southern California (USC) with a bachelor of science degree in Interdisciplinary Studies. The Interdisciplinary Studies program at USC allows students to develop a degree plan spanning at least two disciplines. My degree plan included courses in computer science, marketing, and technical communication. In addition to university courses, I have completed courses in team dynamics, project management, and C, C++, and C# programming offered by the training department at PrintCom, a manufacturer of high-end laser printers.

Work-experience paragraph

Throughout last summer, I worked as an intern in the quality-assurance department of PrintCom. I assisted quality-assurance engineers in testing printer drivers, installers, and utilities. In addition, I maintained a database containing the results of these tests and summarized the results in weekly reports. This experience gave me valuable knowledge of the principles of quality assurance and of the techniques used in testing software.

Concluding paragraph

I would appreciate the opportunity to discuss further the education, skills, and abilities I could bring to Santa Clara Technology. You can reach me any workday after 3 p.m. (PDT) at (907) 555-1234 or by e-mail at sstur17@axl.com.

Sincerely yours,

Shelley Sturman

Shelley Sturman

Enclosure: résumé

FIGURE 22.5   A Sample Job-Application Letter

HTML (hypertext markup language) is the standard language used for creating Web pages. Software programs called **HTML editors** provide novices with an easy way to create Web pages, and most word processing programs allow a document to be converted into HTML and saved as a Web page.

As you design a Web page, beware of letting unnecessary graphics and multimedia elements distract from your message. Yes, you *can* add a textured background to the screen that will make it look like marble or cloth, but will that background make reading the text easier? Will a sound file improve communication of your main points, or are you adding sound simply because you can? Consider the following guidelines when designing a Web page:

- *Make sure your text is easy to read.* Many Web pages are difficult to read because of textured and brightly colored backgrounds. Keep the background of a Web page light in tone so that your text can be read with ease. Because color type can also be difficult to read, avoid vibrant colors for long blocks of text. Bear in mind that most readers are used to reading dark (typically black) text on a light (typically white) background.

- *Chunk information carefully, and keep your Web pages short.* Because many people have difficulty reading long documents on a computer screen, be sure to chunk your information into concise paragraphs. Also, readers often find it difficult to read a Web page that requires extensive scrolling down the screen. Break up long text blocks into separate Web pages that require no more than one or two screens of scrolling. Use hypertext links to connect the text blocks and to help readers navigate across the pages.

- *Include date posted or updated.* To help readers who will want to know whether your Web site has been updated recently and who may need to cite your Web site in the list of references, always include the date you post or update your Web page.

- *Limit the file size of your Web pages.* A Web page that is filled with visuals and sound files can be slow and clunky to load, especially for users with old computers or dial-up connections to the Internet. Limiting your use of visuals and sound files so that your pages load quickly will help ensure that your documents are read.

- *Use hypertext links effectively.* Make sure that all of your links work correctly and that all the pages of your Web site include a link back to your home page, so that readers can access it easily. You can make your text easier to read by judiciously limiting the number of links you embed in it. In addition to embedded text links, consider including a list of important links on a separate page for readers' convenience.

- *Use the elements of document design.* Most principles of good print document design apply to Web page design as well.

For more on document design, see Chapter 21.

Lab Reports

A **lab report** is written to summarize the results of an experiment or test and to provide a road map for others who wish to repeat the experiment; it generally consists of the following five sections:

1. **Introduction:** Provides background information: the hypothesis of the experiment, the question to be answered, how the question arose

2. **Methods:** Describes how the research was conducted or the experiment performed

3. **Results:** Describes what happened as a result of your research or experiment

4. **Discussion:** Explains your results

5. **References:** Cites the sources used in conducting the research, performing the experiment, or writing the report

The content, style, and format of a lab report may vary from discipline to discipline or from course to course. Before writing a lab report, be certain that you understand your instructor's requirements, and look at sample lab reports in your field. The sample in Figure 22.6 (see pp. 662–63) shows excerpts from a lab report written by two students in a soils science course. It uses the documentation format advocated by the Council of Science Editors (CSE).

Bulk Density and Total Pore Space

Joe Aquino and Sheila Norris
Soils 101
Lab Section 1
February 22, 2012

Introduction

Background information that
the reader will need to
understand the experiment

Soil is an arrangement of solids and voids. The voids, called pore spaces, are important for root growth, water movement, water storage, and gas exchange between the soil and atmosphere. A medium-textured soil good for plant growth will have a pore-space content of about 0.50 (half solids, half pore space). The total pore space is the space between sand, silt, and clay particles (micropore space) plus the space between soil aggregates (macropore space).[1]

[The Introduction continues with a discussion of the formulas used to calculate bulk density, particle density, and porosity.]

Methods

Detailed explanation of the
methods used

To determine the bulk density[2] and total pore space of two soil samples, we hammered cans into the wall of a soil pit (Hagerstown silt loam). We collected samples from the Ap horizon and a Bt horizon. We then placed a block of wood over the cans so that the hammer did not smash them. After hammering the cans into the soil, we dug the cans, now full of soil, out of the horizons; we trimmed off any excess soil. The samples were dried in an oven at 105°C for two days and weighed. We then determined the volume of the cans by measuring the height and radius, as follows:

volume = $1/4$ r^2h

We used the formulas noted in the Introduction to determine bulk density and porosity of the samples. Particle density was assumed to be 2.65 g/cm^3. The textural class of each horizon was determined by feel; that is, we squeezed and kneaded each sample and assigned it to a particular textural class.

FIGURE 22.6   A Sample Lab Report

Presents the results of the experiment, with a table showing quantitative data

Results

We found both soils to have relatively light bulk densities and large porosities, but the Bt horizon had greater porosity than the Ap. Furthermore, we determined that the Ap horizon was a silt loam, whereas the Bt was a clay (see Table 1).

Table 1 Textural class, bulk density, and porosity of two Hagerstown soil horizons

Textural Class	Ap Silt Loam	Bt Clay
Bulk density (g/cm^3)	1.20	1.08
Porosity	0.55	0.59

Explains what was significant about the results of the research

Discussion

Both soils had bulk densities and porosities in the range we would have expected from the discussions in the lab manual and textbook. The Ap horizon is a medium-textured soil and is considered a good topsoil for plant growth, so a porosity around 0.5 is consistent with those facts. The Bt horizon is a fine-textured horizon (containing a large amount of clay), and the bulk density is in the predicted range.

The references are in the format recommended by the Council of Science Editors (CSE). They begin on a new page.

References

1. Brady NC, Weil RR. The nature and properties of soils. 11th ed. New York: Prentice-Hall; 1996. 291 p.

2. Blake GR, Hartge KH. Bulk density. In: Klute A, editor. Methods of soil analysis. Part 1. 2nd ed. Agronomy 1986; 9:363-376.

23

Planning a Research Project

To research a topic effectively at the college level requires a plan. A clear sense of your rhetorical situation, as well as the practical needs of your research task (such as the due date and the level of detail required), will help you create one. Figure 23.1 lists common elements that you will need to consider as you plan your research project, and also as you continue to find and evaluate sources and draft your project.

Define your research task and set a schedule.

Analyze your rhetorical situation.

- Determine your purpose.
- Analyze your audience to understand the interest and background your readers bring to the project, and analyze your attitude to determine how you want your readers to think of you.
- Determine the genre, or type, of research project you are creating, such as a proposal or laboratory report, and the expectations for research, writing, and design associated with this genre.

Understand the assignment.

- Check your syllabus or consult your instructor about the number and types of resources required, the length of the project, and so forth.
- Determine the final due date, and assign interim due dates to keep your project on track.

Establish a research log.

- Create a list of keywords.
- Create a working bibliography, and annotate entries.
- Take notes on your sources.

Choose a topic, get an overview, and narrow your topic.

Choose a topic that is appropriate to the assignment and of interest to you and your readers.

- Consult with your instructor.
- Review textbooks and other course materials.
- Explore newspapers, magazines, and Internet sites.

Get an overview, and narrow your topic (if necessary).

- Consult subject guides or a librarian to determine the availability of sources on your topic.
- Get necessary background by consulting encyclopedias and other general reference sources.
- Start a working bibliography (list of sources) to keep track of the sources you are beginning to explore.
- Draft questions to guide your research.

FIGURE 23.1 Overview of a Research Project

Search for in-depth information on your topic.

Conduct a search for sources, using carefully selected search terms.

- Check the library's resources (such as the catalog, databases, or home page) for books, articles, and multimedia.
- Check Internet sites for relevant Web sites, blogs, groups.

- Keep a list of search terms in a research log, and annotate your working bibliography to keep track of sources.
- Add relevant sources to your working bibliography, and annotate entries to record the sources' main points and how you would use the source.
- Refine your research questions, and draft a thesis.

REFINE YOUR SEARCH.

Ask yourself questions like these:

- Is this what I expected to find?
- Am I finding enough?
- Am I finding too much?
- Do I need to modify my keywords?

- Do I need to recheck background sources?
- Do I need to revise my research questions?
- Do I need to modify my thesis statement?

Continue searching for relevant and reliable sources in response to your answers.

Evaluate your sources.

Determine the relevance of potential sources.

- Does the source explain terms or concepts or provide background?
- Does the source provide evidence to support your claims?
- Does the source offer alternative viewpoints or lend authority?

Determine the reliability of potential sources.

- Who wrote it?
- When was it published?
- Who published it?
- Is the source scholarly or popular (or something else)?
- Is the source printed or online?
- What does the source say?

Continue to evaluate and refine your search strategy based on your research results.

Use your research to support your ideas.

Use evidence from sources to support your ideas.

- Synthesize ideas from multiple sources.
- Support your ideas with summaries, paraphrases, and quotations as appropriate.

Avoid plagiarism.

- Paraphrase carefully to avoid plagiarism.
- Carefully integrate source material into your text.
- Cite sources using an appropriate citation style.

Analyzing Your Rhetorical Situation and Setting a Schedule

Making your research project manageable begins with defining the scope and goals of your research project. Begin by analyzing your *rhetorical situation:*

- What is your *purpose*? Is it to explain a concept, report on or argue for a position, or analyze the causes of an event or a behavior?
- Who is your *audiences* and what will their interests, attitudes, and expectations for the project be? How many and what kinds of resources does your audience expect you to consult? (For college research projects, your audience will likely be your instructor.)

To learn more about primary and secondary research, see Chapter 24.

▪ What *genre* is the research project, and how will that affect the kinds of sources you use? An observational report in the social sciences may demand mainly *primary research,* whereas an argument essay for a history course may require a variety of *secondary* and primary sources.

Also be sure you consider the following practical issues before you begin your research project:

▪ How long should the research project be?

▪ When is it due?

▪ Are any interim assignments required (such as an outline or an annotated bibliography)?

If you're not sure of the answers to these questions, ask your instructor to clarify the assignment or define any confusing terms so that you can work most efficiently.

Finally, set a schedule. Be sure to take into consideration the projects you have due for other classes as well as other responsibilities (to work or family, for example) or activities. A sample schedule is shown in Figure 23.2.

Sunday	Monday	Tuesday	Wednesday	Thursday	Friday	Saturday
	1 Analyze writing situation & choose topic	2	3 Check resources available and get an overview	4	5 Draft research questions & narrow topic further (?)	6
7	8 Set up a working bibliog.	9 List search terms and start searching for sources	10 Topic and working bib with 3 sources due!	11 Evaluate the sources I've found so far	12	13 Draft a thesis statement
14 Write a first draft	15 Peer review—in class	16 More research? Revise research questions and search terms?	17 Don't forget to evaluate new sources!	18 Start revising!	19	20
21	22 Draft the works-cited list	23	24 Revise the 2nd draft	25	26	27
28 Edit, spell-check, and proofread	29 Final project due in class today!	30	31			

FIGURE 23.2   Sample Schedule for a 3- to 5-Page Research Project

Some library Web sites may offer an online scheduler to help you with this process. Look for a link on your library's Web site, or try out an assignment calculator, such as the one found at the University of Minnesota library's Web site, www.lib.umn.edu/help/calculator/.

Choosing a Topic and Getting an Overview

Often students will be assigned a topic for a research project. If you are free to choose your own topic, consult course materials, such as textbooks and handouts, to get ideas, and consult your instructor to make sure your topic is appropriate. Sometimes conducting an Internet search may give you an idea for a topic.

Once you've chosen an appropriate topic, an overview can help you determine the kinds of issues you should consider.

General Encyclopedias

General encyclopedias, such as *Britannica Online* and the *Columbia Encyclopedia,* provide basic information about many topics. Your library will likely have one or more general encyclopedias, available either on the shelf or through the library's digital portal. Often, encyclopedias are part of an online reference package. *Wikipedia,* too, offers a wealth of information, and it is often the first stop for students who are accustomed to consulting the Internet first for information. Be aware, though, that *Wikipedia* is user generated rather than traditionally published, and for this reason, the quality of information found there can be inconsistent. Many instructors do not consider *Wikipedia* a reliable source, so you should ask your teacher for advice on consulting it at this stage. Whichever general encyclopedia you consult, bear in mind that general encyclopedias should be used only for an overview of a topic; the information is not sufficiently in-depth to be an appropriate resource for college research.

Specialized Encyclopedias and Other Overview Resources

Specialized, or **subject-specific, encyclopedias** cover topics in more depth than general encyclopedias do. Here are some examples:

> *Encyclopedia of Computer Science and Technology*
>
> *Encyclopedia of Addictions*
>
> *Encyclopedia of Global Warming and Climate Change*
>
> *Encyclopedia of Human Rights*
>
> *The Encyclopedia of Punk*
>
> *Grove Dictionary of Art* or *Grove Art Online*

In addition to providing an overview of a topic, specialized encyclopedias often include an explanation of issues related to the topic, definitions of specialized terminology, and selective bibliographies of additional sources. As starting points, specialized encyclopedias have two distinct advantages:

1. They provide a comprehensive introduction to your topic, including the key terms you will need to find relevant material in catalogs and databases.

2. They present subtopics, enabling you to see many possibilities for focusing your research.

Frequently, libraries prepare **guides to a subject**—lists of reliable sources on popular topics. A guide can offer very useful suggested resources for research, so check your library to find out if such a guide is available. You may also find resources that provide good overviews of topics, such as *CQ Researcher.* A reference librarian can help point you in the right direction.

Narrowing Your Topic and Drafting Research Questions

After you have gotten a sense of the kinds of sources available on your topic, you may be ready to narrow it. Focus on a topic that you can explore thoroughly in the number of pages assigned and the length of time available. Finding your own take on a subject can help you narrow it as well. The invention strategies in Chapter 11 can help you focus in on one aspect of your topic.

You may also want to write questions about your topic and then focus in on one or two that can be answered through research. These will become the research questions that will guide your search for information. You may need to add or revise these questions as you conduct your search. The answers you devise can form the basis for your thesis statement.

Establishing a Research Log

One of the best ways to keep track of your research is to keep all your notes in one place, in a **research log.** Your log may be digital—a folder on your computer with files for notes, lists of keywords, and your working bibliography—or analog—a notebook with pockets for copies of sources works well).

Listing Keywords

Finding useful sources depends on determining the right **keywords**—words or phrases that describe your topic—to use while searching catalogs, databases, and the Internet. Start your list of keywords by noting the main words from your research question or thesis statement. Look for useful terms in your search results, and use these to expand your list. Then add synonyms (or words with a similar meaning) to expand your list.

For example, student Cristina Dinh might have started with a term like *home schooling.* She might have added *home education* or *home study.* After reading an article in an encyclopedia about her subject, she might have added *student-paced education* or *autonomous learning* to expand her scope.

Creating a Working Bibliography

A **working bibliography** is an ongoing record of the sources you discover as you research your subject. In your final project, you will probably not end up citing all the sources you list in your working bibliography, but recording the information you will need to cite a source—*as you identify it*—will save you time later. (Just be sure to double-check that your entries are accurate!)

Your working bibliography should include the following for each source:

- **Author(s) name(s)**
- **Title and subtitle**
- **Publication information:** A book's edition number (for example, *revised edition, 3rd ed.*), the name and location of the book's publisher, and the page numbers of the section you consulted; a periodical's name, volume and issue number or date, and the article's page numbers
- **Access information:** The call number of a book; the name of the database through which you accessed the source; the URL of the article (if available without a subscription), the URL of the source's home page, or the **DOI** (digital object identifier—a permanent identifying code that won't change over time or from database to database); the date you last accessed the source (for a Web page or Web site)
- **Medium of publication:** *Print* for printed books and articles, *Web* for online books and articles accessed through a database or found online, *DVD* for a film you watched at home, *MP3* for a music file, and so on

You can store your working bibliography in a computer file, in specialized bibliography software, or even on note cards. Each method has its advantages:

- A **computer file** allows you to move citations into order and incorporate the bibliography into your research project easily using standard software (such as Word or Excel).
- **Specialized bibliography software** (such as RefWorks, Zotero, or the Bedford Bibliographer) designed for creating bibliographies helps you create the citation in the specific citation style (such as MLA or APA) required by your discipline. These software programs are not perfect, however; you still need to double-check your citations against the models in the style manual you are using or in Chapter 27 or 28 of this text.
- **Index cards** (one card per source) are easy to arrange and rearrange and allow you to include notes on the cards themselves.
- **A notebook** allows you to keep everything—working bibliography, annotations, notes, copies of chapters or articles—all in one place.

Chapters 27 and 28 present two common documentation styles—one created by the Modern Language Association (MLA) and widely used in the humanities, and the other advocated by the American Psychological Association (APA) and used in the social sciences. Other disciplines have their own preferred styles of documentation. Confirm with your instructor which documentation style is required for your assignment so that you can follow that style for all the sources you put into your working bibliography.

Annotating Your Working Bibliography

An **annotated bibliography** provides an overview of sources that you have considered for your research project. Instructors sometimes ask students to create an annotated bibliography as a separate assignment to demonstrate that each student has done some preparatory research and has considered the usefulness of the sources he or she has found. But researchers frequently create annotated bibliographies for their own use, to keep a record of sources and their thoughts about them, especially when their research occurs over a lengthy period of time. Researchers sometimes also publish annotated bibliographies to provide others with a useful tool for beginning a research project of their own.

What an annotated bibliography includes depends on the researcher's writing situation. If the annotated bibliography is intended for publication, the emphasis is on the source's main claims and major supporting evidence. If the annotated bibliography is for the researcher's use (or if it is for a class assignment), the annotation may also include information about how the source could be used in the research project.

Most annotated bibliographies created for publication or a class assignment also include an introduction that explains the subject, purpose, and scope of the annotated references and may describe how and why the author selected those sources. For instance, an annotated bibliography featuring works about computer animation might have the following introduction:

> Early animations of virtual people in computer games tended to be oblivious to their surroundings, reacting only when hit by moving objects, and then in ways that were not always appropriate—that is, a small object might generate a large effect. In the past few years, however, computer animators have turned their attention to designing virtual people who react appropriately to events around them. The sources below represent the last two years' worth of publications on the subject from the *IEEE Xplore* database.

To annotate your working bibliography, answer these three questions about each source:

- What kind of source is this?
- What does the source say?
- How can I use the source?

    Here are two example annotations:

MLA Style	APA Style
Drennan, Tammy. "Freedom of Education in Hard Times." *Alliance for the Separation of School and State*. Schoolandstate .org, 26 Mar. 2010. Web. 9 May 2012.	Castelvecchi, D. (2008, August 30). Carbon tubes leave nano behind. *Science News, 174*(5), 9-9. Retrieved from http://www.sciencenews.org
This Web page discusses the benefits of brainstorming ideas and tapping the community as options for overcoming economic hardships faced by home-schoolers. I have concerns about the reliability of this source, since it does not identify its members or funding sources. (It seems to be a one-woman show, with all the documents on the site written by Tammy Drennan.) But it's interesting because it is written by a home schooling parent herself. I might be able to use this as evidence of the limitations of home schooling—a lack of resources such as lab equipment and subject-matter experts.	This news article, which describes a new, flexible lightweight material 30 times stronger than Kevlar and possibly useful for better bulletproof vests, provides evidence of yet another upcoming technology that might be useful to law enforcement. I can focus on the ways in which lighter, stronger bulletproof materials might change SWAT tactics—for instance, enabling officers to carry more gear, protect police vehicles, or to blend into crowds better.

Taking Notes on Your Sources

The summaries that you include in a working bibliography or that you make on a printed or digital copy of a source are useful reminders, but you should also make notes that analyze the text, that synthesize what you are learning with ideas you have gleaned elsewhere or with your own ideas, and that evaluate the quality of the source.

For more on synthesizing, see pp. 533–34, 697–98.

You will mine your notes for language to use in your draft, so be careful to

- summarize accurately, using your own words and sentence structures;
- paraphrase without borrowing the language or sentence structure of the source;
- quote accurately and place all language from the source in quotation marks.

You can take notes on a photocopy of a printed text or use comments or highlighting to annotate a digital text. Whenever possible, download, print, photocopy, or scan useful sources, so that you can read and make notes at your leisure and so that you can double-check your summaries, paraphrases, and quotations of sources against the original. These strategies, along with those discussed in Chapter 26, "Using Sources to Support Your Ideas," will keep you from plagiarizing inadvertently.

For more on annotating, see pp. 522–28; for more on avoiding plagiarism, see pp. 698–708.

24

Finding Sources and Conducting Field Research

Students today are surrounded by a wealth of information—in print, online, even face to face! This wealth can make finding the information you need to support your ideas exciting, but it also means you will have to develop a research strategy and sift possible sources carefully. What you are writing about and who will read your writing project will help you decide whether journal articles about your topic written by experts in the field will be most appropriate or whether you should rely on articles from newspapers and magazines you access online, or even whether blog posts or tweets from politicians and other public figures, information about legislation, a historic document, or a video will best help you support your claims. Does your writing project require you to depend mainly on **secondary sources**— works that analyze and summarize a subject—or develop **primary sources,** such as interviews with experts, surveys, or observational studies you conduct yourself? Whatever sources you decide will best help you support your claims, this chapter will help you find or develop the resources you need.

To learn how to devise a research strategy, see Chapter 23; to learn how to evaluate sources, see Chapter 25.

Searching Library Catalogs and Databases

For most college research projects, finding appropriate sources starts with your library's home page, where you can

- use your library's catalog to find books, reference sources (such as encyclopedias and dictionaries), reports, documents, multimedia resources (such as films and audio recordings), and much more;
- use your library's databases to find articles in newspapers, magazines, and scholarly journals.

Your library's home page is also the place to find information about the brick-and-mortar library—its floor plan, its hours of operation, and the journals it has available in print. You might even be able to find research guides, find links to what you need in other libraries, or get online help from a librarian.

Use appropriate search terms.

Just as with a search engine like *Google,* you can search a library catalog or database by typing your search terms—an author's name, the title of a work, a subject term or keyword, even a call number—into the search box. To search successfully, put yourself in the position of the people writing about your topic to figure out what words they might have used. If your topic is "ecology," for example, you may find information under the keywords *ecosystem, environment, pollution,* and *endangered species,* as well as a number of other related keywords, depending on the focus of the research.

Narrow (or expand) your results.

When conducting a search, you may get too few hits and have to broaden your topic. To broaden your search, try the following:

Replace a specific term with a more general term	Replace *sister* or *brother* with *sibling*
Substitute a synonym for one of your keywords	Replace *home study* with *home schooling* or *student-paced education*
Combine terms with *or* to get results with either or both terms	Search *home study or home schooling* to get results that include both *home study* and *home schooling*
Add a wildcard character, usually an asterisk (*) or question mark (?) (Check the search tips to find out which wildcard character is in use.)	Search *home school** or *home school?* to retrieve results for *home school, home schooling,* and *home-schooler*

Most often, you'll get too many hits and need to narrow your search. To narrow a search, try the following:

Add a specific term	Search not just *home schooling* but *home schooling statistics*
Combine search terms into phrases or word strings	Search *Home schooling in California*

In many cases, using phrases or word strings will limit your results to items that include *all* the words you have specified. In a few cases, you may need to insert quotation marks around the terms or insert the word *and* between them to create a search phrase or word string. Check the search tips for the database, catalog, or search engine you are using.

Find books (and other sources) through your library's catalog.

Books housed in academic library collections offer two distinct advantages to the student researcher:

1. They provide in-depth coverage of topics.

2. They are more likely to be published by reputable presses that strive for standards of accuracy and reliability.

To find books (as well as reference works and multimedia resources) on your topic, turn to your library's catalog (see Figure 24.1). You can generally search the online catalog by author's name, title, keyword, or subject heading, and narrow your search by using the catalog's advanced search options.

Though you can search by keywords, most college libraries catalog sources use special *subject headings* devised by the Library of Congress (the national library of the United States). Finding and using the subject headings most relevant to your search will make your research more productive. You can locate the subject headings your library uses by pulling up the record of a relevant book you have already found and looking for the list of words under the heading "Subject" or "Subject headings" (Figure 24.1). Including these terms in your search may help you find additional relevant resources. Ask a librarian for help if you cannot identify the headings.

FIGURE 24.1   A Book's Catalog Record
An item's record provides a lot more information than just the author, title, and call number. You can also find the subject terms by which it was cataloged and perhaps also the item's status (whether it has been checked out) and its location. Some libraries may allow you to place a hold on a book or find similar items. Some libraries, such as the one whose catalog is depicted here, even allow you to capture the book's record with your smartphone or have the information texted or e-mailed to you.

Some library catalogs allow you to search by call number, which makes it easy to find other items on the same or a similar topic. (You might think of a call-number search as the electronic equivalent of looking at books shelved nearby.) For example, typing LC40 (the first part of the call number from the library record shown in Figure 24.1) into the search box calls up the records of other items on the subject of home schooling:

Title	Call number
Well-Trained Mind: A Guide to Classical Education at Home	**LC40**.B39 2004
Love in a Time of Homeschooling: A Mother and Daughter's Uncommon Year	**LC40**.B76 2010
Homeschool: An American History	**LC40**.G34 2008
Family Matters: Why Homeschooling Makes Sense	**LC40**.G88 1992
Home Schooling: Parents as Educators	**LC40**.H65 1995
How Children Learn at Home	**LC40**.T48 2007

If your search for books in your college library turns up little that is useful to you, do not give up. Consider using *WorldCat* (www.worldcat.org), which includes records for many libraries in the United States and worldwide. You may be able to request an item from another library via your library's interlibrary loan service. Inquire at your library for services available to you that can connect you to resources in other libraries.

Though library catalogs are the place to go to find books, you can also use your library's catalog to find

- *Audio:* recordings of music, speeches, plays, and readings
- *Video:* films and documentaries in a variety of formats
- *Art:* drawings, paintings, photographs, and engravings; some libraries may also own collections of artwork

Many libraries also house **archives and special collections** comprising manuscripts, rare books, and specialized materials or resources of local or worldwide interest. Where as some libraries may list these items in their online catalog, others may provide links to these special collections in a different location on their Web sites; still others may provide access only through a catalog in the archives or special-collections room. Ask a librarian whether such materials may be useful to you.

Find articles in periodicals using your library's databases.

Much of the information you will use to write your research project will come from articles in **periodicals,** publications such as newspapers, magazines, or scholarly journals that are published at regular intervals. To locate relevant articles on your topic, start your search with one of your library's databases. Why not just start with a *Google* search? There are two very good reasons:

1. *Google* will pull up articles from any publication it indexes, from freely available personal Web sites to scholarly journals. Results rise to the top of the list based on a number of factors but not necessarily the reliability of the source. A *Google* search will turn up helpful sources, but you will need to spend a good deal of time sifting through the numerous hits you get to find sources that are both relevant and reliable. (*Google Scholar* may help you locate more reliable sources than those you might find through a typical *Google* search.)

2. Sources you find through *Google* may ask you to pay for access to articles, or they may require a subscription. Your library already subscribes to these sources on your behalf. Also, adding databases to your search strategy will round out and diversify your search, and provide you with access to resources not available through a search engine such as *Google*.

Most college libraries subscribe at least to **general databases** and **subject-specific databases** as well as databases that index newspapers. General databases (such as *Academic OneFile, Academic Search Premier* or *Elite* or *Complete,* and *ProQuest Central*) index articles from both scholarly journals and popular magazines.[1] Subject-specific databases (such as *ERIC—Education Resources Information Center, MLA International Bibliography, PsycINFO, and General Science Full Text*) index articles only in their discipline. Newspaper databases (such as *Alt-Press Watch, LexisNexis Academic, National Newspaper Index, and ProQuest Newspapers*) index newspaper articles. For college-level research projects, you may use all three types of databases to find appropriate articles. (Note that many libraries also offer ways to search multiple databases at once.) For the research project on home schooling that appears in Chapter 27, "Citing and Documenting Sources in MLA Style," Cristina Dinh might have consulted both a general database and a subject-specific database like *ERIC*.

If your database search returns too many unhelpful results, use the search strategies discussed at the beginning of this chapter (p. 675) or use the database's advanced search options to refine your search. Many databases allow users to restrict results to articles published in academic journals, for example, or to articles that were published only after a certain date (see Figure 24.2). Use the Help option or ask a librarian for assistance.

Increasingly, databases provide access to full-text articles, either in HTML or PDF format. When you have the option, choose the PDF format, as this will provide you with photographs, graphs, and charts in context, and you will be able to include the page numbers in your citation. If you find a citation to an article that is not accessible through a database, however, do not ignore it. Check with a librarian to find out how you can get a copy of the article.

---

[1] The names of these databases change over time and vary from library to library, so ask your instructor or a reference librarian if you can help identify a general database.

Database

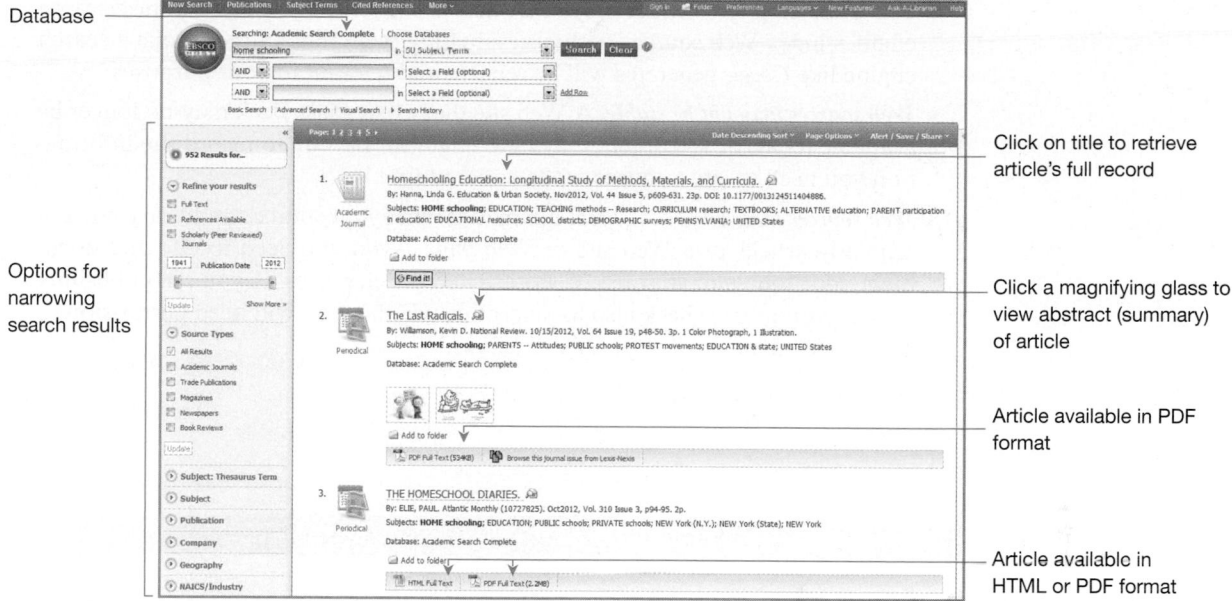

Click on title to retrieve article's full record

Options for narrowing search results

Click a magnifying glass to view abstract (summary) of article

Article available in PDF format

Article available in HTML or PDF format

FIGURE 24.2   Database Search Results
Database search results may allow you to access an article directly or provide the information you need to locate (and cite) it, including the title, the author(s), and the article's publication information. The database may also provide options for narrowing a search by publication date, source type, and so on.

Find government documents and statistical information.

Federal, state, and local governments make many of their documents available directly through the Web. For example, you can access statistical data about the United States through the U.S. Census Bureau's Web site (www.census.gov), and you can learn a great deal about other countries through the Web sites of the U.S. State Department (travel.state.gov) and the CIA (www.cia.gov/library/publications/the-world-factbook).

The Library of Congress provides a useful portal for finding government documents (federal, state, local, and international) through its Web site (www.loc.gov), and the U.S. Government Printing Office provides free electronic access to documents produced by the federal government through its FDsys Web page (www.gpo.gov/fdsys).

Some libraries have collections of government publications and provide access to government documents through databases or catalogs. Your library may also offer statistical resources and data sets. See if your library has a guide to these resources, or ask a librarian for advice. You can also find government documents online using an advanced *Google* search (www.google.com/advanced_search) and specifying *.gov* as the type of site or domain you want to search (see Figure 24.3).

To learn more about the domains of Web sites, see Chapter 25, p. 695.

Find Web sites and interactive sources.

By now, you are likely quite familiar with searching the Web. This section introduces you to some tools and strategies to use it more efficiently. But first, a few cautions:

■ ***Your research project will be only as credible as the sources you use.*** Because search engines index Web sources without evaluating them, not all the results a search engine like *Google* generates will be reliable and relevant to your purposes.

■ ***Web sources may not be stable.*** A Web site that existed last week may no longer be available today, or its content may have changed. Be sure to record the information you need to cite a source when you first find it.

For guidelines on how to cite Web sources, see pp. 727–30 (MLA style); or pp. 747–48 (APA style); for more on evaluating sources, especially Web sources, see Chapter 25.

■ ***Web sources must be documented.*** No matter what your source—a library book, a scholarly article, or a Web site or Web page—you will need to cite and document your source in your list of works cited or references. If you are publishing your report online, check also to determine whether you will need permission to reproduce an image or any other elements.

FIGURE 24.3 An Advanced Google Search
Use *Google's* advanced search (www.google.com/advanced_search) to locate information within specific sites or domains (such as *.edu* or *.gov*) or to narrow results to sites that include or exclude specific words, appear only in English or another language, and so on.

Google Scholar and *Google Book Search*

Although you may use search engines like *Google* with great rapidity and out of habit, as a college researcher you are likely to find it worthwhile to familiarize yourself with other parts of the *Google* search site. Of particular interest to the academic writer are *Google Scholar* and *Google Book Search*. *Google Scholar* retrieves articles from a number of scholarly databases and a wide range of general-interest and scholarly books. *Google Book Search* searches both popular and scholarly books. Both *Google Scholar* and *Google Book Search* offer overviews and, in some cases, the full text of a source.

Note: Whatever search engine you use, always click on the link called *Help, Hints,* or *Tips* on the search tool's home page to find out more about the commands and advanced-search techniques it offers. Most search engines allow searches using the techniques discussed on p. 675. Many also provide advanced searching options that allow you to limit results to those created between specific dates, in specific languages, and so on.

Other Useful Search Options

No matter how precisely you search the Web with a standard search engine, you may not hit on the best available resources. Starting your search from a subject guide, such as those provided by the *Internet Public Library* (www.ipl.org/div/special), *Infomine* (www.infomine.ucr.edu), or the librarians at your school, can direct you to relevant and reliable sources of online information.

Interactive Sources

Interactive sources, including blogs, wikis, RSS feeds, social networking sites (like *Facebook* and *Twitter*), and discussion lists, can also be useful sources of information, especially if your research project focuses on a current event or late-breaking news.

- **Blogs** are Web sites that are updated regularly, often many times a day. They are usually organized chronologically, with the newest posts at the top, and may contain links or news stories, but generally focus on the opinions of the blog host and visitors. Blogs by experts in the field are likely to be more informative than blogs by amateurs or fans.

- **Wikis** — of which *Wikipedia* is the best known example — offer content contributed and modified collaboratively by a community of users. Wikis can be very useful for gleaning background information, but because (in most cases) anyone can write or revise wiki entries, many instructors will not accept them as reliable sources for college-level research projects. Use wikis cautiously.

- **RSS (Really Simple Syndication) feeds** aggregate frequently updated sites, such as news sites and blogs, into links in a single Web page or e-mail. Most search engines provide this service, as do sites such as *NewzCrawler* (www.newzcrawler .com) and *FeedDemon* (www.feeddemon.com). RSS feeds can be useful if you are researching news stories or political campaigns.

- **Social networking sites,** like *Facebook* and *Twitter,* allow users to create groups or pages on topics of interest or to follow the thoughts and activities of newsmakers.
- **Discussion lists** are electronic mailing lists that allow members to post comments and get feedback from others interested in the same topic. The most reliable discussion lists are moderated and attract experts on the topic. Many online communities provide some kind of indexing or search mechanism so that you can look for "threads" (conversations) related to your topic.

Although you need to evaluate the information you find in all sources carefully, you must be especially careful with information from social networking sites and discussion lists. However, such sources can provide up-to-the-minute information. Also be aware that whereas most online communities welcome guests and newcomers, others may perceive your questions as intrusive or naive. It may be useful to "lurk" (that is, just to read posts) before making a contribution.

Conducting Field Research

In universities, government agencies, and the business world, field research can be as important as library research. In some majors, like education or sociology, as well as in service-learning courses, primary research projects are common. Even in the writing projects covered in Chapters 2–9, observations, interviews, and surveys may be useful or even necessary. As you consider how you might use field research in your writing projects, ask your instructor whether your institution requires you to obtain approval, and check Chapters 27 and 28 for information about citing interviews you conduct yourself.

Conduct observational studies.

Observational studies, such as profiling a place (see Chapter 3) for a writing course or studying how children play for a psychology or sociology course, are common in college. To conduct an observational study effectively, follow these guidelines:

Planning an Observational Study

To ensure that your observational visits are productive, plan them carefully:

- **Arrange access if necessary.** Visits to a private location (such as a day-care center or school) require special permission, so be sure to arrange your visit in advance. When making your request, state your intentions and goals for your study directly and fully. You may be surprised at how receptive people can be to a college student on assignment. But have a fallback plan in case your request is refused or the business or institution places constraints on you that hamper your research.
- **Develop a hypothesis.** In advance, write down a tentative assumption about what you expect to learn from your study—your **hypothesis.** This will guide your observations and notes, and you can adjust your expectations in response to

what you observe if necessary. Consider, too, how your presence will affect those whom you are observing, so you can minimize your impact or take the effect of your presence into consideration.

- **Consider how best to conduct the observation.** Decide where to place yourself to make your observations most effective. Should you move around to observe from multiple vantage points, or will a single perspective be more productive?

Making Observations

Strategies for conducting your observation include the following:

- **Description:** *Describe* in detail the setting and the people you are observing. Note the physical arrangement and functions of the space, and the number, activities, and appearance of the people. Record as many details as possible, draw diagrams or sketches if helpful, and take photographs or videos if allowed (and if those you are observing do not object).

- **Narration:** *Narrate* the activities going on around you. Try initially to be an innocent observer: Pretend that you have never seen anything like this activity or place before, and explain what you are seeing step by step, even if what you are writing seems obvious. Include interactions among people, and capture snippets of conversations (in quotation marks) if possible.

- **Analysis and classification:** Break the scene down into its component parts, identify common threads, and organize the details into categories.

For more about narration, description, and classification, see Chapters, 14, 15, and 17.

Take careful notes during your visit if you can do so unobtrusively, or immediately afterwards if you can't. You can use a notebook and pencil, a laptop or tablet, or even a smartphone to record your notes. Choose whatever is least disruptive to those around you. You may need to use abbreviations and symbols to capture your observations on-site, but be sure to convert such shorthand into words and phrases as soon as possible after the visit so that you don't forget its significance.

Writing Your Observational Study

Immediately after your visit, fill in any gaps in your notes, and review your notes to look for meaningful patterns. You might find *mapping strategies,* such as *clustering* or *outlining,* useful for discovering patterns in your notes. Take some time to reflect on what you saw. Asking yourself questions like these might help:

For more about mapping, clustering, or outlining strategies, see Chapter 11, pp. 508–9, 510–14.

- How did what I observed fit my own or my readers' likely preconceptions of the place or activity? Did my observations upset any of my preconceptions? What, if anything, seemed contradictory or out of place?

- What interested me most about the activity or place? What are my readers likely to find interesting about it?

- What did I learn?

Your purpose in writing about your visit is to share your insights into the meaning and significance of your observations. Assume that your readers have never been to the place, and provide enough detail for it to come alive for them. Decide on the perspective you want to convey, and choose the details necessary to convey your insights.

| PRACTICING THE GENRE |

Collaborating on an Observational Study

Arrange to meet with a small group (three or four students) for an observational visit somewhere on campus, such as the student center, gym, or cafeteria. Have each group member focus on a specific task, such as recording what people are wearing, doing, or saying, or capturing what the place looks, sounds, and smells like. After twenty to thirty minutes, report to one another on your observations. Discuss any difficulties that arise.

Conduct interviews.

A successful interview involves careful planning before the interview, but it also requires keen listening skills and the ability to ask appropriate follow-up questions while conducting the interview. Courtesy and consideration for your subject are crucial at all stages of the process.

Planning the Interview

Planning an interview involves the following:

- **Choosing an interview subject.** For a profile of an individual, your interview will be with one person; for a profile of an organization, you might interview several people, all with different roles or points of view. Prepare a list of interview candidates, as busy people might turn you down.

- **Arranging the interview.** Give your prospective subject a brief description of your project, and show some sincere enthusiasm for your project. Keep in mind that the person you want to interview will be donating valuable time to you, so call ahead to arrange the interview, allow your subject to specify the amount of time she or he can spare, and come prepared.

Preparing for the Interview

In preparation for the interview, consider your objectives:

- Do you want details or a general orientation (the "big picture") from this interview?

- Do you want this interview to lead you to interviews with other key people?

- Do you want mainly facts or opinions?

- Do you need to clarify something you have observed or read? If so, what?

Making an observational visit and doing some background reading beforehand can be helpful. Find out as much as you can about the organization or company (size, location, purpose, etc.), as well as the key people.

Good questions are key to a successful interview. You will likely want to ask a few **closed questions** (questions that request specific information) and a number of **open questions** (questions that give the respondent range and flexibility and encourage him or her to share anecdotes, personal revelations, and expressions of attitudes):

Open Questions	Closed Questions
What do you think about _____?	How do you do _____?
Describe your reaction when _____ happened.	What does _____ mean?
Tell me about a time you were _____.	How was _____ developed?

The best questions encourage the subject to talk freely but stick to the point. You may need to ask a follow-up question to refocus the discussion or to clarify a point, so be prepared. If you are unsure about a subject's answer, follow up by rephrasing the subject's answer, prefacing it by saying something like "Let me see if I have this right" or "Am I correct in saying that you feel _____?" Avoid *forced-choice questions* ("Which do you think is the better approach: _____ or _____?") and *leading questions* ("How well do you think _____ is doing?").

During the Interview

Another key to good interviewing is flexibility. Ask the questions you have prepared, but also be ready to shift gears to take full advantage of what your subject can offer.

- **Take notes.** Take notes during the interview, even if you are recording your discussion. You might find it useful to divide several pages of a notebook into two columns or to set up a word processing file in two columns. Use the left-hand column to note details about the scene and your subject or about your impressions overall; in the right-hand column, write several questions and record answers to your questions. Remember that how something is said is as important as what is said. Look for material that will give texture to your writing—gesture, verbal inflection, facial expression, body language, physical appearance, dress, hair, or anything that makes the person an individual.

For an example of a student's interview notes, see Chapter 3, pp. 112–13.

- **Listen carefully.** Avoid interrupting your subject or talking about yourself; rather, listen carefully and guide the discussion by asking follow-up questions and probing politely for more information.

- **Be considerate.** Do not stay longer than the time you were allotted unless your subject agrees to continue the discussion, and show your appreciation for the time you have been given by thanking your subject and offering her or him a copy of your finished project.

Following the Interview

After the interview, do the following:

- **Reflect on the interview.** As soon as you finish the interview, find a quiet place to reflect on it and to review and amplify your notes. Asking yourself questions like these might help: What did I learn? What seemed contradictory or surprising about the interview? How did what was said fit my own or my readers' likely expectations about the person, activity, or place? How can I summarize my impressions?

Also make a list of any questions that arise. You may want to follow up with your subject for more information, but limit yourself to one e-mail or phone call to avoid becoming a bother.

- **Thank your subject.** Send your interview subject a thank-you note within twenty-four hours of the interview. Try to reference something specific from the interview, something you thought was surprising or thought provoking. And send your subject a copy of your finished project with a note of appreciation.

PRACTICING THE GENRE

Interviewing a Classmate

In pairs, practice the genre by interviewing a classmate:

- First, spend five to ten minutes writing questions and thinking about what you'd like to learn. Then, during a ten-minute interview, ask the questions you have prepared, but also ask one or more follow-up questions in response to something your classmate has told you.

- Following the interview, spend a few minutes thinking about what you learned about your classmate and about conducting an interview. What might you do differently when conducting a formal interview?

Conduct surveys.

Surveys let you gauge the opinions and knowledge of large numbers of people. You might conduct a survey to gauge opinion in a political science course or to assess familiarity with a television show for a media studies course. You might also conduct a survey to assess the seriousness of a problem for a service-learning class or in response to an assignment to propose a solution to a problem (Chapter 7). This section briefly outlines procedures you can follow to carry out an informal survey, and it highlights areas where caution is needed. Colleges and universities have restrictions about the use and distribution of questionnaires, so check your institution's policy or obtain permission before beginning the survey.

Designing Your Survey

Use the following tips to design an effective survey:

- **Conduct background research.** You may need to conduct background research on your topic. For example, to create a survey on scheduling appointments at the student health center, you may first need to contact the health center to determine its scheduling practices, and you may want to interview health center personnel.

- **Focus your study.** Before starting out, decide what you expect to learn (your *hypothesis*). Make sure your focus is limited focus on one or two important issues—so you can craft a brief questionnaire that respondents can complete quickly and easily and so that you can organize and report on your results more easily.

- **Write questions.** Plan to use a number of *closed questions* (questions that request specific information), such as *two-way questions, multiple-choice questions, ranking scale questions,* and *checklist questions* (see Figure 24.4). You will also likely want to include a few *open questions* (questions that give respondents the opportunity to write their answers in their own words). Closed questions are easier to tally, but open questions are likely to provide you with deeper insight and a fuller sense of respondents' opinions. Whatever questions you develop, be sure that you provide all the answer options your respondents are likely to want, and make sure your questions are clear and unambiguous.

- **Identify the population you are trying to reach.** Even for an informal study, you should try to get a reasonably representative group. For example, to study satisfaction with appointment scheduling at the student health center, you would need to include a representative sample of all the students at the school—not only those who have visited the health center. Determine the demographic makeup of your school, and arrange to reach out to a representative sample.

- **Design the questionnaire.** Begin your questionnaire with a brief, clear introduction stating the purpose of your survey and explaining how you intend to use the results. Give advice on answering the questions, estimate the amount of time needed to complete the questionnaire, and—unless you are administering the survey in person—indicate the date by which completed surveys must be returned. Organize your questions from least to most complicated or in any order that seems logical, and format your questionnaire so that it is easy to read and complete.

- **Test the questionnaire.** Ask at least three readers to complete your questionnaire before you distribute it. Time them as they respond, or ask them to keep track of how long they take to complete it. Discuss with them any confusion or problems they experience. Review their responses with them to be certain that each question is eliciting the information you want it to elicit. From what you learn, revise your questions and adjust the format of the questionnaire.

Administering the Survey

The more respondents you have, the better, but constraints of time and expense will almost certainly limit the number. As few as twenty-five could be adequate for an informal study, but to get twenty-five responses, you may need to solicit fifty or more participants.

You can conduct the survey in person or over the telephone; use an online service such as *SurveyMonkey* (surveymonkey.com) or *Zoomerang* (zoomerang.com); e-mail the questionnaires; or conduct the survey using a social media site such as *Facebook*. You may also distribute surveys to groups of people in class or around campus and wait to collect their responses.

This is a survey about scheduling appointments at the student health center. Your participation will help determine how long students have to wait to use the clinic's services and how these services might be more conveniently scheduled. The survey should take only 3 to 4 minutes to complete. All responses are confidential.

Two-way question —— 1. Have you ever made an appointment at the clinic?
❑ Yes   ❑ No

Filter —— If you answered "No" to question 1, skip to question 5.

Multiple-choice questions ——

2. How frequently have you had to wait more than 10 minutes at the clinic for a scheduled appointment?
❑ Always   ❑ Usually   ❑ Occasionally   ❑ Never

3. Have you ever had to wait more than 30 minutes at the clinic for a scheduled appointment?
❑ Yes   ❑ No   ❑ Uncertain

4. Based on your experience with the clinic, how would you rate its system for scheduling appointments?

❑ 1 (poor)   ❑ 2 (adequate)   ❑ 3 (good)   ❑ 4 (excellent)

Ranking questions ——

5. Given your present work and class schedule, which times during the day (Monday through Friday) would be the most and least convenient for you to schedule appointments at the clinic? (Rank your choices from 1 for most convenient time to 4 for least convenient time.)

	1 (most convenient)	2 (more convenient)	3 (less convenient)	4 (least convenient)
morning (7 a.m.–noon)	❑	❑	❑	❑
afternoon (noon–5 p.m.)	❑	❑	❑	❑
dinnertime (5–7 p.m.)	❑	❑	❑	❑
evening (7–10 p.m.)	❑	❑	❑	❑

6. If you have had an appointment at the student health center within the last six months, please evaluate your experience.

7. If you have had an appointment at the student health center within the last six months, please indicate what you believe would most improve scheduling of appointments at the clinic.

Open questions ——

8. If you have *never* had an appointment at the student health center, please indicate why you have not made use of this service.

Thank you for your participation.

FIGURE 24.4   Sample Questionnaire: Scheduling at the Student Health Center

Each method has its advantages and disadvantages. For example, face-to-face surveys allow you to get more in-depth responses, but participants may be unwilling to answer personal questions face to face. Though fewer than half the surveys you solicit using survey software are likely to be completed (your invitations may wind up in a spam folder), online software will tabulate responses automatically.

Writing the Report

When writing your report, include a summary of the results, as well as an interpretation of what the results mean.

- **Summarize the results.** Once you have the completed questionnaires, tally the results from the closed questions. (If you conducted the survey online, this will have already been done for you.) You can give the results from the closed questions as percentages, either within the text of your report or in one or more tables or graphs. Next, read all respondents' answers to each open question to determine the variety of responses they gave. Summarize the responses by classifying the answers. You might classify them as positive, negative, or neutral or by grouping them into more specific categories. Finally, identify quotations that express a range of responses succinctly and engagingly to use in your report.

- **Interpret the results.** Once you have tallied the responses and read answers to open questions, think about what the results mean. Does the information you gathered support your hypothesis? If so, how? If the results do not support your hypothesis, where did you go wrong? Was there a problem with the way you worded your questions or with the sample of the population you contacted? Or was your hypothesis in need of adjustment?

- **Write the report.** Reports in the social sciences use a standard format, with headings introducing the following categories of information:

  - **Abstract:** A brief summary of the report, usually including one sentence summarizing each section

  - **Introduction:** Includes context for the study (other similar studies, if any, and their results), the question or questions the researcher wanted to answer and why this question (or these questions) are important, and the limits of what the researcher expected the survey to reveal

  - **Methods:** Includes the questionnaire, identifies the number and type of participants, and describes the methods used for administering the questionnaire and recording data

  - **Results:** Includes the data from the survey, with limited commentary or interpretation

  - **Discussion:** Includes the researcher's interpretation of results, an explanation of how the data support the hypothesis (or not), and the conclusions the researcher has drawn from the research

25

Evaluating Sources

As soon as you start your search for sources, you should begin evaluating what you find not only to decide whether they are *relevant* to your research project but also to determine how *credible* or *reliable* they are.

Choosing Relevant Sources

Sources are **relevant** when they help you achieve your aims with your readers. Relevant sources may

- explain terms or concepts;
- provide background information;
- provide evidence in support of your claims;
- provide alternative viewpoints or interpretations;
- lend authority to your point of view.

A search for sources may reveal many seemingly relevant books and articles—more than any researcher could ever actually consult. A search on the term *home schooling* in one database, for example, got 1,172 hits. Obviously, a glance at all the hits to determine which are most relevant would take far too much time. To speed up the process, resources, such as library catalogs, databases, and search engines, provide tools to narrow the results. For example, in one popular all-purpose database, you can limit results by publication date, language, and publication or source type, among other options. (Check the Help screen to learn how to use these tools.) In this database, limiting the *home schooling* results to articles published in scholarly journals in English over the last ten years, reduced the number of hits to fifty-six, a far more reasonable number to review. (Remember that if you have too few results or your results are not targeted correctly, you can expand your search by removing limits selectively.)

For more on focusing search results and selecting search terms, see Chapter 24, p. 675.

Once you've reduced your search results to a manageable number, click on the remaining titles to look closely at each record. The analysis of an article's detailed record in Figure 25.1 shows what to look for.

After you have identified a reasonable number of relevant sources, examine the sources themselves:

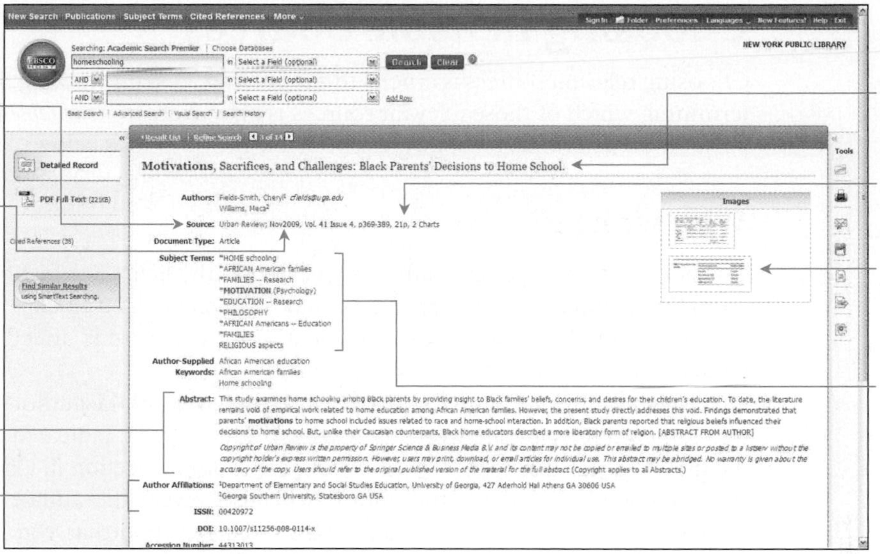

Publication: What do you know about the periodical? Is it well respected?

Date: Is the article recent enough for your area of study, or is it a classic? (Some older, "classic" sources may offer authoritative perspectives, but for current controversies or recent developments, use recent sources.)

Abstract: Does the article address your topic? What angle does it take?

Authors: Are they experts in the field? Do they have relevant background?

Title: Does the article address your topic?

Length: Does the length suggest the topic is treated in depth?

Illustrations: Does the article include illustrations that may illuminate concepts?

Subject terms: Are any of your keywords listed? Should any of these terms be added to your keywords list?

Figure 25.1   Analyzing the Detailed Record of an Article from a Periodicals Database
Analyze the detailed record of an article to determine whether the article itself is worth reading by asking yourself the following questions: Does the title suggest that the article addresses your topic? Are the authors experts in the field? Was the article published in a periodical that is likely to be reliable, was it published recently, and is it lengthy enough to indicate that the topic is treated in depth? Does the abstract (or summary) suggest that the article addresses your topic? If so, what angle does it take?

- Read the preface, introduction, or conclusion of books, or the first or last few paragraphs of articles, to determine which aspect of the topic is addressed or which approach to the topic is taken. To obtain a clear picture of a topic, researchers need to consider sources that address different aspects of the topic or take different approaches.

- Look at the headings or references in articles, or the table of contents and index in books, to see how much of the content relates specifically to your topic.

- Consider the way the source is written: Sources written for general readers may be accessible but may not analyze the subject in depth. Extremely specialized works may be too technical. Poorly written sources may be unreliable. (See Choosing Reliable Sources, p. 692, for more on scholarly versus popular sources and for a discussion of why researchers should avoid sources that are poorly written or riddled with errors.)

If close scrutiny leaves you with too few sources—or too many sources from too few perspectives—conduct a search using additional or alternative keywords, or explore links to related articles, look at the references in a particularly useful article, or look for other sources by an author whose work you find useful.

Choosing Reliable Sources

Choosing relevant sources is crucial to assembling a useful working bibliography. Determining which of those relevant sources is also likely to be *reliable* is even more important. To determine reliability, ask yourself the questions below.

Who wrote it?

Consider, first, whether the author is an *expert* in the field. The fact that someone has a PhD in astrophysics is no indication that he or she will be an expert in military history, for example, so be careful that the area of expertise is directly relevant to the topic.

To determine the author's area of expertise, look for the author's professional affiliation (where he or she works or teaches). This may be indicated at the bottom of the first page of an article or in an "About the Author" section in a book or on a Web site. Frequently, Googling the author will also reveal the author's affiliation, but double-check to make sure the affiliation is current and that you have located the right person. You may also consult a biographical reference source available through your library. Looking to see what other works the author has published, and with whom, can also help you ascertain his or her areas of expertise.

Contributors to blogs, wikis, and online discussion forums may or may not be experts in the field. Determine whether the site screens contributors, and double-check any information taken from sites for which you cannot determine the credentials of contributors.

Also consider the author's *perspective*. Most writing is not neutral or objective and does not claim to be. Knowledge of the author's perspective enables you to assess *bias* and determine whether the author's perspective affects the presentation of his or her argument. To determine the author's perspective, look for the main point and ask yourself question like these:

- What evidence does the author provide to support this point? Is it from authoritative sources? Is it persuasive?

For more details on these argumentative strategies, see Chapter 19.

- Does the author make concessions to or refute opposing arguments?
- Does the author avoid fallacies, confrontational phrasing, and loaded words?

When was it published?

In general, especially when you are writing about science or technology, current events, or emerging trends, you should consult the most up-to-date sources available on your subject. The date of publication for articles you locate should be indicated in your search results. For a print book, look for the copyright date on the copyright page (usually on the back of the title page); for an e-book, look for the copyright date at the beginning or end of the electronic file. If your source is a Web site, consider when it, and the content within it, was last updated (often indicated at the bottom of the Web page or home page).

You may also need older, "classic" sources that establish the principles, theories, and data on which later work is based and may provide a useful perspective for evaluating other works. To determine which sources are classics, note the ones that are cited most often in encyclopedia articles, lists of works cited or references, and recent works on the subject. You may also want to consult your instructor or a librarian to help you determine which works are classics in your field.

Is the source scholarly, popular, or for a trade group?

Scholarly sources (whether books or articles) are written by and for experts in a field of study, frequently professors or academic researchers. They can be challenging to read and understand because they use the language of the field and terminology that may be unfamiliar to those outside the discipline, but they are considered reliable because the contents are written by specialists and peer-reviewed (reviewed by specialists) before publication. Scholarly sources also tend to delve deeply into a subject, often a narrowly defined subject. Scholarly sources may be published by a university press, a scholarly organization, or a commercial publisher (such as Kluwer Academic or Blackwell). Though scholarly sources may provide an overview of the subject, they generally focus on a specific issue or argument and generally contain a great deal of original research.

In contrast, **popular sources** are written to entertain and educate the general public. For the most part, they are written by journalists who have conducted research and interviewed experts. They may include original research, especially on current events or emerging trends. Mainly, though, they report on and summarize original research and are written for interested, nonspecialist readers.

Of course, popular sources range widely along the reliability spectrum. Highly respected newspapers and magazines, such as the *New York Times*, the *Guardian,* the *Economist,* and *Harper's Magazine,* publish original research on news and culture. These newspapers and magazines check facts carefully and are often considered appropriate sources for research projects in entry-level courses (although you should check with your instructor to find out her or his expectations). Magazines that focus on celebrity gossip, such as *People* and *Us Weekly,* are unlikely to be considered appropriate sources for a college-level research project.

Trade publications—periodicals that report on news and technical advances in a specific industry—are written for those employed in the industry and include such titles as *Advertising Age, World Cement,* and *American Machinist.* Some trade publications may be appropriate for college research projects, especially in the sciences, but keep in mind that these publications are intended for a specialist audience and may focus on marketing products to professionals in the field. Table 25.1 summarizes some of the important differences between scholarly journals, popular magazines, and trade publications.

TABLE 25.1   Scholarly Journals versus Popular Magazines and Trade Publications

Scholarly Journals	*Popular Magazines*	*Trade Publications*
Journals are usually published 4 to 6 times per year.	Magazines are usually published weekly or monthly.	Trade publications may be published daily, weekly, monthly, or quarterly, depending on the industry covered.
Articles are usually written by scholars (with *PhD* or academic affiliations after their names).	Authors of articles are journalists but may quote experts.	Articles may be written by professionals or by journalists with quotes from experts.
Many articles have more than one author.	Most articles have a single author.	Authors of articles may or may not be named.
In print journals, the title page often appears on the cover, and the covers frequently lack artwork.	Photographs, usually in color, appear on the covers of most print magazines.	Photographs, usually in color, appear on the covers of most print trade publications.
Articles may include charts, tables, figures, and quotations from other scholarly sources.	Articles frequently include color pictures and sidebars.	Articles frequently include color pictures and sidebars.
An abstract (summary) of the article may appear on the first page.	A headline or engaging description may precede the article.	Headlines often include names or terms familiar only to industry insiders.
Most articles are fairly long—5 to 20 pages.	Most articles are fairly short—1 to 5 pages.	Most articles are fairly short—1 to 5 pages.
Articles cite sources and provide a bibliography (works-cited or reference list).	Articles rarely include a list of works cited or references but may mention or quote experts.	Articles rarely include a list of works cited or references but may mention or quote experts.

Who published it?

Determining who published or sponsored a source you are considering can help you gauge its reliability and ascertain the publication's slant (or point of view). Look to see whether the source was published by a commercial publisher (such as St. Martin's or Random House); a university press (such as the University of Nebraska Press); a corporation, an organization, or an interest group (such as the RAND Corporation, the World Wildlife Fund, or the National Restaurant Association); a government agency (such as the Internal Revenue Service or the U.S. Census Bureau); or the author on his or her own. Determining the publisher or sponsor is particularly important for material published on the Web.

If your source is a Web page, look at the URL (uniform resource locator) to find its top-level domain, which is indicated by a suffix. Some of the most useful ones are listed here:

.gov	U.S. federal government and some state or local government institutions
.org	nonprofit organizations
.edu	educational institutions
.com	businesses and commercial enterprises
.net	usually businesses or organizations associated with networks
.mil	the U.S. military

For the most part, *.gov* and *.edu* are the most likely to offer reliable sources of information for a college research project. However, sources with any of these domains may vary in reliability. For example, a file with a *.com* suffix may offer a highly reliable history of a corporation and be an appropriate source for someone writing a history of corporate America, whereas a file with an *.edu* suffix may have been posted by a student or by a faculty member outside his or her area of expertise. It is essential to look at Web sites carefully. Determine who sponsors the site: Is it a business, a professional group, a private organization, an educational institution, a government agency, or an individual? Look for a link, usually at the top or the bottom of the home page, called something like "Who We Are" or "About Us." If you cannot determine who sponsors a site, carefully double-check any information you find there.

Consider, too, checking how often the Web site has been linked to and the types of links provided by the Web site. That a site has been linked to repeatedly does not guarantee reliability, but the information may be helpful in conjunction with other recommendations in this chapter. To determine the number of times a Web page has been linked to, type *link:* plus the URL into a *Google* search box. To check the links provided, click on them and apply the criteria in this chapter.

If the source was published by a commercial publisher, check out the publisher's Web site, and ask yourself questions like these:

- Does the publisher offer works from a single perspective or from multiple perspectives?
- Do the works it publishes cover a wide variety of topics or focus on a particular array?
- Does the publisher's Web site host links to a particular type of site?

Consider the screen shots in Figure 25.2. The screen shot on the left is from the Web site of the *Nation*; the screen shot on the right is from the online version of the *National Review*. Compare the titles of the articles, and look at the photographs and advertisements. Do you notice any particular slant to the coverage?

The Web sites of book publishers may offer a link to a catalog. If so, look at the works it lists. Does the publisher seem to publish works on a particular topic or from a particular point of view? Does the publisher generally offer popular, academic, or professional works?

If your source is a periodical (a magazine, newspaper, newsletter, or scholarly journal), consider whether it focuses on a particular topic or offers a single point of view. In

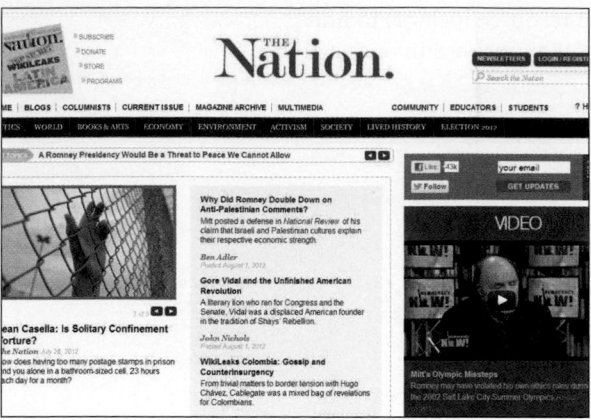 

FIGURE 25.2

Assessing a Publisher's Perspective

Consulting a publisher's Web site can help you determine the publisher's slant or point of view. A careful look at the Web sites of the *Nation* and the *National Review* indicates that one takes a liberal perspective on politics, while the other takes a conservative one. After looking carefully at the Web sites, can you determine which is which?

addition to looking at the article you are considering, visit the publisher's Web site, which may help you determine this.

How is the source written?

Most works that are published professionally (including popular newspapers and magazines, as well as scholarly journals and trade magazines) will have been edited carefully. These sources will generally avoid errors of grammar, punctuation, and spelling. Web sites sponsored by professional organizations, too, will generally avoid these kinds of errors. Personal Web sites, however, are unlikely to have been professionally edited and fact-checked. If a Web site is riddled with errors, be very careful to double-check any information you take from that site.

What does the source say?

Finally, and perhaps most importantly, consider the source itself. Answering the following questions can help you determine whether the source is worth consideration:

- What is the intended audience of the source? Does the source address an audience of experts, or is it intended for a general audience?

- What is the purpose of the source? Does it review a number of different positions, or does it argue for a position of its own? If it makes its own argument, analyze the argument closely.

- What is the tone of the source? Is the tone reasonable? Does the source respond to alternative viewpoints, and are those responses logical and reasonable?

- What evidence is offered to support the argument? Is the evidence relevant and reliable? What kinds of citations or links does the source supply?

To learn more about analyzing an argument, see Chapter 19, pp. 608–25.

26

Using Sources to Support Your Ideas

Writing a college research project requires you to

- analyze sources to understand the arguments those sources are making, the information they are using to support their claims, and the ways those arguments and the supporting evidence they use relate to your topic;
- synthesize information from sources to support, extend, and challenge your own ideas;
- integrate information from sources with your own ideas to contribute something new to the "conversation" on your topic.

Synthesizing Sources

Synthesizing means making connections among ideas from texts and from the writer's own experience. Once you have analyzed a number of sources on your topic, consider questions like the following to help you synthesize ideas and information:

- Do any of the sources you read use similar approaches or come to similar conclusions? What common themes do they explore? Do any of them use the same evidence (facts, statistics, research studies, examples) to support their claims?
- What differentiates their various positions? Where do the writers disagree, and why? Does one writer seem to be responding to or challenging one or more of the others?
- Do you agree with some sources and disagree with others? What makes one source more convincing than the others? Do any of the sources you have read offer support for your claims? Do any of them challenge your conclusions? If so, can you *refute* the challenge or do you need to *concede* a point?

Sentence strategies like the following can help you clarify where you differ from or agree with the sources you have read:

▶ A study by X supports my position by demonstrating that _____ .

▶ X and Y think this issue is about _____ . But what is really at stake here is _____ .

▶ X claims that _____ . But I agree with Y, who argues that _____ .

▶ On this issue, X and Y say _____ . Although I understand and to some degree sympathize with their point of view, I agree with Z that this is ultimately a question of _____ .

To learn more about synthesis, see Chapter 12, pp. 533–34.

The paragraph from Patrick O'Malley's paper on p. 700 shows how ideas and information from sources can be synthesized to support the writer's claim.

Acknowledging Sources and Avoiding Plagiarism

In your college writing, you will be expected to use and acknowledge **secondary sources**—books, articles, published or recorded interviews, Web sites, computer bulletin boards, lectures, and other print and nonprint materials—in addition to your own ideas, insights, and field research. The following information will help you decide what does and does not need to be acknowledged and will enable you to avoid *plagiarizing* from sources inadvertently.

What does and does not need to be acknowledged?

For the most part, any ideas, information, or language you borrow from a source—whether the source is in print or online—must be acknowledged by including an in-text citation and an entry in your list of works cited (MLA style) or references (APA style). The only types of information that do not require acknowledgment are common knowledge (for example, John F. Kennedy was assassinated in Dallas), facts widely available in many sources (U.S. presidents used to be inaugurated on March 4 rather than January 20), well-known quotations ("To be or not to be / That is the question"), and material you created or gathered yourself, such as photographs that you took or data from surveys that you conducted.

Remember that you need to acknowledge the source of any visual (photograph, table, chart, graph, diagram, drawing, map, screen shot) that you did not create yourself as well as the source of any information that you used to create your own visual. (You should also request permission from the source of a visual if your essay is going to be posted online without password protection.) When in doubt about whether you need to acknowledge a source, do so.

For more on citing sources in MLA and APA style, see Chapters 27 and 28.

The documentation guidelines in the next two chapters present two styles for citing sources: MLA and APA. Whichever style you use, the most important thing is that your readers be able to tell where words or ideas that are not your own begin and end. You can accomplish this most readily by taking and transcribing notes carefully, by placing parenthetical source citations correctly, and by separating your words from those of the source with **signal phrases** such as "According to Smith," "Peters claims," and "As Olmos asserts." (When you cite a source for the first time in a signal phrase, use the author's full name; after that, use just the last name.)

Avoid plagiarism by acknowledging sources and quoting, paraphrasing, and summarizing carefully.

When you use material from another source, you need to acknowledge the source, usually by citing the author and page or publication date in your text and including a list of works cited or references at the end of your essay. Failure to acknowledge sources—even by accident—constitutes plagiarism, a serious transgression. By citing sources correctly, you give appropriate credit to the originator of the words and ideas you are using, offer your readers the information they need to consult those sources directly, and build your own credibility.

Writers—students and professionals alike—occasionally fail to acknowledge sources properly. Students sometimes mistakenly assume that plagiarizing occurs only when another writer's exact words are used without acknowledgment. In fact, plagiarism can also apply to paraphrases as well as to such diverse forms of expression as musical compositions, visual images, ideas, and statistics. Therefore, keep in mind that you must indicate the source of any borrowed information, idea, language, or visual or audio material you use in your essay, whether you have *paraphrased, summarized,* or *quoted* directly from the source or have reproduced it or referred to it in some other way.

Remember especially the need to document electronic sources fully and accurately. Perhaps because it is so easy to access and distribute text and visuals online and to copy material from one electronic document and paste it into another, some students do not realize, or may forget, that information, ideas, and images from electronic sources require acknowledgment in even more detail than those from print sources. At the same time, the improper (unacknowledged) use of online sources is often very easy for readers to detect.

Some people plagiarize simply because they do not know the conventions for using and acknowledging sources. Others plagiarize because they keep sloppy notes and thus fail to distinguish between their own and their sources' ideas. If you keep a working bibliography and careful notes, you will not make this serious mistake. If you are unfamiliar with the conventions for documentation, this and the next two chapters will clarify how you can incorporate sources into your writing and properly acknowledge your use of those sources.

Another reason some people plagiarize is that they feel intimidated by the writing task or the deadline. If you experience this anxiety about your work, speak to your instructor. Do not run the risk of failing a course or being expelled from your college because of plagiarism.

If you are confused about what is and what is not plagiarism, be sure to ask your instructor.

Using Information from Sources to Support Your Claims

When writing a research project, remember that the goal is to use the ideas and information you find in sources *to support your own ideas*. Make sure that each of your supporting paragraphs does three things:

1. States a claim that supports your thesis
2. Provides evidence that supports your claim
3. Explains to readers how the evidence supports your claim

Consider this paragraph from Patrick O'Malley's proposal in Chapter 7, "More Testing, More Learning" (pp. 304–10):

States claim

Explains how evidence supports claim

Provides evidence

> The main reason professors should give frequent exams is that when they do and when they provide feedback to students on how well they are doing, students learn more in the course and perform better on major exams, projects, and papers. It makes sense that in a challenging course containing a great deal of material, students will learn more of it and put it to better use if they have to apply or "practice" it frequently on exams, which also helps them find out how much they are learning and what they need to go over again. A 2006 study reported in *Psychological Science* journal concluded that "taking repeated tests on material leads to better long-term retention than repeated studying," according to the study's coauthors, Henry L. Roediger and Jeffrey Karpicke (ScienceWatch.com, 2008). When asked what the impact of this breakthrough research would be, they responded: "We hope that this research may be picked up in educational circles as a way to improve educational practices, both for students in the classroom and as a study strategy outside of class." The new field of mind, brain, and education research advocates the use of "retrieval testing." For example, research by Karpicke and Blunt (2011) published in *Science* found that testing was more effective than other, more traditional methods of studying both for comprehension and for analysis. Why retrieval testing works is not known. A UCLA psychologist, Robert Bjork, speculates that it may be effective because "when we use our memories by retrieving things, we change our access" to that information. "What we recall," therefore, "becomes more recallable in the future" (qtd. in Belluck, 2011).

O'Malley connects this body paragraph to his thesis by beginning with the transition *The main reason* and by repeating the phrase *perform better* from his forecasting statement. He synthesizes information from a variety of sources. For example, he uses quotations from some sources and a summary of another to provide evidence. And he doesn't merely stitch quotations and summary together; rather, he explains how the evidence supports his claim by stating that it "makes sense" that students "apply or 'practice'" what they learn on frequent exams.

For more on synthesis, see Chapter 12, pp. 533–34.

Decide whether to quote, paraphrase, or summarize.

As illustrated in O'Malley's paragraph, above, writers integrate supporting evidence by quoting, paraphrasing, or summarizing information or ideas from sources. This section provides guidelines for deciding when to use each of these three methods and how to quote, paraphrase, and summarize effectively. Note that all examples in this section follow MLA style for in-text citations, which is explained in detail in Chapter 27.

For more on MLA style for citing sources in the body of your research project, see pp. 709–14.

As a rule, quote only in these situations:

- When the wording of the source is particularly memorable or vivid or expresses a point so well that you cannot improve it
- When the words of reliable and respected authorities would lend support to your position
- When you wish to cite an author whose opinions challenge or vary greatly from those of other experts
- When you are going to discuss the source's choice of words

Paraphrase passages whose details you wish to use but whose language is not particularly striking. Summarize any long passages whose main points you wish to record as support for a point you are making.

Copy quotations exactly, or use italics, ellipses, and brackets to indicate changes.

Quotations should duplicate the source exactly, even if they contain spelling errors. Add the notation *sic* (Latin for "thus") in brackets immediately after any such error to indicate that it is not your error but your source's. As long as you signal them appropriately, you may make changes to

- emphasize particular words;
- omit irrelevant information;
- insert information necessary for clarity;
- make the quotation conform grammatically to your sentence.

Using Italics for Emphasis   You may italicize any words in the quotation that you want to emphasize; add a semicolon and the words *emphasis added* (in regular type, not italicized or underlined) to the parenthetical citation:

> In her 2001 exposé of the struggles of the working class, Ehrenreich writes, "The wages Winn-Dixie is offering--*$6 and a couple of dimes to start with*--are not enough, I decide, to compensate for this indignity" (14; emphasis added).

Using Ellipsis Marks for Omissions   You may decide to omit words from a quotation because they are not relevant to the point you are making. When you omit words from within a quotation, use **ellipses**—three spaced periods (. . .) — in place of the missing words. When the omission occurs within a sentence, include a space before the first ellipsis mark and after the last mark:

> Hermione Roddice is described in Lawrence's *Women in Love* as a "woman of the new school, full of intellectuality and . . . nerve-worn with consciousness" (17).

When the omission falls at the end of a sentence, place a period *directly after* the final word of the sentence, followed by a space and three spaced ellipsis marks:

> But Grimaldi's commentary contends that for Aristotle rhetoric, like dialectic, had "no limited and unique subject matter upon which it must be exercised. . . . Instead, rhetoric as an art transcends all specific disciplines and may be brought into play in them" (6).

A period plus ellipses can indicate the omission not just of the rest of a sentence but also of whole sentences, paragraphs, or even pages.

When a parenthetical reference follows the ellipses at the end of a sentence, place the three spaced periods after the quotation, and place the sentence period after the final parenthesis:

> But Grimaldi's commentary contends that for Aristotle rhetoric, like dialectic, had "no limited and unique subject matter upon which it must be exercised. . . . Instead, rhetoric as an art transcends all specific disciplines . . ." (6).

When you quote only single words or phrases, you do not need to use ellipses because it will be obvious that you have left out some of the original:

> More specifically, Wharton's imagery of suffusing brightness transforms Undine before her glass into "some fabled creature whose home was in a beam of light" (21).

For the same reason, you need not use ellipses if you omit the beginning of a quoted sentence unless the rest of the sentence begins with a capitalized word and still appears to be a complete sentence.

Using Brackets for Insertions or Changes   Use brackets around an insertion or a change needed to make a quotation conform grammatically to your sentence, such as a change in the form of a verb or pronoun or in the capitalization of the first word of the quotation. In this example from an essay on James Joyce's short story "Araby," the writer adapts Joyce's phrases "we played till our bodies glowed" and "shook music from the buckled harness" to fit the grammar of her sentences:

> In the dark, cold streets during the "short days of winter," the boys must generate their own heat by "play[ing] till [their] bodies glowed." Music is "[shaken] from the buckled harness" as if it were unnatural, and the singers in the market chant nasally of "the troubles in our native land" (30).

You may also use brackets to add or substitute explanatory material in a quotation:

> Guterson notes that among Native Americans in Florida, "education was in the home; learning by doing was reinforced by the myths and legends which repeated the basic value system of their [the Seminoles'] way of life" (159).

Some changes that make a quotation conform grammatically to another sentence may be made without any signal to readers:

- A period at the end of a quotation may be changed to a comma if you are using the quotation within your own sentence.
- Double quotation marks enclosing a quotation may be changed to single quotation marks when the quotation is enclosed within a longer quotation.

Adjusting the Punctuation within Quotations   Although punctuation within a quotation should reproduce the original, some adaptations may be necessary. Use single quotation marks for quotations within the quotation:

Original from David Guterson's **_Family Matters_ (pp. 16–17)**	**Quoted Version**
E. D. Hirsch also recognizes the connection between family and learning, suggesting in his discussion of family background and academic achievement "that the significant part of our children's education has been going on outside rather than inside the schools."	Guterson claims that E. D. Hirsch "also recognizes the connection between family and learning, suggesting in his discussion of family background and academic achievement 'that the significant part of our children's education has been going on outside rather than inside the schools' " (16-17).

If the quotation ends with a question mark or an exclamation point, retain the original punctuation:

> "Did you think I loved you?" Edith later asks Dombey (566).

If a quotation ending with a question mark or an exclamation point concludes your sentence, retain the question mark or exclamation point, and put the parenthetical reference and sentence period outside the quotation marks:

> Edith later asks Dombey, "Did you think I loved you?" (566).

Avoiding Grammatical Tangles   When you incorporate quotations into your writing, and especially when you omit words from quotations, you run the risk of creating ungrammatical sentences. Avoid these three common errors:

- Verb incompatibility
- Ungrammatical omissions
- Sentence fragments

Verb incompatibility occurs when the verb form in the introductory statement is grammatically incompatible with the verb form in the quotation. When your quotation has a verb form that does not fit in with your text, it is usually possible to use just part of the quotation, thus avoiding verb incompatibility:

▶ The narrator suggests his bitter disappointment when "~~I saw myself~~ as a creature
he describes seeing himself "

driven and derided by vanity" (35).

As this sentence illustrates, use the present tense when you refer to events in a literary work.

Ungrammatical omissions may occur when you delete text from a quotation. To avoid this problem, try adapting the quotation (with brackets) so that its parts fit together grammatically, or use only one part of the quotation:

▶ From the moment of the boy's arrival in Araby, the bazaar is presented as a

commercial enterprise: "I could not find any sixpenny entrance and . . .
hand[ed]
~~handing~~ a shilling to a weary-looking man" (34).

▶ From the moment of the boy's arrival in Araby, the bazaar is presented as a

He "   *"*
commercial enterprise: "~~I~~ could not find any sixpenny entrance ~~and~~
so had to pay a shilling to get in
~~. . . handing a shilling to a weary-looking man~~" (34).

Sentence fragments sometimes result when writers forget to include a verb in the sentence introducing a quotation, especially when the quotation itself is a complete sentence. Make sure you introduce a quotation with a complete sentence:

leads
▶ The girl's interest in the bazaar ~~leading~~ the narrator to make what amounts to a sacred

oath: "If I go . . . I will bring you something" (32).

Use in-text or block quotations.

Depending on its length, you may incorporate a quotation into your text by enclosing it in quotation marks or by setting it off from your text in a block without quotation marks. In either case, be sure to integrate the quotation into your essay using the strategies described here:

In-Text Quotations   Incorporate brief quotations (no more than four typed lines of prose or three lines of poetry) into your text. You may place a quotation virtually anywhere in your sentence:

At the Beginning

"To live a life is not to cross a field," Sutherland, quoting Pasternak, writes at the beginning of her narrative (11).

In the Middle

Woolf begins and ends by speaking of the need of the woman writer to have "money and a room of her own" (4)--an idea that certainly spoke to Plath's condition.

At the End

In *The Second Sex*, Simone de Beauvoir describes such an experience as one in which the girl "becomes an object, and she sees herself as object" (378).

Divided by Your Own Words

"Science usually prefers the literal to the nonliteral term," Kinneavy writes, "--that is, figures of speech are often out of place in science" (177).

When you quote poetry within your text, use a slash (/) with spaces before and after to signal the end of each line of verse:

> Alluding to St. Augustine's distinction between the City of God and the Earthly City, Lowell writes that "much against my will / I left the City of God where it belongs" (4-5).

Block Quotations   In MLA style, use the block form for prose quotations of five or more typed lines and for poetry quotations of four or more lines. Indent the quotation an inch from the left margin, as shown in the following example:

> In "A Literary Legacy from Dunbar to Baraka," Margaret Walker says of Paul Lawrence Dunbar's dialect poems:
>> He realized that the while world in the United States tolerated his literary genius only because of his "jingles in a broken tongue," and they found the old "darky" tales and speech amusing and within the vein of folklore into which they wished to classify all Negro life. This troubled Dunbar because he realized that white America was denigrating him as a writer and as a man. (70)

In APA style, use block form for quotations of forty words or more. Indent the block quotation half an inch.

In a block quotation, double-space between lines just as you do in your text. *Do not* enclose the passage within quotation marks. Use a colon to introduce a block quotation unless the context calls for another punctuation mark or none at all. When quoting a single paragraph or part of one in MLA style, do not indent the first line of the quotation more than the rest. In quoting two or more paragraphs, indent the first line of each paragraph an extra quarter inch. If you are using APA style, indent the first line of subsequent paragraphs in the block quotation an additional half inch from the indention of the block quotation.

Note that in MLA style the parenthetical page reference follows the period in block quotations.

Use punctuation to integrate quotations into your writing.

Statements that introduce in-text quotations take a range of punctuation marks and lead-in words. Here are some examples of ways writers typically introduce quotations:

Introducing a Quotation Using a Colon   A colon usually follows an independent clause placed before the quotation:

> As George Williams notes, protection of white privilege is critical to patterns of discrimination: "Whenever a number of persons within a society have enjoyed for a considerable period of time certain opportunities for getting wealth, for exercising power and authority, and for successfully claiming prestige and social deference, there is a strong tendency for these people to feel that these benefits are theirs 'by right' " (727).

Introducing a Quotation Using a Comma   A comma usually follows an introduction that incorporates the quotation in its sentence structure:

> Similarly, Duncan Turner asserts, "As matters now stand, it is unwise to talk about communication without some understanding of Burke" (259).

Introducing a Quotation Using *That*   No punctuation is generally needed with *that*, and no capital letter is used to begin the quotation:

> Noting this failure, Alice Miller asserts that "the reason for her despair was not her suffering but the impossibility of communicating her suffering to another person" (255).

Paraphrase sources carefully.

In a **paraphrase,** the writer restates in his or her own words all the relevant information from a passage, without any additional comments or any suggestion of agreement or disagreement with the source's ideas. A paraphrase is useful for recording details of the passage when the order of the details is important but the source's wording is not. Because all the details of the passage are included, a paraphrase is often about the same length as the original passage. It is better to paraphrase than to quote ordinary material in which the author's way of expressing things is not worth special attention.

Here is a passage from a book on home schooling and an example of an acceptable paraphrase of it:

Original Source

Bruner and the discovery theorists have also illuminated conditions that apparently pave the way for learning. It is significant that these conditions are unique to each learner, so unique, in fact, that in many cases classrooms can't provide them. Bruner also contends that the more one discovers information in a great variety of circumstances, the more likely one is to develop the inner categories required to organize that information. Yet life at school, which is for the most part generic and predictable, daily keeps many children from the great variety of circumstances they need to learn well.

—David Guterson, *Family Matters: Why Homeschooling Makes Sense,* p. 172

Acceptable Paraphrase

According to Guterson, the "discovery theorists," particularly Bruner, have found that there seem to be certain conditions that help learning to take place. Because individuals require different conditions, many children are not able to learn in the classroom. According to Bruner, when people can explore information in many different situations, they learn to classify and order what they discover. The general routine of the school day, however, does not provide children with the diverse activities and situations that would allow them to learn these skills (172).

The highlighting shows that some words in the paraphrase were taken from the source. Indeed, it would be nearly impossible for paraphrasers to avoid using any key terms from the source, and it would be counterproductive to try to do so, because the original and the paraphrase necessarily share the same information and concepts. Notice, though, that of the total of eighty-five words in the paraphrase, the paraphraser uses only a name (*Bruner*) and a few other key nouns and verbs for which it would be awkward to substitute other words or phrases. If the paraphraser had wanted to use other, more distinctive language from the source—for example, the description of life at school as "generic and predictable"—these adjectives would need to be enclosed in quotation marks. In fact, the paraphraser puts quotation marks around only one of the terms from the source: "discovery theorists"—a technical term likely to be unfamiliar to readers.

Paraphrasers must, however, avoid borrowing too many words and repeating the sentence structures from a source. Here is an unacceptable paraphrase of the first sentence in the Guterson passage:

Unacceptable Paraphrase: Too Many Borrowed Words and Phrases

Apparently, some conditions, which have been illuminated by Bruner and other discovery theorists, pave the way for people to learn.

Repeated sentence structure

Repeated words

Here, the paraphrase borrows almost all of its key language from the source sentence, including the entire phrase *pave the way for*. Even if you cite the source, this heavy borrowing would be considered plagiarism.

Here is another unacceptable paraphrase of the same sentence:

Repeated words
Synonyms
Repeated sentence
structure

Unacceptable Paraphrase: Sentence Structure Repeated Too Closely

Bruner and other *researchers* have also *identified circumstances* that *seem to ease the path* to learning.

If you compare the source's first sentence and this paraphrase of it, you will see that the paraphraser has borrowed the phrases and clauses of the source and arranged them in an almost identical sequence, simply substituting synonyms for most of the key terms. This paraphrase would also be considered plagiarism.

Summaries should present the source's main ideas in a balanced and readable way.

Unlike a paraphrase, a **summary** presents only the main ideas of a source, leaving out examples and details.

Here is one student's summary of five pages from Guterson's book *Family Matters.* You can see at a glance how drastically summaries can condense information, in this case from five pages to five sentences. Depending on the summarizer's purpose, the five pages could be summarized in one sentence, the five sentences here, or two or three dozen sentences.

> In looking at different theories of learning that discuss individual-based programs (such as home schooling) versus the public school system, Guterson describes the disagreements among "cognitivist" theorists. One group, the "discovery theorists," believes that individual children learn by creating their own ways of sorting the information they take in from their experiences. Schools should help students develop better ways of organizing new material, not just present them with material that is already categorized, as traditional schools do. "Assimilationist theorists," by contrast, believe that children learn by linking what they don't know to information they already know. These theorists claim that traditional schools help students learn when they present information in ways that allow children to fit the new material into categories they have already developed (171-75).

Summaries like this one are more than a dry list of main ideas from a source. They are instead a coherent, readable new text composed of the source's main ideas. Summaries provide balanced coverage of a source, following the same sequence of ideas and avoiding any hint of agreement or disagreement with them.

27

Citing and Documenting Sources in MLA Style

When using the MLA system of documentation, include both an in-text citation and a list of works cited. **In-text citations** tell your readers where the ideas or words you have borrowed come from, and the entries in the **works-cited list** allow readers to locate your sources so that they can read more about your topic.

In most cases, include the author's last name and the page number on which the borrowed material appears in the text of your research project. You can incorporate this information in two ways, often used together:

SIGNAL PHRASE   By naming the author in the text of your research project with a signal phrase (*Simon described*) and including the page reference (in parentheses) at the end of the borrowed passage:

author's last name   *appropriate verb*

> Simon, a well-known figure in New York literary society, described the impression Dr. James made on her as a child in the Bronx: He was a "not-too-skeletal Ichabod Crane" (68).

page number

PARENTHETICAL CITATION   By including the author's name and the page number together in parentheses at the end of the borrowed passage:

author's last name + page number

> Dr. James is described as a "not-too-skeletal Ichabod Crane" (Simon 68).

WORKS-CITED ENTRY   Simon, Kate. "Birthing." *Bronx Primitive: Portraits in a Childhood.* New York: Viking, 1982. 68-77. Print.

In most cases, you will want to use a *signal phrase* because doing so lets you put your source in context. The signal-phrase-plus-page-reference combination also allows you to make crystal clear where the source information begins and ends. Use a parenthetical citation alone when you have already identified the author or when citing the source of an uncontroversial fact.

The in-text citation (with or without a signal phrase) should include only as much information as is needed to lead readers to the source in your list of works cited and allow them to find the passage you are citing in that source. In most cases, that means the author's last name and the page number on which the borrowed material appears. In some cases, you may need to include other information in your in-text citation (such as a brief version of the title if the author is unknown or if you cite more than one work by this author). In a few cases, you may not be able to include a page reference, as, for example, when you cite a Web site that does not include page numbers. In such cases, you may include other identifying information, such as a paragraph number or section heading.

The most common types of in-text citations follow. For other, less common citation types, consult the *MLA Handbook for Writers of Research Papers,* Seventh Edition. Most libraries will own a copy. If the handbook does not provide a model citation, use the information here to create a citation that will lead your readers to the source.

Citing Sources in the Text

Directory to In-Text-Citation Models

One author   When citing most works with a single author, include the author's name (usually the last name is enough)* and the page number on which the cited material appears.

author's last name + appropriate verb   *page number*

SIGNAL PHRASE   Simon describes Dr. James as a "not-too-skeletal Ichabod Crane" (68).

author's last name + page number

PARENTHETICAL CITATION   Dr. James is described as a "not-too-skeletal Ichabod Crane" (Simon 68).

---

* But see entries for "Two or More Works by the Same Author," "Two or More Authors with the Same Last Name," and "Work without Page Numbers or a One-Page Work" on pp. 711, 712, and 713.

BLOCK QUOTATION   In Kate Simon's story "Birthing," the description of Dr. James captures

author's name

both his physical appearance and his role in the community:

> He looked so much like a story character—the gentled Scrooge
> of a St. Nicholas Magazine Christmas issue, a not-too-skeletal
> Ichabod Crane. . . . Dr. James was, even when I knew him as a
> child, quite an old man, retired from a prestigious and lucrative
> practice in Boston. . . . His was a prosperous intellectual family,
> the famous New England Jameses that produced William and Henry,
> but to the older Bronx doctors, *the* James was the magnificent old
> driven scarecrow. (68)

page number

(A works-cited entry for "Birthing" appears on page 709.)

More than one author   To cite a source by two or three authors, include all the authors'
last names. To cite a source with four or more authors, model your in-text citation on
the entry in your works-cited list: Use either all the authors' names or just the first
author's name followed by *et al.* ("and others" in Latin, not italicized).

SIGNAL PHRASE   Dyal, Corning, and Willows (1975) identify several types of students,
including the "Authority-Rebel" (4).

PARENTHETICAL   The Authority-Rebel "tends to see himself as superior to other
CITATION   students in the class" (Dyal, Corning, and Willows 4).

The drug AZT has been shown to reduce the risk of transmission
from HIV-positive mothers to their infants by as much as two-thirds
(Van de Perre et al. 4 5).

Unknown author   If the author's name is unknown, use a shortened version of the
title, beginning with the word by which the title is alphabetized in the works-cited list.

An international pollution treaty still to be ratified would prohibit ships from dumping
plastic at sea ("Plastic Is Found" 68).

The full title of the work is "Plastic Is Found in the Sargasso Sea; Pieces of Apparent
Refuse Cover Wide Atlantic Region."

Two or more works by the same author   If you cite more than one work by the
same author, include a shortened version of the title.

When old paint becomes transparent, it sometimes shows the artist's original plans:
"a tree will show through a woman's dress" (Hellman, *Pentimento* 1).

Two or more authors with the same last name   When citing works by authors with the same last name, include each author's first initial in the citation. If the first initials are also the same, spell out the authors' first names.

> Chaplin's *Modern Times* provides a good example of montage used to make an editorial statement (E. Roberts 246).

Corporation, organization, or government agency as author   In a signal phrase, use the full name of the corporation, organization, or government agency. In a parenthetical citation, use the full name if it is brief or a shortened version if it is long.

SIGNAL PHRASE	According to the Washington State Board for Community and Technical Colleges, a tuition increase . . . from Initiative 601 (4).
PARENTHETICAL CITATION	A tuition increase has been proposed for community and technical colleges to offset budget deficits from Initiative 601 (Washington State Board 4).

Literary work (novel, play, poem)   Provide information that will help readers find the passage you are citing no matter what edition of the novel, play, or poem they are using. For a novel or other prose work, provide the part or chapter number as well as the page numbers from the edition you used.

NOVEL OR OTHER PROSE WORK	In *Hard Times,* Tom reveals his utter narcissism by blaming Louisa for his own failure: " ' You have regularly given me up. You never cared for me'" (Dickens 262; bk. 3, ch. 9).

For a play in verse, use act, scene, and line numbers instead of page numbers.

PLAY (IN VERSE)	At the beginning, Regan's fawning rhetoric hides her true attitude toward Lear: "I profess / myself an enemy to all other joys . . . / And find that I am alone felicitate / In your dear highness' love" (*King Lear* 1.1.74-75, 77-78).

For a poem, indicate the line numbers and stanzas or sections (if they are numbered) instead of page numbers.

POEM	In "Song of Myself," Whitman finds poetic details in busy urban settings, as when he describes "the blab of the pave, tires of carts . . . the driver with his interrogating thumb" (8.153-54).

If the source gives only line numbers, use the term *lines* in your first citation and use only the numbers in subsequent citations.

> In "Before you thought of spring," Dickinson at first identifies the spirit of spring with a bird, possibly a robin--"A fellow in the skies / Inspiriting habiliments / Of indigo and brown" (lines 4, 7-8)--but by the end of the poem, she has linked it with poetry and perhaps even the poet herself, as the bird, like Dickinson "shouts for joy to nobody / But his seraphic self!" (15-16)

Work in an anthology   Use the name of the author of the work, not the editor of the anthology, in your in-text citation.

SIGNAL PHRASE	In "Six Days: Some Rememberings," Grace Paley recalls that when she was in jail for protesting the Vietnam War, her pen and paper were taken away and she felt "a terrible pain in the area of my heart--a nausea" (191).
PARENTHETICAL CITATION	Writers may have a visceral reaction--"a nausea" (Paley 191)-- to being deprived of access to writing implements.

Religious work   In your first citation, include the element that begins your entry in the works-cited list, such as the edition name of the religious work you are citing, and include the book or section name (using standard abbreviations in parenthetical citations) and any chapter or verse numbers.

> She ignored the admonition "Pride goes before destruction, and a haughty spirit before a fall" (*New Oxford Annotated Bible,* Prov. 16.18).

Multivolume work (one volume, more than one volume)   If you cite only one volume of a multivolume work, treat the in-text citation as you would any other work, but include the volume number in the works-cited entry (see p. 719).

ONE VOLUME	Forster argued that modernist writers valued experimentation and gradually sought to blur the line between poetry and prose (150).

When you use two or more volumes of a multivolume work, include the volume number and the page number(s) in your in-text citation.

MORE THAN ONE VOLUME	Modernist writers valued experimentation and gradually sought to blur the line between poetry and prose (Forster 3: 150).

Indirect citation (quotation from a secondary source)   If possible, locate the original source and cite that. If not possible, name the original source but also include the secondary source in which you found the material you are citing, plus the abbreviation *qtd. in.* Include the secondary source in your list of works cited.

> E. M. Forster says, "the collapse of all civilization, so realistic for us, sounded in Matthew Arnold's ears like a distant and harmonious cataract" (qtd. in Trilling 11).

Entire work   Include the reference in the text without any page numbers or parentheses.

> In *The Structure of Scientific Revolutions,* Thomas Kuhn discusses how scientists change their thinking.

Work without page numbers or a one-page work (with/without other section numbers)   If a work (such as a Web page) has no page numbers or is only one page long, omit the page number. If it uses screen numbers or paragraph numbers, insert a comma after the author's name, an identifying term (such as *screen*) or abbreviation (*par.* or *pars.*), and the number.

WITHOUT PAGE OR OTHER NUMBERS   The average speed on Montana's interstate highways, for example, has risen by only 2 miles per hour since the repeal of the federal speed limit, with most drivers topping out at 75 (Schmid).

WITH OTHER SECTION NUMBERS   Whitman considered African American speech "a source of a native grand opera" (Ellison, par. 13).

Two or more works cited in the same parentheses   If you cite two or more sources for a piece of information, include them in the same parentheses, separated by semicolons.

A few studies have considered differences between oral and written discourse production (Scardamalia, Bereiter, and Goelman; Gould).

If the parenthetical citation is likely to prove disruptive for your reader, cite multiple sources in a footnote or an end note.

Creating a List of Works Cited

Directory to Works-Cited-List Models

In your MLA-style research paper, every source you cite must have a corresponding entry in the list of works cited, and every entry in your list of works cited must correspond to at least one citation in your research project.

Follow these rules when formatting your list of works cited in MLA style:

- Double-space the whole works-cited list.

- Alphabetize entries by the first word in the citation (usually the first author's last name, or the title if the author is unknown, ignoring *A, An,* or *The*).

- Use a "hanging indent" for all entries: Do not indent the first line, but indent second and subsequent lines of the entry by half an inch (or five spaces).

- Shorten publishers' names: Abbreviate compound or hyphenated names to the first name only (*Bedford/St. Martin's* becomes *Bedford,* for example); omit words like *Company* or *Books;* and for university presses, shorten the words *University* and *Press* to *U* and *P*.

Nowadays, many print sources are also available in an electronic format, either online or through a database your school's library subscribes to. For most online versions of a source, follow the form of the corresponding print version. For example, if you are citing an article from an online periodical, put the article title in quotation marks and italicize the name of the periodical. If the source has also been published in print (as with most e-books and many magazines and newspapers that appear online), include the print publication information if it is available. Also include information specific to the version of the source you used.

For sources accessed through a database, include the following:

- Title of the database (in italics)

- Medium of publication (*Web*)

- Date you last accessed the source

For other online sources, include the following:

- Title of the Web site (in italics)

- Version or edition used (if any)

- Publisher or sponsor of the site; if not available, use *N.p.*

- Date of publication or last update; if not available, use *n.d.*

- Medium of publication (*Web*)

- Date you last accessed the source

Content on the Web frequently changes or disappears, and because the same information that traditionally published books and periodicals provide is not always included for Web sources, giving your reader a complete citation is not always possible. Always keep your goal in mind: to provide enough information so that your reader can track down the source. If you cannot find all of the information listed here, include what you can.

Author Listings

One author   List the author last name first (followed by a comma), and insert a period at the end of the name.

> Isaacson, Walter.

Two or three authors   List the first author last name first (followed by a comma). List the other authors in the usual first-name/last-name order. Insert the word *and* before the last author's name, and follow it with a period.

> Saba, Laura, and Julie Gattis.

> Wilmut, Ian, Keith Campbell, and Colin Tudge.

Four or more authors   List the first author last name first (followed by a comma). Then either list all the authors' names (in the usual first-name/last-name order, with a comma between authors, the word *and* before the last name, and a period after it) *or* insert *et al.* (which means *and others* in Latin) in regular type (not italics). Whichever you decide to do, be sure to use the same format in your in-text citation.

> Hunt, Lynn, Thomas R. Martin, Barbara H. Rosenwein, R. Po-chia Hsia,
>   and Bonnie G. Smith.

> Hunt, Lynn, et al.

Unknown author   Begin the entry with the title.

> *Primary Colors: A Novel of Politics.*

> "Out of Sight."

Corporation, organization, or government agency as author   Use the name of the corporation, organization, or government agency as the author.

> RAND Corporation.

> United States. National Commission on Terrorist Attacks.

Two or more works by the same author   Replace the author's name in subsequent entries with three hyphens, and alphabetize the works by the first important word in the title:

> Eugenides, Jeffrey. The Marriage Plot.

> ---. Middlesex.

> ---. "Walkabout."

Books (Print, Electronic, Database)

Basic format (print, e-book, database)

Author, last name first   *Title (and subtitle, if any), italicized*   *Publication info*   *Medium*

PRINT   Eugenides, Jeffrey. *The Marriage Plot*. New York: Farrar, 2011. Print.

City of publication   *Publisher (abbreviated)*   *Year of publication*

Print publication info   *Medium*

E-BOOK   Eugenides, Jeffrey. *The Marriage Plot*. New York: Farrar, 2011. Kindle e-book file.

Print publication info   *Database name, italicized*

DATABASE   Whitman, Walt. *Leaves of Grass*. Philadelphia: McKay, 1900. *Bartleby.com*. Web. 28 Nov. 2011.

Medium   *Access date*

Figure 27.1 (p. 718) shows you where to find the source information you will need to create a works-cited entry for a book.

Anthology or edited collection   If you are referring to the anthology as a whole, put the editor's name first.

> Masri, Heather, ed. *Science Fiction: Stories and Contexts*. Boston: Bedford, 2009. Print.

Work in an anthology or edited collection   If you're referring to a selection in an anthology, begin the entry with the name of the selection's author.

> Hopkinson, Nalo. "Something to Hitch Meat To." *Science Fiction: Stories and Contexts*. Ed. Heather Masri. Boston: Bedford, 2009. 838-50. Print.

If you cite more than one selection from an anthology or collection, you may create an entry for the collection as a whole (see the model above) and then cross-reference individual selections to that entry.

Selection author   *Selection title*   *Anthology editor*

Hopkinson, Nalo. "Something to Hitch Meat To." Masri 838-50. Print.

Selection pages in anthology

Introduction, preface, foreword, or afterword

> Murfin, Ross C. Introduction. *Heart of Darkness*. By Joseph Conrad. 3rd ed. Boston: Bedford, 2011. 3-16. Print.

Translation

> Tolstoy, Leo. *War and Peace*. Trans. Richard Pevear and Larissa Volokhonsky. New York: Vintage, 2009. Print.

Graphic narrative   If the graphic narrative was a collaboration between a writer and an illustrator, begin your entry with the name of the person on whose work your

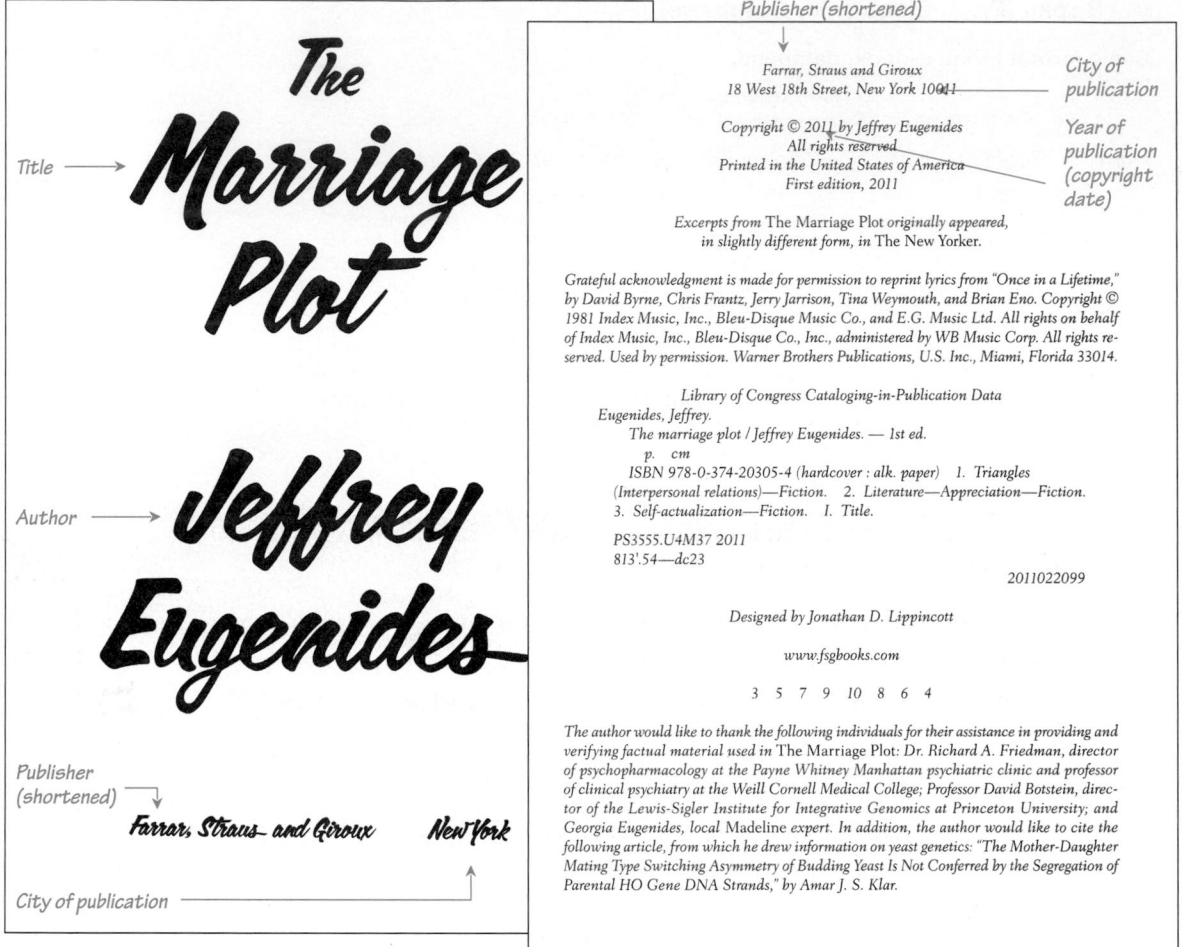

FIGURE 27.1   Documentation Map for a Book   Look for the author, title, publisher, and city of publication on the title page (at the front of the book) and the year of publication (or copyright date) on the copyright page (usually on the back of the title page in print books). The title page and copyright page may appear in a different location or look a little different in an e-book or a book accessed through a database, but the information provided should be the same.

research project focuses. If the author also created the illustrations, then follow the basic model for a book with one author (p. 716).

> Pekar, Harvey, and Joyce Brabner. *Our Cancer Year*. Illus. Frank Stack. New York: Four Walls Eight Window, 1994. Print.

Religious work   Include an entry in the list of works cited only if you cite a specific edition of a sacred text.

> *The Qu'ran: English Translation and Parallel Arabic Text*. Trans. M. A. S. Abdel Haleem. New York: Oxford UP, 2010. Print.

Multivolume work   If you use only one volume from a multivolume work, indicate the volume number after the title. If you use more than one volume, indicate the total number of volumes after the title.

One volume cited

Sandburg, Carl. *Abraham Lincoln*. Vol. 2. New York: Scribner's, 1939. Print.

More than one volume cited

Sandburg, Carl. *Abraham Lincoln*. 6 vols. New York: Scribner's, 1939. Print.

Later edition of a book   Include the edition name (such as *Revised*) or number following the title.

Rottenberg, Annette T., and Donna Haisty Winchell. *The Structure of Argument*. 6th ed. Boston: Bedford, 2009. Print.

Republished book   Provide the original year of publication after the title of the book, followed by publication information for the edition you are using.

Original publication date

Alcott, Louisa May. *An Old-Fashioned Girl*. 1870. New York: Puffin, 1995. Print.

Republication information

Title within a title   When a title that is normally italicized appears within a book title, do not italicize it. If the title within the title would normally be enclosed in quotation marks, include the quotation marks and also set the title in italics.

Hertenstein, Mike. *The Double Vision of* Star Trek: *Half-Humans, Evil Twins, and Science Fiction*. Chicago: Cornerstone, 1998. Print.

Miller, Edwin Haviland. *Walt Whitman's "Song of Myself": A Mosaic of Interpretation*. Iowa City: U of Iowa P, 1989. Print.

Book in a series   Include the series title and number (if any) after the medium of publication. If the word *Series* is part of the name, include the abbreviation *Ser.* before the series number. (This information will appear on the title page or on the page facing the title page.) Abbreviate any commonly abbreviated words in the series title.

Zigova, Tanya, et al. *Neural Stem Cells: Methods and Protocols*. Totowa: Humana, 2002. Print. Methods in Molecular Biology 198.

Dictionary entry or article in another reference book (print, online, database)   If no author is listed, begin with the entry's title. (But check for initials following the entry or article and a list of authors in the front of the book.) If the reference work is familiar, omit the publication information.

PRINT   "Homeopathy." *Webster's New World College Dictionary*. 4th ed. 1999. Print.

PRINT   Trenear-Harvey, Glenmore S. "Farm Hall." *Historical Dictionary of Atomic Espionage.*
Lanham: Scarecrow, 2011. Print.

Web site (italics)   *Site sponsor*   *Medium*

ONLINE   "Homeopathy." *Merriam-Webster.com.* Merriam-Webster, Inc., 2011. Web.
29 Nov. 2011.

Access date

DATABASE   Powell, Jason L. "Power Elite." *Blackwell Encyclopedia of Sociology.* Ed. George
Ritzer. Wiley-Blackwell, 2007. *Blackwell Reference Online.* Web. 29 Nov. 2011.

Database (italics)   *Medium*   *Access date*

Government document (print, online)   If no author is named, begin with the government
and agency that issued the document. If the author is named, include that information
either before or after the document's title (introduced with the word *By*). In the United
States, the publication information for most print government documents is *Washington:
GPO.* (*GPO* stands for *Government Printing Office.*) But most government documents are
now published online.

Issuing government   *Issuing department*

PRINT   United States. Dept. of Health and Human Services. *Trends in Underage
Drinking in the United States, 1991-2007.* By Gabriella Newes-Adeyi et al.
Washington: GPO, 2009. Print.

Authors

Issuing agency

ONLINE   United States. Centers for Disease Control. "Youth Risk Behavior Surveillance—
United States, 2009." *Morbidity and Mortality Weekly Report.*
Centers for Disease Control. Dept. of Health and Human Services.

Web site (italics)   *Site sponsor*

4 June 2010. Web. 30 Nov. 2011.

Publication date   *Medium*   *Access date*

Published proceedings of a conference   If the name of the conference is part of the
title of the publication, it need not be repeated. If it isn't part of the title, insert the
name of the conference following the title. Use the format for a work in an anthology
to cite an individual presentation (see p. 717).

Conference name included in title

Duffett, John, ed. *Against the Crime of Silence: Proceedings of the International War Crimes
Tribunal.* Nov. 1967, Stockholm. New York: Clarion-Simon, 1970. Print.

Pamphlet or brochure

U.S. Foundation for Boating Safety and Clean Water. *Hypothermia and Cold Water Survival.*
Alexandria: U.S. Foundation for Boating, 2001. Print.

Doctoral dissertation (published, unpublished)   Cite a published dissertation as you would a book, but add pertinent dissertation information before the publication data. Enclose the title of an unpublished dissertation in quotation marks.

Title in italics

PUBLISHED   Jones, Anna Maria. *Problem Novels/Perverse Readers: Late-Victorian Fiction and the Perilous Pleasures of Identification.* Diss. U of Notre Dame, 2001. Ann Arbor: UMI, 2001. Print.
Dissertation information

Title in quotation marks

UNPUBLISHED   Bullock, Barbara. "Basic Needs Fulfillment among Less Developed Countries: Social Progress over Two Decades of Growth." Diss. Vanderbilt U, 1986. Print.
Dissertation information

Articles (Print, Online, Database)

Articles appear in periodicals—works that are issued at regular intervals such as scholarly journals, newspapers, and magazines—Most periodicals today are available both in print and in electronic form (online or through an electronic database); some are available only in electronic format. If you are using the online version of an article, use the models provided here. If no model matches your source exactly, choose the closest print match, and add the site sponsor, the medium, and the date you last accessed the site, along with any other information your reader will need to track down the source.

From a scholarly journal (print, online, database)   Scholarly journals are typically identified using their volume and issue numbers, separated by a period.

Author, last name first   *Title of article (in quotation marks)*

PRINT   Garas-York, Keli. "Overlapping Student Environments: An Examination of the Homeschool Connection and Its Impact on Achievement." *Journal of College Admission* 42.4 (2010): 430-49. Print.
Title of journal (in italics)   *Volume* *Issue* *Year*   *Pages*   *Medium*

ONLINE   Saho, Bala S. K. "The Appropriation of Islam in a Gambian Village: Life and Times of Shaykh Mass Kay, 1827-1936. *African Studies Quarterly* 12.4 (2011): n pag. Web. 12 Dec. 2011.
No page numbers   *Medium*   *Access date*

DATABASE   Garas-York, Keli. "Overlapping Student Environments: An Examination of the Homeschool Connection and Its Impact on Achievement." *Journal of College Admission* 42.4 (2010): 430-49. *Academic Search Complete.* Web. 13 Dec. 2011.
Database (italics)
Medium   *Access date*

If a journal does not use volume numbers, provide the issue number only.

For help distinguishing between scholarly journals and magazines, see Chapter 25, pp. 693–94.

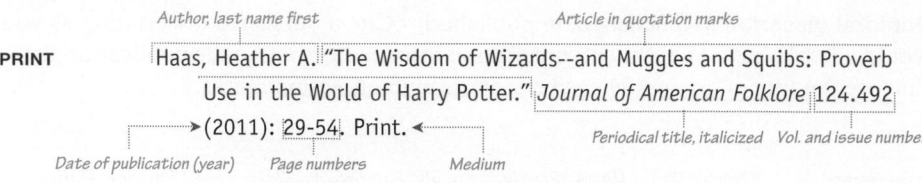

PRINT　Haas, Heather A. "The Wisdom of Wizards--and Muggles and Squibs: Proverb Use in the World of Harry Potter." *Journal of American Folklore* 124.492 (2011): 29-54. Print.

Author, last name first　　*Article in quotation marks*

Periodical title, italicized　*Vol. and issue number*

Date of publication (year)　*Page numbers*　*Medium*

ONLINE　Markel, J. D. "Religious Allegory and Cultural Discomfort in Mike Leigh's *Happy-Go-Lucky*: And Why *Larry Crowne* Is One of the Best Films of 2011." *Bright Lights* 74 (2011): n. pag. Web. 29 Nov. 2011.

Issue number only　　*No page numbers*　*Medium*　*Access date*

DATABASE　Haas, Heather A. "The Wisdom of Wizards--and Muggles and Squibs: Proverb Use in the World of *Harry Potter*." *Journal of American Folklore* 124.492 (2011): 29-54. *Academic Search Complete.* Web. 29 Nov. 2011.

Database (italics)

Online journals may not include page numbers; if paragraph or other section numbers are provided, use them instead. Otherwise, insert *n. pag.* (for *no page numbers*). If the article is not on a continuous sequence of pages, give the first page number followed by a plus sign. (See entry for a print version of a newspaper for an example.)

Figure 27.2 shows where to find the source information you will need to create a works-cited entry for three of the journal articles cited here.

From a newspaper (print, online, database)　Newspapers are identified by date, not volume and issue numbers, with the names of months longer than four letters abbreviated. If the article is from a special edition of the newspaper (*early ed., natl ed.*), include the edition name after the date. If articles are not on a continuous series of pages, give only the first page number followed by a plus sign. For unpaginated articles accessed through a database, use *n. pag.*

PRINT　Stoll, John D., et al. "U.S. Squeezes Auto Creditors." *Wall Street Journal* 10 Apr. 2009: A1+. Print.

Noncontinuous pages

ONLINE　Medina, Jennifer, and Brian Stelter. "Police Clear Occupy Encampments in Two Cities." *New York Times.* New York Times, 30 Nov. 2011. Web. 30 Nov. 2011.

Web-site (italics)　*Site sponsor*　*Publication date*　*Medium*　*Access date*

DATABASE　Lopez, Steve. "Put Occupy L.A. on the Bus." *Los Angeles Times* 30 Nov. 2011, Home ed.: n. pag. *LexisNexis Academic.* Web. 30 Nov. 2011.

Edition name　*No page numbers*　*Database (italics)*

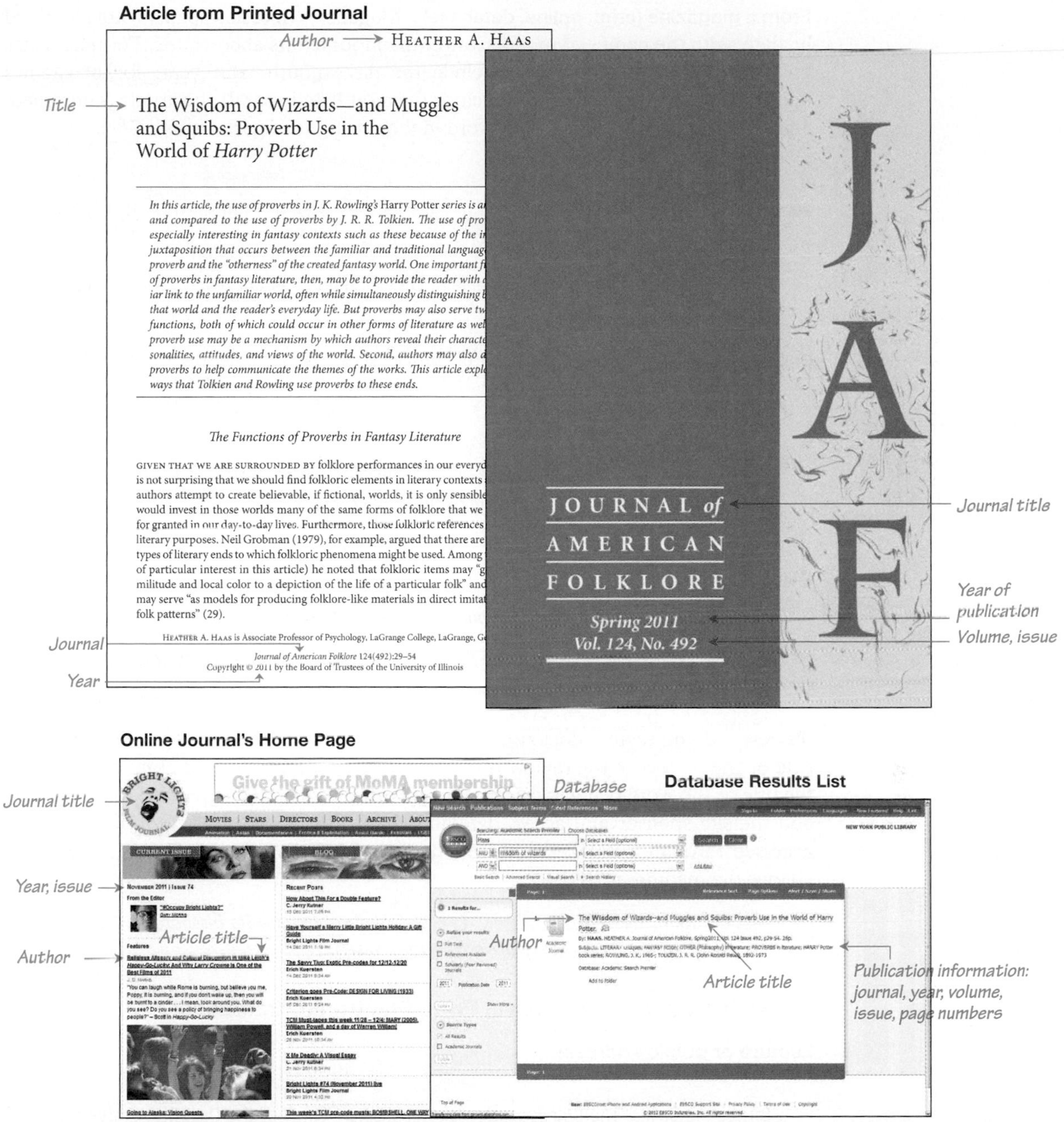

Article from Printed Journal

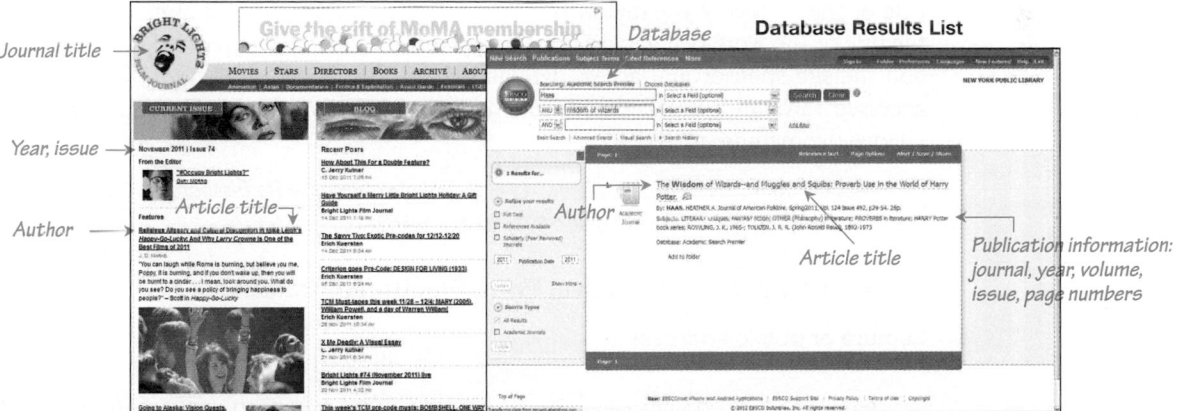

Author ⟶ HEATHER A. HAAS

Title ⟶ The Wisdom of Wizards—and Muggles and Squibs: Proverb Use in the World of *Harry Potter*

In this article, the use of proverbs in J. K. Rowling's Harry Potter series is a and compared to the use of proverbs by J. R. R. Tolkien. The use of pro especially interesting in fantasy contexts such as these because of the i juxtaposition that occurs between the familiar and traditional languag proverb and the "otherness" of the created fantasy world. One important f of proverbs in fantasy literature, then, may be to provide the reader with iar link to the unfamiliar world, often while simultaneously distinguishing that world and the reader's everyday life. But proverbs may also serve tw functions, both of which could occur in other forms of literature as wel proverb use may be a mechanism by which authors reveal their characte sonalities, attitudes, and views of the world. Second, authors may also proverbs to help communicate the themes of the works. This article expl ways that Tolkien and Rowling use proverbs to these ends.

The Functions of Proverbs in Fantasy Literature

GIVEN THAT WE ARE SURROUNDED BY folklore performances in our everyd is not surprising that we should find folkloric elements in literary contexts authors attempt to create believable, if fictional, worlds, it is only sensible would invest in those worlds many of the same forms of folklore that we for granted in our day-to-day lives. Furthermore, those folkloric references literary purposes. Neil Grobman (1979), for example, argued that there are types of literary ends to which folkloric phenomena might be used. Among of particular interest in this article) he noted that folkloric items may "g militude and local color to a depiction of the life of a particular folk" and may serve "as models for producing folklore-like materials in direct imitat folk patterns" (29).

HEATHER A. HAAS is Associate Professor of Psychology, LaGrange College, LaGrange, Ge

Journal ⟶ Journal of American Folklore 124(492):29–54

Year ⟶ Copyright © 2011 by the Board of Trustees of the University of Illinois

Journal title ⟶ JOURNAL *of* AMERICAN FOLKLORE ⟵ Journal title

Spring 2011 ⟵ Year of publication
Vol. 124, No. 492 ⟵ Volume, issue

Online Journal's Home Page

Journal title ⟶

Year, issue ⟶

Article title ⟶

Author ⟶

Database ⟶   **Database Results List**

Author ⟶   Article title ⟶

The Wisdom of Wizards—Muggles and Squibs: Proverb Use in the World of Harry Potter.

Publication information: journal, year, volume, issue, page numbers

FIGURE 27.2 Documentation Map for a Journal Article   For a print journal, look for the title of the journal on the front cover or in the table of contents. The author and article title will also be listed there; they will, of course, appear on the first page of the article (shown here) as well. The information you will need to cite an article you access through a database will appear in the list of results, the detailed record of the article, and the PDF (or HTML) version of the article itself. For an article published in an electronic journal, look for the information you need to create the works-cited entry on the journal's home page or on the page on which the article appears.

From a magazine (print, online, database)   Magazines (like newspapers) are identified by date, with the names of months longer than four letters abbreviated. For magazines published weekly or biweekly, include the day, month, and year; for magazines published monthly or bimonthly, include the month and year. If the article is unsigned, alphabetize by the first important word in the title (ignoring *A, An,* and *The*).

Publication date (weekly)

PRINT   Harrell, Eben. "A Flicker of Consciousness." *Time* 28 Nov. 2011: 42-47. Print.

Publication date (monthly)

Branch, Taylor. "The Shame of College Sports." *Atlantic* Oct. 2011: 80-110. Print.

Web site (italic)   Site sponsor

ONLINE   Harrell, Eben. "A Flicker of Consciousness." *Time.* Time, Inc. 28 Nov. 2011.
Web. 30 Nov. 2011.
Medium   Access date

DATABASE   Harrell, Eben. "A Flicker of Consciousness." *Time* 28 Nov. 2011: 42-47.
Academic Search Complete. Web. 7 Dec. 2011.
Database (italics)   Medium   Access date

Editorial or letter to the editor

"Stay Classy." Editorial. *New Republic* 1 Dec. 2011: 1. Print.

Wegeiser, Art. "How Does He Know?" Letter. *Pittsburgh Post-Gazette* 30 Nov. 2011:
B6. Print.

Review   If the review does not include an author's name, start the entry with the title of the review. If the review is untitled, begin with *Rev. of* and alphabetize under the title of the work being reviewed. For a review in an online newspaper or magazine, add the site sponsor and access date and change the medium to *Web*. For a review accessed through a database, add the database title (in italics) and access date and change the medium to *Web*.

Cassidy, John. "Master of Disaster." Rev. of *Globalization and Its Discontents,* by Joseph
Stiglitz. *New Yorker* 12 July 2002: 82-86. Print.

Multimedia Sources (Live, Print, Electronic, Database)

Lecture or public address

Title of lecture   Conference title

Birnbaum, Jack. "The Domestication of Computers." Conf. of the Usability Professionals
Association. Hyatt Grand Cypress Resort, Orlando. 10 July 2002. Lecture.
Location   Date of lecture   Medium

Letter   If the letter has been published, treat it like a work in an anthology (p. 717), but add the recipient, the date, and any identifying number after the author's name. If the letter is unpublished, change the medium to *MS* ("manu-script") if written by hand or *TS* ("typescript") if typed.

Sender   *Recipient*   *Date*   *Medium*

DuHamel, Grace. Letter to the author. 22 Mar. 2008. TS.

Map or chart (print, online)

PRINT *Map of Afghanistan and Surrounding Territory*. Map. Burlington: GiziMap, 2001. Print.

ONLINE "North America, 1797." Map. *Perry-Castañeda Library Map Collection*. U of Texas, 21 June 2011. Web. 1 Dec. 2011.

Cartoon or comic strip (print, online)
Provide the title (if given) in quotation marks directly following the artist's name.

PRINT Cheney, Tom. Cartoon. *New Yorker* 10 Oct. 2005: 55. Print.

ONLINE Hunt, Tarol. "Goblins." Comic strip. *Goblinscomic.com*. Tarol Hunt, 29 Sept. 2011. Web. 30 Nov. 2011.

Advertisement (print, broadcast, online)

PRINT Hospital for Special Surgery. Advertisement. *New York Times* 13 Apr. 2009: A7. Print.

BROADCAST Norweigian Cruise Line. Advertisement. *WNET.org*. PBS, 29 Apr. 2012. Television.

ONLINE Volkswagen Passat. Advertisement. *Slate*. Slate Group, 1 Dec. 2011. Web. 1 Dec. 2011.

Work of art (museum, print, Web site)
Include the year the work was created, the medium (*Oil on canvas*), and the museum or collection and its location. If the work was accessed online, include the Web site name and your date of access and change the medium to *Web*.

MUSEUM Palmer Payne, Elsie. *Sheep Dipping Time*. c. 1930s. Oil on canvas. *(Medium)*
Nevada Museum of Art, Reno. *(Location)*

PRINT Chihuly, Dale. *Carmine and White Flower Set*. 1987. Glass. Tacoma Art Museum, Tacoma. New York: Abrams, 2011. 109. Print. *(Print publication information)*

WEB SITE Sekaer, Peter. *A Sign Business Shop*, New York. 1935. International Center of Photography, New York. *International Center of Photography*. Web. 5 Dec. 2011. *(Web site)*
(Medium) (Access date)

Musical composition

Beethoven, Ludwig van. *Violin Concerto in D Major, Op. 61*. 1809. New York: Edwin F. Kalmus, n.d. Print.

Gershwin, George. *Porgy and Bess*. 1935. New York: Alfred, 1999. Print.

Performance

The Agony and the Ecstasy of Steve Jobs. Writ. and perf. Mike Daisey. Dir. Jean-Michele Gregory. Public Theater, New York. 25 Nov. 2011. Performance.

Television or radio program   Include the network, local station, and broadcast date. Treat a show you streamed as you would a Web page, but include information about key contributors (host or performers, for example) as you would for a broadcast television or radio program. If you downloaded the program as a podcast, include the information as for a broadcast program, but change the medium to match the type of file you accessed (*MP3, JPEG file*).

BROADCAST	*Frontline*. Prod. Greg Barker. PBS. WNET, New York, 22 Nov. 2011. Television.
STREAMED	"A Perfect Terrorist." *Frontline*. Writ., prod., and dir. Thomas Jennings. *WNET.org*. PBS, 22 Nov. 2011. Web. 1 Dec. 2011.
DOWNLOADED	"Patient Zero." *Radio Lab*. Host. Jad Abumrad and Robert Krulwich. Natl. Public Radio. WNYC, New York, 14 Nov. 2011. MP3.

Podcast (streamed, downloaded)   Treat a podcast you listened to or watched online as you would an online television or radio program (see "A Perfect Terrorist" entry above). Treat a podcast you downloaded as you would a television or radio program you downloaded (see "Patient Zero" entry above).

Film (theater, DVD, streamed)

THEATER	*Space Station*. Prod. and dir. Toni Myers. Narr. Tom Cruise. IMAX, 2002. Film.
DVD	*Casablanca*. Dir. Michael Curtiz. Perf. Humphrey Bogart, Ingrid Bergman, and Paul Henreid. 1942. Warner Home Video, 2003. DVD.
STREAMED	*The Social Network*. Dir. David Fincher. Writ. Aaron Sorkin. Perf. Jesse Eisenberg, Justin Timberlake, and Andrew Garfield. Columbia Pictures, 2010. iTunes. Web. 1 Dec. 2010.

Online video

> Film School. "Sunny Day." *YouTube*. YouTube, 12 June 2010. Web. 1 Dec. 2010.

Music recording

> Beethoven, Ludwig van. *Violin Concerto in D Major, Op. 61*. U.S.S.R. State Orchestra. Cond. Alexander Gauk. Perf. David Oistrakh. Allegro, 1980. CD.

> Maroon 5. "Moves Like Jagger." *Hands All Over*. A&M/Octone Records, 2011. MP3.

Interview (print, broadcast, personal)   If a personal interview takes place through e-mail, change "Personal interview" to "E-mail interview."

PRINT   Ashrawi, Hanan. "Tanks vs. Olive Branches." Interview by Rose Marie
               Berger. *Sojourners* Feb. 2005: 22-26. Print.

BROADCAST   Dobbs, Bill. "Occupy Wall Street." Interview by Brooke Gladstone. *On
               the Media*. Natl. Public Radio. WNYC, New York, 7 Oct. 2011. Web. 1
               Dec. 2011.

PERSONAL   Ellis, Trey. Personal interview. 3 Sept. 2008.

Other Electronic Sources

Online sources have proliferated in the last ten years. With that proliferation has come access to more information than ever before. But not all of that information is of equal value. Before including a source found on *Google* in your research project, be sure that it is appropriate for a college-level writing project, and evaluate its reliability carefully.

For help evaluating online sources, see Chapter 25.

If you are using the online version of a source for which there is no model shown here, choose the model that best matches your source, change the medium as appropriate, add the date you last accessed the source, and add any other information that readers will need to find the source themselves.

Web page or other document on a Web site

Author/editor, last name first   *Document title (in quotation marks)*

McGann, Jerome J., ed. "Introduction to the Final Installment of the Rossetti Archive."

Title of site (italicized)

The Complete Writings and Pictures of Dante Gabriel Rossetti: A Hypermedia Archive.

Sponsor

Institute for Advanced Technology in the Humanities, University of Virginia,

Publication date/last update   Access date

2008. Web. 16 Oct. 2012.

Figure 27.3 (p. 728) shows where to find the source information you will need to create a works-cited entry for the Web page cited here.

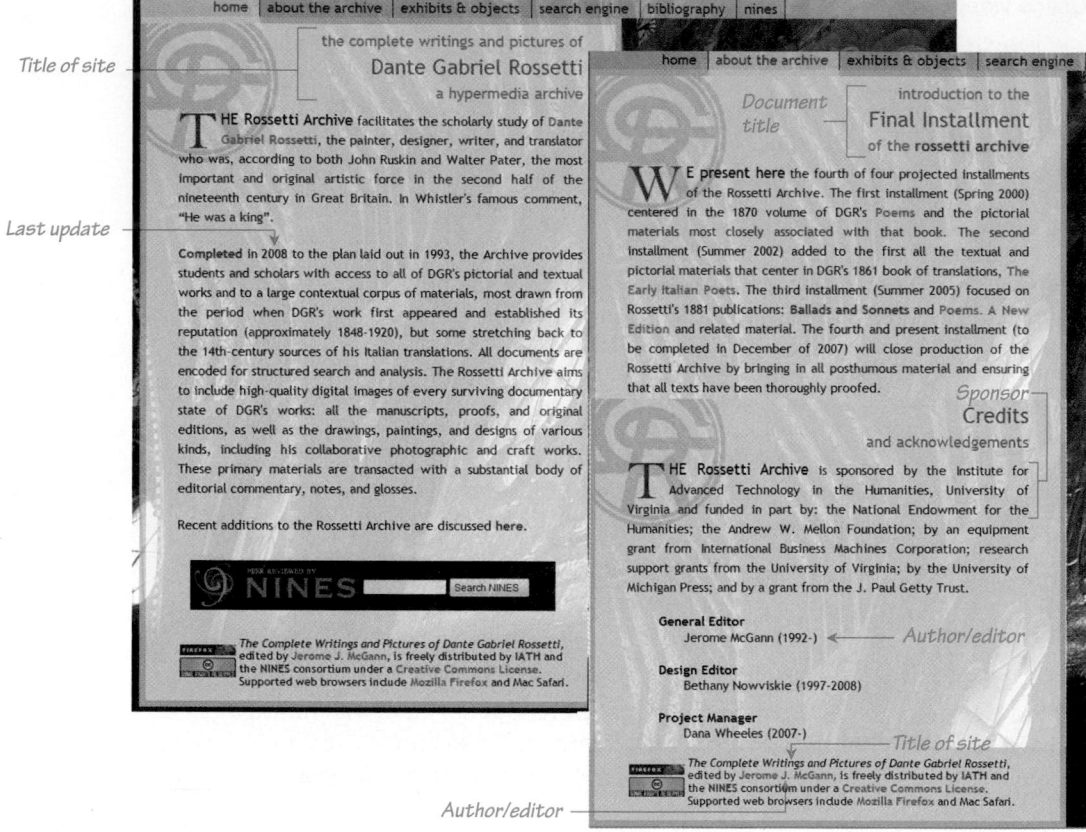

FIGURE 27.3   Documentation Map for a Web Page

Look for the author or editor and title of the Web page on the Web page itself. The title of the Web site may appear on the Web page, on the site's home page, or both. The sponsor may be listed at the bottom of the Web page, on the home page, or somewhere else. (Look for a page entitled "About Us," "Who We Are," or "Contact Us.") If no publication or copyright date or "last update" appears on the Web page, the home page, or elsewhere on the site, insert *n.d.* in its place.

Entire Web site   If the author's name is not given, begin the citation with the title. For an untitled personal site, put a description such as *Home page* where the Web site's title would normally appear (but with no quotation marks or italics). If no site sponsor or publisher is named, insert *N.p.* (for *No publisher*).

Gardner, James Alan. *A Seminar on Writing Prose*. N.p., 2001. Web. 1 Dec. 2011.

The Complete Writings and Pictures of Dante Gabriel Rossetti: A Hypermedia Archive. Ed. Jerome J. McGann. Institute for Advanced Technology in the Humanities, University of Virginia, 2008. Web. 16 Oct. 2012.

Chesson, Frederick W. Home page. N.p., 1 Apr. 2003. Web. 26 Apr. 2008.

Online scholarly project   Treat an online scholarly project as you would a Web site, but include the name of the editor, if given.

> *The Darwin Correspondence Project.* Ed. Janet Browne. American Council of Learned
>   Societies and U Cambridge, 2011. Web. 1 Dec. 2011.

Book or a short work in an online scholarly project   Treat a book or a short work in an online scholarly project as you would a Web page or another document on a Web site, but set the title in italics if the work is a book and in quotation marks if it is an article, essay, poem, or other short work, and include the print publication information (if any) following the title.

> Heims, Marjorie. "The Strange Case of Sarah Jones." *The Free Expression Policy Project.*
>   FEPP, 2 Nov. 2011. Web. 1 Dec. 2011.

> *Original publication information*
>
> Corelli, Marie. *The Treasure of Heaven.* London: Constable, 1906. *Victorian Women Writer's*
>   *Project.* Ed. Percy Willett. Indiana U, 10 July 1999. Web. 10 Sept. 2008.

Blog (entire blog, blog post)   If the author of the blog post uses a pseudonym, begin with the pseudonym and put the blogger's real name in brackets. Cite an entire blog as you would an entire Web site (see p. 728).

> *Blog title*   *Sponsor*
> *Talking Points Memo.* Ed. Josh Marshall. TPM Media, 1 Dec. 2011. Web. 1 Dec. 2011.
> *Pseudonym*   *Real name*
> Negative Camber [Todd McCandless]. *Formula1blog.* F1b., 2011. Web. 1 Dec. 2011.
> *Post author*   *Post title*
> Marshall, Josh. "Coke and Grass at Amish Raid." *Talking Points Memo.* TPM Media, 1 Dec.
>   2011. Web. 1 Dec. 2011.

Wiki article   Since wikis are written and edited collectively, start your entry with the title of the article you are citing. But check with your instructor before using information from a wiki in your research project; because content is written and edited collectively, it is difficult to assess its reliability and impossible to determine the expertise of the contributers.

> "John Lydon." *Wikipedia.* Wikipedia Foundation, 14 Nov. 2011. Web. 1 Dec. 2011.

Discussion group or newsgroup posting   Use the subject line of the posting (in quotation marks) as the title, and include the name of the discussion or newsgroup.

> *Post author*   *Subject line*   *Group name* *Site sponsor*
> Martin, Francesca Alys. "Wait--Did Somebody Say 'Buffy'?" *Cultstud-I.* U of S Fl,
>   8 Mar. 2000. Web. 8 Mar. 2008.
>   *Post date*

E-mail message

Sender   Subject line   Recipient   Date sent

Olson, Kate. "Update on State Legislative Grants." Message to the author. 5 Nov. 2008.
E-mail.

Medium

Nonperiodical publication on a CD-ROM

Picasso: The Man, His Works, the Legend. Danbury: Grolier Interactive, 1996. CD-ROM.

Computer software

How Computers Work. Indianapolis: Que, 1998. CD-ROM.

Student Research Project in MLA Style

On the following pages is a student research paper speculating about the causes of a trend—the increase in home schooling. The author, Cristina Dinh, cites statistics, quotes authorities, and paraphrases and summarizes background information and support for her argument. She uses the MLA documentation style.

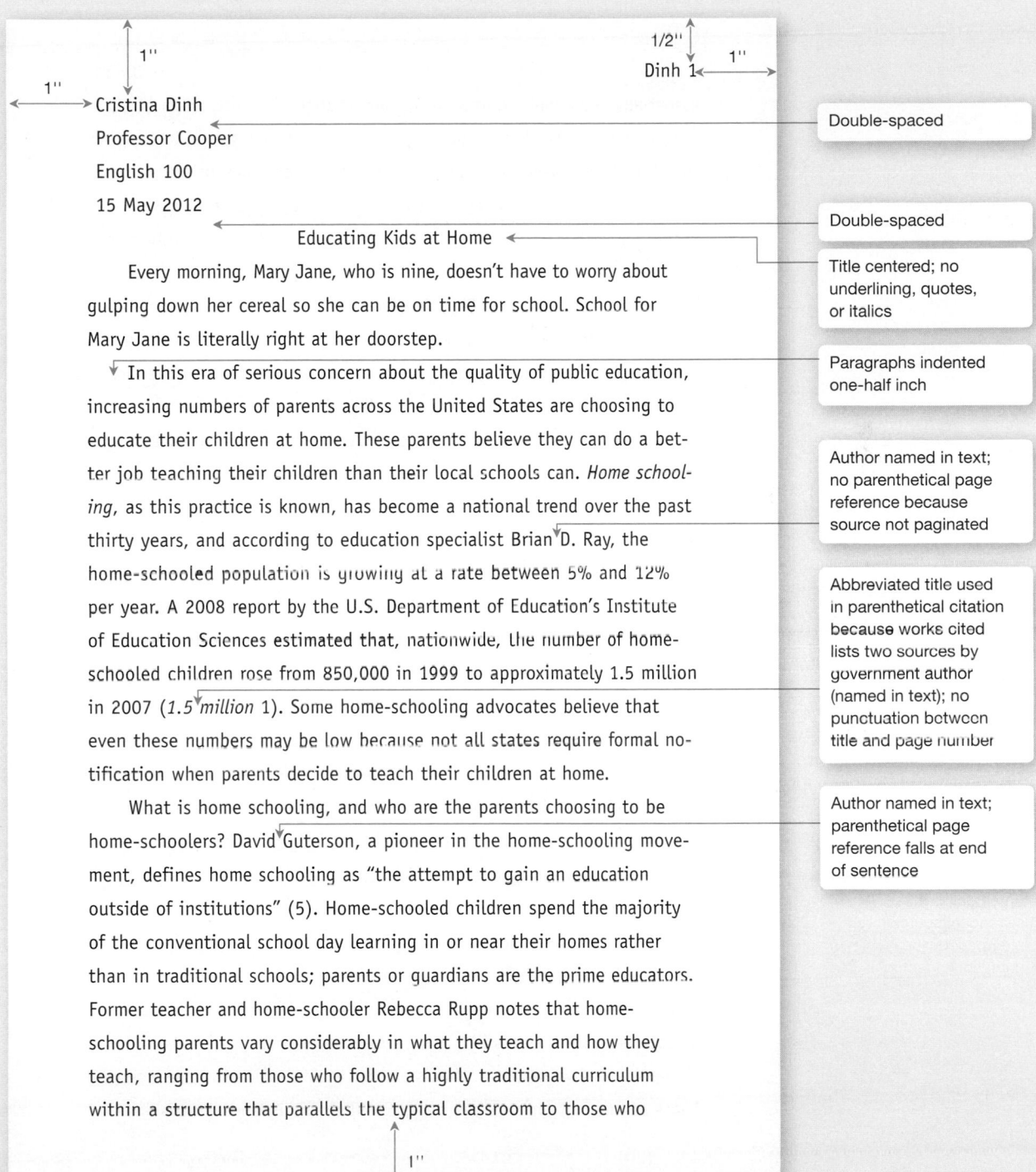

1/2"

Dinh 1

1"

1"

1"

Cristina Dinh

Professor Cooper

English 100

15 May 2012

Educating Kids at Home

Every morning, Mary Jane, who is nine, doesn't have to worry about gulping down her cereal so she can be on time for school. School for Mary Jane is literally right at her doorstep.

In this era of serious concern about the quality of public education, increasing numbers of parents across the United States are choosing to educate their children at home. These parents believe they can do a better job teaching their children than their local schools can. *Home schooling*, as this practice is known, has become a national trend over the past thirty years, and according to education specialist Brian D. Ray, the home-schooled population is growing at a rate between 5% and 12% per year. A 2008 report by the U.S. Department of Education's Institute of Education Sciences estimated that, nationwide, the number of home-schooled children rose from 850,000 in 1999 to approximately 1.5 million in 2007 (*1.5 million* 1). Some home-schooling advocates believe that even these numbers may be low because not all states require formal notification when parents decide to teach their children at home.

What is home schooling, and who are the parents choosing to be home-schoolers? David Guterson, a pioneer in the home-schooling movement, defines home schooling as "the attempt to gain an education outside of institutions" (5). Home-schooled children spend the majority of the conventional school day learning in or near their homes rather than in traditional schools; parents or guardians are the prime educators. Former teacher and home-schooler Rebecca Rupp notes that home-schooling parents vary considerably in what they teach and how they teach, ranging from those who follow a highly traditional curriculum within a structure that parallels the typical classroom to those who

1"

Double-spaced

Double-spaced

Title centered; no underlining, quotes, or italics

Paragraphs indented one-half inch

Author named in text; no parenthetical page reference because source not paginated

Abbreviated title used in parenthetical citation because works cited lists two sources by government author (named in text); no punctuation between title and page number

Author named in text; parenthetical page reference falls at end of sentence

Dinh 2

essentially allow their children to pursue whatever interests them at their own pace (3). Home-schoolers commonly combine formal instruction with life skills instruction, learning fractions, for example, in terms of monetary units or cooking measurements (Saba and Gattis 89). According to the U.S. Department of Education's 2008 report, while home-schoolers are also a diverse group politically and philosophically-- libertarians, conservatives, Christian fundamentalists--most say they home school for one of three reasons: they are concerned about the qual- ity of academic instruction, the general school environment, or the lack of religious or moral instruction (*1.5 million* 2).

The first group generally believes that children need individual at- tention and the opportunity to learn at their own pace to learn well. This group says that one teacher in a classroom of twenty to thirty children (the size of typical public-school classes) cannot give this kind of atten- tion. These parents believe they can give their children greater enrich- ment and more specialized instruction than public schools can provide. At home, parents can work one-on-one with each child and be flexible about time, allowing their children to pursue their interests at earlier ages. Many of these parents, like home-schooler Peter Bergson, believe that

> home schooling provides more of an opportunity to continue the natural learning process that's in evidence in all children.
>
> [In school,] you change the learning process from self-directed to other-directed, from the child asking questions to the teacher asking questions. You shut down areas of potential interest. (qtd. in Kohn 22)

This trend can be traced back to the 1960s, when many people began criticizing traditional schools. Various types of "alternative schools" were created, and some parents began teaching their children at home (Friedlander 150). Parents like this mention several reasons for their disappointment with public schools and for their decision to home school. A lack of funding, for example, leaves children without new textbooks.

Work by two authors cited

Quotation of more than four lines typed as a block and indented ten spaces (1 inch)

Brackets indicate alteration of quotation

Parenthetical citation of secondary source falls after period when quotation indented as a block

Dinh 3

In a 2002 survey, 31% of teachers said that their students are using textbooks that are more than ten years old, and 29% said that they do not have enough textbooks for all of their students (National Education Association). Many schools also cannot afford to buy laboratory equipment and other teaching materials. At my own high school, the chemistry teacher told me that most of the lab equipment we used came from a research firm he worked for. In a 2006 Gallup poll, lack of proper financial support ranked first on the list of the problems in public schools (Rose and Gallup).

  Parents also cite overcrowding as a reason for taking their kids out of school. The more students in a classroom, the less learning that goes on, as Cafi Cohen discovered before choosing to home school; after spending several days observing what went on in her child's classroom, she found that administrative duties, including disciplining, took up to 80% of a teacher's time, with only 20% of the day devoted to learning (6). Moreover, faced with a large group of children, a teacher ends up gearing lessons to the students in the middle level, so children at both ends miss out. Gifted children and those with learning disabilities particularly suffer in this situation. At home, parents of these children say they can tailor the material and the pace for each child. Studies show that home-schooling methods seem to work well in preparing children academically. Lawrence Rudner, director of the ERIC Clearinghouse on Assessment and Evaluation at the University of Maryland and a researcher on home schooling, found that testing of home-schooled students showed them to be between one and three years ahead of public school students their age (xi). Home-schooled children have also made particularly strong showings in academic competitions; since the late 1990s, 10% of National Spelling Bee participants have been home schooled, as have two National Spelling Bee and two National Geographic Bee winners (Lyman). More and more selective colleges are admitting, and even recruiting, home-schooled applicants (Basham, Merrifield, and Hepburn 15).

Corporate author's name cited

Dinh 4

Parents in the second group--those concerned with the general school environment--claim that their children are more well-rounded than those in school. Because they don't have to sit in classrooms all day, home-schooled kids can pursue their own projects, often combining crafts or technical skills with academic subjects. Home-schoolers participate in outside activities, such as 4-H competitions, field trips with peers in home-school support groups, science fairs, musical and dramatic productions, church activities, and Boy Scouts or Girl Scouts (Saba and Gattis 59-62). In fact, they may even be able to participate to some extent in actual school activities. A 1999 survey conducted by the U.S. Department of Education's Institute of Education Sciences found that 28% of public schools allowed home-schooled students to participate in extracurricular activities alongside enrolled students, and 20% allowed home-schooled students to attend some classes (*Homeschooling* 12).

Many home-schooling parents believe that these activities provide the social opportunities kids need without exposing their children to the peer pressure they would have to deal with as regular school students. For example, many kids think that drinking and using drugs are cool. When I was in high school, my friends would tell me a few drinks wouldn't hurt or affect driving. If I had listened to them, I wouldn't be alive today. Four of my friends were killed under the influence of alcohol. Between 1992 and 2008, the number of high school seniors surveyed who had used any illicit drug in the last year climbed from 27.1% to 36.6% (Johnston et al. 59).

Another reason many parents decide to home school their kids is that they are concerned for their children's safety. Samuel L. Blumenfeld notes that "physical risk" is an important reason many parents remove their children from public schools as "[m]ore and more children are assaulted, robbed, and murdered in school" and a "culture of violence, abetted by rap music, drug trafficking, . . . and racial tension, has engulfed teenagers" (4). Beginning in the mid-1990s, a string of school

Work by four more authors cited

Dinh 5

shootings--including the 1999 massacres in Littleton, Colorado, and Conyers, Georgia, and the 2001 massacre in Santee, California--has led to increasing fears that young people are simply not safe at school.

While all of the reasons mentioned so far are important, perhaps the single most significant cause of the growing home-schooling trend is Christian fundamentalist dissatisfaction with "godless" public schools. Sociologist Mitchell L. Stevens, author of one of the first comprehensive studies of home schooling, cites a mailing sent out by Basic Christian Education, a company that markets home-schooling materials, titled "What Really Happens in Public Schools." This publication sums up the fears of fundamentalist home-schoolers about public schools: that they encourage high levels of teenage sexual activity and pregnancies "out of wedlock"; expose children to "violence, crime, lack of discipline, and, of course, drugs of every kind"; present positive portrayals of communism and socialism and negative portrayals of capitalism; and undermine children's Christian beliefs by promoting "New Age philosophies, Yoga, Transcendental Meditation, witchcraft demonstrations, and Eastern religions" (51).

As early as 1988, Luanne Shackelford and Susan White, two Christian home-schooling mothers, were claiming that because schools expose children to "[p]eer pressure, perverts, secular textbooks, values clarification, TV, pornography, rock music, bad movies . . . [h]ome schooling seems to be the best plan to achieve our goal [to raise good Christians]" (160). As another mother more recently put it:

> I don't like the way schools are going. . . . What's wrong with Christianity all of a sudden? You know? This country was founded on Christian, on religious principles. [People] came over here for religious freedom, and now all of a sudden all religious references seem to be stricken out of the public school, and I don't like that at all. (qtd. in Stevens 67)

Although many nonfundamentalist home-schoolers make some of these same criticisms, those who cite the lack of "Christian values" in

Dinh 6

public schools have particular concerns of their own. For example, home-schooling leader Raymond Moore talks of parents who are "'sick and tired of the teaching of evolution in the schools as a cut-and-dried fact,' along with other evidence of so-called secular humanism" (Kohn 21), such as textbooks that contain material contradicting Christian beliefs. Moreover, parents worry that schools undermine their children's moral values. In particular, some Christian fundamentalist parents object to sex education in schools, saying that it encourages children to become sexually active early, challenging values taught at home. They see the family as the core and believe that the best place to instill family values is within the family. These Christian home-schooling parents want to provide their children not only with academic knowledge but also with a moral grounding consistent with their religious beliefs.

Still other home-schooling parents object to a perceived government-mandated value system that they believe attempts to override the values, not necessarily religious in nature, of individual families. For these parents, home schooling is a way of resisting what they see as unwarranted intrusion by the federal government into personal concerns (*Alliance*).

Armed with their convictions, parents such as those who belong to the Christian Home School Legal Defense Association have fought in court and lobbied for legislation that allows them the option of home schooling. In the 1970s, most states had compulsory attendance laws that made it difficult, if not illegal, to keep school-age children home from school. Today, home schooling is permitted in every state, with strict regulation required by only a few (Home School). As a result, Mary Jane is one of hundreds of thousands of American children who can start their school day without leaving the house.

Single quotation marks indicate a quotation within a quotation

Citation placed close to quotation, before comma but after quotation marks

Internet source cited by shortened form of title; author's name and page numbers unavailable

Shortened form of corporate author's name cited

Works-cited entries begin on a new page; entries are in alphabetical order.

Title centered

Double-spaced

Entries begin flush with left margin; subsequent lines indent half an inch.

Periods separate author, title, publication information, medium, and date of access.

1''

1/2''

Dinh 7

1''

Works Cited

Alliance for the Separation of School and State. Home page. Alliance for the Separation of School and State, 26 Feb. 2009. Web. 10 Apr. 2012.

Basham, Patrick, John Merrifield, and Claudia R. Hepburn. *Home Schooling: From the Extreme to the Mainstream*. 2nd ed. Vancouver: Fraser Institute, 2007. Studies in Education Policy. *Fraser Institute*. Web. 13 Apr. 2012.

Blumenfeld, Samuel L. *Homeschooling: A Parent's Guide to Teaching Children*. Bridgewater: Replica, 1999. Print.

Cohen, Cafi. *And What about College? How Home-Schooling Leads to Admissions to the Best Colleges and Universities*. Cambridge: Holt, 1997. Print.

Friedlander, Tom. "A Decade of Home Schooling." *The Home School Reader*. Ed. Mark Hegener and Helen Hegener. Tonasket: Home Education, 1988. 147-56. Print.

Guterson, David. *Family Matters: Why Homeschooling Makes Sense*. San Diego: Harcourt, 1992. Print.

Home School Legal Defense Association. "State Action Map." HSLDA, 2009. Web. 5 Apr. 2012.

Johnston, Lloyd D., et al. *Monitoring the Future: National Results on Adolescent Drug Use, Overview of Key Findings, 2008*. Bethesda: National Institute on Drug Abuse, 2009. Web. 20 Apr. 2012.

Kohn, Alfie. "Home Schooling." *Atlantic Monthly* Apr. 1988: 20-25. Print.

Lyman, Isabel. "Generation Two." *American Enterprise* Oct./Nov. 2002: 48-49. *InfoTrac OneFile*. Web. 10 May 2012.

National Education Association. *2002 Instructional Materials Survey*. Sept. 2002. Association of American Publishers, 2002. Web. 21 Apr. 2012.

Ray, Brian D. "Research Facts on Home Schooling." *National Home Education Research Institute*. NHERI, 2008. Web. 10 Apr. 2012.

Dinh 8

Rose, Lowell C., and Alec M. Gallup. "The 38th Annual PDK/Gallup Poll of

the Public's Attitudes toward the Public Schools." *Phi Delta Kappan*

88.1 (2006): n. pag. *Phi Delta Kappa International*. Web.

1 May 2009.

Rudner, Lawrence. Foreword. *The McGraw-Hill Home-Schooling Companion*.

By Laura Saba and Julie Gattis. New York: McGraw, 2002. Print.

Rupp, Rebecca. *The Complete Home Learning Source Book*. New York: Three

Rivers, 1998. Print.

Saba, Laura, and Julie Gattis. *The McGraw-Hill Home-Schooling Companion*.

New York: McGraw, 2002. Print.

Shackelford, Luanne, and Susan White. *A Survivor's Guide to Home

Schooling*. Westchester: Crossway, 1988. Print.

Stevens, Mitchell L. *Kingdom of Children: Culture and Controversy in the

Homeschooling Movement*. Princeton: Princeton UP, 2001. Print.

United States. Dept. of Education. Institute of Education Sciences.

Homeschooling in the United States: 1999. Washington: GPO, 2001.

National Center for Education Statistics. Web. 23 Apr. 2009.

- - -. *1.5 Million Homeschooled Students in the United States in 2007*.

Washington: GPO, 2008. *National Center for Education Statistics*. Web.

23 Apr. 2009.

Source with no pagination marked *n. pag.*

Untitled section labeled

For multiple sources by the same author, replace author's name with three hyphens followed by a period. (The name of this government source has three separate components.)

28

Citing and Documenting Sources in APA Style

When using the APA system of documentation, include both an in-text citation and a list of references at the end of the research project. **In-text citations** tell your readers where the ideas or words you have borrowed come from, and the entries in the **list of references** allow readers to locate your sources so that they can read more about your topic.

The most common types of in-text citations follow. For other, less common citation types, consult the *Publication Manual of the American Psychological Association,* Sixth Edition. Most libraries will own a copy.

Citing Sources in the Text

Directory to In-Text-Citation Models

When citing ideas, information, or words borrowed from a source, include the author's last name and the date of publication in the text of your research project. In most cases, you will want to use a *signal phrase* to introduce the works you are citing, since doing so gives you the opportunity to put the work and its author in context. A signal phrase includes the author's last name, the date of publication, and a verb that describes the author's attitude or stance:

Smith (2011) complains that . . .

Jones (2012) defends her position by . . .

Use a parenthetical citation—*(Jones, 2012)*—when you have already introduced the author or the work or when citing the source of an uncontroversial fact. When quoting from a source, also include the page number: *Smith (2011) complains that he "never gets a break" (p. 123)*. When you are paraphrasing or summarizing, you may omit the page reference, although including it is not wrong.

One author

SIGNAL PHRASE	Upton Sinclair (2005), a crusading journalist, wrote that workers sometimes "fell into the vats; and when they were fished out, there was never enough of them left to be worth exhibiting" (p. 134).
PARENTHETICAL CITATION	*The Jungle*, a naturalistic novel inspired by the French writer Zola, described in lurid detail the working conditions of the time, including what became of unlucky workers who fell into the vats while making sausage (Sinclair, 2005).

author's last name + date

REFERENCE-LIST ENTRY	Sinclair, U. (2005). *The jungle*. New York, NY: Oxford University Press. (Original work published 1906)

More than one author   In a signal phrase, use the word *and* between the authors' names; in a parenthetical citation, use an ampersand (&). When citing a work by three to seven authors, list all the authors in your first reference; in subsequent references, just list the first and use *et al.* (Latin for *and others*).

SIGNAL PHRASE	As Jamison and Tyree (2001) have found, racial bias does not diminish merely through exposure to individuals of other races.
PARENTHETICAL CITATION	Racial bias does not diminish through exposure (Jamison & Tyree, 2001).
FIRST CITATION	Rosenzweig, Breedlove, and Watson (2005) wrote that biological psychology is an interdisciplinary field that includes scientists from "quite different backgrounds" (p. 3).
LATER CITATIONS	Biological psychology is "the field that relates behavior to bodily processes, especially the workings of the brain" (Rosenzweig et al., 2005, p. 3).

For works with more than seven authors, list the first six, an ellipsis (. . .), and the last author.

Unknown author   To cite a work when the author is unknown, the APA suggests using a shortened version of the title.

An international pollution treaty still to be ratified would prohibit all plastic garbage from being dumped at sea ("Plastic Is Found," 1972).

The full title of the article is "Plastic Is Found in the Sargasso Sea; Pieces of Apparent Refuse Cover Wide Atlantic Region."

Two or more works by the same author in the same year   When your list of references includes two works by the same author, the year of publication is usually enough to distinguish them. Occasionally, though, you may have two works by the same author in the same year. If this happens, alphabetize the works by title in your list of references, and add a lowercase letter after the date (2005a, 2005b).

> Middle-class unemployed workers are better off than their lower-class counterparts, because "the white collar unemployed are likely to have some assets to invest in their job search" (Ehrenreich, 2005b, p. 16).

Two or more authors with the same last name   Include the author's initials.

> F. Johnson (2010) conducted an intriguing study on teen smoking.

Corporation, organization, or government agency as author   Spell out the name of the organization the first time you use it, but abbreviate it in subsequent citations.

> (National Institutes of Health, 2012)

> (NIH, 2012)

Indirect citation (quotation from a secondary source)   To quote material taken not from the original source but from a secondary source that quotes the original, give the secondary source in the reference list, and in your essay acknowledge the original source and cite the secondary source.

> E. M. Forster said "the collapse of all civilization, so realistic for us, sounded in Matthew Arnold's ears like a distant and harmonious cataract" (as cited in Trilling, 1955, p. 11).

Two or more works cited in the same parentheses   List sources in alphabetical order separated by semicolons.

> (Johnson, 2010; NIH, 2012)

Creating a List of References

Directory to Reference-List Models

Author Listings

Books (Print, Electronic)

Author Listings

When the list of references includes several works by the same author, the APA provides the following rules for arranging these entries in the list:

- Same-name single-author entries precede multiple-author entries:

  Zettelmeyer, F. (2000).

  Zettelmeyer, F., Morton, F. S., & Silva-Risso, J. (2006).

- Entries with the same first author and a different second author are alphabetized under the first author according to the second author's last name:

  Dhar, R., & Nowlis, S. M. (2004).

  Dhar, R., & Simonson, I. (2003).

- Entries by the same authors are arranged by year of publication, in chronological order:

  Golder, P. N., & Tellis, G. J. (2003).

  Golder, P. N., & Tellis, G. J. (2004).

- Entries by the same authors with the same publication year should be arranged alphabetically by title (according to the first word after *A, An,* or *The*), and lowercase letters (*a, b, c,* and so on) should be appended to the year in parentheses:

  Aaron, P. (1990a). Basic . . .

  Aaron, P. (1990b). Elements . . .

One author

Ehrenreich, B. (2001). *Nickel and dimed: On (not) getting by in America*. New York, NY: Metropolitan.

More than one author

Saba, L., & Gattis, J. (2002). *The McGraw-Hill homeschooling companion*. New York, NY: McGraw-Hill.

Hunt, L., Po-Chia Hsia, R., Martin, T. R., Rosenwein, B. H., Rosenwein, H., & Smith, B. G. (2001). *The making of the West: Peoples and cultures*. Boston, MA: Bedford.

If there are more than seven authors, list only the first six, insert an ellipsis (. . .), and add the last author's name.

Unknown author   Begin the entry with the title.

Communities blowing whistle on street basketball. (2003). *USA Today*, p. 20A.

If an author is designated as "Anonymous," include the word *Anonymous* in place of the author, and alphabetize it as "Anonymous" in the reference list.

Anonymous. (2006). *Primary colors*. New York, NY: Random House.

Corporation, organization, or government agency as author

American Medical Association. (2004). *Family medical guide*. Hoboken, NJ: Wiley.

Two or more works by the same author

When you cite two or more works by the same author, arrange them in chronological (time) order.

Pinker, S. (2005). So how does the mind work? *Mind and Language, 20*(1): 1-24. doi:10.1111/j.0268-1064.2005.00274.x

Pinker, S. (2011). *The better angels of our nature: Why violence has declined*. New York, NY: Viking.

When you cite two works by the same author in the same year, alphabetize entries by title and then add a lowercase letter following each year.

Pinker, S. (2005a). *Hotheads*. New York, NY: Pocket Penguins.

Pinker, S. (2005b). So how does the mind work? *Mind and Language, 20*(1), 1-24. doi: 10.1111/j.0268-1064.2005.00274.x

Books (Print, Electronic)

When citing a book, capitalize only the first word of the title and subtitle and any proper nouns (*Dallas, Darwin*). Book titles are italicized.

Basic format for a book

<table>
<tr><td></td><td>*Author*</td><td>*Year*</td><td>*Title*</td></tr>
<tr><td>**PRINT**</td><td colspan="3">Pinker, S. (2011). *The better angels of our nature: Why violence has declined.*</td></tr>
<tr><td></td><td colspan="3">New York, NY: Viking.</td></tr>
<tr><td></td><td>*City, State (abbr)*</td><td>*Publisher*</td><td></td></tr>
</table>

E-BOOK   Pinker, S. (2011). *The better angels of our nature: Why violence has declined*.
New York, NY: Viking. [Nook Book Edition].

E-publication information

DATABASE   Darwin, C. (2001). *The origin of species*. Retrieved from http://bartleby.com
(Original work published 1909-14)   *Database information*

If an e-book has been assigned a **digital object identifier** (or *doi*) — a combination of numbers and letters assigned by the publisher to identify the work — add that information at the end of the citation.

Author and editor

Arnold, M. (1994). *Culture and anarchy* (S. Lipman, Ed.). New Haven, CT: Yale University Press. (Original work published 1869)

Edited collection

Waldman, D., & Walker, J. (Eds.). (1999). *Feminism and documentary*. Minneapolis, MN: University of Minnesota Press.

Work in an anthology or edited collection

Fairbairn-Dunlop, P. (1993). Women and agriculture in western Samoa. In J. H. Momsen & V. Kinnaird (Eds.), *Different places, different voices* (pp. 211-226). London, England: Routledge.

Translation

Tolstoy, L. (2002). *War and peace* (C. Garnett, Trans.). New York, NY: Modern Library. (Original work published 1869)

Dictionary entry or article in another reference book

Rowland, R. P. (2001). Myasthenia gravis. In *Encyclopedia Americana* (Vol. 19, p. 683). Danbury, CT: Grolier.

Introduction, preface, foreword, or afterword

Graff, G., & Phelan, J. Preface (2004). In M. Twain, *Adventures of Huckleberry Finn* (pp. iii-vii). Boston, MA: Bedford.

Later edition of a book

Axelrod, R., & Cooper, C. (2013). *The St. Martin's guide to writing* (10th ed.). Boston, MA: Bedford.

Government document

U.S. Department of Health and Human Services. (2009). *Trends in underage drinking in the United States, 1991-2007*. Washington, DC: Government Printing Office.

Note: when the author and publisher are the same, use the word *Author* (not italicized) as the name of the publisher.

Unpublished doctoral dissertation

Bullock, B. (1986). *Basic needs fulfillment among less developed countries: Social progress over two decades of growth* (Unpublished doctoral dissertation). Vanderbilt University, Nashville, TN.

Articles (Print, Electronic)

For articles, capitalize only the first word of the title, proper nouns (*Barclay, Berlin*), and the first word following a colon (if any). Omit quotation marks around the titles of articles, but capitalize all the important words of journal, newspaper, and magazine titles, and set them in italics. If you are accessing an article through a database, follow the model for a comparable source.

From a scholarly journal

PRINT

Author   Year   Article title

Tran, D. (2002). Personal income by state, second quarter 2002. *Current Business, 82*(11), 55-73.

Journal title   Volume (issue) Pages

Shan, J. Z., Morris, A. G., & Sun, F. (2001). Financial development and economic growth: A chicken and egg problem? *Review of Economics, 9,* 443-454.

Volume only Pages

Include the digital object identifier (or *doi*) when available. When a doi has not been assigned, include the journal's URL.

ELECTRONIC

Tharp, R. G. (1989). Psychocultural variables and constants: Effects on teaching and learning in schools. *American Psychologist, 44*(2), 349-359. doi:10.1037/0003-066X.44.2.349

DOI

Houston, R. G., & Toma, F. (2003). Home schooling: An alternative school choice. *Southern Economic Journal, 69*(4), 920-936. Retrieved from http://www.southerneconomic.org

URL

From a newspaper

PRINT

Year Month Day

Peterson, A. (2003, May 20). Finding a cure for old age. *The Wall Street Journal*, pp. D1, D5.

ELECTRONIC

Barboza, D., and LaFraniere, S. (2012, May 17). 'Princelings' in China use family ties to gain riches. *The New York Times*. Retrieved from http://www.nytimes.com

From a magazine If a magazine is published weekly or biweekly (every other week), include the full date following the author's name. If it is published monthly or bimonthly, include just the year and month (or months).

Weekly or biweekly

PRINT   Gross, M. J. (2003, April 29). Family life during war time. *The Advocate*,
                            42-48.

Monthly or bimonthly

              Shelby, A. (2005, September/October). Good going: Alaska's glacier
                            crossroads. *Sierra*, 90, 23.

ELECTRONIC   Marche, S. (2012, May). Is Facebook making us lonely? *The Atlantic*. Retrieved
                            from http://theatlantic.com

Editorial or letter to the editor

      Kosinski, T. (2012, May 15). Who cares what she thinks? [Letter to the editor]. *The Chicago
           Sun-Times*. Retrieved from http:// www.suntimes.com/opinions/letters/12522890-474/
           who-cares-what-she-thinks.html

Review

"Review of" + item type + title of item reviewed

      Cassidy, J. (2002, July 12). Master of disaster [Review of the book *Globalization and its
           discontents*]. *The New Yorker,* 82-86.

If the review is untitled, use the bracketed information as the title, retaining the brackets.

Multimedia Sources (Print or Electronic)

Television program

Label

      Charlsen, C. (Writer and producer). (2003, July 14). Murder of the century [Television series
           episode]. In M. Samels (Executive producer), *American Experience*. Boston, MA: WGBH.

Film, video, or DVD

Label

      Nolan, C. (Writer and director). (2010). *Inception* [Motion picture]. Los Angeles, CA: Warner Bros.

Sound recording

PODCAST   Dubner, S. (2012, May 17). Retirement kills [Audio podcast]. *Freakonomics
                      Radio*. Retrieved from http://www.freakonomics.com

Label

RECORDING   Maroon 5. (2010). Moves like Jagger. On *Hands all over* [CD]. New York, NY:
                    A&M/Octone Records.

Interview   Do not list personal interviews in your reference list. Instead, cite the interviewee in your text (last name and initials), and in parentheses give the notation *personal communication* (in regular type, not italicized) followed by a comma and the date of the interview. For published interviews, use the appropriate format for an article.

Other Electronic Sources

A rule of thumb for citing electronic sources not covered in one of the preceding sections is to include enough information to allow readers to access and retrieve the source. For most online sources, provide as much of the following as you can:

For more information on finding sources, see Chapter 25, pp. 69–96.

- Name of author
- Date of publication or most recent update (in parentheses; if unavailable, use the abbreviation *n.d.*)
- Title of document (such as a Web page)
- Title of Web site
- Any special retrieval information, such as a URL; include the date you last accessed the source only when the content is likely to change or be updated (as on a wiki, for example)

Web site   The APA does not require an entry in the list of references for entire Web sites. Instead, give the name of the site in your text with its Web address in parentheses.

Web page or document on a Web site

American Cancer Society. (2011, Oct. 10). *Child and teen tobacco use*. Retrieved from http://www.cancer.org/Cancer/CancerCauses/TobaccoCancer/ ChildandTeenTobaccoUse/child-and-teen-tobacco-use-what-to-do

Heins, M. (2003, January 24). The strange case of Sarah Jones. *The Free Expression Policy Project*. Retrieved from http://www.fepproject.org/commentaries/sarahjones.html

Discussion list and newsgroup postings   Include online postings in your list of references only if you can provide data that would allow others to retrieve the source.

Label

Paikeday, T. (2005, October 10). "Esquivalience" is out [Electronic mailing list message]. Retrieved from http://listserv.linguistlist.org/cgi-bin/wa?A1=ind0510b&L=ads-1#1

Label

Ditmire, S. (2005, February 10). NJ tea party [Newsgroup message]. Retrieved from http://groups.google.com/group/TeaParty

Blog post

Label

Mestel, R. (2012, May 17). Fructose makes rats dumber. [Web log post]. Retrieved from http://www.latimes.com/health/boostershots/la-fructose-makes-rats-stupid-brain-20120517,0,2305241.story?track=rss

Wiki entry   Start with the article title and include the post date (or *n.d.,* if there is no date), since wikis may be updated frequently, as well as the retrieval date.

> Sleep. (2011, November 26). Retrieved May 21, 2011, from Wiki of Science: http://
> wikiofscience.wikidot.com/science:sleep

E-mail message   Personal correspondence, including e-mail, should not be included in your reference list. Instead, cite the person's name in your text, and in parentheses give the notation *personal communication* (in regular type, not italicized) and the date.

Computer software   If an individual has proprietary rights to the software, cite that person's name as you would for a print text. Otherwise, cite as you would for an anonymous print text.

> *Label*
> How Computers Work [Software]. (1998). Available from Que: http://www.howcomputers
> work.net

A Sample Reference List

To see the complete text of this student research project in APA style, see Chapter 7, pp. 304–9.

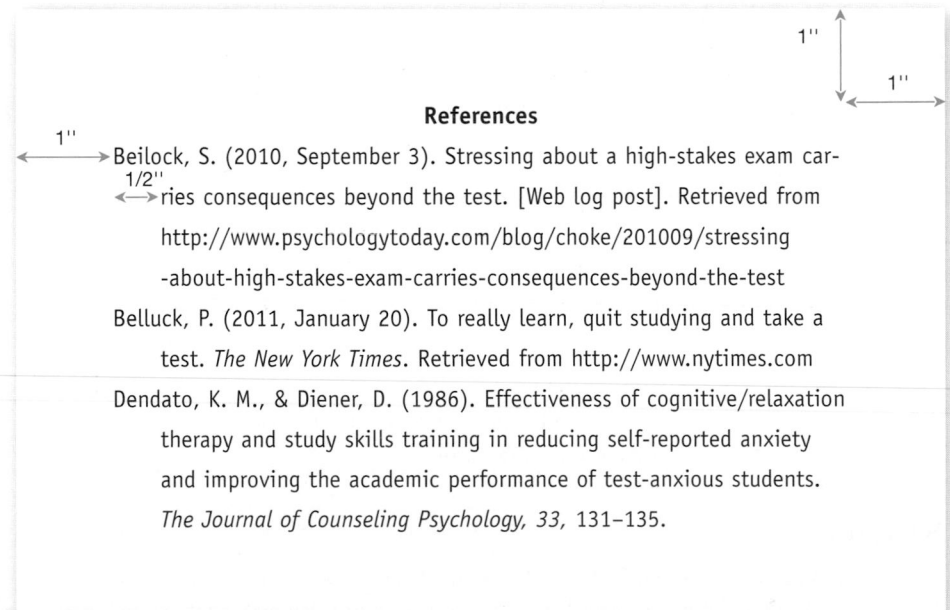

References

Beilock, S. (2010, September 3). Stressing about a high-stakes exam carries consequences beyond the test. [Web log post]. Retrieved from http://www.psychologytoday.com/blog/choke/201009/stressing -about-high-stakes-exam-carries-consequences-beyond-the-test

Belluck, P. (2011, January 20). To really learn, quit studying and take a test. *The New York Times.* Retrieved from http://www.nytimes.com

Dendato, K. M., & Diener, D. (1986). Effectiveness of cognitive/relaxation therapy and study skills training in reducing self-reported anxiety and improving the academic performance of test-anxious students. *The Journal of Counseling Psychology, 33,* 131–135.

Frederiksen, N. (1984). The real test bias: Influences of testing on teaching and learning. *American Psychologist, 39*, 193–202.

Karpicke, J. D., & Blunt, J. R. (2011, January 30). Retrieval practice produces more learning than elaborative studying with concept mapping. *Science Online*. doi: 10.1126/science.1199327

Light, R. J. (1990). *Explorations with students and faculty about teaching, learning, and student life*. Cambridge, MA: Harvard University Graduate School of Education and Kennedy School of Government.

Rothblum, E. D., Solomon, L., & Murakami, J. (1986). Affective, cognitive, and behavioral differences between high and low procrastinators. *Journal of Counseling Psychology, 33,* 387–394.

ScienceWatch.com (2008, February). Henry L. Roediger and Jeff Karpicke talk with ScienceWatch.com and answer a few questions about this month's fast breaking paper in the field of psychiatry/psychology. [Interview]. Retrieved from http://sciencewatch.com/dr/fbp/2008/08febfbp/08febfbpRoedigerETAL

Writing
for Assessment

29

Essay Examinations

Many instructors believe that essay exams are the best way to find out what you have learned and, more important, help you consolidate and reinforce your learning. Essay exams demonstrate that you can sort through the large body of information covered in a course, identify what is significant, and explain your decision. They show whether you understand basic concepts and can use those concepts to interpret specific materials, make connections, draw comparisons and find contrasts, and synthesize information in support of an original assertion. They may even ask you to justify your own evaluations and argue for your opinions with convincing reasons and supporting evidence. All instructors want students to think critically and analytically about a subject; many feel that an essay exams provide the best demonstration that you can do so.

As a college student, then, you will face a variety of essay exams, from short-answer identifications to take-home exams. The writing activities and strategies discussed in Parts One and Three of this book—particularly narrating, describing, defining, classifying, comparing and contrasting, and arguing—as well as the critical thinking strategies in Part Two will help you do well on these exams. This chapter provides specific guidelines for you to follow in preparing for and writing essay exams, and analyzes a group of typical exam questions and answers to help you determine which strategies will be most useful.

Preparing for an Exam

The best way to ensure that you will do well on essay exams is to keep up with readings and assignments from the very start of the course: Do the reading, go to lectures, take careful notes, participate in discussion sessions, and organize study groups with classmates to explore and review course material throughout the term. Trying to cram weeks of information into a single night of study will never allow you to do your best.

As you study, avoid simply memorizing information aimlessly. Instead, clarify the important issues of the course and use these issues to focus your understanding of specific facts and particular readings. Try to see relations among topics; concentrate on the central concerns of each study unit, and see what connections you can discover; and place all you have learned into a meaningful context.

As an exam approaches, find out what you can about the form it will take. No question is more irritating to instructors than "Do we need to know this for the exam?" but it is generally legitimate to ask whether the questions will require short or long answers, how many questions there will be, whether you may choose which questions to answer, and what kinds of thinking and writing will be required of you. Some instructors may hand out study guides for exams or even lists of potential questions.

If yours does not, make up questions you think the instructor might ask and then plan answers to them with classmates. Returning to your notes and to assigned readings with specific questions in mind can help enormously in your process of understanding. The important thing to remember is that an essay exam tests more than your memory of specific information; it requires you to use this information to demonstrate a comprehensive grasp of the material covered in the course.

Taking the Exam

Doing well on an essay exam begins with a plan of attack. Once you analyze the questions to determine what is wanted, apportion your time.

Read the exam carefully.

Before you answer a question, read the entire exam so that you can apportion your time realistically. Pay particular attention to how many points you may earn in different parts of the test; notice any directions that suggest how long an answer should be or how much space it should take up. As you are doing so, you may wish to make tentative choices of the questions you will answer and decide on the order in which you will answer them. If you have ideas about how you would organize any of your answers, you might also jot down scratch outlines. But before you start to complete any answers, write down the actual clock time you expect to be working on each question or set of questions. Careful time management is crucial to your success on essay exams; devoting some time to each question is always better than using up your time on only a few.

Before beginning to write your first answer, analyze the question carefully so that you can focus your attention on the information that will be pertinent to your answer. Consider this question from a sociology final:

> Drawing from lectures and discussions on the contradictory aspects of American values, the "bureaucratic personality," and the behaviors associated with social mobility, discuss the problems of attaining economic success in a relatively "open," complex, post-industrial society such as the United States.

Though the question looks confusing at first, once you sort it out, you will find that it contains the key terms for the answer's thesis, as well as the main points of development. Look first at the words that give you directions: *draw from* and *discuss*. The term *discuss* invites you to list and explain the problems of attaining economic success. The categories of these problems are already identified in the opening phrases: "contradictory . . . values," "bureaucratic personality," and "behaviors associated with social mobility." Therefore, you would begin with a thesis that includes the key words in the final clause ("attaining economic success in a relatively open, complex, post-industrial society") and then take up each category of problem—and perhaps other problems you can think of—in separate paragraphs.

Typical Essay Exam Questions

The next section presents questions in nine common categories (on the left) with an explanation of how students should respond to each question (on the right). All the examples are drawn from short quizzes, midterms, and final exams for a variety of first- and second-year courses. These questions demonstrate the range of writing you may be expected to do on exams. Pay particular attention to how the directions and key words in each case help you define the writing task.

Notice that each question indicates the amount of time students should devote to their answer. In reality, students are often expected to determine how much time to spend, depending on the number of points allocated to the question—for example, students should spend half the exam period answering a question that could earn half the exam's points. In general, instructors expect students to need the entire exam period to write an effective essay exam. If you find that you have finished the exam in half the time, review your answers: You probably have not included all the information your instructor was looking for.

Define or Identify   Questions that require you to write a few sentences defining or identifying material from readings or lectures may ask for a brief overview of a large topic, or a more detailed definition or identification of a more narrowly defined topic. In composing a *definition* or identification, always ask yourself why this item is important enough to be on the exam.

See Chapter 16 for more on defining.

Question 29.1 (15/100 points; 15 minutes)

What are the three stages of African literature?	This question asks for a brief overview of a large topic. Answering this question would involve naming the periods is historical order and then describing each period in a sentence or two.

Question 29.2 (20/100 points; 20 minutes)

Define and state some important facts concerning each of the following: a. demographics b. Instrumental model c. RCA d. telephone booth of the air e. penny press	With no more than three or four minutes for each part, students answering Question 29.2 would offer a concise definition for each item (probably in a sentence) and add facts relevant to the main topics in the course.

Recall Details of a Specific Source   Sometimes instructors will ask for a straightforward *summary* or *paraphrase* of a specific source—for example, a book or a film. To answer such questions, the student must recount details directly from the source without interpretation or evaluation. In the following example from a sociology exam, students were allowed about ten minutes to complete the answer on one lined page provided with the exam.

Question 29.3 (100/100 points; 50 minutes)

In his article "Is There a Culture of Poverty?" Oscar Lewis addresses a popular question in the social sciences: What is the "culture of poverty"? How is it able to come into being, according to Lewis? That is, under what conditions does it exist? When does he say a person is no longer a part of the culture of poverty? What does Lewis say is the future of the culture of poverty?

The phrasing in Question 29.3 invites a fairly clear-cut structure: Each of the five questions can be turned into an assertion and supported with examples from Lewis's article. For example, the first two questions could become assertions like these: "Lewis defines the culture of poverty as ____," and "According to Lewis, the culture of poverty comes into being through ____." The important thing in this case is to summarize accurately what the writer said and not waste time evaluating or criticizing his ideas.

For more on paraphrasing and summarizing, see Chapter 12, pp. 532–33, and Chapter 26, pp. 706–8.

Explain the Importance or Significance   Another kind of essay exam question asks students to explain the importance of something covered in the course. Such questions require specific examples as the basis for a more general discussion of what has been studied. This type of question often involves *interpreting* a literary or cinematic work by concentrating on a particular aspect of it.

Question 29.4 (10/100 points; 15 minutes)

In the last scene of *Paths of Glory,* the owner of a café brings a young German woman onto a small stage in his café to sing for the French troops, while Colonel Dax looks on from outside the café. Briefly explain the significance of this scene in relation to the movie as a whole.

In answering this question, a student's first task would be to reconsider the whole movie, looking for ways in which this one brief scene illuminates or explains larger issues or themes. Then, in a paragraph or two, the student would summarize these themes and point out how each element of the scene fits into the overall context.

Question 29.5 (10/100 points; 20 minutes)

Chukovsky gives many examples of cute expressions and statements uttered by small children. Give an example of two of the kinds of statements that he finds interesting. Then state their implications for understanding the nature of language in particular and communication more generally.

For Question 29.5 (on a communications exam), students would start by choosing examples of children's utterances from Chukovsky's book. These examples would then provide the basis for demonstrating the student's grasp of the larger subject. Questions like these require students to decide for themselves the significance of the information and to organize the answer so that the general ideas are clearly developed.

Apply Concepts   Very often, courses in the humanities and the social sciences emphasize significant themes, ideologies, or concepts. A common type of essay exam question asks students to apply the concepts to works studied in the course.

See Chapter 4 for more on explaining a concept.

Question 29.6 (45/130 points; 40 minutes)

Several works studied in this course depict scapegoat figures. Select two written works and two films, and discuss how their authors or directors present and analyze the social conflicts that lead to the creation of scapegoats.

The answer to Question 29.6 would provide an introductory paragraph defining the concept "scapegoat" and referring to the works to be discussed. Then the student would devote a paragraph or two to the works, pointing out specific examples to illustrate the concept. A concluding paragraph would probably attempt to bring the concept into clearer focus.

Comment on a Quotation   On essay exams, an instructor will often ask students to comment on a quotation they are seeing for the first time. Usually, such quotations will express some surprising or controversial opinion that complements or challenges basic principles or ideas in the course. Sometimes the writer being quoted is identified, sometimes not. In fact, it is not unusual for instructors to write the quotation themselves.

Question 29.7 (75/100 points; 90 minutes)

"Some historians believe that economic hardship and oppression breed social revolt, but the experience of the United States and Mexico between 1900 and 1920 suggests that people may rebel also during times of prosperity."

Question 29.7, from a midterm exam in a history course, asks students to "comment," but the three questions make clear that a successful answer would require an *argument:* a clear *thesis* stating a position on the views

Comment on this statement. Why did large numbers of Americans and Mexicans wish to change conditions in their countries during the years from 1900 to 1920? How successful were their efforts? Who benefited from the changes that took place?

expressed in the quotation, specific *reasons* for that thesis, and *support* for the thesis from readings and lectures. In general, such questions do not have a "correct" answer: Whether students agree or disagree with the quotation is not as important as whether they can argue their case reasonably and convincingly, demonstrating a firm grasp of the subject matter.

See Chapter 19 for more on these components of an argument.

Compare and Contrast   Instructors are particularly fond of essay exam questions that require a *comparison and contrast* of two or three principles, ideas, works, activities, or phenomena. To answer this kind of question, you need to explore fully the relations between the things to be compared, analyze each one separately, and then search out specific points of likeness or difference. Students must thus show a thorough knowledge of the things being compared, as well as a clear understanding of the basic issues on which comparisons and contrasts can be made. Whether the point of comparison is stated in the question or left for you to define for yourself, your answer needs to be limited to the aspects of similarity or difference that are most relevant to the general concepts or themes covered in the course.

Question 29.8 (50/100 points; 1 hour)

Compare and analyze the views of colonialism presented in Memmi's *Colonizer and the Colonized* and Pontecorvo's *Battle of Algiers*. What are the significant differences between these two views?

Often, as in Question 29.8, the basis of comparison will be limited to a particular focus; here, for example, students are asked to compare two works in terms of their views of colonialism.

See Chapter 18 for more on comparing and contrasting.

Question 29.9 (50/100 points; 1 hour)

What was the role of the United States in Cuban affairs from 1898 until 1959? How did its role there compare with its role in the rest of Spanish America during the same period?

Sometimes instructors will simply identify what is to be compared, as in Question 29.9. In this question from a Latin American history exam, students are left the task of choosing the basis of the comparison.

Synthesize Information from Various Sources   In a course with several assigned readings, an instructor may ask students to pull together, or *synthesize,* information from several or even all the readings.

For more on synthesizing, see Chapter 12, pp. 533–34,. and Chapter 26, pp. 697–98, 700–701.

Question 29.10 (25/100 points; 30 minutes)

On the basis of the articles read on El Salvador, Nicaragua, Peru, Chile, Argentina, and Mexico, what would you say are the major problems confronting Latin America today? Discuss the major types of problems with references to particular countries as examples.

Question 29.10, from the final in a Latin American studies course, asks students to decide which major problems to discuss, which countries to include in each discussion, and how to use material from many readings to develop their answers, all in half an hour. To compose a coherent essay, a student will need a carefully developed *forecasting statement*.

For more on forecasting statements, see Chapter 13, pp. 547–48.

Analyze Causes   In humanities and social science courses, much of what students study concerns the causes of trends, actions, and events. Hence, it is not surprising to find questions about causes on essay exams. In such cases, the instructor expects students to *analyze* causes of various phenomena discussed in readings and lectures.

See Chapter 9 for more on analyzing causes.

Question 29.11 (25/100 points; 30 minutes)

Given that we occupy several positions in the course of our lives and given that each position has a specific role attached to it, what kinds of problems or dilemmas arise from those multiple roles, and how are they handled?

Question 29.11 comes from a midterm exam in sociology. The question requires students to develop a list of causes in the answer. The causes would be organized under a thesis statement, and each cause would be argued and supported by referring to lectures or readings.

Criticize or Evaluate   Occasionally, instructors will include essay exam questions that invite students to *evaluate* a concept or a work. They want more than opinion: They expect a reasoned, documented evaluation based on appropriate standards of judgment. Such questions test students' ability to recall and synthesize pertinent information and to understand and apply criteria taught in the course.

See Chapter 8 for more on evaluation.

Question 29.12 (10/85 points; 20 minutes)

Eisenstein and Mukerji both argue that movable print was important to the rise of Protestantism. Cole extends this argument to say that print set off a chain of events that was important to the history of the United States. Summarize this argument, and evaluate any part of it if you choose.

Question 29.12 appeared on a communications course midterm that asked students to answer "in two paragraphs." The question asks students to summarize and evaluate an argument that appears in several course readings. The students would probably use the writing strategies of comparison and contrast to analyze and evaluate the authors' views.

Write your answer.

Your strategy for writing depends on the length of your answer. For short identifications and definitions, start with a general identifying statement and then move on to describe specific applications or explanations. Two complete sentences will almost always suffice.

See Chapter 13 for more on forecasting and transitions.

For longer answers, begin with a clear and explicit thesis statement. Use key terms from the question in your thesis, and use the same key terms throughout your essay. If the question does not supply any key terms, provide your own. Outlining your answer will enable you to forecast your points in your opening sentences. Use transitions such as *first, second, moreover, however,* and *thus* to signal clear relations among paragraphs.

As you write, you will certainly think of new ideas or facts to include. If you find that you want to add a sentence or two to sections you have already completed, write them in the margin or at the top of the page, with a neat arrow pointing to where they fit in your answer. Strike out words or even sentences you want to change by drawing through them neatly with a single line. If you run out of time when you are writing an answer, jot down the remaining ideas, just to show that you know the material and with more time could have continued your answer.

Model Answers

Here we analyze several successful answers and give you an opportunity to analyze one for yourself. These analyses, along with the information we have provided elsewhere in this chapter, should greatly improve your chances of writing successful exam answers.

Short Answers   A literature midterm opened with ten items to identify, each worth 3 points. Students had about two minutes for each item. Here are three of Brenda Gossett's answers, each one earning her the full 3 points:

> Rauffenstein: He was the German general who was in charge of the castle where Boeldieu, Maréchal, and Rosenthal were finally sent in *The Grand Illusion*. He, along with Boeldieu, represented the aristocracy, which was slowly fading out at that time.

> Iges Peninsula: This peninsula is created by the Meuse River in France. It is there that the Camp of Hell was created in *The Debacle*. The Camp of Hell is where the French army was interned after the Germans defeated them in the Franco-Prussian War.

> Pache: He was the "religious peasant" in the novel *The Debacle*. It was he who inevitably became a scapegoat when he was murdered by Loubet, La poulle, and Chouteau because he wouldn't share his bread with them.

The instructor said only "identify the following" but clearly wanted students both to identify the item and to indicate its significance to the work in which it appeared. Gossett does both and gets full credit. She mentions particular works, characters, and events. Although she is rushed, she answers in complete sentences.

She does not misspell any words or leave out any commas or periods. Her answers are complete and correct.

Paragraph-Length Answers   The following question is from a weekly literature quiz. With only a few minutes to respond, students were instructed to "answer in a few sentences." Here is the question and Camille Prestera's answer:

> In *Things Fall Apart*, how did Okonkwo's relationship with his father affect his attitude toward his son? (20/100 points)

> Okonkwo despised his father, who was lazy, cowardly, and in debt. Okonkwo tried to be everything his father wasn't. He was hardworking, wealthy, and a great warrior and wrestler. Okonkwo treated his son harshly because he was afraid he saw the same weakness in Nwoye that he despised in his father. The result of this harsh treatment was that Nwoye left home.

Prestera begins by describing Okonkwo and his father, contrasting the two sharply. Then she explains Okonkwo's relationship with his son Nwoye. Her answer is coherent and straightforward.

Long Answers   Many final exams include at least one question requiring an essay-length answer. John Pixley had an hour to plan and write this essay for a final exam in a literature course in response to the following question applying a concept:

> Many American writers have portrayed their characters or their poetic speaker as being engaged in a quest. The quest may be explicit or implicit, it may be external or psychological, and it may end in failure or success. Analyze the quest motif in the work of four of the following writers: Edwards, Franklin, Hawthorne, Thoreau, Douglass, Whitman, Dickinson, James, Twain.

1   Americans pride themselves on being ambitious and on being able to strive for goals and to tap their potential. Some say that this is what the "American Dream" is all about. It is important for one to do and be all that one is capable of. This entails a quest or search for identity, experience, and happiness. Hence, the idea of the quest is a vital one in the United States, and it can be seen as a theme throughout American literature.

2   In eighteenth-century colonial America, Jonathan Edwards dealt with this theme in his autobiographical and personal writings. Unlike his fiery and hard-nosed sermons, these autobiographical writings present a sensitive, vulnerable man trying to find himself and his proper, satisfying place in the world. He is concerned with his spiritual growth, in being free to find and explore religious experience and happiness. For example, in *Personal Narrative*, he very carefully traces the stages of religious beliefs. He tells about periods of abandoned ecstasy, doubts, and rational revelations. He also notes that his best insights and growth came at times when he was alone in the wilderness, in nature. Edwards's efforts to find himself in relation to the world can also be seen

Key term, quest, is mentioned in introduction and thesis.

First writer is identified immediately.

Edwards's work and the details of his quest are presented.

in his "Observations of the Natural World," in which he relates various meticulously observed and described natural phenomena to religious precepts and occurrences. Here, he is trying to give the world and life, of which he is a part, some sense of meaning and purpose.

3   Although he was a contemporary of Edwards, Benjamin Franklin, who was very involved in the founding of the United States as a nation, had a different conception of the quest. He sees the quest as being one for practical accomplishment, success, and wealth. In his *Autobiography*, he stresses that happiness involves working hard to accomplish things, getting along with others, and establishing a good reputation. Unlike Edwards's, his quest is external and bound up with society. He is concerned with his morals and behavior, but as seen in part 2 of the *Autobiography*, he deals with them in an objective, pragmatic, even statistical way, rather than in sensitive pondering. It is also evident in this work that Franklin, unlike Edwards, believes so much in himself and his quest that he is able to laugh at himself. His concern with society can be seen in *Poor Richard's Almanac*, in which he gives practical advice on how to find success and happiness in the world, how to "be healthy, wealthy, and wise."

4   Still another version of the quest can be seen in the mid-nineteenth-century poetry of Walt Whitman. The quest that he portrays blends elements of those of Edwards and Franklin. In "Song of Myself," which is clearly autobiographical, the speaker emphasizes the importance of finding, knowing, and enjoying oneself as part of nature and the human community. He says that one should come to realize that one is lovable, just as are all other people and all of nature and life. This is a quest for sensitivity and awareness, as Edwards advocates, and for great self-confidence, as Franklin advocates. Along with Edwards, Whitman sees that peaceful isolation in nature is important; but he also sees the importance of interacting with people, as Franklin does. Being optimistic and feeling good--in both the literal and the figurative sense-- are the objects of this quest. Unfortunately, personal disappointment and national crisis (i.e., the Civil War) shattered Whitman's sense of confidence, and he lost the impetus of this quest in his own life.

5   This theme of the quest can be seen in prose fiction as well as in poetry and autobiography. One interesting example is "The Beast in the Jungle," a short story written by Henry James around 1903. It is interesting in that not only does the principal character, John Marcher, fail in his lifelong quest, but his failure comes about in a most subtle and frustrating way. Marcher believes that something momentous is going to happen in his future. He talks about his belief to only one person, a woman named May. May decides to befriend him for life and watch with him for the momentous occurrence to come about, for "the beast in the jungle" to "pounce." As time passes, May seems to know what this occurrence is and eventually even says that it has happened; but John is still in the dark. It is only long after May's death that the beast pounces on him in his recognition that the "beast" was his failure to truly love May, the one woman of his life, even though she gave him all the encouragement that she possibly,

---

Marginal annotations:

Transition sentence identifies second writer. Key term (*quest*) is repeated.

Contrast with Edwards adds coherence to essay.

Another key term from the question, *external*, is used.

Franklin's particular kind of quest is described.

Transition sentence identifies third writer. Key term is repeated.

Comparison of Whitman to Edwards and Franklin sustains coherence of essay.

Whitman's quest is defined.

Transition: Key term is repeated, and fourth writer is identified.

Quest of James character is described.

decently could. Marcher never defined the terms of his quest until it was too late. By just waiting and watching, he failed to find feeling and passion. This tragic realization, as someone like Whitman would view it, brings about John Marcher's ruin.

Conclusion repeats key term.

6   As seen in these few examples, the theme of the quest is a significant one in American literature. Also obvious is the fact that there are a variety of approaches to, methods used in, and outcomes of the quest. This is an appropriate theme for American literature, seeing how much Americans cherish the right of "the pursuit of happiness."

Pixley's answer is strong for two reasons: He has the information he needs, and he has organized it carefully and presented it coherently.

EXERCISE 29.1

The following essay was written by Dan Hepler. He answered the same essay exam question as his classmate John Pixley. Analyze Hepler's essay to discover whether it meets the criteria of a good essay exam answer. Review the criteria mentioned earlier in this chapter (in the section Write Your Answer, p. 759) and in the annotated commentary of John Pixley's answer. Try to identify the features of Hepler's essay that contribute to or work against its success.

Dan Hepler's Answer

The quest motif is certainly important in American literature. By considering Franklin, Thoreau, Douglass, and Twain, we can see that the quest may be explicit or implicit, external or psychological, a failure or a success. Tracing the quest motif through these four authors seems to show a developing concern in American literature with transcending materialism to address deeper issues. It also reveals a drift toward ambiguity and pessimism.   1

Benjamin Franklin's quest, as revealed by his *Autobiography*, is for material comfort and outward success. His quest may be considered an explicit one because he announces clearly what he is trying to do: perfect a systematic approach for living long and happily. The whole *Autobiography* is a road map intended for other people to use as a guide; Franklin apparently meant rather literally for people to imitate his methods. He wrote with the assumption that his success was reproducible. He is possibly the most optimistic author in American literature because he enjoys life, knows exactly *why* he enjoys life, and believes that anyone else willing to follow his formula may enjoy life as well.   2

By Franklin's standards, his quest is clearly a success. But his *Autobiography* portrays only an external, not a psychological, success. This is not to suggest that Franklin was a psychological failure. Indeed, we have every reason to believe the contrary. But the fact remains that Franklin *wrote* only about external success; he never indicated how he really felt emotionally. Possibly it was part of Franklin's overriding optimism to assume that material comfort leads naturally to emotional fulfillment.   3

Henry David Thoreau presents a more multifaceted quest. His *Walden* is, on the simplest level, the chronicle of Thoreau's physical journey out of town and into the woods.   4

But the moving itself is not the focus of *Walden*. It is really more of a metaphor for some kind of spiritual quest going on within Thoreau's mind. Most of the action in *Walden* is mental, as Thoreau contemplates and philosophizes, always using the lake, the woods, and his own daily actions as symbols of higher, more eternal truths. This spiritual quest is a success in that Thoreau is able to appreciate the beauty of nature and to see through much of the sham and false assumptions of town life and blind materialism.

Thoreau does not leave us with nearly as explicit a "blueprint" for success as Franklin does. Even Franklin's plan is limited to people of high intelligence, personal discipline, and sound character; Franklin sometimes seems to forget that many human beings are in fact weak and evil and so would stand little chance of success similar to his own. But at least Franklin's quest could be duplicated by another Franklin. Thoreau's quest is more problematic, for even as great a mystic and naturalist as Thoreau himself could not remain in the woods indefinitely. This points toward the idea that the real quest is all internal and psychological; Thoreau seems to have gone to the woods to develop a spiritual strength that he could keep and take elsewhere on subsequent dealings with the "real world."

The quest of Frederick Douglass was explicit in that he needed physically to get north and escape slavery, but it was also implicit because he sought to discover and redefine himself through his quest, as Thoreau did. Douglass's motives were more sharply focused than either Franklin's or Thoreau's; his very humanness was at stake, as well as his physical well-being and possibly even his life. But Douglass also makes it clear that the most horrible part of slavery was the mental anguish of having no hope of freedom. His learning to read, and his maintenance of this skill, seems to have been as important as the maintenance of his material comforts, of which he had very few. In a sense, Douglass's quest is the most psychological and abstract so far because it is for the very essence of freedom and humanity, both of which were mostly taken for granted by Franklin and Thoreau. Also, Douglass's quest is the most pessimistic of the three; Douglass concludes that physical violence is the only way out, as he finds with the Covey incident.

Finally, Mark Twain's *Huckleberry Finn* is an example of the full range of meaning that the quest motif may assume. Geographically, Huck's quest is very large. But again, there is a quest defined implicitly as well as one defined explicitly, as Huck (without consciously realizing it) searches for morality, truth, and freedom. Twain's use of the quest is ambiguous, even more so than the previous writers', because while he suggests success superficially (i.e., the "happily ever after" scene in the last chapter), he really hints at some sort of ultimate hopelessness inherent in society. Not even Douglass questions the good or evil of American society as deeply as Twain does; for Douglass, everything will be fine when slavery is abolished; but for Twain, the only solution is to "light out for the territories" altogether--and when Twain wrote, he knew that the territories were no more.

Twain's implicit sense of spiritual failure stands in marked contrast to Franklin's buoyant confidence in material success. The guiding image of the quest, however, is central to American values and, consequently, a theme that these writers and others have adapted to suit their own vision.

EXERCISE 29.2

Analyze the following essay exam questions to decide what kind of writing task they present. What is being asked of the student as a participant in the course and as a writer? Given the time constraints of the exam, what plan would you propose for writing the answer? Following each question is the number of points it is worth and the amount of time allotted to answer it.

1. Cortazar is a producer of fantastic literature. Discuss first what fantastic literature is. Then choose any four stories by Cortazar as examples, and discuss the fantastic elements in these stories. Refer to the structure, techniques, and narrative styles that he uses in these four stories. If you like, you may refer to more than four, of course. (Points: 30 of 100. Time: 40 of 150 minutes.)

2. During the course of the twentieth century, the United States experienced three significant periods of social reform—the progressive era, the age of the Great Depression, and the decade of the 1960s. What were the sources of reform in each period? What were the most significant reform achievements of each period as well as the largest failings? (Points: 35 of 100. Time: 75 of 180 minutes.)

3. Since literature is both an artistic and an ideological product, writers comment on their material context through their writing.

   a. What is Rulfo's perspective of his Mexican reality, and how is it portrayed through his stories?

   b. What particular themes does he deal with, especially in these stories: "The Burning Plain," "Luvina," "They Gave Us the Land," "Paso del Norte," and "Tell Them Not to Kill Me!"?

   c. What literary techniques and structures does he use to convey his perspective? Refer to a specific story as an example.

   (Points: 30 of 100. Time: 20 of 50 minutes.)

4. Why is there a special reason to be concerned about the influence of television watching on kids? In your answer, include a statement of the following:

   a. Your own understanding of the *general communication principles* involved for any television watcher.

   b. What is special about television and kids.

   c. How advertisers and producers use this information. (You should draw from the relevant readings as well as lectures.)

   (Points: 20 of 90. Time: 25 of 90 minutes.)

5. Analyze the autobiographical tradition in American literature, focusing on differences and similarities among authors and, if appropriate, changes over time. Discuss four authors in all. In addition to the conscious autobiographers—Edwards, Franklin, Thoreau, and Douglass—you may choose one or two figures from among the following fictional or poetic quasi-autobiographers: Hawthorne, Whitman, Dickinson, and Twain. (Points: 50 of 120. Time: 60 of 180 minutes.)

6. How does the system of (media) sponsorship work, and what, if any, ideological control do sponsors exert? Be specific and illustrative. (Points: 33 of 100. Time: 60 of 180 minutes.)

7　Several of the works studied in this course analyze the tension between myth and reality. Select two written works and two films, and analyze how their authors or directors present the conflict between myth and reality and how they resolve it, if they resolve it. (Points: 45 of 130. Time: 60 of 180 minutes.)

8　*Man's Hope* is a novel about the Spanish Civil War written while the war was still going on. *La Guerre Est Finie* is a film about Spanish revolutionaries depicting their activities nearly thirty years after the civil war. Discuss how the temporal relationship of each of these works to the civil war is reflected in the character of the works themselves and in the differences between them. (Points: 58 of 100. Time: 30 of 50 minutes.)

9　Write an essay on one of these topics: The role of the narrator in *Tom Jones* and *Pride and Prejudice* or the characters of Uncle Toby and Miss Bates. (Points: 33 of 100. Time: 60 of 180 minutes.)

30

Writing Portfolios

A writing **portfolio** displays your work. Portfolios for college composition courses usually include a selection of your writing for the course and an essay reflecting on your writing and on what you learned in the course. The contents of a portfolio will, of course, vary from writer to writer and from instructor to instructor. This chapter provides some advice for assembling a writing portfolio using the resources in *The St. Martin's Guide to Writing*.

The Purposes of a Writing Portfolio

Portfolios are generally used to display an individual's accomplishments. Artists present portfolios of their best work to gallery owners. Designers and architects present portfolios of their most successful work to potential clients. Writing students may be asked to submit a portfolio of their work for evaluation. No matter what the occasion, a portfolio presents a rich opportunity to show what you can do.

Creating a portfolio for a composition course enables you to present your best, most representative, or most extensively revised writing. Your instructor will assign the final grade, but how you select the materials included in your portfolio and describe them in your introductory essay may have some influence on your instructor's judgment. Most important, selecting your work and composing an introductory reflective essay give you an opportunity to review, reinforce, and therefore better remember and apply what you have learned. Reviewing your work can increase your satisfaction with the course, give you insights into your intellectual development, and help you recognize your strengths and weaknesses.

Assembling a Portfolio for Your Composition Course

Some instructors give students free rein in deciding what to include in their portfolio, but most specify what the portfolio should include. Instructors usually ask students to select a certain number of essays, and they may specify that certain types of essays be included, such as one based on personal experience or observation and another based on library and Internet research, along with other materials like in-class writing or responses to readings. Many instructors also ask students to include materials that reflect their writing process (such as invention work, drafts, and critical responses). In addition to a selection of course materials, instructors usually require a reflective essay or letter that introduces the portfolio and evaluates the writer's own work.

Instructors who require portfolios often do not assign grades to individual drafts or revisions but wait until the end of the term to grade the entire portfolio. In such cases, instructors may ask students to submit a midterm portfolio for an in-progress course evaluation. A midterm portfolio usually includes plans for revising one or more of the essays included.

There are many ways to assemble portfolios, and you will need to determine exactly what your instructor expects your portfolio to include. Here are some of the variables to consider:

- How many essays should be included in the portfolio?

- May essays be revised further for the portfolio?

- What other material should be included (such as invention or research notes, exercises, notes from collaborative activities, analyses of readings, or downloaded Web pages)?

- May material from other courses, workplace projects, or service-learning projects be included? For more on service learning, see Chapter 33.

- Should the portfolio be introduced by a reflective essay or letter? If so, how long should it be? Are there any special requirements for it?

- How should the portfolio be organized?

The following sections review specific resources in the *Guide* that can help you compose your portfolio.

Select your work.

Even if your instructor specifies what to include in your portfolio, you have some important decisions to make. Here are some suggestions to help you:

- If you are asked to select only your best essays, begin by rereading them to see how well each one develops the basic features of its genre. Also review any feedback you received from your instructor, classmates, writing center tutors, or other readers.

- If you are asked to make further revisions to one or more of your essays, reread the essay, using the Critical Reading Guide for that genre, or get a response to it from your instructor, a classmate, or a writing center tutor. It may also help to review any responses you received on earlier drafts as well as the Troubleshooting Guide for that genre to see what else you could do to improve the essay. Be sure to edit and proofread your essays carefully.

- If you are asked to select an essay based on personal experience, you might choose the remembered event essay you wrote for Chapter 2. If you are asked for essays based on firsthand observation and analysis, look at what you wrote for the profile (Chapter 3), the concept explanation (Chapter 4), finding common ground (Chapter 5), or the story analysis (Chapter 10). If you are asked to include argument essays, review the writing you did for Chapters 6–9.

- If you are asked to select essays incorporating library or Internet research, look at the essays you wrote for Chapters 4–9.

- If you are asked to select essays with a range of different purposes and audiences, you might begin by reviewing the Determining the Writer's Purpose and Audience sections of the Part One chapters you used. Then reread your invention notes defining the particular purpose and audience for each essay you wrote.

- If you are asked to include examples of your writing process work, look for your most thoughtful invention work, for a first draft and one or more revisions showing significant rethinking or reorganization, for your critical reading response to another student's draft showing perceptive criticism and helpful suggestions, or for a draft you edited heavily.

- If you are asked to include a complete process for one essay, you should choose process materials that show the quality as well as quantity of work you have done. Look for examples of thoughtful invention and substantive revision you can point out in your reflective essay.

- If you are asked to select essays that show the progress you have made in the course, you may want to choose essays that underwent radical change during the term.

Reflect on your work and what you have learned.

Many instructors require a written statement in the form of an essay or letter introducing the portfolio. Some ask for a simple description of the work presented in your portfolio; others prefer an evaluation of your work; still others may want you to connect your learning in this course to other courses and to work you hope to do in the future. Keeping the following considerations in mind will help you write a thoughtful, well-organized statement to your instructor about what you have learned:

- ***Introduce and describe your work.*** Because you will need to refer to several works or parts of a work, name each item in your portfolio in a consistent way. In describing an essay, give its title, genre (using the title of the chapter in *The St. Martin's Guide*), purpose, audience, and topic.

- ***Justify your choices.*** When you justify what you see as your "best" work, you think critically about the standards you are using to evaluate good writing in each genre. The *Guide* sets forth clear criteria for each kind of writing in the Use the Basic Features and Critical Reading Guide sections in Chapters 2–10. Review these sections as you judge the success of your essay, and refer to them as you explain your analysis.

If you need help writing an evaluation, review Chapter 8.

- ***Illustrate your growth as a writer with specific examples.*** You may have selected work to show how you have grown as a writer, but you should not assume your readers will read the portfolio as you do without some guidance. You need to show them where they can find evidence that supports your analysis by citing relevant examples from the work included in your portfolio. Summarize or quote your examples, and be sure to tell readers what you think the examples illustrate. Also refer to them in a way that will help readers locate them with ease — perhaps by page and paragraph number (see the next section for some suggestions for organizing your portfolio).

- *Use the* **Guide** *to help you reflect on your learning.* Your instructor may ask you to consider what you learned in writing and revising a particular essay as well as what you learned about the process of writing that essay. In either case, it will help you to anchor your reflections in the specific work you have done using this book. Consider what you have learned analyzing and discussing the readings, drafting and researching, participating in groups, getting and giving critical comments, and revising and editing. Look again at the Thinking Critically sections in Chapters 2–10. There you will find questions that will help you reflect on how you solved problems when revising an essay and how your writing can be situated and understood in a larger social context. You may well be able to use your responses to these questions in your portfolio's reflective essay.

Organize your portfolio.

Some instructors prescribe the portfolio's design and organization, while others allow students to be creative. Portfolios may be presented in an inexpensive manila folder, in a looseleaf binder, or on a Web site. Follow your instructor's specific guidelines. Here are some possibilities for organizing your portfolio:

- *Include a cover or front page.* The design of the front page may be left up to you, but be sure to indicate the class section number, the instructor's name, your own name, and the date.

- *Include a table of contents.* Portfolios, like books, need a table of contents so that readers can see at a glance what is included and where it is located. The table of contents should appear at the beginning of the portfolio, identifying all of the parts and specifying the page on which each part begins. You may decide to renumber all of the pages in the portfolio consecutively, even though some of the material already has page numbers. If you add new page numbers, consider using a different color, putting the new page numbers in a new place, or using a letter- or word-number sequence (such as *Event-1, Position-1*, etc.). Whatever you decide, be consistent.

- *Label each item.* If your instructor does not specify how you should label your work, you need to develop a clear system on your own. You may need to explain your system briefly in a note on the table of contents or in your introductory reflective essay, where you refer to particular items in your portfolio. For example, you could use the *Guide* chapter number to identify each essay assignment. To indicate process materials, consider using the chapter number and title and the relevant heading from that chapter's Guide to Writing section (such as Chapter 2, Writing a Draft). To identify different drafts, you could write on the top left margin of every page the chapter number, essay title, and draft number. For drafts that received a critical reading, you might want to add the notation "Read by *S*." You should also date all of your work.

- *Sequence the material.* If your instructor does not indicate how you should order the work included in your portfolio, you will have to decide yourself. If your instructor asks you to present two or more examples of your best work, you may want to begin with the essay you consider your very best. If your instructor asks you to show the progress you have made in the course, you could begin with your weakest essay and either show how you improved it or present later essays that were stronger. If your instructor asks you to demonstrate growth, you might organize your work by the particular areas that improved. For example, you could show that you learned to rework your writing substantially by presenting multiple drafts. Or to show that you learned to edit effectively or to avoid certain sentence errors, you could give examples of a particular error you made one or two times early on but avoided in later drafts.

PART 6

Writing and Speaking to Wider Audiences

31

Oral Presentations

At some point in your academic career, you will probably be asked to give an oral presentation. In fact, you may give many oral presentations before you graduate, and you almost certainly will give oral presentations on the job. This chapter contains practical suggestions for preparing and giving effective oral presentations.

Preparing

Many people are terrified at the thought of public speaking, particularly people who have little experience with it. Even experienced public speakers can become jittery before giving an oral presentation. The key to defeating nervousness and anxiety is to research and prepare. If you have researched your subject thoroughly and have planned your presentation in detail, then you should be able to relax. If you find that you are still anxious, take a few slow, deep breaths before starting your presentation. It is also helpful not to think of your presentation as a performance. Remember that you are communicating a message. Think of your presentation as simply talking to an audience.

Understand the kind of oral presentation you have been asked to give.

The list that follows identifies the four basic types of oral presentations:

- *Impromptu presentation.* An impromptu oral presentation is given without preparation. In a history class, for example, your instructor may call on you to explain briefly a concept you are studying, such as "manifest destiny." As best you can, you would recall what you have read and summarize the information. Although impromptu presentations are given without preparation, they do require knowledge of the subject matter.

- *Extemporaneous presentation.* In an extemporaneous presentation, you prepare beforehand and speak from notes or an outline. For example, in a management class, you might prepare a report on a business that you recently visited. In most academic and business situations, extemporaneous talks are preferred because they are informal yet well organized. Extemporaneous presentation often includes outlining your major points using presentation software, such as PowerPoint.

- *Scripted presentation.* Reading from a script is one way to ensure that you say exactly what you want to say—and that you take no more than the time you have been allotted. Because you read to your audience, a scripted presentation can be stiff and boring unless it is carefully planned and rehearsed. Scripted presentations also need to be written so that the audience can easily follow the presentation by just hearing it. Sentences should be kept short, with explicit transition words and phrases. You will also need to provide more transitions and cues than in documents that are read (see Use Cues to Orient Listeners, below). A simple guideline to remember is that if your writing is difficult for you to read aloud, it will be difficult to listen to as well.

- *Memorized presentation.* This type of oral presentation is written and committed to memory beforehand. For instance, at a sales meeting, you might evaluate a new product in relation to its competition. However, most people prefer scripted talks because of the difficulty of memorizing a lengthy oral presentation.

Assess your audience and purpose.

To give effective oral presentations, you need to assess your audience and your purpose. Even for an impromptu presentation, you should take a few moments to think about why and to whom you are speaking. To assess your audience, ask the same questions you would ask about readers: Why are the members of my audience here? What do they already know about my subject? How do they feel about my topic? What objections might they have to my argument?

Define your purpose by completing the following statement:

▶ In this oral presentation, I want to _____."

For instance, you may want to speculate on the causes of companies' hiring part-time instead of full-time workers, or you may want to argue your position on the ethics of this new hiring policy.

Determine how much information you can present in the allotted time.

Your presentation should be exactly as long as the time allotted. Using substantially less time will make your presentation seem incomplete or superficial; using substantially more time may alienate your audience. Plan your presentation to allocate sufficient time for an introduction, concluding remarks, and follow-up questions (if a question-and-answer session is to be part of the presentation). If you are giving a scripted presentation, each double-spaced page of text will probably take two minutes to deliver. Time yourself to be sure.

Use cues to orient listeners.

Listening is one of the most difficult ways to comprehend information, in part because listeners cannot look back at previous information or scan forward, as readers can. To help your audience follow your oral presentation, use the same cues you would use to orient readers—but use them more frequently and overtly. Here are four basic cues that are especially helpful for listeners:

- *Thesis and forecasting statements.* Begin your presentation with thesis and forecasting statements that announce to audience members what you intend to communicate (your thesis) and the order in which you will present your material (your forecast). For instance, if you will present an argument about deregulation in the telecommunications industry, you can begin by asserting your position and preview the reasons you will offer to support your position.

- *Transitions.* Provide transitions when you move from one point to the next to help your audience follow the twists and turns of your presentation. For example, when you have finished discussing your first reason, state explicitly that you are now turning to your second reason.

- *Summaries.* End your oral presentation with a summary of the main points you have made. Also look for opportunities to use summaries throughout the presentation, particularly when you have spent a long time discussing something complicated. A brief summary that indicates the point you are making and its relation to your overall thesis can help listeners understand how the parts of your argument fit together to support your thesis.

- *Visuals.* Visual presentation of these cues will reinforce them. An outline of your presentation, including your thesis and main topics (in a bulleted or numbered list), can all be presented on a PowerPoint slide.

For further discussion and illustration of orienting cues, see Chapter 13.

Prepare effective and appropriate visuals.

For planned presentations, you can use a variety of visuals—from simple lists and graphs to sophisticated computer demonstrations—to help both you and your audience. As mentioned previously, presentation software, such as PowerPoint or Prezi, allows you to list the major points of your presentation, helping your listeners understand and remember what you say.

But there are other ways to incorporate visuals. Writing on a board or flip chart has several advantages: low cost, high visibility, and simplicity for composing or altering on the spot. To present a long passage or detailed graphic, photocopied handouts are preferable, although they can be distracting.

Presentation software slides, such as the one in Figure 31.1, can be created and displayed with relative ease. Presentation software has the advantage of allowing the use of animation, video, and audio. Just be sure that the bells and whistles don't drown you out.

If you use presentation software, think of it as integral to your presentation, not just decorative. The text you include should be concise, easy to read, and uncluttered. You may use it to list the main points of your presentation, to signal transitions from one topic to another, to provide multimedia examples, or to summarize information you have presented.

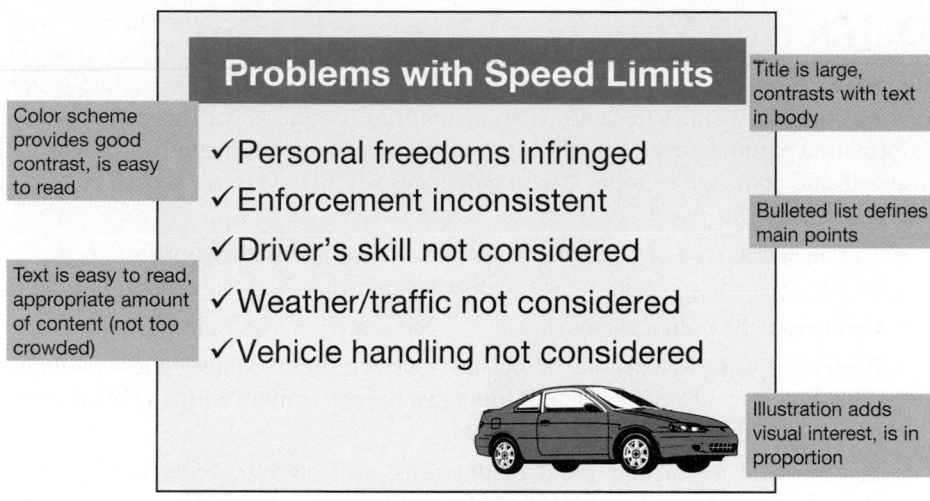

FIGURE 31.1   Sample PowerPoint Slide

As you prepare visuals of any kind, keep in mind that they must be legible to everyone in your audience, including people seated in the back of the room. Use a large, easy-to-read font and generous amounts of space around text.

For more on designing documents, see Chapter 21.

Verify that you will have the correct equipment and supplies.

Well before your presentation is scheduled to begin, verify that the presentation room contains all of the equipment and supplies you will need. For example, if you plan to use a projector, make sure it is in the room, placed correctly, and working well. Anticipating your needs as well as potential problems (for example, by bringing a backup copy of any files you need) will make your presentation go smoothly and help reduce your anxiety.

Rehearse your presentation.

Rehearsing will help you become more familiar with your material, fit the material into the allotted time, and feel more confident about speaking in public. If possible, rehearse in the same room in which you will give the presentation, using the same equipment. Also try to rehearse before an audience of colleagues or friends who can give you feedback. Rehearsing a script or memorized presentation will enable you to plan your delivery. For a scripted talk, mark cues selectively on your printed text to remind yourself when to pause or emphasize a word or phrase.

Delivering Your Oral Presentation

Before your presentation, try to relax: Take a few deep breaths, drink some water, or step outside for some fresh air. If someone is to introduce you, give that person information about yourself and your presentation. Otherwise, begin by introducing yourself and your title or topic. These guidelines will help you make a professional impression:

- As you speak, try to make eye contact with the people in the room.

- If you are behind a lectern, avoid slouching, leaning on it, or gripping it tightly throughout the presentation.

- If you are using visuals, be careful not to block the audience's view of them. After introducing a new visual, resume making eye contact with audience members; talk to the audience, not the visual.

- Try to avoid distracting vocal mannerisms, such as repeatedly saying "uh," "like," or "you know," or fidgeting with your hair or clothes.

- Speak loudly enough that all members of the audience can hear you, and speak clearly and distinctly. Nervousness may cause you to speak too rapidly, so watch your pace.

- Do not speak in a monotone. Instead, let the pitch of your voice rise and fall naturally, especially when giving a scripted presentation, and use your hands naturally, gesturing as you would in a conversation.

- Dress appropriately for your audience and the formality of the situation in which you are speaking. The focus should be on your message, not on how you are dressed.

End the presentation by thanking your audience for giving you the opportunity to speak. If appropriate, offer to answer any questions in a question-and-answer session following the presentation, in a private conversation, or in a follow-up correspondence.

32

Working with Others

Writers often seek advice and feedback from friends, colleagues, or mentors on individual writing projects. For instance, they may consult a librarian for advice on research, try out an argument on a coworker or fellow student, or ask a trusted friend to check for grammar errors. On some occasions, writers also work in small groups to research, plan, and compose joint writing projects.

Working with others is often referred to as *collaboration*. Collaborating with others on individual projects and especially on joint writing projects can be challenging but also rewarding. The following advice will help you anticipate the difficulties so that you can get the most out of the collaboration.

Working with Others on Your Individual Writing Projects

This book assumes that you will collaborate with others, at least with your instructor and classmates, to write your essays. Class discussion of the readings will help you understand more about the genres you will be writing, and responses to your invention work and to drafts of your essays will give you ideas for writing more effectively.

Collaboration is also built directly into the activities in the writing assignment chapters. In every assignment chapter, four activities ask you to collaborate with other students in a purposeful way. Chapter 6, Arguing a Position, for example, has these activities:

Practicing the Genre: Debating a Position. This activity asks you to get together with a small group of your classmates to practice asserting a position, offering reasons and support for it, and anticipating likely objections to it. Afterward, your group is encouraged to discuss the process, reflecting on what parts presented the biggest challenges, and why.

Make connections. This activity, following each of the professional readings, invites you to examine some of the important ideas and underlying assumptions of the reading. In small-group discussion, you can explore your responses and develop your understanding.

Test Your Choice. At the point where you need to frame your position, you can get feedback to determine whether your choice will be effective with readers.

Critical Reading Guide. Once you have a draft of your essay, anyone using the Critical Reading Guide can give you a comprehensive evaluation of your work, and you can do likewise for others. Because the Chapter 6 Critical Reading Guide reflects the particular requirements of an essay arguing a position, anyone using it to evaluate your draft will be able to give you focused, relevant advice.

In these four activities, you collaborate with others to develop your individual writing by discovering what you may know about a project before you get very far into it, assessing your progress after a period of initial work, and evaluating your first attempts to draft a complete essay. There are many other occasions for fruitful collaboration in the assignment chapters. For instance, in Chapter 6 you might work with other students to complete the Analyze & Write activities that follow the readings. You and another student might exchange revisions of your essays to help each other with final editing and proofreading. Or you might meet or exchange e-mail messages with two or three other students to work on the Reflecting on the Genre section that concludes the chapter. Working collaboratively on these activities may not only make them easier or more enjoyable but also make them more productive, through the exchange of many more ideas than you might have come up with on your own.

Following are guidelines for successful collaboration on individual writing projects:

- Whenever you read someone else's writing, have the writer inform you about his or her purpose and readers. Collaboration is always more effective when writers focus on helping other writers achieve their purposes for their particular readers. If a writer is explaining a concept to readers who know nothing about it, as might be the case in Chapter 4, Explaining a Concept, your comments are likely to be unhelpful if you assume the essay is addressed to someone who shares your understanding of the concept.

- Know the genre the writer is working in. If a writer is proposing a solution to a problem and you are evaluating the writing as though it were an essay arguing a position, your advice is likely to be off the mark.

- When you evaluate another writer's work, be sure you know the stage of its development. Is it a set of tentative notes for a first draft? A partial draft? A complete draft? A revision? If it is a draft, you want to focus on helping the writer develop and organize ideas; if it is a revision, you might focus exclusively on cueing and coherence or editing and proofreading.

- When you evaluate someone's writing, be helpful and supportive but also frank and specific. You do a writing partner no favor if you shrink from criticizing and giving advice. If your criticism seems grounded in the purpose, audience, and genre, it will probably not seem arbitrary or personal to your partner.

- Bring as much writing as possible to a scheduled meeting with other writers. The further along your writing is, the more you can learn from the collaboration.

- Try to be receptive to criticism. Later, you can decide whether to change your essay, and how.

Working with Others on Joint Writing Projects

In addition to collaborating with others on your individual writing projects, you may have the opportunity to collaborate to produce a single essay. For instance, in Chapter 6, Arguing a Position, you could collaborate to construct a persuasive argument for a position you share with two or three other students. In Chapter 4, Explaining a Concept, you could work with a few other students to research and explain a concept, perhaps using graphics or hands-on activities to help others grasp the concept and its implications. In Chapter 7, Proposing a Solution, you have an opportunity to practice researching and writing proposals, by far the most common type of joint writing project in college, the workplace, and the community.

When people collaborate on joint projects, they often share responsibility for the final product but divide up tasks for the preparation of the final draft. For example, each team member might take on responsibilities related to his or her areas of expertise. Someone who knows the problem firsthand might work on developing ways to explain the problem to those who have not experienced it directly. People who have experience making forecasts and planning budgets might be assigned to research and draft those aspects of the proposal. Everyone in the group might suggest ways of improving the draft, and individuals might be assigned parts to strengthen and clarify. When a final draft seems near, one person might be assigned the job of improving cueing and coherence, another might be in charge of editing and proofreading, and a third might work on document design. Because the team shares responsibility for the final document, most teams collectively review the final draft so that errors do not slip through the cracks.

Consider the following workplace writing example. A pharmaceuticals company decided to invest time and money in finding a solution to a problem the company saw as damaging to its business as well as to the community. The company assigned a team of seven division managers and a technical writer, gave them a budget to pay for outside consultants, and asked them to present a written proposal to the state legislature and local school board in six months' time. The pharmaceuticals team divided the project into a series of research and writing tasks like those outlined in the Guide to Writing in Chapter 7. The team members scheduled due dates for each task and progress reports to identify problems as they arose. They assigned responsibility for each task and identified which tasks might need consultation with outside experts.

Writing collaboratively on a joint project certainly has benefits. Collaboration not only draws on the expertise and energy of different people but also creates an outcome that is greater than the sum of its parts. One difficulty of collaborative writing projects, however, is that learning how to work effectively with others takes time and effort. Writers working on a joint project need to spend a lot of time communicating with one another. They must learn to anticipate conflicts and resolve them constructively. They should be realistic in scheduling and complete their assigned tasks responsibly. They have to be flexible in their writing processes and open to different points of view.

If you are assigned a joint project in a college course, your instructor may decide how large your group should be and may even assign students to particular groups. If you are unhappy being in a particular group, discuss the situation with your instructor as soon as possible. To help group members work together constructively on joint writing projects, here are some ground rules you will want to discuss and implement:

- Begin by establishing clear and easy means of communicating with one another. Exchange e-mail addresses, but also exchange phone numbers as a backup.

- Expect to spend a lot of time planning the project together and discussing who will do what and when. Discuss how the group should divide responsibilities. Remember, however, to remain flexible and keep lines of communication open to deal with problems as they arise.

- Set a schedule of regular meetings, and agree on how to run the meetings. For example, should someone lead each discussion? Should the role of discussion leader fall to one person or rotate among group members? Should each meeting have an agenda? If so, how and when should it be set?

- Make sure each team member has a say in major decisions, such as choosing a topic and devising a thesis statement. This isn't always easy: Some team members might be inclined to agree with whatever the team seems to want, even if they privately have concerns. However, you can get frank input from every person on the team if you periodically collect comments or votes anonymously.

- Treat each other with respect and consideration, but do not be surprised by disagreements and personality conflicts. Arguing can stimulate thinking—inspiring creativity as well as encouraging each person to explain ideas clearly and systematically—but arguing can also encourage aggressiveness in some people and withdrawal in others. If there is a problem in the way the group interacts, address it immediately, perhaps by calling a special meeting to work out a solution. Try to avoid placing blame. Consider, for example, whether taking turns would ensure that everyone contributes to the discussion and no one dominates. Urge everyone to refrain from characterizing other people and instead to speak only about what they themselves think and feel by making "I" rather than "you" statements.

- Keep track of everyone's progress. Consider creating a chart so that all members can see at a glance what they need to do and when. Schedule regular progress reports so that any problems can be identified immediately.

- If the group will make an oral presentation of the final proposal, plan it carefully, giving each person a role. Rehearse the presentation as a group to make sure it satisfies the time limit and other requirements of the assignment.

For more on oral presentations, see Chapter 31.

33

Writing in Your Community

Service learning combines classroom education with life experience. In service-learning programs, students are most often placed in off-campus positions with government bureaus such as local parks and recreation departments or nonprofit organizations that offer community support services such as tutoring or computer skills. In these positions, students have an opportunity to apply what they are studying in class. Here are a few examples:

- Nursing students teach expectant mothers about prenatal and infant care.
- Chemistry students tour local elementary schools demonstrating science "magic."
- Botany students teach fourth graders about plants native to their region.
- Zoology students help researchers gather samples for a study of local amphibian populations.
- Political science students work with the local government to increase voter turnout.
- English-speaking students tutor grade school children who are having trouble learning to read and write English.

Though you will probably find much to write about in your community service experience, you may also find writing to a wider audience to be part of your service.

Using Your Service Experience as Source Material

For many of the writing assignments in Part One, you might draw on your service experience for source material.

Find a topic.

One of the many advantages of service learning is that it can present numerous topics that might be fruitfully explored through your writing. To generate a substantial list of ideas, you need only ask yourself some simple questions:

- Who is most affected by the situation, and how are these people affected?
- How long has this situation existed?
- What forces shape the situation? Can anything be done to alter them?
- How have other organizations handled this issue? How might the situation be improved?
- What common perceptions do people hold about this situation? What are my own perceptions?
- If perceptions are inaccurate, how might they be changed?

Gather sources.

For most college writing projects, research is often limited, by time and availability, to what one can find in the library or on the Internet. A service-learning environment can provide field research sources that would otherwise be difficult to tap. The most significant of these potential sources is the people who run the organization in which you are doing your service. If you have focused your writing on the kinds of issues that are relevant to your service, these people can provide expertise. Many of the people you work with will have years of experience and specialized training and probably will have researched the subject themselves. Take advantage of your opportunity to tap their knowledge. When approached courteously, people are often more than willing to share what they know.

For suggestions on making observations, conducting interviews, and creating questionnaires, see Chapter 24.

Depending on the situation, your service site might also be a good place to circulate a questionnaire or conduct a survey to help you gather information about your subject. Of course, your own observations and experiences as you perform your service will be valuable as well. You might consider keeping a daily journal in which you record these experiences and observations. When you are ready to begin writing, you will have already done some early invention work.

The service organization itself might also be a good source of information. Such organizations often collect and produce literature that is relevant to their mission. Your organization might even maintain its own small library of resource materials. Frequently, such organizations are also part of a network of similar groups that share their expertise through newsletters, trade journals, Web sites, or online discussion groups. Explore these unique resources.

Keep in mind the ethical considerations that are involved. Many service-learning environments, such as those that involve counseling, tutoring, or teaching, can give you access to information that should be kept confidential, especially if you are working with minors. Be sure that you are open about your information gathering and that everyone whom you might use as a source knows your intentions. Any questionnaires should state what you intend to do with the information gathered. Any information gained from interviews should be properly attributed, but obtain your subjects' explicit permission before using their names. Err on the side of caution and consideration, and ask your instructor for guidance if you have any questions about how to treat sensitive material.

Writing *about* Your Service Experience

Writing in a service-learning program is really no different from other writing situations. You must still identify for yourself the kind of writing you are doing, generate ideas through invention, and refine those ideas through a process of drafting and revision. Service learning, however, may put you in a position to write for a nonacademic audience. For example, you might write an editorial for your campus or local newspaper in which you argue for increased support for your service organization or project. You might craft a letter to local government officials or even representatives to the state or national legislature suggesting a solution to a specific problem. Here are some ideas for using the writing activities discussed in Part One of this textbook:

Chapter 2: Remembering an Event

- Write about your first day of service. What happened? How did you feel? What did you learn? How did it differ from what you expected to learn?

- Write about a particularly difficult day. Why was it difficult? How did you handle the situation? What would you do differently? What did you learn from the experience?

Chapter 3: Writing Profiles

- Write about the place where you are doing your service. What does it look like? How does it make you feel? How does the location reflect or affect what goes on there? What does go on there?

- Write about one of the people you have met doing your service. What is he or she like? How is he or she typical (or atypical) of other people in the same position? What makes this person special or different?

Chapter 4: Explaining a Concept

- Write about a concept with which you were unfamiliar before you did your service. What does the concept mean? How is it important in the context of your service experience? How does what you learned about this concept make you think differently now?

- Write about a concept that you knew but now understand differently because of your service. How has your understanding of the concept changed? What caused that change? How might you explain that change to someone who does not share your experience?

Chapter 5: Finding Common Ground

- Write about a debate that is relevant to the type of service you are doing, and briefly describe each position in the debate. (Note that there may be more than two.) Who are the major proponents of each position? What are the main reasons and evidence given to support each position? Where is it possible to establish common ground between the positions?

Chapter 6: Arguing a Position

- Write an argument in support of the service organization you are working with. Why should people support it? How can they support it? Why is it a worthwhile endeavor?

- Write an argument about the value of service learning. What have you gained from this experience? Who should participate? What are the advantages of service learning to individuals and the community?

Chapter 7: Proposing a Solution

- Write about a process or procedure within or affecting the organization you are working with that you think needs to be improved. Why does it need to be improved? How might it be improved?

- Write about a policy, law, or practice that you think should be eliminated or revised because it negatively affects the organization you are working with. What would be the benefit of eliminating or revising it? What steps would need to be taken in order to change the policy, law, or practice?

Chapter 8: Justifying an Evaluation

- Write about how effectively the organization you are working with satisfies its objectives. How do you measure its effectiveness?

- Write about your school's service-learning program. In what ways is it most successful? In what ways could it be improved?

Chapter 9: Speculating about Causes

- Write about the causes for a problem or situation that you have encountered through your service-learning experience. What brought the problem about? What circumstances perpetuate it?

- Write about why service-learning programs have become common. What function do they serve that traditional education models do not? What demands do they meet?

Writing *for* Your Service Organization

Some service-learning situations will put you in a position not just to write *about* your service experience but also to write *for* your service experience. You might be asked to create flyers, brochures, press releases, or Web pages for a community organization. You might help craft presentations or reports. Though these may not be academic writing activities, the strategies presented in this text still apply. You might be asked, for example, to write a brochure that explains the purpose and function of the organization. In effect, you would be writing an explanation, and you would need to keep in mind the basic features of this genre outlined in Chapter 4.

In such writing situations, it is important to consider your rhetorical situation: What is your purpose? Who is your audience? How do you want readers to think of you or the organization you represent? In what medium will you be communicating? While in class you might be asked to select a topic and write an essay in which you argue a position (Chapter 6) or propose a solution (Chapter 7), in your service experience you might be asked to create a flyer that explains the importance of a no-kill animal shelter to potential donors or a brochure that urges commuters to carpool to reduce traffic congestion. Identifying your rhetorical situation will help you communicate your goals more effectively.

Writing in organizations is frequently a collaborative process. Everyone involved in the process is expected to do his or her part. When your written document will be used to represent your organization in any way, respect the expertise of the staff, especially when their assessment of the audience differs from your own. In some situations, your service writing may be heavily edited—or not used at all. Make sure your instructor and service-learning program administrators are aware of any instances in which you and members of the organization are having difficulty reaching a consensus.

For suggestions on how to make such collaboration run smoothly and successfully, see Chapter 32.

Finally, remember that nonacademic writing often requires greater attention to presentation than most kinds of academic writing. One-inch margins and double-spaced text are simply not enough when you are trying to create eye-catching documents such as brochures and press releases. Document design can not only make a piece of writing more visually attractive and thereby stimulate readers' interest but also help readers with different needs identify which parts of the document are most relevant. Therefore, carefully consider the layout and configuration of your document, and take advantage of the flexibility that even a simple word processing program can give you.

For more on document design, see Chapter 21.

Acknowledgments

United States. The printing, copying, redistribution, or retransmission of the Material without express written permission is prohibited. www.nytimes.com

Linda Hasselstrom. Excerpt from "Why One Peaceful Woman Carries a Pistol" from *Land Circle*. Copyright © 1991, 2008 by Linda Hasselstrom. Reprinted by permission of Fulcrum Publishing, Inc.

Dan Hurley. "Can You Make Yourself Smarter?" from *The New York Times*, April 22, 2012. Copyright 2012 The New York Times. All rights reserved. Used by permission and protected by the Copyright Laws of the United States. The printing, copying, redistribution, or retransmission of this Content without express written permission is prohibited. www.nytimes.com

Nate Jackson. "The N.F.L.'s Head Cases" from *The New York Times*, October 23, 2010. Copyright © 2010 The New York Times. All rights reserved. Used by permission and protected by the Copyright Laws of the United States. The printing, copying, redistribution, or retransmission of this Content without express written permission is prohibited. www.nytimes.com

Martin Luther King Jr. Excerpt from "Letter from Birmingham Jail." Copyright © 1963 by Dr. Martin Luther King, Jr.; copyright renewed 1991 by Coretta Scott King. Reprinted by arrangement with the Heirs to the Estate of Martin Luther King, Jr., c/o Writers House as agent for the proprietor New York, NY.

Stephen King. "Why We Crave Horror Movies." Copyright © Stephen King. All rights reserved. Originally appeared in *Playboy* (1982). Reprinted with permission.

Karen Kornbluh. "Win-Win Flexibility." Originally published in *The Atlantic Monthly* (January/February 2003) from New America Foundation, June 29, 2005. Reprinted by permission of the author.

National Kidney Foundation. "Financial Incentives for Organ Donation," February 1, 2003. Reprinted by permission of National Kidney Foundation.

Christine Rosen. "The Myth of Multitasking." From *The New Atlantis*, Number 20, Spring 2008. Copyright © 2008 The New Atlantis. Reproduced by permission.

Hanna Rosin. "Mother Inferior?" from *The Wall Street Journal*, January 15, 2011. The Wall Street Journal by News Corporation; Dow Jones & Co. Copyright © 2011. Reproduced with permission of Dow Jones & Company, Inc., in the formats Textbook/Other Book via Copyright Clearance Center.

Tom Ruprecht. "In Too Deep" from *The New York Times*, July 7, 2011. Copyright © 2011 The New York Times. All rights reserved. Used by permission and protected by the Copyright Laws of the United States. The printing, copying, redistribution, or retransmission of this Content without express written permission is prohibited. www.nytimes.com

Sally Satel. "Yuan a Kidney?" from *Slate*, June 13, 2011. Copyright © 2011 The Slate Group. All rights reserved. Used by permission and protected by the Copyright Laws of the United States. The printing, copying, redistribution, or retransmission of the Material without express written permission is prohibited. www.slate.com

Gabriel Thompson. "A Gringo in the Lettuce Fields" from *Working in the Shadows: A Year of Doing the Jobs That (Most) Americans Won't Do*. Copyright © 2010 by Gabriel Thompson. Reprinted by permission of Nation Books, a member of the Perseus Books Group.

Anastasia Toufexis. "Love: The Right Chemistry" from *Time*, February 15, 1993. Copyright © 1993 by Time Inc. Reprinted by permission. TIME is a registered trademark of Time Inc. All rights reserved.

Shankar Vedantam. "The Little Dog Lost at Sea" from *The Hidden Brain: How Our Unconscious Minds Elect Presidents, Control Markets, Wage Wars, and Save Our Lives* by Shankar Vedantam. Copyright © 2010 by Shankar Vedantam. Used by permission of Spiegel & Grau, an imprint of The Random House Publishing Group, a division of Random House, Inc.

Lane Wallace. "Do Sports Helmets Help or Hurt?" from *The Atlantic*, February 19, 2011. Copyright © 2011 by Lane Wallace. All rights reserved. Reprinted by permission of the author.

David Weisman. "Disposable Heroes" from *Seedmagazine.com*, January 11, 2011. Copyright © 2011 by David Weisman. Reprinted by permission of author.

William Carlos Williams. "The Use of Force" by William Carlos Williams from *The Collected Stories of William Carlos Williams*. Copyright ©1938 by William Carlos Williams. Reprinted by permission of New Directions Publishing Corp.

Picture Credits

7 © Jahi Chikwendiu/The Washington Post via Getty Images; **8** © Yellow Dog Productions/Getty Images; **9** (left) Library of Congress, Prints & Photographs Department, LC-USZ62-113601; (right) © Jonathan Kirn/Getty Images; **17** Phyllis Rose; **22, 23** Courtesy of Jenée Desmond-Harris; **27** Courtesy of Tom Ruprecht; **31** Courtesy of Kate Beaton; **58** © Bill Aron/PhotoEdit; **59** (left) © H. Lorren Au Jr./The Orange County Register/ZUMAPRESS.com/Alamy; (right) © Michael Newman/PhotoEdit; **64** © Scott Ryan; **67** REUTERS/Mario Anzuoni/Landov; **69** © Kyle Hood; **70** © Shannon Brinkman; **74** Courtesy of Amanda Coyne; **81, 82** Courtesy of Gabriel Thompson; **116** © Visage/Stockbyte/Getty Images; **117** (left) © Comstock/Alamy; (right) © Doug Nicholson/Media Source; **124** Fraley, R. Chris and Phillip R. Shaver. "Adult Romantic Attachment: Theoretical Developments, Emerging Controversies, and Unanswered Questions." Review of General Psychology, 2000, 4(2): 132–154. American Psychological Association, publisher. Adapted with permission; **126, 167** Photo by Nina Leen/Time Life Pictures/Getty Images; **128** Courtesy of Anastasia Toufexis; **130** Diagram by Nigel Holmes for TIME Magazine; **134** Photograph by Rob Fraser; **142** © Rex Features via AP Images; **149** National Geographic.com; **172** AP Photo/Nati Harnik; **173** (left) © Librado Romero/The New York Times/Redux; (right) © Image Source/Alamy; **192** Graph courtesy Human Rights First. Source: Parents Television Council; **196** Courtesy of Bloggingheads.tv;

219 (top) © Peter Z. Mahakian; (bottom) © Erin Patrice O'Brien; 220 Courtesy of Amy Chua; 222 © Jona Frank; 223 © Stephen Voss; 225 Photo by Susan Chalifoux/The Boston Globe via Getty Images; 226 Photo by Barry Chin/The Boston Globe via Getty Images; 227 © Getty Images; 229 Photo by Mia Weisman; 231 Courtesy of Lane Wallace; 234 Courtesy of American Enterprise Institute; 238 © Mike Lovett/Brandeis University; 242 AP Photo/Eric Risberg; 243 (left) © Michael Newman/PhotoEdit; (right) © Proehl Studios/Corbis; 246 © Patrick Ward/Alamy; 255 Courtesy Dallas Morning News; 260 Jessica McConnell Burt/The George Washington University; 266 © Dirk Anschütz; 273 U.S. Department of Transportation/ National Highway Traffic Safety Administration; 289 Courtesy of the Death Penalty Information Center; 296 © Children's Television Workshop/Getty Images; 297 (left) © David Young-Wolff/PhotoEdit; (right) © Blend Images/Alamy; 310 © JB Reed; 312 Melanie Gordon Photography; 316 Courtesy of Yale Rudd Center for Food Policy & Obesity; 317 Centers for Disease Control and Prevention; 318 (top) Reprinted from American Journal of Preventative Medicine, 2004; 27: 205–210. Nielsen SJ, Popkin BM. Changes in beverage intake between 1977 and 2001 with permission from Elsevier; (bottom) U.S. Bureau of Labor Statistics; 322 Courtesy of © Organisation for Economic Co-Operation & Development; 329 Courtesy of the Ad Council; 350 Photo by Jaap Buitendijk/© 2011 Warner Bros. Ent. Harry Potter publishing rights © J.K.R. Harry Potter characters, names and related indicia are trademarks of © Warner Bros Ent. All rights reserved/Courtesy Everett Collection; 351 (left) © ClassicStock/Alamy; (right) © Stockbyte/Getty Images; 359, 360, 362, 397 © Universal/Courtesy Everett Collection; 363 (top) Copyright Guardian News & Media Ltd 2012; (bottom), 364, 365 L.A. Noire Screenshots Courtesy of Rockstar Games, Inc. All Rights Reserved; 368 Photo by Theo Wargo/WireImage for Bragman Nyman Cafarelli/Getty Images; 374 © Matthew Cavanaugh; 382 Courtesy of Yelp.com; 402 NOAA/Florida Keys National Marine Sanctuary Staff; 403 (left) Chicago Tribune/MCT/Landov; (right) © Randy Faris/Corbis; 404 Data provided by Johnston, L.D., O'Malley, P.M., Bachman, J. G. & Schulenberg, J.E. (December 14, 2011). "Decline in teen smoking resumes in 2011." University of Michigan News Service: Ann Arbor, MI. Table 1: "Trends in Prevalence of Use of Cigarettes in Grades 8, 10, and 12." The Monitoring the Futures Study. Institute for Social Research, University of Michigan, 2011. Web. 13 April 2012; 411 Courtesy of Pew Research Center, Social & Demographic Trends Project. In the Battle of the Bulge, More Soldiers than Successes. http://pewresearch.org/pubs/310/in-the-battle-of-the-bulge-more-soldiers-than-success. http://pewresearch.org/ pubs/?ChartID=114; 415 © Julia Vitullo-Martin, Honolulu Star-Advertiser; 422 © BERTRAND LANGLOIS/AFP/Getty Images; 426 © Naum Kazhdan/The New York Times/Redux; 428 (left) © Ozier Muhammad/The New York Times/Redux; (right) © Peter DaSilva/The New York Times/Redux; 433 © Jonathan Jarvis; 471 Courtesy of Natalie Grace George, Lacey Iris Patzer, and Sam Williams; 488 © The Irish Image Collection/Design Pics/Newscom; 495 Missouri History Museum, St. Louis. Photo by J.A. Scholten; 497 The Granger Collection, New York; 501 Library of Congress, Prints & Photographs Division, LC-USZ62-109601; 504 © ZUMA Press/Newscom; 507 © Marek Uliasz/Alamy; 522 Photo by Howard Sochurek/Time Life Pictures/Getty Images; 545 © 2009 Angela Butler Photography/Getty Images; 562 Library of Congress; 570 From Newsweek © February 8, 1999, p. 50. The Newsweek/Daily Beast Company LLC. All rights reserved. Used by permission and protected by the Copyright Laws of the United States. The printing, copying, redistribution, or retransmission of the Material without express written permission is prohibited; 571 From *Home Repair Handbook* (Menlo Park, Calif.: Sunset, 1999), pp. 156–157; 626 © Amanda Hall/Robert Harding/Newscom; 627 Courtesy WWF; 630 (left), 635 Library of Congress, Prints & Photographs Division, LC-USF34-013407-C; 630 (right) Grant Wood American, 1891–1942, American Gothic, 1930, Oil on Beaver Board, 78 x 65.3 cm (30 3/4 x 25 3/4 in.), Friends of American Art Collection, 1930.934, The Art Institute of Chicago. Photography © The Art Institute of Chicago. Art © Figge Art Museum, successors to the Estate of Nan Wood Graham/Licensed by VAGA, New York, NY; 631, 634 Photograph courtesy of the Gordon Parks Foundation Copyright The Gordon Parks Foundation; 638 Library of Congress, Prints & Photographs Division, LC-USZ62-42810; 639 (top left) Courtesy of Agency: Freight Train. Photographer: Dan Bishop, Model: Jemme, Ford Models; (top right) © Andrew Burton/Getty Images; (bottom left) Courtesy of Novopelle. Carlos Cortinas, Art Director; Glen Day, Writer; 650 (2nd from top) LALO ALCARAZ © 2002. Dist. by UNIVERSAL UCLICK. Reprinted with permission. All rights reserved; (3rd from top) © JH Pete Carmichael/Getty Images; (bottom) Microsoft product screen reprinted with permission from Microsoft Corporation; 665 © Greg Gard/Alamy; 676 Used by permission of the UCR Libraries, University of California, Riverside; 679, 691, 723 (bottom right) Courtesy of EBSCO Publishing; 680 Courtesy of Google; 694 (left & center) © Bill Aron/PhotoEdit; 694 (right) Courtesy of World Cement, Palladian Publications; (right) Courtesy of District Administration, Professional Media Group; (right) Courtesy of Advertising Age, Crain Communications; 696 (left) Reprinted with permission from the February 6, 2012, issue of *The Nation*. Portions of each week's *Nation* magazine can be accessed at http://www.thenation.com; (right) Courtesy of National Review; 718 Title and Copyright pages from THE MARRIAGE PLOT by Jeffrey Eugenides. Copyright © 2011 by Farrar, Straus and Giroux, LLC. Reprinted by permission of Farrar, Straus and Giroux, LLC.; 723 (top left & right) From *Journal of American Folklore*. Copyright 2011 by the Board of Trustees of the University of Illinois. Used with permission of the authors and the University of Illinois Press; (bottom left) Courtesy of Bright Lights Film Journal http://www.brightlightsfilm.com; 728 Courtesy of Rossetti Archive www.rossettiarchive.org; 751 © Charlie Newham/Alamy; 771 © Liz Boyd/Alamy.

e-Pages Credits

Juliane Koepcke. *How I Survived a Plane Crash*. AP Photo, BBC World Service, Outlook © 2012; Sally Williams— The Telegraph, 22nd March 2012 © Telegraph Media Group Limited.

Andrew Lam. *Waterloo*. Courtesy of Heyday.

Kate Beaton. *Treasure*. Courtesy of Kate Beaton.

Veronica Chambers. *The Secret Latina*. Courtesy of Veronica Chambers.

Index

Entries followed by an **e** symbol may be found online at **bedfordstmartins.com/theguide/epages**.

Submitting Your Essays for Publication

We hope that we'll be able to include many new essays by students in the next editions of *The St. Martin's Guide to Writing* and its companion collections. Please let us see the best essays you've written using the *Guide*. Send them with this submission form and copies of the agreement form on the back of this page (one for each essay you submit) to English Editor—Student Essays, Bedford/St. Martin's, 33 Irving Place, 10th Floor, New York, NY 10003, or submit them online at **bedfordstmartins.com/theguide**.

PAPER SUBMISSION FORM

Student's Name _____

Instructor's Name _____

School _____

Department _____

Writing Assignment (circle one)

Remembering an Event   Proposing a Solution

Writing Profiles   Justifying an Evaluation

Explaining a Concept   Speculating about Causes

Finding Common Ground   Analyzing Stories

Arguing a Position

Agreement Form

I hereby assign to Bedford/St. Martin's ("Bedford") all of my right, title, and interest throughout the world, including without limitation all copyrights, in and to my essay, _____, and any notes and drafts pertaining to it (the sample essay and such materials being referred to as the "Essay").

I understand that Bedford in its discretion has the right but not the obligation to publish the Essay in any form(s) or format(s) that it may desire; that Bedford may edit, revise, condense, or otherwise alter the Essay as it deems appropriate in order to prepare the same for publication. I understand that Bedford has the right to use and to authorize the use of my name as author of the Essay in connection with any work that contains the Essay (or a portion of it).

I represent that the Essay is wholly original and was completely written by me, that publication of it will not infringe on the rights of any third party, and that I have not granted any rights in it to any third party.

In the event Bedford determines to publish any part of the Essay in one of its print books, I will receive one free copy of the work in which it appears.

Student's signature _____

Name _____ Date _____

Permanent address _____

_____

Phone number(s) _____

E-mail address(es) _____

A Note to the Student:

When a writer creates something—a story, an essay, a poem—he or she automatically possesses all of the rights to that piece of writing, no trip to the U.S. Copyright Office needed. When a writer—a historian, a novelist, a sportswriter—publishes his or her work, he or she normally transfers some or all of those rights to the publisher, by formal agreement. The form above is one such formal agreement. By entering into this agreement, you are engaging in a modern publishing ritual—the transfer of rights from writer to publisher. If this is your first experience submitting something for publication, you should know that you are in good company: every student who has published an essay in one of our books entered into this agreement, and just about every published writer has entered into a similar one.

Thank you for submitting your essay.